PSYCHOLOGY

The science of mind and behaviour

Richard D. Gross

Edward Arnold

A division of Hodder & Stoughton

LONDON   NEW YORK   MELBOURNE   AUCKLAND

© 1987 Richard D. Gross

First published in Great Britain 1987
  Fifth impression 1988

British Library Cataloguing in Publication Data

Gross, Richard D.
  Psychology: the science of mind and behaviour.
  1. Psychology
  I. Title
  150   BF139

ISBN 0-7131-3623-5

Typeset in 10/11pt Plantin by Mathematical Composition Setters Ltd, Salisbury, Wilts.
Printed and bound in Great Britain for Edward Arnold, the educational, academic and
medical publishing division of Hodder and Stoughton Limited,
41 Bedford Square, London WC1B 3DQ, by Richard Clay Ltd, Bungay, Suffolk.

Contents

Dedication

To Jan, my wife, Tanya and Joelle, my daughters, for giving me the time and space necessary to undertake this project.

To my late father, who just missed sharing with me the satisfaction of completing this book.

Preface

This book aims to provide a self-contained introduction to all major aspects of psychology. The content is based on the revised Associated Examining Board (AEB) A-level psychology syllabus, but it should also be useful if you are studying for the Joint Matriculation Board (JMB) A-level or an International Baccalaureate examination in psychology, or if you are starting a psychology degree or studying psychology as a subsidiary subject in some other area of higher education.

In writing the book I have made use of many years' teaching of A-level to attempt to give an up-to-date coverage of all aspects of the AEB syllabus in a way that avoids either superficiality or excessive detail.

I have tried to raise all the important questions about each topic discussed, to help you get a firm grasp of the topic as a whole. Summaries of relevant research are given and some of the most important sources given in the text are found in the list of references; specific references that I consider particularly important have been asterisked in the list of references to provide pointers to further reading if you wish. (You will sometimes find that a date quoted in the text for a specific reference differs from the date given in the list of references. Often the same work will be published by different publishers or in different editions—the date in the text normally refers to the original date of publication, while that in the list of references indicates the particular editions which I consulted. Such discrepancies do not, of course, arise in the case of journal/magazine articles.)

The book is not intended to be read in sequence from cover to cover, like a novel. Instead, each chapter can be regarded as a self-contained 'unit', to suit different sequences of tackling the overall subject-matter. Extensive cross-referencing between chapters has been included both to facilitate this and to show how different topics and parts of the syllabus are interrelated—I am sure that your class discussions will soon show that to divide human behaviour and experience into separate 'bits' is quite artificial but not to divide them up in some way seems to make things impossibly difficult for students, teachers and textbook writers alike. (The details given in the Contents list are only a very general guide to what each chapter discusses—a full index has been included to help locate specific points and details.)

I have tried to make the tone as light-hearted as I could without detracting from the basic seriousness of the topics under discussion. I have also tried not to 'preach' or talk *at* you, the reader, but to address you as directly as possible, asking you questions from time to time, and to present the subject-matter in a way that will both help you write your essays and/or seminar papers and also stimulate discussion with fellow students and teachers.

Compare this work with others. Write to the publishers about it, if you wish. In short, *use* it.

Richard D. Gross

Acknowledgements

The publishers would like to thank the following for their permission to reproduce copyright material:

Academic Press for Figures 6.10 and 6.11; American Psychological Association for Figures 6.5 and 7.1; British Psychological Society for Figures 4.3 f and g and 10.1; Brooks /Cole Publishing Company for Figure 27.2; Professor R. B. Cattell for Figure 25.3; Collins Publishers for Figures 5.8 and 19.5; W. H. Freeman and Company for Figures 5.1, 5.3, 5.4, 5.6 and 6.3; Methuen & Co for Figures 25.2 and 27.1; Thomas Nelson and Sons Ltd for Figure 19.9; Oxford University Press for Figure 14.2; Penguin Books Ltd for Figure 25.1; Pergamon Press for Table 17.1; Stanford Alumni Association for Figure 16.1; Van Nostrand Reinhold for Figure 25.4; Weidenfeld (Publishers) Limited for Figure 2.2; West Publishing Company for Figure 5.7.

1

What is Psychology?

Definitions

When a psychologist meets someone for the first time at, say, a party, and replies to the standard 'opening line', 'What do you do for a living?', the reaction of the newly made acquaintance is likely to fall into one of the following categories:

a) 'Oh, I'd better be careful what I say from now on,' (partly defensive, partly amused);
b) 'I bet you meet some right nutters in your work,' (partly intrigued, partly sympathetic);
c) 'What exactly is psychology?' (partly inquisitive, partly puzzled).

What these betray (especially the first two) is an inaccurate and incomplete understanding of the subject. The first reaction seems to imply that psychologists are mind-readers and have access to other people's thoughts. *They do not.* The second reaction seems to imply that psychologists work only or largely with people who could variously be described as 'mentally ill', 'emotionally disturbed' or 'insane'. *They do not.* The third reaction perhaps implies that the borderline between psychology and other subject disciplines is not clearly drawn. *It is not,* and what this chapter attempts to do is provide a general answer to (c) by doing three things:

i)   Looking at some changing definitions of psychology (as given by psychologists themselves) and some of the major schools of thought within psychology as a whole;
ii) Outlining the major subdivisions of the subject-matter of psychology, and seeing what different psychologists actually do;
iii) Looking at the relationship between psychology and common sense.

1) *Do psychologists agree among themselves as to what psychology is?*
   The word *psychology* is derived from two Greek words, *psyche* (mind, soul or spirit) and *logos* (discourse or study) which, put together, produce 'Study of the mind'.
   The appearance of psychology as a subject discipline in its own right is

1

generally dated at 1879, when Wilhelm Wundt opened the first psychology laboratory, at the University of Leipzig in Germany. Wundt and his co-workers were attempting to investigate 'the mind' through *introspection*, that is, observing and analysing their own conscious mental processes (thoughts, images, feelings) as they occurred. They recorded and measured the results of their introspections under *controlled* conditions, ie under the same physical surroundings, using the same 'stimulus' (eg a clicking metronome), giving the same verbal instructions to each person (subject) who participated, and so on. It was this emphasis on measurement and control which really marked the separation of the 'new psychology' from its parent discipline of philosophy.

For hundreds of years philosophers had been reflecting on and speculating about 'the mind'. Now, for the first time, scientists (Wundt was actually a physiologist by training) were applying some of the basic methods of scientific investigation to the study of mental processes.

> Psychology is the Science of Mental Life, both of its phenomena and of their conditions...The Phenomena are such things as we call feelings, desires, cognition, reasoning, decisions and the like. (William James, 1890)

However, by the second decade of the twentieth century, the validity and usefulness of this method were being seriously questioned, in particular by an American psychologist, John B. Watson. He believed that introspection produced results which could never be proved or disproved, eg if my introspection produces different results from *yours*, how can we ever decide whose is correct? Of course, we cannot, because there is no objective way of doing so; we cannot 'get behind' the introspective report to check its accuracy. Introspection is subjective and only the individual can observe their own mental processes—no one else can do it for them. Consequently, Watson proposed that psychologists should confine themselves to what is measurable and observable by more than one person, namely *behaviour*.

> For the behaviourist, psychology is that division of Natural Science which takes human behaviour—the doings and sayings, both learned and unlearned—as its subject matter. (John B. Watson, 1919)

So a new brand of psychology had emerged, known as *behaviour-ism*. It largely replaced Wundt's Introspectionism, advocating that human beings should be regarded as complex animals and studied using the same scientific methods as used by chemistry and physics. This was the only way, Watson believed, that psychology could make any claims to being a science itself: to emulate the natural sciences, psychology must adopt its objective methods. The study of inaccessible, private, mental processes was to have no place in a truly scientific psychology.

Behaviourism (in one form or another) was to remain the dominant force within psychology for the next thirty years or so, especially in the USA and, to a lesser extent, in Britain. The emphasis on the role of learning (in the form of *conditioning*) was to make that topic one of the central areas of research in psychology as a whole. Behaviourist theories of learning are often referred to as Stimulus–Response (S–R) theories, because of their attempt to analyse all behaviour into stimulus–response units, no matter how complex the behaviour. A reaction against Behaviourism came in the form of the *Gestalt* school of psychology which emerged in in the 1920s and '30s in Austria and Germany. The Gestalt psychologists were mainly interested in perception and believed that perceptions could not be broken down in the way that behaviourists advocated for behaviour; one of their central beliefs was that 'the whole is greater than the sum of its parts' (see Chapter 4).

Starting in 1900, in Austria, Sigmund Freud was beginning to publish his theory of personality in which the *unconscious mind* was to play such a crucial role. Freud's *psychoanalytical theory* also represented a challenge, and a major alternative, to behaviourism.

During the 1950s and '60s, many psychologists began to look to the work of computer scientists in trying to understand the more complex behaviour which, they felt, Learning Theory had either neglected altogether or greatly oversimplified. The behaviour in question was what Wundt and the early scientific psychologists had called 'Mind' or mental processes, but which were now referred to as *cognition* or Cognitive Processes (see W. James's 1890 definition opposite). This involves all the ways in which we come to *know* the world around us, particularly *memory, perception, language, thinking, problem-solving, reasoning and concept-attainment.*

The cognitive psychologist compares the 'Mind' to a computer in an attempt to gain some understanding of the former which might be impossible without the latter. So, for example, 'What if people perceive objects in the way that computers are programmed to?' is one kind of question that may be asked and is based, of course, on what we already know about how computers work.

As we noted earlier, what makes mental (or cognitive) processes different from behaviour is that they are essentially 'private' in that, at best, you can only *infer* from, say, a person's furrowed brow or head-scratching that they are trying to puzzle out a problem or make up their mind about something. You can also ask them what they are doing, but ultimately you cannot prove or disprove their account of what is going on inside their head, because nobody else can get inside their head to find out.

Thus we have come full circle—back to the behaviourists' original criticisms of introspection. However, mental processes are now accepted as being valid subject-matter for psychology, providing we can objectify or externalize them (make them 'public'), as in memory tests or problem-solving tasks. Consequently, what a person says and does are perfectly acceptable sources of data (information) *about* their cognitive processes, although the processes themselves remain inaccessible to the observer, who can study them only indirectly.

> Psychology is usually defined as the scientific study of behaviour. Its subject matter includes behavioural processes that are observable, such as gestures, speech and physiological changes, and processes that can only be inferred, such as thoughts and dreams. (K. Clark & G. Miller, 1970)

2) How can we divide up the work that psychologists do?

As we have seen, behaviourist and cognitive psychology have been very influential in determining the general direction that psychology has taken in the last sixty or seventy years, and this is reflected in the definitions of their subject which psychologists have given. However, there is much more to what

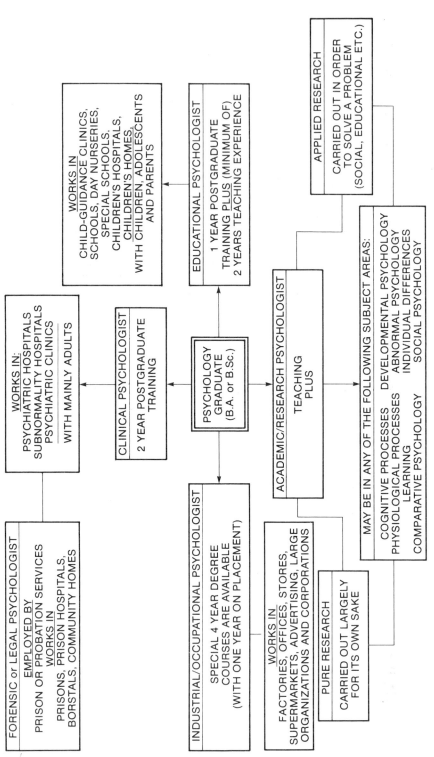

Figure 1.1 The major areas of academic and applied psychology open to psychology graduates

goes on under the general heading of 'psychology' than what we have outlined so far: there are other schools of thought, other aspects of human (and animal) activity that constitute the special focus of study, and finally different kinds of work that different psychologists do.

A distinction which may prove helpful is that between the *academic* and the *applied* branches of the subject (see Figure 1.1). The academic psychologist carries out research (scientific investigation) in a particular area (eg perception) and is attached to a university, polytechnic or research establishment where they will also teach first degree students (undergraduates) and may supervise the research of postgraduates.

Research is of two major kinds: *pure*, ie done for its own sake and intended, primarily, to increase our knowledge and understanding; and *applied*, ie aimed at solving a particular problem, usually a social problem such as alcoholism or juvenile delinquency. Applied psychology is usually funded by a government institution, like the Home Office or the Department of Education and Science, or by some commercial or industrial institution. (As will be seen later, many applied psychologists are also engaged in research.)

The range of topics that may be investigated is as wide as psychology itself, but a way of classifying them has been suggested by Legge (1975), namely, those which focus on the *processes* or *mechanisms* underlying various aspects of behaviour, and those which focus more directly on the *person*.

The Process Approach (Experimental Psychology)

This category itself divides into four main areas—cognitive processes, physiological processes, comparative psychology, and learning—and collectively is known as *experimental psychology*. (This is something of a misnomer, since the experimental method is used in almost all areas of psychology, including the person-oriented approach; it was originally used to distinguish scientific psychology from the philosophy from which it emerged. Sometimes the term general is used instead of 'experimental.')

1) Cognitive Processes (Chapters 4 to 7)
'Cognition' means knowing, so cognitive (or mental) processes refer to all those ways in which knowledge of the world is attained, retained and used, including *attention, memory, perception, language, thinking, problem-solving, reasoning* and *concept-attainment* ('higher-order' mental activities). As we have seen, these are processes which can only be inferred and which cannot be seen directly. Although these are often studied for their own sake, they may have very important practical implications too, for example, understanding the memory processes involved in eye-witness testimony (see Chapter 6). Much social psychology (listed here as belonging in the Person-category) is cognitive in flavour, that is, concerned with the mental processes involved in interpersonal perception (eg stereotyping) and attitude change (eg cognitive dissonance) and is known as *social cognition*. Also, Piaget's theory of development (again, belonging to the Person category) is concerned with cognitive development (see Chapter 19).

2) Physiological Processes (Chapters 15 to 17)

Physiological psychologists are interested in the physical basis of behaviour, how the functions of the nervous system (in particular the brain) and the endocrine (hormonal) system are related to and influence behaviour and mental processes. For example, are there parts of the brain specifically concerned with particular behaviours and abilities (localization of brain function)? What role do hormones play in the experience of emotion and how are these linked to brain processes? What is the relationship between brain activity and different states of consciousness (including sleep)? What changes occur in the brain when we say that learning has taken place or that a memory has been established? These are just some of the questions that physiological psychologists try to answer.

However, we must be aware of the philosophical issue of reductionism which, although it does not apply just to the physiological psychology, has become focused on the 'Mind-Body' issue (see Chapter 2). Briefly, some physiologists believe that the 'mind' can be 'reduced' to or explained (in principle) totally in terms of brain processes etc. The implication is that, once we know enough about how the brain works, psychology will no longer have a role to play!

Related to interest in physiological processes is interest in the biological process of genetic transmission (the science of *genetics* exists in its own right). The Heredity–Environment issue, which runs right through psychology, makes use of what geneticists have discovered about what kinds of characteristics can be passed from parents to offspring, how this takes place and how genetic factors can be influenced by environmental ones (see Chapters 5, 14, 20, 22, and 27).

3) Comparative Psychology (Chapter 14)

This is often used synonymously with *animal* psychology, but the word 'comparative' implies the original purpose of studying animals, namely to increase our understanding of human behaviour. The study of animal behaviour was inspired by Darwin's (1859) theory of evolution and it seems quite reasonable to believe that, by studying more simple species from which we have evolved, we should learn more about ourselves.

However, there is a great temptation to extrapolate directly from non-human species to ourselves (an issue that is discussed in Chapter 2). Moreover, much study of animal behaviour takes place for its own sake and is perhaps more appropriately called 'animal' psychology, although animals continue to be used as experimental subjects when for moral and practical reasons humans cannot.

Ironically, the study of animals was first taken up by psychologists (as opposed to biologists, which Darwin was) and much of their research took place in the laboratory (this includes Watson's work and that of the behaviourists that followed him). More recently (especially since the 1950s) zoologists have been advocating the 'naturalist' approach to the study of animal behaviour, observing animals in their natural habitat and sometimes manipulating or modifying aspects of their environment. This *ethological* approach is associated particularly with Konrad Lorenz, Niko Tinbergen, and Robert Hinde. Interestingly, some developmental psychologists are adopting an ethological approach to the study of child development and an eminent child psychiatrist, John Bowlby, has been greatly influenced by the work of Lorenz in his theories of attachment (see Chapter 18).

4) Learning (Chapter 3)

Just as cognitive processes make an important appearance in social and developmental psychology, so the learning process permeates most other subdivisions of psychology. This is partly a reflection of the impact of behaviourism on psychology as a whole (at least up to the 1950s), since learning plays such a central part in behaviourist theory where it is studied in the form of *Conditioning*. But there is much more to learning than conditioning. We shall be discussing the work of Social Learning theorists who, while sharing many of the basic principles of Conditioning theory, also believe that conditioning alone cannot account for much human behaviour. They have focused on *Observational Learning* (Modelling) as an important additional learning process—especially in children. (See also Chapter 21.)

Learning which is closely related to cognitive processes, such as language and perception, is also considered to be different from conditioning; thus Gestalt psychology's *Insight* learning and the learning by rats of 'mental maps' (Tolman) are examples of *Cognitive* learning. All three kinds of learning (plus others) will feature prominently in the discussion of development, and the applications of theories of learning are important in treatment of behaviour disorders (see Chapter 29).

Note We should perhaps make a distinction between (a) 'theories of learning', which include all three types mentioned above, and (b) 'learning theory', which usually refers to the behaviourist theories of conditioning, eg Pavlov, Watson and Skinner.

The Person Approach

This second category of psychology also covers four major areas of research—Developmental, Abnormal, Individual Differences, and Social.

1) Developmental Psychology (Chapters 18 to 24)

Developmental psychology studies the physical, intellectual, social and emotional changes that occur in the individual over time. One very significant change that has occurred within developmental psychology during the past ten to fifteen years is the recognition that development is not confined to childhood and adolescence, but is a lifelong process (referred to as the *Lifespan Approach*). While the ageing process has been studied for many years, the emphasis has tended to be on physical aspects and the associated psychopathology (or mental illness, especially senile dementia); it has not had the 'flavour' of a stage of development, unlike pregnancy, infancy, toddlerhood and so on. Also, 'growing old' has, traditionally, had very negative connotations, compared with 'growing up', which is normally taken to be something desirable and almost an end in itself (see Chapter 24). It is now widely accepted, however, that adulthood is a developmental stage, quite distinct from adolescence (see Chapter 23).

The first major theorist to acknowledge the lifelong nature of development ('cradle-to-grave') was Erik Erikson, who described the 'Eight Ages of Man', each of which presents the individual with a new developmental task to be worked on.

As we have already seen, developmental psychologists draw heavily on basic research findings from other major areas of psychology (especially 'experimental' or general psychology). Developmental psychology is not an isolated or independent field and advances in it depend on progress in the entire realm of psychology, for example, behavioural genetics, physiological psychology, learning, perception and motivation. This is reflected in the wide-ranging methods and techniques of study that are used. But developmental psychology also contributes to other areas of psychology; for example, although Piaget's theory of cognitive development was meant to map the changes that take place up to about fifteen years of age, he is considered to have made a massive contribution to psychology as a whole.

Developmental psychology also provides an important 'testing ground' for general psychological principles, many of which have derived from laboratory studies on animals; the study of developmental changes can indicate just how valid these principles are when applied to human beings in the real world. It was Darwin's *Origin of Species* (1859) which inspired the view that the child is a rich source of potential information about the nature of the human species as a whole. By careful observation of the developing infant and child, the evolution and development of the human species (*Phylogeny*) can be traced. (*Ontogeny* is the evolution and development of the individual.) The developing organism can be regarded as a microcosm of the species as it developed. (A microcosm is a smaller-scale example of some larger process or situation, eg the family is a microcosm of society.)

2) Abnormal Psychology (Chapter 28)

This studies the underlying causes of what are variously called mental illness, behaviour disorders, emotional disturbance and forms of deviancy (which may include criminality, sexual perversions, drug abuse and alcoholism); it is closely linked with one of the applied areas of psychology, namely, clinical psychology (see below). Clearly, there is also overlap between abnormal psychology and the study of (normal) personality: we have to know what the range of individual differences is before we can begin to classify people (or their behaviour) as abnormal or deviant.

3) Individual Differences (Chapters 25 to 27)

As the name suggests, this is concerned with the ways in which people can differ from one another, in particular sex or gender (see Chapter 22), personality and intelligence.

Personality can be thought of as those relatively stable and enduring aspects of an individual which distinguish them from other people, making them unique, but which at the same time permit a comparison between individuals. Within that general definition, there are several different theoretical approaches, including the trait and type approach (Eysenck and Cattell), the psychoanalytic (Freud, Jung, Adler), the humanistic (Maslow, Rogers), the social learning approach (Mischell) and the cognitive (Kelly). The first of these, the trait and type approach, is closely related to *psychometrics* ('mental measurement'), since this approach makes great use of standardized tests of personality on which to compare large numbers of individuals and groups or classes of individuals.

Similarly, the study of *intelligence* is very much concerned with differences between individuals and groups (eg racial and age-groups) and a great deal of time and money has been invested since 1905 (when the Frenchmen Binet and Simon devised the first intelligence test) in constructing new tests and refining old ones. One of the most hotly debated issues in psychology is how to account for differences in measured intelligence between different racial groups in terms of genetic factors (nature or heredity) or environmental factors (nurture or environment). The status of the tests used is problematic, as is the attempt to define the term 'intelligence' itself (see Chapter 27).

4) Social Psychology (Chapters 8 to 13)

Some psychologists would claim that 'all psychology is social psychology' since all behaviour takes place within a social context and, even when we are alone, our behaviour continues to be influenced by others (eg their potential response to what we are doing). Our own self-concept, as we shall see (Chapter 9) is in large measure a reflection of how others have treated us and responded to us in the past, but others may have a more immediate and direct influence upon us when we are actually in their presence (see Chapter 12).

Social psychology is also concerned with interpersonal perception (forming impressions of others), interpersonal attraction (why we like some people more than others), attitudes and attitude change, prejudice and pro- and anti-social behaviour (including aggression). Social psychologists tend to draw on the work of general psychology in order to see how this can help them understand the behaviour that goes on between people.

Is there a real difference between the Process and the Person approaches after all? I have tried to show how different research areas overlap with others and how, in practice, it is very difficult to separate them, even if it can be done theoretically.

However, there are differences (mainly of degree) which are worth mentioning:

The Process approach is much more confined to the laboratory, makes far greater use of animals as subjects, and makes the general and basic assumption that psychological processes (particularly learning) are essentially the same in *all* species; any differences that are found between members of different species are only *quantitative* (differences of degree). In contrast, the Person approach makes much greater use of field studies (eg observing subjects in their natural environments) and of non-experimental methods (e.g. correlational studies). In the main, human subjects are used and it is assumed that *qualitative* differences (differences in kind) exist between humans and other animals.

Our discussion of the Person/Process approaches has been concerned with the academic branch of psychology. Fortunately, the situation is a little more straightforward as far as *applied* psychology is concerned, partly because of the special training required (over and above the minimum requirement that all psychologists must possess a psychology degree) and partly because of the place and type of work involved. The three major areas of applied psychology are Educational, Clinical, and Industrial (or Occupational).

Educational Psychology

The educational psychologist has had at least two years teaching experience and has gained a postgraduate qualification in educational or child psychology. The main areas of responsibility include:

a) Administering psychological tests, particularly intelligence or IQ tests, as part of the assessment of learning difficulties;
b) The planning and supervision of remedial teaching;
c) Research into teaching methods, the curriculum (subjects taught), interviewing and counselling methods and techniques;
d) The planning of educational programmes designed to meet the needs of mentally and physically handicapped (including the visually handicapped and autistic) and other groups of children and adolescents who are not attending ordinary schools (ie *special education*).

Educational psychologists are usually employed by the Local Education Authority (LEA) and work in one or more of the following: child guidance clinics (usually staffed by a psychiatrist, one or more educational psychologists, several psychiatric social workers, one or more child psychotherapists, and, sometimes, a speech therapist); the Schools Psychological Service; hospitals, day nurseries, nursery schools, special schools (day and residential) and residential children's homes. The age of clients is up to 18 years, but most will fall into the 5 to 16 age-group.

Clinical Psychology

Clinical psychologists are by far the most numerous single group of psychologists: more than a third of all psychologists classify themselves as clinical and a further 10 per cent or so call themselves 'counselling psychologists' (they tend to work with younger clients in colleges and universities rather than in hospitals).

The clinical psychologist has trained for two or three years as a postgraduate and is qualified to:

a) Administer tests of personality and intelligence as part of the assessment and diagnosis of mental disorder (including mental handicap and mental illness) and behavioural and emotional disorders.
b) Plan and carry out programmes of therapy, usually *behaviour therapy/modification* (both derived from Learning theory principles), but occasionally they may choose *psychotherapy* (group or individual) in preference to, or in addition to, behavioural techniques. (See Chapter 29.)

Psychotherapy is usually carried out by psychiatrists or psychotherapists and is based on the psychoanalytic (psychodynamic) theories of personality associated with Freud (see Chapters 26 and 29). Patients may be of any age but are usually adults, of whom many will be elderly; the clinical psychologist works in psychiatric and subnormality hospitals, psychiatric wards in general hospitals and psychiatric clinics. Many are engaged in conducting research into abnormal psychology.

A special sub-group of clinical psychologists is that of the *forensic* or *legal* psychologists who are employed by the prison or probation service. The forensic psychologist may be called as an expert witness in court trials to testify regarding: (a) the credibility of witnesses and defendants; (b) the fitness of individuals to stand trial; (c) any other matter seen as requiring the expert opinion of a psychologist (eg handwriting). They may work in community homes (once called approved schools), detention centres, youth custody centres, and prisons or prison hospitals (for the criminally insane) such as Broadmoor and Rampton.

Industrial or Occupational Psychology

The responsibilities of the industrial or occupational psychologist include:

a) The selection and training of individuals for jobs and vocational guidance, which often involves giving aptitude tests and tests of interest and is sometimes the responsibility of individuals trained in personnel management, which has a large psychology component.
b) Industrial rehabilitation, ie helping people, who for reasons of illness, accident or redundancy, need to choose and re-train for a new career.
c) Designing training schemes, as part of 'fitting the person to the job'; this is particularly important at a time when new technology is replacing old methods and sometimes taking over totally the jobs done by particular workers. Teaching machines and simulators (eg of an aeroplane cockpit) often feature prominently in such training schemes.
d) 'Fitting the job to the person' (*engineering psychology*) whereby applications from experimental psychology are made to the design of equipment and machinery, in order to make the best use of human resources and to minimize accidents and fatigue. Examples of how engineering psychologists have been consulted include telephone dialling codes (memory and attention) and the design of decimal coinage (tactile and visual discrimination); these illustrate very well the interplay between applied and pure research where the former very often depends on the latter and any complete separation between them is not possible.
e) Advising on working conditions so as to maximize productivity; this represents part of ergonomics, officially defined as 'the study of man in his working environment'.
f) Helping the flow of communication between departments or sections in government institutions or 'industrial relations' in commerce and industry (often called *organizational psychology*). So here the emphasis is on the social, rather than the physical or practical, aspects of the working environment.
g) Helping to sell products and services through advertising and promotions. Many psychologists are employed in the advertising industry, where they draw on what experimental psychologists say about human motivation, attitudes, cognition and so on.

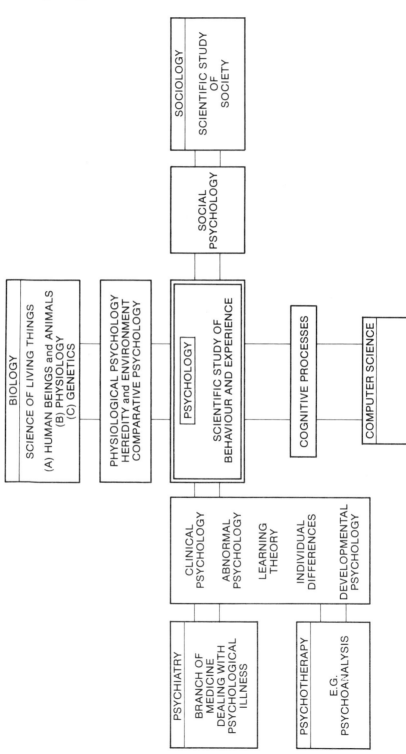

Figure 1.2   The relationship between psychology and other scientific disciplines

Schools of Thought or Theoretical Approaches

Throughout our discussion so far, we have had cause to refer to behaviourist, or psychoanalytic, or cognitive theories or perspectives; it should be apparent by now that we cannot talk about psychologists as if they all shared some basic theory about 'what makes people tick', nor indeed, do they agree about what sort of terminology or methodology to use when carrying out their research or formulating their theories.

Different psychologists make different assumptions about what particular aspects of a person are worthy of study, sometimes to the exclusion of any others, and this helps to determine an underlying *model* or *image* of what human beings are like. In turn, this model or image determines a view of psychological normality, the nature of development, preferred methods of study, the major cause(s) of abnormal behaviour and the preferred methods and goals of treatment. These issues and the position of five major theoretical approaches (psychoanalytic, behaviourist, humanistic-existential, neurobiological and cognitive) regarding them are summarized in Table 1.1 overleaf.

These (together with different versions of each) are the major theoretical approaches that will make their appearance throughout the book (particularly in relation to development). It should be evident from even a cursory glance at the table how different and distinctive is the *language* used by each approach. So let us now take a closer look at some of the language used in psychology as a whole.

The Language of Psychology

As in all sciences, there is a special set of technical terms (jargon) to get used to and this is generally accepted as an unavoidable feature of studying the subject. But over and above these technical words which only scientists speak to fellow scientists, psychologists use words that are familiar to us from everyday speech and it is here that 'doing psychology' can become a little confusing.

Some examples of this are 'behaviour' and 'personality'. For a parent to tell their child to 'behave yourself' is meaningless to a psychologist's ears since behaving is something we are all doing all the time (even when asleep) and to say someone 'has no personality' is equally meaningless, because as personality refers to what makes a person unique and different from others you cannot help but have one! Other terms, which denote large portions of the research of experimental psychology, such as memory (Chapter 6), learning (Chapter 3) and intelligence (Chapter 27) are called *hypothetical constructs*, that is, they do not refer to anything that can be directly observed but can only be inferred from observable behaviour. Equally important, they seem to be necessary in order to account for the behaviour that is observed; but there is a danger of thinking of them as 'things' or 'entities', rather than as a way of trying to make sense of behaviour.

Another way in which psychologists try to make sense of something is by comparing it with something else (often something complex is compared with something more simple), that is, they use an *analogy* (or analogue). Since the 1950s and the development of computer science, the *computer analogy* has

Table 1.1 Five major theoretical approaches in psychology

	(a) Psychoanalytic or psychodynamic (eg Freud)	(b) Behaviourist or Stimulus-response (eg Skinner)	(c) Humanistic-existential (eg Maslow)	(d) Neurobiological or Biogenic	(e) Cognitive
1. Nature of human beings	Individual is in conflict due to opposing demands made by different parts of the personality – ID, EGO, SUPEREGO. Behaviour is largely determined by unconscious forces.	Human behaviour is shaped by environmental forces (REINFORCEMENT) and is a collection of learned responses to external stimuli. The key learning process is conditioning (classical and operant)	The individual is unique, free, rational and self-determining. Free-will and Self-actualization make human beings distinct from animals. Present experience is as important as past experience.	Behaviour is determined by genetic, physiological and neurobiological factors and processes. The influence of the Central Nervous System (especially the Brain) is crucial.	The human mind is compared to a computer. People are INFORMATION-PROCESSORS, selecting information, coding it, storing it and retrieving it when needed. Memory, perception and language are central.
2. Nature of psychological normality	Adequate balance between Id, Ego, Superego. But conflict is always present to some degree.	Possession of an adequately large repertoire of adaptive responses.	Ability to accept oneself, to realize one's potential, to achieve intimacy with others, to find meaning in life.	Properly functioning nervous system.	Proper functioning of cognitive processes and the ability to use them to monitor and control behaviour.
3. Nature of psychological development	PSYCHOSEXUAL stages: Oral (0–1); Anal (1–3); Phallic (3–5/6); Latency (5/6–Puberty) Genital (Puberty–Maturity) Sequence determined by Maturation. The individual is shaped by early	None as such. No stages of development. Different behaviour is selectively reinforced at different ages but the differences between a child and an adult are merely QUANTITATIVE.	Development of self-concept, in particular self-regard (self-esteem). Satisfaction of lower-level needs as pre-requisite for higher-level (growth) needs.	Stages of behavioural/ psychological development based on changes in brain growth which are genetically determined (i.e. maturation).	① Stages of Cognitive Development (e.g. Piaget): Sensorimotor (0–2); Pre-operational (2–7); Concrete operational (7–11); Formal operational (11–15). ② Information-Processing approach – development of memory, perception, language, attention, etc.

4. Preferred method(s) of study	*Case-study* (Clinical method)	*Experiment* (Animals and humans)	*Case-study*	*Experiment* (Animals and humans)	*Experiment* (Mainly humans) *Computer simulation*
5. Major cause(s) of abnormal behaviour	Emotional disturbance or Neurosis caused by unresolved conflicts stemming from childhood. Abnormal behaviour is symptomatic of such conflicts. Main feature is Anxiety.	The learning of maladaptive responses or the failure to learn adaptive ones in the first place. No distinction between symptoms and the behaviour disorder.	Inability to accept and express one's true nature, to take responsibility for one's own actions and to make authentic choices. Anxiety stems from denying part of Self. Referred to as Identity crisis or Ontological insecurity.	Genetic disorders, organic (bodily) disorders (e.g. brain disease or injury), chemical imbalance, food allergies. MENTAL ILLNESS gives rise to behavioural and psychological symptoms.	Unrealistic or irrational ideas and beliefs about self and others. Inability to monitor or control behaviour through appropriate cognitive processes.
6. Preferred method(s) of treatment	Insight-oriented Psychotherapy (e.g. Psychoanalysis). The unconscious is revealed through Dream interpretation, Free-association, Transference.	Behaviour therapy or modification. E.g. Systematic desensitization, Aversion therapy, Flooding, Behaviour shaping, Token economy.	Client-centred therapy; insights come from the client as present experiences are explored with the therapist.	Physical treatments. E.g. Chemotherapy (Drugs), Electro-convulsive Therapy (E.C.T.), Psychosurgery.	E.g. Cognitive-Behaviour Therapy, Rational-emotive Therapy, Zen meditation and Behavioural Self-control.
7. Goal(s) of treatment	To uncover and work through unconscious conflicts to make them conscious. To achieve reasonable balance between id, ego and superego.	To eliminate maladaptive responses and to acquire adaptive ones.	To rediscover the *Whole self*, which can then proceed towards Self-Actualization.	To alleviate symptoms and/or to actually reverse the underlying cause(s) of the illness.	To correct these unrealistic/irrational ideas and beliefs so that thinking becomes an effective means of controlling behaviour.

become very popular as a way of trying to understand how the brain works; as we have seen, the language of computer science has permeated the cognitive view of man as an information processor. A *model* is a kind of metaphor; so, for instance, 'man the information processor' is not meant to be taken too literally but is more of a suggestion as to how we might think of people's behaviour, again in order to understand it better. A model entails a single, fundamental idea or image and is not as complex as a theory (although sometimes the terms are used interchangeably).

In Chapter 2, a *theory* is defined as a complex set of interrelated statements which attempt to explain certain observed phenomena. (But this is only one of many definitions that you might come across in your reading!) Although, strictly speaking, the role of theory is to explain, in practice, when we refer to a particular theory (e.g. that of Freud or Piaget), we often include description as well.

R. Murray Thomas (1985) defines a theory as 'an explanation of how the facts fit together' and he likens a theory to a lens through which to view the subject matter, filtering out certain facts and giving a particular pattern to those it lets in.

A *hypothesis* is defined in Chapter 2 as a testable statement about the relationship between two or more variables. The term is sometimes used to mean something very similar to 'theory' but these two meanings should be kept separate.

What is a Definition?

This is not as straightforward as it may first seem—like most things, definitions come in a variety of shapes and sizes. Bell and Staines (1981) identify at least four different kinds—Descriptive, Stipulative, Circular and Operational.

Descriptive definitions aim to spell out the conventional (everyday) meaning of a term and can be right or wrong, accurate or inaccurate. For example, 'a behaviourist is someone who studies behaviour' is inaccurate because it is too wide; 'a behaviourist is someone who studies rats in Skinner boxes' is inaccurate because it is too narrow. So descriptive definitions can be 'right' or 'wrong'.

Stipulative (or *nominal*) definitions cannot be 'right' or 'wrong' because they refer to how the author stipulates a term should be used. This can be confusing if the author is giving a definition of a term already familiar in common parlance (eg the examples of 'behaviour' and 'personality' above); it is more common for stipulative definitions to be used when new terms are coined to suit a particular theoretical purpose (eg 'proactive inhibition' or 'fixed interval schedule') where the term has virtually no precise meaning outside its technical usage. Although not 'right' or 'wrong', it might still be thought unclear, too narrow or idiosyncratic (eg 'IQ' for 'intelligence' or 'superego' for 'conscience').

Circular definitions are those in which what is being defined is included in the definition itself—it 'chases its own tail'. For example, 'intelligence is what intelligence tests measure' begs the question of just what intelligence is, since if we ask 'Well, what do intelligence tests measure?' the definition's reply is 'Intelligence' and so we are back to where we started—we have come full circle! Sometimes debates about the 'evidence' may actually be about definitions!

This definition of intelligence is not only circular but is also an *operational* definition, ie it tells us *how* to measure something or classify something in a certain way (eg someone of average intelligence has an IQ of 100). But this does not help to define the concept or enlighten us as to the nature of intelligence, what is involved in being intelligent, what it *means*!

Finally, we should be aware of the distinction between operational definitions and the related, but separate, concept of *operationalization* of variables in psychological research, which refers to the way in which, for the purpose of a particular experiment, the investigator is going to define or measure the variables in question. How could we translate, for example, the idea of 'the influence of TV on children's behaviour' into a form which would enable us to collect some data? We might formulate the hypothesis, 'watching TV violence increases the child's level of aggression' and operationalize 'TV violence' as 'the use of knives and/or guns to kill or injure' and 'aggression' as 'the number of times the child uses its own body or some physical object to strike another child during an hour's play session'. There are many other ways we could operationalize these two variables so we are offering a 'definition' of them only in the context of a particular investigation.

Psychology and Common Sense

A common reaction among psychology students, when discussing the findings of some piece of research, is to say 'But we knew that already' implying that 'It's only common sense'. Alternatively, they might say 'But that's not what we normally understand by such-and-such', implying that the research is in some way wrong. So it seems that psychology is often in a 'Catch-22' position—either it merely *confirms* common sense or it *contradicts* it, in which case psychology seems to be the less credible.

Whereas only a few of us would think of ourselves as physicists or doctors, engineers or novelists, unless we had received a special education, or training, or had special talent, we all consider that we know something about people and why they behave as they do. So there is a sense in which we are all psychologists!

This is a theme explored at length by Joynson in *Psychology and Common Sense* (1974). He begins by stating that human beings are not like the objects of natural science—we understand ourselves and can already predict and control our behaviour to a remarkable extent. This creates for the psychologist a paradoxical task: what kind of understanding can you seek of a creature which already understands itself?

For Joynson, the fundamental question is 'If the psychologist did not exist, would it be necessary to invent him?' For Skinner, 'it is science or nothing' and Broadbent, another leading behaviourist, also rejects the validity of our everyday understanding of ourselves and others (Joynson calls it 'the behaviourists' prejudice'). Yet it seems inevitable that we try to make sense of our own and other people's behaviour (by virtue of our cognitive abilities and the nature of social interaction) and to this extent we are all psychologists. (This is discussed further in relation to Interpersonal Perception—see Chapter 8.)

Heather (1976) points to ordinary language as embodying our 'natural' understanding of human behaviour; in his view, as long as human beings have lived they have been psychologists, and language gives us an 'elaborate and highly refined conceptual tool, developed over thousands of years of talking to each other'. So how can we resolve the dilemma? Legge (1975) and others resolve it by distinguishing between *formal* and *informal* psychology (or professional versus amateur, scientific versus non-scientific). Our common sense, intuitive or 'natural' understanding is unsystematic and does not constitute a body of knowledge; this makes it very difficult to 'check' an individual's 'theory' about human nature as does the fact that each individual has to learn from their own experience. So part of the aim of formal psychology is precisely to provide such a systematic body of knowledge, which represents the unobservable bases of our 'gut-reactions'.

But it could be argued that informal psychology does provide a 'body of knowledge' in the form of proverbs or sayings or folk wisdom, handed down from generation to generation, for example, 'birds of a feather flock together', 'too many cooks spoil the broth' and 'don't cross your bridges before you come to them'. Perhaps these contain at least a grain of truth. But the problem is that for each of them we can find yet another proverb which states the opposite—'opposites attract', 'many hands make light work' and 'time and tide wait for no man' (or 'nothing ventured, nothing gained'). Common sense does not help us to reconcile these contradictory statements—but formal psychology can! Indeed, there does seem to be some evidence to support both proverbs in the first pair (see Chapter 10 on Interpersonal Attraction); formal psychology tries to identify the *conditions* under which each statement holds true—they only appear contradictory if we assume that only one or the other can be true! In this way, we can see scientific psychology as throwing light on our everyday, informal understanding, not necessarily as negating or invalidating it.

Legge believes that most psychological research should indeed be aimed at demonstrations of 'what we know already' but that it should aim to go one step further; only the methods of science, he believes, can provide us with the public, communicable body of knowledge that we are seeking. According to Allport (1947), the aim of science is 'Understanding, prediction and control above the levels achieved by unaided common sense' and this is meant to apply to psychology as much as it does to the natural sciences. Just what science involves, and how appropriately we can study people scientifically, is the subject of the next chapter.

2

Is Psychology a Science?

Philosophy and Psychology

In trying to answer the important and complex question of whether psychology is a science, it is instructive to take a brief look at some of the major philosophical influences that helped to create psychology as a separate discipline and which help to explain what psychology is today. 'Is psychology a science?' is essentially a philosophical question; it cannot be answered without taking the meaning of certain concepts into account, in particular, the concept of a science. The two major philosophical influences I will describe here are *Empiricism* and *Positivism*.

Empiricism

The *Empiricists* were seventeenth-century British philosophers (notably Locke, Hume and Berkeley) who believed that the only source of true knowledge about the world is sensory experience, that is, what comes to us through our senses or what can be inferred about the relationships between such sensory facts. This fundamental belief proved to be one of the major influences on the development of physics and chemistry. Indeed, the word 'empirical' ('through the senses') is often used synonymously with 'scientific', implying that what is at the heart of scientific activity is the observation and measurement of the world and the collection of data. Empiricist philosophers were usually contrasted with Rationalists or Nativists who believed that knowledge of the world is largely innate or inborn.

Although Wundt had been influenced by empiricism through its impact on science as a whole (including physiology) it was behaviourism which was to embody empiricist philosophy within psychology. Locke maintained that the mind at birth was a *tabula rasa*, a blank slate on which experience made its imprint, and this extreme environmentalism is built into the behaviourist view of learning, whereby the child is totally malleable and can be made into anything the environment wants it to become. According to George Miller (1967), the implications of empiricism for psychology, in addition to the emphasis on the senses as the 'doors to the mind', include (a) the analysis into *elements* (eg conscious mind into simple ideas or overt behaviour into Stimulus–Response units); and (b) a theory of *association* necessary for explaining how simple elements can be combined to form more complex elements or compounds.

Thus empiricism provided for psychology both a theory ('tabula rasa' view of the mind) and a methodology (central role of observation and measurement), and this corresponds to a very important distinction between two kinds of behaviourism—philosophical and methodological. *Philosophical behaviourism*, in its most extreme form, is Watson's rejection of mind, the view that, for example, thinking is nothing but a series of vocal or sub-vocal verbal responses; less extreme is Skinner's belief that mental concepts are irrelevant in trying to predict and control human behaviour. *Methodological behaviourism* refers to the emphasis on observation, the collection and measurement of data, the importance of the experiment and so on. Despite the decline of philosophical behaviourism, methodological behaviourism has continued to exert its influence—most psychologists today are behaviourists in this second sense and it underlies the way psychology is taught.

Positivism

The philosophy of Auguste Comte (1842), positivism was directly influenced by the achievements of the natural sciences during the seventeenth, eighteenth and nineteenth centuries. In essence, Comte advocated the application of the methods and principles of natural science to human behaviour, institutions and political organizations (which is why he is regarded as the father of sociology).

According to Heather (1976), there are two significant events that marked the impact of positivism on psychology; first, the publication in 1859 of Darwin's *Origin of Species*, outlining his theory of evolution, and which enabled psychology to be placed firmly within the biological sciences ('man as organism'); and, secondly, the opening of the first psychology laboratory by Wundt in 1879, which created the precedent for the experimental basis on which academic psychology has rested ever since.

The work that Comte began in 1842 culminated in the 1920s in the formation of the Vienna Circle, a group of philosophers (including A. J. Ayer), mathematicians and scientists who attempted to rid philosophy of any statements which could not be publicly verified or empirically tested (ie metaphysical statements). They believed that the scientific path was the only one that could lead to 'the truth' and advance human progress. These *Logical Positivists* were strong supporters of early behaviourism which, in rejecting introspectionism and the study of private, subjective, experience, was trying to put psychology on a public footing, whereby any number of observers could agree about 'the facts'. (We shall discuss later some of the consequences of the behaviourist attempt to confine 'the data' to purely 'objective' facts.) Related to logical positivism is *Materialism* (or *Physicalism*), the belief that all valid propositions (including those to do with consciousness) must be capable of being translated into the language of physics. From this it follows that, eventually, psychology will be 'swallowed up' in the universal science of physics (having first been replaced by physiology and biochemistry etc). This represents an extreme form of *Reductionism* which we shall discuss in detail later in the chapter.

What is Science?

A science may be defined in various ways, but there are certain criteria that must be met:

a) There must be a definable *subject-matter*, that is, what the science is *about*, the range of objects or phenomena it studies;

b) There must be some kind of *theory* construction and *hypothesis* testing. A theory is a complex set of interrelated statements which attempts to explain certain observed phenomena; from a theory, particular statements can be inferred which constitute testable statements about the relationship between two or more variables. These testable statements usually take the form of predictions about what will happen under certain specified conditions and are known as *hypotheses*; it is hypotheses, rather than whole theories, which are empirically tested in scientific research.

c) Facts cannot be established through rational argument (despite the attempts of philosophers or 'armchair' psychologists) but through the use of *empirical* methods of investigation, that is, observation, measurement and other *objective* ways of gathering information (data-collection). The major methods used in psychology are summarized in Figure 2.1 on page 22.

d) Science should attempt to discover general *laws* or principles that govern, in the case of psychology, human behaviour and mental processes and which are intended to be applicable to every member of the human species (ie *universal*).

Induction and Scientific Method

What we have said so far about what constitutes a science would probably be agreed by most psychologists and philosophers of science. But this does not necessarily tell us how scientific activity proceeds, the sequence of 'events' or the precise relationship between theory, hypothesis-testing and the collection of data.

The classic picture of how scientific method goes on is called *induction* (the Inductive Method). Briefly, as a form of reasoning, it involves moving from the particular to the general, that is, drawing general conclusions from a number of separate observations. Medawar (1963) describes the inductive method as a process of scientific discovery in this way: it begins with simple, unbiased, unprejudiced observation and out of this sensory evidence, embodied in the form of simple propositions or declarations of fact, generalizations will grow up and take shape—'Out of the disorderly array of facts an orderly theory, an orderly general statement will somehow emerge'. But three main problems arise from this picture:

a) There is no such thing as 'unbiased' or 'unprejudiced' observation—our perception is always selective and we always interpret what we see (see Chapter 4). As Popper (1972) says, observation is always pre-structured and directed and this is as true of physics as it is of psychology.

b) Induction does not enable us to *prove* general statements, although it may enable us to discover relationships among sense-data, ie, what is observed. (We shall discuss this further when we take a closer look at the psychological experiment.)

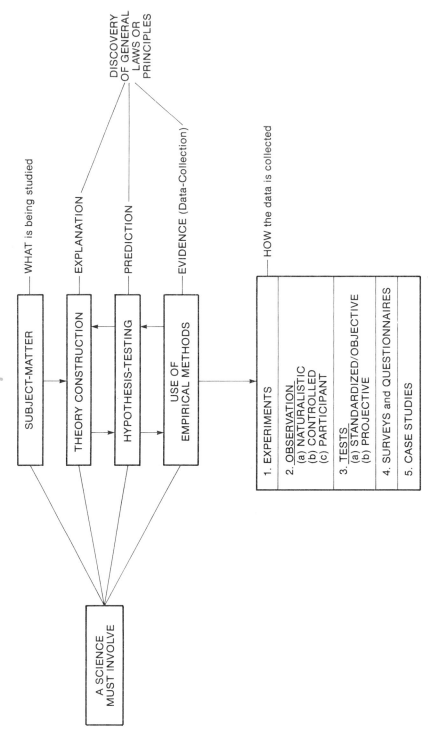

Figure 2.1   The major criteria of a science and the empirical methods used in psychology

c) The sum of inductive statements (separate observations) is unable, logically, to lead to generalizations which are more than the sum of those statements. (This too is discussed later.)

The first problem in particular has led Popper to revise the stages of the scientific process as presented by the inductive method and it may be useful to compare Popper's revised version with the original:

Table 2.1 Comparison of the classical, inductive view of science and Popper's revised version

Inductive method (Classical view of science)	*Popper's version*
1. Observation and Method 2. Inductive Generalization 3. Hypothesis 4. Attempted verification of hypothesis 5. Proof or disproof 6. Knowledge	1. Problem (usually a refutation of an existing theory or prediction), see page 26 2. Proposed solution or new theory 3. Deduction of testable statements from the new theory (ie hypotheses) 4. Tests or attempts to refute by methods including observation and experiment 5. Establishing a preference between competing theories

Popper's version shows quite clearly that observation does not go on in a 'theoretical vacuum' but is related, more or less directly, to some theory.

This point is discussed at length by James Deese (1972), who argues that, despite the essential reliance (like all science) on observation, empirical information (data) plays a more modest role than is normally supposed. The function of empirical observation is *not* to find out what causes what or how things work in some ultimate sense but simply to provide justification for some particular way of looking at the world. In other words, observation justifies (or not) a theory that we (or someone else) already hold and it is theories which determine what kinds of data are collected.

The interdependence between theory and data is shown in Deese's belief that: (a) theory in the absence of data is *not* science; and (b) data alone do not make a science. So both theory and data are necessary for science. But 'data' are not 'facts' in the ordinary sense—they are part of the information needed to establish psychological facts, which depend on the interpretation of data in the light of a theory. 'Data' in Deese's sense correspond to the 'unbiased' observation of the classic, inductive, view of science; 'facts' in Deese's sense correspond to Popper's alternative view. So for Deese, a *Fact* equals *Data* plus *Theory*. When we talk about 'evidence' we normally mean measurement, numbers, recordings etc, which are interpretable in terms of a particular theory, *not* 'pure observations'. (This relates to the issue of objectivity which we shall discuss below.)

Let us now return to the criteria of a science and see how easily (or otherwise) they can be satisfied in the case of psychology.

The Subject-matter of Psychology—What is it About?

As we saw in Chapter 1, definitions of psychology have changed during the past hundred years or so. However, even if there were a single definition that all or most psychologists could agree about, the fact would remain that different schools of thought define the subject-matter rather differently. In particular, each school rests upon a different image of what human beings are like, which in turn determines *what* it is important to study as well as *how* to study it. Consequently, not only do different schools represent different facets of the same discipline but they seem to comprise self-contained disciplines (eg Beloff, 1973). In the words of Kuhn (1962), this state of affairs amounts to the lack of a *paradigm*. According to Kuhn, a philosopher of science, the role of theory is absolutely central to the definition and state of a science and a field of study can only be properly considered a science if a majority of its workers subscribe to a common global theory or perspective, that is, a paradigm. Specifically, a paradigm provides answers to the following questions:

a) What are the fundamental entities which constitute the subject-matter?
b) How do these (fundamental entities) interact with one another and with the human senses?
c) What questions may be legitimately asked about such entities and what techniques used in seeking solutions to them?

In the case of biologists, it is Darwin's theory of evolution which unites them and helps to give them an identity which distinguishes them from say, physicists, whose unifying theory is Einstein's relativity theory. This shared set of assumptions, methods and 'language' is clearly lacking in psychology.

Kuhn identifies three historical stages in the development of a science:

Pre-science	Here no paradigm has been developed and there are several schools of thought.
Normal science	Here a paradigm has emerged and this dictates the kind of research carried out; the results are interpreted so as to be consistent with it. The details of the theory are filled in and workers explore how far the theory can go; disagreements may arise but these can be resolved within the limits allowed by the paradigm.
Revolution	A point is reached, in almost all established sciences, where the conflicting evidence becomes so overwhelming that the old paradigm has to be abandoned, and a new one takes its place (paradigm-shift); for example, Copernican physics was replaced by Newtonian, which itself was displaced by Einstein's theory. When this paradigm-shift occurs, there is a return to normal science.

In terms of these stages, psychology is still pre-scientific; Warren (1971) also takes this view. But Palermo (1971) believes that psychology has already gone through several paradigm shifts. The original paradigm was *Structuralism*, represented most clearly in Wundt's introspectionism, with its emphasis on identifying the elements of the conscious thoughts and feelings of normal human adults. This was replaced by *Behaviourism*, with its emphasis on the objective observation of the behaviour of adults, children and animals. More recently, the rise of *Cognitive Psychology* has once again put 'mind' back on the psychological map; while recognizing that cognitive processes can only be inferred from observable behaviour, it is understood that they can nonetheless be studied using experimental techniques.

Finally, Valentine (1982) claims that behaviourism comes as close to a paradigm as anything could, it provides: (i) a clear definition of the subject-matter, namely behaviour as opposed to mental/cognitive processes or experience; (ii) fundamental assumptions in the shape of the central role of learning (in particular, conditioning) and the analysis of behaviour in stimulus-response terms, the emphasis on the *functional analysis* of behaviour, allowing prediction and control (as opposed to explanation or understanding); and (iii) a methodology, with the controlled experiment at its core.

But a number of points need to be made about Valentine's position. In terms of the distinction made earlier between philosophical and method-ological behaviourism, the strongest claim that could be made is that what unites psychologists is methodological behaviourism. However: (a) clearly not all psychologists are methodological behaviourists, eg psychoanalytic and humanistic psychologists; and (b) methodological behaviourism, as already explained, refers to a way of conducting research and is *not* a theory about the subject-matter of psychology! It seems difficult not to agree with Kuhn that psychology is still in a pre-scientific stage of its development.

There is also a rather ironic twist to Valentine's claim about behaviourism being a paradigm, and that is that the most famous and influential behaviourist, B. F. Skinner, is an 'enemy' of theories in psychology! He maintains (1950) that psychology should aim to predict and control behaviour, not to explain it by use of theory. Theories, he claims, whether they deal with mental processes, physiological processes, or anything else, are not only unnecessary but can create new problems of explanation which can then become 'covered up' and may generate wasteful research. Instead he advocates a much more direct approach which stresses the pursuit of func-tional laws based directly on empirical research.

Skinner's empirical approach rests on the assumption that 'facts' can exist without theory ('pure' facts) and that observation can be non-selective or 'unprejudiced'. But we saw earlier that this is a mistaken view. Also, it seems that prediction of behaviour pre-supposes some theory as to what 'underlies' the behaviour but this is precisely what Skinner's *a-theoretical* approach denies.

Popper (1959) believes that, 'Theories are nets cast to catch what we call "the world", to rationalize, to explain and to master it.' Valentine (1982) believes that theories are both logically and psychologically necessary. But they also serve a very important practical (*heuristic*) function, that is, they guide research; as Allport (1955) puts it, 'theory is the stage upon which experiments are conducted' and it allows us to select from an infinite number of possible experiments.

What makes a Good Theory?

Having discussed the crucial role of theory in scientific activity, we are still left with the complex question of how to decide whether a particular theory is 'good' or not.

R. Murray Thomas (1985) lists nine criteria for evaluating a theory. Taken as a whole, these are not limited to *scientific* criteria, that is, a 'good' theory is not simply one that is 'scientific' and there are other important dimensions of a theory that are taken into account.

1) Perhaps the most important of the scientific criteria is to do with *falsifiability* or *refutability*. The logical positivists advanced the principle of *verification*, which maintains that for a statement to be factually 'true', it must be possible to know how to demonstrate its truth, that is, what observations would lead us, under certain conditions, to accept the statement as being true or reject it as being false. So they believed that science should only concern itself with that which can be completely 'nailed down' or tested— anything else is a pseudo-problem or pseudo-statement (and included in this latter category was Freud's psychoanalytic theory).

However, Popper (1959) argued that the principle of verification was invalid as a way of distinguishing between science and non-science. He maintained that it was too easy to obtain evidence to support a theory; this is precisely the appeal of Freudian theory, according to Popper, because it can explain anything! Since, as we have already seen, observational statements and statements of experimental results are always interpretations of the data in the light of theories, it is deceptively easy to verify a theory. A more stringent and meaningful requirement, according to Popper, is to attempt to *falsify* the theory. But whereas for the logical positivists a non-scientific statement was a meaningless statement, Popper never dismissed non-scientific theory as having no value (as the logical positivists had misinterpreted him as saying). On the contrary, he thought that non-scientific observations might be of considerable importance and he realized that science in the past had emerged from metaphysical or mythical-religious conceptions of the world.

2) A second major criterion is that a good theory should accurately reflect the reality it is trying to explain—this is to do with its *truth value*. The danger with this is that, if used alone or as the major criterion, it forces us to choose between competing theories; for if, for instance, Freudian theory is 'correct' or 'true', then how can Skinner's also be correct or true? Perhaps the solution to this dilemma is to say that these theories are sufficiently different for us to regard both as being 'partially true', they each 'tell the truth' but only about part of the total 'jigsaw'. (See Table 1.1, page 14). In relation to what we said in Chapter 1 about informal psychology, a further requirement of a good theory connected to its truth value is that it should be *reflexive*. This means that any theory of human behaviour must be able to explain how the theory itself came about, because formulating theories is part of the human behaviour the theory is attempting to explain in the first place. Everything that goes under the name of 'scientific activity' is part of the totality of human activity, so psychologists are in the unique position of having to account not only for the behaviour of those they are studying but at the same time having to account for their *own* behaviour in so doing! The psychologist as scientist is engaging in the very same (or at least very similar) activity that the objects

of study are also engaged in—they are part of their own subject-matter. As Heather (1976) puts it, the psychologist is making observations about observers, experimenting with experimenters and theorizing about theorizers.

This conundrum was solved very neatly by George Kelly in his *Personal Construct Theory* in which he proposes the model of 'man the scientist' (see Chapter 25). Heather (1976) believes that the acid test of any psychological theory is whether or not it is capable of explaining its own creation and no behaviourist theory, he maintains, can pass the test!

3)   A good theory should be stated in such a way that it can be clearly understood by anyone who is reasonably competent in English, maths and logical reasoning. Many students complain that psychology textbooks are too wordy and use unnecessarily complex language, and many psychologists criticize certain theories (eg those of Piaget and Freud) for being too vague or imprecise or complex.

4)   A good theory should be able to explain not only past events but also accurately predict future events. In addition, it should enable us to make accurate predictions about the behaviour of a particular individual rather than dealing with general statements about groups of people. This relates to the distinction between *idiographic* and *nomothetic* approaches. Idiographic (from the Greek *idio* meaning 'own', 'personal' or 'private') refers to the study of individuals, while 'nomothetic' ('law-giving' or law-like) refers to the study of groups.

The case study, clearly, is the idiographic method par excellence; Freud used it exclusively (although this did not prevent him formulating a theory meant to apply to *all*). But the case study method makes the use of statistical analysis impossible and mainstream experimental psychology is rooted in the nomothetic approach of natural science, which is concerned with trying to discover general laws. The idiographic approach is concerned with people as unique individuals, as 'singular events' rather than instances of universal laws, and as such, it does not enable generalization beyond the single case, although it may suggest hypotheses that can be tested with other subjects. The nomothetic approach, as it involves several subjects, does enable us to make generalizations about people; it also requires verification through experimental replication and the results to be analysed statistically. Perhaps the most crucial difference is that the nomothetic approach enables us to *predict* with some accuracy future *group* results but it *cannot* help predict the behaviour of an *individual*—the uniqueness of each response is to a large degree 'swallowed up' in the group score. By contrast, the idiographic approach deals with events which never recur in the same form—they can neither be replicated nor predicted!

Allport (1961) believes that psychology should be concerned with the study of the *individual*, not the group, with uniqueness and not commonalities. He used a biographical-type case study which some critics would say is more suitable for history and literature than science. To the extent that scientific psychology must be (predominantly) nomothetic, Allport would conclude that psychology cannot (or should not) be a science. (See Chapter 25.)

5)   A good theory should be *internally consistent*, that is, the different parts of the theory should all fit together to form a coherent structure; there should not be any contradictions between one part of the theory and another, and the terms and concepts used should be logically connected.

6) A good theory should also be *economical*, in the sense that it is based on as few unproven assumptions as possible. Also, the mechanisms it suggests to explain the phenomena in question should be as simple as possible. These requirements are sometimes summed up in 'the law of parsimony' or 'Occam's razor', that is, if we have to choose between two theories which are equally 'good' in all other respects, we should choose the simpler, more economical, theory.

7) A good theory generates a great deal of new research and stimulates general interest and discussion. This is known as the 'fertility criterion' and can take several forms, eg direct replication studies, testing certain assumptions or principles not previously tested, verification studies (to test whether some theoretical assumption is borne out in real life), 'population applicability' (for example, cross-cultural research), and 'extended theorizing' (developing and modifying the original theory, for example, the Neo-Freudians, such as Jung, Adler and Erikson, and Neo-Behaviourists, such as the Social Learning Theorists).

8) A good theory is one we find self-satisfying; this has to do with its intuitive or even aesthetic appeal, which can in no way be measured. It has to do with a feeling that the theory has captured the essence of what it is trying to explain, it 'feels right'. Clearly this is the least scientific of all the nine criteria.

9) A good theory should offer practical guidance in solving everyday problems (eg child-rearing, crime, mental illness); this is related to the *aims* of psychology.

In 1969, the American Psychological Association took at its annual conference the theme of 'Psychology and the problems of Society'. George Miller, who was then president, took as the title of his address 'Psychology as a means of promoting human welfare'. In it, he made the distinction between psychology as a natural science and as a means of changing our image of ourselves.

Psychology as a natural science aims, theoretically, at providing the 'true' view of man's psychological nature and, practically, at applying the theoretical principles discovered to provide behavioural technologies, that is, ways of manipulating our circumstances and behaviour to make them fit our desires and goals. (Examples can be found in behaviour therapy and modification and intelligence testing.) In this context, psychologists become 'the experts', the professionals, who present their findings to the rest (the public at large) and apply these findings in the form of behavioural control. But Miller is unhappy with the idea of psychologists as experts; he believes that of the three aims of psychology as a science, understanding and prediction are more appropriate than control, with understanding being the primary goal.

In its other role, often implicit and unconscious, psychology seems to work to change our beliefs about what we are like as human beings. Rather than discovering means to ends, it may have the effect of influencing the very nature of those ends themselves, helping to create a 'new and different public conception of what is humanly possible and what is humanly desirable,' (George Miller, 1969).

This suggests a tenth criterion of a theory to add to the nine already discussed: a good theory is one which has had a distinct impact upon our image of ourselves, what we think we are like and are capable of, and—in this indirect way—a good theory is one which has an impact upon the way we behave. Indeed, Miller cites Freud's theory in exactly this context and sums up by saying, 'the impact of Freud's thought has been due far less to the instrumentalities he provided than the changed conception of ourselves that he implied'. Freud could be seen as having changed the nature of the problems human beings face and it is in this way, rather than through providing practical solutions to those problems we already have, that psychology in general, and theories in particular, might exert their most powerful and significant influence.

The Methodology of Psychology

In this section, I shall focus on the *experiment*, as this is usually taken to be the most scientific of all methods, the 'method of choice'. This is for three main reasons: (i) it is *replicable*; (ii) it allows us to make statements about *cause* and *effect*; (iii) it permits a considerable degree of *control* which helps to make it the most *objective* method.

How applicable is the experimental method to the study of people?

Replicability (Repeatability)
A fundamental requirement of all scientific research is that workers in the field should be able to check each others' findings; the purpose of publishing a detailed report of a piece of research is precisely so that others can see for themselves exactly what was done. This is not because of a lack of trust, but because we cannot *generalize* from the results of a single experiment; this may be due to the fact that the sample used in a particular study was unusual or a-typical in some way and hence was *unrepresentative*. (This often happens in A-level experiments because of the difficulty of finding a wide range of subjects.) Since most scientific theories are intended to apply to *all* cases of a similar kind (eg all situations in which two chemicals are combined or where human subjects have to recall a list of words in any order), we must try to ensure that the results reflect the theory rather than the particular sample of subjects used. The more often an experiment is repeated (which necessarily entails different samples being used each time), with the same results obtained, the more confident one can be that the theory being tested is valid.

Perhaps a more fundamental reason for repeating a study is that no one test of a theory can ever completely *prove* it. The concept of proof in science (as opposed to, say, maths) is very complex and to ask 'Is theory X true?' or 'Has theory Y been proven?' is really to ask the wrong kinds of questions. More usefully, we should ask 'How much, or what kind of, evidence is there to support the theory?' In practice, what often happens is that part of a theory finds fairly consistent support while another part does not. (Remember, only *parts* of a theory are tested at one time, not the whole theory.) The important point here is that there is no such thing as absolute proof in psychology or any other science: there can only be a series of tests of a particular hypothesis (sometimes with variations), an accumulated series of results which, on balance, tend to support (or otherwise) the theory from which the hypothesis has been derived.

Use of statistics

Once we have collected our data it has to be interpreted: what do our facts and figures mean, what do they tell us, how do they relate to our hypothesis? Usually, this interpretation involves the use of statistical procedures which both *describe* the data, thus making it easier to understand, and, through the use of tests of significance, tell us the *probability* of our results having occurred by chance alone. It is important to note here that probability is the best we can hope for—there is no certainty in science; in any particular study, the most we can conclude is that the hypothesis has been supported *on this occasion*. The more times that different researchers produce evidence to support the hypothesis, the more 'faith' we can put in it; belief in the validity of a theory is very much a matter of faith, but it is faith based on 'public' evidence.

Returning to our original theme of replicability, another fundamental reason for repeating experiments is that all scientific method is based on induction, the basis of which is reasoning from the *particular* to the *general*, from particular observations to general conclusions. Yet however many observations of the 'same' phenomenon are made, each observation (which can include an experiment to test a hypothesis) is only a *specific* observation and there can be no logical certainty that the observation will be made again even under 'identical' conditions. A classic philosophical example is that although the sun has always risen in the past, there is no certainty that it will rise tomorrow! (But there's a very good chance that it will.) Therefore we need as many demonstrations of a particular hypothesis as possible, since there is no logical guarantee that the same results will be obtained next time.

But in what sense is a replication a test of the same hypothesis? Clearly, there is a sense in which any experiment can only be carried out *once* (just as a teacher can only give the 'same' lesson once or a cook make the 'same' meal once); it is a unique event. What is being repeated is a test of the *essential characteristics* of the experiment, but just what these are can be a matter of interpretation. This can be seen by asking the following three questions:

i)   How typical of people in general are the human *subjects* used by psychologists?

ii)   How typical of real-life situations are the *situations* in which psychologists study people?

iii) How typical of human behaviour is the behaviour of *non-human subjects* used by psychologists?

i) We said earlier that one reason for replication is that we cannot generalize from the results of a single experiment, often because the subject sample is unrepresentative. It is certainly much more difficult to generalize about people than it is about, say, chemicals; in other words, particular human subjects are much *less representative* of people in general than a particular sample of a certain chemical is of that chemical. This raises the question of *biased* or unrepresentative sampling.

George Miller (1967) estimated that 90 per cent of American experiments have used college students (who are accessible and 'cheap') and yet the results still tend to be generalized to the American population as a whole, and often beyond that to the British, Western Europe etc. But there is no reason to believe that American college students are typical of any group, in terms of gender, intelligence, age, personality, social class background or any other *subject variables* which can influence how subjects will perform in an experimental situation.

Again, volunteers for psychology experiments are a self-selected group. Ora (1965), for instance, found that volunteers tend to be abnormally insecure, dependent on and influenced by others, aggressive, neurotic and introverted.

ii) Most experiments are conducted in laboratories—strange and contrived environments in which people are asked to perform unusual or even bizarre tasks. How can we be sure that the way people behave in the laboratory is an accurate indication of how they behave outside, in 'real life?' Heather (1976) believes that we cannot. In his view, 'Psychologists have attempted to squeeze the study of human life into a laboratory situation where it becomes unrecognizably different from its naturally occurring form.' The artificiality of the lab, together with the 'unnatural' things that the subjects may be asked to do, jointly produce a distortion of behaviour. The very term 'subject' implies that the participant is being treated as something less than a person, a de-humanized and de-personalized 'object' that fits the mechanistic view of man which is at the root of empirical (methodological) behaviourism. (We should note that experiments *can* be conducted in natural settings, in which case they are called *field experiments*. An experiment is defined not by where it is conducted but by how—it is the experimenter's manipulation of the independent variable, plus the control of all the other relevant variables, that makes an investigation experimental. But for practical reasons, experiments are usually carried out in a laboratory setting).

iii) The question of *animal experiments* is important because of the extent to which they are used in many areas of psychology; clearly, although a great deal of animal research is conducted for its own sake, much is also under-taken in order to help us to understand human behaviour. How can it do this?

a)   There is an underlying evolutionary continuity between man and other species which gives rise to the assumption that differences between man and other species are merely *quantitative* (as opposed to qualitative), ie other species may display more simple behaviour and have more primitive nervous systems than humans but they are not of a different order from humans. So, it is believed, it is valuable to study these more simple cases in order to understand the more complex ones.

b)   Animals are smaller and therefore easier to study in the laboratory: they have much shorter life-spans and periods of gestation and maturation, so it is much easier to study their development—many generations can be studied in a relatively short time.

c)   Animal studies can provide useful hypotheses for subsequent testing on human subjects and, equally important, animals can be used to test cause-and-effect relationships where the existing human evidence is only corre-lational (eg the relationship between smoking and lung-cancer).

d)   It is legally permitted to use much more rigorous experimental controls with animals than with humans, for example, inter-breeding (to study genetic influences), subjecting young animals to all kinds of deprivation (sensory, perceptual, maternal, social etc), surgically, and in other ways, interfering with their brains etc. The ethical status of these experiments is often very dubious. However, we can never be *certain* that the mechanisms involved in the behaviour of one species are the same as those involved in the behaviour of others; ultimately, we have to test the particular species whose behaviour we are trying to explain and this is true even when the species being compared are very closely related on the evolutionary scale. Humans are *not* chimpanzees, rats or pigeons, and even if human behaviour appears to be very similar to that of some simpler species, we cannot be sure that it 'works' in exactly the same way. When we try to explain human behaviour in terms of how rats perform in Skinner boxes, for example, we are committing the sin of *ratomorphism* (Koestler 1970). The opposite, but equally sinful, error is that of *anthropomorphism*, that is, attributing human-like qualities or motives to non-human organisms or objects.

Cause and Effect

This represents another aspect of induction, as well as another 'symptom' of the positivistic/mechanistic nature of academic psychology. According to Heather (1976), to say that psychology is mechanistic in nature implies a view of people as some complex piece of machinery, inert and passive, propelled into motion only by the action of some force (either external or internal) upon them; their behaviour is fully explicable, in principle, in terms of 'causes' over which they have no control.

The notion of cause is a complex one and there are different opinions regarding exactly what constitute the logical grounds for inferring a cause-and-effect relationship for some empirical observation. But it is generally agreed that a 'cause' cannot be *directly* observed; strictly speaking, all that can be observed are two events appearing close together in space and/or time (the principle of *contiguity*).

One view is that the cause must be both a *necessary* and *sufficient* condition for the appearance of the effect and (usually) the cause must *precede* the effect. To take the biological example of the knee-jerk reflex, the reflex will only occur when the knee is struck in a particular spot (corresponding to the tap-on-the-knee as a *necessary* condition) and it occurs every time the knee is tapped (corresponding to the tap-on-the-knee as a *sufficient* condition). The tap-on-the-knee, of course, also precedes the leg shooting up in the air.

To put it more formally: (i) A (the tap-on-the-knee) *must* occur for B (the reflex) to occur, and in the absence of A, B never happens; (ii) B always occurs when A occurs—A never happens without B following. This relationship must, of course, be demonstrated on several occasions, and the more often this happens, the more confident we can be that a cause-and-effect relationship does exist.

According to Watson's early brand of behaviourism, the cause (or antecedent events) was presumed to be limited to events in the outside world, the 'stimuli' which elicited responses (effect) from the passive organism (see Chapter 3). Although this philosophical behaviourism has now largely been replaced by methodological behaviourism, the basic mechanistic notion of cause still tends to dominate. Sometimes the Independent Variable (IV) is thought of as a cause and the Dependent Variable (DV) as the effect. But the IV and DV are much more general than cause and effect: the IV is what the experimenter manipulates (systematically varies), for example, the amount of sleep subjects have, and the DV is some aspect of the subject's behaviour (which varies as a function of differences in the IV), for example, the ability to recall a poem.

Using the necessary and sufficient condition criteria, we could not say (assuming that subjects with no sleep do significantly worse than the others) that lack of sleep is a *necessary* condition of poor recall (since other factors could also account for the poor recall, eg alcohol), but it could be a *sufficient* condition (the lack of sleep alone produced poor recall). The lack of sleep also preceded the poor recall. However, as alcohol could produce similar results as well, lack of sleep can hardly be thought of as a sufficient condition of poor recall in the way that a tap on the knee is a sufficient condition of the knee-jerk reflex. Most human behaviour has multiple causes.

Because of the complexity of the notion of cause, as well as the complexity of most behaviour, psychologists tend to avoid the terms cause and effect altogether. More commonly they talk about 'variable X systematically vary-ing as variable Y is varied' or 'changes in variable X producing changes in variable Y' or 'the conditions under which such-and-such behaviour occurs'.

Deese (1972) makes the important point that, ultimately, what is taken as a cause and an effect is an inference arising *not* from direct observation but from the theory from which the hypothesis being tested has been derived: it is the theory which states what is necessary and sufficient for the production of certain events, it is the theory which states what is supposed to influence what.

An alternative view altogether is put forward by Heather (1976), namely, that human beings are the causes of their own behaviour. This view regards people as *agents*, in sharp contrast to the mechanistic view described at the beginning of this section.

Control and Objectivity

The purpose of control is to enable the experimenter to isolate the one key variable which has been selected (the IV), in order to observe its effect on some other variable (the DV); control is intended to allow us to conclude that it is the IV and nothing else which is influencing the DV.

But how do we know when we have controlled *all* the variables? It is fairly easy to control the more obvious ones (eg *situational* variables such as room temperature, noise levels, and instructions, and *subject* variables, such as gender, age, and intelligence), but for every variable that is controlled there is probably at least one which is not! It is the purpose of different kinds of *experimental design* to control subject variables. But it is never possible to control these completely; it is the *variability* of human beings that makes them so much more difficult to study scientifically than, say, chemicals. (See Miller, 1984.) The important point here is that what is controlled and what is not is based on the judgement and intuition of the experimenter—what they think is important (and possible) to control. This is hardly the kind of degree of objectivity normally associated with the scientific experiment!

Clearly, control and objectivity are matters of *degree* only and it is unreasonable and unrealistic to expect total objectivity in any science, even physics. As Popper (1972) has said, it is unrealistic—because impossible—to regard any observation as being totally objective, value-free or uninfluenced by the experimenter's interests, preferences or expectations.

In addition to the impossibility of complete control, there is a problem involved in assuming that the IV (or 'stimulus' or 'input') is identical for *all* subjects and that the DV (or 'response' or 'output') is dependent on what the former is, in some objectively definable sense. Many psychologists are very critical of this assumption (eg Joynson, 1974, Heather, 1976, Lewis 1977). The notion of a stimulus (as defined by behaviourists, anyway) implies that it can be defined independently of the particular subject presented with it and that it has a standard effect on all subjects; but it seems in practice very difficult to give a completely objective definition.

One such attempt is made by Broadbent (1961), a leading British behaviourist, who defines a stimulus in terms of the physical stimulation impinging on the subject's sense organs; but this completely ignores the distinction between sensation—what 'the eye' sees—and perception—what 'the seer' sees (see Chapter 4). Perception involves an interpretation of the sense-data provided by the stimulus; the subject's past experience, motivational state, expectations and so on help to determine the *meaning* of the stimulus for the subject and, in turn, the meaning helps determine the subject's response. There is a sense in which, in a purely objective way, the stimulus does not exist: what the stimulus really is, is how it is interpreted by the subject and this will differ from subject to subject.

If the stimulus has meaning for the subject, then it follows that the response is not a passive reaction produced by the stimulus but is itself meaningful; and it acquires this through what the subject is trying to do. Heather (1976) argues that a 'science of persons' would stress that human action is always directed to the *future*, rather than being reactions to past events (ie the stimulus). Broadbent gives an objective definition of a response as 'events at those parts of the body which act on the outer world' or 'muscular contractions'. But 'muscular contractions' or movements have no meaning in themselves—they only acquire their meaning when they form part of a series of movements intended to achieve some goal (in which case we call them *actions*). It is no easy matter trying to describe what we do except in terms of what we are trying to achieve by doing it, whether it is scratching your back, writing an essay, or eating. The further we go in trying to break these actions down into their component parts (ie the muscle movements involved), the further removed we become from the categories we normally use to think about human behaviour. And the further we go, the less meaningful the descriptions become, for example we could analyse 'eating' by describing the individual action of picking up the fork, moving it down towards the plate, piercing a piece of food etc, but could we analyse each of these further and still be describing actions (as opposed to movements)? What Broadbent is advocating is a form of Reductionism, an attempt to 'reduce' actions to muscle movements in the name of objectivity. (We shall take a closer look at Reductionism below.)

The Psychology Experiment as a Social Situation

Another way of exploring the issue of objectivity is to look more closely at what is involved in an experiment where a human experimenter tests a human subject. Clearly, the situation is not equivalent to that in which a human experimenter investigates some part of the physical world—people are *not* inanimate objects but animate, conscious, thinking beings.

A more accurate way of thinking about the psychological experiment is as a *social situation*, which entails mutual expectations by participants. How are the expectations of the subject and the experimenter related?

The Subject's Expectations
On the subject's side are what Orne (1962) has called the *demand characteristics* of experiments. Whereas in the mechanistic model the emphasis is usually on what is *done to* the (passive) subject, Orne is interested in what the human subject *does*. The subject's performance in an experiment could almost be conceptualized as problem-solving behaviour since, at some level, they see it as their task to ascertain the true purpose of the experiment and to respond in a manner which will support the hypothesis being tested. In this context, the totality of *cues* which convey an experimental hypothesis to the subject become significant determinants of the subject's behaviour and it is the sum total of those cues that Orne labels the 'demand characteristics of the experimental situation'.

So the subject is on a constant 'look-out' for cues about how to behave— what do these cues include? As well as the actual communication during the experiment itself (both explicitly in the form of instructions and implicitly in the form of non-verbal communication), cues include whatever the subject might already have heard about the experiment (eg from other subjects), the way the subject is approached initially and asked to volunteer, the person of the experimenter, and the setting of the experiment. It is very difficult in practice to find truly naïve subjects who do not believe they have at least some familiarity with psychology, or who cannot infer the purpose of the experiment from the procedure. The central point is that the subject is not a passive responder but is actively engaged in trying to work out what is going on and how they should perform.

This tendency to identify the demand characteristics is related to the tendency to play the role of 'a good experimental subject', wanting to please and co-operate with the experimenter and not to 'upset the experiment'. It is mainly in this sense that Orne sees the experiment as a 'social situation'. The demand characteristics of the situation help define what the role of 'good experimental subject' is and the subject's responses are a function of the role that is created.

The Experimenter's Expectations
On the other hand, the experimenter unconsciously conveys to the subject how the subject should behave; this is referred to as *experimenter bias*. The point is that the experimenter is unaware of the influence he may be exerting (often in the form of non-verbal messages) on the subject. This was demonstrated by Rosenthal (1966) who put hundreds of his psychology students in the role of experimenter with rats as subjects. He told half the experimenters that they would be studying a strain of 'maze-bright' rats (bred from intelligent stock) and the other half that they would be studying 'maze-dull' rats. In fact, the rats were all 'average' and were randomly allocated to the two groups, yet the first group of experimenters reported

significantly better performance on maze-learning for their rats than the second group.

With human subjects, the experimenter's expectations are likely to be all the more important since, as we have seen, they are looking for all the available cues to help them successfully play their 'role'; and so, unwittingly, the experimenter may be influencing the subject's actual behaviour!

Removing Bias
Can anything be done to prevent these sources of bias?

The answer is 'Yes', first by making sure that the subjects do not know under what conditions they are being tested. This, in fact, is standard practice but will never eliminate the impact of demand characteristics altogether. Perhaps the clearest example of where this can be effective is in tests of drug-effects, where control subjects are given a sugar pill or other 'placebo' while the experimental subjects receive the real drug (*single-blind technique*).

Better still, as a way of reducing experimenter bias, is to ensure that the experimenter also does not know which subjects have been given the drug and which the placebo; for example, the experimenter who administers the drug or placebo is not the one who measures the effects (*double-blind technique*).

However, by using these two methods of control, we have not changed the nature of the experimental situation from a social to a non-social one: we have merely altered certain aspects of the situation in which subjects try to make sense of an often bewildering and apparently senseless experience. Perhaps by removing some of the potential sources of bias, the experience is made all the more bewildering and their need to search for demand characteristics is made all the more necessary.

Reductionism

We have criticized the attempt by extreme behaviourists to 'reduce' actions to 'muscular contractions' by pointing out that, whereas actions are meaningful (and purposeful), muscle movements are not. What Broadbent advocates stems from his attempt to make psychology objective, to rid it of all 'mentalistic' language, since 'muscle movements' are publicly observable while 'thoughts' and 'intentions' etc are private and inaccessible to others. So we can say that philosophical behaviourists are trying to reduce 'the mind' to a series of muscle movements (often they make do with talking about stimulus –response or S–R connections). The logical conclusion of this is to explain mental processes and behaviour in terms of physiology (especially neurophysiology), biochemistry, chemistry, and ultimately, physics (the primary science). If we want to get to the 'ultimate truth' of something, we must seek more minute units of analysis; even to talk about 'S–R connections' represents a much 'larger' unit of analysis than, for instance, a description of the neurons (brain-cells) involved in those connections, with 'muscular contractions' representing an intermediate unit. Similarly, an account of the neurons represents a 'larger' unit of analysis than an account of the atoms and molecules of which they are composed.

According to this view, behaviourism could be regarded as an intermediate or transitional stage in the ultimate rejection of traditional, mentalistic, psychological concepts; that is, ultimately psychology (in any form) will be reduced to (and replaced by) microphysics.

But is this reductionist approach acceptable or even meaningful? Can a thorough knowledge of the primary sciences (even if this is attained) ever replace the need for psychological explanations? There are several objections which have been raised by psychologists and others. First, Legge (1975) considers the example of signing our name. Although this could (in principle) be explained in terms of nerve activity and muscle movement, the real importance of a signature is its *social* (psychological) meaning. As we saw above, only actions are meaningful and the vast majority of our actions derive their meaning from their relevance to our interactions with others (see Chapter 8).

Secondly, even if we could reduce signing our name in this way, we would only be specifying what nerve activity and muscle movements are involved in a *particular instance* of name-signing, and not every possible instance. The point is that we can sign our name in many different ways, for example, by holding the pen in our mouth, or using a stick in the sand or using chalk on a wall, and each involves a different combination of brain and muscle activity; the 'act' of signing our name is largely independent of any particular physiological activity that may be involved. Clearly, even with a complete knowledge of physiology, a psychological explanation is more appropriate and useful, which raises the issue of *levels* of *explanation*.

Rose (1976) argues that the controversy surrounding the reductionist issue stems from a semantic confusion (a confusion over word-meanings), namely, an equation of 'explaining' and 'explaining away'. If we are trying to get rid of psychological explanations altogether, replacing them with neurophysiological ones, then this is the 'unacceptable face' of reductionism. But if an explanation of brain function is used to enhance or complement our psychological explanation, then this is no threat to psychology.

Rose believes that the confusion between 'explaining' and 'explaining away' can be removed by introducing the concept of a *hierarchy of levels of explanation*.

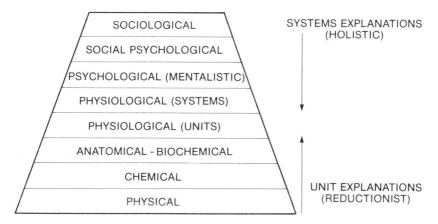

Figure 2.2   Hierarchical levels of explanation (from Rose, 1976)

These different hierarchical levels correspond to different scientific disciplines; as you move up the hierarchy, the size of the unit of description increases (*holistic*) but there is an inverse relationship between size and complexity, so that as you move up the units also become less complex. By the same token, as you move down the hierarchy, the units become smaller and more complex (*reductionist*). Also, the fundamental explanations in a particular discipline can be found at some lower or more basic level. For example, what physics can tell us about atoms can provide explanations relevant to chemistry (eg how atoms are joined to form molecules), and psychology can be seen as providing 'basic' explanations for sociology (eg how memory and perception work).

Rose's major point is that each level involves a different 'universe of discourse', that is, a different set of concepts and terminology, a different way of conceptualizing the 'same' phenomena, and because they are different, one cannot be substituted for another. Levels lower down in the hierarchy cannot replace levels higher up because they are doing essentially different jobs; each is valid in its own right and what makes one level of explanation the 'right' one is the *purpose* of the explanation at any particular time, what sort of answer we want and why we want it. For example, since the larger, higher-level explanations are more 'economical' than the smaller, lower-level ones (ie it is easier and faster to talk about 'signing our name' than to describe all the brain and muscle activity involved), the former will generally be more effective for the purposes of communication, either between individuals or within one's own head.

The Reductionist controversy has probably generated more heat over the *mind–body* problem than any other, and to this we now turn.

The Mind–Body Problem (Or the Problem of Mind and Brain)

This is concerned with the relationship between mind (or consciousness) and neurophysiological processes, in particular, brain activity. Much of the controversy within psychology regarding the place of 'mind' in a scientific psychology, culminating in the rise of behaviourism in America, stems from the *dualism* of the seventeenth-century French philosopher, Déscartes. He distinguished between 'mind' and 'body', the latter being 'reduced' to a machine driven by a hydraulic system of vital liquids running through the nerves. According to Déscartes, the mind (or soul) was located in the brain's pineal gland, and was seen as driving the body through the brain and nerves, but it is qualitatively different from the body, non-physical and non-material. His famous '*cogito ergo sum*' ('I think, therefore I am') implied that what makes human beings different from animals is the possession of a mind or soul and this is the essence of man. Dualism remained the dominant view of the mind–body issue until Watson's behaviourist manifesto in 1913.

If we accept that mind and body are fundamentally different, the problem remains as to how we are to understand their relationship. The major proposed solutions are summarized in Figure 2.3.

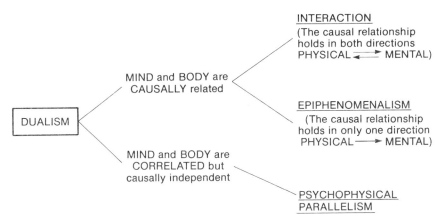

Figure 2.3 The dualism between mind and body

Interaction

Both common sense and ordinary language seem to attribute both mental and physical events with causal power. For instance, we talk about 'mind over matter' and there seems to be some medical support for this view—as in the case of cancer patients who help to beat their disease through their determination to get better. Psychosomatic illness is usually defined as caused by stress or other psychological factors, although the physical symptoms are very real, eg stomach ulcers; and the whole concept of voluntary actions and movements depends upon the belief that willing or deciding to move our arm, for example, will result in our arm moving. Similarly, we often attribute changes in our perceptions to 'mind-changing' drugs (eg the hallucinogens) through their effect on brain chemicals, or changes in intelligence or personality to brain damage or surgery.

But despite these examples, it is difficult to understand how something physical and spatial can influence something that is non-physical and non-spatial (and vice-versa). Where, for instance, does the interaction occur?

Valentine (1982) believes that in the case of apparent interaction (as in the examples above), we simply choose to focus attention on one aspect of the cause and the other aspect of the effect, and this does not preclude the existence of the other correlated aspect. For example, we may choose to say that some psychological stress has caused a stomach ulcer, but this does not preclude some unmentioned physiological state that is correlated with the stress.

Boden (1972) prefers to think of 'the mind' as guiding, rather than causing, physical movements.

Epiphenomenalism

While granting that mental and physical events are different, epiphenomenalists argue that mental experiences or processes are non-causal by-products of physical processes; only physical processes have causal power. A consequence of this view is that mental processes have no part to play in the explanation of behaviour and so can be disregarded for that purpose; this is a view adopted by B. F. Skinner, although he is often taken to reject the concept of mind altogether (as did Watson).

Psychophysical Parallelism

It was the philosopher Leibniz (in 1714) who first argued that mental and physical events occur simultaneously (like two synchronized clocks or orchestras) but do not causally influence each other. In psychology, Wundt was one early advocate of this view, as were the Gestalt psychologists (see Chapter 4) who maintained that there is a one-to-one correspondence between how a stimulus is perceived and how it is represented in the brain, a correspondence they called *isomorphism*. A good deal of physiological psychology also assumes this view.

But clearly, any kind of simple correlation is often missing; for example, depression could be associated with a variety of physical states and, conversely, the same physical state (e.g. arousal) could be associated with a number of psychological states.

If we reject Dualism, the main alternative is Monism, which can take two major forms, as seen in Figure 2.4.

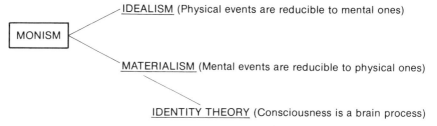

Figure 2.4   Monism

Idealism

According to this view, only mental phenomena are real. Berkeley (1710) argued that *'esse'* is *'percipi'* (to be is to be perceived); the universe is occupied only by minds, physical objects being entirely dependent on these and existing solely as ideas in someone's mind.

Most psychologists and philosophers would not accept this view and it also seems to be anti-commonsense. But humanistic psychologists, strongly influenced by phenomenology, do stress the fundamental nature of experience and the dependence of our knowledge of the external world on how we interpret and define it. It is, of course, a view which is rejected out of hand by philosophical behaviourists.

Materialism (or Physicalism)

This maintains the opposite of idealism, namely, that only physical phenomena are real, and lies at the heart of the Reductionist approach; Watson favoured this view. But how would it explain, for instance, non-organic psychological disorders (eg neurosis)? Psychiatrists tend to be materialists and assume that, eventually, organic causes will be found for all kinds of disorder (see Chapter 28) but, interestingly, Freud started out as a materialist but had to acknowledge the reality of psychic phenomena which form the very basis of psychoanalytic theory.

Identity Theory

This is a recently popular form of materialism which claims that consciousness *is* a brain process, in the same way that 'heat is mean kinetic energy' or a 'gene is a section of the DNA molecule'. This form of identity is contingent (true as a matter of fact) as opposed to logical (true by definition), the latter being stronger; but contingent identity is stronger than correlation. When we say that consciousness is a brain process, what is implied is that both consciousness and the brain process refer to the same thing (contingent identity), but they do not have the same meaning (as do 'brother' and 'male sibling', for example).

An important difference between Materialism and Identity Theory is that, if mental processes are contingently identical with brain processes (as the latter maintains), then mental processes, as much as brain processes, are capable of causally influencing behaviour.

Joynson (1972) believes that Identity Theory represents a 'purely verbal solution which dissolves into what is effectively dualism, at any attempt to put it into practice'. Borst (1970) claims that Identity Theory could hardly apply to all mental concepts, eg promising, and Gray (1971) rejects it on the grounds of not being very fruitful for research—if identity is assumed, it precludes further investigation and the possible discovery of non-identity.

Finally, more radical solutions have been proposed by those who reject both Dualism and Monism. For example, Ryle (1949) believes that the distinction between mind and body is purely grammatical, whereby matter is usually described using nouns and pronouns, and mind using verbs, adverbs and adjectives. So all language describing states of mind can be shown, on analysis, to be behaviour and possible behaviour (Ryle's position is known as *logical behaviourism*).

Valentine (1982) believes that the best solution may be the *double-aspect theory*, a sophisticated variant of parallelism, which gives credence to the reality of mental and physical processes but claims that these are merely two aspects of the same fundamental underlying reality. The main philosophical objection to this view is that the 'underlying reality' remains essentially unknowable. In terms of the hierarchical levels of explanation that we discussed above, Rose (1976) believes that the concept of mind resides at a higher hierarchical level than the concept of brain processes.

Free Will Versus Determinism

Like the mind–body issue, free will versus determinism is one of the most intractable philosophical problems that still 'haunts' psychology. It also seems to capture the basic conflict between the commonsense view of ourselves and the view that is offered by scientific psychology.

Our everyday, intuitive, commonsense understanding is that people have the ability to choose their own course of action, to determine their lives and, to this extent, have free will. At the same time, this freedom is exercised only within certain limits set by physical, political, sociological and other environmental factors.

The concept of free will is also inextricably linked to the concept of responsibility; we normally think of people as being *morally responsible* for what they do since they are the 'cause' of what they do—they are not driven by powerful outside forces. This view is embodied in the law, of course, which also allows for exceptional cases, such as 'diminished responsibility' or 'unfit to plead because of insanity' (see Chapter 28).

Yet the positivistic/mechanistic nature of scientific psychology implies a very different view, namely that behaviour is determined by external events or stimuli and that people are passive responders and, to this extent, are not free. Determinism also implies that behaviour occurs in a regular, orderly manner which is totally predictable (at least in principle) and that every human action has a cause.

Several points need to be made here:

a) First, from our discussion above of the inductive nature of science, it should be clear that total predictability is impossible (Popper, 1950). The past does not logically guarantee the future; and if this is true of classical physics, how much more true is it of human behaviour? So if determinism's main requirement is that behaviour should be completely predictable, it does not seem to pose the same 'threat' to the free-will view as it might seem to.

b) We have already argued that the free-will view regards people as the cause of their own behaviour, so the two views are not opposed on the grounds of whether or not behaviour is *caused*, but rather in relation to the source and nature of the cause. (The opposite of 'caused', strictly speaking, is 'random' and no one would seriously argue that human nature is random; indeed, it would be difficult to reconcile moral responsibility with the idea of randomness.)

c) An important distinction can be made between coercion or compulsion on the one hand and determinism on the other. Free acts are free from coercion or compulsion, but this is consistent with them being determined (this view is called *soft determinism*).

So 'soft determinism' represents one attempt to reconcile the free will and determinism arguments. Another is provided by Heather (1976) who points out that we can describe human behaviour in lawful terms and still 'give man his freedom'. How? By thinking of man as a rule-following animal. Much of our social behaviour is highly predictable and there is a great deal of regularity about it; for instance, 'Would you pass the salt, please?', followed by, 'Yes certainly'. Although the response is very predictable it is far from being inevitable, nor is it 'caused' by the initial request; in principle, at least, we are free to ignore the request or we may give an unexpected reply, such as 'Why, what's wrong with my cooking?'.

The 'rules' of social interaction are, of course, often *implicit* and should not be equated with the formal or explicit rules of a game of football. Nonetheless, to see human behaviour as governed by rules allows us to: (a) predict it, within certain limits; and (b) continue to think of humans as fundamentally free.

Skinner's Rejection of Free Will

Probably the most outspoken advocate of the view that man is *not* free is B. F. Skinner (see Chapters 3 & 29). In *Beyond Freedom and Dignity* (1971) he argues that behavioural freedom is an illusion.

When negative reinforcers (ie consequences that an organism will work to escape from or avoid) are considered along with positive ones ('rewards'), then almost *all* behaviour is controlled by the contingencies of reinforcement which occur constantly in the environment. When we believe we are behaving 'freely' we are merely free of negative reinforcement or its threat; our behaviour is still *determined* by the pursuit of things that have been positively reinforcing in the past, and consists of responses that have previously been positively reinforced. When we perceive others as behaving 'freely' we are merely unaware of their reinforcement histories and the contingencies that govern their behaviour. So, for Skinner, the doctrine of 'autonomous man', upon which so many social institutions are based, is illusory.

Based on his work with rats and pigeons, which shows that behaviour is more efficiently controlled through the use of positive reinforcement (rather than negative reinforcement or punishment), Skinner advocates that we should abandon our illusory beliefs in behavioural freedom, accept the inevitability of control, and design an environment in which behaviour will be directed towards socially desirable ends exclusively through the use of positive reinforcement. This is the key to Skinner's imaginary utopia described in his 1948 novel *Walden Two*.

If Skinner is advocating positive reinforcement as a *means* to achieving a socially desirable goal, the question still remains as to who is to say what those goals should be. Skinner urges psychologists themselves not to be shy about participating in the shaping of policies of control; but in so doing, would they not be exercising their free will? For Skinner, there seems to be no contradiction in the idea of a few, more powerful, individuals deciding to create a totalitarian society in which the majority is controlled, externally, through conditioning techniques, which is what he describes in *Walden Two* and is advocating now for the 'real' world.

Ethics of Psychological Research

Space only permits a brief discussion of this important issue, but there must be at least some recognition of the often subtle ethical problems raised by research involving human subjects.

These problems are often especially pertinent in the case of non-adult subjects. Both the American Psychological Association (1972) and the Society for Research in Child Development (1973) have produced written guidelines and principles for research in general and with children in particular. For example, the researcher should respect the child's freedom to choose to participate in research and to discontinue participation at any time. Also the researcher must obtain the 'informed consent' of the parents if the child cannot choose (by virtue of age or handicap) and must not use any research that may harm the child in any way, physically or psychologically.

The British Psychological Society (1978) has also approved a set of ethical principles, similar to the American ones. The welfare of the child or adult must always be put before the researcher's needs or interests, the identity of subjects must be concealed, and deceiving the subject as to the true purpose of the research (especially experiments) must be avoided unless absolutely necessary (in which case the subject must be 'de-briefed' at the conclusion of the study).

3

Learning

We have already seen how the behaviourist approach has exerted a major influence in psychology. In view of the central role of learning in philosophical behaviourism, it is not surprising that the topic of learning should itself be one of the most researched and discussed in the whole of psychology.

However, the concept of learning illustrates very well the discrepancy between the everyday, commonsense use of a term and its technical, scientific, use (see Chapter 1).

Learning as 'What is Learned' and as 'How it is Learned'

When the layperson talks about learning the emphasis is usually on *what* has been learned, for example, learning to drive or to use a computer, learning French or learning about the causes of the Vietnam war. But when psychologists use the term, their focus is on the *process* of learning itself, almost irrespective of the end product; they ask 'How does it work?' rather than, 'What does it lead to?'.

Another important difference is that when we focus on the end-product we tend to judge the learning to be deliberate; when you learn to drive, for example, you pay to acquire certain specific skills which will get you your driving licence. But for the psychologist, learning can take place without there being a 'teacher' as such: we can learn by merely observing others who may not even know they are being watched, let alone trying to teach us anything. We can also learn without other people being involved at all; for example, if two 'events' occur often enough in the environment (eg lightning followed by thunder) then we can learn about how they are related without anyone trying to teach us.

How Can Learning be Defined?

As we saw in Chapter 1, learning is a hypothetical construct, that is, it cannot be directly observed but can only be inferred from observable behaviour. So, for example, if a person's performance on a task at Time 1 differs in any particular way or to some degree from performance on the task at Time 2, we may infer that learning has taken place. But if that change is observed on just that one occasion we would be much more hesitant about making such an inference. Learning, therefore, normally implies a fairly permanent change in a person's behavioural performance. Again, temporary fluctuations in behaviour can occur as a result of fatigue, drugs, temperature changes, and so on, and this is another reason for taking *permanence* as a minimum requirement for saying that learning has taken place.

However, permanent changes in behaviour can also result from things that have nothing to do with learning, for example, the effects of brain damage on behaviour, or the changes associated with puberty and other maturational processes. So to call behavioural change a case of learning, the change must be linked in some way to past experience of some kind (regardless of whether there was any attempt to bring about that change).

For these reasons, psychologists usually define learning as, 'a relatively permanent change in behaviour due to past experience' (Coon, 1983), or, 'a relatively permanent change in behavioural potential which accompanies experience but which is not the result of simple growth factors or of reversible influences such as fatigue or hunger' (Kimble, 1961).

Learning Versus Performance

Kimble's definition has one major advantage over Coon's, namely, it implies a distinction between learning (behavioural potential) and performance (actual behaviour). Think of all the things you know and can do but which you are not displaying at this present moment—if you can swim you are almost certainly not doing so as you read this chapter but you could readily do so if faced with a pool full of water! So what you could do (potential behaviour based on learning) and what you are actually doing (current performance) are two different things, but ultimately, of course, the only proof of learning is a particular kind of performance (such as exams).

We can relate the learning-performance distinction to what we said earlier about what counts as learning: performance, but not learning, can fluctuate due to fatigue, drugs, emotional factors etc, and so is much more variable than the more permanent learning. (Exams come to mind again, many students have left the exam room knowing what they could not demonstrate during the exam itself.)

Learning and Other Abilities

A rather different kind of definition is offered by Howe (1980), for whom learning is, 'a biological device that functions to protect the human individual and to extend his capacities'. In this context, learning is neither independent of nor entirely separate from several other abilities, in particular memory and perception; indeed, learning and memory may be regarded as two sides of the same coin (see Chapter 6).

According to Howe, learning is also *cumulative*, that is, what we learn at any time is influenced by our previous learning, so that developmental and learning processes are closely interlinked. Also, most instances of learning take the form of adaptive changes whereby we increase our effectiveness in dealing with the environment; this has undoubted survival value.

Some Basic Questions about Learning

If it is generally agreed by psychologists that learning is: (i) relatively permanent, and (ii) due to past experience; there is much less agreement about
(a) exactly what changes when learning takes place and (b) what kinds of past
experience are involved. Put in another way, how do the changes occur and
what mechanisms are involved?

A dimension along which psychologists differ regarding (a) and (b) is the
extent to which they focus on the overt, behavioural changes as opposed
to the covert, cognitive changes. As we have seen in Chapters 1 and 2,
behaviourists such as Watson and Skinner emphasize the former to the exclusion of the latter, while cognitive psychologists are more interested in the
latter as they are reflected in the former.

We will now take a detailed look at different theories of learning.

Behaviourist Approaches—Learning Theory
(Classical and Operant Conditioning)

Figure 3.1 shows the major figures in the behaviourist tradition and how they
relate to each other. Historically (or chronologically) Skinner does not belong
at the top but at the bottom—he was born several years after the others and
is still alive. But he appears at the top because of the distinction he made (in
1938) between *respondents* (or respondent behaviour), which are triggered

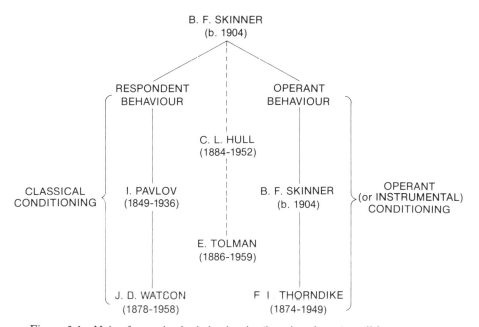

Figure 3.1   Major figures in the behaviourist (learning theory) traditions

automatically by particular environmental stimuli, and *operants* (or operant behaviour) which are not tied to stimuli in that way and which are essentially voluntary.

Related to this distinction is that between Classical (or Pavlovian) conditioning and Operant (or Instrumental) conditioning; although they both represent the behaviourist Stimulus–Response (S–R) approach to learning, there are some important differences between them too, hence Skinner's distinction. Neither Hull nor Tolman fit easily into either of the two major types of conditioning, which is why they are placed between the others. (I will not discuss Hull's theory in this chapter but will do so in relation to motivation in Chapter 17.)

Classical Conditioning

Or, why do dogs drool over bells?

Ivan Pavlov was a physiologist interested in the process of digestion in dogs, for which research he was awarded the Nobel Prize in 1904 (the year Skinner was born). He developed a surgical technique whereby a dog's salivary secretions could be collected in a tube attached to the outside of its cheek so the drops of saliva could be easily measured. In the course of his physiological investigations Pavlov noticed that the dogs would often start salivating *before* any food was given to them, for example, when they looked at the food, or saw the feeding bucket or even when they heard the footsteps of the approaching laboratory assistant who was coming to feed them.

These observations led to the study of what is now called Classical Conditioning (or Pavlovian Conditioning), whereby a stimulus (eg a bell) which

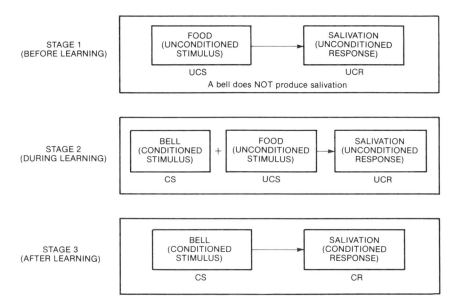

Figure 3.2 The basic procedure involved in classical conditioning

would not normally produce a particular response (eg salivation) eventually comes to do so by being paired with another stimulus (food) which normally does produce the response. The basic procedure is summarized in Figure 3.2.

Before conditioning the taste of food will naturally, and automatically, make the dog salivate but the sound of a bell will not ; so the food is referred to as an Unconditioned Stimulus (UCS) and the salivation is an Unconditioned Response (UCR), an automatic, reflex, biologically built-in response. The dog does not have to learn to salivate in response to food, it can do so naturally. During conditioning the bell is paired with the food. Because the bell does not naturally produce salivation it is referred to as a Conditioned Stimulus (CS), ie it is *neutral* with respect to salivation.

If the bell and food are paired a sufficient number of times the dog starts to salivate as soon as it hears the bell and before the food is presented. When this occurs we say that conditioning has occurred and the salivation is now referred to as a Conditioned Response (CR) since it is produced by a conditioned stimulus (CS), the bell.

This basic procedure can be used with a variety of conditioned stimuli; eg buzzers, metronomes, lights, geometric figures and so on. The exact relationship between the CS and the UCS can also be varied to give different kinds of conditioning; for example, in the example shown in Figure 3.2, the CS is presented about half a second before the UCS and is called Delayed or Forward Conditioning. This and three other alternatives are shown in Table 3.1.

Table 3.1 Four types of classical conditioning based on different CS-UCS relationships

1. *Delayed or forward*	The CS is presented before the UCS and remains 'on' while the UCS is presented and until the UCR appears. Conditioning has occurred when the CR appears before the UCS is presented. A half second interval produces the strongest learning — as the interval increases so the poorer the learning becomes. This is the kind of conditioning typically used in the laboratory, especially with animals.
2. *Backward*	The CS is presented after the UCS; generally, this produces very little, if any, learning in laboratory animals. However, much advertising uses backward conditioning (eg the idyllic, tropical, scene is set and then the coconut bar is introduced).
3. *Simultaneous*	The CS and UCS are presented together; conditioning has occurred when the CS on its own produces the CR. This kind of conditioning occurs frequently in real-life situations (eg the sound of the dentist's drill accompanies the contact of the drill with your tooth).
4. *Trace*	The CS is presented and removed before the UCS is presented, so that only a 'memory trace' of the CS remains to be conditioned. The CR is usually weaker than in Delayed or Simultaneous conditioning.

Higher Order Conditioning

Pavlov demonstrated that a strong CS could be used in place of food to produce salivation in response to a new stimulus which had never been paired with food. For example, if the CS is a buzzer, it can be paired with, say, a black square in such a way that after ten pairings (using delayed conditioning) the dog will salivate a small but significant amount at the sight of the black square before the buzzer is sounded.

Remember that the black square had never been associated with food directly, but only indirectly, through association with the buzzer which had been; it is as if the CS were functioning as a UCS. The buzzer and food situation is referred to as *first order* conditioning and the black square and buzzer situation as *second order* conditioning. Pavlov found that, with dogs at least, learning could not go beyond third or fourth order conditioning; even so, conditioning is beginning to look a rather more complex process than it did when we first described it.

Generalization and Discrimination

Other phenomena involved in classical conditioning (as well as operant) which make it a more complex and versatile process are generalisation and discrimination.

In *generalization* the CR transfers spontaneously to stimuli that are similar to, but different from, the original CS. For example, if a dog is trained using a bell of a particular pitch and it is then presented with a bell a little higher or lower in pitch, it will still salivate, although only one bell (the original CS) was actually paired with food. However, if the dog is continually presented with bells that are increasingly different from the original, the CR will gradually weaken and eventually stop altogether; the dog is showing *discrimination*. (See Figure 3.3.)

In addition to spontaneous discrimination, as in the above example, Pavlov trained dogs to discriminate in the original conditioning procedure. For example, if a high-pitched bell is paired with food but a low-pitched bell is not, the dog will start salivating in response to the former but not to the latter (Discrimination Training).

An interesting phenomenon related to discrimination is what Pavlov called *experimental neurosis*. He trained dogs to salivate to a circle but not to an ellipse and then gradually changed the shape of the ellipse until it became

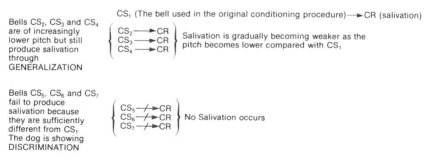

Figure 3.3 An example of discrimination occurring spontaneously as a result of generalization stopping

almost circular. As this happened the dogs started behaving in 'neurotic' ways-whining, trembling, urinating and defecating, refusing to eat and so on. It was as if they did not know how to respond: was the stimulus a circle (in which case, through generalization, they 'ought' to salivate) or was it an ellipse (in which case, through discrimination, they 'should not' salivate)?

Extinction and Spontaneous Recovery
After dogs had been conditioned to salivate to a bell, if the bell was repeatedly presented without food, the CR of salivation became gradually weaker and eventually stopped altogether; this is called *extinction*.

When this happens it might seem as if the association between the bell and the food has faded so that the dog has 'unlearnt' the original connection. But this is not the case: when dogs were removed from the experimental situation, following extinction, and then put back a couple of hours or so later, and Pavlov re-presented the bell, the dogs started salivating again. Although there had been no further pairing of the bell and food, the CR of salivation reappeared in response to the bell, a phenomenon called *spontaneous recovery*. It shows that extinction does not involve an 'erasing' of the original learning but rather a learning to inhibit or suppress the CR when the CS is continually presented without a UCS.

Does Classical Conditioning Apply to Human Behaviour?

Certainly, there have been many laboratory demonstrations with human subjects and the basic procedure is useful as a way of thinking about how certain fairly automatic responses may be acquired in real life. Also, as we shall see in Chapter 29, the impact of conditioning principles (both classical and operant) within clinical psychology has been considerable, ie they can be used deliberately to change people's behaviour in a certain direction. (See also Table 1.1, page 14, comparing different theoretical approaches.)

The Experiments
The first attempt to apply Pavlov's findings with dogs to humans was made by J. B. Watson, the founder of Behaviourism. Working with Rosalie Rayner (1920), Watson succeeded in inducing fear in a young child through classical conditioning.

The Case of Little Albert (Watson and Rayner, 1920)
Albert B's mother was a wet nurse in a children's hospital; the baby was described as, 'healthy from birth' and, 'on the whole stolid and unemotional'. When he was about nine months old his reactions to various stimuli were tested—a white rat, a rabbit, a dog, a monkey, masks with and without hair, cotton wool, burning newspapers, and a hammer striking a four-foot steel bar (just behind his head); only the last of these produced a fear response in the baby and so constituted the UCS (with the fear the UCR). The other stimuli were neutral since they did not produce fear.

When Albert was just over eleven months old the rat and the UCS were presented together; this occurred seven times altogether over the next seven weeks by which time the rat (CS) on its own came to produce the fear response (now a CR).

The CR transferred spontaneously to the rabbit, the dog, a sealskin fur coat, cotton wool, Watson's hair and a Santa Claus mask but it did not generalise to Albert's building blocks or to the hair of two observers (ie Albert showed discrimination).

Five days after conditioning the CR produced by the rat persisted; ten days after conditioning it was 'much less marked' but one month after conditioning it was still evident.

Whether or not Watson and Rayner had intended to remove the CR, Albert's mother did not give them the opportunity because she removed him from the hospital.

Watson and Rayner might have attempted to remove little Albert's fear using the method of 'direct un-conditioning' employed by Mary Cover Jones (1924) to treat *Little Peter*.

The Case of Little Peter

Little Peter was a 2-year-old living in a charitable institution. Jones was mainly interested in those children who cried and trembled when an animal (eg a frog, rat or rabbit) was shown to them and Peter, who in other respects was regarded as well-adjusted, had an extreme fear of rats, rabbits, fur coats, feathers, cotton wool, frogs and fish. (It was not known how this fear had arisen.)

Jones, supervised by Watson, put the rabbit in a wire cage in front of Peter while he ate his lunch and, forty sessions later, Peter ate his lunch with one hand and stroked the rabbit (now on his lap) with the other. By a series of 17 steps, the rabbit in the cage was brought a little closer each day then was let free in the room and eventually sat on Peter's lunch tray.

This represents an early example of a method of removing fears (or phobias) called systematic desensitisation, which is used a great deal today.

If a fear of rats can be deliberately induced (as in Little Albert's case) or removed (as in Little Peter's), does classical conditioning also help to explain how fears are acquired, spontaneously, in everyday life?

We can see how, for example, a fear of the dentist could be learnt in this way, eg:

Drill hitting a nerve (UCS) → pain/fear (UCR)
Sound of drill (CS) + drill hitting nerve (UCS) → Pain/fear (UCR)
Sound of the drill (CS) → Fear (CR)

You could become conditioned to more than one CS in the same 'sitting'—it all depends on what you notice at the time. For example, if you are looking at the dentist peering into your mouth, you may become afraid of 'faces seen upside down' or if the dentist is wearing a mask you may acquire a fear of masks too. Also through generalization, you can come to fear all drill-like noises or white coats worn by medical personnel or lab technicians and so on.

Generalization may be useful up to a point but discrimination may be just as important; a carpenter needs to use an electric drill and it is necessary for them to do so without trembling through fear. (Of course, not everyone's conditioned fear responses are of equal strength—mine could be extreme compared with yours, although we may both have acquired the fear through classical conditioning.)

As we shall see in Chapter 28, human fears may often be kept going through avoiding the object of our fears, ie we do not give the fear a chance to undergo extinction. (This occurs in conjunction with operant conditioning whereby the avoidance behaviour becomes strengthened through negative reinforcement, which will be discussed later in this chapter.)

Experimental Studies of Classical Conditioning with Humans

Because of the reflex nature of the UCR (and the biological link between the UCS and UCR) the range of the CRs that can be induced in the laboratory is largely confined to those controlled by the Autonomic Nervous System or ANS (see Chapter 15) and over which we have little—if any—conscious control, for example, salivation, the knee-jerk reflex, the eye-blink response (to a puff of air, for instance), the finger-flexing reflex (a response to a mild electric shock), and vasoconstriction (constriction of the blood vessels).

In an early study, Menzies (1937) conditioned vasoconstriction to the sound of a buzzer by pairing the buzzer with the UCS of immersing the hand in cold water. More recently, Woods and Kulkosky (1976) and Woods (1979) conditioned hypoglycaemia (a lowering of blood-sugar level) to a number of conditioned stimuli, including a bright light, a sound, and the experimental room itself.

An interesting study by Volkova (1953) demonstrated the phenomena of semantic conditioning, generalization and discrimination. The UCS was cranberry purée, delivered to a child's mouth via a chute, producing salivation as the UCR. The Russian word for 'good' was spoken by the experimenter as the purée was delivered and the word itself eventually came to produce salivation (as a CR). The experimenter then recited various sentences, some of which could be construed as expressing something 'good' and others which could not. Salivation was elicited by, 'The pioneer helps his comrade' and, 'Leningrad is a wonderful city' but not by, 'The pupil was rude to the teacher' or, 'My friend is seriously ill'.

Classical conditioning has been demonstrated in very young babies, although there are certain problems in interpreting the findings from such young subjects. Marquis (1931) conditioned eight babies, during the first nine days after birth, to a buzzer sounded for five seconds while their feeding bottle was presented, giving the UCR of sucking. It took between 100 and 250 joint presentations of the buzzer and bottle to produce sucking to the buzzer alone. (Note that the UCS was itself based on prior conditioning— association of the sight of the feeding bottle and its contact with the baby's lips—and so is an example of second order conditioning.)

Lintz and Fitzgerald (1966) used a puff of air as the UCS producing the eye blink response (UCR) in babies of 33-days-old and over; the puff of air was preceded by an auditory tone which eventually came to produce the eye blink response on its own (but only after 25 pairings of the CS and UCS over several days).

Fitzgerald and Brackbill (1976) conclude that only a small number of reflexes (eg sucking and blinking) can be classically conditioned during the first few weeks of life and for this to happen the baby must be alert and attentive.

Operant or Instrumental Conditioning

Why do rats press levers?

When Skinner drew the distinction between respondent and operant behaviour, he was not rejecting the discoveries of Pavlov and Watson but arguing that most animal and human behaviour is not elicited by specific stimuli in the way they described. Instead, he was interested in how animals *operate* on their environment and how this operant behaviour is *instrumental* in bringing about certain *consequences* which then determine how probable that behaviour is to be repeated.

Skinner's view of learning saw the learner as much more *active* than Pavlov or Watson had, for whom behaviour was automatically brought about by stimuli—unconditioned stimuli before learning and conditioned stimuli after learning. In classical conditioning, there is a certain necessity and inevitability about the response—the animal has no choice but to respond in a particular way. But in operant conditioning things are much less certain: behaviour is *emitted* by the organism (not *elicited* by the stimulus) and so is essentially *voluntary* (as opposed to reflex or involuntary) and the likelihood of a particular behaviour being emitted is a function of the past consequences of such behaviour.

Just as Watson's ideas were based on the earlier work of Pavlov, so Skinner's study of operant conditioning grew out of the earlier work of another American, Edward Thorndike.

Thorndike and the Law of Effect

Thorndike built puzzle-boxes for use with cats; their task was to operate a latch which would automatically cause the door to spring open. Each time they managed to escape there was a piece of fish waiting for them which was visible from inside the puzzle-box. (The cats were deprived of food for a considerable time before the experiments began and so were highly motivated.) Each time, after eating the fish, they were put straight back in and the whole process was repeated.

At first the cats struggled to get out, behaving in a purely random fashion, and it was only by chance that the first escape was made. But each time they were returned to the puzzle-box it took them less time to operate the latch and make their escape. For instance, with one of the boxes, the average time for the first escape was five minutes but after ten to twenty trials this was reduced to about five seconds. How did Thorndike account for this?

The learning, he said, was essentially random or *trial-and-error*; there was no sudden flash of insight into how the releasing mechanism worked but rather a gradual reduction in the number of errors made and hence escape time. As to exactly what was being learned in this trial-and-error way, Thorndike proposed a 'connection between the situation and a certain impulse to act', or between the stimulus (the manipulative components of the box) and the response (the behaviour which allowed the cat to escape). Further, the stimulus response connection is, 'stamped in when pleasure results from the act, and stamped out when it doesn't'; this is Thorndike's famous *law of effect* (1898).

The Law of Effect is crucially important as a way of distinguishing classical and operant conditioning (as Skinner was to do forty years later):

i)   It points out that what happens *as a result* of behaviour will influence that behaviour in the future, whereas in classical conditioning it is, in a sense, what happens before behaviour (pairing of the CS and UCS) that is crucial and which determines the behaviour.

ii) It points out that the animal is not indifferent to the nature of those consequences—responses that bring about 'satisfaction' or pleasure are likely to be repeated, those which bring about 'discomfort' are likely not to be; while in classical conditioning the UCS works essentially in the same way whether it is food (something pleasant) or electric shock (something unpleasant or aversive) since the response is produced *by* it and not vice-versa.

Skinner's 'Analysis of Behaviour'

We saw in Chapter 1 that Skinner's approach was a-theoretical, that is, he was attempting to control and predict behaviour, not explain it. He used a form of puzzle-box known as a Skinner box, which was designed for a rat or pigeon to do things in rather than escape from. This box has a lever (in the case of rats), under which is a food tray, and the experimenter decides exactly what the relationship shall be between pressing the lever and the delivery of a food pellet; in this sense, the experimenter has total control of the animal's environment but it is the rat that has to do the work.

Another modification of Thorndike's work was Skinner's use of the term *strengthen* in place of 'stamping in' and *weaken* in place of 'stamping out' in Thorndike's Law of Effect; for Skinner, Thorndike's terms were too mentalistic and his own more objective and descriptive. The analysis of behaviour, according to Skinner, requires an accurate but neutral representation of the relationship (or *contingencies*) between: (a) *antecedents* (the stimulus conditions, eg the lever, the click of the food dispenser, a light that may go on when the lever is pressed); (b) *behaviours* (or *operants*, eg pressing the lever); and (c) *consequences* (what happens as a result of the operant behaviour). We shall look at (a) and (c) in more detail.

'Behaviour is Shaped and Maintained by its Consequences'

This quote from Skinner represents his version of the Law of Effect; the consequences of operants can be: (i) a *positive reinforcement*, (ii) a *negative reinforcement*, or (iii) a *punishment* and their effects on behaviour can be summarized as in Figure 3.4 on page 56.

You will see from Figure 3.4 that positive and negative reinforcement have the same effect on behaviour, namely *strengthening* it (making it more

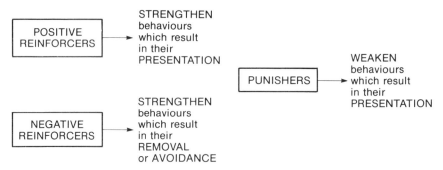

Figure 3.4   The consequences of behaviour and their effects

probable), but each works in a different way, from the opposite direction. *Positive reinforcement* involves presenting something the animal likes (eg food) while *negative reinforcement* involves the removal or avoidance of some 'aversive' (literally 'painful') state of affairs (eg electric shock).

Punishment has the opposite effect on behaviour—it *weakens* it (making it less probable)—through the presentation of an aversive stimulus.

Let us take the example of a rat pressing a lever in a Skinner box (Figure 3.5).

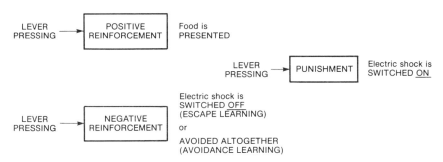

Figure 3.5   3 possible consequences of lever-pressing in a Skinner box

The difference between negative reinforcement and punishment should now be clear: in the former, an aversive stimulus comes to an end or is avoided altogether, while in the latter, the aversive stimulus begins.

What is the Difference Between a Reinforcer and Reinforcement?

You may have spotted that in Figure 3.4 the term Reinforcer (and Punisher) is used while in Figure 3.5 I have referred to Reinforcement (and Punishment); the difference is between a thing and a process. Food itself is a reinforcer, electric shock a punisher; the process whereby food is presented as a result of lever-pressing is (positive) reinforcement and when electric shock is presented instead it is called punishment.

But we should note here just how Skinner defines these terms or, more accurately, how he decides that something is or is not a reinforcer or a punisher. It is, in fact, a decision that must be made retrospectively, that is, after food or shock etc, has been made contingent on, say, lever-pressing, on a number of occasions. So, if the behaviour is strengthened when followed by food, we can call the food a reinforcer, and if the shock weakens it we can call the shock a punisher; therefore, reinforcers and punishers cannot be defined independently of the effects they have on behaviour.

This kind of definition could be accused of circularity ('a reinforcer is whatever strengthens behaviour' and 'whatever strengthens behaviour is a reinforcer') and it seems to make the task of predicting behaviour rather tricky, since Skinner is saying that we have to 'wait and observe' just what the effects on behaviour are.

A partial solution (of an empirical if not a logical kind) is to ensure that rats and pigeons are highly motivated to learn the relationship between pressing levers or pecking discs and receiving food by starving them for several hours before the experiments begin!

A partial justification for 'waiting and seeing' is that, according to Skinner, this is a more rather than a less scientific way of going about things, since the intended effect may not always coincide with the actual effect. Take an example from parent-child interaction: if a child who feels deprived of its parents' attention finds that they respond when it is naughty, the child is more likely to go on being naughty, even if the parents' response is to shout or smack. Being shouted at, or being smacked, is at least a form of attention and is preferable to being ignored; so, whereas the parents' intention is to stop the child being naughty, the actual effect may be the opposite, ie an intended punishment may turn out to be a positive reinforcement!

Similarly, a positive reinforcement can only loosely be called a reward as 'reward' implies that the rewarder expects to strengthen behaviour, whereas 'positive reinforcement' refers to what has been shown to strengthen the behaviour of the rewarded person or animal.

Primary and Secondary Reinforcers

As well as the distinction between positive and negative reinforcement, an important distinction also exists between two types of reinforcer, primary and secondary. Primary reinforcers (eg food, water, sex) are naturally reinforcing, reinforcing in themselves, whereas secondary reinforcers acquire their reinforcing properties through association with primary reinforcers, that is, we have to *learn* (through classical conditioning) to find them reinforcing.

Examples of human secondary (or conditioned) reinforcers are money, trading stamps, cheques and tokens (see Chapter 29 for a discussion of token economy programmes used with psychiatric patients and other groups).

In a Skinner box situation, if a click accompanies the presentation of each pellet of food, the rat will eventually come to find the click on its own reinforcing; this is demonstrated by using the click as a reinforcer for getting the rat to learn some new response.

A famous demonstration of the power of secondary reinforcers is the study by Wolfe (1936). He used the Chimp-O-Mat machine which chimpanzees learned to operate in order to obtain poker chips as a secondary reinforcement for solving problems.

Table 3.2 Common reinforcement schedules and associated patterns of response and resistance to extinction

Reinforcement schedule	Example	Pattern and rate of responding	Resistance to extinction	Human behaviour
1. Continuous Reinforcement (CRF)	Every single desired response is reinforced.	Response rate is low but steady.	Very low — the quickest way to bring about extinction.	TV set which is very reliable and works every time it's turned on.
2. Fixed Interval (FI)	A reinforcement is given every 30 seconds (FI 30) — provided the response occurs at least once during that time.	Response rate speeds up as the next reinforcement becomes available; a pause after each reinforcement. Overall response rate fairly low.	Fairly low — extinction occurs quite quickly.	1. Being paid regularly — every week or month. 2. Receiving a regular weekly test or timed essay.
3. Variable Interval (VI)	A reinforcement is given on average every 30 seconds (VI 30) — but the interval varies from trial to trial. So the interval on any one occasion is unpredictable.	Response rate is very stable over long periods of time. Still some tendency to increase response rate as time elapses since the last reinforcement.	Very high — extinction occurs very slowly and gradually.	Many self-employed people receive payment irregularly — depends when the customer pays for the product or service.
4. Fixed Ratio (FR)	A reinforcement is given for a fixed number of responses — however long this may take. E.g. one reinforcement for every 10 responses (FR 10).	There is a pronounced pause after each reinforcement and then a very high rate of responding leading up to the next reinforcement.	as Fixed Interval.	1. Piecework — the more work done, the more money earned. 2. Commission — extra money for so many goods made or sales completed.
5. Variable Ratio (VR)	A reinforcement is given on average every 10 responses (V.R. 10) but the number varies from trial to trial. So the number of responses required on any one occasion is unpredictable.	Very high response rate — and very steady.	Very high — the most resistant of all the schedules.	Gambling.

Secondary reinforcers are often important because they 'bridge the gap' between the response and the primary reinforcer which may not be immediately forthcoming.

Schedules of Reinforcement

Another important aspect of Skinner's work (eg Ferster and Skinner, 1957) is concerned with the effects on behaviour of how frequently and how regularly (or predictably) reinforcements are presented. He identified five major schedules, each of which is associated with a characteristic pattern of responding and, as Walker (1984) observes, this part of Skinner's research is in large measure counter-intuitive, which makes it all the more interesting.

To summarize, first, rats and pigeons (and probably most mammals and birds) typically 'work harder' (eg press the lever at a faster rate) for scant reward: when reinforcements are (i) relatively few and far between, and (ii) relatively irregular or unpredictable, not only will they go on working but will do so long after the reinforcement has actually been withdrawn altogether!

So each schedule can be analysed in terms of: (a) pattern and rate of response; and (b) resistance to extinction. This is summarized in Table 3.2.

A convenient way of displaying visually the rate of response is to plot responses cumulatively, as steps along a vertical axis, against the time when they are made along the horizontal axis; Skinner called this a 'cumulative record' and it is shown in Figure 3.6.

Usually, a continuous schedule is only used when some new response is being learned; once it is being emitted regularly and reliably it can be maintained by using one of the four *partial* or *intermittent* schedules. But, of course, this change must be gradual: if the animal is used to being reinforced

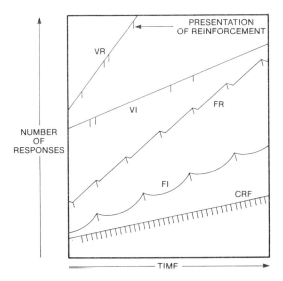

Figure 3.6   Typical cumulative records for a response (such as lever-pressing) reinforced using 5 schedules of reinforcement

every time it makes a certain response, and it is then switched to a Variable Ratio (VR) 50, it will soon stop responding.

Skinner (1938) originally used an interval schedule because a reinforcement is guaranteed, sooner or later, so long as one response is made in the interval.

Shaping—the Reinforcement of Successive Approximations

Reinforcement can also be used to build up relatively complex behaviour—behaviour which the animal does not normally display or which is not part of its natural repertoire—by reinforcing closer and closer approximations to the desired behaviour.

First, the behaviour must be broken down into a number of small steps, each of which is reinforced in sequence, so that gradually what the animal can do is much more what the experimenter is trying to teach it. This is what animal trainers have been doing for hundreds of years and is the method of reinforcement Skinner used to teach pigeons to play ping-pong or turn a full (anticlockwise) circle. Most skills in humans are learned in this step-by-step manner, whether this happens deliberately and consciously (as in driving) or spontaneously and unconsciously (as in acquiring speech).

Shaping also provides an important foundation for behaviour modification, used to teach mentally handicapped children and adults to use the toilet, feed and dress themselves and other social skills. It has been used also to develop speech in autistic children.

Superstitious Behaviour

An interesting example of the role of reinforcement is the situation where a certain behaviour is strengthened, by chance, because it happens to precede a reinforcement; the relationship between the behaviour and the reinforcer is accidental (not contingent), ie the reinforcer would have occurred anyway.

Skinner (1948) first noticed this phenomenon while training pigeons to peck at a disc. Sometimes they would engage in some irrelevant behaviour (eg turning in circles, hopping from side to side) just before pecking the disc and the resulting reinforcer would strengthen both the disc-pecking *and* the irrelevant response. Of course, so long as the required response of pecking was emitted the reinforcer would follow, whether or not the pigeon turned around or hopped from one side to another.

Whenever we 'keep our fingers crossed' or engage in any type of ritual (as is quite common amongst sportsmen and women, while 'warming up' for competition, or actors) we, in Skinner's terms, are displaying superstitious behaviour.

Negative Reinforcement—Escape and Avoidance Learning

Figure 3.5 has shown that two forms of negative reinforcement are Escape and Avoidance Learning; these are the two major ways in which negative reinforcement has been studied in the laboratory. Escape learning is relatively simple; for example, rats can learn to press a lever in order to turn off electric shock. Avoidance learning is more complex and more relevant to certain aspects of human behaviour.

Most laboratory studies have used a 'shuttle box', a box divided into two compartments, sometimes with a barrier or door between the two compartments, and electric shock can be delivered through the floor of either compartment independently of the other. Neither side is permanently safe, but only one is electrified at a time; the problem for the animal is to find which is the safe side on any one occasion. A warning signal is given whenever the electrified side is to be changed, so the animal can always avoid being shocked if it switches sides when it hears (or sees) the warning signal. But why should it? According to Walker (1984) the only theory of avoidance learning worth considering is the Two Factor Theory (Mowrer, 1960) or the Two Process Theory (Gray, 1975), the two processes or factors being classical and operant conditioning. According to Mowrer, the animal first learns to be afraid (through classical conditioning the light or buzzer warning signal elicits an anticipatory emotional response of fear or anxiety) and then learns a response to reduce the fear (jumping the barrier is negatively reinforced through avoiding the shock before it is switched on).

Miller (1948) attempted to separate out the classical from the operant factors. At first he trained rats to run out of a white room, through a small door, into a black room by giving them shocks in the white room. After pre-training, the door was closed and could only be opened by the rat turning a wheel. Even though no further shocks were given, the residual 'aversiveness' of the white room (acquired through classical conditioning) was sufficient to motivate the rats to learn quickly to turn the wheel so that they could run through into the 'safe' room, thus relieving their anxiety (negative reinforcement).

An interesting and important difference can now be seen between positive and negative reinforcement in relation to extinction. If we try to teach a rat to learn a new response in order to get it into a black box which used to contain food, it will soon stop responding; but if a rat successfully escapes from a white room which used to be dangerous, it may go on escaping indefinitely. In the former case it soon 'discovers' that the food is no longer available but in the latter it does not stay around long enough to 'discover' that the shock is no longer available.

Therefore, responses which are motivated by conditioned fear or anxiety should persist longer (take longer to extinguish) than those motivated by positive incentives. Avoidance learning prevents the learner from 'testing reality' and this has been found in dogs and humans (eg Solomon and Wynne, 1953, Turner and Solomon, 1962). In humans, phobias may be seen as becoming persistent in this way and one therapeutic attempt to bring about extinction through forced reality testing is called flooding or implosion therapy (eg Yates, 1970, see Chapter 29).

Punishment

Skinner has always maintained that positive reinforcement (and, to a lesser extent, negative reinforcement) is a much more potent influence on behaviour than punishment, both with animals and humans, largely because the latter can only make certain responses less likely—you cannot teach an animal or a person anything new by punishment alone.

Other psychologists either disagree with Skinner or emphasize different reasons for the ineffectiveness of punishment.

Campbell and Church (1969) argue that punishments are, if anything, a stronger influence on behaviour than the incentive effects of reinforcements (at least as far as laboratory animals are concerned). The problem, however, is the unpleasant side-effects of stress, anxiety, withdrawal, aggression and so on (see Chapter 21 for discussion of this in relation to children).

Estes (1970) trained two groups of rats to press a lever for food, after which they were given extinction trials. For Group A, the first few extinction trials involved strong electric shock every time they pressed; from then on, the food was simply withheld. For Group B, food was withheld on all the extinction trials (and no shocks).

In the first stage of extinction, Group A rats did make fewer responses but they later resumed their previous rate of responding and by the end of the experiment had made as many responses as Group B. Estes concluded that punishment merely *suppressed* the lever pressing in the short term, but did not weaken it.

Other experiments have shown that the strength and duration of the suppression effect depend on the *intensity* of the punishment (eg Bow and Church, 1967) and the degree of deprivation. However, the response is still suppressed rather than un-learned.

Howe (1980) points out that when alternative ways of obtaining reinforcers are available, punishment has a more powerful suppressive effect on the punished behaviour. For example, Azrin and Holtz (1966) combined punishment and reinforcement so that response A was punished while response B, incompatible with A, was positively reinforced. This is something that Skinner advocates with human beings.

The Antecedents of Behaviour—Stimulus Control

A crucial difference between classical and operant conditioning is to do with the role of the stimulus in relation to the response. Whereas in classical conditioning the stimulus elicits or triggers the response in an automatic way, in operant the stimulus indicates the likely consequence of emitting a particular response, ie the operant behaviour is more likely to occur in the presence of some stimuli rather than others. If the rat has been reinforced for pressing the lever, it is more likely to go on emitting that response as the lever becomes associated both with reinforcement and the action of pressing (probably through classical conditioning). Technically, lever pressing has now come under the control of the lever stimulus—but there is still no inevitability about pressing it, only an increased probability.

Similarly, drivers' behaviour is brought under the stimulus control of traffic signals, road signs, other vehicles, pedestrians and so on. Much of our everyday behaviour can be seen in this way; sitting on chairs, answering the telephone, turning on the television etc. are all operants which are more likely to occur in the presence of those stimuli because of the past consequences of doing so.

A special case of stimulus control is a *discriminative stimulus*. In the Skinner box, for example, if a rat is reinforced for lever pressing *only* when a light is on, the light soon becomes a discriminative stimulus, ie the rat only presses when the light is on. If you learn to ask your teacher questions only when they are sitting at their desk (and not when standing by the board) because this has been the occasion for discussion in previous lessons, then your question-asking behaviour is under the stimulus control of your teacher's behaviour.

Does Conditioning Work in the Same Way for all Species?

According to Walker (1984), the fact that many experiments involving a variety of species can all be described as classical conditioning (since in all cases a response comes to be elicited by a new stimulus) does *not* in itself mean that there is only one mechanism involved or only one explanation which applies, equally, to all species and all cases.

Although conditionability seems to be an almost universal property of nervous systems (including those of sea snails, flatworms and fruit flies) many psychologists have argued that there can be no general laws of learning (eg Seligman, 1970). But what might such laws be?

One example is the law of *contiguity*: events (or stimuli) which occur close together in time and space are likely to become associated with each other. Most of the examples of conditioning we have considered so far would appear to 'obey' the law of contiguity. But can we find exceptions and, if so, how can we explain them?

A famous and important exception are *taste aversion* studies (Garcia and Koelling, 1966, Garcia et al, 1966, Riley and Baril, 1976). Rats were given a novel-tasting solution, eg saccharine-flavoured water (the CS), prior to a drug, eg apomorphine (the UCS), which has a delayed action, inducing severe intestinal illness (the UCR). Rats were conditioned to the water (ie producing the CR of intestinal illness) after only a single trial and, more significantly, even when there was a five to ten hour delay between the taste of the water and the illness; illness seems to be naturally attributed to tastes.

However, although rats quickly develop aversions to new tastes, it is very difficult to condition them to new odours and it is impossible to deter pigeons from water. For other species, taste aversions are very difficult to establish even if the animal is made very ill and in almost all species aversions are learned more easily to new flavours than to familiar ones.

Thus there seems to be definite biological limitations on the ability of animals to develop a conditional aversion. Similarly, the average rat will learn very quickly to avoid shock in a shuttlebox and will also learn very quickly to press a lever for food. However, rats do not learn very readily to press a lever to avoid shock. Again, pigeons can be trained quickly to fly from one perch to another in order to avoid shock but it is almost impossible to train them to peck a disc to avoid shock.

Findings like these have led Bolles (1980) and others to conclude that we cannot regard the basic principles of learning as applying equally to all species in all situations; we must take into account the evolutionary history of the species as well as the individual organism's learning history.

An important idea in this context is Seligman's concept of *preparedness* (1970). Animals are biologically prepared to learn actions that are closely related to the survival of their species (eg learned water or food aversions) and these prepared behaviours are learned with very little training. By the same token, there are also 'contra-prepared' behaviours which are contrary to an animal's natural tendencies and so are learned with great difficulty, if at all. Seligman believes that most of the behaviour studied in the laboratory falls somewhere in between these two extremes.

Oakley (1983) believes that preparedness in conditioning is an inherited characteristic. If, in the history of a species, individuals have often been exposed to certain biologically significant kinds of association, then the ability to learn rapidly about such associations becomes genetically transmitted. These genetic constraints apply to both classical and operant conditioning.

What about preparedness in humans? Much of the relevant data relates to how easily certain conditioned fear responses can be induced in the laboratory or how common certain phobias are compared with others (the 'naturally occurring ones'). For instance, Ohman (1975) and Hygge and Ohman (1978) paired slides of snakes and spiders with strong electric shock and quickly established conditioned emotional responses to the slides but not so with slides of flowers, houses or berries.

Seligman (1972) observed that human phobias tend to fall into certain narrow categories, most of them being of animals or dangerous places. Most common of all were fear of snakes, spiders, the dark, high places and closed-in places and often there is no previous evidence for the fear actually having been conditioned.

Another interesting finding is that classically conditioned responses extinguish faster in humans than animals. According to Weiskrantz (1982) this is because the CRs are modulated by more complex human memories. Lowe et al (1978) explained the difference in patterns of responding on a fixed interval schedule between humans and animals by referring to the 'cognitive overlay' shown by humans.

These findings in turn raise further questions, including (i) what exactly is learned during conditioning and (ii) what is the role of cognitive factors in conditioning? I shall treat these as two parts of the same question.

Is Conditioning More Complex than it Seems? The Role of Cognition

According to Mackintosh (1978), conditioning is *not* reducible to the strengthening of S–R associations by the automatic action of a process called reinforcement. It is more appropriate to think of it as a matter of detecting and learning about *relations between events*, whereby animals typically discover what signals or causes events that are important to them, such as food, water, danger or safety. Mackintosh goes on to say that instead of treating salivation or lever-pressing as what is learned, we could regard it simply as a convenient *index* that the subject has detected certain relationships in its environment.

Indeed, Pavlov himself described the CS as a 'signal' for the UCS, the relationship between CS and the UCS as one of 'stimulus substitution' and the CR as an 'anticipatory' response, suggesting that his dogs were *expecting* the food to follow the bell etc.

To support this interpretation, Rescorla (1968) presented two groups of animals with the same number of CS–UCS pairings, but the second group also received additional presentations of the UCS on its own without the CS. The first group showed much stronger conditioning than the second, indicating that the most important factor (in classical conditioning anyway) is how *predictably* the UCS follows the CS, not *how often* the CS and UCS are paired.

Again, Rescorla (1967) presented the CS at irregular intervals both before and after the UCS (eg five seconds before, then five seconds after, then ten seconds before etc.) so that the animal 'learnt' that the CS is not related to the UCS in any systematic way; and this may make it difficult to condition the animal to the same CS in later experiments since it has already learned that it is not systematically related to past events.

Hulse et al (1978), Dickinson (1980), Roitblat et al (1983) and Walker (1983) all regard conditioning as involving the formation of central representation of causal relations (or, at least, predictive ones) between events: stimulus event A predicts stimulus event B (the CS predicts the UCS). But the learning may also take the form: stimulus event A predicts that stimulus event B will *not* occur; this is called *conditioned suppression* or *inhibition*.

Pavlov (1927) first trained a dog with three separate stimuli: a flashing light, the tone of C sharp and a rotating disc; all of these were signals for food. Then an 'inhibitory combination' was formed by sounding a metronome along with the rotating disc, this combination never being followed by food; and the dog learned not to salivate. Then the metronome was sounded along with the tone and flashing light which produced a virtual elimination of salivation. Pavlov concluded that the metronome had become a 'conditioned inhibitor'.

Another demonstration of the complexity of conditioning is the phenomenon of *blocking* (Kamin, 1969). If, for example, an animal is shown a light, quickly followed by an electric shock, the light soon comes to elicit fear as a CR. If a noise is then added (Noise + Light + Shock), then the noise should also soon become a CS, since it too is being paired with shock.

However, this is not what happens; if the noise is later presented alone, it fails to produce a CR. Why? It seems that the noise has somehow been 'blocked' from becoming a CS because of the previous conditioning to the light; in cognitive terms, since the light already predicts shock, the noise is irrelevant, it provides no additional information—the animal already 'knows' that shock will follow the light.

Turning now to operant conditioning, the complexity of learning is well illustrated by *learned helplessness* (Seligman, 1974, 1975). Dogs were strapped into a harness and given a series of shocks from which they could not escape. They were later required to learn avoidance behaviour in a shuttlebox—they had to jump a barrier within 10 seconds of a warning signal or suffer 50 seconds of painful shock. Whereas control dogs, which had not been subjected to the inescapable shocks, learned the avoidance response very quickly, about two-thirds of the experimental dogs seemed unable to do so. They seemed passively resigned to suffering the shock and even if they did successfully avoid the shock on one trial, they were unlikely to do so on the next. Some dogs had to be pushed over the barrier 200 times or more before this learned helplessness wore off.

So the dogs, according to Seligman, learned that no behaviour on their part had any effect on the occurrence (or non-occurrence) of a particular event (ie the shock). This has been demonstrated using human subjects by Miller and Norman (1979) and Maier and Seligman (1976) have tried to explain depression in humans in terms of learned helplessness (see Chapters 17 and 28).

Skinner's claim that reinforcements and punishments automatically strengthen and weaken behaviour has been challenged by many, including Bandura (1977). He maintains that: (i) they provide the learner with *information* about the likely consequences of certain behaviour under certain conditions, that is 'what leads to what', and whether we are 'right' or 'wrong' (*feedback*); and (ii) they motivate us by causing us to *anticipate future outcomes*—our present behaviours are largely governed by the outcomes in which we expect them to result.

While Bandura is addressing his comments primarily to human behaviour, one of the earliest challenges to Skinner's view came from a fellow student of learning in rats, Edward Tolman.

Tolman's Cognitive Behaviourism—Latent Learning and Cognitive Maps

Tolman, although working within the behaviourist tradition in the 1920s, '30s and '40s, would today be regarded as a cognitive psychologist, since he explained the learning of rats in terms of inferred cognitive processes, in particular 'cognitive' or mental maps. He also distinguished between learning and performance (or 'knowing' and 'doing').

Tolman and Honzik (1930) showed that learning *can* take place in the absence of reinforcement (contrary to Skinner's position) in the following way: Group 1 were reinforced every time they found their way through a maze to the food box; Group 2 were never reinforced; and Group 3 received no reinforcement for the first ten days of the experiment but did so from day eleven onwards.

Group 1, as you might expect, learned to run the maze quickly and made fewer and fewer mistakes. Again, not surprisingly, Group 2 never decreased the time it took them to find the food and they wandered the same maze aimlessly much of the time. Group 3, however, having apparently made no progress during the first ten days (of no reinforcement) showed a sudden decrease in the time it took to reach the goal-box on day eleven when they received their first reinforcement and caught up almost immediately with Group 1.

Clearly the Group 3 rats had been learning their way through the maze during the first ten days but that learning was *latent* (or 'behaviourally silent'), that is, it did not show up in their actual behaviour (performance). With the incentive of the reinforcement on day eleven, that previously 'hidden' learning was demonstrated, allowing Group 3 rats to catch up very quickly with the Group 1 rats which had been reinforced from the beginning. So Tolman and Honzik had produced evidence for the view that reinforcement may be important in relation to *performance* of learned behaviour but that it is not necessary for the learning itself.

Having established the role of reinforcement, Tolman wanted to know exactly what it is that is learned (and which does not require reinforcement). Tolman's theory (1948) of *sign-learning* (or place-learning) maintains that rats learn something *about* 'what leads to what' in the maze, that is, they learn *expectations* as to which part of the maze will be followed by which other part of the maze. These expectations Tolman called '*cognitive maps*' and they represent a primitive kind of perceptual map of the maze, an understanding of the spatial relationships that constitute the maze (much like the mental map you or I have of familiar streets, those that lead to your home or to college). What's the evidence?

Of course, like all cognitive processes, a cognitive map cannot be directly observed but only inferred from actual behaviour. However, it is difficult to know how else to explain the findings that rats, which have originally learned to run through a maze, could then swim through it if it was flooded or roll through it, or how they could take short-cuts or how, if the maze were rotated, they could find the usual food location from several different starting points.

These findings suggest that it is *not* the individual movements of walking or swimming etc. that constitute the learning of the maze (as the Chain Response or Reflex theory would maintain) but rather something to do with the geographical characteristics of the maze (Sign Learning Theory). In a direct test between these two opposed theories, Restle (1957) flooded a maze immediately after a group of rats had learnt to run it and they were able to swim to the goal-box with no more errors than when they had walked. This clearly supports Tolman's theory of sign learning.

Applications of Conditioning

The three major ways in which conditioning principles have been put to practical use with people are:

i) *Behaviour therapy* or *modification*, which constitutes a major form of treatment of behaviour disorders (and which is discussed in detail in Chapter 29).

ii) *Biofeedback*, a way of bringing automatic, physiological processes under voluntary control (and which is discussed in detail in Chapter 16).

iii) *Programmed learning* or *instruction*, 'a method of instruction that systematically applies the principles of operant conditioning to the learning situation' (Haber and Runyon, 1983).

The first 'teaching machine' was devised by Pressey, an educational psychologist, in 1926; it basically consisted of a series of multiple choice questions used for testing what students had already been taught. Skinner (1954, 1958) advocated the extension of this technique for initial *learning*.

Not only did Skinner believe that all learning (human and animal) takes place according to the principles of (operant) conditioning but that the usual classroom situation is not an ideal situation for learning to happen: the teacher typically has little control over crucial variables such as students paying attention, their motivation and the reinforcements they receive, and often it is the aversive consequences of the classroom which dominate (such as trying to avoid failure or the teacher's disapproval).

Skinner also believed that much conventional teaching-learning is slow and inefficient. Programmed instruction can remove these obstacles to learning on the basis of six principles:

i) The material to be learned is broken down into a number of elements— separate items of information (or frames).

ii)   The material is presented in a pre-determined sequence, such that each step or increment is so small that the probability of making errors is almost zero; this continuous reinforcement schedule ensures a high level of *motivation*.

iii) For every correct response, an immediate reinforcement is provided in the form of the learner being told that the response is correct (*immediate feedback*); an incorrect response takes the learner back to that item (usually after a brief account of why the answer is incorrect). In either case, the learner is checking their own progress.

iv)   At each step, the learner must emit (or voluntarily produce) a correct answer in order to receive a reinforcement; in this way, reinforcement is *contingent* upon appropriate behaviour and the learner is *actively participating* in their learning.

v)   The reinforcement of correct responses to a number of small steps (successive approximations) making up the material to be learned represents a form of *shaping*.

vi)   The learner works at their own pace, which allows for any individual differences in speed of learning.

Linear Versus Branching Programmes

The kind of programmed learning which Skinner devised and advocated is *linear*; it comprises a predetermined sequence of steps which is the same for all students and each must be correctly answered before moving on to the next. By contrast, *branching* programmes (Crowder, 1961) usually comprise larger frames (chunks of information and explanations rather than very short, simple, questions and bits of information) and they allow alternative routes through the material depending on the accuracy of the learner's answers. This allows more able students to skip familiar material and move on to more advanced material. Branching also enables a learner who makes an error to find out *why* the answer is wrong by directing them to branch off from the main stem of the programme and work through some special review material.

Both linear and branching programmes can take the form of: (a) *books* (programmed texts); (b) *teaching machines* (in which, for example, a frame is exposed in the left-hand window and the student writes the answer in the right-hand window, and pulling a lever moves the answer under a perspex cover, revealing the correct answer and the next frame); or (c) *Computer Assisted Instruction* (CAI). CAI usually involves an elaborate, complex, branching programme; the learner either operates a teletype keyboard or uses a special probe to indicate their answer on a monitor.

How Effective is Programmed Instruction?

To compare programmed instruction (often called self-instruction) with traditional teaching methods is no simple matter, partly because each can vary so much and each may interact with a number of other variables. Ellson et al (1968) found that one or two sessions a day with individual tutors made no significant improvement in the reading performance of slum children, but two sessions a day of CAI did; and Suppes and Morningstar (1969) also found that CAI was more effective than traditional classroom instruction. However, Seltzer (1971) discovered that some of the superiority of CAI over conventional methods in socially-depressed areas could be attributed to the apathy and incompetence of some classroom teachers rather than reflecting a fundamental difference in the two methods.

Schramm (1964) reviewed 165 studies and concluded that students do learn from programmed instruction but, in general, it is neither superior nor inferior to conventional teaching methods. It seems that both the type of material and the type of students will have a major bearing on the relative effectiveness of methods of instruction.

Social Learning Theory and Observational Learning

In other words, learning through watching rather than doing.

A major alternative to conditioning (as an attempt to understand learning) comes from Social Learning Theory. This originated in the USA in the 1940s and '50s as an attempt to re-interpret certain aspects of Freud's psycho-analytic theory in the terms of conditioning theory (or Orthodox Learning Theory) (eg Dollard and Miller, 1950). This was carried on in the 1960s and 1970s, notably by Albert Bandura, who tried to make Freud's concept of identification more objective and scientifically viable by studying it in the laboratory in the form of imitation.

How are Social Learning Theory and Orthodox Learning Theory Related?

i) Along with other behaviourist psychologists, the Social Learning theorists (SL theorists) believe that all behaviour is learned through the same mechanisms, according to the same principles of learning. However, where they differ significantly from Pavlov, Watson, Skinner and so on, is in their interest specifically in human learning, especially the acquisition of social and moral behaviour. (We shall be discussing both theories in relation to moral development in Chapter 21.) According to McLoughlin (1971), social learning is 'behaviour learned in interpersonal situations and linked to the needs that require for their satisfaction the mediation of other people'.

ii) Although SL theorists agree that we should observe what is observable, they also believe that there are important cognitive or mediating variables which intervene between stimulus and response without which we cannot adequately explain behaviour. These cognitive variables cannot be directly observed but can only be inferred from observing actual behaviour. We shall hear more about this later on.

iii) SL theorists do not deny the importance of classical and operant conditioning but they do think that these learning processes cannot adequately account for the appearance of *novel* behaviour, that is, behaviour which the individual has not displayed before; classical conditioning can explain how a response shifts from one stimulus to another (stimulus substitution) while operant can explain how spontaneously-produced responses, through selective reinforcement and shaping, become more likely to be repeated. But if these were the *only* two kinds of learning, the child's behavioural repertoire would be very limited indeed.

Consequently, the SL theorists have emphasized a kind of learning that is distinct from conditioning, namely *observational learning*, that is, learning through watching the behaviour of another person. There are several important points to note about the concept of observational learning:

a) The person whose behaviour is observed is called the *model*; hence 'modelling' is normally used synonymously with 'observational learning'.

b) The learning takes place spontaneously, with no deliberate effort on the learner's part or any intention to teach on the model's part.

c) Both fairly specific behaviours (eg nailbiting) and more general, emotional states (eg fear of the dentist) can be modelled (the latter through facial expressions, body posture etc.).

d) Observational learning, as such, takes place without any reinforcement (eg Bandura, 1965); for learning to occur, mere exposure to the model is sufficient. However, whether the learning actually reveals itself in the child's behaviour (ie *imitated*) depends, among other things, on the *consequences* of the behaviour, both for the model and the child (eg Bandura, Ross and Ross, 1963). So, whereas for Skinner the role of reinforcement is central to the learning process itself, for the SL theorists it is important only in so far as it determines the likelihood of learned responses actually being demonstrated. This, of course, is the crucial distinction between learning and performance which we came across when discussing Tolman's cognitive behaviourism.

e) Much of the SL theorists' research has centered on the characteristics of models which make them more or less likely to be imitated and the conditions under which the learning will be performed.

Reinforcement as Information about the Future

We noted above that Bandura takes a very different view of how reinforcement works to Skinner and this relates directly to the learning-performance distinction which Bandura makes but which Skinner does not.

According to Skinner, reinforcement works *automatically*; the strengthening of a response simply 'happens' and the learner, human or animal, is not required to assess or evaluate the effects of their behaviour. Bandura (1977), on the other hand, maintains that, 'Reinforcement serves principally as an informative and motivational operation rather than as a mechanical response strengthener.' By *informative* he means that the consequences of our behaviour (reinforcement or punishment) tell us under what circumstances it would seem wise to try a particular behaviour in the future, that is, they improve our prediction of whether a given action will lead to pleasant or unpleasant outcomes in the future. While Skinner believes that a consequence exerts its influence in *reverse* (ie strengthening the behaviour that *preceded* the reinforcement or punishment), Bandura argues that the consequence exerts its influence forwards, *into the future*, by giving the learner information about what effects can be expected if they behave that way again in similar circumstances.

For these reasons, we can learn from observing others (as well as from our own behaviour), since watching others can provide the same information as to what kind of behaviour leads to which consequence.

By *motivational*, Bandura means that we are more likely to try to learn the modelled behaviour if we value the consequences related to that behaviour. But since Bandura also makes the distinction between learning and performance, the motivational effect of reinforcement (as we noted above) may be greater in relation to demonstration of learning rather than the learning itself.

The Role of Cognitive Factors in Observational Learning

The learning process is a much more complex one according to Bandura than it is for Skinner; in Bandura's view, 'contrary to mechanistic metaphors, outcomes change behaviour in humans through the intervening influence of thought' (1974). Bandura believes that there are five major functions involved in observational learning:

i) Paying *attention*—the learner must attend to the pertinent clues in the stimulus situation and ignore those aspects of the model and the environment that are incidental and do not affect the performance the learner seeks to learn. Especially with complex behaviour, failure to reproduce the behaviour properly later on is often due to misdirected attention at the time of modelling.

ii) Recording in memory a *visual image* or *semantic code* for the modelled behaviour, as without an adequate coding system the learner fails to store what has been seen or heard (see Chapter 6). There are obvious developmental trends in the ability to learn from models; whereas an infant's use of modelling is confined mainly to immediate imitation, the older child can defer (postpone) imitation because of its superior use of symbols. The codes must, of course, be suitable for transforming into overt actions.

iii) *Memory permanence*—this refers to devices such as rehearsal and use of multiple codes to help *retain* the stored information over long periods.

iv) *Reproducing the observed motor activities accurately*—this usually requires a number of trials in order to get the muscular *feel* of the behaviour (through feedback). Again, there are developmental trends involved here, whereby the older child enjoys greater muscular strength and control.

v) *Motivation*—behaviourists have traditionally equated this with the role of the *consequences of behaviour* and we have already discussed above the differences between Bandura's and Skinner's interpretation of the nature of reinforcement and how it works. Some evidence for the role of cognitive factors is provided by a study by Bandura et al (1963) in which children were asked to reproduce the actions of a model seen on a film. Group 1 simply watched the film, Group 2 were asked to describe the model's actions as they saw them on the film and Group 3 were asked to count while watching the film (an interfering task). It was found that Group 2 children were able to reproduce the behaviour of the model most accurately and thoroughly through the aid of verbalization; as expected, Group 3 children did worst of all, with Group 1 children somewhere in between.

We shall have more to say about the role of cognitive factors in modelling in Chapter 21 on moral development.

Insight Learning

Insight learning represents a view of learning as 'purely cognitive' and stems from a theoretical approach in psychology which is diametrically opposed to the S–R approach, namely, the *Gestalt* school. The Gestalt psychologists are best known for their work on perception (see Chapter 4) and their view of learning is directly linked to their view of perception; indeed, insight learning can be defined as a perceptual restructuring of the elements that constitute a problem-situation, whereby a previously missing 'ingredient' is supplied and all the parts are seen in relationship to each other, forming a meaningful whole.

For example, imagine a chimpanzee, in its cage, reaching for a banana which lies outside the cage; its arm is not long enough to get the banana, but also outside the cage is a stick which the chimp can reach and which is long enough to reach the banana. After reaching with its arm unsuccessfully, it suddenly reaches for the stick and uses it to rake in the banana.

Kohler (1925), one of the leading Gestalt psychologists, used this and similar problems to demonstrate insight learning, which he saw as opposed to the trial-and-error learning involved in S–R approaches. In the latter, stimulus and response become associated when, by chance, the animal produces the correct response (or 'solves the problem') and is reinforced for doing so. However, the correct response does not appear suddenly, it merely takes less and less time to be made on each subsequent trial and there is no 'understanding' involved.

By contrast, in insight learning a sudden solution is the rule (usually preceded by long pauses, during which there is inspection of the whole visual field) and once the solution has appeared, it can be repeated immediately the next time the problem is confronted. What is learned is not a specific set of conditioned associations but a cognitive relationship between a means to an end, and this makes *transfer* to other, similar, problem situations easier.

For example, Sultan (Kohler's most intelligent chimp) was able to pull into the cage the longer of two sticks by using the shorter one and then, with the longer one, was able to pull in a piece of fruit. Again, he was able to join two sticks together in order to make a stick long enough to rake in some fruit. In a different kind of problem, he learned to stack boxes, one on top of the other, in order to reach bananas suspended from the ceiling.

However, a couple of qualifications need to be made:

a) Animals do not usually demonstrate insight learning very easily unless all the elements that constitute the problem are in their field of vision at the same time; for example, the chimp has to be able to see the fruit and sticks (or boxes) together before it can grasp their relationship and solve the problem. People, by contrast, could immediately *think* of a stick and go looking for one; language is an important tool for thinking in this kind of problem-solving situation.

b) Kohler has been criticized for his belief that insight involves a sudden re-structuring of the situation independent of the animal's past experience. There is evidence that insightful solutions can be facilitated by 'hints' or cues, especially if the elements of the problem situation are already familiar to the learner. This is captured especially well in another solution that Sultan found to the banana-problem; he succeeded in breaking off a branch from a sawn-off castor-oil bush, located inside the cage, which he used to rake in a banana lying outside the cage. Although Kohler described this as happening in 'one single quick chain of action', and despite its appearance as a 'flash of insight', it did not come 'out of the blue', out of nowhere. Sultan was very familiar with bananas and with castor-oil bushes, as well as sticks.

According to Arthur Koestler (1970), all acts of 'creation', whether in painting, humour, poetry or science, share one basic characteristic, namely the juxtaposition of two concepts or ideas or images which were previously separate. When two things, previously unrelated, are seen as belonging together in some way, a joke or a scientific discovery is made. He cites the story of Archimedes who was asked to judge whether a beautiful crown, allegedly made of pure gold, had in fact been adulterated with silver. Short of melting it down, he was stumped—he knew the specific weight of gold (its weight per volume unit) but how was he to measure the volume of such a complicated and ornate object as the crown?

One day, while getting into his bath, Archimedes noticed the familiar sight of the water-level rising and, in a flash ('Eureka!') he realized that the volume of water displaced was equal to the volume of his immersed body and that here was a way that the volume of the crown could also be measured. So, two already familiar pieces of knowledge, first the specific weight of gold, and, secondly, water displacement equalling object immersion, were, for the first time, related to each other and in that moment a discovery was made. Only someone with Archimedes' knowledge could have made such a discovery; in Koestler's terms, he was *ripe* to make the discovery.

In the case of chimpanzees, their ripeness includes their manual dexterity and their advanced sensory motor co-ordination (biological) and their familiarity with sticks, bananas etc (experiential or environmental); the former are reminiscent of Scligman's concept of preparedness (see page 63) and the latter is demonstrated by a study of Birch (1945). Monkeys which were allowed to play with sticks for three days solved the food-raking problem faster than monkeys without such experience.

Do We Have to Choose Between Trial-and-Error and Insight?

In other words, is it either Thorndike or Kohler?

Koestler believes that the debate between the S–R and the cognitive psychologists derives to a large extent from a refusal to take seriously the notion of ripeness. Rats and cats have generally been presented with tasks for which they are biologically ill-fitted and so the resulting learning was bound to appear gradual, piecemeal, and at first quite random.

Kohler and the Gestalt school, by contrast, set chimps problems for which they were (almost) ripe and so gave the impression that all learning is based on insight.

So, is there a middle ground?

Gagné's Hierarchy of Learning

Gagné (1970) has attempted to answer the question regarding the relationship between simple and complex forms of learning. Is there a continuity between them and, if so, what form does this take? His solution is to regard eight major varieties of learning as *hierarchically* related, each building on earlier, more simple abilities, which, therefore, represent prerequisites for later, more complex abilities. These are summarized in Table 3.3.

Table 3.3   Gagné's hierarchy of learning

1. *Signal learning*	The establishment of a simple connection in which a stimulus takes on the properties of a signal. *(classical conditioning)*
2. *Stimulus-Response learning*	The establishment of a connection between a stimulus and a response where the response is a voluntary movement and the connection is instrumental in satisfying a need or motive. *(operant conditioning)*
1 and 2 are prerequisites for: 3. *Chaining*	The connecting of a sequence of two or more previously learned stimulus-response connections.
4. *Verbal association*	The learning of chains that are specifically verbal, important for the acquisition and use of language. Enables a number of learned connections involving words to be emitted in a single sequence.
3 and 4 are prerequisites for: 5. *Discrimination learning*	Making different responses to similar stimuli. Involves more than simply making isolated stimulus-response connections because it is necessary to deal with the problem of interference between similar items.
5 is a prerequisite for: 6. *Concept learning*	Learning to make a common response to stimuli that form a class or category but which differ in their physical characteristics. Requires representing information in memory, classifying events and discriminating between them on basis of abstracted properties.
6 is a prerequisite for: 7. *Rule-learning*	A rule is a chain of two or more concepts (eg 'if A then B').
7 is a prerequisite for: 8. *Problem-solving*	Involves re-combining old rules into new ones, making it possible to answer questions and solve problems, especially important for real-life human problem-solving situations.

Harlow's Concept of Learning Sets

According to Harlow (1949), S–R learning and insight learning are related; essentially, they are two different phases of the same, continuous process, with S–R learning predominant in the early stages and insight developing out of prior S–R connections. He suggests that the concept of a *learning set* (or 'learning to learn') represents an intervening process between S–R and insight learning; the greater the number of sets, the better equipped the learner is to adapt to a changing environment, and a very large number of different sets 'may supply the raw material for human thinking'.

To study learning sets, Harlow gave monkeys a variety of discrimination tasks. In the simplest, the monkey had to choose between two objects, one of which was designated the 'correct one'; in a more complex task the monkey had to find the 'odd-one-out' of three objects. In both types of task, the pair of objects or set of three was changed each time a correct discrimination was made. So, for example, the monkey might be shown a small red square and a large blue circle and would be given six trials in which to choose the 'correct' one (for which a food reward was given). When this had been achieved a different pair of objects (eg, a green triangle and a black circle) was presented and once again the monkey had six trials in which to make the correct discrimination.

In one study, involving 344 of these two-object tasks, the results were dramatic. Learning the first few discriminations was difficult but it gradually became easier as the number of different tasks increased, until after 300 the solution was immediate (solved on the first trial). Remember that the same pair of objects was never used more than once.

There were certain kinds of errors to which different monkeys were prone that made it quite systematic. For example, choosing the object on the right, or alternating sides from trial to trial, or always choosing the larger object. Such errors gradually dropped out as the monkey realized that none of these was relevant to the solution; once this happened, it could adopt a new strategy that was appropriate to *all* the tasks and which did not depend on the specific stimuli used. According to Harlow, a learning set involves learning a general skill applicable to a whole new class of problems, or again, it consists of learning a simple rule or code, based on a *conceptual* (not a perceptual) relationship (1959). To this extent, Harlow demonstrated that insightful learning itself is (at least partially) learned and grows out of more random, trial-and-error learning.

Bruner (1966) reported similar findings in rats running mazes: after learning to take the route involving a series of left/right/left/right turns, they took substantially less time than before to learn to reverse the sequence (right/left/right/left), that is, they had learned to alternate.

Learning Set and Transfer of Learning

Learning set represents a special case of a more general phenomenon known as transfer of learning (or training). Essentially, transfer refers to the influence of earlier learning on later learning which we saw, when defining learning at the beginning of the chapter, to be an inherent feature of the learning process in general (eg Howe, 1980).

Howe maintains that some kinds of transfer take the form of simple stimulus generalization (equivalent to Gagné's Signal Learning) while in more complex learning situations transfer may depend on the acquisition of rules or principles that apply to a variety of different circumstances (Gagné's Concept and Rule Learning and Problem-Solving). Learning sets can be viewed as intermediate between simple generalization and the more complex transfer phenomena involved in hierarchically organized skills.

It used to be thought that certain disciplines (such as Latin or maths) were so general in their transferability that they could 'train the mind' to cope with almost any demand that might subsequently be made of it. (This was the thinking behind the 'classical' education of the public schools.) However, it is now recognised (especially for motor skills) that the effect of training is much more limited and is restrained by the degree of similarity of the components of different tasks; and yet the notion of similarity itself is a complex one.

For instance, in a *mirror-drawing* task, practice under one condition (eg drawing the outline of a star without the mirror) *interferes* with performance under the other conditions (drawing using only the mirror-image of the star) producing *negative transfer*. Yet tracing patterns of very different appearance might seem to constitute dissimilar tasks but in fact there is considerable *positive transfer* from practising one pattern using only the mirror-image to being able to trace another under the same conditions. Positive transfer also occurs when subjects practise with their non-preferred hand. The normal laboratory procedure for studying transfer is as follows:

Experimental group	Learns A	Learns B	Tested on B
Control group		Learns B	Tested on B

If learning A enhances the learning of B, then we say that positive transfer occurs; if A interferes with B then we speak of negative transfer and if A makes no difference either way then there is no transfer.

Transfer is commonly analysed in S–R terms: (i) where the S–R relationships are the same (eg A and B require the same response) then we expect to find positive transfer; (ii) where the S–R relationships are different (A requires one response and B a different, incompatible response) then we expect negative transfer.

Again, when an *old* response is required by a *new* stimulus there is positive transfer; when a *new* response is required by an *old* stimulus there is negative transfer. Learning sets, of course, are one form of positive transfer and positive transfer in general illustrates the cumulative nature of learning, whereby new learning builds on prior learning. Not only is learning cumulative but, as we said early in the chapter, it is closely intertwined with other processes, particularly perception and memory and it is to these that we now turn in the next three chapters.

4

Sensory Processes, Perception and Attention

When we move our eyes or our heads, the objects we see around us remain stable; similarly, when we follow an object that is itself moving, we attribute the movement to the object and not to ourselves. When we approach somebody in the street, we do not experience them as gradually growing 'before our very eyes'; and objects seen from various angles are still recognized as 'the same' object as they are when seen from head-on.

These examples of how we experience the world may seem so commonplace as not worth mentioning until we realize what is actually taking place physically. If we compare what we experience (namely, a world of objects that remain stable and constant) with what our sense organs receive in the form of physical stimulation (an almost continuous state of flux) it is almost as if there are two entirely different worlds involved: the one we are consciously aware of is a world of 'things' and people (*perception*) and the one we are not aware of is a world of sense-data (*sensation*).

How are Sensation and Perception Related?

Essentially, perception cannot occur in the absence of sensation, but the sense-data constitute only the 'raw material' from which our conscious awareness of objects is constructed. So, to the extent that we perceive the world as it really is, we do this *indirectly*, through analysing, interpreting and trying to make sense of sensations. It seems that we are in direct and immediate contact with the world as we do not have to work out consciously what objects are (not usually, at least). However, our awareness of things is the end-product of a long and complex process, which begins with physical energy stimulating the sense-organs (light in the case of vision, sound waves in the case of hearing and so on) and ends with the brain interpreting the information that it has received from the sense organs. (We shall look later at how the visual system processes visual information.) So whereas the visual system as a whole is involved in (visual) perception, in sensation only the sense-organs (the eyes) are directly stimulated; but, of course, the sense-organs are part of the perceptual system as a whole.

Definitions of Perception

Gregory (1966) brings out this difference when he states that, 'Perception is not determined simply by stimulus patterns; rather it is a dynamic searching for the best interpretation of the available data . . . perception involves going beyond the immediately given evidence of the senses.'

Coon (1983) defines perception as, 'the process of assembling sensations into a useable mental representation of the world'. Again, 'perception creates faces, melodies, works of art, illusions etc, out of the raw material of sensation'.

Defining perception in terms of sensory stimulation makes it necessary to distinguish between perception proper and experiences which are indistinguishable from these but which do not involve stimulation of the sense-organs, namely, hallucinations (see Chapter 28), eg 'seeing pink elephants' in the absence of any.

Coon's reference to illusions suggests another distinction, namely between accurate perception, whereby our interpretation matches the objective nature of the object or stimulus (true or *veridical* perception), and mistaken or *false* perception, where we in some way mis-interpret what is presented to the senses. Illusions, of course, are examples of mistaken perception. But whereas in hallucinations the sense-organs are not involved (only the brain), in illusions it is the interpretation of the sense-data that results in a mis-perception. (We shall discuss illusions later in the chapter.)

The Senses—Providing the Raw Material of Perception

According to Ornstein (1975) we do not perceive objective reality but, rather, our *construction* of reality; our sense organs gather information which the brain modifies and sorts and this 'heavily filtered input' is compared with memories, expectancies and so on until, finally, our consciousness is constructed as a 'best guess' about reality.

In a similar vein, William James (1902) maintained that, 'the mind, in short, works on the data it receives much as the sculptor works on his block of stone'. However, different artists use different materials and, similarly, different sensory systems provide different kinds of sense-data for the perceiver-sculptor to 'model'. Perhaps it is unnecessary to spell out that each of our various sensory systems is only designed to respond to a particular kind of stimulation but a related, and equally important point (often overlooked) is that they also function as *data-reduction systems* (eg Ornstein, 1975).

To the extent that something cannot be sensed (ie, our senses are not responsive or sensitive to it) it does not exist for us; while we normally regard our senses as the 'windows' to the world, a major job they perform is to discard 'irrelevant' information and to register only what is likely to be of practical value (clearly, something which has occurred as a result of evolutionary forces). We would be overwhelmed if we responded to the world as it is; different forms of energy are so diverse that they are still being discovered and all species have developed particular sensitivity to certain of these which have aided their survival.

The frog is a useful example here: in the visual system there are specialized kinds of detectors, one of which responds only to small, dark, objects coming into the field of vision and which move quite close to the eye (a net convexity detector). Clearly, the frog has evolved its own specialized 'bug-perceiving' sub-system (Lettvin et al, 1965).

The human eye responds to radiant electromagnetic energy in the visible spectrum; although the entire spectrum ranges from less than 1 billionth of a metre to more than 100 metres, we can 'see' only the tiny portion between 380 and 780 billionths of a metre (nanometres) which we call light. Infra-red radiation, ultrasonics, pressure, mechanical vibrations in the air and other forms of energy are all around us and yet, by design, the eye only responds to that very limited part of the visible electromagnetic spectrum. (Although pressure on the eyeball produces sensations of light, it is external sources of light which normally produce the sensation.)

Classification of Sensory Systems

The senses have been classified in several ways. For example, Sherrington (1906) identified three kinds of receptors: (i) *exteroceptors* (which tell us about the external environment); (ii) *interoceptors* (which tell us about the internal environment); and (iii) *proprioceptors* (which deal with the position of our body in space and its movement through space). *Exteroception* includes the five 'traditional' senses of *sight* (vision), *hearing* (audition), *smell* (olfaction), *taste* (gustation) and *touch* (cutaneous or skin senses). *Interoception* includes the internal receptors for oxygen, carbon dioxide, blood glucose and so on. *Proprioception* is usually sub-divided into: (i) the *kinaesthetic sense*, which monitors movements of the limbs, joints and muscles; and (ii) the *vestibular sense*, which responds to gravity and the movements of the head.

Gibson (1966) rejected proprioception as a distinct sensory system (and saw taste and smell as representing the same system), and Legge (1975) includes proprioception under the general heading of interoception.

Characteristics of Sensory Systems

However we classify them, sensory systems (or modalities) have certain characteristics in common:

i) as we have already seen, they each respond to particular forms of energy or information:

ii) they each have a *sense organ* (or accessory structure) which is the first 'point of entry' for the information which will be processed by the system (the sense organ, as it were, 'catches' the information);

iii) they each have *sense-receptors* (or transducers), specialized cells which are sensitive to particular kinds of energy and which then convert it into electrical nerve impulses, the only form in which this physical energy can be dealt with by the brain (see Chapter 15).

Table 4.1 Sense organs, sense receptors and brain areas for the 6 major sensory systems/modalities

Sense modality	Sense organ (Accessory Structure)	Sense receptor (Transducer)	Brain area (Cortex unless otherwise indicated)
Vision (Sight)	Eye (in particular, the lens)	Rods and cones (in the retina)	Occipital lobe (via Optic Nerve)
Audition (Hearing)	Outer ear (Pinna) Middle ear (Eardrum and Ossicles) Inner ear (Cochlea)	Specialized hair cells in the organ of corti situated in the cochlea	Temporal lobe (via Auditory Nerve)
Gustation (Taste)	Tongue (in particular, the taste buds and papillae, the ridges around the side of the tongue)	Special receptors in the taste buds which connect with sensory neurons (nerve-cells)	Temporal lobe (via Gustatory Nerve)
Olfaction (Smell)	Nose (in particular, the olfactory mucosa of the nasal cavity)	Transducers in the olfactory mucosa	Temporal lobe and limbic system (via olfactory bulb and olfactory tracts)
Skin or cutaneous senses (Touch)	Skin	There are about 5 million sensors of at least 7 types, eg: 1. Meissner's corpuscles (Touch); 2. Pacinian corpuscles (Stretching and vibration) 3. Krause end bulbs (Cold)	Parietal lobe (somatosensory cortex) and cerebellum
Proprioception — kinaesthetic and vestibular senses	Inner ear (semicircular canals) (in particular, the vestibular sacs)	Vestibular sensors or otoliths ('earstones'), tiny crystals attached to hair cells in vestibular sacs which are sensitive to gravity	Cerebellum (via Vestibular nerve)

iv) they each involve a specialized part of the brain which interprets the messages received from the sense-receptors and (usually) results in conscious awareness of an object, a person, a word, a taste etc. (ie, we perceive).

v) a certain minimum stimulation of the sense receptors is necessary before any sensory experience will occur; this is known as the *absolute threshold*. In practice, instead of finding a single intensity value below which a subject never detects the stimulus and above which they always detect it, a *range* of values is found and the absolute threshold is taken to be the value at which the stimulus is detected 50 per cent of the time.

Unfortunately, there is only space to discuss vision in any detail; Table 4.1 summarizes the major sense organs, sense receptors and brain areas involved in the six major sensory systems.

Not only does the absolute threshold vary from individual to individual but it varies for the same individual at different times, depending on physical state, motivation, physical conditions of presentation and so on.

The *difference threshold* is the minimum amount of stimulation necessary to discriminate between two stimuli and is also known as the *just noticeable difference* (jnd). Weber's law states that the jnd is a constant value but this, of course, will differ from one sense modality to another; for example, 1/133 is the value needed to tell apart the pitch of two different tones and 1/5 for discriminating between saline solutions.

Fechner (1860) reformulated Weber's law and the Weber-Fechner law, as it has come to be known, states that large increases in the intensity of a stimulus produces smaller, proportional, increases in the perceived intensity. Fechner's was one of the first attempts to express mathematically a psychological phenomenon and was an important contribution to *psychophysics*, which studies the relationship between physical stimuli and the subjective experience of them and which is of enormous historical importance in the development of psychology as a science.

The Weber-Fechner law holds only approximately through the middle ranges of stimulus intensities and an alternative approach is *signal detection theory*, which rejects the notion of thresholds altogether. Each sensory channel always carries *noise* (any activity which interferes with the detection of a signal); the stronger the stimulus, the higher the signal-to-noise ratio and the easier it is to detect the stimulus. The detection of a stimulus, therefore, then becomes a statistical matter.

The Visual System

i) The Sense-organ—The Eye
Ornstein (1975) describes the eye as, 'the most important avenue of personal consciousness' and it is estimated that 90 per cent of the information we receive about the external world reaches us through the eyes. The great majority of research interest has focused on vision, both as a sensory system and a perceptual system.

The sense organ of vision is the eye and its major structures are shown in Figure 4.1 on page 82.

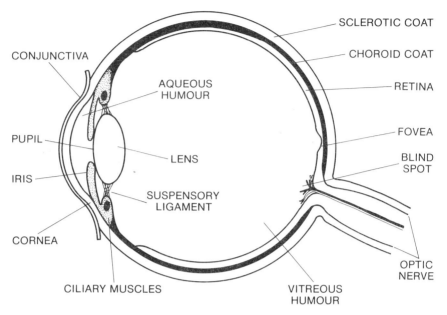

Figure 4.1   The major structures of the human eye

The *conjunctiva* is a transparent, delicate membrane, covering the inside of the eyelids and the front of the eye. It contains nerves and many tiny blood vessels which dilate (expand) if the eye is irritated or injured (the eye becomes bloodshot). The *cornea* is a transparent membrane which protects the lens and through which light enters the eye.

The *pupil* regulates the amount of light entering the eye, via the *iris* (the coloured part of the eye) which has tiny sets of muscles that dilate and contract the pupil. (Pupil size is also regulated by the ciliary muscles.) In bright light, the pupil contracts to shut out some of the light rays; when light is dim or we are looking at distant objects, the pupil dilates to let more light in. Ultimately, pupil size is controlled by the Autonomic Nervous System or ANS (and so is outside conscious control); the parasympathetic branch of the ANS controls change in pupil size as a function of change in illumination, while the sympathetic branch dilates the pupils under conditions of strong emotional arousal (eg, an 'emergency' situation when we need to see 'better'). (See Chapter 15.)

The *lens*, situated just behind the iris, is enclosed in a capsule held firmly in place by the *suspensory ligaments*. It focuses light on the retina as an inverted (upside-down) image and its shape is regulated by the *ciliary muscles*. Between the cornea and the lens is the *anterior chamber* filled with *aqueous humour*, a clear, watery fluid, and behind the lens is the *posterior chamber* (larger than the anterior) and filled with *vitreous humour*, a jelly-like substance. Both fluids give the eyeball its shape and help to keep it firm.

The *sclerotic coat* is the thickest layer of the eyeball and forms the outer, white part of the eye. It consists of a strong, fibrous membrane, except in the front where it bulges to form the cornea. The *choroid coat* is a dark layer containing black colouring matter which darkens the chamber of the eye and prevents reflection of light inside the eye; in front, it becomes the iris which is seen through the transparent cornea.

The *retina* is the innermost layer of the eyeball, formed by the expansion of the optic nerve which enters at the back and a little to the nasal side of the eye. It is a delicate membrane, comprising three main layers:

i)   *Rods* and *cones*, photosensitive cells which convert light energy into electrical nerve impulses (and forming the rear layer of the retina);
ii) *Biopolar cells*, which are connected to the rods and cones and which are also connected to;
iii) *Ganglion cells*, whose fibres (axons) form the beginning of the *optic nerve* leading to the brain.

ii) The Receptors—Rods and Cones

Most of the eye's structures are, in fact, accessory structures and Gregory (1966) has estimated that only about 10 per cent of the light entering the eye actually reaches the transducers (rods and cones), the rest being absorbed by the accessory structures.

The *rods* are one thousand times more sensitive than cones and are far more numerous—in each retina there are 125 million rods and 6 million cones. Their distribution around the retina also differs: *cones* are much more numerous towards the centre of the retina, in particular, the *fovea*, where there is a concentration of about 50 000 cones, while the rods are distributed fairly evenly around the periphery (but none is to be found in the fovea). The rods are specialized for vision in dim light (including night-time vision) and contain a photosensitive chemical (rhodopsin) which changes structure in response to low levels of illumination; they help us see black, white and intermediate greys (achromatic colour) and this is referred to as scotopic vision. The cones are specialized for bright light vision (including daylight) and contain iodopsin; they help us see chromatic colour (red, green, blue etc.) and provide photopic vision.

When focusing on objects in bright light, the most sharply-defined image is obtained by looking directly at them, thereby projecting the light onto the fovea (which, remember, is packed with cones); in night-light, however, the sharpest image is actually produced by looking slightly to one side of the object (eg, a star in the sky), thereby stimulating the rods which are found in the periphery of the retina.

The chemical difference between the rods and cones also explains the phenomenon of *dark adaptation*: if you go into a dark cinema from bright sunlight, you will experience near blindness for a few seconds because the rods need a little time to take over from the cones which were responding outside (ie, the rhodopsin in the rods is being regenerated or re-synthesized, having been 'bleached' by the bright sunlight). It takes 30 minutes for the rods to reach their maximum level of responding.

The 131 million rods and cones are 'reduced' to one million ganglion cells which make up the optic nerve; this means that information reaching the brain has already been 'refined' to some extent compared with the relatively 'raw' information received from other sensory nerves. However, the degree of 'reduction' or *summation* differs considerably for different areas of the retina: in the periphery, up to 1200 rods may combine to form a single ganglion cell and thus to a single axon in the optic nerve, providing only very general visual information; while at the fovea, perhaps only ten to twelve cones are summed for each ganglion cell and this provides much more detailed information. Two other kinds of cell, *horizontal* and *amacrine*, interconnect with groups of the other cells and connect them together, which increases further the degree of information-processing which takes place in the retina itself.

iii) Colour-Vision and Colour-Blindness

Colour is composed of three *primary colours*, red, blue and green (yellow is sometimes included as a fourth), and there are three corresponding types of cone—red-sensitive, blue-sensitive and green-sensitive (they each contain different photopigments and are maximally sensitive to light in short, medium and long wavelengths, S, M and L cones respectively).

Any chromatic light hitting the retina is composed of different amounts of these primary colours (eg, turquoise might be 70 per cent blue and 30 per cent green) so blue-sensitive cones would 'fire' fairly quickly and green-sensitive cones fairly slowly—and red-sensitive ones would not fire at all.

However, *perceived* colour is not solely determined by the wavelength composition of the light reflected from the object; other influences include:

a) *Prior stimulation* of the retina (as shown by negative after-images; if you stare at, say, a bright red surface and then look at a white wall, the after-image will normally be bluish-green, which is complementary to red);

b) *Nature of the surroundings*, such as the simultaneous contrast created by adjacent areas of different colour or brightness, eg, a grey square will appear brighter set against a black background than against a white background;

c) Our familiarity and knowledge of an object's colour (this relates to perceptual *constancy*, which we shall discuss in more detail later in the chapter, but it shows the artificiality of distinguishing, in practice, between sensation and perception).

The normal eye can discriminate three systems of colour: (i) *light-dark*; (ii) *yellow-blue*; and (iii) *red-green* (ie, it is *trichromatic*). The absence of (ii) or (iii) produces *dichromatic* vision (partial colour blindness) and the absence of both produces *monochromatic* or *achromatic* vision (total colour-blindness). Most common is red-green blindness (about 7 per cent of males and less than 1 per cent of females), the next most common is monochromatic vision (but still confined to fewer than 1 in 40 000 people), and least common of all is yellow-blue blindness (Hilgard et al, 1979).

iv) Visual Pathways—from Eye to Brain

As we have seen, the 131 million receptors in each eye are combined to form the 1 million optic nerve fibres which means that there is a massive integration and channelling of information.

As you can see from Figure 4.2, the pathway from the half of each retina closest to the nose crosses over at the *optic chiasma* (or chasm) and travels to the *opposite* hemisphere (crossed pathways), while the pathway from the half

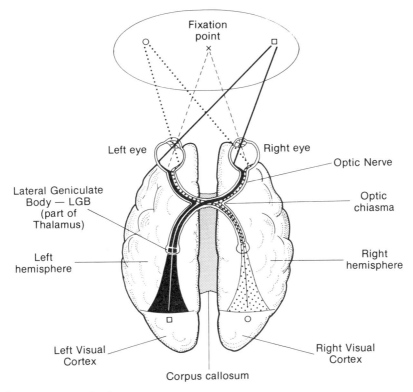

Figure 4.2 The visual system

of each retina furthest from the nose (uncrossed pathways) travels to the hemisphere on the *same* side as the eye. This means that if somebody fixates on a point straight ahead of them, so that the eyes converge, the image of an object to the *right* of fixation falls on the left half of each retina and information about it passes along the crossed pathway from the right eye and the uncrossed pathway from the left eye to the *left* hemisphere—no information is passed directly to the right hemisphere. For an object to the *left* of fixation, all these relationships are reversed so that information is passed directly only to the *right* hemisphere. Therefore it follows that any damage to the visual area of just one hemisphere will produce blind areas in *both* eyes; however, the crossed pathway ensures that complete blindness in *either* eye will *not* occur.

Before reaching the occipital cortex, the optic nerve travels through the *lateral geniculate body* (LGB), which is located in the thalamus, and visual pathways also travel to other sub-cortical areas, including the *superior colliculus*.

The LGB is divided into six layers of cells, three responding to input from the left eye and alternating with three from the right eye. Each cell responds only to light on a specific part of the retina called its *receptive field*: the receptive fields of LGB cells are spread across the entire retina with a great deal of overlap.

The thalamus as a whole functions as a relay station for information travelling to the cortex but, according to Lindsay and Norman (1972), the LGB is unlikely to be simply a passer-on of unaltered information. They point out that the LGB receives input from the reticular formation (a structure in the brain-stem which determines the general level of arousal—see Chapters 15, 16 and 17) which suggests that the LGB may serve to decide whether signals are sent on for higher processing (possibly with help from feedback from the cortex) (Dobson et al, 1981).

The *superior colliculus* is situated in the roof of the midbrain (below the cortex) and receives visual information directly from the retina but is also interconnected to the visual cortex. It seems to play an important role in the control of several visual reflexes, including eye movements and perception of the location of objects. The receptive fields of cells in this area are larger than most of those in the cortex and they are more evenly spread in the periphery of the retina, an area which is particularly sensitive to moving stimuli. Schiller and Stryker (1972) found that direct stimulation of the superior colliculus produced eye movement.

The visual *cortex* is the final destination for most visual information and interprets the incoming signals; it also inverts the retinal image so that the world is seen the 'right way up'. Also, the position of visual information on the cortex approximates the locations of the real world in that adjacent areas of the visual world fall side-by-side on the cortex. However, the *amount* of cortex devoted to different areas of the world differs—that portion of the visual field falling on the fovea is greatly emphasized, with the peripheral areas receiving relatively little cortical representation (Frisby, 1980).

Perception—an Active Process

The definitions of Gregory and Coon, considered earlier, make it clear that perception is not the passive process that it might seem—if our perceptions were a copy of what our senses received by way of stimulation from external objects, objects and people would appear to be constantly changing size, shape, colour, location and so on. But our experience is of a mostly stable and predictable world of objects and we achieve this through an *active* process of interpretation.

According to Gregory (1966), what we perceive is not the data but the interpretation of it, 'a perceived object is a hypothesis, suggested and tested by sensory data', a construction from physical sources of energy. To understand how this process works we must consider three main principles of perception.

Principles of Perception—Selection, Inference and Organization

i) Perception is Selective
Much of what arrives at the senses is never perceived, that is, we are not aware of it at any particular moment. Given the amount of stimulation that

surrounds us, and the limited capacity of the brain to process and interpret information at one time, it seems inevitable (and highly desirable) that we should only be able to attend to some things and not others. Think of how chaotic things would be if, for example, we were constantly aware of the clothes on our body, or the sound of our own breathing, or the sight of our arms and legs as we walk—quite apart from all the stimulation provided by other people and the physical world.

Although it is generally agreed that perception is selective, exactly how this selection process works, and just how much and how many things we can attend to at the same time, is a matter of debate and we shall devote a separate section of this chapter to the topic of attention.

ii) Perception Involves Inference—Going Beyond the Information Given

It might be necessary to attend to only a fraction of all the incoming information, but it is often just as necessary to supplement it, because the total information that we might need could be missing (not directly available to our senses).

We often view objects from angles such that their 'true' shape and size is not reflected in the retinal image they project; for example, rectangular doors often project trapezoid-shaped images, round cups often project elliptical-shaped images and people of normal size often project very small images, and yet we usually perceive them as rectangular, round and normal-sized respectively. These are examples of shape and size *constancy*, the ability to perceive objects as we know them to be despite changes in the sensory stimulation which they produce; whether this ability is learned or inborn is discussed in the next chapter.

An impressive demonstration of the mechanisms which produce constancy is *after-images*. If you stare at a bright light for a few seconds, the after-image this causes has a fixed size, shape and position on the retina. But if you quickly look at a nearby object and then at one further away, the after-image seems to shrink and swell, seeming largest when we are looking at the most distant object. Why should this happen? A real object casts a smaller image the further away it is and to maintain perceptual constancy, the image is 'scaled up' by the brain (*constancy scaling*); the same scaling effect is applied to after-images, producing changes in their apparent size. Another easy but quite convincing demonstration is to draw your outline in the mirror in a steamy bathroom (closing one eye as you do so)—the image which appears life-size as you drew it (guided by constancy) seems half the normal size as you stand back from it.

However much you incline your head, you still perceive trees or telegraph poles as vertical and, similarly, with horizontal lines. But do *size* and *shape constancy* always work?

Clearly, there are times when they do not: your conceptual knowledge that those things moving about down there are cars and people does not convince your perceptual experience when you look down from a very tall building— they do *look* more like ants than people! But this is an exception to the rule.

As we move our heads around, we, in fact, produce a constantly changing pattern of retinal images and yet we do not perceive the world spinning around; kinaesthetic feedback from the muscles and the organs of balance in the ear is integrated with the changing retinal stimulation by the brain so as to *inhibit* perception of movement—this is called *location constancy*. To keep the world from swinging crazily every time we move our eyes, the brain subtracts the eye-movement commands from the resulting changes on the retina and this helps to keep people and objects 'in their place'. (Demonstrations of how location constancy might be learned through experience rather than inborn are discussed in Chapter 5, page 124.)

In *colour constancy*, familiar objects retain their colour (strictly, they retain their hue) under a variety of lighting conditions (including night light), provided there is sufficient contrast and shadow. Again, this is not a fool-proof process, and we do sometimes make mistakes, but clearly, there is not a one-to-one correspondence between wavelength of light and colour perception.

Related to colour constancy is *brightness constancy*; for example, we perceive coal as black even in bright sunlight and paper as white even in deep shadow, although the coal may actually be reflecting more light than the paper (as measured by a photometer or light meter).

Another example of inference is when we attribute to an object characteristics which we could only know directly if we were to use one or more senses other than the one we are using at the time—for example, we choose an apple because it *looks* sweet, juicy, crisp and so on.

A fundamental difference between sensation and perception in the case of vision is that the retinal image is two-dimensional but perception is three-dimensional; whether we learn to perceive depth or it is innate is discussed in Chapter 5 and we shall say more about 3-D perception later. Similarly, the image projected onto the retina is inverted (upside-down) but we see the world the right-way-up.

Illusions represent yet another example of how we go beyond the information given, whereby what we perceive may not be physically present in the stimulus (and hence not present in the retinal image). Gregory (in a BBC TV programme, 'States of Mind', 1983) has identified four types of illusion:

i)   *Distortions*, such as the Müller–Lyer, Horizontal-Vertical, Ponzo and Circle illusions (See Figure 4.3 (a), (b), (c) and (d)); here we are genuinely mis-perceiving, that is, making a perceptual *mistake*.

ii)   *Ambiguous figures*, such as the Rubin Vase (see Figure 4.6 (j)) and the Necker Cube (see Figure 4.3 (e)); here, the *same* input results in *different* perceptions through a switch of attention.

iii) *Paradoxical figures*, such as the Penrose impossible objects (see Figure 4.3 (f) and (g)); in the case of the 'impossible triangle', we make the false assumption that the three corners are all the same distance away from us. A three-dimensional 'version' of the triangle can be made, but the corners are not actually touching—they may appear to do so, however, when viewed from a particular angle.

iv)   *Fictions*, such as the Kanizsa triangle (see Figure 4.3 (h)) in which we see what is literally not there, not 'given' in the stimulus (an absence of data).

As you might expect, Gregory explains illusions in terms of a perceptual hypothesis which is not confirmed by the 'data', that is, our attempt to interpret the stimulus figure turns out to be misplaced or inappropriate, resulting in the experience of an illusion. It is our attempt to construe the stimulus in

Figure 4.3 Common illusions
(a) Müller–Lyer illusion
   The arrow with the outgoing fins is seen as longer, but they are the same length
(b) Horizontal–vertical illusion
   The vertical line is seen as longer, but they are the same length
(c) Ponzo illusion
   The top line of the 2 central lines is seen as longer, but they are the same length
(d) The circles illusion
   The central circle in the left-hand group is seen as larger than that in the right-hand group, but they are the same size
(e) Necker cube
   The crosses can be seen as being drawn either on the back side of the cube or on the top side (looking down)
(f) The Penrose impossible triangle

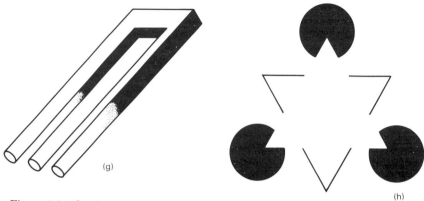

Figure 4.3   *Continued*
(g) Another impossible object
(h) The Kanizsa triangle

keeping with how we normally construe the world which misleads us, in particular, reading depth and distance cues into two-dimensional drawings, and the most famous case is the Müller–Lyer illusion (page 89).

According to Gregory, the arrow with the *ingoing fins* provides linear perspective cues which suggest it could be the *outside corner* of a building; the ingoing fins, accordingly, are seen as walls receding away from us so that the shaft is *closer* to us. For the arrow with the *outgoing fins*, the situation is reversed; perspective cues suggest it could be the *inside corner* of a room, so that the outgoing fins are seen as walls approaching us, in which case the shaft is in some sense *further away* from us. (See Figure 4.4.)

However, the retinal images produced by the shafts are *equal* and, according to *size constancy*, if equal-sized images are produced by two lines, one of which is further away from us than the other, then the line which is further away *must actually be longer*!

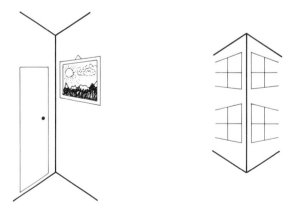

Figure 4.4   A representation of Gregory's explanation of the Müller–Lyer illusion in terms of depth cues and size constancy

All this interpretation is, of course, taking place quite unconsciously and so quickly that we perceive the illusion immediately. There is support for Gregory from the fact that when the arrows are removed from their flat paper background and presented in the dark as a luminous model, they are seen as three-dimensional. However, Eysenck (1984) believes that Gregory was mistaken when he claimed that *everyone* perceives it this way.

The role of learning in perception of the illusion also tends to support Gregory's interpretation as evidenced by the study of cataract patients and cross-cultural studies (both discussed in Chapter 5).

However, if (as in Figure 4.5), the perspective cues are removed but the illusion remains, then this strongly suggests that Gregory's 'mis-applied size constancy theory' is itself mis-applied. Eysenck (1984) concludes that the line may seem longer or shorter than its actual length simply because it is part of a larger or smaller object. Day (1980) believes that probably more than one factor contributes to the experience of an illusion and that different illusions may require explanations.

We should also note here that not all psychologists would agree with Gregory's interpretation of the Müller–Lyer illusion in terms of perspective cues and constancy scaling, *not* because these are not involved but because they are not the active, unconscious, processes of inference which Gregory says they are.

Probably the most noteworthy champion of the view that the senses should be thought of as 'perceptual systems' is J. J. Gibson (1950, 1966, 1979). Gibson believes that the third dimension is available to the senses as directly as the other two dimensions and neither depth nor constancy is 'computed'; these so-called 'higher order' features (which include linear perspective,

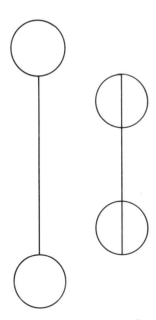

Figure 4.5 The Müller–Lyer illusion with the depth cues removed

texture gradient and motion parallax) are immediate cues for depth, *automatically* processed by the sense receptors and automatically producing the perceptual experience of depth.

Gibson's belief that these depth cues are automatically combined to produce an experience of depth represents a '*bottom up*' approach, while Gregory's emphasis on 'hypothesis testing' (based on past experience, expectations and context) is a '*top-down*' approach. Again, Gibson seems to be equating sensation and perception; if all perception were *veridical*, his case might be stronger than many believe it actually is but our discussion of illusions demonstrates that our perception is often mistaken.

Eysenck (1984) maintains that, in a sense, Gibson's theory is too good because he is arguing that stimulation of the sense organs and receptors provides so much valuable information that space perception is essentially perfect (which, clearly, it is not). However, perception usually involves the combined influence of 'bottom-up' and 'top-down' processes (Eysenck, 1984). Even if Gibson were right about veridical perception (and Wilding, 1982, for one, believes the evidence to support Gibson is lacking), his theory could not account for illusions; Gregory's theory seems much better able to deal with perception that 'goes wrong' because the same processes of inference and hypothesis-testing are involved as are involved in perception *in general*.

We have been talking about illusions so far in a very restricted and special sense, namely, visual stimuli which have been deliberately created to be illusions; however, we are surrounded by illusions which we do not normally think of in this way, partly, perhaps, because they are so commonplace:

a) All drawings, paintings etc are two-dimensional but because of perspective cues used by the artist, we *infer* depth and distance (the third dimension); we add something which is not physically present in the stimulus. This applies to the images projected onto our television and cinema screens too and they also employ another kind of illusion, namely (b).

b) *Illusions of movement.* Just as it is possible for changes in patterns of stimulation on the retina not to be accompanied by perception of movement, so it is possible to perceive movement *without* a successive pattern of retinal stimulation (ie, *apparent movement* or *motion*).

If you look at a spot of light in an otherwise completely dark room, the light will appear to move (even though it is stationary); this is called the *autokinetic effect*. However, if other lights are introduced, the effect disappears (because a frame of reference has been introduced).

Moving pictures are based upon *stroboscopic motion*, where a succession of stationary images is projected onto a screen sufficiently quickly to produce an illusory impression of continuous movement. A simpler form of this is the *phi phenomenon*, much researched in the lab, whereby a number of separate lights turned on and off in quick succession will create the impression of a *single* light moving from one position to another.

Finally, when the only information we have about movement is visual (that is, there are no proprioceptive cues), we tend to assume that larger objects remain stationary while smaller ones move. A famous demonstration of this was carried out by Duncker (1939) who shone a light onto a screen and then moved the screen to one side; most subjects reported that they saw the light move (in the opposite direction to the actual movement of the screen). This is an example of *induced movement*. Other examples include the moon seen through a thin cover of moving clouds (where it is the moon—the smaller object—which is seen to move) and the common experience of sitting in a train alongside another train and not being sure which one has started to pull out of the station.

Veridical Perception of Movement

What these movement illusions show is that the brain normally uses more than just retinal images when perceiving *real* movement. The assumption that larger objects are less likely to be moving than smaller ones is one extra 'rule' that is used, so that judgements about relative size are important extra bits of information; however, as we have seen, this can mislead us as much as it can inform us.

Clearly, there must be changes in the retinal image; indeed, it seems that the receptors only respond to *changes* in the environment and the eyes are constantly making minute, oscillatory, movements which keep the receptors stimulated. A device for stabilizing the retinal image (Cornsweet, 1970) shows that these movements are necessary for seeing things *at all*! A tiny slide projector, mounted on a contact lens, is attached to the cornea and a slide projected onto a screen; since the lens and the projector move with the eye, the retinal image is stabilized (ie, eye movements and the movement of the image on the screen 'cancel each other out' and so the retinal image stays in the same place). After initially seeing the picture with normal acuity, within a few seconds it begins to fade and after a minute disappears altogether.

As we have said, if you turn your head slowly around with your eyes open, you will create a succession of different retinal images—but you will *not* perceive movement; clearly, therefore, changes in the retinal image cannot be a sufficient basis for the perception of movement. Conversely, when an unchanging object moves across your visual field and you follow it with your eyes, the retinal image remains the same but you *do* perceive movement.

Another important cue to movement is *configuration change*. Objects moving in the environment usually do so against a background of stationary (or differently moving) objects, and the nose and other anatomical borders to the visual field also provide a stationary reference point against which to judge movement (which causes a configuration change or change in the overall pattern and interrelationship between objects). However, although in practice this is often an important source of information, it may not be a necessary one. Gregory (1973) points out that if a lighted cigarette is moved about in a dark room it will be perceived as moving even though there are no background cues or frame of reference.

It seems that the brain is capable of distinguishing between eye movements which signal movement of objects (real movement) and eye movements (and movements of the head) which do not (as when you scan a stationary scene and things stay in their proper place). Probably the superior colliculus plays an important role in making this distinction. Gregory (1973) describes two systems: (i) the image-retina system which responds to changes in the visual field which produce changes in the retinal image; and (ii) the eye-head system, which responds to movements of the head and eyes. He argues that the perception of movement is the product of an interplay between the two systems.

iii) Perception is Organized

This is best demonstrated by the work of the *gestalt* psychologists who argued that if you try to analyse experiences into their constituent parts, you tend to destroy them; we perceive objects *not* as accumulations or combinations of isolated sensations (colours, shapes, sizes etc) but as *organized wholes* or *gestalts*. (The German word 'Gestalt' is sometimes translated as configuration, pattern or form).

The way in which we form *gestalten* is to apply certain principles which can be subsumed under the *law of prägnanz*, which states that, 'psychological organization will always be as "good" as the prevailing conditions allow' (Koffka, 1935). But what is 'good'? According to Attneave (1954), a 'good' figure is one with a high degree of internal *redundancy*, that is, the structure of any unseen part is highly predictable from the visible parts and Hochberg's (1978) 'minimum principle' maintains that if there is more than one way of organizing a given visual stimulus, the one most likely to be perceived is the one requiring the *least* amount of information to describe it.

In practice, the 'best' way of perceiving is the most simple, symmetrical, uniform and stable and this is achieved through *proximity, closure, continuity* and *symmetry, similarity, figure-ground* and the *part-whole relationship.*

a) Proximity

Elements which appear close together—in space or time—tend to be perceived together, so that Figure 4.6(a) is normally seen as three pairs of parallel lines and 4.6(b) as a group of three dots, followed by a pair, followed by a single dot.

(a)   (b)

Figure 4.6   The Gestalt principles of organization
(a) Proximity
(b) Proximity

An auditory example would be the perception of a series of musical notes as a melody because they occur soon after one another in time.

b) Closure

Closed figures are more easily perceived than open or incomplete ones, so that we tend to close incomplete figures, as in Figure 4.6(c) and 4.6(d), in order to give their familiar meaning.

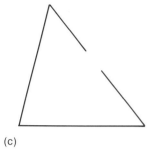

(c)   (d)

Figure 4.6 *Continued*
(c) Closure
(d) Closure

c) *Continuity and Symmetry*

Similar parts of a figure which appear in straight or curved lines tend to stand out; when they make recognizable shapes (such as circles and squares) they become conspicuous. So, for example, the crosses in Figure 4.6(e) are seen as composing a square, those in 4.6(f) a circle and those in 4.6(g) a straight line. Again, music is perceived as continuous rather than a series of distinct, separate sounds and the same applies to speech.

(e)   (f)   (g)

Figure 4.6 *Continued*
(e) Continuity and symmetry
(f) Continuity and symmetry
(g) Continuity and symmetry

d) *Similarity*

Like-elements tend to be perceived together, as belonging to the same pattern. In Figure 4.6(h), for example, we tend to see alternating rows of dots and crosses (rather than columns of dots and crosses intermingled); if we turn it on its side (4.6(i)), we now see columns of dots alternating with columns of crosses.

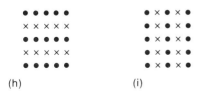

(h)   (i)

Figure 4.6 *Continued*
(h) Similarity
(i) Similarity

When we hear all the separate voices in a choir as one entity, the principle of similarity is operating.

e) Figure-ground
Some part of a stimulus always stands out as being in the foreground (the Figure) and everything else as background (Ground); the figure is what we attend to at any particular time and the ground represents the context in which the figure is presented and from which it derives its meaning.

According to Rubin (1921), the figure has 'thinglike' qualities, while the ground is relatively uniform; the figure also seems to be nearer and the ground extends unbroken behind it.

(j)

Figure 4.6 *Continued*
(j) A reversible figure-ground: a vase or 2 profiles?

Figure 4.6(j) (the famous Rubin vase) illustrates the Figure-Ground principle and is also *reversible*, ie, it can be seen in two ways—when we attend to the vase, the profiles constitute ground and when we switch attention to the profiles, they become the figure.

Figure 4.7 Leeper's ambiguous lady

Another famous example of a reversible Figure-Ground phenomenon is Leeper's Ambiguous Lady (Figure 4.7). Can you seen an attractive young lady and an old hag? Objectively, they are both present in the picture—but it is impossible to see them both simultaneously. A map is another example— we normally see the land as figure and the sea as ground, since we are more familiar with the shape of Africa, for example, than the shape of the Atlantic.

An auditory example is following one conversation out of several going on in a 'cocktail party' situation (usually the one we are involved in); but a reversal can occur if, for example, our name is mentioned by someone on the other side of the room. Try repeating 'over-run' out loud and you will find the two words alternating as figure and ground.

f) Part-Whole Relationship

Figures 4.6(e), 4.6(f) and 4.6(g) illustrate the principle that, 'the whole is greater than the sum of its parts': each pattern is composed of 12 crosses but the gestalts are different despite the similarity of the parts (and are determined largely through proximity and continuity/symmetry).

Another example is the case of water (H_2O) which is composed of a mixture of hydrogen (H) and oxygen (O) but the properties of water are very different from those of hydrogen or oxygen taken separately. Again, the notes in a musical scale played up the scale produce a very different sound compared with the same notes played down the scale and the same melody can be recognized when hummed, whistled or played with different instruments and in different keys.

An Evaluation of Gestalt Principles

Eysenck (1984) believes that Gestalt principles make reasonable intuitive sense but are merely *descriptive* with little or no explanatory power; he also thinks they are rather limited in that they are only directly applicable to two-dimensional representation—with 3-D scenes, figure-ground separation can be facilitated by depth cues and movement information.

However, Navon (1977) demonstrated the principle of 'the whole is greater than the sum of its parts' by presenting subjects with large ('global') letters composed of several smaller ('local') letters and finding that global features were perceived more easily than local features. He concluded that it is difficult (if not impossible) to avoid perceiving the whole and that global processing occurs before any more detailed perceptual analysis.

Similarly, Palmer (1977) argues that visual form is analysed *hierarchically*, from overall configuration and moving down to basic features or elements; at each level, Gestalt principles were found to help determine how the low-level units are combined to form more organized gestalten at that level. Marr (1976) also found the Gestalt principles useful in achieving accurate *segmentation*, that is, how visual information is used to decide which regions of a visual scene belong together and form coherent structures. He devised a computer program aimed at achieving segmentation (of a teddy bear, for example) using the Gestalt principles and obtained very encouraging results; however, additional knowledge of the object is sometimes necessary (Marr, 1982).

Perceptual Set and Schemas

As we have seen, perception is distinct from sensation although it is dependent on it; while perception is an active process which involves selection, inference and organization, sensation is a relatively passive process involving the stimulation of the sense-organs.

A concept which lies at the heart of this active process of perception is that of *set* and the related concept of a *schema*. Allport (1955) defined perceptual set as, 'a perceptual bias or predisposition or readiness to perceive particular features of a stimulus', that is, the tendency to perceive or notice some aspects of the available sense-data and ignore others.

Bartlett (1932) defined a schema as 'an active organization of past reactions and of past experiences which must always be supposed to be operating in any well-adapted organic response' and Vernon (1955) defined schemas as, 'persistent and deep-rooted, well-organized classifications of ways of perceiving, thinking and believing'. Vernon maintains that set works in two ways: first as a *selector*, whereby the perceiver has certain expectations which help focus attention on particular aspects of the incoming sensory stimulation; and, secondly, as an *interpreter*, whereby the perceiver knows how to deal with the selected data, how to classify, understand and name it and what inferences to draw from it.

What Determines Set?

There are several factors which can influence or induce set, most of which are to do with the perceiver (*perceiver* or *organismic variables*), some of which are to do with the nature of the stimulus or the conditions under which it is being perceived (*stimulus* or *situational variables*). However, whether they arise primarily within the perceiver or from outside, they only indirectly influence perception through directly influencing set which, as such, is of course itself a perceiver variable or characteristic. (See Figure 4.8.)

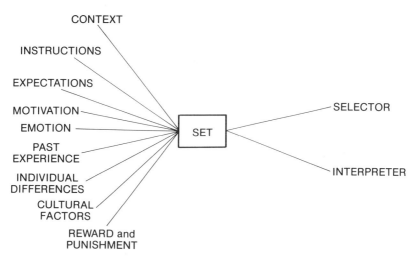

Figure 4.8 The indirect influence of perceiver and stimulus variables on perception through their direct influence on set

Context, Instructions and Other Situational Variables

In Russia, one school of psychology, stemming from the work of Uzuadze (1886–1950) has attached great importance to the study of set. A typical experiment involves the subject being given two wooden balls, a large one in the right hand and a small one in the left hand; after several such presentations, two balls of equal size are placed one in each hand. This produces a *contrast-effect*, whereby the ball in the right hand is perceived as smaller than the one in the left, since set had been induced previously through experience with the different-sized balls. (Running one hand under cold water and the other under hot and then immersing them both in warm water will also produce a contrast-effect.)

A classic demonstration of how instructions can induce set was done by Chapman (1932). Subjects saw a series of cards on which were printed several capital letters; the cards varied according to—(a) the number of letters (four to eight), (b) the identity of the letters, and (c) their spatial arrangement. They were presented tachistoscopically (ie, for very brief measured periods of time) so that ability to recognize them would be less than perfect and set was manipulated by instructing subjects to report on one of the three characteristics of a card on each exposure (number of letters, which they were, and spatial arrangement). Compared with subjects given instructions after exposure (which, presumably, had no influence on set), those given instructions before exposure made far fewer errors, on all three attributes.

The way that instructions create set is, essentially, through inducing *expectations* on the perceiver's part. There are many examples of selective perception outside the laboratory where set is a key variable: a great deal of occupational and professional training can be seen as equipping the trainee with a system of sets which will enhance performance in various ways, such as a policeman being trained to notice and remember car registration numbers, or the physical characteristics of (potential) law-breakers.

Often, there is an interaction between *expectation* and *context*, as in the letter/number series below:

E D C 13 A   16 15 14 13 12

The physical stimulus '13' is the same in each case but is perceived differently because of the context in which it appears; we expect it to be a letter B when in a sequence of other letters and the number 13 when in a sequence of other numbers (Minturn and Bruner, 1951).

We may fail to notice printing errors or writing errors for the same reason, for example, 'The cat sat on the map and licked its whiskers'. If you can't spot the deliberate mistake, look at Figure 4.9 overleaf.
What do you read in the triangles? What words are actually written in the triangles? What you perceive and what is physically present should, in each case, be different.

These last three examples demonstrate the interaction between *expectation* and *past experience*; a classic experimental demonstration of this is a study by Bruner and Postman (1949).

They presented subjects with unusual playing cards, with the colour and

Figure 4.9

suit combinations reversed (eg, black hearts and red spades). The cards were presented tachistoscopically and, not surprisingly perhaps, at very short exposures the subjects tended to report that the cards were normal (basing their reports on one feature and assuming that the other matched it). But at longer exposures, they sometimes reported 'brown or purple hearts' or 'cards in black with red edges', which suggested a genuine perceptual distortion ('compromise perceptions', an almost literal blending of stimulus information and stored information). A whole theory of perception has been built around the belief that what we perceive depends on past experience. The *transactionalists* (eg Ames) argue that, because the sensory input is always ambiguous, the interpretation selected is the most likely one in the light of what has been perceived in the past. A famous demonstration is the Ames Room, which is constructed in such a way that when viewed with one eye through a special viewing hole, a person at one end may look like a dwarf and a person at the other end like a giant and if a person crosses the room they appear to change size (see Figure 4.10). Of course, the perceiver is put into a situation of having to choose between two different beliefs about the world built up through past experience: (i) rooms are rectangular and consist of right angles etc.; and (ii) people are usually of 'average' height. Most subjects choose the former and so judge the people to be odd but the famous

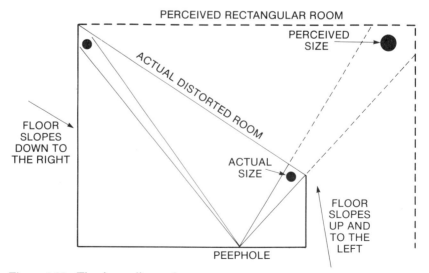

Figure 4.10 The Ames distorted room

case of the wife who saw her husband in the Ames room and judged the room to be odd shows that particular past experience can override more generalized beliefs about the world.

The Effects of Motivation and Emotion on Perception

Allport (1955) distinguished six types of motivational-emotional influence on perception: bodily needs (normally studied as the effects of physiological deprivation), reward and punishment, emotional connotation, individual values, personality, and the value of objects.

Before we can consider the relevant empirical studies, we should mention two principles of perception related to the concept of set, namely *perceptual accentuation/sensitization*, whereby things that are relevant or salient for us are perceived as larger, brighter, more attractive, more valuable etc. and *perceptual defence*, whereby things that are threatening or anxiety-provoking in some way are more difficult to perceive at a conscious level (McGinnies, 1949).

i) Effects of Physiological Deprivation

Cannon's Homoeostatic Drive theory (1929) maintained that we have a number of basic bodily (biogenic) drives (eg, hunger, thirst, warmth and sex) and that if these are not satisfied the body's internal environment becomes imbalanced and we are driven to satisfy these needs and hence restore the balance (see Chapter 17). Individuals who endure prolonged and extreme physiological deprivation may hallucinate the objects they need to satisfy their needs (eg, water in the desert) or they may mis-interpret stimuli that are physically present (eg, mistaking a rattle-snake's rattle for the sound of an ice-cream van!).

Sandford (1936) deprived subjects of food for up to four hours and then showed them ambiguous pictures; as the period of deprivation increased, so the tendency to perceive the pictures as food or food-related objects also increased. The same subjects a year later were deprived for up to 24 hours and similar results were produced. Sandford also found that there was a fluctuation in the tendency to perceive food or food-related objects which reflected the subjects' normal meal-times. Similar results were found by Levine et al (1942) but only up to six hours of food deprivation, and by Lazarus et al (1953) up to three to four hours.

Gilchrist and Nesberg (1952) found that hungry and thirsty subjects perceived pictures of food and drink as being brighter than pictures of non-food and drink objects after up to eight hours of deprivation. When they were allowed to eat and drink at will, estimates of brightness immediately returned to pre-deprivation levels. This last study also illustrates perceptual accentuation/sensitization.

ii) Effects of Reward and Punishment

A famous study by Schafer and Murphy (1943) used pictures of two juxtaposed faces. (See Figure 4.11 overleaf.)

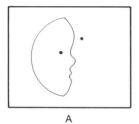 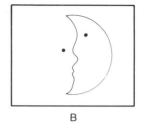 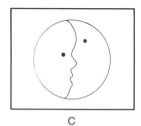

A   B   C

Figure 4.11. Schafer and Murphy's juxtaposed faces

Whenever A was shown, the subject was rewarded with money and whenever B was shown, the money was withdrawn (as a punishment). Subjects were encouraged to learn to name and recognize the faces and when C was presented there was a pronounced tendency to see A rather than B.

Rock and Fleck (1950) failed to produce Schafer and Murphy's results in a replication but Solley and and Sommer (1957) found that five- to nine-year-olds perceived the rewarded face as happier, nearer, brighter and as having stronger contours; and this was confirmed by Engel (1960) using five-year-olds.

Synder and Synder (1956) presented subjects with two simultaneous voices, one of which had been associated with a reward of money and the other with loss of money and found that subjects reported more from the rewarded voice.

Lazarus and McCleary (1951) used electric shocks as punishment when certain nonsense syllables were shown on a tachistoscope along with other, non-punished syllables. Although subjects were unable to perceive consciously many of the syllables, their Galvanic Skin Response or GSR (a measure of the skin's resistance to electricity which decreases as anxiety increases through greater sweating) changed significantly in response to the previously punished syllables.

iii) Effects of Emotional Connotation—Perceptual Defence

McGinnies (1949) coined the term 'perceptual defence' to refer to the findings from laboratory experiments that subliminally-perceived words (below the threshold of consciousness) which evoke unpleasant emotions take longer to perceive at a conscious level than neutral words.

The Lazarus and McCleary study described above demonstrated that recognition can occur before perception enters conscious awareness ('autonomic discrimination without awareness' or the 'subception effect'); somehow enough information is transmitted to the Autonomic Nervous System (ANS) to determine different levels of GSR but insufficient information reaches the brain centres responsible for correct verbal classification. (See Chapter 26 for a discussion of Freud's concept of repression to which perceptual defence is related.) Bruner and Postman (1947) reported a significant difference between the times taken to recognize neutral words compared with sexual and other taboo words, but there were important individual differences between subjects.

McGinnies (1949) presented subjects, on a tachistoscope, with eleven emotionally neutral words (such as 'apple', 'broom' and 'glass') and seven emotionally-arousing, taboo words (such as 'whore', 'penis', 'rape', 'bitch'). Each word was presented for increasingly long durations until it was named and there was a significantly higher recognition threshold for the taboo words (ie, it took longer for subjects to name them). The taboo words also produced a greater GSR and more of them were distorted when being named.

But the perceptual defence explanation put forward by McGinnies has been questioned. For example, Solomon and Howes (1951) argued that the neutral words are simply more familiar (in written form, at least) than the taboo words and this alone could explain the differences in recognition threshold. Vernon (1962) pointed out that several of the words used were sexual slang words (including 'balls' and 'screw') so some subjects would be more familiar with these than other subjects.

Another criticism has been that subjects are not failing to recognize the taboo words as quickly as the neutral words but that they may feel too embarrassed to say them out loud (at least, until they are absolutely sure what the word is). Some support for this hypothesis comes from a study by Aronfreed et al (1953) in which female subjects were tested by a male experimenter; longer recognition thresholds and greater emotional responses were produced for the taboo words compared with those produced when other combinations of subjects and experimenters were used. Support also comes from a study by Bitterman and Kniffin (1953) who found that there was no perceptual defence effect if subjects were allowed to write down their answers instead of saying them out loud.

It has been suggested, too, that subjects may find it difficult to 'believe their eyes' because they do not expect taboo words to be used in a serious, scientific experiment. Postman et al (1953) found that warning subjects about the words eliminated the perceptual defence effect, but Cowen and Beier (1954) found that a warning made no difference.

McGinnies and Sherman (1952) found that clearly presented taboo words raised the threshold for neutral words which followed them, demonstrating that arousal of unpleasant emotions could have an effect independently of the object to be perceived. Dixon (1958) and Hardy and Legge (1968) found a similar effect of taboo or unpleasant emotive words on the detection of a light.

Worthington (1969) tried to settle the argument by asking 160 subjects to say which of two faint spots of light, presented successively on a screen, was brighter (in fact, there was no difference). Embedded in each spot of light was a very faint subliminal word (too faint to be consciously perceived); nine different words were used, all previously rated for emotionality. The spots of light containing the words rated high on emotionality were consistently perceived as dimmer than those containing low-rated words. Given that subjects were not consciously aware of the existence of the words, Worthington's results seem to support the perceptual defence explanation. Hardy and Legge (1968) also found evidence for the view that perceptual defence is a *perceptual* (as opposed to a response bias) phenomenon. The concept of perceptual defence in particular (and subliminal perception in general) becomes more acceptable if perception is thought of *not* as a unitary event but involving multiple processing stages and mechanisms with consciousness perhaps representing the final level of processing (Dixon, 1981, Erdely, 1974).

iv) Effect of Individual Values

Bruner, Postman and McGinnies (1948) rated subjects on the Allport–Vernon Scale of Values (Theoretical, Social, Aesthetic, Political, Economic and Religious) and found that those rated high on a particular value were more sensitive to related words than to non-related words. Mistaken guesses tended to be made from the same area of interest but this implies a response-bias effect rather than a perceptual-bias effect.

Similarly, McClelland and Liberman (1949) found that subjects rated high on Need for Achievement (nAch) perceived words related to success and mastery at a lower level of illumination than subjects low in nAch.

v) Effect of Personality

Eriksen (1951) reported that aggressive subjects more quickly perceived pictures depicting acts of aggression than less aggressive subjects and in 1965 showed that some subjects respond more readily to anxiety-arousing material (*sensitizers*) than others (*repressors*); the latter finding represents an important qualification to the perceptual defence data.

Witkin et al (1954) and Witkin and Price-Williams (1974) identified two kinds of 'cognitive style', associated with certain personality characteristics. In the Rod-and-Frame Test, subjects have to adjust a rod to a vertical position when it is viewed inside a frame which is tilted away from the vertical; and in the Embedded Figure Test, subjects have to find a geometrical figure which is concealed within some more complex picture or diagram. On the basis of these, Witkin and Price-Williams identified *field-independent* perceivers, who can more easily perform those tasks successfully, are more analytical, deal with the environment more actively and can more easily ignore misleading cues, and *field-dependent* perceivers, who display the opposite tendencies.

Field-independents have a positive body-image, higher self-esteem, are less afraid of sexual and aggressive impulses and are less prepared to submit to external authority or social pressure than field-dependents. Interestingly, there is a tendency for field-independents to be male and for field-dependence generally to decline during childhood (but less so for girls).

A similar distinction was made by Holzman and Klein (1950) between *levellers*, who tend to minimize the differences between stimuli and are much more influenced by context and *sharpeners* who work in the opposite direction.

vi) Effect of the Value of Objects

This relates to the phenomenon of Perceptual Accentuation/Sensitization. In a famous study, Bruner and Goodman (1947) required children to turn a knob which controlled a circular patch of light on a screen, so that the patch of light was the same size as coins of various denominations. All children tended to over-estimate the coins (compared with a control group who estimated the size of cardboard discs) but children from poor families did so to a greater extent than wealthy children. Presumably, money is perceived as more valuable by children who have less of it.

In a replication study, Carter and Schooler (1949) found that over-estimation of coins only occurred when judgements were made from memory, not when direct matching was required; this was in fact the

Table 4.2 Summary of studies demonstrating the effects of motivation and emotion on perception

1) Physiological deprivation	2) Reward and punishment	3) Emotional connotation – Perceptal defence	4) Individual values	5) Personality	6) Value of objects – Perceptual accentuation
Sandford (1936) Levine et al (1942) Lazarus et al (1953) Gilchrist and Nesberg (1952)	Schafer and Murphy (1943) Rock and Fleck (1950) Solley and Sommer (1957) Engel (1960) Snyder and Snyder (1956) Lazarus and McCleary (1951)	Bruner and Postman (1947) McGinnies (1949) Solomon and Howes (1951) Vernon (1962) Aronfreed et al (1953) Bitterman and Kniffin (1953) Postman et al (1953) Cowen and Beier (1954) McGinnies and Sherman (1952) Dixon (1958) Hardy and Legge (1968) Worthington (1969)	Bruner, Postman and McGinnies (1948) McClelland and Liberman (1949)	Eriksen (1951, 1965) Witkin et al (1954) Witkin and Price-Williams (1974) Holzman and Klein (1950)	Bruner and Goodman (1947) Carter and Schooler (1949) Ashley et al (1951) Lambert et al (1949) Solley and Haigh (1958)

opposite of what Bruner and Goodman had found. Ashley et al (1951) confirmed the original findings when subjects were hypnotized into believing that they were rich or poor.

Lambert et al (1949) divided nursery school children into two groups and they were shown how to turn a handle to obtain a poker chip; the experimental group could exchange the chips for sweets, while the control group simply received a sweet when they turned the handle. Before the experiment, both groups had over-estimated the size of poker chips by about 5 per cent, but after ten days of exchanging the chips for sweets, the experimental group were over-estimating by 13 per cent, while the control group's over-estimation remained steady.

Finally, Solley and Haigh (1958) asked four- to eight-year-olds to draw pictures of Santa Claus at intervals during the month before Christmas and the two weeks following. As Christmas approached, so the pictures became larger, as did Santa's sack of toys, but afterwards his toys shrank and so did Santa.

(A summary of these studies is found in Table 4.2 on page 105.)

Depth Perception

Since the retina is only a two-dimensional surface, how do we manage to perceive depth, the third dimension?

Depth cues can be classified in terms of, (i) *monocular–binocular* and (ii) *pictorial–non-pictorial* (or secondary-primary) and these are summarized in Table 4.3. *Monocular* cues are those which can be detected with one eye only and so are not primarily dependent on biological processes—except in the case of accommodation. The vast majority of monocular cues are *pictorial*, that is, they are features of the visual field itself (and they are also *static*) but *binocular* cues depend upon the structure and function of the *two* eyes.

Table 4.3   A classification of depth cues

	Monocular	*Binocular*
Pictorial (secondary)	1. Relative size 2. Relative brightness 3. Superimposition (overlap) 4. Linear perspective 5. Aerial perspective 6. Height in the horizontal plane 7. Light and shadow 8. Texture gradient 9. Motion parallax	
Non-Pictorial (Primary)	Accommodation	1. Retinal disparity 2. Convergence

Monocular—Pictorial Cues

1) *Relative size*: in an array of different-sized objects, smaller ones are usually seen as more distant, (particularly if they are known to have a constant size).

2) *Relative brightness*: brighter objects normally appear to be nearer.

3) *Superimposition* (or overlap): an object which blocks the view of another is seen as being nearer.

4) *Linear perspective*: parallel lines (eg railway tracks) appear to converge as they recede into the distance.

5) *Aerial perspective*: objects at a great distance appear to have a different colour (eg, the hazy, bluish, tint of distant mountains).

6) *Height in the horizontal plane*: when looking across a flat expanse (eg, across the sea), objects which are more distant seem 'higher' (ie, closer to the horizon) than nearer objects which seem 'lower' and closer to the ground.

7) *Light* and *shadow*: three-dimensional objects produce variations in light and shade (eg, we normally assume that light comes from above).

8) *Texture gradient*: sand, for instance, is perceived as being more textured close-to but as it stretches away from us it looks more uniform, smooth and fine-grained.

9) *Motion parallax*: this is the major *dynamic* cue to depth (either monocular or binocular) and refers to the speed of apparent movement of objects nearer or further away from us; generally, objects further away seem to move more slowly than nearer objects (eg, telegraph poles seen out of a train window flash by when they are close to the track).

Monocular–Non-Pictorial Cues

Accommodation: refers to the change in the shape of the lens depending on the distance of the object—it flattens for distant objects and thickens for closer ones (and provides depth cues within about 4 feet).

Binocular–Non-Pictorial Cues

1) *Retinal disparity*: because our eyes are (approximately) 6 cm apart, they each receive slightly different retinal images; the superimposition of these two images is *stereoscopic vision*. (Close each eye in turn and you'll see the difference!) Related to this is convergence.

2) *Convergence*: refers to the simultaneous orienting of both eyes towards the same object—when we look at a distant object (25 feet or more) the line of vision of our two eyes is parallel but the closer the object, the more our eyes turn inwards towards each other. (Of course, if the object is too close, we go 'cross-eyed' and cannot focus properly.)

Pattern Recognition—What makes a 'T' a 'T'?

In a sense, pattern recognition is the central problem of perception and is almost synonymous with perception itself—how are we able to recognize, identify and categorize objects? What are the processes by which sensory information is converted into a psychologically meaningful perception?

Eysenck (1984) defines pattern recognition as 'assigning meaning to visual input by identifying the objects in the visual field' and believes that the ease with which we normally succeed in identifying objects in fact conceals the, 'amazing flexibility of the human perceptual system as it copes with a multitude of different stimuli', a quite remarkable achievement.

A common way of illustrating the problem is to think of all the different ways in which a particular stimulus might be presented; for instance, letters of the alphabet, as in Figure 4.12.

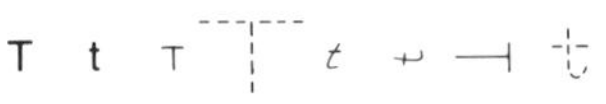

T   t   т   ｜   𝑡   ↵   ⊣   ᴛ̈

Figure 4.12   What makes a 'T' a 'T'?

What do all these marks on the page have in common? To say that obviously they are all letter 'T's is too easy and, in a sense, begs the question. How are we able to recognize them as 'T's, what makes them identifiable in this way, what makes a 'T' a 'T'? These are what theories of pattern recognition (PR) attempt to answer.

Theories of Pattern Recognition

There are three major kinds of theory: (i) *template-matching*; (ii) *prototype*; and (iii) *feature detection*.

i)   Template Matching Hypothesis

As with all PR theories, the template matching hypothesis (TMH) sees PR as the comparison of information which has just stimulated the sense organs (retained in sensory memory) with the relatively permanent information acquired during our lifetime; when a match is made between the coming sensory information and something in our long-term stores, then PR takes place. But what exactly is this something? According to the TMH, the memory system stores a large number of constructs or internal representations (*templates*) and we compare incoming stimulus information with these miniature copies of previously presented patterns or objects. But if there is an unlimited number of ways of presenting the letter 'T' for example, it follows that there would have to be an unlimited number of templates, one for each *particular* instance of the letter.

The TMH seems unable to explain how we could recognize even slightly unfamiliar patterns, and not only would the number of templates required be neurologically impossible, since it would have to be infinite, the hypothesis ends up *assuming* what it is trying to explain (Donahoe and Wessells 1980). (Incidentally, template matching is the basic technique used by computers to 'read', which is one reason why they are so bad at recognizing any slight deviation from the highly specific configurations in their memories—see Chapter 7. It is also the basis of price-coding in supermarkets—each packet has a special code which identifies the item for which the computer supplies the price; this is then entered on the cash-register tape.)

ii) Prototype Theories

Instead of proposing that what we store is a template for each individual pattern, we could suggest a smaller number of *prototypes*, 'abstract forms representing the basic elements of a set of stimuli' (Eysenck, 1984). Whereas template theories treat each stimulus as a separate entity, prototype theories maintain that similarities between related stimuli play an important part in PR, whereby each stimulus is a member of a *category* of stimuli and shares certain basic properties with other members of the category (eg Posner, 1969, Reed, 1972).

While the idea of a prototype is intuitively appealing, the precise nature of prototypes and the matching process is not very explicit and prototype theories fail to explain how PR is affected by the context as well as by the stimulus itself (Eysenck, 1984). Just what those properties are which are shared by a category of stimuli is what we want to know but what prototype theories fail to tell us; this is where the third type of theory comes into its own.

iii) Feature Detection Theories

By far the most researched and influential theories of PR maintain that each stimulus pattern can be thought of as a configuration of elementary features; letters of the alphabet, for example, are composed of combinations of about twelve basic features (including straight vertical lines, horizontals and closed curves) so an 'A' may be analysed into two diagonals, one horizontal, a pointed head and an open bottom. The evidence for this is of two main kinds, behavioural and neurological.

a) Behavioural Studies

A common experimental technique is a visual scanning task in which subjects search lists of letters as rapidly as possible in order to find a specified target letter which occurs in unpredictable positions in the lists. Clearly, finding the target letter involves recognizing a particular pattern and rejecting others and if recognition entails the detection of elementary features, then the task should be more difficult the more features the target and non-target letters have in common.

This was confirmed by Neisser (1964) and Rabbitt (1967). Subjects found 'Z' much faster in a list comprising C, G and O than when M, X and E were the non-target letters. Similarly, Gibson et al (1968) found that it took longer to decide that P and R are different than to distinguish between G and W.

b) Neurological Studies

There is considerable evidence that the visual systems of a wide variety of vertebrates contain both peripheral (retinal) and central (cortical) cells that respond only to particular features of visual stimuli (eg Barlow et al, 1972, Hubel and Wiesel, 1959, '62, '63, '68).

Hubel and Wiesel, for example, using cats and monkeys, identified three kinds of cortical cells.

i)   *Simple cells* respond only to particular features of a stimulus (eg straight lines, edges and slits) in particular *orientations* and in particular *locations* in the animal's visual field. For example, a bar presented vertically may cause a particular cell to 'fire' but if the bar is moved to one side or out of vertical it will not respond.

ii) *Complex cells* also respond to lines of particular orientations but location is no longer important; in other words, a vertical line detector will respond wherever in the visual field it is. It seems that complex cells receive inputs from larger numbers of simple cells sharing the same orientation–sensitivity.

iii) *Hypercomplex cells* are 'fed' by large numbers of complex cells and are similar to complex cells but they take *length* into account too.

But do these different kinds of cell constitute the feature detectors postulated by feature detection theories?

Marr (1982) tried to construct a computerized feature-detection system and found that the activity in any one cell is too variable and ambiguous to be thought of as feature detection as such; however, it might provide the first step in the analysis of features present in the visual input. Perhaps these neurological detectors are a necessary pre-condition for any higher-level (cognitive) pattern analysis taking place.

However, there are also some more basic criticisms. Eysenck (1984), for example, argues that feature theories typically assume a *serial* form of processing, with feature extraction being followed by feature combination and, finally by PR. Hubel and Wiesel (1962), for example, saw the sequence of simple, complex and hypercomplex cells representing a serial flow of information, whereby only particular information is processed at any one time before being passed on to the next level upwards and so on.

However, Lennie (1980) reviewed the literature and concluded that a great deal of non-serial processing takes place in the visual cortex and that the relationship between the three kinds of cell is more complex than originally thought.

An interesting and famous example of non-serial processing is Selfridge's (1959) computer program for the recognition of Morse code and a small set of hand-written letters, which he called *Pandemonium* (the capital of Hell in 'Paradise Lost'). The components are four kinds of *demons*:

a) *Image* demons who simply copy the pattern—much as the retina records visual patterns;

b) *Feature* demons, who analyse the information from the image demons in terms of combinations of features;

c) *Cognitive* demons who are specialized for particular letters and will 'scream' according to how much the input from the feature demons matches their special letter;

d) A *decision* demon, who chooses the 'loudest scream' and, hence, the *name* of the letter.

Because it is able to deal with many options simultaneously (eg, is this letter an A, B, C or D etc.?), Pandemonium is an example of *parallel processing* (as opposed to serial processing).

The Importance of Context

A number of writers have pointed out that feature detection theories do not take sufficient account of the *context* and certain perceiver variables, such as expectations (eg Eysenck, 1984, Massaro et al, 1978, Norman, 1976, Palmer, 1975) and we saw some examples of their influence earlier in this chapter. Clearly, the same features can produce different patterns (especially if they are ambiguous) and different features can produce the same pattern depending on context, which can tell us what pattern are *likely* to be present and hence what to expect. Indeed, we may *fail* to notice the absence of something or a distorted form of a stimulus (eg typographical errors) because of its high predictability.

This influence of context and expectation on the analysis of sensory features illustrates what is called *conceptually-driven processing*; processing which begins with the elementary features and works 'upwards' towards PR is *data-driven* and most feature detection theories to date seem to fall into this latter category.

Attention

One effect of context on PR may be to allow a partial and selective analysis of the stimuli to be recognized, that is, PR involves selectively attending to some aspects of the presented stimuli but not others. PR and selective attention, therefore, can be seen to be closely related, (Solso, 1979).

Attention in this sense of selectivity is, in fact, just one of several senses in which the term has been used; Moray (1970), for example, identified six meanings but for our present purposes, two main senses should be stressed (following Wilding, 1982):

i)   Attention as the mechanisms which reject some information and take in others (whether or not the latter enters conscious awareness)—*selective attention*;

ii) Attention as some upper limit to the amount of processing that can be performed on incoming information at any one time—*capacity*.

We shall consider (i) and (ii) together in the remainder of this chapter. (Wilding points out that the term has also been used to refer to arousal level, vigilance and the ability to stay alert and concentrate. These will be discussed in Chapters 16 and 17.)

Methods of Studying Attention

Eysenck (1984) identifies two basic experimental techniques used to study attention:

i)   Subjects are presented with two or more simultaneous 'messages' and are instructed to process and respond to only one of these. The most popular way of doing this is to use *shadowing*, whereby one message is fed into the left ear and a different message into the right ear (through headphones) and the subject has to repeat one of those messages aloud as they hear it.

The shadowing technique is really a particular form of *dichotic listening* (eg Broadbent, 1952) which refers to the simultaneous receipt of two different stimulus inputs, one to each ear. Shadowing was first used by Cherry (1953) who wanted to study the *cocktail party situation*, in which the individual manages to select one or two voices to listen to from the hubbub of numerous conversations taking place at the same time and in the same room. The subject is instructed to select, which can tell us something about the selection process and what happens to unattended stimuli (ie, it is more directly concerned with *selective attention*).

ii) In the *dual-task* technique, the subject is asked to attend and respond to *both* (or all) the messages; whereas shadowing focuses attention on a particular message, the dual task method deliberately *divides* the subject's attention and this provides useful information about a person's processing limitations and also about attention mechanisms and their *capacity*.

Theories of Selective Attention

A number of theories, based largely on the shadowing technique, have tried to account for selective attention by proposing that somewhere in the processing of information there is a 'bottleneck' or *filter* (partly due to neurological limitations), at which point the attended message is passed on for further processing and the non-attended message is either filtered-out altogether (and so has no effect on behaviour) or is processed only to a limited degree.

These *single channel models* (Broadbent, 1958, Treisman, 1964, Deutsch and Deutsch, 1963 and Norman, 1968, 1969, 1976) differ essentially over the *position* of the filter and hence how much (and what kind of) processing of the non-attended message takes place.

Broadbent's 'Filter Model' (1958)

This model sees the bottleneck occurring very early in processing and is based on the gross *physical* properties of the incoming stimuli. For example, much early research suggested that very little, if any, of the non-attended message could be recalled, except: (i) the speaker's gender; and (ii) whether it consisted of words or pure tones (Cherry, 1953, Cherry and Taylor, 1954, Treisman, 1964). Subjects were unable to identify its content, the language in which it was spoken, whether it changed from English to German or whether it was English played backwards. Even a word repeated 35 times was not recalled (Moray, 1959). The filter is also 'tuned' to other physical characteristics, such as volume, brightness, intensity and novelty.

However, as important as a predisposition to respond to novel stimuli may be, Broadbent's model could not account for a feature of the 'cocktail party situation', whereby we can be engaged in one conversation but can switch our attention if we hear our name mentioned in another. Moray (1959) found this happened about a third of the time in a shadowing task.

Gray and Wedderburn (1960) presented to alternate ears the syllables composing a word plus random digits, so that when a syllable was 'heard' by one ear, the other ear would 'hear' digits. For example:

Left ear: OB   2   TIVE
right ear: 6   JEC   9

According to Broadbent, when subjects were asked to repeat what they had heard in one ear (or channel) they should have reported 'ob-two-tive' or 'six-jec-nine'; this is nonsense, of course, but the filter model maintains that it is the physical nature of the auditory signal (ie which ear receives which input) and not meaning which determines what is attended to and, hence, what is recalled.

However, Grey and Wedderburn's subjects reported 'objective', thus demonstrating their capacity to switch attention rapidly from channel to channel; Broadbent argued that we can only attend to one channel at a time. Similarly, when the left ear heard 'Dear/5/Jane' and the right heard '3/Aunt/4', subjects tended to report the whole phrase ('Dear Aunt Jane') and so were grouping the bits of the message in terms of meaning.

Treisman (1960) played 'crept out of . . . flowers' as the shadowed message and 'brightly coloured . . . the swamp' as the non-shadowed, and found that subjects often reported 'crept out of the swamp'. In all these examples, the subject's experience with grammatical and semantic aspects of language override the instructions to attend only to one ear.

Again, because subjects are usually not asked about the non-shadowed message until the end of the experiment, it is possible that they have *forgotten* what they have actually noticed during the shadowing task (which would also contradict Broadbent's model). Norman (1969) stopped subjects—without warning—in the middle of a shadowing task and they were able to recall the last few words of the non-shadowed message if questioning occurred within 30 seconds of being interrupted (see Chapter 6).

A number of studies have shown that when certain words in the shadowed message are followed by electric shock and then later appear in the non-attended message, there is an associated change in GSR (cg Moray, 1970, Corteen and Wood, 1972, Corteen and Dunn, 1974) and von Wright et al (1975) found that not only the conditioned word but synonyms and words which sounded like it also produced the change in GSR.

Treisman's Attenuator Model (1964)

This model retains much of the 'architecture' of Broadbent's, but sees the bottleneck as being much more flexible. Whereas Broadbent's model is an all-or-none model (input is either allowed through or is filtered out, attended to or not attended to), Treisman's stimulus-analysis system proceeds through a hierarchy. First, initial screening evaluates the signal on the basis of gross physical characteristics (much like Broadbent's) but instead of 'irrelevant' messages being excluded, the *attenuator* ('perceptual filter') 'turns their volume down' so that they are still 'available for higher level processing'. 'The channel filter attenuates irrelevant messages rather than blocks them completely,' (Treisman, 1964). Secondly, further analysis is based on individual words, grammatical structure and word-meaning.

Clearly, Treisman's model can account for the 'cocktail-party situation' (while Broadbent's cannot) and it does seem to provide a logical explanation of how we can 'hear' something while not attending to it and how we attend to the meaning rather than the physical characteristics of the message alone.

However, there remains the problem of how the executive decisions are made: does a simple attenuator have the capacity to analyse the intricate features of a message and check them with some master control to see whether they should or should not pass through and can it do so as quickly as is necessary? (Solso, 1979.)

The Pertinence Model

This model, originally proposed by Deutsch and Deutsch in 1963 and revised by Norman in 1968, 1969 and 1976, puts the bottleneck much nearer the response end of the processing system by proposing that *all* signals are initially analysed and *then* passed on to an attenuator, which passes on the message for further processing in a toned-down form. Compared with Treisman's model, the decision as to the *pertinence* or relevance of a message occurs much *earlier*.

If every signal is initially analysed, this would seem to make the model very uneconomical (Solso, 1979) and it also makes it rather rigid and inflexible (Eysenck, 1984). But is there any evidence that *all* incoming information is initially analysed?

Treisman and Geffen (1967) used a shadowing task in which subjects had to repeat the shadowed message aloud but also had to indicate (by tapping) when they heard a certain 'target' word, which could occur in *either* ear. The Pertinence model would predict that the target item should be detected and produce a response in whichever ear it appeared while the Filter model would predict that it would not be detected if it appeared in the non-shadowed ear. What were the results?

Subjects detected 87 per cent of the target words in the shadowed ear but only 8 per cent in the non-attended ear, which seems to represent unequivocal support for Broadbent. However, Deutsch and Norman (1967) rejected the experiment as a valid test of the pertinence model on the grounds that subjects had to shadow *and* tap in one message but only tap in the other and this made the shadowed target words more important than the non-shadowed ones. However, when Treisman and Riley (1969) removed this bias by telling subjects to stop shadowing and to tap as soon as they detected a target in either message, there was still a greater detection of shadowed target-words than non-shadowed (although it was a less dramatic difference than in the 1967 experiment).

Other studies have also failed to support the Pertinence Model (eg Kahneman, 1973, Moray and O'Brien, 1967, Moray, 1970 and Neisser 1976).

Johnston and Heinz (1978) have proposed a more flexible model, whereby selection is possible at several different stages of processing and in a 1979 experiment found that the amount of processing of a non-shadowed message varies as a function of task-demand in a way which is more consistent with Treisman's model than that of Deutsch and Deutsch and Norman. Johnston and Wilson (1980) found that non-target words were processed semantically when subjects did not know at which ear target-words would arrive (divided attention condition), but they were not semantically processed when they did know (focused attention condition). This suggests that the amount of processing received by non-target stimuli is often only as much as is required to perform the experimental task.

An Evaluation of Single Channel Models

Wilding (1982) believes that more is known about non-attended messages than either Broadbent's or Treisman's models can accommodate, but not as much as proposed by the Pertinence model.

Many researchers have begun to question whether any filter theory which assumes a single, general purpose, limited-capacity central processor, can, in principle, account for the complexities of selective attention (eg Allport, 1980, Hirst et al, 1978, Neisser, 1976, Norman and Bobrow, 1975) and much of the relevant evidence comes from *dual-task* studies which are more directly concerned with processing *capacity*.

Studies of Processing Capacity—Limited or Unlimited?

Many of the earlier shadowing experiments overlooked a number of critical variables which can influence performance on these tasks, including practice, degree of similarity between competing tasks, the difficulty of tasks and so on.

Allport (1980) cites a number of examples of people demonstrating a capacity to handle two inputs simultaneously which are sometimes quite astonishing. Allport et al (1972), for instance, found that musicians of reasonable competence could shadow a prose message while sight-reading music. Peterson (1969) found that subjects were able to read letters aloud and add digits presented auditorally (although not as efficiently as when either was performed alone) and Japanese abacus operators could answer general knowledge questions while operating (Hatano et al, 1977). Tierney (1973) and Shaffer (1975) found that copy-typing and shadowing were possible together (but not audio-typing and reading aloud).

Automatic Versus Controlled Processing
Of course, these examples involve tasks which are very different from each other, while most of the shadowing experiments on which the single channel models were based involve highly similar messages. The subjects involved are also often highly skilled and thoroughly practised in one of the tasks; in Shiffrin and Schneider's terms (1977), these subjects are displaying *automatic processing*. This operates when stimuli are consistently mapped onto responses; stimuli 'attract attention and initiate responses automatically, immediately and regardless of other inputs or the memory load' by triggering existing sequences of operations in long-term memory. In other words, there are *no* capacity limitations for such tasks, they do not require attention and they are very difficult to modify once they have been acquired. *Controlled processing*, on the other hand (which corresponds to focused attention) is of limited capacity, requires attention and can be used flexibly in changing circumstances.

Learning to drive a car clearly results in *automaticity*; at first focused attention is required for each component part of the skill but the experienced driver is able to engage in interaction with the environment in the relative absence of awareness (Norman, 1976).

As useful as the concept of automatic processing may be, it is certainly not without its critics. For instance, La Berge (1981) points out that many different criteria have been used for establishing automatic processing, including: (a) unavoidability; (b) occurring without awareness; (c) high efficiency; (d) without capacity limitations; and (e) resistance to modification.

Eysenck (1984) maintains that it is quite possible to conclude mistakenly that a process satisfies one or more of these criteria, as in the *Stroop effect*, in which colour words are presented (eg 'blue') in a conflicting coloured ink (eg 'blue' written in red ink) and the subject's task is to name the colour (ie red). The colour words usually interfere with the task and the interpretation usually made is that they are processed automatically and unavoidably (even though they are irrelevant to the task).

However, Kahneman and Henik (1979) found that the effect was much greater when the distracting information was in the same *location* as the colour which was to be identified, rather than in an adjacent location within the central fixation area and this suggests that the Stroop effect may not be automatic and unavoidable after all.

Furthermore, Treisman and Gelade (1980) argue that some processes may be intrinsically incapable of automatic processing.

Conclusions

Spelke et al (1976) argue that people's ability to develop skills in specialized situations is so great that it may never be possible to define the general limits of cognitive capacity and so the concept of attention-as-capacity is largely redundant.

Allport (1980) rejects the concept of a general purpose, limited-capacity processor altogether; the concept of attention, he says, is often used synonymously with 'consciousness' with no proper specification of how it is supposed to operate and it has done little, if anything, to increase our understanding of the problems it is meant to explain. Instead, he proposes a number of different specific processing mechanisms; when two simultaneous tasks are highly similar, they compete for the *same* specific mechanisms and this leads to mutual interference but dissimilar tasks involve different mechanisms and so no interference occurs.

However, Eysenck (1984) believes this could lead to chaos; some central control is necessary if behaviour is to be purposeful and co-ordinated. So what is the solution?

One possibility is the proposal by Baddeley and Hitch (1974) of two specific systems (an articulatory loop and a visuospatial scratch pad) in addition to a central capacity processor (which is modality-free). This could explain why overt repetition of an over-learned sequence of digits (which uses an articulatory loop) does not interfere with verbal reasoning (which uses the central processor). Eysenck (1982 a) advocates a combination of the approaches of Allport and Baddeley and Hitch, seeing a hierarchical structure of processes, with a central processor at the top and more specific resources below it; those at the top tend to be more non-automatic, while those lower down tend to be automatic.

5

Perception: The Nature–Nurture Debate

The heredity-environment (or nature-nurture) aspect of perception has been hotly debated in psychology. In this chapter we shall consider the evidence supporting both sides of the argument.

However, we should not expect any simple answers. As we saw in Chapter 4, perception is a complex set of different but interconnected and overlapping abilities (eg, perception of depth, colour and movement) and several sense modalities are involved. To ask whether perception is learnt or innate is to oversimplify the issue. Philosophers, who considered this question long before psychologists began to study it scientifically, tended to oversimplify their questions and, consequently, produced oversimplified answers, which were of two distinct types. The *Nativists* believed that we are born with certain capacities to perceive the world in particular ways; these capacities are often immature or incomplete at birth but develop gradually thereafter. Psychologists of a Nativist persuasion believe that this development after birth proceeds through the genetically-determined process of maturation, with learning playing only a minor role—or none at all. This type of psychology is best illustrated by the Gestalt school. The *Empiricists* maintained that all our knowledge and abilities are acquired through experience, that is, are learned (the word 'empirical' means 'through the senses'); the Transactionalists are one school of psychology embodying the empiricist philosophy.

Most present-day psychologists would consider themselves neither Nativists nor Empiricists but rather *Interactionists*, understanding that we may be born with capacities to perceive the world in certain ways but stimulation and environmental influences in general are crucial in determining how—and even whether—these capacities actually develop. Different perceptual abilities may be more or less affected by genetic or environmental factors, but it is certain that any perceptual ability is the product of an interaction between both sets of factors; both are always involved, although it is not always obvious exactly what part they play.

117

The Study of Perceptual Development

What kind of evidence is relevant?

a) *The perceptual abilities of newborn babies* are the most direct way of investigating the nature–nurture issue. In general, the earlier a particular ability appears, the more likely it is to be under the influence of genetic factors; however, the fact that it develops some time after birth does not necessarily mean it has been learnt, since it could take time to mature. There are other special difficulties involved in studying speechless subjects, as we shall see below.

b) *Animal experiments* often involve depriving animals in some way of normal sensory and perceptual stimulation and recording the long-term effects of this deprivation on their sensory and perceptual abilities. Some studies reverse this and actually provide the animals with 'extra' experience and stimulation; still others study the animal's brain to see how it controls perceptual abilities. From a research point of view, the main advantage of studying animals is that we can manipulate their environments in ways which are not permissible with human subjects. Deprivation studies can tell us how much and what kinds of early experience are necessary for normal perceptual development in those species being studied, but we must be very cautious about generalizing these findings to humans.

c) *Studies of human cataract patients* represent the human counterpart to animal deprivation studies. These patients have been deprived of normal visual experience through a physical defect, rather than through experimental manipulation or interference, and constitute a kind of 'natural experiment'. Their vision is restored through surgical removal of the cataract and the abilities that are evident immediately after removal of the bandages are normally taken to be innate and unlearned. However, there are special problems involved here too; generalizing from 'unusual' adults to 'normal' babies can be hazardous and it is not always obvious whether abilities that do not appear have to be learned or are 'present' but not being used.

d) In *studies of perceptual adaptation* or *readjustment*, human subjects wear special goggles which distort the visual world in various ways. If they can adapt to such a distorted-looking world then human 'perceptual habits' cannot be as fixed or rigid as they would be if they were under genetic control—perhaps the way we perceive is itself originally learned. However, we need to ask what kind of adaptation is taking place: is it actually perceptual or is it merely motor, that is, learning to move about successfully in a very different-looking environment? If the latter is the case, then we cannot conclude necessarily that our perceptual 'habits' are habits at all (ie, learned in the first place) but only that we are good at changing our body movements to 'match' what we see.

e) *Cross-cultural studies* attempt to test whether or not the way that we, in Western culture, perceive things is universal, that is, perceived in the same way by people who live in cultures very different from our own. The most common method of testing is to present members of different cultural groups with the same stimulus material, usually visual illusions.

We can be fairly confident that any differences between members of different cultures reflect different learning experiences and, to that extent, our perceptual abilities can be thought of as shaped by our cultural environment. However, as we shall see, psychologists disagree as to the identity of the key variables involved.

An Overview of the Evidence

Having said that most psychologists regard perceptual abilities as the product of an interaction between genetic factors (nature) and environmental factors (nurture), some attempts have been made to test directly the merits of the Nativist and Empricist positions and we shall discuss some of these when we look at the work of Tom Bower with infants.

By the same token, most of the evidence which supports the Nativist theory derives from infant studies; as we said above, the earlier a particular ability appears, the less opportunity there has been for learning to have occurred and so the more likely it is that the ability is under genetic control.

Although the bulk of the evidence supports the Interactionist position, there are grounds for concluding that relatively simple perceptual abilities are more under genetic control and less susceptible to environmental influence, while the situation is reversed in the case of more complex abilities. The most clear-cut demonstration of this comes from human cataract patients and so we shall start with these.

Studies of Human Cataract Patients

These really represent the 'natural' counterpart in humans of the animal experiments described above. They are based on case-studies of patients who have undergone an operation for the removal of cataracts to 'restore' their sight (a cataract is a film over the lens of the eye and can either be present at birth or develop any time afterwards). Most of the evidence comes from the work of Von Senden, a German doctor who, in 1932, reported on 65 cases of people who had undergone cataract-removal surgery; the earliest case was reported in 1700, the latest in 1928.

Von Senden's original data was taken up again by Hebb in 1949, who analysed the findings in terms of: (i) *figural unity*, the ability to detect the presence of a figure or stimulus; and (ii) *figural identity*, being able to name or in some other way identify the object, to 'say' what it is. Hebb concluded that while (i) seems to be innate, (ii) seems to require learning.

Initially, cataract patients are typically bewildered by an array of visual stimuli (rather like the 'blooming, buzzing confusion' which William James believed was the perceptual experience of newborn babies). However, they can distinguish figures from ground (ie some object from its background), fixate objects, scan them and follow moving objects with their eyes. But they cannot identify by sight alone those objects which are already familiar through touch (and this includes faces), distinguish between various geometrical shapes without counting the corners or tracing the outline with their fingers, or say which of two sticks is longer without feeling them (although they can tell there is a difference).

They also fail to show perceptual constancy, that is, the recognition and perception of things as the same despite changes in their appearance (compare with Piaget's concept of conservation, see Chapter 19). For example, even after visual identification has occurred (ie, things are recognized through sight alone) there may be little generalization to situations other than that in which the object was originally recognized, eg a lump of sugar held in someone's hand may not be identified as such when suspended from a piece of string. Another example would be the failure to recognize a triangle as being the same geometrical shape when its white side is turned over to reveal a red side or when viewed under different lighting conditions. (Interestingly, as we shall see later in the chapter, Bower believes that size and shape constancy are probably innate; Hebb's findings suggest this is not so.)

So the more simple ability of figural unity seems to be available very soon after cataract removal and seems not to be dependent on prior visual experience, while the more complex figural identity seems to require a long period of training. Hebb believes that this is how these two aspects of perception normally develop.

Further evidence comes from a single case, that of a man named S. B., reported by Gregory and Wallace in 1963. S. B. was 52 when he received his sight after a corneal graft operation. His judgement of size and distance were good, provided that he was familiar with the objects in question. He could recognize objects visually if he was already familiar with them through touch while blind so, unlike most of the 65 cases analysed by Hebb, he displayed good cross-modal transfer, ie, recognition through one sense modality (touch) being substituted by another (vision). However, he seemed to have great difficulty in identifying objects visually if he was not already familiar with them in this way: a year after his operation he still could not draw the front of a bus although the rest of the drawing was very well executed. S. B. was never able to use his new-found ability to see to its fullest extent; for instance, he did not bother to turn on the light at night but would sit in the dark all evening.

Although these 66 cases seem to underline the importance of experience as far as all but the most simple perceptual abilities are concerned, there are certain problems related to these studies:

a) Adult patients are not the same as babies; while the sensory systems of babies are all relatively undeveloped, adults have other well-developed sensory modalities which tend to compensate for the lack of vision (touch and hearing in particular). These other channels may actually hinder visual learning since the patient, in order to use vision, may have to actually 'un-learn' previous experience. Since people tend to find it easier to use the channel they already know best, or use most often, S B.'s poor cross-modal transfer (his continued preference for touch over vision) may reflect this tendency to stick with what is familiar rather than experiment with the unknown. This may be a safer conclusion to draw than Hebb's, which is that figural identity is (normally) largely learned.

b) It seems that, traditionally, cataract patients have not been very adequately prepared for their 'new world of vision'; their resulting confusion and general emotional distress following the operation may result in a rather inaccurate picture of what they can and cannot actually see. Referring to S. B. again, when blind he would cross the street on his own, but once he could see the traffic it frightened him so much that he refused to cross on his own. He, in fact, died three years after his operation, at least partially from depression. (Depression was also common amongst Von Senden's cases.)

c) We do not know what physical deterioration of the visual system may have occurred during the years of blindness and so cannot be sure that the absence of figural identity is due to lack of visual stimulation and learning (which Hebb believes are responsible) rather than to some physical damage.

d) The reliability of the case histories themselves is open to doubt; presumably the standards for reporting in 1700 were not as strict as they are today, so that there is great variability in the ages of the patients when they underwent surgery, and when their cataracts first appeared, hence in the amount of visual experience prior to the defect.

Animal Experiments

Riesen (1947) deprived one group of chimps of light by raising them in darkness, except for several 45-second periods of exposure to light while they were being fed; this continued until they were 16 months old and they were compared with a group of normally-reared chimps. The deprived group showed markedly inferior perceptual abilities when tested at 16 months: while they did show pupil constriction to light and were startled by sudden, intense illumination, they did not blink in response to threatening movements made towards their faces or show any interest in their toys unless they accidentally touched them with some part of their bodies.

But as Weiskrantz (1956) pointed out, the visual deficiencies in the deprived group were probably due to failure of the retinas to develop properly; when the retina is not stimulated by light, fewer of the retinal cells develop and the visual cortex too may begin to degenerate. So, Riesen's experiment may show only that a certain amount of light is physically necessary to maintain the visual system and to allow it to mature normally. In an effort to overcome these objections to his original study, Riesen later reared three chimps, from birth until they were seven months old, under three different conditions:

i) *Debi* spent the whole time in darkness.
ii) *Kova* spent 1½ hours per day exposed to diffuse or unpatterned light by wearing translucent goggles; the rest of the time was spent in darkness.
iii) *Lad* was raised in normal lighting conditions.

As expected, Debi suffered retinal damage but neither of the other two did. Lad was no different, perceptually, from any other normally-reared chimp. It was Kova who was of special interest since, while she did not suffer any retinal damage, she was only exposed to unpatterned light, so that she did not see 'objects' as such but only patches of light, different colours and brightnesses, but not distinguishable shapes or patterns. She was noticeably retarded; for example, she needed six days of training (receiving two electric shocks per day from a yellow and black striped disc) before she even whimpered when the disc was shown. Again, she was very slow to follow a moving object just with her eyes.

In 1965 Riesen fitted translucent goggles to monkeys, chimps and kittens for the first three months of their lives. Some simple perceptual abilities remained intact, such as differentiating colours, size and brightness, but more complex abilities did not, eg following a moving object, differentiating between geometrical shapes, perceiving depth and distinguishing a moving object from a stationary one. Riesen's studies as a whole suggest that:

a) Light is necessary for normal physical development of the visual system (at least in chimps, some monkeys and kittens);
b) Patterned light is also necessary for the normal development of some of the complex visual abilities (in those species).

Therefore, environmental stimulation of certain kinds seems to be essential for normal perceptual development. If perception were wholly innate, environmental factors (over and above those which can actually harm the developing organism or actively prevent maturation from taking place) should not have any effect; Riesen has shown, however, that they do.

Other animal experiments have also shown the impact of early experience on perceptual abilities.

Hubel and Wiesel (1962/3) used cats reared in full or partial blindfolds (translucent goggles). The receptive fields of the latter failed to develop normally (receptive fields are groups of perhaps several thousand retinal cells, each of which registers a line at a specific angle making up the image projected from the object onto the eye—this information is then transmitted to the brain).

In a later study, Hubel (1979) found evidence that the brain itself can be affected by visual deprivation. He surgically closed either the left or right eyelid of several monkeys when they were two weeks old. This reduced the amount of light striking the retina; the eyelid remained closed until 18 months of age. He then opened the eye and injected into the non-deprived eye a radioactive substance which would be transported to the visual cortex soon after the injection. Pictures were taken of slices of cortex with radiation-sensitive film, allowing a study of the *ocular dominance columns*, which are groups of cells in the cortex that respond to input from either the right or the left eye. The columns of the open eye were greatly expanded while those of the closed eye had shrunk dramatically. Also, there seems to be a critical period for the development of these areas of the visual cortex, lasting from three to six weeks after birth.

Blakemore and Cooper (1970), and Blakemore (1973), looked at more specific environmental effects. They raised kittens from birth in darkness, except for a five-hour period each day when they were placed in a large drum or round chamber which had either vertical or horizontal stripes on the walls. A collar prevented the kittens from seeing their own bodies, so that the stripes were the only visual stimuli they encountered.

At five months old, the kittens were tested for line recognition by being presented with a moving pointer held either vertically or horizontally. Those reared in the 'vertical world' would only reach out to touch a vertical pointer, while those reared in the 'horizontal world' reached only for a horizontal pointer. Depending on what kind of visual experience they had had for the first five months, they acted as if they were blind in the presence of the other kind of visual stimulus. This 'behavioural blindness' mirrored the 'physiological blindness': by placing microelectrodes into individual cells in the visual cortex, Blakemore and Cooper found that for those kittens raised in a vertically-striped environment there were no cells that fired in response to bars of light moved horizontally, and the reverse was true for the kittens raised in the horizontally-striped environment. The only receptive fields to have developed were those which reflected the kind of early visual experience the kittens had had.

However, this does not show conclusively that responding to lines at different angles develops solely through environmental influence: it is possible that receptive fields for all angles are present at birth and that where a kitten sees only vertical lines, those fields which would otherwise have responded to horizontal lines are 'taken over' by vertical fields. Another possibility is offered by Leventhal and Hirsch (1975). They found that exposure to horizontal and vertical lines prevents the appearance of any cells responsive to diagonals, but cells responsive to horizontals and verticals can be found even after exposure to diagonal lines only. This suggests that the horizontal and vertical cells are in some way more basic and robust than diagonal cells.

However, these findings do seem to suggest very strongly that the type of environment is important in the development of at least certain kinds of perceptual ability in some species: in kittens, perception does seem to be at least partly learned.

Held and Hein (1963) were concerned with the effects of deprivation on the ability of kittens to guide their movements through vision. Given that a kitten's perceptual abilities are not entirely innate, to what extent is the acquisition of these abilities dependent on exposure to visual stimulation *and* motor activity? They found that only by moving about in a visually rich environment will normally sensory-motor co-ordination develop—passive exposure to such an environment is not sufficient.

Held and Hein used an apparatus called the kitten-carousel (see Figure 5.1). For the first eight weeks after birth, kittens were kept in darkness and then spent about three hours each day in the carousel (the rest of the time being spent in the dark). The 'active' kitten could move itself around (its legs

Figure 5.1   The kitten carousel (from Held, 1965)

were free) and its movements were transmitted to the 'passive' kitten via a series of pulleys, ie every time the active kitten moved the passive kitten moved the same distance, at the same speed etc. The significant thing to note is that both kittens had exactly the same visual experience (both type and amount) but one could move itself about while the other was dependent on the first one's movements.

After several weeks of this arrangement, they were tested for 'paw-eye co-ordination'. The active kittens were markedly superior; for example, after thirty hours exposure they all showed visually-guided paw placement (if gently lowered towards the floor, they extended their paws, which is a typical response for normally-reared kittens). But none of the passive kittens could do this after thirty hours, nor did they blink in response to an approaching object. Also, they did not show the normal reluctance to step onto the deep side of the visual cliff apparatus (see below). But does this mean that they could not actually perceive depth?

It seems that this would be a premature conclusion as the 'passive' kittens soon learned the normal avoidance responses when allowed to run around in a lighted environment. This suggests that, rather than having failed to learn depth perception as such, they simply had not learned the correct motor responses associated with depth perception. Indeed, Miller and Walk (1975), in a modification of Held and Hein's study, concluded that depth perception is innate but can be improved with experience.

So we must distinguish between perception on the one hand and sensory-motor co-ordination on the other (see the next section on Perceptual Readjustment studies).

A general problem with animal studies (as with studies of human infants) is that we can only infer what their perceptual experiences are through observing their behaviour or their physiological responses—they cannot tell us more directly what they can see or cannot see. We cannot be certain that animals deprived in particular ways do not perceive particular stimuli, only that they do not behave as if they do. It is possible that certain perceptual abilities have developed, but if they have not become linked to the animal's behaviour we may have no way of knowing.

Perceptual Adaptation/Readjustment Studies

The basic hypothesis being tested in these studies is that human beings are capable of perceiving the world in a different way from normal and adjusting to this altered perception, thus demonstrating that perception is largely learned. The greater the degree of adaptation to a new perceptual world, the more significant the role of learning is taken to be. (Compared with other species that have been tested, human beings come out on top as far as this adaptability is concerned.)

It follows that the less adaptation a particular species shows, the greater the control of genetic factors in the perceptual abilities of that species. This has been clearly demonstrated by Sperry's experiment (1943) with salamanders and Hess's experiment (1956) with chickens.

Sperry rotated the eyes of salamanders through 180 degrees so that images on the retina were inverted (upside-down) compared with the normal eye.

When presented with a stimulus moving upwards, the salamanders moved their heads downwards—they moved according to what they saw. But they showed no tendency to adapt over time and had to be force-fed, or fed in the dark.

Hess's subjects were chickens; he fitted them with prisms which shifted the image seven degrees either to the left or the right. Chickens which wore left-shifting prisms always pecked to the left of the grain by seven degrees; similarly, those fitted with right-shifting prisms always pecked to the right by seven degrees. Like the salamanders, the chickens did not show any signs of adapting, however many times they pecked.

One of the earliest recorded human studies was that of George Stratton (in 1896), an American who fitted himself with a telescope on one eye which 'turned the world upside down'. (The other eye was kept covered, since if both eyes had worn telescopes it would have proved too much of a strain, especially to the eye-movement muscles.) He wore the telescope for a total of 87 hours over an eight-day period; he wore blindfolds at night and at other times when not wearing the inverting lens. As far as possible he went about his normal routine. For the first three days he was aware that part of his environment—the part not in his immediate field of vision but on the periphery—was in a different orientation. But by the fourth day he was beginning to imagine unseen parts as also being inverted, and by the fifth day he had to make a conscious effort to remember that he actually had the telescope on. He was able to walk round the house without bumping into furniture and when he moved, his surroundings looked 'normal'; however, when he concentrated hard and remained still, things still appeared upside down. By the eighth day, everything seemed 'harmonious'; he began to 'feel' inverted but this was quite normal and natural to him.

When Stratton removed the telescope, he immediately recognized the visual orientation as the one that existed prior to the start of the experiment. He found it surprisingly bewildering, although definitely *not* upside-down. This absence of an inverted after-image or after-effect is quite a crucial finding: it means that Stratton had not actually learnt to *see* the world in an upside-down fashion, otherwise removal of the telescope would have caused the now normal (right-way-up) world to look upside-down again! Instead, it suggests that the adaptation has taken the form of learning the appropriate motor responses in an upside-down-looking world. (Compare this with the question of depth-perception in Held and Hein's kittens that we discussed earlier.)

Having said this, Stratton did experience an after-effect which caused things before him to 'swing and sweep' as he moved his eyes, showing that location constancy (seeing things as stable and remaining in the same place) had been disrupted. In another experiment, Stratton made goggles which visually displaced his body so that he always appeared horizontally in front of himself—wherever he walked he 'followed' his own body image, which was suspended at right angles to his actual body. When he lay down, his body would appear above him, vertically, again at right angles. After three days, he was able to go out for a walk on his own—and lived to tell the tale!

More recently, Snyder and Pronko (1952) made goggles which inverted and reversed the visual world. Their subjects wore them continually for thirty days and were able to adapt to the changes. Two years after the experiment, these subjects coped just as well, when refitted with the goggles, as subjects who were first-timers, at the end of the thirty-day period. This shows that motor adaptations are extremely resistant to forgetting.

Kohler (1962) used an optical device which inverted the image without reversing left and right (more like Stratton's than Snyder and Pronko's). His subjects were disoriented and even nauseous at first but after several days adjusted and lived reasonably normally. Kohler concluded that upright vision could be achieved if the subject moved about and touched objects in the environment and the more familiar the object was, the easier this could be achieved. The fact that some of the subjects had an inverted after-effect when they removed the apparatus also suggests that the adaptation may actually be visual in nature and not simply sensory-motor. However, the after-effect lasted only for the first few minutes, which suggests that any purely perceptual learning that did occur was not very substantial. Similarly, when subjects wore goggles, such that the left half of each lens was red and the right half green, the visual world at first looked red when the subject looked to the left and green when the subject looked to the right. But adaptation to this occurred after only a few hours. Upon removal of the goggles, the visual world seemed to be coloured in the opposite direction to that experienced when the goggles were being worn. Yet, as with the inverting goggles, this after-effect lasted only a short time.

The importance of moving about in the physical environment when adapting to a perceptually distorted world was confirmed by Held. Based on his work with the kitten carousel, discussed earlier, he got one human subject to push another around on a trolley inside a large drum, while both wore goggles that shifted everything to one side. They both had identical visual experiences (as did the active and passive kitten) but the one who did the pushing made a faster and more efficient adjustment (as did the active kitten).

So what can we conclude from these studies?

a) It seems that when subjects adapt to a distorted perceptual world, they are not, for the most part, actually learning to see 'normally' but instead are developing the appropriate motor behaviour which helps them to get around and function efficiently in their environment. What is learnt is not a new way of perceiving the world but a new set of body movements.

b) The visual system, at least in adults, is extremely flexible and can adjust to distorted conditions. This strongly suggests that learning plays an important role in perceptual development, since a totally or largely innate system would not allow such adaptation to occur.

c) Because the subjects are adults, who have already undergone a great deal of learning, and in whom maturation has already taken place, it is difficult to generalize from these studies to how babies develop under normal circumstances. Just because an adult is able to learn to perceive the world in a different way, we cannot automatically assume that babies originally have to learn to perceive the world as they do.

Cross-cultural Studies

These have mainly involved testing members of different cultural groups using the same test materials, usually visual illusions. The two most commonly used have been the Müller-Lyer and the Horizontal-Vertical (see Chapter 4).

The pioneering study was carried out by Rivers et al in 1901. They went to the Murray Islands, a group of islands situated in the Torres Straits (between New Guinea and Australia); they found that the Murray Islanders were less prone to the Müller-Lyer illusion than Europeans, but more prone to the Horizontal-Vertical illusion than Europeans.

Probably the largest study was that of Segall, Campbell and Herskovits (1963) who spent six years studying African children and adults, and inhabitants of the Philippines, and comparing them with each other as well as with South Africans of European descent and Americans from Illinois (in the Midwest of the USA). On the Müller-Lyer illusion, the Africans and Philippinos were much less susceptible than the other two groups, but there were some interesting results for the Horizontal-Vertical illusion.

Two of the African tribes studied, the Batoro and the Bayankole, were at the top end of the illusion scale, that is, they were most likely to see it. They both live in high, open country where you can see for miles without 'interference'; hence, vertical objects, such as trees or mountains, become important focal points and are used to estimate distances.

A third tribe, the Bete, who live in a jungle environment, were at the bottom end of the scale—they were least likely to see the illusion of all the groups. Europeans and Americans tended to come somewhere in between the three African tribes.

The implication is that ecology, ie the physical environment which a cultural group occupies, is closely tied to the susceptibility of that group to visual illusions; as we shall see below, some psychologists believe that ecology actually determines susceptibility.

Another illusion that has been used in cross-cultural research, but less often than the other two, is the rotating trapezoid: it is attached to a motor and revolves in a circle. It has horizontal and vertical bars fixed to it to give the impression of a window. (See Figure 5.2 on page 128.)

Most Western observers report seeing a rectangle that oscillates to and fro, backwards and forwards, rather than a trapezoid revolving through 360 degrees (which is what it actually is and does). This seems to be based on the assumption that it is a window (or window-type object). (This effect is reduced when it is viewed binocularly, that is, with both eyes rather than monocularly, that is, with one eye closed; it is also reduced when the horizontal bars are removed.)

On the assumption that it is normally interpreted as a window by people who are used to seeing windows, and who bring with them expectations of rectangularity, we might expect that people from cultures where windows (as we know them) are not an everyday sight might see the rotating trapezoid for what it is.

One such cultural group are the Zulus, who not only do not have western-style windows but tend to live in a rather circular environment. Allport and Pettigrew (1957) compared urban and rural Zulus with each other and with Europeans.

Under optimal conditions (using one eye and further away) there were no differences between the three groups. But under less-than-optimal conditions (using both eyes and being closer in) the rural Zulus—who live in the tradi-

Figure 5.2   The rotating trapezoid window (as used by Allport and Pettigrew, 1957)

tional circular culture—were less likely to perceive an oscillating rectangle than the other two groups and were more likely to perceive a rotating trapezoid.

Stewart (1973) found that rural Tonga children were less likely to see the Ames 'distorted room' as being normal compared with both children living in the city of Lusaka (Zambia) and European children. She found the same differences for other illusions (including the Müller-Lyer) and, interestingly, the greater the exposure to a 'rectangular' environment, the greater the susceptibility to the Müller-Lyer illusion. How can we account for the differences?

One of the first attempts to explain the results of cross-cultural studies was Segall et al's (1963) 'carpentered world hypothesis'; referring to members of Western culture they say:

> We live in a culture in which straight lines abound and in which perhaps ninety per cent of the acute and obtuse angles formed on our retina by the straight lines of our visual field are realistically interpretable as right angles extended in space. (Segall et al, 1963)

What they are saying, in effect, is that we tend to interpret illusion figures, which are two-dimensional drawings, in terms of our past experiences, so that in Western culture (which is a 'carpentered world') we add a third dimension (depth) which is not actually present in the drawing. This misleads us as to the true nature of the stimulus, resulting in what we call an illusion. We are more or less likely to experience the illusion depending on what our cultural experience tells us the drawing *could* represent; if we are not used to straight lines and right angles, why should we think there is any difference in the length of the shafts of the arrows in the Müller-Lyer figure? Similarly, if we live in a circular environment, why should we see the rotating trapezoid as an oscillating rectangle? (We shall see later that the very tendency to interpret two-dimensional diagrams or pictures in three-dimensional terms may itself be something that is culturally determined.)

However, apart from certain theoretical and methodological criticisms of the carpentered world hypothesis, there is also substantial evidence which does not support it. Mundy-Castle and Nelson (1962) studied the Knysma forest dwellers, a group of isolated, white, illiterate South Africans. Despite the rectangularity of their environment, they were unable to give appropriate 3-D responses to 2-D symbols on a standard test, and on the Müller-Lyer figure their responses were not significantly different from non-Europeans.

However, they did differ significantly from literate, white adults. Again, Jahoda (1966) found no support for the hypothesis that groups living in open country would be more susceptible to the Horizontal-Vertical illusion compared with groups living in dense, tropical rain forest (using Ghanaian subjects).

Finally, Gregor and McPherson (1965) found no significant differences between two groups of Australian aborigines on the two illusions, despite one group living in a relatively urbanised, carpentered environment and the other living primitively out of doors.

Consequently, Mundy-Castle and Nelson, Jahoda, and Gregor and McPherson, have suggested that Campbell et al exaggerated the influence of ecology on cultural differences in perception. Jahoda, for example, has stressed the importance of considering the possible effects of exposure to Western education and other cultural variables (which were largely overlooked in the Segall, Campbell and Herskovits study). He believes that many of the findings may reflect the inability of some cultural groups to interpret 2-D drawings or other representations of the 3-D world, something which we take so much for granted since we encounter them from birth onwards. But it may be very difficult for people who are not familiar with them through a lifetime of exposure to interpret them in this way: the tendency to see pictures as depicting objects in the real world may itself be culturally determined.

It seems there are two separate processes involved when we 'read' pictures: first, we must learn to make perceptual inferences about the real world (what is the picture of?) and secondly, we must learn the conventions which the picture-maker is using in order to assess the real world (for instance, all the depth cues, such as linear perspective, relative size and superimposition). (See Chapter 4.)

Cross-cultural research, mainly in Africa, shows that the interpretation of pictures is far from automatic; rather than an inborn ability, it is a skill of considerable complexity.

We will finish this section by looking at some relevant findings. Turnbull (1961) studied the Bambuti pygmies who live in the dense rain forests of the Congo, a closed-in world without vast open spaces. Turnbull brought a pygmy out to a vast plain where a herd of buffalo was grazing in the distance. The pygmy said he had never seen one of those insects before; when told they were buffalo, he was offended and Turnbull was accused of insulting his intelligence. Turnbull drove the jeep towards the buffalo; the pygmy's eyes widened in amazement as he saw the insects 'grow' into buffalo before him. He concluded that witchcraft was being used to deceive him.

This is a good illustration of lack of size constancy, an important cue we use to 'read' pictures. The sight of the buffalo from such a distance was so far removed from the pygmy's experience that he could only believe that they were small animals (insects) rather than much larger ones (buffalo) which only *looked* smaller (by virtue of the small retinal image produced by large objects viewed from a distance). He could not apply size constancy for such great distances (but presumably he could for shorter ones) and if he could be deceived in this way when looking at real, live buffalo, how much more insulted would have felt if he had been shown a photograph of the same scene?

Directly relevant to this question is a study by Deregowski (1972) who describes an African woman who slowly discovered that a photo she was shown portrayed a human profile. According to Deregowski, 'She discovered in turn the nose, the mouth, the eye, but where was the other eye? I tried turning my profile to explain why she could see only one eye, but she hopped around to my other side to point out that I possessed a second eye which the picture lacked.' The woman was treating the picture as an object rather than as a 2-D representation of an object—she had not learnt to 'infer' the depth in the picture, the parts that were not immediately visible (which clearly she could do when looking at a real face). Her 'object' turned out to have only two dimensions and this is what she found bewildering.

Many other studies confirm this general picture, involving various tribal and linguistic groups. However, picture-less environments are fast disappearing all over the world and certainly it is becoming increasingly difficult to find 'naïve' subjects.

But Deregowski did manage to find a group of people, the Me'en tribe, living in a remote part of Ethiopia, who are still largely unaffected by Western culture. Members of the tribe were shown drawings of animals. They responded by feeling, smelling, tasting or rustling the paper and showed no interest in the visual content of the picture itself.

When the unfamiliar paper was replaced by pictures painted on cloth (which was familiar to them), they responded to the drawing of the animal without exception. Although we must be careful about generalization from just one small sample, the responses of the Me'en suggest that familiarity with pictures, photographs and so on may *not* after all be the essential pre-requisite for 'reading' pictures (as representations of the 3-D world) that Jahoda and others have maintained . Yet the response of the Me'en to the unfamiliar paper brings to mind a baby's typical response to its first picture book—it goes in the mouth like everything else, long before the baby shows any interest in the pictures themselves. It is to babies that we now turn.

Studies of Human Infants

To repeat a point made earlier, these represent the most direct way of trying to settle the nature-nurture issue. But, of course, the fact that the baby cannot tell us what it sees and hears etc presents problems of its own, the most important being that the investigator has to *infer* what the baby perceives; we can never be sure that the inference is correct.

Again, if newborns do not show a particular ability this does not necessarily mean that such abilities have to be learnt—they may develop sometime after birth through the action of genetic 'time switches' involved in the process of maturation. The general rule is that the earlier an ability appears, the more likely it is to be genetically controlled and not the result of learning. Clearly, as was pointed out at the beginning, perception is not a single ability but a series of abilities. (Vision has been most widely studied, both in infants, adults and animals, and most of this chapter so far has concentrated on this sense modality. We shall be emphasizing vision in this section too).

Vision involves perception of colour, shape, size, depth, movement etc. Some of these may be largely innate, while others may be largely due to the effects of experience. We must be specific about which aspect of perception we are talking about when trying to establish to what extent, and in what ways, genetic and environmental factors have their influence.

Asking the Right Questions

In 1890 William James, the famous American psychologist and philosopher, wrote, 'the baby, assailed by eyes, ears, nose, skin and entrails at once, feels it all as one great blooming, buzzing confusion'.

Until quite recently, many people (including psychologists) agreed with James that the baby's perception of the world is hazy, poorly defined, unstructured, even chaotic. Many have gone so far as to believe that babies are born blind. But studies of newborns in the last fifteen to twenty years have taught us to ask, 'Can the baby see or not, or hear or not?' is the wrong kind of question. Instead, we should ask; 'What and how well can the baby see and hear?'

Methods of Studying Infant Perception
Psychologists make inferences about infants' perception in two ways: first, by looking at what the baby *possesses* by way of sensory equipment (its structural and physical attributes); and secondly, by observing what the baby *does* (including physiological changes in the presence of various stimuli). In both cases we ask, 'What is the baby likely to be seeing or hearing?' and, 'How soon can particular abilities be expected, or seem to, develop?'

More specifically, what are some of the methods used to study infant perception? (These relate mostly to what the baby does rather than what it possesses.)

a) A general and widely used method is to present, simultaneously, two stimuli. If the infant spends more time looking at one than the other, then it is inferred that: (i) it can actually tell the difference (discriminate) between them; and (ii) that it prefers the one it looks at longer. This is called the *spontaneous visual preference technique.*

b) Another method involves reflecting light on the cornea to monitor the baby's vision and then filming the reflection of the cornea. This gives the researcher a more precise reading of what the baby is looking at than is possible from simply noting the orientation of the head or the general direction of the gaze (as in (a)).

c) Another approach is to measure the baby's sucking rate, via a dummy or pacifier, as a response to different stimuli. A baseline rate is recorded before the stimulus is presented (ie, the baby's normal or spontaneous sucking rate). When the stimulus is presented, the baby at first tends to suck noticeably slower or faster but after a while habituation sets in (that is, the baby stops responding to it as a novel stimulus) and a return to the baseline rate occurs.

The stimulus is then changed in some way and if there is another increase or decrease in sucking rate, it is inferred that the baby can tell the difference—it is responding to the change as a novel stimulus.

d) A fourth method, again using a dummy or nipple, is to attach it to audio-visual equipment so that when the baby sucks, a tape-recording is switched on, or an image projected onto a screen can be brought into sharper focus the harder the baby sucks.

e) Two important physiological measures are the baby's heart rate and breatning rate—usually a decrease in these is taken to indicate that something has caught the baby's attention.

These methods may be combined with each other and also with study of the visual apparatus (or any other) itself to help us infer what the baby actually perceives.

Studying What the Baby Possesses

What can we tell about the infant's visual perception from studying its visual apparatus?

We know that the nervous system as a whole is still immature (as we might expect). The optic nerve, connecting the eye to the visual cortex, is thinner and shorter than that of an adult and is only partially myelinated (insulated by a myelin sheath), so that visual information is transmitted inefficiently to a similarly undeveloped cortex for interpretation. However, myelination is complete by about 4 months after birth. (Without myelination of the optic nerve, we could probably only see diffuse flashes of light.)

The human eye at birth is about half the size and weight of an adult's; the eyeball is shorter and this reduces the distance between the retina and the lens, making vision less efficient. However, the newborn's eyeball is anatomically identical to the adult's—all the parts are there but the relationship to each other is different and they do not all develop at the same rate; for example, the cornea is much closer to its final form than the iris.

Perception of Colour
The retina is fairly well developed at birth; the rods and cones, which are the light-sensitive cells in the retina, are also fairly well developed, so the basis for colour vision is present in the newborn. (These two kinds of retinal cells become differentiated by the seventh month of pregnancy at the latest.) By three to four months after birth, the baby can distinguish blue, green, yellow, and red, and there seems to be a preference for reds and blues over greens and yellows. Babies can also discriminate brightness differences (within the same colour) of as little as 5 per cent—for adults the figure is 1 per cent.

Perception of Brightness
The fovea (which is packed with cones and thus provides the clearest image of an object when viewed in daylight or other bright light) is fairly well developed at birth; by four months after conception it has become structurally differentiated.

We know that babies react to bright light while still in the womb—if a bright light is shone on a pregnant woman's belly, the baby may move towards it. (Perhaps some of the baby's movements in the womb, known as 'quickening', which usually begin around the fourth month, stem from this attraction to light.) Also, the pupillary reflex (a response to bright light whereby the pupil contracts, thus reducing the amount of light that enters the eye) is present in even premature babies. Similarly, the blink reflex to bright light is present at birth.

So clearly, the neonate is sensitive to differences in the intensity of light. A five-day-old infant will look for different amounts of time at stimuli of different brightnesses; as it gets older, less intensity is needed to produce the pupillary reflex. Even when a newborn is asleep, it will screw up its eyes, frown and tense its muscles if a bright light suddenly shines on its face. But if it is awake and brought near a window but not into bright sunlight, it will often turn towards the light, indicating that it knows where the light is coming from and that it is attracted to it.

Hershenson (1964) found that newborns, when presented with a dim, medium and bright light, all preferred the medium, followed by the bright and finally the dim light.

Perception of Movement

The ability to follow a moving stimulus depends upon a reflex called the optokinetic reflex (or optic nystagmus), which consists of a series of back-and-forth eye movements called visual saccades (you can spot them if you watch the eyes of somebody who is reading). This reflex is present soon after birth; for instance, within forty-eight hours of birth, babies can track a slowly moving object. It is only about half as efficient as an adult's at this time, but it improves rapidly during the next three months.

Neonates usually visually explore or scan their surroundings five to ten per cent of their waking time. They seem to prefer moving objects to stationary ones; for example, they reduce their sucking rate when they see moving lights and even if the movement is apparent rather than real, three to five-day-olds prefer this to non-movement (Haith, 1966).

If a series of fine, vertical stripes is passed across the baby's field of vision, they will produce visual saccades; if the stripes are made finer and finer (so that eventually they appear grey) the saccades stop. Babies are more successful at tracking horizontal than vertical movement but even then it will be jerky—they re-fixate often, gazing at the moving object and then shifting their gaze to a different spot. One possible reason for this jerkiness is that *convergence* is absent at birth, although it usually appears two days after birth and is fully developed by two to three months. Convergence is essential for fixation and depth perception (see Chapter 4).

Also essential for the efficient vision is *accommodation*. At birth, the eye operates rather like a fixed focus camera, that is, the baby only sees clear-cut images of objects that are about 20 cm from its face and anything nearer or farther will tend to look blurred. (The baby must also be looking directly at the object.) There is no real accommodation at all at first, which is due to the immaturity and weakness of the ciliary muscles which focus the lens by changing its shape.

However, 20 cm, conveniently, is approximately the distance between the baby's face and the face of the person feeding it, which gives the baby plenty of opportunity to examine the adult face and become familiar with it.

By 2 months, the baby is beginning to accommodate to the distance of objects and by 4 months the ability to accommodate has reached adult standards. This improvement, like many of the others we have noted above, seems to be very largely due to maturation.

Visual Acuity

Related to the ability to see clear, well-defined images is the baby's visual acuity, ie its ability to distinguish clearly the parts of a stimulus. (In a more general sense, visual acuity refers to how well or efficiently an individual can see.)

The average one-day-old has a visual acuity of 20:150; an adult with the same acuity would be able to identify a letter from 20 feet away that a person with near perfect vision (20:20) could identify from 150 feet. Individual differences range from about 20:150 to 20:800. But despite this imperfect vision, the baby likes to see an image in as clear a way as possible. Kalnins and Bruner (1973) found that one- to three-month-olds will learn to operate the focus on a projector in order to make the picture clearer; the focus was connected directly to a nipple and was arranged so that appropriate sucking rates would bring the blurred picture into focus. Also they looked less at an out-of-focus image than when it was clear-cut.

Visual acuity improves rapidly during the first four to six months and between six and twelve months will come within adult ranges. But it may not reach 20:20 until ten or eleven years of age. Again, there are important individual differences as to the eventual attainment of 20:20 vision: it seems to depend a great deal on the genes that determine the eventual shape of the eyes. Some babies will have 20:20 vision by the time they are six months old, others will never attain it.

A method of investigating acuity is through visually-evoked potentials (VEPs): electrodes are attached to the scalp, above the visual cortex, and a visual stimulus is presented. If the electrical activity changes then the baby is judged to be perceiving the stimulus. Atkinson et al (1979) found VEPs in newborns, showing that some degree of acuity is present then. Soko (1978) noted the steady development of acuity during the first six months, as indicated by the elicitation of VEPs to finer and finer grids.

Studying What the Baby Does

What can we tell about the infant's visual perception from studying its behavioural response to stimuli?

Perception of Pattern or Form

Fantz (1961) presented thirty babies, aged one to fifteen weeks, with a variety of stimuli and used the time spent looking at each of these as an index of the baby's visual preferences. They were shown, at weekly intervals, pairs of stimuli comprising: bullseyes, horizontal stripes, checkerboards, two sizes of plain square, a cross, a circle and two triangles (of the same area). (See Figure 5.3.)

There was a distinct preference, at all ages, for the bullseye over the stripes and for the checkerboard over the plain square; the bullseye was most looked at of all the stimuli, and next most popular was the checkerboard.

So, there seems to be a very early, if not inborn, preference for more complex over less complex stimuli, that is, stimuli which contain more information, in which there is more 'going on'. However, this preference for complexity also seems to be a function of age. Fantz's babies, tested weekly, were presented with progressively narrower stripes, and as they got older

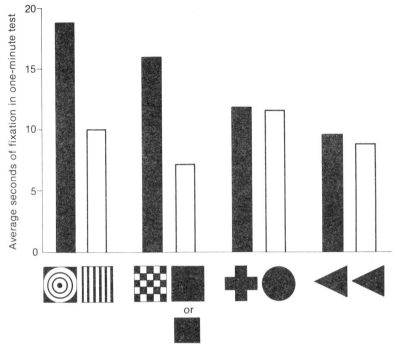

Figure 5.3 The bars indicate looking time for each of the stimulus patterns presented in pairs (from R. L. Fantz, 'The origin of form perception', 1961)

they could distinguish targets with narrower and narrower stripes. For instance, at two weeks, they could distinguish between (and seemed to prefer) stripes 1/8 inch thickness from a distance of nine inches, and a plain grey square. By three months, they looked longer at stripes 1/64 inch thickness, ten inches away, than at a plain grey square.

Other researchers have also found this preference for complexity as a function of age. For example, Brennan et al (1966) studied three-, eight- and fourteen-week-old babies. The youngest preferred a 2×2 checkerboard, the middle group an 8×8 and the oldest a 24×24. In another experiment, Fantz (1961) showed that two- to four-month-olds prefer patterns to colour or brightness. Six discs were shown; one was plain red, one plain white and one plain yellow. The others were a face, printed matter and a bullseye. At all ages there was a preference for the face over either the printed matter or the bullseye and all three were preferred to the plain discs (see Figure 5.4 on page 136).

The preference for increasing complexity seems to indicate that the capacity for differentiation steadily improves, possibly because the ability to scan becomes more efficient and thorough.

Studies of eye movements give precise indications of what subjects are looking at. At first, when a baby finds a stimulus interesting, it continues to scan it but it tends to limit itself to the focus of interest; for example, Kessen (1966) and Salapatek (1975) found that very young infants confine their scanning to one corner of a triangle which seems to indicate a preference for areas of greatest contrast. (Another example is the eyes and hairline of the face.)

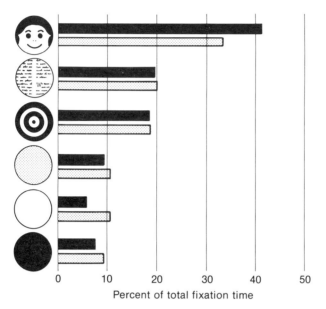

Figure 5.4   The upper bar of each pair indicates looking time for 2- to 3-month-olds, the lower bar for babies of 4 months old (from R. L. Fantz, 1961)

Only later does the baby begin to explore all around the stimulus and inside it (eg, all corners of the triangle or the nose and mouth of the face); in other words, the baby now attends to the *whole* pattern and not just to specific parts.

Bower (1966) experimentally tested the question, 'How much can babies take in?' by training infants to respond to the stimulus, shown in Figure 5.5, for a reward of 'peek-a-boo'. When they were responding consistently, they were shown each component separately (the circle, the 'X' and the two dots) and they continued to respond in the same way as they had to the whole stimulus. This suggests that they did not notice the difference and that, when presented with the original stimulus, they were only attending to a particular part of it; their capacity for processing information is limited and remains so up until about three months.

Figure 5.5   'Whole' stimulus used by Bower (1966)

Facedness

This ability to process the whole stimulus, rather than just parts of it, has particular significance for the perception of human faces or representations of faces (facedness).

One of the first studies of facedness was conducted by Ahrens in 1954. He presented various dots and angles, drawn on round or oval contours, partial and complete drawings of faces, 3-D models of faces and actual, live faces, in order to discover how much detail is needed to elicit smiling at different ages. He found that at six weeks (when the first social smile usually occurs, see Chapter 18) a crude, two-dot representation of the eyes is most effective and contour is unimportant. Between six weeks and three months, the eye-pattern is still most effective but a realistic, as opposed to a schematic (diagrammatic) representation is becoming more important. (During this period, smiling is indiscriminate—the baby smiles at all faces, familiar and unfamiliar. See Chapter 18 again.) By about four months, the eyes are still necessary but no longer sufficient. Now the nose and mouth must be present. Also, a real face is most effective of all, followed by a realistic drawing and least effective of all is a schematic drawing. (At about three or four months, the baby shows that it recognizes familiar faces by smiling more at them than at unfamiliar ones. This is consistent with Ahrens' and Bower's findings that at about three to four months the *whole* face or pattern becomes important and the baby can now process the entire stimulus.)

Therefore it would appear that only gradually do babies come to recognize faces as faces, since they are not capable of processing all the information that constitutes a face until they are three to four months old (probably brain development has much to do with this increasing capacity but, of course, coming to recognize particular faces is something that has to be learnt).

Fantz, however, takes a different view, namely that babies are born with a preference for facedness. In a famous 1961 study, he presented four-day to six-month olds with all possible pairs of three stimuli which were black against a pink background and the approximate shape and size of an adult's head (see Figure 5.6).

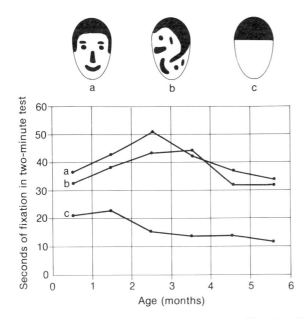

Figure 5.6 Looking time for each of 3 face-like stimuli (from R. L. Fantz, 1961)

At all age levels, infants looked more at the schematic representation than they did at the scrambled face, while the control stimulus was largely ignored. Even though the difference in the time spent looking at (a) and (b) was slight, Fantz concluded that, 'there is an unlearned, primitive meaning in the form perception of infants', such that there is an innate preference for facedness.

However, Hershenson (1965) pointed out that (a) and (b) are both more complex than (c) and that may account for their preference over (c), as opposed to their resemblance to human faces. So he presented newborns with all possible pairs of three equally complex stimuli:

i)   a real female face;
ii) a distorted picture, which retained the outline of head and hair but altered the position of the other features;
iii) a scrambled face, as in Fantz's experiment (stimulus (b)).

He found no preference for any of these three and concluded that a preference for real faces is not inborn and usually does not appear until about four months of age.

However, some recent findings seem to support Fantz's view. Jirari (1970) found that newborns were more likely to turn their heads to follow a face with at least some of the features in the correct position than one with completely scrambled features. Whether we accept Fantz's view or Hershenson's, the role of biological factors seems to be quite important: either it is present at birth (in which case learning could not be responsible) or it makes its appearance between three and four months, suggesting the role of maturation.

However, clearly the baby has to learn to recognize particular faces—the biologically-determined preference is for faces in general not specific ones. (This is similar to Bowlby's view that there is an innate tendency to become attached to one person—but the child must learn who that person is. See Chapter 18.) Therefore, the environment must offer the opportunity for looking at the same faces fairly often and regularly; where this opportunity is missing the preference for facedness may be retarded. For example, Ambrose (1960) found that a preference for a real over a scrambled face appeared, on average, one month later in children reared in institutions compared with home-reared children. Again, Fantz and Nevis (1967) confirmed Ambrose's findings when they followed up institutionalized children from two to twenty-four weeks.

In trying to draw conclusions about the perception of facedness, we should perhaps look back over our previous discussion of movement, complexity and pattern or form perception. We have seen that babies prefer stimuli that move to stationary ones, stimuli that have a distinct pattern and those which are more rather than less complex. However, complexity is a function of age and it seems that not until three or four months can a baby take in all the information contained in a stimulus and look 'inside' it (and not just at the points of greatest contrast). Somewhere between three and four months babies begin to recognize particular human faces.

Rheingold (1961) suggests that human beings should be thought of as stimulus objects: they have built-in features which make them particularly likely to become attractive to infants—they are in almost constant movement, are complex, have a distinct pattern, are a source of sound (the voice) and are often responsive to the infant's own behaviour which leads to a continuous, reciprocal interchange.

Instead of taking the view that there is a genetically-determined preference for the human face per se, Rheingold believes that infants develop a selective responsiveness to it (and things that resemble it) as it embodies all the stimulus dimensions that babies seem, innately, to prefer, conveniently 'packaged' in a very attractive and stimulating form. For this reason, she calls the human face a *supernormal stimulus* (see Chapter 14).

Perception of Depth and 3-D Objects

This has been one of the most researched aspects of infant perception and has perhaps become the focus for the heredity-environment issue. If babies can perceive depth at birth or very soon afterwards, this suggests that the ability is genetically determined; the earlier it develops the more likely it is that learning does not play a very important role.

It has been investigated in rather different ways, but probably the most famous study, and one of the earliest, was carried out by Gibson and Walk (1960) using the 'visual cliff' apparatus. As you can see from Figure 5.7, it consists of a central platform, on one side of which is a sheet of plate glass and immediately below this a black and white checkerboard design (the shallow side). On the other side is another sheet of plate glass, this time with the checkerboard design placed on the floor, a distance of about four feet, giving the appearance of a drop or 'cliff' (the 'deep side'). The baby is placed on the central platform and its mother calls to it and beckons it, first from one side, then from the other.

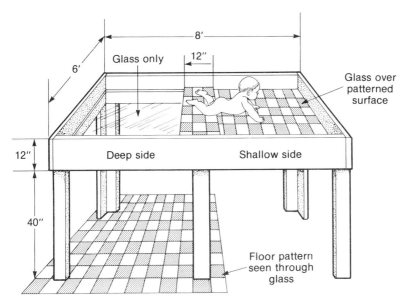

Figure 5.7 The visual cliff (from John P. Dworetzky, *Introduction to Child Development*)

Gibson and Walk used babies aged six to fourteen months; most of them would not crawl onto the 'deep side' and this was interpreted as indicating depth perception (that is, they perceived the visual cliff or apparent drop and therefore did not venture onto it). The few who did venture onto the cliff (either by backing onto it or resting one foot on it for support) did so 'accidentally'—their poor motor control was responsible rather than their inability to perceive depth.

But can we be sure that a baby old enough to crawl has not learnt to perceive depth? Gibson and Walk took their findings as strong support for the view that depth perception is (probably) inborn, but since they only used babies who could already crawl, we cannot be certain how early this ability normally appears.

Gibson and Walk also tested other species on the visual cliff and found supporting evidence. Chicks less than a day old never hopped down onto the deep side, goat kids and lambs, tested as soon as they could stand, also avoided it, rats, if they could feel the glass with their very sensitive whiskers, stepped down on either side, and four-week-old kittens avoided the deep side unless they were reared in the dark (in which case they tended to fall down on either side). If forcibly placed on the deep side, these young animals would freeze in terror.

A more direct test of depth prediction in infants was conducted by Campos et al (1978). Their subjects were two-, three-and-a-half-, and five-month-olds and they used heart rate as the index of depth perception. Even the youngest showed a drop in heart rate, showing interest, when placed on the deep side; they were also less likely to cry and were more attentive to what was underneath them and they clearly were not frightened by what they saw. There were no such changes when they were placed on the shallow side. Therefore it seems that even two-month-olds can perceive depth and that avoidance behaviour is probably learnt (perhaps after the baby has had a few experiences of falling).

Another way of investigating depth perception is to observe how babies react when an object approaches their faces from a distance. Bower et al (1970) found that babies just 20 days old put their hands in front of their faces as a looming disc approached, indicating some very early depth perception. If a large box is moved towards the baby's face, from the visual information that the box is getting larger it seems to understand that it is getting closer and would be harmful and, accordingly, puts its arm in front of its face to protect itself. (This occurs even with one eye closed but not when equivalent pictures were seen on a screen, showing that motion parallax is the critical cue for distance.)

It also suggests that the baby sees the box as a solid, 3-D object and Bower (1979) investigated this hypothesis by presenting 'solid' objects which were not solid at all but illusions of 3-D objects created by using special polarizing filters and goggles. Babies aged sixteen to twenty-four weeks old were sat in front of a screen. A plastic, translucent object is suspended between lights and the screen so that it casts a double shadow on the back; when the screen is viewed from the front, using polarizing goggles, these double shadows merge to form the image of a single 3-D object.

None of the babies showed any surprise when they grasped the real, solid objects but when they reached for the apparent objects and discovered there was nothing solid to get hold of, they all expressed surprise and some even showed distress. Clearly, they expected to be able to touch what they could 'see'. Bower believes that this ability is innate.

Mary Sheridan has pointed out that blind babies do not show the defensive reaction to an approaching object (discussed above), even though the object displaces the air (causes a draught) as it gets closer. Bower demonstrated the importance of vision in this defensive reaction by testing babies under three conditions: (i) an object was moved towards the baby, accompanied by displacement of the air; (ii) displacement of air alone; (iii) an object was brought towards the baby without any displacement. As predicted (i) produced the strongest defensive reaction, followed by (iii); (ii) produced no response at all.

Size Constancy

Empiricists would argue that size constancy is learned and that babies and young children are likely to be 'tricked' by the appearance of things—if something *looks* smaller (projects a smaller retinal image) then it *is* smaller.

Nativists, on the other hand, would claim that, like all perceptual abilities, constancy is innate, so that the baby can judge the size of an object regardless of the retinal image produced by the object.

Bower (1966) tested these two opposing hypotheses experimentally. Initially, he trained two- to three-month-olds to turn their heads at the sight of a 30 cm cube, at a distance of 1 metre (when they turned their heads in the desired direction, an adult popped up in front of the baby and cried 'peek-a-boo', a very powerful reinforcer for babies). When they were looking at the cube consistently, it was replaced by: (i) a 30 cm cube at a distance of 3 metres (this would produce a retinal image one-third the size of the original; (ii) a 90 cm cube at a distance of 1 metre (this would produce a retinal image three times the size of the original); or (iii) a 90 cm cube at a distance of 3 metres (this would produce exactly the same sized image as the original).

How often the baby turned its head towards each of these three cubes could be used as a measure of how similar to the original the baby considered it to be; ie, if the baby generalized its head-turning response mainly to (i), this would be evidence for size constancy. This is what the Nativists predict: the baby will respond to the actual size of the cube, regardless of distance. If the head-turning response generalized mainly to (iii), this would be evidence for lack of size constancy: as predicted by the Empiricists, the baby at first would 'compare' retail images and base its perception of similarity on these, regardless of distance.

What Bower found was that, compared with 98 head-turns produced by the original cube, (i) produced 58, (ii) produced 54 and (iii) produced 22. This seems to represent clear support for the nativists: babies responded most to the cube of the same *size*, regardless of distance, next came the cube the same distance away as the original but of a different size, and last of all came the cube of a different size and distance, but giving the same retinal image as the original. It is the difference between (i) and (iii) which constitutes the critical findings.

Table 5.1 Findings of major studies of (visual) perception in connection with the nature-nurture debate

← Less complex · Perceptual ability · More complex →

Studies	Pupil constriction to light	Startle response to sudden light	Blink response to approaching object	Brightness discrimination	Colour	Fixation of objects	Following a moving object with eyes/ scanning	Figure/ ground	Sensory-motor co-ordination	3-D perception (object solidity)	Depth	Form —Geometric shapes —Illusions —Faces	Constancy —Size —Shape
Cataract patients Hebb (1949)						Innate	Innate	Innate				Learnt	Learnt
							(Figural unity)					(Figural identity)	
Animal experiments Riesen (1947, 1965)	Light stimulation NOT required		Light stimulation required				Requires patterned light				Requires patterned light	Requires patterned light	
Blakemore and Cooper (1970)												Specific experience necessary	
Held and Hein (1963)			ACTIVE sensory experience necessary						ACTIVE sensory experience necessary		ACTIVE sensory experience necessary for correct motor responses		
Miller and Walk (1975)											Innate — but can be improved with experience		

Adaptation/ readjustment Sperry (1943) salamanders Hess (1956) chickens	Innate — 'wired in'	
Stratton (1896) Snyder and Pronko (1952) Kohler (1962)	Learnt. Adaptation involves new motor movements not perceptions.	
Cross-cultural Rivers et al (1901) Segall et al (1963) Allport and Pettigrew (1957) Stewart (1973) Mundy-Castle and Nelson (1962) Jahoda (1966) Gregor and McPherson (1965) Turnbull (1961) Deregowski (1972)		Susceptibility to illusions is learnt. But lack of agreement as to what factors are involved. Interpreting 2-D pictures etc. is learnt
		Turnbull (1961) — Size Constancy is learnt

Table 5.1 (Continued)

Infant studies						
1. Visual apparatus	Innate	Innate	Rods and cones functioning at birth	Innate		Neither convergence nor accommodation present at birth
2. Behavioural studies Fantz (1961) Brennan et al 1966						Innate preference for more complex and patterned stimuli
Kessen (1966) Salapatek (1975) Bower (1966)				Scanning limited to one part of stimulus. Whole object scanned by 3–4 months		
Ahrens (1954)						2 dots sufficient to produce smiling

Fantz (1961)	Innate preference for faces
Jirari (1970)	Innate preference for faces
Hershenson (1965)	Complexity is what is preferred
Ambrose (1960) Fantz and Nevis (1967)	Preference for faces can be retarded by e.g. institutionalization
Gibson and Walk (1960)	Innate
Campos et al (1978)	Innate
Bower et al (1970)	Innate
Bower (1979)	Innate
Bower (1966)	Innate
Bower (1966)	Gestalt principle of closure is innate

Shape Constancy

Using a similar procedure to the one described above for size constancy, Bower (1966) studied shape constancy. If a two-month-old was trained to turn its head to look at a rectangle, it would continue to do so when the same rectangle was turned slightly (to produce a trapezoid retinal image). However, Gollin (1965) and Murray and Szymczyk (1978) suggest that experience with particular shapes is necessary for certain kinds of shape constancy; for example, if you show children pictures of objects that have been partially erased, they have more difficulty than adults in figuring out what the objects are.

Organization

Finally, Bower was interested in how the infant's perception is organized in terms of certain Gestalt principles (see Chapter 4). He wanted to find out if closure is an inborn characteristic (as the Gestalt psychologists claim) by training two-month-olds to respond to a black wire triangle with a black iron bar across it and then presenting them with the four triangle-stimuli shown in Figure 5.8.

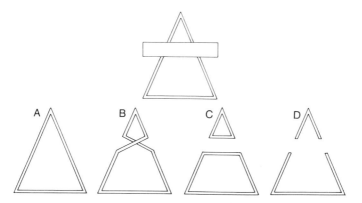

Figure 5.8. The stimulus figures used in Bower's study of closure (after T. Bower, 1977)

The fact that they generalized their response to a complete triangle suggests that they 'understood' that underneath the black iron bar lay a complete, unbroken triangle and given that they were unlikely to have encountered many triangular stimuli in their lifetime, Bower's findings support the view that closure is an inborn feature of infant perceptual ability.

6

Memory

The Concept of Memory

As we saw in Chapter 3, learning is defined in terms of relatively permanent changes due to past experience and memory is a crucial part of the learning process—without memory, experiences would be 'lost' and we could not benefit from past experience. Unless, in some way, our prior learning can be 'recorded' it cannot be used at a later date and so we are not in a position to benefit from our past experience. However, trying to define learning and memory independently of each other is very difficult as they represent two sides of the same coin: (i) learning depends on memory for its 'permanency'; and, conversely, (ii) memory would have no 'content' if learning were not taking place.

Therefore, we could define memory as the *retention* of *learning* or *experience*; this shows how interdependent the two processes are.

The Study of Memory

As we saw in Chapter 1, memory (like learning) is a hypothetical construct and, as such, is an abstract concept which refers to three distinguishable but interrelated processes: (i) *registration* (or reception); (ii) *storage*; and (iii) *retrieval* (see Figure 6.1).

Registration can be thought of as a necessary condition for storage to take place but, as we shall see below, it is not a sufficient condition, ie not everything which registers on the sense receptors is stored. The topic of selective attention was discussed in Chapter 4.

Similarly, storage can be seen as a necessary, but not a sufficient, condition for retrieval, ie you can only recover information which has been stored (you cannot remember something you do not know), but the fact that you know it is no guarantee that you will remember it on any particular occasion. This is the crucial distinction between *availability* (whether or not the information has been stored) and *accessibility* (whether or not it can be retrieved), which is especially relevant in relation to theories of forgetting.

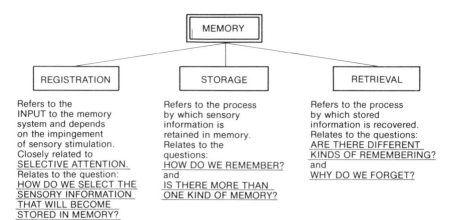

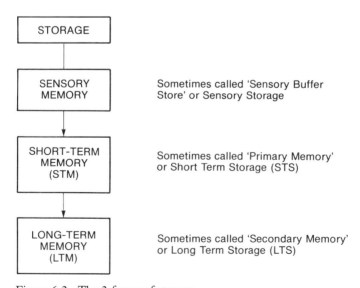

Figure 6.1   The 3 processes of memory

In practice, the way in which storage is studied is through testing the subject's ability to retrieve and this is equivalent to the distinction we made in Chapter 3 between learning and performance: learning corresponds to the storage aspect of memory, while performance corresponds to the retrieval aspect of memory. (This again shows how closely related the two processes of learning and memory are.)

However, there are several kinds of retrieval; so, as tested by recall, for example, storage may seem not to have occurred (no learning) but as tested by recognition, storage (and hence learning) might be demonstrated. In this chapter, we shall be concentrating on memory as storage and memory as retrieval, but it is important to regard memory as a whole as a function of all three.

Figure 6.2   The 3 forms of storage

The distinction between Primary Memory and Secondary Memory was originally made by William James in 1890, although Ebbinghaus (1885), one of the pioneers of memory research, would have accepted the distinction. Hebb (1949), Broadbent (1958), Waugh and Norman (1965) and many others have also made the distinction but perhaps the most elaborate version is built into Atkinson and Shiffrin's 'Two-Process Model' (1968, 1971). Strictly speaking, Short-Term Memory (STM) and Long-Term Memory (LTM) refer to experimental procedures for investigating primary and secondary memory respectively, which are assumed to underlie them; however, we shall use 'STM' and 'LTM' to refer to both (see Figure 6.2). Although most research and theorizing has concentrated on these second and third stages of the storage process, logically the place to start is with Sensory Memory.

Sensory Memory

If, after being shown something for a fraction of a second, we did not retain an impression of it in a fairly literal way for a rather longer time, in most cases we would not be able to understand or process it adequately and it would not be remembered. It seems that we process information both from the stimulus itself and our subsequent memory of it.

Sensory memory gives us an accurate account of the environment as experienced by the sensory system. When we receive a visual input, for example, its image remains with us for one or two seconds in a relatively unanalysed form; after this, any information which is not attended to or processed further is forgotten. So clearly, sensory memory and registration are very closely related and it is misleading to consider it a form of storage as opposed to a necessary requirement for storage proper (ie STM).

Sensory memory seems to be *modality specific*, that is, the storage (such as it is) occurs *within* the sensory system that received the information, and not at some central location. Additional information entering the *same* sensory channel immediately disrupts the storage; for example, if shortly after a visual array is presented a second visual stimulus is flashed, the memory of the initial array may be lost. However, if the second stimulus is a sound or smell it will not interfere with memory of the visual stimulus.

Sperling (1960, 1963) studied the *visual* modality (or the *iconic store*) and showed that more information is available *immediately* after visual stimulation than can be recalled even a few seconds later. He showed subjects an array comprising three rows of four letters (a 4×3 matrix) for 50 m/secs ($\frac{1}{20}$ of a second). When they had to recall as many as possible from the whole matrix (*whole reports* or span of apprehension), subjects recalled, on average, 4.32 letters (out of 12), although they commonly reported having seen more than they could actually remember.

In another condition, subjects were required to recall the top, middle or bottom row depending on whether they heard a high-, medium- or low-pitched tone. Although subjects could not know in advance which tone would be heard, they succeeded in recalling an average of 3.04 of the letters from each row, which meant that between nine and ten words were available immediately after presentation. Clearly, the information must have been lost rapidly in the first condition: in the time it took to try to recall the whole array approximately five words were lost, and this was supported by the finding that the advantage of *partial reports* (just one row) was lost if the auditory signal was delayed for a second or so.

Similar effects have been reported for the *auditory* modality (what Neisser, 1967, called the *echoic store*) by several researchers, including Broadbent (1958), Treisman (1964), Bliss et al (1966). It seems that iconic memory involves storage of stimuli which have been discriminated in terms of *physical* features only (eg size, shape, colour, location) as distinct from their meaning, and Morton (1970) reported that the echoic store (what he called the Pre-Categorical acoustic store) works in the same way.

Short-Term Memory (STM)

According to Lloyd et al (1984) probably less than one-hundredth of all the sensory information that impinges every second on the human senses reaches consciousness, and of this, only one-twentieth achieves anything approaching stable storage.

Clearly, if memory ability were limited to sensory memory, our capacity for retaining information about the world would be extremely limited as well as very precarious. However, according to models of memory such as Atkinson and Shiffrin's Two-Process Model (1968, 1971), some information from sensory memory is successfully passed on to STM, which allows us to store information long enough to be able to *use* it and for this reason it is often referred to as 'Working Memory'. (However, 'working memory' has different connotations as used by Baddeley and Hitch, 1974 and Hitch, 1980—see below.)

We can analyse STM (as we can LTM) in terms of three dimensions: (i) *capacity* (how much information can be stored); (ii) *duration* (how *long* the information can be held in storage); and (iii) *coding* (in what *ways* sensory input is transformed or processed so that it can be stored, ie how it is *represented* by the memory system).

i) Capacity

Ebbinghaus (1885) and Wundt (in the 1880s) were two of the first psychologists to maintain that STM is limited to six or seven bits of information; but the most famous account is given by George Miller in 'The Magical Number Seven, plus or minus two: some limits on our capacity for processing information' (1956). In that article Miller showed how *chunking* can be used to expand the limited capacity of STM by using already-established memory stores to categorize or encode new information.

If we think of STM's capacity as seven 'slots' (plus or minus two), each slot being able to accommodate one bit or unit of information, then seven individual letters would each fill a slot and there would be no 'room' left for any additional letters. However, if the letters are chunked into a word, then the word would constitute a unit of information and there would still be six free slots.

In the example, the 25 bits of information can be chunked into (or reduced to) six words, which could quite easily be reduced further to one 'bit' (or chunk) based on prior familiarity with the words:

S	A	V	A	O
R	E	E	E	G
U	R	S	Y	A
O	O	D	N	S
F	C	N	E	R

To be able to chunk, you have to know the 'rule' or the 'code' which in this case is: starting with *F* (bottom left-hand corner) read upwards until you get to *S* and then drop down to *C* and read upwards until you get to *A*, then go to *N* and read upwards and so on. This should give you 'four score and seven years ago'.

Whenever we reduce a larger to a smaller amount of information we are chunking and this not only increases the capacity of STM but also makes it more likely that the information will be stored for longer. It also represents a form of encoding information by imposing a *meaning* on otherwise meaningless letters or numbers etc: (a) arranging letters into words, words into phrases, phrases into sentences; (b) converting 1066 (four bits of information) into a date (one chunk), so a string of 28 numbers could be reduced to seven dates; (c) using a *rule* to organize information, eg the series 149162536496481100121 (21 bits) is generated by the rule by which $1^2 = 1$, $2^2 = 4$, $3^2 = 9$ and so on. The rule represents a single chunk and that is all that has to be remembered.

These examples demonstrate how chunking allows us to bypass the seven-bit 'bottleneck'; although the amount of information contained in any one chunk may be unlimited (eg the rule in (c) above can generate an infinitely long set of digits), the number of chunks which can be held in STM is still limited to 7 plus or minus 2.

ii) Duration

It seems that we can hold information in STM for between 15 and 30 seconds (according to Atkinson and Shiffrin, 1971) unaided, but this can be extended through *rehearsal* or repetition. Rehearsal seems to require some kind of speech (either overtly or mentally) whereby the subject 'says' the information to keep it 'circulating' within STM (eg repeating a telephone number out loud until you dial it), but it is easily disrupted by either external distractions (eg someone asking you for change while you are repeating the number) or internal ones (eg thinking about your own telephone number).

Therefore it seems that in rehearsal information is maintained in the memory system *acoustically* (the *sounds* of the items are repeated and stored); although, according to Weber and Castleman (1970) it *can* be visual, this is likely to be slower than acoustic rehearsal.

iii) Coding

As we have seen in relation to rehearsal, coding in STM seems to be primarily acoustic, ie information from sensory memory (including visual) is converted into sound and is stored in this form.

Table 6.1   Summary of major differences between STM and LTM

	Capacity	*Duration*	*Coding*
STM	7 bits of information. Can be increased by chunking.	15 to 30 seconds (un-aided). Can be in-creased by rehearsal.	Acoustic
LTM	Unlimited	From a few minutes to several years (perhaps permanently).	(i) Semantic (ii) Visual (iii) Acoustic

Long-Term Memory (LTM)

i) Capacity
It is usually thought that LTM has unlimited capacity. It can be seen as the repository of all things in memory which are not currently being used but which are potentially retrievable. It enables us to deal with the past and to use that information to deal with the present; in a sense; LTM allows us to live in the past and present simultaneously.

Bower (1975) has identified some of the classes of information contained in LTM; these include: (a) a spatial model of the world around us: (b) know-ledge of the physical world, physical laws and properties of objects; (c) beliefs about people, ourselves, social norms, values and goals; (d) motor skills, problem-solving skills and plans for achieving various things; (e) perceptual skills in understanding language, interpreting music etc.

ii) Duration
Information can be held for between a few minutes and several years (which may in fact span the individual's entire lifetime).

iii) Coding
There are at least two forms of coding in LTM: (i) *semantic code*, which deals with material in terms of verbal meaning; (ii) *imagery* or *visual code*, which takes a pictorial form. The former seems to be more common, especially when we have to deal with abstract material for which it is difficult to conjure up appropriate images. However, it has also been suggested that an acoustic code is used in LTM.

The Two-Process Model
(Atkinson and Shiffrin, 1968, 1971)

So far, we have been discussing STM and LTM differences without looking specifically at Atkinson and Shiffrin's model (see Figure 6.3). This is called the Two-Process Model because of the emphasis on STM and LTM in which stored information has been coded, in contrast with sensory memory which

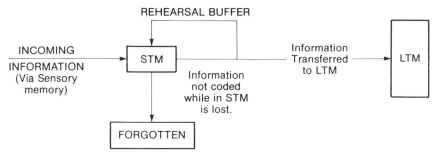

Figure 6.3 The '2-process model' of memory (based on Atkinson and Shiffrin, 1971)

holds information from the environment in roughly its original or 'sensory' form.

Sensory memory, STM and LTM are referred to by the model as permanent *structural components* of the memory system and represent intrinsic features of the information-processing system of humans. In addition to these structural components, the memory system comprises relatively transient processes called *control processes*, of which one is rehearsal. Rehearsal serves two main functions (i) to act as buffer between sensory memory and LTM by maintaining incoming information within STM; and (ii) to transfer information to LTM.

Finally, how does information transfer from sensory memory to STM? According to Atkinson and Shiffrin, it is scanned and matched with information in LTM and if a match occurs (ie *pattern recognition*) the information from sensory memory might then be fed into STM along with a verbal label from LTM. (Pattern recognition was discussed in Chapter 4.)

What is the Evidence for the Two-Process Model?

a) Two-Component Tasks

In the laboratory, performance on certain memory tasks seems to be most conveniently explained in terms of a STM–LTM distinction; for example, if subjects are shown 20 words in succession and then asked immediately to recall them in any order (*free-recall*), typical results would be as shown in Figure 6.4 overleaf.

The probability of recalling any word depends on its position in the list (its serial position) and hence the graph shown in Figure 6.4 is called a *serial position curve*. Subjects typically recall those items from the end of the list first and get more of these correct than earlier items (the *recency effect*). According to Murdock (1962), this is true no matter how long the list. Also, slower rates of presentation improve recall of the earlier items relative to the later items (the *primacy effect*), and Craik (1969) and Murdock and Walker (1969) found that faster rates of presentation, if anything, enhance the recency effect. Recall for words in the middle of the list is worst.

The implication is that the recency effect reflects words being retrieved from STM, whereas the primacy effect reflects retrieval from LTM. The last

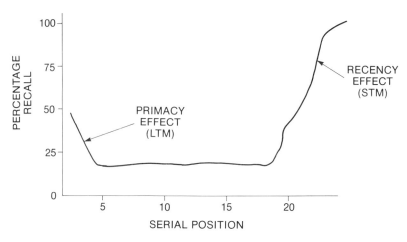

Figure 6.4   A typical serial position curve

items are only remembered if recalled first and tested immediately, as demonstrated by Glanzer and Cunitz (1966); when recall is delayed for a few seconds by, for example, getting subjects to count backwards (thus preventing rehearsal) the recency effect disappears while recall of earlier items is comparatively unaffected. Two groups of subjects were presented with the same list of words: one group recalled the material immediately after presentation while the other group recalled after 30 seconds. The first group showed a recency effect (indicating STM retrieval) and the second group showed a primary effect (indicating LTM retrieval).

A second kind of task involves what has become known as the *Brown–Peterson* technique (Brown, 1958, Peterson and Peterson, 1959) and is concerned specifically with the effects of the length of the recall interval on recall (see Figure 6.5).

Peterson and Peterson (1959) gave subjects short series of letters (eg CPQ) to see the effects of a distracting task, such as counting backwards in threes, on recall. (Counting backwards is an interfering task which prevents rehearsal, thus reducing the time the letters can be kept in STM.) Even with very small amounts of material, 90 per cent is forgotten if recall is delayed for 15 to 20 seconds; the remaining 10 per cent is thought to be retained over a longer period (and is processed by LTM).

This rapid loss of information from memory when rehearsal is prevented is usually taken as evidence for the existence of a STM with rapid decay of the memory trace or displacement; the kind of forgetting involved in LTM is thought to be different and this difference in forgetting represents further support for the Two-Process model. (See pages 163–70.) However, not everyone accepts this interpretation of the findings. For example, Gruneberg (1970) argues that they could be a feature of *any* memory system and do not imply a distinction between two separate stores.

The concept of rehearsal itself, so important in Atkinson and Shiffrin's model, has also been criticized as both unnecessary and too general. Craik and Watkins (1973), for example, asked subjects to remember only certain

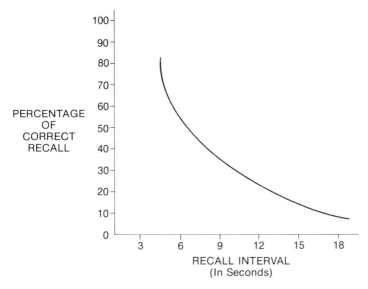

Figure 6.5 The effects of interfering tasks on recall (based on Peterson and Peterson, 1959)

words (those beginning with a particular letter) from lists presented either rapidly or slowly; the position of critical words relative to non-critical ones determined the amount of time a particular word spent in STM and the number of potential rehearsals given to it. Retention over long periods was found to be unrelated to *either* duration in STM *or* the number of explicit or implicit rehearsals.

An earlier study (Glanzer and Meinzer, 1967) had shown that the apparent effectiveness of rehearsal in enhancing retention may not just be a function of verbal repetition. Subjects who were required to repeat items aloud recalled fewer of them than subjects allowed an equal period of silent rehearsal; perhaps in silent rehearsal the subject is not merely repeating the material but may actually be re-coding it into a different form which enhances recall.

Craik and Watkins (1973) distinguished between: (a) *maintenance* (or rote) *rehearsal*; and (b) *elaborative rehearsal*. Maintenance rehearsal involves repeating the items in the form in which they are presented and is sufficient to retain them in the short-term; elaborative rehearsal involves elaboration of the items, for example, semantic recoding (giving them a meaning) or associative linking of words with pre-existing knowledge, and this is necessary for long-term retention.

Maintenance rehearsal seems not to be necessary for storage, as illustrated by Jenkins's study (1974) in which subjects showed they could remember material even though they were not expecting to be tested and so were not predisposed to rehearse. (This is Incidental Learning.)

Therefore it seems that it is the *kind* of rehearsal or processing that is crucial rather than the amount and this idea has been investigated in particular by Craik and Lockhart (1972).

Levels or Depths of Processing

According to Craik and Lockhart (1972) it is not rehearsal as such which is important but what is done with or to the material during rehearsal. They take a very different view of the memory system from Atkinson and Shiffrin.

As we have seen, the Two-Process model distinguishes between structural components (sensory memory, STM and LTM) and control processes (eg rehearsal, attention, coding), with the latter being tied to the former and the emphasis on the sequence of stages that information goes through as it passes from one structural component to another when being processed.

The levels or depths of processing approach, on the other hand, begins with hypothesized processes and then formulates a memory system (the structural components) in terms of these operations.

Craik and Lockhart (1972) and Neisser (1976) see memory, essentially, as the *by-product* of the processing of information; the durability of memory (or trace persistence) is a direct function of the depth of processing. Incoming stimuli are subjected to a series of analyses, starting with a shallow, sensory analysis, passing through an intermediate, phonetic level and finishing with a deeper, semantic analysis. Which level is used depends on both the nature of the stimulus and the time available for processing; the general rule is that the deeper the level of processing used, the less likely the material is to be forgotten.

Table 6.2   The three levels or depths of processing (based on Craik and Lockhart, 1972)

1. Structural or shallow level	Is the word written in capital letters—or not? [What does it *look* like?]
2. Phonetic or phonemic level	Does the word rhyme with some other word? [What does it *sound* like?]
3. Semantic level	Does the word mean the same as some other word? [What does it *mean?*]

With words, shallow processing corresponds to physical features while deep processing corresponds to meaning.

Craik and Tulving (1975) presented subjects with words via a tachistoscope and were asked one of four questions about each word: (i) Is the word in capital letters? (eg TABLE/table); (ii) Does the word rhyme with *wait*? (eg hate or chicken); (iii) Is the word a type of food? (eg cheese or steel); (iv) Would the word fit the sentence 'He kicked the — into the tree'? (eg ball or rain).

Of these, (i) corresponds to structural processing (ii) to phonetic processing and (iii) and (iv) to semantic processing. Subjects had to answer 'yes' or 'no' to each question and were subsequently given an unexpected test of recognition, which involved presentation of the words they had seen intermixed with the same number of words they had not seen; subjects had to say which they had seen before.

There was a significantly better recognition with deeper levels of processing. Also, recognition was superior if the answer was 'yes' than if it was 'no'.

A number of subsequent studies have confirmed these results, eg Diagostino et al (1977), Klein and Saltz (1976) and Schulman (1974), using recognition and recall.

In studies by Bower and Karlin (1974) and Strnad and Mueller (1977), subjects were shown pictures of faces and had to make judgements about: (a) the honesty, (b) likeability; and (c) gender of each face. Later recognition was much better after (a) and (b) than after (c), implying that the former required deeper processing.

Criticisms of the Depths of Processing Approach
Baddeley (1978) asks whether it represents anything more than a useful rule of thumb. More specifically:

i) It seems to say little more than that meaningful events are well remembered, which he considers to be a rather mundane conclusion;
ii) It is vague and generally untestable;
iii) Perhaps most seriously, is there any way of independently measuring depth of processing apart from the percentage of recognition or recall? Since any material that is well remembered is described as 'deeply processed' the definition of 'depth' is rather *circular*.

In view of these and other criticisms, there has recently been a move away from the notion of 'depth' towards the *qualitative features* of *encoding*. Contrary to Craik and Lockhart's view, there is no conclusive evidence that semantic features are forgotten more slowly than physical features. Nelson and Vining (1978), for example, found that physical and semantic features are forgotten at the same rate if they are initially learned to the same degree. Again, Hunt and Elliot (1980) found that 'low-level' features of words can sometimes be well remembered; for example, words with unusual spellings may be remembered better than words with common or predictable spellings.

So it seems that the difference between levels of processing is more general than the distinction between encoding in terms of perceptual characteristics or meaning. Deep processing involves greater *elaboration* of memories during the encoding phase than shallow processing, and this involves creating more associations between the new material and existing memories (Ellis and Hunt, 1983). This view cuts across the structural–semantic distinction of Craik and Lockhart because even superficial perceptual information can be richly elaborated.

b) Coding

Returning to the evidence bearing on the Two-Process model, many studies have produced results which suggest that STM and LTM code information in different ways.

If we take again the familiar example of trying to remember a telephone number, we keep it in STM by auditory rehearsal (using an acoustic code), that is, we *say* it over and over, regardless of whether we have looked it up in the directory or the operator has given it to us. Experimental findings tend to support this view of STM.

Conrad (1963, 1964) presented subjects with sequences of six consonants and found that the errors they made in trying to remember them were similar in *sound* to the correct item (eg b/d, p/v, m/n) despite the fact that they had been presented *visually*. In fact, they made the same kind of acoustic errors as they did when trying to detect similar spoken consonants against a noisy background.

Hull (1964) asked subjects to recall visually-presented letters that either sounded alike (eg d, c, b, t, p, v) or different (eg l, w, k, f, r, t) and found that more errors were made in the former condition.

Wickelgren (1965) asked subjects to read four letters followed by a list of eight letters and they then had to recall the original four letters. They had more difficulty in doing this when the second list comprised letters of similar *sound* than when they were acoustically different. This was found to be true for digits too.

Baddeley (1966) found that immediate recall of the order of short lists of unrelated words was seriously impeded if the words were acoustically similar (eg caught/short/taut/nought) but not if they were semantically similar (eg huge/great/big/wide). After a delay, however, exactly the opposite effect occurred.

Kintsch and Buschke (1969) used a probe technique which is able to separate STM and LTM components. They found that phonemic or acoustic similarity influenced only STM while semantic similarity influenced only LTM.

According to Sachs (1967) the phonemic or grammatical features of prose sentences were forgotten almost immediately, while the semantic features were well remembered even after a long delay. Finally, Craik and Levy (1970) found that material which is highly related conceptually (eg north/south/east/west) is beneficial to LTM but does not affect STM.

Therefore, there is considerable support for the view that STM uses an acoustic code and LTM a semantic code. However, not everyone accepts this view.

Bearing in mind what we said earlier about chunking in STM, we used the term 'meaning' to describe what is involved in reducing large amounts of information to smaller and more manageable amounts so as to increase the capacity of STM. According to Miller (1956), chunking represents a linguistic re-coding which seems to be the 'very lifeblood of the thought process'. He says that it is not surprising that such compression of information can occur when you consider how lexical information is normally processed: our capacity to read and understand is largely based on the chunking of letters into words, words into phrases and phrases into sentences. Therefore, the capability of STM to handle a vast amount of information is facilitated by our ability to chunk information; however, this cannot occur until certain information in LTM is activated and a match made between the incoming items and its representation in LTM.

This is illustrated by an experiment by Miller and Selfridge (1950) in which subjects were presented with a number of 'sentences' (of varying lengths) which represented different approximations to true English sentences. Subjects had to recall the words in their correct order; immediate recall was greater the closer the sentence approximated normal English. This suggests that subjects used knowledge of semantic and syntactic structure (presumably stored in LTM) to facilitate immediate memory.

More recently, Bower and Springston (1970) presented subjects with a letter sequence which they had to recall. In one condition, letters were read so that they did not form a well-known group and so could not be matched with information stored in LTM (eg fb, iph, dtw, aib, m), while in another they did (eg fbi, phd, twa, ibm). The latter were more readily recalled; they were clearly clustered along the lines of acronyms familiar to most college students and, in effect, the pause after 'fbi' etc allowed subjects to 'look it up' in their mental lexicon and so encode the letter in a chunk.

Letter recognition is another way of demonstrating a semantic code in STM. Posner (1970) used response time as a measure of how easy it was to identify two letters as being the same or not. For example, using AA, Aa, AB and Ab, Aa took longer than AA. Why? Identical letters are judged by physical (or visual) characteristics while letters with the same name but with different visual features (Aa) are compared in terms of their *verbal* characteristics; the latter takes longer. Shepard (1975) has found evidence of a *visual* code used by STM to perform complex transformations of visual stimuli which are very difficult (if not impossible) to encode acoustically.

So, clearly, an acoustic code is *not* the only one used in STM. Equally, you only have to think of all the voices and melodies, for example, which we can remember over long periods of time and which are, presumably, acoustically coded, and of all the faces, scenes, skills and so on which are difficult to process verbally, to recognize that a single, semantic code is *not* the only one used by LTM, (eg Wickens, 1972).

Ball et al (1975) found that subjects took just as long to identify the meaning of sentences as they did to recognize the acoustic or phonetic properties, that is, the sentences were coded in LTM both semantically and phonetically, and Morris (1978) points out that Conrad's study (1964) showed only that the phonetic code is used in STM and the semantic code in LTM, *not* that these are the *only* ones used by each system.

Shulman (1972) argues that acoustic and other non-semantic features often achieve LT storage while transiently remembered information may be semantically encoded.

Finally, Wickelgren (1973) says that it could be that the mode of coding reflects the processing which has occurred in a given context, rather than being a property of the memory store itself.

c) **Brain-damaged Patients**
A third major kind of evidence relevant to the Two-Process model is to do with brain damage and its effects on memory: if STM and LTM are indeed distinct, then there should be some kind of brain damage which impairs the latter but leaves the former intact.

Such a form of brain damage is *anterograde amnesia* and a famous case that of H.M. (Milner et al, 1978).

The Case of H.M. (after Milner et al, 1978)
H.M. began suffering major epileptic seizures when he was 10 and at 27 underwent surgery which destroyed several forebrain structures, including the hippocampus. The surgery dramatically reduced the epilepsy but left him with severe anterograde amnesia: he had near-normal memory for anything

which he had learned *prior* to the surgery but he had severe memory deficits for events which occurred *after* the surgery.

His STM was generally normal; for instance, he could retain verbal information for about 15 seconds without rehearsal and for much longer with rehearsal. However, he could not transfer information into LTM or, if he could, he could not retrieve it.

He had almost no knowledge of current affairs because he forgot all the news almost as soon as he had read about it; he had no idea what time of day it was unless he had just looked at the clock; he could not remember that his father had died or that his family had moved house; and he would re-read the same magazine without realizing he had already read it.

Although he could recognize friends, tell you their names and relate stories about them, he could do so only if he knew them before the surgery. People he met after the operation remained, in effect, total strangers to him and he had to 'get to know them' afresh each time they came to his house.

However, he was able to learn and remember perceptual and motor skills; but he had to be reminded each day just what skills he knew how to do.

Cases of anterograde amnesia like that of H.M. have been interpreted by Milner and Atkinson and Shiffrin as supporting the STM–LTM distinction, since the memory impairment seems to be to do with the *transfer* of information from STM to LTM.

However, there is evidence that the problem in these patients is not one of transfer but one of *retrieval* (eg Warrington and Weiskrantz, 1968, 1978), that is, the information is successfully transferred and stored in LTM but it cannot easily be recovered when required. This interpretation is more consistent with Craik and Lockhart's depth of processing approach (1972)—the amnesiac may not be able to process most kinds of new information deeply enough for retrieval from LTM but can do so to allow STM retrieval.

Finally, the other major kind of amnesia is *retrograde amnesia* where the patient fails to remember what happens *before* the surgery or accident which causes it. According to Russell and Nathan (1946), it can be caused by head injuries, Electro-Convulsive Therapy (ECT), carbon-monoxide poisoning and extreme stress. As in anterograde, there is typically little or no disruption of STM and the period of memory loss may be minutes, days or even years.

Usually, when retrograde amnesia is caused by brain damage it is accompanied by anterograde, so in this respect, H.M. was an exception. Similarly, patients who are suffering from Korsakov's Syndrome (caused by severe, chronic alcoholism involving general brain damage) usually experience both kinds of amnesia.

What seems to be involved in retrograde amnesia is a disruption of the *consolidation process*, whereby, once new information has entered LTM, a consolidation time is needed for it to become firmly established physically in the brain (see page 168). An interesting demonstration of this is that of Lynch and Yarnell (1973) who interviewed American football players within 30 seconds of a head trauma (and following a brief neurological examination). They were interviewed again three to five minutes afterwards and (where possible) every five to twenty minutes after that. In the immediate interview, they accurately recalled the event but five minutes later they had forgotten it completely.

Alternatives to the Two-Process Model

There have been several attempts to modify and revise Atkinson and Shiffrin's Two-Process model, one of which is the *working memory hypothesis* (Baddeley and Hitch, 1974) which relates specifically to STM. They proposed that STM comprises a number of independent *sub-systems*, each of which is involved in a different cognitive 'job of work'; they do not have to be thought of as distinct stores but merely as independent capacities or capabilities of STM.

According to Hitch (1980), working memory can be divided into four subsystems (i) an *output system* (or Articulatory Loop) which retains speech output; (ii) an *input system*, which retains recently spoken language; (iii) a *non-verbal system*, which briefly retains visuospatial information; and (iv) a *general purpose central executive* which can 'juggle' with most kinds of information.

Another alternative to the Two-Process model is proposed by Wickelgren (1974), who argues that all the available experimental findings can be explained by a *single store model*—acoustic, semantic and visuospatial information can all be held in the same store and how quickly they are forgotten will depend on their strength of storage and the number of similar competing items in memory.

Tulving's division (1972) of LTM into *semantic memory* and *episodic memory* also represents an important modification of the original Two-Process model. Semantic memory is like a 'mental thesaurus' and acts like a dictionary, enabling us to understand language in general (including words, concepts, rules and abstract ideas): 'semantic memory does not register perceptible properties of inputs, but rather cognitive referents of input signals'.

By contrast, episodic memory involves the storage of personal experiences, it 'receives and stores information about temporally dated episodes or events and relations among those events' and it is always stored in terms of 'autographical reference'. It is quite susceptible to change and loss but is important for being able to recognize people, places and events that we have encountered in the past.

Some support for this distinction comes from studies of amnesia: no matter how much personal information an individual might forget, including, in extreme cases, a complete loss of personal identity (episodic memory), they never forget how to speak their native tongue (semantic memory). However, there are many models of semantic memory which we shall discuss in a later section.

Retrieval

'Remembering' can take many different forms, as shown in Figure 6.6 overleaf. However, they are all ways of recovering or locating information which has been stored; they also represent different ways of measuring memory in the laboratory.

1   *Recognition* is a sensitive form of remembering, whereby some thing or

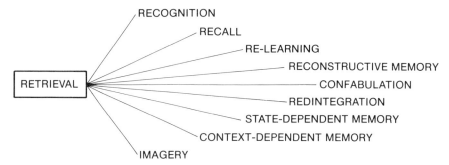

Figure 6.6   Different forms of remembering or retrieval

somebody strikes us as familiar without our being able to name or otherwise identify it. Or we may recognize certain objects or faces as having been 'present' in a test situation when the 'target' items are present with other 'distractor' items (which were not originally present). This is the kind of remembering involved in multiple choice tests—the answers from which you have to choose one can be regarded as retrieval cues.

2   *Recall* is a more stringent form of remembering and usually involves the active searching of our memory stores. When we recall, we reproduce something learned some time earlier and often the retrieval cues are missing or very sparse. This is the kind of remembering involved in timed essays.

3   *Re-learning* is the most sensitive measure of all—even though something may seem to be totally 'forgotten', it may be easier to learn second time around than it was originally. In experiments it is usually expressed as a

$$Savings \ score = \frac{Original \ Trials - Relearning \ Trials}{Original \ Trials} \times \frac{100}{1}$$

4   *Re-constructive memory* is the kind of remembering involved when information is passed from one person to another, often by word-of-mouth, as in the spreading of rumours or gossip. It is not simple reproduction of the past but interpretation of the past in the light of our beliefs, schemas, expectations and so on, and so often involves a *distortion* of objective truth. (We shall look at this in greater detail below).

5   *Confabulation* refers to a kind of memory error often made under conditions of high motivation or arousal—if we are unable to recall a certain item, we may manufacture something that seems appropriate. For example, the detailed accounts that hypnotized subjects give of their childhood birthdays often turn out to be confabulations; they seem to combine several birthdays and 'fill in' the missing details. Patients with Korsakov's Syndrome are very prone to confabulation.

6   *Redintegration* is the recollection of past experiences on the basis of a few cues, which might be souvenirs, particular smells, melodies—almost anything, in fact, which serve as reminders. Only a portion of the information is immediately available and a search of memory gradually leads to the redintegration of knowledge into some kind of coherent whole. The search is fairly systematic, rather like a detective's investigation, but every so often some item will 'pop up', quite unrelated to what is currently being

Table 6.3 Some of the most commonly used mnemonic devices

A   Method of loci ('method of places' or the 'house' technique) You have to imagine a short walk through a series of locations, perhaps a journey through a familiar street, past well-known buildings or through the rooms in your house or college.   Take each of the (unrelated) words to be remembered in turn (eg the items on a shopping list) and associate it with each of your locations. The more bizarre the association, the greater the probability of recalling the words when needed.
B   Associations You find a relationship between the unrelated words by weaving them into a sensible story.
C   Rhyme and rhythm Eg 'Thirty days hath September . . . etc.

D   Numeric pegword system ('Pigeonhole technique')
Numbers are associated with a rhyming object and you picture the items to be remembered in relation to the relevant pegword.
 	
Eg   One   —   bun   Egg   ('Egg on a bun')
      Two   —   shoe   Sausage   ('Sausage in a shoe')
      Three   —   tree   Potatoes   ('Potatoes growing on a tree')
 	
The items to be remembered are hooked onto the pegword by constructing an image which includes the first item with the bun, the second with the shoes etc.

consciously thought about. This kind of remembering is involved in eye-witness testimony and the recollection of childhood involved in psychoanalysis (as is reconstructive memory).

7 *State-dependent memory* and

8 *Context (or cue-)dependent memory* refer to the similarity or difference between the state (eg alcohol or no-alcohol) or the context (eg the room) in which the original learning took place and in which the learning is remembered. Generally, if two different states or contexts are involved, retrieval is poor. We shall return to this in relation to Forgetting.

9 *Imagery* is the basis of many kinds of *mnemonic* devices ('memory aids') and there is much evidence that we can remember verbal material better if we can 'hook it' onto some visual image—this relates both to initial learning (how the material is encoded) and retrieval (see Table 6.3 above).

Theories of Forgetting

To understand why we forget, we must consider the distinction made earlier between *availability* and *accessibility*; the former refers to whether or not material has been *stored* in the first place, while the latter refers to being able to *retrieve* what has been stored (the question of retrievability). In terms of the Two-Process model, since information must be transferred from STM to

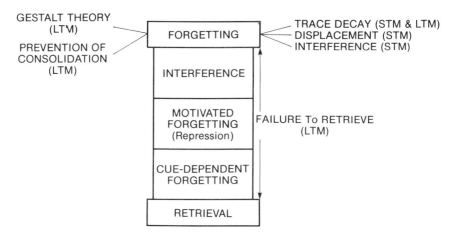

Figure 6.7   Different theories of forgetting, including retrieval failure

LTM for permanent storage, availability has to do mainly with STM and the transfer of information from STM into LTM, while accessibility has to do mainly with LTM.

Therefore one way of looking at forgetting is to ask what prevents information staying in STM long enough to be transferred to LTM (some answers are trace decay, displacement and interference) and another is to ask what prevents us from locating the information that is in LTM (some answers being interference, motivated forgetting and cue-dependent forgetting, which are all to do with failure to retrieve).

Other theories of forgetting, which try to explain long-term forgetting, are not concerned with either availability or accessibility as such but are to do with what happens to long-term memories once transfer from STM has occurred—these are trace decay, Gestalt theory and prevention of consolidation.

Trace Decay

Essentially this is an attempt to explain why forgetting increases with time. William James (1890) claimed that the limiting factor in STM is simply the passage of time: a stimulus decays from STM as its neural after-effects decay. Modern supporters of this view include Brown, 1958, Peterson and Peterson, 1959 and Wingfield and Byrnes, 1972.

The underlying assumption is that learning leaves a 'trace' in the brain, that is, there is some sort of physical change after learning that was not there before, and forgetting is due to a spontaneous fading or weakening of the neural memory trace over time.

Hebb (1949) argued that the physiological basis of memory is dualistic, that is, there are two phases involved in the formation of memory: (i) a group of nerve cells excite each other, resulting in a very brief memory trace; (ii) with repeated neural activity, a structural neural change occurs. The first phase corresponds roughly to STM and forgetting is due to neural decay, the second phase corresponds roughly to LTM and forgetting must be due to the intervention of some other information. So, for Hebb, trace decay applies only to STM.

This belief represents a major argument in support of the Two-Process model. However, the idea of trace decay has been extended to LT forgetting, in the form of decay-through-disuse; that is, if certain knowledge or skills are not used or practised for long periods, the memory trace corresponding to them will fade and hence they will be forgotten. Yet a good deal of remembering goes on when we think decay might have eradicated it, especially in the case of motor skills (eg driving, typing, playing the piano) with no intervening practice. The ability of the elderly to recall their youth, or of a delirious person remembering a foreign language not spoken since childhood, also testify against any simple decay-through-disuse explanation. But how satisfactory is trace decay as an account of ST forgetting?

Waugh and Norman (1965) used a *serial probe technique* in which sequences of 16 digits are presented, at the rate of one to four per second and one of the 16 is then selected (the probe) and the subject has to name the digit which *follows* the probe. Simple trace-decay would predict much better retention of the rapidly presented digits since there is less time between presentation and test. However, they found no such relationship.

In a famous earlier study, Jenkins and Dallenbach (1924) found that when subjects were allowed to sleep during the interval between learning and recall of nonsense syllables, they remembered many more of them than subjects who stayed awake for an equivalent period. Two groups of subjects learnt a ten-item list of nonsense syllables either late at night or early in the morning. The night subjects were woken after one, two, four or eight hours and tested for recall (as well as being tested immediately after learning). The day subjects reported back to the lab at the same intervals but continued their daily activities. In both groups, recall declined with time *but* it declined to a greater extent in the day group.

If decay is a natural result of the passage of time alone, then we should have expected equal forgetting in both groups. The results suggest that it is what *happens* in between learning and recall which determines forgetting in STM, not time as such (and this would seem to apply to LT forgetting too). The major alternative to trace decay is *interference* (see below).

Displacement

In a limited capacity ST store, new items tend to displace old ones; this, of course, rests on the assumption of a limited number of 'slots' into which new material can be inserted ('the magic number seven, plus or minus two') so that when a new piece of information is to be introduced, one of the existing seven slots would need to release its existing material to make way for it. (In terms of memory traces, new material will have *high* trace-strength and older items *low* trace-strength). Glanzer et al (1967) tested the trace decay, displacement and interference theories and found displacement to be a *major* factor, but they also found a small effect of time delay, suggesting a possible decay component.

Shallice (1967) found that although rapidly presented digits did show less marked forgetting (suggesting trace decay), elapsed time was *less* important than the number of subsequent items in determining the probability of recall (which suggests displacement).

Finally, Reitman (1971, 1974) found evidence for both trace decay *and* displacement. However, he argues that it is far from clear that displacement refers to a process distinct from either decay, on the one hand, or interference, on the other (or some mixing of the two).

Interference

According to this theory, forgetting increases with time *solely* because of increasing interference between competing memories; as our store of information grows, it becomes increasingly difficult to identify or locate a particular item and this constitutes a failure to retrieve from LTM. Near the beginning of the storage process, interference from extraneous material can prevent new information from passing from STM into LTM.

Interference is conceptualized in Stimulus–Response (S–R) terms and is commonly studied experimentally using *paired associate* learning, that is, the first member of the pair is a stimulus for the second member of the pair (the response) and subjects are presented with one list (or more) comprising several such pairs (often nonsense syllables).

The usual procedure for studying interference in the lab is shown in Figure 6.8.

Normally, the first member of each pair in list A is the same as in list B but the second member of each pair is different in the two lists. In Retroactive Inhibition (RI) the learning of a second, later, list (B) interferes with the recall of the original list A (so the interference works *backwards*) while in Proactive Inhibition (PI) list A interferes with the recall of later learned list B (and so works *forwards*).

McGeoch (1942) concluded that the greater the similarity between the two lists, the greater the interference, for example, a list of numbers learned before or after a list of adjectives is likely to interfere very little. However, if the *same* stimulus is associated with a *different* response, interference will be very marked (compare this with negative transfer of learning which we discussed in Chapter 3).

In an early study by McGeoch and McDonald (1931) subjects learned a list of words and then were given an interfering task before being re-tested on the first list—if they had to read jokes, recall was 43 per cent, if they had to

RETROACTIVE INHIBITION (Retro = BACKWARD) A ◄──── B	EXPERIMENTAL GROUP	LEARN A	LEARN B	RECALL A
	CONTROL GROUP	LEARN A	REST (or Unrelated task)	RECALL A

PROACTIVE INHIBITION (Pro = FORWARD) A ────► B	EXPERIMENTAL GROUP	LEARN A	LEARN B	RECALL B
	CONTROL GROUP	REST (or Unrelated task)	LEARN B	RECALL B

Figure 6.8 The usual procedure for studying interference in the laboratory

read a list of numbers it was 37 per cent, nonsense syllables 26 per cent, unrelated adjectives 22 per cent, antonyms of the original list 18 per cent, and synonyms of the original list 12 per cent.

Melton and von Lackum (1941), using nonsense syllables, found evidence that the effects of RI were greater than those of PI (using an immediate test of recall). However, Underwood (1948) found that if there was a time interval between the original learning and the recall test, the difference disappeared.

It seems that PI *increases* with time while RI *decreases* with time and Underwood (1957) believes that PI is the more important of the two: the amount of forgetting in any one set of material is an increasing function of the amount of similar material subjects have learned in the past.

But why should RI decrease with time? Both Melton and Irwin (1940) and Underwood (1957) argue that RI is affected by two factors: first, response competition at recall; and secondly, *unlearning*, that is, a process similar to the extinction involved in conditioning, whereby the responses on the first list are not 'reinforced' during the learning of the second list. But the responses on the first list undergo spontaneous recovery and so RI decreases over time. While RI involves both response competition and unlearning, PI involves only the former—the first list is increasingly able to exert response competition on the second and so PI increases over time.

An interesting study by Ekstrand (1973) investigated the influence of sleep on both kinds of interference. Sleep facilitated recall in both RI and PI but to a greater extent in the former. Ekstrand suggested that the role of sleep is not merely to reduce interference but to facilitate consolidation and dreaming may, in fact, constitute a cause of interference (see Chapter 16).

Evaluation of Interference Theory

Although experimental demonstrations of interference are quite plentiful, real-life situations in which we must learn incompatible responses to the same stimulus are quite rare. Most of the experimental support has used nonsense syllables but interference is much less easy to demonstrate when meaningful material is used.

For example, the subject has to learn the response *bell* to the stimulus *woj*. The word *bell* is not actually 'learned' in the lab but is already part of the subject's semantic memory; what is learned is 'bell-as-a-response-to-woj', events which are dependent on the specific laboratory situation (and which are stored in episodic memory). If studies of RI and PI are largely studying episodic memory, then the 'laws' of interference are also largely based on episodic as opposed to semantic memory and it is likely that, whereas episodic memory is susceptible to interference, semantic memory is much more resistant since it is more stable and structured.

As a complete theory of forgetting, interference faces severe difficulties. For example, how could it account for the results of a study by Tulving (1967) who used a modified free-recall technique, whereby each presentation of a list of words was followed by three successive recall trials? Although the number of words recalled on each trial remained fairly constant, the *specific words* recalled change from trial to trial; only about 50 per cent of words recalled were remembered on all three trials.

This is a clear demonstration of storage (or availability) outstripping retrieval (accessibility) which could not be accounted for either by interference (how could a word that was 'unlearned' on trial one be present on trial two or three?) or trace decay (since more time has elapsed by trial three). The best explanation is in terms of different retrieval cues being used on different trials.

Baddeley (1976) regards trace decay as the main cause of forgetting, with interference only a minor contributory factor. He points out that it has been very difficult to demonstrate significant PI outside the lab, one reason being that when learning of potentially interfering material is spaced out over time, interference is greatly reduced and in the lab it is rather artificially compressed in time, thus increasing the probability of interference. So the major problem is generalizing the results to real-life situations.

The Gestalt Theory of Forgetting

Not surprisingly, the Gestalt account of forgetting is closely related to the Gestalt theory of perception (see Chapter 4). It is the only theory of forgetting which proposes that memories undergo *qualitative* changes over time: complex memories change so as to become more internally consistent in the direction of 'good form'. For example, irregular shapes will increasingly be remembered as more regular and symmetrical. Although there is no convincing evidence of such changes in shape memory, some supporting evidence comes from reconstructive distortions of memory for stories towards greater simplicity and consistency; however, the latter changes are not spontaneous as the Gestalt theory would require.

Prevention of Consolidation

Once new information has entered LTM, a consolidation time is needed for it to become firmly recorded (this is the *consolidation process*): changes occur in the nervous system, as a result of learning, which are time-dependent.

We saw earlier that patients who have been the victims of concussion or brain injury or who have undergone brain 'surgery' or ECT commonly suffer retrograde amnesia, that is, loss of memory of events which have occurred prior to the accident.

Hudspeth et al (1964) found that retention of a learned response increases with increase in the interval between training and ECT; an hour's delay permits almost perfect retention. McGaugh (1970) reports that certain drugs (strychnine, nicotine, caffeine and amphetamine) given immediately after a learning trial seem to speed up the consolidation process (see Chapter 15).

Cue-dependent Forgetting—Failure to Retrieve

Tulving (1974) used the term 'cue-dependent forgetting' to refer jointly to: (a) state-dependent; and (b) context-dependent forgetting. According to Tulving, accessibility (ie retrievability) is governed by *retrieval cues* or *routes* which can either be encoded with the to-be-remembered material (at the time of learning) or can be provided later as prods or pointers which govern where in the memory the search will take place. Psychological or physiological *states* represent internal cues while environmental or *contextual* variables represent external cues.

Goodwin et al (1969) found that memory loss was greater for subjects going from an alcohol to a non-alcohol state, compared with those going from a non-alcohol to an alcohol state. Darley et al (1973) found similar results using marijuana, as did Baddeley (1982) with subjects taking drugs or under hypnotic suggestion to influence mood. Interestingly, Zechmeister and Nyberg (1982) found that these effects can be reduced if subjects are encouraged to re-create imaginatively the conditions of learning.

Regarding context, Abernethy (1940) got one group of subjects to learn *and* recall in the same room, while a second group learned and recalled in different rooms; the recall of the first group was much better. Godden and Baddeley (1975) had divers learn word lists either on land or 15 feet under water; recall later was either in the same context or a different one and in the latter conditions there was a 30 per cent decrement in recall. They repeated the study in 1980 using recognition as the measure of remembering and found no effect; they, therefore, concluded, that context-dependent forgetting applies to recall only.

A different kind of contextual variable is that used by Tulving and Pearlstone (1966) which took the form of the category name of words that subjects had to learn. They were read lists of varying numbers of words (12, 24, or 48) containing categories of 1, 2, or 4 exemplars per list with the exemplars along with the category name; they were asked only to memorize the exemplars.

Half the subjects free-recalled by writing the words on a blank piece of paper but the other half were provided with the category names as cues and they recalled more words. However, when the first group were later given the category names, their recall improved, which illustrates very well the distinction between availability and accessibility; the category-name cues helped make accessible what was, in fact, available, so they knew more than they could retrieve under the cue-less conditions. These results were confirmed by Tulving and Psotka (1971).

But how closely related to the recall cue must the encoding cues be in order to operate as effective retrieval cues? Tulving's *Encoding Specificity Principle* (ESP) is one answer to this question (eg Tulving and Osker, 1968) and maintains that cues only help retrieval if they have been encoded *at the time of learning*: in the Tulving and Pearlstone experiment described above, the category names were presented along with the exemplars and so, presumably, were encoded at the time of learning. The ESP, according to Tulving, explains why recall is sometimes superior to recognition (even though, generally recognition is considered to be easier than recall, eg Tulving, 1979, Zechmeister and Nyberg, 1982).

However, not everyone accepts the ESP. For example, Jones (1979) distinguishes between two kinds of cues: (i) those which may *not* have been encoded in the original learning and so do not form part of the information to be recalled (based on *extrinsic knowledge*); and (ii) those which *have* been encoded during learning and which do (based on *intrinsic knowledge*). They *both* aid recall but probably work in different ways. Supporting evidence is provided by Bahrick (1969) and Santa and Lamners (1976).

The problem is being able to define a cue encoded at learning independently of its ability to stimulate recall of information. An effective recall cue is inferred to have been encoded while an ineffective one is inferred not to have been and this is rather circular.

Motivated Forgetting—Repression

As we shall see in Chapter 26, Freud believed that forgetting is motivated, that is, we forget for a reason (or reasons). In the case of repression, painful, disturbing or threatening thoughts or ideas are actively pushed out of our conscious minds and are made unconscious in order to protect ourselves against them. So the unconscious, according to Freud, is largely composed of these repressed memories which are exceedingly difficult to retrieve (are inaccessible) but remain 'in storage' and continue to exert a great influence over us even though we have no awareness of them (and so are available).

Repression is very difficult to demonstrate experimentally (although, of course, there is considerable clinical 'evidence'), for example, both Glucksberg and King (1967) and Bradley and Morris (1976) found that recall of words associated with electric shock is poorer than for words not associated with shock but the effect is only short-lived (see Chapter 26).

Even if it could be more reliably demonstrated, repression could not easily explain either (a) why forgetting increases with time, or (b) why we forget pleasant as well as unpleasant experiences.

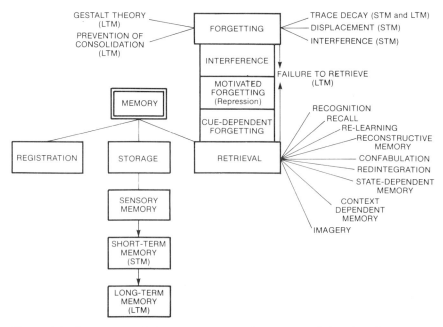

Figure 6.9   A summary of the 3 components of memory and theories of forgetting

Special Issues

a) Semantic Memory

We discussed earlier Tulving's distinction (1972) between episodic and semantic memory and have also seen the very close relationship between semantic coding and LTM.

Semantic memory (SM) refers to the store of knowledge which underlies cognitive ability, its capacity is vast (probably unlimited) and it is also impressive by virtue of the speed with which we can retrieve information from it, which suggests that it is highly structured and *organized*. More specifically, it is involved in the use of language, problem-solving, logical reasoning, asking and answering questions and our ability to understand and predict events based on laws, principles, regularities etc.

The study of SM has focused on our long-term conceptual and linguistic knowledge of the world and there are many different models that have been proposed. Perhaps the best known of these, and the one which has generated most research and debate, is the *hierarchical network model* (Collins and Quillian 1969, 1972).

This is concerned with our memory for words and their meanings and the information involved is organized hierarchically, as shown in Figure 6.10. SM is portrayed as a network of concepts which are connected with other concepts by pointers; each word or concept is represented by a particular node in the network. The meaning of a particular word is given by the configuration of pointers that connect that word with other words.

Some pointers indicate the *properties* of a word, eg a canary 'can sing' and 'is yellow'; other pointers indicate the *category* the word belongs to, at a lower, more specific level, the category of *bird* and at a higher, more general level, the category *animal*. Since all birds (or almost all) have certain properties in common (eg have wings, can fly, and have feathers) these are stored together with the concept 'bird'; it would be unnecessary (redundant) for

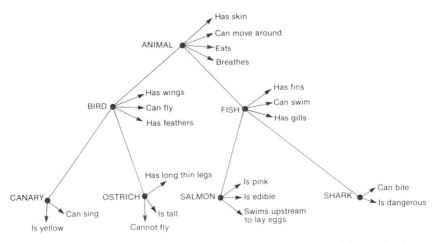

Figure 6.10 Part of the semantic memory network for a 3-level hierarchy (from Collins and Quillian, 1969)

them to be stored with each kind of bird. Similarly, the properties shared by canaries, birds and animals need only be stored at the highest level, that of animal—this is the most economical way of storing a great deal of information. Since, by implication, whatever is stored at a higher level (eg animal) applies to lower level words (eg canary), a hierarchical organization involves little redundancy, ie a relatively large amount of information can be stored in a relatively small space.

How does the model explain the way we go about comprehending and verifying simple sentences? If we were asked whether the statement, 'A canary can sing' is true, we would only need to find the word 'canary' and retrieve the properties stored with that word. However, to verify 'a canary can fly' we would first have to find 'canary' and then move up one level to 'bird' before retrieving the property 'can fly'. Assuming that it takes time to move from one level to another, it should take longer to verify 'a canary can fly' than to verify 'a canary can sing' and it would take even longer to verify 'a canary has skin'. The model assumes that the various properties stored with each word are scanned simultaneously so these are not assumed to be a critical variable.

Collins and Quillian presented subjects with various sentences, including the examples given above, which subjects had to judge as true or false, by pressing an appropriate button as quickly as possible; reaction time was used as a measure of difficulty.

The main finding was that the time taken to decide that a statement is true increased as function of the number of levels the subject had to go through to verify it. Thus, more time was needed to verify 'a canary is an animal' than 'a canary is a bird', which is what the model, of course, predicts.

However, it is not without its critics. For example, Landauer and Meyer (1972) argue that it takes longer to verify 'a canary is an animal' because there are *more animals* than birds. So the findings of Collins and Quillian could be accounted for in terms of the relationship between category size and reaction time.

Again, some members of a category are judged as more typical than other members, eg 'robin' and 'chicken' both belong to the category 'bird' but a robin is judged to be a more typical bird than a chicken. So when determining whether instances belong to a category, subjects respond faster to typical instances ('a robin is a bird') than to atypical ones ('a chicken is a bird'), as demonstrated by Smith (1967) and Wilkins (1971). That should not happen according to the hierarchical model—presumably the same distance has to be travelled in both cases.

Rips et al (1973) and Smith et al (1974) found that subjects took longer to verify 'a bear is a mammal' than 'a bear is an animal' which is the *opposite* of what the hierarchical model predicts, since 'animal' is *higher* up in the hierarchy than 'mammal'. Conrad (1972) found evidence that response time may be due to the frequency with which certain words appear together rather than the number of levels which have to be crossed.

The findings could be explained in terms of how easy (or difficult) it is to imagine concepts at different levels: the higher up the hierarchy you go, the more abstract the category becomes and the more difficult it becomes to form a mental image of it, eg it is easier to picture a canary than 'an animal'. This could explain the findings at least as well as the distance as such that must be crossed (eg Jorgansen and Kintsch, 1973).

In view of these and other criticisms, Collins and Loftus (1975) have revised the model of SM so that it is no longer structured hierarchically. Instead, the memory system is seen as a network of interconnected concepts and clusters of concepts: the more closely related two concepts are, the more links there are between them. The path between two concepts is short if they are closely related with regard to a particular property but longer if they are less closely related. This revised model can account for typicality effects much better than the original model.

Other advantages are: (a) it does not define the memory network in terms of logical, hierarchical relationships—human memory may simply not be as logical and systematic as the original model proposes; and (b) it allows for an individual's personal experience and the structure of the environment to which they are exposed to determine, at least partly, the relationship between concepts.

b) Organization

We have already mentioned organization when discussing semantic memory and in fact it represents a way of encoding information. For example, Sperling and Speelman (1970) found that some subjects reported actively organizing letters in lists which they had to remember, while others just tried to rehearse them; the latter made acoustic confusional mistakes, whereas the former did not. So the same material can be coded in different ways involving different systems and, hence, different degrees of retention.

According to Meyer (1973), to remember is to have organized. Organization may occur either at *storage* or *retrieval*: at storage, it serves to reduce the amount of material to be remembered by hierarchically grouping or chunking it; while at retrieval, organized items have greater uniqueness and, therefore, an increased number of retrieval routes or 'tags' associated with them.

Organization can either be imposed by the experimenter (EO) or spontaneously by the subject, which Tulving (1980) called 'subjective organization' (SO). He was attempting to account for the findings, from many studies, that in free-recall of randomly selected words, subjects consistently tend to recall groups of words in the *same* order, despite changes in the order of presentation on each trial (eg Jenkins and Russell, 1952, and Bousfield, 1953). The earlier interpretation was that the organization simply reflected pre-existing associations, the results, therefore, being consistent with a passive, associationistic view. Tulving (1962), on the other hand, saw subjects as *actively* imposing their own organization on the lists.

Mandler (1967) found that instructions to organize will facilitate learning, even though the subject is not trying to remember the material. He used a pack of 52 cards, with a word printed on each; experimental subjects were told to place the cards into seven columns. Half of each group was told to try to remember the words, but not the other half. After five sorting trials, recall was tested; those instructed to organize the cards recalled as many words as subjects instructed to remember them, which suggests that organization was equivalent to learning.

Segal (1969) found that if category labels are presented randomly among a list of exemplars, the category labels preceded the exemplars at recall, and Cohen (1966) found, using categorizable lists, that either several exemplars from a particular category are recalled—or none at all.

A classic study of organization is that of Bower et al (1969). Subjects had

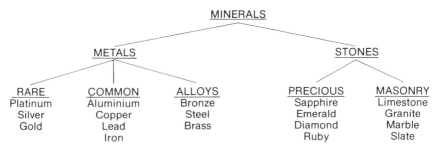

Figure 6.11   An example of a conceptual hierarchy used in Bower et al's (1969) experiment

to learn a list of 112 words arranged into conceptual hierarchies (see Figure 6.11).

For experimental subjects, the words were organized in hierarchical form (28 on each of four trials) while control subjects were shown 28 words on each of four trials but they were selected randomly. The experimental subjects recalled almost all 120 words correctly while control subjects recalled only half as many correctly. Clearly, organization can facilitate retention. Conversely, disrupting the organization of items may impair retention (eg Bower et al, 1969). Restle (1974) proposed the 'degree of organization' principle: the better we can organize new material (relate it to existing knowledge) the better it will be retained. Memory is seen as bound up with our thinking, perception and other cognitive processes; explanations of memory for digits, letters and other 'bits and pieces' of information are likely to be inadequate as explanations of memory for complex and meaningful material.

c) **Imagery**

Imagery is another, much researched, form of organization and, as was mentioned earlier, it plays a very important role in 'memory aids' or *mnemonics*. What they all have in common is either the reduction or elaboration of the way we encode information; we either strip away irrelevant information in order to have as little as possible to remember, or we elaborate the information to be stored (either verbally or through imagery).

An example of (verbal) reduction is the acronym ROYGBIV, an aid to remembering the colours of the spectrum (Red/Orange/Yellow/Green/Blue/Indigo/Violet); of course you must be able to remember the code and also decode it. Alternatively, an elaboration of this acronym is 'Richard of York Gave Battle in Vain' which is decoded in the same way.

According to Paivio (1969), probably the most powerful predictor of the ease with which words will be learned is their 'concreteness', that is, how easily the word evokes a mental image. Richardson (1972) has also stressed the importance of imagery as an aid to memory and regards it as a process of organization, for to produce an image of a single stimulus will not improve recall. In a 1974 experiment, Richardson tested subjects' free recall of a series of 'concrete' and 'abstract' words, and by varying the interval between presenting the stimulus and recalling it, he concluded that the 'effect of imageability lies in secondary memory; in other words, 'concrete' words were recalled significantly more efficiently from LTM (compared with 'abstract' words) whereas there was no difference with recall from STM.

Bower (1972) showed that asking subjects to form a mental image of pairs of unrelated nouns (eg 'dog' and 'hat') where the two words were interacting in some way, resulted in significantly better recall than when subjects were instructed merely to memorize the words. Bower considers that the more unusual the details of the image the better, a view shared by Horowitz et al (1969). Paivio (1971) believes that a general theme or principle, rather than specific content, is more easily retrieved by converting information into visual images. Whenever abstract material can be converted into concrete ideas, recall is enhanced. Exclusive reliance on the verbal system for encoding and retrieving information is a mistake.

A dramatic illustration of the role of imagery is the man with the exceptional memory documented by Luria in *The Mind of a Mnemonist* (1968). He could recall, without error, a list of words that increased up to 30, 50 and eventually 70 and he could remember nonsense material after days, months and even years. His recall was accompanied by extreme *synaesthesia*, that is, sensory information from one modality evokes a sensation in another, for example, colours are associated with tastes. He once said to Luria, 'What a crumbly yellow voice you have'. These synaesthetic components seemed to provide a background for each item to be recalled and he used the method of loci some of the time (see Table 6.3 page 163).

d) Reconstructive Memory and Eye-Witness Testimony

Because of the large amount of work on the organizational aspects of memory, and because of the need to study meaningful material (as opposed to lists of words etc.), there has been a 're-discovery' of the work of Bartlett on Constructive and Inferential Memory (*Remembering*, 1932). Bartlett used two main methods (i) *repeated reproduction*; and (ii) *serial reproduction*.

In repeated reproduction, the same subject is presented with a story or argumentative prose passage or a picture and has to recall it some days, weeks or even years later. If the reproductions were given frequently, and at short intervals, they rapidly became fixed and changed very little; however, if the intervals were sufficiently long, the material could go on being transformed almost indefinitely.

In serial reproduction, one subject reproduces the original story etc, then a second subject has to reproduce the first reproduction, then a third subject has to reproduce the second reproduction and so on until six or seven reproductions have been made. The method was meant to duplicate, to some extent, the process by which rumours or gossip are spread or legends passed from generation to generation.

One of the best-known pieces of material Bartlett used was a North American Indian folk-tale called 'The War of the Ghosts', which is difficult for British non-Indian peoples because of its style and some of its unfamiliar content and underlying beliefs and conventions. Ian Hunter (1972) used 'The War of the Ghosts' (and a serial reproduction method) and found similar characteristic changes to those reported by Bartlett, including:

i)   The story becomes noticeably shorter; eg Bartlett found that after 6 or 7 reproductions, it shrank from 330 to 180 words.

ii) Despite it becoming shorter, and details being omitted, the story becomes more coherent; no matter how distorted it might become, it remains a story because subjects are interpreting the story as a whole, both listening to it and retelling it.
iii) It also becomes more conventional, that is, it retains only those details which can be easily assimilated to the shared past experience and cultural background of the subjects.
iv) It becomes more clichéd, that is, any peculiar or individual interpretations tend to be dropped.

Bartlett concluded that *interpretation* plays a large and largely unrecognized role in the remembering of stories and past events. We *reconstruct* the past by trying to fit it into our existing *schemata*; the more difficult this is to do, the more likely it is to be forgotten or distorted so that it does. Bartlett refers to *'efforts after meaning'*, that is, trying to make the past more logical, more coherent, and generally, more 'sensible', which involves making *inferences* or deductions about what could or should have happened. Rather than human memory being computer-like, with the output matching the input, Bartlett and Hunter believe that we process information in an active attempt to understand it. Memory is an 'imaginative reconstruction' of experience (Bartlett, 1932).

This view of memory as reconstructive in nature is also taken by Elizabeth Loftus who has investigated it mainly in relation to *eye-witness testimony* (which is also the title of a book she had published in 1979). She argues that the evidence given by witnesses in court cases is highly unreliable; her research strongly suggests that it is the form of questions that witnesses are asked which mainly influences how they 'remember' what they 'witnessed'. 'Leading questions' are of special interest, because they can introduce new information which can alter the witness's memory of an event—by their form or content they suggest to a witness the answer that *should* be given, as in the classic, 'Have you stopped beating your wife?' Lawyers, of course, are skilled at deliberately asking such questions, and undoubtedly, police also use such questioning when interrogating suspects and witnesses to a crime.

Loftus studied the influence of questioning in the lab using students as eyewitnesses and films of automobile accidents as the events they had to remember and report. In one study, 100 students saw a film of a multiple-car accident and were then asked to complete a 22-item questionnaire, six of which were 'critical' questions. For half the subjects, the critical questions began, 'Did you see *a* (broken headlight)?' and for the other half, they began, 'Did you see *the* (broken headlight)?', the only difference being in the form of the article, *the* or *a*.

Of course, usually when we use the definite article we are assuming the existence of the denoted object, but when we use the indefinite article no such assumption is being made and the influence of the form of question was reflected in the results. When asked about something which had not in fact appeared in the film, 15 per cent in *the* group said 'Yes' compared with only 7 per cent in the *a* group, who were also more likely to say 'Don't know', both when the object had been present and when it had not.

In a second experiment, Loftus explored the influence of changing a single word in certain critical questions on the subject's judgement of speed. For some subjects, the critical question was 'About how fast were the cars going when they *hit* each other?'; for others, 'hit' was replaced by 'smashed', 'collided' 'bumped' or 'contacted'. These different words have very different connotations regarding speed and force of impact and, again, these were borne out in the judgements of speed: 'smashed' produced an average speed estimate of 40.8 mph, 'collided' 39.3 mph, 'bumped' 38.1 mph, 'hit' 34.0 mph and 'contacted' 31.8 mph.

Loftus wanted to find out if subjects were truly mis-remembering, ie does memory itself undergo change as a result of misleading questions or is the existing memorial representation of the accident merely being supplemented by the misleading questions? Theoretically, this is a very important issue—the idea of *memory as reconstruction* is that memory itself is transformed, at the time of retrieval, that is, what was encoded originally changes when it is recalled.

Loftus tested this again by showing subjects a short film of a traffic accident. One-third of them answered the question, 'About how fast were the cars going when they smashed into each other?'; another third were asked the same question with 'hit' substituted for 'smashed'; and the remaining third, acting as a control group, were not asked about speed of the cars. Once again, those whose question used the word 'smashed' gave higher estimates than those whose question used 'hit'.

A week later, the subjects answered a new series of questions (without seeing the film again). This time the critical question asked whether the witness had seen any broken glass (although there was none in the film). If 'smashed' really influenced subjects to remember the accident as more serious than it was, then they might also 'remember' details that were not shown but which are consistent with an accident occurring at high speed, such as broken glass.

The results showed that more than twice as many subjects who had earlier been asked a 'smashed' question reported seeing the non-existent glass than those who had been asked a 'hit' question. Clearly, the answer to the question about the glass was determined by the earlier question about speed, which had changed what was originally encoded when seeing the film.

Finally, Loftus believes that hypnosis and 'truth serums' can produce as much fiction as fact. Hypnosis encourages a person to relax, to co-operate and to concentrate and suggestibility is so heightened that people may 'remember' events that never occurred. Putnam (1979) believes that subjects who are hypnotized to help them remember a witnessed crime are especially susceptible to leading questions (see Chapter 16).

7

Language and Thought

In Chapter 19 we shall see that one major difference between Piaget and Bruner concerns the role played by language in shaping the course of a child's cognitive development. Briefly, Piaget believes that children can only use words correctly after the appropriate mental structures have developed; consequently, language training will have no effect unless the child's thinking has matured sufficiently.

Bruner takes the opposite view; the transition from the iconic to the symbolic mode of representation is due to the development of language, and without language thought would be limited to what can be learned through actions or images. It follows that cognitive development can be significantly speeded up by training in the use of symbols.

In Chapter 19 we shall be looking at how thinking changes during childhood and adolescence according to these two theorists and, in Chapter 20, discussing the main stages of language development. But now we shall try to put some of these theories and areas of research together by focusing on the relationship between language and thought.

Clearly, thinking and language both become more complex and sophisticated together, although a child's understanding of language usually exceeds its ability to use it. Also, a child may use a word correctly before it grasps the underlying concept. As adults, our thinking often goes on through the medium of imagery and we express our thoughts and feelings through gestures and facial expressions and other non-verbal ways. Artists 'think' non-linguistically. We have all had the experience of knowing what we want to say but being unable to find the right words to say it (students often do poorly in essays because they cannot put into words what they 'know').

From all of these examples, it would appear that thinking is possible without language. But psychologists differ greatly as to the exact relationship between the two; their views fall into three main categories:

i) Bruner and also Edward Sapir, Benjamin Lee Whorf, John Watson, and Basil Bernstein, see thought as being dependent on, or caused by, language.
ii) A second view, as represented by Piaget, takes the opposite position, namely that language is dependent on, and reflects, the level of cognitive

development. (See chapter 19 for a discussion of Piaget's and Bruner's views.)

iii) A third view regards thought and language as originally quite separate activities which come together and interact at a certain point of development (about two years old) and is associated mainly with L.S. Vygotsky, the eminent Russian psychologist.

Does Language Determine Thought?

The philosopher, Ludwig Wittgenstein, claimed that, 'the limits of my language mean the limits of my world'; by this he meant that we can only think about and understand the world through language, so that if our language does not possess certain ideas or concepts, then they cannot exist for us.

Many psychologists argue that language may determine the way we think about objects or events. Others contend that language is not merely a means of expression but actually determines our very ideas, thoughts and perceptions, that is, not simply *how* but *what* we think and perceive depends upon language.

Among those who adopt this latter view are Benjamin Lee Whorf, an amateur linguist, and Edward Sapir, a linguist and anthropologist (someone who studies and compares different societies and cultures). They reached very similar conclusions quite independently of each other, but their theory has become known as the Sapir-Whorf Linguistic Relativity Hypothesis (often their names are dropped and it is understood that Whorf is the major figure whose theory is being discussed). To give a flavour of what this viewpoint entails, let us consider quotes from both men; first Sapir (1929):

> We see and hear and otherwise experience very largely as we do because the language habits of our community predispose certain choices of interpretation. Philosophically, this is very radical, it undermines the possibility of man's access to the real world.

In the above, Sapir is making a very similar point to Wittgenstein. According to Whorf (1941):

> The categories and types that we isolate in the world of phenomena we don't find there because they stare every observer in the face; we cut nature up, organize it into concepts and describe significances as we do, largely because we are party to an agreement which holds in the pattern of our language.

What they are both saying is that language determines our concepts and we can think only through the use of concepts (this is *linguistic determinism*). It follows that acquiring a language involves acquiring a world-view (that is, how we 'cut nature up'—it does not come 'ready sliced') and that people with different languages have different world-views, that is, they cut nature up differently (this is, strictly speaking, what the *Linguistic Relativity Hypothesis* maintains). We shall be discussing below differences in the way the spectrum is cut up linguistically; the analogy of thin, medium and thick-sliced is not as outrageous as it might first sound!

What sort of thing are Sapir and Whorf describing?

Vocabulary determines the categories we use to perceive and understand the world. For instance, whereas in English we have a single word for snow, the Eskimos have more than twenty specific words (including one for fluffy snow, one for drifting snow, another for packed snow, and so on). The Hopi Indians (whose language Whorf studied for several years) have only one word for 'insect', 'aeroplane' and 'pilot', and the Zuni Indians do not distinguish, verbally, between yellow and orange.

But it is not only the vocabulary of a language that determines how and what we think and perceive but also the grammar. In the Hopi language, no distinction is made between past, present and future; it is a 'timeless language' (compared with English), although it does recognize duration, ie how long an event lasts.

In European languages, 'time' is treated as an objective entity, as if it were a ruler with equal spaces or intervals marked off, and there is a clear demarcation between past, present and future (corresponding to three separate sections of the ruler). We say 'ten days' in much the same way as we say 'ten men', although we cannot experience ten days simultaneously. By contrast, the Hopi Indians do not talk about an objective period of time but only as it appears subjectively to the observer. For example, they say, 'I stayed until the sixth day' or, 'I left on the sixth day' (instead of, 'I stayed for six days').

Again, the Hopi Indians get by without tenses for their verbs and have no words or grammatical forms which refer directly to 'time'. Instead, they use different verb endings according to how certain the speaker is about an event (whether they have actually seen it or have just heard about it), or different voice inflections which express whether the speaker is reporting an event, expecting an event or making a generalization about events.

In English, we think of nouns as denoting objects and events and verbs as denoting actions. But in the Hopi language, 'lightning', 'wave', 'flame', 'meteor', 'puff of smoke' and 'pulsation' are all verbs, as events of necessarily brief duration must be verbs; so, for example, 'it lightened', 'it smoked' and 'it flamed'.

All these differences, according to Sapir and Whorf, determine differences in how native speakers think about, perceive and remember the world: the world *is* different according to what language we speak (or perhaps, more accurately, the language we 'think in').

The Strong Version of the Linguistic Relativity Hypothesis

Some support for this comes from a study by Carroll and Casagrande (1958). They compared Navaho children (both those who spoke only Navaho, Navaho-Navaho, and those who spoke English and Navaho, English-Navaho) and American children (of European descent, who spoke only English) on the development of form or shape recognition.

The Navaho language stresses the importance of form. For example, verbs of handling involve different words according to the type of object being handled, so that long and flexible objects (such as string) have one word form, while long, rigid objects (like sticks) have another and flat and flexible objects (like cloth) have still a different word form. It is also known (from other research) that American children of European descent develop object recognition in this order: size, colour and form or shape.

If the Navaho language has influenced cognitive development (as Sapir and Whorf predict it would) then the developmental sequence of the Navaho-Navaho children should differ from that of the American children—they should be superior. And this, indeed, was what Carroll and Casagrande found: the Navaho-Navaho children were best at form recognition and showed it earliest, next came the American children, and last of all the English-Navaho children.

So this seems to lend support to the Sapir-Whorf view. But why did the American children come second and not third? According to the researchers, they were atypical, having had a great deal of experience of shape classification at nursery school.

Perhaps the most directly relevant studies are those which have looked at the ways in which different languages 'code' the colours of the spectrum. According to the Linguistic Relativity Hypothesis, if a language does not make certain discriminations in its verbal labels, then native speakers of that language will be unable to make the corresponding perceptual discriminations. In other words, taking a previous example, since the Zuni language does not distinguish between yellow and orange, Zuni speakers should not be able to perceive the difference between these two colours—they would be 'blind' for these two colours. Does this reflect the way things really are?

Brown and Lenneberg (1954) compared English with Shone (a language of Zimbabwe) and Bassa (a language of Liberia), each of which divides up the spectrum very differently. They found that colours (hues) for which there is no single name in the language are not easily recognized by speakers of that language. However, this seems to be a result of storage, or the way that information is coded, rather than a result of the direct influence of language on the perception of colours. When subjects were forced to place greater emphasis on verbal cues when remembering colours they had seen, the colour was more accessible and easily picked out of a large array. That is, by stressing the name of the colour, it became easier to code and hence more easily recognized.

Lenneberg and Roberts (1956) found that the number of errors made by bilingual Zuni-English speakers in distinguishing orange and yellow fell midway between that of monolingual Zuni and monolingual English speakers. This suggests that the two languages do not determine two different sets of perceptions which in some way conflict, but rather two sets of labels for essentially the same colour perceptions.

Other studies show that speakers can learn new labels for colours, indicating that there are no differences in what is actually perceived by native speakers of different languages. Instead, language serves to draw attention to differences in the environment and acts as a label to help store these differences in memory; sometimes the label we apply to what we see may distort our recall of what was seen, since the label determines how we code our experiences into memory storage.

This was well illustrated in a famous experiment by Carmichael, Hogan and Walter (1932). Two separate groups of subjects were given identical stimulus figures but two different sets of labels. After a period of time, both groups were asked to reproduce the figures. The drawings of both groups were distorted in comparison with the original stimulus according to which label had been presented. (See Figure 7.1 overleaf.)

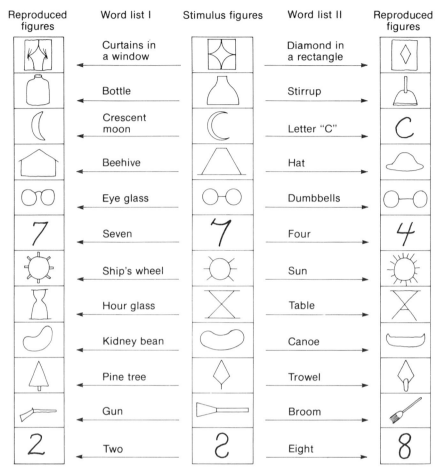

Figure 7.1 Stimulus figures, word lists and reproduced figures (from the experiment by Carmichael, Hogan and Walter, 1932)

So there seems to be very little direct evidence to support the original (strong) form of the Linguistic Relativity Hypothesis, but quite a lot to support the 'weaker' version which states that language determines how easily we recognize an object or situation, how much attention is paid to it, how codeable certain concepts are and, hence, how 'available' these concepts are to speakers of a language. According to Brown (1956), language merely predisposes people to think or perceive in certain ways, or about certain things—it does not determine these thoughts and perceptions.

Again, is it reasonable to believe that, say, Hopi Indians really think differently from ourselves? Judith Greene (1975) asks us to imagine a Hopi linguist doing a Whorfian analysis of English: would they think that we have 'primitive' beliefs that ships are really female or that mountains have feet or that 'driving a car', 'driving off in golf' and 'driving a hard bargain' all involve the same activity? Of course not; we do distinguish between the grammar of a language and our perceptual experience of it. The fact that we can translate from Hopi into English, and vice versa, implies that there is a universally-shared knowledge of the world, which is independent of the particular language in which it is expressed.

Many psychologists now believe that Whorf overestimated the significance of language differences. For example, Furth (1966) maintains that the extent to which a language actually limits thought seems to be small. And there is evidence that some types of thought are completely independent of language.

Universal Linguistic Structures

Quite recently, interest has shifted to how thought influences language. Specifically, the question being asked is whether there are universal characteristics of human thought processes that produce universal linguistic structures.

Berlin and Kay (1969) conducted a survey of a wide variety of languages. Despite a diversity of terms denoting colour, all languages apparently select colour terms from the 11 basic colour categories of black, white, red, green, yellow, blue, brown, purple, pink, orange and grey. In English, all 11 are used. But the Ibibio of Nigeria use only four and the Jalé of New Guinea only two. However, this does not indicate an arbitrary division of the colour spectrum: if a language has fewer than the 11 terms, the terms it lacks come from categories lower down in the list. For example, Jalé names only the first two categories (black and white) and Ibibio the first four (black, white, red and green) and so on down the list. Of course, the smaller the number of terms, the wider the range of colours they apply to. So, for example, green in Ibibio encompasses the English green, yellow and blue. Therefore, according to Whorf, speakers of Ibibio should be unable to perceive the same colour differences that English speakers can. Do the findings bear him out?

Berlin and Kay devised a chart with 320 small squares of colour, comprising virtually all the hues that the human eye can discriminate. They then asked native speakers of dozens of languages to point our the best example of colour terms in their language. The choices were virtually the same from language to language—basic colours seem to correspond across languages.

However, the boundaries of basic colour categories (whether, say, pink is included in the red category or given a separate label) vary according to the number of colour terms a particular language has. It seems that people find certain basic colours more salient or meaningful than others (these are called 'focal colours'). Even when a language does not possess a term for every focal colour, speakers of that language can easily learn the missing ones and can borrow terms for them from other languages. For example, Rosch (1973) studied the Dani of New Guinea who (like the Jalé) distinguish only black ('mili') and white ('mola'). They quickly picked up arbitrary names for eight other focal colours which Rosch invented.

Finally, Bornstein et al (1976) found that infants seem able to perceive differences between focal colours long before they learn verbal labels for them. This represents a very important contradiction of Whorf's theory, at least as far as the perception of colour is concerned.

Peripheralism

Another theory which maintains that language determines thought is that of John B. Watson (1912), the founder of Behaviourism (see Chapter 1). He claimed that all thought processes are really no more than the sensations produced by tiny movements of the speech apparatus which are too small to produce audible sounds. In fact, he was trying to deny thought altogether and so 'reduce' it to silent speech. His theory is known as Peripheralism, that is, thinking does not occur centrally in the brain but peripherally in the voice box. In 1912 his theory was very speculative since there were no instruments precise enough to detect such movements. However, movements of the larynx have since been detected. Yet this does not tell us that these movements *are* thoughts or even that they are necessary for thinking to occur, only that they accompany thinking. An experiment by Smith et al (1947) leaves little doubt that, in fact, these movements are not necessary. Smith injected himself with a drug (curare) which causes total paralysis of the skeletal muscles and complete respiratory paralysis too, so that he had to be kept breathing artificially. He was later able to report the thoughts and perceptions he had during his paralysis.

Also, Furth (1966) demonstrated experimentally that people who are born deaf and mute, and who do not learn any sign language, are of average ability in thinking and intelligence as adults; Watson would have predicted that such individuals would be incapable of thinking.

Does Language Reflect Cognitive Development?

Synpraxic Speech
A strong claim for the importance of language in higher thinking processes was made by Luria and Yudovich in 1956. They studied a pair of five-year-old identical twin boys in Russia, whose home environment was unstimulating and who played almost exclusively together. They had only a very primitive level of speech development, received very little encouragement to speak from adults and made little progress towards a symbolic use of words.

Luria described their speech as *synpraxic*, a primitive form of speech in which the child cannot detach the word from the object or action which it denotes. Their communication with each other consisted of words and actions inextricably mixed. Words on their own had no permanent meanings and could only be understood in a concrete situation; also, their meanings changed according to the situation in which they were used and the tone of voice in which they were spoken. (Usually, words as such are used fairly consistently across different situations—this is really part of the definition of a word, as opposed to a babbled sound. Certainly, adults do have to interpret a child's early speech in light of the context in which it is used but you would not expect to have to do this with a 5-year-old.) For example, one of their names (Lioshia) could mean:

'I (Lioshia) am playing nicely' *or*
'Let him (Lioshia) go for a walk' *or*
'Look (Lioshia) what I have done'.

They hardly ever used speech to describe objects or events, or to help them plan their actions, they could not understand other people's speech, and their own represented a private system of communication, a kind of signalling (rather than symbolic) system. However, they were normal in most other ways and did not appear to be mentally retarded. Yet they never played with other children and when they played with each other the content was always very primitive and monotonous; for example, there was never any attempt to build or construct things. Their language deficiency seemed to underline their backwardness in powers of abstraction and generalization which are so crucial in the organization of planned, complex activity.

The twins were separated and placed in different nursery schools. One was given special remedial training for his language deficiency and the other was not. Although the twin given special treatment did make more rapid progress, and ten months later was still in advance of his brother, equally significant is the fact that *both* made progress and the synpraxic speech died away. So we must be cautious in drawing any firm conclusions about the effects of the special training that only one twin received.

However, Luria and Yudovich conclude by saying:

> The whole structure of the mental life of both twins was simultaneously and sharply changed. Once they acquired an objective language system, the children were able to formulate the aims of their activity verbally and after only three months we observed the beginnings of meaningful play. (Luria and Yudovich, 1956)

Also, many other studies have shown that retarded children who are given special language training will not only increase their language ability but also their IQ score.

Language, Race and Social Class—Deprived or just Different?

A related but much more general issue is that of cultural deprivation, which includes linguistic deprivation. Hess and Shipman (1965) studied 163 American mothers and their four-year-olds and found social class-related differences in communication which seemed to influence the child's intellectual development. In particular, they drew attention to 'a lack of meaning in the mother-child communication system' for low-status families; that is, language was used much less to convey meaning (to describe, explain, express and so on) and much more to give orders and commands to the child. Hess and Shipman claim that, 'the meaning of deprivation is a deprivation of meaning'. (See Chapter 27.)

Bernstein's (1961) theory of Restricted and Elaborated codes has much in common with Hess and Shipman's findings but is more complex and probably more controversial also.

Essentially, Bernstein, an English sociologist, claims that working-class and middle-class children speak two different kinds of language (codes)—a Restricted Code and an Elaborated Code respectively. Since the relationship between potential and developed intelligence is mediated through language, the lack of an Elaborated Code prevents the working-class child from developing their full intellectual potential. These language codes, according to Bernstein, underlie the whole pattern of relationships (to objects and people) experienced by middle-class and working-class families, as well as the patterns of learning which their children bring with them to school.

Bernstein studied the effect of social class differences in language on the child's intellectual ability by comparing the performance of boys from lower working-class homes with boys from famous public schools on tests of verbal and non-verbal intelligence (see Chapter 27). Working-class boys who scored high on the non-verbal test scored lower on the verbal test (sometimes there was a difference of up to 26 points) but scores for the public school boys did not show this pattern. These differences in verbal and non-verbal IQ for the working-class boys were attributed to their poor linguistic background, that is, their Restricted Code (or 'Public Language').

So what are the characteristics of these two codes? The Restricted Code is syntactically crude, repetitive, rigid, limited in its use of adjectives and adverbs, uses more pronouns than nouns, and involves short, grammatically simple and incomplete sentences. It is context-bound, that is, the meaning is not made explicit but assumes that the listener is familiar with the situation being described. For example, a conversation might start with the words 'He gave me it', when the listener cannot be expected to know who 'he' or what 'it' is. 'I' is rarely used and much of the meaning is conveyed non-verbally. Frequent use is made of uninformative but emotionally reinforcing phrases such as, 'you see', 'you know', 'wouldn't it' and 'don't I'; it tends to emphasize the present, the here and now, is poor at tracing causal relationships, and does not permit the expression of abstract or hypothetical thought.

By contrast, the Elaborated Code is syntactically more complex and flexible, sentences are longer and more complex. It makes use of a range of subordinate clauses, as well as conjunctions, prepositions, adjectives and adverbs, and allows the expression of abstract thoughts. 'I' is often used, more nouns than pronouns are used, and it is context-independent, so that it does not assume the listener is familiar with the situation being described but makes the meaning explicit (for example, 'John gave me this book'). Also, it emphasizes the precise description of experiences and feelings, as well as the speaker's intentions. Finally, it tends to stress past and future, rather than the present.

Stones (1971) gives examples of imaginary conversations on a bus between a mother and child:

Mother: Hold on tight.
Child : Why?
Mother: Hold on tight.
Child : Why?
Mother: You'll fall.
Child : Why?
Mother: I told you to hold on tight, didn't I?

This would be a fairly typical Restricted Code type of conversation: the words are being used more as signals than symbols, with very little attempt to explain or reason on the mother's part. Now contrast this with an Elaborated Code mother and her child:

Mother: Hold on tight, darling.
Child : Why?
Mother: If you don't you'll be thrown forward and you'll fall.
Child : Why?
Mother: Because if the bus suddenly stops, you'll jerk forward onto the seat in front.

Child : Why?
Mother: Now, darling, hold on tightly and don't make such a fuss.

Bernstein's theory has important implications for education.

a) Although lower working-class pupils can achieve a good deal of mechanical learning, they are much more handicapped in attempting academic work: the Restricted Code acts as a filter to restrict what gets through from the teacher who, by definition, is an Elaborated Code user. But the middle-class child has access to both codes.

b) Schooling is conducted almost entirely in an Elaborated, formal, code. Hence the middle-class child merely has to develop their language skills, while the working-class child has to change theirs; put another way, school is *continuous* with the home for the middle-class but not for the working-class child. The latter may be able to give correct answers but they may not spring from an understanding of the basic concepts involved; instead they may be 'surface' responses which have been learned fairly automatically. The older the child gets, the more difficult it becomes to overcome this disadvantage since the educational system becomes more and more abstract.

c) The middle-class child is used to attending long speech sequences (middle-class parents place more emphasis on verbal explanations as part of their disciplinary techniques), while the working-class child, (often used to communicating in a noisy, even chaotic environment) may find concentrating very difficult and may even have learnt how *not* to attend.

d) Middle-class parents encourage their children to ask questions and if they cannot answer them themselves will consult a book or refer the child to one. The world is presented as rational and knowable—it can be mastered and understood. Working-class parents, on the other hand, are generally less responsive to their child's questions and may be unable or unwilling to 'point the child in the right direction'. The working-class child might then come to regard the world as largely unknowable or only knowable by others. Clearly, asking and answering questions, using books and other reference materials, and generally being inquisitive and wanting to find out about the world are all fundamental parts of formal schooling.

If true, these implications of having only a Restricted Code are of quite crucial importance. They amount to the impossibility of upward social mobility (moving 'up' from working-class status to middle-class status). How could a working-class child (limited to a Restricted Code) ever grow up to become a teacher, who is a middle-class Elaborated Code User? But we know this does happen.

Clearly, any theory formulated in terms of two basic types tends to over-simplify things as they really are, so that a more helpful way of thinking about language codes may be to see Restricted and Elaborated Codes as two ends of a continuum. Perhaps there are some working-class children who are 'stuck' at the Restricted Code end but many will be able to move varying degrees along the scale. Bernstein himself acknowledges that middle-class children can use the Restricted Code under appropriate circumstances and perhaps some never reach the Elaborated Code end of the scale.

Perhaps the most serious criticism of Bernstein's theory is to do with the very terms 'restricted' and 'elaborated': they imply an evaluation of middle-class speech as being in some way 'superior', that is, it resembles 'standard' (or 'the Queen's') English much more than working-class speech does. But this is very difficult to defend on objective grounds.

In a similar fashion, the English spoken by black children and adults, according to Bernstein, is a Restricted Code, and this makes their thinking less logical than that of white, middle-class, children and adults.

Labov and Black English

Bereiter and Englemann (1966) point out that certain inner-city, black dialects of American English are often called 'substandard' rather than 'non-standard' and are often attacked as illogical. One reason given for this attack is that speakers of these dialects often omit the present tense *copula* (the verb 'to be'), producing such sentences as, 'He a fool' instead of the standard, 'He is a fool'. But which version is more logical?

Labov (1970) showed that speakers of both dialects are in fact expressing the same ideas and understand each other equally well. Also, many prestigious world languages, such as Russian and Arabic, like black English, also omit the present tense of the verb 'to be', yet they are never called illogical. This suggests that black English dialects are frowned upon as a matter of convention, or prejudice, and not because they are poorer vehicles for expressing meaning and thinking logically.

Again, the structure of black English (phonology, syntax etc.) differs in important ways from standard English, and as intelligence tests are administered in standard English, black children are clearly under a linguistic handicap. (This applies to the white, working-class child too.) Lahey (1973) observed that black English speakers are not making grammatical 'errors' but are correctly using a separate dialect of English; black English is different from standard English but is just as logical. Bernstein based his view of black English on a limited sample; in addition, many children from low-income black families simply would not or could not speak freely and comfortably in their full language when around whites.

Similarly, Labov has pointed out that the social situation is a powerful determinant of verbal behaviour. He describes the dramatic changes that can take place when the testing conditions are changed. A young black boy was shown a toy and asked, by a friendly white interviewer, to tell him everything he could about it. The boy said very little and remained silent for much of the time. In a second situation, Leon, the eight-year-old boy, was interviewed by a black interviewer. This time, he answered the questions with single words or indistinct sounds. However, when sitting on the floor, sharing a bag of crisps with his best friend, and with the same black interviewer introducing topics in the local dialect, Leon emerged as a lively conversationalist. If the first two situations had been relied upon, Leon would have been labelled 'non-verbal' or 'linguistically retarded'. (In the same way, the nature of the testing situation might be partly responsible for Bernstein's conclusions about the white, working-class, child's Restricted Code.)

The picture that is emerging is that black children are actually bilingual. At home, in the playground, in their neighbourhoods, they speak an accepted vernacular; but in the classroom, they are forced to use another form of the English language in which they are little practised.

Houston (1970) studied black children in rural northern Florida, USA, and found that they have at least two language 'registers'—one for school and one for out of school. The school register was also used when the children talked to people who seemed to be in authority and only when using the register did they use short sentences, simple syntax and strange intonation; what they said was limited and concealed their thoughts, attitudes and feelings. Once out of school their natural register was easy, fluent, creative and even gifted. It was unquestionably non-standard English (not substandard); in fact, it was another language, with its own grammar. Houston's findings certainly do not support the view that such children lack the language needed for abstract thinking.

Williams (1972) devised the BITCH test (Black Intelligence Test of Cultural Homogeneity), a test specifically designed to measure the true ability of black children, written in the dialect in which they are skilled instead of the usual standard English. Significantly, Genshaft and Hirt (1974) found that when white children were tested using black dialect sentences, they did very poorly indeed! Black and white children matched for social class and non-verbal IQ did equally well on tests of standard English sentences.

Many would argue that it is unfair to give white children tests written in black English since they are not skilled in this language register. But it is equally unfair to test black children using standard English since this is often their second language. (See Chapter 27.)

Are Language and Thought Separate and Independent?

Piaget believes that, 'language and thought are links in a genetic circle . . . in the last analysis both depend on intelligence itself, which antedates language and is independent of it'. This is a convenient way of leading into the third and final major view of the language-thought relationship, which is best represented by the late Russian psychologist, L. S. Vygotsky.

According to Vygotsky, thought and language start out as separate and independent activities. In very young children (as in animals) thought precedes language (it is pre-verbal, as in sensorimotor intelligence) and language is devoid of thought (for example, when the baby cries or makes other sounds with its vocal apparatus, it is usually expressing feelings or trying to attract attention to fulfilling some other social aim).

Then, at about two years, there is a crucial moment when pre-linguistic thought (actions, perceptions, images etc) and pre-intellectual language (crying, babbling etc) 'meet and join to initiate a new kind of behaviour . . . thought becomes verbal and speech rational' (Vygotsky, 1962).

Vyogotsky's theory can be represented as two overlapping circles, one representing pre-linguistic thought, the other pre-intellectual language; where they overlap represents verbal thought and rational speech. (see Figure 7.2 overleaf.)

Between the ages of two and seven, language performs two functions: (i)

Figure 7.2 Summary of Vygotsky's theory of language and thought

an internal one of monitoring and directing internal thought; and (ii) an external one, namely communicating the results of the child's thinking to others. But the child cannot yet distinguish them, which results in egocentric speech – the child talks out loud about its plans and actions and is neither thinking privately nor communicating publicly to others but is caught somewhere in between. Another way of putting this is that the child cannot distinguish between speech for itself (what Piaget called autistic speech) and speech for others (which Piaget called socialized speech).

Then at about seven years (when concrete operational thought usually begins) the child starts to restrict its overt language to the purposes of communication, while the thought function of language is now internalized as internal speech or verbal thought. Piaget originally claimed that egocentric speech is just a kind of running commentary on the child's behaviour and that when it declines at around seven it 'disappears' to be replaced by socialized speech (communicative speech). Vygotsky, on the other hand, noted that egocentric speech becomes more and more unlike social speech just as it begins to disappear. His experiments showed that when six- or seven-year-olds are trying to solve a difficult problem, or are thwarted in their attempts to do something (for example, their pencil breaks in the middle of drawing a picture), so that they have to revise their plans, they often revert to overt verbalization. (Adults, too, often 'think out loud' in similar situations; for example, 'Now where did I put it?' or 'Now what am I going to do?' especially if they believe there is no one around who can hear them.)

These findings convinced Vygotsky that the function of egocentric speech is similar to that of inner speech: it does not merely accompany the child's activity but serves 'mental orientation, conscious understanding; it helps in overcoming difficulties, it is speech for oneself, intimately and usefully connected with the child's thinking. In the end it becomes inner speech.'

The positions of Piaget and Vygotsky can be summarized as seen in Figure 7.3.

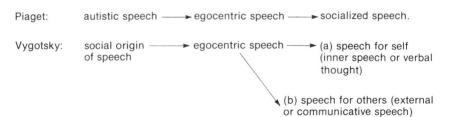

Figure 7.3 Piaget's and Vygotsky's views on egocentric speech

By 1962, Piaget had come to share Vygotsky's view regarding the function and fate of egocentric speech. Both inner speech and egocentric speech differ from speech for others in that they do not have to satisfy the grammatical conventions: they are both elliptical (abbreviated) and incomplete, concerned more with the essential meaning rather than how it is expressed. Inner speech, Vygotsky says, is a 'dynamic, shifting, unstable thing, fluttering between word and thought.'

It is interesting to note that overt speech can sometimes resemble inner speech, in its abbreviated nature, long after egocentric speech has been replaced. For instance, people who know each other very well, like married couples, may often talk in a kind of shorthand which would not be used with anybody else: 'Tea?' asked with a rising inflection, and perhaps at a certain hour of the day, will be interpreted correctly as, 'Would you like a cup of tea, dear?' (This is reminiscent of the child's one-word sentences or holophrases which adults have to interpret according to the context—see Chapter 20). Friends or colleagues often share a vocabulary which would be meaningless to an outsider; the more familiar we are with others, the more shared experiences we have in common, and the less explicit our speech has to be. In Bernstein's terms, we slip into a Restricted Code when we are talking to familiar people in familiar surroundings and whom we assume see things as we do.

In conclusion, although we have considered apparently different theories about the relationship between language and thought, there are points of overlap between them. If we superimpose them on top of each other we may have a more comprehensive and accurate picture of the nature of that relationship than any one on its own can provide.

Artificial Intelligence

In other words—can machines think?

Solso (1979) defines Artificial Intelligence (AI) as the ability of machines to do things that require 'intelligence'. Although much of the research is devoted to developing machines that act as if 'intelligent', this is not usually designed with the intention of mimicking human cognitive processes. However, there are some workers in the field who are concerned with the development of 'intelligent' machines that model human thought and this approach is known as *Computer Simulation* (CS) and we shall be primarily concerned with this approach in the rest of this chapter.

Computer Simulation and Cognitive Psychology

Solso believes that AI in general, and CS in particular, have a kind of symbiotic relationship with man. To develop artificial ways of reproducing human perception, memory, language, thought and so on, we need to know how these processes work in humans, but, equally, developments in CS can also add to our understanding of those very processes.

We have seen that there are several views about the relationship between language and thought. But there is widespread agreement that language is a prime manifestation of (other) underlying cognitive processes and, more than any other category of human response variables, it is language that reflects thought, perception, memory, problem-solving and so on.

One of the earliest and most influential studies on computer 'thinking' as reflected in language processing was that of Alan Turing (1950), an English mathematician, who posed the fundamental question, 'Can machines think?' He formulated it as, 'Can a computing machine behave in the way we behave when we say we are thinking?,' and to make it even more specific, he focused on the criteria of linguistic communication. The idea was that in order for a computer to fool us into thinking it is human, it must be able to understand and generate a response that effectively mimics human conversation. Accordingly, Turing proposed the *Imitation Game*, where a computer is compared with a human being in terms of the answer it gives to an interrogator: if the interrogator cannot determine when they are communicating with a human being and when with a computer, then, Turing would say, the machine must be behaving in a human way. And that, he implied, is all anyone should ever mean by the question, 'Can machines think?'

Turing carried his proposal even further by allowing the interrogator to communicate with the human and computer via a tele-typewriter, in order to by-pass the problems produced by natural speech with all its intonations, inflexions, hesitations etc. This would simplify and clarify the problem as Turing saw it, since the significant human achievement is to be able to string words together to make meaningful, grammatical, sentences. Turing proposed that within fifty years there would be computers that could successfully play the Imitation Game; but even Turing would have been amazed at the sophistication of HAL (*H*euristically programmed *A*lgorithmic computer), the on-board spaceship computer in *2001: A Space Odyssey*.

Some more down-to-earth examples of actual simulations are those of Weizenbaum (1966) and Colby et al (1972). Weizenbaum produced one of the first conversational programs (*Eliza*) which, in one specific form (Doctor) involves Eliza assuming a role very similar to that of a psychiatrist; and Colby et al wrote a program which simulated a paranoid patient (Parry).

Despite the fact that some of the computer's conversations are good enough to fool some of the people some of the time, they cannot fool all the people all of the time. This is not because of their lack of memory for words (which is almost infinite) or because of their inability to produce meaningful sentences (which is extensive), but because basically they lack the understanding of what language is all about (Solso, 1979).

Miller (1976) believes that Turing's proposed game illustrates how intimately related are computers, communication and cognition: human intelligence is best demonstrated when we communicate, so for a machine to be considered an 'equal', it must communicate as we do.

But is this conceivable, given the way that computers are constructed and how they work (or 'think')? Should we think of computers as giant brains and of human brains as 'nothing but' organic computers? These are some of the central issues that we shall now turn to.

How do Computers Work?

Most general purpose computers are based on binary (two-state) logic, that is, an on-or-off, active-or-non-active, yes-or-no principle. (This has been compared with the all-or-none principle of the neuron—see Chapter 15.)

Beyond this, how computers operate is completely determined by two constraints: first, the physical structure of the computer itself (the make, model, storage capacity, kind of display etc), known as the *hardware*; and secondly, the program (a particular set of instructions which 'tell' the computer what operation(s) to carry out), known as the *software*. Of course, whereas the hardware is fixed and unchanging, the software is constantly changing and may be infinitely flexible.

Whatever the nature of a particular program, it must spell out each step that must be taken in order to perform the operation; the computer can only obey instructions that are explicit, precise and rigorous, so no assumptions can be left for the machine to infer—there must be exact specification. This is often represented in the form of a flow diagram/chart and it embodies the programmer's model of how the operation might be carried out by a human thinker.

Of course, the fact that a computer can successfully solve certain problems (which at one time could only be solved by people) does not in itself prove that the computer 'thinks' in the same way as a human. We know that computers can play chess and other games very skilfully, and they are particularly good at solving problems of a purely deductive nature, so that, given the rules, the computer can work through exhaustively until it produces the correct answer (eg arithmetical calculations or all possible moves in a game of noughts and crosses). But in a sense these are not problems at all because there is no doubt about how to find the correct solution (and what constitutes a correct solution). So just how instructive about human cognitive processes is the information-processing capacity of most computers?

The General Problem Solver (GPS)

Many psychologists date the 'birth' of cognitive psychology from 1956, when Newell and Simon devised their 'Logic Theorist' computer program (with a further paper by Newell, Simon and Shaw in 1958), which was then extended into the General Problem Solver or GPS (Simon and Newell, 1964).

It was designed to simulate the entire range of human problem-solving and represented the first major attempt to mirror human cognitive activity (including the proof of theorems in symbolic logic, namely those from Whitehead and Russell's *Principia Mathematica* (1925)). But to understand the significance of what Simon and Newell were attempting, we must look at the distinction between two kinds of strategy that a computer may be programed to use—the *algorithmic* and *heuristic*.

An *algorithm* is a procedure that guarantees a solution to a given problem by systematically testing every alternative in order, until the correct response is produced and verified. (The flow diagram is an example of an algorithmic approach.)

A *heuristic* is a strategy, trick, simplification, empirical rule or any 'rule of thumb' which drastically cuts down the amount of 'work' that must be carried out, thereby reducing a problem to manageable proportions through increasing the selectivity of the program regarding which operations to perform.

If we take the case of chess, for example, it has proved impractical to write an exhaustive program whereby every single *possible* move is represented and then systematically tested—the number of possible moves is simply too vast. So an algorithmic approach is inappropriate. Instead, a heuristic approach is adopted. For example, Miller, Galanter and Pribram (1960) discussed the kinds of considerations that might be involved when programming a computer to select chess moves. The program might contain instructions for looking at a set of goals such as, 'Check the safety of the king', 'Check the material balance of the pieces', 'Control the centre of the board' and so on. Each goal is checked in turn and if it needs attention then certain possible moves are initiated, while at the same time checking that their consequences over the next few moves will not endanger any of the other goals. (So far, chess-playing computers have not proved a match for even moderate human chess-players.) Heuristics do not guarantee solutions (as algorithms do) but when they do work, they greatly reduce the amount of search time required.

The General Problem Solver is a heuristic program and was based on the assumption that much human problem-solving is of this type. (Newell and Simon, in an attempt to ensure that the GPS reflects accurately how a person might solve particular problems, rely on subjects' verbalizations about the thoughts going through their heads when working on problems.) Not only do heuristics seem to be a better model of how people solve problems, but they save a great amount of sometimes needless computation and can be used in situations where the algorithm is either inappropriate or unknown.

An Evaluation of Computer Simulation

As indicated above, there seem to be two interrelated questions involved in the mind/brain-computer debate: firstly, are brains 'nothing but' computers; and, secondly, can computers think/are they intelligent?

As far as the first question is concerned, Rose (1976) sees it as a symptom of *Machinomorphia* (cf 'ratomorphism' discussed in Chapter 1) and it represents a form of Reductionism (see Chapter 2). To think of brains as computers, Rose says, is part of the process of thinking of people as machines which can be controlled, programmed and manipulated, an extreme form of the mechanism (*machine-ism*) of which Heather (1976) is so critical.

Miller (1976) maintains that, 'Whatever else a brain may be it most certainly is not a digital computer.' We simply do not know enough about how the brain works to be able to compare it with a computer in this way and, besides, a brain is an organic, living, organ, not a gadget that humans have conceived and built. By the same token, we could not begin to contemplate building a brain-like computer until we knew the principles by which the brain operates. Also, it would have to be made of analogous units which are 'connected in a similar way, capable of analogous plastic modifications and with analogous responses to incoming sensory data, both from outside the computer and from within its own works' (Rose, 1976).

The second question is concerned not so much with possible biocomputers ('brains in a bottle') but with the computers we have already. Can we meaningfully call them intelligent? And do they really help us to understand how we ourselves think any better?

i) To some extent, whether or not we consider a computer to be intelligent hinges on our definition of intelligence; to the extent that playing chess is an intelligent activity, then a chess-playing computer may be considered intelligent.

We have also seen that Miller believes that human intelligence is best demonstrated when we communicate, but there are still so many different definitions of intelligence (see Chapter 27) that it is impossible to give a simple answer to the question. A way around it is to say that the intelligence of the machine is merely an expression of the intelligence of the human programmer.

ii) It is sometimes argued that, while computers are very useful and very efficient as high-speed and accurate *calculators* (this is the purpose for which they were originally designed—to compute is to calculate) and as solvers of logical problems, they are not very good at the kind of thinking that human brains do best, namely, creative and original thinking —whether displayed in art or science, humour, insight etc. Even allowing for the heuristic program of GPS (which was intended to reflect the intuitive problem-solving of humans based on 'hunches' derived from past experience but which do not, logically, guarantee a solution), 'computer thinking' is often too efficient and logical to constitute a valid model of human thinking. Depending on the program and its input, a computer's output is usually absolutely predictable; this contrasts sharply with the workings of the brain, which is vastly more complex and unpredictable.

iii) Related to this are two further points. Firstly, computers do not get bored, or tired, or anxious etc, and this lack of emotion represents perhaps the most basic reason for not making any direct comparison. Secondly, computers do not forget, they have perfect recall, i.e, they can retrieve any information stored within their memory (provided they are programed appropriately) and in the identical form to how it went in. But human memory is much more fallible, our retrieval is typically less than perfect, and it is also often distorted in some way. (See Chapter 6.)

iv) Usually, computers are doing only one, or a few, specific jobs at any one time (corresponding to individual programs), while the brain is performing a vast number of separate tasks simultaneously. According to Rose, intelligence, if anything, must involve *all* the activities of the brain and not just the computer-like (see (i)). This is the difference between *sequential functioning* (computer) and *parallel processing* (brain).

v) Finally, Dreyfus, in a famous paper called 'Why computers must have bodies in order to be intelligent' (1967), argues that the question of whether an artificial or mechanical intelligence is possible boils down to whether there can be an artificial embodied agent and he refers to what Polyani (1958) says about tool-using. Our knowledge of something as a tool is quite different from our knowledge of it as an object and this can include a hammer and parts of our own body. It is the same with language—in talking, we need to know how to use our words as instruments in 'pointing to' our goals and to do this, we need a knowledge of words as 'tools' and not as objects. For computers, by contrast, there is only one kind of knowledge, one way to deal with information—it must be presented as an object.

Again, for the embodied agent there is a second possibility—we can build up skills and assimilate instruments as extensions to our body. We do not need to know everything objectively in order to know how to act, since we are using things to satisfy our needs—that is, we need only know things as *means*, not ends.

According to Shotter (1975), machines, compared with organisms—let alone persons—are rather limited.

8

Interpersonal Perception

In many ways, it would be quite appropriate to begin a textbook of psychology with a chapter on Interpersonal Perception, as this is concerned with how we all attempt to explain, understand and predict the behaviour of other people. To this extent, we all do in our everyday lives what the professional psychologist does as a scientist (see Chapters 1 and 2), since it is impossible to interact with people and not try to make sense of their actions and to anticipate how they are likely to behave in the future. So here we shall be examining the key processes involved in our day-to-day attempts to understand and predict the behaviour of others. Probably in no other area of psychology does the unique nature of the discipline as a whole become so apparent, namely, the fact that psychologists are studying 'themselves', they are part of the subject matter, and in order to study human behaviour they must utilize the very same processes they are attempting to explain!

To make this a little more clear, let us think of what the psychologist does when choosing to study a particular aspect of behaviour. Firstly, a *selection* is made from the vast range of behaviour that could be studied. Secondly, the theoretical statements and all the evidence that is collected must be *organized* so that they constitute a coherent whole (eg one theory should be distinguishable from another). Thirdly, there are always elements of *inference* or 'going beyond the information given', that is, making theoretical assumptions about what cannot be directly observed or measured (including generalizing to situations that have not yet been observed and making predictions).

Selection, organization and inference represent three fundamental principles of perception. In any kind of psychological (or other scientific) research, the very same processes are used which some psychologists have chosen to study explicitly; not all psychologists study perception, of course, but they must all engage in the act of perceiving as part of their 'scientific behaviour'. (See Chapter 4.)

Two important questions have been raised by this discussion:

i)   What is the relationship between perception (in general) and interpersonal perception (in particular)?
ii) What is the difference between the professional psychologist and the amateur (lay person)?

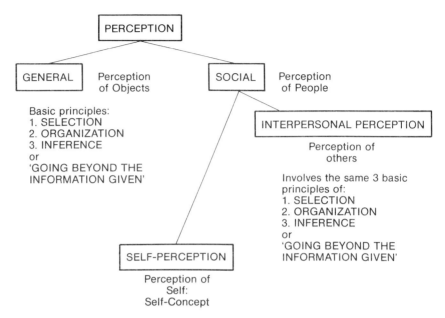

Figure 8.1   General and social perception

To answer the first question, consider Figure 8.1. As you can see, inter-personal perception is the perception of others (sometimes called 'person perception'); the other component of social perception is the perception of self (see Chapter 9 on Self-Concept).

As we shall see, the way we perceive others involves: (*a*) selection (eg focusing on someone's physical appearance or on just one particular aspect of their behaviour; (*b*) organization (eg trying to form a complete, coherent impression of a person); and (*c*) inference (eg attributing to someone certain characteristics for which there is no direct or immediate evidence, as in stereotyping).

So interpersonal perception, like general (object) perception, is based on these three principles. But, of course, there are also fundamental differences between perceiving inanimate objects and perceiving other people:

i)   People *behave* (but objects do not); it is often behaviour which provides the data for making inferences about what people are like;
ii) People *interact* with other people (but we do not interact with objects or they with each other); one person's behaviour can influence another's, so that each one's behaviour towards the other is at least partly a product of the other's behaviour towards them;
iii) People *perceive* and *experience* (but objects cannot); one person's perception can influence the other's (probably through their behaviour, especially their non-verbal behaviour), so that each person's perception of the other is at least partly a product of the other's perception of them.

Some psychologists (particularly the phenomenological psychologists) regard experience as the major source of 'data' (as opposed to behaviour) in social interaction; eg R. D. Laing (1967) argued that the task of social phenomenology is to relate my experience of your behaviour to your experience of my behaviour, so that it studies the relationship between experience and experience.

In Laing's book *Knots*, (1972), he dramatically (and often humorously) demonstrates the kind of tangles that human relationships can get into, in the form of short prose poems and diagrammatic poems. Here are two of the shorter and more straightforward examples:

Jack frightens Jill he will leave her because he is frightened she will leave him.

Jack You are a pain in the neck
To stop *you* giving me a pain in the neck
I protect my neck by tightening my neck muscles,
Which gives me the pain in the neck you are.
Jill My head aches through trying to stop you giving me a headache.

For Laing, 'knots' like these illustrate how my experience of another is a function of the other's experience of me—and vice versa.

As far as the question of how the amateur and professional psychologist differ, let us look at what Judy Gahagan (1975/84) has to say on the matter:

(i) The layperson uses their theories for pragmatic (or practical) and immediate purposes, as opposed to gaining knowledge for its own sake. (Remember the distinction between pure and applied research discussed in Chapter 1; most research into interpersonal perception is pure research but it sometimes has implications for practical situations, such as interviews.)

(ii) The layperson is rarely a disinterested observer of others' behaviour—we usually have a vested interest in what is going on and are usually emotionally involved to some extent. The professional, as a scientist, has to be 'detached' and objective (although complete detachment is impossible; the very fact that a psychologist has chosen one topic to investigate rather than another demonstrates this).

(iii) The layperson may be completely unaware of the reasoning they have followed when making inferences about others, and this reasoning may change from one situation to another. So the layperson's theories are not spelt out or articulated (hence 'implicit' personality theories) and may not be consistent. But psychologists must try to be consistent and must make their reasoning explicit so that other psychologists can examine it.

Definitions and Models of Interpersonal Perception

Judy Gahagan (1984) defines interpersonal perception as 'the study of how the layperson uses theory and data in understanding people'. She breaks this definition down further into three main components:

i) The study of how people perceive others as *physical objects* and form impressions of their physical appearance, actions and the social categories to which they can be assigned. Often the first thing we notice about someone is some aspect of their appearance (eg clothes, hair) and to this extent we are treating them as no more than 'things'. This is usually the first step involved in stereotyping, since it is usually on the basis of their physical appearance that we assign people to groups.

ii) The study of how people perceive others as *psychological entities*—we form impressions of what kind of person they are or we infer what their feelings, motives, personality traits etc, might be (having already identified them as belonging to a particular group—sexual, racial, occupational).

iii) The study of the layperson as a *psychologist*—we have already dealt with this above.

According to Cook (1971), interpersonal perception is 'the study of the ways people react and respond to others, in thought, feeling and action'. He goes on to summarize all the research under one of two headings, what he calls the Intuition Model and the Inference Model.

The Intuition Model is mainly concerned with the idea of *global perception*, that is, how we form overall impressions of others and it is based on the work of the Gestalt psychologists; what we said earlier about organization (as a basic principle of perception) is based largely on their work. Applied to people, it means that we try to perceive people as whole entities, in as complete a way as possible; people are not simply a collection of separate traits or characteristics ('the whole is greater than the sum of its parts').

The Inference Model is mainly concerned with 'implicit personality theories', that is, our beliefs, held unconsciously, about how certain traits belong together, so that if a person displays one of these, it is inferred that they also have (some of) the others. Stereotypes illustrate such implicit theories. The Inference Model is also concerned with how we make judgements about the causes of people's behaviour (including our own) and whether, therefore, they can be held responsible for it; the study of how people make such judgements is called the Attribution Process.

Forming Impressions of Others—Global Perception (Intuition Model)

The two major explanations of how global perception takes place are: (i) Central versus Peripheral Traits; and (ii) the Primary-Recency Effect.

i) Central versus Peripheral Traits

The basic idea here is that certain information which we have about a person (ie certain traits we believe they possess) is more important in determining our overall impression of that person than any other information.

The classic study is that of Asch (1946). He presented subjects with a list of adjectives describing a fictitious person. One group had the following list: intelligent, skilful, industrious, warm, determined, practical, and cautious. A second group had the same list, except that the word 'cold' replaced the word 'warm'. These lists were called the Stimulus lists.

Both groups were then presented with a second list (the Response list) of 18 trait words (different from the Stimulus list) and they were asked to underline those which described the 'target' person. The two groups chose significantly and consistently different words from the second list. For example, the 'warm' group saw the character as generous, humorous, sociable and popular, while the 'cold' group saw him as having the opposite traits. There were also certain qualities attributed to him equally by both groups—eg reliable, good-looking, persistent, serious, restrained, strong and honest.

The words 'warm' and 'cold' seemed to have a major effect on the overall impression of the target person for the two groups. When Asch used 'polite' and 'blunt' (instead of 'warm' and 'cold') subjects underlined almost identical words in the response list. Asch concluded from this that 'warm-cold' represented a *central* trait or dimension, while 'polite-blunt' represented a *peripheral* trait or dimension. And the central traits which seem to influence our global perception in this way are implicitly *evaluative*, that is, they are to do with whether the person is liked or disliked, popular or unpopular, friendly or unfriendly, kind or cruel etc.

Based on Asch's study, Kelley (1950) set out to: (a) check Asch's findings; and (b) see whether the description of the target person as 'warm' or 'cold' would influence subjects' behaviour towards him. The subjects were students at the Massachusetts Institute of Technology and the target person was a male member of staff not known to the students. Before he arrived, Kelley explained to the students that their regular teacher would not be coming and they would be having Mr X instead; he also told them that they would be asked to assess him at the end of the session. They were then given some biographical notes about the substitute teacher; for some subjects these included the description 'rather warm' and for others 'rather cold' – otherwise the biographies were identical.

A 20-minute discussion followed between the teacher and the students, during which Kelley recorded how often each student attempted to interact with the teacher. After he left the room students assessed him on 15 rating scales (eg 'knows his stuff—doesn't know his stuff', 'good natured—irritable'). It was found that subjects who had read the 'warm' description constantly responded more favourably to him than those who had read the 'cold' description. The two groups also responded differently when asked to write a free description. Fifty-six per cent of the 'warm' group participated in the discussion, compared with 32 per cent of the 'cold' group. So not only had Kelley confirmed Asch's findings regarding the 'central' nature of the 'warm-cold' dimension, but he had also demonstrated a relationship between how students perceived the target person and their attempts to interact with a real person (as opposed to Asch's fictitious person).

However, Wishner (1960) cast doubt on both Asch's and Kelley's results by claiming that 'warm-cold' is no more important than any other pair of adjectives or traits, and that Asch's results were entirely due to the particular combination of the 'critical pair' ('warm-cold'/polite-blunt') with all the other trait-words (in both the stimulus and response lists).

Wishner used all the trait words that Asch had used (the stimulus list, plus the critical pairs, plus the response list) and gave them all to 214 psychology students—but he rearranged them so that some from the response list were transferred to the stimulus list, and vice versa, and different critical pairs were inserted.

He predicted that he would get the same results as Asch and what this would mean is that 'warm-cold' is *not* central. (If it were, its exclusion from the list would remove the differences between the two groups in what traits they chose from the response list.) He did, in fact, get the same results as Asch and so concluded that 'warm-cold' is no more important in colouring our overall impression of people than any other pair of opposites.

There had been a considerable amount of work based on Asch's original study. Some of this tends to support Asch by demonstrating what is called the halo effect: if we are told that a person has a particular favourable characteristic (eg 'warm', which suggests the person is likeable), then we tend to attribute them with other favourable characteristics. The reverse is true if we are told the person is 'cold' (and, therefore, unlikeable).

The halo effect seems to illustrate very well two of the principles of perception discussed earlier:

i) We like to see people in as consistent a way as possible; it is simpler to regard someone as having either all good or all bad qualities than a mixture of good and bad. Perhaps the most extreme example of this is when lovers regard each other as perfect and faultless—'love is blind' is just an instance of the halo effect.

Similarly, the 'us' and 'them' mentality, whereby our enemies are seen as personifying evil while we are all good, seems to demonstrate our need to organize or structure our perceptions in as coherent and 'complete' a way as possible.

ii) Certain groups of traits seem to belong together, e.g. warm, intelligent, capable, generous, popular. If we know someone is warm, we also perceive them as possessing these other traits (so the halo effect is similar to individual stereotypes, to be discussed below under the Inference Model.)

ii) The Primacy-Recency Effect

The other major explanation of global perception concentrates on the *order* in which we learn things about a person: the primacy effect refers to the greater impact of what we first learn about someone ('first impressions count'); and the recency effect to the greater impact of what we learn later on.

One of the most famous studies was that of Luchins (1957). Subjects were matched on measures of personality and then allocated to one of four groups: group 1 heard a straightforward description of an extrovert character called Jim; group 2 heard a straightforward introvert description. (These were control groups used to establish that subjects could accurately identify extroverts and introverts—there was a 75 per cent success rate). Group 3 heard the first half of the extrovert description followed by the second half of the introvert description; and group 4 heard the reverse of group 3 (so for groups 3 and 4 the descriptions were contradictory).

All the subjects were then asked to rate Jim in terms of introversion-extroversion. Group 1 subjects judged him to be the most extroverted and group 2 the most introverted (as you would expect); and, although the judgements of groups 3 and 4 were less extreme, group 3 subjects did rate Jim as being more extrovert than group 4 subjects. Remember, they all received the same information about Jim, only the order was different.

Luchins concluded that the earlier elements of the description had a greater impact than the later elements, so he had found evidence for the primacy effect.

Support for this view came in an earlier study, again by Asch (1946). He used two lists of six adjectives describing a hypothetical person (intelligent, industrious, impulsive, critical, stubborn and envious), one in the above order and the other in the reverse order. Subjects given the first list (where the first words denoted desirable qualities) formed a favourable overall impression, while subjects given the second list (where the first words denoted undesirable qualities) formed an unfavourable overall impression.

Both the Luchins and Asch studies involved hypothetical people. In Jones et al's study (1968), an actual person was used (a stooge of the experimenters). Subjects watched a student trying to solve a series of difficult multiple-choice problems and were then asked to assess his intelligence. It was arranged so that the student always solved 15 out of 30 correctly; but some subjects saw him get most of the right answers at the beginning of the series, while others saw him get most of the right answers at the end of the series. (The problems were all of equal difficulty.)

The commonsense prediction would be that when the student improved as the series went on (ie got most right towards the end) he would be judged as more intelligent than when he seemed to be getting worse as the series went on (got most right towards the beginning); in the first case he would seem to be learning as he went along, in the second case his early successes could be attributed to guesswork or 'beginner's luck'. Jones et al made the commonsense prediction that there would be a *recency effect*. However, the opposite was found—the student under the first condition was judged as being more intelligent and so there was a primacy effect. Significantly, subjects' memories were distorted in the same direction—when asked to recall how many problems the students had solved correctly, those who had seen the 15 bunched at the beginning said 20.6 (on average) while those who had seen them bunched at the end said 12.5 (on average), so these over- and under-estimations also reflected the impact of the primacy effect.

How can we account for this?

Luchins himself says that when later information is discrepant with earlier information, people tend to regard the first information as revealing the 'real' person and to explain away or dismiss the later information as not representative or typical. Anderson (1974) maintains that people pay more attention to information that is presented when they are first trying to form an impression about someone and, having formed some initial impression, they pay less attention to any subsequent information.

But does the primacy effect always prove more powerful than the recency effect? The answer seems to be, that it does, but only under certain conditions.

Luchins reasoned that if the primacy effect is due to decreased attention being paid to later information, then it should be possible to destroy the effect by warning subjects against making snap judgements. He found that warning subjects did have this effect and that it was particularly effective if it was given between the presentation of the two inconsistent pieces of information about the same individual.

In a similar vein, Hendrick and Constanini (1970) found that primacy seems to prevail unless subjects are specifically instructed to attend closely to all the information. Also, when subjects performed some irrelevant task in between the two pieces of information, the recency effect proved more powerful and the longer the time-interval between the two, the greater the recency effect proved to be.

Hodges (1974) found that a negative first impression is more resistant to change than a positive one. Why should this be? One explanation may be that negative information carries more weight because it is likely to reflect socially undesirable traits or behaviour and, therefore, the observer can be more confident in attributing the trait or behaviour to the person's 'real' nature. Another explanation may be that it is more adaptive for us to be aware of negative traits than positive ones, since the former are potentially harmful or dangerous to us.

It can be argued that in the Asch and Luchins studies the situation is an extremely artificial one—subjects are obliged to use data selected for them, they are not free to form impressions by selecting information that *they* think is relevant. But Roger Brown points out that few subjects hesitated to formulate an impression or to answer questions about Jim, even on the basis of very limited information. This supports the view that we characteristically 'go beyond the information given' and seek ways of organizing and structuring our impressions of others using any available 'data'.

Finally, Luchins found that, although the primacy effect may be important in relation to strangers, as far as friends and other people whom we know well are concerned, the recency effect seems to be stronger. For example, we may discover something about a friend's childhood, or something that happened to them before we knew them, which might change our whole perception of them. This raises the fundamental question, 'How well do we (or can we) know anybody?'. This is related to the question of the *accuracy* of our perception of others. (How well we can know ourselves is discussed in Chapter 9 on Self-Concept.)

Accuracy of Perception

There are a number of questions involved here, eg does it make sense to measure accuracy at all? And do individuals differ in how accurately they perceive others?

As far as the first question is concerned, it seems quite clear that we cannot measure accuracy in any absolute way but only relative to some criterion, that is, there is no 'ultimate truth' about a person, no sense in which we can say this is what person X is 'really like'. Indeed, to talk about 'the real person' at all seems to presuppose that people actually do possess enduring qualities and characteristics, something which has been questioned by many sociologists and social psychologists. (See Chapter 25.) For example, sociologists such as Goffman (see Chapter 9), who represent the Symbolic Interactionist school, believe that humans are actors and that our behaviour is a series of performances, controlled and managed in conformity with the 'definition of the situation'. Part of the definition of the situation involves allocation of roles—to ourselves and to others; once we know what is expected of us and what we expect of others, then interaction can proceed reasonably smoothly (assuming, of course, that all the actors agree on the definition of the situation and hence their respective roles).

From this point of view, the 'real self' ('under the mask') either does not exist at all or is not 'visible' or accessible—people *are* simply the roles they play in different situations and so it is meaningless to talk about the enduring qualities of people.

But personality theorists, of course, do believe that we possess these enduring qualities which, to a large extent, determine our behaviour in different situations. How else can we account for the fact that different individuals may vary in how they interpret the 'same' situation or the same role? Definition of the situation, while important, may itself reflect the personality of the individual, as much as it does 'the situation'. Common sense also seems to assume the existence of these fairly permanent qualities and characteristics, although sometimes the role we are playing may be a relatively more important determinant of our behaviour than our personality. We shall look at roles in more detail later on.

Assuming that we can talk meaningfully about accuracy in perceiving people, are some people better judges of personal qualities than other people? Are some of us more accurate perceivers than others? Is perception of others a general skill or is it specific to particular types of situation?

There is a considerable amount of research bearing on those questions, but the evidence is very mixed and, therefore, inconclusive—Vernon (1933) found no evidence for a general accuracy skill, nor did Crow and Hammond (1957). But Cline and Richards (1960) concluded that judges were accurate when asked to make different kinds of judgements involving different subjects (implying that accuracy is a general skill).

Common sense might suggest that some people are more likely to be accurate judges (in general) by virtue of the kind of work they do and the kind of training they have received for it, for example, psychologists and psychiatrists. But the evidence here is also mixed.

Cline (1964) found that individuals with more than ten years of psychiatric or psychological training were more accurate at predicting how another group of individuals would describe themselves but less accurate at predicting how this group would behave in real life, compared with colleagues who had had less than three years experience.

Kremers (1960) found no difference in accuracy between professional psychologists and laypeople in their ability to assess personality characteristics; in fact, the trained professional may be *less* accurate as they will tend to concentrate on the finer details of personality rather than on the overall personality. So do good judges (if they exist) tend to be particular kinds of people themselves, ie do they have any distinguishable characteristics?

Intelligence does not seem to be correlated with the ability to judge others (eg Taft, 1955) but characteristics that are likely to be important include;

a) A certain degree of detachment;
b) Wide experience with people from a diversity of backgrounds;
c) Being well-adjusted, emotionally stable and socially skilled;
d) Having self-insight (self-understanding).

There is also some evidence that we are more accurate in judging people who are similar to ourselves.

Social Roles

As we shall see in Chapter 9, social roles represent a major part of the individual's self-image and this becomes increasingly true as we get older. What are social roles?

Judy Gahagan's definition (1984), is simple but useful, namely, 'the slots or positions that we occupy in society'. These slots or positions in a sense exist independently of any particular individual who might occupy them (which is partly why symbolic interactionists emphasize 'roles' as opposed to 'personality') and associated with each slot or position are expectations about how the occupant should behave (and sometimes should think, feel and look also) which are called *norms* (the 'oughts' of roles).

One reason why it is so important to conform to these expectations is that most social roles are interdependent, that is, they do not exist in isolation but constitute social systems or *role sets*. An occupant of a particular role, therefore, has at least one role partner (member of the role set) and if society is to function properly each member of the role set must be able to rely on all the others behaving in an appropriate way.

This interdependence is particularly striking in the case of *complementary* roles (eg parent-child, teacher-student, doctor-patient); here, one role implies the other, it cannot really exist in the absence of the other and so for each occupant to play their role efficiently so must the other.

Whether or not the roles are complementary, the importance of role behaviour (the actual behaviour of the role occupant) corresponding to role expectations (norms) is that this expectation makes other people's behaviour more predictable (assuming, of course, that the role is understood in the same way by all the role partners). The more predictable other people's behaviour is, the 'smoother' the social interaction becomes. Also, many roles are universal, that is, they are found in all societies and cultures, because they derive directly from the components of social structure that are universal, eg gender, age, kinship (family relationships) and occupation.

Roles may vary in how far they extend in time and space; for example, a bank clerk's role is very much confined to a particular building and to particular times of the day, but a parent's role is not confined in either of these two ways—while there is a sense in which the bank clerk stops being a bank clerk at 5.00 or 5.30, a parent is always a parent.

Roles also vary in the extent to which role expectations involve large sectors of an occupant's behaviour, for example, a priest's behaviour is almost completely determined (directly or indirectly) by the fact that he is a priest, and he is expected to behave like one at all times. Shop assistants, however, are much less role-governed in this way—outside their place of work, they are free (within the law, of course) to do and be whatever they choose.

Perhaps both these aspects of roles (extension in time and space, and the sectors of the occupant's behaviour covered by the role expectations) can be understood by reference to the notion of being 'on/off duty'. In the shop assistant's case it is relatively clear compared with, say, a member of the police force, who, even if officially off-duty, is expected to be morally impeccable at all times, and a crime committed by them is always judged more harshly than the same crime committed by a member of 'the public'. Equally clear, but at the opposite end of the spectrum, are the cases of the parent and the priest—they are never off duty.

Role Conflict

However, a social system rarely works perfectly and roles can easily come into conflict.

The major categories of conflict are—(a) *intra-role* (within the same role), and (b) *inter-role* (between different roles). Related to these are three important sources of conflict:

i) Role expectations are not sufficently clear to guide the occupant's behaviour and interactions with others; this can make a person feel at a loss to know how to act and might be experienced as 'not knowing what is expected of me'. (This is an example of intra-role conflict.) An example of this is the study by Schwartz (1957), where the role of nurses in psychiatric hospitals was changed from a traditional and clearly defined custodial one to a much vaguer 'therapeutic' role.

ii) The role partners have conflicting expectations of the role occupant: a child might have conflicting demands made on it by parents, or a teacher may have conflicting loyalties to students and colleagues (eg being asked to show solidarity with colleagues staging a walk-out because of inadequate heating while students are in the middle of an exam). This is also an example of intra-role conflict.

iii) Occupying more than one role simultaneously (eg father, husband and son) can in itself produce conflict because different people may be making demands on the same role occupant at the same time, eg a man's boss wants him to stay late at work to discuss an urgent matter while his wife has been complaining recently about how little time she spends alone with him. This is inter-role conflict.

These fairly common sources of conflict do not reflect anything about the qualities or capabilities of the occupant, but rather they reflect a social system which is not functioning properly. But, of course, role strain can also arise from the incompetence of the occupant or their unsuitability to the role.

Where the symbolic interactionists seem to have overstated their case is that there is usually some room for individuals to express their personality while fulfilling the prescribed, explicit, shared role expectations; no two individuals play out their role expectations in identical ways and, as Gahagan points out, to a degree roles are re-created by their occupants. So actual role behaviour would seem to reflect both something about the role itself (independent of particular occupants – what different occupants all have in common) and the personality of the particular occupant (how different occupants 'interpret' the role differently). The relative balance between the two will vary from one role to another.

Making Judgements About Others (Inference Model)

The Inference Model deals with two main issues (i) how we account for social behaviour, that is, how we attribute causes to people's behaviour (the attribution process); and (ii) implicit personality theories, that is, our beliefs about what characteristics tend to belong together, in particular, stereotyping.

The Attribution Process
Most of our impressions of others are based on what they actually do—their overt behaviour—and the setting in which it occurs. Sometimes, of course, we only know about someone's behaviour from someone else, so that our impressions may be based on second-hand information, and in many psychology experiments subjects are merely informed (verbally or in writing) about the behaviour of some hypothetical person.

In all these cases, we usually try to explain why the person behaved as they did by identifying the cause of the behaviour; in particular, was it something to do with the person, for instance, their motives, intentions or personality (an *internal* cause) or was it something to do with the situation, including some other person or some physical feature of the environment (an *external* cause)? Unless we can make this sort of judgement, we cannot really use the person's behaviour as a basis for forming an impression of them, and although we might mistakenly attribute the cause to the person instead of the situation, attribution still has to be made.

The process by which we make this judgement is called the *attribution process* and was first investigated by Fritz Heider (1958). He demonstrated the strength of the human tendency to explain people's behaviour in terms of their intentions by showing that we sometimes attribute intentions to inanimate objects!

In a famous study, Heider and Simmel (1944) showed animated cartoons of three geometrical figures (a large triangle, a smaller triangle, and a disc) moving around, in and out of a large square. Subjects tended to see them as having human characteristics, and, in particular, as having intentions towards each other. A common perception was to see the two triangles as two men in rivalry for a girl (the disc), with the larger triangle being seen as aggressive and a bully, the smaller triangle being seen as defiant and heroic and the disc as timid. (It is interesting to compare the notions of intentionality in adults and what Piaget calls *animism* in the child—see Chapter 19—which refers to the belief that objects and aspects of nature, such as the sun and moon, can decide to do things and are 'alive' in the way that people are.)

Jones and Davis's Correspondent Inference Theory (1965)

Jones and Davis, very much influenced by Heider, investigated the issue of how we decide that someone's behaviour is intentional when the information we have at our disposal is so often ambiguous. They believe that the goal of the attribution process is to be able to make *correspondent inferences*, that is, to infer that both the behaviour and the intention that produced it correspond to some underlying, stable, feature of the person (ie a disposition); for instance, knowing that John has an argumentative disposition, we are in a better position to predict that he will intentionally start an argument and to account for one which actually takes place.

Agreeing with Heider, Jones and Davis maintain that before we can begin to attribute intentions, we have to be confident that, firstly, the actor is capable of having deliberately performed the act and that, secondly, they knew the effects that their behaviour would produce. Having made these preliminary decisions, how do we then proceed to infer that the intended behaviour is related to some underlying disposition?

One answer suggested by Jones and Davis is the *analysis of uncommon effects*: when more than one course of action is open to a person, a way of understanding why they chose one course rather than another is to compare the consequences of the action that *is* taken with the consequences of those which are not, ie, what is distinctive (or uncommon) about the effects of the choice that is made? For instance, if you have a strong preference for one polytechnic or university, even though they are all similar with regard to type of course, number of students, reputation, and so on, the fact that all the others require you to be in residence during your first year suggests that you have a strong preference for being independent and looking after yourself.

Generally, the fewer the differences between the chosen and the unchosen alternatives, the more confidently we can infer dispositions, as in the above example; and the more negative elements that are involved in the chosen alternative, the more confident still we can be of the importance of the distinctive consequence. (If living out of residence means a lot of extra travelling, or is more expensive, then the desire to be self-sufficient assumes even greater significance.)

However, the analysis of uncommon effects can lead to ambiguous conclusions, and other cues must also be made use of, in particular, choice, social desirability, social role and prior expectations.

i) *Choice* is self-explanatory: is the actor's behaviour situationally constrained or a result of free will?

ii) *Social desirability* relates to the *norms* associated with different situations. Much of the time, the need to explain other people's behaviour does not actually arise—to the extent that we 'conform', there is 'nothing to explain'. We base our impressions of others more on behaviour that is in some way unusual, novel, bizarre or antisocial, than on behaviour which is expected or conventional; the former seems to provide more information about what the person is like, largely because when we behave unconventionally we are more likely to be ostracized, shunned or disapproved of.

For example, since we are expected to dress soberly, look sad and talk respectfully of the person who has died at a funeral, when we see people behaving in this way we can easily attribute their behaviour to the situation ('that's how one acts at funerals'); but if somebody arrives in brightly-coloured clothes, making jokes and saying what a lout the deceased was, they are 'breaking the rules', their behaviour needs explaining and is likely to be attributed to characteristics of the person who is acting in this socially undesirable way.

This was demonstrated in an experiment by Jones, Davis and Gergen (1961) in which subjects listened to a tape-recording of a job interview where the applicant was, supposedly, applying to be an astronaut or a submariner. Prior to hearing the tape, subjects were informed of the ideal qualities for the job: astronauts should be inner-directed and able to exist without social interaction, while submariners should be other-directed and gregarious—and the subjects believed that the candidates also understood these ideal qualities.

The tape presented the candidate as behaving either in accordance with these qualities, or in the opposite way, and subjects had to give their impressions of the candidate. When the candidate behaved in the opposite way, subjects more confidently rated the candidate as actually being like that, compared with subjects who heard a 'conforming' candidate.

iii) *Roles* refer to another kind of conformity: when people in well-defined roles behave as they are expected to, this tells us relatively little about their underlying dispositions (they are 'just doing their job'). But when they display out-of-role behaviour, we can use their actions to infer 'what they are really like'.

iv) *Prior expectations* are based on past experiences with the same actor. The better we know someone, the better placed we are to decide whether their behaviour on a particular occasion is 'typical' or not and if it is 'atypical', we are more likely to dismiss it or play down its significance or explain it in terms of situational factors.

Kelley's Co-variation Model (1967)

Also based on Heider's early work, Harold Kelley has investigated the attribution process, concentrating on how we make judgements about internal and external causes. His co-variation model is intended to explain causes where we have knowledge of how the person being studied usually behaves in a variety of situations and how others usually behave in those situations. The principle of co-variation states that, 'an effect is attributed to one of its possible causes with which, over time, it co-varies'; that is, if two events repeatedly occur together, we are more likely to infer that they are causally related than if they very rarely occur together. If the behaviour to be explained is thought of as an effect, the cause can be one of three kinds and the extent to which the behaviour co-varies with each of these three kinds of possible cause is what we base our attribution upon. So what are the three kinds of causal information which Kelley identifies?

To explain this, we will take the hypothetical example of a student, called Sally, who is late for her psychology class:

Consensus refers to the extent to which other people behave in the same way, ie are other students late for psychology class? If all (or most) other students are late then we have *high* consensus, but if Sally is the only one, we have *low* consensus.

Distinctiveness refers to the extent to which Sally behaves in a similar way towards other, similar, 'stimuli' or 'entities', i.e. is Sally late for other subjects? If she is, then we have *low* distinctiveness, but if she is only late for psychology, then we have *high* distinctiveness.

Consistency refers to how stable Sally's behaviour is over time and place, ie is Sally late in all sorts of contexts, in and out of college? If she is, we have *high* consistency, if she is not, then consistency is *low*.

Kelley believes that a combination of low consensus (Sally is the only one late), low distinctiveness (she is late for all her subjects), and high consistency (she is late for dates as well as college), will lead us to make a *person* attribution, that is, the cause of Sally's behaviour is 'inside' Sally, she is a poor time-keeper. However, any other combination would normally result in an *external* attribution, eg if Sally is generally punctual (low consistency), or if most students are late for psychology (high consensus), then the cause of Sally's lateness might be the subject, or the teacher, or both.

Is there any empirical support for Kelley? Although there is some support for the co-variation model (eg Ferguson and Wells, 1980, McArthur, 1972, Zuckerman, 1978), there is also a number of qualifications that need to be made. Firstly, not all three types of causal information are used to the same extent by subjects in laboratory studies; for example, Kruglanski (1977) found that consistency is preferred to distinctiveness, and both of these are preferred to consensus (Kruglanski, 1978, Major, 1980). Secondly, when given the opportunity, subjects seek additional information about the actor (eg personality) or about the situation (eg norms) as opposed to the types of information suggested by the co-variation model (Garland et al, 1975).

Thirdly, and perhaps most seriously, Kelley seems to have over-estimated people's ability to assess co-variation. He originally compared the social perceiver to a naïve scientist, trying to draw inferences in much the same way as the formal scientist draws conclusions from data; more significantly, it is a *normative* model, which states how, *ideally*, people should come to draw inferences about the behaviour of others. However, the actual procedures that people adopt when inferring causality seem to fall short of this idealized picture—we are not as logical, rational and systematic as the model suggests.

More recently, Kelley (1972, 1973) has offered an alternative model which is meant to cover those situations (perhaps the majority) in which we do not have information about consensus, distinctiveness and consistency; indeed, often the only information we have is a single occurrence of the behaviour of a particular individual. In such cases, we must rely on what Kelley calls *causal schemata*, which are general ideas about 'how certain kinds of causes interact to produce a specific kind of effect' (Kelley, 1972). Fiske and Taylor (1984) argue that causal schemata provide the social perceiver with a 'causal shorthand' for accomplishing complex inferences quickly and easily. They are based on our experience of cause-effect relationships, and what we have been taught by others about such relationships, and they come into play when causal information is otherwise ambiguous and incomplete.

The two major kinds of causal schemata are: (i) Multiple Necessary Causes; and (ii) Multiple Sufficient Causes. Experience tells us that, for example, to win a marathon, you must not only be fit and highly motivated, but you must have trained hard for several months beforehand, you must wear the right kind of running shoes, and so on. Only if all these causes are present is success guaranteed and the absence of any one of them is likely to produce failure; so, in this sense, success is more informative than failure. This is an example of *multiple necessary causes*.

In the case of *multiple sufficient causes*, any one of several causes is sufficient to produce a particular outcome. For example, a film star or sporting personality might promote a particular brand of coffee or aftershave either because they genuinely believe in the product or because of the fee—either is a sufficient cause. As Lloyd et al (1984) argue, it is reasonable to assume that it is the fee which accounts for the appearance in the commercial, in which case we discount the other cause (that they 'believe' in the product) according to the *discounting principle* (Kelley 1973).

Sources of Error and Bias in the Attribution Process

We have already seen that perceivers do not always infer causes as prescribed by Kelley's co-variation model; for example, research into sources of error and bias seems to provide a more accurate account of how people actually make causal attributions than the normative models which are commonly used to assess their accuracy.

a)   The Fundamental Attribution Error

Even though almost all behaviour is the product of *both* the person and the situation, our causal explanations tend to emphasize one or the other. Why should this be?

According to Jones and Nisbett (1971), a possible answer is that it is part of human nature to act in this way: we all want to see ourselves as competent observers and interpreters of human behaviour, and to achieve this end we naïvely assume that simple explanations are better than complex ones. To try to analyse the interactions between personal and situational factors would take time and energy, and usually (as we have seen) we seldom have all the relevant information anyway. The *fundamental attribution error* refers to the tendency to attribute behaviour to a person's dispositional qualities (ie *internal* causes) as opposed to situational factors (Heider, 1958, Jones and McGillis, 1976) and this seems to be true even when the actor has been assigned to a role or coerced into behaving in a particular way (eg Jones et al, 1971, Miller et al, 1981).

Why should this happen? In relation to Jones and Nisbett's suggestion that we prefer simple to complex explanations, the preference for internal causes could be understood in terms of making the behaviour of others more predictable which, in turn, enhances our sense of control over the environment as well as making us feel more competent observers.

Heider (1958) believed that behaviour represents the 'figure' against the 'ground', comprised of context, roles, situational pressures and so on, that is, behaviour is conspicuous and situational factors are (comparatively) less easily perceived.

Yet under some conditions, people over-emphasize the role of situation factors. For example, Kulik (1983) found over-attribution to the situation when an actor's behaviour is inconsistent with prior expectations about their dispositions and Quattrone (1982) found the same effect when people's attention is focussed on situational factors.

For these reasons, Fiske and Taylor (1984) suggest that we should call the Fundamental Attribution 'Error' a 'bias' instead.

b)   *The Actor-Observer Effect*

Related to the Fundamental Attribution Error is the tendency for actors and observers to make different attributions about the same event. The actor usually sees their own behaviour as primarily a response to the situation and so quite variable from situation to situation (the cause is external), while the observer typically attributes the *same* behaviour to the actor's intentions and dispositions and so quite consistent across situations (the cause is internal). (The observer's attribution to internal causes is, of course, the Fundamental Attribution Error.)

Take the example of a man entering a room full of people, tripping up and spilling his drink; the others will probably be more aware of the behaviour itself, and so judge him to be a 'clumsy clot', while the unfortunate person himself will be more aware of the uneven carpet or the slippery glass. So what is perceptually salient or vivid for the actor (the carpet or the glass) is not what is perceptually salient or vivid for the observer (the tripping and spilling of the drink).

c)   *Self-serving Attributional Bias*

Of course, no one wants to admit to being clumsy, so we are more likely to 'blame' tripping over on something external to ourselves; but we are quite happy to take the credit for our successes. This is referred to as Self-serving Attributional Bias. There is some evidence that positively valued outcomes (eg altriusm) are more often attributed to people, and negatively valued outcomes (eg being late) to situational factors, regardless of who committed them (Tillman and Carver, 1980). However, when either the self or someone closely associated with the self has committed the action, credit for positive events (*self-enhancing bias*) and denial of responsibility for negative ones (*self-protecting bias*) are even stronger (Taylor and Koivumaki, 1976).

An interesting exception to this general rule is the case of very depressed people; Abramson et al (1978) found that they tend to explain their failures in terms of their own inadequacies and their successes more in terms of external factors, such as luck and chance.

The Importance of the Consequences
The more serious the *consequences* of the actor's behaviour, the more likely the Fundamental Attribution Error is to be made: the more serious the outcome, the more likely we are to judge the actor as responsible, regardless of the perceived intentions of the actor.

For example, Walster (1966) gave subjects an account of a car accident in which a young man's car had been left at the top of a hill and then rolled down backwards. One group was told that very little damage was done to the car and no other vehicle was involved; a second group was told that it collided with another car, causing some damage; while a third group was told that the car crashed into a shop, injuring the shopkeeper and a small child. When they had to assess how responsible the car owner was, the third group found him more 'guilty' or morally culpable than the second group, and the second group found him more guilty than the first.

Similarly, Chaikin and Darley (1973) found that if someone spills ink over a large and expensive book, subjects are more likely to hold the person responsible than if it is spilt over a newspaper. Another facet of the consequences of behaviour is how these consequences affect us personally (*personal* or *hedonic relevance*): the more they affect us (the greater the hedonic relevance), the more likely we are to hold the actor responsible. For example, if someone spills ink over *our* large and expensive book, the more likely we are to blame them than if the book belonged to somebody else.

Jones and Charms (1957) got subjects to participate in an experiment where small groups were engaged in a problem-solving task. In each group was a stooge who behaved quite incompetently at the task; half the subjects in each group were told they would receive prize money based on their individual performance, while the other half were told they would be rewarded according to the group's performance (so if one member failed they would all fail to receive any prize money). Afterwards, each subject had to rate all the other group members: the stooge was rated more negatively if he prevented the subjects from receiving prize money (ie if his behaviour had hedonic relevance for them) even though he behaved identically under both conditions.

Going one step further than hedonic relevance is *personalism*, which is the perceiver's belief that the actor *intended* to harm the perceiver; in terms of Jones and Davis's model (see page 208), this increases the making of a correspondent inference.

The Fallacy of Representative Behaviour
Finally, Nisbett and Ross (1980) have pointed out that one of the commonest traps we fall into is assuming that behaviour is much more representative

than it actually is of the actor's 'repertoire'. This means that distinctiveness is under-estimated and consistency is over-estimated, resulting in an increase in the tendency to attribute internal causes to behaviour.

Implicit Personality Theory: Stereotyping

Having decided whether an action tells us something about the actor (internal attribution) rather than something about the stimulus or context (external attribution), we usually go on to make further inferences about the actor which go well beyond the 'evidence' (ie the person's behaviour).

As we saw earlier, we all have 'implicit' theories about what makes people 'tick' and one kind of implicit theory is to do with how personality is structured, and what traits tend to go together or cluster; these particular theories are known as stereotypes. The term was coined by Walter Lippmann (1922); he defined it as a schema (a mental map or picture in our head) which associates a set of personality traits with members of a particular group (group stereotype) or a schema which associates a set of personality traits as belonging together in a particular individual (individual stereotype). (Most definitions (and most of the research) have been aimed at group stereotypes but we shall discuss both types.)

Tagiuri (1969) defined stereotyping as, 'the general inclination to place a person in categories according to some easily and quickly identifiable characteristic such as age, sex, ethnic membership, nationality or occupation, and then to attribute to him qualities believed to be typical to members of that category'. Judy Gahagan (1984) defines stereotypes as beliefs about the characteristics possessed by some group and possessed, therefore, by any member of that group.

Individual Stereotypes

Our names are a part of the central core of our self-image, and names can sometimes form the basis for being stereotyped, which, in turn, lead us to expect certain kinds of behaviour from people. Harari and McDavid (1973) pointed out that first names, like surnames, are often associated with particular characteristics, partly determined by the media (eg the hero and heroine are often called Stephen and Elizabeth, and the villains and fall guys Elmer and Bertha).

Experienced teachers were asked to evaluate a set of short essays, written by eleven-year-olds who were identified by first name only. Some essays were randomly associated with four names stereotyped by the teachers as attractive and favourable (David, Michael, Karen and Lisa) and four stereotyped as unattractive and unfavourable (Elmer, Hubert, Bertha and Adelle). Although the same essays were associated with different names for different teachers, those by 'attractive' names were graded a full letter grade higher than those by 'unattractive' names, and, significantly, the effect was stronger with boys' names than with girls'.

Wiggin et al (1969) presented subjects with details concerning a hypothetical person (background, social status, school achievement, emotional stability, etc) all except his IQ, and then asked them to estimate it. Two-thirds used his vocabulary and academic achievement as the main indicators of his intelligence, but a substantial minority used social status or industriousness, and one even used emotional stability, as the sole criterion of high intelligence. We can say from this that different subjects had different implicit personality theories concerning which characteristics are associated with intelligence.

Another kind of individual stereotype involves inferring what somebody is like psychologically from certain aspects of their physical appearance. Allport pointed to popular stereotypes of this kind, such as the totally unfounded beliefs that fat people are jolly, high foreheads are a sign of superior intelligence, eyes too close together is a sign of untrustworthiness, and redheads have fiery tempers.

Gibbins et al (1969) showed women subjects a series of photographs of fashion models wearing different dresses. The women were immediately willing to provide extensive accounts of each model's personality, level of education, morality, hobbies and so on. Similarly, Dion et al (1972) found that photos of attractive people are consistently credited with more desirable qualities—more intelligent, more moral, better adjusted, warmer, more poised, more sexually responsive, happier and more successful. (This is an example of a positive halo effect.)

Berscheid and Walster (1974) also found that physically attractive people are perceived as happier, nicer and more competent than physically unattractive people. However, it is possible to be 'too attractive for your own good'. Dermer and Thiel (1975) found that very attractive women were judged as being egotistic, vain, materialistic, snobbish and less likely to be successfully married. it also seems that physical size in men works in a very similar way to physical attractiveness (especially facial) in women—tall men (with a good physique) are often seen as having more desirable qualities and being of higher status, than smaller, shorter, fatter or skinnier men. (See Chapter 10.)

Clearly, our readiness to attribute characteristics to photos of people on the basis of their physical appearance is related to our stereotypes of males and females generally; the above findings suggest that we have a generalized notion of what defines attractiveness in men and women and then apply this to particular cases. So a tall woman would be perceived differently from a short woman and a tall man—in all three cases, their psychological characteristics are equally 'hidden', but we are usually prepared to describe them very differently based on what we believe makes a man or woman attractive. This represents a kind of interaction between individual and group stereotypes, to which we now turn.

Group Stereotypes

The basis for applying group stereotypes is similar to that for individual stereotypes: we may infer what qualities a person possesses either by being told what group they belong to (homosexual, Turk, Jew etc.) or by observing their physical appearance and using one (or more) of these 'clues' to categorize them as belonging to a particular group (policeman, punk, 'old person' etc.).

Essentially, a group stereotype is an over-generalization about what characteristics are shared by *all* members of a group; in reality, it is impossible for every single member of a group to share even one psychological characteristic. Why should every person with, say, a particular skin colour, have the same (or even similar) personality traits?

But according to Allport (1954), most stereotypes do contain a 'grain of truth'. Clearly, the degree of generalization involved is too great to make a stereotype factually true; no group is completely homogeneous and individual differences are the norm. But it may represent the 'best guess' in the absence of any other information.

The process of stereotyping itself involves the following reasoning; (i) we assign someone to a particular group (eg on the basis of their physical appearance); (ii) we bring into play the belief that all members of the group share certain characteristics (the stereotype); (iii) we infer that this particular individual must possess these characteristics.

What evidence is there that people do actually apply group stereotypes? Karr (1975/8) found that homosexual males are usually rated as being more tense, shallow, yielding, impulsive, passive and quiet than men labelled as heterosexual; they are also rated less honest, fair, healthy, valuable, stable, intellectual, friendly and clean as a result of their homosexuality.

The basic method of studying ethnic stereotypes is that used by Katz and Braly (1933) in one of the best known and earliest studies of its kind. One hundred undergraduates at Princeton University in America were presented with a list of ethnic groups (Americans, Jews, Negroes, Turks, Germans, Chinese, Irish, English, Italians and Japanese) and 84 words describing personality. They were asked to list, for each ethnic group, the five or six traits most characteristic of that group. The aim was to find out whether traditional social stereotypes (as typically portrayed in papers and magazines) were actually held by Princeton students. The result showed that, in fact, they showed considerable agreement, especially about derogatory traits. One of the rather disturbing aspects of the findings was that most of the students had no personal contact with any members of most of the ethnic groups they had to rate; presumably, they had absorbed the images of those groups prevalent in the media.

In 1951, Gilbert studied another sample of Princeton students and this time there was less uniformity of agreement (especially about unfavourable traits) than in the 1933 study. Many expressed great irritation at being asked to make generalizations at all.

In 1967, Karlins, Coffman and Walters repeated the study. Again many students objected to doing the task but there was greater agreement on the traits they did assign compared with the 1951 study. There seemed to be a re-emergence of social stereotyping but in the direction of a more favourable stereotypical image.

Another feature of stereotyping is that it can influence how we interpret and classify behaviour we have observed and, in turn, how we recall that behaviour, ie it can determine what we select to notice in the first place and hence what we later remember. Clearly, this has great relevance to eye-witness testimony, that is, what witnesses say about a crime or accident they have witnessed. (See Chapter 6.)

Duncan (1976) showed subjects a video of a discussion between two males and told them it was a 'live' interaction over closed circuit television; they had to classify various pieces of behaviour. At one point, the discussion became heated and one actor gave the other a shove—the screen then went blank. Duncan wanted to see how subjects classified the shove, and they could choose from 'playing around', 'dramatizing', 'aggressive behaviour' and 'violent behaviour'. Subjects saw a version of the same film which differed only in the race of the two actors, either two whites, two blacks, a white who shoved a black, or a black who shoved a white. Many more subjects classified the black man's shove as violent behaviour, especially if he shoved a white man!

Rothbart et al (1979) found that people often recall better those facts that support their stereotypes (a case of selective remembering); and Howard and Rothbart (1980) found that people have better recall of facts which are critical of the minority than facts which are favourable (a case of negative memory bias). These findings help to explain why prejudices tend to remain fairly stable over time (although stereotypes represent only one component of prejudice—the cognitive or 'belief' component).

Stereotypes may also result in polarized judgements, that is, the tendency to exaggerate the significance of a trait if it does not fit our stereotype of a certain ethnic or other group. Rubovits and Maehr (1973) gave 66 white female student teachers descriptions of 264 children (both black and white) whom they would be meeting—they were described as either 'gifted' or 'non-gifted' and these false descriptions were allocated randomly. When they did meet, less attention was given to the black children and they were criticized more often than the whites. Those who received the best treatment were the 'gifted' white children, but the 'gifted' black children were treated *worse* than the 'non-gifted' blacks (and, therefore, worst of all). Was this because 'giftedness' did not coincide with the stereotype of a black child?

Similarly, Linville and Jones (1980) gave subjects written descriptions of applications to law school. One group was told that one particularly impressive applicant was black; another group was told that the same applicant was white. Subjects judged the black applicant far more positively than the white—it made him seem all the more exceptional and, therefore, all the more impressive. When the situation was repeated with a particularly poor applicant, the black was judged far more harshly—it made him seem all the more typical and, therefore, unimpressive. Similar results were found when men judged female applicants.

Stereotypes and Behaviour

Our expectations of people's personalities or capabilities may influence the way we actually treat them, which in turn may influence their behaviour in such a way that our expectation is confirmed. This is known as the *self-fulfilling prophecy* and is an illustration of how stereotypes can (although unwittingly) influence our behaviour, and not just our perception and memory.

The children in the Rubovits and Maehr study could, over a period of time, have developed the high or low self-esteem or self-confidence which might have influenced their academic performance in the direction predicted or expected by the teachers. As we shall see in Chapter 9, the reactions of others can become a part of our own self-concept and this will be reflected in our actual behaviour. This is particularly dangerous in relation to racial and sexual discrimination; for example, poor housing and education can produce low self-esteem, poor academic achievement, laziness and so on, which are then taken as justification of the continued provision of poor housing and education.

Denzin (1968) tested the hypothesis that the more favourable a patient's attitude towards psychiatric hospitals and treatment (as assessed by the psychiatrist), the more favourable the prognosis, the more therapy the patient would receive and the sooner they would leave the hospital—the hypothesis was confirmed.

Meichenbaum et al (1969) selected 6 girls out of a class of 14 adolescents in a school for juvenile offenders, and their teachers were told they had high academic potential and were late developers. Observers' ratings showed subsequent differences in the teachers' behaviour towards those girls and on later objective examinations the six girls (matched with others on actual potential, classroom behaviour and the amount of attention normally received from teachers) performed significantly better. The teachers' expectations had actually influenced their behaviour towards the 'late developers' which had then influenced the girls' performances.

Finally, according to Campbell (1967) stereotypes can produce serious social problems. They involve : (a) the over-estimation of differences between groups, making groups appear vastly more different from each other than they really are; (b) the underestimation of variations within a group, since they regard groups as homogeneous, that is, every single member of the group is the same; (c) distortions of reality, since, like all generalizations, they appear to be factually true; and (d) so long as the stereotype is in the forefront of consciousness, the individual never has to question it or examine the reasons underlying it—the stereotype can then, through the self-fulfilling prophecy, be used to justify hostility, discrimination and oppression.

9

Self-Concept

When you look into the mirror at your face, you are both the person who is looking and that which is being looked at. In a less tangible or concrete way, when you think about the kind of person you are, or something you have done, you are both the person doing the thinking and what is being thought about. In other words, you are both *subject* (the thinker or looker) and *object* (what is being looked at or thought about). We use the personal pronoun 'I' to refer to us as subject and 'me' to refer to us as object and this represents a rather special relationship that we have with ourselves, namely *self-consciousness* or *self-awareness*.

While other animal species have consciousness (ie they have sensations of cold, heat, hunger, thirst, and can feel pleasure, pain, fear, sexual arousal etc.), only humans have self-consciousness. The term 'self-conscious' is often used to mean embarrassment or shyness and certainly we do feel like this in situations where we are made to feel object-like, or exposed in some way, eg if we get on the bus in the morning to discover we are wearing odd socks or have our sweater on back-to-front. But this is a secondary meaning – the primary meaning refers to this unique relationship whereby the same person, the same *self*, is both subject and object, knower and known, thinker and thought about, seer and seen etc.

Dobzhansky (1967), an eminent geneticist, claims that self-awareness is a fundamental characteristic and evolutionary novelty of humans as a species.

What is the Self?

There are many definitions of self as it is a term that is very difficult to define in any precise way. Also, as we shall see, there are many 'self' terms which are often used interchangeably but which have fairly distinct meanings (eg 'self-image', 'self-esteem', 'ideal self', 'self-identity'). 'Self' and 'self-concept' are used interchangeably to refer to an individual's overall self-awareness. According to Murphy (1947), 'the self is the individual as known to the individual', and Burns (1980) defines it as, 'the set of attitudes a person holds towards himself'.

Certainly, in our everyday interactions with others, it is a great advantage to know something about their self-concept, since this makes their behaviour both more understandable and more predictable. When we say we know someone well, part of what we mean is that we know what they think of themselves; behaviour that is apparently the same may have two different meanings if performed by two individuals with different self-concepts. For example, if two children both choose very difficult problems to solve instead of easier ones, it could reflect the genuine self-confidence of one child, while for the other child it could be a defence against fear of failing at easier problems (since the child could not be criticized for failing on very difficult ones). So we cannot fully understand a person's behaviour unless we also understand what that behaviour means for the person.

Components of the Self-Concept

The self-concept is a general term that refers to three major components: (i) self-image; (ii) self-esteem; (iii) ideal-self.

Self-Image (or Ego Identity)
This refers to the way in which we would describe ourselves, the kind of person we think we are (whether we like what we are or not). One way of investigating self-image is to ask people to answer the question, 'Who am I?' 20 times (Kuhn 1960), which, typically, produces two main categories of answers—social roles and personality traits. Social roles are usually quite objective aspects of our self-image (eg son, daughter, brother, sister, student etc), they are 'facts' and can be verified by others. Personality traits, on the other hand, are more a matter of opinion and judgement and what we think we are like may be different from how others see us (eg we may think we are quite friendly but others may see us as cold or a little aloof). But, as we said earlier, the better we know someone, the more we know how they see themselves and so the more likely it is that our perception of them and their perception of themselves coincide.

As well as social roles and personality traits, people often make reference to their physical characteristics in response to the 'who am I?' question, such as tall, short, fat, thin, blue-eyed, brown-haired etc. These are part of our *body image* or *bodily self*, the bodily *me*, which also includes bodily sensations (usually temporary states) of pain, cold, hunger and so on.

A more permanent feature of our body-image is concerned with what we count as part of our body (and hence belonging to *us*) and what we do not. Gordon Allport (1955), a very eminent self-theorist, gives two rather dramatic and vivid examples of how intimate our bodily sense is and just where we draw the boundaries between 'me' and 'not me':

a)   Imagine swallowing your saliva—or actually do it! Now imagine spitting it into a cup and drinking it! Clearly, once we have spat out our saliva, we have disowned it—it no longer belongs to us.

b)   Imagine sucking blood from a cut in your finger (something we do quite automatically, assuming the cut is relatively slight). Now imagine sucking the blood from a plaster on your finger! Again, once it has soaked into the plaster it has ceased to be part of ourselves.

Interestingly this rule does not always apply; for example, we might feel we have lost part of ourselves when we have very long hair cut off and lovers often keep a lock of each other's hair as a constant (and tangible) reminder that the other exists.

Clearly, whenever our body changes in some way, so our body-image changes. In extreme cases, where a limb is lost, or the person is scarred due to an accident, or undergoes cosmetic surgery to, say, change the shape of their nose, we would expect a correspondingly dramatic change in body-image, sometimes favourable, sometimes not.

But throughout our lives, as part of the normal process of maturation and ageing, we all experience growth spurts, changes in height, weight and the general appearance and 'feel' of our body, and each time we have to make an adjustment to our body-image. In Chapter 23 we shall look at puberty and how the bodily changes involved affect the adolescent's body-image and, hence, their self-concept; and in Chapter 24 we shall be discussing how the physical (as well as the social and intellectual) changes involved in ageing can influence the self-image of the ageing individual.

Another fundamental aspect of body-image is to do with our biological sex. As we will see in Chapter 22, gender is the social equivalent or the social interpretation of sex, and our gender, or gender identity, is another part of the central core of our self-image.

Other aspects of the central core include our name, age, occupation and race or ethnic group. Some of these will be more salient or relevant at certain times and in particular situations; for example, we will be very conscious of our gender if we are the only male in an otherwise all-female group, and very aware of our race if we are the only minority person in our group. A study by McGuire et al (1978) found that six to twelve year-olds whose ethnic group was the minority in their school all spontaneously mentioned it as part of their self-concept. Taking this a step further, there are parts of ourselves of which we may be totally unaware, at all times, ie our self-concept (as a whole) may be partly unconscious. We shall return to this theme later in the chapter.

Self-esteem (Self-regard)

While the self-image is essentially descriptive, self-esteem is essentially evaluative: it refers to the extent to which we like and accept or approve of ourselves, how worthwhile a person we think we are. Coopersmith (1967), whose important study of self-esteem we shall be describing in detail later on, defined it as, 'a personal judgement of worthiness, that is expressed in the attitudes the individual holds towards himself'.

How much we like or value ourselves can be an overall judgement or it can relate to specific areas of our lives. For example, we can have a generally high opinion of ourselves and yet not like certain of our characteristics or attributes, such as our wavy or curly hair (when we want it straight) or our lack of assertiveness (when we want to be more assertive). Alternatively, it may be impossible or certainly very difficult to have high overall esteem if we are very badly disfigured or are desperately shy. Again, we may regard ourselves highly as far as our academic abilities are concerned but not think we are 'up to much' when it comes to athletics.

Our self-esteem can be regarded as how we evaluate our self-image, ie how much we like the kind of person we think we are. Clearly, certain characteristics or abilities have a greater value in society generally and so are likely to influence our self-esteem accordingly, for example, being physically attractive as opposed to unattractive. But, of course, there are degrees of attractiveness, and physical appearance will be more important to some individuals than to others.

Also, certain characteristics or abilities will have differing values according to the society we live in or the particular groups we belong to, whether we are male or female, young or old, working class or middle class, and so on. Thus being tall may be an advantage if you are male but not if you are female, being intelligent may have a positive 'loading' if your peer group is academically orientated but not if your peers think that being tough and going out are what matter in life.

Our self-esteem will also be partly determined by how much our self-image differs from our ideal-self, the third component of the self-concept.

Ideal-self (Ego Ideal or Idealized Self-image)
If our self-image is the kind of person we think we are, then our ideal-self is the kind of person we would like to be. Again, this can vary in extent and degree—we may want to be different in certain respects or we may want to be a totally different person. (We may even wish we were someone else!)

We might be very dissatisfied with what we are like and want to be different for this reason, or we may basically like ourselves and want to develop and extend ourselves along essentially the same lines.

Generally, the greater the gap between our self-image and our ideal-self, the lower our self-esteem. We shall discuss this relationship between self-image and ideal-self in more detail when examining Rogers's (1959) theory of self, later in the chapter.

Theories of Self

C. H. Cooley and G. H. Mead
One of the earliest and most influential theories of self was propounded by Mead (1934) who was influenced both by James's distinction between 'I' (self as knower) and 'Me' (self as known) and by Cooley's (1902) theory of the 'looking-glass self'.

Cooley's theory maintains that the self is reflected in the reactions of other people, who are the 'looking-glass' for oneself, ie in order to understand what we are like, we need to see how others see us, and this is how the child gradually builds up an impression of what it is like. At first, the infant is not aware of self and others and makes no distinction between 'me' and 'not me'; it simply experiences a 'stream of impressions' which gradually become integrated and discriminated so that the distinction is finally made.

Mead also believed that knowledge of self and others develops simultaneously, both being dependent on social interaction; self and society represent a common whole and neither can exist without the other. According to Mead, the human being is an organism with a self and this converts him into a special kind of actor, transforms his relation to the world and gives his actions a unique character. The human being is an object to himself, that is, he can perceive himself, have conceptions about himself, communicate with himself and so on; in summary, he can interact with himself (address himself, respond to the address and address himself anew). This self-interaction is a great influence upon his transactions with the world in general and with other people in particular.

Mead stresses that the self is a *process* and not a structure (it is not equivalent, for example, to Freud's ego, nor is it an organized body of needs and motives, nor a collection of attitudes, norms and values). What makes a self what it is, is a *reflexive* process, whereby it acts upon and responds to itself. (This is Mead's way of making the 'I'/'Me' distinction—the experiencing 'I' cannot be an object, it cannot itself be experienced, since it is the very act of experiencing; what we experience and interact with is our 'me'.)

Self-interaction means that the person ceases to be a mere responder, whose behaviour is the product of what acts upon him from outside, or inside, or both; instead, he acts towards his world, interprets what he encounters and organizes his actions on the basis of this interpretation. Mead says the person is 'over against' their world and not merely 'in' it, they define their world rather than merely responding to it and construct their action rather than merely 'releasing' it.

An important feature of interaction is language, which represents a fundamental means by which we come to represent ourselves to ourselves (and which, according to Mead, is more powerful than non-verbal communication, eg gestures, facial expressions and body posture). This, together with our learning to regard ourselves from the point of view of others, determines our self-concept.

Initially, the child thinks about his conduct as 'good or bad only as he reacts to his own acts in the remembered words of his parents'; 'me' at this stage is a combination of the child's memory of his own actions and the kind of reaction they received.

In the next stage, the child's pretend play, in particular 'playing at mummies and daddies', or 'doctors or nurses', helps the child to understand and incorporate adult attitudes and behaviour. Here, the child is not merely imitating but also 'calls out in himself the same response as he calls out in the other', that is, he is being, say, the child *and* the parent, and, as the parent, is responding to himself as the child. So, in playing with a doll, the child 'responds in tone of voice and in attitudes as his parents respond to his cries and chortles'.

In this way, the child acquires a variety of social viewpoints or 'perspectives' (mother, father, nurse, doctor etc.) which are then used to accompany, direct and evaluate its own behaviour. This is how the socialized part of the self (Mead's 'me') expands and develops. At first, these viewpoints or perspectives are based upon specific adults, but in time, the child comes to react to itself and its behaviour from the viewpoint of a 'typical mother', a 'typical nurse' or 'people in general'; Mead called those the perspectives of 'generalized others' and the incorporation of the generalized other marks the final, qualitative change in 'the me'. To quote Mead again, 'it is this generalized other in his experience which provides him with a self'.

Grammatically, our 'me' is third person (like 'she' or 'he') and it is an image of self seen from the perspective of a judgemental, non-participant observer. By its very nature, 'me' is social, because it grows out of this role-playing, whereby the child is being the other person.

Carl Rogers (1959)

Carl Rogers is one of the leading Humanistic or Phenomenological psychologists who, as mentioned in Chapter 1, reject both the Psychoanalytic and the Behaviourist (or Stimulus-Response) approaches. They emphasize the individual's uniqueness and freedom to choose a particular course of action in contrast to the rather deterministic nature of both psychoanalysis and behaviourism—behaviour is *not* a response to unconscious forces (Freud) or to external stimuli (S-R theory) but to the individual's perception, interpretation and comprehension of external stimuli. Since no one else can know our perception, we are the best experts on ourselves.

Related to this emphasis on how we perceive and interpret reality is the importance of a person's current, moment-to-moment experience, what we are thinking and feeling *now*, in contrast to Freud's belief that our present behaviour is largely determined by our past, in the form of repressed childhood experiences. Freud also believed that human nature is fundamentally destructive and irrational and he took a very pessimistic view of human beings. Rogers, on the other hand, sees human nature in a very positive and optimistic light: 'there is no beast in man; there is only man in man'.

The forces that direct behaviour reside within us and when social conditions do not block or distort them, these forces direct us towards *self-actualization*, which Rogers defines as, 'the inherent tendency of the organism to develop all its capacities in ways which serve to maintain or enhance the organism'. Like the other major humanistic psychologist, Abraham Maslow, Rogers believes that self-actualization is an innate tendency, a basic motivating force which makes us different from other animal species and therefore peculiarly human.

Central to Rogers's theory (and to his form of psychotherapy, known as client-centred therapy) is the concept of self. The self is an 'organized, consistent set of perceptions and beliefs about oneself'. It includes my awareness of 'what I am', 'what I can do', and influences both my perception of the world and my behaviour; we evaluate every experience in terms of it and most human behaviour can be understood as an attempt to maintain consistency between our self-image and our actions.

But this consistency is not always achieved and our self-image (and related self-esteem) may differ quite radically from our actual behaviour and from how others see us. For example, a person may be highly successful and respected by others and yet regard herself as a failure! This would be an example of what Rogers calls *incongruence*—being told you are successful is incongruent or inconsistent with the fact that you do not hold this view of your self. Incongruent experiences, feelings, actions and so on, because they conflict with our (conscious) self-image, and because we prefer to act and feel in ways that are consistent with our self-image, may be threatening and so are denied access to awareness (they may remain *unsymbolized*) through actual denial, distortion or blocking.

These defence mechanisms prevent the self from growing and changing and widen the gulf between our self-image and reality (ie our actual behaviour or our true feelings). As the self-image becomes more and more unrealistic, so the incongruent person becomes more and more confused, vulnerable, dissatisfied, and, eventually, seriously maladjusted.

The self-image of the congruent person is flexible and realistically changes as new experiences occur; the opposite is true of the incongruent person.

When your self-image matches what you really think and feel and do, you are in the best position to realize your potential (self-actualize); the greater the gap between self-image and reality, the greater the likelihood of anxiety and emotional disturbance. Similarly, as we noted earlier, the greater the gap between self-image and ideal-self, the less fulfilled the individual will be.

To show how two different examples of a rigid and inflexible self-image may work, let us suppose that a young man's self-image requires that every woman he meets will find him irresistible and fall head-over-heels in love with him. He meets a woman whom he finds attractive but she shows no interest in him; this represents an incongruence between his self-image and his experience. How does he deal with the threat this represents for him? He might say, 'She's just playing hard to get' or, 'She has no taste' or, 'She must be crazy—thank goodness I found out before she fell hopelessly in love with me'.

Now let us look at the opposite extreme, a young man who believes that he is totally unattractive to women. If an attractive woman shows an interest in him, this will produce incongruence and hence threat and he might deal with it by rationalizing that, 'She's just feeling sorry for me' or he might deliberately do something (eg be rude to her) to sabotage the relationship and so remove the threat.

Of course, most of us will not have such an extreme self-image as either of these two hypothetical young men, whether positive or negative, and most of us are sufficiently flexible and realistic to recognize that just as we are not 'God's gift to the opposite sex' nor are we sexually hopeless; indeed, our self-image regarding our sexual appeal has been learned from our past successes and failures ('you win some, you lose some').

How does our self-concept develop?

Many of Rogers's therapeutic clients had trouble accepting their own feelings and experiences; they seemed to have learned during childhood that in order to obtain the love and acceptance of others (particularly their parents), they had to feel and act in distorted or dishonest ways, ie they had to deny certain parts of themselves. (Rogers calls this *conditional positive regard*.)

This applies, in varying degrees, to almost every child—love and praise are withheld until the child conforms to parental and social standards of conduct. So the child (and later the adult) learns to act and feel in ways that earn approval from others, rather than in ways which may be more intrinsically satisfying and more 'real'. In order to maintain conditional positive regard, we suppress actions and feelings that are unacceptable to others who are important to us (significant others), instead of using our own spontaneous perceptions and feelings as guides to our behaviour. Rogers says that we develop *conditions of worth* (those conditions under which positive regard will be forthcoming) which become internalized—we perceive and are aware of those experiences that coincide with the conditions of worth but distort or deny those that do not. This denial and distortion leads to a distinction between the *organism* and the *self*, whereby the organism is the whole of one's possible experience (everything we do and feel and think) and the self is the recognized, accepted and acknowledged part of a person's experience. Ideally, the two would refer to one and the same thing, but, for most of us, they do not.

Corresponding to the need for positive regard (the universal wish to be loved and accepted by significant others) is the need for *positive self-regard*, the internalization of those values and behaviour of which others approve, so that we think of ourselves as good and lovable and worthy. (This corresponds to high self-esteem, while negative self-regard corresponds to low self-esteem).

In order to experience positive self-regard, our behaviour and experience must match our conditions of worth; the problem here is that this can produce incongruence through the denial of our true thoughts and feelings. But since the need for positive regard and positive self-regard is so strong, these conditions of worth can supersede the values associated with self-actualization. Consequently, we come to behave and think and feel in particular ways because others want us to and many adult adjustment problems are bound up with an attempt to live by other people's standards instead of one's own.

Congruence and self-actualization are enhanced by substituting organismic values for conditions of worth, so that the distinction between the self and organism becomes more and more blurred. The greater the *unconditional positive regard*, the greater the congruence between: (a) self-image and reality; and (b) self-image and ideal-self. It is precisely this unconditional positive regard which the therapist offers the client in Rogers's client-centred therapy, ie the therapist creates an atmosphere of total acceptance and support, regardless of what the client says or does, and which is non-judgemental, so that the client, in turn, comes to accept certain feelings and thoughts as their own, instead of denying, distorting and disowning them (illustrated by such responses as, 'I don't know why I did that' or 'I wasn't feeling myself'). Finally, positive self-regard is no longer dependent upon conditions of worth.

(Rogers has also been responsible for the growth of encounter groups, whereby people who are basically mentally healthy can be helped to grow and develop and achieve self-actualization by interacting with others in a free and unrestricted atmosphere of mutual acceptance.)

Gordon Allport (1955)

Allport wanted to avoid the emotional connotations of terms like 'self' and 'ego' and so he coined the term 'proprium' instead, which, 'includes all aspects of personality that make for inward unity; it refers to the sense of what is peculiarly ours'. For Allport, there are eight major components of the proprium:

i) Bodily Sense We have already discussed this in relation to body-image (which is part of self-image), but a few additional points deserve mention: firstly, Allport says that our bodily sense is heightened during physical exercise, pain, and sensual pleasure; and secondly, he asks us to locate our self physically, ie where do 'you' reside in your body—are you in your heart or somewhere between your eyes or somewhere else?

The answer we give may say a good deal about our self-image and self-concept as a whole.

ii) Self-identity This is also part of self-image and can be broken down into four major aspects:

a) I am a person in my own right, I am an individual (*individuality*);

b) I am a separate person from all others, there is only one me (*uniqueness*);

c) I continue to exist as (a) and (b) above, (*continuity*);

d) I have private, unshareable, experiences (*private experience*).

iii) Ego Enhancement This is equivalent to self-esteem (or self-regard) and refers to self-love, self-respect, wanting to survive, self-assertion, self-satisfaction, pride and so on.

iv) Ego-extension This is also part of our self-image and refers to those things and people (significant others) that are not the individual but which constitute, psychologically, part of the individual and which we call 'mine':

a) Material possessions, especially those which have particular personal and emotional significance;

b) Love-objects, both people (individuals and groups we belong to or would like to belong to) and things, for which we feel great affection and whose loss would cause us great sadness and even grief;

c) Non-material possessions, such as ideals, beliefs, attitudes, values and so on.

v) Rational Agent This refers to the rational, logical, reasoning part of the self (very similar to Freud's ego).

vi) Self-image Allport also refers to this as the phenomenal self which comprises: (a) how I assess my own abilities, status and so on; and (b) my aspirations, ambitions, hopes and so on (which really corresponds to ideal-self or ego-ideal).

vii) Propriate Striving This is concerned with motivation, which is much more than the reduction of tension or the satisfaction of our basic needs. Motivation has a future reference and implies a striving for goals and objectives, planning, problem solving and intention, and includes interests, tendencies, disposition and expectation. Self-actualization would feature here too. (See Chapter 17.)

viii) The Knower The knowing self transcends all these other components of the proprium and is aware of them, as well as recognizing itself as the knower. It corresponds to James's 'I' and is the centre of the proprium, the core around which the other 'propriate functions' gather.

Bannister and Fransella (1980) put forward a working definition of self which overlaps a great deal with Allport's theory. But there are some points that are worth developing a little further.

First, in a fundamental sense, we continue to be the same person throughout our lives: you wake up in the morning and you are the same you who went to bed the night before and who will be going to bed that night. Similarly, you are the same person you were ten years ago and will be the same person in ten years time. Clearly, memory is a vital process involved in this continuing sense of 'I' or 'me', but our ability to think about ourselves continuing into the future suggests that is is neither a necessary nor a sufficient condition of this continuity. (Of course, this is not to deny that we can and do change in certain respects—we develop new skills, let others lapse, become more cynical or less self-confident and so on. But these changes are changes within the same particular individual.)

Secondly, we are *causes* of our own behaviour, in that we have purposes, intentions, motives, reasons and so on, and to acknowledge these is to accept responsibility for the consequences of our actions.

Thirdly, we assume that other people have selves, just as we do—by analogy with ourselves, other people must have comparable, subjective, experiences. Although, of course, these experiences are private, so that we cannot have somebody else's experiences and they cannot have ours, these experiences are nonetheless shareable—mainly through language, spoken and written, but also through art forms, such as painting and sculpture.

Fourthly, we are conscious and have self-awareness. Psychology itself is a direct expression of consciousness, in that it is an attempt to explain and reflect on what people do and experience.

Bannister (1981) also raises the question as to how, and how completely, we know ourselves. We sometimes behave in ways that surprise even ourselves (eg 'I had a second helping so I must have been hungrier than I thought' or, 'I found myself crying at a sentimental film, something I never usually do'), which shows that we cannot predict our behaviour 100 per cent accurately.

Again, not all aspects of ourselves are equally accessible to us; for instance, recollection of our own past can be more or less difficult to get at. An extreme instance is Freud's notion of the unconscious, whereby things of which we may be totally unaware (eg repressed childhood events) may still affect our feeling and behaviour. But we do not have to accept all the details of Freud's theory, only the more general point that we have much more going on inside us than we can name or readily become aware of. A great deal of psychotherapy, as well as individual soul-searching, is aimed at bringing to the surface hitherto unrecognized consistencies in our lives.

As to *how* we get to know ourselves, there seems little doubt that this is a developmental process. Bannister and Agnew (1977) made tape-recordings of groups of children answering a variety of questions about their school, home, favourite games and so on. Test tapes were transcribed and then re-recorded in different voices so as to exclude circumstantial clues (such as name, parents' occupation) as to the identity of the children. Four months after the original recording, the children were asked to identify their own statements, to point out statements that were definitely not theirs and to give reasons for their choice.

The children's ability to recognize their own statements increased steadily with age and the strategies used became more complex: at five, they relied heavily on their (often inaccurate) memory or used simple clues such as whether they themselves participated in the kinds of activity mentioned in the statement; by nine, they were using psychologically more complex methods of identifying which statements they had made and which they had not.

Any theory or attempt to explain how we come to be what we are and how we change, involves us in the question of what kind of evidence we use. Kelly (1955), in a similar vein to Cooley and Mead, believes that we derive our picture of ourselves through the picture we have of other people's picture of us. So the central evidence is the reaction of others to us, both what they say of us and the implications of their behaviour towards us; we filter others' views of us through our view of them. We build up a continuous and changing picture of ourselves out of our interaction with others.

In relation to change, and the fear of change, Fransella (1972) explored the way in which stutterers who seem to be on the verge of a cure, often suddenly relapse. They know how to live as 'stutterers' and understand how people react and relate to them in that role; nearing cure, they are overwhelmed by fear of the unknown and the strangeness of being a fluent speaker, a non-stutterer. (This can probably be extended to other cases where people continue to play familiar roles despite their apparent—or indeed real—suffering and hardship. It is a case of 'better the devil you know . . .'.)

The paradox of self-knowing is that, if I come to learn something about myself, then that knowledge immediately changes me, to some degree or other: we can never be exactly the same again because we know something we did not know before!

Factors Influencing the Development of the Self-Concept

Michael Argyle (1969) believes that there are four major factors which influence the development of the self-concept, namely: (i) the reaction of others; (ii) comparison with others; (iii) social roles; and (iv) identification.

We shall look at each of these in turn.

i) Reaction of Others

We have already seen in the theories of Cooley and Mead how central the reactions of others are in the formulation of our self-concept and there is considerable support.

Many studies have found that self-ratings correlate with ratings by others, but self-ratings are usually more favourable; this represents evidence that the reactions of others do affect our self-image. Videbeck (1960) asked subjects to read poems aloud, some of which were evaluated favourably, others unfavourably, by a supposed speech-expert; self-ratings on the ability to recite poems shifted accordingly, so the more (un)favourable the expert's rating, the more (un)favourable the subject's self-rating. (What is important here is the belief that the other is an expert in an activity where the subject has little experience or expertise.)

Guthrie (1938) told the story of a female student, a dull and unattractive girl. Some of her classmates decided to play a trick on her by pretending she was the most desirable girl in the college and drawing lots to decide who would take her out first, second and so on. By the fifth or sixth date, she was no longer regarded as dull and unattractive—by being treated as attractive, she had, in a sense, *become* attractive (perhaps by wearing different clothes and smiling more etc) and her self-image had clearly changed; for the boys who dated her later, it was no longer a chore! 'Before the year was over, she had developed an easy manner and a confident assumption that she was popular.'

During the pre-school years children are extremely concerned with how adults view them and few things are more relevant than how significant others react to them, that is, parents and older siblings, and other people whose opinions the child values. Strictly speaking, it is the child's perception of others' reactions that makes such an important contribution to how the child comes to perceive itself. After all, the child has no frame of reference for evaluating parental reactions—parents are all-powerful figures as far as the pre-schooler is concerned, so what they say is 'fact' (eg Swift, 1964). If a child is consistently told how beautiful she is, she will come to believe it, it will become part of her self-image; similarly, if a child is repeatedly told how stupid or clumsy he is, this too will become accepted as the 'truth' and the child will tend to act accordingly. The first child is likely to develop high self-esteem, and the second low self-esteem.

Argyle explains this in terms of *introjection* (a process very similar to identification) whereby we come to incorporate into our own personalities the perceptions, attitudes and reactions to ourselves of our parents, and it is through the reactions of others that the child learns its conditions of worth, ie which behaviours will produce positive regard and which will not.

When the child starts school, the number and variety of significant others increases, to include teachers and peers. At the same time, the child's self-image is becoming more differentiated, that is, it has more parts to it, and significant others then become important in relation to different parts of the self-image; for example, the teacher is important as far as the child's academic ability is concerned, parents as far as how lovable the child is, and so on.

A good deal of research has been conducted in connection with self-esteem and the reaction of others and the study by Coopersmith (1967) is one of the most important. He assessed hundreds of nine- and ten-year-old boys for their level of self-esteem by combining their scores on his Self-Esteem Inventory (comprising 58 questions about peers, parents, school and personal interests), with teachers' evaluations of the boys (their reactions to failure, self-confidence in new situations, sociability with peers and need for encouragement and reassurance) and with their scores on the Thematic Apperception Test (TAT), in which the subject is shown a standard series of pictures, in a definite sequence, and is asked to invent a story for each picture. In particular, the subject is asked to say: (i) what events have led up to the situation depicted in the picture; (ii) what the character(s) is (are) thinking and feeling; and (iii) what the outcome will be. The stories can then be analysed for such things as need for achievement and self-esteem.

Of the large original sample, Coopersmith selected five groups, including those who scored high on all three measures of self-esteem and those who scored low on all three measures (17 per group). They were studied in depth, using a variety of tests, and it was found that the high-esteem boys were confident about their own perceptions and judgements, expected to succeed at new tasks and to influence others, and readily expressed their opinions. They were also doing better in school and were more often chosen as friends by other children than the low-esteem boys; they had a realistic view of themselves and their abilities, were not unduly worried by criticism and enjoyed participating in things. By contrast, the low-esteem boys were a 'sad little group', isolated, fearful, reluctant to join in, self-conscious, over-sensitive to criticism, consistently underrated themselves, tended to under-achieve in class and were pre-occupied with their own problems.

Interestingly, there were no measurably significant differences in intelligence or physical attractiveness between the two groups; they were all white and from middle-class homes and were free from any obvious emotional disturbance. So how did Coopersmith account for their differences in self-esteem?

He gave the boys' mothers a questionnaire to complete, gave them in-depth interviews, and the boys were also asked about their parents' child-rearing methods; he found significant differences between the two sets of parents. (see Table 9.1 on the next page.)

The optimum conditions for the development of high self-esteem seem to involve a combination of firm enforcement of limits on the child's behaviour plus a good deal of acceptance of the child's autonomy and freedom within those limits. Firm management helps the child to develop firm inner controls, and a predictable and structured social environment helps the child to deal effectively with the environment and hence to feel 'in control' of the world (rather than controlled by it.) Clear and firmly enforced rules help the child to establish clear self-definitions—the child is forced to acknowledge powers outside itself and to recognize the needs and rights of others, thereby learning to distinguish between wish and reality, self and others, me and not-me. Also, parental restrictions (although sometimes frustrating) prove to the child that they are concerned about its welfare.

Coopersmith followed the boys through into adulthood and found that the high-esteem boys consistently out-performed the low-esteem boys and proved more successful educationally and vocationally.

But we must be careful not to infer from Coopersmith's findings that certain kinds of child-rearing methods actually produce different levels of self-esteem in the child. Coopersmith's data are only correlational, that is, he found an association between the two variables, and so we cannot be sure that one is the cause of the other. Remember, too, that his subjects were white middle-class boys and therefore were not representative of the American population as a whole—what about working-class, black and female children?

Research has shown that, generally, working-class children suffer from lower self-esteem, as do delinquent groups; the latter's 'toughness' and antisocial behaviour are often an attempt to protect self-esteem by demonstrating their power to destroy what society values and so to prove that they do matter after all.

Lang (1969) reviewed 13 studies of black high- and low-achievers (four to sixteen-year-olds) and singled out self-esteem as an important factor separating the two groups. Confidence and a sense of personal control help minority students to do well in school.

Girls, generally, have lower self-esteem than boys. For instance, when paired with boys in problem-solving tasks, they sometimes artificially depress their performance so as not to outshine their male partners (boys very rarely do this!). Some girls seem to feel uncomfortable in the superior role, as if this is inconsistent with their 'true' position in life. (See Chapter 17.) They also tend to rate themselves less highly than boys on written tests of self-esteem, set themselves lower goals in life and are more inclined to underestimate their abilities than boys even in primary school, where in reading and language skills they often tend to surpass boys.

However, Sears (1970), studying boys and girls, confirmed Coopersmith's results for boys—but not for girls; children with at least one warm and accepting parent had higher self-esteem than children with cold and unaccepting parents.

An interesting contrast with the parents of high-esteem boys in Coopersmith's and Sear's studies is the study of interaction between parents

Table 9.1 The main characteristics of parents in Coopersmith's 1967 study of self-esteem

PARENTS OF HIGH-ESTEEM BOYS	PARENTS OF LOW-ESTEEM BOYS
1. Also had high self-esteem.	(No corresponding findings)
2. Were emotionally stable, self-reliant and resilient.	(No corresponding findings)
3. Had clear definitions of each parent's areas of authority and responsibility.	(No corresponding findings)
4. Had high expectations of their children but also provided sound models for them and gave consistent encouragement and support.	4. Seemed unclear what their standards and expectations for their children were and so could not enforce them in any systematic way.
5. Regarded their children as important and interesting people and respected their opinions. Indeed, they often sought the child's opinion and stressed his rights and encouraged discussion. Reasoning was strongly valued as a method of obtaining co-operation and compliance.	5. They seemed to consider their sons as not being very significant and not deserving the respect owed to adults. They tended to use autocratic measures and stressed their rights and powers as parents.
6. They tended to punish promptly and consistently.	6. Their discipline was very unpredictable and inconsistent and so their sons were not sure where they stood.
7. They were neither very punitive nor very permissive, tended not to use physical punishment, gave rewards for good behaviour and occasionally withdrawal of love or approval for bad behaviour.	7. They fluctuated between over-strictness and over-permissiveness, preferred punishment to reward, did use physical punishment, and were more likely to use love-withdrawal as punishment.
8. They were more accepting of their children and expressed this through specific everyday concern, physical affection and close rapport. They also seemed to know a great deal about their children (eg interests, friends' names).	8. They tended to withdraw from their children, were inattentive and neglectful, were relatively harsh and disrespectful towards them, and provided a physically, emotionally and intellectually rather impoverished environment. They knew significantly less about their children and treated them almost as if they were a burden.
9. They were regarded by their sons as being 'fair' towards them.	9. They were often regarded as being 'unfair' by their sons.

and their schizophrenic children. Lennard et al (1965) and Mishler and Waxler (1968) found that these parents tend to deny communicative support to the child, and often do not respond to the child's statements and demands for recognition of its opinions. When the parents do communicate with the child it is often in the form of an interruption or an intrusion, rather than a response to the child. In fact, they respond selectively to those of the child's utterances which they themselves have initiated rather than those initiated by the child. At the same time, interaction proceeds in a rather stereotyped way—making spontaneity almost impossible.

R. D. Laing suggests that the kinds of communication patterns within the family make the development of ego boundaries in the child very difficult, ie there is a confusion between self and not-self (me and not-me). This impaired autonomy of the self (or self-identity) and impaired appreciation of external reality are often found to be fundamental characteristics of schizophrenic adolescents and adults. (See Chapter 28.)

Finally, we should not forget the role of social and cultural influences on self-esteem. LeFley (1974) found that American Indian children had a lower self-esteem than American white children. Yet others have found the opposite: for instance, Calhoun et al (1978) studying Portuguese-Mexicans, Soares and Soares (1969), studying black and Puerto Rican children, and Trowbridge and Trowbridge (1972), studying low-income children, found that these groups all had higher self-esteem than white, middle-class, American children.

ii) Comparison with Others

According to Bannister and Agnew (1976), the personal construct of 'self' is intrinsically *bipolar*, that is, having a concept of self implies a concept of not-self. (This is similar to what Cooley and Mead say about self and society being unable to exist without each other—they are really two sides of the same coin.) So one way in which we come to form a picture of what we are like is to see how we compare with others.

Indeed, there are certain parts of our self-image which only take on any significance at all through comparison with others; for example, 'tall' and 'fat' are not absolute characteristics (like, say, 'blue-eyed'), and we are only tall or fat in comparison with others who are shorter or thinner than ourselves. This is true of many other characteristics, including intelligence.

Part of the reaction of parents and other adults to a child often takes the form of a comparison between the child and other siblings (or unrelated children). If the child is told repeatedly that it is 'less clever than your big sister', it will come to incorporate this as part of its self-image and will probably have lower self-esteem as a result. This could adversely affect the child's academic performance so that it does not achieve in line with its true ability: a child of above average intelligence who has grown up in the shadow of a brilliant brother or sister may be less successful academically than an average or even below average child who has not had to face these unfavourable comparisons.

Rosenburg (1965) studied large numbers of adolescents in New York State and found that those with the highest self-esteem tended to be of higher social class, to have done better at school and to have been leaders in their clubs, all of which represent the basis for a favourable comparison between self and others. Adults also continually compare themselves with others in order to put their abilities and achievements into some sort of perspective. For example, Latané (1966) found that subjects in experiments are most interested to know about other subjects who are slightly better than themselves. So the performance of others forms a frame of reference for our own and gives meaning to 'poor', 'average' and 'good' students.

This seems to make sense in terms of our everyday experience. If we are trying to assess our ability or our improvement in some skill, we would normally, and most usefully, compare ourselves with others who are comparable, those who are 'in the same league' as ourselves (eg other A-level students rather than degree level students). And if we play tennis, although we may fantasize about being Wimbledon champion, a realistic comparison would be with others who belong to our tennis club or with players we compete against. Our ideal-self (as far as tennis is concerned) should then involve becoming a player who wins more matches than are lost or whose back-hand is reasonably good (when at present it is non-existent). Anything else (such as wanting to be best in the world) is likely to create the conditions for disappointment and low self-esteem.

iii) Social Roles

As mentioned earlier when discussing the central core of the self-image, social roles are what people commonly regard as part of 'who they are'. Kuhn (1960) asked seven-year-olds and undergraduate students to give 20 different answers to the question, 'Who am I?'. The seven-year-olds gave an average of five answers relating to roles, while the undergraduates gave an average of ten.

Clearly, individuals incorporate more and more roles into their self-image as they grow up; and this is what we would expect since as we get older we assume an increasing number and variety of roles. The pre-schooler is a son or daughter, perhaps a brother or sister, and has other familial roles, and may also be a friend to another child, but the number and range of roles are limited compared with the older child or adult. As we grow up and venture into the 'big wide world', our duties and responsibilities, as well as our choices, involve us in all kinds of roles and relationships with others (eg occupational roles, groups and organizations we belong to and so on).

Roles are important because they help us to define social situations by providing *norms* for behaviour—we know how we are supposed to behave as well as what to expect from others. Also, roles are complementary, that is, one role implies another, so that one cannot exist without the other (eg doctor and patient, teacher and student, parent and child); this helps to make our interactions more predictable. (See Chapter 8.) Often, the most difficult thing is knowing what our role is in a particular situation, being unsure about what is expected of us. But even when we do know, we may still feel strange and uncomfortable in the role (as when wearing clothes that do not quite fit properly) and this usually occurs when the role is a new one for us.

Goffman (1956) points out that in order to perform effectively in a new role, the newcomer must put on a mask, as if acting the part, so as to give the impression of possessing the qualities needed. But when the role has been played for long enough, and others have responded appropriately to the actor, the role becomes an integral part of their personality and so is no longer a mask. At first, we are very self-conscious (in the literal sense) and then our 'automatic pilot' takes over. Burns (1980) refers to studies of medical students who come to see themselves as doctors as their training progresses —31 per cent in the first year compared with 83 per cent by the fourth year. The effect is particularly marked when patients start treating them like doctors (as opposed to students).

When people are promoted within their occupational hierarchy, they change their self-concept in a direction that is consistent with their new position. The crucial experience again seems to be playing the role and having others respond to you accordingly ('taking you seriously' in the role). (This is another example of how self and others are inextricably linked.)

iv) Identification

We shall be discussing this at length in Chapter 21 (in relation to moral development), Chapter 22 (in relation to the development of gender identity and gender role identity) and in Chapter 26 (in relation to personality development). We can say here that we have already seen in this chapter how the related concept of introjection can account for the impact of the reaction of others (including their comparison of us with others) in the formation of our self-concept.

Developmental Changes in the Self-Concept

It is generally agreed by psychologists that at first the infant cannot differentiate between self and not-self and that the self-concept (or sense of self) is something acquired gradually during childhood as the result of experience. But does this mean that the baby does not have any sense of self at all?

Maccoby (1980) maintains that babies do have ample basis for making a distinction between themselves and others on two counts: (i) their own fingers hurt when bitten (but they do not have any such sensations when they are biting their rattle or their mother's fingers); and (ii) probably quite early in life they begin to associate feelings from their own body movements with the sight of their own limbs and the sounds of their own cries. These sense impressions are bound together into a cluster that defines the bodily self (a part of body image) so this is probably the first aspect of the self-concept to develop.

Other aspects of self-concept develop by degrees, but there do seem to be fairly clearly-defined stages of development. Young children may know their own names, understand the limits of their own bodies, and yet be unable to think about themselves as coherent entities—so self-awareness or self-consciousness develops very gradually. According to Piaget, an awareness of self comes through the gradual process of adaptation to the environment (see Chapter 19); as the child explores objects and accommodates to them (thus developing new sensorimotor schemas) it simultaneously discovers aspects of its self, for example, trying to put a large block into its mouth and finding that it will not fit is a lesson in self-hood as well as a lesson about the world of objects.

1) Self-Recognition

One way in which the development of bodily self has been studied is through self-recognition and this involves more than just a simple discrimination of bodily features. In order to determine that the person in a photograph, or a film, or the reflection in a mirror, is oneself, certain knowledge seems to be necessary: first, at least a rudimentary knowledge of oneself as continuous through time (necessary for recognizing ourselves in a photograph or movie) and space (necessary for recognizing ourselves in mirrors); and secondly, knowledge of particular features (what we look like).

This means that recognizing a visual representation of oneself presupposes at least some kind of knowledge of self. Although other kinds of self-recognition are possible (eg one's voice or feelings), only visual self-recognition has been studied extensively, both in animals and humans.

Self-Recognition in Non-human Species

Many animals (including fish, birds, chickens and monkeys) react to their mirror-images as if they were other animals, that is, they do not seem to recognize it as their reflection at all. But self-recognition has been observed in the higher primates—chimpanzees and other great apes.

Gallup (1977) studied pre-adolescent, wild-born chimps and placed a full-length mirror on the wall of each animal's cage. At first they reacted as if another chimp had appeared—they threatened, vocalized or made conciliatory gestures; but this quickly faded out and by the end of three days had almost disappeared. They then used the image to explore themselves, eg they would pick up a piece of food and place it on their face, which could not be seen without the mirror.

After ten days exposure, each chimp was anaesthetized and a bright red spot was painted on the uppermost part of one eyebrow ridge and a second spot on the top of the opposite ear, using an odourless, non-irritating dye. When the chimp had recovered from the anaesthetic, it was returned to its cage, from which the mirror had been removed, and it was observed to see how often it touched the marked parts of its body. The mirror was then replaced and each chimp began to explore the marked spots 25 times more often than it had done before.

The procedure was repeated with chimps which had never seen themselves in the mirror and they reacted to the mirror-image as if it were another chimp (they did not touch the spots). So it seems that the first group had learned to recognize themselves, supporting Cooley's and Mead's theories which stress interaction with others and the reactions of others as crucial to the development of self-concept.

Lower primates (monkeys, gibbons and baboons) are unable to learn to recognize their mirror-image, whether they are raised in isolation or normally.

Self-Recognition in Human Infants

a) Mirrors

A number of researchers (including Lewis and Brooks, 1974, Bertenthal and Fischer, 1978, Lewis and Brooks-Gunn, 1979) have used modified forms of

Gallup's technique with 6–24 month olds. The mother applies a dot of rouge to the child's nose (pretending to wipe the baby's face) and the baby is then observed to see how often it touches its nose. It is then placed in front of a mirror and again the number of times it touches its nose is recorded. At about 18 months, there is a significant change. For example, in the Lewis and Brooks-Gunn (1979) study, touching the dot was never seen before 15 months; between 15 and 18 months, 5 to 25 per cent of infants touched it, while 75 per cent of the 18–20 month olds did.

Bertenthal and Fischer (1978) traced the steps leading up to this change at 18 months. At six months, the infants reached out and touched some part of the mirror-image (perhaps indicating that they thought it was another baby, much like other species do). By 10 months, they usually passed the 'hat-test', where a hat was attached to a special vest by a rod so that each movement of the baby produced a movement of the hat. They tended to look up at the real hat or reached for it (not the image in the mirror), showing: (i) that they understood that movement of the hat was somehow connected with movement of their own body; and (ii) that they could use the mirror to locate the place where the movement was occurring.

In order to use the mirror-image to touch the dot on its nose, the baby must also have built up a schema of how its face should look in the mirror before it can notice the discrepancy created by the dot, and it seems this does not develop before about 18 months. This is also about the time when, according to Piaget, object permanence is completed, so object permanence would seem to be a necessary condition for the development of self-recognition. (See Chapter 19.)

b) *Photographs*
Self-recognition in photographs is usually confined to the face (even adults have trouble with their bodies, let alone infants and young children). Preverbal children's ability to recognize their faces is best inferred by comparing their response to photographs of themselves with their response to photographs of others (making the photographs as similar as possible).

Lewis and Brooks-Gunn (1979) studied 9–24 month olds with 35 mm slides of themselves, same-sex peers and opposite-sex peers, with only the faces and shoulders showing. Under 24 months (and in some cases under 12 months), babies reacted differently to themselves (by, for example, smiling more). Some of the youngest differentiated between photos of themselves and those of opposite-sex infants but *not* between photos of themselves and infants of the same sex.

When asked to point out and label their own photo in a set that included their own and those of others, it was found that comprehension preceded production (a common feature of development which we will note, for example, in Chapter 20, in connection with language development). Almost all the infants could point to their own photo by 18 months but did not label their own photo until 21–24 months.

Self-Recognition in Older Children and Adults
Older children can recognize themselves in mirrors, except for the severely mentally retarded (a mental age of below two years) and some emotionally disturbed children.

Nolan and Kagan (1980) studied 2½ to 5½ year olds and found that almost all of them could pick out the photo of themselves from a set of photos of faces with the eyes blackened. They also found that recognition of hands increased with age: 26 per cent of 2½ year olds compared with 48 per cent of 5½ year olds recognized their hands with the palms up. So visual recognition is not confined to the face.

The only adults who have trouble recognizing their own faces are those suffering from certain Central Nervous System (CNS) disorders, the severely mentally retarded and some psychotics (schizophrenia is a major type of psychotic illness).

2) Self-Definition

Piaget and many others have pointed to the importance of language in consolidating the early development of self-awareness by providing labels which permit distinctions between self and not-self ('I', 'you', 'me', 'it' and so on); these labels can, of course, then by used by the toddler to communicate notions of selfhood to others.

Before we look at the development of the personal pronouns 'I' and 'you', it is worth mentioning a very important label which, at first, is applied by others to the child but which the child then uses to label itself and which is part of the central core of the self-image, ie the child's *name*. Usually, names are not chosen arbitrarily—either the parents particularly like the name, or they want to name the child after a relative or famous person and so on; certainly, names are not neutral labels in terms of how people respond to them and what they associate with them. (We may, for example, be more or less favourably disposed to people by virtue of their name alone. See Chapter 8.)

Jahoda (1954) described the naming practices of the Ashanti tribe of West Africa. Children born on different days of the week are given names accordingly, because of the belief that they have different personalities. Police records showed that among juvenile delinquents, there was a very low percentage of boys born on Monday (believed to have a quiet and calm personality) but a very high rate of Wednesday-born boys (thought to be naturally aggressive).

This is an example of the self-fulfilling prophecy, whereby, on the basis of some label that is applied, people are treated in such a way that they actually develop the characteristics and behaviour which the label says they (should) have. It is reasonable to believe that these Ashanti boys were treated in a way consistent with the name given to them and that, as a result, they 'became' what their name indicated they were 'really' like. In English-speaking countries, days of the week (eg Tuesday) and months of the year (April, May and June) are used as names and they have associations which may influence others' reactions. (For example, 'Monday's child is fair of face, Tuesday's child is full of grace . . . .')

When children refer to themselves as 'I' (or 'me') and others as 'you', they are having to reverse the labels that are normally used to refer to them by others ('you', 'he', 'she'). Also, of course, they hear others refer to themselves as 'I' and not as 'you', 'he', 'she'. This is a problem of *shifting reference*.

But, despite this, most children do not invert 'I' and 'you' and this requires the child to decide on a working rule of usage, in order to solve the problem of shifting reference (Clark 1976).

'I' sometimes refers to the child's mother, father or assorted others, and the child may use one of two hypotheses:

i) 'I' means an adult who is speaking and 'you' means the child;
ii) 'I' means whoever is speaking and 'you' whoever is spoken to.

Only the second takes into account the shifting reference. Some children adopt the first but then discard it after a few months.

It seems that some kind of rule must be involved since, if the child's use of pronouns were based on imitation of the speech it hears, it would almost certainly refer to itself as others do, namely 'you', 'he' or 'she'. Admittedly, most children do go through a stage of referring to themselves by their name but it seems that toddlers focus on the consistencies in speech and use 'you' and 'I' appropriately at a time when the tendency to imitate is still very strong.

According to Charney (1978), 'I' (plus 'me', 'mine' and 'my') appear first between the ages of 20 and 22 months, while 'you', 'he' and 'she' appear two months later. When asked 'Where is my hair?', 'Where is your hair?' and 'Where is her hair?', young children responded to the second and third earlier than to the first, even though in spontaneous conversation they used 'I' correctly earlier than 'you'.

An interesting observation (eg Fraiberg and Adelson, 1976) is that autistic and blind children often use personal pronouns incorrectly, using 'I' for others and 'you' for self. (This may be associated with the abnormal interactions and relationships that these children experience which, in turn, would further support Cooley and Mead.)

3) The Psychological Self

Maccoby (1980) has asked what exactly children mean when they refer to themselves as 'I' or 'me'. Are they referring to anything more than a physical entity enclosed by an envelope of skin?

Flavell (1978) investigated development of the psychological self in 2½ to 5 year olds. In one study, he placed a doll on the table in front of the child and explained that dolls are like people in some ways—arms, legs, hands and so on (pointing as he did so). Then the child was asked how dolls are different from people, whether they know their names and think about things etc. Most children said a doll does not know its name and cannot think about things, but people can. They were then asked, 'Where is the part of you that knows your name and thinks about things?' and 'Where do you do your thinking and knowing?'. Fourteen out of twenty-two children gave fairly clear localization for the thinking self, namely, 'in their heads', while others found it very difficult. The experimenters then looked directly into the child's eyes and asked, 'Can I see you thinking in there?'. Most children thought not.

These answers suggest that by 3½ to 4 years, children have a rudimentary concept of a private, thinking self that is not visible even to someone looking directly into their eyes; they can distinguish this from the bodily self which they know is visible to others.

4) The Categorical Self

We have already noted that age and gender are parts of the central core of the self-image; they represent two of the categories regarding the self which are also used to perceive and interpret the behaviour of others. So we shall now look at age in a little more detail.

Age is probably the first social category to be acquired by the child (and is so even before a concept of number develops). Perceptual factors like facial, vocal and size changes, language usage, dress and body movements, make age a fairly obvious way of categorizing and classifying people (and hence of discriminating between them). Social factors related to age (eg status, control, roles) may also be perceived by the young child.

Lewis and Brooks (1974) found that babies respond differently to child and adult strangers, and Lewis and Brooks-Gunn (1979) found that 6 to 12 month olds can distinguish between photographs, slides and papier-maché heads of adults and babies. By 12 months, they prefer interacting with strange babies to strange adults. Also, as soon as they have acquired labels like 'mummy' and 'daddy' and 'baby', they almost never make age-related mistakes.

The ability of pre-schoolers to classify others by age becomes even more sophisticated. However, the concept of 'old' is very relative: to the three-year-old, the seven-year-old is old, while to the twenty-year-old, the seven-year-old is young. So how we classify people into age-groups depends on our own age. (See Chapter 24.)

Another important category that emerges in infancy is that of *efficacy*, the belief in the self's ability to control and affect the environment (Lewis and Goldberg, 1969); this represents the self as a *causal agent*. As the child gets older, the variety of categories used to describe oneself multiplies.

For instance, Keller et al (1978) asked three-, four- and five-year-olds to talk about themselves and to complete sentences by choosing from eight categories—actions, relationships, body image, possessions, personal labels, evaluation and personal characteristics and preferences. Between one-third and one-half of all the responses were in the Actions category (eg go to school, help mummy) for all three age groups and its use increased between the ages of three and five. Very few of the other seven categories were used more than 10 per cent of the time. Montmayor and Eisen (1977) gave 10-, 13-, 14- and 18-year-olds the twenty statements test; with age, answers became less concrete and more abstract, less present and more future-oriented. Older children/adolescents are more likely to use: occupational role, ideology, sense of self-determinism, a sense of unity, interpersonal style, beliefs and personal characteristics. Younger children are more likely to refer to age, address, appearance, favourite activities, possessions and resources, citizenship and physical self or body-image.

According to Broughton (1978), before the age of seven, children tend to define the self in physical terms—hair colour, height, favourite activities—while inner, psychological, experiences and characteristics are not described as being distinct from overt behaviour and external, physical characteristics. During middle childhood, descriptions shift gradually to more abstract descriptions of facts and from 'physicalistic' to psychological (eg Damon and Hart, 1982 and Harter, 1983).

Livesley and Bromley (1973) analysed self-report data from 320 British children. Those categories which became less important with age were those relating to objective information about themselves, eg appearance, information and identity, possessions, family and friends. Those which became more important were concerned with personal attributes, interests, beliefs, values and relationships with, and attitudes towards, others. These general trends are shown by the responses of 6-, 8- and 11-year-olds to questions about what would change if they 'became' their best friend, or when they grow up, or what had changed since they were a baby (Mohr, 1978). Six-year-olds most often mentioned external characteristics (name, age, possessions), while older children described their typical behaviour. Some 11-year-olds also referred to internal thoughts and feelings.

Special Issues

1) Self-Disclosure

How accurately others perceive us is determined partly by how much we reveal to them about ourselves, and this special kind of communication is called *self-disclosure*. According to Jourard (1971), we disclose ourselves in many ways—through what we say and do (as well as what we omit to say and do) and this includes facial expressions, gestures and other forms of non-verbal communication (NVC). This means that we have greater control over some aspects of self-disclosure than others, since, generally, we have greater control over verbal than non-verbal behaviour. However, Jourard believes that the decision to self-disclose (or to become 'transparent') is one taken freely and the aim in disclosing ourselves is to 'be known, to be perceived by the other as the one I know myself to be' (1971).

Jourard believes that we can learn a great deal about ourselves through mutual self-disclosure and our intimacy with others can be enhanced. It is a way of both achieving and maintaining healthy personality (1964) but only if the self-disclosure meets the criterion of *authenticity* (or honesty) (1968). People with low self-esteem are often unable or unwilling to be open with others and, if they self-disclose at all, they tend to say things about themselves which they do not mean and which have been chosen more for their impact on how others see them ('impression management') than for their 'truth'.

What factors influence how much we disclose to others? Five major factors have emerged from the research: (i) reciprocity; (ii) norms; (iii) trust; (iv) quality of the relationship; and (v) gender.

i) Jourard and Friedman (1970) found that the more personal information we disclose to someone, the more personal information they are likely to disclose to us. Sometimes, we might feel the other person is 'overdoing it' and giving too much away but we are still likely to reveal more about ourselves than we otherwise would.

ii)   The situation we are in often determines how much (or what kinds of) disclosure are appropriate; for instance, it is acceptable for someone whom we meet at a party to tell us about their job but not to reveal details about medical problems or political beliefs.

iii)   Generally, the more we trust someone, the more prepared we are to self-disclose to them.

iv)   Altman and Taylor's 'Social Penetration Theory' maintains that the more intimate we are with somebody, the greater the range of topics we disclose to them and the more deeply we discuss any particular topic. Equally, a high degree of mutual self-disclosure can enhance the intimacy of the relationship.

v)   Cozby (1973) found that women generally disclose more than men and Jourard (1971) argues that men's limited self-disclosure prevents healthy self-expression and adds stress to their lives.

2)   Self-Monitoring

This refers to the extent to which people normally attend to external, social, situations as guides for their behaviour, as opposed to their own, internal states (eg Snyder, 1979).

High self-monitors assess their behaviour with respect to the situation they are in and seem to blend easily into the social situation, knowing exactly what to say and do; if faced with an unfamiliar situation, they will ask, 'What's the ideal person for this situation and how can I be it?'. By contrast, *low self-monitors* remain themselves regardless of the situation and rarely bend or adapt to the norms of the social setting. If faced with an unfamiliar situation, they will ask, 'How can I best be me in this situation?'.

Again, high self-monitors are concerned with behaving in a socially appropriate manner and so are more likely to monitor the situation (rather than themselves), looking for subtle cues as to 'how to behave'. According to Ickes and Barnes (1977) they are also on the watch for cues as to how others might be trying to manipulate or deceive them. For low self-monitors, the reverse is true; what they are monitoring is their behaviour in relation to their own enduring needs and values and the watch-word is consistency. Perhaps not surprisingly, high self-monitors are found to be more socially skilled; for instance, they learn how to behave in new situations faster, are more likely to initiate conversations and can interpret NVC more accurately compared with low self-monitors (Ickes and Barnes, 1977, Snyder, 1979).

According to Ajzen et al (1982), low self-monitors are more prone to the effects of temporary mood-states or fatigue, that is, their behaviour is more likely to reveal their feelings, while highs are better at concealing these sources of internal interference. Because highs are more responsive to the demands of particular situations, their behaviour shows greater cross-situational inconsistency, that is, they behave differently in different situations. In contrast, lows are more consistent in different situations, because their behaviour is governed much more by personal characteristics, which are more enduring than the norms associated with different situations.

Finally, highs see themselves as flexible, adaptable and shrewd and point to situational factors when accounting for why they behave as they do, while lows tend to explain their behaviour in terms of personality characteristics, values, principles and so on. (This is relevant to the Attribution Process that we discussed in the last chapter.)

3) Impression Management

It is difficult to think of a social situation in which we are not trying (consciously or otherwise) to influence how others perceive us. This fundamental aspect of social interaction is referred to as *impression management* and is closely related to the concept of Self-presentation.

Sometimes we may be trying to influence particular people on a particular occasion (eg a job interview) or we may be trying to maintain an image of ourselves which we believe is shared with other people in general (eg that we are caring or competent or attractive). Yet whatever the situation, it does seem that impression management is going on all the time, and this is consistent with what we have already said about the influence of other people's reactions to us on the development of our self-concept.

Because behaviour is the vehicle for conveying impressions, a number of writers have likened the process of impression management to that of *acting*. To create a successful impression requires the right setting, props (eg the way you are dressed), skills and a shared understanding of what counts as 'backstage'; the person who takes self-disclosure too far, for instance, may be regarded as bringing onto the stage what should be kept 'backstage' and so creates an unfavourable impression. Erving Goffman, a Canadian sociologist, is one of the best known exponents of this 'dramaturgical' analysis of social interaction, in books such as *Stigma* (1963) and *The Presentation of Self in Everyday Life* (1971).

Impression management requires us to 'take the role of the other' (see Cooley and Mead's theory of self), that is, we must be able, psychologically, to step into someone else's shoes in order to see how the impression looks from their viewpoint and to adjust our behaviour accordingly.

How do we do it? How do we try to impress another person favourably? Fiske and Taylor (1984), in a review of the literature, identify five major components:

i) In *behaviour matching*, we try to match the target person's behaviour; an example would be that if they are self-disclosing, we will, too, to a comparable degree.

ii) When we *conform to situational norms*, we use our knowledge of what is appropriate behaviour in a particular situation to adopt that behaviour ourselves. For every social setting, there is a pattern of social interaction which conveys the best identity for that setting—what Alexander and Knight (1971) call the 'situated identity'. High self-monitors, in this respect, are more likely to be successful in making a favourable impression.

iii) *Appreciating* or *flattering others* can sometimes produce a favourable response from the target person, especially if the appreciation is sincere. But flattery, if seen for what is it, can backfire on the flatterer who will be seen as deliberately trying to achieve their own ends.

iv) If we show *consistency among our beliefs*, or between our beliefs and behaviour, we are more likely to impress other people favourably, since inconsistency is generally taken as a sign of weakness.

v)   Our *verbal* and *non-verbal behaviour* should match, which they usually do if we are being sincere. However, if we are flattering, for instance, or in some other way being dishonest, the non-verbal channel will often 'leak', giving away our true feelings (eg DePaulo and Rosenthal, 1979). When people perceive an inconsistency between what we are saying and what we are conveying with our body, the non-verbal channel is usually taken as conveying the 'true' message (Argyle et al, 1972, Mehrabian, 1972).

Finally, there are certain exceptions to the rule regarding trying to convey positive impressions:

a)   We may feel constrained by the impressions which others already have of us and we act in order to 'muddy the waters' (Snyder and Wickland, 1981). For instance, if you are continually being told how good a son or daughter you are, the responsibility this places on you might encourage you to behave in the opposite fashion, so that you 'free yourself' from the expectation that you will go on behaving dutifully and respectfully etc.

b)   You might protect yourself from anticipated failure by blaming, in advance, things about yourself which could explain the failure apart from your lack of competence. For example, teachers at exam time get quite used to students telling them how badly they are going to do, because of lack of sleep, not having been well, having been unable to revise, always getting anxious about exams and so on. These 'excuses' must be plausible, not too damaging and not very easy for anyone else to check out if they are to be successful in terms of impression management; of course, indirectly they are attempts to convey a positive impression but they make use of negative attributes and these are 'centre stage'. There is a danger that these 'excuses' become internalized and then form part of our self-image, affecting both our behaviour and our self-esteem.

10

Interpersonal Attraction

According to popular belief, it is love that makes the world go round, but according to Rubin and McNeil (1983) liking perhaps more than loving is what keeps it spinning. How are liking and loving related and how are they different? What determines our choice of friends, partners, lovers and spouse? Is it possible to measure how much we like or love someone and is it possible to predict the kind of choices we are likely to make? These are some of the major questions we shall try to answer.

Interpersonal attraction is really a facet of interpersonal perception: one of the major influences on choice of friends and the permanence of love-relationships seems to be the perceived similarity between oneself and others; another, physical attractiveness, was discussed in Chapter 8 in relation to stereotyping. The other major determinants of attraction are proximity, familiarity, reciprocal liking, complementarity and competence.

Relationships Must be Rewarding

This is the first law of interpersonal attraction.

Before we discuss each of the seven major influences on interpersonal attraction in detail, it is important that we should consider the main theoretical approach to attraction overall, namely Exchange Theory (Thibaut and Kelley, 1959, Blau, 1964, Homans, 1974). (Exchange Theory is discussed further in Chapter 13.)

In trying to answer the question, 'What do all the important relationships in my life have in common?' you may say something to the effect that they are all rewarding, that is, they provide you with security, happiness, content-ment, fun and so on and (if you are honest) you will probably also acknowledge that they can be complex, demanding and, at times, even painful. If all relationships involve both positive and negative, desirable and undesirable, aspects, what determines our continued involvement with them (if we have that kind of choice) or how much we value them (if we don't)?

According to Homans (1974), we view our feelings for others in terms of *profits*, that is, the amount of reward obtained from the relationship minus the cost—the greater the reward and lower the cost, the greater the profit and the greater the attraction.

According to Blau (1964), our interactions are 'expensive'; they take time, energy, commitment and may involve unpleasant emotions and experiences, and so what we get in return must outweigh what we put in. Similarly, Berscheid and Walster (1978) argue that in any social interaction, people exchange rewards (eg information, affection, status, money, skills and attention) and the degree of attraction or liking will reflect how each person evaluates the rewards they have received relative to those they have given.

But is it appropriate to think of relationships with other people in these economic—capitalistic terms? There is no doubt that Exchange Theory sees people as fundamentally selfish and human relationships as based primarily on self-interest. Are we really like this?

Like many attempts in psychology to explain behaviour, Exchange Theory offers a metaphor for human relationships and it should not be taken too literally. However, according to Rubin in *Liking and Loving* (1973), although we like to believe that the joy of giving is as important as the desire to receive, 'we must face up to the fact that our attitudes toward other people are determined to a large extent by our assessments of the rewards they hold for us'. At the same time, he believes that Exchange Theory is not an adequate, complete account, 'Human beings are sometimes altruistic in the fullest sense of the word. They make sacrifices for the sake of others without any consideration of the rewards they will obtain from them in return'; and altruism is most often and most clearly seen in close interpersonal relationships. Douvan (1972) and Wexler (1980) agree. (See Chapter 14.)

Indeed, some psychologists make the distinction between 'true' love and friendship, which are altruistic, and less admirable forms which are based on considerations of exchange (Brown, 1986). Erich Fromm, for instance, in *The Art of Loving* (1956) defines true love as giving, as opposed to the false love of the 'marketing character' which depends upon expecting to have the favours returned. Is there any empirical support for such a distinction?

Mills and Clark (1980) identified two kinds of intimate relationship: (i) the *communal* couple, in which each partner gives out of concern for the other; and (ii) the *exchange* couple, in which each keeps mental records of who is 'ahead' and who is 'behind'. Such a scorekeeping mentality in a close relationship guarantees that both parties will be dissatisfied and Murstein (1978) has designed a scale (the Exchange Orientation Scale) which is intended to identify individuals who are preoccupied with 'getting their "fair" share'. These exchange types are suspicious, fearful, paranoid and insecure compared with the giving and trusting types (Murstein et al, 1977).

The Matching Hypothesis (Getting the Best Deal We Can)

According to Roger Brown (1986), Exchange Theory clearly predicts that individuals who are willing to become romantically involved with each other will be fairly closely matched in their ability to reward one another.

Ideally, we would all have the most beautiful/handsome, charming, generous, and in other ways desirable, partners because we are all perfectly selfish (according to the theory). But, of course, this is impossible and so we have to find a compromise solution. The best general bargain that can be struck is a value-match, that is, a subjective belief that our partner is the most rewarding we could realistically hope to find—this is the matching hypothesis.

One of the major ways in which the matching hypothesis has been empirically investigated is the 'computer dance'. Men and women independently buy tickets for a dance (usually at a university or college at the start of an academic year) and complete detailed questionnaires about themselves which the computer, supposedly, uses in order to make ideal matches. The student subjects are rated (without their knowledge, of course) for physical attractiveness and are, in fact, assigned a partner purely randomly.

The earliest such study was carried out by Hatfield et al (1966) and they wanted to know how many men would ask their partner for a second date and on what basis. It turned out that the single most important factor that determined how likely it was that a woman would be asked out again was her physical attractiveness—regardless of the man's.

This is contrary to what the matching hypothesis predicts. If we settle for a value-match (as the hypothesis predicts), then only those men who happened to be matched (by chance) with a date whose attractiveness level closely resembled their own would have asked for a second date. But it seems that the men acted on pure selfishness: the more attractive the woman, the greater the probability that she would be asked out again, regardless of the man's own attractiveness. So the matching hypothesis seems to have been contradicted.

However, according to Brown (1986), these results reflect the rather artificial nature of the design and later computer dance studies have tended to support the matching hypothesis. For example, Berscheid et al (1971) gave subjects the chance to specify characteristics they hoped to find in their dates, including physical attractiveness measured on a nine-point scale. They were told the computer would be able to meet this specification because the number of students was so large. Those rated as less attractive actually *asked* for less attractive dates, the moderately attractive asked for moderately attractive dates and the most attractive asked for the most attractive dates. This matching phenomenon results from a well-learned sense of what is 'fitting' rather than a fear of being rebuffed (Brown, 1986); that is, we learn to adjust our expectations of rewards in line with what we believe we have to offer others. This matching for physical attractiveness was also found by Berscheid and Walster (1974).

Clearly, matching for physical attractiveness is a major determinant of couple-formation and is even stronger in the case of 'real couples' than with the randomly-created couples of the computer dance. Murstein (1972) asked subjects to rate the photos of the male and female members of 99 engaged or steady couples for physical attractiveness when these were presented in a random order; he found that they were rated as being much closer in attractiveness than computer-dance couples.

Compatibility

As we have seen, physical attraction is the major predictor of liking in the short term—at least as measured by the wish to date again—and there are several other supporting studies (eg Brislin and Lewis, 1968, Tesser and Brodie, 1971, Walster et al, 1966). But not only is there a matching phenomenon involved in physical attractiveness, according to the matching hypothesis, genuine couples will be more alike than random couples on *any* dimension which enters into a calculation of social value (Brown, 1986) and there is evidence suggesting that matching is an important ingredient of compatibility. Hatfield et al (1978), in a review of the literature, concluded that couples tend to be similar with respect to IQ, education and other characteristics.

Hill, Rubin and Peplau (1976) studied 231 steadily-dating couples over a two-year period, at the end of which 103 couples had broken up (45 per cent). The surviving couples tended to be more alike in terms of age, intelligence, educational and career plans, as well as physical attractiveness, while those who split up often mentioned differences in interests, background, sexual attitudes and ideas about marriage. Certain other characteristics seemed irrelevant in that they did not distinguish between the couples who split up and those who survived, namely height, religion and father's occupation.

Could the splitting up or staying together have been predicted from the initial questionnaire data? It seems they could to a significant degree: about 80 per cent of the couples who described themselves as being 'in love' at the start stayed together, compared with 56 per cent who did not so describe themselves. Interestingly, whether or not they had had sexual intercourse, and whether or not they were living together, was completely unrelated to whether or not they were still together two years later.

Can the findings throw any light on Exchange Theory? Of couples in which both members initially reported being equally involved in the relationship, only 23 per cent broke up, but where one member was much more involved than the other, 54 per cent did so. The latter type is a highly unstable couple in which the one who is more involved (putting more in but getting less in return) may feel dependent and exploited, while the one who is less involved (putting less in but getting more in return) may feel restless and guilty.

Scales have been developed to measure the 'returns' for each member of a couple. The Hatfield Global Measure of Equity-Inequity (Hatfield et al, 1978), for example, attempts to identify individuals who feel that their relationship is *equitable*, that is, they get as much as they give (a scale value of 0), those who feel severely underbenefitted, that is, they get much *less* than they give (a scale value of -3) and those who feel extremely overbenefitted, that is, they get much *more* than they give (a scale value of $+3$).

Hatfield, Walster and Traupmann (1978) interviewed 537 college men and women who were dating, either casually or seriously, and asked them if they expected to be together in one and five years time. Those who felt the relationship was equitable were much more likely than either the under or overbenefitted to believe they would still be together (as predicted by Exchange Theory) and a follow-up $3\frac{1}{2}$ months later confirmed these expectations. Those in equitable relationships were the most happy and contented, the underbenefitted felt angry and the overbenefitted felt guilty; and these findings were confirmed by Traupmann, Hatfield and Wexler (1983).

According to Murstein and MacDonald (1983), although the principles of exchange and equity play a significant role in intimate relationships, a great *conscious* concern with 'getting a fair deal', especially in the short term, makes compatibility very hard to achieve, both in friendship and, especially, in marriage. (This corresponds to the 'Exchange' couple, described by Mills and Clark, 1980, mentioned above.)

What might people do if they believe they are not getting a fair deal in order to restore equity? One course of action is to have an extra-marital affair; Hatfield, Traupmann and Walster (1978) found that, of 2 000 married people they studied, those who felt deprived, cheated or underbenefitted had extra-marital affairs sooner into their marriage, and had more of them, than those who felt either fairly treated or overbenefitted (Brown, 1986).

Specific Factors Influencing Attraction

There is a number of important factors which influence interpersonal attraction and we will now consider each of these in turn.

1) Proximity, Exposure and Familiarity

This really represents a minimum requirement for attraction because it represents a minimum requirement for interaction. Clearly, the further apart two people live, the lower the probability that they will ever meet, let alone become friends or marry each other; and in extreme cases (eg living in different countries) this does not tell us a great deal about why we like some people more than others.

More informative are sociological studies which show that the closer a man and woman live within the same town or city, the more likely they are to marry one another (eg Katz and Hill, 1958, Kerckhoff, 1974); this is known as the Propinquity Effect. Perhaps most instructive of all are studies which show that we are more likely to be friends with people we live next-door to, sit next to in class or work next to in an office or factory, than those who are physically further away.

Byrne and Buehler (1955) asked their students to sit according to alphabetical order for the first term of their course; at the start, only 8 per cent knew each other's names but this had increased to 21 per cent by the end of the term. More importantly, 74 per cent knew the names of those who sat next to them or nearby. Segal (1974) asked students at a state police academy to name their closest friends on the force. Nearly half those named were immediately next to the name in the alphabet and it turned out that they had been assigned dormitories and classroom seats according to their position in the alphabet.

Festinger et al (1950) studied friendship patterns in a university campus housing complex for married students. People were more friendly with those who lived next door (41 per cent), next most friendly with those living two doors away and least friendly with those who lived at the end of the corridor (10 per cent). Families separated by four flats hardly ever became friends and in two-storey blocks of flats, the residents tended to interact mainly with others living on the same floor. On any one floor, people who lived near stairways had more friends than those living at the end of the corridor. Similar friendship patterns have been reported for a new suburban community (Whyte, 1956), student dormitories (Evans and Wilson, 1949) and residents of a home for the elderly (Simon and Lawton 1967).

Clearly, what all these cases of proximity have in common is the increased opportunity for interaction, what Zajonc (1968) calls *exposure*. According to Argyle (1981), the more two people interact, the more polarized their attitudes towards each other become, usually in the direction of greater liking which, in turn, increases the likelihood of further interaction, but only if the interaction is as equals. (Equal status interaction has important implications for reducing prejudice—see Chapter 11.)

However, we still have not really explained why greater proximity increases attraction; could not increased exposure just as easily decrease attraction? A crucial variable related to exposure is *familiarity*; it seems that we like people and things which are familiar and dislike or distrust the unfamiliar (and so, to this extent, familiarity does not breed contempt!).

Newcomb (1961) offered male students free board and lodging at a rented boarding house at Michigan University if they participated in a study of the acquaintance process. They were randomly assigned a room and during the first year of the study it seemed that it was similarity of attitudes, beliefs and values which was the strongest determinant of liking. In the second year, using different subjects, Newcomb assigned each student a room-mate who was either highly similar to him, or as different as possible, on a wide range of attitudes, beliefs and values. It was predicted, based on the first year's results, that similarity would again be the major influence, but it turned out to be familiarity that was the key factor—room-mates became friends far more often than would have been expected on the basis of their characteristics.

Similarly, Priest and Sawyer (1967) found a striking tendency for students to like the person next-door more than the person two doors away and to like that person more than the one three doors away, and so on.

Saegert et al (1973) found that female subjects who were 'incidentally' exposed to other women (that is, there was no actual talking or other interaction) on a number of occasions during a 'liquid-tasting experiment' came to prefer these women to those whom they only saw once. Despite having to taste unpleasant laboratory solutions, the mere repeated exposure to other people seems to be a reason for liking them.

Zajonc et al (1971, 1974) asked subjects to evaluate photographs of strangers and those which appeared more often were rated more positively than those which appeared less often. Similar results were found when female students rated slides of male students for attractiveness (Wilson and Nakajo, 1965), when subjects had to rate paintings (Zajonc et al, 1972), Pakistani music (Heingartner and Hall, 1974) and political candidates (Stang, 1974). Grush et al (1978) found that the amount of exposure given to political candidates by the media was a very reliable predictor of their eventual success in American primary elections.

Nor is the 'exposure–familiarity' effect confined to humans, it seems. Cross et al (1967) raised rats from birth, exposing them to one or other musical experience (Mozart, Schoenberg or nothing) for the first 52 days of life. After a 15-day break, they were tested for their musical preferences and a marked exposure effect was found (although the control group had a preference for Mozart).

So it seems that we like what we know and what we are familiar with, perhaps because it is predictable and causes us very little in the way of anxiety.

On the other hand, repeated exposure to something or somebody may reveal the less acceptable and desirable qualities, so that familiarity will 'breed contempt'. However, most of the research on familiarity has supported the positive outcome of repeated exposure.

Personal Space

Or—when proximity breeds contempt—too close for comfort.

As we have seen, it is not proximity as such which accounts for increased liking but the greater opportunity for interaction with those who are physically accessible to us. In Exchange Theory terms, proximity can bring about rewards at low costs and this interpersonal 'profit' is translated into liking; if we do not have to make great effort to find people whom we like, then we can 'invest' more of ourselves in those who are available, close at hand and 'on tap'.

However, it seems that sometimes mere physical closeness (especially if accompanied by bodily contact) can be unpleasant and cause us to dislike the person concerned, even to the point of physically removing ourselves from their vicinity. If we are sitting in an otherwise empty row of seats in a train, for instance, and someone comes and sits right next to us, we may well feel uneasy and suspicious (especially if the stranger is of the opposite sex), whether or not we do anything about it. In a series of studies by Sommer, the experimenter deliberately sat close to unsuspecting subjects when there was plenty of other available space in order to see how likely they were to react to this invasion of their personal space. In the Library Study (Felipe and Sommer, 1966), the subjects were female students studying at a large table with six chairs on either side of the table; there were at least two empty chairs on either side of each subject and one opposite, and there were a number of experimental conditions in which, for example, the experimenter: (i) sat next to the subject and moved his chair nearer to hers (ii) sat two seats away from her (leaving one chair between them); (iii) sat three seats away; and (iv) sat immediately opposite her.

Subjects were more likely to leave, move away, adjust the chair or erect barriers (such as putting a bag on the table between themselves and the 'intruder') when he sat next to them, as in condition (i). Similar results were found for psychiatric patients (Felipe and Sommer, 1966) and for people sitting on park benches (Sommer et al, 1969); in the latter study, the experimenter sat six inches away from subjects on an otherwise empty bench and these subjects were much more likely to move away—and sooner—than control subjects who were not joined by the over-friendly stranger.

We have all had the experience of accidentally making body contact with a stranger, which usually produces an immediate apology, and even when forced into very close proximity (such as on a crowded tube train or in a crowded lift) we somehow manage to take 'diversionary action'; that is, we look away, ensuring that we do not make eye-contact, look down or up, anywhere but *at* the stranger (we may even pretend to cat-nap if there is nowhere or nothing to look at!).

It seems that we are very sensitive to others'—and our own—need for personal space. This term was first used by the anthropologist Edward T. Hall (1959, 1966) to describe the human behaviour which resembled the 'individual distance' of zoo animals (Hediger, 1951); that is, the distance which two individuals of the same species try to keep between each other. According to Hall, we learn *proxemic rules*, which prescribe: (a) the amount of physical distance that is appropriate in daily relationships; and (b) the kinds of situations in which closeness or distance is proper. Our feelings for others may depend on whether these culturally determined rules are followed and these rules are themselves influenced by the nature of the relationship; for instance, relatives and intimate friends are allowed much closer proximity —and bodily contact—than mere acquaintances or strangers. As far as bodily contact is concerned, there are different rules for different relatives, depending on their gender and this applies to friends too.

One famous study by Jourard (1966) asked college students to report which parts of their body were touched by their fathers, mothers, same-sex friends and opposite-sex friends. Not surprisingly, opposite-sex friends turned out to be allowed the most intimate bodily contact, especially in terms of the total body area of contact but also which particular parts of the body are touched. (See Figure 10.1.)

Hall identifies four main regions or zones of personal space, which are summarised in Table 10.1.

Table 10.1 Hall's four zones of personal space (1959, 1966)

1 *Intimate distance* (0–18 inches)	This may involve actual bodily contact and is reserved for our most intimate relationships.
2 *Casual–personal distance* (1½ feet–4 feet)	This is the distance in which we usually interact with close friends, trusted acquaintances, at parties, or with those who share special interests with us.
3 *Social–consultative distance* (4 feet–12 feet)	This is the distance commonly found between colleagues at work, and is used for most business and formal contacts.
4 *Public distance* (12 feet and beyond)	This is used for large, public meetings and lectures, and meetings with high-ranking persons.

It is important to note that there may be certain exceptions to these proxemic rules or they may be modified under certain circumstances:

i)   We sometimes allow strangers (or near-strangers) to enter our intimate zone, eg doctors, dentists, hairdressers, where bodily contact is expected or necessary as part of our respective roles.

ii) Children are much less sensitive to the rules of proxemics and often embarrass strangers by how freely they enter other people's intimate zone; clearly, these rules are acquired in the course of socialization although they are usually implicit and not explicit (like the rules of grammar).

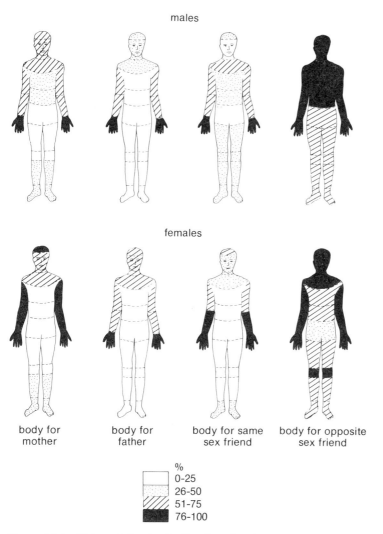

Figure 10.1   Male and female 'bodies for others', as experienced through the amount of touching received from others (Jourard, 1966)

iii)   There are important cultural differences regarding proxemic rules; each zone allows the use of different cues of touch, smell, hearing and seeing, which are more important in some cultures than others. Watson and Graves (1966) observed discussion groups of Americans or those from Arab countries; in the latter there was more direct face-to-face orient-ation, greater closeness and touching. South Americans and Arabs have been called 'contact cultures' while the Scots and Swedes have been called 'non-contact cultures'.

iv)   Proximity is but one kind of social act which makes up the degree of intimacy which exists between two people. According to Argyle and Dean (1965), we all have a tendency to approach others, to be in contact with them, to seek the company of others, and at the same time we have an opposing tendency to avoid others, to remain separate and independent of others. The balance between these two opposing tendencies is 'negotiated', non-verbally, in each social situation in which we find ourselves, so that we try to find a mutually acceptable level of intimacy, that is, a level with which we feel comfortable. Clearly, the subjects in the studies of Sommer and his colleagues felt uncomfortable when the experimenter sat himself right next to them—he was making the situation too intimate as far as they were concerned. Similarly, when we are squeezed against fellow-passengers in the tube, we look away from those nearest to us to prevent the level of intimacy from increasing any further—it is already psychologically (as well as physically) uncomfortable enough by this stage!

v)   Hildreth et al (1971) found that criminals convicted of violent crimes were much more sensitive to physical closeness with others than non-violent criminals. Nicholson (1977) refers to the concept of a 'body-buffer zone', defined as the point at which a person begins to feel uncomfortable when approached by another (a concept similar to Hall's 'personal space'). Violent criminals compared with non-criminals, and schizophrenics compared with other kinds of psychiatric patients, tend to have larger body-buffer zones, that is, they more easily begin to feel uneasy when others walk towards them.

According to Altman and Taylor (1973), successful friendships may *require* an initial establishment of boundary understandings; that is, in Hall's terms, strangers must be 'invited' into our intimate zone and not 'trespass' from an initial casual-personal distance, while in Argyle and Dean's 'equilibrium model' of intimacy, strangers who make a situation uncomfortably intimate, too soon, are unlikely to become friends.

2)   Similarity—Do Birds of a Feather Flock Together?

We have already discussed this to some extent in relation to the matching hypothesis.

Most studies suggest that the critical similarities are those to do with beliefs, attitudes and values. Newcomb (1943) in a famous study of Bennington College, an expensive East Coast women's university college with a liberal tradition amongst the teaching staff and senior students, found that many students coming from conservative backgrounds adopted liberal attitudes in order to gain the liking and acceptance of classmates.

In his 1961 study described above, Newcomb found that similarity of attitudes, values and beliefs was the major determinant of liking among room-mates, at least when they were randomly assigned. Support comes from several studies, including Byrne (1971), Byrne and Griffitt (1973) and Griffitt and Veitch (1974).

In the last of these, Griffitt and Veitch (1974) paid 13 males to spend ten days in a fall-out shelter: those with similar attitudes and opinions liked each other most by the end of the study, particularly if they agreed on highly salient issues. Duck (1973) found that similarity of cognitive constructs used for describing other people was an especially strong determinant of liking (see Chapter 25).

However, it seems that the importance of similarity may depend on how long-standing or otherwise a relationship is. For example, Kerckhoff and Davis (1962) tested and interviewed young couples at college who were contemplating marriage. Those who had been together for less than 18 months tended to have a stronger relationship when the partners' values coincided but with couples of longer-standing, similarity was *not* the most important factor.

This led Kerckhoff and Davis (1962) to propose that relationships pass through a series of 'filters': at first, similarity of sociological variables will determine the likelihood of individuals meeting in the first place; then consensus on certain basic values is necessary for the couple to become relatively stable and permanent; finally, complementarity of needs becomes important (see below).

Why should similarity be so important? According to Rubin (1973), similarity is rewarding because:

a) Agreement may provide a basis for engaging in joint activities;
b) A person who agrees with us helps to increase our confidence in our own opinions, which enhances our self-esteem; according to Duck (1979), the validation that friends give us is experienced as the evidence of the accuracy of our personal constructs;
c) Most people are vain enough to believe that anyone who shares their views must be a sensitive and praiseworthy individual;
d) People who agree about things that matter to them generally find it easier to communicate;
e) We may assume that people with similar attitudes to ourselves will be like us—and so we like them in turn (this is called reciprocal liking, see below).

Our self-esteem may be increased by winning someone over to our point of view; according to Sigall (1970), we like converts to our opinions more than those who agree with us in the first place, and further evidence comes from a study by Aronson and Linder (1965) which we shall discuss below.

3) Complementarity—Do Opposites Attract?

We have seen that similarity may be especially important during the early stages of a relationship, but that complementary needs may become relatively more important as the relationship persists (Kerckhoff and Davis, 1962).

According to Winch (1955, 1958), happy marriages are often based on each member's ability to fulfill the needs of the other. A classic example is that of a dominant person who would not be likely to choose as a partner someone who was equally dominant; this is probably a good recipe for disaster and Winch (1954) found some empirical support for this view. Other support comes from Katz et al (1960), Levinger (1964) and Tharp (1966).

Snyder and Fromkin (1980) go so far as to suggest that, because we like to see ourselves as unique individuals, others whom we see as being highly similar to ourselves may be disliked for that reason. However, Rubin and

McNeil (1983) cannot agree. They argue that, although diversity is valuable and enriching and, under certain circumstances we might actively seek it, people with fundamentally different approaches to life are unlikely to become friends. Thus, 'For a human being to adapt to a rapidly changing world, he needs the companionship and support of others with whom he may sometimes disagree, but nevertheless feels a fundamental bond of likemindedness.' (Rubin and McNeil, 1983.)

4) Reciprocal Liking

Or, I like you because you like me.

It is certainly very flattering when someone pays us compliments and generally seems to like us; perhaps it also puts us under a certain obligation to reward the other person in turn.

According to Aronson's reward-cost principle (1976), we are most attracted to a person who makes entirely positive comments about us over a number of occasions and least attracted to one who makes entirely negative comments about us over a number of occasions. This in itself may seem rather obvious. More interesting, however, is Aronson and Linder's 'gain-loss' theory of attraction (1965). According to this, someone who starts off by disliking us and then changes their feelings in our favour will be liked *more* than someone who likes us from the start; equally, someone who begins by liking us and then adopts a negative attitude towards us will be disliked *more* than someone who dislikes us from the start.

Aronson and Linder (1965) told subjects that the experiment was concerned with verbal conditioning and that the learner (a confederate) had to be deceived by being told it was about interpersonal attraction; in fact, the naïve subject believed she was the confederate. She assisted the experimenter by monitoring the learner's performance during seven separate conversations between the experimenter and the learner, in which the latter described her impressions of the subject (whom she had met during the course of the experiment) and then had to rate how much she liked the learner. As predicted, when the learner changed from disliking to liking (*gain condition*), she was liked much more than when she liked the subject from the start; and when the learner changed from liking to disliking (*loss condition*) she was disliked much more than when she disliked the subject from the start.

In a similar study (Clore et al, 1975) subjects had to rate how attracted a woman was to a man in a video on the basis of her non-verbal communication only; as in the Aronson and Linder experiment, the gain condition (in which she first acted rather coolly towards him and then 'warmed up') produced the highest attractiveness rating and the loss condition the lowest.

5) Competence

Although we generally admire and respect people who show themselves to be capable and competent, it seems that we prefer competent people who are at the same time fallible: we do not like people who seem perfect and so when their 'human slip' shows, we like them more, not less.

In one famous study, Aronson et al (1966) played tape recordings of a 'Quizbowl' (the equivalent of the British 'University Challenge' TV programme). Some subjects heard a tape of a 'superior' contestant, who answered 92 per cent of the very difficult quiz questions correctly, was editor of the college yearbook, was a member of the athletics teams and so on; while other subjects heard a tape of an average contestant, who answered 30 per cent of the very difficult questions correctly, was a proofreader on the yearbook staff and so on. For each group (superior and average), half the contestants made a 'spilt coffee blunder' and subjects were asked to rate how much they liked the contestant. What were the findings?

Regardless of whether he spilled his coffee, the superior contestant was liked more than the average one *but* the superior contestant who spilled the coffee was the most liked of all; the least-well liked was the clumsy, average contestant.

Showing himself to be fallible (and, to that extent, more human), the competent person may be perceived as more like ourselves and, therefore, more attractive for that reason. However, this assumes that we regard the competent person as being superior to ourselves in the first place; if we think of ourselves as superior, the clumsiness may then have the effect of making the person seem less like ourselves, and, hence, less likeable.

A critical influence, therefore, on how we respond to the fallibility of other people is our own initial level of self-esteem. Aronson et al (1970) repeated the experiment and confirmed that spilling coffee only enhanced the attractiveness of the superior contestant for subjects of average self-esteem; those with very high *or* very low self-esteem, liked him less. So it is *relative*, rather than absolute, competence or superiority which is related to attraction (Mettee and Wilkins, 1972), which was confirmed by Helmreich et al (1970).

Deaux (1972) reported an interesting sex difference: while males were attracted to a competent man who made a blunder, women preferred competent people who did not blunder (whether male or female). (What does this suggest to you about the relative self-esteem of men and women?)

Finally, a fascinating political example is given by Rubin and McNeil (1983): after President Kennedy had approved the ill-fated Bay of Pigs invasion of Cuba in 1961 (which led to the Cuban missile-crisis), an opinion poll taken immediately afterwards showed that his popularity actually *increased*. It seems that we do not like even our national leaders to appear perfect!

6) Physical Attractiveness

We have said much about this already in relation to the 'matching hypothesis'; but there is a great deal of research which is revealing about the influence of physical appearance on attraction which goes beyond the dimension of similarity.

We saw in Chapter 8, when discussing individual stereotypes, that people who are physically attractive are perceived as being psychologically attractive also; that is, they are judged to have a whole host of positive characteristics even in the absence of any evidence about the kind of person they are, simply on the basis of what they look like. But can it work the other way round, that is, if we hear of a person having certain positive qualities, will our rating of their physical attractiveness be increased?

Gross and Crofton (1977) found that the more favourably someone was described as a person, the higher their photographs would be rated for physical attractiveness. This represents one way in which perception of physical attractiveness is not objective but is influenced by a number of factors, including culture, gender, context and personality.

Culture

Different cultures have different criteria of what constitutes physical beauty; according to Garfield (1982), chipped teeth, body scars, artificially elongated heads and bound feet have all been regarded as beautiful, and even in our own culture definitions change over time, as in the 'ideal' figure for women. Facial beauty is generally regarded as more important in women than men, while in men it is their stature, particularly height, which influences how attractive they are judged to be.

Feldman (1971) has observed that every American President elected between 1900 and 1968 was taller than his major opponent. It is possible, of course, that taller men have other characteristics that make them more desirable than shorter men, but certainly the perception of a man's height is correlated with liking him. Two-thirds of a Californian sample who planned to vote for Kennedy in the 1960 presidential election perceived him as being taller than Nixon and a majority of those planning to vote for Nixon saw him as being at least as tall as Kennedy; Kennedy was actually a few inches taller (Hilgard et al, 1979).

Gender

It seems that men are more responsive to beauty than women; they generally seem to prefer an attractive woman, whether to work with, to date, or to marry, whereas women generally consider similarity of interests to be as or more important (Stroebe et al, 1971).

Physically attractive women have significantly more frequent dates than less attractive women but this is not true of men (Krebs and Adinolfi, 1975), and after a dance, men are more likely to report feelings of attraction based on physical appearance than are women (Berscheid and Walster, 1974). These differences seem to be symptomatic of the pervasive difference in gender roles which exist in our society (see Chapter 22), in which, traditionally, a woman has been regarded as the property of a man, whereby her beauty increases his status and respect in the eyes of others (Sigall and Landy, 1973). Again, the reverse does not seem to apply—the attractiveness of a man does not seem to enhance a woman's standing among other women (Bar-Tal and Saxe, 1976).

Context

According to Gergen and Gergen (1981), perceived beauty can wax and wane according to circumstances; for example, a person who disagrees with us might suddenly lose their physical appeal—and vice-versa (Walster, 1971).

Several studies have looked at the interaction between a person's physical attractiveness and their chances of being found guilty of a crime. Do good-looking criminals get off lightly?

Monahan (1941) found that beautiful women were less likely to be convicted and Efran (1974) found that we tend to be more lenient when punishing good-looking criminals; this was confirmed by Landy and Armstrong (1969). However, a criminal's good looks can actually work to their disadvantage depending on the nature of the crime: if the crime is one in which the criminal's good-looks played a part (eg fraud in which a woman charms a man into giving her money for a non-existent cause), they are likely to be more severely punished than a less attractive person committing the same crime. When the crime is not related to good looks (eg burglary), an unattractive person is likely to be more severely punished than an attractive one. These predictions were confirmed in an experiment by Sigall and Ostrove (1975).

Similarly, adults (including parents) may treat children differently according to their physical appeal (quite unconsciously, of course). Adults may also expect that good-looking children will be better behaved than less attractive ones; when the former do behave badly they may have their behaviour excused by adults making situational—as opposed to dispositional—attributions (see Chapter 8).

Dion (1972), in an experimental study, used photographs of seven-year-old children plus accounts of their misbehaviour (either mild or severe) and found that adult subjects were more likely to attribute antisocial tendencies to the unattractive children if the misbehaviour were serious. Subjects also thought that the attractive children were less likely to have behaved badly in the past and were thought less likely to be naughty again (even if the present behaviour were serious). Unattractive girls were evaluated more leniently than unattractive boys, which suggests the interaction of attractiveness and gender role.

Physically attractive children are generally more popular with their peers (Dion and Berscheid, 1974), and Adams (1977) and Snyder et al (1977) suggest that physically attractive children may become friendly and self-confident as a consequence of people's response to their good looks, which may become a source of power over other children (Dion and Stein, 1978). Good looks in adults may also become a source of power over other adults (Chaiken, 1979).

However, as we saw in Chapter 8, it is possible to be too good-looking for your own good. For instance, Krebs and Adinolfi (1975) found that it was the attractive, but not the most attractive, students, who were most popular among their peers. Reis et al (1980) report that physically attractive males may be avoided by other males, while moderately attractive females are more likely to be satisfied with their social relationships than more or less attractive peers.

Personality

Authoritarian members of juries tend to be generally biased against the defendant (eg Mitchell and Byrne, 1972/3, Kirby and Lambeth, 1974). However, it is important who the defendant is; Mitchell (1973) found that authoritarian jurors are influenced by attractiveness when the defendant is an ordinary member of the public but not when they are an authority figure.

Liking and Loving

To end the chapter, we will return to the theme of liking and loving which we touched on earlier.

In *Liking and Loving* (1973), Rubin defines liking as positive evaluation of another; loving is more than an intense liking and is qualitatively different, comprising three main components:

i)   *Attachment*: the need for the physical presence and emotional support of the loved one. (On the Love Scale, an attachment item is 'If I could never be with ____ I would feel miserable'.)

ii) *Caring*: a feeling of concern and responsibility for the loved one. ('If ____ were feeling badly, my first duty would be to cheer him/her up'.)

iii) *Intimacy*: the desire for close and confidential contact and communication, wanting to share certain thoughts and feeling with the loved one more fully than with anyone else. ('I feel that I can confide in ____ about practically everything'.)

Caring corresponds to Fromm's definition of love (1956) as, 'the active concern for the life and growth of that which we love'.

The Love Scale can be applied to same-sex friends too and Rubin found that females reported loving their friends more than men, but there was no differences in scores on the Liking Scale. Caldwell and Peplau (1982) found that women's friendships tend to be more intimate than men's, engaging in more spontaneous joint activities and more exchange of confidences. Rubin and McNeil (1983) suggest that loving for men may be channelled into single, sexual relationships while women may be better able to experience attachment, caring and intimacy in a wider range and variety of relationships.

Couples who score high on the Love Scale tend to stare a great deal into each other's eyes (Rubin, 1970) and Love Scores are much more highly correlated with marriage scores than Liking Scores (Rubin and McNeil, 1983). It has been suggested that love is a label that we learn to attach to our own state of physiological arousal (see Chapter 17) but most of the time love does *not* involve intense physical symptoms; love, therefore, is more usefully thought of as a particular sort of attitude that one person has towards another (Rubin and McNeil, 1983).

Attitudes, Attitude Change and Prejudice

According to Fiske and Taylor (1984), the study of attitudes is the corner-stone of social psychology. Much of the impetus came from attempts to change people's attitudes during the Second World War and the more general concern with the influence of the mass media on the individual. The mass media were becoming an increasingly powerful force in the 1940s, particularly the United States.

Much of this chapter will be concerned with attitude change, reflecting the context in which the study of attitudes originally developed. We shall do this in three main ways, by looking at: (i) persuasive communication, that is, study of deliberate attempts to change attitudes as carried out at Yale University during the 1940s and '50s by Hovland (who had started his research while employed by the US War Department's Information and Education Department) and his colleagues; (ii) theories of attitude change, in particular, Festinger's Cognitive Dissonance Theory (1957); and (iii) attempts to reduce prejudice, which is commonly regarded as an extreme attitude.

We shall begin by looking at the nature of attitudes and different ways of measuring them, and we shall also be discussing the nature of prejudice and some theories of its origins.

What are Attitudes?

There is no single definition on which all psychologists would agree and a sample of definitions is given over the page in Table 11.1. According to Secord and Backman (1964), most definitions comprise three components, namely: (i) the *cognitive*, what a person believes about the attitude object, what it is like, objectively; (ii) the *affective*, what a person feels about the attitude object, how favourably or unfavourably it is evaluated, reflecting its place in the person's scale of values; and (iii) the *behavioural*, how a person actually responds to the attitude object based on (i) and (ii).

Most psychologists would probably agree with Secord and Backman regarding the three components, although this is not without its problems, in particular, the assumption that they are highly correlated; we shall return to the attitude–behaviour relationship below.

Table 11.1 Some definitions of attitudes

Allport 1935	'An attitude is a mental and neural state of readiness, organized through experience, exerting a directive or dynamic influence upon the individual's response to all objects and situations with which it is related.'
Rokeach 1968	'A learned orientation, or disposition, toward an object or situation, which provides a tendency to respond favourably or unfavourably to the object or situation.' [The learning may not be based on personal experience but may be acquired through observational learning and identification.]
Warren and Jahoda 1973	'...attitudes have social references in their origins and development and in their objects, while at the same time they have psychological reference in that they inhere in the individual and are intimately enmeshed in his behaviour and his psychological make-up.
Mednick et al 1975	'An attitude is a predisposition to act in a certain way towards some aspect of one's environment, including other people.'
Bem 1979	'Attitudes are likes and dislikes.'

Attitudes, Beliefs and Values: What is the Difference?

It is easy to use these terms interchangeably and there is no doubt that they are overlapping concepts; Campbell (1963) argues that attitudes and values are one and the same, for instance. However, a distinction is normally made between them and an attitude can be thought of as a kind of blend or integration of beliefs and values (Elms, 1976).

Beliefs represent the knowledge or information we have about the world (although they may be inaccurate or incomplete) and, in themselves, are non-evaluative. According to Fishbein and Ajzen (1975), 'a belief links an object to some attribute' (eg 'America' and 'capitalist state') and in Morgan and King's terms (1971), a belief is 'the acceptance of some proposition'. To convert a belief into an attitude, a 'value' ingredient is needed which, by definition, is to do with an individual's sense of what is desirable, good, valuable, worthwhile and so on.

Allport (1935) defined a value as, 'a belief upon which a man acts by preference' and, according to Rokeach (1968), 'a value is an enduring belief that a specific mode of conduct or end-state of existence is personally or socially preferable to an opposite or converse mode of conduct or end-state of existence.' While most adults will have many thousands of beliefs, they have only hundreds of attitudes and a few dozen values.

Rokeach distinguishes between *terminal values* (desirable end-states or goals, for example, wisdom, an exciting life, equality, peace of mind and brotherhood) and *instrumental values* (desirable attributes, for example, competence, helpfulness and intellectualism); the former are desirable in themselves while the latter are desirable as means to the achievement of the former.

Probably the best known classification of values is that of Allport, Vernon and Lindzey (1951). Their scale of values attempts to measure the relative importance for an individual of six value orientations, namely *theoretical* (truth), *aesthetic* (harmony), *political* (power), *economic* (usefulness), *social* (altruistic love) and *religious* (unity). These value orientations may be regarded as corresponding to Rokeach's terminal values.

Whereas beliefs have an 'is-ness' about them (ie a belief *that* something is so), values have an 'oughtness' about them (ie a belief *in something*). Beliefs are, in themselves, neutral whereas values, by definition, are not: they provide standards and motives which guide our actions towards the achievement of those values.

Finally, it is important to make the point that attitudes, beliefs and values are hypothetical constructs and cannot be directly measured or observed but must be inferred from behaviour, including responses to tests and questionnaires. Also, they are all learned through interaction with the social environment.

Attitudes and Behaviour—How are they Related?

Given that attitudes can only be inferred from what a person says and does, once we have established a person's attitudes, are we then in a position to predict accurately their behaviour? As we saw when discussing the three components of attitudes proposed by Secord and Backman, the behavioural component would seem to be highly correlated with the cognitive and affective components. But is this true in practice? Do people's expressed attitudes (cognitive and affective components) coincide with their overt actions (behavioural component)?

An early, classic study which shows the inconsistency of attitudes and behaviour is that of La Piere (1934). He travelled around the USA with a Chinese couple, expecting to encounter anti-Oriental attitudes which would make it difficult for them to find accommodation. But in the course of 10,000 miles of travel they were discriminated against only once and there appeared to be no prejudice. However, when each of the 251 establishments visited was sent a letter asking whether they would provide food and lodging to members of the Chinese race, over 90 per cent of the 128 which responded gave an emphatic 'No', one establishment gave an unqualified 'Yes', and the rest said their decision would depend on the circumstances. In a review of the literature, Wicker (1969) painted a general picture of inconsistency. How can we account for these inconsistencies?

It is generally agreed that attitudes are only one determinant of behaviour; they represent *predispositions* to behave but how we actually act in a particular situation will depend on the immediate consequences of our behaviour, how we think others will evaluate our actions and habitual ways of behaving in those kinds of situations. (Cook and Selltiz, 1964.) In addition, there may be *situational factors* influencing behaviour; for example, in the La Piere study, the high quality of his Chinese friends' clothes and luggage and their politeness, together with the presence of La Piere himself, may have made it more difficult to show overt prejudice, and, besides, to turn away three guests is clearly against the financial interests of a hotel (at least in the short-term). Thus, sometimes we experience a *conflict* of *attitudes* and behaviour may represent a compromise between them; or, alternatively, the *strength* of one attitude relative to others may dictate a particular course of action.

Again, the same attitude may be expressed, behaviourally, in a variety of ways and in varying degrees; for example, having a positive attitude towards the Labour party does not necessarily mean that you actually become a member or that you attend public meetings. However, if you don't vote Labour in a general or local election, people may question your attitude. In other words, an attitude should predict behaviour to some extent, even if this is extremely limited and specific.

Indeed, Ajzen and Fishbein (1977) argue that attitudes *can* predict behaviour if and when appropriate attitude-measurement techniques are used; the key to success is to ensure a high degree of *specificity* of attitude and behaviour. For example, if we want to predict whether a person will participate in an anti-litter campaign, we must measure their attitude towards reducing litter, rather than their general attitude towards protecting the environment, that is, the measures of attitude and behaviour must *correspond*.

For example, when married women's attitudes towards birth control were correlated with their actual use of oral contraceptives during the two years following the study, Davidson and Jaccard (1979) found virtually no relationship (0·08); clearly, the correspondence here was very low. However, when 'attitudes towards oral contraceptives' were measured, the correlation rose to 0·32 and when 'attitudes towards oral contraceptives during the next two years' were measured, the correlation rose still further to 0·57; in both these cases, correspondence was much higher.

Another factor which influences the relationship between attitude and behaviour is to do with direct behavioural experience (Lloyd et al, 1984). According to Fazio and Zanna (1981), a number of studies have shown that attitudes which are based on direct experience have greater predictive value than those based only on indirect experience. Direct experience, of course, provides us with more information about the attitude object and our attitude may also be more easily retrieved from memory compared with one not based on personal experience (Fazio and Zanna, 1981).

Measurement of Attitudes

Many of the problems of attitude measurement are the same as those associated with other kinds of mental measurement, in particular personality (see Chapter 25) and intelligence (see Chapter 27); the general problems of reliability, validity and standardization are discussed in detail there.

However, one or two points should be made here. Most attitude scales rely on verbal reports and usually take the form of standardized statements which clearly refer to the attitude being measured. Such scales make two basic assumptions: (i) that the same statement has the same meaning for all subjects; and (ii), more fundamentally, that attitudes, when expressed verbally, can be quantified.

One source of bias is *social desirability*, that is, giving answers which the subject thinks are expected or 'proper' rather than giving honest answers; incorporating a *lie scale* can help detect this tendency to give socially desirable answers. Reassuring subjects that their answers will remain anonymous and stressing the importance of giving honest answers can also help reduce social desirability; similarly, introducing irrelevant items ('red herrings') can help to make the true purpose of the scale less obvious and so less susceptible to distorted responses.

Another source of bias is *response set*, the tendency to agree or disagree with questions consistently or to give answers which are consistently in the middle of the scale (rather than at the extremes).

Both kinds of bias detract from the reliability of attitude scales and, to the extent that a test is not reliable, it cannot be valid (ie actually measure the attitude it claims to measure).

Some of the major methods of attitude measurement are shown in Table 11.2 below.

Persuasive Communication

How easy (or difficult) is it to change someone's mind? According to Laswell (1948), in order to understand and predict the effectiveness of one person's

Table 11.2 Some major methods used in attitude measurement

1 *The Bogardus Social Distance Scale (1925)* This is really a measure of racial prejudice and comprises a series of statements representing degrees of social distance between the subject and a large number of ethnic/national groups which the subject would find tolerable. Statements range from 'to close kinship by marriage' through 'to my street as neighbours' and 'to citizenship in my country' to 'would exclude from my country'. The subject has to tick or cross one or more of these.
2 *Likert Scale (1932)* This is the most commonly used formal procedure. It comprises a number of statements, for each of which subjects must indicate whether they: (a) strongly agree, (b) agree, (c) undecided, (d) disagree, (e) strongly disagree.

3 *Thurstone Scale (1929)*
This is not itself an attitude scale but a method for devising such a scale. A series of statements, each implying a certain evaluation of the attitude object, is collected; they must cover a wide range of views and be worded as unambiguously as possible.
    They are then given to a number of 'judges' who estimate the degree to which each statement (or item) implies a positive or a negative attitude (on an 11-point scale); any items which produce substantial disagreement are discarded, until about 20 remain. Each item will have a numerical rating, assigned by a consensus of judges, ranging from 'extremely favourable' to 'extremely unfavourable' as opposite poles.
    The questionnaire is then piloted (tested) on subjects who indicate which items they agree with; their responses can then be scored and a mean attitude score calculated.
<div align="right">*Continued*</div>

Table 11.2 *(Continued)*

---

4 Semantic Differential (Osgood, Suci and Tannenbaum, 1957)
This constitutes at least nine pairs of *bi-polar* adjectives, for each of which
there is a seven-point scale (with a value of seven usually being given to the
positive pole, eg good, strong, active, and one to the negative pole). The
subject has to tick or cross at some point along the scale for each pair of
adjectives. Single words (rather than statements) are used to denote the
attitude object, eg *father*. Examples of bi-polar scales are:

```
good    — — — — — — —  bad
strong  — — — — — — —  weak
active  — — — — — — —  passive
```

'Good-bad' illustrates the *evaluative* factor, 'strong-weak' the *potency* factor and
'active-passive, the *activity* factor; for each factor there would be least two
bi-polar scales, with the evaluative factor being the most important.

---

5 Sociometry (Moreno, 1953)
This can be used with any 'natural' group (at school, college, work etc). Each
group member is asked to name another who would be their preferred partner
for a specific activity or as a friend. The product of these choices is a *sociogram*
which charts the friendship group (sub-groups), who are the popular and
unpopular members, who are the isolates, who are the leaders and so on:

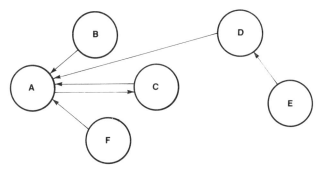

Each circle represents a group member, the arrows indicating direction of
preference (ie who prefers whom). Can you identify the most popular (and the
most likely leader)?

---

6 Interviews
These can be either: (a) *open-ended* (or unstructured), where the subject is
simply asked to express attitudes towards a particular attitude object; or (b)
structured, where a pre-determined set of questions is asked of each subject
(like a verbal questionnaire).

---

attempt to change the attitude of another, we need to know 'who says what
to whom and with what effect'.

In the terms of Hovland and Janis (1959), we need to study: (a) the *source*
of the persuasive communication, that is, the communicator (Laswell's
'who'); (b) the *message* itself (Laswell's 'what'); (c) the *recipient* of the
message, or the audience, (Laswell's 'whom'); and (d) the *situation* or *context*.
Figure 11.1 shows each of these four factors together with the major

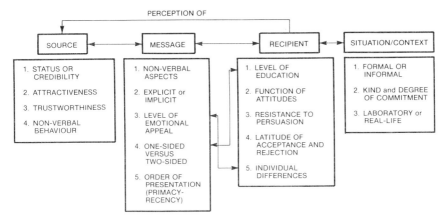

Figure 11.1 The 4 major factors involved in persuasive communication (arrows between boxes indicate examples of interaction between variables)

aspects of each which have been investigated. Two important points about Figure 11.1 are, first, that as far as the impact of the source is concerned, it is how the recipient *perceives* the source which is crucial (although the experimenter usually assumes that the manipulation of source variables will determine how the source is perceived) and, secondly, that the four factors *interact* with each other and it is quite artificial to investigate them in isolation from each other.

In some studies which we shall be discussing, this interaction becomes evident; for example, the impact of a one- or two-sided message (message-variable) seems to depend on the recipient's level of education (recipient variable) and, similarly, the effect of a fear-arousing message (message-variable) will depend on the recipients' normal level of anxiety (recipient-variable).

How is attitude change measured? The basic paradigm in attitude-change research involves three steps or stages: (i) measure subjects' (recipients') attitude towards the attitude object (pre-test); (ii) expose subjects to a persuasive communication (manipulate a source, message or situational variable or isolate a recipient-variable as the independent variable); (iii) measure subjects' attitudes again (post-test). If there is a difference between pre- and post-test measures, then the persuasive communication is judged to have 'worked'.

McGuire (1969) sees this dependent variable of 'attitude change' as being too vague and instead proposes that we should be asking about the recipient, have they: (i) *attended* to the message; (ii) *comprehended* it; (iii) *yielded* to it; (iv) *retained* it; and (v) *acted* as a result?

The Source

1) Status or Credibility
An important ingredient of status or credibility is whether the source is perceived as being an expert (or at least knowledgeable) in relation to the

attitude object; in general, the more expert the source, the more likely we are to be persuaded.

Hovland and Weiss (1951) asked American subjects to read a statement about the practicality of atomic submarines: those who were told it was written by J. Robert Oppenheimer were more convinced of its truth than those who were told its source was *Pravda*. A similar effect was found when the article concerned antihistamine drugs and the source was either the *New England Journal of Medicine* or a mass-circulation magazine.

Hovland and Weiss collected additional questionnaire data which confirmed that subjects saw the medical journal as more credible (in the sense of trustworthy) but there were no differences in how well the articles were remembered (and, therefore, attended to originally).

Kelman and Hovland (1953) found similar results when subjects heard a lecture on juvenile delinquency which advocated a lenient attitude towards juvenile delinquents; when the speaker was a 'juvenile court judge' attitude change was much greater than when the speaker was either a 'dope peddler' or a 'randomly chosen member of the studio audience'.

However both studies produced what is called the '*sleeper effect*', that is, when subjects were re-tested three to four weeks later, the original differences between different sources greatly decreased, so that there was an increasing acceptance of the message from the low-status source and a decreasing acceptance of the high-status source. However, this only occurs if subjects are *not* reminded of the identity and characteristics of the source, so, presumably, the source's identity becomes detached from the actual message with time; according to Hovland, the connection between the arguments and the conclusion of a message is remembered longer than the connection between a 'cue' (such as communicator credibility) and the conclusion.

According to Johnson and Scileppi (1969), credibility is only important in relation to attitude issues with which the subject is only mildly involved; but when ego involvement is high, the effect vanishes, perhaps because more attention is paid to the content of the message. Also, the more important the attitude issue is to our self-concept, the more suspicious we are of attempts to influence us about it (Reich and Adcock, 1975), which points to another interaction between source and recipient variables. (We shall say more about the function of attitudes below.)

In the laboratory, if there is a conflict between a powerful expert figure and the subject's peers, the former is usually more influential, but in real-life situations, the reverse seems to be true. Furthermore, some peers appear to be more influential than others. In a study by Lazarsfeld et al (1948) of voting behaviour in the USA, it emerged that the majority of voters were not being directly influenced by the media but indirectly through peers (relatives, friends, colleagues etc) considered to be 'in the know' regarding political matters. These peers were referred to as *opinion leaders* and Lazarsfeld put forward the 'Two-step Flow Hypothesis', whereby influences stemming from the media first reach opinion leaders, who, in turn, pass on what they have read and heard to their everyday associates for whom they are influential.

Menzel and Katz (1955) wanted to know how doctors decide to use a new drug and found that doctors who were opinion leaders tended to be influenced by journal articles and professional meetings and conferences etc to a greater degree than non-opinion leader colleagues. However, opinion leaders may themselves look to colleagues of even higher status, so that there may be three or four steps between the media and the majority of the target population instead of the two originally proposed by Lazarsfeld.

Another component of credibility is the *similarity* between the source and the recipient (as perceived by the latter), as demonstrated by, for example, Berscheid (1966) and Burnstein et al (1961).

2) Attractiveness

A source who is charming, humorous and has a pleasant manner is more persuasive (everything else being equal) than one who does not have these qualities. An unattractive or unlikeable source might produce a 'boomerang effect' whereby the audience responds by adopting attitudes which are contrary to those being advocated.

3) Trustworthiness

This relates to the perceived *intentions* and *motives* of the source, in particular, are they deliberately trying to influence me and is there an ulterior motive for doing so?

Walster and Festinger (1962) found that if subjects believe they are 'merely overhearing' a message they are more likely to be influenced by it than subjects who hear the same message presented directly to them; this seems to depend on (i) the subject being interested in the issue to begin with, and (ii) the subject being initially favourably disposed towards the position being advocated (Brock and Becker, 1965).

An overheard source is less likely to be suspected of ulterior motives and, to this extent, is more trustworthy. Also, when the source is perceived as trying to persuade, counter-arguments are provoked in the subject to a greater extent than if the message is 'overheard' (Brock, 1967) and if subjects are actually warned in advance of the source's attempt to change their mind on some issue, the chances of any attitude change occurring are considerably reduced.

Finally, a message is very effective if it is seen as actually being contrary to the source's self-interest. In a study by Walster et al (1966), subjects were presented with arguments advocating more or less power for the courts and which, supposedly, came from either a criminal or a prosecutor. The criminal was less effective when advocating a reduction in the courts' power and more effective when advocating an increase in power, the latter being the opposite of what subjects expected him to advocate. Compared with the prosecutor who argued for an increase in the courts' power, the criminal who did so was seen as both more honest and more persuasive. (If we believe that someone is [sincerely] advocating a position which is opposed to their own self-interest, we may come to regard the argument as worth taking seriously for that reason.)

4) Non-verbal Behaviour

This is important largely because of how it contributes to the source being perceived as attractive and trustworthy. One especially pertinent dimension of non-verbal behaviour is proximity, which we discussed in Chapter 10.

In an experimental study, Albert and Dabbs (1970) found that most attitude change was produced when the source stood 14 to 15 feet away and least at a distance of 1 to 2 feet; probably, subjects in the latter condition felt that their intimate zone was being encroached and resented this.

Abelson and Zimbardo (1970) advised campaigning candidates and door-to-door canvassers to keep a distance of 4 to 5 feet, a respectful distance when talking to strangers, especially when you are on the stranger's 'territory'; this corresponds to Hall's social–consultative distance.

The Message

1) Non-verbal Aspects

Following on from what we have said about the source, face-to-face communication may be more effective than attempts by the media to change attitudes because when the source receives feedback from the recipient (in the form of facial expressions, eye contact, body posture and so on) they are in a better position to anticipate objections and to modify the message and present counter-arguments.

Maslow et al (1971) found that over-and-above the content of a message, how confidently it is presented is a crucial variable. In an experiment, subjects read details of a law case intended to help them judge whether or not the accused was guilty; some subjects read a confidently presented argument in favour of the accused (using phrases such as 'obviously', 'I am quite sure', 'I believe'), while others read a much more tentative argument ('I don't know', 'I'm not positive', 'I'm unsure') and, as predicted, significantly more subjects judged in favour of the accused in the former case. In the same study, subjects saw an actor make lip movements to a neutral sounding tape of a non-guilty plea in a confident, neutral or doubtful way (through facial expression etc) and similar results were found. (Confidence could just as easily be discussed as a source-variable as opposed to a message-variable.)

2) Explicit or Implicit

The question here is whether the argument should be clearly spelt-out (so that no one is left in any doubt as to the conclusions to be drawn) or whether an implicit message is more effective, leaving the recipient to work out the conclusions on their own.

McGuire (1968) believes that implicit messages may be more effective if the recipient is capable of, and likely to, draw the conclusions; but for recipients of low intelligence or motivation, explicit messages may be preferred (Hovland and Mandell, 1952).

3) Level of Emotional Appeal

Can subjects be frightened into changing their minds?

One of the most famous attempts to induce attitude change through the manipulation of fear was by Janis and Feshbach (1953). American high-school students were randomly assigned to one of four groups, one control and three experimental. The message was concerned with dental hygiene and degree of fear-arousal was manipulated by the number and nature of consequences of improper care of teeth which were referred to (and shown in colour slides); each message also contained factual information about the causes of tooth decay and some advice about caring for teeth.

The *high fear* condition made 71 references to unpleasant effects, including toothache, painful treatment and possible secondary diseases, including blindness and cancer; the *moderate fear* condition made 49 references; and the *low fear* condition just 18. (Control subjects heard a talk about the eye.)

Before the experiment, subjects' attitudes to dental health—and their dental habits—were assessed as part of a general health survey; the same questionnaire was given again immediately following the fear-inducing message and one week later.

As far as how worried subjects were about their teeth (an index of attitude change), it seemed that fear had worked, that is, the stronger the appeal to fear, the more anxious subjects were. However, as far as actual changes in dental behaviour were concerned, the high-fear condition proved to be the least effective; 8 per cent of the high-fear group had adopted the recommendations (changes in toothbrushing and visiting the dentist in the weeks immediately following the experiment), compared with 22 per cent and 37 per cent in the moderate- and low-fear conditions respectively. Similar results were reported by Janis and Terwillinger (1962) when they presented a mild- and strong-fear message concerning the relationship between smoking and cancer.

It would seem that, in McGuire's terms you can frighten people into attending to a message, comprehending it, yielding to it and retaining it but not necessarily into acting upon it; indeed, fear may be so great that action is inhibited rather than facilitated. However, this general conclusion needs to be qualified in three main ways.

First, if the audience is told *how* to avoid undesirable consequences and believes that the preventative action is realistic and will be effective, then even high levels of fear in the message can produce changes in behaviour—and the more specific and precise the instructions, the greater the behaviour change. The presence of such instructions is referred to as the *high availability* factor (Leventhal et al, 1965, Leventhal, 1970) and a number of studies have demonstrated that while making subjects afraid is in itself counterproductive, if fear-inducement is combined with reassuring recommendations as to how the potential threat can be averted, then behavioural change can take place (eg DeWolfe and Governdale, 1964, Harris and Jellison, 1971).

Secondly, in situations of minimal or extreme fear, the message may fail to produce any attitude change, let alone any change in behaviour. According to McGuire (1968), there is an inverted U-shaped curve in the relationship between fear and attitude change (see Figure 11.2 overleaf). In segment 1 of the curve, the subject is not particularly interested in (aroused by) the message; it is hardly attended to and may not even register. In segment 2, attention and arousal increase as fear increases, but the fear remains within manageable proportions. In segment 3, attention will decrease again but this time because defences are being used to deal with extreme fear, for example, the message may be denied ('it couldn't happen to me') or repressed (made unconscious and, hence, forgotten).

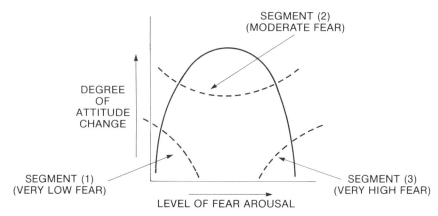

Figure 11.2   Inverted ∪ curve showing relationship between attitude change and fear arousal (based on McGuire, 1968)

Thirdly, there are important individual differences regarding normal levels of anxiety (either as a personality trait or in connection with the issue in question, which McGuire calls 'initial level of concern'). Clearly, a person who has a high level of initial concern will be more easily pushed into sector 3 (see Figure 11.2) than someone with a low level of initial concern; the former may be overwhelmed by a high-fear message (in which case defences are used against it) while the latter may become interested and aroused enough for the message to have an impact. So different degrees of fear will have different effects upon different individuals depending on their initial level of anxiety (another important interaction).

Janis and Feshbach (1953) re-analysed their original data and found that high-anxiety subjects (who reported frequent shortage of breath, heart-pounding etc) were less influenced by a high-fear message than low-anxiety subjects, but were more influenced by a low-fear message.

Finally, another interesting interaction effect between fear-arousal and recipient-variables is the finding by Insko et al (1965) that moderate fear arousal was more effective for smokers, while a high fear arousal was more effective for strengthening the resolve of non-smokers never to start.

4)   One-Sided Versus Two-Sided Arguments

Whether or not advertisers should make any kind of reference to rival products, or politicians to their opponents, seems to depend on the audience; again we have an interaction effect.

Hovland, Lumsdaine and Sheffield (1949) presented two groups of over two hundred soldiers with a series of radio transcripts, arguing that it would take at least two years to end the war with Japan: one group received a strictly one-sided message and the other a strictly two-sided message.

Overall, the two messages produced the same net change in attitudes. However, when education was taken into account, important differences emerged: those who were better educated (had at least completed high school) were more influenced by a two-sided argument; while those who were less well educated were more influenced by a one-sided presentation. Hass and Linder (1972) suggest that this might be related to the recipients' knowledge of counter-arguments; recipients who are aware of arguments opposed to the speaker's point of view are most persuaded by two-sided messages which explicitly refute these arguments.

Hovland et al also found evidence that soldiers whose initial attitude was similar to the message were more influenced by a one-sided argument (keeping education constant) while the opposite held true for those initially opposed to it. These results were confirmed by Chu (1967) who also found that a two-sided argument is more effective if subjects are already familiar with the topic.

5) Order of Presentation (Primacy–Recency)

Having decided to make a two-sided presentation, which side of the argument should come first—the one you want your audience to hold or the counter-position? This, of course, is another instance of the *primacy–recency* issue which we first saw when discussing memory (Chapter 6) and then in interpersonal perception (Chapter 8).

Early research (Lund, 1925) showed a primacy effect but Hovland et al (1957) thought primacy was more powerful only under certain conditions: (i) if both sides are presented by the same person and the subject is not initially aware that conflicting arguments will be presented; (ii) if the subject makes some kind of public commitment at the end of the first message (eg they agree to their views being published in a magazine).

McGuire (1957) attempted to persuade subjects to accept an educational course by presenting the desirable features first and the undesirable ones second, and found evidence of a primacy effect; if the order of presentation is reversed, the subject 'switches off' from the rest of the message and so the desirable features are not 'heard'.

Rosnow and Robinson (1967) found that when subjects are not very familiar with the issue, or not very interested in it, a recency effect tends to occur, but if the subject is very involved (eg the issue is highly controversial) a primacy effect predominates.

Another important factor is the time interval between the two messages. Miller and Campbell (1959) used material from a simulated jury trial and their findings are shown in Figure 11.3.

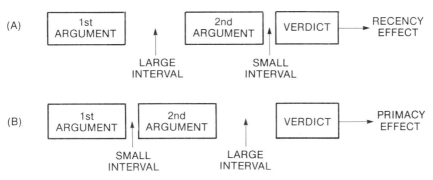

Figure 11.3 The influence of time on primacy-recency in a 2-sided argument (based on Miller and Campbell, 1959)

Finally, Hass and Linder (1972) advocate that when there are no delays at all, the opposing argument should be given first and then strongly refuted; in this way attention is drawn to the speaker's viewpoint for most of the presentation.

The Recipient

1) Level of Education

We have discussed this already in relation to the Hovland et al study of soldiers (1949) but without saying why the better educated should be more influenced by a two-sided argument. Perhaps they are intellectually better equipped to handle conflicting arguments and are more used to doing so; they might find a two-sided argument more challenging and also may not want to think of themselves as being easily persuaded (as in a one-sided argument).

2) The Function of Attitudes

Given what we have said about attitudes comprising three major components, and given the interconnection between attitudes, values and beliefs, it is perhaps not surprising that many psychologists take the view that not all attitudes have all the same significance for the individual and that they serve different functions.

If we accept this, it follows that some attitudes will be harder to change than others and a major classification of the functions of attitudes is that of

Table 11.3 Four major functions of attitudes (Katz, 1960)

(i) *Knowledge function:* We seek a degree of predictability, consistency and stability in our perception of the world (corresponding to the *cognitive* component of attitudes); attitudes give meaning and direction to experience, supplying frames of reference for judging events and objects.
(ii) *Adjustive (instrumental or utilitarian) function:* We obtain favourable responses from others by displaying socially acceptable attitudes, so attitudes become associated with important rewards (such as the approval and acceptance of others). These attitudes may be publicly expressed but not necessarily believed, as in compliance (see Chapter 12).
(iii) *Value-expressive function:* We achieve self-expression through cherished values. The reward may not be gaining social support but confirmation of the more positive aspects of one's own self-concept (of course, self-concept can also be affected by culturally-based stereotypes, eg gender roles). Particularly important for a sense of personal integrity.
(iv) *Ego-defensive function:* Attitudes help us to be protected from admitting personal deficiencies. For example, denial permits us to defend our self-concept. Prejudice helps to sustain our self-concept by maintaining a sense of superiority over others. Ego-defence often means avoiding and denying self-knowledge (so this function of attitudes comes closest to being unconscious in Freud's sense). (See Chapter 26.)

Katz (1960). He is concerned with the motives which attitudes serve and sees some of these motives as conscious and others unconscious; his approach is probably the closest that modern theories come to a Freudian, psycho-dynamic view of attitudes.

So what are the psychological needs met by holding and changing attitudes? According to Katz, the two principal functions of attitudes are: (i) they provide a ready basis for interpreting the world and processing new information; and (ii) they provide a way of gaining and maintaining social identification. Beyond this, he proposes four motivational functions which are summarized in Table 11.3.

Katz's functional approach is especially important in trying to account for prejudice and attempting to reduce it. A similar classification was proposed by Smith et al (1956): (a) *object appraisal* refers to the adaptive function of attitudes in meeting day-to-day problems (corresponding to Katz's knowledge function); (b) *social adjustment* refers to the usefulness of an attitude in social relationships (corresponding to Katz's adjustive function); (c) *externalization* involves responding to an external event in terms of some unresolved internal conflict, thus distorting it (corresponding to Katz's ego-defensive function); and (d) *quality* of *expressiveness* which is more concerned with how attitudes reflect an individual's deeper pattern of life, a person's expressive nature or style of operating, and so is not really about functions at all (Reich and Adcock, 1976).

3) Resistance To Persuasion

In general, it seems that resistance is strongest when counter-arguments are available and weakest when they are not. According to McGuire and Papageorgis (1961), people can be 'innoculated' against attempts to persuade them; by analogy with medical immunization, the subject is given a mild 'dose' of an argument against their own opinion, sufficient to activate a defensive counter-argument. Subjects were first exposed to an opposing argument and then were given statements countering these arguments and reinforcing their initial attitudes; a week later, they read a different message which also challenged their initial attitude and they were then less likely to be persuaded by it than subjects who had not been innoculated (including some who had received support for their opinion but no attack).

Does simply warning someone in advance help them resist persuasive communications? Freedman and Sears (1965) found that it did when teenagers were warned about a speech which would be arguing against young people being allowed to drive, but Hass and Mann (1976) found that it did not when subjects were warned about an argument which would oppose their own regarding the chances of an economic recession. How can we account for this discrepancy?

According to Kiesler and Jones (1971) the more committed we are to an issue, the more resistant we are likely to be, regardless of any advance warning; when a warning does have an effect it does so by drawing on that commitment and, perhaps, by prompting us to anticipate counter-arguments and prepare arguments against these (a kind of 'self-innoculation'). Also, the better-informed we are about a topic, the more resistant we are likely to be; Hass and Mann (1976) warn us against being caught in a situation where we have to defend a view which we cannot defend intelligently, in an informed way. (An excellent way of learning how to defend a particular viewpoint is, paradoxically, to argue for its *opposite*, that is, to play 'devil's advocate', in that way, you can discover the weakness in your position and try to prepare defensive arguments. You might like to have a class debate in which you deliberately choose to defend the view which is opposed to your own.)

4) Latitude of Acceptance and Rejection

The greater the discrepancy between the attitude a person already holds, and the one which the communicator wants the person to hold, the less likely it is that any shift in attitude will occur. Another way of saying this is that if the persuasive message lies outside a person's *latitude of acceptance* (arguments they are prepared to accept) then it will be rejected (and so will fall within the person's *latitude of rejection*).

Sherif and Hovland (1961) found that unacceptable statements tend to be perceived as even more hostile or unfavourable than they really are (*contrast*) while those which are not so extreme may be gradually incorporated into the person's latitude of acceptance (*assimilation*). The more extreme the person's initial position, and the greater the ego-involvement in it: (i) the smaller the latitude of acceptance; (ii) the greater the latitude of rejection; (iii) the greater the contrast effect; and, consequently, (iv) the less the attitude change.

Himmelfarb and Eagly (1974) have pointed out that laboratory experiments normally use issues which are relatively unimportant, together with a high-credibility source; compared with field studies, this has the effect of increasing the latitude of acceptance and hence making attitude change more likely.

5) Individual Differences

We have discussed anxiety in relation to the impact of messages which appeal to fear, but we need to say something about gender, self-esteem, persuasibility and intelligence.

Many early studies suggested that women are more easily persuaded (eg Janis and Field, 1956, 1959) but this may simply have been the product of the experimenters' choice of 'male-dominated' issues, such as politics and the economy (Aronson, 1976). Indeed, studies carried out more recently have shown that while women may be more easily persuaded about 'male' issues, men are equally persuasible in relation to 'female' issues, such as home management and family relationships (Sistrunk and McDavid (1971)).

High self-esteem subjects tend to try to influence others and are less easily persuaded by others compared with low self-esteem subjects, at least in the case of men. In women, there is some evidence that low self-esteem subjects may actually move even further away from the message (probably as a form of ego-defence) while women of medium self-esteem are the most persuasible.

Is there a personality factor which can be called persuasibility? McGuire (1968) thinks there is but that it may not manifest itself equally in relation to both comprehension and yielding, and he makes a similar point in relation to intelligence: we would expect a negative correlation between intelligence and persuasibility if the latter is thought of in terms of yielding, *but* since there is a positive correlation between intelligence and comprehension, the overall relationship between intelligence and persuasibility is not a straight-line but a *curvilinear* one (as is the inverted-U curve in Figure 11.2).

Table 11.4 Summary of all the studies cited in relation to the 4 major factors involved in persuasive communication

Source	Message	Recipient	Situation/context
1. Status or credibility Hovland and Weiss (1951) Kelman and Hovland (1953) Johnson and Scileppi (1969) Lazarsfeld et al (1948) Menzel and Katz (1955) Berscheid (1966) Burnstein et al (1966)	**1. Non-verbal aspects** Maslow et al (1971)	**1. Level of education** Hovland et al (1949)**	**1. Formal or informal** Kelly (1955) Janis and Mann (1965)
2. Attractiveness	**2. Explicit or implicit** McGuire (1968) Hovland and Mandell (1952)	**2. Function of attitudes** Katz (1960) Smith et al (1956)	**2. Kind and degree of commitment**
3. Trustworthiness Walster and Festinger (1962) Brock and Becker (1965) Brock (1967) Walster et al (1966)	**3. Level of emotional appeal** Janis and Feshbach (1953) Janis and Terwilliger (1962) Leventhal et al (1965) Leventhal (1970) DeWolfe and Governdale (1964) Harris and Jellison (1971) McGuire (1968) Iusko et al (1965)	**3. Resistance to persuasion** McGuire and Papageorgis (1961) Freedman and Sears (1965) Hass and Mann (1976) Kiesler and Jones (1971)	**3. Laboratory or real-life**
4. Non-verbal behaviour Albert and Dabbs (1970) Abelson and Zimbardo (1970)	**4. One-sided versus two-sided arguments** Hovland et al (1949)** Hass and Linder (1972)* Chu (1967)	**4. Latitude of acceptance and rejection** Sherif and Hovland (1961) Himmelfarb and Eagly (1974)	
	5. Order of presentation Lund (1925) Hovland et al (1957) McGuire (1957) Rosnow and Robinson (1967) Miller and Campbell (1959) Hass and Linder (1972)*	**5. Individual differences** Janis and Field (1956, 1959) Aronson (1976) Sistrunk and McDavid (1971) McGuire (1968)	

Situation or Context

Informal situations, such as group discussions, often prove more effective than *formal* situations, such as speeches and lectures, partly because of differences in the perception of who is trying to influence whom and for what motives. Role-play is another kind of informal situation which has been found effective, both in a therapeutic setting (Kelly, 1955) and experimentally (Janis and Mann, 1965). In the latter, subjects who played the role of cancer patients showed significantly greater changes in their attitudes *and* their smoking behaviour than subjects who heard information via a tape-recorder or controls, who did neither.

In a group context, subjects may be obliged to make some kind of public *commitment* to a particular attitude which may initially reflect pressures to conform (see Chapter 12) but which may then bring about genuine attitude change through the reduction of cognitive dissonance (see below); opinions which are expressed privately or anonymously are far less likely to bring about attitude change.

Finally, as we have already noted, *laboratory* studies are much more likely to produce attitude change than *real-life* situations, for a variety of reasons. (See Table 11.4 for a summary of all the major studies cited.)

Theories of Attitude Change—The Need for Consistency

The most influential theories of attitude change have concentrated on the principle of *cognitive consistency*, whereby human beings are seen as internally active information processors who sort through and modify a large number of cognitive elements in order to achieve some kind of cognitive coherence.

Three of the best known consistency theories are: (i) Heider's *balance theory* (1958), according to which people seek harmony among their various attitudes and beliefs and tend to evaluate in similar ways things that are related to each other; (ii) Osgood and Tannenbaums' *congruity theory* (1955), which maintains that when two attitudes or beliefs are inconsistent with each other, it is the one that is less firmly held which will be the one that changes; and (iii) Festinger's *cognitive dissonance theory* (1957), which we shall now examine in detail.

Cognitive Dissonance

The central idea is that whenever an individual simultaneously holds two cognitions which are psychologically inconsistent, they experience dissonance, which is a negative drive state, a state of 'psychological discomfort or tension' which motivates the individual to reduce it by achieving consonance; attitude change is seen as a major way of reducing dissonance.

Cognitions are 'the things a person knows about himself, about his behaviour and about his surroundings' (Festinger, 1957) and any two cognitions can be consonant (A implies B), dissonant (A implies not–B, the obverse of A) or irrelevant to each other.

A classic example of when dissonance is likely to arise is if we smoke and also believe that smoking causes cancer; assuming that we would rather not have cancer, the cognition 'I smoke' is psychologically inconsistent with the cognition 'smoking causes cancer'. Perhaps the most efficient (and certainly the healthiest!) way to reduce dissonance is to stop smoking, but most of us will work on the other cognition; for example, we might:

a) Belittle the evidence about smoking and cancer (eg the human data is only correlational);
b) Associate with other smokers (eg, 'If so-and-so smokes, then it can't be very dangerous');
c) Smoke low-tar cigarettes;
d) Convince ourselves that smoking is an important and highly pleasurable activity;
e) Make a virtue out of it by developing a romantic, devil-may-care image and flaunting danger by smoking etc.

All these possible ways of reducing dissonance demonstrate that dissonance theory regards the human being not as a rational creature but a *rationalizing* one, attempting to *appear* rational both to others and to oneself.

1) Dissonance Following a Decision

If we have to choose between two equally attractive objects or activities, then one way of reducing the resulting dissonance is to emphasize the undesirable features of the one we have rejected; in this way we are trying to add to the number of consonant cognitions and reduce the number of dissonant ones.

This was demonstrated in a study by Brehm (1956) in which female subjects had to rate the desirability of several household appliances on an eight-point scale. When they had done this, they had to choose between two of the items (their reward for participating), which for half the subjects were $\frac{1}{2}$ to $1\frac{1}{2}$ points apart on the scale (*high-dissonance* condition) and for the other half were a full three points apart (*low-dissonance* condition). When subjects were asked to re-evaluate the items they had chosen and rejected, they showed increased liking for the chosen item and decreased liking for the rejected one. So far, so good.

The theory also predicts that we will tend to actively *avoid* information which emphasizes the desirable qualities of the item we have rejected (because that will add to the dissonance) as well as actively *seeking* information which praises the desirable qualities of the item we have chosen (because that will reduce dissonance by increasing consonance). So if we have had a difficult time deciding which new car to buy, we will avoid advertisements for other cars and go out of our way to find advertisements for our own. Is there evidence to support this prediction?

A study by Ehrlich et al (1957) suggested that there is a tendency to prefer advertisements showing the car subjects had recently bought but no corresponding avoidance of advertisements showing other cars; this was confirmed by Freedman and Sears (1965) and Sears (1968).

Dissonance theory predicts that there will be *selective exposure* to consonant information, that is, seeking consistent information which is not present at the time. However, there is more to selective perception: other aspects include *selective attention* (looking at consistent information which is present) and *selective interpretation* (perceiving ambiguous information as being consistent with our other cognitions). Each of these has been investigated and in a review of the literature Fiske and Taylor (1984) conclude that the evidence overall is stronger for selective attention and interpretation than for selective exposure.

2) Dissonance Resulting from Effort

In one of the classic dissonance experiments (Aronson and Mills, 1959), female college students volunteered for a discussion on the psychology of sex, with the understanding that the research was concerned with the dynamics of group discussion. Each subject was interviewed individually and asked if she could participate without embarrassment; all but one said yes. If she had been assigned to the *control* condition, she was simply accepted; but for acceptance to the *severe embarrassment* condition she had to take an 'embarrassment test' (reading out loud to a male experimenter a list of obscene words and some explicit sexual passages from modern novels—remember the year was 1959!); and for acceptance to the *mild embarrassment* condition she had to read aloud words like 'prostitute' and 'virgin'. They then all heard a tape-recording of an actual discussion (by a group which they believed they would later join) which was about lower animals and extremely dull. Subjects then had to rate the discussion and the group members in terms of how interesting or dull and intelligent or unintelligent they found them.

As predicted, the Severe Embarrassment subjects gave the most positive ratings—because they had experienced the greatest dissonance! These results have been confirmed by Aronson (1961), Gerard and Matthewson (1966), Lewis (1964) and Zimbardo (1965).

So, when a voluntarily chosen experience turns out badly, the fact that we chose it motivates us to try to think that it actually turned out well: the greater the sacrifice or hardship associated with the choice, the greater the dissonance and, therefore, the greater the pressure towards attitude change.

3) Engaging in Counter-attitudinal Behaviour

Probably the most famous of all the dissonance experiments is the one carried out by Festinger and Carlsmith (1959). College students were brought, one at a time, into a small room to work for 30 minutes on two extremely dull and repetitive tasks (stacking spools and turning pegs). Later, they were offered either one dollar or twenty dollars to enter a waiting room and to try to convince the next 'subject' (in fact, a female stooge) that the tasks were interesting and enjoyable. Commonsense would predict that the twenty-dollar group would be the more likely to change their attitude in favour of the tasks (they had more reason to do so) and this is also the prediction which would be made by Reinforcement or Incentive theory (Janis et al, 1965) which maintains that the greater the reward or incentive, the greater the attitude change (liking for the tasks).

However, Festinger and Carlsmith found, as predicted by dissonance theory, that it was, in fact, the one-dollar group which showed the greater attitude change. Why? The large, twenty-dollar incentive gave those subjects ample *justification* for their counter-attitudinal behaviour and so they experienced very little dissonance; by contrast, the one-dollar subjects experienced considerable dissonance since they could hardly justify their counter-attitudinal behaviour in terms of the negligible reward, hence, the change of attitude to reduce the dissonance.

These findings have been confirmed by several studies in which children are given either a mild or a severe threat not to play with an attractive toy (Aronson and Carlsmith, 1963, Freedman, 1965, Turner and Wright, 1965). If children obey a mild threat, they will experience greater dissonance because it is more difficult for them to justify their behaviour than it is for children who are given a severe threat, and so the mild threat condition produces greater reduction in liking of the toy.

But does counter-attitudinal behaviour always and inevitably produce dissonance and attitude change? It seems not—dissonance only occurs when *volitional* (voluntary) behaviour is involved, that is, when we feel we acted of our own free will; if we believe we had no choice, there is no dissonance and, hence, no attitude change. A study by Freedman (1963) shows that dissonance theory and reinforcement or incentive theory are not necessarily opposed to each other—their respective predictions may *both* be confirmed when applied to the conditions of voluntary or involuntary behaviour.

Freedman asked subjects to perform a dull task after *first* informing them that either: (a) the data would definitely be of *no* value to the experimenter since his experiment was already completed; or (b) that the data would be of *great* value to him. Subjects in (a) enjoyed the task to a much greater extent than those in (b), because the former experienced greater dissonance (*dissonance effect*). However, in a parallel set of conditions, he withheld information about the value of the task until *after* subjects had completed the task and found the opposite effect, that is, those in (b) enjoyed the task much more (they received the reward of his gratitude), while those in (a) could reason, 'If I'd known I wouldn't have done it' and so experienced no dissonance (*incentive effect*).

Another variable which influences dissonance, and which interacts with voluntary or involuntary behaviour, is degree of *commitment*. Carlsmith et al (1966) used a procedure similar to that of Festinger and Carlsmith's one dollar/twenty dollar experiment and also found that the smaller reward produced the greater attitude change.

However, this dissonance effect was only found under conditions where subjects lied to another person in a highly committing, face-to-face situation (they had to make an identifiable video recording); where subjects merely had to write an essay and were assured of complete anonymity, then an incentive effect was found (ie the bigger the reward, the greater the attitude change). (In the Festinger and Carlsmith study, this face-to-face variable was not manipulated.)

According to Brehm and Cohen (1962), both volition *and* commitment are necessary for the arousal of dissonance and the greater one of these (or both), the greater the dissonance. Similarly, Collins and Hoyt argue that we must perceive our behaviour as having serious consequences if we are to experience dissonance; for instance, in the Festinger and Carlsmith experiment, dissonance would only occur if subjects believed they really had convinced the next subject how enjoyable the task was.

Kelman and Baron (1974) distinguish between two *kinds* of dissonance: (i) *moral*, in which counter-attitudinal behaviour is related to a value so that greater reward produces more dissonance (and greater effort produces less dissonance); and (ii) *hedonic*, in which lesser reward produces greater dissonance (and greater effort produces greater dissonance). Hedonic dissonance is involved in the one dollar/twenty dollar experiment.

Evaluation of Dissonance Theory

Alternative Explanations

Not only do dissonance effects occur under certain specified conditions (eg volition and commitment), but some critics have argued that even under those conditions it is possible to explain the findings in other ways.

For instance, in the Aronson and Mills (1959) experiment, the severe embarrassment condition effectively masked the true purpose of the experiment and also seemed to cause genuine embarrassment—blushing, hesitation, looking down at the floor and so on. According to Chapanis and Chapanis (1964), the use of sexual material suggests at least two plausible alternative explanations:

i) While reciting the material, the female subjects became sexually aroused which could have increased the attractiveness of the group;
ii) They felt relief (from sexual anxiety) when they discovered how banal the group discussion really was, also increasing the group's attractiveness.

Gerard and Matthewson (1966) tested these alternative explanations by operationalizing 'unpleasant effort' as electric shocks, so that the initiation into the group had nothing to do with sexual arousal or relief from sexual anxiety. What subjects thought would be a discussion about 'college morals' turned out to be one about cheating in exams and, consistent with Aronson and Mills's results, subjects who underwent severe shock came to rate the discussion far more favourably than mild-shock subjects. Both studies show that dissonance is only experienced when severe initiation is endured *in order* to get into a group which turns out to be dull.

According to Bem (1965) dissonance as such is neither a necessary nor sufficient explanation and he rejects any reference to hypothetical, intervening variables. According to his Self-Perception theory (1965, 1972), there is no evidence that we have an internal need for consistency or that we are bothered about violating our principles or attitudes—we come to know about our own internal states in the same way that we learn to attribute feelings and attitudes to others, namely, through observation of behaviour. Since the internal cues we experience are often weak or ambiguous, in order to determine what it is we are thinking or feeling we have to scan our overt behaviour and the situation in which it occurs and then to infer our attitudes and values.

Applied to the one dollar/twenty dollar experiment, the twenty-dollar subjects could easily attribute their behaviour to external factors, (the large financial reward) and so make a *situational attribution* ('I did it for the money') while the one-dollar subjects inferred that they must have enjoyed the task otherwise why else would they have tried to convince the next subject ('I did it because I really enjoyed it') making a *dispositional attribution*. So who is right, Festinger or Bem?

There is additional evidence to support both theories and Fazio (1977) suggests that each most accurately describes attitude change under different circumstances—Bem's when the attitude is consistent with behaviour and Festinger's when behaviour is inconsistent with an attitude.

There is no doubt that we do sometimes 'work backwards' from behaviour to 'internal states', eg our stomach rumbles or we have 'second helpings' at a meal and then infer how hungry we must have been, or we shout at someone and infer that we are angry. However, dissonance does not only arise in an attitude-behaviour conflict—the conflict may be between two attitudes or beliefs. Gergen and Gergen (1981) conclude that self-perception theory is a plausible and provocative alternative to dissonance theory.

Again, Tedeschi et al (1971) maintain that in terms of impression management, dissonance experiments demonstrate the human need to *appear* consistent rather than a drive to actually *be* consistent; yet Zanna and Cooper (1974) believe that dissonance is an arousal state with aversive emotional properties and Cooper et al (1978) found that subjects given tranquillizers show little attitude change compared with non-tranquillized subjects (suggesting that dissonance is associated with physiological changes).

Individual Differences
People seem to differ with regard to their preferred methods of reducing dissonance and also what is dissonant for one person may not necessarily be dissonant for another—self-concept must be taken into account.

It has also been found that chronic anxiety is related to the 'need for balance', so that people rated as highly anxious show behaviour consistent with dissonance theory, while those rated low on anxiety show behaviour consistent with reinforcement or incentive theory (Steiner and Rogers, 1963). The theory also assumes that once a particular threshold of tension or psychological discomfort is reached, the individual will inevitably act to reduce the inconsistency which produced it. However, most people seem to be able to tolerate a great deal of (logical) inconsistency among their actions and beliefs and only a few individuals reveal a strong integration of their belief system (Katz, 1968). Mills et al (1959) believe that dissonant information can sometimes be positively valuable.

Cognitive Dissonance Theory as a Notion
According to Bannister and Fransella (1980), cognitive dissonance theory is a *notion*, 'the sort of idea which coffee-table conversation amongst psychologists might produce'. They believe it is over-simple and vague and that it functions in psychology in much the same way as folk tales do in literature: it can form the plot for endless experiments but it cannot be legitimately called a theory. However, there is no doubt that it has generated an enormous amount of both research and theorizing.

Prejudice

As an extreme attitude, prejudice comprises the components of all attitudes:

i)   The *cognitive* component is the *stereotype* (which, in itself, is neutral, neither favourable nor unfavourable, see Chapter 8);

ii)   The *affective* component is a strong feeling of hostility *or* liking (prejudice, as such, is not necessarily prejudice *against* but can also be *for* a particular group or kind of person);

iii) The *behavioural* component can take different forms. Allport (1954) proposed five stages of this component:

    a) *Anti-locution*—hostile talk, verbal denigration and insult, racial jokes etc.;

    b) *Avoidance*—keeping a distance but without inflicting any harm;

    c) *Discrimination*—exclusion from housing, civil rights, employment etc;

    d) *Physical attack*—violence against the person and property;

    e) *Extermination*—indiscriminate violence against an entire group.

As with all attitudes, the cognitive and affective components may not necessarily be manifested behaviourally (as in the La Piere, 1934, study discussed above). But it is just as important to recognize that discrimination does not necessarily imply the presence of cognitive and affective components —people may discriminate if the prevailing social norms dictate that they do so and if their wish to become or remain a member of the discriminating group is stronger than their wish to be fair and egalitarian etc. As far as definitions of prejudice are concerned, they almost without exception stress the hostile, negative, kind (rather than the favourable kind) and the research which tries to identify how prejudice arises, and how it might be reduced, also concentrates on hostile prejudice. Coon (1982) defines prejudice as 'a negative attitude or prejudgment tinged with unreasonable suspicion, fear, or hatred' and Allport (1954) as, 'an antipathy based on faulty and inflexible generalization directed towards a group as a whole or towards an individual because he is a member of that group. It may be felt or expressed.'

Some Demonstrations of Prejudice

A quite dramatic (and alarming) demonstration of the *creation* of prejudice is the 'blue eyes–brown eyes' field experiment described in Box 11.1.

Allport and Kramer (1946) demonstrated an important relationship between racial prejudice and perception. They found that people with strong anti-Semitic prejudice were able to distinguish Jews from non-Jews more accurately than unprejudiced people. Because of the salience of Jews for the prejudiced subjects, they pay attention to the cues which indicate Jewish-ness (whatever these may be) and ignore other features.

The prejudiced person (or society) must be able to classify everybody as a member of the 'good' or 'bad' race. This can produce ludicrous situations, as in South Africa where Japanese are classified as white and Chinese as coloured.

The denial of objects at the boundaries of well-defined classes is a feature of normal perception, for, assuming that objects fall into discrete groups, we have an economic (convenient) description of the world. (A relevant study —although not concerned with prejudice—is that of Bruner and Postman, 1949, in which subjects were shown unusual playing cards—see Chapter 4.)

Taylor et al (1978) reported that surveys taken between 1970–76 indicated increasing support for integration in education and housing in the USA. However, many studies of whites' behaviour in the same period (including

---

Box 11.1 'The Blue Eyes–Brown Eyes' Experiment

(Reported by Aronson and Osherow, 1980)

Aronson and Osherow (1980) reported an experiment with third graders (nine-year-olds) in the USA, conducted by their teacher, Elliott.

She told her class one day that brown-eyed people are more intelligent and 'better' people than those with blue eyes. Brown-eyed students, though in the minority, would be the 'ruling class' over the inferior blue-eyed children , given extra privileges, and the blue-eyed students were 'kept in their place' by such restrictions as being last in line, seated at the back of the class and given less break time.

Within a short time, the blue-eyed children began to do more poorly in their schoolwork and became depressed and angry and described themselves more negatively. The brown-eyed group grew mean, oppressing the others and making derogatory statements about them.

The next day, Elliot announced that she had lied and that it was really blue-eyed people who are superior. The pattern of discrimination, derogation and prejudice quickly reversed itself; she then de-briefed the children.

Several similar studies have replicated this scenario with other populations.

---

many studies of college students) have shown that anti-black sentiment remains stronger than the survey data suggest (Crosby et al, 1980)

In a study by Benson et al (1976), a completed application to graduate school was 'planted' in an airport telephone booth. Half the time the applicant (shown in a photograph) was white, the other half black. In all cases, a stamped, addressed, envelope, and a note asking 'Dad' to post the form were attached. The context made it clear that 'Dad' had lost the letter in the airport. More of the white subjects who found the application bothered to post it when the applicant was white than when they were black.

In another study (Word et al, 1974) , white Princeton students met and interviewed a black or white high school student (the latter were confederates, trained to behave in a standard fashion). Although subjects did not discriminate against black students in any overt fashion, they sat further away from them, made more speech errors and terminated the interviews more quickly.

Poskocil (1977) found that whites may feel anxious or uneasy when dealing with blacks, which produces differential treatment (as shown in the Word et al study); and Crosby et al (1980) found that whites were less likely to help stranded black motorists, less likely to make an emergency phone call for a black, and more likely to report black shoplifters (but see discussion of Bystander Intervention in Chapter 13).

Origins of Prejudice

Theories of the origins of prejudice fall into two major categories: (i) those which see prejudice as stemming from *personality* variables; and (ii) those which emphasize the interaction between personal (individual) and social variables (and which can be called *social psychological theories*).

1) Personality Theories

The Authoritarian Personality

In 1950, Adorno, Frenkel-Brunswick, Levinson and Sanford proposed the concept of the authoritarian personality, a type of person who is prejudiced by virtue of specific personality traits which predispose them to be hostile towards ethnic, racial and other minority or 'out' groups.

They began by studying anti-semitism in Nazi Germany in the 1940s and drew on Freud's theories to help understand the relationship between 'collective ideologies' (such as Fascism) and individual personality (Brown, 1985). After their emigration to the USA, studies began with 2 000 college students and other native-born, white, non-Jewish, middle-class Americans, which involved interviews concerning their political views and childhood experiences and the use of projective tests designed to reveal unconscious attitudes towards minority groups.

A number of scales were developed in the course of their research designed to measure: (a) anti-Semitism; (b) ethnocentrism (the belief that one's own ethnic—or other membership—group is superior to others and the tendency to judge all other groups from the standpoint of one's own); and (c) political-economic conservatism. Out of these emerged the famous F scale (F for Fascism), which measures anti-democratic tendencies *indirectly* by not mentioning specific minority groups or ideological beliefs; what it reveals is that anti-Semitism is part of a general factor rather than an isolated prejudice, so that the authoritarian personality is prejudiced in a very generalized way. What other characteristics do they have?

Typically, the authoritarian personality is hostile to people of inferior status, servile to those of higher status, contemptuous of weakness, rigid and inflexible, intolerant of ambiguity and uncertainty, unwilling to introspect feelings, and an upholder of conventional values and ways of life (as represented by religion, for example). This belief in convention and intolerance of ambiguity combine to make minorities 'them' and the authoritarian's membership group 'us'; 'they' are by definition 'bad' and 'we' are by definition 'good'.

Authoritarians have often experienced a harsh, punitive, disciplinarian upbringing, with little affection and they often reveal considerable latent hostility towards their parents. Such unconscious hostility may be *displaced* onto minority groups (so that they become the objects of the authoritarian's hostility) and/or *projected* onto these groups (whereby the authoritarian feels threatened *by* them). Is there any evidence to support this account of prejudice?

As far as the relationship between the authoritarian personality and upbringing is concerned, Byrne (1965) found a correlation between the F-scores of college students and their parents, and Levinson and Huffman (1955) reported that authoritarian parents are more likely to stress discipline, conventionalism and submission in their child-rearing methods compared with non-authoritarian parents.

In the laboratory, they have been shown to be intolerant of ambiguity (Milton, 1957, Harvey, 1963), and outside they have been shown to: (a) have a positive bias towards the police (Larsen, 1968, Mitchell, 1973; (b) be anti-pornography (Byrne et al, 1973, Griffitt, 1973); (c) be highly susceptible to social influence, especially in relation to people of higher status (Crutchfield, 1955, Nadler, 1959—see Chapter 12); and (d) more likely to give a verdict of guilty and recommend longer sentences when serving on juries (Bray and Noble, 1978).

The Open and Closed Mind

However, the work of Adorno et al has been criticized because it assumed that authoritarianism is a characteristic of the political right and so implied that there is no equivalent authoritarianism on the left (eg Shils, 1954).

The best known attempt to redress this balance is that of Rokeach (1960), who has developed a *dogmatism scale*; '*ideological dogmatism*' refers to a relatively rigid outlook on life and intolerance of those with opposing beliefs. High scores on the dogmatism scale reveal: (i) closedness of mind; (ii) lack of flexibility; and (iii) authoritarianism, regardless of particular social and political ideology.

So an individual with left-wing or progressive beliefs can espouse them in just as rigid and dogmatic a way as someone with right-wing or reactionary views—they can be equally *extreme* (and closed) regardless of their particular content.

The dogmatic individual tends to accentuate differences between 'us and them' (eg 'The USA and USSR have just about nothing in common'), displays self-aggrandizement (eg 'If I had to choose between happiness and greatness, I'd choose greatness'), a paranoid outlook on life ('I often feel people are looking at me critically') and is uncompromising in their beliefs and intolerant of others. These characteristics serve as defences against the dogmatic person's self-inadequacy.

In fact, Rokeach found it difficult to find closed-mindedness in people with left-wing views; but, as Brown (1985) points out, such views were generally much more unacceptable in the USA in the 1950s even than they are today and required people who held them to show open-mindedness and cognitive flexibility.

Tough-Mindedness and Tender-Mindedness

Similarly, Eysenck (1954) distinguishes between: (i) Radicalism–Conservatism (the R factor), corresponding to right/left-wing political beliefs; and (ii) Toughmindedness–Tendermindedness (the T factor), corresponding to authoritarianism (Adorno et al) and dogmatism (Rokeach). A tough-minded person will be attracted to extreme political ideologies, be it Fascism or Communism; the authoritarian person is tough-minded and conservative, while the humanitarian is tender-minded and radical.

2) Social Psychological Theories

Adorno et al recognized that, as important as personality dynamics are, it is *society* which provides the content of attitudes and prejudice and it is society which defines who are the 'out-groups'. Also, as we noted earlier, discrimination does not necessarily imply prejudice, and by the same token, authoritarianism. According to Brown (1985), 'cultural or societal norms may be much more important than personality in accounting for ethnocentrism, out-group rejection, prejudice and discrimination.'

The Impact of Social Norms—Prejudice as Conformity

Although research on the authoritarian personality has been valuable, individual bigotry can explain only a small proportion of racial discrimination. For example, even though overt discrimination has been, traditionally, greater in the South of the USA, white Southerners have not scored higher than whites from the North on measures of authoritarianism (Pettigrew, 1959). So, clearly, conformity to social norms can prove more powerful as a determinant of behaviour than personality factors.

Minard (1952) found that black and white coal miners in West Virginia followed a pattern of almost complete integration below ground but almost complete segregation above! This only makes sense when viewed in terms of conformity to the norms which operated in those different situations.

Pettigrew (1971) also found that Southern Americans are not more anti-Semitic than those from the North (as the authoritarian personality explanation would require). Again, women are more anti-black than men in the South, but not in the North; those affiliated to a political party are more anti-black in the South than independents, but no such differences exist in the North. These differences cannot be explained in terms of personality differences.

Contrary to the claims of the authoritarian personality, the traditional anti-black attitudes in the southern USA have *not* been combined with anti-Semitism or prejudice against other minority groups, ie prejudice is not the generalized attitude which Adorno et al claim it is.

According to Reich and Adcock (1976), the need to conform and to not be seen as different may cause milder prejudices, but active discrimination against, and ill-treatment of, minorities is best seen as reflecting a prejudice which already exists and which is maintained and legitimized by conformity.

If prejudice is *not* a generalized attitude to all out-groups, it suggests that we *learn* to become prejudiced against particular groups in the same way that we learn other kinds of attitudes, eg through observational learning involving parents, peers, the media and so on. (In Chapter 22 we shall be discussing how television and books etc can influence children's attitudes towards male and female gender roles, which can provide the basis for the prejudice we call sexism.)

Inter-Group Conflict

Campbell (1947) found a strong relationship between dissatisfaction with their financial position and the general political state of the country, on the one hand, and anti-Semitism on the other, on the part of 300 non-Jewish Americans; of those who were generally satisfied, only 22 per cent showed any form of prejudice, while 62 per cent of the dissatisfied were prejudiced against Jews. Also, as prosperity declined between 1880 and 1930 in the USA, the number of lynchings of blacks in the South increased; during the more prosperous years, the lynchings decreased.

These findings are consistent with data from many other nations and historical periods—the greater the competition for scarce resources, the greater the hostility between various ethnic groups; Selznick and Steinberg (1969) and Maykovich (1975), for example, found high levels of racism among lower-class whites who felt that blacks were taking away their jobs.

Sherif (1966) argues that inter-group conflict arises as a result of a conflict

---

Box 11.2 The Robber's Cave Experiment (Sherif et al, 1961)

The setting was Robber's Cave State Park in Oklahoma, where 22 white, middle-class, Protestant, well-adjusted boys, spent two weeks at a summer camp; they were randomly assigned to two groups of 11, each occupying a separate cabin, out of sight of each other. None of the boys knew any of the others prior to their arrival at the camp.

During the first stage of the experiment, each group co-operated on a number of activities (eg pitching tents, making meals, a treasure hunt) and soon a distinct set of norms emerged which defined the group's identity; one group called itself the 'Rattlers' and the other called itself the 'Eagles'. Towards the end of the first week, they were allowed to become aware of the other's existence and an 'us and them' language quickly developed.

The second stage began with the announcement that there was to be a grand tournament between the two groups, comprising 10 sporting events, plus points awarded for the state of their cabins and so on; a splendid trophy, medals and four-bladed knives for each of the group members would be awarded to the winning group.

Before the tournament began, the Rattler's flag was burned and the camp counsellors (the experimenters) had to break up a fight between the two groups. With some 'help' from the counsellors, the Eagles won and later the Rattlers stole their medals and knives.

There was a strong preference for the in-group: Rattlers stereotyped all Rattlers as brave, tough, and friendly and (almost) all Eagles as sneaky, stinkers and smart alecks; and the Eagles stereotyped themselves and the Rattlers in a similar fashion.

---

of interests; when two groups want to achieve the same goal but cannot both have it, hostility is produced between them. Indeed, he claims that conflict of interest (or competition) is a *sufficient* condition for the occurrence of hostility or conflict and he bases this claim on one of the most famous field experimenters in social psychology, the Robber's Cave experiment, described above in Box 11.2, which Brown (1986) describes as the most successful field experiment ever conducted on inter-group conflict.

Clearly, the competition threatened an unfair distribution of rewards (the trophy, medals and knives) and the losing group inevitably saw the winners as undeserving. Sherif et al's results were confirmed by Blake and Mouton (1962, 1979) with adults from industrial organizations meeting for two-week periods.

However, Tyerman and Spencer (1983) challenged Sherif et al's conclusions that competition is a sufficient condition for inter-group conflict by observing scouts at their annual camp. The boys knew each other well before the start of camp and much of what they did there was similar to what the Rattlers and Eagles did at Robber's Cave. They were divided into four 'patrols' who competed in situations familiar to them from previous camps, but the friendship ties which existed prior to arrival at camp were maintained across the patrol groups; competition remained friendly and there was no increase of in-group solidarity. Tyerman and Spencer believe that the four groups continued to see themselves as part of the whole group (a view deliberately encouraged by the leader) and concluded that Sherif et al's results reflect the transitory nature of their experimental group; the fact that the boys knew each other beforehand, had established friendships, were familiar with camp life and had a leader who encouraged co-operation, were all important contextual/situational influences on the boys' behaviour. It seems that 'competition' may not, after all, be a sufficient condition for inter-group conflict and hostility.

If we accept this conclusion, the question arises whether it is a *necessary* condition. In other words, can hostility arise in the *absence* of conflicting interests?

According to Tajfel et al (1971), the answer is *yes*. They believe that the mere *perception* of the existence of another group can in itself produce discrimination: when people are arbitrarily and randomly divided into two groups, knowledge of the other group's existence is a sufficient condition for the development of pro-in-group and anti-out-group attitudes; this is known as the *minimal* group.

Tajfel et al argue that, before any discrimination can occur, people must be categorized as members of an in-group or an out-group (making categorization a necessary condition); but more significantly, the very act of categorization by itself produces conflict and discrimination (making it also a sufficient condition).

These conclusions are based on the creation of artificial groups among 14 to 15-year-old Bristol schoolboys; the criteria which were used were arbitrary and superficial and differed from experiment to experiment. They included: (i) chronic 'overestimators' or 'underestimators' on a task involving estimating the number of dots appearing on slide projections; (ii) preference for paintings by Klee or Kandinsky; (iii) the toss of a coin.

Once these arbitrary groups had been formed, the boys worked alone in cubicles on a task which required them to allocate points, as in a game, which could be exchanged at the end for one-tenth of a penny each. The points could be allocated: (a) to themselves; (b) to fellow group-members; or (c) members of the other group. The only option which was taken up was (b). The only information each boy had about another boy was whether or not he was a member of the same group or the other group, otherwise he was anonymous, unknown, unseen and unidentified. The allocation of points was always to the advantage of in-group members and to the detriment of out-group members—even when a co-operative strategy would have maximized the outcome for the in-group.

Brown (1986) sees this in-group favouritism as a form of ethnocentrism and cites a number of studies which show that the in-group is always rated as more likeable and fair than the out-group; the work of the in-group is rated more highly and 'good' deeds are attributed to the in-group and 'bad deeds' to the out-group (eg Brewer and Silver, 1978, Locksley et al, 1980).

In the Tajfel et al experiments, the actual group-assignments were always made randomly whatever the boys believed to be the basis for the categorization; but Billig and Tajfel (1973) and Locksley et al (1980) went even further in the creation of minimal groups by actually *telling* the subjects that they were being randomly assigned, tossing the coin in front of them and giving them obviously meaningless names (such as *A*s and *B*s or 'Kappas' and 'Phis'). These most minimal of all groups *still* showed a strong in-group preference.

A number of studies have ruled out the possibility of perceived similarity, nature of the task, experimenter-effects and demand characteristics as explanations of minimal group effects; and the findings have been replicated using a wide range of subjects in a wide range of cultures, including Welsh adults (Branthwaite and Jones, 1975), female undergraduates in California (Brewer and Silver, 1978), male and female undergraduates in Oregon (Howard and Rothbart, 1980) and New York (Locksley et al, 1980), students in Switzerland (Doise and Sinclair, 1973), soldiers in the West German army (Dann and Doise, 1974) and Maori children in New Zealand (Vaughan, 1977). (However, Wetherall, 1982, maintains that inter-group conflict is *not* inevitable. She studied white and Polynesian children in New Zealand and found the latter to be much more generous towards the out-group, reflecting cultural norms which emphasized co-operation.) How can we account for the minimal group effect?

Tajfel and Turner (1979) and Tajfel (1981) offer an explanation in the form of *Social Identity Theory* (SIT). According to SIT: (i) individuals strive to achieve or maintain a positive self-image; and (ii) the self-image has two components, *personal identity* and *social identity* (see Chapter 9). In fact, each of us has several social identities, corresponding to the number of different groups with which we identify and, in relation to each one, the more positive the image of the group, the more positive will be our own social identity and, hence, our self-image. By emphasizing the desirability of the in-group(s) and the undesirability of the out-group(s) and focusing on those distinctions which enable one's own group to come out on top, we help to create for ourselves a satisfactory social identity and this can be seen as lying at the heart of prejudice.

Members of minimal groups in the laboratory (compared with controls who are not assigned to a group) show higher self-esteem (eg Oakes and Turner, 1980) and prejudice seems to bolster self-esteem (eg Gergen, 1971) through bolstering group-esteem.

Some individuals may be more prone to prejudice because they have an intense need for acceptance by others; for such individuals, personal and social identity may be much more interlinked than for those with a lesser need for social acceptance. The need for a sense of security and superiority can be met by belonging to a favoured in-group and showing hostility towards out-groups; this is seen very clearly in majority–minority group relations where, for example, almost any white may feel superior to any black, no matter how well-educated or economically well-off.

Allport (1954) noted that many cases of prejudice are part of the conformity found in 'polite' social chatter. Affiliation needs can readily produce anti-social effects—an otherwise upstanding citizen may feel it necessary to show the strength of their affiliation by 'putting down' members of out-groups. This pattern may be especially intense in the case of converts to a new group.

Prejudice can be seen as an adjustive mechanism which bolsters the self-concept of individuals who have feelings of personal inadequacy; it becomes a 'prop' for these individuals (but with potentially undesirable social implications).

Scapegoating

This theory of prejudice as an outlet for frustration, combines two ideas: first, Freud's concept of *displacement*, whereby substitute objects or targets for aggression are found when it is impossible to express the hostility towards its real target (see Chapter 26); and secondly, the *frustration-aggression* hypothesis which maintains that frustration always gives rise to aggression—and aggression is always caused by frustration (see Chapter 13).

The substitute object is, of course, the scapegoat, and there are usually socially-approved (legitimized) groups which serve as targets for frustration-induced aggression; in England, during the 1930s and '40s it was predominantly the Jews, who were replaced by West Indians during the 1950s and '60s and, during the 1970s and '80s, predominantly Pakistani Asians.

Scapegoating can account for the non-experimental findings on inter-group conflict discussed in the previous section, and an interesting laboratory demonstration of this was the experiment by Weatherley (1961). He gave an anti-Semitism scale to subjects and divided them into high and low scorers; half of each group were subjected to very insulting remarks (while filling in a second questionnaire) and then given picture-story tests and asked to tell a story about each picture. Some pictures showed people with Jewish-sounding names and it was found that high scorers directed more aggression towards 'Jewish' pictures than low scorers *and* this difference was confined to the 'Jewish' pictures. This shows that hostility is not indiscriminate (or 'blind') but requires a target which is an already-disliked out-group (which tends to contradict the authoritarian personality theory).

The Reduction of Prejudice

According to Brown (1986), two factors seem to be more effective than any others in trying to reduce inter-group conflict and racial (and other kinds of) prejudice: (i) non-competitive contact of an *equal status*; and (ii) the pursuit of common (*superordinate*) goals which are only attainable by co-operation. These are interrelated as this quote from Allport shows:

> Prejudice (unless deeply rooted in the character structure of the individual) may be reduced by equal status contact between majority and minority groups in the pursuit of common goals. The effect is greatly enhanced if this contact is sanctioned by institutional supports (ie by law, custom or local atmosphere)... (Allport, 1954).

Equal Status Contact

It is generally agreed that increased contact by itself is not sufficient to reduce prejudice; despite what we said in Chapter 10 about preferring people who are familiar, if this contact is between people who are consistently of the same, unequal status, then 'familiarity may breed contempt'. Aronson (1980) points out that many whites (in the USA) have always had a great deal of contact with blacks—as dishwashers, toilet attendants, domestic servants, and so on; such contacts may simply reinforce the stereotypes held by whites of blacks as being inferior.

One early study of equal-status contact was that of Deutsch and Collins (1951) who compared two kinds of housing projects, one of which was thoroughly integrated (blacks and whites were assigned houses regardless of race) and the other segregated. Residents of both were intensively interviewed and it was found that both casual and neighbourly contact were greater in the integrated housing with a corresponding decrease in prejudice among whites towards blacks; so it appeared to be environmental support which was sustaining prejudice in the segregated project.

Similarly, Jahoda (1961) found that, although a majority of American whites stated a preference for residential segregation in a survey, the preference was cut by half where whites had the experience of working with blacks and having them as neighbours. However, was this reduction confined to the black neighbours with whom the whites interacted or was it a more generalized reduction of anti-black prejudice?

The Minard study of miners in West Virginia (1952) suggests that the change was confined to situations in which it was socially permissible to be unprejudiced, and Stouffer (1949) and Amir (1969) found that inter-racial attitudes improved markedly when blacks and whites served together as soldiers in battle and on ships, although relationships were not so good at base camp.

It might be thought that de-segregation of American schools would provide a major test of the effectiveness of equal-status contact in reducing prejudice and a number of studies have been carried out to this end. However, the results are very discouraging. Gerard and Miller (1975) found in their longitudinal study in Riverside, California, that white, black and Hispanic–American students continued to 'hang-out' together in a clear ethnic structure.

Stephan (1978) reviewed a number of studies and concluded that de-segregation as such seems *not* to have reduced white prejudice towards blacks, and black prejudice towards whites seems to have increased. Schofield (1982) studied a 'model' integrated school and found that, at first, interaction and friendship were totally governed by group attitudes and then slowly started to take account of personal qualities over a three-year period. However, racial attitudes changed very little; Wax (1979) found a similar pattern in a study of five de-segregated schools. Brown and Turner (1981) argue that if inter-group contact does reduce prejudice, it is *not* because it encourages interpersonal friendship (as Deutsch and Collins would claim) but because of changes in the nature and structure of *inter-group* relationships. So why does de-segregation not reduce prejudice?

According to Brown (1986), institutional support from families, school boards and the community is often lacking but, more seriously, equal-status contact in pursuit of common goals is *not* what actually goes on in de-segregated schools. While formal status in the classroom may be equal, the socio-economic status differences still exist, as do differences in achievement status and, far from co-operating in pursuit of common goals, students are competing in pursuit of individual goals.

Pursuit of Common Goals

In a co-operative situation, the attainment of one person's goal enhances the chances of attainment of the goals of other group members; and this reverses the situation where competition prevails (Brown, 1986).

One of the few attempts to alter the classroom experience in order to realize equal-status contact *and* mutual co-operation is the *jigsaw classroom* technique of Aronson et al (1978). Children are assigned to small, inter-racial learning groups, in which each member is given material which represents one piece of the lesson to be learned. Each child must learn its part and then communicate it to the rest of the group and, at the end of the lesson, each child is tested on the *whole* lesson and is given an individual score. Each child must, therefore, learn the full lesson but each is dependent on the others in the group for parts of the lesson that can only be learned from them, hence, there is complete mutual interdependence. What are its effects?

Aronson et al (1978) believe that the jigsaw method enhances students' self-esteem, improves academic performance, increases liking for classmates and improves some inter-racial perceptions. However, although the children of different racial groups who had actually worked together came to like each other better as individuals, their reduced prejudice did *not* generalize to those ethnic groups as a whole; similar limited effects have been found amongst co-operative groups by Cook (1978). However, most experiments of this type are small-scale and relatively short-term interventions (Brown, 1986).

In the Robber's Cave field experiment, Sherif et al (1961) introduced a third stage in which seven equal-status contact situations were created (including filling out questionnaires together, seeing movies and having meals together); none of these, nor all of them in combination, did anything to reduce friction.

However, it was also arranged that the camp's drinking water supply was cut off and the only way of restoring it was by a co-operative effort by the Rattlers and Eagles. Similarly, in order to afford to hire a movie, the two groups agreed to make an equal contribution and on a trip to Cedar Lake, one of the trucks got stuck and they all had to pull on a rope together to get it started again. Other co-operative tasks involved making meals and pitching tents. In the final few days, the group divisions disappeared and they actually suggested travelling home together in one bus; 65 per cent of their friendship choices now were made from the other group and their stereotypes changed too, becoming much more favourable.

Conclusions

Despite what we have said about the ineffectiveness of mere contact, it nonetheless provides the opportunity for getting to know members of different racial groups as individuals (eg Deutsch and Collins, 1951, Wilner et al, 1955, Hamilton and Bishop, 1976).

When people are separated and segregated, the stage is set for *autistic hostility*, that is, ignorance of others which leads to a failure to understand the reasons for their actions; lack of contact means there is no 'reality testing' against which to check your own interpretations of others' behaviour.

Autistic hostility can produce a *mirror-image phenomenon* (Bronfenbrenner, 1960), whereby both sides come to see themselves as being in the right and honourable and the other as threatening and unworthy. By increased contact, the out-group loses its strangeness and becomes more differentiated, that is, it no longer consists of interchangeable 'units' but a collection of unique individuals.

Even when we do not get to know individuals on a personal basis, we may revise our prejudices if we come into contact with people who violate our stereotypes (especially if they seem similar to ourselves). According to

Gurwitz and Dodge (1977) even contact with a single person who contradicts previous stereotypes may reduce prejudice and Blanchard et al (1975) found that the white worker who realizes that their black co-workers may share many of the same aspirations, grievances and attitudes towards the company begins to discard stereotyped images of blacks (and vice-versa).

However, as we have found in a number of studies discussed in this section, changes in prejudice arising from the work situation may not generalize to other situations (eg blacks as parents, or citizens) and until prejudice is reduced in society at large (eg through education and consciousness-raising, eg Mednick, 1975) particular cases of prejudice-reduction will represent nothing more than what a democratic and just society could be.

12

Social Influence

Most, if not all, human behaviour can only be properly understood if it is thought of as social in nature, that is, as being directly or indirectly bound up with and influenced by the behaviour of others.

Social influence, as studied by psychologists, can take several different forms; Hollander (1981) maintains that it represents the central process of concern in social psychology. He states that social influence occurs whenever an individual responds to the actual or implied presence of one or more others, and that influencing others, for whatever end, is basic to social life.

Simply being in the presence of others will normally affect our behaviour compared with our private behaviour (think of all the things you do when you are in your own home that you would not dream of doing in public!), and psychologists have studied this as *social facilitation*. (We should note, however, that even our private behaviour has been acquired through contacts with others, for example, imitating or identifying with models, being reinforced for behaving in particular ways and so on, so our actions still have a social meaning even in the absence of other people; behaviour always goes on within a social context.)

A more direct form of social influence involves not merely being in the presence of others but interacting with them and making some attempt to change the behaviour of one or more of those involved in a particular direction. This could be a key member of a group exerting their influence over the group as a whole, in order to solve a problem or complete a task (*leadership*), a group trying to influence its members to adopt a particular attitude or dress code (*conformity*), or an authority figure trying to make someone comply with their demands (*obedience*).

1) Social Facilitation

Triplett (1898) carried out what is widely considered to be the first social psychology experiment and it involved the effects of competition on the average time it took children to complete 150 winds of a fishing reel. Each child was tested under two conditions, working alone and working in pairs, each child competing against the other member of the pair; performance was clearly superior in the pairs condition.

However, it seems that it is the mere presence of others which is the crucial variable (*social facilitation*) not the element of competition. F. H. Allport (1924) instructed his subjects not to try to compete against one another (and also prevented any collaboration) while engaging on a variety of tasks, which included crossing out all the vowels in a newspaper article, multiplication and finding logical flaws in arguments; he still found that subjects performed better when they could see others working than when they worked alone and he called this form of social facilitation, the *co-action effect*. Social facilitation can also be seen when an individual performs a task in front of an audience (other people who are not doing what the person is doing) and this is called the *audience effect*. (Social facilitation has also been found in non-human species, including ants, chickens and rats—Cottrell, 1972.)

Other studies have shown that social facilitation can occur by simply telling subjects that others are performing the same task elsewhere (Dashiell, 1935).

However, whether or not social facilitation occurs depends on the nature of the task, in particular, how simple and well-learned it is. According to Zajonc (1966), 'an audience impairs the acquisition of new responses and facilitates the emission of well-learned responses'. In other words, things a subject already knows how to do (eg cancelling numbers and letters and simple multiplication) are done better when others are present, but things which are complex or which the subject is required to learn, are done less well when others are present. These findings have been confirmed by Cottrell (1972) and Geen and Gange (1977). Why should this be?

According to Zajonc (1966), the presence of others (in whatever capacity) increases the subject's drive level or level of arousal and since, up to a certain level, arousal enhances the performance of well-learned behaviour, the presence of others will facilitate performance on simple tasks. However, when the task is complex, the effect of increased arousal is to make it more likely that incorrect or irrelevant responses will be performed and, hence, more errors are made; the arousal produced by the presence of others, together with that produced by the task itself, produce a level beyond the optimum level for ideal performance (Zajonc's explanation is based on Hull's learning theory—see Chapter 17).

Gahagan (1975) suggests that, strictly, there is no such thing as the *mere* presence of others. She cites a study by Laird (1923) in which the audience was overtly hostile to the subjects; the effect for most subjects was a decline in performance, even on a simple task, but a few actually improved.

2) **Leaders and Leadership**

Are leaders born or are they made? Is it trait or situation?

The study of leadership is another example of the nature–nurture issue, for two of the major approaches have been the trait approach, which tries to identify the personality traits and the characteristics which make a person a leader, and the situational approach, which is concerned with the leader's dependence on the group and views leadership as a complex social process. (These two approaches are also found in discussion of personality—see Chapter 25.)

To an extent, focus on 'the leader' implies a trait approach (ie, what is it about leaders *as individuals*, and compared with other individuals, which explains their 'success'?); while to talk about 'leadership' implies a situational approach (eg, under what circumstances will an individual assume the role of leader?).

The Trait Approach

This represents the first major approach, and the broad aim was to determine those personal attributes which make a person a leader (Cowley, 1928). A number of characteristics have been proposed as being advantageous (at least in men) including height, weight, an attractive appearance, self-confidence, and being well-adjusted and intelligent. As far as intelligence is concerned, several studies and reviews have shown that the typical leader is only slightly more intelligent than the average member of the group (eg Gibb, 1969, Mann, 1959 and Stogdill, 1974). Gibb (1969) also concluded that leaders are neither extremely authoritarian nor extremely egalitarian but somewhere in between.

The findings overall, however, are inconclusive, that is, leaders are not consistently found to be particular kinds of people who differ in predictable ways from non-leaders. According to Brown (1985), for example, although personal qualities are important, it has proved impossible to make a list of attributes or traits which fits a wide range of leaders without considering these leadership qualities 'in relation to the situations and the problems to be faced by the membership of the group in question'.

However, 'personality' has been studied in various guises, one major one being that of leadership style. An early and famous study of leadership style is that of Lewin, Lippitt and White (1939) which is described in Box 12.1.

Although the findings of the Lewin et al study strongly suggest that it is style of leadership (which is not necessarily a fixed characteristic) rather than personality (which is), Brown (1985) argues that individuals, their groups and leaders can only be understood in the context of the wider society of which they form a part. The 'democratic' style is, implicitly, the favourable and acceptable one of the three studied by Lewin et al because that was the one prevalent in American society during the 1930s.

Sayles (1966) reviewed both experimental and survey studies of leadership styles in industry. He found that no one style was consistently superior to any other in experimental studies of supervisors; but survey studies showed that democratic leadership was associated with greater productivity, and was more acceptable, than an autocratic style. However, Sayles argued that the tasks used in the experimental studies were so boring and limited that people did not get involved and, consequently, differences in leadership style were not given the chance to show up. He also made the point that democratic supervisors probably also differ in other ways apart from their leadership style (eg intelligence) compared with autocratic colleagues.

The Situational Approach

This began to emerge in the 1950s and was an attempt to rectify some of the shortcomings of the trait approach. For instance, the situational approach acknowledges that leadership involves leaders and followers in various role relationships and that there are several paths to becoming validated as a leader.

Box 12.1: Lewin, Lippitt and White's (1939) Study of Leadership Styles

Lewin et al wanted to investigate the effects of three kinds of adult behaviour on a group of 10-year-old boys attending after-school clubs. The clubs were led by adults who acted in one of three ways: *autocratic, democratic* or *laissez-faire*.

The Democratic group met two days before the other two groups, and what they chose to do (they were concerned with model-making) the other two groups were told to do, thus providing a basis for comparing the boys' output, experience and behaviour.

i) Autocratic leaders told the boys what sort of models they would make and with whom they would work; they sometimes praised or blamed them for their work but did not explain their comments and, although friendly, were aloof and impersonal.

ii) Democratic leaders discussed various possible projects and allowed the boys to choose work-mates and generally to make their own decisions. They explained their comments and joined in with the group activities.

iii) Laissez-faire leaders left the boys very much to their own devices, only offered help when asked for it (which was not very often) and gave neither praise nor blame.

What were the findings?

i) Boys with an autocratic leader became aggressive towards each other when things went wrong and were submissive in their approaches to the leader (which were often attention-seeking). If he left the room, the boys stopped working and became either disruptive or apathetic. However, the models they made were comparable, both in quantity and quality, to those of the boys in the democratic group.

ii) Boys with a democratic leader got on much better with each other and seemed to like each other more than the boys in (i). Although slightly less work was actually done, approaches to the leader were usually task-related. When he left the room, the boys carried on working, showing greater independence and they co-operated with each other when things went wrong.

iii) Boys with a laissez-faire leader were aggressive towards each other, although less so than in (i). Very little work was done, whether the leader was present or not and they were easily discouraged when things were not going exactly right.

Each leader was then instructed to adopt one of the other kinds of leadership; the boys' behaviour was shown to depend on the style of leadership and *not* on the personality of the leader. Significantly, two of the most aggressive boys from the autocratic group were switched to the democratic group and quickly became co-operative and involved.

The question of *validation* is to do with how the leader comes to occupy the role, that is, how do they achieve legitimacy as a leader? In a formal group structure, the leader is *assigned* by an external authority and is imposed on the group (an *appointed* leader); while in an informal group structure, the leader *achieves* their authority from the group members, who may withdraw their support just as they gave it, and is called an *emergent* leader.

Bavelas et al (1960) suggests that the question, 'Who is leader?' might be better put as, 'What functions are to be fulfilled?'. He proposes that an appointed leader is one who performs certain kinds of tasks rather than someone who possesses certain characteristics or styles of social interaction, and some leaders may be primarily decision-makers who do not have interpersonal relationships as a major requirement of their role.

Conversely, even in formal structures there are emergent (or 'informal') leaders who exert influence among their peers by virtue of their personal qualities, especially how verbal they are (eg Hare, 1976, Sorrentino & Boutillier, 1975).

Even in the case of appointed leaders, leadership is a complex social process, involving a transaction or exchange between the group members; the leader is dependent on the rest of the group for liking and approval and their attitudes towards the leader will influence the process of leadership. This was demonstrated in an experiment by Rice et al (1980), whose subjects were military cadets at West Point Academy. Groups of male cadets had to complete tasks under the leadership of either a male or female cadet; the 'followers' were assigned so that half the groups were composed of followers with liberal attitudes towards women's rights and half of followers who held traditional attitudes. The liberal cadets responded in a very similar way to male and female leaders, while the traditionalists preferred the group atmosphere when the leader was male; the latter also attributed the success of the women-led groups to luck and that of the men-led groups to hard work and the co-operation of the group members.

While not ignoring the leader's characteristics, the situational approach stresses their appropriateness to a group in a given situation and a major feature of the situation is the group's *primary task*, that is, what the group is in existence to do. So the leader's competence in enabling the group to achieve its purpose is a crucial feature of their role.

Fiedler's Contingency Model of Leader Effectiveness

In the 1960s there was a revival of interest in the leader's personality characteristics, but it was a much more sophisticated approach than the trait approach and one which also represented an extension of the situational approach.

A major figure in this new approach was Fiedler (1967, 1968, 1971, 1972, 1974) whose *Contingency Model* for the analysis of leadership effectiveness is mainly concerned with the fit or match between a leader's personal qualities or leadership style, on the one hand, and the requirements of the situation, on the other.

He began by measuring the extent to which leaders distinguish between their most and least preferred co-worker (LPC) and developed a scale which gives an LPC score. Someone with a high LPC score still sees their least preferred co-worker in a relatively favourable light and also tends to be more accepting, permissive, considerate and person-oriented in relationships with group members (*relationship-oriented*). By contrast, someone with a low LPC score sees their least-preferred co-worker very differently, with the latter regarded very unfavourably, and also tends to be directive, controlling and dominant in relationships with group members (*task-oriented*).

Fiedler then investigated the fit between these two styles of leadership and the needs of the situation; the basic hypothesis being tested is that the effectiveness of a leader is contingent upon the fit between (a) the leader's style and (b) the quality of leader-member relationships, task structure and the position-power of the leader. The *quality* of *leader–member relationships* refers to the extent to which the leader has the confidence of the group and to the general psychological climate of the group. *Task structure* refers to the complexity of the task and the number of possible solutions: the more unstructured the task, the more the leader must motivate and inspire members to find solutions rather than rely on the backing of their superiors. The leader's *position–power* refers to the power inherent in the role, for example, the rewards and punishments at their disposal and the organizational support from superiors.

The model predicts varying degrees of effectiveness for different combinations of leader and situational variables and Fiedler tested it in a number of countries and a variety of organizations, including boards of directors, basketball teams and bomber crews. He predicted that task-oriented leaders perform most effectively *either* under very favourable *or* very unfavourable conditions (ie extremes of the three situational variables) while relationship-oriented leaders are most effective under conditions which are neither extremely favourable nor extremely unfavourable. He has reported considerable support for his contingency model.

However, it has not gone uncriticized. For example, Kerr (1977) found that the LPC score is unstable and shows changes over time; similarly, Offerman (1980) found changes in the LPC score following group interactions, depending on whether the leaders were of the same or opposite gender from the other group members. Rice (1978), in an extensive review of studies using the LPC, concluded that it is not altogether clear what the LPC is actually a measure of and he also criticizes the model for largely ignoring the group members and for assuming that the leader's position is fixed.

Leadership and Communication Networks

Fiedler in fact saw leadership style as a relatively fixed personality characteristic but Brown (1985) refers to studies which, like that of Lewin et al (1939), suggest that leadership is *not* an inborn personality characteristic. A number of laboratory studies have imposed a particular communication network on a group of subjects (eg a five-person wheel, or 'Y', or chain) in each of which one person is randomly assigned to the central position, so that the other group members can only communicate via that central person and not directly with each other (eg Leavitt, 1951, Davis and Hornseth, 1967).

From studies like these, Brown (1985) concludes that when people are put into positions where the group has to depend on their efforts, they tend to accept the challenge and behave like leaders; just as crucially, they are recognized as leaders by the rest of the group. Compared with people occupying peripheral positions, they tend to send more messages, to solve problems more quickly, to make fewer errors and to be more satisfied with their own and the group's efforts. Although recognizing that not anyone can fill any role, Brown (1985) concludes that finding oneself in a position of leadership may bring out hidden talents; certainly as far as laboratory studies are concerned it seems to be primarily the position in the network, and not personality, which accounts for the assumption of the leadership role.

Leadership and Power

We have referred several times to the notion of power when discussing leadership and clearly they are closely related concepts, but just as there are different kinds of leader (eg appointed and emergent) so there are different kinds of power. A comprehensive classification has been proposed by French and Raven (1960) and is summarized in Table 12.1.

In the context of the trait approach, might we have inadvertently stumbled across a characteristic which is consistently displayed by every leader, namely

Table 12.1   Five kinds of power as proposed by French and Raven (1960)

1 *Legitimate power:*	The formal power invested in a particular role (eg President of USA, Prime Minister, headteacher, bank manager) regardless of the personality of the particular occupant.
2 *Reward power:*	The power an individual possesses by virtue of their control over valued resources ('rewards'), including salary or wages, food, love, respect, co-operation (eg parents, colleagues, bosses, friends, shop-keepers).
3 *Coercive power:*	The power an individual possesses by virtue of their control over feared consequences ('punishments'), including the withdrawal of rewards, demotion, dismissal (eg the same as for Reward Power). [In both 2 and 3, the power is to a large extent inherent in the role itself but personality of the role-occupant can play a greater part than in 1.]
4 *Expert power:*	The power an individual possesses by virtue of their possession of special knowledge, skills and expertise (eg doctors, teachers, plumbers, electricians, car mechanics). (Related to this is *informational power* which is to do with *access* to important sources of information, such as that available through the media.)
5 *Referent power:*	The power an individual possesses by virtue of their personal qualities (eg charm, magnetism, ability to persuade and 'win' people over). The *charismatic* leader has great referent power (which may be more important than their legitimate power) but parents, teachers, friends and others may also possess this kind of power.

the lust for power? If we accept Adler's theory of the 'will to power', that is, the tendency in each of us to overcome our fundamental feeling of inferiority (see Chapter 26), then leaders could be seen as satisfying their will to power in that particular way and this would lend further support to the notion of desire for power as a characteristic of all leaders.

However, Gergen and Gergen (1981) warn us against this conclusion; although leadership does imply power, it would be a mistake, they argue, to assume that everyone who possesses power is highly motivated to achieve it. They claim that many political leaders, for example, are recruited and encouraged by others who promote them to powerful positions and their needs for affiliation may be far stronger than their needs for power.

3) Conformity

Crutchfield (1962) defined conformity simply as, 'yielding to group pressures'. Aronson (1976) defined it as, 'a change in a person's behaviour or opinions as a result of real or imagined pressure from a person or group of people'. Mann (1969) said that, 'the essence of conformity is yielding to group pressures but it may take different forms and be based on motives other than group pressure.' These motives we shall consider later in the chapter.

What these definitions have in common is the reference to group pressure; they do not specify particular groups with particular beliefs or practices but any group which is important for the individual at the time. The group may be composed of people who are significant others for the individual, for example, family or peers, or it may be a reference group, whose values the individual admires or aspires to but which does not involve actual membership.

So conformity does not imply adhering to any particular set of attitudes or values, for instance, traditional middle class or bourgeois, but yielding to the pressures of a group, regardless of its majority or minority status.

Empirical Studies of Conformity

An early study by Jenness (1932) could be regarded as one of the very first empirical studies of conformity, although it is usually discussed in the context of social facilitation. Jenness (a student of Allport's) asked students individually to estimate the number of beans in a bottle and then had them discuss it to arrive at a group estimate. When they were asked individually to make a second estimate, there was a distinct shift towards the group's estimate.

Sherif (1935)

Using a similar procedure to Jenness, Sherif used a visual illusion called the autokinetic effect, whereby a spot of light seen in an otherwise dark room appears to move.

He told his subjects that he was going to move the light and that their task was to say how far they thought the light moved. They were tested individually at first, being asked to estimate the extent of movement several times; the estimates of individual subjects fluctuated to begin with but then 'settled down' and became quite consistent. However, there were wide differences between subjects. Subjects then heard the estimates of other subjects and this represented the group situation (there were usually 3 per group). Under these conditions, the estimates of different subjects converged, that is, they became more alike; a group norm developed.

To illustrate what happened, let us suppose that when tested individually, four subjects gave fairly consistent estimates of 8, 6, $3\frac{1}{2}$ and $2\frac{1}{2}$ inches respectively. In the group situation, when hearing the estimates of the other three, the estimates of the four subjects changed to 6, 5, 4 and 5 inches, much closer to each other than their original, individual estimates. (In this hypothetical example, the average or mean score is 5 inches, both for the individual and the group estimates, but the first set of scores differs from each other much more than the second set. So when subjects are tested in a group, scores converge towards the average of their individual scores. In practice, it did not always work out quite as neatly as this.)

Just as different individuals produced different estimates, so did different groups; this happened both under the conditions already described and also when subjects were tested in small groups right from the start. Two further points need to be made: (i) subjects were not in any way instructed to agree with the others in the group, yet their estimates still converged, even when there were wide differences to begin with between individuals; (ii) when subjects were tested again individually, their estimates closely resembled the group estimate or norm (rather than their original, individual, estimates).

Comparing Sherif's and Jenness's experiments, whereas Jenness's subjects were instructed to arrive at a group estimate, there were no such instructions for Sherif's subjects, who were quite unaware of being influenced; indeed, in interviews they hotly denied being affected by the others' estimates. Even though they did not think of themselves as being engaged in a common task, Sherif's subjects nonetheless adjusted their judgements to bring them into line with those of others.

According to Brown (1985), at least in Western culture, to be in agreement with others satisfies an important psychological need, especially in situations where people are uncertain. Clearly, in an ambiguous situation such as the autokinetic effect represented, subjects were only too willing to validate their own estimates by comparing them with those of other subjects, 'and through such a "social comparison" process (Festinger, 1954) a common social reality is established and validated'. (Brown, 1985.)

A later study using the autokinetic effect (Sherif and Sherif, 1969) took place in a monastery and instead of convergence taking place between novices and monks, there was conflict between them. Clearly, the need to be in agreement with others can itself be influenced by other social and psychological variables. (What do you think these might have been in this case?)

Asch (1951, 1952, 1956)

While Sherif believed that he had shown that conformity does indeed take place, others, notably, Asch, were very critical of his findings. According to Asch, the fact that the task used by Sherif was ambiguous (ie, there was no right or wrong answer) made it difficult to draw any definite conclusions about conformity: conformity should be measured in terms of the individual's tendency to agree with other group members who unanimously give the wrong answer on a task where the solution is obvious or unambiguous. If people yield to group pressure when the answer is obvious, this is a much stricter test of conformity than where there is no correct or incorrect answer to begin with, as in Sherif's autokinetic effect (where the light does not actually move at all!).

In a series of experiments, beginning in 1951, Asch gave subjects the simple perceptual task of matching one line (a standard line) with another (a comparison line), each presented on a separate card. See Figure 12.1 below.

The subject has to say which of A, B or C is the same length as the standard line.

A group of 36 control subjects, who were tested individually, made only three mistakes when tested 20 times each (using different standard and comparison lines), showing that the task was simple—the answer was obvious and unambiguous.

In the original experiment, students were tested in groups of seven to nine, in which only one person was a 'real' (naïve) subject, the others being confederates or accomplices of Asch, who had been instructed beforehand to give the same wrong answers on certain trials ('critical' trials).

They were seated either in a straight line or round a table and it was arranged so that the real subject was always the last to answer (or the last but one). On the first two trials, the confederates all gave the right answer, as did the real subject. But on the third trial, all the confederates agreed on the 'wrong' answer. During the next 20 minutes, there were six more critical trials. Thirty-two per cent of the real subjects agreed with the wrong answer, that is, conformed, on *all* the critical trials, while 74 per cent conformed on at least *one* of the critical trials.

When interviewed at length following the experiment, the real subjects said that they had been influenced to some extent by the opposition of the rest of the group. But there were more specific reasons that subjects gave for conforming. Some wanted to act in accordance with the experimenter's wishes and wanted to convey a favourable impression of themselves by not

STANDARD LINE

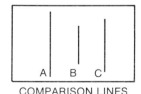

COMPARISON LINES

Figure 12.1   Stimulus cards used in Asch's conformity experiments (1951/52/56)

'upsetting the experiment', which they believed they would have done by disagreeing with the majority. They thought some obscure 'mistake' had been made. Others said that they wanted to be like everyone else, did not want to 'appear different', 'be made to look a fool', a 'social outcast' or 'inferior'.

So, for many subjects there was a discrepancy between what answer they gave in the group and what they privately believed; they knew the 'wrong' answer was wrong but went along with it nonetheless. Contrast this with the subjects in Sherif's experiment for whom there was no conflict between the group's estimate and their own, individual, estimates.

However, there were some of Asch's subjects who seemed to believe that the majority opinion was actually correct on the critical trials (and that the majority is usually correct, regardless of the issue in question). A few, who had no reason to believe that there was anything wrong with their eyesight, genuinely doubted the validity of their own judgements by wondering if they were suffering from eye strain or if their chairs had been moved so that they could not see the cards properly. So the reasons for conforming can be several, yet whatever the particular reason(s), the kind of conformity here (for the majority of subjects, anyway) is different from that involved in Sherif's experiment, where there was no majority wrong answer to conflict with the individual's, privately-held, right answer.

It was clear that many subjects did experience a good deal of stress as a result of the conflict and a subsequent study by Bogdonoff et al (1961) actually measured the physiological stresses associated with the Asch experiments. They found that increase in the level of plasma-free fatty acid (an indicator of central nervous system arousal) was correlated with the subjects' state of conflict when they realized that there was a discrepancy between their judgement and that of the majority. This high level was maintained for those who stuck to their judgement but dropped sharply if they conformed.

So far this was the basic experiment that Asch carried out in 1951; in 1952 and 1956, he varied the basic situation and manipulated different variables in order to see what the crucial influences on conformity were:

a)   Does the rate of conformity go on increasing as the size of the majority goes on increasing?

It seems not. Where there is a real subject and just one confederate, the conformity rate is very low indeed, as you might expect ('it's my word against yours'). Where there are two confederates and one subject, conformity begins to increase, and it is higher still when there are three confederates and one subject. But beyond three, conformity does not continue to rise; so, for example, 13 confederates to one real subject does not produce more conformity than a ratio of 3 to 1. Why does three seem to be a critical number?

Judy Gahagan (1975) suggests that where there are more than three the subject might suspect that some of the confederates are simply following each other, so that their credibility as a source of information would be reduced. However, some more recent studies have reported that conformity goes on increasing as the majority increases up to 7 (Gerard et al, 1968, Gerard and Conolley, 1972).

b)   What is the effect of having another member of the group agree with the real subject?

It is to reduce conformity from 32 per cent to 6 per cent, whether the member who agrees is another real subject or a confederate. This could be either because it strengthens the subject's belief that their judgement is correct or because it provides moral support against a potentially 'critical' experimenter and other group members. A similar effect was found by Allen and Levin (1968).

Faucheux and Moscovici (1967) suggest that the non-conforming group member offers another view to the subject, although this is not necessarily the one which the subject adopts. For example, Asch found that, regardless of whether the non-conforming member's answer coincided with the subject's, conformity rate still dropped; and Kimball and Hollander (1974) found that, even when the non-conforming member was believed to be experienced in the kind of ambiguous problems which were being presented, subjects were still more likely to disagree with the majority than they were to agree with the so-called 'expert'.

c) In the original experiment, were subjects justified in fearing that they would be ridiculed by the rest of the group if they gave the answer they believed to be correct?

It seems they were. A group of naïve subjects participated with a single confederate, who gave the wrong answer on the critical trials as happened in the original experiment. The dramatic reaction of the naive subjects was sarcasm, exclamations of disbelief and ridiculing laughter!

d) What happens when the real subject has a 'supporter' at the beginning and then loses that support?

In one situation, the fourth confederate to answer gave the correct answer on the first half of the critical trials but then switched to the incorrect majority answer for the second half. Under these conditions, conformity increased from about 6 to 29 per cent.

e) Will task difficulty affect conformity?

When Asch made the comparison lines more similar in length, so that the task was more difficult, subjects were more likely to yield to the incorrect majority answer, and this is especially true when subjects feel confident that there is a right answer. When tasks are more ambiguous, in the sense that they involve expressing opinions or stating preferences (so there is no objectively correct answer), conformity actually decreases. (But there are some interesting, if not alarming, exceptions to this—see below.)

f) If we think we are in some way less competent than the other group members in relation to the task at hand, are we more likely to conform?

Ross, Bierbrauer and Hoffman (1976) ask us to imagine the naïve subject thinking, 'If I didn't know better, I'd think these guys were blind or crazy. But if they all agree, they'll think *I'm* blind or crazy if I disagree.' So the subject conforms in order to avoid being labelled in that way.

But now imagine that the confederates are all wearing dark glasses. The subject can now easily 'understand' their errors and if they believe that the others know that they can see perfectly well, the subject will have no qualms about reporting the right answer. So, if the difference between the answers of the majority and the real subject can be attributed to some clear difference in ability, or to a difference in perspective, the pressure to conform will be greatly reduced (provided, of course, that subjects believe it is *they* who have the greater ability).

You will remember that some subjects in the original post-experiment interview attributed a more advantageous seating position to the majority or attributed eye-strain to themselves and conformed for this reason. So conformity will be either increased or decreased depending on the nature and direction of the attribution.

Critics of Asch's experiment have pointed out that the subjects may conform because they are reluctant or too embarrassed to expose their private views in face-to-face situations. If so, the level of conformity should decrease if subjects are allowed to write their answers down, or where there is no face-to-face contact between the group members, or where subjects remain anonymous in some other way.

For example, Deutsch and Gerard (1955) used partitions which shielded subjects from the other participants whose response showed up on a light panel in front of them—the real subject had to press one of three buttons. Under these conditions, conformity was lower than in Asch's face-to-face situation. Other support comes from Mouton et al (1956), Argyle (1957) and Crutchfield (1954, see below).

However, it must be remembered that the participants in the Asch experiments were complete strangers to the real subjects, with no special claim to their loyalty or affection. The subjects, therefore, had little reason to fear the social repercussions of not conforming. Yet conformity occurred despite this *and* when the correct answers were so obvious.

Would we expect conformity to be higher still among friends because the social cost of being different is greater? Or might it be lower since we are not so afraid of losing face or looking silly with people we know and trust?

Replications of Asch's Experiments

The Asch studies have stimulated a great deal of research, including many fairly recent attempts to replicate the original findings, and some very interesting results have emerged.

Larsen (1974) found significantly lower conformity rates than Asch had found among groups of American students and suggested that this was because of a changed climate of opinion in America in the 1970s towards independence and criticism and away from conformity. However, in a later (1979) study, Larsen found results very similar to those of Asch. Perhaps the pendulum had begun to swing back again.

Perrin and Spencer (1981) found very low rates of conformity (one out of 396 trials) for a group of British students; but they were engineering, maths and chemistry students and so were perhaps better able to resist conformity pressure because of their special knowledge and experience. Significantly, in the same study, young offenders on probation showed very similar rates of conformity to Asch's; the confederate majority consisted of probation officers and the experimenter was an 'authority figure'.

Brown (1985) makes the interesting suggestion that it may not be just students who have changed since the 1950s but the experimenters too, that is, they may not *expect* so much conformity; 'even when Asch's paradigm is apparently faithfully replicated, the experimenter may, unwittingly, convey

to the subjects certain expectations as to the outcome of the experiment'
(Brown, 1985). (See Chapter 2 on 'experimenter effects'.)

Crutchfield (1954)

Crutchfield criticized Asch's experiments for being time-consuming and
uneconomical, since only one subject could be tested at a time. He, therefore,
changed the experimental situation so that several (usually five) real subjects
could be tested at the same time. Altogether, he tested over 600 subjects.

Each subject sat in an open cubicle which had a panel with an array of
lights and switches; subjects could not see neighbouring panels. Questions,
pictures and other kinds of stimulus were projected on to the wall in front
of the subject and each subject believed that they were the last to respond.
The subject was also told that the lights on the display panel indicated the
answers of the other subjects; in fact, each subject saw an identical display
and so received the same information. The answers were wrong on approximately half the trials.

Crutchfield presented a variety of tasks, and conformity to the wrong
answers differed according to the type of task involved:

i) On the Asch-type perceptual judgement, he found 30 per cent
conformity.
ii) When asked to complete a series of numbers (as in IQ tests) he also
found 30 per cent conformity.
iii) When he presented a star which was obviously smaller in area than a
circle (by about one-third, in fact), there was 46 per cent agreement that
the circle was smaller than the star.
iv) Some of his subjects were army officers attending a three-day assessment programme. Thirty-seven per cent of them agreed with the
statement, 'I doubt whether I would make a good leader' when it was
presented in the booth but, significantly, none of them agreed with it
when tested privately.
v) A substantial proportion of college students agreed with statements
which, under more 'normal' circumstances, they would not be expected
to. For example: (a) 60 to 70 percent of the population of the USA is
aged 65 or over; (b) American males are, on average, taller than
American females, by eight or nine inches; (c) the life expectancy of
American males is only about 25 years; (d) Americans sleep four to five
hours per night, on average, and eat six meals a day; (e) free speech
being a privilege rather than a right, it is proper for a society to suspend
free speech when it feels itself threatened.
Tuddenham and McBride (1959) found similar results for other
groups of subjects.
vi) Some subjects conformed to all of the above tasks, others did not agree
to any; most conformed to some.
vii) Apart from these individual differences, it was found that individuals
were more prepared to conform to difficult items (as in the Asch
experiment).

For most of the different kinds of tasks, the tendency to conform dropped considerably when subjects were re-tested individually. However, there were differences in how much it dropped between submissive and self-confident subjects. For the former, when they were assured that the majority judgements were false, conformity dropped only by 15 per cent and when assured that the majority judgements were correct, conformity actually rose by 25 per cent.

Individual Differences in Conformity

Is there a conforming personality?

Crutchfield (1955) found that people who tend to conform have the following characteristics: they are intellectually less effective, have less ego strength, less leadership ability, less mature social relationships, have feelings of inferiority, tend to be authoritarian, are less self-sufficient, are more submissive, narrow-minded and inhibited and have relatively little insight into their own personalities compared with those who tend not to conform.

But can we say that there is a conforming personality, ie is a person who conforms in one situation also likely to conform in other situations?

Vaughan (1964) found that 20 per cent of subjects exposed to pressures to conform in four separate situations conformed in all four, which suggests that the conforming personality may exist. But McGuire (1968) concluded that consistency across situations is not high. The authoritarian personality (Adorno et al, 1950) is perhaps as close to such a personality type as can be found (this was discussed in the last chapter in relation to prejudice). Elms and Milgram (1966) described the authoritarian personality as having an 'unquestioning respect for convention'.

De Charms and Rosenbaum (1957) and Rosenburg et al (1960) found that men of low self-esteem tend to conform more often than those who are self-assured, suggesting that the former may be motivated by the need for acceptance and security. Strickland and Crowne (1962) and Crowne and Liverant (1963) found that people with a high need for social approval conform more readily than those with a low need. Again, conforming seems to be a way of gaining the approval of others.

These latter findings suggest that conformity is a means of fulfilling a variety of psychological needs; if approval or acceptance is the real motive underlying conforming behaviour, then instead of talking about a conforming personality, we should talk about conformity as a means to an end, a means of satisfying certain needs which are more important to some people than to others.

Apart from personality, *gender* and *culture* represent important sources of individual differences which have been found to influence conformity. Traditionally, females have been found to conform more than males, especially in traditionally male domains (Crutchfield, 1955, Nord, 1969); this seems to be associated with females being more conservative.

However, Crutchfield also found that American women who had attended college were actually less likely to conform than their male counterparts and a more recent study (Eagly, 1978) found no significant differences in overall levels of conformity between men and women (see Chapter 22 on sex and gender roles). Perhaps any differences that have existed in the past are, slowly and gradually, beginning to disappear, and we should always be aware of the important differences that exist *within* each sexual group (see Chapter 22 again).

As far as culture is concerned, Crutchfield concluded that members of ethnic minorities conform highly when working in groups where they are the only minority-group person. This is not perhaps a very surprising finding; we might expect that a white person would also conform highly in an otherwise all-black group, even though the former belongs to the dominant cultural group.

We might also expect, based on the Asch studies, that the presence of one other member of a minority group would significantly reduce the conformity rate, whether there were two different minority groups represented or just one. (Remember that even when the confederate disagrees with both the real subject and the majority, the conformity level drops sharply.)

Riesman (1950) maintained that conformity tends to be higher in stable societies where there are low birth and death rates.

Milgram (1961) studied French and Norwegian students by giving them an Asch-type task which involved matching a standard tone with a comparison tone in terms of the duration of the sound. They were tested in groups of six, where there was only one real subject, but they only heard the judgements of the others on a tape-recorder.

Milgram obtained similar overall results to Asch's but there were some interesting differences between the groups—the Norwegian subjects were significantly more conformist (62 per cent) than the French (50 per cent). When the taped voices began criticizing the non-conforming subjects for failing to accept the judgement of the majority, conformity amongst the Norwegians rose to 75 per cent and they rather passively accepted the criticism. The French, on the other hand, did not take very kindly to the criticism and expressed their disapproval by swearing etc. But despite this, their conformity level rose to 59 per cent. How can we account for these differences?

Milgram suggests that the Norwegians are more uniform in their political and religious beliefs, as well as in their physical appearance, than the French, partly because they have not had the history of invasions and occupations by other nations; they also seem to identify more closely with their country than the French. But we must remember that Milgram's sample was small and students are unlikely to be representative of the Norwegian and French peoples as a whole.

One other relevant cross-cultural study is that of Shouval et al (1975) who studied a much larger sample of 12-year-old Russians and Israelis, who were compared on conformity to peer-group pressures. In Russia, childhood is viewed as a period of obedience, formal learning and discipline, while in Israel, it is a time of preparation for the self-confidence and independence needed for adult life and the emphasis is on adventure. As predicted, the Russian 12-year-olds were found to be influenced by their peers significantly more than their Israeli counterparts.

Conformity and Non-conformity

Are all non-conformers alike? To counter-balance the emphasis that has been placed so far on conformity, it is important that we now look at non-conformity.

According to Willis (1963), two dimensions are necessary in order to construct an adequate representation of conformity and non-conformity, namely: (i) *dependence–independence*; and (ii) *conformity–anti-conformity*. Taken together, these produce three major patterns of behaviour over a series of interactions:

a) *Conformity* which involves a consistent movement *towards* social expectancy:
b) *Independence* which involves a *lack* of consistent movement either towards or away from social expectancy;
c) *Anti-conformity* which involves a consistent movement *away* from social conformity.

Both (b) and (c) represent *non-conformity* but they differ, particularly in relation to the dimension of independence. Whereas (a) and (c) both reveal dependence on others, (b), as the word 'independent' implies, is (relatively) free of such dependence, and (c) is still tied to the norms of some minority group which they put forward in opposition to those of the majority.

Willis saw conformity and non-conformity *not* as personality characteristics but as the outcomes of interaction in a particular situation; the degree of independence, for example, is not fixed even for the same individual. Just as there are different cultural valuations made of different kinds of leadership style, so anti-conformity has a more negative valuation in our culture than independence; 'independence is probably seen as a more authentic, self-motivated, form of response than is the negativism of anticonformity' (Hollander, 1981).

Hollander and Willis (1964) found that subjects responded differently to co-workers (when jointly engaged on a task) according to whether they behaved in a conforming, independent or anti-conforming way. Even when co-workers were presented as being more competent than the subject with respect to the task, subjects were more influenced by the independent, competent co-worker than by the anti-conforming and equally competent co-worker. This lends empirical support to Willis's argument that independence and anti-conformity represent essentially different kinds of non-conformity.

According to Brown (1985), it is virtually impossible to classify behaviour at all as conformist or independent unless we understand the *meaning* the situation has for the individual and the implications it has for their self-image. She concludes that, 'both a person's disposition and situational variables would appear to determine the *degree* of an individual's dissent from or agreement with a group' (Brown, 1985.)

Different Kinds of Conformity

Now that we have looked at some of the major studies of conformity and the factors which influence it, we are in a better position to look at the distinctions that have been made between different kinds of conformity, ie public or private acceptance or both.

Kelman (1958, 1961) distinguished between Compliance, Internalization and Identification.

a) In *compliance*, people yield to group pressure in order to avoid 'punishment' for non-conformity. Publicly, the individual agrees with the majority but privately disagrees. In Asch's experiments, as we have seen, many subjects agreed verbally with the wrong answers knowing them to be wrong, in order to avoid being laughed at, or being the odd-one-out, or upsetting the experiment. Crutchfield's subjects also tended to give one answer in the group situation and another when tested individually.

b) In *internalization*, the individual's opinion comes to resemble the group's and will eventually coincide, so that there is no discrepancy between them and hence no conflict. This was the case with Sherif's subjects who, when tested individually after being in the group, gave estimates which closely reflected the group norm.

Again, the individual incorporates the group opinion or preference or behaviour into their own value or belief system—there is both public and private acceptance.

c) *Identification* involves the individual yielding to pressure because the group has characteristics which the individual finds attractive and wishes to adopt. Like (b), the group preference or belief is accepted both publicly and privately. Identification has been found to be generally more temporary and transient than internalization.

Because the participants in the experiments we have considered were strangers (whether confederates or other real subjects) and did not constitute 'proper' groups, identification does not really apply or help us understand the conformity that took place.

Mann (1969) also distinguished three types of conformity, which overlap with Kelman's (see Table 12.2).

i) *Normative*: here, group pressures force the individual to yield to group norms under threat of rejection or the promise of reward.

It can take two forms—(a) Compliance, which corresponds to Kelman's Compliance, and (b) True Conformity, which corresponds to Kelman's Internalization.

Clearly, in order to be sure which of these is operating we must observe the individual both with the group and away from it.

Table 12.2 The major kinds of conformity involved in the 3 main conformity studies

Kind of conformity		Experimental study of conformity
Normative (Mann)	Compliance (Kelman and Mann)	Asch (1951, 1952, 1956) Crutchfield (1954)
	True conformity (Mann) Internalization (Kelman)	Sherif (1935)
Informational conformity (Mann)		Sherif (1935)
Ingratiational conformity (Mann)		—
Identification (Kelman)		—

ii) *Informational*: this occurs when the individual is in a novel or ambiguous situation and is uncertain how to respond and so looks to the behaviour or opinion of others for guidance. It is a way of trying to avoid appearing stupid or ignorant in front of others.

Judy Gahagan (1975) cites the tendency of highly educated, intelligent and mature people to rely on the critics to find out how they 'should' react to a new play or art exhibition etc. when they feel unsure within their own minds.

When the individual believes that other members of the group have superior knowledge relevant to the task, or are actually perceived as experts, or where the task is highly ambiguous (as in Sherif's experiment), they are said to be under informational pressure. So informational conformity is similar to true conformity and to internalization (as well as to identification) in that there is a correspondence between the individual's opinion and that of the group. However, the underlying motives are different.

iii) *Ingratiational*: here the individual agrees with others in order to impress them or gain their acceptance, for example, a low-status employee agreeing with the boss, or a child being 'good' for its parents. In these examples, there might be public agreement but private disagreement (especially if it is a callous, 'boot-licking' employee in the first example, where conformity is a deliberate means to an end, in which case it is similar to compliance), or there may be true conformity or internalization (which is likely to happen in the second example, where we may also talk about identification, but in a Freudian sense—see Chapters 21, 22 and 26).

Table 12.2 indicates the main kind of conformity involved in the three major studies discussed in the chapter. But there were, for some subjects, other kinds involved as well; for example, in the Asch and Crutchfield experiments, there were elements of true conformity, internalization and informational conformity, where subjects were either not aware of a discrepancy between their own and the group's opinion, or believed the majority had access to information which they did not. The classification is based on the majority of subjects in each study.

Criticisms of Conformity Experiments

a) They fail to isolate the motive underlying the conformity behaviour, ie what kind of conformity is involved. We have put this right by analysing the findings in terms of Kelman's and Mann's distinctions.

b) There is the implicit assumption that independence is 'good' and conformity is 'bad'. Asch (1952) in fact made this value judgement quite explicit. However, as Gahagan (1975) points out, conformity can be highly functional, facilitating the satisfaction of social and non-social needs; it is also necessary, to some extent, for social life to proceed at all.

c) Their relevance to everyday life is questionable, to say the least. Again, Gahagan (1975) explores this criticism. She says that there are 2 main questions that need to be asked:

i) To what extent, if any, is our knowledge of the world defined in terms of other people's beliefs and opinions? Many kinds of knowledge that we take for granted, as 'facts', are actually culturally determined so that different cultures define 'the truth' differently. It is all the more likely that where there is room for disagreement and shades of opinion, as in politics, religion, sport etc, that we will take note of others' reactions and assess 'the truth' accordingly. In practice, the majority opinion is often the one that individuals identify as 'fact'.

ii) Should we view the naïve subject in the Asch experiment as the individual fighting for 'the truth' against the social pressure of the majority (as, for example, some scientists have had to fight to get their views accepted, such as Darwin and Freud) or in some other way?

Moscovici and Faucheux (1972) advocate that we think of the naïve subject as embodying the 'conventional', self-evident opinion of the majority (for example, the conviction that the earth is flat or that man was created in the Garden of Eden), while the confederates giving false answers represent unorthodox, unconventional, eccentric and even outrageous viewpoints or theories (for example, the earth is round, man evolved from apes). Looked at in this way, the conformity experiments seem to provide evidence relating to the question 'How do new ideas come to be accepted?' rather than, 'What processes operate to maintain the status quo?'.

4) Obedience

We have defined conformity as yielding to group pressure; obedience can be defined as complying with the demands of an authority figure. Hedy Brown (1985) sees both conformity and obedience involving an abdication of personal responsibility but there are important differences between them: conformity has to do with the psychological 'need' for acceptance by others and entails going along with one's peers in a group situation, but obedience has to do with the social power and status of an authority figure in a hierarchical situation. While we may deny that we conform (because this seems to detract from our sense of individuality), most of us would be willing to make excuses for ourselves by saying that we were 'obeying orders'.

Roger Brown (1986) makes a similar distinction; he says that conformity behaviour is affected by *example* (from peers or equals) while obedience is affected by *direction* (from somebody in higher authority).

Milgram (1963, 1965, 1974)

In the conformity experiments of Sherif, Asch and Crutchfield, subjects showed conformity by giving a verbal response of some kind or pressing buttons representing answers on various tasks. In what is the most famous and controversial obedience experiment, Milgram's subjects were required to 'kill' another human being.

Milgram was attempting to test the 'Germans are different' hypothesis. This hypothesis has been used by historians to explain the systematic destruction of millions of Jews, Poles and others by the Nazis during the 1930s and 1940s. It maintains that: (i) Hitler could not have put his evil plans into operation without the co-operation of thousands of others; and (ii) the Germans have a basic character defect, namely a readiness to obey authority without question, regardless of the acts demanded by the authority figure, and that it is this readiness to obey which provided Hitler with the co-operation he needed. It is really the second part of the hypothesis which Milgram was trying to test. He had originally planned to take his experiment to Germany, once it was completed at New Haven, Connecticut, but, as we shall see, that proved unnecessary.

The subjects in the original experiment were 20- to 50-year-old men, from all walks of life. They answered advertisements in local newspapers, or that came by post, which asked for volunteers for a study of learning, to be conducted at Yale University. It would take about one hour and there would be a payment of $4.50.

The experiment was later repeated many times, involving about 1 000 people, including housewives, blue-collar workers, college professors and social workers.

The Basic Experiment

When the subject arrived at the 'Yale Interaction Laboratory', they were met by a young, crew-cut man in a laboratory coat, who introduced himself as Jack Williams, the experimenter. Also present was a Mr Wallace, supposedly another subject, in his late fifties, Irish face, an accountant, a little overweight and generally a very mild and harmless-looking man. In fact, Mr Wallace was an assistant of Milgram, and everything that happened after this was pre-planned, staged and scripted; everything, that is, except the degree to which the real subject obeyed the experimenter's instructions. It was as if the whole experiment was a play with the script of the leading character left unwritten—they were to write the script as they went along. The irony is that the subject was the only character who did not know that they were in a play at all!

The subject and Mr Wallace were told that the experiment was concerned with the effects of punishment on learning and that one of them was to be the teacher and the other the learner. Their roles were determined by each drawing a piece of paper from a hat; both, in fact, had 'teacher' written on them. Mr Wallace drew first and called out 'learner', so, of course, the real subject was always the teacher.

They all went into an adjoining room where the learner (Mr Wallace) was strapped into a chair with his arms attached to electrodes which would deliver a shock from the shock generator situated in an adjacent room. When asked if he had any questions, Mr Wallace said he thought he should let them know that he had recently been in hospital for a heart condition, although it was not anything serious. The experimenter assured him that although the shocks might be painful, they would not cause any permanent damage. The teacher (subject) and experimenter (Williams) then moved next door where the generator was situated; the teacher was, in fact, given a 45-volt shock to convince him that it was real, for he was to operate the generator during the experiment. However, that was the only real shock that either the teacher or the learner was to receive.

The generator (which Milgram himself had built and which looked authentic) had a number of switches, each clearly marked with voltage levels and verbal descriptions, starting at 15 volts and going up to 450 in intervals of 15:

15–60	*slight shock*
75–120	*moderate shock*
135–180	*strong shock*
195–240	*very strong shock*
255–300	*intense shock*
315–360	*intense to extreme shock*
375–420	*danger: severe shock*
435–450	*XXX*

The teacher had to read out a series of word pairs (eg 'blue–girl', 'nice–day', 'fat–neck') and then the first of one pair (the stimulus word) followed by five words, of which one was the original paired response. The learner had to choose the correct response to the stimulus word by pressing one of four switches, which turned on a light on a panel in the generator room. Each time he made a mistake, the teacher had to deliver a shock, and each successive mistake was punished by a shock 15 volts higher than the one before.

Milgram had asked 14 psychology students to predict what would happen for 100 subjects in this situation. They thought that a few would break off early on, most would stop somewhere in the middle and a few would continue right up to 450 volts. The highest single estimate for those who would go right to the end was three. He also asked 40 psychiatrists who predicted that less than one per cent would administer the highest voltage.

The astoundingly high figure for those subjects who actually went on giving shocks up to and including 450 volts was 65 per cent. This happened despite a tape-recorded series of responses which the 'teacher' believed were spontaneous reactions to the increasing shock levels. The learner convincingly increased his 'distress' as the severity of the shock increased. This is how it went:

At 75 volts, he started to grunt, moan and groan;
At 125 volts, he shouted 'That really hurts!'
At 150 volts, he started to complain and asked to be excused from the experiment;
At 180 volts, he shouted, 'I can't stand the pain, don't do that!'
At 195 volts, he yelled, 'Let me out! My heart's starting to bother me now!'
At 285 volts, he let out an agonized scream;
At 300 volts, he kicked and banged on the wall and begged to be released;
At 315 volts, there was ominous silence!

(The teacher was instructed to treat no response as if it were an incorrect response, so the shocks could continue beyond 315 volts.) In addition, the experimenter had a script prepared for whenever the teacher refused to continue or showed any resistance or reluctance to do so:

On the first refusal, he would say, 'Please continue'.
On subsequent refusals, he would say, 'The experiment requires that you continue' or, 'It's absolutely essential that you go on'. As a last resort, he would say, 'You have no choice but to go on'.

There were also 'special prods' to reassure the subject that he was not doing the learner any 'permanent tissue damage' and that the experimenter would accept responsibility for anything that might happen.

As we have seen, 65 per cent of subjects went all the way to 450 volts. All subjects who began giving shocks continued up to at least 300; some refused at stages between 300 and 375, but all those who went as far as 375 carried on up to 450!

Before the impression is given that a large percentage of subjects quite callously gave shocks of such high intensities to an innocent 'victim' through blind obedience, we should note that many subjects displayed great anguish, verbally attacked the experimenter, twitched nervously, or broke out into nervous laughter. Many were observed to, 'sweat, stutter, tremble, groan, bite their lips and dig their nails into their flesh. Full-blown, uncontrollable seizures were observed for three subjects.' One experiment had to be stopped due to the subject having a violently convulsive seizure.

Why was there such a high level of obedience?

Milgram tried to answer this crucial question by devising some variations to the basic experiment in order to identify the critical variables.

Variations of the Basic Experiment

i) In post-experimental interviews, many subjects said that they had continued giving shocks because the experiment was being carried out at Yale, a very prestigious and highly respected American university. Milgram therefore transferred the experiment to a run-down office building located in downtown Bridgeport, Connecticut. In this setting, the obedience rate was 50 per cent (for those continuing up to 450 volts), indicating that the awe-inspiring nature of the original location was not a crucial factor, although it clearly played some part.

ii) The proximity of the teacher to the learner proved to be of greater significance than the physical setting. Remember that in the original experiment the teacher and learner were in separate but adjoining rooms, so that the teacher heard the learner (via a tape-recorder) but could not see him.

When they were in the same room (about $1\frac{1}{2}$ feet apart), so that the teacher could see as well as hear the learner, the obedience level dropped to 40 per cent. It dropped further still to 30 per cent when the teacher was required to force the learner's hand onto the shock plate. Clearly, it became much more uncomfortable to see the effects of their obedience, so that considerably fewer subjects were prepared to go all the way. However, these figures of 40 and 30 per cent are still rather high.

iii) Another variation involved giving the teacher social support for refusing to obey. The real subject was teamed with two other 'teachers' (confederates of Milgram). After 150 volts, one of the accomplices announced that he was not going to continue and moved to another part of the room.

After 210 volts, the second one also refused. In all cases, the experimenter continued to order the real subject to proceed as described above.

Only 10 per cent of real subjects then continued all the way to 450 volts— they stopped obeying either immediately after one of the confederates did so or very shortly afterwards. The real subject made very revealing remarks afterwards, such as, 'I didn't realize I could' (ie, refuse to obey). So the 'demands of the situation' seem to be crucial, that is, how the subject interprets and defines what is possible or permissible.

iv) When the teacher was paired with another, confederate, teacher, whereby the real subject only had to read out the word-pairs and the confederate threw the switches, there was 95 per cent obedience. Clearly, it was easier to shift responsibility from themselves to the confederate for what the learner was suffering since 'their hand was not on the button'.

v) The proximity of the experimenter to the teacher was also found to be crucial. When the experimenter left the room, having given the initial instructions, and issued subsequent instructions by telephone, the obedience level dropped to almost zero.

In another variation, instructions were given via a tape-recorder and the experimenter was not seen at all. Under these conditions, obedience rate was about 22 per cent. Subjects often pretended to press the shock button or pressed the button for a lower voltage than they were meant to. This suggests that they were trying to compromise between what their conscience was telling them to do and what the experimenter was telling them to do; in his absence, it was easier to disobey him and to obey the dictates of conscience!

Another way of looking at this is to say that in the experimenter's absence, the subject was forced to accept responsibility for their own actions, while in his presence, with all the prods and prompts and his assurances that he would accept responsibility for anything that might happen to the learner, it was much easier for the subject to deny personal responsibility (they were merely 'doing what they were told').

But clearly it was not as cut and dried as this; we saw earlier that in the original experiment many subjects showed obvious signs of distress and conflict. The experimenter was, it seems, being seen as a legitimate authority in that situation, which was totally convincing and very real for the subjects. The conflict is between two opposing sets of demands, the external authority of the experimenter, who says, 'Shock' and the internal authority of the conscience, which says, 'Don't shock'. The point at which conscience triumphs is, of course, where the subject (finally) stops obeying the experimenter—at that point, the experimenter, in a sense, ceases to be a legitimate authority in the eyes of the subject. Thirty-five per cent of subjects in the original experiment reached that point somewhere before 450 volts; for many of those subjects, the crucial 'prod' was when the experimenter said, 'You have no choice but to go on'. They were able to exercise the choice which, of course, they *did* have and so at that point they stopped obeying.

The experimenter wore a grey, not a white, laboratory coat, which was meant to be ambiguous (eg white might have suggested a medical technician) but which indicated his position as an authority figure. Other studies have shown that the fact that someone is wearing a uniform is often reason enough for them to be obeyed. For example, in a study by Bickman (1974), researchers approached people on the streets of New York and ordered them either to pick up a paper bag or give a coin to a stranger. Half of the researchers were dressed in neat street clothes and half in a guard's uniform. Under 40 per cent obeyed the civilians but more than 80 per cent obeyed the 'guard', even when he walked off after giving the order so that, as far as the 'subjects' were concerned, he could not see whether they had complied or not.

Milgram, of course, had already shown that the 'Germans are different' hypothesis had no foundation, hence his decision not to repeat the experiment in Germany, as originally planned. He concluded that:

A substantial proportion of people do what they are told to do, irrespective of the content of the act and without limitations of conscience, so long as they perceive that the command comes from a legitimate authority. (Milgram, 1974)

Criticisms of Milgram

i)   The main criticisms are to do with the ethics of Milgram's experiments. Baumrind (1964), for example, claims that it is unethical and, therefore, unacceptable, to place innocent and naïve subjects under great emotional strain and pressure in selfish obedience to his quest for knowledge. Their distress during the experiment and the subsequent psychological damage cannot be justified. Milgram defends himself in several ways.

First, clearly, the experiments were not intended to induce as much stress as they did: it simply was not anticipated. He expected most subjects to disobey much sooner than they did. Also, all the subjects were told the purpose of the experiment at the end and re-united with the learner to assure them that he was unharmed.

Secondly, he points out that unlike the learner, who, in the subject's mind, is helplessly strapped in, the subject is free to leave at any time (at least in the theoretical, philosophical sense).

Thirdly, he believes that, even in the extreme cases, no permanent psychological harm was done to the subjects. (This seems to parallel the experimenter's reassurances that the shocks may be painful but not danger-ous.) After the experiments, Milgram sent a summary of the results to each of his subjects, asking whether they had any regrets about having partici-pated: almost 80 per cent were either glad or very glad to have participated, another 15 per cent had no strong feelings one way or another, and just over 1 per cent were either sorry or very sorry to have participated. Furthermore, 80 per cent said that there should be more research of this kind and 74 per cent said they had learned something of lasting value.

This tends to confirm the suggestion made by Rosnow (1978) that this type of experiment may help people to review their value systems and they may emerge from it as better people. We could perhaps vindicate Milgram by saying that the more people who read about his experiments, the better; if we are alerted to our tendency to obey authority figures in ways that may be harmful to others, we may be less likely actually to do it if the situation arose.

Erikson (1968) believes that Milgram made a valuable contribution to our understanding of human behaviour: it needed a man of strength and scientific faith to demonstrate that it is man himself who is responsible for controlling his potentially harmful behaviour.

Etzioni (1968) praised Milgram's attempt to combine humanistic study and empirical research.

Roger Brown (1986) believes that Milgram is ethically 'in the clear' and deserves to be praised, 'for doing research of the highest human consequence while showing great concern for the welfare of his subjects'. (Brown, 1986).

Other major criticisms are more to do with the methodology rather than the ethical issues.

ii)   The charge that the subjects were atypical of the American population seems to be unjustified. As we have noted above, 1 000 subjects were tested, representing a cross-section of the population of New Haven, thought to be a fairly typical small American town. However, Milgram admits that those who went on obeying up to 450 volts were more likely to see the learner as responsible for what happened to him and not the teacher! They seemed to have a stronger authoritarian character and a less advanced level of moral development. But this was a matter of degree only. As Rosenthal and Rosnow (1966) and others have found, people who volunteer for experiments are considerably less authoritarian than those who do not.

Also, Mantell (1971) repeated the experiment in Germany and found an even higher obedience rate than Milgram (85 per cent); Shanat and Yahya (1977) found 80 per cent obedience in Jordan, and Ancona and Pareysin (1968) in Italy and Kilham and Mann (1974) in Australia also found high levels of obedience.

iii) We have already touched on the question of how realistic the situation was for the subject. The obvious, and at times extreme, distress of many subjects itself seems to confirm that they genuinely believed that the learner was, indeed, receiving the shocks. In fact, a follow-up questionnaire one year later showed that three-quarters of the subjects believed that they had been delivering harmful shocks while only one-fifth had any real doubts.

iv) Finally, it has been claimed that what happened to Milgram's subjects in the laboratory cannot be generalized to real-life outside the 'Yale Interaction Laboratory'.

Milgram defends himself by maintaining that the essential process involved in complying to the demands of an authority figure is the same, whether the setting is the artificial one of the laboratory or a naturally occurring one outside it.

A study of great relevance to this issue was conducted by Hofling et al (1966), which aimed to discover whether nurses would comply with an instruction which would involve them having to infringe both hospital regulations and medical ethics (see Box 12.2 overleaf).

In interviews, 22 graduate nurses who had not participated in the actual experiment were presented with the same situation as an issue to discuss; 21 said that they would not have given the drug without written authorization, especially as it exceeded the maximum daily dose. This brings to mind the predictions of the psychology students and psychiatrists that very few subjects would go on giving shocks up to 450 volts in Milgram's experiments. How many of the subjects themselves would have said that they would do so? Rather fewer than 65 per cent, no doubt!

There is, of course, an important difference between the two situations. Milgram's subjects were being asked to inflict pain upon another human being, while the nurses in the Hofling study were being asked to do something quite consistent with their role and, presumably, in the patient's best interests. Or was it?

The 21 nurses who complied probably did not question that it was, since the request came from a Dr Smith from the Psychiatry Department; 11 said they had not even noticed that the 20 mg request exceeded the maximum daily dose. What of the other 10 who did?

In a way, because of the real-life setting of the experiment, and because of

---

Box 12.2: Obedience in a Natural Setting (based on Hofling et al, 1966)

Identical boxes of capsules were placed in 22 wards of both public and private psychiatric hospitals. The capsules were, in fact placebos (consisting of glucose). But the containers were labelled '5 mg capsules of Astrofen'; the labels also indicated that the normal dose is 5 mg with a maximum daily dose of 10 mg.

While the nurse was on duty, a 'doctor' (a confederate 'Dr Smith from the Psychiatric Department') instructed the nurse, by telephone, to give 20 mg of Astrofen to his patient, a Mr Jones, as he was in a desperate hurry and the patient needed the capsules. He said that he would come in to see Mr Jones in 10 minutes time and that he would sign the authorization document for the drug when he got there.

To comply with this request, the nurse would be breaking three basic procedural rules:

i)   The dose was above the maximum daily dose of 10 mg;
ii) Drugs should only be given after written authority has been obtained;
iii) The nurse must be absolutely sure that 'Dr Smith' is a genuine doctor.

A real doctor was posted nearby, unseen by the nurse, and observed what the nurse did following the telephone call—did she comply, did she refuse, or did she try to contact another doctor?

Whatever her course of action, the observer-doctor then revealed to her what was really going on.

21 out of 22 nurses complied unhesitatingly! Eleven later said that they had not noticed the dosage discrepancy.

---

the implications of what would transpire had it not been an experiment, these results are more disturbing than Milgram's. Admittedly, the sample was much smaller than Milgram's and, since 1966, the role of the nurse may have become less 'obedient' and deferential towards doctors and more questioning and critical. But it seems that built into our social roles is a polarity (pair of opposites) which might be expressed as domineering–servile, powerful–powerless, dominant–submissive. Rather than asking what makes some people more obedient than others, or how we would have reacted if we had been one of Milgram's subjects, we should be asking how we would behave if we were put into a position of authority ourselves. How easily could we assume the role and use the power that goes with it? And if we could, how might we explain our ability to do so?

An intriguing but also rather frightening experiment by Zimbardo et al (1973) explored these questions. Their famous Prison Simulation Experiment is described in Box 12.3.

Social power became the major dimension on which everyone and everything was defined. The primary forms of interaction on the part of the guards were commands, insults, degrading comments, verbal and physical aggression and threats. The counterpart by the prisoners were resistance, giving information when asked questions, questioning and (initially) insulting the guards.

Every guard at sometime or another behaved in an abusive, authoritarian way; many seemed positively to enjoy the new-found power and the almost total control over the prisoners which went with the uniform.

Box 12.3 The Prison Simulation Experiment (Zimbardo et al, 1973)

The subjects were recruited through advertisements placed in a city newspaper asking for student volunteers for a two-week study of prison life. They would be paid 15 dollars a day (210 dollars in all, quite a lot of money for a poor student) and over 100 volunteers came forward initially.

They were given clinical interviews and 25 were eventually selected: they were judged to be emotionally stable, physically healthy, 'normal to average', on the basis of extensive personality tests, and also law-abiding (they had no history of convictions, violence or drug-abuse). They were told that their assignment to the role of either prisoner or prison-guard would be determined by the toss of a coin. They all stated a preference for being prisoners.

So at the start of the study there were no measurable differences between those who were to be assigned to one or other role; they were a relatively homogeneous sample of white, middle-class college students from all over the USA and Canada. They all had an equal chance of being either prisoner or guard.

The intention was not to make a literal copy of a real prison setting but to achieve some equivalent psychological effects; the 'mock prison' represented an attempt to simulate functionally some of the significant features of the psychological state of imprisonment.

The basement of Stanford University in California was converted into a mock prison and the experiment began one Sunday morning when the students who had been allocated to the prisoner role were 'arrested', by the Palo Alto police, charged with a felony, told their constitutional rights, searched, handcuffed and taken in the back seat of a squad car to the police station to be booked. After being fingerprinted and having identification forms prepared for his 'jacket' (central information file), the prisoner was taken, blindfold, to 'Stanford County Prison' (the basement of Stanford University), where he was stripped naked, skin-searched, deloused, issued a uniform, bedding etc.

Prisoners wore a loose-fitting smock, with an identification number, front and back, plus a chain bolted around one ankle; they also wore a nylon stocking to cover their hair (instead of being shaved). The guards wore military khaki-style uniforms, silver reflector sunglasses (which made eye-contact impossible) and they carried clubs, whistles, handcuffs and keys to the cells and main gate.

Orders were shouted and the guards pushed the prisoners around if they did not comply quickly enough, but any other physical violence was forbidden. There were visits from a former prison chaplain, a public defender, and relatives and friends of some of the prisoners, as well as disciplinary and parole hearings before a board comprising a group of 'adult authorities'.

Although the guards worked eight-hour shifts, the prisoners were imprisoned in their cells around the clock, allowed out only for meals, exercise, toilet privileges, head-counts and work.

In a remarkably short time, a perverted relationship developed between the prisoners and guards. After an initial rebellion had been crushed, the prisoners reacted passively as the guards stepped up their aggression each day, which made the prisoners even more passive and dependent, and made them feel helpless, that they were no longer in control of their life. In less than 36 hours, one prisoner had to be released because of uncontrolled crying, fits of rage, disorganized thinking and severe depression. Three more developed similar symptoms and had to be released on successive days. A fifth prisoner developed a rash over his whole body which was triggered when his 'parole' had been rejected.

The entire experiment, planned to run for two weeks, was stopped after six days because of the pathological reactions of the prisoners who had originally been selected for their normality.

For example, Guard A said:

> I was surprised at myself—I made them call each other names and clean the toilets out with their bare hands. I practically considered the prisoners cattle and I kept thinking I have to watch out for them in case they try something.

Guard B (preparing for the visitors' first night):

> I made sure I was one of the guards on the yard, because this was my first chance for the type of manipulative power that I really like—being a very noticed figure with complete control over what is said or not.

Guard C:

> Acting authoritatively can be fun. Power can be a great pleasure.

How can we account for such behaviour?

As we have already noted, we cannot attribute the behaviour to any pre-existing personality traits, such as 'psychopathic' or 'sadistic' guards or 'criminal, weak impulse–control' prisoners.

As Zimbardo and Ruch (1977) point out, the abnormal behaviour of both groups is best viewed as a product of transactions with an environment that supports such behaviour. Since they were randomly assigned their roles, showed no prior personality pathology and received no training, how was it that the subjects assumed their roles as quickly and completely as they did?

First, presumably, they had learned stereotypes of guard and prisoner roles from the mass media as well as from social models of power and powerlessness (for example, the parent–child, teacher–student, employer–employee relationships). We are able to draw on our experience and knowledge of other role relationships whenever we are faced with new ones, whether we are called upon to be 'in charge' or to be the submissive or powerless one.

Secondly, environmental conditions facilitate role-playing: a brutalizing atmosphere, like the 'mock' prison, produces brutality and perhaps this kind of aggression is potential in all of us. Had the roles been reversed, those who suffered as the prisoners may just as easily have inflicted suffering on those who were randomly chosen as guards. (In contrast to the Milgram experiment, there seemed to be no conflict for the guards; quite the reverse, in fact. Clearly, the role of teacher and the requirement that they should deliver painful electric shocks were seen by the subjects as inconsistent with each other. But a guard is someone who is meant to behave in an aggressive and brutal way; hence, no conflict.)

Zimbardo and Ruch conclude by saying that, 'this research illustrates not only what a prison-like environment can bring out in relatively normal people, but also how they have been socialized by their society' (Zimbardo and Ruch, 1977.).

Conclusions

Zimbardo et al have, like Milgram, come under severe criticism for the ethics of their research: Savin (1973), for example, argues that their subjects were 'deceived, humiliated or maltreated'. Yet however valid these criticisms might be, is it possible that underlying them is a rather different response which is more difficult to articulate, namely the shock and horror at what Hannah Arendt called 'the banality of evil' (the sub-title of her book, in 1963, about the Israeli trial of Adolf Eichmann, the Nazi war criminal)? To believe that 'ordinary people' could do what Eichmann did, or what Milgram's or Zimbardo's guard-subjects did, is far less acceptable than that Eichmann was an inhuman monster or that experimental subjects have been put under immorally high levels of stress.

Following the trial of William Calley for the Mi Lai massacre during the Vietnam war, a national survey was made of the reaction of the American public to the trial: 51 per cent said that they would follow orders if commanded to shoot all inhabitants of a Vietnamese village. Kelman and Lawrence (1972), who conducted the survey, concluded that many Americans regard Calley's actions at Mi Lai as, 'normal, even desirable, because (they think) he performed them in obedience to legitimate authority'.

As Hedy Brown (1985) observes, both Milgram's and Zimbardo's research shows how easily people can come to behave in 'uncharacteristic' ways when placed in new physical and social situations and given the chance to assume new roles, even temporarily. Both studies testify to 'the power of social institutional forces to make good men engage in evil deeds.' (Zimbardo, 1973.)

13

Pro- and Anti-Social Behaviour

Kidney donors and rabbits banging their feet on the ground have very little in common at first sight. However, on closer inspection, they do seem to share the element of doing something for the benefit of others: this is self-evident in the case of one person donating a kidney to another person, in the case of the rabbit, banging the feet is used as a warning to other rabbits of some threat or danger.

These are both examples of *altruism*, which is really the opposite of selfishness; however, is it possible for an apparently unselfish act to be motivated by basically selfish ends, whether in people or rabbits?

Doing things for others represents a basic social value and so, by definition, is *pro*-social; aggression represents a major form of *anti*-social behaviour because, as it is normally defined, it is harmful to, and may even destroy, the person at whom it is directed.

To arrive at a more complete understanding of both altruism and aggression we shall look at them from a number of perspectives, in particular, social psychology, which makes heavy use of laboratory experiments, and ethology, which studies behaviour (mainly that of animals) in its natural environment.

Biological and Psychological Altruism

An important distinction is that between biological and psychological altruism, which roughly apply to non-human species and human beings respectively. We could not normally attribute the rabbit which warns its fellow-rabbits of an approaching hunter with altruistic *motives* or *intentions* (we would be guilty of anthropomorphism if we did); in a sense this is simply part of its biologically-determined repertoire of behaviour to start banging its feet under certain environmental conditions.

Conversely, in the case of a human kidney donor, we would normally expect the decision to donate to be based on a number of considerations and values; there is certainly no necessity or inevitability about it, and as well as arousing strong feelings, the matter will raise many moral, religious and practical questions. We usually infer altruistic motives and intentions from altruistic acts.

326

If we accept this distinction, then clearly psychological altruism applies only to people and biological altruism mainly to animals, although we shall be asking if it can apply to people also.

Biological Altruism

Are rabbits as unselfish as they seem?

According to Brown (1986), the biological world abounds in examples of altruism, which he defines in terms of the prospects for survival and reproductive success of the altruistic organism relative to the 'beneficiaries' of the altruistic behaviour. By drumming its feet on the ground, the altruistic rabbit increases the chances of other rabbits escaping and, ultimately, producing offspring while at the same time reducing its own chances (by, for example, drawing attention to itself or wasting valuable seconds before it makes its getaway).

Other examples include alarm calls among most species of songbirds (which are all rather similar so that all species will respond when any one of them raises the alarm) and the screeching of monkeys, also an alarm call. Perhaps the ultimate in altruism is the case of bees, wasps and ants in which specialized castes of workers or soldiers are produced which are completely sterile; sterile worker bees, for example, forsake their ability to reproduce in favour of helping their mother, the queen, to do so (Trivers and Hare, 1976).

The Paradox of Altruism

Aren't animals naturally selfish?

From the point of view of Darwin's theory of natural selection, it is truly remarkable for members of a species to help each other in such a way and quite the opposite of what could be considered 'natural'. According to Darwin (*The Origin of Species*, 1859) individual animals survive if they are able to adapt to their environment by virtue of physical (and behavioural) characteristics they possess and which are produced by random genetic variation, or mutation. These better-adapted individuals will, on average, have more offspring and, since those offspring will tend to carry the genes for those adaptive characteristics and behaviours, those genes and characteristics become more and more commonplace in the population.

In this way animal populations become differentiated and when different strains become so different that they can no longer interbreed (because their genotypes are too dissimilar), a new species has evolved. This process of natural selection, therefore, 'operates single-mindedly and relentlessly in favour of traits that improve the chances of survival and the number of offspring of the *individual* animal acting' (Brown, 1986). But surely this is the complete reverse of what happens when an animal acts altruistically? Any animal which regularly acted in a way which benefited others by risking its own safety and survival would be drastically reducing its own chances of having any offspring at all—these individuals would not last long enough to reproduce successfully! Natural selection predicts that individuals will act to the benefit of themselves alone and *not* their group or species.

The 'paradox of altruism' refers to this apparent contradiction between Darwin's theory of natural selection and observed facts about altruistic behaviour in a number of species. Is it possible for an animal to behave altruistically *and* in accordance with the laws of natural selection at the same time? It seems so, because altruism turns out to be only *apparent*, that is, altruistic behaviour is only selfish behaviour in disguise and in order to understand this, we need to shift our attention away from the individual, self-contained, organism to the *gene* as the fundamental unit of evolution (Roediger et al, 1984). This is the approach of sociobiology, the selfish gene instead of the selfish rabbit.

Sociobiology

Sociobiology represents an extension of Darwin's evolutionary theory and was defined by Wilson (1975), one of its most prominent exponents, as 'the systematic study of the biological basis of all social behaviour'; it attempts to understand all types of social behaviour (including altruism, aggression, dominance and sexual behaviour) in evolutionary terms and this extends to human social behaviour.

Hinde (1982), a leading British ethologist, believes that Wilson's 1975 book called *Sociobiology* represents a landmark in biology, integrating population biology, ecology, ethology and related disciplines and helping to bring evolutionary theory and behavioural biology together. However, Hinde is also very critical of Wilson's claims that, eventually, sociobiology would engulf ethology and comparative psychology and that behaviour should be reduced to neurophysiology and sensory physiology. As Hinde points out, altruism, for example, can, by definition, only apply to a dyad or larger group and *not* to an individual (see Chapter 2). So how does sociobiology resolve the 'paradox of altruism'?

The most general explanation of apparent altruism is Hamilton's theory of *kin selection* (1964). If we think of an individual animal as a set of genes rather than as a separate, 'bounded' organism, then it should be regarded as *distributed across kin*, that is, it shares some proportion of its genes with relatives, according to how close the relationship is. It follows that it is possible for an individual to preserve its genes through its own self-sacrifice—if a mother dies in the course of saving her three offspring from a predator, she will have saved $1\frac{1}{2}$ times her own genes (since each offspring inherits one half of its mother's genes). So, in terms of genes, an act of apparent altruism can turn out to be extremely selfish—surrendering your own life as an individual may reap a net profit as far as the survival of your genes in your relatives is concerned. (See *The Selfish Gene* by Dawkins, 1976.)

This means that individuals are selected to act *not* to maximize their own fitness (measured in terms of their own survival and reproduction) but to maximize their *inclusive fitness* (measured in terms of their own survival and reproduction *and* that of relatives) (Hinde, 1982). He asks us to imagine a gene which, in some way, programmed an individual to give its life for others; one copy of the gene would disappear from the population when the altruist died but if the act saved the life of more than two offspring or siblings (each having 50 per cent of its genes in common with the altruist), then the altruistic gene would *still* increase in frequency.

Thus we seem to have resolved the paradox presented by examples of self-sacrifice; when a male lion dies defending his mate, or a honey bee dies when stinging an enemy, or a mother bird attracts a predator away from her off-spring by feigning a broken wing, we can invoke the principle of inclusive fitness to explain apparently altruistic behaviour which is, fundamentally, selfish.

However, we are left with another difficulty—what should we make of cases of altruism on the part of animals which are *not* related? Clearly, kin selection cannot accommodate such cases. Trivers (1971) has proposed the principle of 'delayed reciprocal altruism', by which animals will 'return favours' to other animals which have done them a good turn, or, a good turn is worth-while because it is likely to be reciprocated. For example, male baboons who do not have a female partner sometimes form a temporary alliance with another solitary male baboon; while the latter attacks a male who is 'courting' a female and so distracts the male's attention, the former mates with the female. Those males who often give this kind of help seem to be more likely to receive help in return, so that reciprocation occurs (Packer, 1977).

Similarly, young baboons direct their grooming behaviour towards indi-viduals who will later benefit them. Young females tend to groom dominant adult females who may be powerful allies in the troop in the future, while young males, who will later leave the troop, tend to groom the more subor-dinate females, with whom they are likely to be allowed to practise mating (Cheney, 1978, Crook, 1980).

According to Hinde (1982), other examples are best understood as indi-viduals achieving better results if they make a joint effort (almost a case of 'two heads are better than one'). For instance, it pays two pied wagtails to defend a winter feeding territory together, even though they are not related, because in this way they can achieve a higher feeding-rate (Davies and Houston, 1981).

Biological Altruism in Humans

In terms of kin selection, the situation is far more complex among humans than it is with animals. One reason for this, according to Brown (1986), is that the closeness of kinship is construed very differently from one society to another, so there is no simple correspondence between perceived and actual (genetic) kinship. If altruistic behaviour directly reflected actual kinship, rather than learned conceptions of kinship, it would be impossible for adoptive parents to give their adopted children the quality of care they do.

Taking this argument a step further, whole professions and occupations can be seen as aimed at helping other, unrelated, people (while at the same time providing a living for those who do the helping). As a species, much of our behaviour is altruistic and kin selection can only account for a small portion of our total behaviour-for-others; some principle such as delayed reciprocal inhibition is also needed. However, we are still trying to impose a biological explanation on human social behaviour and this may not be the most appropriate way of trying to understand it; as Roger Brown (1986) says, 'human altruism goes beyond the confines of Darwinism because human evolution is not only biological in nature but also cultural, and, indeed, in recent times primarily cultural'. This brings us to psychological altruism.

Psychological Altruism

Is it possible to be totally unselfish?

Strictly defined, altruism is an act performed for the sake of another person without any personal gain or self-interest. But is there such a thing as a completely unselfish act?

According to Brown (1986), when someone donates a kidney to a relative, they are likely to be rewarded both extrinsically (for example, praise and gratitude of the recipient) and intrinsically (the satisfaction of having saved a relative's life, for instance) and, to this extent, is not being a true—or pure—psychological altruist (although donating an organ *is* an act of biological altruism.)

However, Fellner and Marshall (1981) believe that what such donors do is quite extraordinary; about 88 per cent report having made the decision to donate, if asked, immediately upon being notified by the doctor that they might be required to do so and the decision is often made before being informed of the costs or risks. So what about kidney donors to unrelated strangers?

They are clearly biological altruists as is anyone who risks their life for another, but are they psychologically altruistic? Sadler et al (1971) believe they are not—is it possible to donate one of your bodily organs and not feel some sense of pride or satisfaction?

However, Brown (1986) believes that 'rewards' are not all on the same moral level; in general, extrinsic rewards (eg money) are considered less morally worthy than intrinsic ones (eg satisfaction at doing one's duty).

> We must conclude that cultural evolution, not biological, has produced moral principles that can powerfully reward actions that are in accord with them (Brown, 1986).

Bystander Intervention—Altruism or Apathy?

One of the major ways in which social psychologists have investigated altruism is by studying people's readiness to go to the aid of someone who is in danger or has suffered an accident of some kind. Two of the original researchers in this area were Latané and Darley (1968) whose inspiration was a real event involving a murder victim, Kitty Genovese:

> In 1964, in the Queen's district of New York City, Kitty Genovese was attacked and murdered. The murder took place at around 3.00 a.m. and the murderer left the scene three times before returning to finish off his victim. She crawled to her apartment door, repeatedly screaming that she was being murdered and pleading for help.
>
> Two weeks after the event, the *New York Times*, following up a police tip, carried the horrifying news that 38 neighbours had witnessed the event from their windows and none had responded, even to 'phone the police'.

So the concept of the 'unresponsive bystander' was born and soon after this event, which horrified the American nation, Latané and Darley began their 'scientific' investigation of the phenomenon. Before we look at the research in detail, one major conclusion should be mentioned: while the American media thought it remarkable that out of 38 witnesses not a single one did anything to help, Latané and Darley believed that it was precisely *because* there were so many that Kitty Genovese was not helped.

Latané and Nida (1981) reviewed the 56 experimental studies which had been carried out up to that time and concluded that the most consistent finding (which held true across a variety of situations) was that the presence of others inhibits helping. Why?

It seems that in the presence of others we are less likely to define a situation as an emergency—a situation requiring our intervention—and even if we do define it as an emergency, we may still decide that it is not our responsibility to take action and go to the aid of the victim (diffusion of responsibility). Quite apart from the inhibiting effect of the presence of others (contrast this with social facilitation discussed in Chapter 12) there are other factors which come into play in emergency situations, namely those to do with the relative rewards and costs of intervening; this is what Exchange Theory (eg Thibaut and Kelley, 1959) is concerned with and we shall discuss it in more detail below (see Chapter 10).

Defining the Situation

In other words when is an emergency not an emergency?

In one of the first of the bystander experiments (Latané and Darley, 1968), subjects were shown into a room in order to complete some questionnaires; in one condition they were alone, in another condition there were others present. After a while, steam (resembling smoke) began to pour through a vent in the wall. The test was to see how quickly subjects reacted.

They reacted most quickly when alone and the more people in the room, the slower they were to react; sometimes no one reacted until the steam was so thick that it was very difficult to see the questionnaires. Latané and Rodin (1969) obtained similar results when subjects heard the female experimenter, in an adjoining room, fall, cry out and moan; subjects were much faster to react when alone than when others were present. In post-experimental interviews, each subject reported feeling very hesitant about showing anxiety to the other subjects, so they looked to other subjects for signs of anxiety but since everyone was trying to appear calm, these signs were not found and each subject defined the situation as 'safe'.

In a variation of Latané and Rodin's experiment, 70 per cent of subjects on their own responded within 65 seconds; two friends together responded within a similar time; two strangers together were less likely to react at all, but more slowly if they did; and if a subject was paired with a confederate who had been instructed not to intervene at all, they showed the least and slowest reaction of all.

Diffusion of Responsibility

When does an emergency oblige me to intervene?

Darley and Latané (1968) recruited female subjects to discuss the personal problems of college life with other students—instead of face-to-face discussion, they communicated via an intercom system. One participant (a confederate) mentioned that she was epileptic and later in the discussion she had a 'mock' seizure and begged for help. Of the subjects who believed they were the only other participant, 85 per cent intervened; of those who believed there were two others (three altogether), 62 per cent intervened; and of those who believed there were five others (six altogether), only 31 per cent intervened. The most responsive group was also the fastest to respond. These findings were confirmed by Latané et al (1981).

So while the presence of others may make it less likely that we will define a situation as an emergency in the first place ('if the others look calm and aren't rushing around there can't be anything wrong'), when we do so define it, we may nevertheless decide that somebody else will probably do what is necessary, and the more bystanders that are present (or believed to be present), the lower the probability that any one of them will accept responsibility. Clearly, it is much more difficult to deny responsibility if you are (or think you are) the only witness!

Another aspect of diffusion of responsibility is that, everything else being equal, we may attribute others with greater expertise to cope with the emergency than ourselves; this may sometimes be a rationalization (in which we try to justify to ourselves our inaction) or it may be based on a known fact about a person. For example, Schwarz and Clausen (1970) found that when an additional onlooker was known to be a pre-medical student with experience of working in a hospital emergency ward, a medical emergency (such as a seizure) was especially likely to be left to him.

Piliavin et al (1981) pointed out what they believe is a confusion between *diffusion*, which occurs when responsibility is accepted by the subject but shared by all the witnesses, and *dissolution* which occurs when the behaviour of other witnesses cannot be observed and the subject 'rationalizes' that someone else must have already intervened. However, whichever label is applied, all the studies confirm the original finding that the presence of others inhibits an individual from intervening (Piliavin et al, 1981), and yet there are limits to diffusion of responsibility. Piliavin et al (1969) found that help was offered on crowded subways in New York and Philadelphia as frequently as on relatively empty ones; as Brown (1985), suggests, perhaps it is more difficult to refuse help in a face-to-face situation and in an enclosed space.

The Cost of Intervention—What's in it for me?

Many studies of bystander intervention have manipulated the characteristics of the person in need of help and have interpreted the findings in terms of Exchange Theory (Thibaut and Kelley, 1959), which applies the concepts of rewards, costs and profits to social interaction, in particular to bystander intervention and interpersonal relationships (see Chapter 10).

Rewards (benefits or positive outcomes) are anything which is desirable and the avoidance of anything undesirable (a negative reinforcement in operant conditioning terms) while costs (or negative outcomes) are anything which is undesirable and the deprivation or foregoing of rewards. Profit (or net benefit or outcome) is calculated according to the formula $P = R - C$.

According to Exchange Theory, the tendency to engage in a social action will increase as the promise of its profitability increases (relative to alternative actions). A witness to an emergency (whether it is an accident or a crime) finds they are in a situation where there is much to lose and little to gain; costs can include being assaulted, being late for work and having to appear in court to give evidence, while the rewards may amount to little more than a possible 'thank you'. According to Brown (1986), this is a profitless situation from which most of us would want to escape; he argues that a 'Good Samaritan Law' (which does not exist in Britain or the USA but which does in Germany, France, Italy and Russia) must, to be effective, change the reward–cost matrix for witnesses either by increasing the rewards (eg financially) or by increasing the costs of *not* helping (eg a fine or prison sentence).

Certain kinds of low-cost altruism seem to be fairly common, such as giving a stranger directions or telling them the time. Latané and Darley (1970) had psychology students approach a total of 1500 passers-by in New York to ask them such routine, low-cost, favours; depending on the nature of the favour, between 34 and 85 per cent of New Yorkers proved to be 'low-cost altruists'. However, most people refused to tell the student their name.

Going to a person's aid (having defined the situation as an emergency and accepted the responsibility) seems to depend to a significant degree on the characteristics of the person needing help, since how the 'victim' is perceived contributes greatly to the net profit (or loss) expected from the intervention.

In a study by Piliavin et al (1969), student experimenters pretended to collapse in subway train compartments—they fell to the floor and waited to see if they were helped. Sometimes they would be carrying a cane, sometimes they would wear a jacket which smelled very strongly of alcohol and would be carrying a bottle in a brown paperbag. As predicted by Exchange Theory, help was offered much *less* often in the 'drunk' condition than the 'lame' condition (20 per cent compared with 90 per cent within 70 seconds). In a second study, the person who 'collapsed' bit off a capsule of blood-like dye and this trickled down his chin; the helping rate dropped from 90 per cent to 60 per cent. People were much more likely to get someone else to help, especially someone they thought would be more competent in an emergency (Piliavin and Piliavin, 1972).

Similarly, Piliavin et al (1975) found that when the victim had an ugly facial birthmark, the rate of helping dropped to 61 per cent, and in a different series of experiments, Graf and Riddell (1972) reported that a stranded motorist who is dressed smartly and is well groomed is far more likely to receive help from passing motorists than one who is casually dressed and has long hair.

In general, it seems that the greater the victim's distress, injury or disfigurement, or the more disapproving we are of them (especially if we blame their plight on their undesirable behaviour), the more likely we are to perceive them as being different from ourselves, which, in turn, makes it *less* likely that we will offer them help. The psychological costs of helping someone perceived as being different from ourselves seem to be greater than the same help offered to someone perceived as being similar. On this basis, we would expect help to be offered less often to someone of a different racial group from the bystander; however, the evidence is not as clear-cut as this (Piliavin et al, 1981). They argue that whatever a person's racial attitudes, they may want to project an unprejudiced self-image or may genuinely believe that they are not prejudiced (even if tests suggest otherwise), so that to not offer help because of the victim's race might incur greater psychological costs than to do so.

In Exchange Theory terms, we can predict the likelihood of someone

Table 13.1   The costs of helping and not helping in an emergency and the likelihood of help being offered (Based on Piliavin et al, 1975)

The costs of helping are *low* (eg you are not likely to be injured yourself, the victim is only shocked). The costs of *not* helping are *high* (eg you would feel guilty, others would blame you). *Likelihood of intervention: very high (and direct)*
The costs of helping are *high* (eg you do not like the sight of blood, you are unsure what to do). The costs of *not* helping are *high* (eg it is an emergency, the victim could die). *Likelihood of intervention: fairly high* (but indirect, eg 'phoning for ambulance or police or asking some other bystander to assist).
The costs of helping are *high* (eg 'This drunk could turn violent or over-friendly'). The costs of *not* helping are *low* (eg 'Who would blame me for not helping?'). *Likelihood of intervention: very low* (a common response is to turn the other way or change seats or even compartments).
The costs of helping are *low* (eg 'It wouldn't hurt me to see this blind man across the street'). The costs of *not* helping are *low* (eg 'He seems capable of looking after himself and there are plenty of other people crossing anyway'). *Likelihood of intervention: fairly high* (although people will vary considerably).

giving help by comparing the costs of helping and not helping and this has been done by Piliavin et al (1975), see Table 13.1. We should be aware that what is high cost for one person may be low cost for another (and vice-versa) and this may differ, for the same person, from one situation to another (and even from one occasion to another, depending on mood, for example).

Aggression

We all seem to recognize aggression when we witness it but defining it often proves much more difficult. When used as a noun, aggression usually conveys some behaviour which is intended to harm another (or at least which has this effect); yet even this is too broad a definition, since self-defence and unprovoked attack may both involve similar 'amounts' and types of aggression but only the latter would normally be considered 'anti-social' (and the law also recognizes this distinction).

When used as an adjective, aggression sometimes conveys an action carried out with energy and persistence (Lloyd et al, 1984), something which may even be regarded as socially desirable.

It is almost exclusively in the former sense that psychologists and ethologists have studied aggression and it is also largely aggressive *behaviour* which is the object of study, partly because it is easier to observe and measure than, say, the subjective emotion of aggression.

A number of other important distinctions have been made; eg *hostile* aggression is aimed solely at hurting another ('aggression for the sake of aggression', and so would exclude self-defence) while *instrumental* aggression is a means to an end (and so would include self-defence eg Buss, 1961, Feshbach, 1964).

Humanistic psychologists (eg Maslow, 1968) have distinguished between: (i) *natural* or positive aggression, which is aimed largely at self-defence or combating prejudice and other social injustice; and (ii) *pathological* aggression or violence, which results when our inner nature has become twisted or frustrated.

The distinction between aggression and violence is commonly made. Brown (1985), for example, maintains that, whereas aggression does not necessarily involve physical injury, violence involves the use of great force or physical intensity. Similarly, Moyer (1976) argues that aggression may be no more than verbal or symbolic but violence denotes, 'a form of human aggression that involves inflicting physical damage on persons or property'.

If we combined Moyer's definition with Ruch's (1984) definition ('behaviour intended to harm another person who does not wish to be harmed') we should have a pretty good idea of what psychologists have in mind when they write about aggression, although they do not always make it clear how they conceptualize the concept (Brown, 1985).

The Nature and Nurture of Aggression

Although aggression has been studied in the context of gender differences (see Chapter 22), here it will be discussed as another example of the nature–nurture issue; the question being asked is whether aggression, as a characteristic of human beings, is biologically determined or the product of learning and environmental influences, and we shall be drawing on a number of theoretical approaches, namely the Ethological, the Neurophysiological, the Psychoanalytic and Learning Theory.

a) The Ethological Approach

Schuster (1978) defined ethology as, 'a branch of behavioural biology concerned with the evolution and function of species-specific behaviour'.

According to Hinde (1982), when ethologists consider any class of behaviour, they are concerned with four issues:

i) What immediately causes it. (This would include specific stimuli called *releasers* which trigger instinctive patterns of behaviour, some of these being called *Fixed Action Patterns* or FAPs).

ii) How such behaviour has developed over the animal's life-cycle (*ontogeny*).

iii) What the useful consequences of such behaviour are (its *function*).

iv) How the behaviour has evolved within the species (*phylogeny*).

As far as aggression is concerned, it is instinctive in all species and is clearly important in the evolutionary development of the species, allowing individuals to adapt to their environment, survive in it and, hence, successfully reproduce. When space or food are scarce, many species limit their reproduction and survive by marking off living space which they defend against 'trespassers'; this is known as *territoriality* (Smith et al, 1982). Aggressiveness is clearly important in competing successfully for limited resources, in defending territory and for basic survival. Are there any human parallels?

According to Ardrey (1966), in *The Territorial Imperative*, people strive to acquire land and possessions, form strong attachments to them and are willing to defend (sometimes violently) what they believe is rightfully theirs. However, to infer from these superficial similarities that a fundamentally similar territorial instinct is at work is greatly to over-simplify human behaviour, which is vastly more complex than any comparable animal behaviour.

Probably the most famous and most comprehensive ethological account of human aggression is that of Konrad Lorenz in *On Aggression* (1966). He believes that it is legitimate to make direct comparisons between different species, although his theory of human aggression is based on the study of non-primates and mainly non-mammals, in particular, fish and insects. He defines aggression as, 'the fighting instinct in beast and man which is directed *against* members of the same species'; in animals and humans it is basically constructive, but in humans it has become distorted. In what ways?

Probably the major differences between animal and human aggression is to do with *ritualization*, which refers to a way of discharging aggression in a fixed, stereotyped, pattern whereby fights between members of the same species result in relatively little physical harm to either victor or vanquished but at the same time allowing a victor to emerge. For instance, the fighting that takes place between stags is highly ritualized and the triumphant one is the male who 'makes his point' rather than the one who kills or incapacitates his opponent. In the same way, wolves will end their fight with the loser exposing its jugular vein—but its exposure is sufficient and no blood is spilled. (This is rather like two sword-fighters, one of whom loses their sword and faces the victor, inviting them to 'run me through'; but, by this stage, the fight has already been won and lost.)

Sometimes, antagonists may approach each other in a threatening manner but not actually engage in combat—one will show *appeasement rituals* (or gestures) which prevent the other from actual conflict. For example, in one species of jackdaws, individuals live in close proximity and to prevent mutually destructive conflict, a very effective appeasement gesture has developed: the nape section at the bottom of the head is clearly marked off from the rest of the body by its plumage and colouring and when one bird 'offers' its nape to an aggressor, the latter will never attack, even if on the verge of doing so. Similarly, in many species, a male never 'seriously' attacks a female because the female displays the appropriate appeasement rituals when the male begins to show aggressive 'intent'.

So through these various kinds of ritual, animals avoid destroying each other. But in human beings, according to Lorenz, although aggression remains basically adaptive, it is no longer *under the control* of rituals; this does *not* mean that human appeasement responses are not effective (eg smiling, cowering, cringing, or begging for mercy) and, indeed, Lorenz and Eibl-Eibesfeldt believe that they are normally *very* effective. So what is it about human beings that makes them appear so aggressive?

According to Lorenz, it is their *technology*. However naturally aggressive human beings are as a species compared with other species, their superior brains have enabled them to construct weapons which remove combat from the eye-to-eye situation and so the effectiveness of appeasement rituals is reduced. Indeed, the deadliest weapons (as measured by the number of victims who can be killed or injured at one time) are precisely those which can be used at the greatest distance from the intended victims (eg bombs and intercontinental nuclear missiles). According to Lea (1984), 'We have developed a technology which enables our intentions to override our instincts'.

Criticisms of Lorenz

1. In keeping with his belief that humans are naturally highly aggressive, Lorenz maintains that their 'natural condition' is that of 'warrior'. However, he seems to be in a minority of one in this respect; it is generally agreed that early man was not a warrior but a 'hunter-gatherer' (such as the present-day Eskimos, Pygmies of the Ituri forest, Aborigines, Kalahari Bushmen, the Punan of Borneo and so on), who live in small clans which hardly ever come into contact with other groups of people (Siann, 1985).

2. If early man was, indeed, a warrior, we would expect his close evolutionary relatives to be highly aggressive also; however, the evidence is certainly mixed here. According to Helmuth (1973), behaviour within and between groups of primates is predominantly peaceful, while Horn (1978) argues that it is not obvious that man's ancestors were any less deadly than other species—even without the most primitive weapons, other primates, including chimps, can and do kill each other.

Goodall (1978) describes warfare between two colonies of chimps which ended in the killing of every male in one of the groups and Lea (1984) points out that infanticide is one of the commoner kinds of unrestrained aggression among animals. He cites Hardy's (1977) study of Hanuman langurs, an Indian monkey species, in which incoming males commonly kill infants despite the attempts of females to resist this male aggression.

Infanticide is not confined to primates: male lions that succeed in taking over a 'pride' of females (so displacing other adult males) will often attack and kill any cubs that are present (which then makes the females more available for mating) (Schaller, 1972, Bertram, 1978). So Lorenz seems to have greatly overstated the case when he claimed that animal aggression always stops before an animal is killed. Lea (1984) believes that, although there is some truth in Lorenz's claim, it is basically a myth.

According to Leakey and Lewin (1977a), cultural influences are far more important determinants of human aggression than biological factors; whatever potential for aggression we may have inherited as a species, it is culturally-overridden and re-packaged into forms which fit current circumstances. In most cases, cultural forces teach or support non-aggression but when pro-social aggression is necessary (including disciplining children and wrong-doers, assertiveness, self-defence and even warfare), cultural processes teach and sustain it.

Siann (1985) argues that primates and man are characterized by their responsiveness and adaptiveness to the world around them (eg food, weather, terrain); their behaviour is, typically, not stereotyped and unpredictable and man is unique in being able to pass on the experience of each generation to future generations through language and customs.

3. Lorenz's view of aggression, in humans and animals, as being spontaneous rather than reactive, has been criticized. Like the other three instincts or drives (namely, hunger, sexuality and flight, which collectively he calls the 'big four'), aggressive behaviour occurs *not* in response to environmental stimuli but spontaneously when instinctive aggressive energy builds up and demands discharge. The evidence for this energy-model is very sparse indeed; according to Siann (1985) it amounts to the male cichlid fish which attacks its female mate and an anecdote about Lorenz's maiden aunt. This view of aggression as being inevitable because aggressive energy builds-up, unrelated to external events, has come under fire from many contemporary biologists and ethologists, who believe that aggression in animals is reactive and modifiable by a variety of internal and external conditions (eg Hinde, 1974). (Lorenz's 'hydraulic' model of instinct is discussed further in the next chapter.)

If Lorenz is correct, it should be possible to show specific changes in certain physiological measures before and after aggression (Siann, 1985); but it has proved impossible to do so (Swanson, 1976).

4. Although it is generally agreed that fighting between animals of the same species is highly ritualized (Wilson, 1975), some critics of Lorenz (eg Shuster, 1978) have pointed out that he did not take account of how the *goals* of behaviour influence the degree of ritual; for example, antelopes are much more likely to use rituals when fighting over territory than when competing for a sexual partner.

5. Learning plays no part in Lorenz's theory of aggression which, at least when applied to primates and human beings, makes it inadequate. Cultures differ in the degree and kind of aggression which are permissible and socializing influences can override any innate differences which may exist between males and females. (See Mead's study of three New Guinea tribes—Chapter 22.)

b) The Neurophysiological Approach

Much of the evidence for the role of the brain in aggression is based on animal experiments and so any generalization to human beings must be cautiously made.

According to Green (1980), the study of emotion in animals has been concerned almost exclusively with the study of aggression and much of the experimental study of aggression has concentrated on the *limbic system*. The limbic system (see Chapter 15) comprises a number of structures, including the thalamus, hypothalamus, hippocampus, amygdala, septum, cingulate gyrus, olfactory bulbs and mammillary bodies. These are situated in the upper brain-stem and inner surfaces of the cerebral hemispheres, and the limbic system as a whole plays a major role in regulating emotional and sexual behaviour; in vertebrates it is also involved in fight and flight ('emergency') responses.

Early twentieth-century studies showed that if parts of the cortex of cats and dogs are destroyed, 'sham rage' is produced (so named, by Masserman, because the cat could be stroked and even purr while simultaneously showing all the signs of rage); this suggests that the cortex normally acts as an inhibitor of sub-cortical structures (including the limbic system).

Bard (1928) found in cats that this sham-rage produced by removal of the cortex largely disappeared if the hypothalamus is also removed (it in fact becomes fragmented with unsheathed claws but without an arched back). Conversely, the whole of the cerebral cortex could be removed without destroying the rage response and stimulation of the hypothalamus would produce attack behaviour.

So it appears that the hypothalamus is essential for the full expression of aggression (and, indeed, of all emotional behaviour).

Later research has shown that stimulation or destruction of the amygdala can produce either placidity or rage, depending on the precise location; according to Lloyd et al (1984), this suggests that the amygdala plays a controlling or moderating role and that the hypothalamus plays an integrative role. Destruction of the septum produces aggressiveness and hyper-emotionality (lack of emotional control). Papez (1937) claimed that the limbic system includes a set of interconnected pathways and centres (since known as the Papez Circuit) which play a vital role in aggressive behaviour; his research included post-mortems of the brains of people (who had suffered from emotional disorders) as well as rabid dogs.

A great deal of research has been concerned with the effects of the part played by the amygdala. Rosvold et al (1954) removed the amygdala from the dominant monkey in a social group and found, on its return to the colony, that it quickly lost its place in the hierarchy and Downer (1962) also found that the removal of the amygdala had the effect of making a monkey more docile.

Many studies have confirmed that amygdala damage produces placidity (it has a 'taming effect') which is part of the Kluver-Bucy (1937) syndrome which also includes hypersexuality and hyperorality (putting objects in the mouth). This represents the obverse of septal damage, although there are important species differences; for example, it is very difficult to produce septal aggression in monkeys. By stimulating the septum of a bull (using radio-control), Delgado (1969) stopped it in mid-charge.

Moyer (1968, 1971) has identified a number of different kinds of aggression (based on ethological studies), including instrumental, inter-male, predatory, fear-provoked, territorial, irritable, maternal and hierarchical and each may have its own precise control centre in the limbic system. Some support comes from a study by Flynn et al (1970) of cats' response to rats; they found that a majority of cats do not spontaneously attack rats but will do so if appropriate areas of the hypothalamus or other specific parts of the limbic system are stimulated and different kinds of attack are related to specific areas of the hypothalamus. Moyer (1976) has reported similar findings.

Despite studies like those of Moyer and Flynn et al, research has failed to show conclusively that 'aggression centres' exist, as Siann (1985) says, and even in rats and cats the elicitation of aggressive behaviour usually depends on aspects of the experimental situation (such as whether or not other animals or objects are present, the strength of the electrical stimulation) and the state of the experimental animal itself, such as whether it is hungry or not (eg Desisto, 1970 and Johnson, 1972).

According to Shah and Roth (1974), there is no single area in the limbic system of primates which functions autonomously or which directs all the other areas. It is also known that the limbic system of primates is massively interconnected with the brain's thinking and reasoning centres which are located in the cortex (Siann, 1985); those areas involved in aggression are closely related to those which process information from the environment.

Delgado (1967, 1971) implanted electrodes in the brains of several members of a monkey colony and the 'aggression area' of selected monkeys was stimulated (through radio transmission). A monkey's position in the hierarchy had a strong influence on how it behaved when its brain was stimulated—when a dominant male was stimulated, he would attack subordinate males but not females while when a subordinate male was stimulated, he would show cowering and submissive behaviour in the presence of a dominant male *but* would attack a submissive partner.

Clearly, these monkeys possess brain mechanisms which allow them to behave aggressively, but the triggering of these mechanisms depends upon other areas of the brain which receive and process information from the environment (Smith et al, 1982). What about humans?

Heath (1962) found that stimulating the limbic system of certain patients can produce fear and anger and in a study of 46 epileptic patients, Jasper and Rasmusson (1958) found that stimulating their amygdala produced fear in just two, while the rest reported confusion or did not respond at all.

Only in a few cases has stimulation of the amygdala actually produced aggressive outbursts or violent attacks of rage and overall the evidence from these kinds of studies is very inconclusive.

Shah and Roth (1974) have cited a number of reports of abnormalities of the limbic system (eg atrophy, tumours and lesions) being associated with abnormal behaviour (including extremely irritable and even explosive behaviour) and there is some evidence that limbic tumours are associated with abnormally aggressive behaviour (Mark, 1978).

According to Siann (1985), the evidence linking temporal lobe epilepsy and violent behaviour is weak and controversial, as is all the evidence regarding brain abnormalities and aggression or violence. Even if there were a strong and consistent relationship found, this would not show that particular abnormalities actually *cause* violent behaviour or that specific brain areas are responsible for the control of aggression; other physical, psychological, social and environmental factors may be involved.

Siann (1985) also reviews studies of biochemical and genetic influences. She concludes that no particular chemical messenger, neural transmitter, hormone or other substance (such as alcohol or drugs) has been shown to have an 'invariant specific effect on the predisposition to aggressive emotion or violent behaviour'; the evidence regarding the role of genetic reactors is equally weak. (In Chapters 28 and 29 we shall be looking at the effects of psychosurgery as treatment for mental illness, including extreme violence, as well as at the causes of psychopathy.)

c) The Psychoanalytic Approach

Freud's theory will be discussed in detail in Chapter 26 where we shall see that his personality theory is normally regarded as an instinct theory.

It was not until late in his life that Freud recognized aggression as an instinct distinct from sexuality (libido) and it was the horrific carnage of World War I (1914–18) which provided the impetus for the re-working of his theory of aggression. In *Beyond the Pleasure Principle* (1922) and *The Ego and the Id* (1923) he distinguished between the Life Instincts (or *Eros*), including sexuality, and the Death Instinct (*Thanatos*).

Thanatos represents an inborn destructiveness and aggression, directed primarily against the self. The aim (as with all instincts in Freud's view) is to reduce tension or excitation to a minimum and, ultimately, to its total elimination; this was the idyllic state we enjoyed in the womb, where our needs were met as they arose and, for a while, at our mother's breast, but after this, the only way of achieving such a Nirvana is through death.

However, self-directed aggression conflicts with the Life Instincts (particularly the self-preservative component), so we either eroticise it by combining it with libido (producing sadism, masochism and sado-masochism) or we direct it towards others, or we take some of this outwardly-directed aggression back into our own personality in the form of the superego (the moral part of personality—see Chapter 21).

Freud believed that we must destroy some other thing or person if we are not to destroy ourselves, so strong is the impulse to self-destruction; paradoxically, conflict with the Life Instinct results in our aggression being displaced onto others. More positively, aggression can be sublimated into sport, physical occupations, and domination and mastery of nature and the world in general.

Like Freud, Lorenz also argued that we need to acknowledge our aggressiveness and to control it through sport (eg the Olympics), expeditions, explorations and so on, especially if international co-operation is involved (activities which Lorenz called 'displacement' activities). Another similarity between them is the view of aggression as spontaneous and not reactive, that is, aggressive energy builds up until eventually it has to be discharged in some way.

Some support for Freud (and Lorenz) is provided by studies of people who commit brutal crimes. Megargee (1966), for example, reported that brutally aggressive crimes are often committed by *overcontrolled* individuals; they repress their anger and over a period of time the pressure to be aggressive builds up. Often it is an objectively trivial incident which provokes the destructive outburst, with the aggressors returning to their previously passive state and once more seeming incapable of violence.

Megargee found that male juveniles who had been convicted of extremely brutal crimes (eg the murder of their parents or the particularly savage murder of strangers) seemed to be overcontrolled to a far greater extent than boys convicted of moderately aggressive crimes. The former usually had no record of antisocial aggression and were rated as being more friendly and co-operative by prison counsellors. A test has been designed which is meant to identify such overcontrolled individuals before they explode into violence (Megargee et al, 1967, Lane and Kling, 1979).

Ultimately, of course, Thanatos always wins its struggle with Eros and sometimes it enjoys a premature victory in the form of suicide.

Unlike his ideas on sexuality, Freud's ideas on aggression made little impact either on the public imagination or on other psychologists (including other psychoanalysts) until the publication of *Frustration and Aggression* by Dollard et al (1939), *Human Aggression* by Storr (1968) and *The Anatomy of Human Destructiveness* by Fromm (1977).

Storr, a psychoanalyst, dedicated his book to Lorenz. He identified four forms of psychopathology attributable to the inadequate resolution of the aggressive drive, namely depression, schizoid behaviour, paranoia and psychopathy (see Chapter 28).

Fromm, also a psychoanalyst, sees 'aggression' as covering emotions and behaviour motivated to enable the 'aggressor' to preserve or enhance their own position. Human beings, like most other animals, have a 'built-in' potential for defensive aggression which is fundamentally harmless; pathological aggression (eg cruelty and destructiveness) are not due to this inbuilt potential but to aggression-producing conditions in the environment. These pathological aspects of aggression can be woven into the individual's character structure by early emotional experiences, as evidenced by intensive explorations of historical figures such as Stalin, Himmler and Hitler.

d) The Learning Theory Approach

Intended partly to 'translate' some of Freud's psychoanalytic concepts into learning theory terms, Dollard, Doob, Miller, Mowrer and Sears published *Frustration and Aggression* (1939) in which they proposed their *Frustration–Aggression Hypothesis*. According to this, frustration *always* causes aggression and aggression is *always* a consequence of frustration; while agreeing with Freud that aggression is an innate response, Dollard et al argued that it would only be triggered by frustrating situations and events.

Some support for this view comes from the displacement of aggression, where a substitute object is found for the expression of aggressive feelings because they cannot be vented openly and directly towards their real target (see Chapter 26). An example of this displacement of aggression is the scapegoating found in prejudice (see Chapter 11) and a study by Barker et al (1941) found that children who were deliberately frustrated by being denied access to attractive toys behaved aggressively towards toys with which they were allowed to play.

However, it soon became apparent that the frustration–aggression hypothesis, in its original form, was an overstatement. Miller (1941) revised it by claiming that frustration is an *instigator* of aggression but situational factors (eg learned inhibition, fear of retaliation) may prevent actual aggressive behaviour from occurring; in other words, although frustration may make aggression more likely, it is far from being a sufficient cause of aggression.

Frustration can produce a variety of responses (of which aggression is but one), including regression (see Chapter 26), depression and lethargy

(Seligman, 1975—see Chapter 17). Frustration may also produce different responses in different people in different situations; Kulik and Brown (1979), for example, found that frustration was more likely to produce aggression if subjects believed that the person responsible for frustrating them did so deliberately, and without good reason, showing the importance of cognitive factors as cues for aggressive behaviour.

Bandura (1973) has argued that frustration might be a source of *arousal*, but frustration-induced arousal (like other types of arousal) could have a variety of outcomes of which aggression is only one; whether it actually occurs is more the result of learned patterns of behaviour triggered by environmental cues.

A similar line of argument is that of Berkowitz, who has proposed a number of modifications to the original frustration-aggression hypothesis (1962, 1969, 1978, 1979, 1980). His major argument is that frustration produces *anger* rather than aggression; what is important about frustration is that it is psychologically painful and anything which is psychologically (or physically) painful can lead to aggression.

For anger or psychological pain to be converted into actual aggression, certain *cues* are needed; these are environmental stimuli associated either with aggressive behaviour or with the frustrating object or person.

Green and Berkowitz (1967) had a confederate insult and berate subjects for failing to complete a jigsaw. They then watched a film in which Kirk Douglas was brutally beaten. After the film, subjects were given the chance to electrically shock the confederate, by which time they had learnt that his name was either Bob or Kirk—they used higher intensity shocks if his name was Kirk, the name acting as a cue to aggressive behaviour.

Berkowitz and Le Page (1967), in a similar experiment to the one just described, found that subjects delivered more shocks to the confederate if a rifle and revolver were nearby than when neutral objects such as badminton rackets were present. (This is known as the 'Weapons Effect'.) Leyens and Parke (1975) found that even photos of guns could intensify retaliatory attacks.

Berkowitz (1978) also believes that other situational cues which remind the subject of previous painful experiences or prior reinforcements for aggression can contribute to aggressive behaviour. What about physical pain?

Pain and aggression seem to be linked for many animal species as well as humans (Berkowitz, 1979, Moyer, 1976, Ulrich, 1966). If two animals are cooped up in a small cage and given electric shocks, or hit, they often begin fighting. Since it occurs with great regularity, emerges without training and persists even without reward, some believe that aggression is an unlearned response to pain, a reflexive reaction (Ulrich and Azrin, 1962).

Berkowitz et al (1979) had subjects sit with one hand in a tank of water, either a cold 42° F or a comfortable 63° F and at the same time they could deliver monetary rewards or punishments (blasts of noise) to a partner in the next room. The 'cold water' subjects delivered the most 'hurt' to their partners. Rotton et al (1978) had found similar results using foul smells instead of cold water. However, not everyone agrees with these conclusions. Baron (1977), for example, argues that in the experimental situation, frustration is a relatively weak instigator of aggression and its effect depends on a variety of other variables. One of these is the gender of the subject

(Buss, 1963) and another is the knowledge or belief that aggression will be useful in 'ridding oneself of frustration' (ie unless the aggressive behaviour is instrumental in achieving other goals) (Buss, 1966). Gentry (1970) found that male subjects frustrated by the experimenter (who repeatedly interfered with their attempts to complete an IQ test) later delivered *lower* shocks to the experimenter than subjects who were not so frustrated.

One final criticism of the frustration–aggression hypothesis is that many cases of aggression occur in situations where frustration is *not* present. Baron and Lawton (1972) found that subjects working in a hot, stuffy room showed more aggression than controls working in more pleasant surroundings—but only when both groups had seen an aggressive model. Even pleasant arousal (eg physical exercise or watching erotic films) can increase aggression towards people who have previously been sources of frustration.

Social Learning Theory: The Influence of Observing Aggression

In Chapter 21 we shall look in detail at the work of Bandura and other Social Learning Theorists who believe that observational learning (or modelling) is a fundamental form of social learning over and above conditioning (see Chapter 3). A number of different kinds of evidence point towards the importance of models, including laboratory experiments (see Chapter 21) and field (real-life) correlational studies. Bandura (1973) and Baron (1977) both report that aggressive and delinquent children tend to have parents who frequently model aggressive behaviour and Strauss et al (1980) confirm the widely-held belief that parents who abuse their children have often been the victims of parental abuse themselves.

Perhaps the most important feature of social learning theory is how it has alerted us to the power of television as a source of modelling, especially for children, including, of course, the modelling of aggression and violence. Apart from the learning and imitation of the model's behaviour, two mechanisms which may be involved in the influence of televised aggression on behaviour are: (i) the *reduction of inhibitions* against behaving aggressively by coming to believe that aggression is a typical or permissible way of solving problems or attaining goals; and (ii) *desensitization*, whereby the more aggression and violence are witnessed, the less disturbing they become. What is the evidence that television violence and violent behaviour are related?

Hundreds of studies have been conducted in this area and have been reviewed both in academic reviews (eg Siann, 1985) and in reports resulting from government-sponsored research (eg the 1972 Surgeon-General's Report in the USA and Home Office reports in the UK, such as the 1977 report on film censorship and violence). The American National Institute of Mental Health published, in 1982, its findings, based on a ten-year research programme in which 2,500 studies were reviewed. The main conclusion was that watching violence on television causes children and adolescents to behave more aggressively.

Since 1967, the percentage of programmes shown on American television containing violent episodes has remained about the same but the number of violent episodes per show has steadily increased. Despite a 1979 agreement by television networks to a code limiting the amount of violence in cartoons, Cramer and Mechem (1982) found that there had been no decrease; indeed, if anything, the new cartoons are even more violent. Saturday morning children's television comprises mainly one violent cartoon after another in USA and these show an estimated 18 violent acts per hour; the percentage of children's television in the UK which is made up of American cartoons has been steadily increasing in recent years.

In 1965/6, the average American household watched $5\frac{1}{2}$ hours of television per day and by 1980/1 this figure had increased to over $6\frac{1}{2}$ (Burger, 1982).

The studies which have been reviewed are of three major kinds; (i) laboratory experiments (ii) field studies; and (iii) experimental field studies. The limitations of the first two methods apply here as much as they do to other aspects of behaviour (see Chapter 2) but the three methods combined do seem to offer quite persuasive evidence. In one laboratory study (Liebert and Baron, 1972), children were randomly assigned to one of two groups: they either watched a violent programme ('The Untouchables') or an equally engaging and arousing but non-violent sporting event. When they were subsequently allowed to play, the 'Untouchables' group was rated as playing more aggressively. But how permanent are such effects likely to be?

Hundreds of field (correlational) studies suggest that children who watch more television at home behave more aggressively. Lefkowitz et al (1972) studied several hundred subjects over 10 years and found that boys who watched more television violence at age 9 were rated as being more aggressive by peers and teachers at age 19.

Similarly, Eron et al (1972) and Huesmann (1983) studied a group of 8-year-olds and followed them up until they were 18. They found that aggressive behaviour at 18 (based on peer ratings) could be predicted from knowledge of viewing habits at age 8.

It is possible that boys who watch more violent television differ in other important respects from those who watch less (for instance, it may be something to do with their personality and/or their family environment which accounts for their attraction to televised violence in the first place) in which case we cannot be sure that it is the observation of violence which causes their greater behavioural aggression.

One study which meets some of these criticisms is a field experiment by Parke et al (1977), whose subjects were Belgian and American male juvenile delinquents living in small-group cottages in low-security institutions. Their normal rate of aggressive behaviour (using a number of categories) was assessed and then the boys in one cottage were exposed to five commercial films involving violence over a period of one week, while boys in another cottage saw five non-violent films during the same period; the former showed significant increases in aggressive behaviour for most of the categories used but the latter showed no such increases.

Television Violence and Catharsis

One argument in defence (if not in favour) of watching television violence is that witnessing others being aggressive will help the viewer to 'get it out of their system' (strictly, this is *vicarious catharsis*), thus making the viewer *less* likely to behave aggressively. The argument is based partly on Freud's and Lorenz's theory of aggression but the evidence appears to contradict it (Tavris, 1983).

The basic research paradigm involves angering one group of subjects and not angering a control group (usually by a confederate insulting the subject), after which half of the subjects in each group is shown either a violent programme or a non-violent programme. Finally, all subjects are ostensibly given the chance to deliver electric shocks to the confederate who insulted them.

The results of several such experiments show that: (a) regardless of the level of anger aroused, subjects who witness aggression deliver *more* shocks than those who witness non-violent programmes; (b) anger–aroused subjects generally respond *more* punitively than non-aroused subjects; and (c) anger-aroused subjects who witness violence respond *most* punitively of all. This last finding in particular contradicts the vicarious catharsis hypothesis and instead supports a social learning theory explanation.

Television and Pro-Social Behaviour

If social learning theorists are correct in what they say about the harmful effects of watching television, it follows that watching television can also be beneficial by promoting pro-social behaviour. It seems only fair that we 'balance the books' and end this section by briefly mentioning some research which shows the positive side of television's influence.

O'Connor (1969) found that 'loners' in nursery schools, that is, children who tended to isolate themselves, who watched a specially prepared film portraying nursery children interacting with reinforcing consequences, became much less isolated than loners who did not watch the film; the improvements persisted.

Friedrich and Stein (1973) found that pro-social programmes (as opposed to 'Superman' or 'Batman' or a neutral programme) helped four-year-olds with self-control (comprising obedience to rules, tolerance of delay and persistence at tasks).

Aggression and De-individuation

We saw in Chapter 12 that being in the presence of others may enhance an individual's performance on a task (social facilitation) and this is usually regarded as a positive influence. But is it possible that being in the company of other people will have a detrimental influence on a person's behaviour, including the tendency to behave more aggressively?

The concept of *de-individuation* has been used to try to explain why it is that people in groups may behave in an uncharacteristically aggressive way (and in other anti-social ways) relative to their individual behaviour. If people believe that they will be identified, and consequently punished, they will inhibit their aggressive impulses (Donnerstein and Donnerstein, 1975, Rogers, 1980, Wilson and Rogers, 1975) but Gergen and Gergen (1981) suggest that in urban settings identification may be difficult and this may reduce people's fear of punishment, with the effect that they are more 'free' to behave in anti-social ways. When an individual's identity is lost in the mass of people and when the markers of personality are reduced, the individual is said to be de-individuated (Gergen and Gergen, 1981).

One of the earliest studies of crowd behaviour was that of Le Bon (1895) and based on his work, Festinger et al (1952) first introduced the concept of de-individuation, defining it as, 'a state of affairs in a group where members do not pay attention to other individuals *qua* individuals and, correspondingly, the members do not feel they are being singled out by others'. Could this be a motive for becoming a part of certain groups in the first place?

In *Escape from Freedom* (1941), Fromm argued that what makes people free is their individuality, uniqueness and self-awareness but these are the very attributes which may also isolate people from each other so that they come to fear their freedom. Not only can groups provide people with a sense of identity and belongingness (see Maslow's hierarchy of needs—Chapter 25) but they can allow individuals to merge with the group, to forego their individuality and to become anonymous—in other words, to de-individuate. Is there any evidence to support this view?

Most relevant studies have been laboratory experiments but one interesting field-study was conducted by Diener et al (1976), who observed 1300 trick-or-treating children on Halloween night. When they were completely anonymous (for instance, wearing costumes which prevented them from being recognized and going from house to house in large groups) they were most likely to steal money and candy.

In an early experimental study, Festinger et al (1952) ran discussion groups in which male undergraduates were asked to discuss their feelings towards their parents. They found a correlation between how often negative statements about parents were made and the extent to which subjects failed to remember who had said what in the discussion group. This was taken as evidence for the hypothesis that de-individuation produces a lowering of inhibitions.

Festinger et al also found that those groups in which more hostility towards parents was expressed were also more attractive to the participants (as expressed by their willingness to return for a further discussion) which was interpreted as indicating that 'submergence' in a group is one of the attractions of group membership.

However, Brown (1985) believes the study is not a very convincing one. For one thing, rather than de-individuation being the cause of uninhibited behaviour in groups, could it not be caused *by* it, so that the perceived similarity of the members increases and less attention is paid to individuals as they engage in uninhibited behaviour?

Singer et al (1965) stressed the importance of internal psychological processes rather than group processes and defined de-individuation as 'a subjective state in which people lose their self-consciousness'. They found that de-individuation produced a greater number of obscene comments being made by female subjects under conditions of anonymity when discussing pornography. They also found, as did Festinger et al, that increased de-individuation was complemented by greater liking for the group.

Zimbardo (1969) also emphasized the absence of self-awareness and self-evaluation as well as lowered social evaluation; under certain conditions, an individual changes their self-perception and that of others and engages in uninhibited behaviour and this is de-individuation.

Zimbardo regarded anonymity as a major source of de-individuation and was the first to operationalize anonymity by having subjects wear hoods and masks. In one study, female students had to deliver electric shocks to another student as an aid to learning. Half the subjects wore bulky lab coats and hoods that hid their faces, were spoken to in groups of four and were never referred to by name; the other half wore their normal clothes, were given large name tabs to wear and were introduced to each other by name and could see each other dimly while giving the shock. The student who received the shock was seen through a one-way mirror and pretended to be in extreme discomfort—writhing, twisting, grimacing and finally tearing her hand away from the strap. The hooded, de-individuated subjects gave twice as much shock as the individuated subjects; if they were told that the student receiving the shock was honest, sincere and warm she did not receive any less shock than those who believed she was conceited or critical; by contrast, the individuated subjects did adjust the shock they administered according to the victim's character.

However, manipulating anonymity has not always proved very easy (as Brown, 1985, points out). Belgian soldiers who wore hoods did not behave more aggressively; instead they became self-conscious, suspicious and anxious and the apparently individuated controls retained their 'normal' level of de-individuation related to their status as uniformed soldiers.

One of the functions of uniform in the 'real world' is precisely to reduce individuality and hence, at least indirectly, to increase de-individuation: a standard uniform is a clear sign for others, at least, that the wearer belongs to the group or the institution and, to that extent, the uniqueness of the individual is rendered less important or apparent. De-possessing someone of their 'civilian' clothes is a major technique of de-personalizing the inmate in 'total institutions' such as prisons and psychiatric hospitals (Goffman, 1968, 1971).

As Brown (1985) observes, the victims of aggression are often dehumanized by, amongst other things, shaving their heads and dressing them in ill-fitting clothes so that they appear less human and so can be humiliated and abused more easily. (See the 'Prison Simulation Experiment' by Zimbardo et al— Chapter 12.) While it may be true that the de-individuation produced by wearing military or police uniform increases the likelihood of brutality, it can just as easily work the other way—the anonymity of massed ranks of police or soldiers may make them appear less human and thus make them a more obvious target for a rioting crowd's violence.

Finally, just as television need not produce harmful effects, so de-individuation does not necessarily produce anti-social behaviour; both Zimbardo (1969) and Johnson and Downing (1979) have pointed out that under proper circumstances, de-individuation can be liberating. This was well illustrated by the 'Black Room' experiment (Gergen et al, 1973), which involved subjects spending an hour together, either in a completely dark room or in a normally-lit room. In the dark room, subjects at first chatted in a lively manner and explored the physical space and then began to discuss serious matters before conversation faded to be replaced by physical contact: 90 per cent of subjects deliberately touched other subjects, almost 50 per cent hugged and 80 per cent admitted to being sexually aroused. By comparison, control subjects talked politely, in the light, for the whole hour.

It seems that we can become uninhibited in the dark where the usual norms of intimacy no longer prevail—we feel less accountable for our behaviour in such situations but this state of de-individuation can be to the mutual benefit of all participants (Gergen and Gergen, 1981).

14

The Ethological Approach to the Study of Animal Behaviour

Experimental and Naturalistic Approaches

In Chapter 1 a distinction was made between the experimental study of animals (comparative or animal psychology) and the ethological approach; while the former is laboratory-based, is associated largely with the behaviourists' attempts to investigate the process of learning and has used 'convenient' species, in particular, rats and pigeons (see Chapter 3), the latter emphasizes the importance of studying animals in their natural habitat, tends to see instinctive (unlearned) behaviour as playing a central role and tries to use as wide a range of species as possible.

Ironically, it was Darwin's theory of evolution which helped to shape behaviourism; if more complex species have evolved from less complex ones so that the differences between them are merely quantitative, it made sense to study the simpler ones (eg rats) in order to enhance our understanding of the more complex ones (ie humans). This was conveniently carried out in laboratories and the natural world of Darwinian theory became virtually forgotten—or at least irrelevant.

Ethology also has its roots in evolutionary theory, specifically in the work of the nineteenth and early twentieth century naturalists (Thorpe, 1979), but Konrad Lorenz and Niko Tinbergen, two of the key European founders and popularizers of ethology, were trying to redress the 'unnatural' balance created by the study of rats in laboratories by putting behaviour back into its natural context and bringing evolutionary theory back into the centre of the attempt to understand that behaviour.

Ethological Questions and Methods

We saw in Chapter 13 that there are four basic questions which ethologists ask about any instance of behaviour, briefly they are (Hinde, 1982): (i) what was the immediate cause (or trigger)? (ii) How has it developed during the animal's lifetime (Ontogeny)? (iii) What is the behaviour for (*function*)? And (iv) how has it evolved within the species (Phylogeny)?

Clearly, (iii) and (iv) are directly derived from evolutionary theory: the purpose of behaviour is central to evolution because a basic assumption is that behaviour which has no purpose will disappear and that the behaviour shared by all members of a species (or, for example, all the males or all the females within a species) has been retained because, ultimately, it has helped the species survive. Precisely how it evolved can be at least partly investigated by comparing species which are known to be related morphologically (ie structurally).

The ethologists, as biologists, believe that behaviour can be studied in the same way as any other aspect of life; just as different species have different skeletons, so they have different behaviour, and if species with similar skeletons also display similar behaviour, this is strong evidence in favour of the view that behaviour is *inherited* or *instinctive*.

Although the concept of instinct plays a crucial role in ethology, it does not necessarily exclude learning from the explanation of behaviour; indeed, a great deal of research and theorizing has focused on the learning process called *imprinting* (Lorenz, 1935) which we shall discuss in detail later in the chapter. Again, although ethologists are primarily zoologists, they are not averse to studying animals in the laboratory (especially in relation to question (i)), but the findings are always put back into the animal's natural context of behaviour.

The word *ethology* simply means 'study of behaviour' and, of course, many psychologists are equally interested in this subject-matter. However, ethology represents a special way of studying behaviour, namely treating it as a biological entity, so that it is the study of behaviour as part of zoology (as distinct from social science, for example) (Lea, 1984).

Hinde (1982) believes that Lorenz and Tinbergen were not carving out a new set of problems but were pioneering a new approach to old ones already being studied in established disciplines. He points out that there are still very few university departments of ethology; most ethologists work within the traditional departments of biology, psychology, veterinary studies, physiology and so on.

Crook (1970) has distinguished between three kinds of ethology: (i) *comparative ethology*, the oldest and best known and represented by Lorenz and Tinbergen; (ii) *social ethology*; and (iii) *behavioural ecology*.

While comparative ethologists study the behaviour of individual animals towards each other and try to build up a picture of animal *society* from this, social ethologists take the animal society as their starting point and regard it as a biological entity in its own right (just as the comparative ethologists take behaviour as an entity in its own right) and then try to make sense of individual behaviour in terms of its relation to the whole society. Crook believes that comparative ethology has paid too little attention to the social environment which generates the most important selective pressures that are brought to bear on a social animal.

Within social ethology in particular, and ethology in general, Wilson's *Sociobiology* (1975) and Dawkins's *The Selfish Gene* (1976) sparked a revolution; we discussed sociobiology in the last chapter in relation to altruism and, by the same token, all social behaviour, and whole societies themselves, can be explained, according to the sociobiologist, in terms of evolution by natural selection. Wilson (1975) believes that socio-cultural behaviours (including aggression, altruism, sexuality, ambition and religion) are largely inherited and the kinds of society and culture created by human beings are constrained by the influence of genes, selected during the past few million years when our ancestors were hunter-gatherers. For instance, he believes that we are genetically predisposed to classify people as friends or aliens, to suspect and fear the actions of strangers and to resolve conflicts with them by means of aggression (Hinde, 1982).

Lea (1984) distinguished social ethology, a field of study, from socio-biology, a theoretical system which is applied to social ethology; the basic *method* of sociobiology, he says, is to ask of every behaviour, what would be the evolutionary fate of a gene which produced that behaviour, given the environment in which the organism bearing it must live?

Sociobiology also overlaps with the third kind of ethology identified by Crook, namely behavioural ecology, which is primarily concerned with how behaviour contributes to an animal's equilibrium with its environment; one major point of overlap is the study of *territoriality* (see below and Chapter 13).

Ethology and Psychology

As we have seen, both psychologists and ethologists are interested in behaviour, although in different ways and for different reasons. Beyond this, why should psychologists be interested in a biological approach? Lea (1984) believes there are three major reasons:

i)   There have been many attempts to explain human behaviour in terms of the evolutionary history of homo sapiens and so psychologists should take account of such explanations.
ii) An evolutionary explanation is often a good place to begin; it helps us to understand the functions and mechanisms involved which can then provide hypotheses to be tested with human subjects.
iii) We cannot properly understand what it is to be human unless we understand what it is to be non-human.

Lea also points to a number of ways in which ethology may be *applied*: (a) practically, to help us breed endangered species, for example; (b) methodologically, particularly in the naturalistic observation of babies and young children; (c) conceptually, by using ideas and concepts from ethology and incorporating them into psychological theory (eg 'personal space', see Chapter 10); and (d) empirically, by direct extrapolation of the results from the study of animals to humans (eg human infants becoming attached to their mother through imprinting as studied in goslings, see Chapter 18).

Evolutionary Theory

Darwin claimed that all living things are related and that more complex forms of life are derived from the forms which preceded them by a process of adaptation through natural selection, called *evolution*. The earliest of earth's life-forms were single-celled, asexual micro-organisms which reproduced simply by asexual cell division; this meant that offspring were genetically identical to parents so that there was no genetic variability and little room for adaptive selection.

In the course of evolution, the process of *sexual* (diploid) *reproduction* appeared, which enabled offspring to be genetically quite different from either parent or from other offspring, because (except for identical twins) every individual has a unique combination of genes. This greater variability allows more efficient selection, because the greater the variability, the greater the availability of individuals who will survive new or changed environmental conditions; the survivors will then reproduce and pass on to their offspring those genes responsible for the characteristics which enabled them to survive. Gradually, more and more individuals with particular characteristics will emerge and when these individuals can no longer mate with other individuals who have a different set of characteristics, a new species has evolved. (See Chapter 13.)

Another crucial evolutionary development was *mobility*: this facilitates adaptation by helping animals, 'to cope with the daily cycles of sun, tide and darkness, to protect themselves against seasonal changes by migrating, to seek out new sources of food and shelter, and to colonize new territory' (Latané and Hothersall, 1980).

Lea (1984) summarizes some of the major terms used in evolutionary theory:

Evolution, of course, implies a gradual rather than a sudden change (and is usually contrasted with 'revolution'); species do not appear 'out of the blue' but emerge from other species by a series of linked steps. However, evolution is not going on at a more or less constant rate: the history of life is characterized by 'punctuated equilibria', long periods during which relatively little is going on by way of new species appearing, followed by 'adaptive radiations' when whole new groups evolve.

Natural selection refers to the natural occurrence of a process performed deliberately by human breeders, perpetuating some lines in preference to others, thus producing new varieties of animal. A *fit* animal is one which leaves more offspring and *adaptedness* means being well-suited to the environment the organism lives in. The precise environment to which an animal is adapted is called its *ecological niche* (and any one ecological niche can only be occupied by one species at any one time).

Selective pressure is any property of the environment (especially of the ecological niche) which tends to favour one form of a species over another, that is, it is a factor which makes some animals fitter than others. Finally, a *species* is the range of *gene* exchange and the field within which evolution can operate.

The Concept of Instinct

As we mentioned earlier, the concept of instinct is central to ethological explanations of behaviour and opposes it to the extreme environmentalism of the behaviourists; Tinbergen's *The Study of Instinct* (1951) represents one of the key landmarks in the history of ethology. What is an instinct?

Essentially, it is an inherited behaviour pattern which is common to all members of a species (hence, it is often used synonymously with *species–specific* behaviour); it is innate as opposed to learnt and it tends to be stereotyped, that is, it appears in the same form every time it is displayed. An instinct is what motivates behaviour and makes it purposeful and goal-directed, and associated with each instinct (eg hunger, reproduction, aggression) is an *action–specific energy*. This might sound plausible enough, but a major problem with a term like 'instinct' is that it sounds deceptively like an explanation for behaviour when, in fact, it is nothing more than a label, a description.

Partly for this reason, and partly because it is impossible to investigate an instinct without investigating particular manifestations of it, Tinbergen, Lorenz and other ethologists define instincts in terms of *Fixed Action Patterns* (FAPs). These are readily identifiable units of behaviour which break up the stream of behaviour and can be treated like morphological characteristics; every species has a repertoire of FAPs which are as much characteristic of the species as are its structural characteristics (Hinde, 1982), ie FAPs are species–specific.

Fixed Action Patterns

Before defining an FAP in more detail, we will look at two commonly-quoted examples: (a) the egg-rolling of the greylag goose (Lorenz and Tinbergen, 1938); and (b) the begging-response of the herring-gull chick (Tinbergen and Perdeck, 1950).

a) Whenever an egg rolled away from her nest, a greylag goose always retrieved it in the same way, by turning to face it, stretching out her neck, walking slowly towards it, hooking her beak over it and rolling it slowly back into the nest. This did not seem the most efficient way of going about it—it sometimes took several attempts and on occasions she failed completely.

b) Herring-gulls nest on the ground and the parents go off to find food at sea, on local rubbish tips or some other distant source. When they return, they land on their small nesting territory and stand close to the chick (or even over it), pointing their beaks at the ground. The chick then pecks at the parents' beak which stimulates the parent to regurgitate the food it has collected, allowing the chick to be fed.

Based on these and numerous other examples (mainly from birds and fish), the concept of an FAP emerged; based on Lorenz, Lea (1984) proposes six major characteristics shared by all FAPs (some of which we have already touched on in discussing the concept of 'instinct'):

i) They are *stereotyped*, that is, the behaviour always occurs in the same form;

ii) They are *universal*, that is, they occur in all the members of a species (or at least, all members of a defined class, eg geese as distinct from ganders and goslings), and, therefore, there should be intra-specific similarity. FAPs are *species–specific*.

iii) They are *independent of individual experience*, that is, they are unlearnt and so they should occur regardless of an animal's particular history. This can be demonstrated by 'isolation' experiments, where an animal is reared, from birth, entirely on its own, so that its behaviour cannot have been learned through its contact with other members of the species; any FAPs it displays must, therefore, have been inherited. However, as we shall see below, this does not rule out the role of learning and environmental factors altogether.

iv) They are *ballistic*, that is, they cannot be varied if conditions change once the FAP has been 'launched'; once triggered, it runs its course. Although (see (vi) below) there must be a stimulus which triggers the FAP, its particular characteristics seem to be irrelevant; for instance, Lorenz and Tinbergen presented a greylag goose with a giant, cardboard, Easter egg, painted with the same sort of markings as a real goose egg and in her attempt to roll it in, it got stuck between her beak and her breast and she stayed like that for several seconds. In this sense, the behaviour is totally inflexible (so there is overlap with (i)).

v) They have a *singleness* of *purpose*, that is, they have only one function and are only shown in specific situations (eg the greylag goose only uses her FAP for egg-retrieval to retrieve eggs—and for nothing else).

vi) They are *triggered* by *specific stimuli*, which constitute the immediate cause of the FAP. These trigger stimuli can be considered both a necessary and sufficient condition for the appearance of the FAP; the greylag goose will only show her egg-rolling if she sees an egg within reach of the nest and if she does see one will always attempt to roll it in. (The egg is an example of *sign stimulus*.)

Sign Stimuli, Releasers and Supernormal Stimuli

Just how specific does the trigger have to be? In the above example (iv), it would seem that a real goose egg and the giant cardboard Easter egg have enough in common for the latter to 'count' as a trigger for egg-rolling. What seems to be critical is that the trigger has certain characteristics and any others it does or does not have seem to be largely irrelevant. Many famous examples of ethological 'experiments' (often, literally, in the field) involve the presentation of artificial stimuli which resemble the natural trigger stimulus, to a greater or lesser degree, in various ways.

Tinbergen and Perdeck (1950) presented herring-gull chicks with a life-like 3-D model of a gull's head and a simple cardboard cut-out (two-dimensional, with just an eye and a beak) and found that both were sufficient to produce the begging response. So what specific features of the parent's head are important?

They tried a number of variations based on three characteristics of the adult herring gull: namely (a) its white head; (b) its yellow beak; and (c) a small red spot one-third of the way from the end of its lower mandible. Three series of cardboard cut-out heads were used, thus manipulating each of three variables:

i) *Spot Colour*: all models had yellow beaks with spots on. The chicks pecked most at the red spot but black, blue and white spots also produced many responses.

ii) *Spot–beak contrast*: all models had medium-grey beaks with the spot colour varying from white through shades of grey to black. Medium-grey spots were the least effective; black and white the most effective.

iii) *Beak colour*: the models were of different colours and all were lacking spots. A yellow beak (the natural colour) was actually *less* effective than a red one and the nearer to red it was, the more effective it was.

Tinbergen and Perdeck concluded that it is the redness of the beak (how close to red it is) and the contrast between the beak and the spot which are the key features that produce the begging response in herring-gull chicks.

Another example is the size and speckled-ness of an oystercatcher's eggs. A herring-gull's eggs in fact look very much like an oystercatcher's except that they are twice the size; Tinbergen (1948) put a gull's egg near an oystercatcher's nest and found that the returning oystercatcher would choose to brood the outsize gull egg in preference to its own. It would also choose an absurd giant egg (which was as speckled as a real egg) in preference to both its own and the herring gull's egg.

Herring-gulls themselves seem to go for size. Baerends and Kruijt (1973) used models to study the egg-rolling of herring-gulls and found that larger models were preferred to smaller, speckled to plain, and green to a variety of other colours; shape seemed to make little difference.

Therefore the most effective stimulus is not necessarily the one which is most like the natural stimulus and such artificial stimuli are known as *super-normal* stimuli (or *super-releasers*) which Hinde (1982) describes as a kind of caricature of the natural sign stimulus.

Although the terms 'sign stimulus' and 'releaser' are often used interchangeably, there is an important difference, as Lea (1984) points out. Although both the speckles on the oystercatcher's egg and the red spot on the herring gull's beak are sign stimuli (because they help to trigger particular FAPs), the former seems to have another, more important function, namely, to help camouflage the eggs. The red spot, however, seems to have evolved for the sole purpose of acting as a sign stimulus which makes it a *releaser*; so while all releasers are sign stimuli, not all sign stimuli are releasers and true releasers are often found in one species but not in another, closely related, species.

The Role of Environmental Factors

Another famous example of a releaser is the bright red underbelly of the male three-spined stickleback studied by Tinbergen but, interestingly the precise FAP it triggers depends on whether the fish is on its own territory or another's. The red belly of an intruder will release *attack* behaviour if the stickleback is on 'homeground' but when it is 'trespassing' the same stickleback will *flee*. (Exactly how it 'knows' whether it is inside or outside its own territory is itself an important and complex issue).

This tells us that the probability that an FAP will be elicited is *not* determined solely by the presence or absence of a releaser (or sign stimulus) which means that it may not, after all, be a sufficient condition (see above).

Apart from territory, what other environmental factors may influence the appearance of FAPs?

When discussing the criteria of FAPs above, we referred to isolation experiments as one way of demonstrating the innateness of such behaviour. One famous isolation experiment is that of Eibl-Eibesfeldt (1975) who took some baby squirrels, still on a liquid diet, and brought them up in bare cages. The cages were quite warm but there was no nesting material to burrow into or hide things in. When they were fully grown, they were given a supply of nuts and, despite having no solid food before and not having seen a nut before (or another squirrel eating one), they ate the nuts quite easily, in much the same way as normally-reared adults. When they had eaten their fill, they attempted to bury the surplus nuts, pushing them into a corner with their noses and stamping them down with their back feet, just as wild squirrels stamp earth over their stores of nuts.

Clearly, the squirrels could not have learned this behaviour—'recognizing' the nuts seems to be part of the squirrels' innate repertoire of behaviour and the nut-burying behaviour an FAP. (This example also seems to demonstrate the stereotyped, species–specific and ballistic nature of FAPs.)

Similarly, female rats reared in isolation developed the normal maternal behaviours of nest-building and retrieval and licking of their pups (Reiss, 1951). However, Reiss also found that if rats were reared so that they were prevented from carrying anything in their paws (eg faeces fell through the floor-grid of the cage and they were given only powdered food instead of pellets), when they came to have litters, they did not build nests, nor did they retrieve their young. It seems that early experience of carrying things is essential for normal maternal behaviour to develop. Birch (1948) reported that if female rats are prevented from licking their own genital organs (to obtain salt) they fail to lick or retrieve their pups and will actually eat many of them; and Kinder (1927) found that nest-building and temperature are inversely related, so that the higher the temperature, the less the nest-building.

Laughing gulls (like herring gulls) have a red spot on their beak which is a releaser for pecking by chicks. However, the accuracy of pecking improves with time, partly due to learning; week-old chicks, for example, have learned to distinguish the shape of the parent's beak and so they peck selectively, whereas before this, pecking seems to be rather 'hit and miss' (Hailman, 1969),

Another classic study of its kind is Thorpe's study of the chaffinch (Thorpe, 1956, 1963, 1972). Using an acoustic spectograph (which converts sound into a 'sound picture'), Thorpe discovered that only some features of the chaffinch's song are inherited; birds reared in isolation will only produce the 'basic' song but the 'dialect', that is, the full refinements and temporal pattern, are learned from other chaffinches in the locality and this learning has to take place not later than the bird's first spring. Once learned, the dialect remains invariant throughout the bird's life.

Similar findings were reported by Marler and Tamura (1964) and Konishi (1965) for the American white-crowned sparrow. Konishi removed the cochlea of fledgelings and found that they need to hear their own song in order to produce even the inherited standard song (so acoustic feedback mediates the effects of genetic factors). However, deafening the birds made no difference *after* they had already produced a song.

Evans (1980) likens the inherited, 'basic' song to a *template*—the bird has to use this as a guide and, ultimately, must match its own singing to it; in the white-crowned sparrow, anyway, it must receive acoustic feedback to be able to do this.

The Role of Hormonal Factors and Their Interaction With the Environment

Just as the influence of sign stimuli and releasers are mediated by environmental factors, so hormonal factors also help determine their effect.

Achievement of successful reproduction, for example, depends upon a complex series of changes in the endocrine system which are related to changes in the external situation, themselves partly determined by the endocrine and behavioural changes (Hinde 1982).

In the female canary, for instance, environmental factors, such as long day length and the male canary's song, influence the hypothalamo-pituitary-gonad system and result in gonadal development and the release of oestrogen (see Chapters 15 and 22), which has a positive influence on nest-building behaviour. The external factors themselves also influence the effectiveness of oestrogen in influencing behaviour.

Nest-building results in a nest, and stimuli from the nest produce a change in selection of nest material (from grass for the outside to feathers for the lining), a decrease in nest-building and further reproductive development; stimuli from the nest are received through the ventral areas of the skin (Hinde, 1965, Hinde and Steel, 1966).

Similar findings have come from studies of mammals. For example, stimuli from a female monkey influence the levels of sex hormone in a male (Bernstein et al, 1977) and not only does testosterone promote the mating behaviour of male rats, but mating increases testosterone levels (Thomas and Thomas, 1973).

Innate Releasing Mechanisms

So far we have considered the actual, overt, behaviour (FAPs) and the stimuli which, under certain environmental and hormonal conditions, trigger them (sign stimuli or releasers). Somewhere within the animal's nervous system there must be a mechanism which mediates between the two and this hypothetical 'centre' is known as an *Innate Releasing Mechanism* (IRM).

IRMs, together with the *psycho-hydraulic model* of *motivation*, can help to explain two apparently contradictory findings: firstly, a herring-gull chick that has just eaten will not peck at a cardboard model of a parent gull's head (so clearly the releaser is not sufficient); and secondly, a whole sequence of behaviour may take place in the absence of any obvious releasing stimulus and so is quite spontaneous (*vacuum activity*), in which case the releaser does not even seem to be necessary.

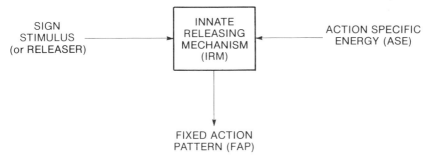

Figure 14.1 The Innate Release Mechanism (IRM) can be activated either by accumulation of ASE or by a strong stimulus or by the combined effect of both

The IRM has to be sufficiently stimulated for the corresponding FAP to occur and whether or not a releaser will be either necessary or sufficient to produce it will depend on the amount of *Action–Specific Energy* (ASE) which has built up in the hypothetical reservoirs of the psycho-hydraulic model.

For each instinct and FAP there is assumed to be a specific kind of energy which powers or energizes the behaviour (this is the ASE); in the case of the herring-gull chick which has just eaten, all its pecking-ASE has been 'used' up and the releaser is not sufficient to 'switch on' the IRM. By contrast, in the case of vacuum activity, there is such a build-up of ASE that the IRM is activated and the behaviour occurs *without* a releaser being needed. (See Chapter 13 for a discussion of Lorenz's view of human aggression, which sees it as being primarily a form of vacuum activity based on the psycho-hydraulic model.)

So Lorenz's psycho-hydraulic model takes account of both the strength of releasing stimuli and the quantity of accumulated energy; the threshold of response is a changing one, depending on environmental and internal factors. (See Figure 14.1.)

Criticisms of the Ethological Approach

1. Although ethologists generally have become increasingly willing to acknowledge the importance of environmental factors in the modification of behaviour patterns, they have always seen instinct as of primary importance. Evans (1975) believes that this has resulted in an over-simplified picture of behaviour, especially when instinct-explanations are applied to human behaviour (see Chapter 13).

2. A specific, and famous, example, of a misplaced ethological explanation is Lorenz and Tinbergens' account of the alarm reaction in young turkeys. They found that the most effective alarm-raiser was the silhouette shown in Figure 14.2. Only when it was moved from right to left did it elicit an alarm reaction; under these conditions the short neck preceded the long tail and so resembled the shadow that would be cast by a bird of prey, such as a hawk; when it was moved from left to right, it resembled a long-necked bird, such as a goose.

Figure 14.2   The hawk-goose silhouette used by Lorenz and Tinbergen

Lorenz and Tinbergen believed that they had demonstrated an IRM especially adapted in the course of evolution to a certain characteristic of birds of prey. However, Schneirla (1965) pointed out that all animals tend to withdraw from any source of stimulation which suddenly changes and even if Lorenz and Tinbergen had used a plain triangle, they would have obtained a similar result; that is, the short-neck presented first represents a sudden change while the long-neck presented first represents a gradual and, consequently, less alarming, change in stimulation.

Schneirla is, therefore, arguing that Lorenz and Tinbergens' explanation is more complicated than it needs to be. However, Green et al (1966, 1968) have subsequently confirmed the original findings.

3. Evans (1980) has criticized the concept of an IRM itself. His reasons are as follows: (a) the very term 'releasing' is itself problematic, because of cases such as young turkey chicks which emit certain specific vocalizations that are designed to *inhibit* a response in the adult bird, not to release one (namely, attacking and killing the chick); (b) stimuli may orientate behaviour (as in the greylag goose's egg-retrieval) and arouse the animal, and not just release or trigger responses; (c) the sign stimulus is often much more complex than the term 'mechanism' implies (or in the begging-response of herring gull chicks), and what is needed is a thorough knowledge of how the animal processes information, how stimuli are filtered in the nervous system and how only the key characteristics are selected and attended to.

    In defence of the IRM concept, Lea (1984), argues that it is only intended as a *description* of instinctive behaviour (and not an explanation). He suggests that systems which can be described in terms of IRMs should be called 'micro-instincts' (to distinguish them from broad tendencies such as hunger, sex and aggression) and believes that the IRM concept has made instinct a scientifically respectable concept, making it coherent and recognizable.

4. The psycho-hydraulic model has also been criticized, most seriously because it does not fit the facts. The model maintains that energy can only be released through the performance of instinct-related behaviour; if this were so, then *consummatory* behaviour (sequences of responses made when the goal is actually reached, eg drinking) cannot be by-passed, that is, the ASE associated with drinking could only be reduced by actually drinking. However, studies of animals in which water is placed directly into their stomachs (eg Adolph, 1939) shows that they do *not* start drinking (following a 10–15 minute interval to allow the water

to be absorbed) which is contrary to what Lorenz's model would predict. (See Chapter 17.)

Evans (1975) points out that the model has been discredited not only in relation to eating and drinking. In another famous example of FAPs, Tinbergen (1951) describes the courtship behaviour of the stickleback. Normally, when a female swims into a male's territory, he swims up to her in a series of loops called a 'zigzag dance'; she swims round in front of him, then he turns round and swims down the nest (which he has built) and she follows him down. This, in turn, causes him to point his head at the nest entrance; she enters and this releases a quivering response in the male who then thrusts his snout at the female's rump, causing her to spawn eggs. Finally, he fertilizes the eggs, and while he is doing this, she swims away.

It seems that merely *seeing* the newly-laid eggs is enough to 'satisfy' the male's mating ASE—actually fertilizing them does not seem to be necessary, contrary to what the hydraulic model would predict.

The Social Nature of FAPs

In the stickleback's mating behaviour just described, the initial sign stimulus is the female's swollen belly; this then sets in motion a series of FAPs, each of which serves as a sign stimulus for the next FAP.

Both Lorenz (1950) and Hinde (1982) believe that FAPs often function as *signals*, from one animal to another; while 'sign stimulus' implies a selective responsiveness on the part of the responder, 'social releaser' 'implies the evolution of especially effective stimulus features, involving movements or structures or both in the signaller' (Hinde, 1982). In other words, in the course of evolution, many FAPs have developed which are triggered by social releasers (which may, themselves, be FAPs triggered by other social releasers as in the stickleback's mating behaviour) and which are primarily concerned with *communication* between members of the same species; these tend to be either predominantly male–male encounters (as in threat behaviour, territoriality, competition over a female, etc) or male–female encounters (as in mating and courtship). How have such patterns of social communication evolved?

According to Hinde (1982), there are three main sources: (i) displacement activity (ii) intention movements; and (iii) the consequences of activity in the autonomic nervous system (eg movements of hair, feathers, urination and defecation, changes in skin colour). We shall concentrate here on (i).

Conflict and Displacement Activity

Animals will sometimes find themselves in a situation where a source of food and a source of threat are in the same place at the same time (eg the food is cheese, the threat is a cat and the animal caught in the middle is a mouse). Alternatively, they may face a conflict between aggression (a rival male should be approached and attacked) and fear (the other male is quite capable of inflicting injury itself).

Another example of *approach–avoidance* conflict is mating in 'distance species' (Hediger, 1951), such as most common garden birds and gulls; members of these species normally like to maintain distance from other members, but, of course, their sexual drive requires that they come into close proximity with another animal. What do animals do when faced with such conflicts?

Often, some third kind of behaviour appears which seems to be entirely irrelevant to the situation. For example, two cocks facing each other and preparing for a fight may suddenly break off and start pulling up the grass, or hungry rats put in an unfamiliar cage may start to wash themselves rigorously (Lea, 1984).

These *displacement activities* often involve preening, washing or other activities associated with care of the body surface (eg the chaffinch wipes its beak or its feathers); alternatively, they may involve nest-building, feeding or even sleeping! They all have in common the fact that they are *readily available* behaviours, that is, they are all behaviours the animal engages in frequently and regularly.

Almost by definition, displacement activities only arise when another animal is involved in some way, which tells us that the conflict involves aggression, fear and sex; they are also generally themselves FAPs, which is important if they are to be used as social signals, since their 'meaning' should be unambiguous for members of the same species.

The psycho-hydraulic model maintains that displacement activity occurs when two mutually incompatible IRMs are released simultaneously and, as a result, inhibit each other; the ASE associated with each overflows into another, stimulating it and producing some behaviour which is unrelated to either of the original IRMs (displacement activity is, therefore, a kind of vacuum activity). This implies that the presence or absence, or relative strength, of an appropriate sign stimulus is irrelevant; however, Raber (1948) found that turkey cocks showed displaced feeding or drinking only if food or water were available and Rowell (1961) reported that chaffinch preening is increased if its feathers are sprayed with water. Similar observations have been made in nesting terns.

Often, the inhibition of one activity by the other produces *intention movements*, that is, the incomplete preparatory phases of a movement (for example, a bird crouches before take-off), or there may be a rapid alternation between the two behaviours that are in conflict. Alternatively, elements of both kinds of behaviour may be combined to produce an ambivalent form of behaviour; or, again, one kind of behaviour (eg aggression) may be displayed but with some other animal or object as the target (this kind of displaced aggression is described by Freud as a means of ego defence—see Chapter 26).

Displacement Activity, FAPs and Evolution

According to Lorenz (1950) and, as we have seen, Hinde (1982), many FAPs are social in character and many have probably evolved from displacement reactions. Lea (1984) describes the two stages of evolution involved:

i) The form of displacement reaction would become standardized, so as both to display any relevant body features most effectively and because any animal without such characteristics can be more easily identified and rejected. If a characteristic body structure is involved, there will be a selective advantage for animals who have it in a larger, brighter or exaggerated form or who display it sooner or more vigorously. These structures serve to enhance the signal (eg the stickleback's red belly). The standard form of the displacement reaction is usually exaggerated compared with the original, 'functional' form of the response; this is called *ritualization* (Huxley, 1914).

ii) The response, now in full use as a signal, would lose its connections with its original sign stimuli and motivation; for example, preening becomes attached to the sex drive instead of the care-of-body-surface drive and would be released by some releaser from the female. In effect, a new IRM would have been formed and the process is called *emancipation* (Lorenz, 1950).

Is there any evidence to support Lorenz?

According to Hinde (1982), comparisons across several species often show correlations between the extent to which a signal has been developed and the development of accompanying structures which serve to enhance that signal; they seem to have evolved in parallel.

In zebra finches, beak-wiping is a fairly common displacement reaction to approach–avoidance conflicts; but in two other grass finches (striated and spice), the *same* beak-wiping has become ritualized and emancipated and it functions as an effective courtship response in the male when the female sexually presents herself. (Other important examples of ritualization are described in Chapter 13 in relation to aggression.)

Courtship and Mating: How do Animals Fall in Love?

There are many parallels between sexually-motivated postures and appeasement postures; any behaviour implying subservience is quite likely to be adopted as part of a courtship display. It follows, therefore, that a great deal of courtship ritual involves the reduction of aggression necessary for mating to take place. (Conversely, some appeasement displays involve triggering behaviour in the attacker which is incompatible with aggression; for instance, baboons adopt the female sexual presentation posture causing the aggressor to mount them!)

Males and females, of course, are both necessary for reproduction but each contributes a different size and type of sex-cell or gamete; the female ovum contains both genetic information *and* a food store (source of nourishment and energy) for the new organism while the male sperm is a source of genetic information only. Consequently, the female commits more resources to her offspring and this puts her under greater selective pressure to provide care, both pre- and post-natally: this is why, according to the sociobiologists, female mammals have evolved so that they retain their offspring inside their bodies for the duration of the pregnancy.

To a great extent, this difference in the size of male and female gametes (*anisogamy*) determines the different roles of males and females. Where fertilization is *internal* (as in birds and mammals), anisogamy has produced physiological adaptations in the female such that she provides the food and parental care: as Dawkins (1976) puts it, they have lost the 'race to desert' the offspring long ago in their evolutionary past. Where fertilization is *external* (as in fish), the balance is more equal; the male can be sure of his paternity and so the incentive to desert is weaker; indeed, the female has to release her eggs first which gives her the opportunity to leave, and in several species (such as the stickleback) it is the male who builds the nest and cares for the eggs until they hatch—or even beyond.

For widely-dispersed, solitary animals, it may not be easy for males and females actually to find each other. To overcome this, many species have evolved auditory signals (such as the cuckoo's call) or chemical communication; for example, many insects and mammals have a wide range of secretory cells which emit substances called *pheromones* into the environment.

However, in most species there are several males and females present in the same vicinity and the problem there becomes how particular males come to mate with particular females. Usually, there are two or more males competing for the attentions of the same female and, as we saw when discussing the evolution of FAPs from displacement activity, the male who shows the appropriate courtship display, in the most exaggerated form and with the greatest persistence, and who also possesses the brightest releasing stimuli, will be chosen.

Once they have 'found each other', what sort of relationship do they form?

Sometimes, copulation is the first and last contact they have with each other (the animal equivalent of a 'one-night-stand', or casual sex) which is what normally happens when no parental care is actually needed; but it may occur where the one-parent family is the normal pattern (eg female cats and male sticklebacks).

Some females (such as chimps) are *promiscuous*, that is, they will mate with any and all available males, while in a *pair-bond* (especially common among birds), one male and one female remain more or less 'faithful' to each other for one mating season or several and both may play a substantial part in the care of the offspring. Perhaps more common is for the male and female to play different roles, for instance, the male is the nest-builder and the female does the egg-sitting. In pair-bonds, the male and female are usually similar in size and also in appearance.

In *polygyny*, one male has exclusive access to a group of females (his 'harem') as in red deer, or a small group of males has access to a larger group of females (eg lions). The males tend to be larger than females and often quite different in appearance; care of the young is almost exclusively left to the females. Although not very common, a single female sometimes has access to several males, as in the American jacana or the Tasmanian native hen.

Social Structure

Why do animals live in groups?

According to Lea (1984) there are two ways of trying to answer the question why animals live in groups: either we can start with simple behaviours which go on between individuals and see how these 'add up' to a social structure (the 'bottom-up' approach); or we can start with whole societies and ask how they influence the behaviour of individuals and how they are produced by natural selection (the 'top-down' approach.)

Within non-solitary species, the range of social organization is enormous, varying from flocks of seed-eating birds which form in autumn and are really no more than aggregations of individuals to *eusocial* insects, where there is a highly structured division of labour—different body structures equip different ants, bees and wasps to perform different but interdependent roles, namely, worker, soldier and queen. (These are among the most altruistic species too—see Chapter 13.) According to Lea (1984), there are about 170,000 species of such social insects ('Hymenoptera') who live in elaborate, differentiated societies.

Living in a group has a number of advantages for an individual animal, in particular, it makes a mate readily accessible. Equally important, finding food may be easier in a group; for instance, members can report to each other where food is available (a famous example being the 'waggle dance' of the honey bee, described by Von Frisch, 1966, which informs other bees of the exact location of food, who then go in increasing numbers to the food supply to collect it and bring it back to the hive).

A group may also be able to tackle larger prey than an individual animal could (as in lions) and the group has a better chance of spotting a predator and 'sounding the alarm'. Most predators take only one victim (or a very small proportion of the whole group) and so the larger the group the greater the probability that any one individual will survive an attack. However, a large group is more likely to be spotted in the first place.

For groups to remain fairly permanent and stable (and to survive as groups), there needs to be some kind of *dominance hierarchy*, an arrangement whereby some members have precedence over others for such things as access to mates, food etc. This ensures that at least some members of the group would survive a severe food shortage, because each 'knows its place'; energy is not wasted fighting over scarce resources.

Dominance hierarchies are common among species which live *within* territories and were originally observed by Schjelderup-Ebbe (1922) who discovered a literal pecking-order among hens; 'pecking-order' is now used almost synonymously with 'dominance hierarchy'. They represent a simple kind of social structure and have been found in species ranging from red jungle fowl (an ancestor of the domestic chicken) and wild Barbary apes.

Most animal societies are more complex than is implied by a dominance hierarchy and even strictly territorial animals usually have at least a minimal social grouping comprising a mother and her young (territoriality will be discussed separately below).

Often a key factor in more complex social groupings is the temporary or permanent nature of sexual relationships between males and females, which we discussed earlier in relation to courtship and mating. However, there are other important kinds of relationship, such as sibling groups and 'matriline'. All the females in a pride of lions or a larger group are, at least, first cousins (Bertram, 1976, Hardy, 1977) and in brush turkeys, females are courted by pairs of brothers, only one of which will ultimately mate with her (Watts and Stokes, 1971); these are examples of *sibling groups*.

A *matriline* is a group comprising a dominant female, sexually mature daughters (and possibly granddaughters) and the dependent young of all of them, and it is found in almost all primates.

Territoriality

Basically, a territory is an area of space which is held and defended by a solitary animal, or a family group, and in which food is found and the young are reared.

Territoriality is common among birds, many coastal and river fish and many mammals but is less common among invertebrates. Territories may vary enormously in size and there is no simple correlation between size of territory and the availability of food (one of the major explanations for the evolution of territoriality, eg Lack, 1966, and Wynne-Edwards, 1962). For example, birds of prey have very large territories (about 1 square mile) from which they obtain all their food, while herring-gulls have a limited territory within a colony but they obtain all their food elsewhere (at sea, for instance).

Manning (1973) compares territory to an elastic disc, the centre of which is well-defined as a particular animal's territory and any intruder who enters this space will provoke an extremely aggressive response by the territory owner. As one moves out from the centre, the owner's threat behaviour becomes less pronounced until a point is reached where it becomes quite half-hearted; it is at this peripheral 'no-man's-land' that threat displays are most in evidence, which suggest that they are essentially a compromise when the tendencies to attack and to escape are finely balanced and, as predicted by Lorenz's hydraulic model, displacement activities also commonly occur in this 'border-area'. According to Manning, therefore, territories do *not* have fixed boundaries.

A related concept is that of a 'home range', a defined place in which an animal lives but which may overlap with the living space of one or more others. For instance, herring gulls defend a small area around their nesting sites but their home range also includes various feeding places which they visit in common with many other gulls; at feeding sites *agonistic* encounters (ie attack, threat, fight, flight, submission and appeasement behaviour) may occur over food but *not* over the use of space as such.

Another way in which space may be shared is in terms of time; cats, for example, operate a 'time-share' system, by which the freshness of the urine smell acts as a signal as to whose territory it is at that particular time. Similarly, many primates which live in groups share overlapping home-ranges; by using special vocal signals (as in howler monkeys) groups can avoid each other and, consequently, can avoid disputes over ownership. So the same territory can be owned by several individuals (or groups) but at different times.

Territoriality, therefore, is a much more flexible and varied feature of animal social behaviour than was once thought.

Parental Care and Imprinting

A large number of instinctive behaviour patterns are concerned with inter-actions between parents and their young who need to 'know', for instance, what to do in order to elicit food (as in herring-gull chicks). It may also be vital for the young animal's survival that it stay close to its parent(s) if they belong to a *precocial* species, in which the new-born are capable of locomotion and possess well-developed sense-organs. A mobile young animal needs to stay close to its parents and, if it has to *learn* to recognize them, this learning needs to be rapid, and this is one of the characteristics of a form of learning which Lorenz (1935) called *imprinting*.

Lorenz defined imprinting as the learning which occurs in a young bird when following a moving object; specifically, what the bird learns is the characteristics of the object (which, in the wild, will usually be the mother) so that it discriminates the object from others and, in this way, it becomes attached to the imprinted object. This attachment is manifested as a tendency to follow the familiar object, so that following is both a cause and effect of imprinting.

This tendency to become imprinted (*imprintability*) is genetically determined (and species–specific) and the following response is an FAP: the sign stimuli include movement, size and general conspicuousness and since young birds do not innately recognize their mothers, any object which combines these properties can be a potential 'target' for imprinting. Lea (1984) maintains that instinct gives the chick a 'concept' of the mother, but the environment has to supply the details.

Indeed, in a very famous ethological experiment, Lorenz took a large clutch of goose eggs and kept them until they were about to hatch out. Half were then placed under the goose mother and the other half Lorenz kept beside him for several hours. After hatching, the first group followed the mother and the second group followed Lorenz; he then put them altogether under an upturned box to allow them to mix and when the box was removed, the two groups separated to go to their respective guardians.

So what characterizes imprinting as a form of learning?

Lorenz believed that imprinting is unique for the following reasons:

i) It only occurs during a brief *critical period*, early in the bird's life.
ii) Once it has occurred, it is *irreversible*.
iii) It is *supra-individual*, that is, it is to do with a *class* of objects (a species) rather than an individual.
iv) It influences patterns of behaviour which have not yet developed in the animal's repertoire (for example, the selection of a sexual partner).

We should add as a fifth characteristic that Lorenz believed that imprinting only occurred in a group of ground-nesting (nidifugous) birds called *precocial* (see above), in particular, ducks, geese and chickens. (Precocial species are contrasted with *altricial* species, including human beings, in which newborns are incapable of mobility and are totally dependent on others.)

What is the evidence?

Critical and Sensitive Periods

Lorenz borrowed the term 'critical period' from embryology, implying that there are periods in development during which the individual is especially impressionable or vulnerable, that is, when particular experiences exert a profound and lasting influence on later behaviour.

In relation to imprinting, 'critical' implies that *unless* learning occurs during a particular period after hatching, it will *never* occur; (it also conveys the second major characteristic of imprinting, namely, irreversibility). Imprintability, according to Lorenz, is genetically 'switched on' and then 'switched off' again at the end of the period; in the case of mallard ducklings the critical period lasts for the first few hours after hatching (Lorenz, 1935) and, more precisely, between 5 and 24 hours after hatching, with a peak between 13 to 16 hours (Ramsay and Hess, 1954). Hess (1958), studying chicks, ducklings and goslings, maintains that although imprinting *could* occur as early as one hour after hatching, the strongest responses occurred between 12 to 17 hours ('critical period peak'); after 32 hours, it was extremely unlikely to happen and it became increasingly difficult after 20 hours. Gottlieb (1961) reported a critical period of 8 to 27 hours (with no peak) for Peking ducklings.

Are these periods switched on and off in the way Lorenz believed?

Many researchers have shown that if a young bird is kept in isolation, it remains unimprinted (and still imprintable) beyond the end of the normal critical period (for instance, Sluckin, 1961 and Bateson, 1964, with ducklings). Also, if chicks are kept in an unstimulating environment (especially if it is visually unstimulating) they could imprint well after the critical period normally ends (Guiton, 1958); similar results were found by Moltz and Stettner (1961) who fitted translucent hoods to ducklings, thus preventing perception of patterned light.

In view of this evidence that the young bird's experience can extend the period of imprintability, Lorenz's original proposal that the termination (as well as the onset) of the critical period is under genetic control seemed untenable and this led Sluckin (1965) to coin the term *sensitive period* instead. A sensitive period is one during which learning is most *likely* to happen and will happen most *easily* but it is not as 'critical' or 'once-and-for-all' as the critical period concept suggests. It seems more useful to think in terms of the *probability* that imprinting will occur rather than 'whether-or-not' it will occur.

Hinde (1966) defines a sensitive period as, 'a time during an organism's development when a particular influence is most likely to have an effect', while according to Dworetzky (1981), 'there could be times in our life when we are genetically primed to respond to certain influences and other times when those influences would have little or no effect'.

Hinde (1966) believes that once imprinting has occurred, the young bird is likely to respond with fear to every other object it encounters and so will avoid them, thus ensuring that no new imprinting occurs.

Reversibility

Lorenz believed that once imprinting had taken place, it could not be 'undone' or reversed. However, there are many experimental demonstrations of reversibility, such as those of Guiton (1966), Salzen and Sluckin (1959) and Salzen (1967).

Guiton (1966), for example, found that ducklings imprinted on farmyard chickens still tried to mate with other ducks when they became sexually mature, and ducklings imprinted on a pair of yellow rubber gloves showed normal sexual preferences after being familiarized with other ducks. Domestic cocks would only try to mate with a yellow rubber glove if they had been reared alone; early imprinting on the glove was clearly reversed if this was followed by contact with females of the species.

Irreversibility is probably more a feature of imprinting in natural settings than the laboratory.

So what kind of learning is imprinting?

1. As far as the 'following' element is concerned, it seems that even if this is prevented, imprinting will still occur. Baer and Gray (1960) individually exposed 32 domestic chicks to a guinea-pig, separated by a glass wall, thus preventing any bodily contact or overt following. A few days later, they chose the familiar guinea-pig significantly more often than an unfamiliar one.

Similar results were found by Moltz (1960). Baer and Gray (1960) concluded that, 'imprinting is not a learning to follow, but a learning of the characteristics of the parent-object'.

In a similar vein, Sluckin (1965) argues that 'exposure learning' is the essential process involved; this is similar to the 'perceptual learning' described by Bateson (1966) who found that exposing chicks to a colour pattern in their home pens both subsequently facilitated imprinting to that pattern *and* discrimination learning involving that pattern. Bateson concludes that both perceptual learning and imprinting involve S-S (stimulus-stimulus) associations, independent of any response–contingent reinforcement; in other words, the young bird is learning *about* the stimulus, to recognize it, not to follow it as such and any following which does occur does so *as a consequence* of this perceptual learning.

Lorenz would certainly agree that imprinting is a different kind of learning altogether from conditioning, but he argued that imprinting is more or less instantaneous; however, it is now clear that the longer a bird is exposed to an object the stronger its preference for that object becomes (eg Salzen and Sluckin, 1959).

2. As far as imprinting being *supra*-individual, there can be no doubt that, when a young bird learns the characteristics of its parent and follows it, the learning is of a *particular* parent bird and so cannot be described as supra-individual (characteristic of the species in general).

Schutz (1965) claimed that learning an attachment to the parent precedes the learning which will determine its sexual preferences when mature; the latter, according to Bateson (1978 b), involves learning the characteristics of siblings as well as those of the parent and serves to ensure that the individual will both breed with a mate of the same-species and also *not* breed with a very close relative.

3. As originally defined by Lorenz, imprinting did not seem to be a very wide-spread phenomenon but confined to a few species of precocial birds. However, since the 1970s, the way ethologists and developmental psychologists have come to regard imprinting has changed considerably— Lorenz's examples are now seen as extreme cases of a far more general phenomenon.

According to Immelmann and Suomi (1981), sensitive periods occur much more frequently in many species (including many breeds of fish, insects, sheep, deer, buffalo, dogs and goats, higher primates and human beings) and can apply to a much wider range of behaviour than just attachment, for example, choice of habitat, preferences for specific foods, learning communication signals, choice of sexual partner and control of aggression.

The existence of sensitive periods probably constitutes a general psychobiological principle of development and will be discussed in relation to human attachment (Chapter 18), language development (Chapter 20), gender identity (Chapter 22) and personality development (Chapter 26).

15

The Nervous System

The biological basis of behaviour is an integral part of the study of psychology. The important point to remember is that psychologists are interested in biology *not* for its own sake but for what it can tell them about behaviour and mental processes.

A few other important points should be made about the relationship between psychology and biology:

a) The kind of behaviour of which an animal species is capable depends very much on the kind of *body* it possesses; humans can flap their arms as much they like but they will never fly (unaided) because arms are simply not suited to flight, they are not designed for it, while wings are. However, we are very skilled at manipulating objects (particularly small ones) because that is how our hands and fingers have developed during the course of evolution.

b) The possession of a specialized body is of very little use unless the nervous system is able to control it; of course, evolution of the one usually mirrors evolution of the other. The kind of behaviour of which a species is capable is determined by the kind of *nervous system* it possesses.

c) The kind of nervous system also determines the extent and the nature of the *learning* of which a species is capable. As you move along the phylogenetic-evolutionary-scale, from simple, one-celled amoeba, through insects, birds, mammals, to primates, including homo sapiens, the nervous system becomes gradually more complex and behaviour becomes increasingly the product of learning and environmental influence, as distinct from instinct and other innate, genetically-determined factors.

An Overview of the Human Nervous System (NS)— Structure and Function

As you can see from Figure 15.1, the NS involves a number of sub-divisions. Before looking at these in detail, we need to look at some of the general

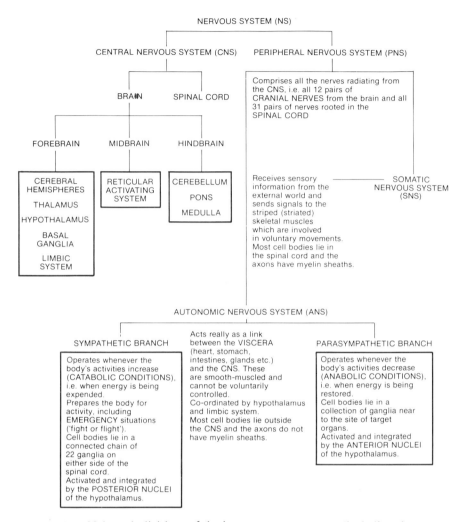

Figure 15.1 Major sub-divisions of the human nervous system (including the main sub-divisions of the brain)

characteristics of the NS:

1. The NS as a whole comprises between 10 and 12 billion (ie 10 to 12 thousand million) nerve cells or *neuron(e)s*; these are the basic structural units or building blocks of the NS.

2. Other kinds of cell in the NS include *glia* ('glue') cells, which are mostly smaller than neurons and ten times more numerous; they supply nutrients and structural support to the neurons and provide a barrier to certain substances from the bloodstream.

3. About 80 per cent of all neurons are found in the brain, in particular, in the cerebral cortex, the topmost outer layer.

4.   Information is passed from neuron to neuron in the form of *electro-chemical impulses* and these constitute the 'language' of the NS.

5.   Neurons are of three main kinds: (i) *sensory* (or afferent) which carry information from the sense organs to the CNS; (ii) *motor* (or efferent) which carry information from the CNS to the muscles and glands; and (iii) *inter* (or connector) which connect neurons to other neurons and integrate the activities of sensory and motor neurons. Interneurons are the most numerous and constitute about 97 per cent of the total number of neurons in the CNS, which is the only part of the NS in which they are found.

6.   Although no two neurons are identical, most share the same basic structure and they work in essentially the same way. Figure 15.2 shows a typical motor neuron.

The *cell body* houses the nucleus (which contains the genetic code), the cytoplasm (which feeds the nucleus) and the other mechanisms common to all living cells. The *dendrites* branch out from the cell body and it is through

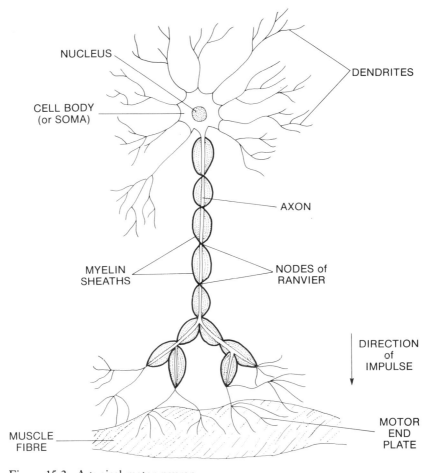

Figure 15.2   A typical motor neuron

the dendrites that the neuron makes electrochemical contact with other neurons by *receiving* incoming signals from neighbouring neurons. The *axon* is a thin cylinder of protoplasm which projects away from the cell body and carries the signals, received by the dendrites, to other neurons. A *myelin sheath* is a white fatty substance (made from specialized Schwann cells) which insulates the axon and speeds up the rate of conduction of signals down the axon and towards the *terminal buttons* (or boutons or synaptic knobs).

As Figure 15.3 shows, the terminal buttons house a number of tiny sacs or *synaptic vesicles* which contain between 10 and 100,000 molecules of a chemical messenger called a *neurotransmitter*. When an electrochemical impulse has passed down the axon and arrives at a terminal button, the vesicles discharge their contents into the minute gap between the end of the terminal button (referred to as the *presynaptic membrane*) and the dendrite of the receiving neuron (the *postsynaptic membrane*) called the *synaptic cleft* (or gap).

The neurotransmitter molecules cross the gap and combine with special receptor sites in the post-synaptic membrane of the dendrite of the receiving neuron. The *synapse*, therefore, refers to the junction between neurons (there is no actual physical contact between them) at which signals are passed from a sending to a recipient neuron through the release of neurotransmitters.

However, some neurons use a form of direct electrical influence, although these 'electrotonic' synapses are not well understood (MacVicar and Dudek, 1981), and synapses are sometimes found between dendrite and dendrite, axon and cell body and between axon and axon. However, the most common arrangement is for neurons to interconnect at synapses where a form of chemical communication is used (Iversen, 1979).

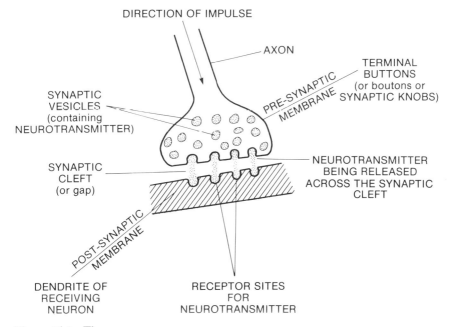

Figure 15.3   The synapse

7.   The electrochemical signal which passes down the axon is called an *action potential*. Before the action potential occurs, an inactive neuron has concentrations of positively charged *potassium* (K+) ions (electrically charged potassium atoms) and large, negatively charged protein molecules. Outside the neuron, in the surrounding fluid, there are concentrations of positively charged *sodium* ions (Na+) and negatively charged *chloride* ions (Cl−). The large, negatively charged, protein ions are trapped inside the neuron, while the positively charged sodium ions are kept out by the action of the sodium-potassium pumps which allow potassium (and chloride) ions to move in and out fairly freely.

The overall effect of this uneven distribution of ions is that the *inside* of the cell is electrically *negative* relative to the outside (by about 70 millivolts); the neuron is said to be *impermeable* to positively charged sodium ions and this describes its resting state or *resting potential*.

When an action potential occurs, the inside of the neuron momentarily changes from negative to positive (+40 millivolts), sodium channels are opened (for 1 millisecond) and sodium ions flood into the neuron (it is now permeable to sodium ions). This sets off a chain reaction, whereby the sodium channels open at adjacent membrane sites all the way down the axon; but almost as soon as the sodium channels are opened, so they close again and potassium channels are opened instead, allowing potassium ions *out* through the membrane and restoring the negative resting potential.

Because the myelin sheath is not continuous but segmented (so that at the *Nodes* of *Ranvier* the axon is actually exposed), the action potential jumps from one node to another down the axon; this is called *saltatory conduction* and is actually faster than if the sheaths were continuous. (See Figure 15.2.)

8.   Some synapses are *excitatory* (they 'instruct' the receiving neuron to 'fire', ie to conduct an action potential) while others are *inhibitory* (they 'instruct' the receiving neuron *not* to 'fire'). Because each neuron may have between 1000 and 10, 000 synapses, some of which will be excitatory and some inhibitory, the 'decision' to fire or not to fire will depend on the *combined* effect of all its receiving synapses; if enough excitatory synapses are active, their combined effect may add up to exceed the threshold for firing of the receiving neuron (this is called *summation*).

9.   Inhibitory synapses are important because they help control the spread of excitation through the highly interconnected NS and so keep activity channelled in appropriate networks or 'circuits'; epileptic seizures or fits, for example, may be caused by excitation of many different brain circuits at the same time and if it were not for inhibition, we might all be having seizures much of the time.

10.   The stimulus to the neuron must be intense enough to produce an action potential, that is, it must exceed the *threshold of response*, but once this has been passed, it travels, at the same speed, to the end of the axon. So an impulse is either present or absent (the *all-or-none rule*).

11.   Action potentials are all of the same strength (amplitude), so the intensity of the stimulus is measured by: (a) the *frequency* of firing, whereby the stronger the stimulus, the more often the neuron will fire (a *very* strong stimulus producing a volley of impulses); and (b) the *number* of neurons

stimulated, whereby the stronger the stimulus, the greater the number of neurons stimulated.

12. However strong the stimulus, there is always a very short interval after each firing (one or two milliseconds) during which no further impulse can pass; this is the *absolute refractory period*. This is followed by a *relative refractory period*; the stronger the stimulus, the shorter the interval between the absolute refractory period and the next impulse.

13. Neurons vary considerably in size; for example, a neuron in the spinal cord may have an axon two or three feet long running from the tip of the spine down to the big toe, while in the brain, neurons are only a few one-thousandths of an inch long.

14. Axons of motor neurons which terminate in muscles end in a series of branches, tipped by motor end plates, each of which is attached to a single muscle fibre; impulses at the motor end plate cause the muscle to contract (eg the arm is raised).

15. A *nerve* is a bundle of elongated axons belonging to hundreds or thousands of neurons; they spread out to every part of the body, sense receptors, skin, muscles and internal organs. Twelve pairs of *cranial nerves* leave the brain through holes in the skull and 31 pairs of *spinal nerves* leave the spinal cord through the vertebrae; together, they constitute the nerves of the PNS.
Nerves are usually large enough to be seen with the naked eye, while neurons can only be seen with the help of a powerful microscope.

16. What makes a synapse either excitatory or inhibitory is the particular *neurotransmitter(s)* contained within the vesicles of the synaptic button.
As we have seen, neurotransmitter molecules cross the synaptic cleft and then attach themselves to specific receptor sites in the post-synaptic membrane; these sites actually consist of large protein molecules. A region on the surface of the receptor site is precisely tailored to match the shape of the transmitter molecule (in a lock-and-key fashion). The effect of the transmitter is brought to an end either by *deactivation* (where it is destroyed by special enzymes) or by *re-uptake* (where it is pumped back into the pre-synaptic axon, either for destruction or re-cycling).
According to Iversen (1979) and Rosenzweig and Leiman (1982) there are at least 30 different neurotransmitters in the brain, each with its specific excitatory or inhibitory effect on certain neurons; the various chemicals are localized in specific groups of neurons and pathways and are not randomly distributed throughout the brain. Some of the major transmitters and their effects are shown in Table 15.1 overleaf.
There is some evidence that more than one kind of transmitter may be released from the same synaptic button depending on the pattern of action potentials reaching it (Lloyd et al, 1984).
A distinction is sometimes made between: (i) *neurotransmitters* which have a fairly direct influence on receiving neurons; and (ii) *neuromodulators*, which 'tune' or 'prime' neurons so that they will respond in a particular way to later stimulation by a neurotransmitter.
Included among this group of neuromodulators are certain neuropeptides

Table 15.1 Major neurotransmitters and their effects

Neurotransmitter	Effect on receiving neuron	Related behaviour
1. Acetylcholine (ACh)	Generally *excitatory* but can be *inhibitory*, depending on the type of receptor molecule involved.	Voluntary movement of muscles, behavioural inhibition, drinking, memory.
2. Norepinephrine (Noradrenaline)	*Inhibitory* (in CNS) and *excitatory* (in ANS)	Wakefulness and arousal — behavioural and emotional, eating. Some forms of recurrent *depression* associated with low levels and *mania* with high levels.
3. Dopamine	*Inhibitory* and *excitatory*	Voluntary movement, emotional arousal. *Parkinson's disease* caused by atrophy of dopamine–releasing neurons (which link the midbrain to the corpus striatum). *Schizophrenia* may be caused by over-activity of dopamine in the hypothalamus, limbic system and medial forebrain bundle which mediate emotion and thought. Abnormally high concentrations of dopamine and dopamine receptors in brains of deceased schizophrenics (Snyder, 1980).
4. Serotonin	*Inhibitory* and *excitatory*	Sleep, temperature regulation.

Neurotransmitters 2, 3 (and 4) are grouped as: Monoamine Transmitters

5. GABA (gamma-amino butyric acid).	*Inhibitory* It is the most common inhibitor in the CNS (up to one third of all the brain's synaptic buttons) and is found in all parts of the CNS.	Motor behaviour. The inherited disease *Huntington's chorea* may result from degeneration of GABA cells in the corpus striatum which is involved in motor control. (Perry et al, 1973.)
6. Glycine	*Inhibitory* Found in the spinal cord.	Spinal reflexes and other motor behaviour.
7. Glutomate	*Excitatory*	Unknown
8. Aspartate	*Excitatory*	Unknown
9. Peptides	*Inhibitory* and *excitatory*	Sensory transmission, especially pain.

Table 15.2 The effect of major psychoactive drugs on neurotransmitters, physiology, mood and behaviour

Drug	Neurotransmitters affected	Effects on physiology, mood and behaviour
1. Curare (used by South American Indians to poison their arrows).	Acetylcholine (ACh) Prevented from acting because the curare molecules cover up the postsynaptic receptor sites of the muscle neurons	Fatal muscular paralysis. The brain is not affected — but all other muscles, including respiratory muscles, are paralysed
2. Botulinum toxin (present in improperly-prepared food)	Acetylcholine (ACh)	Paralysis which is often fatal (= botulism)
3. Nerve gases and insectisides	Acetylcholine (ACh)	Fatal muscular paralysis
4. Amphetamines ('Speed or Uppers') eg Benzedrine Dexedrine Methedrine Drinamyl ('Purple Hearts')	Dopamine and Norepinephrine — their re-uptake is blocked, making them effective for longer.	Seem to act more as psychomotor stimulants than antidepressants (which is how they are often presented). Increase alertness, counteract fatigue and lethargy and produce feelings of confidence and decisiveness. Suppress appetite. (Through stimulation of Reticular Activating System which controls overall level of arousal and 'mimicking' the sympathetic branch of the ANS). But high doses can induce symptoms identical with paranoid schizophrenia
5. Antidepressants A. Tricyclics Imipramine (Tofranil) Amitriptyline (Tryptizol)	Work by blocking the breakdown of norepinephrine and serotonin	Feeling of euphoria. They block Rapid Eye Movement (REM) sleep.
B. Monoamine oxidase (MAO) Inhibitors Phenelzine (Nardil) Tranylcypromine (Parnate)	These inhibit the enzyme Monoamine oxidase (MAO) which breaks down the monoamine transmitters subsequent to their release.	

6. L-DOPA	Dopamine The body converts the drug into dopamine.	Prescribed for patients with Parkinson's disease. Can sometimes produce symptoms of schizophrenia.
7. *Major tranquillizers* Phenothiazines ('Antischizophrenic Drugs') Chlorpromazine (Largactil or Thorazine). Trifluoperazine (Stelazine).	Dopamine They bind to dopamine receptor sites (they are dopamine-antagonists) and so prevent dopamine from reaching those receptor sites.	Reduce schizophrenic — and other psychotic — symptoms. The Reticular Activating System is *not* affected, nor the Electroencephalogram (EEG). But electrical activity in hypothalamus and limbic system is suppressed.
8. *Minor tranquillizers* Benzodiazepines ('Antianxiety Drugs' or Anxiolytic sedatives) Diazepam (Valium) Chlordiazepoxide (Librium) Meprobamate (Miltown)	Inosine (which might be a neurotransmitter modulator) binds with the same receptor sites as these drugs. It could be the body's own anxiety reliever (Skolnick, 1979). GABA	A calming effect, reducing anxiety and tension without depressing the level of alertness. Valium prescribed to patients with Huntington's Chorea may help by stimulating GABA receptors
9. *Hallucinogenic drugs* LSD (lysergic acid diethylamide) Psilocybin ('magic mushroom')	Structurally similar to serotonin	Produce feelings of calm, contentment, inner peace, increased appetite and possible disorientation (cannabis); illusions, hallucinations, distortions of time perception and contact with 'reality' (LSD).
Mescaline	Structurally similar to norepinephrine and dopamine	
Cannabis (marijuana, hashish, pot, weed, grass, etc.).	They seem to work by blocking the effects of *serotonin*, which usually inhibits thought processes and emotions	Overdoses of LSD can cause psychotic reactions and could kill.
Phencyclidine (PCP or 'Angel Dust')	May attach themselves to serotonin receptor sites, preventing the sites from receiving it. The result is that consciousness becomes flooded with remote associations and feelings (Siegel and Jarvik, 1975).	LSD, *psilocybin* and *mescaline* are also referred to as 'Psychedelics'. All hallucinogenic drugs are also called 'Psychotomimetic', which means 'imitation of psychosis', because some produce effects very similar to schizophrenia.

(*Continued*)

Table 15.2 (*Continued*)

Drug	Neurotransmitters affected	Effects on physiology, mood and behaviour
10. *Sedatives (or depressants)* Barbiturates (Luminal — phenobarbitone Amytal — amylobarbitone Nembutal, Seconal, Pentothal) Alcohol	In large quantities these are sleep-inducers (*hypnotics*) and may act in a similar way to certain anaesthetics. In smaller doses, they act more like (minor) tranquillizers combined with alcohol, they can be fatal.	In small amounts, barbiturates and alcohol can act as stimulants by reducing anxiety and reducing inhibitions. Larger quantities induce sedation, stupor (sleep), anaesthesia, loss of consciousness and death (Ornstein, 1977). Larger amounts may cause people to become belligerent and abusive, disorientated and confused and may experience hallucinations. Addicts who are withdrawn from alcohol often suffer 'delirium tremens' (the D.T's) which can be fatal.
Opiates (Narcotics) (Codeine, Morphine, Heroin)	Opium comes from the juice of certain types of poppy, its active ingredients are *codeine* and *morphine*. Morphine is stronger than codeine and *heroin* (derived from morphine) is the strongest narcotic of all. Neural tissue is eventually destroyed after prolonged use of heroin and the *endorphins* are under-produced.	At first, heroin produces intense pleasure but repeated use produces *tolerance* — ie. ever-increasing amounts must be taken to achieve the same effect. Tolerance soon gives way to physical and psychological *dependence*, otherwise known as *addiction*.
11. *Stimulants* Caffeine Nicotine Cocaine	Caffeine is found in tea and coffee and many carbonated drinks, particularly colas.	*Nicotine* may have a relaxing or stimulating effect, depending on circumstances. It is addictive. Effects of *cocaine* similar to those of amphetamines but former is addictive.

(which are included in Table 15.1), notably the *encephalins* ('in the head') and the *endorphins* ('morphine-within'), which are also known as *optoids* because functionally they resemble the opium drugs morphine, heroin and opium itself.

Morphine is commonly used for the relief of severe, intractable pain and the discovery of 'opiate receptors' in the neurons (Pert et al, 1974) strongly suggested that the brain creates its own powerful pain-killer; encephalins and endorphins seemed to fit the bill and they may work by interfering with the release of transmitters from the pre-synaptic membrane of neurons which transmit information about pain.

It is thought that they are released during acupuncture (eg Watson, 1980) and hypnosis, producing a reduction in perceived pain, but pain-information probably still reaches the brain (since it is not the pain receptors which are directly influenced). (See Chapter 16.)

It is also believed that placebos ('dummy drugs') work by influencing the release of endorphins (Fields, 1979, Watkins and Mayer, 1982) and they may be important in how animals deal with pain and stress (Riley et al, 1980).

Other neuromodulators are the *prostoglandins* which cause long-term shifts in neuronal sensitivity (Lloyd et al, 1984); it is believed that a deficiency in prostoglandins may cause schizophrenia (Harrobin, 1980).

Other neuropeptides are found as *hormones*, including: (i) *vasopressin*, which is thought to play a role in memory; (ii) *corticosteroids* ('stress hormones') and *adrenocorticotrophic hormone* (ACTH) which are involved in stress reactions and emotional arousal; and (iii) *androgens* (male sex hormones) which regulate sex drive in both sexes. (See the later section on the Endocrine System.)

17. The *effect* of *drugs* on *behaviour* is mediated by their effect on neurotransmitters. The drugs which psychologists are particularly interested in are *psychoactive* drugs, those which produce mental effects ('active' in the 'psyche') and directly alter the level of activity in one or more brain systems (either increasing or decreasing it) (Cooper et al, 1982). Table 15.2 summarizes the effects on mood and behaviour of some major drugs, together with effects on neurotransmitters.

The Central Nervous System (CNS)

Methods of Studying the Brain
How do we know what we know?

1) One of the earliest methods used was the study of patients who had suffered brain damage, either as the result of an accident or a stroke or tumour. A famous and early use of this method led to the discovery of a specialized area of the brain for speech.

In 1869, a French physician, Paul Broca, reviewed evidence from a number of cases of brain damage and concluded that injury to a certain part of the left cerebral hemisphere caused the patient's speech to become slow and laboured but ability to understand speech was almost completely unaffected. What is now called *Broca's Area* seems to control the ability to produce speech and damage to it causes *motor* (or expressive) *aphasia*.

In 1874, Carl Wernicke reported that injury to a different part of the left hemisphere caused *receptive aphasia*, that is, the inability to understand speech (one's own or someone else's).

These *clinical* studies of the brain have usually been conducted in parallel with *anatomical* studies, usually during the course of post-mortems where human beings are involved. Studying *structure* and *function* in a complementary way is essential for an adequate understanding of such a complex organ as the brain.

2) Where *animal experiments* are concerned (as in other areas of psychology), parts of the brain may be *surgically removed* (either through cutting or burning out with electrodes—a method called *ablation*) or an area of the brain may be damaged (rather than removed), in which case a *lesion* is produced. An early user of the first method was Karl Lashley, working with rats in the 1920s, and it has been used extensively to study the role of the brain in eating (see Chapter 17).

One major exception to the rule that the subjects in these surgical experiments are always animals is *split-brain* patients, who have undergone surgery for epilepsy when all other treatments have failed. The surgery involves cutting the tissue which connects the two halves of the brain (the corpus callosum) and Roger Sperry and his colleagues in the 1960s and 1970s made full use of the unique opportunity to study these 'split brains'. Their work will be discussed in detail later in the chapter.

3) Instead of surgically removing or damaging the brain, it can be *stimulated*, either chemically (using micro-pipettes to drop transmitter substances onto specific areas of the brain) or, more commonly, electrically, using *micro-electrodes*, whereby precise locations can be stimulated. Again, where humans are the subjects, they are usually already undergoing surgery for a brain tumour or some other abnormality (such as epilepsy) and the neurosurgeon takes advantage of the fact that the patient is conscious, alert and able to report memories, sensations and so on produced by the stimulation. Wilder Penfield pioneered this kind of research in the 1950s.

4) *Microelectrodes* are also used to *record* the electrical activity in individual neurons when the subject (usually a cat or monkey) is presented with various kinds of stimuli; this was the method used by Hubel and Wiesel in the 1960s to study visual feature detectors. (See Chapters 4 and 5.)

5) The electrical activity of the brain can also be recorded from the outside by fitting electrodes to the scalp; this can be traced on paper and typical brainwave patterns associated with various states of arousal have been found. This is the *electroencephalogram* (EEG) which records action potentials for large groups of neurons and has been used extensively in the study of states of consciousness, including sleep (see Chapter 16).

A brief change in the EEG may be produced by the presentation of a single stimulus but the effect may well be lost (or obscured) in the overall pattern of waves. However, if the stimulus is presented repeatedly, and the results averaged by a computer, other waves cancel out and the evoked response can be detected. This technique is known as the *Average Evoked Potential* and has shown, for example, that an identical visual stimulus yields different AEPs according to the meaning the subject attaches to it (Johnston and Chesney, 1974).

6) A relatively recent method involves *radioactive labelling* which takes advantage of the brain's flexible use of blood-carried oxygen. A radioactive isotope is added to the blood, causing low levels of radioactivity which increase as greater blood flow occurs to more active areas of the brain. A scanner next to the head feeds radiation readings to a computer, which produces a coloured map of the most and least active brain regions; different regions change colour as the person attempts a variety of tasks or is presented with a variety of stimuli (Lassen et al, 1978).

7) Another use of computers is the CAT-scan (Computerized Axial Tomography); a moving X-ray beam takes pictures from different positions around the head which are converted by the computer into 'brain slices', apparent cross-sections of the brain. It is used primarily for the detection and diagnosis of brain injury and disease but is not as efficient as the more recent PET (Position Emission Tomography). This uses the same computer-calculation approach as CAT but uses radiation for the information from which the brain-slices are computed (Ter-Pogossian et al, 1980). A radio-active tracer is added to a substance used by the body (eg oxygen or glucose); as the marked substance is metabolized, PET shows the pattern of its use, for example, more or less use of glucose could indicate a tumour and changes are revealed when the eyes are opened or closed (Phelps et al, 1981).

More recently still, Nuclear Magnetic Resonance Imaging (NMR) (Schulman, 1983) applies a magnetic field and measures its effects on the rota-tion of atomic nuclei of some element in the body; again, a computerized cross-sectional image is produced. So far only hydrogen nuclei have been used.

What can these various methods tell us?

As psychologists, of course, we must not lose sight of the significance of these methods—we are not interested in the brain for its own sake (as fascinating as this may be) but for what it can tell us about the control of psychological functions and abilities, both subjective and behavioural. It is tempting to infer that if damage to (or loss of) a particular brain area is associated with the loss of (or reduction in) a particular ability, that part of the brain normally controls that ability; unfortunately, there are other possibilities. For example, the damaged area might itself be controlled by a different (undamaged) area or the damage may have disrupted the normal functioning of nearby, or related, intact areas. We shall return to some of these issues later when we discuss split-brain patients.

Development of the Brain

One of the most remarkable things about the human brain is not its size or even the number of neurons of which it is composed but rather the staggering complexity of the interconnections between the neurons; given that there are somewhere between 8 to 10 billion neurons, each of which may have between 1,000 and 10,000 synaptic connections with other neurons, it has been estimated that there are more possible ways in which the neurons of a single human brain can be interconnected than there are atoms in the known universe!

It is the development of synaptic connections which accounts for much of the increase in brain weight after birth. At birth, the baby has almost its full complement of neurons and the brain is closer at birth to its adult size than any other organ. (It represents 10 per cent of the baby's total body weight compared with 2 per cent of the adult's.)

At 6 months, it is already half its eventual adult weight, at 12 months, 60 per cent, at 5 years, 90 per cent and at 10 years 95 per cent; the increase in weight is almost 200 per cent in the first three years and reaches its maximum weight by about 20 years. The average male adult brain weighs 1375 grammes (about 3 pounds) and the female 1250 grammes. While the major development before birth is the growth of neurons, brain growth after birth is the result of four major changes:

i)   We have already mentioned the growth of *synaptic* connections between neighbouring neurons. The continued growth or survival of any given neuron in fact depends on the establishment of synaptic connections with other neurons, and the death of individual neurons is extremely common during brain development (Oppenheim, 1981, Wolff, 1981). Indeed, the period of *peak* development in any one brain area is marked by the *greatest* rate of cell death in that area which will occur during the lifetime of the organism, a much higher rate than is associated with ageing, for example (see Chapter 24).

ii) The neurons do actually increase in *size* (but not in number).

iii) *Glial* cells develop (and are ten times more numerous than neurons); they 'pad out' the space in between neurons and supply them with vital nutrients.

iv) *Myelin sheaths* grow around the axons to insulate the neuron and speed up the conduction of action potentials.

Once fully grown, the brain loses weight by about 1 gramme each year.

If it were the absolute size of brains which determined level of intelligence, then humans would certainly be surpassed by many species, and even if we take *brain size : body size* ratio, we would still find that house mice, porpoises, tree shrews and squirrel monkeys come higher in the intelligence league than ourselves.

Clearly, it is the *kind* of brain which is important and what seems to be unique about the human brain is the proportion of it which is *not* devoted to particular physical and psychological functions and which is, therefore, 'free' to facilitate our intelligence, our general ability to think, reason, use language and learn.

The Major Structures and Functions of the Brain

Figure 15.1 (on page 371) shows that the brain is normally subdivided into: (i) the Forebrain; (ii) the Midbrain; and (iii) the Hindbrain. We shall discuss them in this order. (See Figure 15.4.)

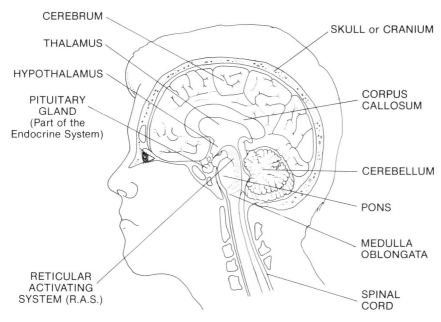

CEREBRUM

THALAMUS

HYPOTHALAMUS

PITUITARY
GLAND
(Part of the
Endocrine System)

RETICULAR
ACTIVATING
SYSTEM (R.A.S.)

SKULL or CRANIUM

CORPUS
CALLOSUM

CEREBELLUM

PONS

MEDULLA
OBLONGATA

SPINAL
CORD

Figure 15.4 A cross-section of the human brain, showing the inner face of the right cerebral hemisphere

1) The Forebrain

a) The Cerebral Hemispheres (or Cerebrum)
The cerebral hemispheres are the two large structures at the top of the brain which enfold (and, therefore, conceal from view) most other brain structures—if you were to remove an intact brain, its appearance would be dominated by the massive hemispheres, with just the cerebellum and brain-stem showing at the back.

The top layers of the cerebrum (about 1 cm at its deepest) is the *cerebral cortex* (usually just called 'cortex' which means 'bark'); it is highly con-voluted or wrinkled (see Figure 15.5(a)) which is necessary in order to pack its 2½ square feet surface area into the relatively small space inside the cranium.

It is pinkish-grey in colour (hence 'grey matter') but below the cortex the cerebrum consists of much thicker white matter which consists of myelinated axons (the cortex consists of cell bodies).

There is a large crevice running along the cerebrum from front to back (the *longitudinal fissure* or *sulcus*) which divides the two hemispheres, but further down they are connected by a dense mass of commissurial ('joining') fibres called the *corpus callosum* (or 'hard body').

In each hemisphere, there are two other natural dividing lines: (i) the *lateral fissure* (or fissure of Sylvius); and (ii) the *central fissure* (or fissure of Rolando). The lateral fissure separates the *temporal lobe* from the *frontal lobe* (anteriorly) and from the *parietal lobe* (posteriorly), while the central fissure separates the frontal and parietal lobes. The *occipital lobe* is situated behind the parietal lobe and is at the back of the head (see Figure 15.5 (a)).

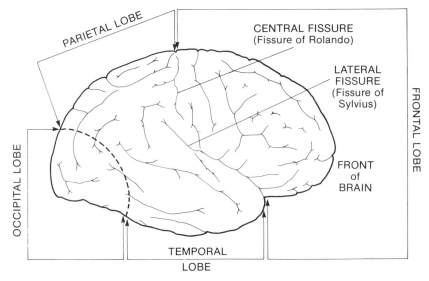

Figure 15.5(a) The major structural sub-divisions of the cerebral cortex

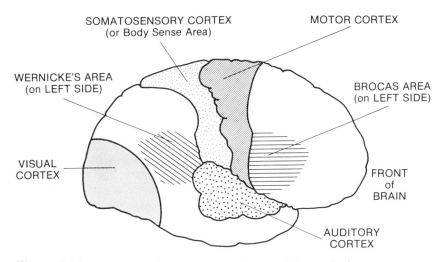

Figure 15.5(b) The major functional sub-divisions of the cerebral cortex

(Remember, this division of the cortex into four lobes—named after the bones beneath which they lie—is a feature of *both* hemispheres, which are mirror-images of each other.)

As Figure 15.5 (b) shows, the *visual cortex* is found in the occipital lobe, the auditory cortex in the temporal lobe, the *somatosensory* (or body-sense) *cortex* in the parietal lobe and the *motor cortex* in the frontal lobe.

The somatosensory cortex and motor cortex are perhaps the most well-defined areas and both show *contralateral control*, that is, areas in the *right* hemisphere receive information from and are concerned with the activities of the *left* side of the body—and vice-versa. The crossing over takes place in the medulla (part of the brain stem) and is called corticospinal decussation. These areas represent the body in an upside-down fashion, so information from the feet, for example, is received by neurons at the top of the area.

Furthermore, the *amount* of cortex taken up with the motor activities of, or sensory information from, different parts of the body is associated *not* with the size of that body part but with the degree of precise motor control or the sensitivity of that part of the body. So fingers have much more cortex devoted to them than the trunk, for example, in the motor cortex and the lips have a very large representation in the somatosensory cortex.

Broca's area is found in the frontal lobe and Wernicke's area borders the temporal and parietal lobes but in the *left* hemisphere only. (We shall say more about this under *localization* of brain function.)

About three-quarters of the cortex does not have an obvious sensory or motor function and is known as the *association cortex*; this is where the 'higher mental functions' (cognition)—thinking, reasoning, learning etc—probably 'occur' but except for certain aspects of memory and perception these aspects of human intelligence have resisted attempts to localize them. However, there is no doubt that the cortex is not necessary for biological survival (this is controlled by various *sub*-cortical structures), since some species do not have one to begin with (eg birds) and in those that do, surgical removal does not prevent the animal from displaying a wide range of behaviour—although it becomes much more automatic and stereotyped. Also, the human brain has a greater proportion of association cortex than any other species.

According to Suomi (1982), what makes the cortex of special interest to the developmental psychobiologist is: first, that it is the last part of the brain to stop growing and differentiating; secondly, it undergoes greater structural change and transformation *after* birth than any other part of the brain; and, thirdly, a greater number of neural interconnections are made *after* birth than during the pre-natal period.

According to Conel (1959), the sequence of cortical development is: (i) the motor area; (ii) the somatosensory area; (iii) the visual area; and (iv) the auditory area. It is interesting to try to relate this sequence to the nature-nurture debate on perception (see Chapter 5) and Piaget's theory of cognitive development, in which motor activity plays such a vital part (see Chapter 19).

b) The Thalamus ('deep chamber')

There are actually two thalami, situated deep in the forebrain (between the brain-stem and the cerebral hemispheres). Each is an egg-shaped mass of grey matter and represents a crucial link between the cerebrum and the sense organs. *All* sensory signals pass through the thalamus, which serves as a relay station or major integrator of information flowing in from the sense organs to the cortex; each contains nuclei which are specialized to handle particular types of signal:

i)   The *ventrobasal complex* which takes information fed in from the body via the spinal cord;

ii) The *lateral geniculate* ('bent') *body* (LGB) which processes visual information (see Chapter 4);

iii) The *medial geniculate body* which processes auditory information.

The thalamus also receives information from the cortex, mainly dealing with complex limb movements, and these are directed to the cerebellum. Another part of the thalamus plays a part in sleep and waking.

c)   The Hypothalamus ('under the thalamus')
For its size (which is about the size of the tip of your index finger) the hypothalamus is a remarkable and extremely important part of the brain. It plays a major part in homoeostasis (control of the body's internal environment) and motivation, including eating and drinking, sexual behaviour and emotional arousal.

Seven areas can be identified, each with its own special function: (i) *posterior* (sex drive); (ii) *anterior* (water balance): (iii) *supraoptic*, also water balance: (iv) *presupraoptic* (heat control): (v) *ventromedial* (hunger): (vi) *dorsomedial* (aggression); and (vii) *dorsal* (pleasure).
(The role of the hypothalamus, particularly in relation to hunger and eating, is discussed in detail in Chapter 17.)

The hypothalamus works basically in two ways: (i) by sending electro-chemical signals to the entire ANS, so that it represents a major link between the CNS and the ANS; and (ii) by influencing the *pituitary gland*, to which it is connected by a network of blood vessels and neurons. You can see from Figure 15.4 that the pituitary gland is situated in the brain, just below and to one side of the hypothalamus, but it is not part of the CNS; it is in fact part of the *endocrine* (hormonal) *system* which we shall discuss later in the chapter (and see Chapter 17).

d)   Basal Ganglia ('nerve knots')
These are embedded in the mass of white matter of each cerebral hemisphere and are themselves small areas of grey matter, in fact comprising a number of smaller structures: (i) the *corpus striatum* ('striped body'), composed of the lentiform nucleus and caudate nucleus; (ii) the *amygdala* ('almond'); and (iii) the *substantia nigra*. These structures are closely linked to the thalamus and they seem to play a part in muscle tone and posture by integrating and co-ordinating the main voluntary muscle movements which are the concern of the great descending motor pathway (the *pyramidal system*). Information from the cortex is relayed to the brain stem and cerebellum.

e)   The Limbic System ('bordering')
This is not a separate structure but comprises a number of highly interrelated structures which, when seen from the side, seem to nest inside each other, encircling the brain-stem in a 'wishbone'.

The major structures are: (a) the thalamus; (b) hypothalamus; (c) mamillary body; (d) anterior commissure; (e) septum pellucidum; (f) cingulate gyrus; (g) hippocampus; (h) amygdala; (i) fornix; and (j) olfactory bulb.

The limbic system is very similar to that of primitive mammals and so is often called 'the old mammalian brain'. It is also sometimes called the 'nose brain' because much of its development seems to have been related to the olfactory sense (and, of course, the olfactory bulb is one of its components).

It is closely involved with behaviours which satisfy certain motivational and emotional needs, including feeding, fighting, escape and mating and its role in relation to aggression was discussed in detail in Chapter 13.

The hippocampus is involved in memory; someone whose hippocampus is damaged is very easily distracted and they will be unable to carry out an intended sequence of actions (eg making a cup of tea) because they have forgotten what they had planned to do. (See Chapter 6.)

The limbic system as a whole serves as a meeting place between the cortex (or 'neocortex', in evolutionary terms the most recent part of the brain to have developed) and older parts of the brain, such as the hypothalamus. From the cortex it receives interpreted information about the world and from the hypothalamus information about the body's internal state; these are integrated and the 'conclusions' are fed back to the cortex and to the older, sub-cortical areas.

2) The Midbrain

This is really an extension of the brain stem and connects the forebrain to the spinal cord. The main structure is the *Reticular Activating System* (RAS) which ascends from the spinal cord to the forebrain carrying mainly sensory information (the ARAS) and descends from the forebrain to the spinal cord carrying mainly motor information.

The ARAS is vitally important in maintaining our general level of arousal or alertness (and is often called the 'consciousness switch') and plays an important part (but by no means the only one) in the sleep–waking cycle (see Chapter 16). It also plays a part in selective attention; although it responds unselectively to all kinds of stimulation, it helps to screen extraneous sensory information, by, for example, controlling *habituation* to constant sources of stimulation and making us alert and responsive mainly to *changes* in stimulation (see Chapter 4).

The sleeping parent who keeps 'one ear open' for the baby who might start to cry is relying on their ARAS to let only very important sensory signals through, so it acts as a kind of sentry for the cortex. Damage can induce a coma-like state of sleep.

The midbrain also contains important centres for visual and auditory reflexes, including the *orienting reflex*, a general response to a novel stimulus. Birds which sight, track and capture prey in flight have very prominent and bulging areas in their midbrain and bats have a very prominent auditory area in the midbrain.

3) The Hindbrain

a) Cerebellum ('little brain')

Like the cerebrum, this consists of two halves or hemispheres and is even more convoluted than the cortex. It synthesizes all sensory information from vision, the inner ear (which controls balance), the muscles and the joints and can calculate the movements required in a particular sequence of behaviour. So the cerebellum plays a vital role in the co-ordination of voluntary (skeletal) muscle activity, balance and fine movements (such as reaching for things); motor commands which originate in higher brain centres are processed here before transmission to the muscles.

Damage to the cerebellum can cause hand tremors, drunken movements, loss of balance and the inability to reach for objects normally (*ataxia*) and hand tremors are quite common amongst the elderly.

The cerebellum also controls the intricate movements involved in the swimming of a fish, the flying of a bird and playing a musical instrument or driving a car. Once learned, complex movements such as are involved in signing our name, picking up a glass, walking, even talking, seem to be 'programmed' into the cerebellum, so that we can do them 'automatically', without having to think consciously about what we are doing; the cerebellum acts like an 'automatic pilot' inside the brain.

The cerebellum accounts for about 11 per cent of the entire brain weight and only the cerebrum is larger. Its grey matter in fact consists of three layers of cells, the middle layer of which, the *purkinje* cells, can link each synapse with up to 100,000 other neurons, more than any other kind of brain cell.

b) The Pons ('bridge')
This is a bulge of white matter which connects the two halves of the cerebellum. It is an important connection between the midbrain and the medulla and is vital in integrating the movements of the two sides of the body. Four of the twelve cranial nerves (which originate in the brain) have their nuclei ('relay stations') here, including the large trigeminal nerve. It is the middle portion of the brain stem.

c) The Medulla Oblongata ('rather long marrow')
This is a fibrous section of the lower brain stem (about 2 cm long) and is really a thick extension of the spinal cord. In evolutionary terms, it is the oldest part of the brain and it is the site of the crossing over of the major nerve tracts coming up from the spinal cord and coming down from the brain.

It contains vital reflex centres, which control breathing, cardiac function, swallowing, vomiting, coughing, chewing, salivation and facial movements.

(The midbrain, pons and medulla together make up the *brain-stem*.)

The Spinal Cord
About the thickness of a little finger, the spinal cord passes down the whole length of the back from the brain-stem, encased in the vertebrae of the spine. The spinal cord is the main communication 'cable' between the brain (CNS) and the PNS, providing the pathway between body and brain.

Messages enter and leave the spinal cord by means of 31 pairs of spinal nerves; each pair innervates a different and fairly specific part of the body and are 'mixed', that is, they contain both motor and sensory neurons for most of their length. However, at the junction with the cord itself, the nerves divide into two roots—the *dorsal root* (towards the back of the body) which contains sensory neurons, and the *ventral root* (towards the front of the body) which contains motor neurons.

The spinal cord constitutes a simplified model (compared with the brain) of a neurological system which receives sensory information, processes it and then delivers impulses to the muscles for the initiation and co-ordination of motor activity. The basic *functional* unit of the NS is the spinal reflex arc, for instance, the *knee-jerk reflex* involves just two kinds of neurons: a sensory neuron conveys information about stimulation of the patella tendon to the spinal cord and this information crosses a single synapse within the grey 'butterfly' (which runs inside the centre of the cord), which causes a motor neuron to stimulate the appropriate muscle groups in the leg which causes the leg to shoot up in the air.

However, most spinal reflexes are more complex than this; for example, withdrawing your hand from a hot plate will involve an interneuron (as well as a sensory and motor) and two synapses. Commonly, the experience of pain follows one or two seconds after you have withdrawn your hand—this is how long it takes for sensory information to reach the cortex.

The Localization of Brain Function

So far we have said about the cerebral hemispheres that: (a) they are mirror-images of each other; (b) they both divide into four lobes; but (c) Broca's area and Wernicke's area (which deal with speech production and comprehension respectively) only appear in the *left* hemisphere.

This (and other evidence) has led to the view that the hemispheres are functionally different (*functional lateralization*) and much of the discussion has focused on language. From studies of stroke victims in particular it is generally agreed that for the majority of *right*-handed people their *left* hemisphere is *dominant* for speech (and language ability in general); someone who is paralysed down their *right* side must have suffered damage to the *left* hemisphere and if they have also suffered *aphasia*, then we can infer that language is normally controlled by the *left* hemisphere.

A small proportion of right-handed people have their right hemisphere dominant for language and a few left-handed people have their right hemisphere dominant; however, it is more common for left-handed people and ambidextrous people *not* to have one or other hemisphere as dominant.

In the majority of right-handed people, anyway, is the dominance of the left hemisphere a built-in characteristic or is it modifiable?

According to Zaidel (1978), the two hemispheres are fairly equal up until about five years old. In general, a child's brain is much more *plastic* (or flexible) than an adult's (eg Rose, 1976); for example, in children up to three years, brain trauma produces similar effects regardless of which site is damaged. Provided the lesion is not too severe, or if it occurs on one side only, considerable recovery is possible—the corresponding area on the other side takes over the function of the damaged area and this seems to be especially true of speech.

This seems to support the conclusions of Lashley who (in the 1920s) studied the effects of brain destruction on rats' learning ability. His (1929) *law of mass action* states that the learning of difficult problems depends upon the *amount* of damage to the cortex and *not* the position or site of the damage; the *greater* the cortical damage, the *greater* the learning difficulty but he could not find *specific* neural circuits related to the learning of, or memory for, particular types of problem. The *law* of *equipotentiality* states that corresponding parts of the brain are capable of taking over the function normally performed by the damaged area.

Similarly, the *principle* of *multiple control* maintains that any particular part of the brain is likely to be involved in the performance of many different types of behaviour. Teitelbaum (1971), for example, found that rats with lesions in their lateral hypothalamus show deficits in certain learning situations as well as impaired feeding. Conversely, the same behaviour (eg aggression, emotion) normally involve a number of brain sites and the logical conclusion of this seems to be that the brain functions as a complete unit, an integrated whole.

However, the fascinating studies of split-brain patients suggests a very different picture.

Split-Brain Patients: One Brain or Two? One Mind or Two?

Remember that split-brain patients have undergone surgery (normally in the treatment of epilepsy) to cut their corpus callosum which normally joins the two hemispheres and allows an exchange of information from one to another. While the surgery may relieve the suffering it has a major side-effect, namely, the two hemispheres become functionally separate, ie they act as two separate, independent brains.

Sperry (based on a number of studies in the 1960s and 1970s, for which he was awarded the Nobel Prize for Medicine in 1981) and Ornstein (1975) believe that split-brain studies reveal the 'true' nature of the two hemispheres and that each embodies a different kind of consciousness (see Chapter 16).

In a typical experiment (eg Sperry and Gazzaniga, 1967), the subject sits in front of a screen with their hands free to handle objects behind the screen but which are obscured from sight by the screen. While fixating on a spot in the middle of the screen, a word (eg 'key') is flashed onto the *left* side of the screen for one-tenth of a second to ensure that the word is only 'seen' by the *right* hemisphere.

If asked to pick out the key from a pile of objects with the *left* hand (still controlled by the *right* hemisphere), this can be done quite easily; however, the subject is unable to *say* what word appeared on the screen (since the *left* hemisphere did not receive the information from the right as it would in a normal subject). The subject literally does not know why they choose that object.

Again, a word (eg 'heart') is flashed on a screen, with 'he' to the left and 'art' to the right of the fixation point. If asked to *name* the word, subjects will say 'art' (because this is the portion of the word projected to the *left* hemisphere) but when asked to point with the left hand to one of two cards on which 'he' and 'art' are written, the left hand will point to 'he' (because this was the portion projected to the *right* hemisphere).

These examples show that the right hemisphere is not completely without language ability—otherwise subjects could not successfully point or select, but it clearly lacks the left hemisphere's ability to name and articulate what has been experienced. In the second example, both hemispheres are hand-icapped if information is not conveyed from one to the other—the whole word ('heart') is not perceived by either!

A similar but perhaps more dramatic example involved sets of photographs of different faces—a beautiful young female model, a podgy-cheeked boy, an old man and so on. Each photo was cut down the middle and the halves of two different faces were pasted together. They were then presented to subjects in such a way that the left side of the photo would only be visible to the right hemisphere and vice-versa. So, for example, with an old man on the right and young boy on the left, if subjects were asked to *describe* what they had seen (the *left* hemisphere responding) they would say 'old man' but if asked to *point* with their left hand to the complete photo of the person they had seen (the *right* hemisphere responding) they would point to the 'young boy'. It seems that two completely separate visual worlds can exist within the same head!

These and many more, equally dramatic, experiments led Sperry and Ornstein to conclude that each of the separated hemispheres has its own private sensations, perceptions, thoughts, feelings and memories, in short, they constitute two separate minds, two separate spheres of consciousness (Sperry, 1964).

So while the 'consciousness of the left' is linguistic, mathematical, rational, logical and analytical, the 'consciousness of the right is non-verbal, musical, visuo-spatial, intuitive and emotional (see Chapter 16). However, not everyone accepts these conclusions.

Cohen (1975) argues that longstanding pre-surgical pathology might have caused an abnormal reorganization of the brains of these split-brain patients, so that generalizing to normal people might not be valid. She cites a study by Kinsbourne in which the left hemisphere of aphasic patients was anaesthetized but they continued to speak fluently but unintelligibly, suggesting that the abnormal speech is produced by the non-specialist *right* hemisphere. This seems to contradict the conclusions of split-brain studies that the right hemisphere has some understanding of language but is *mute*!

Also because there is not a straightforward relationship between handedness and lateralization of brain function, it is difficult to predict the effects of injuries or operations with any certainty, even when hand preference is clear. Cohen observes that although most individuals reflect the basic, language—left, visuo-spatial—right, pattern typical of right-handers, about 10 per cent of right-handers and 30 per cent of left-handers show either the opposite pattern or show functional symmetry (bilaterality or mixed-brainedness).

Cohen is also critical of studies of hemispheric lateralization using normal subjects. She concludes by arguing that the two sides of the brain do not function in isolation but form a highly integrated system. Most everyday tasks involve a mixture of 'left' and 'right' skills—in listening to speech, for instance, we analyse both the words *and* the intonation pattern, while in the appreciation of opera, an integrated perception of linguistic and musical elements occurs, and in reading, analysis of visual shapes and linguistic knowledge are both required and these may be accompanied by imagery and subvocal speech. Far from doing their own thing, the two hemispheres work very much together (Cohen, 1975).

The Autonomic Nervous System (ANS)

As Figure 15.1 shows, the ANS is the part of the PNS which controls the internal organs and glands of the body over which we have little (or any) voluntary control.

It comprises two branches, the *sympathetic*, which takes over whenever the body needs to use its energy, as in an emergency situation (the 'fight or flight'

Table 15.3 Major sympathetic and parasympathetic reactions

Organ or function affected	Sympathetic reaction	Parasympathetic reaction
1. Heart-rate	Increase	Decrease
2. Blood-pressure	Increase	Decrease
3. Secretion of saliva	Suppressed (mouth feels dry)	Stimulated
4. Pupils	Dilate (to aid vision)	Contract
5. Limbs (and trunk)	Dilation of blood vessels of the voluntary muscles (to help us run faster, for example)	Contraction of these blood vessels
6. Peristalsis (Contractions of stomach and intestines)	Slows down (You don't feel hungry in an emergency)	Speeds up
7. Galvanic Skin Response (GSR) (Measure of the electrical resistance of the skin)	Decreases (due to increased sweating, associated with increased anxiety)	Increases
8. Bladder muscles	Relaxed (there may be temporary loss of bladder control)	Contracted
9. Adrenal glands	Stimulated to secrete more adrenaline and noradrenaline	Reduced secretion
10. Breathing rate	Increased (through dilation of bronchi)	Decreased
11. Liver	Glucose (stored as glycogen) is released into the blood to increase energy	Sugar is stored
12. Emotion	Experience of strong emotion	Less extreme emotions

syndrome) and the *parasympathetic*, which is dominant when the body is at 'rest' and energy is being built up.

Essentially, therefore, the two branches work in opposite ways but they are both equally necessary for the maintenance of the delicately balanced internal state called homoeostasis, (see Chapter 17).

Sometimes a sequence of sympathetic and parasympathetic activity is required; in sexual arousal in men, erection is primarily parasympathetic while ejaculation is primarily sympathetic (Katchadourian and Lunde, 1979).

The ANS produces its effects in two ways: (i) by direct neural stimulation of body organs; and (ii) by stimulating the release of hormones from the endocrine glands; in both cases, the *hypothalamus* is the orchestrator. Table

Table 15.4 Major pituitary hormones and their effects

Hormone	Endocrine gland or organ stimulated	Effects
Growth hormone (somatotropin)	Body tissues	Increases growth of bones and muscles, particularly in childhood and adolescence. Too little produces *pituitary dwarfism* and too much *gigantism*.
Gonadotrophic hormones 1. Luteinizing hormone (LH)	Gonads (Testes — Male, Ovaries – Female)	Development of sex (germ) cells ⟨Ova (Female) / Sperm (Male)⟩ Production of sex homones ⟨Oestrogen and Progesterone (Female) / Testosterone (Male)⟩
2. Follicle-stimulating hormone (FSH)	Ovaries	Production of follicles in ovary during ovulation.
Thyrotrophic hormone (TTH)	Thyroid gland	Secretion of *thyroxin* which controls metabolic rate — too little causes lethargy and depression, too much causes hyperactivity and anxiety.
Lactogenic hormone (Prolactin)	Breasts	Milk production during pregnancy.
Adrenocorticotrophic hormone (ACTH)	Adrenal glands 1. Adrenal medulla 2. Adrenal cortex	Secretion of adrenalin and noradrenaline Secretion of adreno-corticoid hormones (or corticosteroids), eg cortisol and hydrocortisone (important in coping with stress) (see Chapter 17).
Oxytocin	Uterus (Womb)	Causes contractions during labour and milk release during breast-feeding.
Vasopressin (Also a neurotransmitter)	Blood vessels	Causes contraction of the muscle in the walls of blood vessels and so raises blood pressure.
Antidiuretic hormone (ADH)	Kidneys	Regulates the amount of water passed in the urine.

Anterior pituitary — spans from Growth hormone through Adrenocorticotrophic hormone (ACTH).

Posterior pituitary — spans from Oxytocin through Antidiuretic hormone (ADH).

Other endocrine glands include:

(A) *Thymus* — situated in the chest; functions are unknown but thought to involve production of antibodies (see Chapter 17).

(B) *Pancreas* — secretes *insulin* (Anti-Diabetic hormone), given in the treatment of diabetes. Controls the body's ability to absorb and use glucose and fats.

(C) *Pineal body/gland* — situated near corpus callosum, functions unknown but may play a role in sleep–waking cycle (see Chapter 16).

15.3 summarizes the major sympathetic and parasympathetic effects on the organs and glands and the ANS will be discussed further in Chapter 17 in relation to emotional stress.

The Endocrine System

As we have said, many of the bodily reactions which result from the ANS are produced by its effect on the *endocrine* glands, which secrete *hormones* (chemical messengers which, unlike neurotransmitters, are released directly into the bloodstream and are carried throughout the body).

The effect of hormones is much slower than that of neurotransmitters: an electrochemical impulse can convey a message in a matter of milliseconds while several seconds may be required for the stimulation, release and arrival of a needed hormone at its destination. Consequently, where an immediate behavioural reaction is required (eg a reflex action), the NS plays the major role: hormones are better suited to communicating steady, relatively unchanging, messages over prolonged periods of time (eg the bodily changes associated with puberty).

Endocrine glands are ductless and are contrasted with *exocrine* glands (such as salivary, sweat and tear glands) which do have ducts and secrete fluids directly onto the body surface or into body cavities; their influence is, consequently, much less widespread than that of endocrine glands.

The major endocrine gland is the *pituitary* which, as we have seen, is physically (but not functionally or structurally) part of the brain (situated just below the hypothalamus). It is often called the 'master gland' because it produces the largest number of different hormones and also controls the secretion of several other endocrine glands.

The pituitary comprises two independently functioning parts: (a) the *posterior* and (b) the *anterior*; the former passes on hormones which are thought to be manufactured in the hypothalamus, while the latter is stimulated by the hypothalamus to produce its own hormones. The major hormones of the posterior and anterior lobes of the pituitary are shown, with their effects, in Table 15.4.

Other important endocrine glands are the *adrenals* (situated just above the kidneys), each of which comprises the adrenal *medulla* (inner core) and the adrenal *cortex* (outer layer). As Table 15.4 shows, the medulla secretes adrenaline and noradrenaline which are the transmitter substances for the sympathetic branch of the ANS; consequently, the 'fight or flight' syndrome is often kept going by a 'closed circuit', whereby the sympathetic NS stimulates the adrenals to produce adrenaline and noradrenaline (initiated by the hypothalamus, which stimulates the pituitary gland to secrete ACTH which, in turn, stimulates the adrenals) which then stimulate the sympathetic nerves and so on. This closed circuit explains why your heart continues to pound for several seconds after a dangerous or stressful situation has passed. (See Chapter 17.)

16

Consciousness and Awareness

Consciousness and Self-Consciousness

When discussing the self-concept in Chapter 9 it was suggested that, whereas animals may be said to have consciousness, only human beings have self-consciousness, a special relationship we have with ourselves whereby we are able to treat ourselves as if we were objects or things through thought and reflection.

Consciousness is usually discussed in relation to humans and nothing more will be said in this chapter about the consciousness of other species; but because of the diverse ways in which psychologists have studied the topic (including animal experiments), some of what we say will have direct bearing on animal consciousness.

Meanings of 'Consciousness'

We use the term in a variety of ways in everyday language, for example: (a) when we are awake we are conscious but when we are asleep, or in a coma, or we have been 'knocked out' by a punch to the head, we are unconscious (the term 'unconscious' is often reserved for the last two examples but, as we shall see, when we fall asleep, we do 'lose consciousness') (b) when we do something consciously we do it deliberately or knowingly but to do something automatically or without having to think about it (eg an experienced driver or typist) is to do it unconsciously; (c) advertising campaigns (eg anti-drug) are aimed at increasing public consciousness or awareness of the risks and dangers associated with taking drugs.

Similarly, psychologists and other scientists interested in trying to understand consciousness define it in different ways. Freud, for example, saw consciousness as a whole comprising three levels; (i) the conscious, which refers to what we are fully aware of at any one time; (ii) the pre-conscious, which refers to what we could become aware of quite easily if we switched our attention to it; and (iii) the unconscious, which refers to what we have pushed out of our conscious minds, through repression, making it extremely inaccessible, although it continues to exert an influence on our thoughts, feelings and behaviour. (See Chapter 26.)

Although most psychologists would agree that thoughts, feelings, memories, etc differ in their degree of accessibility (that is, they could all be placed on a *continuum* of consciousness, with 'completely conscious' at one end and 'completely unconscious' at the other), most would not accept Freud's formulation of the unconscious (based on repression). Indeed, other psychodynamic theorists, in particular Jung, disagreed fundamentally with Freud's view of the unconscious; although he admitted the existence of repression, Jung distinguished between the personal and the collective unconscious, the former being based on the individual's personal experiences, the latter being inherited and common to all human beings (or at least to all members of a particular cultural or racial group — see Chapter 26).

Rubin and McNeil (1983) define consciousness as, 'our subjective awareness of our actions and of the world around us'; Ruch (1984) gives it a much more cognitive emphasis by defining it as, 'a process of experiencing the external and internal environment in ways that separate immediate stimuli from immediate responses, that is, stimuli are processed and 'understood' in some sense as against leading directly to mechanical responses'.

Both definitions share a view of consciousness as pointing inwards, towards our thoughts, feelings, actions etc and outwards, towards external, environmental, events (including other people). Emphasis on the internal world is, of course, where psychology began as a separate discipline with Wundt's study of conscious thought through introspection, but this was soon replaced by a dramatic shift in the opposite direction, when Watson rejected consciousness as a valid object of scientific investigation as part of his 'behaviourist manifesto' (see Chapter 1).

Since the late 1960s, the pendulum has begun to swing back towards an interest in consciousness, particularly in exploring different states of awareness and how changes from one state to another take place. While humanistic psychologists such as Maslow may be primarily concerned with a person's subjective experience, physiological psychologists are more interested in trying to correlate subjective states of awareness with objective, physiological measures of consciousness, such as electroencephalograms, or EEGs, ('brain waves'), breathing and heart rates, blood pressure, and so on.

Consciousness, Arousal and Alertness

These physiological measures described above (and other correlates of consciousness) are often described as measures of level of *arousal* or *alertness*. Both subjectively and in terms of overt behaviour there is an obvious difference between being sleepy and being wide-awake in terms of degree of arousal or alertness; less obvious are the smaller changes which occur during normal wakefulness and which of two kinds, tonic and phasic, mediated by different brain systems (Lloyd et al, 1984).

Tonic Alertness
Changes in *tonic alertness* reflect intrinsic (and usually quite slow) changes of the basic level of arousal throughout a 24-hour period (or even across a

lifetime) and so are closely related to various biological rhythms, in particular the circadian rhythm (see below). It was originally thought that the Reticular Formation or Reticular Activating System (RAS) was solely responsible for arousing and maintaining consciousness (in Chapter 15 the RAS was described as a 'consciousness switch'); for instance, if the brain-stem is severed below the RAS, the animal will be paralysed but will remain fully alert when awake and will show normal sleep-wake EEG patterns, but if it is sectioned above the RAS the animal will fall into a state of continuous slow-wave sleep.

Again, Moruzzi and Magoun (1949) found that electrical stimulation of the RAS of anaesthetized cats produced long-lasting signs of arousal in their EEGs; in cats that were not anaesthetized, the effect of RAS stimulation was to produce behavioural signs of arousal, alertness and attention. According to Moruzzi and Magoun, sleep occurs when the level of activity of the RAS falls below a certain critical level.

However, it is now known that other brain structures (both in the thalamus and hypothalamus) are involved in the sleep-wake cycle and the co-ordination of all these systems is necessary for the initiation and maintenance of conscious awareness (Lloyd et al, 1984).

Both during wakefulness and during sleep, there are periodic, fairly predictable, changes in the degree of alertness; the day-time changes are referred to as governed by a *diurnal rhythm* and the sleep (night-time) changes by an *ultradian rhythm*.

Phasic Alertness

Changes in *phasic alertness* involve short-term, temporary, variations in arousal, over a period of seconds, initiated by novel and important environmental events. An important component of these changes is the *orienting response* to arousing stimuli (which involves a *decrease* in heart-rate and breathing rate, pupil dilation, a tensing of the muscles and characteristic changes in the EEG, which becomes desynchronized); if the stimuli are continuously presented, the orienting response is replaced by *habituation*, whereby the person or animal stops responding to them.

Habituation is, in fact, a form of adaptation; it is more important from a survival point of view to respond to novel stimuli rather than constant ones and since most stimuli are relatively constant, we need to be able to attend selectively to those which are different and/or unexpected. So it is the *changing* aspects of the environment which demand, and usually receive, our attention and the nervous systems of animals and humans have evolved in such a way as to make them especially responsive to change.

Consciousness and Attention

Another way in which experimental psychologists have studied consciousness is through the concept of attention. Although consciousness is difficult to describe because it is fundamental to everything we do (Rubin and McNeil, 1983), one way of trying to 'pin it down' is to study what we are *paying attention* to, that is, what is in the forefront of our consciousness, and according to Allport (1980a), 'attention is the experimental psychologists' code name for consciousness'.

Focal attention (or focal awareness) is what we are currently paying deliberate attention to and what is in the centre of our awareness (this corresponds to Freud's 'conscious'); all those other aspects of our environment, or our own thoughts and feelings which are on the fringes of our awareness but which could easily become the object of our focal attention, are within our *peripheral attention* or awareness (which corresponds to Freud's 'pre-conscious'). (Selective attention is discussed in the context of perception in Chapter 4.) How important is focal attention?

We do seem capable of doing many things quite unconsiously (ie automatically, without having to think about what we are doing) and this perhaps is best illustrated by our perceptual abilities; as we saw in Chapter 4, the complex cognitive processes of inference, organization and selection go on without our being aware of them and our perception is mostly direct and immediate. Indeed, it is difficult to imagine what it would be like if we were aware of how we perceive; in order to select consciously one version of the ambiguous lady cartoon, for example, we must either know that there are a young and an old lady 'in' the picture or we must have already *perceived* both versions (in which case, how did the original perception come about?). You may have had difficulty yourself perceiving the old lady if your immediate perception was of the young lady, even though you consciously 'searched' for and tried to see the alternative version. (This underlines the very important difference between *conception* and *perception*.)

Using a rather different (but popular) example, something which we normally do quite automatically (such as walking down stairs) might well be disrupted if we try to bring it into focal awareness. Again, this makes sense in terms of freeing us to attend to those environmental events which are unfamiliar or threatening in some way; if we had to think about our bodily movements when walking, this would add to the long list of sources of stimulation competing for our attention!

Perhaps only when first negotiating stairs as a toddler did we ever have to attend focally to ascending and descending them; but even with skills which do require focal attention when they are first acquired (eg driving, playing the piano), once they have been mastered, they become automatic, and, as Lloyd et al (1984) put it, unconscious processes seem to be 'precipitates' of earlier conscious processes.

Nisbett and Wilson (1977) go so far as to claim that all psychological activities (including social behaviour) are governed by processes of which we are unaware. If people are asked about what they think governed their behaviour after participating in a social psychology experiment, the answers they give do not usually correspond very well with the explanations which psychologists offer for the same behaviour (and which they believe are the *real* reasons). Nisbett and Wilson argue that our belief that we can account for our own behaviour ('commonsense' or intuitive explanations) is illusory because what really guides our behaviour is not available to consciousness (compare this with Freud's distinction between 'our' reasons and 'the reasons'—see Chapter 26).

However, as we saw in Chapter 1, many psychologists take the view that people are psychologists and that commonsense explanations may be as valid as theoretical, scientific ones (eg Joynson, 1974, Heather, 1976), which seems to be in direct conflict with that of Nisbett and Wilson.

The Functions of Consciousness

Like perception, many cases of problem-solving seem to involve processes which are 'out of consciousness'; for example, answers often seem to 'pop into our head' and we do not know how we reached them. If what is important is the solution (as opposed to the process involved in reaching it), then consciousness may be seen as incidental to information-processing.

The complexity of our nervous system which makes our consciousness possible provided our ancestors with the flexibility of behaviour which helped them survive; however, it is less obvious whether consciousness was *itself* adaptive or simply a side-effect or by-product of a complex nervous system (Humphrey, 1982).

Some psychologists and biologists believe that consciousness is a powerful agent for controlling behaviour which has evolved in its own right. Accordingly, non-conscious problem-solving systems are seen as the *servants* of consciousness; they are guided and integrated by consciousness but carry out automated routines (Ruch, 1984).

According to Hilgard's (1977 b) 'neo-dissociation' theory, the consciousness which *solves* a problem may be different from that which *reports* the solution; neither is 'higher' or 'lower' than the other, they are simply different. This theory is based on Hilgard's work with hypnosis and consistent with the work on split-brain patients (discussed in Chapter 15).

Two Kinds of Consciousness

As we saw in Chapter 15, the two cerebral hemispheres are specialized (although they share the potential for many functions and both participate in most psychological activities), so that each is dominant with respect to particular functions. According to Ornstein (1975), the *left hemisphere* is analytical, thinks logically (especially in verbal and mathematical functions), processes information *sequentially* (one item at a time) and its mode of operation is primarily *linear* (straight-line). By contrast, the *right hemisphere* thinks in a *holistic* way, its language ability is limited, it specializes in space perception, the perception of body image and recognition of faces and artistic endeavour, it processes information more *diffusely* than the left and integrates several inputs at once.

Ornstein (1975) believes that these two modes of operation represent two distinct modes of consciousness; in daily life we normally just alternate between the two and, although they might complement each other, they do not readily substitute for one another (as when you try to describe a spiral staircase or how you tie a shoe-lace).

Galin and Ornstein (1972) recorded changes in subjects' EEGs when presented with either verbal or spatial tasks. On *verbal* tasks, alpha rhythms (associated with a waking adult with their eyes closed) in the right hemisphere *increased* relative to the left, while on *spatial* tasks, the reverse was true. The appearance of alpha rhythms indicates a 'turning off' of information processing in the area of the brain involved, so, on verbal tasks, information processing is being turned off in the right hemisphere, which is the side of the brain not being used (as if to reduce the interference between the two conflicting modes of operation of the two hemispheres).

Similarly, Simernitskaya (1974) found that people with damage to the left hemisphere had greater problems with consciously-executed writing, while those with right-hemisphere damage had greater problems with more automatic writing, such as signing their name. He concluded that the left hemisphere may be more involved in highly conscious processes which require intentional behaviour and the focusing of attention, while the right may be more involved with automatic or unconscious actions and more sensitive to material outside the conscious focus of attention.

Finally, Klein and Armitage (1979) found that performance on verbal and spatial tasks varied (for the same subject) on an approximately 90-minute (*ultradian*) cycle, so that, depending on when they were tested, they would be more efficient at one or other kind of task; these waking ultradian cycles may reflect a shift in balance between the two hemispheres.

Consciousness and the Electroencephalogram (EEG)

As we saw in Chapter 15, a major way (since the 1930s) of studying the working of the brain is to monitor the electrical activity of the brain; exactly the same information can be used to throw light on consciousness, because particular patterns of electrical activity are correlated with other indices of arousal and alertness.

Electroencephalography (literally, 'electric-in-head-writing') detects the output of minute electrical 'ripples', caused by changes in the electrical charges in different parts of the brain (usually the synchronized activity of large groups of neurons); although there are characteristic patterns which are common to all individuals of a particular age or developmental stage, each individual's brain-activity is as unique and distinctive as their fingerprints.

The EEG machine has wires, an amplifier, electromagnetic pens and paper revolving on a drum. One end of each wire is attached to the scalp (with the help of special jelly) and the other to the amplifier, which can register impulses of 100 microvolts (1/10,000 of a volt) or less and magnifies them 1 million times; the impulses are traced on paper by pens and appear as rows of oscillating waves (see Figure 16.1). The waves vary in frequency and amplitude: (i) *frequency* is measured as the number of oscillations per second and the more oscillations, the higher the frequency; one complete oscillation is a *cycle* and the frequency is expressed as cycles per second (cps); (ii) *amplitude* is measured as half the height from the peak to the trough of a single oscillation. Frequency is the more important of the two measures.

The four major types of wave (measured in frequency) are:

1) *Beta* (1 cps and over)—these are found mainly in adults who are awake, alert, whose eyes are open and who may be concentrating on some task or other. They are most reliably recorded from the front and middle of the scalp and are related to activity in the sensory and motor cortex.
2) *Alpha* (8 to 13 cps)—these are found mainly in adults who are awake, relaxed and whose eyes are closed. They are most reliably recorded from the back of the scalp.

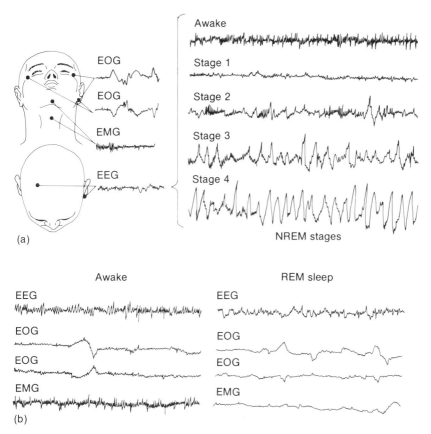

Figure 16.1 Comparison of physiological measures for different types of sleep
(a) The NREM stages are represented in typical order of appearance; in reality
each one gradually blends into the next
(b) REM is in some ways similar to waking but in others quite different; the EEG
is more similar to waking than to that of any NREM stage and REMs are
present, but the body muscles are deeply inhibited

3)   *Theta* (4 to 7 cps)—these are found mainly in children aged 2 to 5 years
     and psychopaths and may be evoked by frustration.
4)   *Delta* (1 to 3 cps)—these are found mainly in infants, sleeping adults
     or adults with brain tumours.

Computerized electroencephalography has recently been used to detect
evoked potentials, minute voltage changes induced in the brain by fairly
specific visual and auditory stimuli; often the average of a number of
responses to similar kinds of stimuli is used (the Average Evoked Potential
or AEP) in order to amplify the signal-to-noise ratio. AEPs are used to study
newborns, some children with learning problems, patients in a coma, stroke
victims, tumour patients and patients with multiple sclerosis, but for certain
brain conditions, brain-scanning has largely replaced the EEG in the past few
years. (The Diagram Group, 1982.)

Sleep

1) Sleep and the Circadian Rhythm

According to Rose (1976), stability in many dynamic biochemical and physiological systems is achieved by some kind of oscillatory process in which the concentration of some substance, activity or process varies rhythmically round some mean value. So what sets the period of the rhythm?

It might seem that the 24-hour clocks provided by the day–night–day sequence would represent an obvious timing mechanism for living organisms but there is a good deal of evidence that it is not the primary means of timing. Rose refers to studies of volunteers who spend long periods in mines or caves without any time-cues and yet who manage to maintain their rhythms of eating, excreting, sleeping and wakefulness within a (roughly) circadian (24 hour) cycle. (In fact their internal clock runs a little slow—25 to 26 hours —which is why they underestimate the time they have spent underground.)

Therefore, in human adults, at least, it appears that the circadian rhythm does not depend primarily on external cues (although, presumably, it can be adjusted if necessary, using these external cues). But could not the rhythm have been learnt as a result of years of environmental experience?

Animal experiments, in which the length of 'day' can be manipulated, show that this is true but only up to a point; animals can be adjusted to cycles which vary by up to four or five hours above or below 24 but there are limits beyond which the cycle cannot be environmentally manipulated, just as hibernation cycles cannot be adjusted to fit experimentally manipulated 'seasons' (Harker, 1964, Aschoff, 1965, Brady, 1968). (The circadian rhythm is discussed again in relation to stress, see Chapter 17.)

The circadian rhythm (or 'biological clock'), therefore, seems to be predominantly an *internal* property of the system, and sleep is part of that rhythm. So if external cues are largely irrelevant, what are the internal events which cause sleep?

2) The Physiology of Sleep

First, we must qualify what we have said about the role of environmental cues. When darkness falls, the eyes indirectly inform a biological clock, the *pineal gland*, a tiny structure at the top of the brain-stem which keeps track of the body's natural cycles and registers external factors such as light and darkness. It secretes melatonin, a hormone that affects brain cells which use serotonin, a sleep-related transmitter substance; in turn, serotonin is concentrated in the *raphe nuclei* (situated near the pons) which secrete a substance which acts on the RAS to induce light sleep. Jouvet (1967) found that lesions of the raphe nucleus in cats produce severe insomnia and naturally-occurring lesions in humans seem to have a very similar effect.

Also, the retina projects directly onto the *suprachiasmatic nucleus* (in the hypothalamus) which ensures that the sleep-wake cycle is tuned to the rhythm of the night and day; if the connection with the retina is severed, the sleep-wake cycle goes 'haywire'.

Another important sleep centre is the *locus coeruleus*, a small patch of dark cells situated in the brain-stem which is thought to secrete a substance which initiates active (or REM) sleep (see below), and we have already discussed the role of the RAS in maintaining a general level of arousal; if the level of activity in the RAS falls below a certain critical level, sleep will occur (Moruzzi and Magoun, 1949) and it is quite clear that in sleep, sensory input to the RAS is reduced and the electrical activity sweeping from it up through the cortex drops below the level required to keep us awake (the Diagram Group, 1982).

Finally, there is evidence that a substance called *factor* S accumulates gradually in the brains of animals while they are awake and if this is removed from the fluid surrounding the brain and transferred into another animal, sleep will be induced. It is likely that factor S contributes to our feelings of sleepiness (the Diagram Group, 1982).

3) The Varieties of Sleep and the Ultradian Rhythm
In the typical sleep laboratory, a subject settles down for the night with not only EEG wires attached but also wires from an electrooculogram or EOG ('oculo' meaning 'eye') and from an electromyogram or EMG ('myo' meaning 'muscle').

A typical night's sleep comprises a number of ultradian cycles (approximately 90 minutes duration) and each cycle comprises a number of stages:

Stage 1:   When we first fall asleep, we enter stage 1 sleep; the EEG is irregular and lacks the pattern of alpha waves which characterize the relaxed waking state. Our heart-rate begins to slow down, our muscles relax and it is easy to wake someone up. (The transitory stage from being awake to entering stage 1 sleep is called the *hypnogogic period* and is sometimes used to include stage 1 (eg Schachter, 1976).)

Stage 2:   This is a deeper state of sleep than stage 1 but it is still fairly easy to wake someone. The EEGs show bursts of activity called 'spindles'.

Stage 3:   Sleep is becoming deeper, the spindles disappear and are replaced by long slow delta waves. The sleeper is now quite unresponsive to external stimuli and so is difficult to wake; heart-rate, blood pressure and body temperature all continue to drop.

Stage 4:   The sleeper now enters 'delta sleep' (deep sleep or 'quiet sleep') and will spend up to 30 minutes in stage 4; about an hour has elapsed since stage 1 began.

The cycle then goes into reverse, so the sleeper re-enters stage 3, then stage 2, but instead of re-entering stage 1, a different kind of sleep (Active sleep) appears: pulse and respiration rates increase, as does blood pressure, and all three processes become less regular, EEGs begin to resemble those of the waking state (showing that the brain is active) and yet it is even more difficult to wake someone from this kind of sleep than the deep stage 4 sleep, and for this reason it is referred to as 'paradoxical' sleep (Aserinsky and Kleitman, 1953). Another characteristic of active sleep are the rapid eye movements (the eye-balls moving back and forth, up and down, together) under the closed lids (hence 'rapid eye movement' sleep, or REM sleep). Finally, while the brain may be very active, the body is not; REM sleep is characterized by muscular paralysis (especially the muscles of the arms and legs) so that all the tossing and turning and other typical movements associated with sleep in fact

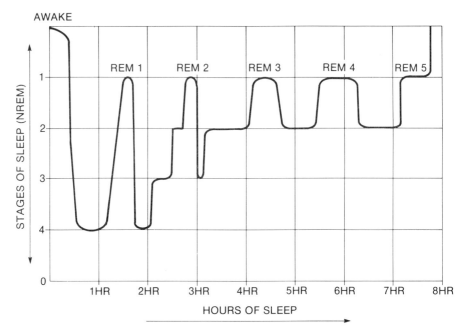

Figure 16.2 A typical night's sleep (note the disappearance of stages 3 and 4 and the relative increase in the length of REM periods)

occur during stages 1 to 4, which, collectively, are called NREM sleep, ie non-rapid-eye-movement. (The distinction between REM and NREM sleep was originally made by Dement and Kleitman, 1957).

See Figure 16.1 on page 403.

After ten or so minutes in REM sleep, we re-enter NREM sleep (stages 2 to 4) and so another ultradian cycle begins. However, with each 90 minute cycle, (of which there are four or five on average per night) the duration of the REM sleep increases and that of NREM sleep decreases; the first cycle normally provides the deepest sleep and the shortest REM period as the night goes on, we spend relatively more time in REM and less in NREM sleep. In later cycles, it is quite common to go from REM to stage 2 and then straight back into REM sleep (by-passing stages 3 and 4) and natural waking usually occurs during a period of REM sleep. (See Figure 16.2.)

4) Sleeping and Dreaming

The sleeping subject, if woken during REM sleep, will report that they have been dreaming about 80 per cent of the time, while being woken from NREM sleep only produces a 15 per cent 'dreaming rate' (Dement, 1978).

REMs seem to be a very reliable indicator that someone is dreaming (especially in combination with the fairly high frequency and low amplitude brain waves). To some extent, the nature of the REMs reflects the content of the dream (for instance, dreaming about a tennis match and a back-and-forth movement of the eyes—as would happen in waking life), but it is now generally agreed that there is no one-to-one correspondence between dream action and eye-movement, although cues about the general nature of the dream can often be gleaned by a look at the REM record. For example, if the eye movements are small and sparse, we are probably having a peaceful, fairly passive dream, whereas larger and more continuous REMs suggest a more active and emotional dream (Faraday, 1972). (Faraday also notes that research has shown that movements of the inner ear also occur during sleep and may be correlated with the auditory content of dreams.)

Not only is there a difference in the number of times that dreams are reported when subjects are woken from REM and NREM ('orthodox') sleep, but the *kind* of mental activity associated with each is very different. Subjects woken from NREM sleep tend to report dreams which are shorter, less vivid and less visual than REM dreams and, in fact, subjects often describe themselves as having been 'thinking' rather than dreaming; NREM sleep is also associated with sleep-walking (somnambulism), sleep-talking and some types of nightmare.

REM sleep has been called 'dream sleep' or the 'D-state' and some have gone as far as to call it the 'third state of existence', because it is in many ways as different from NREM sleep (the 'S-state') as it is from waking. This leads us to ask why we need to dream.

If REM sleep is dream sleep, then how do we account for the loss of muscle tone (ie the paralysis)?

According to Chase (1981), the loss of movement is intended to prevent us from acting out our dreams. In cats (whose sleep physiology is almost indistinguishable from our own), damage to the brain-stem (which is responsible for the inhibition of movement) causes them to act out their dreams in a full-blooded way (Morrison, 1983); typically, they groom themselves, get up and 'chase' a mouse but do both in a manner which shows that they are actually dreaming and real mice will be ignored.

According to the Activation-Synthesis Model (Hobson and McCarley, 1977), a dream is a process which begins with the periodic firing of *giant cells* (neurons found in the brain stem) which trigger REMs and characteristic EEGs plus high levels of *activation* in other parts of the brain, including those concerned with sensation (especially vision), motor activity and emotion. This neural firing also reduces the tone of the major skeletal muscles (arms and legs, in particular) producing the temporary paralysis.

Of course, the activation of sensory areas does not correspond to actual environmental events (the dream is hallucinatory) and the muscle paralysis prevents the acting out of the motor impulses. Instead, we *synthesize* a dream mentally, creating a dream content which corresponds to the pattern of brain stimulation. According to Hobson and McCarley, it is the unusual intensity and rapidity of brain stimulation (often involving the simultaneous activation of areas which are not usually activated together when we are awake) which accounts for the highly changeable and sometimes bizarre content of dreams.

In a similar vein, Rose (1976) explains dreaming in terms of the relatively random inputs which trigger memory sequences at a time when 'waking' control mechanisms (which normally keep a fairly close watch over these sequences) are either reduced or absent.

This *neural* theory of dreaming might account for 'where dreams come from' but not 'what dreams are for'. Psychological theories of dreaming focus on the 'synthesis' component of Hobson and McCarley's model (rather than the activation component) and try to explain its significance for the dreamer. Freud's dream theory is probably the best known (and the most controversial) and is discussed in detail in Chapter 26; he saw all dreams as wish-fulfilments, an expression of repressed, sexual, 'forbidden' desires in a disguised form, thus enabling the dreamer to to go on sleeping (hence, 'dreams are the guardians of sleep'). Jung disagreed with Freud about the wish-fulfilment and the sexual nature of dreams, but both shared the view that symbolism is of central importance and that dreams can put the dreamer in touch with parts of the self which are usually concealed during waking life.

Calvin S. Hall (1966) described dreams as, 'a personal document, a letter to oneself' and, like Jung, advocated the study of dream *series* rather than single, isolated dreams.

5) The Need for REM Sleep—the Effects of REM Deprivation

When subjects are deprived of REM sleep (as distinct from NREM), the effects are usually detrimental to their well-being and psychological functioning. Dement (1960) woke subjects from their REM sleep on five successive nights (while a control group were only woken during NREM sleep periods). The former became nervous, grumbly, irritable, unable to concentrate and some even began to hallucinate; when they were allowed to sleep uninterruptedly, they did 60 per cent more dreaming until they had made up their lost REM time. For as many as five nights following their REM deprivation, they spent more time in REM than usual and on some nights they doubled their REM time. (This is called the REM *rebound*.)

In cats too, it seems that NREM alone is inadequate. Jouvet (1967) placed cats on a small island surrounded by water and allowed them either to remain awake or to go into NREM sleep. However, whenever they entered REM sleep, they tended to slip into the water and woke up; prolonged deprivation of REM produced abnormal behaviour, including hypersexuality and, eventually, death.

Many drugs, including alcohol and various sleeping pills, suppress REM sleep without affecting NREM sleep (which is ironic, because the body seems to need REM more). If people or cats are deprived of *all* sleep for a period of days, they will eventually go to sleep standing up, but the body seems to have a specific need for REM and after REM deprivation, subjects go straight into REM sleep.

How can we account for the REM rebound? Evans and Newman (1964) see the human brain as a computer which, during REM sleep, goes 'offline' and sifts through the mass of data which has bombarded the senses during the day; dreams represent the brain's attempt to interpret the computer-like information-processing going on in the sleeping mind. REM represents an opportunity to 'clear the stores', discard redundant information and to rehearse and check various programme routines.

Only gradually do we acquire sleep–wake patterns which we associate with the circadian rhythm; during much of their first year, babies are sleeping for about 18 hours per 24, by about 12 months they have two periods of sleep every 24 hours (one daytime and one night-time) and not until about 5 years has an 'adult' pattern become established (probably as a result of both environmental and maturational factors).

Within these changing patterns, the relative proportions of REM and NREM sleep change quite dramatically: whereas the newborn spends half of its 18 hours in REM sleep, adults usually spend only one-quarter of their 8 hours in REM sleep; babies' brains, it has been suggested, need to process and assimilate the flood of new stimuli pouring in from the outside world and REM sleep helps them to achieve this.

6) The Need for NREM Sleep—Why Sleep at All?

While sleep has the features of a *primary drive* (such as hunger and sex), what makes it unique as a primary biological drive is that the need for sleep is reflected in *decreased* levels of arousal and its satisfaction is associated with further decreases. Sleep, therefore, represents a serious exception to the view that organisms seek a single optimal level of (non-specific) arousal (Lloyd et al, 1984). (See Chapter 17.)

Different species characteristically sleep for different periods; those at risk from predators, which cannot find a safe place to sleep, or which spend large parts of each day searching for and consuming food and water (such as herd animals), sleep very little, while predators who sleep in safe places and can satisfy their food and water needs fairly quickly (such as lions), sleep for much of the day (Lloyd et al, 1984).

The *Evolutionary theory* of sleep (eg Meddis, 1977, 1979) maintains that sleep is an advantage because it keeps the animal *immobilized* for long periods and in this way less conspicuous for would-be predators and, therefore, safer. The safer the animal from predators, the longer it is likely to sleep, as we noted above.

Meddis also argues that the long sleep periods of babies have evolved in order to prevent exhaustion in their mothers and, in this sense, sleep is still functional—at least for mothers of babies and small children! As for the need for immobilization, this no longer seems viable as an explanation of sleep in humans and so may be regarded as a remnant of our evolutionary past.

A variant of the evolutionary theory is *Hibernation theory* (eg Rogers, 1981) which argues that elaborate mechanisms of sleep have evolved solely to keep us quiet in the dark; animals hibernate in order to conserve energy and to stay out of possible danger during the winter months.

The *Restoration theory* (eg Oswald, 1966, 1974) maintains that both REM and NREM sleep serve a restorative, replenishing, function. NREM restores bodily processes which have deteriorated during the day, while REM sleep is a time for replenishing and renewing brain processes through the stimulation of protein synthesis. The REM rebound is explained as an attempt to compensate for lost brain-repair time: the eight-week rebound period (which is commonly found following the withdrawal of drugs which interfere with REM sleep) approximates the time required for repair to brain cells to occur.

The theory also accounts for the large proportion of babies' sleeping-time spent in REM sleep; as we noted earlier, the developing brain needs a great deal of protein synthesis for cell manufacture and growth.

There is some evidence to support the Restoration theory; for example, sleep time has been found to increase following daytime exercise (eg Shapiro et al, 1981) and the deeper stages of NREM sleep are specifically correlated with the release of growth hormone, which is important for tissue growth, protein and RNA synthesis, and the formation of red blood cells.

However, cell repair goes on 24 hours a day (even though it does reach a peak at night) but a more serious objection to the theory is that far from being a restful state, REM sleep, as we have seen, is an active state (at least as far as the brain is concerned) and probably burns up a substantial amount of energy. Indeed, blood flow to the brain increases during REM sleep and this would actually *prevent* high levels of protein synthesis. In view of this kind of evidence, Oswald (1974) maintains that *both* types of sleep are involved in the process of restoring *bodily* tissue.

Finally, it has been suggested that REM sleep plays a critical role in the stabilization of certain kinds of memory, especially those which have emotional significance; retention may be disturbed if learning is followed by a period of REM deprivation, suggesting that REM sleep involves the stimulation of the consolidation process (see Chapter 6).

Daydreaming

Dream research shows that we all dream and that people who claim 'I never dream' are simply failing to remember their dreams. Although on a much smaller scale, research into daydreaming suggests that we all indulge in this kind of daytime, waking fantasy and one of the pioneers of this research is Singer (1975) who interviewed hundreds of people and identified three kinds of daydreams:

● *Type 1* are rather anxious daydreams, often centred on fear of failure; they tend to be unorganized, fleeting and vague;
● *Type 2* are self-critical and self-doubting and may sometimes be quite hostile;
● *Type 3* are 'happy daydreams', reflecting a positive self-image and self-acceptance.

Men and women daydream equally often and in similar ways. However, there is a slight tendency for women to have personal, passive and body-orientated fantasies, while men often fantasize about athletic and heroic achievement.

We daydream less as we get older although 'happy daydreamers' are the most likely to carry on into old age and, interestingly, daydreaming seems to peak every 90 minutes, thus following an ultradian rhythm (Lavie and Kripke, 1975, Chase, 1979).

Finally, Singer (1976b) believes that daydreaming is necessary for optimum intellectual functioning, self-control and a peaceful inner life; it can help us to cope with boredom and help relax us when engaged in some demanding intellectual work.

Hypnosis

Rubin and McNeil (1983) define hypnosis as, 'an altered state of consciousness, in which the hypnotized subject can be influenced to behave and to experience things differently than she would in the ordinary waking state'. Elsewhere, they define it as, 'a state of increased suggestibility (or willingness to comply with another person's directions) that is brought about through the use of certain procedures by another person, the hypnotist.'

This notion of *suggestibility* is often thought to be at the core of hypnosis and a great deal of research has attempted to identify personality types which are high and low in 'hypnotizability'. Hilgard (1970) believes that people can be classified in this way; Morgan et al (1970) found that, among student subjects, 'highs' are often humanities majors and are able to lose themselves in individual pursuits (such as reading) while 'lows' are often science majors and are more likely to participate in group activities. (Compare this with Eysenck's description of introverts and extroverts—see Chapter 25.)

About 5 per cent of the population can be induced to a deep hypnotic trance and about 10 per cent do not respond at all, with the majority falling somewhere in between these two extremes.

The Hypnotic Procedure

According to Hilgard (1975), hypnosis is, 'the state of consciousness caused in a subject by a systematic procedure for altering consciousness, usually carried out by one person (the hypnotist) to alter the consciousness of another (the subject).'

The typical procedure begins with a ten to fifteen minute induction of verbal suggestions designed to induce a passive, sleeplike (but waking) state. For the next 45 minutes or so, the subject is asked to perform a number of tasks which may be based on the Stanford Hypnotic Susceptibility Scales (Weitzenhoffer and Hilgard, 1965). These scales are heavily weighted with: (a) ideomotor ('thought-movement') tasks, such as 'postural sway' (falling without forcing), 'arm immobilization' (the arm rises less than one inch in 10 seconds) and 'verbal inhibition' (not being able to give their name within 10 seconds); but also include (b) sensory hallucinations (eg imagining a fly is in the room and behaving in some appropriate way); (c) temporary amnesia (only being able to recall three or fewer items from a longer series); (d) age regression (eg the subject is taken back in time and asked to describe events and people in their childhood); and (e) posthypnotic suggestion (eg after being 'awakened' the subject opens the window when the hypnotist gets out his handkerchief, a signal given to the subject while in the hypnotic state).

The more items the subject 'passes', the higher their susceptibility score; using these scales, men and women have been found to be equally hypnotizable and people with vivid imaginations and who feel comfortable taking orders from others also tend to be hypnotized more easily. Susceptibility seems to reach a peak up to the age of ten years and declines steadily after that (Morgan and Hilgard, 1971).

Trance or Role-Playing?

What is the evidence that the hypnotic state constitutes a qualitatively different state of consciousness, as Hilgard claims?

There is no doubt that the hypnotic state is *not* a state of sleep (using EEGs and other criteria), although subjects often report dream-like imagery and may show REMs while 'dreaming'. Some report feeling bored but relaxed, others seem to attain a kind of controlled hypnogogic state (neither fully awake nor asleep) and almost all remain aware of who and where they are; some of the more responsive subjects, however, may not remember what they did and may think only a few minutes have passed (Ruch, 1984).

Some of the evidence seems quite convincing; for example, touching the skin with a pencil may cause blisters if the subject has been told it is red hot and touching the skin with a Japanese wax-plant may fail to cause a skin reaction if the subject believes it is a harmless chestnut leaf.

Again, telling a subject that they have just eaten a large, fatty, meal causes the body to secrete lipase (a fat-digesting enzyme); when they think the meal was rich in protein, pepsin and tryspin are secreted (protein-digesting enzymes). Hypnosis can also affect breathing rate, heart-rate and various kinds of glandular activity (the Diagram Group, 1982).

However, Barber (1970) believes that all hypnotic phenomena are due to motivational and social-psychological factors. The 'hypnotic trance' does not constitute a unique state, he says (there is no distinctive EEG, for instance) and the 'hypnotized' person is simply highly motivated to co-operate with the hypnotist's suggestions and is good at 'role-playing'; anything that can be done in the hypnotized state can be done while 'awake'.

A similar argument is made by Orne (1970) who paid a group of subjects (and trained them) to pretend they were hypnotized; an experienced hypnotist could not tell them apart from a group who had actually been hypnotized, despite sticking them with pins and asking them to engage in all sorts of unusual behaviour.

Hypnosis and Pain

It has been claimed by many critics of hypnosis that the only distinctive psychological change which it produces is *relaxation* (which can just as easily be produced by other techniques, such as meditation, relaxation exercises etc).

However, Hilgard, one of the leading researchers in the field, believes that hypnosis has been successfully used with dental patients, burn victims, women in childbirth and terminal cancer patients to reduce their pain. One experimental technique for studying pain is the *cold pressor response*, where the subject immerses their arm in freezing water and is asked to report how painful it is over a 30-second period.

Hypnotized subjects are told that the experience will not be painful and usually report very little pain (a 'slight tingle', for example). However, physiological measures of pain (such as heart-rate and blood pressure) are usually extremely high and this led Hilgard to propose his Neo-Dissociation Theory (1975b). Dissociation refers to a separation between different aspects of consciousness; in the case of pain, there are at least two components: (a) a sensory component; and (b) an emotional component and hypnosis only influences the latter. Unlike drugs, hypnosis does not prevent pain information from reaching the brain — so the pain information is available and, if pressed, the hypnotized subject may be able to report the pain.

Hypnotized subjects who reported no pain were asked if some other part of themselves (a *hidden observer*) might know more; if such a hidden observer were contacted, it often reported knowledge of some degree of pain (although this was usually less than for the same subject when not hypnotized). (Hilgard, 1978a.)

Hypnosis has been successfully used in psychotherapy (Frankel and Zamansky, 1978) and has also been used as a memory enhancer for witnesses to accidents and criminal cases (Block, 1976). However, because of the possibility of accidentally creating pseudo-memories (Hilgard, 1981), testimony given under hypnosis is usually inadmissable in court.

Meditation

Meditation has been defined by Golsman (1977) as a clearing or emptying of the mind through a narrowly focused thought process; the special word or phrase (the *mantra*) used in Transcendental Meditation is an example of this.

According to Burns and Dobson (1984), the different forms and varieties of meditation are all ways of achieving an inner quiet and a heightened awareness and can be thought of as the art of being in the 'here and now'.

Meditation, originally practised in India and other Eastern countries, became popular in the late 1960s in the West as part of the 'flower power' phenomenon which was, among other things, a rejection by the youth of traditional materialistic values which were seen as severely limiting people's individual freedoms.

Since then, meditation has been studied by psychologists as a state of consciousness (and a technique for bringing that about) using fairly traditional, scientific techniques (which is ironic when you consider that Western science was one of the institutions rejected by 'flower power').

There are many reported cases of yogis who manage to control their autonomic functions quite voluntarily through meditation, enabling them to endure all kinds of injury and deprivation, without suffering any apparent physical harm. A famous example is Ramanand Yogi, a 46-year-old Hindu who, through the practice of yoga ('union'), managed to survive for over five hours in a sealed metal box in 1970. He was filmed and various physiological measures were taken while he was inside: he used just over one-half of the calculated minimum amount of oxygen needed to keep him alive (and during one hour, he was averaging just one-quarter).

The secret of yogis' science-defying feats seem to be the *trance*-like state which is induced by meditation techniques, whereby the body's metabolism is slowed down considerably. However, others believe that meditation (like hypnosis) is simply an elaborate way of inducing quite normal *relaxation responses* and that there is nothing unique or magical about meditation (eg Benson, 1975).

Benson believes that, over and above any religious beliefs surrounding it, meditation requires: (i) a quiet environment where the meditator will not be interrupted; (ii) a mental device on which to concentrate (such as the mantra, which is repeated continuously); (iii) a passive attitude as opposed to an active, striving one; and (iv) a comfortable position. Regular use of this simplified form of meditation encourages a relaxation response, which triggers the parasympathetic branch of the ANS. (Benson et al, 1977, Hoffman et al, 1982.) Ornstein (1977) has suggested that meditation is primarily a right hemisphere 'intuitive' activity and practising meditation for long periods may induce a relative shift in hemisphere dominance (Pagano and Frumkin, 1977). Some research has shown that meditators do better than non-meditators on certain right-hemisphere tasks, such as remembering musical tones, but they do worse on verbal problem-solving tasks (Schwartz, 1974); however, we cannot be sure that these differences arose *because* of meditation, since this was a correlational study and there have been other important differences between meditators and non-meditators apart from meditation.

Biofeedback

What yogis seems to be able to do through meditation can apparently be achieved in a much more scientifically-orientated way through biofeedback; simply, the individual is provided with information (feedback) about specific aspects of their biological functioning (eg heart-rate, breathing rate, blood pressure, EEG and GSR) and on the strength of that information is trained to control those biological functions (of which we are normally completely unaware) at will.

In a typical training session, a subject is connected up to various recording machines and when, say, blood pressure falls within a certain pre-determined range, a signal is given (a buzzer sounds or a flashing light is switched on); this signal, of course, is the feedback.

Biofeedback techniques grew out of experiments with rats by Miller and Dicara (1967), and Dicara and Miller (1968), in which, it was claimed, involuntary, autonomic, responses were brought under control using operant conditioning. (Briefly, paralysed rats were rewarded by hypothalamic electrical stimulation whenever their breathing rate—and other autonomic functions—changed in the desired direction.) This was quite a startling finding because until then it had been believed that autonomic behaviour could only be conditioned using classical methods and that operant conditioning could only be applied to voluntary behaviour (see Chapter 3).

However, the results have always been considered highly controversial and have never been replicated (Walker, 1984); indeed, Miller himself (1978) has spoken out against accepting the results from any experiments using curarized (paralysed) animals.

Nevertheless, research into biofeedback has continued, with mixed fortunes. Many studies have claimed that a wide range of autonomic functions can be brought under voluntary control. Early biofeedback experiments seem to show that subjects could control their EEGs without any specific training (Hart, 1968, Kamiya, 1968) and many studies have attempted to get subjects to produce alpha waves, with apparent success (Brown, 1970, Knowlis and Kamiya, 1970).

High blood pressure, migraine headaches, some types of vomiting and secretion of stomach acids which can cause ulcers can all be modified by biofeedback (Blanchard and Young, 1974, Shapiro and Schwartz, 1972) as can skin temperature and salivation (Plotkin, 1979).

However, these results have not always been replicated and the results may turn out to be artificial. For instance, eye-movements can produce changes in the electrical field which block input to an ordinary alpha recorder (Hardt and Kamiya, 1976), that is, the apparent control of alpha waves may be the result of changes in eye movements as opposed to actual changes in brain activity.

Similarly, Anand and Chhina (1961) examined yogis who claimed to be able to stop their heart and, indeed, no heartbeat could be found. However, electrocardiograms (ECGs) showed that their hearts were beating *faster* than normal; they had learnt to control pressure in the thoracic cavity and could shut off the return of blood to the heart, thereby eliminating the characteristic heartbeat noise.

Other studies have shown that blood pressure and heart-rate can be controlled through subtle muscular movements or sometimes through breathing changes (Levenson, 1976). So the learning of blood pressure and heart-rate control etc might, in fact, be a *consequence* of control over muscular responses.

Biofeedback has been applied to an enormous variety of clinical problems but there is serious doubt about its effectiveness, especially compared with other procedures (Yates, 1980). Beiman (1978), for example, believes that simple training in voluntary muscle relaxation is often at least as effective— and sometimes more so—as biofeedback in the control of tension.

LeFrançois (1983) argues that the application of biofeedback in medicine has tremendous, but largely unproven, potential, and Miller (1978), whose studies of rats provided the stimulus, believes that most biofeedback research has been conducted at the first stage of scientific research, namely, pilot studies which have shown promise; what is needed now, he says, are controlled comparisons, where new treatments, such as biofeedback, are compared with other treatments and with placebos.

17

Motivation, Emotion and Stress

1) Motivation: The 'Why' of Behaviour

Trying to define *motivation* is a little like trying to define psychology itself; each major theoretical approach tries to account for what causes human behaviour and the underlying image of human beings implicit in each theory is, in essence, a theory of the causes of behaviour (see Table 1.1, page 14.) Motives are a special kind of cause which, 'energize, direct and sustain a person's behaviour (including hunger, thirst, sex and curiosity)' (Rubin and McNeil, 1983). The word motive comes from the Latin for 'move' and this is captured in George Miller's definition:

> The study of motivation is the study of all those pushes and prods — biological, social and psychological — that defeat our laziness and move us, either eagerly or reluctantly, to action (George Miller, 1967).

Motivated behaviour is goal-directed, purposeful, behaviour and it is difficult to think of any behaviour (animal or human) which is not motivated in this sense. However, exactly how the underlying motives are conceptualized and how they are investigated depends very much on the persuasion of the psychologist; for instance, a *psychoanalytic* psychologist will try to discover *unconscious* motives and wishes, a *behaviourist* will search for *reinforcement schedules*, a *humanistic* psychologist will relate behaviour to *self-actualization*, a *neurobiological* psychologist will look for processes taking place in the *nervous system* and a *cognitive* psychologist will try to relate behaviour to the person's *thinking*.

Even these superficial examples will indicate that motives may differ with regard to a number of features or dimensions, including: (i) internal or external, (ii) innate or learned, (iii) mechanistic or cognitive, (iv) conscious or unconscious; and a number of attempts have been made to classify different kinds of motives which loosely correspond to the major psychological theories outlined above.

Murray (1938) identified 20 different human motives (which he called needs), including dominance, achievement and autonomy. Rubin and McNeil (1983) classify motives into two major categories, (i) survival or physiological motives, and (ii) competence or cognitive motives, with social motives representing a third category. Clearly, humans share survival motives with all other animals and, as we shall see below, we also share certain competence motives; but others are peculiarly and uniquely human, notably self-actualization, which lies at the peak of a 'hierarchy of needs' in Maslow's (1954) humanistic theory. (This is discussed in detail in Chapter 25.)

In Chapter 26 we shall discuss Freud's psychoanalytic theory (together with other related theories) as a theory of personality but since the emphasis is upon dynamic forces which operate within each one of us (rather than how people differ) it can just as well be regarded as an account of human motivation.

In Chapter 3, we discussed laboratory studies of learning, in particular, of conditioning; for Skinner, 'motivation' is too mentalistic a term to be acceptable and, besides, behaviour can be analysed in terms of reinforcement schedules which leave nothing 'behind' the behaviour to be explained. However, not all learning theorists agree with Skinner; we noted in Chapter 3 some of the important differences between orthodox learning theorists and social learning theorists and in this chapter we shall discuss the Drive-Reduction theory of Clarke L. Hull, which also differs from Skinner's in important ways.

We shall take a close look at physiological theories of motivation (on which Hull's drive-reduction theory is partly based) as well as competency motives, including what Murray called achievement motivation or need for achievement (nAch). Another of the needs identified by Murray was affiliation, that is, the need for the company of, and the interaction with, other people; social needs have been discussed, in various ways, in Chapters 8 to 13.

Philosophy and Psychology in The Study of Motivation

As with many other aspects of psychology, the study of motivation has its roots in philosophy. *Rationalists* saw human beings as free to choose between different courses of action and so, in a sense, the concept of motivation becomes unnecessary—we behave as we do because we have chosen to do so and it is our reason which determines our behaviour. This idea of freedom and responsibility is a basic premise of both humanistic and cognitive approaches.

The seventeenth-century British philosopher, Hobbes, proposed the theory of *hedonism*, which maintains that all behaviour is determined by the seeking of pleasure and the avoidance of pain—these are the 'real' motives (whatever we believe our motives to be) and this basic idea is an important one in Freud's psychoanalytic theory. Similarly, the basic principles of positive and negative reinforcement can be seen as corresponding to the seeking of pleasure and avoidance of pain respectively and, of course, these are central to Skinner's operant conditioning.

Freud's theory is often referred to as an instinct theory and the concept played a major role in early psychological approaches to motivation. Largely inspired by Darwin's (1859) theory of evolution (which argued that humans and animals differ only quantitatively and not qualitatively), a number of psychologists (including William James and William McDougall), identified human instincts meant to explain human behaviour. McDougall (1908), for example, originally proposed twelve and by 1924 over 800 separate instincts had been identified; but to explain behaviour by labelling it is to *explain* nothing (eg 'We behave aggressively because of our aggressive instinct' is a circular statement) and this, combined with the sheer proliferation of instincts, seriously undermined the whole approach. (However, the concept of instinct—with certain important modifications—remains a central feature of the *ethological* approach to behaviour, in particular, animal behaviour, which we discussed in Chapter 14.)

During the 1920s the concept of instinct was largely replaced by the concept of *drive*, a term first used by Woodworth (1918), who compared human behaviour with the operation of a machine; the mechanism of a machine is relatively passive and drive is the power applied to make it 'go'.

The concept of drive has taken two major forms: (i) the *homoeostatic drive* theory (Cannon, 1929), which is a physiological theory; and (ii) the *drive-reduction* theory (Hull, 1943) which is primarily a theory of learning.

i) Homoeostatic Drive Theory

The term *homoeostasis* was coined by Cannon in 1929 to refer to the process by which an organism maintains a fairly constant internal (bodily) environment, that is, how body temperature, blood-sugar level, salt-concentration in the blood etc are kept in a state of relative balance or equilibrium. The basic idea is that when a state of imbalance arises (eg through a substantial rise in body temperature) something must happen to correct the imbalance and restore equilibrium (eg sweating); in this case, the animal does not have to 'do' anything because sweating is completely automatic and purely physiological. However, in the case of the imbalance which is caused by the body's need for food or drink (tissue-need), the hungry or thirsty animal has to behave in a way which will procure food or water and it is here that the concept of a homoeostatic *drive* becomes important: tissue need leads to internal imbalance, which leads to homoeostatic drive, which leads to appropriate behaviour, which leads to restoration of internal balance, which leads to drive reduction.

As Simon Green (1980) points out, the internal environment requires a regular supply of raw materials from the external world but while oxygen intake, for example, is involuntary and continuous, eating and drinking are voluntary and discontinuous (or spaced) and while we talk about a hunger and thirst drive, we do not talk about an 'oxygen drive'. Because of the voluntary nature of eating and drinking, hunger and thirst have been the homoeostatic drives most researched by physiological psychologists.

Hunger
Hunger arises from the body's need for nutrients used in growth, bodily repair, the maintenance of health and the production of energy. Cannon originally believed that the hunger drive is caused by stomach contractions ('hunger pangs') and that food reduces the drive by stopping the contractions.

In an experiment by Cannon and Washburn (1912), Washburn swallowed a balloon so that his stomach contractions could be measured; as predicted, there was a high correlation between contractions and hunger. However, this hardly proves that the contractions actually *caused* the hunger and, indeed, the balloon itself may have been the cause of the contractions (Davis et al, 1959).

There are several other important objection to Cannon's theory of hunger: (i) people whose stomachs have been surgically removed still get hungry and hunger persists even when neural pathways from the stomach to the brain are cut; (ii) even a full stomach can 'feel' hungry if the passage to the small intestine is blocked (LeFrançois, 1983); (iii) the duodenum is probably more involved in hunger feelings than the stomach (Schachter, 1971); and (iv) people in affluent societies like our own very rarely experience hunger pangs (even though we may express our hunger by saying 'I'm starving').

Green (1980) refers to studies with rats in which the oesophagus is cut (producing an 'oesophagael fistula') so that food may be taken in through the mouth (so by-passing the stomach) or placed directly into the stomach (so by-passing the mouth). The results suggest that short-term regulation of food intake (as measured by how much food is eaten and over what length of time) could be controlled by either oral or gastric (stomach) factors; although neither is actually necessary, the presence of food in the stomach and small intestine is more important and yet being able to taste and chew our food seems to be essential for a feeling of being full and sated.

Compared with these 'peripheral' influences on the hunger drive, most recent research has focused on 'central' influences, that is, the role of brain centres which respond to change in blood-sugar level and fat content in the bloodstream and, in particular, the hypothalamus.

Research with rats in the 1940s identified the hypothalamus as playing a crucial role in eating behaviour. Hetherington and Ranson (1940, 1942), for example, found that lesions in the lower, central, portion of the hypothalamus (the *ventro-medial* nucleus or VMH) would cause *hyperphagia*, that is, the rat would carry on eating until it became grotesquely fat, doubling or even trebling its normal body weight. This suggests that the normal function of the VMH is to *inhibit* feeding when the animal is 'full'; hence the VMH became known as the 'satiety centre' and it has been found in rats, cats, dogs, chickens and monkeys (Teitelbaum, 1967).

Just as there is a centre which stops feeding, so there seems to be a part of the hypothalamus which normally *stimulates* feeding in the first place: the lateral hypothalamus (LH), if damaged, would cause the animal to starve (even in the presence of food) to the point of death; this failure to feed is called *aphagia* (Anand and Brobeck, 1951).

An interesting finding is that the *taste* of food seems to be especially important in hyperphagic rats; whereas most animals will eat even bad-tasting food ('you'll eat anything if you're hungry enough'), hyperphagic rats are very fussy and will refuse their regular food if quinine is added to it, even if this means that they become underweight (Teitelbaum, 1955). Similar results were found with obese humans (Nisbett, 1968 and Deck, 1971).

Internal and External Cues for Eating
One possible explanation is that the VMH lesion reduces the rat's sensitivity

to *internal* cues of satiation (eg blood-sugar level and body fat content) and instead it becomes more responsive to *external* cues (eg taste). Schachter (1971) reports that overweight people also seem to pay little attention to internal cues (eg hunger pangs) and base their eating habits more on external cues (eg the availability and taste of food); although there is some evidence that hypothalamic tumours are associated with obesity in obese humans (Grossman, 1967), there is no evidence that the hypothalamus does not function properly in overweight people generally. However, it is still possible that it works *differently* in 'fat' and 'thin' eaters.

Schachter et al (1968) found that while normal weight subjects respond to the internal cue of stomach distention ('feeling bloated') by refusing any more food, obese subjects tend to go on eating. Similarly, when a group of normal subjects and a group of obese subjects were deprived of one meal and then half of each group was given a roast-beef sandwich and the other half left hungry, only the normal weight subjects who had eaten the sandwich ate fewer crackers when allowed to eat their fill—it made no difference to the obese subjects whether or not they had eaten a sandwich as to how many crackers they ate.

Schachter (1971) suggests that it is the *availability* of food to which the obese subjects were responding and similar findings were reported by Nisbett (1968). However, both researchers found that obese subjects are less prepared than normal weight subjects to make an effort to find food (eg go into the next room to get sandwiches) or to prepare the food in some way (eg shell peanuts); so the former tend to keep on eating as long as food is in sight or ready-to-eat, regardless of whether their physiological needs have been met, while the latter are more willing to search for food but only if they are genuinely hungry.

Overweight people also tend to report that they feel hungry at prescribed eating times even if they have eaten a short while before; normal weight individuals tend to eat only when they feel hungry and this is relatively independent of clock-time.

Needs Without Specific Drives—Learning What to Eat

Clearly, with persistent deprivation, the resulting drive can come to dominate all aspects of a person's behaviour. Keys et al (1950) studied a group of volunteer subjects who spent six months in a state of semi-starvation (less than half their normal caloric intake). Their thoughts, dreams and conversations soon became dominated by food; their gum-chewing, coffee-drinking and smoking all increased markedly and, as time went on, they spent more and more time collecting 'pin-ups' of recipes and cooking utensils and devising elaborate menus.

These subjects' drive for food and their physiological need for food were clearly highly correlated, but often this connection is not always so evident; a good example of this is how we (and animals) know what to eat for a nutritionally-balanced diet. While we all need vitamin C, for example, we do not actively seek it out if we are deprived of it, nor, if we did, would we have any easy way of detecting it with any of our senses in the food we eat.

Stefanson (1938) reported that many Arctic explorers died of scurvy (a severe vitamin C deficiency) while the Eskimos were thriving (by eating animal fat, for example, which is rich in vitamin C); the explorers tended to retain their practice of eating lean meat even in a situation which necessitated a change.

Richter (1942, 1943) found that if specific glands in rats were removed (eg pancreas), they compensated by eating increased or decreased amounts of appropriate foods (eg decrease in sugar intake). Rozin et al (1968) made the diet of rats deficient in certain essential vitamins and minerals and found that they soon developed an aversion to this diet and came to prefer new food; the aversion persisted even after the deficiency was corrected. So rats, at least, seem to learn (presumably through taste and odour cues) which diets best meet their biological needs (Barker et al, 1977).

Presumably, we can do the same and cultural evolution helps the selection of balanced diets. Rozin (1977) points out that Mexicans increased the calcium in their diet by mixing small amounts of mineral lime into their tortillas and the Chinese cook spare ribs with vinegar. In Britain and the USA, by contrast, we seem to prefer diets which are fundamentally detrimental to our health, although in recent years there has been a strong campaign in favour of healthy eating.

Needs Without Specific Drives—Learning How Much to Eat

Keesey and Powley (1975) maintain that even people who do not continuously monitor their weight manage to keep it within a range of a few pounds, despite great variations in physical activity and the nutritional value of various foods they eat.

Similarly, laboratory animals with access to unlimited amounts of food will regulate their body weights very precisely within a certain range and the hypothalamus seems to play a vital role in this process of weight regulation. While hunger seems to be initiated by low blood-sugar levels, it usually stops before any increase could register in the hypothalamus; the hypothalamus also monitors fat content and when this rises above a certain point eating is inhibited (Nisbett, 1972), thus enabling humans and other mammals to maintain a remarkably stable weight.

Despite the importance of the hypothalamus, it is now generally accepted that to think of the VMH as a satiety centre and the LH as a feeding centre is not the most useful or accurate way of characterizing the role of the hypothalamus. Hyperphagia is probably the result of interruption of nerve fibres passing through the hypothalamus, since obesity may be produced by cutting these fibres behind the hypothalamus; similarly, LH aphagia may be 'mimicked' by damage to a bundle of fibres running from the brain-stem to the corpus striatum in the forebrain (Green, 1980).

Gold (1973) argues that the hypothalamus is probably a neural transmitting station to other parts of the brain and so it is the severing of neural pathways which seems to cause aphagia and hyperphagia rather than the destruction of a specific brain structure.

There is also some evidence that neurotransmitters are centrally involved in the control of appetite. Woods et al (1981) found that appetite in obese rats was reduced by one of a number of hormones belonging to the *peptides* group and injections of *beta-endorphins* (opiate-like chemicals produced by the brain which reduce the perception of pain) have been found to increase appetite (Margules et al, 1978). (See Chapter 15.)

Thirst

We can go without food substantially longer than water; while pangs of hunger may fade after a few days, sensations of thirst soon become maddening and thirsty rats will learn to find a reward of water faster than an equally hungry rat will learn to find a food-reward.

A dry mouth and throat are obvious cues to thirst but there are, like hunger, delicate biochemical processes within the body. A lesion in the LH causes adipsia (a prolonged refusal to drink) and, conversely, stimulation of parts of the hypothalamus by angiotensin (a neurotransmitter) causes a previously water-sated rat to start drinking within seconds (Green, 1980).

The hypothalamus contains specialized cells (osmoreceptors) which are sensitive to osmotic pressure and others which detect changes in salt concentration; Anderson (1971) injected a small amount of salt solution into the hypothalamus of a goat, which then proceeded to drink several gallons of water.

Exercise or increase in body temperature causes us to sweat which, as well as cooling the body, also takes water from the blood; with less water, the concentration of salt in the blood increases (since the same amount of salt is dissolved in less water) and this high salt concentration stimulates the specialized cells in the hypothalamus—which causes drinking.

The hypothalamus also stimulates the posterior lobe of the pituitary gland to release the antidiuretic hormone (ADH), which in turn stimulates the kidneys to reduce the excretion of water (ie more concentrated urine). (It is thought that ADH is actually manufactured in the hypothalamus itself.)

Like hunger, thirst and drinking seem to stop long before enough time has elapsed for the body to have absorbed the water from the stomach and for the water–salt balance in the blood to have been restored. So what makes us stop drinking?

Stomach distention is one important factor; Deaux (1973) observes that cold water is more thirst-quenching because it moves out of the stomach much more slowly and so provides a clearer stomach-distention signal to the brain. Another is the mouth-metering mechanism, which gauges the amount of water being ingested and compares the amount needed to restore the water balance (Bellows, 1939).

ii)   Drive–Reduction Theory

As indicated earlier, Hull's motivational theory must be considered in the context of his theory of learning. Drive-reduction was intended to explain the fundamental principle of reinforcement, both positive (the reduction of a drive by the *presentation* of a stimulus) and negative (the reduction of a drive by the *removal* or *avoidance* of a stimulus).

As we have seen in discussing homoeostasis, a physiological or tissue-need gives rise to a corresponding drive and behaviour which removes the need and consequently reduces the drive. The needs and drives in which Hull was interested were the primary (physiological), homoeostatic, needs and drives of hunger, thirst, air, avoiding injury, maintaining an optimum temperature, defecation and urination, rest, sleep, activity and propagation (reproduction) and Hull believed that *all* behaviour (human and animal) originates in their

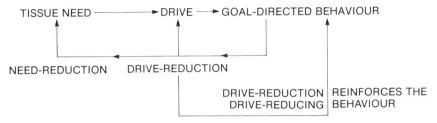

Figure 17.1 Summary of drive-reduction theory

satisfaction. The essence of drive-reduction theory can be represented as in Figure 17.1.

While the terms need and drive are often used interchangeably, there is a fundamental difference between them—whereas needs are physiological and can be defined objectively (eg in terms of hours without food or blood-sugar level), drives are psychological (behavioural) and constitute hypothetical constructs (although drives are operationalized as hours of deprivation in Hull's equations—see below). Hull proposed a number of equations which were meant to be testable in laboratory experiments and perhaps the most important of these was:

$$sEr = D \times V \times K \times sHr$$

where sEr stands for the intensity or likelihood of any learned behaviour which can be calculated if four other factors are known, namely D (the drive or motivation, measured by some indicator of physical need, such as hours of deprivation), V (the intensity of the signal for the behaviour), K (the degree of incentive, measured by the size of the reward or some other measure of its desirability), and sHr (habit strength, measured as the amount of practice given, usually in terms of the number of reinforcements). (Walker, 1984.)

Criticisms of Homoeostatic Drive–Reduction Theory

Hull's basic premise that animals (and, by implication, people) *always* learn through primary drive-reduction and *never* learn if drive-reduction does not occur can be criticized from several directions:

a) Even in the case of primary drives, their relationship to *needs* is very unclear, as we saw when discussing the eating behaviour of obese people; at its simplest, drives *can* occur in the absence of any obvious physiological need.

One example of a non-homoeostatic drive in animals is electrical self-stimulation of the brain (ESB). Olds and Milner (1954) found that a rat stimulated by an electrode implanted near its septum (part of the limbic system) would return again and again to the area of the cage where it had been stimulated and Olds (1958) found that rats which normally press a lever 25 times per hour for a food reward will press 100 times per *minute* for a reward of electrical stimulation.

So powerful a reinforcer is brain stimulation that a male rat with an electrode in its LH will self-stimulate in preference to eating if hungry, drinking when thirsty or having access to a sexually receptive female. This effect has been found in rats, cats, monkeys and pigeons (and humans, occasionally). According to Green (1980), the main reward site for ESB is the median forebrain bundle or MFB, a fibre tract which runs from the brain stem up to the forebrain through the LH and the effect seems to depend on the presence of the synaptic transmitters dopamine and noradrenaline (the catecholamines). There are also brain sites which, when stimulated, motivate the animal to *terminate* stimulation.

These reward centres are generally thought of as the neural substrate of 'pleasure', so that any behaviour defined as pleasurable involves their activation; as Green (1980) puts it, ESB is seen as a 'short-cut' to pleasure, 'eliminating the need for natural drives and reinforcers'.

b) As we saw in Chapter 3, Tolman's cognitive behaviourism challenged Skinner's S–R psychology because it showed that learning could take place in the absence of reinforcement (latent learning); since Hull was defining reinforcement in terms of drive-reduction, and was claiming that learning could not occur without drive-reduction, it follows that Tolman was also showing that learning *could* take place in the absence of drive-reduction.

c) Hull's theory was also inadequate in that it emphasized primary (homoeostatic) drives to the exclusion of secondary (non-homoeostatic) drives: primary drives are based on primary (innate) needs while much human (and, to a lesser extent, animal) behaviour can only be understood in terms of secondary (acquired) drives. A number of researchers, notably Neal Miller (1948), Mowrer (1950) and Dollard and Miller (1950) modified Hull's theory to include acquired drives (in particular, that of anxiety) which led in the 1950s to a great deal of research on avoidance learning (see Chapter 3).

The attachment of babies to their mothers has been explained in terms of a secondary drive (acquired through classical conditioning by associating her with the reduction of the primary hunger drive). (See Chapter 18.) Phobias can be understood in terms of avoidance learning (whereby avoiding the feared object or situation reduces the fear and so, through negative reinforcement, makes avoidance more likely. (See Chapters, 3, 28 and 29.)

For Mowrer (1950), the secondary drive of anxiety is one of the main instigators of behaviour; striving for social approval, success, power and money can all be seen as being motivated by the wish to *avoid* the unpleasant consequences which, early in life, became associated with loss of parental love, failure or weakness.

d) Although not everyone would agree with this interpretation, it does underline the inadequacy of drive–reduction theory, which in Maslow's terms, only deals with *survival* needs and ignores completely the *self-actualization* (or 'growth') needs, which make human motivation distinctively different from that of animals. However, just as ESB cannot be accommodated by drive-reduction when considering only animal motivation, so animals seem to have other non-homoeostatic drives which they share, to some degree, with humans. The rest of this part of the chapter will be devoted to these important, and pervasive, non-homoeostatic needs and drives.

Competence Motives—Motives Without Specific Primary Needs

According to White (1959), the 'master reinforcer' which keeps most of us motivated over long periods of time is the need to confirm our sense of personal competence; competence is defined as our capacity to deal effectively with the environment. It is *intrinsically* rewarding and satisfying to feel that we are capable human beings, to be able to understand, predict and control our world (which, as you may have spotted, also happen to be the major aims of science—see Chapter 2).

Unlike hunger, which comes and goes, competence seems to be a continuous, on-going, motive; we cannot satisfy it and then do without it until it next appears because it is not rooted in any specific physiological need and for this reason it is not very helpful to think of the competence motive as a drive which pushes us into seeking its reduction.

Another important difference between competence motives and homoeostatic drives is that the former often involves the *search for stimulation* rather than an attempt to reduce them as in the latter.

One way of seeking stimulation is through *curiosity* and *exploration*, which has been demonstrated in a number of species. Dember (1956) and Fowler (1958) found that if rats are allowed to become thoroughly familiar with a maze and then the maze is changed in some way, they will spend more time exploring the altered maze, even in the absence of any obvious *extrinsic* reward, such as food; they are displaying a *curiosity drive* (Butler, 1954).

Butler (1954), Harlow (1953) and Harlow et al (1950, 1956) gave monkeys mechanical puzzles to solve (eg undoing a chain, lifting a hook and opening a clasp) which they did, over and over again, for hours at a time, with no other reward; they were displaying their *manipulative drive* (Harlow et al, 1950).

Play and Motivation

Much of the behaviour normally described as play can be thought of in terms of the drives for curiosity, exploration and manipulation (eg Piaget, 1952); indeed, play and exploration are often equated. But is this valid?

Hutt (1966) distinguished between *specific* and *diverse* exploration and believes that play may be similar to the latter, but not the former; however, as Fisher (1980) points out, these are difficult to distinguish in practice in babies and young children, partly because both are facilitated by novelty and complexity. It seems that, almost from birth, babies show a preference for novel and more complex stimuli, although the level of complexity which is preferred is a function of the baby's age (which, of course, is correlated with perceptual and other aspects of development—see Chapter 5).

The purpose of play from the child's point of view is simple enjoyment; it does not consciously engage in play in order to find out how things work or try out adult roles or exercise its imagination but because it is fun and intrinsically satisfying. Any learning which does result is quite incidental, although for the young child there is no real distinction between 'work' and 'play' in an adult sense. Piaget (1951) distinguishes between play, which is performed for its own sake (and which allows the child to practise its skills and abilities in a relaxed and carefree way) and 'intellectual activity' or learning, in which there is an external aim or purpose; this distinction is meant to apply to the three major types of play he identifies (mastery, symbolic or make-believe and play with rules) but is more blurred in the first. (Piaget's theory is discussed in more detail in Chapter 19, and two other major theories, those of Freud and Erikson, are both discussed in Chapter 26.)

It is not just humans who play—the young of many species engage in activities which seem to have little to do with the homoeostatic or survival needs; however, the higher up the evolutionary scale the species is, the more apparent and purposeful the play becomes and the more the nature of play changes as the young animal develops. As Fontana (1983) points out, even in monkeys, play is mainly confined to physical movement of some kind, such as chasing and romping, and it usually involves other young monkeys; but in humans, play goes through a series of stages (see Piaget, 1951) and there is a great variety of types of play, including manipulation of physical objects, physical play with other people, symbolic or imaginative play and so on.

Motivation and Adaptation

Piaget saw play as essentially an adaptive activity and, throughout development, play helps to consolidate recently acquired abilities as well as aiding the development of additional cognitive and social skills (Rubin et al, 1983).

In the same way, the competence motives of curiosity, exploration and manipulation undoubtedly have adaptive significance for an individual and, ultimately, for the species. Although the internal conditions which give rise to competence motives are not apparent (in contrast with physiological drives) and although they do not have any obvious, immediate, consequences for the fulfilment of biological needs, investigating and exploring the environment equips an animal with 'knowledge' which can be used in times of stress or danger (Bolles, 1967).

According to *optimal-level* (or *arousal*) theories (Berlyne, 1969, Arkes and Garske, 1977), these kinds of behaviours are based on an in-built tendency to seek a certain 'optimum' level of stimulation or activity (not unlike a homoeostatic model of drive reduction).

According to Berlyne (1969), exploring the unfamiliar increases arousal but if it is too different from what we are used to, arousal will be too high (we feel anxious and tense) while if it is not different enough, arousal is too low (we soon become bored). Our optimum level of arousal is partly determined by how relaxed we are feeling initially: when we are relaxed we are more likely to welcome novel and challenging experiences (to increase arousal) whereas when we are already tense, we prefer to deal with what is already familiar and relatively undemanding. (This applies to animals too.)

A number of *sensory deprivation* experiments, involving mature animal and human subjects, lend support to optimum-level theories. Butler (1954) kept monkeys in small, barren cages and pressing a button brought the reward of opening a small observation window, through which they could see, for example, an electric train. The human subjects in an equivalent situation listened to the same stock-market report over and over again (Smith and Myers, 1966). In the classic experiments on sensory deprivation carried out by Hebb and his colleagues at McGill University in the 1950s (Bexton et al, 1954, Heron, 1957), subjects almost completely cut off from their normal sensory stimulation (by wearing blindfolds, ear-muffs, cardboard tubes on their arms and legs etc) soon began to experience extreme psychological discomfort, reported hallucinations and could not tolerate their confinement for usually more than three days.

Conversely, Ludwig (1975) reported that excessive stimulation ('sensory overload') is also debilitating and could be responsible for some kinds of psychological disorders in our highly urbanized society.

Arousal and Personality

Clearly, different individuals can tolerate different levels of arousal; one person's optimum may be 'overload' for another person and 'deprivation' for someone else. Perhaps those who can tolerate (indeed, seek) the highest levels of arousal are those who take life-threatening risks (by climbing mountains, parachuting, performing stunts, etc).

Ogilvie (1974) interviewed a group of top international athletes and found them to be: (i) strongly in need of success and recognition; (ii) highly autonomous and needing to dominate; (iii) self-assertive and forthright; (iv) loners, preferring transitory relationships to deep emotional ties; and (v) very low in anxiety, very realistic and having a high degree of emotional control. In sum, they are 'stimulus addictive', needing to extend themselves periodically to the limits of their physical, emotional and intellectual capacities, 'in order to escape from the tensionless state associated with everyday living'.

Zuckerman (1978) gave personality tests to over 10,000 people and divided them into *augmenters*, whose brains become more responsive the greater the stimulation, and *reducers*, whose brains exercise some kind of inhibition, whereby they become less responsive with increased stimulation.

Thus some people tend to thrive on stimulation and actively seek to increase it while others seek to reduce it (compare this with Eysenck's theory of Introversion-Extroversion, see Chapter 25).

The Need for Control

Another major kind of competence motive is the need to be in control of our own destiny and not at the mercy of external forces (Rubin and McNeil, 1983). The need for control is closely linked with the need to be free from the controls and restrictions of others, to dictate our own actions and not be dictated to; according to Brehm (1966), when our freedom is threatened, we tend to react by reasserting our freedom, which he called *psychological reactance*.

When people initially expect to have control over the outcomes of their actions, the first experience of not being in control is likely to produce reactance (Wortman and Brehm, 1975) but further bad experiences are likely to result in *learned helplessness* (Seligman, 1975), which was discussed briefly in Chapter 3 and to which we shall return in the section on stress.

Again, there are important individual differences. Rotter (1966) proposed the *locus* of *control* concept to refer to our beliefs about what controls events in our everyday lives and how we get reinforced for our actions. Locus of control was first assessed by the Locus of Control Scale (Rotter, 1966, Rotter et al, 1962) a self-administered questionnaire comprising 23 pairs of opposed statements; the scale contrasts *internals* (eg 'People's misfortunes result from the mistakes they make' or, 'What happens to me is my own doing') who believe they are responsible for what happens to them, with *externals* ('Many of the unhappy things in people's lives are partly due to bad luck' or, 'Sometimes I feel that I don't have enough control over the direction my life is taking') who believe that luck, fate and other people and events control most aspects of their lives.

Cognitive Motives—Consistency and Achievement

Perhaps one of the most researched cognitive motives is the need for *cognitive consistency* which we discussed in Chapter 11 in relation to attitudes and attitude change.

Another which has generated an enormous amount of research and theorizing is *achievement motivation* or Need for Achievement (nAch), which was one of the 20 human motives identified by Murray in 1938. He drew a sharp distinction between 'psychogenic' or psychological needs which are learned and 'viscerogenic' or physiological needs which are innate.

Based on his acceptance of Freud's belief that people express their true motives more clearly in free-association than in direct self-reports (or questionnaire-type personality lists), Murray devised the Thematic Apperception Test (TAT), which consists of a series of three or four pictures, each shown for about four minutes, about which the subject has to write a story based on the following questions:

a) What is happening and who are the people?
b) What has led up to the situation?
c) What is being thought and what is wanted and by whom?
d) What will happen, what will be done?

The pictures are sufficiently ambiguous to allow a wide range of interpretations and how a person interprets them reveals their unconscious motives; hence the TAT is a major *projective* test used in motivation and personality research. Its inter-judge reliability is quite high but test–retest reliability is lower. A person who scores high on nAch is concerned with standards of excellence, high levels of performance, recognition of others and the pursuit of long-term goals (ie they are ambitious).

McClelland and his colleagues (eg McClelland et al, 1953, 1958) is the major figure associated with nAch research and has found that high scorers tend to perform better on a number of tasks, including anagram puzzles, are generally more persistent and prefer an 'expert' to a 'friendly' work partner, compared with low scorers.

High scorers also tend to attribute their performance to *internal* factors (ability, effort etc) while low scorers are more likely to attribute theirs to *external* factors (ease of the task, luck etc). Two very important variables which interact with nAch are (i) Fear of Failure and (ii) Fear of Success. Atkinson (1964) argued that achievement-related behaviour is powerfully affected not just by nAch but also by *fear of failure*; he proposed a modified theory of achievement behaviour, incorporating nAch, fear of failure and certain contextual variables, in particular the perceived probability of success or failure and the incentive associated with success or failure.

Atkinson predicted that subjects whose nAch is greater than their fear of failure will show a real preference for tasks of intermediate degrees of difficulty, while subjects for whom fear of failure is greater than nAch will prefer either very easy or very difficult tasks and will avoid tasks of intermediate difficulty.

The prediction has been confirmed in the lab using a game of hoop-la, choice of options amongst degree students and career choice amongst students (high nAch ones being more realistic about their choice of career).

It has been found consistently that nAch scores do not predict the actual behaviour of females as well as that of males. Why should this be? According to Maccoby (1963), females, traditionally, have not been encouraged to be successful in those areas in which men are expected to excel (and which are reflected in nAch scores), but Horner (1970, 1972), using a story completion task, found that female students showed significantly greater *fear of success* than male students. This fear of success is likely to influence behaviour in competitive situations and situations in which success is seen by women as coming into conflict with their relationships with men and their success as women.

Hoffman (1977) followed up Horner's subjects and found that the high fear of success scorers married and had children sooner than low scorers; having a baby reaffirms their sense of femininity, removes them from the competitive arena and re-establishes their dependency on their husbands. Significantly, many become pregnant when faced with the possibility of success in an area where they might have been in competition with their husbands.

Finally, McClelland (1961) was also interested in the relationship between the economic growth or decline of certain societies and the level of nAch as reflected in each society's literature, folk-tales, etc. With the help of trained scorers, he found a positive correlation between the number of achievement-orientated themes and measures of economic activity within a particular society at different historical periods, including 350 years in the history of England and Greece from 900 to 100 BC.

2) Emotion: Adding Flavour to Behaviour

Mr Spock in 'Star Trek' is often pointing out to Captain Kirk how much energy human beings waste through reacting emotionally to things when a more logical and rational approach would be more productive. But would we be human at all if we did not react in this way? This is not to advocate 'being emotional' in the sense of losing control of our feelings or being unable to consider things in a calm and detached way; however, it is the richness of our emotions and our capacity to have feelings as well as to think and reason which makes us unique as a species. Emotions set the tone of our experience and give life its vitality and, like motives, they are internal factors which can energize, direct and sustain behaviour (Rubin & McNeil, 1983).

Many attempts have been made by psychologists to *classify* emotions:

1) Wundt (1896) believed that emotional experience can be described in terms of combinations of three dimensions—pleasantness/unpleasantness, calm/excitement and relaxation/tension, based on introspection;
2) Schlosberg (1941) also identified pleasantness/unpleasantness, together with acceptance/rejection and sleep/tension, based on photos of posed facial expressions;
3) Osgood (1966) also saw pleasantness as one dimension plus activation and control, which correspond to the evaluative, activity and potency factors of the semantic differential—see Chapter 11—based on live emotional displays;
4) Ekman et al (1972) and Ekman and Friesen (1975) identified six primary emotions (surprise, fear, disgust, anger, happiness and sadness) which they believe are universal, that is, they are expressed facially in the same way, and recognized as such, by members of a diversity of cultures and so are probably innate, based on photos of posed facial expressions;
5) Plutchik (1980) identifies eight primary emotions (which correspond to Ekman and Friesen's six, except that 'joy' and 'sorrow' are used for 'happiness' and 'sadness' respectively, plus acceptance and expectancy).

For each emotion that we may identify, there are three *components*: (i) the *subjective experience* of happiness, sadness, anger etc; (ii) the *physiological changes* which occur, involving the nervous system and the endocrine system, over which we have little, if any, conscious control although we may become aware of some of their effects (such as 'butterflies in the stomach', gooseflesh, sweating etc, see Chapter 15); (iii) the *behaviour* associated with a particular emotion, such as smiling, crying, frowning, running away, being frozen to the spot etc.

How these three components are related, and the relative emphasis given to one or more of them, is what distinguishes competing theories of emotion, to which we now turn.

Theories of Emotion

The James–Lange Theory

If there is a common-sense theory of emotion, it is that something happens which produces in us a subjective emotional experience and, *as a result* of this, certain bodily and/or behavioural changes occur. William James (originally in 1878 and then in 1890) and Lange, a Dane, at first quite independently of James, turned this common-sense view on its head and argued that our emotional experience is the *result*, not the cause, of perceived bodily changes. To give an example used by James, the common-sense view says that we meet a bear, are frightened and run; the James–Lange theory maintains that we are frightened *because* we run! Again, 'We feel sorry

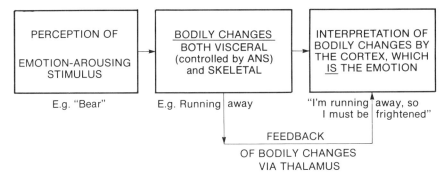

Figure 17.2   The James–Lange theory of emotion

because we cry, angry because we strike, afraid because we tremble . . .'
(James, 1890); indeed, the perception of bodily changes *is* the emotion.
(Lange and James, 1922).

The crucial factor in the James–Lange theory is *feedback* from the bodily
changes (see Figure 17.2); we label our subjective state by *inferring* how we
feel based on perception of our own bodily changes ('I'm trembling so I must
be afraid') which is rather similar to Bem's self-perception theory (see
Chapter 11). How feasible is this theory?

You may be able to think of situations in which you have reacted in a fairly
automatic way (eg you've slipped coming down the stairs) and only after you
have grabbed the bannisters do you become aware of feeling frightened (and
a little shaken)—it is almost as if the sudden change in your behaviour has
caused the fear, quite apart from *why* you grabbed the bannisters.

The theory implies that by controlling (deliberately altering) our behaviour
we can control our emotional experiences. Try smiling—do you feel any
happier? A crucial test (which James admitted would be very difficult to
perform) would be to examine the emotional experience of someone who is
completely anaesthetized but not intellectually or motor-impaired.

An interesting laboratory experiment which may seem to support the
James–Lange theory is that of Laird (1974), when 32 students were falsely
told that they were to participate in an experiment to measure activity in the
facial muscles. Bogus electrodes were attached to their faces (as if to measure
physiological responses) and the subjects were instructed to raise their
eyebrows, contract the muscles in their forehead and make other facial
expressions without their realizing the emotional significance of what they
were doing. Cartoons were then projected onto a screen and, regardless of
their content, subjects rated as funnier those they saw while 'smiling'; also,
when rating their own emotion, subjects described themselves as happier
when they were smiling, angrier when frowning and so on.

So, to some extent, overt behaviour can serve as a *cause* of subjective
feelings, and yet in the James–Lange theory, these bodily changes occur
spontaneously, not consciously and deliberately, so perhaps we cannot draw
too many conclusions from studies like Laird's. Besides, there are other,
equally serious objections to the theory, in particular, those made by Cannon
in 1927.

The Cannon–Bard Theory

According to Cannon, there are four major faults with the James–Lange theory:

1) The theory implies that for each subjectively distinct emotion there is a corresponding set of physiological changes enabling us to label the emotion we are experiencing. But is there any evidence that such physiological differences actually exist?

According to Wolf and Wolff (1947), although it is possible to make physiological distinctions between certain emotions (eg anger is generally associated with an increase in gastric activity and fear with an inhibition of gastric activity), efforts to find clear-cut physiological differences between some of the more subtle emotions have not been as successful (eg depression, feeling overwhelmed).

Ax (1953, 1957) reported that fear is associated with increased heart-rate, skin conduction level, muscle action potential frequency and breathing rate (corresponding to the effects of *adrenaline*) while anger is accompanied by increased diastolic blood pressure, frequency of spontaneous skin conduction responses and action potential size (indicating the greater influence of *noradrenaline*).

Ax's findings have been confirmed by Funkenstein (1956), Elmadjian et al (1957) and Frankenhaeuser (1975). Schachter (1957) confirmed that fear is influenced largely by adrenaline but found that anger produces a mixed adrenaline–noradrenaline response and pain produces a noradrenaline-like pattern.

Lang et al (1972) noted that even the general patterns of bodily response identified for anger and fear may vary from individual to individual and from situation to situation for the same individual.

According to Lloyd et al (1984), the research does not allow us to distinguish between the effects of general autonomic feedback and differentiated arousal patterns but, to be fair to James, he was probably more concerned with *expressive* behaviour (running away, trembling etc) than he was with visceral responses (which is what the research we have just reviewed has focused on) and it could be argued that Cannon's first criticism is, therefore, not strictly relevant. (Indeed, since we are almost completely unaware of these visceral changes, it would have been very difficult for James to have claimed that it is 'visceral feedback' which constitutes the emotion.)

2) Even if there were identifiable patterns of physiological response associated with different subjective emotions, Cannon argued that such physiological changes themselves do not necessarily produce emotional states.

He based this on a famous study by Marañon (1924) who injected 210 subjects with adrenaline: 71 per cent said they only experienced physical symptoms, but with no emotional overtones at all, and most of the rest reported '*as if*' emotions; the few who experienced genuine emotion had to imagine (or remember) a highly emotional event. More recently, Hohmann (1966) studied 25 adult males with spinal cord injuries who suffered corresponding damage to their autonomic nervous system and who reported significant changes in the nature and intensity of certain emotional experiences, particularly, anger, fear and sexual feelings. Generally, the higher up

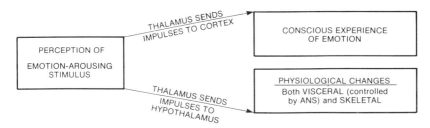

Figure 17.3 The Cannon–Bard theory of emotion

the spinal cord the lesion, the greater the disruption of visceral responses and the greater the disturbance of normal emotional experiences; like Marañon's subjects, they too reported 'as if' emotions, a 'mental kind of anger', for example.

Therefore it would seem that physiological changes, although not sufficient for the experience of 'full-blooded' emotions, are *necessary*. However, even though Marañon's and Hohmann's subjects did not experience 'real' emotions, it is significant that they experienced *particular* 'as if' emotions rather than a generalized state of arousal; clearly, perception of an eliciting stimulus is needed to give an emotion a full-bodied flavour.

3) A third criticism is to do with whether or not the physiological changes associated with emotion are even necessary (let alone sufficient). Cannon (1927) removed the sympathetic nervous system of cats and Sherrington (1900) severed the spinal cord and vagus nerves of dogs; in both cases, feedback from the viscera to the brain was prevented but the animals showed apparently normal emotional reactions. However, as Lloyd et al (1984) point out, we do not know about their emotional experience.

Yet Dana's (1921) study of a patient with a spinal cord lesion lends support to Cannon—despite having no sympathetic functioning and extremely limited muscular movement, the patient showed a range of emotions, including grief, joy, displeasure and affection.

4) Cannon also argued that, as we often feel emotions quite rapidly, and as the viscera are quite slow to react, how could the physiological changes be the source of such sudden emotion (as required by the James–Lange theory)?

So what is different about Cannon's theory (known as the Cannon–Bard theory)?
As Figure 17.3 shows, the subjective emotion is quite *independent* of the physiological changes involved: the emotion-producing stimulus is processed by the thalamus which sends impulses (i) to the cortex where the emotion is consciously experienced and (ii) to the hypothalamus, which sets in motion certain autonomic physiological changes.

Schachter's Cognitive Labelling Theory
According to Schachter (1964), Cannon was wrong in thinking that bodily changes and the experience of emotion are independent and the James–Lange theory is mistaken in claiming that physiological changes cause the feeling of emotion. However, he shares the James–Lange belief that physiological changes *precede* the experience of emotion because the latter depends

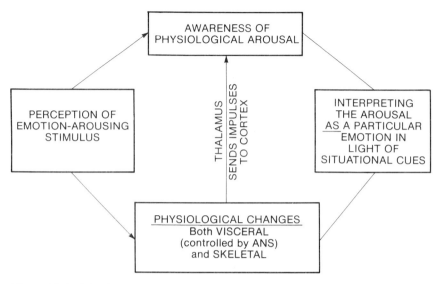

Figure 17.4   Schachter's cognitive labelling theory (or 2-factor theory)

on *both* physiological changes *and* the interpretation of those changes—we have to *decide* which particular emotion we are feeling, and which label we attach to our arousal depends on to what we *attribute* that arousal. (See Figure 17.4.) (Schachter is saying that physiological arousal is *necessary* for the experience of emotion but the nature of arousal is immaterial—it is how we interpret that arousal that matters and so the theory is also known as the 'Two factor theory of emotion').

The classic experiment which demonstrates the cognitive theory of emotion is that of Schachter and Singer (1962) described in Box 1.

Schacter and Wheeler (1962) confirmed these results by injecting subjects either with adrenaline or chlorpromazine (which inhibits arousal); controls were injected with a placebo. While watching a slapstick comedy, the adrenaline-subjects laughed more, and the chlorpromazine subjects less, than the control subjects.

Another supporting study worthy of mention is that by Dutton and Aron (1974). (See Box 2.) This study confirms Schacter's theory that the autonomic arousal which accompanies all emotions is similar and that it is our *interpretation* of that arousal that is important, even though this sometimes results in our *mis-identifying* our emotions; Dutton and Aron's suspension bridge subjects seemed to be mis-labelling their fear as sexual attraction to the interviewer. (What do you think would have been the outcome if the interviewer had been male?)

However, the theory has not always been confirmed (eg Maslach, 1979, Marshall and Zimbardo, 1979) and Lloyd et al (1984) believe that Schachter failed to manipulate arousal and cognition *independently* of each other, in particular, injections are not likely to be affectively neutral (whether adrenaline or placebo), nor would the effects of adrenaline be experienced without some emotional colouring, and the situation with the confederate does more

Box 1: Shachter and Singer's (1962) Adrenaline Experiment

Subjects were given what they were told was a vitamin injection in order to see its effect on vision; in fact, it was adrenaline. Subjects were tested under one of four conditions:

A   Subjects were told the *real* side-effects of the injection (namely palpitations, tightness in the throat, tremor, sweating, etc);
B   Subjects were given *false* information about the effects of the injection (eg itching and headache);
C   Subjects were given *no* information about any side effects (true or false);
D   Control group subjects were given a saline injection.

While waiting for a 'vision test', each subject (one at a time) sat in a waiting room with another 'subject' (in fact, a confederate of the experimenters). For half the subjects in each condition, the confederate acted in a happy, frivious, way (making paper aeroplanes, laughing out loud and playing with a hula hoop) while for the other half, he acted very angrily (eventually tearing up the questionnaire which he and the subject were both asked to complete).

Subjects' emotional experiences were assessed by: (a) observers' ratings of the degree to which they joined in with the confederate's behaviour; and (b) by self-report scales. What were the results?

As predicted, groups A and D were much less likely to join in with the confederate and to report feeling euphoric or angry, while group B and C subjects assumed the confederate's behaviour and emotion. Why? While group A could attribute their arousal to the injection and so did not need to explain it in emotional terms (thus confirming Marañon's findings), groups B and C attributed *their* arousal to 'emotional' factors, using the confederate's behaviour as a *cue* for identifying their own state of arousal as either euphoria or anger.

Box 2: Falling in Love on a Suspension Bridge (Dutton and Aron, 1974)

The subjects were unsuspecting males, aged 18 to 35, who were visiting the Capilano Canyon in British Columbia, Canada. An attractive female experimenter approached the men and asked them questions as part of a survey she was supposedly conducting on reactions to scenic attractions. One of the things they were asked to do was to invent a short story about an ambiguous picture of a woman, which was later scored for the amount of sexual content, taken to reflect their sexual attraction towards the interviewer.

Some men were interviewed on an extremely unstable suspension bridge, 230 feet above the Canyon (high-arousal condition) and others on a solid wooden bridge upstream (low-arousal condition); as predicted, the stories of the former group contained significantly more sexual imagery.

---

than simply provide a label. Despite these (and other) criticisms, Schachter's theory has been widely accepted; it has also stimulated a good deal of theorizing, including modifications (eg Arnold, 1960, the 'Valins' Effect', (Valins, 1966) the Cognitive Appraisal theory of Lazarus et al, 1970 and Izard, 1977, 1978, 1980).

3)   Stress: When Emotions Become Harmful

While there is no single definition of stress, we have all experienced it at one time or another and, because of its potential harm, physiologically and psychologically, psychologists, psychiatrists and others agree that it is essential that we try to understand it in order to prevent it or at least minimize it.

Cox (1975) identifies three models of stress around which definitions and research have revolved:

a)   The *engineering model* sees external stresses giving rise to a stress reaction, or strain, in the individual, so the stress is located in the stimulus characteristics of the environment; stress is what *happens to* a person (not what happens within a person).

The concept is derived from Hooke's Law of Elasticity in physics which deals with how loads (stress) produce deformation in metals. Up to a point, stress is inevitable and can be tolerated; indeed, moderate levels may even be beneficial and complete absence of stress (as measured, say, by anxiety or physiological arousal) could be positively detrimental (for instance, being so relaxed that you fail to notice the car speeding towards you as you are crossing the road).

There is no doubt that stress helps to keep us alert, providing us with some of the energy required to maintain an interest in our environment, to explore it and adapt to it; in these respects, stress is similar to motivation and emotion (or is a component of both). However, when stress becomes intolerable (when we are stretched beyond our limits of elasticity) it becomes positively harmful.

b)   The *physiological model* is primarily concerned with what happens *within* the person, that is, with the 'response' aspects of the engineering model, in particular the physiological (and, to a lesser extent, the psychological) changes which occur as a result of stress.

The impetus for this view of stress was Hans Selye's (1956) definition that, 'stress is the non-specific response of the body to any demand made upon it'. His original observations were made when he was a medical student and noticed a general malaise or syndrome associated with 'being ill', regardless of the nature of the illness. The syndrome was characterised by: a loss of appetite, an associated loss of weight and strength, loss of ambition, and a typical facial expression associated with illness. Further examination of extreme cases revealed major physiological changes, including enlargement of the adrenal cortex, shrinkage of the thymus, spleen and lymphatics (all involved in the body's immune system), and, eventually, deep bleeding ulcers of the stomach and upper gut (confirmed by Cox, 1978). These changes, representing the non-specific response to illness, were supposed to reflect a genuine phenomenon not embraced by specific responses and Selye called them the *General Adaptation Syndrome* (GAS)—we shall discuss this further below.

c)   The *transactional model* represents a kind of blend of the first two models and sees stress as arising from an *interaction* between people and their environment, in particular, when there is an imbalance between the person's perception of the demand being made of them by the situation and their ability to meet the demand, and when failure to cope is important (McGrath, 1970). Because it is the person's *perception* of this mis-match between demand and ability which causes stress, the model allows for important individual differences in what are sources of stress and how much stress is experienced; people may also differ in terms of characteristic physiological responses to stress (over and above the GAS); for instance, some will typically have migraine headaches, others break out in a rash, others have stomach pains and so on. There are also wide differences in how people attempt to cope with stress, psychologically and behaviourally, and we shall discuss some of these below.

The Engineering model may be seen as primarily concerned with the question 'What *causes* stress?', and the Physiological Model with the question, 'How do we *react* (physiologically) to stress?'. The Transactional model is concerned with both these questions plus the question, 'How do we *cope* with stress?'. We shall now look at these three major issues.

What Causes Stress?

Frustration and Conflict

We saw in relation to the transactional model that it is perceived mis-match between demand and ability which causes stress, and so anything which prevents us from achieving our goals is a potential source of stress; indeed, *frustration* is usually defined as some kind of negative emotional state which occurs when we are prevented from reaching a goal (eg Coon, 1983) and so frustration is a common source of stress. But what causes frustration?

Our own inadequacies can prevent us from achieving our goals and ambitions (eg we want to be a basketball player but are very short or we want to be a doctor but cannot stand the sight of blood). Or we can be thwarted by a whole host of external/environmental factors over which we have little or no control (although no less than we have over some personal factors, eg being short), such as the train being cancelled, the telephone being out of order, or the weather changing for the worse! We shall say more about these everyday hassles below.

Conflicts develop when a person experiences two or more competing or contradictory motives or goals:

i) *Approach–approach* conflicts involve having to choose between two equally attractive alternatives, eg two equally delicious-sounding dishes on the same menu or two equally interesting courses at college or university (see Cognitive Dissonance theory in Chapter 11 for a discussion of how such conflict is resolved once the decision has been made).

ii) *Avoidance–avoidance* conflicts involve having to choose between two equally unattractive alternatives, eg going to the dentist or putting up with awful toothache, deciding whether to do your psychology or your sociology essay first. It is a case of having to choose 'between the devil and the deep blue sea'.

iii) *Approach–avoidance* conflicts involve the same person or situation having both very desirable and undesirable qualities, eg you are really interested in psychology but you are not so sure about the statistics, or you want to go to university but you would also like to be working and earning some money.

Disruption of Circadian Rhythms

The word *circadian* comes from the Latin '*cira dies*' and means 'about one day'. It describes a particular periodicity or rhythm of a number of physiological and behavioural functions which can be seen in almost all living creatures (Aschoff, 1964, Mills, 1966). There are many other daily rhythms with much shorter periodicities, eg breathing, longer monthly ones, eg menstruation, or annual rhythms eg hibernation (Pengelly, 1974).

It seems that most species synchronize their bodily rhythms to the 24-hour cycle of light and dark, so that during a 24-hour period there is a cycle of many physiological functions (eg heart-rate, metabolic rate, breathing rate, body temperature) which all tend to reach maximum values during the late afternoon and early evening and minimum values in the early hours of the morning (Colquhoun and Edwards, 1970). It might seem fairly obvious that such a rhythm would occur since it is likely that physiological functions would increase during the day when we are active and become depressed at night when we are asleep and inactive; however, many studies have shown that these rhythms persist if we suddenly reverse our activity pattern and sleep during the day and are active during the night (Colquhoun and Edwards, 1970).

There is evidence that these rhythms are internally controlled (endogenous) but that their timing synchronizes and coincides with external (exogenous) environmental cues (Aschoff, 1964, Conroy and Miller, 1970). So if we persist with our reversal of sleep and activity, after a period of acclimatization the body's circadian rhythms will have reversed and become synchronized to the new set of exogenous cues.

Individuals differ considerably in how quickly they can reverse their rhythms; it can take 5 to 7 days for some and up to 14 days for others and some may never achieve a complete reversal (Elliot et al, 1972). Also, not all physiological functions reverse at the same time; eg body temperature usually reverses inside a week for most people, while the rhythms of adreno-cortical hormone takes much longer (Van Loon, 1963). During the changeover period all the body's functions are in a state of *internal desynchronization* (Aschoff, 1964) which is very stressful and accounts for much of the exhaustion, malaise and lassitude associated with changing work shifts (Teleky, 1943).

Psychological functions also seem to follow a well-defined circadian rhythm; for instance, we generally perform most psychological tasks most efficiently when our body temperature is highest and least efficiently when it is lowest. However, one notable exception is short-term memory which is negatively correlated with body temperature (Blake; 1967, Colquhoun, 1971, 1972).

So what happens to job performance (and, therefore, job efficiency) when body temperature and other physiological functions alter rhythm as a result of change in work shift? Hawkins and Armstrong-Esther (1978) studied 11 nurses during the first 7 nights of a period of night duty and found that performance was significantly impaired on the first night but improved progressively on successive nights; body temperature had not fully adjusted to night-working after 7 nights. There were significant differences between individual nurses, with some appearing relatively undisturbed by working nights and others never really adjusting at all. (The effects of lack of sleep were discussed in Chapter 16.)

Another occupational group who are very much affected by disruption to their circadian rhythms are airline pilots who experience 'jet-lag' because they cross time-zones during the course of the flight. If you have ever travelled across a time-zone, you will know what it is like to have your biological rhythms 'out of sync' with your surroundings: if you arrive in Washington DC at, say, 9 a.m. (after an eight-hour flight from London) you may be ready intellectually to start the day but as far as your body is concerned, it is still sleeping-time (back in London it is 3 a.m., the middle of the night). Sleep rhythms may become re-established after a few days, while body temperature and hormonal fluctuations seem to need longer to adjust (Goldberg, 1977).

Noise

According to Burns and Dobson (1984), whether or not noise creates a stressful environment to the detriment of task performance and whether or not individuals can adapt to noise while engaged in an activity depends on a number of other variables, including: (a) whether or not other stress variables are combined with the noise (eg lack of sleep); and (b) the predictability or controllability of the noise.

In relation to (a), Broadbent (1971) found that the combination of noise and lack of sleep could actually *improve* performance (probably because it serves to increase overall arousal), and in relation to (b), Glass and Singer (1972) found that subjects exposed to an annoying but predictable noise while working on a task later made fewer errors than subjects exposed to an equally annoying but unpredictable noise.

Life Changes

Holmes and Rahe (1967) examined 5000 patient records and made a list of 43 life events, of varying seriousness, which seemed to cluster in the months preceeding the oneset of their illness; out of this grew the *Social Readjustment Rating Scale* (SRRS), a self-administered pencil-and-paper measure on which the subject checks all those things which have happened to them in some specified time period (usually 6 to 12 months).

As you can see from Table 17.1 overleaf, the life events are ranked from 1 to 43 and each is assigned a mean value (from 100 for 'death of spouse' to 11 for 'minor violations of the law'); these mean values (or item weightings) were obtained empirically by telling 100 judges that 'marriage' had been assigned an arbitrary value of 500 and asking them to assign a number to each of the other events in terms of how much change in someone's life pattern it would involve *relative* to marriage. The average of the numbers assigned each event was divided by 10 and the resulting values became the weighting of each life event; an individual's SRRS score is the sum of the values for each life event which is ticked.

The assumption underlying the scale is that stress is created by events which require change (whether they are desirable or undesirable). Life

Table 17.1   Social Readjustment Rating Scale
The amount of life stress a person has experienced in a given period of time, say one year, is measured by the total number of life change units(LCUs). These units result from the addition of the values (shown in the right column) associated with events that the person has experienced during the target time period (see text).

Rank	Life Event	Mean Value
1	Death of spouse	100
2	Divorce	73
3	Marital separation	65
4	Jail term	63
5	Death of close family member	63
6	Personal injury or illness	53
7	Marriage	50
8	Fired at work	47
9	Marital reconciliation	45
10	Retirement	45
11	Change in health of family member	44
12	Pregnancy	40
13	Sex difficulties	39
14	Gain of new family member	39
15	Business readjustment	39
16	Change in financial state	38
17	Death of close friend	37
18	Change to different line of work	36
19	Change in number of arguments with spouse	35
20	Mortgage over $10,000	31
21	Foreclosure of mortgage or loan	30
22	Change in responsibilities at work	29
23	Son or daughter leaving home	29
24	Trouble with in-laws	29
25	Outstanding personal achievement	28
26	Wife begins or stops work	26
27	Begin or end school	26
28	Change in living conditions	25
29	Revision of personal habits	24
30	Trouble with boss	23
31	Change in work hours or conditions	20
32	Change in residence	20
33	Change in schools	20
34	Change in recreation	19
35	Change in church activities	19
36	Change in social activities	18
37	Mortgage or loan less than $10,000	17
38	Change in sleeping habits	16
39	Change in number of family get-togethers	15
40	Change in eating habits	15
41	Vacation	13
42	Christmas	12
43	Minor violations of the law	11

Source: Thomas H. Holmes and Richard H. Rahe. "The Social Readjustment Rating Scale," *Journal of Psychosomatic Research, II* (1967), 213–218.

changes are a mixed blessing—while we may welcome the variety and novelty they provide they also prevent us from achieving certain (other) goals and may force us into setting ourselves new goals and objectives which we have not anticipated. The SRRS was intended to predict the onset of illness; how well has it fared?

A number of studies have shown that people who experience many significant life changes (ie a score of 300 life change units or over) are more susceptible to physical and mental illness than those with lower scores (Eron and Peterson, 1982, Holmes and Masude, 1974, Rahe, 1974, 1981, Rahe and Arthur, 1977); correlations are usually small but significant and the range of associated symptoms is wide, including sudden cardiac death, heart attacks (non-fatal), TB, diabetes, leukemia, accidents and even athletics injuries.

However, we should be careful not to draw the wrong conclusions from this data, which is only correlational; for instance, rather than claiming that life-events cause illness, it could be that some life-events are themselves early manifestations of an illness which is already developing, eg being fired from work, sexual difficulties, trouble with in-laws, change in sleeping habits (Brown, 1986). Indeed, a study by Hudgens (1974) found that 29 of the 43 items are *not* independent of a developing illness, and Schroeder and Costa (1984) believe that the case for a causal connection will not be proven until such independent 'uncontaminated' measures are used.

The Controllability of Life Events

Just as noise is stressful when it is unpredictable, so life changes may only be stressful if they are unexpected and, in this sense, uncontrollable. Suls and Mullen (1981) asked subjects to classify the undesirable life changes on the SRRS as either 'controllable' or 'uncontrollable' and found that only the latter were significantly correlated with subsequent onset of illness. These results were confirmed by Stern et al (1982).

As Brown (1986) suggests, perhaps it is *perceived* uncontrollability which makes life-change stressful and, hence, dangerous to health. Using Rotter's (1966) Locus of Control Scale, and devising a new scale (the Life Events Scale), Johnson and Sarason (1978) found that life-events stress was more closely related to psychiatric symptoms (in particular, depression and anxiety) among people rated as high on *external* Locus of Control than among those rated as high on *internal* Locus of Control.

Related to Locus of Control is Seligman's (1975) concept of learned helplessness (see Chapter 3): when dogs, mice, cats and people discover that their behaviour and the delivery of electric shock are independent (ie nothing the subject does will make any difference—the shock will be given anyway), this learned helplessness is generalized to other situations in which shock is *in fact* contingent on the subject's behaviour.

Seligman (1975) believes that human depression can be explained in terms of learned helplessness—the original state of anxiety is replaced by depression when the individual realizes that trauma cannot be controlled and is said to be in a state of inaction (inhibition of coping behaviour) which places them in a highly vulnerable biological position. Learned helplessness is also thought to be involved in drug abuse (Berglas and Jones, 1978) and heart attacks (Krantz et al, 1974).

Abramson, Seligman and Teasdale (1978) reformulated this theory in terms of *attribution*; Peterson and Seligman (1980) see the depressed person as characterized by a particular attributional style, whereby *bad* events are attributed to causes which are *internal*, *stable* and *global* (ie high generalization across events) and *good* events to *external*, *unstable* and *specific* causes (eg luck, other people's generosity). (See Chapter 8.)

In Brady's (1958) 'Executive Monkey' experiment, pairs of monkeys were yoked by an apparatus which gave electric shocks; whenever one received a shock, so did the other (and this happened at 20-second intervals for six hours at a time over a period of several weeks). One of the pair (the 'executive') could prevent shock by pressing a lever; the other also had a lever but pressing it had no effect. The executive developed severe ulcers and eventually died; the other member of the pair showed no apparent ill effects. This is in contradiction to the belief that control over the situation usually *reduces* stress.

Two important points need to be made: first, Brady's monkeys were *not* randomly assigned to the executive and non-executive conditions but had been selected on the basis of how quickly they learned to avoid shock (Seligman et al, 1971); and, secondly, in a partial replication of Brady's experiment, Weiss (1972) using rats, preceded the shock by a *warning signal* for the executives who had much *less* stomach ulceration than their partners. By contrast, Brady's executives had to be constantly vigilant—without a warning signal, they could never be sure whether they would be successful in avoiding the *next* shock, very stressful! Human executives (many of whom are Type A personalities—see below) are also particularly prone to stress-related diseases and air-traffic controllers have the highest incidence of stomach ulcers in the USA.

The Hassles and the Uplifts of Everyday Life
The SRRS is useful but, by definition, most of the 43 changes are not an everyday occurrence.

Lazarus and his colleagues (Kanner, Coyne, Schaefer and Lazarus, 1981) designed a 'hassles scale' (comprising 117 items including 'concerns about weight', 'misplacing or losing things', 'rising price of common goods') and an 'Uplift Scale' (135 items including 'relating well with spouse/lover,' 'feeling healthy', 'meeting your responsibilities').

In a study of 100 men and women, aged 45 to 64, over a 12-month period, Lazarus confirmed their prediction that hassles were positively related to undesirable psychological symptoms and that uplifts were negatively related; they also found that hassles were a more powerful predictor of symptoms than life events (as measured by SRRS) ('divorce', for example, may exert stress by any number of component hassles, such as cooking for oneself, handling money matters and having to tell people about it).

Brown (1986) believes that we need to be able to use the Hassles scale to predict *somatic* symptoms, because psychological symptoms occur very close in time to the hassles themselves.

Personality and Stress
Having already discussed depression in relation to learned helplessness, it seems important to describe the *Type A* personality, which, according to

Brown (1986) has become common in twentieth-century, industrialized/ urbanized societies.

The Type A personality (Friedman and Rosenman, 1974) is, typically, a middle-class American male who has a chronic sense of time urgency, an excessive competitive drive and is prone to free-floating but extraordinarily well-rationalized hostility. He is always setting himself deadlines, has 'hurry sickness', cannot bear waiting his turn, has to do several things at once, is insecure about his status and needs the admiration of peers to bolster his self-esteem. The Type B person may be equally ambitious but it seems to steady him, give him confidence, rather than goad and irritate him.

How does this relate to stress?

The Type A personality is seen as being at risk, specifically for high blood pressure and coronary heart disease. A longitudinal study (Rosenman et al, 1975 and Brand et al, 1978) was begun in 1960/1 and involved 3,000 men, aged 35 to 39, all well at the start of the study; it continued for $8\frac{1}{2}$ years. Type A men were almost $2\frac{1}{2}$ times as likely to develop coronary heart disease as their Type B counterparts; when adjustments were made for traditional risk factors (such as age, smoking, blood cholesterol, blood pressure, heart disease in the family), Type A men were still *twice* as likely to suffer heart attacks, etc. These findings have been replicated in Sweden, Belgium, Honolulu, England, New Zealand and Canada.

How Do We React to Stress?

We have already mentioned the General Adaptation Syndrome or GAS which Selye (1956, 1976) believes represents the body's defence against stress.

Selye argues that the initial symptoms of almost any disease or trauma are virtually identical, that is, the body responds in the same way to *any* stress-or (source of stress), whether it is external and environmental or whether it arises from within the body itself. He has defined stress as, 'the individual's psychophysiological response, mediated largely by the autonomic nervous system and the endocrine system, to any demands made on the individual' (Selye, 1976). The GAS comprises three stages:

i) *Alarm reaction*: This involves physiological changes generally associated with emotion: the sympathetic nervous system is activated and in turn stimulates the adrenal medulla to secrete increased levels of adrenaline and noradrenaline. These are associated with sympathetic changes such as increased blood-sugar level, increased heart-rate and blood pressure, increased blood flow to the muscles, pupil dilation and decreased GSR (see Chapter 15).

The amount of adrenaline and noradrenaline (catecholamines) in the urine reflects the degree of sympathetic-adrenomedullary activity taking place and is correlated with how much stress people report experiencing.

The action of the catecholamines is to mimic sympathetic arousal and, in fact, noradrenaline is the transmitter at the synapses of the sympathetic branch of the ANS. Consequently, noradrenaline from the adrenals prolongs the action of noradrenaline released at synapses in the ANS; this means that, even if the stressor is short-lived and even after it has been removed, sympathetic arousal will continue. (This is a 'closed-loop' process, making a stress reaction self-perpetuating.)

ii) *Resistance*: If the stressor is not removed, the body begins to recover from the initial alarm reaction and to cope with the situation. There is a decrease in sympathetic activity, a lower rate of adrenaline and noradrenaline output, but an increase in output from the other part of the adrenal gland, the adrenal cortex.

The adrenal cortex is controlled by the amount of adrenocorticotrophic hormone (ACTH) in the blood; ACTH is released from the anterior pituitary (the 'master' endocrine gland) upon instructions from the hypothalamus. The adrenal cortex is essential for the maintenance of life and its removal results in death.

The glucocorticoid hormones (chiefly cortisol and corticosterone) control and conserve the amount of glucose in the blood which helps to resist stress of all kinds; Selye believes that increases in blood-sugar levels occur as the person or animal is exposed to stress and, if the stress continues, they return to normal levels and remain so during the resistance stage.

iii) *Exhaustion:* The body's resources are now becoming depleted, the adrenals can no longer function properly, blood glucose levels drop and, in extreme cases, hypoglycaemia could result in death. It is at this stage that psychophysiological (or *psychosomatic*) disorders develop, including high blood pressure, heart disease, asthma, ulcers and so on.

Stress, Disease and Personality

An important way in which stress may result in disease is through its influence on the body's immune system, a collection of billions of cells which travel through the bloodstream and move in and out of tissues and organs, defending the body against invasion by foreign agents (eg bacteria, viruses, cancerous cells); the study of the effect of psychological factors on the immune system is called *psychoimmunology* (Borysenko, 1983). People often catch cold soon after a period of stress (eg final exams) because stress seems to reduce the immune system's ability to fight off cold viruses. But there are some interesting personality variables involved: for example, students with hard-driving personality styles (similar to Type A) were the most stressed by exams, had the lowest antibody levels and caught more colds than other students (Jermott et al, 1981).

A study by Greer et al (1979) in England of women who had been diag-nosed as having breast cancer (and actually had a mastectomy) found that those who reacted either by denying what had happened or by showing a 'fighting spirit' were significantly more likely to be free of cancer five years later than women who stoically accepted it or felt helpless.

A powerful stressor is the death of a close relative (it comes at the top of the SRRS) and there is considerable documentation of surviving relatives dying themselves within weeks or even minutes of the death of a spouse or a child. In the 18 months following such a loss, people have a greater risk of death from a variety of illnesses (including heart attacks and cancer) than others of the same age and gender (Engel, 1971, Kraus and Lilienfield, 1959). (See Chapter 24.)

While heart attacks and strokes may involve changes in the ANS, infectious diseases and cancer are more directly associated with impairment of immune functions and bereaved people definitely have reduced resistance to disease (Bartrop et al, 1977, Schleifer et al, 1980). It seems that adrenaline can inhibit the ability of certain lymphocytes to release chemicals that kill invading germs or cells (including cancer cells) which the body recognizes as foreign; corticosteroids also prevent immature lymphocytes from maturing and, therefore, from properly carrying out their disease-fighting functions.

Animals given electric shocks are more susceptible to infection by viruses, bacteria, parasites and cancer (Riley, 1981) and men who were rated as being depressed were more likely to die of cancer 17 years later (Shekelle et al, 1981).

Finally, Locke (1982) found that 'good copers' deal effectively with shocks and challenges while 'poor copers' easily become depressed, anxious and develop a sense of helplessness. At times of major life changes, the latter showed a diminished level of a certain type of white blood cell ('natural killer cells') which normally fight off viruses and cancer cells.

How Do We Cope With Stress?

This final section will deal with coping as a *psychological* process; the GAS describes a physiological attempt to cope with stress but there are other methods of trying to control physiological reactions to stress which are, in themselves, psychological, in particular, meditation and biofeedback (which we discussed in Chapter 16) and progressive relaxation (see Chapter 29).

The major psychological methods of coping to be discussed here are: (i) defence mechanisms and (ii) coping mechanisms.

i)   The *ego defence mechanisms* (discussed in detail in Chapter 26) are mainly associated with the anxiety produced by conflict, as described in Freud's psychoanalytic theory. All we shall say here is that, by their nature, defence mechanisms involve some degree of distortion of reality and self-deception and, while desirable in the short-term, as long-term solutions to stress they are unhealthy and undesirable.

ii) *Coping mechanisms*, by contrast, are conscious ways of trying to adapt to stress and anxiety in a positive and constructive way, by using thoughts and behaviours oriented towards searching for information, problem-solving, seeking help from others, recognizing our true feelings and establishing goals and objectives. Eight major coping mechanisms described by Grasha (1983) are shown in Table 17.2 overleaf, together with the equivalent defence mechanisms.

One important coping mechanism not discussed by Grasha is *control*. Roger Brown (1986) cites several studies in which subjects in a simulated dental surgery have had access to a button to signal to the 'dentist' when their pain becomes intolerable; the effect is usually to reduce anxiety over possible pain and actually to *increase* the amount of pain that subjects will put up with before using the button (if they use it at all).

Being warned of possible pain and other discomforts, and having treatment explained to you, is called *information control* and it seems that not to have informational control can be very stressful, as found by Baum et al (1983) in

Table 17.2   Some major coping mechanisms and their corresponding defence mechanisms

Coping mechanism	Description	Corresponding defence mechanism
1. Objectivity	Separating one thought from another, or our feelings from our thoughts, which allows us to obtain a better understanding of how we think and feel and an objective evaluation of our actions.	Isolation
2. Logical analysis	Carefully and systematically analysing our problems in order to find explanations and to make plans to solve them, based on the realities of the situation.	Rationalization
3. Concentration	The ability to set aside disturbing thoughts and feelings in order to concentrate on the task in hand.	Denial
4. Empathy	The ability to sense how others are feeling in emotionally-arousing situations so that our interactions take account of their feelings.	Projection
5. Playfulness	The ability to use past feelings, ideas and behaviour appropriately so as to enrich the solution of problems and to otherwise add some enjoyment to life.	Regression
6. Tolerance of ambiguity	The ability to function in situations where we or others cannot make clear choices—because the situation is so complicated.	–
7. Suppression	The ability consciously to forget about or hold back thoughts and feelings until an appropriate time and place to express them arises.	Repression
8. Substitution of thoughts and emotions	The ability consciously to substitute other thoughts or feelings for how we really think or feel in order to meet the demands of the situation.	Reaction formation

Sublimation can be thought of as a Coping Mechanism *and* a Defence Mechanism, because it involves chanelling anxiety in socially desirable ways and so is positive and constructive.

a study of the residents of Three Mile Island, in the USA, scene of a nuclear energy plant accident. Fischoff (1983) also concluded that the risks from nuclear radiation that frighten people most are those which are unobservable, unknown to science and which lie in the future (eg leukaemia, which may develop 20 years after exposure). (As I write, the Chernobyl disaster in Russia has recently occurred and the full horror of what happened begins to register a little more each day as further details are revealed.)

Another kind of control is *cognitive control*; Langer et al (1975) asked patients awaiting elective surgery in hospital (eg hernia repairs, hysterectomies) to think about a time when they were too busy to attend to a minor cut and to compare it with a time when they had been free to lavish concern on a comparable cut. They were told that pain is extremely subjective and that stress can be controlled by controlling attention to the negative and positive aspects of surgery (eg being in hospital gives you a chance to withdraw from everyday hassles). These cognitive control patients were compared with a group of patients who were told what was going to happen to them and warned of post-operative discomforts but reassured about their safety and the quality of care they would receive etc (the information-control group).

Both methods were found to help patients cope (compared with a control group) but cognitive control proved more beneficial than information control in reducing anxiety, requesting sedatives etc. Knowing enough so that you do not have to let your imagination run wild, but not knowing too much so that stress is, unwittingly, increased (information control), combined with thinking about the situation in a constructive way which helps you get things in perspective (cognitive control), would seem to be an ideal way of coping with a stressful situation.

18

Attachment and Separation

Concept of Attachment

The concept of attachment is central to any discussion of the role of parenting (or what, traditionally, has been referred to as 'mothering') and so it is necessary to begin by asking why this is considered to be of such importance in the individual's development.

John Bowlby, writing in 1951, maintained that, 'mother love in infancy and childhood is as important for mental health as are vitamins and proteins for physical health'. More recently (1969/73) he has gone so far as to suggest that individuals with any kind of psychiatric disorder *always* show a disturbance in their social relationships (affectional bonding) and that, in many cases, this has been caused by disturbed bonding (selective attachment) in childhood.

The first relationship is generally regarded as crucial for healthy development because it acts as a model (or prototype) of all later relationships, ie a 'good' mother–child relationship teaches the child what it can expect from, and what it must give to, any future relationship. Erik Erikson believes that what the infant learns through its interaction with its mother is a 'basic trust' or a 'basic mistrust' of the world in general and other people in particular. (See Chapter 26.)

But does an attachment always and inevitably develop between every mother and child, or does it depend, at least to some extent, on the *quality* of the mothering the child receives? When it does occur, does it happen immediately or over a period of time? Can a child be attached to only one person at a time (ie the mother) or can it have multiple attachments and how important are fathers as attachment figures? Are there different degrees of attachment or are they all equally strong? Is there a critical or sensitive period for the development of attachments or can they develop at any time during childhood (or even beyond)? These are the major questions which we shall be trying to answer in the first part of this chapter.

The Gradual Development of Attachments

In *Mothering* (1977), Rudolph Schaffer describes the three stages involved in social development in infancy:

i) The first stage is marked by the infant's attraction to other human beings in preference to inanimate features of the environment.

As we saw in Chapter 5, it is initially the complexity of a stimulus which attracts babies, rather than its 'human-ness'. But about six weeks after birth, babies begin to smile more at human faces and voices, which embody all the qualities of objects (including complexity) in an exaggerated and particularly attractive way. The first 'social smile', therefore, occurs, on average, at six weeks.

ii) The second stage is reached when the infant learns to distinguish different human beings, so that the parent is recognized as familiar and strangers as unfamiliar, as shown by its smiling, for example.

However, the baby still allows other people to handle and look after it without becoming noticeably upset; people are still largely interchangeable (ie equivalent) so long as they provide adequate care. This ability to tell strangers from non-strangers appears, on average, at three months.

iii) The third stage is reached when the baby is capable of forming a lasting, emotionally meaningful bond or attachment with certain specific individuals whose company and attention it actively seeks.

This represents the culmination of a process which began at about six weeks, and the major indications that a bond has been formed are: first, the ability to miss the mother when she is absent, so that fretting will occur if she is out of the room (and, therefore, out of sight) even for a few minutes; and secondly, the appearance of the fear response to strangers, whereby being picked up and talked to by an unfamiliar person causes crying and general distress, sometimes even in the mother's presence. However, the mere presence of a stranger is not usually sufficient to induce this fear response—some direct contact is usually necessary. (By contrast, the mere presence of the mother may offer the young child enough security for it to explore and investigate a strange environment.) These two events (actively missing the mother and showing a fear of strangers) mark the establishment of an attachment and occur, on average, at six or seven months.

The Other Side of Attachment

This gradual development of attachments has important implications for understanding how any separation that has to take place between mother and child may affect not only the child but also the mother herself—and the relationship between them.

Psychologists have studied almost exclusively from the point of view of the child but an important exception are Klaus and Kennell (1976) who look at the bonding process from the point of view of the caregiver. Based on studies of premature babies, they concluded that the amount of physical contact ('skin-to-skin') is important, but even more crucial is the *timing* of such contact. Kennell et al (1979) propose that six to twelve hours after birth constitutes a critical period for the mother's emotional bonding to her infant, that is, the contact must take place during that time or the attachment may fail to develop!

However, others disagree; for example, Rutter (1979) and Rode et al (1981) stress that the bonding process builds up slowly over a period of months (rather than hours) just as the baby's does: the idea of a 'maternal instinct' can blind us to the gradual development of the mother's attachment to her infant, which is by no means automatic or immediate.

Attachment, Attachment Behaviour and Bonds

Babies show a general tendency to want to be close to people, to seek attachments, and at first this is directed towards anyone who happens to be around; if familiar figures are absent, babies will soon seek new attachments to other people (Robertson and Robertson, 1971). However, this general tendency is built on to form selective attachments or *bonds*, that is, attachments to particular individuals which persist over time, even during a period of no contact with the attachment figure.

Maccoby (1980) defines an attachment as, 'a relatively enduring emotional tie to a specific other person'. In infancy and early childhood, attachment is shown primarily by four kinds of behaviour: (i) seeking to be near the other person; (ii) showing distress on separation from that person; (iii) showing joy or relief on reunion; (iv) being generally oriented towards the person, even when not in close proximity, through, for example, listening for the person's voice, watching what they do, getting their attention by showing them toys and so on.

Different Kinds of Attachment

Despite this general tendency to seek attachments and the gradual development of selective attachments, there are important differences in the strength and security of children's bonds.

The *strength* of an attachment refers to the intensity with which attachment behaviours are displayed, while the *security* of an attachment refers to how confident the child is of the attachment figure being there when needed and being able to use them as a safe 'base' from which to explore in a strange environment. How are strength and security related?

There are certain examples of how they are *inversely* related. First, a child may be very 'clingy' because it has returned home from hospital or its mother has been in hospital to have another baby. Secondly, Tizard and Rees (1974) found that four-year-old children reared in institutions showed more clinging and following behaviour than family-reared children but were less likely to show selective attachment or deep relationships: although they seemed to be closely attached to someone, they did not seem to care at all when the person left, which seemed to be a defensive reaction to many experiences of loss. When these children were two, they were very clinging, would run and climb on the lap of anybody they knew even slightly, and in this respect were much more like 12 to 18-month olds. When first meeting strangers, they were very shy and frightened but were much more affectionate to a much wider range of people whom they knew just a little compared with most two-year-olds. To look at a third case, Rosenblum and Harlow (1963) found that rejected infant monkeys showed very strong attachments to rejecting 'mothers'—the monkeys were isolated at birth and reared in a cage with a 'cloth mother' which at random intervals blasted the clinging baby with a strong current of compressed air. These 'blasted' infants spent more time clinging to the surrogate (substitute) mother than controls whose cloth mothers did not abuse them in this way. Similar results were found when infant monkeys were abused by their mothers (who themselves had been 'reared' from birth with surrogate mothers).

It seems that the very act of 'rejection' results in more clinging which, in turn, results in more rejection and this pattern of interaction can be seen in the strength of attachment and loyalty of many abused children (eg Bowlby, 1972).

Fourthly, Hinde and Spencer-Booth (1970) studied infant monkeys and found that those which showed most distress after separation were those which had experienced most rejection from their mothers and for whom there was the most tension in the infant–mother relationship. So anxiety appears to increase attachment behaviour regardless of the response of the attachment-object.

There are also examples of a *positive* relationship between them, for instance, Stayton and Ainsworth (1973) found that children of sensitive, responsive mothers showed *more* positive greeting on reunion and *more* following (suggesting *stronger* attachments) than those shown by children of insensitive, unresponsive mothers but the former showed *less* crying and distress on separation (suggesting *more secure* attachments).

Attachment and Detachment

The whole purpose of bonding is to enable the child to feel secure in strange environments, to move further away from the mother, both literally and emotionally, so that attachment behaviours (eg clinging and following) are reduced and exploration and independence increase; this is known as *detachment*. Normally, we would expect attachment behaviour to be at its peak between 12 and 18 months, (although, according to Maccoby, (1980) it is quite common up to 24 months) and to decline gradually after that. Kagan et al (1976) have reported this developmental pattern for a variety of cultures. According to Rutter (1981), the aim of attachment is detachment but for this to happen the bonds must be secure.

Many animal studies show that detachment is actively encouraged by mothers in their young, but the study of detachment in children has been rather neglected. Noteworthy exceptions are studies by Rheingold (1969) and Rheingold and Eckerman (1970).

In the first study, 24 ten-month-olds were left with their mother in one room but could see, and had access to, another larger room. For some infants the larger room was empty, while for others it contained toys; all the children were observed from behind a one-way mirror. All 24 crawled into the larger room and showed no distress but they kept returning to the mother and then crawling off again. However, when they were *placed* alone in the same environment and left there, they became very distressed and almost completely unable to move. It seems that younger infants need to confirm their mental image of their mother by actually having a look at her from time to time.

In the second study, one- to five-year-olds were placed at one end of unfenced lawns, leaving them at the mother's knee but free to roam. The older the child, the greater distance ventured from her, but there were considerable individual differences. Also situational factors, like being able to keep the mother in view, influenced the extent of their separation.

The Study of Attachments: 'The Strange Situation'

Ainsworth and her colleagues (Ainsworth, Bell and Stayton, 1971, Ainsworth et al, 1978) have devised a method of studying attachments called 'The Strange Situation', which consists of a sequence of eight episodes in which the mother (and/or the father) and a stranger come and go from the room, each episode lasting about three minutes. The sequence of comings and goings is pre-determined and is the same for all the children and so the method used is controlled observation; one or more trained observers record the child's attachment behaviour in the mother's presence, when she leaves, when she returns, how the child responds to the stranger and how the child's play is affected throughout.

It has been mostly one-year-old white middle-class children who have been studied (but other groups have been studied too) and Table 18.1 summarizes the major findings.

The Stability of Attachments

Ainsworth et al's classification system is generally regarded as very reliable and has been used in a large number of studies in which attachment has been the major dependent variable. (Types A and C are sometimes grouped together as Anxiously or Insecurely attached and Type A seems to suggest the absence of any kind of emotional relationship at all. However, Sroufe and Waters (1977) monitored infants' heart-rate and found that Type A maintain an accelerated heart-rate during reunion episodes—even when avoiding their mothers!)

Connell (1976) and Waters (1978) tested white middle-class infants in the Strange Situation at 12 months and then at 18 months; when the overall patterns of interactions with mothers and strangers were looked at, Connell found 81 per cent and Waters 96 per cent were classified in the same way.

Vaughn et al (1979) studied mother–infant pairs living in poverty and experiencing frequent changes of accommodation; they were all single-parent families. At 12 months, 55 per cent were assessed as securely attached (the rest evenly distributed between types A and C) while at 18 months, 66 per cent were securely attached. Significantly, 38 per cent were classified differently on two occasions and this seemed to be related to changes in the family's circumstances; for example, those who were securely attached at first, but were anxiously attached by 18 months, had the most stressed mothers and those who shifted from anxious to secure or who were anxious on both occasions had mothers who experienced an intermediate amount of stress.

Children's early attachment patterns, then, are not necessarily permanent characteristics; if important aspects of their life situation change, children can shift from secure to insecure attachments or vice versa.

Table 18.1 Behaviour associated with 3 types of attachment in one-year-olds, based on the 'strange situation' (Ainsworth et al, 1978)

Category	General description	Percentage of sample	Response to mother leaving	Response to mother returning	Response to stranger
Type A	Anxious-avoidant	15	Show little or no distress. Play is little affected by mother's presence or absence or her whereabouts in the room when present. Generally, they don't seek closeness or contact with her; when she initiates it, they neither resist it nor attempt to maintain it.	They avoid closeness to or interaction with her. Typically, they ignore her or only casually greet her. If they make any approach at all, it is tentative, eg after starting to approach they may turn or look away.	Usually they show no distress and play is little affected. Distress comes from being alone (rather than being left by mother) and they are as easily comforted by stranger as by mother. In fact, in general, they treat both adults in a similar way.
Type B	Securely-attached	70	Play happily with toys. They don't stay particularly close to mother before she leaves but they do try to maintain contact. They will often resist being put down. Obviously distressed during her absence and play is considerably reduced.	They go to her immediately, seeking contact. Quickly calm down in her arms and then able to resume play.	They usually react happily to strangers (in mother's presence) but are distressed by her absence (and not only being alone). The stranger can provide some comfort but not as much as the mother. Generally, they treat mother and stranger very differently.
Type C	Anxious-resistant	15	They are generally either angrier or more passive than types A or B. Fussy and wary in pre-separation episode; they cry a lot more and explore much less than types A or B. Have difficulty using mother as secure base for exploration.	Seek contact with her but simultaneously resist contact and show their anger. Eg they may approach her quickly and reach out to be picked up but, once picked up, struggle to get down. They do not return readily to play but remain uninvolved, glancing frequently at mother.	They actively resist the efforts of strangers to make contact during the pre-separation episodes.

Theories of Attachment

Until the mid to late 1950s, the dominant view of why babies become attached was the 'Cupboard Love' idea, ie babies become attached to the mother who feeds them! There are two theoretical strands to this view which normally are diametrically opposed, namely Freud's psychoanalytic theory and learning theory.
According to Freud,

> The reason why the infant in arms wants to perceive the presence of its mother is only because it already knows by experience that she satisfies all its needs without delay (1926).

And again,

> Love has its origin in attachment to the satisfied need for nourishment (1940).

So, for Freud, the primary drive is for food, and through associating the mother with satisfaction of this primary drive, the child acquires a secondary drive for the mother—she eventually becomes desired in her own right.

It is in these terms (Drive–Reduction or Secondary Drive Theory) that Dollard and Miller (1950), Sears et al (1957) and other learning theorists explain the development of attachments. The baby's primary hunger drive is reduced (satisfied) by the mother and, through a process of classical conditioning, the baby acquires a secondary (dependency) drive for the mother herself. While food is a primary reinforcer, the mother is a secondary reinforcer.

How adequate is the cupboard love explanation of attachment?

A number of studies and theoretical developments have helped to expose its shortcomings:

1) Harlow and Zimmerman (1959) raised rhesus monkeys from birth with two surrogate mothers—a wire mother and one covered in terry-towelling; for half the infants, it was the wire mother who supplied milk and for the other half it was the cloth mother. Regardless of who fed it, all the infants became attached to the cloth mother—they used her as a safe base for exploring a new cage and would seek comfort from her when they were frightened by a mechanical toy. The warmth and 'contact comfort' provided by the cloth mother seemed to be a more powerful contributor to the attachment than the milk she supplied (although the cloth mother who also supplied milk represented an even more powerful combination).

2) In a longitudinal study of Scottish infants, Schaffer and Emerson (1964) found that infants become attached to people who do not perform caretaking activities (notably the father) and, conversely, in 39 per cent of cases, the person who typically fed, bathed and changed the child (typically the mother) was *not* even the child's primary attachment object.

Schaffer and Emerson concluded that the two features of an attachment figure's behaviour which best predicted the character of the infant's attachment to them were: (i) responsiveness to the infants' behaviour; and (ii) the total amount of stimulation provided (eg talking, touching and playing).

3) Both Rheingold and Eckerman (1970) and Schaffer (1971) see the infant

as an active seeker of stimulation and not a passive recipient of food and drink (which is the image portrayed by the cupboard love approach). Much of the infant's social interaction, even in the first few months, takes place when it is fed, clean and generally free from obvious 'biological' needs. The need for stimulation, which Schaffer believes is inborn, becomes selective (the infant comes to prefer human sources of stimulation) and eventually focuses on particular individuals (the infant comes to prefer specific attachment figures). According to this view, babies do not 'live to eat' but 'eat to live'.

4) The work of ethologists, beginning with Lorenz's famous studies of imprinting in goslings (1935), found that attachment of young birds (and various mammals too) takes place through mere exposure, without any feeding taking place. (See Chapter 14.) Although there is no direct comparison between imprinting and human attachments, Bowlby (1969), who originally trained as a psychoanalyst, was greatly influenced by the ethological approach. In particular he emphasized: (a) the *instinctive* nature of attachment behaviour, whereby babies are born with the tendency to display certain behaviours which help ensure proximity and contact with the mother or mother-figure (eg crying, smiling, crawling etc); (b) the importance of parental responsiveness to these innate behaviours; and (c) a critical or sensitive period early in the child's life when attachments must develop. From an evolutionary point of view, attachment behaviour makes very good sense. During the evolution of the human species, it would have been the babies who stayed close to their mothers who would have survived to have children of their own and Bowlby hypothesized that both infants and mothers have evolved a biological need to stay in constant contact with each other.

Critical or Sensitive Periods

Bowlby (1951) claimed that, in general, mothering is almost useless if delayed until after $2\frac{1}{2}$ to 3 years and, for most children, if delayed till after 12 months. The implication of what we said earlier about the stages of development of attachments is that they must be undergone in the sequence described and this may become increasingly difficult as the child gets older. We shall discuss the evidence relating to Bowlby's claim when we examine the long-term effects of maternal deprivation.

Monotropy

Bowlby (1969) claimed that the infant displays a strong innate, tendency to become attached to *one* particular individual (monotropy), although this need not be the natural or biological mother, and also that this attachment is different in kind (qualitatively different) from any subsequent attachment the child might form. Although the evidence supports the view that not all the child's attachments are of equal strength or intensity, that is, that there is a persisting hierarchy (eg Ainsworth, 1967, Schaffer and Emerson, 1964), Bowlby seems to be arguing that the relationship with the mother is, somehow, of a different order altogether from other relationships.

Is there any evidence which contradicts Bowlby's monotropy theory?

Rutter (1981) points out that each of several indicators of attachment (protest or distress if the attached person leaves the child, reduction of anxiety and increase in exploration in a strange situation when the attachment figure is present, and following or seeking contact with the person) has been shown for a variety of attachment figures: siblings (Heinicke and Westheimer, 1965), peers (Schwarz, 1972), fathers (Lamb, 1977) and even inanimate objects (as in Harlow and Zimmerman's cloth mothers), as well as mothers (eg Corter, 1973, Stayton et al, 1973, Ainsworth et al, 1978). Significantly, these attachment responses to others occur even in children who have developed their bonds with their mothers—but they are not shown towards strangers.

Attachments With More Than One Person

If the development of multiple attachments is not something Bowlby would dispute, he might still contend that the attachment to the mother is unique in that it is the first to appear and remains the strongest of all. However, on both these counts, the evidence seems to suggest otherwise.

In the Schaffer and Emerson (1964) longitudinal study, referred to above, four-weekly visits were made to the family home during the baby's first year, and then another visit at 18 months. As their measure of attachment they used the amount of protest the baby showed when separated from a familiar person; they also asked mothers whether the baby cried or fussed when left in its crib, outside a shop in its pram or in a room by itself.

At about 7 months, 29 per cent had already formed several attachments simultaneously; in fact, 10 per cent had formed five or more. At 10 months, 59 per cent had developed more than one attachment and by 18 months, 87 per cent had done so (a third had formed five or more). Although there was usually one particularly strong attachment, the majority of the children showed multiple attachments of varying intensity and only half of the 18-month-olds were principally attached to the mother; in nearly a third of cases the main attachment was to the father, and 75 per cent were attached to the father at 18 months. Although the infants when young tended to protest more when the mother left than when the father left, this tendency was short lived and by 18 months most children protested equally at the departure of either parent.

Fathers as Attachment Figures

Is there more to 'parenting' than 'mothering'?

Both Bowlby and Freud believed that the father is a less important and secondary attachment figure than the 'primary' mother; Bowlby argued that the father is of no direct (emotional) significance to the young child but is only of indirect value as an emotional and economic support for the mother.

Margaret Mead, the anthropologist, regarded the father as a 'biological necessity but a social accident' (1949), again implying the relative unimportance of the father as an attachment figure. Traditionally, the influence of parenting on the child's development has been equated with the influence of 'mothering', hence the term 'maternal deprivation' (coined by Bowlby) to refer to failure to form an attachment with a mother-figure or, once formed, an interruption of that attachment.

It is very unusual to hear psychologists discuss 'paternal' or even 'parental' deprivation and the notion of a 'paternal instinct' is even more improbable. However, a number of studies (including the Schaffer and Emerson study) reveal a very real role that fathers play in the social and emotional development of their young children.

Despite the increasing trend towards fathers taking a more equal or even an exclusive share of the upbringing of young children, it seems that fathers make a different kind of contribution from mothers and that the attachments that develop are correspondingly different (although not in the way or for the reasons that Bowlby suggests).

Fathers often relate to their children in an intense and exclusive manner; for instance, they may play together for half an hour or so when he gets home from work and before the child goes to bed. During that time, the child receives the father's undivided attention in a way that is often very difficult or even impossible for most busy mothers.

Clarke-Stewart (1978) found that most children between 7 and 30 months chose their fathers as playmates in preference to their mothers. Parke (1981) reports that even when the mother's and father's style of play are compared, there are important differences; the father usually engages in more vigorous, physically stimulating, games or unusual and unpredictable types of play (which babies seem to enjoy the most) while the mother plays more conventional games (eg pat-a-cake), joins in the child's play with toys and reads to the child.

Similar results were found by Lamb (1977) who observed 7 to 13-month olds at home. Mothers and fathers hold their babies for basically different reasons, mothers for caretaking and restricting, fathers for playful purposes or because the baby wants to be held.

Mothers seem to be preferred as sources of comfort when the infant is distressed, although this is more likely in unfamiliar surroundings (eg the 'Strange Situation', Kotelchuck, 1976); fathers are preferred as playmates and someone to have fun with! Maccoby (1980) maintains that more than one kind of satisfaction can be derived from an attachment figure and a given child will develop qualitatively different attachments with several significant people in its life, who include, of course, the father.

According to Parke (1981),

> Both mother and father are important attachment objects for their infants, but the circumstances that lead to selecting mum or dad may differ.

The father is not just a poor substitute for the mother—he makes his own unique contribution to the care and development of infants and young children.

Factors Influencing Attachment

So far, we have seen that: (a) there is no foundation for the belief that the biological mother is uniquely capable of caring for her child (the 'blood bond' myth); (b) the 'mother' does not even have to be female; (c) multiple attachments rather than a distinct preference for a mother-figure is the rule rather than the exception for even young infants; and (d) attachment is unrelated to the amount of physical caretaking the baby receives from the attachment figure.

So what does determine the number and intensity of a young child's attachments?

1) Intensity of Interaction

As we have seen, Schaffer and Emerson (1964) believe that the total amount of stimulation provided is one of two major predictors of attachment. The evidence relating to infants' attachments to their fathers demonstrates that the sheer amount of time spent with someone is, in itself, no guarantee that an attachment will develop—it is what happens during the interaction that matters.

Similarly, observations of child-parent relationships from Israeli kibbutzim (eg Fox, 1977) suggest that it is the intensity of the contact, rather than the amount, that is important (quality not quantity). In the kibbutzim, babies are often brought up in communial nurseries from when they are four days old and thereafter the parents spend 2 or 3 hours per day with them. The significant feature of this interaction is that there are none of the distractions of housework and demands from other children to 'dilute' the quality of contact—parents can devote all their energies and attention to their child for the time they are together. (Of course, a certain minimum amount of time spent in interaction is necessary for any attachment to develop at all, but beyond this it is quality that matters.)

2) Sensitivity and the Mother's Personality

Ainsworth and her colleagues (eg Ainsworth et al, 1971) have proposed that the crucial feature of the mother's behaviour towards her child is her sensitivity. For example, waking in the middle of the night to hear the baby crying next door is an example of the intent awareness of the baby and anticipation of its needs which facilitate their satisfaction.

The sensitive mother can see things from her baby's point of view and correctly interpret its signals; she makes her responses temporally contingent on the baby's signals and communications, in other words, she responds to her baby's needs and wishes as and when they arise; she is also accepting of the baby, co-operative with it and accessible or available for it.

By contrast, the insensitive mother interacts with the baby almost exclusively in terms of her own wishes, moods and activities; she may distort the implications of the baby's signals and communications or may even ignore them altogether.

Using the 'Strange Situation', Ainsworth et al have concluded that: (i) sensitive mothers have secure babies who can explore strange environments, using the mother as a safe base, and who can also tolerate brief, occasional, separations from her and (ii) babies of insensitive mothers are so insecure that either they become very angry when she leaves or they seem almost indifferent to her presence or absence and do not use her as a safe base. (See Table 18.1 on page 453.)

Similar results were found by Clarke-Stewart (1973) who used three categories of maternal behaviour which overlap with Ainsworth et al's sensitivity: (a) expression of positive emotion (affectionate, touching, smiling, praise and social speech); (b) contingent responsiveness (the proportion of the baby's cries and so on to which the mother responds); and (c) social stimulation (coming close to the baby, smiling, talking and imitating it).

In general, then, attachments probably develop most readily to people (not just mothers) who can adapt their behaviour to the specific needs—and personality—of the individual child; parental apathy and lack of responsiveness tend to inhibit the bonding process.

3) Consistency

Given that the parent-figure is responsive to the child's needs and that the interaction is reasonably intense, he or she must still be a *consistent* figure in the child's world; people must be *predictable* parts of the child's environment. This predictability and regularity of contact are conspicuously absent in long-stay institutions, such as residential nurseries. Tizard and Rees (1974) studying such an institution, found that, on average, 25 different people had worked with each child for at least a week by the time it was two years old, and the emotional atmosphere was described as 'cool'.

Also, predictability should extend to the personality of the attachment figure, including their behaviour and general way of responding to the child; for example, frequent and unpredictable swings of mood may make attachment-formation much more difficult.

4) Social Responsiveness and the Child's Personality

Just as adults differ (with respect to sensitivity, predictability and so on), so there is evidence that babies also differ in their need for physical contact and comfort.

As part of Schaffer and Emerson's (1964) longitudinal study, they found evidence that some babies liked cuddling while others preferred not to be cuddled. Several actively resisted being embraced or hugged or held tight, even when they were tired, frightened or ill and these babies were much more active and restless generally and much more intolerant of such physical restraints as being dressed. By contrast, the 'cuddlers' were quite placid, slept more and showed more interest in cuddly toys.

These differences were evident during the early weeks and did not seem to be related to how much the mother handled them—they were probably part of the baby's temperament. However, the mother was still a 'haven of safety' for the 'non cuddlers'—they tried to establish visual contact with her or held on to her skirt when frightened but would not cuddle up.

Although these babies were still attached to their mothers, it is interesting to ask whether the mothers of non-cuddlers had more difficulty becoming attached to their infants and whether the non-cuddlers would have difficulties in their adult relationships, particularly their sexual relationships and their relationships with their own children.

Attachment and Social Competence

Many studies have shown that there is a positive correlation between attachment as assessed by the 'Strange Situation' and later social behaviour with adults and peers; there is also a correlation with motor and language development and problem-solving skills.

Londerville and Main (1981), Matas et al (1978), Pastor (1981) and Waters et al (1979) have all suggested that a child who is securely attached at 12 months is likely to be more advanced months or even years later.

Arend et al (1979) concluded that at 18 months, the competent infant actively and effectively finds comfort when needed and uses the attachment figure as a secure base for exploring and mastering the physical world. At 24 months, they confront problems enthusiastically and persistently and enjoy mastery; although much more independent now, the child can still use the parents as and when they are needed. Finally the competent pre-schooler is enthusiastically involved with school work and school mates and can deal with problems in an organized, persistent and flexible way. (These findings can be seen as lending support to Erikson's theory of psychosocial development—see Chapter 26.)

However, as Fishbein (1984) points out, we cannot be certain that the early attachment is directly responsible for the later competence of the child—the latter might simply reflect a continuation of the healthy relationship with the parents.

The Effects of Separation: Bowlby's Maternal Deprivation Hypothesis

Bowlby (1951) argued that, 'an infant and young child should experience a warm, intimate and continuous relationship with his mother (or permanent mother-figure) in which both find satisfaction and enjoyment.' This, together with his monotropy theory, led during the 1950s and 1960s to criticism of the 'latchkey child' phenomenon and the general insistence, from many quarters of society, that mothers with young children should not go out to work but devote 24 hours of every day to child care. Bowlby, in fact, never advocated such a policy but if a mother is away from her child regularly (even if she works part-time), this could be interpreted as not fulfilling the requirement that the mother–child relationship be continuous.

Is there any relevant evidence?

Effects of Day-Care on Attachment
A number of American studies have compared the attachments of children (both working and middle class, from one- and two-parent families) who have experienced day-care (usually a day-care centre) with those of children who have not. There seems to be general agreement that what matters is *not* whether or not the child experiences day-care but: (a) the quality of that substitute care, such as how well staffed the institutions are (eg Caldwell et al, 1970, Vaughn et al, 1980); and (b) the stability of the arrangement (eg Moore, 1964/1967)

Although there may be disturbance to the child's social and emotional development, this is usually only temporary and reflects the child's adjustment to being away from the mother (eg Vaughn et al, 1980). Indeed, there may be long-term benefits for the child who experiences day-care; for instance, Rubinstein and Howes (1979) found that infants placed in high quality centres were more socially adept with peers than comparable home-reared infants.

In one of the biggest longitudinal studies, Kagan et al (1980) studied children who experienced day-care for 7 hours a day, 5 days a week, over 5 years. They were thoroughly tested from $3\frac{1}{2}$ to 29 months for intellectual growth (eg language development), social development (eg relationships with other children) and attachment to the mother, and were compared with children raised at home. No significant differences were found between the two groups in any aspect of development, provided that the day-care facility was well staffed and well equipped; but poor centres can be harmful.

Another crucial factor is the role of work in the mother's life as a whole and whether she enjoys what she is doing. Hoffman (1974) reviewed 122 studies of working mothers and concluded that the dissatisfied mother, whether working or not, and regardless of social class, is less likely to be an adequate mother. Working mothers who enjoy their job are more affectionate and less likely to lose their tempers, and their children are likely to have higher self-esteem.

Studies of child-minders (eg Mayall and Petrie, 1977, Bryant et al, 1980) and day-nurseries in Britain (Garland and White, 1980) tend to confirm the American findings, especially in relation to the quality and stability of the substitute care. However, the variety of quality of care, especially among child-minders, and the different beliefs about their function, especially among day nurseries, are perhaps greater than the American studies reveal and direct comparisons with children who do not receive regular substitute care have not been made.

Bad Home or Good Institution?

Even if Bowlby did not advocate 24 hours a day, 7 days a week mothering, he did at one time (1951) maintain that even a 'bad home' is preferable to any institutional upbringing, provided the 'maternal bond' remains unbroken. Of course, Bowlby is not suggesting that the quality of mothering is irrelevant, but rather that the quality and amount of maternal care provided in the *average* institution is much worse than in the *average* family. As Rutter (1981) points out, the care in even the best institutions often falls well short of the average home although it is superior to the worst homes.

Tizard and Rees (1974) attempted to investigate Bowlby's original claim that the best place for a child is in its own home with its natural parents. Their subjects were a group of 65 children who had been placed in a residential nursery at or before four months of age. Between 2 and $4\frac{1}{2}$ years, 24 of the children were adopted, 15 returned home (their mothers were mostly single parents) and the rest stayed in the nursery (which provided plenty of stimulation but there was a regular staff turnover), because their mothers could not be traced and so could not give the necessary permission for adoption.

The children had been placed in the nursery originally either because social workers believed that they would suffer if they continued to live in their deprived homes or because the parents themselves had been unable to cope and had requested that their child be taken into care. They were compared with a group of children of the same age who were living with their parents in London. At age 2 years, the institution children all showed similar developmental scores, but when they were retested at $4\frac{1}{2}$ years, some interesting differences began to emerge.

The group that was most advanced intellectually were those who had been adopted, with the control group children not far behind. But next came the institution children; those who scored lowest of all were those who returned to their natural mothers. However, with regard to social development, the adopted children and those who returned home were at an advantage: they were much more friendly, co-operative and chatty than the other two groups.

When tested again at 7 years (Tizard, 1977), the adopted children were doing better than the returned children in all aspects of development. However, the IQs of the institution children were within normal limits and there was little difference among any of the groups as far as reading age was concerned.

Perhaps the best conclusions to draw are: first, that the child's natural family is not necessarily the most desirable environment for healthy development; secondly, that adoption can be the best long-term arrangement for children who start out under extreme disadvantage; and thirdly, that children can develop within normal limits in an institution, although the quality of the institution is important. We shall return to the issue of adoption below.

The Case for Maternal Deprivation

Bowlby's (1951) claim that the maternal bond could not be broken in the first few years of life without serious and permanent damage to social, emotional and intellectual development, was based largely on the study of children brought up in orphanages, residential nurseries and other large institutions, conducted during the 1930s and '40s.

For instance, Goldfarb (1943a) compared one group of 15 children raised in institutions from about 6 months until $3\frac{1}{2}$ years of age, when they were fostered (the institution group), with another group of 15 children who had gone straight from their mothers to foster homes (the fostered group).

Although they were matched for genetic factors, mothers' education and occupational status, they might have differed in other important respects which may have determined whether they were fostered or placed in an institution initially, for example, how bright or easy-going they seemed, how withdrawn or prone to illness they were. Clearly, they were not assigned randomly.

The institutions were very clean but lacked human contact or stimulation; babies below 9 months were kept in separate cubicles, intended to prevent the spread of infection, and their only contact with other people occurred during feeding and changing. After nine months, they were put into groups of 15 to 20 and were supervised by a single nurse. They lived 'in almost complete social isolation during the first year of life' and their experience in the following two years was only slightly better.

At 3 years they were given intelligence tests, tests of abstract thinking and social maturity, and their ability to follow rules and make friends was also assessed. Not surprisingly, the institution group fell far behind the fostered group on all these measures; for example, all 15 in the fostered group were average in language development compared with only 3 in the institution group, and the latter were characterized by an inability to keep the rules, a lack of guilt, craving for affection and an inability to make lasting relationships.

When they were assessed later, between the ages of 10 and 14, the institution group performed more poorly on tests of intelligence (average IQ was 72 compared with 95 for the fostered group), social maturity, speech and ability to form relationships. Goldfarb attributed all these differences to the time spent in the institutions.

Classic studies by Spitz (1945, 1946) and Spitz and Wolf (1946) concentrated more on the emotional effects of institutionalization. Spitz visited some very poor orphanages in South America where infants, who received only irregular attention from the staff, became extremely apathetic and displayed high rates of 'anaclitic depression', a severe disturbance which involves symptoms such as poor appetite and morbidity. They maintained that after 3 months of unbroken deprivation, recovery is rarely, if ever, complete, and they painted a horrifying picture of developmental retardation and progressive dehumanization. A similar syndrome, which Spitz called 'hospitalism', involving physical and mental deterioration, is caused by prolonged hospital-ization when separation from the mother takes place.

What both these studies, and Bowlby himself, failed to recognize is that the institutions, which were clearly of a very poor quality, not only failed to provide adequate maternal care, but they were also extremely unstimulating environments in which to grow up. Consequently, we cannot conclude that it was 'maternal deprivation' that was responsible for the developmental retardation—we must distinguish between different *kinds* of deprivation and try to relate these to different kinds of retardation (Rutter, 1981).

Also, by using the general term 'maternal deprivation', the early studies failed to distinguish between the effects of being separated from an attach-ment figure and the effects of never having formed an attachment to begin with. As Michael Rutter (1981) points out, the term *deprivation* (de-privation) refers to the *loss* (through separation) of the mother-figure; the effects are usually *short-term* and can be summarized as *distress*. It is *deprivation* which Bowlby has been mainly concerned with since the 1950s. *Privation*, by contrast, refers to the *absence* of any attachment; the effects are usually *long-term* and can be summarized as *developmental retardation*.

In the remainder of this chapter we shall look at some of the most important effects of Deprivation and Privation, and conclude by asking how permanent the long-term effects are.

Effects of Deprivation (Separation)

Typical examples of a short-term separation is a child going into a residential nursery while its mother goes into hospital to have another baby, or a child having to go into hospital itself. It is difficult to define precisely how short a short-term separation is, but as a rough guide, it is days or weeks, rather than months, that we have in mind. Also, there is a permanent kind of separation, namely through the death of a parent, which must be considered.

Bowlby has found that the term 'distress' characterizes the kind of response which young children typically manifest when they go into hospital; it comprises three components or stages:

i) *Protest*—the initial and immediate reaction takes the form of crying, screaming, kicking and generally struggling to escape or clinging to the mother to prevent her leaving. This is an outward and direct expression of everything the child feels—anger, fear, bitterness, bewilderment etc.

ii) *Despair*—the struggling and protest eventually give way to calmer behaviour, the child seems to become apathetic. But internally the child still feels all the anger and fear that were previously displayed to the world; these are now kept locked inside and the child wants nothing to do with other people. The child may appear depressed and sad and may no longer anticipate the mother's return. It barely reacts to offers of comfort from others and prefers to comfort itself—by rocking, thumb-sucking etc.

iii) *Detachment*—if the separation continues, the child begins to respond to people again but will tend to treat everybody alike and rather superficially. However, if reunited with the mother at this stage, the child may well have to 're-learn' the relationship with her and may even 'reject' her (as she 'rejected' her child).

But clearly not every child goes through these stages of distress and the degree of distress is not the same for all children. So what factors mediate to determine the kind of experience the separation is for a child?

a) Age of the Child

Separations are likely to be more distressing between 6 or 7 months (when attachments have just developed) and 3 years, reaching a peak between 12 and 18 months (Maccoby, 1980). One of the crucial variables associated with age is the ability to hold in the mind an image of the absent mother (ie to think of her). Also the child's limited understanding of language, especially concepts like 'tomorrow' and 'only for a few days', makes it very difficult to explain to the child that the separation is only temporary (and why it has to take place). Young children, therefore, may believe that they have been abandoned altogether, that their mother no longer loves them, and that they may in some way be to blame for what has happened ('Because I'm naughty'). This makes it essential to try to compensate for the limitations of the child's understanding by, eg giving the child a photograph of the mother, even a tape-recording of her voice, or some article of her clothing, indeed, anything to keep alive the child's memory of her.

b) Gender and Temperament

Boys are generally more distressed and vulnerable than girls (everything else being equal). But boys vary a great deal in how they react to separations, as indeed do girls, ie some cope better than others. For both genders, any behaviour problems existing prior to separation are likely to become accentuated. For example, those who make poor relationships (with adults and/or children), or who are socially inhibited, uncommunicative or aggressive, are the most likely to be disturbed by admission to hospital (Stacey et al, 1970).

Schaffer (1966) found that more active babies show less drop in developmental quotients during hospitalization than less active babies.

c) Existing Relationship with Mother and Previous Separations

In general, the more stable and less tense the relationship before separation, the better the child appears to cope; for example, there is less chance that the child will blame itself in any way for the separation taking place.

On the other hand, an extremely close and protective relationship, where the child is rarely or never out of its mother's sight for more than a few minutes and where it is unused to meeting new people (children or adults), may cushion the child against separations to its disadvantage; ie the present separation will be more traumatic because the child has never experienced anything like it before!

Indeed, there is evidence that 'good' previous separations may not only help the child cope with subsequent separations but that they help the child become more independent and self-sufficient generally.

Stacey et al (1970) studied four-year-old children in Wales who went into hospital to have their tonsils removed. They stayed four days and their parents were not able to stay overnight. Some coped very well and it was discovered that they had experienced separations before, mostly staying overnight with their grandparents or a friend.

Multiple attachments should also make any separation less stressful, since the child is, by definition, not totally dependent upon any one individual. Kotelchuck (1976), using the 'Strange Situation', found that when fathers are actively involved as caretakers, children are more comfortable when left alone with strangers and the period during which children strongly protested at separation was shorter if they were cared for by both parents (as opposed to mainly the mother).

Again, Spelke et al (1973) found that infants who were least fearful with strangers (and hence most secure) had had the most interaction with their fathers.

However, everything else being equal, the longer the separation lasts, the more stressful it becomes.

d) Unfamiliarity and Stimulating Quality of the Environment

Bowlby's work and that of the Robertsons, who made a series of films in the 1960s on 'children in brief separation', helped bring into effect the policy of allowing mothers to stay with their children in hospital. Quite clearly, young children (and many adults) are distressed by a strange building, a strange bed, a different routine, strange sounds and smells, and unfamiliar faces which are always coming and going.

Many institutions in the past have proved very unstimulating places for young children; Jolly (1969) believes that boredom resulting from understimulation can itself cause distress, so adequate play facilities must be provided by trained workers.

A factor which can offset the effects of separation in general, and strangeness of the environment in particular, is the presence of persons familiar to the child, but not necessarily who provide any kind of substitute mothering. Thus, Heinicke and Westheimer (1965) found that distress was greatly reduced when children were admitted to a residential nursery with a sibling, even if the sibling was too young to take on a caretaking role. Strangeness can also be offset by taking a familiar toy or blanket into hospital and visits before actual admission.

e) Quality of Substitute Care

In the total absence of the mother, the person or persons who take over the care of the child will determine to a large extent how distressed the child becomes. Multiple attachments will make the situation less stressful, especially if the child remains in its own familiar home environment or stays in another setting it knows well. Even institutions can provide high-quality substitute care, a famous example being the Hampstead nursery run by Burlingham and Anna Freud (1942–44), where stability, affection and active involvement were encouraged.

However, many institutions are run in such a way that it is virtually impossible for any kind of substitute attachment to develop: staff rotas and turnover, a large number of children all competing for the attention of a few adults, and sometimes a deliberate policy of no special relationships in order to avoid claims of favouritism and resultant jealousies (eg the residential nurseries studied by Tizard and Rees (1974)) contribute to this.

The Robertson Experiment

If we were to try to predict how distressed a particular child will be as a result of a separation, each of the above factors would have to be taken into account and evaluated in the light of all the others. We could produce a kind of 'iden-tikit' picture of the combination of factors likely to produce the most extreme distress: a boy, aged between 12 and 24 months, who is rather sensitive, has a very close and stable relationship with his mother, is an only child, has had very little contact with other children, is suddenly removed from home to a totally strange environment (a residential nursery, for example) where there is a large number of children fighting for the attention of a small number of staff, who themselves come and go, on and off duty, so that he has little or no opportunity to build up a relationship with any one of them. His mother has gone into hospital to have another baby, and there is no-one to take her place.

Such a child was John, 17 months old, whose traumatic 9 days in a residential nursery were filmed by the Robertsons; the film records quite dramatically the three stages of distress described, particularly his rejection of his mother when she arrives, with the father, to take him home. Their relationship was disturbed for many months afterwards and John's case tends to support certain parts of Bowlby's theory.

However, as part of the same series of films, the Robertsons themselves fostered four other young children, whose mothers were also in hospital to have babies.

Joyce Robertson gave each child her full-time care and tried to preserve the mother's own methods of care as far as possible. During the month or so prior to the separation, the child was introduced to the Robertson house by visits between the two families, and when the child actually moved in with them, its own bed and blankets, familiar toys and the mother's photograph were also brought. As well as this, the father was encouraged to visit daily.

The four children were: Kate (2 years 5 months), who stayed for 27 days owing to her mother's obstetric complications; Thomas (2 years 4 months), 10 days; Lucy (1 year 9 months), 19 days; and Jane (1 year 5 months), 10 days.

Results

Quite clearly the degree of disturbance was far less than was observed in John's case. However, each was noticeably upset, although this differed according to the child's age.

Both the younger children seemed to transfer attachment to their foster mother quite easily and found security in the new setting. Neither showed acute upset but continued to function well, learn new skills, and increase their vocabularies. However, by the fourth day, Jane had become restless and demanded attention and gave the impression of a child who, 'was under strain and at times bewildered'.

Lucy too had bad patches and by the nineteenth day was in a 'highly sensitive state'. In both cases, the relationship with the father had deteriorated as the placement went on.

Interpretation of the Findings

The Robertsons were impressed by the fact that the child's anxiety was kept within a 'manageable' level and that 'positive development' continued; ie their distress was reduced to a minimum. The crucial factor involved was that the fostering situation had prevented bond disruption, ie it provided for a continuing, intense, personal interaction with the same individual(s) over a period of time. This is what had been denied John: he could not predict who would be available to deal with his needs at different times, and therefore, was unable to develop a relationship to take the place of the one with his mother which he had (temporarily) lost.

The Robertsons concluded that this represents a qualitative difference (difference in kind) from the behaviour of institutionalized children (such as John). However, to see bond disruption as the crucial factor is in sharp contrast with Bowlby's belief that is the loss of the *mother* herself, the person, which is crucial; the child in distress, he says, is grieving or mourning for the absent mother. Bowlby pointed to the fact that even in the fostering situation, distress is only reduced and not completely absent. Of course, when the mother is absent *and* there is no adequate substitute care, disturbance will be far greater; but this hardly implies that loss of the mother herself is the key variable. How can we reconcile these two interpretations?

It is possible that they are both true: John's distress was due to loss of his mother plus the absence of a substitute to take her place, while that of the four fostered children was due primarily to loss of the mother. This fits in neatly with the observed difference between John's behaviour and that of the other four children during their separations.

However, there seems to be an age difference also—the younger children (both under 2 years) seemed to miss their mother less than the 2 older children and this may be due to what we said earlier about the difficulty that the younger child has in keeping her image alive mentally. Perhaps for this reason the most useful comparison is between John, and Lucy and Jane; John, remember, was 1 year and 5 months as was Jane.

Long-Term Effects of Separation

Possibly the most common effect is what Bowlby calls *separation anxiety*, namely the fear that separations will occur again in the future. A good example of this is an episode which occurred two weeks after Kate returned home. Her mother took her to enrol at the school she wanted her to attend when Kate was 5 (more than two years ahead) and the following night Kate screamed as if she were having a nightmare. In the morning she was acutely breathless and the doctor diagnosed bronchial asthma. The mother later recalled that the headteacher had said that he would 'take' her.

This psychosomatic reaction is just one way in which separation anxiety may manifest itself. Others include (a) increased aggressive behaviour and greater demands towards the mother; (b) clinging behaviour—the child will not let the mother out of its sight; (c) detachment—the child becomes apparently self-sufficient because it cannot afford to be let down again; and (d) some fluctuation between (b) and (c).

The Robertsons noticed an interesting difference between the behaviour of the two younger children on reunion with their mother compared with the two older ones. Both recognized her immediately and responded pleasurably to her, but they seemed reluctant to 'give up' their foster mother, eg Lucy clung to her mother but also cried bitterly when Joyce Robertson left. Clearly, an attachment to the foster mother had developed in a relatively short time and the mother offered some protection against the feared separation from the foster mother. This can be seen as lending support to the Robertsons' interpretation.

By contrast, the two older children either ignored Joyce Robertson (as in Thomas's case) or stayed close to the mother (as in Kate's), suggesting, perhaps, that the former presented a threat of another separation from the latter, which lends weight to Bowlby's interpretation.

But, whichever interpretation we may favour, we must remember that in the case of all five children, apart from the actual separation experience itself, there was a baby brother or sister to contend with, a threat to the child's exclusive claim to its mother's love and attention.

Separation anxiety expressed as clinging in the child may generalize to relationships in general so that, for example in marriage, a man who experienced 'bad' separations in childhood may be very dependent on and demanding of his wife.

Bowlby regards *school phobia/refusal* as an expression of separation anxiety —the child fears that something dreadful will happen to its mother while it is at school and stays home in order to prevent it. Two major sources of such fears are: (i) actual events (eg the recent illness of the mother or the death of a relative); and (ii) threats by the mother that she will leave home or 'go mad' or 'kill herself' if things do not improve.

Finally, what about the most permanent of all separations, namely death? Of course, to a young child death and separation for any other reason mean exactly the same; it cannot distinguish between temporary separation and permanent loss.

Rutter found that there was a higher rate of loss of parent through death in a sample of children attending a hospital's child psychiatry department compared with a sample (matched for age, sex and father's occupation) attending paediatric and dental clinics. However, the proportion was still small (less than 1 in 12).

Death in the child's third or fourth year seems crucial; this is when parents are most needed as models for identification and there is an association between death of the *same sex* parent in childhood and psychiatric disturbance in adulthood. It is common for the onset of the disturbance to occur five or more years after the actual bereavement itself. However, a group of adolescent boys was referred to the child psychiatry department within six months of the parent's death; they were diagnosed as depressive (resembling adult grief) and antisocial.

In practice, it is very difficult to separate the effects of the death itself from a whole host of factors associated with it, for example, break-up of the family, grief of the remaining parent and their ability to take over the role of the deceased, the actual circumstances of the death (long illness or accident) and so on. In turn, broken homes have been found to be associated with delinquency (eg Yarrow, 1961). But broken homes occur for many reasons —marital breakdown, divorce and delinquency itself may all be the underlying cause; the death of a parent, even if it does lead to family disruption, is rarely associated with delinquency. Delinquency is most often associated with disturbed family relationships and a method of childrearing which combines hostility with permissiveness. In short, a 'broken home' does not simply produce disruption of a parent-child bond but will produce a child who has probably experienced considerable tension and stress in the home situation both prior to, and often after, separation.

Rutter (1970) studied 9 to 12-year-old boys living on the Isle of Wight and in London. He came across several who had been separated from their mothers when young but who seemed quite well-adjusted. Although they had suffered difficulties at the time, they had overcome them when family life returned to normal; however, some were later rated as maladjusted. What differences were there between the two groups?

Rutter discovered that those who became maladusted had been separated due to family discord, caused, for instance, by the psychiatric illness of one or both parents; while those who did not had been separated because of physical illness, housing problems or holidays, and not disturbance of social relationships as such—even the death of a parent had little lasting effect. Clearly, it is *not* separation as such which is harmful but the *reasons* for the separation and the longer the family disharmony lasts, the greater the risk for the child.

Effects of Privation

As we noted earlier, privation refers to the failure to develop an attachment to any individual and is usually, but not necessarily, associated with children reared from birth (or shortly after) in institutions. Dwarfism (failure to grow properly), for example, may result from inadequate diet, but also from maternal rejection (privation in a family setting). As we noted earlier, the studies of Spitz, Spitz and Wolf, and Goldfarb confused the effects of maternal privation and other kinds, namely sensory, and intellectual (all of which are normally referred to as forms of deprivation).

Prior to these studies, Skeels and Dye (1939) had shown a dramatic difference in intellectual functioning between an experimental group of children moved from a state orphanage in the USA to a state school for the mentally retarded, and a control group who stayed behind.

A total of 25 children were raised in an orphanage, where they experienced a minimum of social interaction and stimulation, until they were almost two years old (average age 19 months); 13 of them (average IQ, 64.3) were then transferred to a school for the mentally retarded where they received individual care from older, subnormal girls. They also enjoyed far superior play facilities, intellectual stimulation, staff–child ratios and so on. The other 12 children (average IQ 86.7) stayed behind and represented the control group.

When they were about $3\frac{1}{2}$ years old, the experimental group of children either returned to the orphanage or were adopted; their average IQ had risen to 92.8 while that of the control group had dropped to 60.5. When they were 7 years old, the average gain for the experimental group was 36 IQ points and the average loss for the control group was 21 points.

Skeels (1966) followed them up into adulthood. All the experimental subjects had more education than the controls, they had all finished high school, about one-third had gone to college, had married, had children of normal intelligence and had been self-supporting though their adult lives. The control subjects had mostly remained in institutions and were unable to earn enough to be self-supporting; they were still mentally retarded.

So what can we conclude about the effects of maternal privation?

Affectionless Psychopathy

In the light of what we said earlier about the importance of the child's first relationship, it would not be unreasonable to expect that a failure to develop an attachment of any kind early on in life would adversely affect all subsequent relationships.

The Harlow 'socially deprived' infant monkeys, especially if they were brought up only with surrogate mothers (and not with other infants) were very disturbed in their later sexual behaviour, and unmothered females themselves become very inadequate mothers. (They have to be artificially inseminated because they will not mate naturally.) But what about human infants?

Bowlby's original contention was that maternal deprivation caused affectionless psychopathy, that is, the inability to have deep feelings for other people and the consequent lack of meaningful human relationships. But his evidence for this is rather unconvincing.

In 1946, Bowlby studied 44 juvenile delinquents who were attending a clinic, having been found guilty of theft. They were compared with a control group, similar in number, age and gender and who, like the first group, were emotionally disturbed (but were not guilty of theft).

Bowlby claimed that affectionless psychopathy was strongly linked to separation experiences in early childhood; 14 of the 44 thieves (but none of the control group) showed many characteristics of the affectionless character (including an inability to experience guilt) and seven of them had suffered complete and prolonged separation from their mothers, or established foster-mothers, for six months or more, during the first five years of life. Two others from among the 14 affectionless characters had spent nine months in hospital unvisited during their second year (when attachments are normally being consolidated). Only 3 of the 30 other, non-affectionless, thieves had suffered comparable separations.

This suggests that privation rather than deprivation was the major cause of the affectionless character: the general picture is of multiple changes of mother-figure and home during the early years making the establishment of attachments very difficult.

However, even if we accept this conclusion, there are still problems with the study; it was a *retrospective* study, which means that the delinquents and their mothers had to remember past events and we know that human memory is far from reliable (especially about very emotive experiences). Also, how does Bowlby account for the remainder of the juvenile thieves (the majority) who had *not* suffered complete and prolonged separations? Subsequent studies by Cockburn and Maclay (1965), Cowie et al (1968) and Naess (1969) all failed to support Bowlby.

A further study carried out by Bowlby et al (1956) involved 60 children (41 boys and 19 girls) aged between 7 and 13, who had spent between 5 months and 2 years in a tuberculosis sanatorium, at various ages up to 4 years; about half of them had been separated before they were 2. No substitute mothering was provided in the sanatorium, where 40 to 60 children were in residence at any one time.

Compared with a group of non-separated control children from the same classes at school, few significant differences emerged. For instance, the average IQ score of the sanatorium children was 107, compared with 110 for the controls, and teachers' ratings were only a little less favourable for the sanatorium children. Although the separated children did more daydreaming, showed less initiative, got over-excited, were more rough in their play, were less able to concentrate and less competitive, the overall picture was of two groups who were more similar than different. There was certainly no evidence of the sanatorium children showing more signs of affectionless psychopathy than the controls, regardless of whether the separation had occurred before or after two years of age. Referring to the fact that illness and death were common in the families of the sanatorium children (10 per cent of the mothers had died by the time of follow-up), Bowlby et al themselves admit that, 'part of the emotional disturbance can be attributed to factors other than separation'.

Therefore, Bowlby's claim for a link between affectionless psychopathy and *separation* (bond disruption) seems largely unsubstantiated but, indirectly, he may have provided some evidence to support the view that *privation* (failure to form bonds) may be associated with the affectionless character; Rutter too would support this latter view.

According to Rutter, it is possible that a failure to form bonds in early childhood is likely to lead to, 'an initial phase of clinging, dependent behaviour, followed by attention-seeking, uninhibited, indiscriminate friendliness and finally a personality characterized by lack of guilt, an inability to keep rules and an inability to form lasting relationships' (1981).

Developmental Retardation

The Skeels and Dye (1939) and Skeels (1966) studies suggest that a crucial variable for intellectual development is the amount of intellectual stimulation the child receives, and not mothering, as such, as Spitz, Goldfarb and Bowlby claimed.

Similar findings were reported by Garvin (1963), who studied children moving from unstimulating homes to institutions where they received more stimulation, and Dennis (1960), who studied orphanages in Iran where children were rarely picked up or talked to.

In general, poor, unstimulating environments are associated with mental subnormality and retarded linguistic development (language is crucial for intellectual development generally). Also, Down's Syndrome children make less progress in institutions than at home, and boys again seem more vulnerable than girls to the effects of most kinds of privation. There are very important individual differences within the sexes too.

One difficulty in trying to identify the effects of privation is to be able to pinpoint which type of privation (eg sensory, intellectual, social or emotional) produces which particular long-term effect. A possible solution is to try to identify critical or sensitive periods.

Critical or Sensitive Periods

It seems that the first six to eight months are critical for the rhesus monkey's social development and the first three years for the development of affectionless psychopathy in humans. As we noted earlier, Bowlby went even further and said that mothering is useless for most children after 12 months. Dennis, in the same study mentioned above, concluded that there is a critical period for intellectual development before two years of age: children adopted from orphanages after two years, unlike those adopted earlier, seemed to be incapable of closing the gap in average IQ between themselves and the average child. Again, post-natal brain growth is most rapid in the first two years of life and susceptibility to damage (eg from an inadequate diet) is greatest during periods of most rapid development (see Chapter 15).

So what is the evidence that critical or sensitive periods actually exist? In general, the more difficult it is to *reverse* the effects of privation, the stronger the belief in such crucial early developmental periods.

Reversibility of Long-Term Effects

Clark and Clark (1976), in a review of the relevant studies, came to the conclusion that the effects of early privation are much more easily reversible than it has been traditionally thought.

For example, as far as Dennis's critical period for intellectual development is concerned, they argue that the later age of adoption makes adapting to the new home a totally different process from that experienced by the early-adopted child. Also, the child has had longer in which to develop habits which may interfere with adjustment; the child may be more withdrawn and disturbed and this may have a reciprocal effect on the family. Looked at in this way, the time spent in the institution has not had a direct, irreversible effect on intellectual functioning, but has had effects which may interfere with future learning and development. Again, the early-adopted child may have been brighter to begin with, which may have influenced their selection!

Studies of Adoption

Barbara Tizard in *Adoption—a Second Chance* (1977) and Tizard and Hodges (1978), report their findings on children in care throughout their early years, who, on leaving care, were either adopted or returned to their own families. (This was a continuation of the study first reported by Tizard and Rees in 1974.) None of these children had had the opportunity to form any stable attachment to any adult; Bowlby would have predicted that they would be incapable of forming any emotionally meaningful relationship with their adoptive parents and that they would show all the signs of affectionless psychopathy. However, by $4\frac{1}{2}$, more than half the adopted children had formed an attachment and most of the adoptive parents, as well as being deeply attached themselves, believed the children were deeply attached in return. They did show some deviant symptoms, such as attention-seeking, poor concentration and over-friendliness towards strangers (compared with the control group), but there was no indication of the affectionless character.

When they were $8\frac{1}{2}$, all the parents regarded the children as having formed deep attachments (including one child who was adopted as late as 7) but many were difficult to manage and unnaturally over-affectionate. At school, too, the adopted children (and those returned to their own families) tended to be more restless, fidgety, irritable and quarrelsome and to have problems in making friendships with other children; the earlier adopted children seemed to be at an advantage. However, Tizard and Hodges conclude that there is no reason to believe that children will be 'scarred' for life by earlier misfortunes or bad experiences simply because they occurred early in life. (Bowlby's views seem to reflect his psychoanalytic training where stress is placed very firmly on the events of the first five, formative, years—see Chapter 26.)

In the right kind of environment, even early privation can be successfully overcome. The adopted group did better than the group returned to their own families, both in the initial stages of settling in and in their subsequent progress. Why? The attitudes of the two sets of parents seem to have been a crucial factor—the adoptive parents worked harder at being parents, perhaps because of the fact that the child was adopted. Many other studies of adoption have stressed the high proportion of successful cases, despite the difficulties of the pre-adoption phase and the later discovery of having been adopted by the child.

Tizard concluded that adoption is the best solution to children's needs, compared with the alternatives of continued institutionalization, long-term fostering or return to the natural family.

Kadushin (1970) in the USA followed up 91 children adopted between the ages of 5 and 12 years. The vast majority were perfectly successful when studied at age 14 and the outcome was much better than expected on the basis of their early history of neglect, multiple changes of foster parents and late age of adoption.

Triseliotis (1980) followed up 40 people born during 1956/7 who had experienced long-term fostering (between 7 and 15 years in a single foster home before the age of 16) and interviewed them when they were 20 to 21 years old. Triseliotis concluded that if the quality and continuity of care and relationships are adequate, the effects of earlier disruptions and suffering can be reversed and normal development can be achieved.

Further evidence comes from the classic study by Freud and Dann (1951) of six pre-school children who had lost their parents in Nazi concentration camps in World War II and had remained together as a group despite several changes of camp. They were taken to an English nursery.

They had developed unusually strong ties with each other which seemed to have had a protective influence—they had been the only constant and stable element in one anothers' lives. The children were very poorly developed, both mentally and physically, normal speech had hardly developed, and they were fearful of adults and resisted their approaches. When they were first discovered (between 3 and 4 years) they clung together desperately. But gradually they began to form attachments to specific adult caretakers and, despite being very jealous and possessive of each others' new relationships, this lessened and they showed a spurt in social and language development.

Despite the various emotional problems they had, they did not show the gross disturbance which might be expected on the basis of the complete lack of mothering which they experienced and the extreme rejection and privation they suffered. 'All that I am able to say about their subsequent development, is that none of them developed phobias, either as children or at any time during their 20 year follow-up,' (Goldberger, 1972, in an unpublished manuscript, cited by Fonagy and Higgit, 1984).

However, the Freud and Dann study suggests that it is bond formation which is important for the development of social and emotional relationships in later childhood and adulthood, rather than with whom the bond is formed, and this tends to support the Robertsons' interpretation of their findings of the fostered children as against Bowlby's.

In a similar vein, Harlow found that the rhesus monkeys which had been reared without a mother but with other baby monkeys grew up to be more-or-less normal adults while those reared only with surrogate mothers developed abnormally, being unable to mate properly and, in the case of females, rejecting their offspring. However, this latter finding is hardly surprising; as Morgan (1974) points out, surrogate-only infants are being brought up without a society, apart from any other monkeys, which is a very abnormal state of affairs. Other monkeys, brought up with a mother only (no other babies), were less well adjusted than those reared normally with peers and a mother which is a much more informative finding.

As far as the reversibility of this early privation is concerned, Suomi and Harlow (1972), Novak and Harlow (1975) and Novak (1979) all found that whereas previously isolated monkeys (reared with surrogates) would completely ignore their first offspring, they would care for their second baby in a quite normal fashion. It appears that the first baby acts as a kind of monkey 'therapist' and as a consequence of this observation, previously isolated monkeys (for 6 months) were reared with younger, 3-month-old female monkeys, chosen because they were less likely to be upset or aggressive when faced with an isolate's aggression or lack of response. The younger monkeys were also likely to approach and play on an elementary, rather than a sophisticated, level with the isolates.

After 26 weeks of 'therapy', the isolates' behaviour was virtually indistin-

Box 1: The Case of Isabelle (Davis, 1947)

Davis (1947) reported the case of Isabelle, in Ohio, USA, who was found at $6\frac{1}{2}$ years old with her deaf-mute mother in a dark room cut off from all other social contact. Her behaviour towards strangers, especially men, was 'almost that of a wild animal', she communicated by gestures and the first attempt at assessing her intelligence gave her a mental age of 19 months; her social maturity was that of a $2\frac{1}{2}$ year old.

Then a systematic and skillful training programme was launched and by $8\frac{1}{2}$ (just 2 years after being found) she had reached an educational level normal for her age. Her IQ had trebled in $1\frac{1}{2}$ years and by 14 years she was described as bright, cheerful, energetic and participating well in all school activities.

Box 2: The Case of the Czech Twins (Koluchova, 1972)

Koluchova (1972) reported the case of two identical twin boys in Czechoslovakia, who were cruelly treated by their stepmother and found in 1967 at about 7 years of age. They had grown up in a small, unheated closet, often locked up in the cellar and were often harshly beaten. After their discovery, they spent time in a children's home and a school for the mentally retarded, before being fostered in 1969. At first they were terrified of many aspects of their new environment and communicated largely by gestures; they had little spontaneous speech. They made steady progress, both socially and intellectually. A follow-up study in 1974/5 showed that they had adjusted to their own age group quite satisfactorily in all respects. They had always had a close relationship with each other and this clearly helped them through their early misery. This highlights the fundamental importance of having *somebody* (not necessarily a mother-figure) with whom to form an emotional bond, as well as the reversibility of extreme, long-term privation.

guishable from that of a normally-reared monkey; follow-up of these 'rehabilitated' monkeys showed their behaviour to be perfectly normal two years later (Cummins and Suomi, 1976).

Of course, we must not generalize from animals to humans; however, the general principle may be the same, namely, that only a deliberate programme of adequate and well-organized compensation will tell us if the effects of privation are reversible or not.

Perhaps the most relevant (and dramatic) human evidence of reversibility comes from studies of children who have been found after enduring years of extreme privation and isolation (see Clarke and Clarke, 1976), for example, Isabelle (see Box 1) and the Czech twins (see Box 2).

Conclusions

The Clarkes point out that, traditionally, deprivation (and privation) studies have not looked merely at early experience but also at *continuous* experience; ie children who begin life as disadvantaged in some way tend to remain so.

For example, the insecure, disturbed, institutionalized child placed in a foster family may elicit antagonistic responses which strengthens its insecurity and reinforces the disturbance.

By contrast, attempts to reverse the effects of adverse early experience (such as those in Boxes 1 and 2) have provided grounds for hope for those who get off to a bad start, and the overwhelming picture that emerges is one of the *resilience* of the child. According to Waddington (1966), 'the human organism appears to have been programmed by the course of evolution to produce normal development outcomes under all but the most adverse of circumstances'; Sameroff and Chandler (1975) talk about a 'self-righting and self-organizing tendency' which helps children to develop normally under abnormal circumstances.

Finally, Morgan (1975) believes that for about twenty years many people, both professional and non-professional, including those responsible for social policy making, have been under an illusion that the connection between maternal deprivation and personality damage has been scientifically established. Not only does this scientific support not exist, she says, but there is sufficient evidence to make it decidedly improbable.

19

Cognitive Development

In this chapter we shall be concentrating on the work of Jean Piaget (1896–1980) who, like Freud and Skinner, has made a massive contribution to psychology as a whole and child development in particular.

Born in Neuchâtel, Switzerland, Piaget was trained as a zoologist and, as such, he was especially interested in the question of how animals adapt to their environment; it was in this context that he became involved in the study of human intelligence. He was also very interested in philosophy, particularly with that branch that deals with general questions about the nature of knowledge, called epistemology, and he came to combine these two areas of interest in *genetic epistemology*, the study of how knowledge develops in human beings.

Intelligence: Trait or Process?

Ironically, Piaget's early involvement with intelligence tests, which attempt to compare individuals on what is assumed to be a fixed trait, was to lead him towards his lifelong study of intelligence as a process. He was not concerned with individual differences but with what is common to all individuals as they pass through the same stages of intellectual or cognitive development.

While working in Paris under Binet, on the standardization of Cyril Burt's IQ test for use with French children (see Chapter 27), Piaget became intrigued by the unusual and unexpected replies that children often gave and he wanted to discover the processes by which these wrong answers were arrived at. He believed that children's mistakes were a much better indicator of how they think than their correct answers ever could be; he also became convinced that their errors were not random but systematic, that there was a pattern to them which revealed the underlying mental structures that generated them. Whereas IQ tests are concerned with the *what* of the child's answers (how many are right or wrong), Piaget was concerned with the *how* (especially as suggested by their mistakes).

The Nature of Intellectual Development

As we have seen, Piaget regarded intelligence as a process, something which changes over time; it also represents a fundamental means by which human beings adapt to their environment. The process essentially involves the individual trying to *construct* an understanding of reality through *interacting* with it; knowledge does not come 'ready-made' but has to be actively discovered (or even 'invented'), and the nature of that knowledge and understanding goes through *qualitative changes* during childhood and adolescence. These changes can be summarized as stages and Piaget identified four major stages which we shall look at below.

Underlying these changes, however, are certain *functional invariants*, ie fundamental aspects of the developmental process which remain the same and work in the same way throughout the various stages, in particular, *assimilation, accommodation* and *equilibration*. But before we can properly understand these unchanging features of development, we need to understand exactly what it is that changes, namely schemas (or schemata).

A *schema* can be thought of as the basic unit or building block of intelligent behaviour; more formally, it is a way of organizing our experience which makes the world more simple, more predictable and more 'know-able'. The baby's schemas are largely confined to inborn reflexes, such as sucking, and they tend to operate quite independently of other reflexes; a sucking schema is also a physical, overt, action. But in the course of development, physical (motor) behaviour comes more and more under the voluntary control of the baby and schemas gradually become more and more internal or 'interiorized', that is, they become mental and the child has started to *think* in something approaching the adult sense of the word. But if at birth we are limited to a few, simple, unrelated, reflexes, how do our schemas change in these ways? This is where assimilation, accommodation and equilibration come in.

At first, the baby will suck anything that touches its lips or is put into its mouth, whether this is its mother's nipple (which produces nourishment) or its father's finger (which does not). The baby is applying a schema that it already possesses by (almost literally) incorporating these objects, sucking them in more or less the same way, that is, *assimilating* them.

However, while the baby is still very young, it will gradually change the shape of its lips according to whether it is sucking a nipple or a finger. Later on, when it is given a cup to feed from, it must change the way it sucks (and swallows) yet again; this will not occur without a lot of spilt milk but eventually a 'drinking-out-of-a-cup' schema will have developed and this is *accommodation*. So in assimilation, the individual applies the schemas they already possess and tries to fit the environment into these; it can be thought of as a generalized use of what we can already do. But schemas are not just physical actions or skills but include ideas, concepts, bits of knowledge, verbal labels and so on. In accommodation, we change already-existing schemas to match the requirements of the environment, which brings us to equilibration.

As long as the child is able to deal with all (or most) new experiences by assimilating them, it will be in a comfortable state of balance or equilibrium

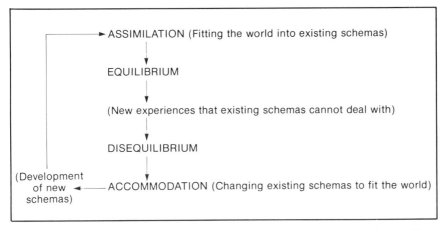

Figure 19.1 Relationship between assimilation, equilibrium, disequilibrium and accommodation in the development of schemas

(brought about by *equilibration*). However, if already-existing schemas are inadequate to cope with new situations, the child is pushed into a less comfortable state of disequilibrium and, to restore the balance, it must change one or more of its schemas, that is, it must accommodate.

So it is through this process of equilibration that development proceeds, a continuous series of assimilations and accommodations, equilibrium and disequilibrium, an ongoing process throughout life but with the most significant developments taking place during the first fifteen years or so. (See Figure 19.1.)

When a schema has recently developed, assimilation ensures that the new learning, which the schema represents, is consolidated, that is, it is practised repeatedly until it can be used easily and even automatically. But assimilation alone would make behaviour very rigid and inflexible and, indeed, very little development would actually take place—this can only happen through accommodation. So assimilation and accommodation are both necessary and complementary and together they constitute the fundamental process of *adaptation*. (Adaptation equals assimilation plus accommodation.)

Stages of Cognitive Development

Having discussed how schemas change and develop in general, we are in a position to look at the characteristic changes that take place during the four major stages that Piaget describes, namely:

i)   The Sensorimotor (0 to 2 years);
ii) The Pre-operational (2 to 7 years);
iii) The Concrete-operational (7 to 11 years);
iv) The Formal-operational (11 to 15 years).

Each stage represents a stage in the development of intelligence (hence 'sensorimotor intelligence', 'pre-operational intelligence' and so on) and is really a way of summarizing the various schemas the individual has at any particular time. But two notes of caution are necessary. First, the ages corresponding to each stage are only approximations or averages; children move through the stages at different speeds, often due to environmental factors. But the *sequence* of stages is invariant and universal (the same for all human beings) and this is based on biological maturation. Secondly, the concept of a 'stage' of development is often interpreted to indicate that development is discontinuous, that is, not a gradual process of change but broken up into 'segments' (ie the stages). This was not the impression Piaget wanted to create and from 1970 he preferred to think of development as a spiral, implying a continuous process. However, later stages build on earlier ones and entail *reconstructing* at a new level what was achieved at the earlier stage; for instance, the operational intelligence of the 7- to 11-year-old originates in the sensorimotor intelligence of the 0 to 2-year-old but they are qualitatively different, ie different kinds of intelligence. (We shall discuss the concept of a stage again when we evaluate Piaget's theory as a whole.)

i)   The Sensorimotor Stage (0 to 2 years)

The baby's intelligence is essentially *practical*, that is, its interactions with the environment consist of overt actions, either *sensory* (seeing, hearing etc) or *motor* (grasping, pulling etc). The baby 'thinks' through acting upon objects and/or perceiving them—a rattle *is* its colour when looked at, its texture when touched or sucked, its sound when shaken—and when it is not being perceived or acted upon in any of these ways, it no longer exists as far as the baby is concerned. This is referred to as a lack of *object permanence*.

This lack of object permanence is part of the baby's profound *egocentrism*, that is, it makes no distinction between itself and the rest of the world, so that nothing (including itself) has any separate, independent, existence. (This should not be confused with egocentrism as it has been studied in the 2- to 7-year-old, where the child cannot distinguish between its own viewpoint and other people's—see page 485).

The development of object permanence is one of the major achievements of the sensorimotor period so we shall discuss it in some detail.

Object Permanence

Between one and four months, when the baby sees its bottle, for example, it begins to suck, apparently for the pleasure of it, even if the teat does not touch its lips. This suggests that the baby has learned to *recognize* its bottle; but it hardly constitutes understanding that the bottle exists independently of the baby itself. The infant will look at a toy if it is within visual range, follow it with its eyes and, between three and four months, try to grasp it. But as soon as it has moved out of sight, the baby acts as if it had ceased to exist; there is no attempt to search for it, with eyes or hands. (It is a case of 'out of sight, out of mind'.)

However, some psychologists believe that Piaget may have been misjudging what babies can do. For example, Bower and Wishart (1972) found that the way an object is made to disappear influences a baby's response, while Piaget believed that it should not make any difference at all. If babies were looking at an object and reaching for it when the lights were turned off, Bower and Wishart found that they would continue to reach for it for up to $1\frac{1}{2}$ minutes. (They used infra-red cameras to observe the babies in the dark.) This strongly suggests that the baby remembers that the object is still there and Bower (1977) believes that the baby's initial difficulty is to do with understanding concepts of location and movement and *not* the object-concept as such.

Also during this stage, according to Piaget, the *whole* object must be visible if the baby is to respond to it at all. However, Bower (1971) claims that if a month-old baby is shown a toy, then a screen is put between the baby and the toy, and the toy is removed and then the screen, the baby shows some surprise or even a startled response, indicating that it expects the toy to be there still. Piaget may have been observing immature motor skills in the infant's failure to 'search' rather than an immature object-concept.

By six to seven months, says Piaget, the baby will reach for a familiar object if only a part of it is visible, suggesting that it realizes that the rest of it is attached to the part that is showing. (Bower, 1974, believes this will happen as early as four months.) However, if you cover up the object completely, even if the baby sees you do it, it will not search for it.

Not until eight months will the baby search for a completely hidden object, but even then, and for a few months after that, the baby will still be 'deceived' by the physical conditions of the search. So, if you hide a toy under a cushion (A) the baby can retrieve it with no difficulty. But if, in full view of the baby, you then place it under a second cushion (B), it will continue to search under cushion (A). Not until about twelve months will the baby search under the cushion where it last saw the toy hidden and do this even when three or four cushions are used. (Gratch and Landers, 1971, suggest this ability appears as early as nine months.)

Another way of testing object permanence is to observe the baby's eye movements to see if it follows a moving object and continues to look along its path even after it has vanished, for example behind a screen. If the baby looks at the other side of the screen where the object would re-appear, the visual search suggests that the baby expects it to re-appear which, in turn, indicates object permanence. (Bower et al, 1971, found that this visual tracking of objects begins between four to eight months.)

During eight to twelve months, the concept of a person as a permanent 'object' develops rapidly and, according to Bell (1970), 'person permanence' may develop at a faster rate than 'physical object permanence', especially in babies whose mothers spend a great deal of time with them in a warm and close relationship.

According to Décarie (1978), it is through realizing the individuality and permanence of the mother that the baby begins to appreciate the permanence of physical objects; and Paraskevopoulos and Hunt (1971) found that infants raised in an institution with a high infant-staff ratio achieved object permanence earlier than those raised in a less well-staffed institution.

Even when the baby can successfully retrieve a hidden object where it was last hidden, object permanence is still not fully developed. For instance, the baby watches you place a toy in a matchbox, after which you place the matchbox under a pillow. When the baby isn't looking, you slip the toy out of the box and leave it under the pillow. Next, you put the now empty box in front of the baby who quickly searches it; on finding no toy inside, it does not search for the missing toy under the pillow.

Before about eighteen months, the young child cannot take into account the possibility that something it has not actually seen might have happened; Piaget refers to this as a *failure to infer invisible displacements*. But once the child can do this, the development of object permanence is complete.

The General Symbolic Function

Apart from object permanence, the sensorimotor stage is important mainly for the development of the *general symbolic function*, one manifestation of which is *language*. But rather than regarding language as the source of thought Piaget saw language as reflecting thought which originates in *action*. (We shall return to the issue of thought and language development at the end of the chapter.)

Piaget distinguished between *symbols*, which resemble the things they represent (eg mental images), and *signs*, which stand for things in a quite arbitrary way and are merely conventional; and language in fact falls into the latter category. When the child begins to represent objects to itself in the form of mental images, it is no longer so dependent on physical exploration and the manipulation of objects; it is now beginning to *think*, working things out in its head. Schemas are now 'interiorized' and this can lead to sudden, insightful solutions. For example, the child might put a cup down on the floor in order to have both hands free to open a door; after looking at the door and then at the cup, it 'realizes', through a mental image of the door opening, that the cup is in the way. So it decides to move the cup to a safer place before trying to open the door.

The other major manifestations of the general symbolic function are: (i) *deferred imitation*, the ability to imitate or reproduce something seen or heard when the 'model' is no longer present, indicating an important advance in the child's capacity to remember; and (ii) *representational* or *make-believe play*, where one object is used as if it were another and this too depends on the child's growing ability to form mental images of things and people in their absence. These developments usually become apparent between 18 and 24 months.

ii) Pre-Operational Stage (2 to 7 Years)

Probably the main difference between this and the sensorimotor stage is the continued development and use of internal images, symbols and language, which is especially important for the child's developing sense of self-awareness (see Chapter 9). At the same time, the child's world is still fundamentally concrete and absolute—things *are* very much as they *seem* and the child tends to be influenced by how things look rather than by logical principles or operations (hence 'pre-operational', the child lacks the logical operations characteristic of later stages).

Piaget in fact subdivided the stage into two: (a) the pre-conceptual (two to four years); and (b) the intuitive (four to seven years).

a) Pre-conceptual

The *absolute* nature of the child's thinking makes it very difficult for it to understand relative terms, such as 'bigger' or 'stronger', and things tend to be 'biggest' or just 'big'.

Classification

If you ask a two to four-year-old to divide apples into 'big red apples' and 'small green apples', the child will *either* put all the red apples together or all the green apples together (regardless of size) *or* all the big ones together or all the small ones together (regardless of colour). In other words, a child of this age can only classify things on the basis of a *single* attribute at a time —in our example, either colour or size but not both at the same time.

Piaget called this concentration on one aspect of an object or situation (to the exclusion of all the others) *centration*; until it can de-centre, the child will be unable to classify things in any kind of logical or systematic way. When the child calls all men 'daddy' or all four-legged animals 'doggie' it is centring on what they have in common and overlooking the differences.

The unsystematic nature of the pre-conceptual child's thinking is well illustrated by what Piaget calls *syncretic thought* (what Vygotsky called 'complexive thinking'), that is, the tendency to link together any neighbouring objects or event on the basis of what individual instances have in common. For example, if a three-year-old is given a box of wooden shapes, of different colours, and is asked to pick out four that are alike, it might pick the shapes shown in Figure 19.2. Here, the characteristic the child focuses on changes with each second shape that is chosen: a red *square* is followed by a *red* circle which is followed by a blue *circle* which is followed by a *blue* triangle, so that only the first and second, second and third, and third and fourth objects have anything in common—there is no one characteristic that all four have in common. A five-year-old would be able to select four of the same shape or four of the same colour—and say what they have in common.

In *transductive reasoning*, the child draws an inference about the relationship between two objects based on a *single* attribute; for example, if A has four legs and B has four legs, then A must be B. If A happens to be a cat and B a dog, the child will draw the wrong conclusion, calling cats 'doggie' for example. This kind of reasoning can lead to what Piaget calls *animistic thinking*, the belief that inanimate objects are alive; for example, because the sun (seems to) follow us when we walk, it must be alive, the reasoning being that if people move and if the sun moves, then the sun is the same as people, ie they are both alive.

The pre-conceptual child also has difficulty with *seriation*, that is, arranging objects on the basis of a particular dimension, such as increasing height.

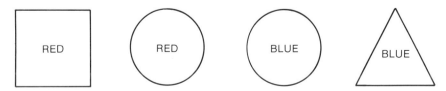

Figure 19.2   Simple example of syncretic thought

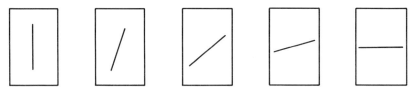

Figure 19.3 The falling-stick card test

Piaget and Szeminska (1941/1952) asked children to put a number of sticks in order of increasing length and found that even five and six-year-olds tended to do this by trial-and-error; they had particular difficulty under-standing that a stick (B) can be both smaller than one stick (A) and larger than another stick (C), and once they have completed the series they are unable to insert an extra stick. The two to four-year-old also cannot easily perceive actions as following a particular order or sequence through time, as in the falling-stick cards test, shown in Figure 19.3.

b) Intuitive
While four- to seven-year-olds may have developed beyond the kinds of thinking described above, they are still very limited in their ability to think logically. Let us look at classification again, this time at what are known as *class-inclusion tasks*.

Class-Inclusion Tasks
Imagine a child is presented with several wooden beads, mostly brown but a few white, and is then asked:

a) 'Are they all wooden?' The child will answer 'Yes';
b) 'Are there more brown or more white beads?' 'Brown';
c) 'Are there more brown beads or more (wooden) beads?' 'Brown'.

According to Piaget, what the child is failing to understand is the relationship between the *whole* (the class of wooden beads) and the *parts* (the classes of brown and white beads); these are referred to as the *superordinate* and the *subordinate class(es)* respectively. The child is still influenced by what it perceives; it can *see* the brown beads, which are more numerous than the white, in a more immediate and direct way than the wooden beads (despite being able to answer the first question correctly).

Piaget took this to be another example of the child's inability to de-centre, but others have challenged his interpretation. Donaldson (1984), for example, asks if the difficulty the child experiences is to do with what is expected of it and how the task is presented. She cites a study by McGarrigle et al which involved four toy cows, three black and one white; they were laid on their sides and children (average age of six) were told they were 'sleeping'. Of those children asked the standard form of the question ('Are there more black cows or more cows?'), 25 per cent answered correctly; while of those asked, 'Are there more black cows or more *sleeping* cows?' 48 per cent answered correctly, the difference being statistically significant.

Again, Markman and Selbert (1976) found that children who failed the standard task had little difficulty if it was posed as a problem of *collections* instead; for example Figure 19.4:

Figure 19.4

i) *Class-inclusion*: 'Who would have the most blocks to play with, someone who owned the orange blocks or someone who owned the blocks?'
ii) *Collection*: 'Who would have the most blocks to play with, someone who owned the orange blocks or someone who owned the pile of blocks?

The only difference between the two tasks is the word 'pile' in the collection task, making it clear to the child that the investigator means '*all* the blocks'; in the standard question, 'the blocks' could mean 'the *remaining* blocks.

Egocentrism

Another predominant feature of the whole pre-operational period is the child's *egocentrism*. The child, according to Piaget, is literally *self-centred*, sees the world totally from its own standpoint and cannot understand that other people might see things differently. Essentially, what the child is unable to do is put itself, psychologically, in somebody else's shoes in order to realize that they do not know everything that it knows, do not perceive what it perceives, do not feel what it feels. One amusing example (Phillips, 1969) is of a four-year-old who is asked, 'Do you have a brother?' to which he replies 'Yes'. Then he is asked, 'What's his name?' to which he replies, 'Jim'. Finally, in response to the question, 'Does Jim have a brother?', he says, 'No'.

One of Piaget's most famous demonstrations of egocentrism involved a three-dimensional model of a Swiss mountain scene (Piaget and Inhelder, 1956). The three mountains were of different colours with snow on top of one, a house on another and a red cross on the third. The child could walk round and explore the model and then sat on one side while a doll was placed at some different location; the child was shown a set of ten pictures taken from different angles around the model and asked to choose the one that represented how the doll saw it.

Four-year-olds were totally unaware of different perspectives from their own and instead chose a photograph which matched how they themselves saw the model; six-year-olds showed some awareness but often chose the wrong photograph; and only seven to eight-year-olds consistently chose the one that represented the doll's view. According to Piaget, children below seven are bound by the 'egocentric illusion'; they fail to understand that what they see is relative to their own position and instead take it to represent 'the world as it really is'.

However, several more recent studies have disputed the conclusion that Piaget drew. Borke (1975), for instance, believes that the three-mountain scene is an unusually difficult way of presenting the problem. He allowed the child to move a second three-dimensional model on a turntable and, under these conditions, even three and four-year-olds could successfully see things as the doll 'saw' them.

Donaldson (1984) cites a study by Hughes using a piece of apparatus meant

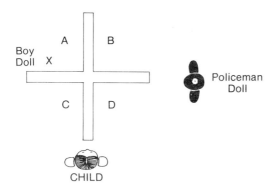

Figure 19.5 Apparatus used by Hughes (from Donaldson, 1984)

to be equivalent to the three-mountain scene, comprising two 'walls' inter-secting to form a cross (see Figure 19.5).

At first, the policeman doll is placed where he could see areas B and D but not A and C (he isn't tall enough to 'see' over the wall). Then the boy doll is put into area A and the child is asked if the policeman can see him, and this is repeated by putting the boy doll in areas B, C and D. Next the policeman is placed where he could see A and C and the child is asked to 'hide the boy so that the policeman can't see him'. If the child makes any mistakes at this stage they are pointed out and the question repeated until the correct answer is given; but very few mistakes were made. The test proper begins with the introduction of a second policeman and the child is now asked to hide the boy from both policeman; this is repeated three times so that each time a different area becomes the only possible hiding place left; for example, with one policeman at the right end of the cross and the other at the top end, the only hiding place for the boy is C. Piaget would predict that children would hide the boy from themselves, that is, where they, the child, could not see him.

However, $3\frac{1}{2}$ to 5-year-olds hid the boy successfully 90 per cent of the time (including 88 per cent of the $3\frac{1}{2}$ to 4-year-olds), even when this meant the boy doll being clearly visible to the child. Even when Hughes used up to six sections of wall and a third policeman, four-year-olds were successful 90 per cent of the time; three-year-olds found it more difficult but still managed 60 per cent success.

How can we account for this discrepancy between Hughes's results and those of Piaget? According to Donaldson, the policeman and boy doll situation enables the child to understand what is being asked of it because there is a meaningful context: it makes 'human sense', even to a three-year-old, because the child can relate to the idea of 'hiding from someone'. By contrast, she thinks the three-mountain situation has no meaningful context, is 'disembedded' (taken out of context), does not make 'human sense' and is 'cold blooded'. Donaldson compares this situation with that in which an American Indian was asked to translate into his native tongue, 'The white man shot six bears today'. 'How can I do that?' he protested, 'No white man could shoot six bears in a day.' It just did not make 'human sense'.

Shatz and Gelman (1973) found that four-year-olds could adjust the complexity of their speech 'downward' if talking to a two-year-old, compared with how they talked to adults; and Shatz (1973) found that they could also choose appropriate toys for themselves and choose less complex ones for two-year-olds. Mossler et al (1976) reported that four to five-year-olds who had recently shared a secret understood that others who had not shared it were unaware of the secret, whereas Piaget would say they would assume that everybody else knew the secret too.

Finally, an intriguing study by Flavell (1978), tested Piaget's egocentric interpretation of the young child who, with its hands covering its eyes, says, 'Now you can't see me'. According to Flavell, children may think of their eyes as 'the window of the soul', so that when somebody is not looking directly into their eyes, they cannot see the child's real self.

Flavell tested these two hypotheses by giving $2\frac{1}{2}$ to 5-year-olds a series of tests concerning what they thought others could see. The experimenter and the child sat on opposite sides of a table on which sat a Snoopy toy. In the simplest procedure, the child was asked to close or cover both eyes and the experimenter said, 'Now your eyes are closed and mine are open', and then asked a series of questions—'Do I see you?', 'Do I see Snoopy?', 'Do I see your head?' and so on.

The youngest children (below the age of $3\frac{1}{2}$) often said that the experimenter could not see them but, without exception, they said that he could see Snoopy and most believed that he could see their head or arm. So the egocentric explanation was ruled out—the children understood that the experimenter could see something which they themselves could not.

Conservation

The other major feature of the pre-operational stage is the child's inability to *conserve*; the child fails to understand that things remain the same (constant) despite changes in their appearance (how they look). It is the perceptual appearance of things that still dominates—things *are* what they *seem* and this is what 'intuitive' is meant to convey.

Piaget's conservation experiments are probably his most famous and have been replicated many times. Let us start with the conservation of *liquid quantity* (or continuous quantity).

In the situation represented in Figure 19.6 although the child agrees that there is the same amount of liquid in A and B, when the contents of B are poured into C, the appearance of C sways the child's judgement so that C is

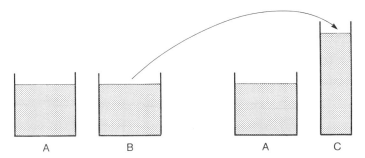

Figure 19.6   The conservation of liquid quantity

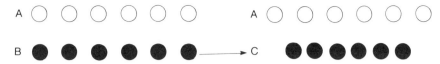

Figure 19.7   Number conservation using counters

now judged to contain more than A ('it looks more' or 'it's taller'). Although the child has seen the liquid poured from B into C and agrees that none has been spilled or added in the process (Piaget called this *identity*), the appearance of the higher level of liquid in the taller, thinner, beaker C is compulsive.

According to Piaget, this is yet another example of centration; here the pre-7 year-old is centring on just one dimension of the beaker C, usually its height, and so fails to take width into account. What the concrete operational child will be able to understand is that as C gets taller it also gets narrower and that these cancel each other out. Piaget calls this *compensation*.

If the water is poured back from C into B, the child will again say that there are equal amounts in A and B; but what it cannot do (which the concrete operational child can) is perform this *operation* mentally, in its head. The ability to perform this mental operation is called *reversibility*.

Other kinds of conservation include number, quantity or substance (discrete quantity), weight and volume. To test number conservation, two rows of counters are put in a one-to-one correspondence and then one row is pushed together as shown in Figure 19.7.

The pre-operational child usually thinks that there are more counters in A than in C because they are 'longer', despite being able to count correctly and agreeing that A and B have equal numbers. In conservation of quantity or substance, two balls of plasticine are used, one of which is rolled into a long sausage and the child typically judges the sausage to have more than the ball. (See Figure 19.8.)

Weight conservation is tested by putting two balls of plasticine on measuring scales and then transforming one of them as in conservation of quantity; and volume conservation involves dropping plasticine into water, and seeing how much is displaced before and after transformation.

As with Piaget's test of egocentrism, many other psychologists have been critical of his methods and, consequently, of his conclusions regarding the pre-operational child's lack of conservation.

Donaldson (1984) has argued that the experimenter may be unwittingly forcing children to produce the wrong answer against their better judgement

Figure 19.8   Substance conservation using plasticine

by the mere fact that they ask the same question twice, once before and once after the transformation. 'If the experimenter pours the liquid from one beaker into another or pushes one row of counters together, they must be doing it for a reason and probably want me to give a different answer,' is how the child's reasoning might run, suggesting that, 'contextual cues might override purely linguistic ones'. How could we test these hypotheses?

One method, used by Rose and Blank (1974), was to drop the pre-transformation question and only ask the child to compare two rows of counters after the transformation: under these conditions six-year-olds often succeeded compared with those tested on the standard form of the task. Significantly, they made fewer errors on the standard task when re-tested a week later. Samuel and Bryant (1984), testing 252 boys and girls aged between 5 and $8\frac{1}{2}$ years confirmed Rose and Blank's findings for conservation of quantity and volume.

Another alternative to Piaget's method was devised by McGarrigle and Donaldson (1974). It was concerned with number conservation and proceeded in the usual way up to the point where the child agreed that there was an equal number of counters in the two rows. Then 'Naughty Teddy' emerges from a hiding place and sweeps over one of the rows and disarranges it, so that the one-to-one correspondence is disrupted. The child is invited to put Teddy back in his box (usually accepted with glee) and the questioning resumes: 'Now, where were we? Ah, yes, is the number in this row the same as the number in that row?' and so on.

Fifty out of 80 four to six-year-olds conserved, compared with 13 out of 80 tested using the standard version. According to Piaget, it should not matter *who* re-arranges the counters (or *how* it happens), but it seems to be relevant to the child as conservation was demonstrated much earlier when Naughty Teddy did it than when the experimenter did it.

But Light et al (1979) criticized the Naughty Teddy study by arguing that the children were, nonverbally and unwittingly, being instructed to 'ignore the rearrangement' and so there is a sense in which the task itself may be 'lost'; this led McGarrigle and Donaldson to conclude that their subjects showed number conservation when, in truth, there was no such evidence.

Perhaps instead of asking *when* children conserve we should question under what *conditions* of attention and memory do they conserve (Miller, 1979). Certainly, conservation is much more complex than Piaget seemed to think.

Other criticisms of Piaget deal with the actual words used in the conservation-task questions. For example, when the liquid is poured from beaker B to beaker C and the child is asked, 'which contains more or are they the same?', how does the pre-operational child interpret 'more'?

Berko and Brown (1960) and Bruner et al (1966) found that some children used 'more' or 'less' when they were really referring to height and length, so in the conservation task they might be quite correct in pointing to beaker C because it is 'taller' than beaker A. As Dworetzky (1981) points out, when a child asks for 'more milk', it observes the level in the glass rise and there may be other similar examples which explain why 'more' is understood as 'tall' or 'taller'; and also why children of up to six or seven regard the vertical dimension as so important when judging the overall size of something. Donaldson and Wales (1970) also observed that children have trouble with words such as 'less', 'more', 'same', 'different from', 'more than', but they claimed that the linguistic bias of the task as a whole creates difficulties for children.

Wheldall and Poborea (1980) tested conservation of liquid quantity *non-verbally*, whereby $6\frac{1}{2}$ year-olds had to press a button when they thought two beakers contained equal amounts of water—significantly more conserved under these conditions than those tested in the traditional way.

iii) Concrete Operational Stage (7 to 11 Years)

In this stage, children develop the mental structure called an *operation*, which is, essentially, an action, performed mentally, comprising (a) *compensation*, (b) *reversibility* and (c) *identity* (see above) and is best seen in the ability to conserve. However, they can only perform the operation in the presence of actual objects—they must be looking at or manipulating the materials (beakers of water, counters etc), hence the name of the stage (ie *concrete*).

Also, some types of conservation are mastered before others; Baer and Wright (1974) point out that the ages at which they normally appear are only approximate and depend on the particular method used to test them. But the order in which they appear tends to be invariant (as is the order of the four major stages), namely: *number* and *liquid quantity* (Continuous Quantity) at six to seven; *substance* or *quantity* and *length* at seven to eight; *weight* at eight to ten; and *volume* at eleven to twelve.

This step-by-step acquisition of new operations is called *décalage* (displacement); in the case of conservation it is *horizontal* (eg a seven-year-old can conserve number but not weight), so that inconsistencies exist within the same kind of ability or operation. *Vertical* décalage refers to inconsistencies between different abilities or operations, eg a child may have mastered all kinds of classification but not all kinds of conservation.

With regard to classification, the concrete operational child can now understand the relationship between super- and sub-ordinate classes, that is, the part-whole relationship; this is closely related to addition and subtraction, for example, adding the parts to make the whole and then subtracting the parts (a form of reversibility).

Other manifestations of the child's growing ability to de-centre include (a) sorting objects on the basis of two or more attributes and (b) a significant decline in egocentrism and the growing relativism of the child's viewpoint.

One remaining problem for the child is concerned with *transitivity* tasks. For example, 'If John is taller than Susan and Susan is taller than Charlie, who is taller, John or Charlie?' Not until the age of eleven or so will the child be able to solve this entirely in its head; the concrete operational child is usually limited to solving the problem when real objects (eg dolls) are physically present.

iv) Formal Operational Stage (11 to 15 Years)

While the concrete operational child is still concerned with manipulating *things* (even if this is done 'in the mind'), the formal operational thinker can manipulate *ideas* or propositions and can reason solely on the basis of verbal statements ('first order' and 'second order' operations respectively). 'Formal' refers to the ability to follow the *form* of an argument without reference to its particular content. In the case of transitivity problems, for example, 'If A is taller than B, and B is taller than C, then A is taller than C', is a form of argument such that the conclusion is logically true, and will always be true, regardless of what A, B or C might refer to.

The adolescent can also think hypothetically, that is, think about situations they have not actually experienced before—or about things which *nobody* has experienced before. For example, Dworetzky (1981) notes that if you asked a formal operational individual what it would be like if people had tails, they might tell you

a) 'Lovers could secretly hold tails under the table', or
b) 'People would leave lifts in a great hurry', or
c) 'Dogs would know when you were happy'.

By contrast, a concrete operational child might tell you not to be so silly, or would tell you where on the body a tail might be, or how funny it would look, showing its dependence upon what has actually been seen.

This ability to imagine and discuss what has never been encountered before is evidence of the continued de-centration that occurs beyond concrete operations. The formal operational person can, therefore, deal with *possibilities* and not just with *actualities*, with 'what is not and what could be', so that they can consider alternatives to existing (concrete) reality as well as notice inconsistencies and contradictions in other people's behaviour (especially that of their parents).

Similarly, adolescents can ask questions about themselves which would have been impossible earlier, such as, 'What or who can I become?'. These kinds of questions form part of the 'identity crisis' of adolescence discussed by Erikson (see Chapter 23).

Finally, adolescents can experiment and search systematically and methodically in order to find the solution to a problem, they can consider all the possible combinations of factors likely to have an effect and through careful reasoning eliminate the irrelevant ones. For example, in the beaker problem (Inhelder and Piaget, 1958), there are four beakers of colourless, odourless liquid (1, 2, 3 and 4) plus a smaller bottle (g) also containing a colourless, odourless liquid; the problem is to find the liquid, or combination of liquids, which will turn yellow when a few drops from bottle g are added to it (the actual combination is 1 plus 3 plus g). Concrete operational children often begin randomly trying various combinations of pairs of liquids, while adolescents systematically consider all the possible combinations.

However, Watson and Johnson-Laird (1972) found that even well-educated adults make all sorts of mistakes on formal reasoning problems, Dulitt (1972) found that only about one-third of average adolescents and adults ever attain formal operations, and Neimark (1979) reviewed several other studies all presenting similar findings.

According to Dasen (1977), formal reasoning does not appear at all in some cultures and even where it does occur it may not be the typical mode of thought; and Flavell (1977) concludes that, while formal operational thinking may emerge during adolescence, it cannot be regarded as the 'characteristic mode of thought for that developmental period'. How can we account for this?

Piaget (1972) suggests that all normal individuals attain formal operations if not by the age of 15 then by 20, but they do so in different areas according to their aptitudes and areas of experience and expertise. Piaget seems to be saying that the specific knowledge and training people have are as important to their cognitive performance as is their general level of cognitive development, which seems to be a rather different position from the one he adopts regarding the first three stages.

Piaget on Play

Piaget (1951) saw play as an *adaptive* activity, which begins early in the sensorimotor period when infants start to repeat actions which they find satisfying or pleasurable. He called these repetitions of actions 'circular reactions' and distinguished three major kinds corresponding to three sub-stages of the sensorimotor period: (i) *primary circular reactions* (one to four months) which are centred on the baby's own body; (ii) *secondary circular reactions* (four to eight months) which are centred on external objects; and (iii) *tertiary circular reactions* (twelve to eighteen months) where the baby experiments in order to find new ways to solve problems or to reproduce interesting outcomes.

As an adaptive activity, play involves both assimilation and accommodation. However, assimilation is often the more important and evident of the two processes and a great deal of play (especially up to the end of the pre-operational period) is 'pure assimilation', whereby the child attempts to fit the world of reality into its own needs and experiences. (By contrast, imitation is an action of almost 'pure' accommodation.) Following on from this, Piaget made a distinction between play, on the one hand, and 'strictly intellectual activity' on the other; in the latter, there is 'adaptation of the schemas to an external reality which constituted a problem', that is, there is an external aim or purpose. But in play, the child, 'repeats his behaviour not in any further effort to learn or investigate but for the mere joy of mastering it and of showing off to himself his own power of subduing reality', that is, it is done for its own sake. So play allows children to practise their competencies in a relaxed and carefree way.

This distinction between play and intellectual activity applies to all three major kinds of play, although it is arguably more difficult to make in the case of *mastery play* than it is in *symbolic* or *make-believe* and *play with rules*. But throughout development, play serves to consolidate recently acquired abilities and also aids the development of additional cognitive and social skills (Rubin et al, 1983).

These three major kinds of play correspond to the major stages of cognitive development like this:

i)   Sensorimotor stage (0 to 2 years): Mastery (or practice) play

ii) Pre-operational stage (2 to 7 years): Symbolic (or make-believe) play

iii) Concrete operational stage (7 to 11 years)⎫
     Formal operational stage (11 to 15 years)⎭ Play with rules

Mastery (or Practice) Play

Essentially this involves repeating new motor schemas in one new context after another and, in a sense, this theme of 'play as mastery' runs through the other kinds of play too: whenever a new skill has been acquired, it tends to be used at almost every opportunity, for the sheer pleasure of doing so, and represents 'pure assimilation'. So play involves the repetition of a schema that has already been mastered, while investigation or exploration involve accommodation to reality and constitute ways in which new schemas develop.

Symbolic (or Make-believe) Play

This type of play involves the child transforming itself or some object into somebody or something else; it begins between $1\frac{1}{2}$ and 2 years and is usually at its height up until about the age of five.

An important feature of make-believe play is role-taking (or role play) which may serve an important function in helping the child to cope with emotional crises and reducing interpersonal conflicts, for example, having rules imposed by parents which it does not fully understand. Piaget and Inhelder (1969) observe that a child may discipline its doll or teddy as the child itself had been disciplined (so *inverting* or reversing roles) or it might re-enact a scene and produce a happy ending. So through make-believe play the child can change the world, internally, into what it wants it to be. (Compare this with Freud's theory of play—see Chapter 26.)

Ungerer et al (1981) hypothesized (based on Piaget's theory) that, since symbolic play develops out of mastery play, younger children, compared with older ones, should: (a) treat objects in a more concrete (less symbolic) way; and (b) use objects in a more active way. These predictions were confirmed for white, middle-class, American children aged 18 to 34 months.

Finally, many psychologists (eg Garvey, 1977) have pointed out the vital role of language in the development of symbolic play; this is shown when a girl talks to her doll in the way that her parents talk to her while feeding her doll and (usually from four onwards) when 'collective symbolism' appears, for example, children playing together and all assuming complementary roles (eg 'cowboys and Indians').

Play with Rules

As the child's thinking becomes more logical, so its games begin to incorporate and be governed by rules. But the child's understanding of rules itself goes through certain developmental changes (see Chapter 21 on moral development).

Evaluation of Piaget's Theory

1) Is Piaget's theory really a *stage* theory at all?

We saw earlier in the chapter that from 1970 Piaget proposed that development should be thought of as a spiral (implying a continuous process) rather than as a step-by-step, discontinuous process (as implied by a stage theory proper). Indeed, the individual may 'straddle' more than one stage at any one time (décalage) which means that cognitive structures do not have to change all at the same time (and to the same extent), which again is implied by a stage theory. Clearly, intellectual development may not be as 'stage-like' as Piaget at first thought (eg Flavell, 1982).

2) Is there any evidence that the *sequence* of stages is as Piaget has described it?

Piaget has always been more interested in the invariant sequence of the stages than, for example, in the timing of stages, which he admitted can be influenced by environmental factors; and there is a great deal of *cross-cultural* evidence to support Piaget's claim that the stages are invariant and universal, at least up to and including the concrete operational stage. For instance, Cowan (1978) and Flavell (1977) both conclude that the order of stages originally observed in Piaget's Swiss sample also describes the course and content for children in hundreds of countries, cultures and sub-cultures.

Conservation tasks have been the most commonly used cross-culturally; for example, Nyiti (1976) tested the Meru of Tanzania, Kamara and Easley (1977) the Themne of Sierra Leone, Kiminyo (1977) the Kamba of Kenya and Nyiti again (1982) compared English-speaking Canadians and the Micmac Canadian Indians. These groups (7 to 12-year-olds) were all tested on conservation of substance, weight and volume and the average ages at which these were correctly solved were highly comparable with those for the USA, Canada and Europe. Significantly, there was some tendency for 11 to 12-year-olds who had never attended school to have more difficulty in volume conservation than their peers who had attended school, but this would be consistent with Piaget's theory.

Fishbein (1984) concludes that the cross-cultural studies seem to indicate that Piaget has identified important, and perhaps universal, aspects of cognitive development.

3) One final point to do with stages is the question of whether there are any stages of cognitive development beyond formal operations. This will be discussed in Chapter 23 on adolescence and adulthood.

4) How scientific are Piaget's methods?

We have already seen how many of his basic ways of testing children's abilities (eg classification, egocentrism, conservation) have been criticized and seem to have resulted in the underestimation of what children can do at particular ages.

But his general 'clinical method' has been criticized on other grounds. Basically, it comprises a question-and-answer technique: the child is presented with a problem of some sort and then invited to respond; once the child answers, the investigator will ask a second question or introduce a variation of the original problem in order to clarify the child's reasoning. All children are asked the same questions to begin with, but how each child responds to these initial probes determines what the investigator does next. The essential problem with this approach is that if the questions and tasks are tailored to individual subjects, how can we compare the answers of different children in order to identify general trends? How reliable are the data when the procedures are basically un-standardized (ie different for different subjects)?

Additional criticisms are that Piaget often did not give details regarding the numbers and ages of his subjects and usually did not present any kind of statistical analysis.

Although aware of some of these shortcomings, Piaget did stress the need for a flexible methodology, that is, one which enables the investigator to probe the child's thinking without distorting it by imposing their own views on the child.

5) Does Piaget's theory explain cognitive development (as a theory should) or does it merely describe?

Despite concepts such as assimilation, accommodation and equilibration, many psychlogists believe that Piaget is not very explicit about exactly *what* the mechanisms are which enable a child to move through the stages. Brainerd (1978), for example, concludes that Piaget's theory is an elaborate description with very little explanatory value.

6) Some critics claim that Piaget over-emphasized cognitive aspects of development to the exclusion of the emotional (and others would say the reverse is true for Freud). But he was familiar with Freud's work and thought it provided valuable clues as to the *content* of children's thinking if not as to *how* they think, which was Piaget's prime concern.

However, in 1972, Piaget expressed his belief that, 'there will be a time when the psychology of the cognitive functions and psychoanalysis will have to blend into a general theory which will improve both by correcting each'.

Elkind (1971) has drawn an interesting parallel between Piaget and Freud by remarking how they both stressed the qualitative differences between children and adults; Elkind says that, relative to adults, the child is a 'cognitive alien' (Piaget) and an 'emotional alien' (Freud).

7) There is no doubt that Piaget's theory has stimulated more research than any other single theory of child development, as well as influencing the theory and practice of the education of young children, particularly the teaching of mathematics and science and the general importance attached to 'discovery learning' (see Chapter 3).

8) One final issue needs discussing, namely the role of language in cognitive development. In order to be able to assess Piaget's views, we need to compare them with the views of another eminent developmental psychologist, Jerome Bruner.

Bruner's Developmental Theory

Bruner has been greatly influenced by Piaget and they share certain basic beliefs, in particular:

a) Children are born with a biological organization that helps them to understand their world, and their underlying cognitive structure matures over time, so that they can think about and organize their world in an increasingly complex way;
b) Children are actively curious and explorative and capable of adapting to their environment through interaction with it.

Bruner's (1966) theory, however, is not about stages of development as such but rather about three ways or *modes* of representing the world, that is, forms that our knowledge and understanding can take, and so he is not concerned exclusively with cognitive growth but also with knowledge in general. The three modes are the enactive, iconic and symbolic, and they develop in this order in the child.

i) Enactive

At first, babies represent the world through actions; any knowledge they have is based upon what they have experienced through their own behaviour (this corresponds to Piaget's sensorimotor stage). Past events are represented through appropriate motor responses; many of our motor schemas, for example, 'bicycle riding, tying knots, aspects of driving, get represented in our muscles, so to speak,' and even when we have the use of language it is often extremely difficult to describe in words *how* we do certain things. Through repeated encounters with the regularities of the environment (ie the same events and conditions repeating themselves) we build up these virtually automatic, abbreviated, patterns of motor activity which we 'run off' as units in the appropriate situation.

Like Piaget, Bruner sees the onset of object permanence as a great leap, a qualitative change in the young child's cognitive development.

ii) Iconic

An icon is an image, so this form of representation involves building up a mental image of things we have experienced. Such images are normally composite, that is, made up of a number of past encounters with similar objects or situations. This mode, therefore, corresponds to the last six months of the sensorimotor stage (where schemas become interiorized) and the whole of the pre-operational stage, where the child is at the mercy of what it perceives in drawing intuitive conclusions about the nature of reality. For example, in the conservation of liquid quantity test, it is the image of the higher level in the taller, thinner, beaker which, according to Piaget, dictates the child's answer.

iii) Symbolic

Bruner's main interest was in the transition from the iconic to the symbolic modes. He and Piaget agree that a very important cognitive change occurs at around six or seven years; while Piaget describes it as the start of logical operations (albeit tied to concrete reality), Bruner saw it as the appearance of the symbolic mode, with language coming into its own as an influence on thought.

The transition from iconic to symbolic modes was demonstrated by Bruner and Kenney (1966). They arranged nine plastic glasses on a 3×3 matrix as shown in Figure 19.6.

Three- to seven- year-olds were familiarized with the matrix. The glasses were then scrambled and the children were asked to put them back the way they had been before; this was the *reproduction task*.

In the *transposition task*, the glasses were removed from the matrix and the glass which had been in the bottom right-hand square was placed in the bottom left-hand square; the child had to rebuild the matrix in this transposed manner.

Children generally could reproduce it earlier than they could transpose it: the reproduction task involved the iconic mode (60 per cent of the five-year-olds could do this, 72 per cent of the six-year-olds and 80 per cent of the seven-year-olds); while the transposition task involved the symbolic mode (the results were nil, 27 and 79 per cent respectively). Clearly, the five-year-olds were dominated by the visual image of the original matrix, while the six

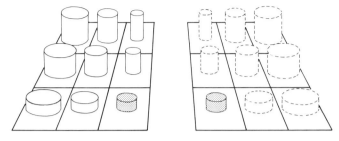

Figure 19.9   The 2 arrangements of glasses used by Bruner and Kenney (1966)

and seven-year olds translated their visual information into the symbolic mode; they relied upon verbal rules to guide them, such as, 'it gets fatter going one way and taller going the other'. So a child using images but not symbols can reproduce but not restructure.

However, the major difference between Bruner and Piaget is to do with the role that language plays in cognitive development.

Language and Cognitive Development

Bruner believes that the leap from the iconic to the symbolic mode is due to the development of language; Piaget, on the other hand, believes that the development of logical thought is due to the acquisition of operations— language is not the cause of cognitive development but a tool to be used in the course of operational thinking. So for Bruner, language and logical thinking are inseparable; without language, human thought would be limited to what could be learned through actions or images. For Piaget, language merely reflects and builds on cognitive structures which have already developed through interaction with the environment. It follows that Bruner believes that cognitive development can be significantly speeded up by training children in the use of symbols; while, as far as Piaget is concerned, it would make no difference.

Does the available evidence help us to choose between these two conflicting views? Two experiments which seem to support Bruner are those conducted by Sonstroem (1966) and Bruner et al (1966).

Sonstroem (1966) tested six and seven year-olds for conservation of substance; those who failed were divided into four groups:

i)   Group A reshaped the plasticine ball themselves and had to describe the new shape—they *manipulated* and *labelled*, using their *inactive, iconic* and *symbolic* modes;

ii)   Group B saw the experimenter reshape the ball and were asked to describe the new shape—they *labelled* without manipulating, using their *iconic* and *symbolic* modes;

iii)   Group C *manipulated* but did not label—using their *enactive* and *iconic* modes;

iv)   Group D neither manipulated nor labelled—using only their *iconic* mode.

They were then re-tested; group A showed a significant improvement while none of the other three groups did. Why?

Inability to conserve is a characteristic of children using the iconic mode —they are dominated by the appearance of the plasticine, but if they are encouraged to use their language skills (symbolic mode), especially in combination with the enactive, the appearance of the plasticine ceases to dominate and they can give a correct conservation response.

In a study of conservation of liquid quantity, Bruner et al (1966) gave four to seven-year olds the orthodox Piagetian task (pre-test): almost all the four and five-year-olds said that there was more liquid in the taller, thinner, beaker, as did about half the six and seven-year-olds.

The children were then shown two standard beakers and a third, wider, beaker and all three were *screened*, so that when the contents of one of the standard beakers was poured into the wider one, the children could not see the level of the liquid but only the tops of the beakers. They were asked which had the most liquid with the screen still covering the liquid level and almost all the five-to seven-year-olds answered correctly, as did about half the four-year-olds. When the screen was removed, all the four-year olds reverted to their pre-screening answer but all the others stuck to the answer given while the screen was in place.

Finally, in the post-test situation, two standard beakers and a taller, thinner, one were used in the orthodox Piagetian way (without a screen): the four-year-olds were unaffected by having seen the beakers screened but the five-year-olds' success rate rose from 20 per cent (pre-test) to 70 per cent (post-test) and for the six and seven-year-olds the figures were 50 (pre-test) to 90 (post-test). What do these results mean?

Activating their speech (symbolic mode) by having them 'say' their judgement when the screen was covering the liquid levels prevented the children of five and over—who normally fail to conserve on the standard Piagetian task—being dominated by the iconic mode. However, the four-year-olds were, clearly, not ready to benefit from this symbolic training and, to this extent, Piaget's view that the mental structures must have already developed before training can help seems to have been supported. Yet the five-year-olds did benefit, contrary to what Piaget would have predicted, and so this finding seems to support Bruner.

Indirect support for Piaget comes from studies of the deaf, who are as capable of operational thinking as the hearing although its appearance is often greatly delayed. Furth (1966) conducted several studies of the development of thinking in the deaf using Piaget-type tasks and concluded that language does not appear to be necessary.

In contrast, according to Hatwell (1966), the blind, who are in full possession of normal language but are impaired in their sensorimotor experiences, are severely delayed in their operational thought development. Piaget takes this as a particularly convincing demonstration that language is not the source of operational thought.

However, studies of the deaf seem to have under-played the delay of operational thought and Cromer (1973) believes that the blind may not, after all, be delayed. Thus the evidence here is mixed.

So what about the more directly relevant question of the effectiveness of language training?

Two studies by Sinclair-de-Zwart seem to support Piaget. In 1967, children were taught the verbal expressions used by other children who had been able to describe how two pencils, two balls of clay and two rows of beads differed. The training sessions, which exposed the children to comparative terms such as 'long', 'thin', 'short', 'fat', 'more' and 'less', proved largely unsuccessful. Although children appeared to understand the language instructions and how to use the words, it was concluded that their level of cognitive maturity prevented them from solving the Piagetian tasks. In a 1969 study, it was shown that children who displayed conservation of volume understood the meaning of words like 'bigger', 'more', 'as much as' and 'same', whereas those who lacked conservation showed no improvement in their ability to use these words correctly after language training. What the latter needed was a grasp of the concept of conservation and until this developed the words would remain relatively meaningless, however well they were taught.

Interestingly, Piaget himself and other Piagetian researchers (eg Inhelder and Karmiloff-Smith, 1978) believe that linguistic interaction with other young children may help the child to advance intellectually, even though verbal training does not. They consider that children's attempts to convince their peers of their own points of view, and the ensuing disputes and conflicts generated by being made aware of contradictions, are all necessary steps in cognitive growth.

What about formal operational thought?

Furth and Younis (1971) believe that language has a 'direct facilitating effect' on formal operational thought, 'precisely because of the close relationship between formal operations and symbolic functioning'. Piaget himself seems to take the view that, while language might be necessary for formal operations, it is not sufficient. Indeed, the language of the formal operational individual does not seem to differ significantly from what it was at some earlier stage.

In conclusion, Piaget believes that, 'language and thought are links in a genetic circle . . . in the last analysis, both depend on intelligence itself, which antedates language and is independent of it.'

20

Language Development

So much of our everyday lives, so many of our interactions with other people, so much of our learning, goes on through the medium of language (spoken and written), that it is almost impossible to discuss any aspect of human behaviour or thinking without taking the role of language into account when studying psychology.

As our brains seem especially designed to enable us to use speech, it is perhaps not surprising that language should play such a central part in our lives. Many psychologists and philosophers have claimed that it is language which makes us unique as a species, it is almost 'what makes us human'.

There are a number of separate but interrelated questions that we need to ask, some of which will be given more emphasis than others in this chapter:

What is language? How can it be defined and what are its major components?

How does language develop and what is the course of language development in the child? Here, we shall be looking mainly at the *stages* of development that have been identified in an attempt to describe it.

Why does language develop in the way it does? Here, we shall be looking at the major *theories* of language acquisition.

What is Language?

Until fairly recently, the study of language was undertaken largely by linguists, who are concerned primarily with the *structure* of language—the sounds that compose it, how these relate to words and sentences, and the rules which govern the relationships between all of these.

But in the last twenty years or so, psychologists have become interested in language, not so much for its own sake, but in how it is acquired, whether it is a human species–specific behaviour, how it affects learning, memory, thinking in general, and so on. The 'marriage' of psychology and linguistics is called *psycholinguistics*, which can be defined as the study of how language is acquired, perceived, understood and produced.

Roger Brown (1965), an eminent American psycholinguist, defines language as an arbitrary system of symbols, 'which taken together make it possible for a creature with limited powers of discrimination and a limited memory to

500

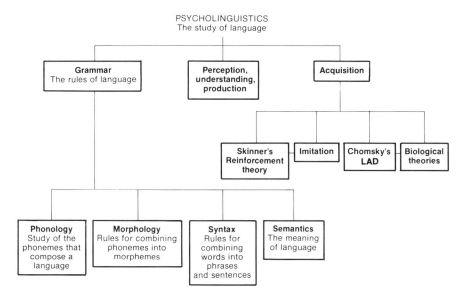

Figure 20.1 Psycholinguistics

transmit and understand an infinite variety of messages and to do this in spite of noise and distraction'. It is, perhaps, this 'infinite variety of messages' that makes human language unique; other species may be able to communicate with each other but it is a very limited system. Successful attempts to teach chimpanzees language (which we shall be considering later) still involve deliberate training; contrast this with children's spontaneous and quite easy mastery of human language within about five years after birth.

In another definition of language, Brown (1973) points out that people do not simply acquire a repertoire of sentences but, 'acquire a rule system that makes it possible to generate a literally infinite variety of sentences, most of them never heard from anyone else'. This rule system is what psycholinguists call *grammar*, but grammar is much more than the parts of speech that we learn about in English at school. It is concerned with the description of language, the rules which determine how a language works, and it comprises *phonology*, *morphology*, *syntax* and *semantics* (see Figure 20.1).

Phonology

This is the study of sounds, the sound system which is the basis of language. The basic sounds of any human language are *phonemes* and different languages are composed of different numbers and combinations of these basic sounds; English, for example, uses 45 distinguishable sounds, some languages use as few as 15 and others as many as 85. When we say that someone speaks English with a foreign accent, we are really saying that they have not yet mastered all the phonemes of English. Similarly, when we recognize a foreign language as, say, French, without being able to speak it or even understand it ourselves, we are recognizing the phonemes as those which 'define' French.

These examples show that phonemes are devoid of meaning—they are just sounds. They correspond roughly to the vowels and consonants of the alphabet, but since there are only 26 of these in English, the same vowel, for example, can represent more than one phoneme (eg the 'o' in '*hop*' is pronounced very differently from the 'o' in '*hope*' and so constitutes a different phoneme).

Morphology
Morphology refers to the rules for combining phonemes into *morphemes* which are the basic units of meaning in a language and consist mainly of words. Other morphemes are prefixes (letters attached to the beginning of a word, such as 'de' or 're') and suffixes (letters attached to the end of a word, such as 's' to make a plural—adding 's' to 'dog' clearly changes the meaning since we now know there is more than one animal). Some morphemes are 'bound' (like the plural 's'), that is, they only take on meaning when attached to other morphemes. But most morphemes are 'free', that is, they have meaning when they stand alone, as most words have; however, single words have only a limited meaning and we usually combine them into longer strings of phrases and sentences.

Syntax
Syntax refers to the rules for combining words into phrases and sentences (and it is often taken to be the same as grammar but, as we have seen, syntax is only one part of grammar). For example, in the sentence 'the dog chased the ____' we know that only a noun can complete it; this is an example of a *syntactic* rule.

Semantics
This is the study of the *meaning* of language. In the above example, 'the dog chased the cat' would be much more meaningful than, say, 'the dog chased the cinema', although both are correct according to the rules of syntax.

Again, 'the academic lecture attracted a limited audience' and, 'the academic liquid became an odorless audience' are both equally correct, but it is difficult to know what the second one means. 'Liquid the an became audience odorless academic' breaks all the rules of syntax and is also incomprehensible.

Describing Language Development

How does language develop in the child? Is there a predictable, orderly sequence of stages, as we saw in Chapter 19?

Many psychologists have pointed out that there seems to be a universal timetable for language development; that is, all children pass through the same stages, regardless of the particular language, culture, geography, cognition or training involved, and at more or less the same age. So maturation seems to play a very important part, but of course environment is equally necessary—the child comes to speak the language it does because that is the one heard spoken around it.

Children seem to be programmed by nature to learn language if they are exposed to it and, as we shall see later, sometimes even when they are *not* (for example, children of deaf–mute parents or congenitally deaf children) they still seem to create some kind of non-verbal language.

Thus language is acquired by every normal person in a predictable, sequential fashion, although the rate of development may differ from child to child.

The major stages that we shall be examining are: the pre-linguistic; the one-word stage; and the stage of two-word sentences; we shall see that this third stage comprises two sub-stages, stage 1 grammar and stage 2 grammar.

a) Pre-Linguistic Stage (up to 1 Year)

The first year of life is really a pre-linguistic phase; the baby makes various sounds with its vocal organs, including crying, long before it can talk. Crying tends to dominate the first month or so, with the baby having different kinds of cries which parents learn to discriminate.

At about six weeks babies begin to coo, producing sounds which seem to be associated with pleasurable states. The vowel sounds that are produced during these early weeks are different from those that will later be made and out of which the first words will be built. During the first six months, the baby's oral cavity and nervous system are not sufficiently mature to enable it to produce the sounds necessary for speech.

The major development to occur during the first year is *babbling*, which usually begins somewhere between six and nine months; the baby now produces phonemes, which take the form of combinations of vowels and consonants (eg *ma, ba, ga, da*). Sometimes these are repeated to produce *reduplicated monosyllables* (*mama, gaga*) and although very different from the earliest cooing sounds, these babbled sounds still have no meaning—it will be another few months before we can say the baby is actually talking.

Two of the main differences between babbling and pre-babbling vocalization are: (i) the baby spends more time making noises, especially when alone in its cot, and seems to enjoy exercising its voice for the sake of it; (ii) babbling has intonational patterns, like speech, with rising inflections and speech-like rhythm.

By 11 or 12 months, the baby often repeats syllables over and over again ('dadadada') and this is called *echolalia*; the baby seems to be echoing itself (the term is also used to refer to the repeating back of other people's speech in autistic children, for example).

At first, only a few phonemes are produced in the baby's babbling. But then *phonemic* (or phonetic) *expansion* occurs, whereby almost every available phoneme is produced. The onset of babbling and phonemic expansion both seem to be based on maturation, independent of experience or learning. Babbling occurs roughly at the same time all over the world, and even deaf babies, or those born to deaf–mute parents (and who, therefore, hear very little speech, if any) babble—and, on average, at the same time as normal babies.

However, by 9 or 10 months, phonetic or phonemic *contraction* begins to take place, whereby phonemes become restricted to those used in the baby's native tongue, so that the influence of the environment is starting to show;

selective reinforcement by parents is probably part of this influence. At this age, therefore, it would be possible to distinguish babies of different nationalities—an English, Chinese and French baby would no longer all sound alike; a speech expert or linguist could correctly identify the baby's native tongue, even though the baby is still only babbling and not yet producing meaningful sounds. Significantly, deaf babies normally stop babbling at around 9 or 10 months, presumably because of lack of feedback, again showing the important interaction between environmental and maturation factors.

Although the baby is now only using phonemes which are 'useful' (those necessary for speech) it will be several years more before *all* the phonemes are mastered. For example, by $2\frac{1}{2}$ years, most children have mastered 27 of the 45 phonemes of English (all the vowels and about two-thirds of the consonants); 3-, 4- and 5-year-olds commonly have trouble pronouncing at least one phoneme. But by 7 years, most English-speaking children have mastered them all.

Also during the babbling stage, babies use gestures, as a kind of pre-language.

Elizabeth Bates et al (1971) studied 9- to 11-month-olds and observed them pointing to an object and then looking at the adult as if to say, 'Look at that' or, 'What's that?' They also 'show' adults the objects they are playing with ('Look at this'). The investigators suggest that these gestures and facial expressions reflect an underlying understanding of the relationships involved, before the child has the words or grammar to express them orally.

b) One-Word Stage (12 to 18 Months)

On average at about one year, the child speaks its first word. (It is interesting to note the word 'infant' comes from the Latin word *infans* which means 'without speech' or 'not speaking'; so perhaps when individuals begin to use words for the first time, they can no longer be considered babies.)

Of course, the baby does not wake up on its first birthday and decide that it is about time it stopped babbling like a baby and started speaking like a child: babbling merges and overlaps with patterned speech (words). Non-word sounds continue for up to another six months (and are called 'jargon'; again note that we often criticize experts in various fields for using jargon or technical language which only they seem to understand—we might describe anyone whom we cannot understand as 'babbling on').

Lenneberg believes that the shift from babbling to words occurs as a result of fundamental developments in the brain; certainly the one-word stage is universal. Since the baby's first words (or articulate sounds) come soon after phonemic contraction, it is not surprising that they involve only a few phonemes. They are often 'invented', not very much like 'adult words' at all to begin with. So what makes a word?

Scollon (1976) defines a word as, 'a systematic matching of form and meaning'. In other words, the baby consistently uses the *same* sound to label the *same* thing or kind of thing and there is now a clear intent to communicate.

Scollon studied the first words of Brenda, a one-year-old. 'Da' was used only when referring to a doll; 'awa', though used in several different situations, always meant something like 'I don't want'; and 'nene' was used to refer to a whole collection of objects or people who had something to do with nurturing or comfort.

The one-year-old may have four or five words, which are sometimes used just as labels for things or people, but, perhaps more importantly, may be used to convey a much more complex message, a whole sentence, in which case they are known as *holophrases*. So, 'milk' might, on one occasion, mean, 'I want some more milk', on another occasion, 'I don't want to finish my milk' and on a third, 'I've just spilt my milk'.

Greenfield and Smith (1976) see holophrases as precursors of later, more complex, sentences: the child uses gestures, tone of voice, and the situation, to add the full meaning to the individual word. Of course, they are still very much dependent on the adult making the 'correct' interpretation (older siblings, too, often take on this interpreter 'role' on behalf of their younger brother or sister; apparently, my older brother was the only other human being who could understand me until I was 5!).

Although limited to one-word utterances, the child clearly understands more complex speech than this, showing some understanding of syntax. For example, Sachs and Truswell (1978) gave 16 to 24-month-olds two-word instructions like, 'kiss duck', 'kiss car' and 'bang duck', 'bang car'. Even when non-linguistic cues were eliminated, they responded correctly most of the time, including being asked to do unfamiliar and strange things like 'tickle book'.

Nelson (1973) studied 18 babies and found that it took from 12 until about 15 or 16 months to achieve a 10-word vocabulary but after that vocabulary builds quite quickly, so that by 19 or 20 months, babies had a 50-word vocabulary. Despite individual differences, all 18 babies showed this spurt after the initial 10 words. What kinds of words are they?

Nelson identified six categories and calculated the percentage of the babies' first 50 words that each category represented in her 18-baby sample:

Category 1: *specific nominals*—names for unique objects, people or animals (14 per cent).

Category 2: *general nominals*—names for classes of objects, people or animals; eg 'ball', 'car', 'milk', 'doggie', 'girl', 'he', 'that' (51 per cent).

Category 3: *action words*—describe or accompany actions or express or demand attention; eg 'bye-bye', 'up', 'look', 'hi' (31 per cent).

Category 4: *modifiers*—refer to properties or qualities of things; eg 'big', 'red', 'pretty', 'hot', 'all gone', 'there', 'mine' (9 per cent);

Category 5: *personal–social words*—say something about the child's feelings or social relationships; eg 'ouch', 'please', 'no', 'yes', 'want' (8 per cent).

Category 6: *function words*—have only a grammatical function; eg 'what', 'where', 'is', 'to', 'for' (4 per cent).

So the nouns (specific and general nominals) compose 65 per cent and action words another 13 per cent, making 78 per cent altogether. Interestingly, even the nouns were related in some way to things the child could do, for example, the names of toys and food. It seems that it is not just the amount of exposure to objects and words that matters but whether the child can play with it, manipulate it, eat it and so on; active involvement with its environment will help determine many of the child's first words.

c) Two-word Stage (About 18 Months)

This stage, like the earlier ones, is universal, but individual differences in the rate of development become increasingly conspicuous.

Like the transition from babbling to one-word sentences, so the move from the one-word to the two-word stage is also gradual—single words are still used for some months after two-word sentences appear, on average at 18 months.

Bee and Mitchell (1980) point out that as well as the continued development of the child's vocabulary, what becomes important now is the growth of understanding of grammar. They subdivide this third stage into two: between 18 and 30 months they call Stage 1 grammar, and from 30 months onwards, Stage 2 grammar.

Stage 1 Grammar (18–30 Months)

The child's speech is typically *telegraphic*, very much like the words found in telegrams. The essence of a telegram, of course, is that as much information as possible is conveyed in as few words as possible, so the words must be very economical. This is exactly what the child's speech is like:

i) Only key words are used, those that contain the most information (Roger Brown calls these *contentives*);

ii) Purely grammatical terms, eg the verb *to be*, plurals, possessives, are omitted (these are known as functional words or *functors*);

iii) There is a rigid word order, which seems to preserve the grammatically correct order and so helps preserve the meaning of the sentence. For example, if a child is asked, 'Does Tanya want to go to sleep?' she might say, 'Tanya sleep' (or, later on, 'Tanya go sleep').

By contrast, adults do not rely exclusively on word order to express meaning; the passive form of a sentence is a good example ('Joelle ate the banana' and, 'The banana was eaten by Joelle' both convey the same meaning, although the word order of each sentence is different).

Again, the child's imitations of adult sentences are simple but retain the word order of the original sentence; eg 'Jessica is playing with the dog' is imitated as 'Play dog'. From the start, the child's sentences are creative; it is as if the child were creating novel sentences based on its own grammar. (Looked at this way, 'errors' only occur when judged from adult standards.)

Braine (1963) tried to write a kind of grammar for the sentences of young children. He observed that certain key words appeared repeatedly and invariably in the same order; these are called *pivot* words ('pivot grammar'). For example, 'see' always came first and 'it' always at the end. The larger group of words which are combined with pivot words he called 'X' words (others call them 'open words').

The basic rule of Braine's pivot grammar seems to be: pick a pivot word and then combine it with any X word. But this is probably an oversimplification. It seems that some pivot words ('bye bye') appear in different places in different sentences, and it also seems to obscure semantic differences. For example, Bloom (1973) observed the same child produce two identical sentences with very different meanings: 'Mommy sock' was used once to mean 'This is mommy's (mummy's) sock'—the child was picking it up—

and again to mean 'Mommy is putting my sock on me'—which is what she was doing at the time. To simply see 'mommy' as a pivot word would tend to overlook these differences.

Again, two-word sentences can express some complex relations, such as: (a) location ('sweater chair'); (b) possessive ('mommy coat'); (c) recurrence ('more milk'); (d) relation between agent and action ('Sarah read'); and (e) relation between object and action ('see sock').

Stage 2 Grammar (From About 30 Months)

This second stage lasts perhaps until 4 or 5 years, and although it may be different for different languages, the rule-governed behaviour in language development is universal in all cultures.

Vocabulary is growing rapidly but also sentences are becoming longer and more complex. The increase in 'Mean Length of Utterance' (MLU) is due largely to the gradual inclusion of the function words that are left out of the telegraphic speech of stage 1 grammar. So stage 2 grammar really begins with the first use of purely grammatical words and continues for several years.

Roger Brown (1973) has found that there is a distinct regularity among English-speaking children in the order in which the grammatical complexities are added.

A study by deVilliers and deVilliers (1973) found that children the world over seem to acquire functional words in the same general order but at different rates. Each function word corresponds to a syntactic rule but when children begin to apply these rules, for example plurals, how do we know that they have actually learned a rule and are not just imitating what they have heard others say?

One demonstration of children's rule-learning ability was carried out by Berko (1958) who showed children a picture of a fictitious creature called a *wug* and told them, 'This is a Wug'.

The children were then shown a second picture in which there were two of these creatures and were told, 'Now there is another one; there are two of them'; and they were asked to complete the sentence 'There are two ____'. Children 3 and 4 years old could successfully supply the correct answer 'wugs', although they had never seen one of these creatures before and certainly could not have been imitating anybody else's speech. Clearly, they were applying a rule about how to form plurals.

Again, in their spontaneous speech, children show that they apply rules that they have inferred or deduced from all the speech going on around them. It is often through their grammatical mistakes (which adults find so amusing) that children demonstrate this rule-governed behaviour, eg 'sheeps', 'geeses', 'mans', 'goed', 'wented'. Since it is extremely unlikely that the child has actually heard these words spoken (by adults), the child could not be simply imitating them. What the child seems to be doing is *overgeneralizing* the rule or *overregularizing* the English language; children from 30 months to about 5 years make language more regular than it really is. This is one of the outstanding characteristics of the child's language development in stage 2 grammar.

A significant fact is that the child is not consciously aware that it has acquired these rules and could not say what the rule is; the rules have not been deliberately taught by parents and yet the child's language is governed by rules. Overgeneralization also applies to word meanings; for example, calling all men 'daddy' or all four-legged animals 'doggie'.

But does this mean that 2- or 3-year-olds cannot discriminate perceptually between a dog and other animals? There is evidence that they can, and that they know much more about word meaning than their semantic errors might suggest. For example, Thompson and Chapman (1977) found that 2-year-olds who call all four-legged animals 'doggie' can often discriminate a dog from other animals if given a set of animal pictures and asked to 'show a doggie'.

According to deVilliers and deVilliers (1979), the 'problem' is often a sheer lack of alternative labels for things. The child is dependent on the labels provided by adults who may consider that a young child does not need to know the difference between say, a dog and a wolf, so they provide a label for those aspects of meaning (or 'semantic features') that the child first notices and can understand.

Clark and Clark (1977) maintain that the child's tendency to overgeneralize (*and* underextend) word meanings suggests that it is forming *hypotheses* about what words signify and then gradually modifying these 'guesses' until their understanding matches that of adults. Clark and Clark refer to this as the *semantic features hypothesis*, whereby children infer meaning from the *perceptual features* of the word referents, that is, their size, shape, texture, taste, sound and so on. Independent support comes from Prawat and Wildfong (1980) and Tomikawa and Dodd (1980).

In the first of these studies, 3- to 4-year olds saw cereal poured into a cup-like container and were asked whether it was a bowl or a cup; most children called it a 'cup', which supported Clark's hypothesis against Nelson's (1978) hypothesis that children infer meanings from the functions of referents.

Clark and Clark (1977) and Bloom (1973 and 1975) have observed the opposite of overgeneralization, namely *underextension*, whereby certain words may be used for very specific reference. For example, one child that Bloom studied used 'car' to refer to cars moving in the road but not to parked cars or when she was riding in one.

According to Miller (1951), by the age of 4 or 5 years basic grammatical rules have been learned and by 5 or 6 a child's language is remarkably like that of an adult. But typically, a 5-year-old will have difficulty understanding passive sentences; if asked to act out 'The horse is kissed by the cow', the child will reverse the meaning, making the horse do the kissing.

Also, there are a great number of irregular words still to be learned and this aspect of grammatical development will take several more years. However, all the basic skills have been acquired.

Theories of Language Acquisition

How can we account for the stages of language development described above?

In trying to answer the question as to *why* children acquire language in the way they do, we are really once again involved in the heredity and environment (or Nature–Nurture) issue.

One type of theory regards language as being learned through essentially the same processes as other behaviour and centres around the concepts of selective reinforcement, shaping and imitation (see Chapter 3); another kind of theory sees language as an inherent, biologically-determined capacity of human beings.

In *Verbal Behaviour* (1957) Skinner applied the principles of operant conditioning to explain language development in children. In essence, he claimed that adults shape the baby's sounds into words and its words into sentences (ie correct grammar is reinforced and incorrect grammar is not), through selective reinforcement. Sometimes, the positive reinforcement comes in the form of the child getting what it asks for; 'May I have some water?' produces a drink which then reinforces that form of words (*'mands'*). Staats and Staats (1963) suggest that parents provide reinforcement by becoming excited, poking, touching, patting and feeding children when they vocalize; a mother's delight upon hearing her child's first real word is exciting for the child and so acquiring language becomes reinforcing in itself.

Skinner also refers to the imitation (*echoic responses*) of verbal labels (*'tacts'*) which receive immediate reinforcement in the form of the approval of parents etc to the extent that they resemble the correct word.

But what is the evidence that parents do actually shape their children's speech? And even if parents are found to reinforce selectively in the way Skinner claims, does it necessarily have any influence on the child's grammar?

Brown, Cazden and Bellugi (1969) wanted to discover whether mothers' responses to their children's language depended on its grammatical correctness or on its presumed meaning. In most cases it was the 'truth value' and not the grammatical correctness or complexity which the mothers responded to; they extract meaning from and interpret the child's incomplete and sometimes primitive sentences.

Braine (1971) and Tizard et al (1972) found that trying to correct grammatical mistakes or teach correct grammar has very little effect. Again, Nelson (1973) found that the children of mothers who systematically corrected their child's poor word pronunciation and rewarded good pronunciation actually developed vocabulary more slowly.

Slobin (1975) found children learn grammatical rules despite their parents, who usually pay little attention to the grammatical structure of their child's speech and often, in fact, reinforce incorrect grammar. He claims that, 'a mother is too engaged in interacting with a child to pay attention to the linguistic form of his utterance'. So, while parents usually respond to (reinforce) true statements and criticize or correct false ones, they pay little regard to their grammatical correctness and even if they did it would have little effect anyway.

As for the role of imitation, it clearly has to be involved in the learning of accent and vocabulary. But when it comes to the complex aspects of language, namely syntax and semantics, the role played by imitation is much less obvious.

When children do imitate adult sentences, they tend to reduce or convert them to their own, currently-operating grammar; as we saw before, between 18 and 30 months the child's imitations are as telegraphic as its spontaneous speech (Brown called this *imitation with reduction*). Again, a good deal of adult language is, in fact, ungrammatical, so that imitation alone could not explain how we ever learn 'correct' English. Even if we do not always speak grammatically ourselves, we still know what is good grammar and what is not.

Lenneberg (1967) cites the case of a boy, who was totally dumb but who could hear and was quite normal mentally; he could understand language and obey verbal instructions etc. But, of course, he could not imitate.

What selective reinforcement and imitation both fail to explain are:

a) Why native speakers of a language have the capacity to produce and understand an indefinitely large number of sentences that they have never heard before and which, indeed, may never have been uttered before by anyone. This is referred to as the *creativity* of language (or its 'open-endedness', in contrast to the 'closed' nature of the vast majority of animal communication—see Chapter 14). 'The normal use of language is innovative, in the sense that much of what we say in the course of normal language use is entirely new, not a repetition of anything that we have heard before . . .' (Chomsky, 1968).

b) The distinction between *competence* (understanding or implicit knowledge of the language) and *performance* (actual use of language on particular occasions); for Skinner, there is only performance. Competence is what underlies the creativity of language.

c) The spontaneous use of *grammatical rules*, which have never been explicitly heard or taught. These rules, as we have seen, are often over-generalized, resulting in linguistic mistakes, but they are clearly not the product of imitation or reinforcement; indeed, we have also seen that children are largely impervious to parental attempts to correct their grammatical errors.

d) The child's ability to understand the meaning of sentences, as opposed to word meaning. The meaning of a sentence is *not* simply the sum of the meaning of individual words; as Neisser (1967) points out, the structure of language is comparable to the structure of perception as described by the Gestalt psychologists (see Chapter 4). Skinner may be able to account for how the child learns the meaning of individual nouns and verbs (since they have an obvious reference) but what about the meaning of grammatical terms ('functors')?

e) The universal sequence of stages of language and development.

The major alternative theory also has two main strands: (i) Chomsky's (1965, 1968) and McNeill's (1970) innate Language Acquisition Device (LAD); and (ii) biological aspects of language.

Chomsky's central idea is that children are born already programmed in some way to learn language. The LAD (whose 'female' counterpart is LAS —Language Acquisition System) is a hypothetical model (that is, an attempt to explain language development by inferring what must be going on in the child's brain but without being able to observe it directly); it is based on the theory that individuals are born with the ability to formulate and understand all types of sentences even though they have never heard them before.

To understand properly what Chomsky is proposing, we must look at what he means by Transformational Grammar, Deep and Surface Structure and how these are connected. When we hear a spoken sentence, we do not 'process' or retain the grammatical structure, the actual words or phrases used (ie the *surface structure*) but instead we transform it into another form, which more or less corresponds to the meaning of the sentence (ie *deep structure*). This understanding or knowledge of how to transform the meaning of a sentence into the words that make up the sentence, and vice-versa (ie *transformational grammar*) is what Chomsky believes is innate, and it is this innate ability which enables us to produce an infinite number of meaningful sentences.

For example, the *same* surface structure can have *different* deep structures; take the sentence, 'They are eating apples'. Can you work out the two meanings of this sentence? Conversely, *different* surface structures can have the *same* deep structure; eg, 'The dog chased the cat' and, 'The cat was chased by the dog'.

Our ability to understand both meanings of the first sentence and the single meaning of the second and third is based on *transformational grammar*, which is essentially what LAD comprises: children are equipped with the ability to learn the rules that transform deep structure into various surface structures (transformations). This is done by looking for certain kinds of linguistic features (*linguistic universals*) which are common to all languages; for example, all known languages make use of consonants and vowels, syllables, subject-predicate, modifier and noun, verb and object. Collectively, these universals provide the 'deep-structure'.

Chomsky argues that these features *must* be universal since all children can learn any language to which they are exposed with equal ease: a child born in England of English parents, if flown over to China soon after birth and brought up by a Chinese family, will learn to speak Chinese just as efficiently as any native-born Chinese (and just as efficiently as it would have learnt English).

Only some kind of LAD, Chomsky argues, can account for the child's learning and knowledge of grammatical rules, in view of the limited and often ungrammatical and incomplete samples of speech that a child hears.

(We should note, as does Lyons (1970), that transformational grammar is *not* intended as a psychological model of how people construct and understand utterances. The grammar of a language, as seen by Chomsky, is an idealized description of the linguistic competence of native speakers of the language; any model of how this competence is applied in actual performance must take into account certain psychologically relevant facts such as memory, attention, the workings of the nervous system and so on.)

Is there any evidence to support Chomsky?

Much of the supporting evidence which does exist comes from study of the biological aspects of language:

a) We have already seen that many of the stages of language development are universal, which suggests the role of maturation. We also saw that deaf babies babble at the same time, and in the same way, as hearing babies—this too implies a maturational underpinning.

b) Our vocal organs, breathing apparatus, auditory system and brain are all highly specialized for spoken communication.

c) As we noted above, adult languages all over the world have certain important features in common (linguistic universals) and transformational grammar is acquired in some form by all human beings, regardless of culture.

This universality of language features may reflect the fact that all human brains are 'built' in a certain way and this matching of language structures and brain structure could account for the ease with which babies learn their native tongue.

d)   Lenneberg (1964, 1967) studied normal and Down's syndrome children and found a consistently strong correlation between *motor* milestones (eg sitting, crawling, standing, walking) and *language* milestones (eg babbling, one-word sentences, two-word sentences). This correlation is much higher than that between language development and age which, in fact, is lacking altogether in Down's children. Although the *rate* of motor and language development is much slower in Down's children, the correlation between them is as high as it is for normal children; this again strongly suggests the role of maturation in language development, which Lenneberg says is much more like learning to walk than learning to read.

e)   The built-in tendency to develop language in some form or other is dramatically illustrated by the case of four congenitally deaf children (Goldin-Meadow and Feldman, 1975). They developed what looked like stage 1 grammar in their gestures; their parents did not know how to use sign language, they were not exposed to any sign language and they could hear no speech.
      The children were observed from the time they were 18 months old and it was found that they created a sign language, first for individual objects and actions (comparable to holophrases) and then later combined them into two-gesture sentences. Although confined to things that were immediately present, they were beginning to use the language process on their own with no encouragement or training from parents. So it seems that LAD may be applied to gestural language as well as to speech. Language is very difficult to suppress, even in adverse environmental circumstances.
      Since adults combine all the pieces of the transformation together, it makes sense that the child goes through stages that are not reflected in adult speech: the child only learns transformational rules one at a time and only gradually do the child's rules come to resemble those of the adult.

f)   Lenneberg also points out that almost all human beings acquire language, regardless of IQ; the only exceptions (apart from individuals who are severely retarded) are 'wild' or 'wolf' children who are thought to have been raised by wild animals (eg Brown, 1958). However, it has been suggested that such children may have been abandoned at birth because they were brain-damaged in some way.

g)   Lenneberg believes that the years leading to puberty (10 to 11) constitute a *critical period* for language development. His argument centres around the relative lack of specialization of the brain while it is still developing, so that brain-damaged children who lose their language abilities can relearn at least some of them as other, non-damaged, parts of the brain seem to take over the language function. By contrast, adults or adolescents, suffering an equivalent amount of damage, will be unable to regain abilities corresponding to the site of the injury since their brains have already 'set', that is, become specialized. For most of us, our left hemisphere is dominant for language (see Chapter 15). However, many of these claims have been disputed. For example, Entus (1977) and Witelson and Pallie (1973) suggest that specialization or localization of brain function may be present at birth.

Also, studies of children reared in conditions of extreme deprivation suggest that the first ten or so years may not necessarily be the critical period that Lenneberg maintains. Curtiss (1977) describes the case of Genie, who was confined to a small back bedroom, harnessed to an infant's potty seat and left, unable to move. She heard no sounds and did not see daylight for years. She was force-fed and deprived of almost all stimulation; she became malnourished and was underdeveloped. She was discovered when she was 13, when she could understand a few words ('rattle', 'bunny', 'red', 'blue', 'green' and 'brown') to which she always responded in the same way. But essentially she had to learn her first language at 13. Genie never developed normal language, it remained constrained and lacked the spontaneity of normal speech; however, she could develop new sentences of her own design. She had to be taught the rules of language long after they are normally (and spontaneously) picked up and so it proved much more difficult for her than for younger children. However, the fact that it was possible at all tends to detract from Lenneberg's idea of a critical period. (Also see the cases of Isabelle and the Czech twins in Chapter 18 on page 475.)

The innateness/biological approach does not deny the importance of interaction with the environment. But language acquisition is seen, essentially, as the acquisition of a series of rules that allow children to generate sentences.

Another way of investigating the nature–nurture issue is to look at attempts that have been made to teach language to non-humans. Until recently, it was generally believed that language ability is confined to humans; Lenneberg, for instance, claims that it represents a species–specific behaviour, common to all humans and found only in humans. But clearly if non-humans can be taught to use language, then they must have the capacity for language (although it does not appear spontaneously, it must be potential in them) and so we would have to revise our ideas as to what makes us different from other species. (Chomsky also believes that language is unique to human beings.)

The obvious subjects for such language-training are our closest evolutionary relatives, chimpanzees and gorillas, the non-human primates. But before considering the findings, we should look again at what defines or characterizes language; clearly, speech and language are not identical (although we often equate them) for parrots can 'talk' but they are not capable of language, since there is no meaning or understanding in the sounds they produce. (This is why we call rote learning 'parrot fashion' learning, because it does not require understanding, just recall.)

In Chomsky's terms, the parrot displays no linguistic *competence*; conversely, a child may display competence without being able to speak (no linguistic *performance*). Lenneberg (1967) studied a child who could not speak but who could 'answer' questions about the content of a short story, couched in a grammatically complex form; he did this by pointing, nodding, shaking his head and so on.

So how can we define language in a way that will prove useful for evaluating the results of studies where humans have tried to teach it to non-humans (who do not speak)?

Brown (1973) has suggested that language (as a form of communication) has three special features: semanticity, displacement and productivity.

Semanticity (meaningfulness): through language we can represent objects, events, and abstract ideas in a symbolic way and this is what makes language meaningful. In general, animal 'vocabularies' are small, the 'words' express emotional states and this makes them more like signals than symbols.

Displacement refers to the fact that language allows us to communicate about things and experiences which may be far away, in time and space, and even things or events which are purely hypothetical. But Von Frisch (1967) has observed that the honeybee performs a dance which informs other bees of the location of a nectar source that may be some distance from the hive. So, while displacement may be a necessary characteristic of human language, it is not a sufficient one (see Chapter 14).

Productivity refers to the capacity of human language for allowing a limited number of individual words to be combined into an unlimited number of sentences. It has been estimated that it would take 10,000 billion years merely to utter all the possible 20 word sentences in English. Displacement does seem to be unique to human language.

Teaching Language to Non-Humans

Early attempts to teach chimps to speak were almost totally unsuccessful.

Kellogg and Kellogg (1933) raised Gua with their own child and treated them exactly alike; although she could understand a total of 70 words or commands, Gua failed to utter a single word.

Hayes and Hayes (1951) used operant conditioning in what was the first deliberate attempt to teach human language to a non-human—Viki, a baby chimp. By age 3, she could say 'up' and 'cup' and (less convincingly) 'mama' and 'papa'.

It became obvious that a chimp's vocal apparatus is unsuited to making English speech sounds, but this does not rule out the possibility that they may still be capable of learning language in some non-spoken form. This is precisely what several psychologists have tried to demonstrate since the 1960s.

The Gardners (1969) took advantage of the fact that chimps are extremely nimble-fingered (they can groom themselves and others, peel fruit, make simple tools, use a screwdriver, wind watches, thread needles and so on) to teach Washoe (a female) American Sign Language (ASL or Ameslan). This is the sign language used by many deaf people in the USA and is based on a series of gestures, each of which corresponds to a word. Many gestures visually represents aspects of the word's meaning. Ameslan also has devices for signalling verb tense and other grammatical structures and it is fully adequate for expressing everything that can be spoken.

Washoe's training began when she was about one-year-old; the Gardners created for her as human an environment as possible (her 'house' was a house trailer), with social companions, objects and daily play activities, including word or sign games. They signed to Washoe and to one another in her presence (just as deaf parents might) and whenever she made a correct sign, she was rewarded. Sometimes her natural gestures were close enough to the correct signs to permit shaping; sometimes her fingers were placed in the correct position. After four years of training Washoe had about 160 signs.

In many ways her progress was similar to a young child learning spoken language. Once she had learned a particular sign she quickly generalized it to appropriate activities or objects; for example, 'more' was signed to request more tickling, more hair brushing, more swinging and a second helping of food. She also over-generalized, as we have seen young children typically do.

Significantly, as soon as Washoe had learned eight to ten signs, she spontaneously began to combine them, forming sentences such as, 'more sweet', 'listen dog', and 'Roger come'. Later she combined three or more. By age 5 her command of language was roughly equivalent to that of a 3-year-old child. It seemed that she did acquire syntax and could combine signs in various ways.

But in other respects, Washoe's progress was quite different from a child's: she was not exposed to sign language until she was a year old and the Gardners had only just acquired Ameslan as a 'second language'. More recently, they began working with chimps that have been exposed since birth to people who are fluent in Ameslan, and the chimps seem to be learning much faster.

Fouts (1972), one of the Gardners' former assistants, has been trying to study how chimps might use Ameslan with each other and whether chimp mothers teach it to their offspring. It was hoped that Washoe might spontaneously teach her own babies, but, unfortunately, they both died soon after birth.

Since then, Washoe has adopted a baby chimp called Loulis; experiments began in 1979 and Washoe began signing to Loulis daily. Loulis has imitated a number of Washoe's signs, but it is not yet clear if he understands what they mean. Savage–Rumbaugh, Rumbaugh and Boysen (1978) reported the 'first instance of . . . symbolic communication between non-human primates'. Each chimp had to depend on the other in order to obtain food; a container was filled with their favourite items, peanut butter and jam sandwiches (they were very American chimps), orange drink and M and Ms (American 'Smarties'). To get food, each chimp had to choose the correct sign and flash it on a projector for the others to view. The requested item could then pass through a hole in the glass from one chimp to the other. The chimp 'team' was accurate 70 to 100 per cent of the time.

Premack (1971) taught Sarah a language based on small plastic symbols of varying shapes and colours; each plastic symbol stood for a word. She learned to construct sentences by arranging symbols on a special magnetized board. (This is easier than learning Ameslan because the symbols were all in front of her and so she did not have to remember them. But she was 'mute' when she did not have her symbols with her.)

Sarah was raised in a cage and then had much less contact with humans than Washoe. Once again, operant conditioning was used: if she correctly chose the symbol for a banana, she would receive the banana as a reinforcement. In this way, she developed a small but impressive vocabulary, making compound sentences and answering simple questions. However, she was unable to generate new sentences of her own.

Rumbaugh, Gill and Glaserfeld (1973) used a different kind of approach again, with Lana. They taught her to operate a special typewriter controlled by a computer. The machine had 50 keys, each displaying a geometric configuration or pattern representing a word in a specially devised language called Yerkish. When Lana typed a configuration it appeared on a screen in front of her. She spontaneously learned to correct herself by checking the sequence of configurations on the screen—she learned to read! Not only did Lana respond to humans who 'conversed' with her via the computer, but she initiated some of the conversations. And when confronted with an object for which she had not been taught a word, she created one. For example, when seeing a ring for the first time she labelled it as a 'finger bracelet' (combining two words she already knew).

Finally, one of the most recent studies involves a female gorilla, Koko (Patterson, 1979). Patterson used Ameslan and after seven years of training, Koko has mastered almost 400 signs. She also understands many equivalent English words for these signs. She has developed syntax and a number of novel sentences; she has also invented 20 of her own combinations for signs for 'nail file', 'eye make-up', 'runny nose' and 'obnoxious'!

Koko's hearing is excellent and she can make subtle auditory language discriminations; for example, one day in a 'discussion' about time, she signed 'lemon'. Her thumb is too short to make the sign for 'eleven', so instead she signed 'lemon o' clock', a like-sounding word: eleven o'clock happens to be the time she has her morning snack!

As Dworetzky (1981) points out, speaking to a gorilla is like glimpsing inside the mind of an alien who sees some things in a different way, sometimes a metaphorically beautiful way, illustrated in Koko's sign for a cigarette lighter, a 'bottle match', 'white tiger' for a zebra, 'quiet chase' for hide-and-seek, 'look mask' for view master, 'false mouth' for nose, 'elephant baby' for a pinnochio doll and 'eye hat' for mask. Koko can use language to express anger ('red mad gorilla') and she has even lied by blaming others, claiming events which never happened and deliberately describing acts differently from how they were. This represents a quite sophisticated use of language.

Some of these findings seem truly remarkable and the conclusion that non-humans do, indeed, have the capacity for language seems quite compelling. They seem to be able to attach meaning to symbols, string the symbols together into meaningful patterns and even create novel, meaningful sentences. But has it been proven that chimps have a grammar which allows them to generate alternative ways of saying the same sentence? (In Chomsky's terms, are they able to transform the same deep structure into various surface structures?) Their language does seem to be usually tied to a fairly specific word order.

Terrace (1979) after five years of working with his own chimp, Nim Chimpsky, concludes that although chimps can acquire a large vocabulary, they are not capable of producing original sentences. But surely the evidence of Washoe and Koko contradicts this conclusion?

Terrace argues that the great apes have been operantly conditioned to make certain signs in order to get what they want and that they are often inadvertently cued by their trainers to produce these signs in sequence; the apes are not really aware of what the signs mean.

Nim Chimpsky's 'utterances' did not increase in length as those of young children do; although she acquired many 'words', she did not use them in longer and longer sentences as time passed. Only 12 per cent of her utterances were spontaneous, the remaining 88 per cent were in response to her teachers. A significantly greater percentage of children's speech is spontaneous. Terrace concludes that there is no evidence that non-humans are grammatically competent, either from his own studies or any of the earlier ones. But what about Brown's criteria of language that we considered earlier?

As far as semanticity is concerned, the non-human primates certainly seem to use symbols meaningfully and accurately, and there is evidence of displacement too; for example, when Washoe signs, 'You me go there in' she is referring to a place she is not in at that moment. In terms of productivity, there is evidence of this too, especially with Washoe and Koko, but this is what Terrace denies.

Premack (1976) argues with Terrace that the rich inventiveness of language displayed by children may be limited in chimps to word substitutions using restricted sentence structures. There seems as yet little evidence of chimps learning and overgeneralization of syntactic rules (as opposed to word meanings), which, as we have seen, is another hallmark of the spontaneously produced language of children.

However, Lana would only receive what she wanted if she pressed the correct keys in the correct order, for example, 'Please machine give piece of apple'. Also, she could tell the difference between 'Lana groom Tim' (one of her trainers) and 'Tim groom Lana', a difference in meaning entirely due to syntax and which young children will confuse before a certain age.

Perhaps the most useful conclusion to draw about the whole issue of language in non-humans is that we simply do not know enough yet to be able to say that they have it or that they do not. Again, the situation may be much more complex than this, so that we may say that they are capable of some aspects of language but not others. Their lack of a specialized area in the brain for language may explain what Terrace sees as the limited findings to date. But perhaps we still have not discovered the best way of allowing non-human primates to show us what they can do. The belief that only we humans have true language ability dies hard!

21

Moral Development

As scientists, psychologists who study moral development are not interested in morality as such (ie those rules and principles for distinguishing right from wrong conduct) or in particular moralities or moral codes, but in the processes by which the individual acquires those rules. The processes are assumed to be the same for all, regardless of the particular moral code the individual acquires.

Roger Brown (1965) compared a morality with the grammar of a language, the latter being a set of rules for forming well-formed as opposed to badly-formed sentences (see Chapter 20). He also pointed out that morality is not static but is always undergoing change—what is considered to be right or acceptable by one generation may not be by the next. But there will always be disagreement between different groups in society, or even between individuals in the same group, regarding certain moral issues.

Eleanor Maccoby (1980) defines moral development as the child's acquisition of rules which govern behaviour in the social world and, in particular, the development of a sense of right and wrong, how the child begins to understand the values that guide and regulate behaviour within a given social system.

As implied by Maccoby's definition, morality has more than one dimension: it is not merely a matter of acquiring an intellectual understanding of society's rules, ie knowing what is right and wrong (*cognitive* component), but also of behaving in accordance with those rules, ie our actual moral conduct (*behavioural* component). Clearly, we often say one thing and behave in a contradictory way—we may know what is right or wrong but we do not necessarily translate this into action. There is also a third component, the feeling aspect, ie guilt, shame, pride and so on (*affective* component); we may behave in a way that most people would judge to be immoral and yet feel no guilt or remorse or, conversely, we may be troubled by a guilty conscience and yet be a law-abiding citizen.

These examples suggest that the three components of morality are, indeed, distinct and that the exact relationship between them is complex and worthy of empirical investigation by psychologists. In practice, psychologists have tended to concentrate on one of the three components, often to the exclusion of the other two. Consequently, no one theory or approach is comprehensive in the sense that it tries to show how moral knowledge, behaviour and feelings are actually interrelated. It is not only in the context of moral development that three or four major theoretical approaches emerge (see Chapter 1) but it becomes particularly clear when discussing this topic just how they differ, each one emphasizing one component and presenting a very different view of what moral development involves:

(i)   Freud's psychoanalytic theory focuses on the affective component; in particular, guilt or moral anxiety, on the one hand, and pride or self-esteem on the other;

(ii) Learning theory, based on classical and operant conditioning, emphasizes the behavioural component;

(iii) Social Learning Theory (outlined briefly in Chapter 3) extends the principles of Learning theory by describing observational learning (or modelling) as well as by relating behaviour to cognitive factors.

(iv) The cognitive–developmental theories of Piaget (see Chapter 19) and Kohlberg concentrate on the cognitive component, ie moral knowledge, understanding and reasoning.

They all have in common the assumption that the acquisition of morality is part of the wider process of socialization, that is, it develops according to the same principles which govern the development of other aspects of socialized behaviour. It follows that, in order to understand moral development in particular, we must understand the process of development in general.

i) Freud's Psychoanalytic Theory

According to Freud, our moral behaviour is controlled by the superego, which comprises the conscience and the ego-ideal. The conscience is that part of our personality which punishes us when we have committed some wrong-doing and so is the source of feelings of guilt; it represents the 'punishing parent' within our personality and is composed of all the prohibitions imposed on us by our parents, the 'thou shalt nots' (see Chapter 26).

The ego-ideal rewards us when we have behaved in accordance with our basic moral values ('thou shalts'); it is the source of our feelings of pride and self-satisfaction and represents the 'rewarding parent' within our personality.

Each part of the superego is acquired through a different process of identification (the conscience through identification with the aggressor, the ego-ideal through anaclitic identification) and the process is completed by age 5 or 6. We will look at these in more detail.

Psychosexual and Moral Development

To appreciate Freud's theory of moral development, it must be seen in the context of personality development, which for Freud proceeds through five psychosexual stages: the Oral (up to 1 year); Anal (1 to 3); Phallic (3 to 5 or 6); Latency (5 or 6 to puberty); and the Genital (puberty to maturity). It is the third of these, the phallic, which is the important one as far as moral development is concerned, since the Oedipus and Electra complexes occur during this stage and the outcome is the acquisition of the superego, through the process of identification.

Oedipus Complex

In the case of boys (who, like girls, take the mother as their first love-object), beginning at about 3, their love for their mother becomes increasingly passionate and this brings them into conflict and rivalry with their father. The little boy does not want to share his mother with anyone and so he is jealous of the father who already 'possesses' her and he wants him dead (which, for a 3-year-old, means 'out of the way').

However, his father is bigger and more powerful and eventually he comes to fear that he may lose the thing he values most in the world, namely, his penis. Partly because he has been punished for masturbating, and may actually have been threatened with all its nasty consequences, and partly because he has observed the absence of a penis in girls, the boy comes to fear that his father will cut off his penis (*fear of castration*).

This situation of jealousy, fear and love Freud called the Oedipus complex, after the mythical King of Thebes, Oedipus, who unwittingly killed his father and married his mother. (When he discovered what he had done, Oedipus blinded himself by gouging out his eyes.)

To resolve the dilemma, the boy represses his desire for his mother (ie makes it unconscious) and identifies with his father, that is, he comes to think, feel and act as if he were his father; this way, at least, he keeps his male organ and can have the mother vicariously, since by becoming like his father, he can indirectly have what his father has.

Electra Complex

The equivalent situation in the case of little girls is the Electra complex, named after another character from Greek mythology, Electra, who induced her brother to kill their mother.

While a little boy's Oedipus complex ends with fear of castration, the girl's Electra complex begins with the belief that she has already been castrated, since little boys have something she does not, namely, a penis. The situation is more complex for girls than boys: while boys have to make one 'move', from a romantic attachment to their mother to identification with their father, girls, who take their mother as their first love-object, become romantically attached to their father before finally identifying with their mother. Why does the girl become attracted to her father?

Freud's answer is *penis envy*. Following her discovery of anatomical sex differences, and her consequent belief that she has already been castrated (for which she blames her mother), a girl feels inadequate for not having a penis and so is attracted to the father who does.

However, as with boys and their fathers, this attraction to the father brings the girl into conflict with her mother; the situation is finally resolved in the same way as the Oedipus complex, that is, through repressing her incestuous desire for her father and identifying with her mother. But what is her motive for doing so?

Freud admitted that he was much less clear about the girl's motive for identifying with the mother than he was about the boy's motive for identifying with the father: if boys fear castration at the hands of their more powerful father, then surely this is sufficient reason to repress desire for the mother and to try to become like the father! It is referred to as *identification with the aggressor* ('If you can't beat them, join them') and the essential motive, therefore, is fear. While the Oedipus complex is brought to an *end* through fear of castration, in the case of the girls the Electra complex *begins* with penis envy. So what do girls have to fear if they believe they have already been castrated? One rather tentative solution proposed by Freud was that, when girls realize that their wish for a penis is unrealistic, they substitute for it the wish for a baby and it is this which makes the mother once again attractive to the little girl. Alternatively, the girl may fear the loss of her mother's love if the 'family romance' continues and so, for girls, *anaclitic identification* may be the more important kind in her moral development.

To ease the pain that results from the fear of loss of love (or its threatened withdrawal), she internalizes the images of the mother and this entails being the 'good' child that her mother would wish her to be ('If I'm not what she wants me to be she'll stop loving me'). This process of internalization is known as anaclitic identification and, like identification with the aggressor, is defensive, since it keeps the mother 'alive' inside the child.

Are males morally superior to females?

If we follow Freud's account through, it would seem that the boy's conscience will be stronger than the girl's because: (a) the conscience represents the punishing parent; (b) it is acquired through identification with the aggressor; and (c) the boy's motive for identifying is much stronger than the girl's (ie the fear of castration). Similarly, we would expect a girl's ego-ideal to be more pronounced than a boy's since: (i) the ego-ideal represents the rewarding parent; (ii) it is acquired through anaclitic identification; and (iii) the girl's motive for identifying is stronger than the boy's (ie fear of loss of mother's love).

Freud did, in fact, maintain that women have weaker superegos than men (although he did not specifically differentiate between the conscience and ego-ideal in this context) but there is *no* evidence to support this view. For example, Hoffman (1975) reviewed a number of studies where children are left alone and so are tempted to violate a prohibition; usually there are no overall gender differences but where they are found, they tend to show girls being the better able to resist temptation.

Freud also saw females as being sexually inferior—they have to make do with babies as a poor substitute for a penis—and he may reasonably be regarded as the father of male chauvinism. Many feminist writers (including Karen Horney (1926) and Clara Thompson (1943), two eminent psychoanalysts) have pointed out that what girls (and women) envy is *not* the penis but the superior status that men enjoy in our society: it is the penis as a *symbol* for that superior status which is envied, not literally the penis as such, and it is men, not women, who equate lack of a penis with inferiority. Horney and Sherman (1971) both report 'womb envy' in men.

There is little evidence that women have more difficulty achieving gender identity than men or that they have an inferiority complex about their bodies (eg Fisher, 1973).

Again, Freud seems to have been largely responsible for the 'Myth of the Vaginal Orgasm' (Koedt, 1974). He claimed that clitoral orgasm is 'adolescent' (ie immature) and when women start having regular sexual intercourse they should transfer the 'site' of the orgasm to the vagina. (This, of course, ties in with his view of the superior, active, 'penetrating' male—the woman is seen merely as the passive recipient of the penis.) Also, whereas for men psychoanalysis aims to develop their capacities, for women the aim, according to Freud, is to help them resign themselves to their limited, inferior, sexuality. Interestingly, Koedt cites evidence that women who do prefer a vaginal orgasm tend to be more anxious and to experience their bodies as more de-personalized (less 'their own').

Evidence for the Oedipus Complex

Is there any evidence to support Freud's account of the Oedipus complex?

One criticism is that, even if true for western cultures, the Oedipus complex may not be universal, that is, it may not apply to all cultures and to all historical periods. For instance, Malinowski (1929), studying the Trobriand Islanders in the South Pacific, reported that the father–son relationship was positive and casual rather than conflict-ridden.

Walters and Thomas (1963) showed that, at least in the laboratory, both adults and children readily imitate aggressive models who pose no threat to them whatsoever; assuming that imitation is some kind of index of identification, this suggests that being in conflict with the model and fearing some kind of punishment from him is neither a necessary nor a sufficient condition for identification to occur.

Kagan and Lemkin (1960) found no evidence of a shift amongst 5- to 6-year-old boys away from their mothers towards their fathers; but Fisher and Greenberg (1977) in one of the major reviews of empirical studies of Freudian theory to date, concluded that children do have to cope with erotic feelings towards the opposite-sex parent and feelings of hostility towards the parent of the same sex.

In the same review, Fisher and Greenberg report that fear of castration (expressed indirectly as concern about physical injury, fear of death, fear of bodily harm or attack) is relatively common in men and is intensified when they are exposed to erotic heterosexual stimulation. Women do seem to be more motivated by fear of loss of love.

Freud's own evidence was clinical, based on case studies of his patients who, with one exception, were adults. A common criticism of his theories is that no valid theory of development in children can be based on studies of adults (see Chapter 26) and so the case of little Hans assumes even greater significance (see Box 1.)

It seems very difficult to regard the case of little Hans as evidence for the Oedipus theory since Freud, and Hans's father, had already made up their minds what was the problem and interpreted all the data accordingly. In addition, there are alternative and equally plausible interpretations, including: (a) the child's own explanation that his fear stemmed from the time he saw a horse collapse in the street; (b) Fromm's (1973) suggestions that the fear stems from two sources, first, his mother's castration threats, and secondly, his fear of death (he had recently seen his first funeral and the collapsed horse which he thought was dead); and (c) Bowlby's (1973) interpretation of the fear of separation from his mother who had threatened to leave home because he was naughty. An interesting postscript is that subsequent to the events described in Freud's paper, Hans's parents separated and later divorced (Bowlby, 1973).

Box 1: 'Analysis of a Phobia in a 5-Year-Old Boy' (1909) — the Case of Little Hans

Hans had a phobia of being bitten by a horse and was especially afraid of white horses with black around the mouth and wearing blinkers; he tried to avoid horses at all costs. [Freud's interpretation: fear of being bitten represented Hans's fear of castration.]

Hans was particularly frightened when he once saw a horse collapse in the street. [Freud's interpretation: seeing the horse collapse reminded him, unconsciously, of his death wish against his father, which made him feel guilty and afraid.]

Is there any reason to believe that Hans saw the horses as symbolizing his father?

i)   Hans once said to his father as he got up from the table: 'Daddy, don't *trot* away from me';

ii)   On another occasion, Hans said: 'Daddy, you are lovely, you're so white'. This suggests he may have thought his father resembled a white horse (as opposed to a dark one);

iii) Hans's father had a moustache;

iv) His father wore glasses which resembled blinkers as worn by horses;

v)   Hans had played 'horses' with his father, with Hans usually riding on his father's back;

Hans claimed that his fear stemmed from the time he saw a horse collapse in the street: 'When the horse in the bus fell down it gave me such a fright really; that was when I got the nonsense (ie the phobia). This was confirmed by Hans's mother. But his father, and Freud, paid little attention to this plausible cause of the phobia.

Freud believed Hans was a 'little Oedipus', loving to be in bed with his mother and going to the bathroom with her, and regarding his father as a rival and wanting him out of the way. But rather than the father being 'the aggressor', it seemed to be the mother who made explicit threats of castration:

a)   'If you do that (touch his penis) I'll send for doctor A to cut off your widdler' (Mother);

b)   She threatened to abandon him; Hans said 'Mummy's told me she won't come back'.

c)   'In the big bath I'm afraid of falling in' (Hans).
'But Mummy bathes you in it. Are you afraid of Mummy dropping you in the water?' (Father).
'I'm afraid of her letting go and my head going in' (Hans).

It seems as though Hans needed his father to protect him from a menancing mother.

Freud also described Hans's desire for his mother as intense, exclusive and spontaneous. But she clearly liked him in bed with her and in the bathroom, and Hans said he preferred his Nanny's company to his mother's.

Hans's father, a convinced Freudian, tried to persuade Hans that his fear of horses was *really* a fear of castration.

Is a Guilty Conscience the Sign of a Moral or an Immoral Person?

Turning now to the relationship between our moral behaviour and our experience of guilt (which has its source in the conscience), Freud's view is counter-intuitive. The common sense view is that the greater the wrong-doing, the greater the guilt, ie the more wrongdoing we do, the more reason we have to feel guilty. But Freud claims that the greater the wrongdoing, the *less* the guilt, or the less the wrongdoing the *greater* the guilt.

How can this be?

The conscience causes us to renounce many of our basic impulses or instinctual wishes, especially our aggressive and sexual urges, and the energy from these renounced desires then becomes available to the conscience. Aggression that is not expressed and directed outwards towards others is instead directed inwards, against the self, a form of self-punishment which is experienced as guilt. So a severe, punitive, conscience is one which has a lot of energy at its disposal to keep in check our basic impulses; hence the more severe our conscience (ie the more guilt we are prone to) the *less* will be our objectively immoral behaviour. (In other words, they are *inversely* related.)

How severe or punitive the conscience is depends on the intensity of the child's aggression felt towards the parent (especially the father) and which does not find an outlet on its original target. It is inevitable that the child will be frustrated and feel hostile towards the parent who punishes it but if the child openly expresses this hostility it is likely to come in for even more severe punishment. So the child turns this aggression in on itself, punishing itself and in this way taking over the parental role—and it is through this process of identification with the aggressor that conscience is acquired.

Strength of conscience, as we have seen, depends on the child's unex-pressed hostility towards the punishing parent and this is only partly deter-mined by the actual severity of the parent's punishment. So the relationship between parents' methods of discipline and the strength of the child's conscience will only be indirect: it is how hostile the child *perceives* the parents to be that is of direct importance and this, in turn, is largely a reflection of the child's own hostility towards the parents.

It follows that a child treated very leniently *could* acquire a very severe conscience and that a son who is brutally beaten by his father *could* have a very weak one.

Is there any evidence to support Freud's belief that guilt and objective wrongdoing are inversely related? And is there any evidence that different kinds of parental discipline are related to strength of conscience?

A relevant study was undertaken by MacKinnon (1938), in which 93 sub-jects were given a series of problems to solve, working alone in a room which contained answer books, some of which they were allowed to use, others not. It was found that 43 cheated; the other 50 did not.

Four weeks later, those who had cheated (and who did not know they had been found out) were asked if they had, in fact, cheated; about 50 per cent of them confessed, while the rest denied it. Those who confessed were asked if they felt guilty about what they had done and those who denied it were asked if they would have felt guilty—25 per cent said they did or would have felt guilty. Of those who had not cheated, 84 per cent said they would have felt guilty.

They were also asked, 'Do you in everyday life often feel guilty about things you have done or not done?' 75 per cent of the non-cheaters said 'Yes', compared with 29 per cent of the cheaters. This seems to confirm Freud's predictions that guilt is not directly proportional to wrongdoing and that, indeed, they are inversely related.

MacKinnon also recorded the incidental behaviour of subjects when they were working on the original problems: 9 of the cheats swore out loud or otherwise cussed at the problem (eg 'You bastard' or, 'These are the God-damnedest things I ever saw') but none of the non-cheats did this. Of the cheats, 31 per cent also performed restless acts such as pounding their fists or kicking the leg of the table, compared with only 4 per cent of the non-cheats.

Could it be that the aggressive energy expressed by the cheats was 'subtracted' from the energy available to the conscience, while the energy unexpressed by the non-cheats could be used to 'fuel' the conscience, as Freud would have suggested?

Sometime after the original experiment, MacKinnon managed to trackdown 28 of the original subjects, all males, 13 of the cheats and 15 of the non-cheats. They were asked to check on a list of common forms of punishment, those most often used by their parent. 78 per cent of the cheaters checked physical punishments (including beatings and deprivation of privileges), compared with 48 per cent of the non-cheats; while 22 per cent of the cheats ticked psychological punishments (eg making the child feel that it had fallen short of some standard or had hurt the parents and lost some of their love) compared with 52 per cent of the non-cheats. (The results are summarized in Table 21.1.)

Although these findings seem to support Freud's contention about the relationship between conscience and wrongdoing, as well as suggesting that a strong conscience is more likely to be caused by psychological methods of discipline, there are a number of cautionary points that we need to make:

i) MacKinnon's data are, of course, only *correlational*, so we cannot be sure

Table 21.1 The percentage of cheats and non-cheats who had been punished physically or psychologically in MacKinnon's (1938) study

	Type of punishment	
	Physical	*Psychological*
Cheats (13)	78%	22%
Non-cheats (15)	48%	52%

that the differences in the strength of conscience were caused by differences in child-rearing. For instance, parents who used psychological methods may have differed in other important respects from those who preferred physical methods and these other differences may have been the critical ones.

Again, the direction of causation could have been the other way round—the children may have forced their parents to use physical methods as a last resort when more psychological methods failed. There is considerable evidence regarding constitutional differences between babies (eg Bell, 1968, Thomas, Chess and Birch, 1970) and it is probably easier (everything else being equal) to use psychological methods of discipline with children who are relatively passive, placid or 'un-demanding' by nature.

ii)   MacKinnon's subjects had to recall their childhood experiences and make judgements about how to classify the kinds of punishment used by their parents; memory is notoriously unreliable, particularly with regard to such emotionally salient matters as this.

iii)   Perhaps the distinction between physical and psychological punishment is rather artificial: from what we have said about identification with the aggressor, it would seem that it is how the child perceives the punishment that is critical, including the intensity of feeling with which it is carried out.

iv)   Can we be sure that the behaviour of MacKinnon's subjects was typical of their moral behaviour in general? This is an issue which we shall come back to shortly.

There is, in fact, a good deal of additional evidence which supports the view that a strong conscience and psychological methods of punishment are positively correlated.

One famous study was carried out by Sears, Maccoby and Levin (1957), who interviewed 379 mothers of 5-year-olds in Boston, USA, both middle and working class. Two main kinds of child-rearing techniques emerged: (a) *love-oriented*, more psychological techniques, which made use of praise and affection as rewards for good behaviour, and isolation and love-withdrawal as punishments for bad behaviour; and (b) *object-oriented*, more physical techniques, which used tangible rewards, deprivation of privileges and actual physical punishment.

Further, the love-oriented parents tended to have children with a more highly developed conscience compared with the children of object-oriented parents. However, the associations were not strong; the strongest were with physical punishment, so that of parents who used it a great deal, 15 per cent had children with a strong conscience compared with 32 per cent of those who used it very little.

Sears et al also found that the mothers most likely to have children with a strong conscience were generally warm and used love-withdrawal as a major disciplinary technique. This is consistent with Danziger's (1971) claim that it may be fear of loss of love, rather than love itself, which motivates the child to behave in socially approved ways (and with Freud's notion of anaclitic identification).

According to Hoffman (1970), excessive use of power-assertive techniques of punishment (physical punishment, withdrawal of privileges, or the threat of either) is associated with low levels of moral development. Hoffman and Saltzstein (1967) and Aronfreed (1969) found that reasoning or explaining tends to be associated with high levels of moral development (as measured by consideration for others, moral reasoning and guilt). Similarly, Leizer and Rogers (1974) found that verbal explanations are more effective than physical punishment and even 6- and 7-year-olds are more amenable to reasoning than to reproaches or chastisement.

Aronfreed and Reber (1965) reported that youngsters seem to learn best how to control their own behaviour if parents explain what they have done wrong, what led up to the misdeed or what the consequences of the misdeed were for the youngster and others.

Glueck and Glueck (1950) found that severe punishment is one of the major factors associated with delinquency in young boys.

Bandura and Walters (1959) compared the attitudes of parents of 26 highly aggressive boys with those of 26 normal boys, matched for intelligence and socio-economic status. Most of the former had been in trouble with the law, felt less guilt and had parents who used physical punishment, compared with the latter; the aggressive boys were also more likely to have been rejected by their parents.

If it is method of punishment which determines the strength of conscience, how does it actually work to produce the effect it does?

One suggestion is that different responses are required in the child in order to end the punishment:

i)   In the case of psychological methods, there must be some kind of symbolic renunciation, an apology, a promise not to do it again etc. In time, these responses become organized into what is normally called conscience.

ii) When the child is punished physically, the response is often more aggression or, at least, feelings of hostility, and the parent may, in fact unwittingly be providing the child with a model of aggressive behaviour to imitate; this does not encourage the inner control implied by conscience.

We shall look in more detail below at the effect of punishment on the child.

An Evaluation of Freud's Concept of Conscience

Freud defined the superego like this:

> This new physical agency continues to carry on the functions which have hitherto been performed by the people in the external world: it observes the ego, gives it orders, judges it and threatens it with punishments, exactly like the parents whose place it has taken (1938).

This way of characterizing the superego serves to reinforce a common way of referring to it in everyday language (or, at least, to a part of it, the conscience). White (1975) points out that we usually tend to personalize conscience (eg we say, 'My conscience would not let me do it' or, 'My conscience got the better of me') as if it had an independent life of its own and existed in its own right.

The word 'conscience' (*con* plus *sciens*) means 'knowing with someone else' and it is often used as if it were an independent witness of our behaviour, an internal judge (as Freud says) of whether our behaviour conforms with our moral code.

Many psychologists have become dissatisfied with the term in recent years, partly for the reasons outlined above and partly also because of the particular form it takes in Freud's theory. One major criticism (Kohlberg, 1969, Hoffman, 1976) is that conscience does not suddenly come into existence at five or six years old, but rather that moral development is a gradual process which begins in childhood and extends into adulthood.

Another criticism is that the belief in an internalized conscience implies that moral behaviour should be consistent across different situations, that is, if our moral conduct is determined by a part of our personality which is unchanging, then the details of the moral situation should be largely irrelevant as far as how we act is concerned. It also follows that people will display 'moral traits', such as honesty, whereby someone who is honest on one occasion, in one type of situation, will be honest on another occasion in other types of situation. But is this what people are like?

Generality versus Specificity in Moral Conduct

The classic study which set out to investigate this issue was the 'Character Education Inquiry', begun in 1928 by Hartshorne and May. They studied 12,000 11- to 14-year olds who were given the opportunity to cheat, lie and steal under conditions in which they were confident of not being found out.

They were observed in a variety of situations—in the classroom, playground, after-school activities, in sports, during party games, and at home. They were also given 20 pencil and paper tests designed to measure moral knowledge (where the questions had objectively right answers) and moral opinion (where they did not). These tests were sometimes scored against adult consensus (what a majority of adults believed) and sometimes against a kind of ideal code supplied by the researchers.

It came as quite a surprise to Hartshorne and May that the results were very inconsistent, so that a child who, say, cheated in one situation would often not cheat in another; for example, a child might cheat in an arithmetic test but not in a spelling test. The overall correlation between bad behaviour in one setting and bad behaviour in another situation was 0.34, much lower than had been expected. Even *within* the same situation (eg school tests in the classroom) children behaved inconsistently, although the consistency was relatively higher than it was *between* situations (eg playground and classroom). So it would appear that a child does not have a uniform, generalized, code of morals to determine behaviour in a variety of situations, but rather the situation is at least as much responsible for the child's moral actions as conscience.

Hartshorne and May concluded that honesty was largely situation–specific and not a general personality trait, ie we cannot say that some people are more honest than others, because this implies consistency across situations which they did not find ('Doctrine of Specificity').

However, subsequent re-analysis of the data (Burton, 1963) showed a significant, if small, tendency for children who were honest on one test to be so on others. And subsequent studies of different measures have tended to confirm that they are positively correlated.

Also Nelson et al (1969) found some consistency for resistance to temptation and Rushton (1980) for altruistic behaviour.

Therefore, in conclusion, it appears that personality, as well as the situation, determines several important aspects of moral behaviour and this represents some measure of support for Freud's concept of the superego.

Freud's approach also limits the child's moral learning to the family which, admittedly, was a much greater influence on the child at the turn of the century, when Freud was first formulating his theories, than it is now. Today's child is exposed to many moral influences in addition to the family, both before and after starting school, including the media, teachers and peers.

Other criticisms have come from learning theorists who, as well as being generally critical of Freud's theories, believe that conscience can be accounted for in terms of the principles of conditioning.

ii) Learning Theory Approach

The Learning Theory (or S–R) approach maintains that moral behaviour is learned according to exactly the same principles of classical and operant conditioning as any other behaviour (see Chapter 3).

The Contribution of Classical Conditioning

Psychologists such as H. J. Eysenck believe that what we normally call conscience is no more and no less than a conditioned response of an emotional type (conditioned emotional response or CER) or, more precisely, a collection of such CERs. How might these CERs come about?

The short answer is, by exactly the same procedure by which salivation becomes a CR to a bell. If, for example, a child is frequently disciplined for being naughty, the negative feelings (mainly anxiety) which the child associates with punishment become associated with the wrongdoing. So the child comes to feel anxious when contemplating doing something naughty and this eventually happens even when the parents are not present.

For instance, if the child is smacked (unconditioned stimulus, UCS), which produces pain and anxiety (unconditioned response, UCR), for stealing, and the child is told, 'You must not steal' (conditioned stimulus, CS) just before it is smacked, eventually the words, 'You must not steal' will come to produce anxiety in the child (CR) and, finally, when the child even thinks about stealing, this CR will be produced.

This anxiety which builds up at the thought of doing wrong and reaches a climax just before the wrongdoing, is a far more effective deterrent than the thought of being caught (which may or may not happen), hence the saying 'conscience makes cowards of us all'. In this sense, the self is generally a better deterent against lawbreaking than police or magistrates.

These feelings of anxiety (CERs) represent our ability to resist temptation.

But conscience, according to Eysenck, also refers to our susceptibility to feelings of guilt, that is, what we feel *after* we have committed some wrong-doing. It seems to be the timing of the punishment which determines whether the resistance-to-temptation component or the guilt component of conscience is affected.

A famous experiment by Solomon, Turner and Lessac (1968) with puppies tends to support the view that resistance to temptation and guilt are not func-tionally equivalent components of conscience (although they are subjectively the same). Puppies were 'punished' (swatted with a newspaper) either just before they began to eat forbidden food or just after they had started to eat it. After being trained in one of these two ways, they were all tested by being made hungry and left alone in a room with the forbidden food. Those puppies punished just before eating, held out much longer against the temptation to eat than those punished just after they had eaten a little during training sessions.

However, once the early-punished puppies had started to eat, they showed little sign of anxiety, in sharp contrast to the second group, which showed all the usual signs of 'doggy guilt'. These differences are explained by assum-ing that the first group were classically conditioned to respond with anxiety to all those stimuli which occurred during the approach to food, while the second group were conditioned to those stimuli occurring after food had been eaten.

So, punishment that is consistently given *before* a misdeed will result in high resistance to temptation but weak guilt when wrongdoing does occur, and the reverse will be true when punishment consistently *follows* the misdeed. (We should note that the anxiety experienced when contem-plating some misdeed is reduced if the temptation is actually resisted; in this way, through negative reinforcement, resistance to temptation can be strengthened—through operant conditioning.)

Several studies have found similar effects to those found with puppies when children are the subjects. For example, Aronfreed (1963) punished a group of young boys verbally for touching attractive toys while still in the act of reaching (as the transgression was about to occur), while boys in a second group were punished a few moments after picking up the toys. They were then left alone in a room with the toys and told not to touch them; as predicted, the first group were better able to resist than the second group. However, even in the relatively simple case of a child who is conditioned to feel anxiety when about to steal, cognitive factors are clearly involved, and if the child is given reasons for not touching forbidden toys, for example, some interesting results emerge.

In studies by LaVoie (1970) and Parke and Murray (1971), children were told that the forbidden toy was: (a) fragile and might break; or (b) that it belonged to another child who did not want them to touch it. Giving a rationale (with a mild punishment) proved to be considerably more effective than just punishment and, significantly, with reasons being given, the timing of punishment became irrelevant.

Based on subsequent studies, Parke (1972,1977) concluded that, when a rationale accompanies punishment:

i)   Mild forms of punishment become just as effective as severe punishment at producing resistance to temptation;

ii)   Delayed punishment becomes as effective as early punishment;
iii) Punishment from an aloof and impersonal adult becomes as effective as
      that from a warm, friendly adult;
iv)   Resistance to temptation is much more stable over time.

There are also interesting developmental factors involved. For instance, Parke (1974) found that 3-year-olds were quite effectively inhibited from touching by being told the toy was fragile and might break (object-oriented rationale) but telling them it belonged to another child (person-oriented rationale) had very little effect. However, 5-year-olds did respond to appeals based on property rights.

Parke concludes that long-term (internalized) moral controls may require cognitively-oriented training procedures as opposed to those which rely solely on the conditioning of anxiety responses.

The Contribution of Operant (or Instrumental) Conditioning

This takes a more active view of the learner; what is being conditioned is not an automatic, physiological response like anxiety but some behaviour of the child which is essentially voluntary. So, while classical conditioning is concerned primarily with the affective or emotional components of morality, operant conditioning is concerned with trying to explain how moral behaviour is acquired. The assumption made is that moral behaviour, like all other operant behaviour, can be made more or less likely to occur depending on its consequences, ie whether it is reinforced or punished. Let us look at some of the evidence.

The Role of Reward and Punishment

Fischer (1963) rewarded one group of children with bubble gum or praise for sharing marbles with other children; they were later more likely to give additional marbles to other children than a second group which had not previously been rewarded.

Midlarsky and Bryan (1967) found that children's generosity increased by hugging them whenever they gave sweets to needy children and Gefand et al (1975) found that praising them had the same effect. Serbin et al (1977) found that children praised for co-operating were more likely to increase their co-operation than children who were not praised.

A number of researchers (eg Garbarino and Bronfenbrenner, 1976, Staub, 1975, and Weissbrod, 1976) have pointed out that reward cannot be applied mechanically: if a parent is not warmly attached to their child, then reward may be of little value in altering the child's behaviour. (This parallels the point we made earlier that the threat of withdrawal of love is only effective if the relationship between parent and child is a warm and close one.)

Similarly, the effect of punishment depends on the relationship between the punisher and the child; if there is already a warm and affectionate relationship between them, the child is much more likely to inhibit unacceptable behaviour than if the same punishment is given by a cold, unaffectionate agent (Parke, 1969, Sears et al, 1957).

The Relative Effectiveness of Reward and Punishment

1) Reward (or positive reinforcement) provides information about which of the many alternatives for action are likely to bring 'happiness' or pleasant outcomes; but punishment only tells us what we should not do, not what we should. So while reward can produce morally acceptable behaviour, punishment, at best, produces an inhibition of morally unacceptable behaviour.

2) Reward may be especially useful in creating high morale or a sense of joy and well-being, while punishment often produces hostility and resentment towards the punisher.

Walters and Grusec (1977) concluded that the individual who is punished may try to break off the relationship or quietly rebel against the punishing agent.

3) The punisher may underestimate the severity and intensity of the punishment and thus abuse it. This is especially likely to occur when an adult physically punishes a child; 'I didn't know my own strength' may be used as an excuse (and sometimes, perhaps, a genuine reason) for a case of child abuse. Also the child may well get used to certain levels of physical punishment, so that the adult has to step up the intensity of the punishment ('smack a bit harder') in order for it to have any effect.

4) As we have noted in relation to modelling and observational learning (see Chapter 3), each time the child is punished (either by an adult or an older child) it is witnessing the meaning of 'social power'. The punisher, by virtue of age, gender, strength or status, is seen as having the right to define what is 'desirable behaviour' and what is not and to perform acts against the powerless child (which, in turn, are condoned by society). So the child learns to follow this model and may well use punishing strategies for controlling the behaviour of others.

5) Usually, punishment only suppresses and inhibits the undesirable behaviour and does not 'eradicate' it. This may explain why physical punishment in particular is often increased in intensity since the weaker smack does not seem to have had any long-term effect.

6) Punishment often occurs in a social situation involving people other than the punisher and the punished. The presence of these others may add to the humiliation felt by the person being punished and they may even 'join in' (as when both parents tell the child off, one after the other). Alternatively, the presence of others may bias the behaviour of the punisher; for example, they may be concerned about their image and use punishment to impress them in some way or to 'keep up appearances' (especially if they are adults) or to teach the others a lesson (if they are children). In the latter case, how effective is the punishment likely to be as far as the originally punished child is concerned?

O'Leary et al (1970) made a study of the spontaneous use of punishment by schoolteachers. Two children from each of five classes were observed for a four-month period; they were quite disruptive in the classroom and were often reprimanded for it publicly by their teacher, usually loudly enough to be heard by most of the class but with little effect on the disruptive behaviour.

The teachers were asked to use 'soft' reprimands, audible only to the child being disruptive. In almost all cases, disruptive behaviour decreased when soft reprimands were directed only at the child in question. When the earlier method was reintroduced, disruptive behaviour again increased, only to fall again when the 'soft' approach was used again.

7) Punishments may, inadvertently, increase the very behaviour they are intended to stop. For example, if a child finds that adults will pay attention to him only when he is being naughty, then the child is more, rather than less, likely to be naughty, since even a smack or a telling off is preferable to being ignored! So what may be intended as a punishment by the adult, may be a reinforcement as far as the child is concerned. (This can be extended to relationships between adults too.)

8) Caroll (1978) maintains that the size of the penalty is only of secondary concern when a crime is being contemplated—of primary concern is the size of the reward the criminal act can reap.

According to Hart (1978), if the penalties are raised, certain groups may come to feel they are being treated unjustly and may increase their unlawfulnesss in retaliation. For example, attempts by the US army to stop crime by increasing punishment seem to have had the reverse effect from those intended by the authorities—lawlessness actually increased, indicating soldiers' resentment against harsh treatment. And Kerr (1978) found that as punishments for crime are increased, so juries tend to convict less often.

9) Is it possible for rewards to decrease the behaviour being rewarded?

The answer is 'yes', when extrinsic (external) rewards are offered for activities which are already intrinsically rewarding, that is, activities which are rewarding in themselves. This is known as the *Paradox of Reward*.

Extrinsic rewards may cause people to change their explanation for their own behaviour. So, from explaining their behaviour in terms of intrinsic rewards (eg 'I enjoy it'), they may come to believe that they were motivated by the desire for the extrinsic reward, and if that is then withdrawn they may decide that the activity is no longer worth doing (Bem, 1972, Lepper and Greene, 1978).

Children's spontaneous motivation to engage in certain kinds of activities is not necessarily facilitated by the knowledge that someone else wants them to do these things. For example, Lepper, Greene and Nisbett (1973) studied children in nursery school who spent most of their time in a large room with tables set out with a variety of toys (eg puzzles, clay, picture books, letter games and beads).

The children had free choice and could spend as much time as they wished with each one. For several days before the experiment, a set of magic markers (which the children did not previously have access to in the school) was put on one of the tables. Records were kept of how long each child spent using them. The children were then taken individually into an adjoining room where they participated in one of three experimental conditions.

One group sat at a table with a set of magic markers. They were shown an impressive-looking 'good player award' and were told they could earn it if they did a very good job of drawing with the markers. When they had worked on drawings for a standard length of time, they were given the award.

A second group worked with the markers for a time equal to the first group. But they were not shown the reward before they started drawing and nothing was said about a reward. At the end of the session, however, they received an award and were told they had done well.

A third group spent an equivalent time using the markers but were neither promised an award nor given one.

About two weeks later, the markers were set out in the classroom again and the researchers recorded the children's spontaneous interest in them. It was found that the first group of children had lost interest compared with the other two groups. Why should this have happened?

Possibly they felt they had been externally controlled in some way and resented this. But Lepper's explanation (which is the more likely) is that an expected reward robs an activity of its intrinsic interest value and makes it seem like a means to an end (not an end in itself).

To support this, he showed that, although the first group of children produced more pictures, the pictures were of lower quality (less detailed, thoughtful and original) than those produced by the children in the other two groups.

These results have been confirmed, using different rewards, by Anderson et al (1976) and Deci (1975).

10) Finally (and in support of Skinner), Perry and Parke (1975) found that a combination of punishment (a loud buzzer sounded whenever 8-year-old boys touched an attractive but forbidden toy) and reward (praise for playing with an unattractive and permitted toy) was more effective than either the reward alone or the punishment alone (the latter being the least effective). It is important that the rewarded behaviour is incompatible with the punished behaviour.

iii) Social Learning Theory

We discussed in Chapter 3 some of the major differences between SL theory and conditioning theory, one of them being the importance of Observational Learning (or Modelling), another being the role of cognitive factors intervening between stimulus and response. We also said that SL theory arose partly as an attempt to 'translate' Freud's theories, in particular his concept of identification, into learning theory terms.

Bandura (1977) believes that the development of self-control is heavily influenced by the models children observe and by patterns of direct reinforcement they encounter (that is, the disciplinary measures used by adults).

Laboratory Studies of Imitation

Albert Bandura, a leading social learning theorist, has conducted several laboratory experiments dealing with imitation.

In one of these (Bandura, Ross and Ross, 1963), nursery school children were exposed to an adult (the model) who spent several minutes mistreating a bobo doll (a large, inflatable, rubber doll) by sitting on it, punching it, pummelling it with a mallet and kicking it about the room. After this, they were shown into a room full of attractive toys and were led to believe that they would be able to play with them, only to be told that the experimenter had changed his mind and had decided to let some other children play with the toys. This experience was meant to make the children feel frustrated which, in turn, was expected to lead to aggressive behaviour (the frustration–aggression hypothesis, see Chapter 13).

Bandura was predicting that children who had watched the aggressive model and who had been frustrated (the experimental group) would imitate the model's aggressive acts, whereas children who had been equally frustrated but who had not seen the aggressive model (the control group) would not. (Of course, they could not imitate what they had not observed; the experiment was simply a demonstration of learning through observation, or observational learning.)

These predictions were confirmed. Children were individually shown into a second room which contained some rather unattractive toys, plus a bobo doll and a mallet, just like those used by the adult model, and they were observed for a 20-minute period. The observers counted the number of aggressive acts each child performed, carefully distinguishing between those which closely resembled the model's (*imitative aggression*) and those which did not (*non-imitative aggression*).

The experimental group showed significantly more imitative aggression and this occurred without any explicit instructions to do so or any real incentive or motivation—it occurred solely through being exposed to the model.

These basic findings have been confirmed in several subsequent experiments, using both live and filmed models (either people or cartoon characters). Interestingly, Bandura (1973) found that observation of a live model produces more imitation of specific aggressive acts (which is how we defined imitative aggression), whereas observation of filmed models (either people or cartoons) produces more aggressive responses of all sorts.

What Characteristics of Models are Important for Imitation?

Evidence from everyday observation tells us that it is not necessary for the model to be known, personally, to the child; and, indeed, the model may not even be a person at all. Although for most children it is parents and siblings who are the most important and frequently imitated models, dogs and cats (and other animals), cartoon super-heroes and even inanimate objects, such as cars and aeroplanes, may all be found sufficiently novel and stimulating for the child to want to reproduce their sounds, movements and actions.

Older children and adolescents choose pop stars, sporting personalities, film stars and other 'remote' people as models. So, clearly, it is not necessary that a model be a human being (although most are) nor that the child has ever actually interacted with the model. But, obviously, observation of the model is necessary for imitation to occur.

Clearly, however, this is not sufficient; if it were, children would spend all their time imitating everything they see (assuming that they can remember and are physically capable of reproducing what they see). But they do not. So who is likely to be imitated?

1) One important factor seems to be the *appropriateness* of the model's behaviour, as perceived by the child. This was demonstrated in an experiment by Bandura et al (1961).

They found that aggressive male models were more readily imitated than aggressive female models.

One probable reason for this is to do with sex roles: it is more acceptable in western culture for men to be aggressive as compared with women, and even by three or four years of age children are learning the dominant stereotypes that relate to sex-role differences (see Chapter 22). So aggressive male models are more likely to be imitated since this is seen by the child as more fitting or appropriate for men (in general) than for women (in general).

2) The same experiment (Bandura et al, 1961) showed that the *relevance* of the model's behaviour, again as perceived by the child, is another important variable. Boys were more likely to imitate the aggressive male model than were girls; the greater relevance of the male model's behaviour for boys lies in the fact that boys perceive the similarity between themselves and the model.

3) Therefore, *similarity* between the model and the child represents another important factor. Perception of this similarity is based upon development of the child's gender identity, that is, the ability to classify itself (and others) as a boy or girl, male or female. (This will be discussed in detail in Chapter 22.) The first stage of this ability is not usually reached until $2\frac{1}{2}$ to 3 years of age and certainly before that there is no preferential imitation of same-sex models.

4) Bandura and Huston (1961) found that nurturant (warm and friendly) adults are more likely to be imitated than unfriendly ones.

In an interesting and instructive demonstration of this, Yarrow et al (1973) exposed children to a model in an attempt to teach them altruism (what might be done to help others in distress). What they learned from the model would only be used in real-life situations if the model had previously established a warm, friendly relationship with them.

5) Bandura et al (1963) showed children films of adults behaving in striking, novel, unusual or aggressive ways. Those who were rewarded for any of these kinds of behaviour were more likely to be imitated than those who were not.

6) They also found that more powerful models were more rapidly imitated than less powerful ones.

7) The *consistency* of a model's behaviour also seems to be a factor that will determine how likely they are to be imitated.

In an experiment by Rosenhan et al (1968), models varied the rewards they gave themselves and others. When the model was good to herself and others, children were likely to adopt her behaviour, but when she rewarded herself and punished others (or vice versa) she was imitated far less often.

Consistency is also important outside the laboratory; many psychologists have observed that inconsistency is one of the consistent characteristics of human behaviour and parents may be as guilty of this as anybody. So what happens when they do not practise what they preach, when they tell their children to behave one way (eg 'You must not shout') and then behave themselves in a contradictory way (eg raising their own voices while telling children not to shout)?

This is an example of how we can, inadvertently, model the very behaviour which we wish to discourage in others.

According to Bryan and Walbek (1970) talking is not enough; children tend to imitate adults exactly, in a rather 'literal' way. So 'do as I say, not as I do' (parent) becomes 'I'll say as you say and do as you do' (child). If the adult's behaviour is at odds with their preaching, then children's behaviour tends to copy this inconsistency.

Learning versus Performance and the Role of Reinforcement

In a study by Bandura (1965), three groups of children were shown a film of an adult who behaved aggressively towards a bobo doll. Group A (the control group) saw the adult kicking, pummelling and punching the bobo doll.

Group B (the model-rewarded group) saw the same adult performing exactly the same aggressive acts, but this time a second adult entered the scene, towards the end of the film, who complimented the model on his aggressive behaviour and gave him helpings of sweets and lemonade to restore his lost energy.

Group C (the model-punished group) saw the same aggressive model as the other two groups but this time a second adult came on at the end of the film and scolded the model and warned him not to be aggressive again.

Thus, the only difference between the three groups was the consequences of the model's behaviour: for group A nothing happened (neither reward nor punishment), for group B the model was rewarded, and for group C the model was punished.

After the film, all the children (one by one) went into a playroom which contained a great number of toys, many of which had not been seen in the film, but which included a bobo doll and a mallet. They were left for 10 minutes in order to see how many acts of imitative aggression each performed. As might be expected, group C children showed significantly less imitative aggression than those in the other two groups.

However, there was no difference between groups A and B. According to the principle of vicarious reinforcement, group B children, who had seen the model rewarded, should have shown much more imitative aggression than group A children, who saw the model neither rewarded nor punished. So it appears that seeing someone else being reinforced is much less powerful an influence than Skinner would have us believe.

But more significant still are the findings from a second stage of the experiment. Each child (from all three groups) was asked to reproduce as much as possible of the model's behaviour and was directly rewarded for each act of imitative aggression. Under these conditions, there was no difference between any of the three groups—they all showed the same high level of imitative aggression. What this means, of course, is that the children in the model-punished group had attended to, and remembered, the model's behaviour (ie learned from the model) to the same extent as those in the other two groups; however, this had not been manifested in their behaviour at first. So the original difference between group C and the other two groups was one of performance (imitation) and not one of learning (acquisition).

Thus rewarding the child's performance was more crucial than whether or not the model had been rewarded. Reinforcing the child for imitating the model merely brought out what the child had already learned through earlier observation of the model—it was *not* the agent or cause of the original learning (as Skinner would maintain).

This means that it is possible for learning to occur but not actually to show up in the child's overt behaviour at the time. The experiment therefore demonstrated the crucial distinction between learning and performance. For learning to occur, mere exposure to the model is sufficient, but whether this learning actually reveals itself in the child's behaviour depends upon factors such as the consequences of the behaviour (both for the model and the child), the child's anticipation of reward or punishment, whether the child is instructed or encouraged to produce the model's behaviour and so on.

It would appear, then, that children may learn equally from all kinds of models (male or female, nurturant or unfriendly, rewarded or punished and so on) but are more likely to imitate models who possess certain characteristics.

Bandura and Walters (1963) found that, if encouraged to do so, children could equally well reproduce the behaviour of a model who had been punished, or who was less powerful, as that of a rewarded model or one who was more powerful.

Evaluation of Experimental Studies of Imitation

Bronfenbrenner (1973) has been one of the most outspoken critics of laboratory studies of imitation. He points out that the basic situation involves the child and an adult model, which is a rather limited social situation and is treated as if it existed in isolation from all other social relationships. Also, there is no actual interaction between the child and the model at any point; certainly, the child has no chance to influence the model in anyway.

Finally, the model and the child are complete strangers and the model is often seen on film and not in the flesh at all. This, of course, is quite unlike 'normal' modelling which takes place within the family.

Bandura would probably reply that television, movie and sporting stars are often important models and are also complete strangers, at least in the sense that there is no interpersonal contact between the child and the model.

This last point can be considered in terms of a distinction made by Danziger (1971) between two kinds of model, namely personal and positional models. A personal model is imitated because of their personal qualities or characteristics, while a positional model is imitated because of the social role that they represent (eg gender, age, occupation).

In the kind of laboratory experiment that Bandura and his colleagues have conducted, a male model represents not only himself but men in general. So, not surprisingly, the aggressive behaviour of a male model is more readily imitated than that of a female model. (We have already discussed this as an example of the appropriateness factor.) Taking over aggressiveness from a female model would involve a more personal kind of imitation and is much less likely to occur in the laboratory where there is no familiarity with the model as a person.

Familiarity, based on previous interaction with the model, may be crucial for personal modelling but clearly is not for positional modelling, where the child need only be familiar with the social role in general (for example, in the case of aggressive behaviour, the child has to have some knowledge of the sex-role stereotype which maintains that, among other things, it is appropriate for men to be aggressive but not for women).

Clearly, personal modelling is much more closely related to the process of identification than it is to imitation.

Imitation and Identification

An interesting finding reported by Baer and Sherman (1964) is that when children are directly rewarded for imitating a model's behaviour, imitation often generalizes to other aspects of the model's behaviour; such *generalized imitation* may play an important part in the learning processes included under the concept of identification. This generalized (spontaneous) imitation may be seen as an important area of overlap between the two concepts of imitation and identification.

The major similarities and differences between imitation and identification are summarized in Table 21.2 over the page.

According to Sears, Rau and Alpert (1965), SL theory represents an S-O-R approach to learning, where 'O' stands for 'organism' and acknowledges the role of cognitive and other intervening variables (between stimulus and response). Identification is seen as one of these intervening variables which, 'very early in life enables the child to learn without the parents having to teach and which creates a self-reinforcing mechanism that competes effectively in some instances with external sources of reinforcement'.

They derived a series of hypotheses about how different sorts of parents might influence children through the models they provide and they tested these through the study of child-rearing practices; we have discussed some of these when discussing Freud's theory earlier in the chapter.

Role of Cognitive Variables

In Chapter 3, we considered some of the important cognitive factors involved in observational learning (attention, memory etc). In this chapter we have also seen the importance of the child's perception of the model and how the model's behaviour is interpreted by the child.

Mischel (1973) described five kinds of cognitive variables which he called *person variables*, which are: (i) *Competencies*—intellectual abilities, social skills, physical skills and other special abilities; (ii) *Cognitive strategies*—

Table 21.2   The major similarities and differences between imitation and identification

Similarities between imitation and identification
1. They are both types of learning.
2. They both involve the reproduction of somebody else's behaviour (the model)
3. They are both examples of observational learning.

Differences	
Imitation	*Identification*
1. Involves fairly specific and overt aspects of the model's behaviour.	1. Involves the child coming to think, feel and act as if it were the model, and so is not confined to overt behaviour but includes the model's attitudes, motives, values, idiosyncrasies, tastes etc.
2. Usually occurs soon after observation of the model's behaviour (minutes or hours rather than days or weeks).	2. Is a process which takes place over an extended period of time, usually years.
3. Does not depend upon any prior interaction or familiarity with the model, who may be a total stranger and who need not even be a person (eg a cartoon character).	3. Depends upon the existence of a personal relationship between the child and the model, based upon previous interaction. The relationship often takes the form of a strong emotional involvement between them (eg parent and child).
4. Involves positional modelling. The emphasis is on *what* is being imitated, that is, the behaviour itself rather than the model as a person. What the model represents is a social role (eg men in general).	4. Involves personal modelling. The emphasis is on *who* is being identified with, that is, the model as a unique individual. Who the model is, is what the child is trying to be.
5. May be conscious or unconscious.	5. By definition, is an unconscious process.

habitual ways of selectively attending to information and organizing it into meaningful categories; (iii) *Expectancies*—about the consequences of different behaviours, about the meaning of different stimuli and about the efficacy of one's own behaviour; (iv) *Subjective outcome variables*—the value we place on the expected outcome or consequences of our behaviour; even if individuals have similar expectancies they may choose to behave differently because of differences in the subjective values placed on the outcomes, ie some rewards are much more rewarding for some individuals than for others.

And what may be a punishment for one child may actually be reinforcing for another (as in the attention-seeking child for whom a smack represents the giving of attention). So rewards and punishments cannot be 'objectively' defined, ie without taking into account the individual concerned. (v) *Self-regulatory systems and plans*—self-imposed standards or rules which the individual adopts for regulating their own behaviour.

This last person variable relates to an important distinction that SL theorists make between *external* and *internal reinforcement* and *punishment* (for Skinner, they are external only); see Figure 21.1.

Internal reinforcement and punishment can be seen as the SL theory equivalent of Freud's superego (ego-ideal and conscience respectively); both theories agree that, eventually, the child no longer needs an outside agency (parents or other adults) to administer rewards and punishments—the child can reward itself (through feelings of pride) and punish itself (through guilt).

Just as both parts of the superego develop through identification, so, as you might expect, self-reinforcement and self-punishment are acquired through observation and imitation of the parents' rewards and punishments: the child's own actions, previously rewarded or punished by the parents, can be reinforced or punished when performed alone, by the child's own *imitative self-approval* ('good girl') and *imitative self-disapproval* ('bad boy').

We set our own standards of conduct and evaluate or respond to our behaviour in the light of these. External reinforcement may only be effective when it is consistent with self-reinforcement, that is, when society approves behaviour which the individual already values highly.

This idea of self-regulation is very similar to that of conscience as an internal judge or policeman, making sure that we 'keep to the straight and narrow'. The ability to reward or punish oneself is an important kind of cognitive or mediating variable.

Whatever the advantages of SL theory compared with orthodox learning theory, one limitation of both approaches is the fact that they say nothing about moral *progress*. Although SL theorists accept that children learn more as they get older and, in that sense, become 'more' moral, they do not see development as having certain laws of its own and so do not see children as changing in similar ways as they get older—the changes that occur are quantitative rather than qualitative.

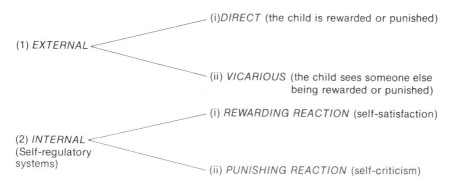

Figure 21.1   External and internal reinforcement and punishment

Again, although SL theorists take cognitive factors (including cognitive development) into account, they represent but one set of factors amongst several (including the situation itself) which determine the child's moral behaviour, and it is still, primarily, behaviour which is of interest.

iv) The Cognitive-Developmental Approach

This fourth and final major approach is the only one which focuses on the cognitive aspect of morality and, hence, on moral development as such, since moral development and overall cognitive development go very much hand in hand. The cognitive-developmental approach, therefore, is the only one which does offer a progressive view of morality: disagreeing with Freud, it sees morality as developing gradually during childhood and adolescence, into adulthood, and disagreeing with the Learning Theory and SL theory approaches, it maintains that there are *stages* of moral development which, like all developmental stages, are qualitatively different (different in kind).

a) Piaget's Theory

Just as Piaget's theory of cognitive development is concerned with how the child's knowledge and understanding change with age, so his theory of moral development is concerned with how the child's moral knowledge and understanding change with age. More specifically, in the *Moral Judgement of the Child* (1932), Piaget investigated: (a) the child's ideas about the rules of the game of marbles; (b) the child's moral judgements; and (c) the child's conception of punishment and justice.

(a)   Piaget chose to study *rules* in the context of a game because he could by-pass the influence of adult teaching and study the child's spontaneous thought directly; this way, he could observe how the child's conception of rules related to its conformity to those rules.

He played the game with a child and pretended not to know the rules; he asked the child to explain them to him and in the course of the game he probed the child's understanding by asking questions such as: 'Where do rules come from?', 'Who made them?' and, 'Can we change them?'.

The idea was to pose the child a problem which it had not had to face before and so throw the child on its own resources. What were his findings?

Children of 5 to about 9 years tended to believe that rules came from the semi-mystical authority of older children, adults, or even God; they are sacred and inviolable and have always existed in their present form and cannot be changed in any way. But in their actual play, children unashamedly bent the rules to suit themselves and saw nothing contradictory in the idea of both players winning.

Children of 10 years and over understood that the rules are invented by children themselves, so that they can be changed. However, since rules are needed to make a game possible, and to prevent quarrelling and to ensure fair play, they can only be changed if all the players agree to the change. At the same time, the older children kept meticulously to the rules, becoming 'lawyers' of the game, discussing the fine points and the implications of any changes that might be made.

(b)   To assess changes in the child's *moral judgements*, Piaget told children pairs of hypothetical stories about children who tell lies or steal or break something:
For example (i):

> A little boy called John is in his room. He is called to dinner. He goes into the dining room. But behind the door there is a chair and on the chair there is a tray with 15 cups on it. John couldn't have known that there was all this behind the door. He goes in, the door knocks against the tray, bang go the 15 cups, and they all get broken.

And (ii):

> Once there was a little boy called Henry. One day, when his mother was out, he tried to get some jam out of the cupboard. He climbed up onto a chair and stretched out his arm. But the jam was too high up and he couldn't reach it and have any. But while he was trying to get it he knocked over a cup. The cup fell down and broke.

or (i):

> There was once a little girl who was called Marie. She wanted to give her mother a nice surprise and cut out a piece of sewing for her. But she didn't know how to use the scissors properly and cut a big hole in her dress.

And (ii):

> A little girl called Margaret went and took her mother's scissors one day when her mother was out. She played with them for a bit. Then, as she didn't know how to use them properly, she made a little hole in her dress.

The child is asked 'who is naughtier?' and 'who should be punished more?'.

Piaget was interested in the reasons the children gave for their answers, rather than the answers themselves. Typically, 5- to 9-year olds said that John or Marie were naughtier, because John broke 15 cups (compared with Henry's one) and Marie made a big hole in her dress (compared with Margaret's little one). Although able to distinguish between intentional and unintentional actions, younger children based their judgement on the severity of the outcome, the sheer amount of damage done (*objective* or *external responsibility*).

Children of 10 years and over, on the other hand, chose Henry and Margaret, because they were both doing something they should not have been and, although the damage done was not deliberate in either case, older children based their judgement on the motive or intention behind the act that resulted in the damage (*internal responsibility*).

What happens when children are asked to make a judgement between a small amount of deliberate damage and a large amount of accidental damage?

This situation was studied by Armsby (1971), who found that even 6-year-olds say that a small amount of deliberate damage is naughtier. However, the answers depend partly on the extent and nature of the damage. For example, if the choice is between the deliberate breakage of a cup and the accidental damage of a television set, 40 per cent of 6-year olds and under 10 per cent of 10-year-olds said the latter was more deserving of punishment. This suggests that young children *can* understand intention (in the sense of deliberate naughtiness) and that they are aware that damage to valued objects is something to be avoided, but also that they have problems weighing up their *relative* importance. As we get older, it becomes easier to weigh up the relative importance of intentions and the damage done, as it does to infer what others' intentions actually are (eg Karniol, 1978).

The Armsby study (and others) suggests that children's understanding of intentions is much more complex than Piaget imagined. Nelson (1980) found that even 3-year-olds can make judgements about intentions regardless of consequences *if* the information about intentions is made explicit; in Piaget's stories, this information was *not* made explicit while the consequences were. Nelson found that in this kind of story 3-year-olds assume that actors who bring about negative consequences must have had negative motives; in this way they are less proficient than older children at discriminating intentions from consequences and using these separate pieces of information to make moral judgements.

Leon (1982) looked at how children's moral judgements are influenced by story-characters giving a rationale following certain accidental or intentional behaviour. Thus 6- and 7-year-olds seem to add together the intention and damage dimensions (one does not replace the other) but the rationale seems to be *more* important than either.

What do children understand by a *lie*? Piaget found that an unintentional falsehood which has serious consequences is judged as naughtier by younger children than a deliberate lie that does not. This too suggests the difficulty that younger children have in weighing up the relative importance of intention, on the one hand, and damage or consequences on the other.

For younger children, the seriousness of a lie is measured by the degree of literal departure from the truth. So, for example, a wild and totally unconvincing fantasy is worse than a realistic and successful deceit; a child who claims to have seen a 'dog as big as an elephant' is naughtier than one who claims to have seen a 'dog as big as a horse' (since elephants are bigger than horses). For the younger child, lies are wrong because they are punished by adults and lying to adults is worse than lying to other children. For the older child, lying is wrong because it betrays the trust without which fruitful and worthwhile social interaction is impossible; lying to adults is not necessarily worse than lying to one's peers.

(c)   The young child feels the need for misdeeds to be punished in some way, but the form of the punishment can be quite arbitrary; what matters is that the individual should pay for their crime with some kind of suffering and, generally, the greater suffering the better (Piaget called this *expiatory punishment*, 'expiatory' meaning 'making amends for' or 'paying the penalty of'). Punishment is decreed by authority and is accepted as just because of its source. So, for example, it is acceptable for a whole class of children to be punished for the misdeed of a single child if the latter does not own up and the others refuse to identify the offender.

A misfortune that closely follows some misdeed that has gone undetected or unpunished is often construed as a punishment, as if natural forces are 'in league' with people in authority to ensure that the disobedient suffer in the end. (This is known as *immanent justice*, 'immanent' meaning 'inherent'.) So if a child tells a lie and gets away with it then later trips and breaks an arm, this is taken by the younger child as a punishment, almost as if God (or some equivalent force) were keeping a constant eye on one's deeds. (This is not very different from the way that 'conscience' is often understood, as we have seen.) The older child, by contrast, sees punishment as bringing home to the offender the nature of the offence and as a deterrent from future misdeeds. Also the 'punishment should fit the crime'; for example, if one child takes another's sweets, the former should be deprived of their sweets or should make it up to the victim in some other appropriate way (the principle of *reciprocity*). (There is currently a trend in Britain, following a lead from the USA, whereby criminals make amends for their crimes in a fairly literal way, by, for example, repairing damage to property, paying for stolen or damaged goods, instead of going to prison.) Some older children go further and say that punishment should take into account the circumstances and needs of the offender (a mild punishment for one person may be severe for another) and some believe that no punishment may be necessary at all if the offender can be reformed without it.

Justice is no longer tied to authority, there is less belief in immanent justice, and punishing innocent persons for the misdeeds of only one is now thought to always be wrong.

Summary of Piaget's Theory

The morality of the 5- to 9-year-old is *heteronomous* ('being subject to another's laws or rules') and that of the child of 10 and over is *autonomous* ('being subject to one's own law or rules').

The younger child's moral knowledge and understanding are objective and absolute: laws, rules, punishment, right and wrong etc exist almost as 'things'; they emanate from external sources and either exist or do not exist, and obedience is a virtue and is good in itself (*moral realism*).

The older child, however, gradually comes to realize that morality is not a matter of obeying external authorities but of evolving and agreeing about principles for achieving mutually agreed and valued ends; ie moral rules grow out of human relationships and we must respect people's differing points of view (*moral relativism*).

However, the moral thinking of any child is always a mixture of heteronomous morality/moral realism and autonomous morality/moral relativism—it is a matter of which one predominates and they are not mutually exclusive. Also, many elements of the latter can be detected in adults' moral thinking (see the discussion of errors in the Attribution Process in Chapter 8).

How did Piaget account for the shift from heteronomous to autonomous morality?

1. It happens partly because of the move from egocentric to operational thought (see Chapter 19), which enables the child to see things from the point of view of others. According to Piaget, remember, this decline of egocentrism usually happens at around seven years, so cognitive development seems to be

a necessary condition for moral development, but not a sufficient condition; moral development lags at least a year or two behind cognitive development and the latter is no guarantee of the former. So what else is involved?

2. There is also a progressive change in social relationships from *unilateral* respect (ie unconditional, absolute and one-way obedience to parents and other adults) to *mutual* respect, within the peer group, where disagreements and disputes between equals have to be negotiated and resolved and a compromise reached. Although they must appear in this order, mutual respect can be delayed or prevented, either by slow cognitive development or by social experience in which unilateral respect predominates. Although adults may be capable of operational thinking, when their relationships have been, and still are, mainly unilateral, they will show marked traces of moral realism.

Is there any evidence to support Piaget?

As regards the existence of general age trends as Piaget described them (ie a general shift from heteronomous to autonomous morality at about nine or ten years), there is quite a lot of cross-cultural support, eg Lerner (1973), Macrae (1954), Hoffman (1970) and Lickona (1976) for the USA, Caruso (1943) for Belgium, Kugelmass et al (1965) for Israel, and Bull (1969) for Hong Kong, the Lebanon and England. There is also some evidence to support the relationship between intelligence and the maturity of moral judgement: the more intelligent the child, the more mature its moral judgement is likely to be, whether an IQ test is used or a Piaget-type test.

But as to why the shift from one type of morality to the other occurs, the evidence is less encouraging for Piaget. Macrae (1954), for instance, did not find that children whose parents were authoritarian were retarded in their moral insights but they were less likely to agree that friendship could take precedence over obedience to a rule.

Kugelmass and Breznitz (1967), studying 1500 adolescents living on Israeli kibbutzim (where the socializing influence of the peer group is considerable) and from conventional family homes, found no differences in the extent to which they used the actors' intentions to form their moral judgements. However, Keasey (1971) found that children who often participate in social activities and assume positions of leadership in their peer group tend to make more mature moral judgements.

Kohlberg (1963) concluded that, overall, the evidence regarding the association between heteronomous morality and unilateral respect on the one hand, and autonomous morality and mutual respect on the other, is very inconclusive.

Piaget has been criticized for not making clear enough what he meant by unilateral and mutual respect and, even allowing for the impact of a child's overall cognitive development on how it may construe a parent's moral tuition (so that two different children could interpret the 'lesson' in two entirely different ways), some psychologists believe that he largely ignored the role of explicit teaching about morality.

According to Wright (1971), Piaget's theory is really intended to explain how *practical* morality develops, ie how an individual conceives those situations in which they are actively involved and which demands a moral response, a moral decision. Yet the evidence which Piaget drew on were samples of the child's *theoretical* morality, ie how an individual thinks about moral problems, real and hypothetical, one's own and others', when not immediately or directly involved. So how are the two related?

According to Piaget, they are related via the concept of *conscious realization* —theory is the conscious realization of the moral principles on which we actually operate. (This is paralleled in the general theory of cognitive development, whereby, 'the child's verbal thinking consists of a progressive coming into consciousness or conscious realization of schemas that have been built up by action'. In other words, we can already *do* things by the time we come to think about them and reflect on them; a good example is the fact that a child learns to talk according to the rules of grammar long before the realization that there are such things as grammatical rules—as we saw in Chapter 20).

It follows that there is always a time-lag between practical and theoretical morality, a delay before a developmental change at the practical level is registered at the theoretical level; this implies that theoretical morality is shaped by practical morality (and not the other way round). Since the adult's theoretical morality (moral theorizing) has an influence only on the child's theoretical morality, it follows that adult theorizing (tuition) will *not* affect the child's practical morality. At best, it can only help theoretical morality to catch up with practical morality (Wright, 1971).

b) Kohlberg's Theory

The other major cognitive-developmental theorist is Lawrence Kohlberg, who in 1955 began to redefine and elaborate Piaget's theory, both longitudinally and cross-sectionally. He has also studied moral development right through to middle age.

Kohlberg was critical of both the concept of a superego or conscience and of the Learning Theory and SLT approaches to morality. He believes that the learning theory approach in particular, which emphasizes overt behaviour, largely ignores or underplays the importance of the way the individual construes the situation and thinks about the issues raised by it, as well as how these cognitive processes change with age. SLT also fails to show developmental changes which even common sense suggests do, in fact, occur.

Kohlberg also believes that research has failed to show any consistent relationship between different patterns of child-rearing and different kinds of moral behaviour. The only way to find any underlying consistency in an individual's moral behaviour and any evidence of developmental trends, Kohlberg believes, is to study the philosophy, logic or reasoning implicit in the cognitive structure which underlies both an individual's thinking and acting (corresponding to Piaget's theoretical and practical morality, respectively). He believes that only the cognitive-developmental approach provides a satisfactory *conceptual* integration of such phenomena as resistance to temptation, pro-social behaviour and so on; the predominant theme of moral development is the understanding of *justice*, which represents the most fundamental moral principle.

The way Kohlberg has studied moral development is to present subjects with moral dilemmas, where there is a conflict between two (or more) moral

Table 21.3   Kohlberg's 3 levels (6 stages) of moral development

Level 1: Pre-Conventional	Stage 1 (Punishment and Obedience Orientation) What is right and wrong is determined by what is punishable and what is not — if stealing is wrong it is because authority figures say so and because they will punish stealing ('might makes right'). So moral action is essentially the avoidance of punishment; things are not right or wrong, good or bad, in themselves.
	Stage 2 (Instrumental–Relativist Orientation) What is right and wrong, good and bad, is now determined by what brings reward and what people want (rather than the more negative avoidance of punishment). Other people's needs and wants come into the picture but only in a reciprocal sense ('You scratch my back, I'll scratch yours').
Level 2: Conventional	Stage 3 (Interpersonal Concordance or 'Good boy—nice girl' Orientation) Good behaviour is whatever pleases others, and being moral is being 'a good person in your own eyes and those of others'. There is emphasis on conformity to stereotyped images of 'majority' or 'natural' behaviour — what the majority thinks is right is right by definition. Intentions begin to be taken into account too. But primarily, behaving morally is pleasing and helping others and doing what they approve of.
	Stage 4 ('Law and Order' Orientation) Being good now comes to mean 'doing one's duty — showing respect for authority and maintaining the social order (status quo) for its own sake. Concern for the common good has gone beyond the stage 3 concern for the good of the family — society protects the rights of individuals and so society must be protected by the individual. Laws are automatically and unquestioningly accepted and obeyed.
Level 3: Post-Conventional	Stage 5 (Social Contract–Legalistic Orientation) Apart from what is constitutionally or democratically agreed upon, what is right is a matter of personal 'values' and 'opinions'. Consequently, there is emphasis on the 'legal point of view' — since laws are established by mutual agreement, they can be changed by the same democratic process. Although laws and rules should be respected, since they protect the rights of the individual as well as those of society as a whole, individual rights can sometimes supersede these laws if they become too destructive or restrictive. The law should *not* be obeyed at all costs, eg life is more 'sacred' than any principle, legal or otherwise.
	Stage 6 (Universal–Ethical Principle Orientation) Moral action is determined by our inner conscience and may or may not be in accord with public opinion or society's laws. What is right or wrong is based upon self-chosen, ethical principles which we arrive at through individual reflection — they are not laid down by society as such. The principles are abstract and universal, such as Justice, Equality, the sacredness of human life and respect for the dignity of human beings as individuals, and only by acting in accordance with them do we ultimately attain full responsibility for our actions.

principles and where the subject has to choose between them. Like Piaget, he is interested not in the actual judgement or choice itself but in the reasons the subject gives for making the choice—*how* people think rather than *what* they think. The reasons represent the structure of the judgement and centre around ten universal moral issues or values; namely, punishment, property, law, roles and concerns of affection and authority, life, liberty, distributive justice, truth and sex.

The most famous of the Kohlberg dilemmas is the one involving Heinz:

> In Europe, a woman was dying from cancer. One drug might save her, a form of radium that a druggist in the same town had recently discovered. The druggist was charging 2,000 dollars, ten times what the drug cost him to make. The sick woman's husband, Heinz, went to everyone he knew to borrow the money, but he could only get together about half of what it cost. He told the druggist that his wife was dying and asked him to sell it cheaper or let him pay later. But the druggist said 'No'. The husband got desperate and broke into the man's store to steal the drug for his wife.

Should the husband have done that? Why?

On the basis of the answers to those two questions, in particular the second, Kohlberg formulated a theory of moral development comprising three levels, each made up of two stages, making six stages in all. So in this sense, Kohlberg's is a more refined and elaborate theory than Piaget's. Two people at the same level and stage could still give two opposing answers: one could say 'Yes, Heinz should have stolen the drug', the other could say 'No, Heinz should not have stolen it'. Remember, it is the underlying *reasons* that determine how mature is a person's moral development. (see Table 21.3.)

Let us see how Kohlberg's stages would apply to a particular moral dilemma, bearing in mind that the same stage can be for or against a particular course of action but based on the same fundamental moral reasoning. Imagine the following dilemma:

> John is seven and has recently been beaten up by an older boy who attends his brother Alan's school. Alan is a very protective older brother and they are very close; Alan decides to avenge John's victimization and to beat up the older boy. But his parents strongly disapprove of physical aggression and he could get into serious trouble with them (as well as the school authorities). One day, after school, Alan waited for the boy and gave him a thorough beating.

Should he have done it? Why?

In Table 21.4 over the page are some typical pro and con answers at each of the six stages.

Cognitive and Moral Development

Like Piaget, Kohlberg believes that cognitive development is a necessary, but not a sufficient, condition of moral development, ie cognitive development does not guarantee a particular level of moral development.

Another way of expressing this relationship is to say that cognitive development sets a limit on maturity of moral reasoning and usually moral development lags behind cognitive development. Table 21.5 shows the relationship between these two aspects of development.

Table 21.4 Responses to a moral dilemma at each of Kohlberg's 6 stages

Pro	Con
Stage 1 It is not really bad to beat him up — so long as he doesn't do him any serious injury. After all, he is only doing what the boy did to John and no one else need find out. He might be called a coward if he didn't do it.	You can't go round beating people up — he might cause him serious injury. If he gets caught he'll be in real trouble — he could be expelled. Even if he's not caught he'll always be afraid of getting beaten up himself — or of John being victimized again.
Stage 2 If he wants to show he really cares for John and can look after him then he should have beaten the boy up. Wouldn't the punishment be worth it if you've proved you can play 'big brother'?	The boy must have had his reasons for beating up John — perhaps he was provoked. What good would it do John anyway? Perhaps he'd prefer Alan to do nothing.
Stage 3 Physical violence is bad but the whole situation is a bad one. He's doing what is natural for a good older brother. You can't blame him for doing something out of caring for and wanting to protect his younger brother. He would have been blamed for not doing it.	If your younger brother gets beaten up, you can't blame yourself for it. Alan showed he cared by *wanting* to beat up the boy — it's the older boy who is the guilty party, not Alan. Alan couldn't have prevented what happened to John and if he gets expelled, this will bring disgrace on the whole family.
Stage 4 The older boy obviously can't get away with bullying younger boys. So it is Alan's duty to look after John and he would always reproach himself for not doing so. But nor can Alan go round beating up people and he must accept the consequences of his actions, even if this means being expelled. Two wrongs don't make it right.	It is natural for Alan to want to avenge John but it is always wrong to be violent. You have to follow the rules regardless of your feelings or special circumstances.
Stage 5 Before you say what Alan did was wrong, you must consider the whole situation. Of course, if an adult were to commit the same act of violence as Alan, they could be prosecuted for assault — the law is quite clear. But it would be quite reasonable for anyone in Alan's situation to do what he did. People will respect him for what he did.	Alan would feel better, and so would John, if the culprit was punished for what he did. But it's not Alan's place to do the punishing — the ends don't justify the means. You can't say categorically it's wrong but even in the circumstances you can't (fully) justify it either. Alan might reproach himself later for acting impulsively.

Continued

Table 21.4 *(Continued)*

Pro	Con
Stage 6 When you have to choose between acting in a caring and protective way towards someone close to you and behaving in a violent way towards a person who aggressed against them, the higher principle of caring and protecting makes it morally right to behave violently — so the end justifies the means. 　Alan had to choose between his own standards of conscience and the dictates of external (social) rules.	The only correct course of action is one that is 'right' for all the parties concerned. Alan's behaviour is the same as the behaviour he is avenging. Others might understand Alan's behaviour but he might condemn himself later on. 　Alan's behaviour should be determined by what he thinks an 'ideally just person' would do in the situation.

When discussing cognitive development, we noted that many adults do not attain formal operations (about 50 per cent in fact) and if this is a necessary condition for reaching the post-conventional level of moral development (stages 5 and 6), then it is not surprising that only about 20 per cent of adults attain the highest level of moral reasoning. Most adults remain at the conventional level (stages 3 and 4), according to Shaver and Strong (1976).

Table 21.5 The relationship between Kohlberg's and Piaget's theories of moral development and Piaget's stages of cognitive development

Kohlberg's theory of moral development	*Age–group included within Kohlberg's levels*	*Stage of cognitive development (Piaget)*	*Stage of moral development (Piaget)*
1. Pre–conventional level (Stages 1 and 2)	Most 9-year-olds and below. Some over 9.	Pre–operational (2 to 7 years)	Heteronomous (5 to 8 or 9 years)
2. Conventional level (Stages 3 and 4)	Most adolescents and adults	Concrete operational (7 to 11 years)	Heteronomous (eg respect for the law and authority figures) *plus* Autonomous (eg taking intentions into account)
3. Post–conventional level (Stages 5 and 6)	About 20% of adults, after 20 years	Formal operational (11 years plus)	Autonomous (10 years and above)

Rest (1983) in a twenty-year longitudinal study of men from early adolescence to their mid-thirties, found that the stages do occur in the order Kohlberg described, but change is very gradual. Over the twenty-year period, these men changed, on average, less than two stages.

Researchers, including Kohlberg himself, have failed to uncover any stage 6 reasoning in the responses of 'ordinary' subjects and considerably less stage 5 reasoning than Kohlberg originally reported. In 1978, he reviewed his theory and concluded that there may not after all be a separate sixth stage —his studies of American and Turkish young people provided no evidence for it. It seems that universal ethical principles guide the reasoning of only a few, very exceptional individuals, such as Martin Luther King, who devote their lives to humanistic causes.

Turiel (1966) found that adults consistently displayed a type of moral reasoning either one stage above, two above, or one below that of child subjects. It was easier to lift children one stage than it was to lift them two stages or to drop them a stage. This indicates that the level of cognitive maturation is an important determinant of moral thinking and that the stages form an invariant sequence. These findings were confirmed by Rest et al (1969), Rest (1982) and Arbuthnot (1975).

In 1957, Kohlberg began a twenty-year longitudinal study of 50 boys in the Chicago area, both working class and middle class. They were initially interviewed when aged 10 to 16 years, then at three yearly intervals; more than half of their thinking was always at the same stage and the rest was at the next adjacent stage (up or down). He also conducted a small, six-year longitudinal study of Turkish village and city boys of the same age. On every re-test, individuals were either at the same stage as three years earlier or had moved up. This was true for the USA too. What determines movement from one stage to the next?

We have already noted that cognitive development is a necessary condition for moral development, and that educational and other socio-cultural factors can influence the rate of moral development and how far it will actually progress. Kohlberg also believes that new and challenging social experience is important.

Since cognitive development is partly under the control of maturation, it follows that moral development is too and, in this sense, morality also has biological roots. This does not mean that specific kinds of moral behaviour or thinking are innate, or that morality is not a cultural phenomenon transmitted across generations, but only that the child is biologically predisposed to acquire this form of thinking in relation to its social experience. (You can compare this with the child's predisposition to acquire language; the actual language the child learns is, of course, the one it is exposed to.)

Compared with Piaget, Kohlberg puts more emphasis on maturation as a determinant of movement through the stages.

Evaluation of Kohlberg's Theory

1. A major problem is that the method used to measure the individual's stage of development is very elaborate and time-consuming. It also involves

a lot of interpretation on the part of the marker, so it is not an objective kind of test.

According to Kurtines and Greif (1974), the scale of moral development lacks standardization, both in administration and scoring—so it could be presented differently by different scorers.

At one time Kohlberg denied that there was ever a scale at all and that his scoring system was never meant to provide consistent results. But in 1978 he produced a 'new' manual, based on his original sample of Chicago boys, which can be thought of as a scale and was intended to provide the consistency and reliability demanded by his critics. However, inter-judge reliability (how often different judges give the same score for the same subject) is only about 75 per cent.

2. Some critics have pointed to the dilemma stories themselves, saying they are unfamiliar to most subjects—children might show more mature reasoning if asked about issues relevant to their day-to-day experience. They are also *hypothetical* and do not involve any serious personal consequences. Would subjects necessarily reason at the same level if they had to think about practical moral issues that could have negative implications for themselves?

Sobesky (1983) presented the Heinz dilemma to high school and college students who were told either that the consequences of stealing the drug were severe (Heinz would definitely be caught and sent to prison) or mild (Heinz could take such a small amount it would not be missed). They were asked to imagine themselves in Heinz's position and describe what they would do and why. In the severe condition, subjects were less likely to advocate stealing and levels of reasoning were lower.

3. If Freud seems to overemphasize the emotional aspects of morality, Kohlberg seems to underemphasize them—or even totally ignore them. Most of our moral responses seem to be more a matter of intuition and feeling than of reasoning and logical deduction—we are not always the rational creatures we would like to be.

4. Some critics believe that Kohlberg has overemphasized justice to the exclusion of other aspects of morality, eg concern for others (Peters, 1971, Puka, 1976). So in this respect it is rather limited.

In a similar vein, the dilemmas tend to deal with prohibitions (laws, rules, authority etc) as opposed to pro-social phenomena (personal sacrifice, conflict between one's own needs and the needs of others etc). Eisenberg-Berg (1979) believe that children's reasoning about pro-social behaviour may be more advanced than their reasoning about prohibitions.

5. Simpson (1964) claims that the stages could be regarded as culturally biased and so not applicable to all non-western cultures; the moral dilemmas are also culture-bound.

Indeed, according to Baumrind (1978), all morality is culturally relative and it is ethnocentric to argue that one kind of moral thought is 'higher' than another; Kohlberg is imposing views derived from his own culture onto other cultures and making value-judgements about what is a more 'mature' or 'desirable' level of moral judgement. (Kohlberg's three levels represent a hierarchy of political ideologies—the conventional level can be seen as conservative or reactionary in nature, while the post-conventional level can be seen as liberal or even radical in nature. Clearly, he favours the latter and regards it as 'superior'.)

6. According to Turiel (1978), Kohlberg has failed to make a basic distinction between *social rules* or *conventions* (arbitrary rules of conduct sanctioned by custom and tradition), eg etiquette and the rules of a game, and *moral rules* (general principles relating to justice fairness and the welfare of others), eg 'it is wrong to steal'. At least within a given culture, conventional rules can be changed but moral rules cannot—the latter seem to be right in themselves.

Turiel asked American 16- and 17-year-olds, 'If a country had no rule against stealing, would it be right for a person to steal in that country?'. Most said it would still be wrong. But they said the rules of a game could be changed if everyone agreed. They also agreed that calling teachers by their first name would be all right if there were no rules forbidding it. Turiel goes as far as to claim that social and conventional thinking are two distinct conceptual systems.

Weston and Turiel (1980) found that 4- to 6-year-olds could recognize the difference. They also read 5- to 11-year-olds two kinds of hypothetical stories, one about a school in which there were no rules about hitting (representing a moral rule) and the other about a school where children were allowed to take their clothes off (representing a social convention); a majority of children at all ages said a school should not allow hitting but it could allow undressing.

Kohlberg views moral judgement and social understanding as one and the same (the 'socio-moral perspective'). (Although Piaget studied children's conceptions of the rules of marbles, this criticism applies equally to him.)

7. Finally, Hoffman (1977) believes that Kohlberg's is the best available approach to understanding the progression from a child's sense of morality (based on the consequences of actions) to the abstract moral code of adults.

22

Sex and Gender

It would probably be true to say that one of the first things that we notice about somebody, if not *the* first thing, is whether they are male or female; it almost seems as if we need to have this information about a person if we are to be able to interact with them properly.

We also expect people to be able to identify us correctly as male or female, and if they cannot, or do not, we would probably be most offended. Our name, age and sex are standard pieces of information on all official forms and our sex, of course, is one of the facts which appears on everyone's birth certificate.

A person's sex, therefore, is a fundamental part of their own self-concept (see Chapter 9) and of their interactions with others. So, given its importance, it is perhaps surprising that there is so much confusion over the terms used to refer to it—sex, gender, sexual identity, sex role and so on. Many of these terms are used interchangeably, but there are crucial differences between them.

In this chapter, we will examine these terms and explore some of the misconceptions and confusions surrounding them. We will also discuss the major theories of sex and gender development.

Terms

1) Of all the terms used, *sex* is the only one which refers to some biological fact about a person. Our sex is our actual physical status, although, as we shall see, it is much more complex than it is often taken to be. For example, there are many ways of defining it apart from our external sexual (genital) organs. (We shall return to this in a moment.)

Sexual identity is an alternative way of referring to our biological status as male or female.

2) Corresponding to our sex (or sexual identity) is our *gender* or *gender identity*, which refers to our classification of ourselves (and others) as male or female, boy or girl etc; a continuous and persistent sense of ourselves as male or female, gender is something which develops gradually through a number of distinct stages. It is the social equivalent, or the social interpretation, of sex.

For most of us, sex and gender correspond, but an important exception is the transsexual (see below). So 'sex' is a biological term and is usually denoted by the terms 'male' and 'female' (which is how we are classified in our birth certificate) while 'gender' is a psychological or cultural term, which does not necessarily reflect biological sex.

3) *Gender role* (often called sex role) refers to the behaviours, attitudes, values, beliefs and so on, which a particular society expects from, or considers appropriate to, males and females on the basis of their biological sex. So to be *masculine*, a male must conform to the male gender role; similarly, for a female to be *feminine*, she must conform to the female gender role.

4) The idea or belief which embodies these expectations is called a *gender role stereotype* (or sex role stereotype). It is a belief about what males and females are supposed to be like, as well as what they are 'naturally' like. Gender role stereotyping, therefore, gives rise to beliefs about *gender differences* (more commonly called *sex differences*).

We shall consider later whether there is any foundation for these stereotypes: are there any significant differences between males and females and, if so, how do these differences arise? (Are they biologically or culturally determined–or both?)

5) If stereotypes refer to what males and females are meant to be like, *gender role behaviour* refers to what they are actually like. So we shall be trying to answer the question of whether gender role behaviour and gender role stereotypes bear any relationship to each other.

6) *Gender role identity* (or sex role identity) refers to the understanding and acceptance of gender roles, that is, understanding and accepting that males and females are expected to be different from each other and to behave in different ways.

7) *Sex typing* refers to the differential treatment of children according to their (biological) sex. If gender differences do exist, then sex typing may be a major determining factor.

8) *Sexual orientation* or *preference* refers to an individual's tastes or preferences in sexual partners: this can be *hetero*sexual (preference for a partner of the opposite sex, 'hetero' meaning 'different'); *homo*sexual (preference for a partner of the same sex, 'homo' meaning 'same'); or *bi*sexual (a choice of both kinds of partner, although there may be a stronger preference for one or the other).

The homosexual is an anatomically normal person, male or female, whose gender identity is, usually, quite consistent with their biological sex and sex of rearing.

9) The *transsexual* is an anatomically normal person who genuinely and very firmly believes that he or she is a member of the opposite sex ('trapped' inside an 'alien' body). Consequently, there is a fundamental inconsistency between their biological sexual identity and their gender identity.

Biological Categories

Biologically, sex is *not* a unidimensional variable, ie there are at least five separate biological categories which can be distinguished, each constituting a (partial) definition:

i)   *Chromosomal sex*—XX female and XY male;
ii) *Gonadal sex*—the sexual or reproductive organs (ovaries in females and testes in males);
iii) *Hormonal sex*—the male hormones are the *androgens*, the most important of which is *testosterone* (secreted by the testes); the ovaries secrete two distinct type of female hormone, namely *oestrogen* and *progesterone*. While the number and range of hormones produced by males and females are virtually the same, females usually produce a preponderance of oestrogen and progesterone, while males usually produce a preponderance of testosterone and androgen, ie we all produce both male and female hormones, but males usually produce more male hormones and females more female hormones.
iv) *Sex of the internal accessory organs*—the Wolffian ducts in males and the Mullerian ducts in females. These are the embryonic forerunners of the reproductive structures (namely, the prostate gland, sperm ducts, seminal vesicles and testes in males, and the fallopian tubes, womb and ovaries in females).
v)   *Function and appearance of the external genitalia*—the penis and scrotum in males, the outer lips of the vagina (labia majora) in females.

Usually, all five of these sexual categories are highly correlated, ie an individual tends to be either male in all these respects or female in all these respects. They also tend to be correlated with non-biological aspects of sex, including the sex to which the baby is assigned at birth, how the child, accordingly, is brought up, gender identity, gender role identity and so on.

However, there are certain disorders which arise during pre- and post-natal development resulting in an inconsistency or lack of correlation between the five sexual categories described above. From these we can learn a great deal about the development of gender identity, gender role and gender role identity; collectively, individuals with such disorders are known as hermaphrodites.

Hermaphroditism

This term is currently used to refer to any discrepancy or contradiction between any of the various components of sexual anatomy and physiology, although, strictly, the term hermaphrodite (from the mythical Greek god/goddess, who had attributes of both sexes) denotes a person who has functioning organs of both sexes (either simultaneously or sequentially).

So included under this heading are:

i)   Chromosome abnormalities, where there is a discrepancy between chromosomal sex and external appearance, including the genitalia (see Chapter 27);
ii) Testosterone insensitivity or testicular feminizing syndrome;
iii) Adrenogenital syndrome;
iv) True hermaphroditism (the others are, strictly, pseudo-hermaphrodites). (See Box 1, page 558.)

Both (ii) and (iii) are the effects of hormones (or lack of them) on the process of sexual differentiation, and we shall concentrate on them now.

Box 1: The Case of Mr Blackwell

In an article called 'The Fight to be Male' (*The Listener*, May 1979), Edward Goldwyn cites the case of Mr Blackwell, only the 303rd patient in all of medical history to be a true hermaphrodite. He is described as a handsome and rather shy 18-year-old Bantu. Although he had a small vaginal opening as well as a penis, he was taken to be a boy and brought up as such. But when he was 14 he developed breasts and was sent to hospital to discover why this had happened. It was found that he had an active ovary on one side of his body and an active testicle on the other. He expressed the wish to remain male and so his female parts were removed.

Goldwyn points out that if his internal ducts had been differently connected, Mr Blackwell could have actually fertilized himself without being able to control it.

Testosterone Insensitivity (Testicular Feminizing Syndrome)

First, see Box 2: the Batista family, on page 563.

At least in the case of Attagracia's descendants, their eventual sexual status is quite unambiguous–by the age of twelve they are, unequivocally, male. But there are many individuals who never complete the route to maleness and end up as neither fully male nor fully female.

Goldwyn describes the case of Daphne Went, a motherly-looking woman, who has inside her two testes where most women have ovaries. She is one of 500 or so 'women' in Britain who have this condition called Testosterone Insensitivity (or Testicular Feminizing Syndrome).

This woman's development began along the male route but it was never finished. The egg was fertilized by a Y-sperm and two normal testes developed. They secreted their first hormone which absorbed the female parts, but when testosterone was produced her body did not respond to it. So, apart from the womb that had gone, everything developed along female lines. When at puberty she developed no pubic hair and did not menstruate (despite breast development and female contours–as a result of the action of oestrogen), there was clearly something wrong! Hormones did not bring on her periods because she had no womb. Chromosomally, Mrs Went is male, in terms of her gonads she is also male (she has testes), but her external appearance is female. She is married, has adopted two children and leads an active and successful life as a woman.

This insensitivity to testosterone is due to a recessive gene and is often diagnosed when a hernia (lump in the abdomen) turns out to be a testis. There is a high probability that the testes will become malignant and so these are usually removed surgically. A 'blind' (very short) vagina is present so that little or no plastic surgery is needed for the adoption of a female appearance and gender role. The Y chromosome tends to give these individuals extra height, which is more typical of males than females.

Adrenogenital Syndrome

This is more common than the Testicular Feminizing Syndrome and is really the converse of it. It is caused by an excessive amount of a testosterone-like substance during the development of a chromosomally normal female. It can happen in one of two ways: either (i) endogenously (originating from within), where androgens (male hormones) are produced by excessive activity of the mother's adrenal glands during pregnancy (the adrenal glands produce oestrogens and androgens in both sexes); or (ii) exogenously (originating from without), where the mother takes progesterone (which is chemically very similar to testosterone) in the form of an artificial hormone preparation called 'progestin', or other steroids, in an attempt to prevent miscarriage.

However it is caused, the adrenogenital syndrome involves the female's external genitalia bearing varying degrees of resemblance to the male external genitalia—usually, there is an enlarged clitoris and fusion of the labioscrotal folds, producing a rather ambiguous genital appearance. Some individuals have even had a complete closure of the urethral groove and a penis capable of becoming erect. The internal organs do not appear to be affected however.

Until fairly recently, sex at birth was assigned on the basis of inspection of the genitalia, so that two individuals with equivalent ambiguities might have been classified differently. More recently, information about the structure of the gonads and the chromosomal make-up of the individual has been acquired, so that females with the syndrome are usually raised as females. The internal structure is usually female and many such individuals are fertile. Therefore, a relatively small amount of cosmetic surgery is all that is required to bring their external appearance into line with other components of their sexual identity.

Those whose adrenals are over-active must also take cortisone to prevent early virilization or masculinization at puberty.

Gender Role Differences

Will boys be boys and girls be girls?

So far, we have been looking at some of the key concepts involved in sex and gender as well as some very important biological aspects of sex, which we shall draw on when discussing the more directly psychological issues. One of these is to do with gender role differences (or psychological sex differences). There are at least two distinct but related questions involved here:

a)   Is there any evidence that boys and girls do actually behave in accordance with gender roles? That is, are boys in fact more masculine than girls and girls more feminine than boys? This is the issue of psychological sex differences.

b)   If such differences do exist, how do we account for them? This is another example of the heredity-environment issue.

Probably the best way of answering the first question is to summarize the conclusions of Eleanor Maccoby and Carol Jacklin in one of the largest reviews of the literature, *The Psychology of Sex Differences* (1974). They set out to show that many of the popular stereotypes about males and females are not borne out by the evidence and concluded that there is a great deal of myth in both popular and scientific views regarding male-female differences (as well as some degree of truth). They spent three years compiling, reviewing and interpreting over two thousand books and articles on sex differences in motivation, social behaviour and intellectual ability. ('Sex' and

'gender' will be used interchangeably when discussing Maccoby and Jacklin's work.)
What are some of the myths?

i)   Girls are more 'social' than boys;
ii) Girls are more suggestible than boys;
iii) Girls have lower self-esteem than boys;
iv) Girls lack achievement motivation relative to boys;
v)   Boys are more 'analytic' than girls;
vi) Girls are more affected by heredity and boys by environment;
vii) Girls are 'auditory' while boys are 'visual'.

What are some of the differences for which Maccoby and Jacklin did find evidence?

a)   Males are more aggressive than females.

In all cultures where aggression has been observed, boys are more aggressive than girls, both physically and verbally. They engage in mock-fighting and aggressive fantasies as well as in direct forms of aggression more often than girls.

The difference manifests itself as soon as social play begins, at about $2\frac{1}{2}$ years. From an early age the primary victims of male aggression are other males, not females. Although both sexes become less aggressive with age, boys and men remain more aggressive during the college years. Little information is available for older adults.

b)   Girls have greater verbal ability than boys.

Girls' verbal abilities probably mature somewhat more rapidly in early life, although a number of recent studies have found no sex differences. From pre-school to adolescence, the sexes are very similar in their verbal abilities. But at about eleven, they begin to diverge and female superiority increases during adolescence and possibly beyond.

Girls score higher on tasks that involve understanding and producing language and on 'high level' verbal tasks (analogies, comprehension of difficult written material, creative writing) as well as 'lower level' measures (fluency and spelling).

c)   Boys excel in visual-spatial ability.

This involves the visual perception of figures or objects in space and how they are related to each other, for example, jigsaw puzzles require this sort of ability. Male superiority does not appear in childhood but is fairly consistent in adolescence and adulthood. The sex differences are roughly equal on analytic and non-analytic tasks.

d)   Boys excel in mathematical ability.

The sexes are similar in the early acquisition of number concepts and the mastery of arithmetic during the primary school years. But beginning at about 12 or 13, boys' mathematical skills increase faster than girls. Different studies tend to reveal differences of different sizes, but overall they are not as great as for spatial ability.

On some issues, Maccoby and Jacklin found ambiguous or inconclusive findings or too little evidence on which to base any definite conclusions—a lot more research is clearly needed into the following areas:

i)   Are there differences in tactile sensitivity?
ii)   Are there differences in fear, timidity and anxiety?
iii) Is one sex more active than the other?
iv)   Is one sex more competitive than the other?
v)   Is one sex more compliant than the other?

There has been a steady stream of research since Maccoby and Jacklin's review was published in 1974. For example, Phillips et al (1978), and Eaton and Keats (1982), concluded that boys are more active than girls, Ginsberg and Miller found that boys are more willing to take risks, and Dipietro (1981) reported that boys are more receptive to bouts of non-aggressive rough-and-tumble play.

Blakemore (1981) and Maccoby (1980) both found that girls and women seem to be more interested in, and responsive to, infants than boys and men; Martin (1980) reported that girls are less demanding than boys, and Gunnar and Donahue (1980) and Hetherington et al (1976) both found that girls are more likely to comply with parental requests.

Finally, Maccoby (1980) suggests that perhaps there is, after all, some truth in the popular belief that boys are harder to bring up than girls.

Maccoby and Jacklin concluded in 1974 that, from their survey of all the data, many popular, widely-held, gender role stereotypes have little or no basis in fact; yet people continue to believe them and to be influenced by them. Why should this be?

One explanation is that our perception is selective—we see what we expect to see—and so myths live on that would otherwise die out under the impact of negative (counter) evidence. Maccoby (1980) argues that even if group gender differences are found in a given area of behaviour (physical, cognitive, emotional or social), the behaviour of individual members of the two genders is often very similar. Men and women, boys and girls, are more alike than they are different.

Gender Role Identity

Before we turn to the question of how we can explain the differences that are found between males and females, we should consider the evidence that children understand and accept gender role differences.

Kuhn et al (1978) found that even $2\frac{1}{2}$- to $3\frac{1}{2}$-year-olds categorize certain behaviours as 'boy' or 'girl' behaviours and Kohlberg (1966) reported that toddlers know that crossing these gender role lines is to be avoided at all costs.

Maccoby (1980) concluded that boys are more likely to avoid 'sissy' behaviours than girls are to avoid 'tomboy' behaviours. This seems to support, and to reflect, the different valuations that these two labels have: to be a 'sissy' (ie to behave in a feminine way if you are male) is a greater sin than to be a 'tomboy' (ie to behave in a masculine way if you are female), implying that masculine behaviour in general is somehow more desirable than feminine behaviour. (We shall return to this issue at the end of the chapter when we consider the concept of androgyny.)

Maccoby and Jacklin (1978) found that by the age of 3, children play more with same gender playmates than those of the opposite gender. Parish and Bryant (1978) found that children aged 5 to 11 tend to be more positive about their own gender and more negative about the opposite gender. They also give higher ratings to male and female peers who excel in subject areas that their gender is known to do well in, for example, girls who did well in reading and boys in mathematics received higher ratings from their 11- and 12-year-old peers than boys who did well in reading and girls in mathematics.

We will now return to second question, ie if psychological sex differences do exist, how can we account for them?

There are a number of competing (and sometimes conflicting) theories that try to explain gender differences and gender role identity, in particular: (a) the biological approach (eg Hutt, 1972); (b) biosocial theory (eg Money and Ehrhardt, 1972); (c) Freud's psychoanalytic theory; (d) social learning theory (eg Bandura 1977); (e) cultural relativism (eg Mead, 1935); and (f) cognitive-developmental theory (eg Kohlberg, 1966).

The Biological Approach

This does not represent a unitary theory (as do the others that we shall be discussing) but rather a way of trying to account for gender differences by concentrating directly on biological aspects of sex differences, such as genetic differences, the process of sexual differentiation, hormonal differences and so on.

As far as sexual differentiation is concerned, Alfred Jost proposed in the 1950s that the natural form of the human is female. This was based on his observation (in rats) that even if the ovaries are removed at the earliest stage of embryonic development, growth still follows a female route, while if the testicles are removed early on, development reverts to the female route. (This was confirmed by Jost in 1970 using rabbits.) So Jost saw male development as the result of interference with the natural (female) developmental course; if a Y chromosome is present, the gonad becomes the testis and male development proceeds, while in the absence of a Y chromosome an ovary is produced and the embryo becomes a female.

Not only does the presence or absence of a Y chromosome determine the course of sexual differentiation, it also seems to be correlated with the biological vulnerability of the sexes, both before and after birth. Although in theory there is a 50:50 chance of a male or female being conceived, in fact there is a preponderance of males: approximately 120 males are conceived for every 100 females, but this ratio reduces to 110:100 for foetuses that survive to full-term (40 weeks of pregnancy), and reduces still further to 106:100 for live births.

This means that more male foetuses are spontaneously aborted and more of them are stillborn or die of birth trauma (including congenital deformities). In fact, throughout life, the male is more vulnerable than the female; for example, in the first year of life, 54 per cent of all deaths involve boys, at the age of 21 the figure rises to 68 per cent, and by 55 it is still as high as 64 per cent. Between 65 and 70 this difference diminishes and after 75, the ratio of women to men is higher—more women survive to older ages, that is, their average life-expectancy is higher (see Chapter 24). Males are also more susceptible to asphyxiation, cerebral palsy, convulsions, virus infections, ulcers, heart disease and some kinds of cancer, and the smaller Y chromosome makes the male more vulnerable to various kinds of inherited diseases and disorders (eg haemophilia).

There is no doubt that males are, biologically, the weaker sex!

Genetic and hormonal differences are responsible for a number of sex-linked characteristics which are apparent at birth or shortly after. For instance, several studies (including Bell et al, 1971, Hutt, 1972, Maccoby, 1980, and Moss, 1967) have shown that female infants are hardier, more regular in their sleeping and eating patterns, more socially responsive, mature faster and are more sensitive to pain, while larger, more muscular males tend to sleep less, cry more, be more active, more irritable and harder to pacify.

Could it be that, if these sex differences are innate, males and females are biologically programmed for certain kinds of activities that are compatible with male and female roles? For instance, might boys be predisposed towards aggression, assertiveness, rough-and-tumble play etc by virtue of higher pain thresholds, higher activity levels, a more muscular physique and their more irritable and demanding temperament? And might docile, undemanding and highly verbal females be ideally suited for adopting nurturant, co-operative, compliant roles? Is there any evidence to support the biological view?

The case of the four Batista boys (see Box 2, below) who were raised as girls from birth and who at puberty suddenly 'became' males seems to support the biological view; inside each female body was a brain which had been masculinized by the testosterone present before birth and which was then activated by another surge at puberty. They have all taken on male roles, do men's jobs, have married women and are accepted as men in spite of the fact that they were reared as girls and, presumably, thought of themselves as girls for the first 10 years or so of their lives (ie had a female

---

Box 2: The Batista Family (Imperato-McGinley et al, 1974)

Imperato-McGinley et al (1974) studied a remarkable family who live in Santo Domingo in the Dominican Republic (in the Caribbean). Of the ten children in the Batista family, four of the sons have changed from being born and growing up as girls, into muscular men. These four children were born with normal female genitalia and body shape but when they were 12, their vaginas healed over, then two testicles descended and they grew full-size penises.

The Batistas are just one of 23 affected families in their village in which 37 children have undergone this change. All these families had a common ancestor, Attagracia Carrasco, who lived in the mid-nineteenth century. She passed on a mutant gene which only shows when carried by both parents.

What happens to these children in the womb?

The egg is fertilized by a Y-sperm and it first develops into a foetus with normal testes. In the normal way, they absorb the female parts and testosterone preserves the male ducts. But the body misses a critical chemical step and so the external anatomy does not change. The step that is missed is the production of a hormone (dihydrotestosterone) which, it is now known, is responsible for creating the male external anatomy.

The change that occurs at puberty is due to the flood of testosterone which, in turn, produces enough dihydrotestosterone to give the normal male appearance (which would normally happen ten to twelve years earlier).

gender identity). However, they may have made the transition as easily as they did because their environment supported their new identity.

Brecher (1970) reports findings for a group of women who had developed a defect of the adrenal gland which causes secretion of male hormones, both before and after birth. If untreated, this can speed up the rate of sexual development and may bring puberty forward to the age of 5 or 6. Cortisone therapy in the 1950s enabled the adrenals to be partially switched off. But compared with a control group, matched for age, intelligence and social class, these women were much more tomboyish.

The claim that the Batista boys could so easily assume male roles because the testosterone had pre-programmed masculinity into their brains itself implies that male and female brains are different. Is there any evidence that they are?

Dorner (1968), who worked with rats, thinks so. He identified a sex centre in the brain such that when a small part of this was destroyed in a newborn male, it would behave as a female. In his terms, it became homosexual. Dorner argues that the same basic differences exist in human brains and that male homosexuals have a female brain. This happens, he claims, due to unusually low levels of testosterone in the womb. In turn, low levels of the male hormone can be induced by high levels of stress in the pregnant mother. But again, this relationship is based on studies of rats. Clearly, generalizing from rats to humans must be done with great caution.

The case of Mrs Went certainly does nothing to support Dorner's hypothesis, nor is there any convincing evidence that there are hormonal differences between homosexuals and heterosexual adults (eg Katchadourian, 1978).

Another case, that of Mr Blackwell (see page 558), also detracts from the biological view. He has a female brain—his hormones used to go through a complete female menstrual cycle and he used to ovulate once a month. Yet, despite his female brain, he wanted to remain a male and does not display the female behaviour predicted by Dorner's theory.

A different kind of evidence relating to brain differences is to do with hemispheric specialization (see Chapter 15). As measured by brainwave patterns, it appears that men have a greater degree of such specialization than women; for example, when performing spatial tasks, a man's right hemisphere tends to be more active while with women both hemispheres are activated (Restak, 1979). In fact, the right hemisphere is generally the dominant one in men and the left in women, which could explain why men are *generally* superior at spatial and mathematical tasks and women at verbal tasks.

However, we should recall Maccoby's observation (1980) that the similarities are greater than the differences between men and women; in other words, the differences *within* each gender are at least as great as the differences *between* them.

Biosocial Theory

Biosocial theory, as the name suggests, takes social factors into account in relation to biological ones. Specifically, it focuses on how babies of different temperaments contribute to their own development by influencing how others treat them; it is the *interaction* between biological and social factors that is important rather than the influence of biology directly.

Intuitively, it is easy to see how these constitutional differences can be reinforced by interaction with adults; adults prefer to spend time with babies who respond to them in 'rewarding' ways, and more demonstrative babies (or 'demanding' ones) tend to receive the adult attention they seek while the more passive baby is more easily 'forgotten'.

However, the baby's sex is just as important as its temperament as far as others are concerned. For instance, Moss (1967) found that even at three weeks after birth, boys are more irritable than girls but, significantly, mothers become relatively less responsive to boys who are crying compared with girls; perhaps they find that attempts to comfort their sons are less effective, or perhaps they believe that boys should not be 'pampered' as much as girls. Whichever of these is true (or even if both apply), we can once again see the reciprocal nature of the parent-child relationship—babies influence their parents at least as much as parents influence them and this is an ongoing process throughout childhood.

The very *fact* of a child's sexual identity is what Money and Ehrhardt (1972) have concentrated on in their biosocial theory. For them 'anatomy is destiny' in the sense that how the infant is labelled sexually determines how the infant is raised or socialized. This, in turn, determines the child's *gender identity* and from this follow gender role, gender role identity and sexual orientation or preference.

Money and Erhardt believe that at first there is considerable flexibility in the process by which the child categorizes itself as boy or girl; the 'sex of rearing' can be changed within the first $2\frac{1}{2}$ to 3 years without any undue psychological harm being done. However, once a child has developed a gender identity, being reassigned to the opposite sex can result in extreme psychological disturbance. Thus the first $2\frac{1}{2}$ to 3 years of life are seen as a critical or sensitive period for the development of gender identity.

Money and Ehrhardt (1972) studied girls who were suffering from the adrenogenital syndrome and who were raised as boys. When the mistake was discovered and their genitals were surgically corrected, and they were reassigned and reared as girls before the age of 3, they easily accepted the gender change; but when all this happened after 3 years, there were many adjustment problems.

Based on their studies of hermaphrodites and pseudo-hermaphrodites, Money and Ehrhardt, Hampson and Hampson, and others, conclude that, despite disparities between an individual's genetic sex, hormonal sex, internal and external organs and the sex or rearing, in the vast majority of cases the individual assumes the gender role consistent with the sex of rearing. In their view, *psychologically*, sexuality is undifferentiated at birth and it becomes differentiated as masculine or feminine in the course of various experiences of growing up.

Money and Ehrhardt (1972) studied ten individuals with the Testicular Feminizing Syndrome, who, remember, are genetically male but who are invariably reared as female because of their female external appearance. These ten showed a high preference for the female role: eight preferred the role of homemaker over an outside job and all reported dreams or fantasies of raising

---

Box 3: The Circumcision That Went Wrong (Money 1974)

A classic piece of evidence relevant to the issue was reported by Money in 1974. It involves a pair of monozygotic twins whose embryonic and foetal development were that of a normal male. An accident during circumcision (by cautery) caused one of the twins to have his penis burned off. Assuming that gender is primarily a social phenomenon, and that identity is learned, it was decided to raise the unfortunate 'penectomized' boy as a girl.

This would seem to be a decisive way of choosing between the learning versus biological arguments, by letting rearing 'compete' with biology, and it would have been a true test case had not as much as possible been done to 'defeat' the male biological realities and to enhance female biological maturation.

At 17 months, 'he' was castrated, ie the androgen-secreting testes were removed, and was given oestrogen (female hormone); also, a vaginal canal was constructed. Much earlier than this, the parents changed 'his' clothes and hairstyle. By the age of 4, 'he' preferred dresses to trousers, took pride in 'his' long hair and was much neater and cleaner this 'his' brother. 'He' sat while urinating, in the usual female fashion, and was modest about exposing 'his' genitals (in contrast to the other twin, for whom an incident of public urination was described by the mother with amusement). 'He' was encouraged to help the mother with the housework, while the brother 'couldn't care less about it'.

At 5 years, 'he' had many tomboyish traits, but was encouraged to be less rough and tough than the other twin, and was generally quieter and more 'ladylike', while the normal twin was physically protective of his 'sister'. At 9 years, although 'he' had been the dominant one since birth, 'he' expressed this by being a 'fussy little mother' to 'his' brother. The brother continued to play the traditional protective, male role.

This seems to support the view that gender identity (and gender role) is learnt. The reversal of original sexual assignment is possible if it takes place early enough and is consistent in all respects, which includes the external genitalia conforming well enough to the new sex. However, the castration and use of oestrogen clearly contributed to the ease of reassignment and probably also accounts for the normal twin being taller.

---

a family. Eight had played primarily with dolls and other typically female toys. They rated themselves high on affection and were fully content with the female role. From other studies it has been shown that such people often find employment in jobs that put a high premium on an attractive female appearance and feminine behaviour, for example, modelling, acting and even prostitution.

The case of Mrs Went, discussed earlier, also tends to support the view that sex of rearing is more important than biological sex.

Money, Hampson and Hampson (1957) studied matched pairs of individuals with the adrenogenital syndrome, the members of each pair having a very similar external genital appearance. The crucial difference between them was that they had been assigned to a different sex. They concluded that psychosexual identity is established more in accordance with the sex of rearing than on the basis of any biological factors. Money (1971) pointed out that requests for sexual reassignment are very rare amongst such individuals. The conformity of most hermaphrodites to their early sex of assignment is so strong that it can withstand ugly virilization in a 'girl' at puberty or breast development and difficulties in having an erection in a 'boy'. In *Man and Woman, Boy and Girl* (1972) Money and Ehrhardt maintain that the human central nervous system is so amenable to the effects of learning that biological contributions to psychosexual identity can be moulded and even reversed by the social influences of early childhood.

However, Diamond (1965/68) points out that to demonstrate that human beings are flexible in their psychosexual identity does not in itself disprove that 'built-in biases' still have to be overcome. Money et al's subjects have been hermaphrodites and, therefore, atypical, not representative of the population as a whole. Is it valid to generalize from an abnormal sample to the 'normal' population? The fact that individuals of ambiguous sex are flexible in their psychosexual orientation and identity does not necessarily mean that the same is true of people in general.

How could we settle the controversy? (See Box 3, page 566).

Freud's Psychoanalytic Theory

We have discussed Freud's theory of psychosexual development in great detail in Chapter 21 (on Moral Development) and will be doing so further in Chapter 26 (on Personality).

You will recall that, according to Freud, sexual identity and sex role are acquired (along with a superego) when the boy's Oedipus complex and the girl's Electra complex are resolved, at 5 or 6 years of age. The role of the traditional mother and father family unit (two-parent family) is, therefore, of crucial importance in Freud's theory of sexual development, whereby the child must identify with the same-sex parent.

So what would Freud have predicted about the psychosexual development of a child who grows up in an 'abnormal', atypical, family, which is becoming increasingly commonplace in contemporary society; for example, single-parent families (where it is often the father who assumes the parental role), unmarried couples who have children, and lesbian couples with children (eg the lesbian mother is given custody of the child or children when a divorce takes place)? Indeed, according to Rutter (1979), the non-traditional family may have become the norm. Is there any evidence that psychosexual development is adversely affected as a result of growing up in an 'un-Freudian' family?

According to Lamb (1977/79), fathers, at the beginning of the child's second year, begin to pay special attention to their sons and withdraw from their daughters. As this happens, boys channel their attention towards their father's behaviour and girls towards their mother's. Through this channelling, children prefer to interact with the same-gender parent and this makes it more likely that identification will occur. So preference for the same-gender parent does seem to be a major factor in the child's acquisition of gender role identity. Research on father absence, for example by Hetherington (1966/72), supports the idea that gender role identity develops within the first two or three years and that fathers are important in this process. If the father is absent before the boy's fourth birthday, he is apt to be less 'masculine', in the sense of being more dependent on his peers, less assertive and less involved in competitive and physical contact sports. But after the age of 4, absence of the father has little effect on the boy's gender role identity. In the case of girls, the effect does not usually show up until adolescence; the most common outcome of father absence for girls is difficulty in adjusting to the female role and in interacting with men. More about fathers when we discuss androgyny.

However, according to Maccoby and Jacklin (1974) and Storms (1980), the expectation that degrees of masculinity or femininity of the parents might influence that of their children is *not* borne out, in heterosexual populations anyway.

The biggest single fear expressed in relation to unconventional families is that if the children are exposed to any combination other than a 'feminine' mother and a 'masculine' father then they are considerably more 'at risk' of becoming homosexual. However, just as exposure to heterosexual relationships between parents does not prevent the child becoming homosexual (indeed, the vast majority of homosexuals grow up in heterosexual families), so exposure to homosexual models seems unlikely to have a decisive impact on sexual orientation either. West (1977), Bancroft (1970) and Keyon (1970) all agree that the evidence suggests that homosexuality, in so far as it is shaped by early life experience, is more likely to be influenced by *poor* relationships with parents, perhaps especially with the same-sex parent.

Hoeffer (1981) and Kirkpatrick et al (1981) compared children raised in homosexual and heterosexual single-mother households and found normal levels of heterosexual development in both groups. Green (1978) studied 37 children (18 males and 19 females), aged between 3 and 20 (average age 11), all of whom were being raised by either a female homosexual or parents who had undergone sex reassignments (21 by homosexual mothers, 16 by transsexual parents); most of the children of the latter were aware that their parents had at one time been a member of the opposite sex. The study was conducted over a two-year period. Green evaluated the younger children's sexual preferences by asking them what toys and games they preferred, about their peer preferences, the roles they chose during fantasy play, their clothing preferences and vocational desires. They were also given the Draw-a-Person Test—children usually draw a person of their own gender before one of the opposite gender. For the adolescents, Green obtained information about their sexual desires and their fantasies about sexual partners as well as about their overt sexual behaviour.

All 37 (with the questionable exception of one child) developed heterosexual preferences and showed a marked desire to conform to the gender roles provided by their culture. None had homosexual or transsexual fantasies. All the young children wanted to play with others of the same gender. Boys wanted to be doctors, firemen, policemen, engineers or scientists, while the girls wanted to be nurses, teachers, mothers or housewives.

Finally, Golombok et al (1983) compared 37 5- to 17-year-olds reared in 27 lesbian households (ie lesbian couples) with 38 of the same age-range raised in 27 heterosexual single-parent households. There were systematic, standardized interviews with the children and the mothers, plus questionnaires given to teachers and the mothers. The two groups did not differ in terms of gender identity, sex role behaviour or sexual orientation, nor did they differ on most measures of emotions, behaviour and relationships (although there was some indication of more frequent psychiatric problems in the single-parent group). It was concluded that rearing in a lesbian household as such did *not* lead to atypical psychosexual development or constitute a psychiatric risk factor.

Social Learning Theory

We have discussed this theory elsewhere (Chapters 3 and 21) and have seen the crucial role played by: (a) observational learning (learning from *models*); and (b) reinforcement. In discussing a study by Bandura et al (1961) (see Chapter 21), we noted that boys were more likely to imitate aggressive male models than girls were (based on perceived similarity and relevance). But how representative are these findings? Are children more likely to imitate same-sex models?

Overall, the evidence is inconclusive. Maccoby and Jacklin (1974), for example, concluded that there is very little evidence that children do actually imitate same-sex models more than opposite-sex models.

One supporting study is that of Wolf (1973) who found that children were more likely to imitate a same-sex model than an opposite-sex model even if the behaviour was sex-inappropriate. But two other studies (Barkley et al, 1977 and Masters et al, 1979) found the reverse to be true, namely, that children preferred to imitate behaviour that is appropriate to their own sex, regardless of the sex of the model!

Perry and Bussey (1979) believe that children imitate same-sex models more than opposite-sex ones when there is no information regarding the sex-appropriateness of the modelled behaviour. However, when there is such information then the sex of the model seems to become relatively unimportant. Grusec and Brinker (1972) conclude that children *attend* equally to *all* models but *imitate* same-sex models more because they are reinforced for doing so. However, while it does appear that children recall more of a model's behaviour when they have previously been reinforced for imitating that model, there is little evidence that children are actually rewarded for imitating models of the same sex.

The Masters et al study (1979) cited above, together with those of Ruble et al (1981) and Slaby and Frey (1975), suggest that, starting at about six or seven years, children *do* begin to pay more attention to same-sex models; significantly, this is when *gender constancy* develops (we shall discuss this in relation to Kohlberg's cognitive theory).

Effects of the Media on Gender Role Stereotypes

Parents, of course, are not the only models that children are exposed to and SL theorists are particularly interested in the way that males and females are portrayed in television, books, films etc. Gender role sterotyping is the belief that it is only natural and fitting for males and females to adhere to traditional gender role patterns; and there is a great deal of evidence that gender role stereotypes are held by parents, pre-school teachers, and the media, including both television and books.

According to Liebert et al (1973), nearly every American child watches two to six hours of television every day, and Brody (1975) estimated that by the age of 18, the average American child has watched 18 000 television murders.

(See Chapter 14.) Even in such programmes as 'Sesame Street' (Gardner, 1970) the child is bombarded by traditional gender role stereotypes. Big Bird is told he is a boy bird and will have to help with men's work, important work, heavy work, and that he should get a girl bird to help Susan with the flower-arranging.

Sternglanz and Serbin (1974) analysed popular children's television. Males outnumbered females by 2 to 1, males were typically aggressive, constructive and rewarded for action, while females were passive, deferential and rewarded for reaction. Weitzman et al (1972) reported similar findings for children's books.

According to Kuhn (1978), as early as 2 years, children have a good deal of knowledge about gender role stereotypes; later on, peers reinforce one another for gender-appropriate behaviour and punish gender-inappropriate behaviour.

Cordua et al (1979) showed 5 and 6-year-olds films of a man and a woman in an occupation characteristic of the opposite gender (for example, a male nurse and a female doctor). When asked who had been the nurse and who the doctor, children usually reversed what they had actually seen; that is, their memory was distorted in the direction of stereotyped roles. Also, there was a stronger tendency to re-label the male nurse than the female doctor, which suggests a double-standard (which we touched on earlier when discussing 'sissies' and 'tomboys') whereby a male in a typically female role is less acceptable or more incongruous than a female in a typical male role.

Reviews of the literature by Greenberg (1982) and Rushton (1982) agreed that about 90 per cent of doctors, lawyers, ministers and business owners are men while women are typically cast as secretaries, teachers, nurses, journalists or entertainers.

Frueh and McGhee (1975) and Rothschild (1979) found that children who watch a lot of commerical television are more traditionally sex-typed themselves (for instance, in their choice of toys) and are more likely to hold stereotyped views of gender roles than classmates who watch little television. Commericals themselves are strongly sex-stereotyped (eg McArthur and Resko, 1975).

Sex-typing

The SL theorists are also interested in child-rearing methods and how differences in those may contribute to gender differences. An important dimension of child-rearing is how parents (and other adults) treat and react to the child by virtue of the child's biological sex, ie *sex-typing*.

Sears et al (1957) found that the greatest and most consistent differences between boys and girls was in the area of aggression, with boys being allowed more aggression in their relationships with other children, while this was discouraged in girls. Boys were also allowed to express aggression towards their parents more than girls were; for some mothers, being 'boylike' meant being aggressive and boys were often encouraged to fight back.

While there do not appear to be any differences at birth (although baby boys may be more restless and less socially responsive than baby girls), by the age of 4 or 5 these differences have become quite clear-cut. Rothbart and Maccoby (1966) also found that mothers were usually more tolerant of their sons' aggressive acts than their daughters'.

Condry and Condry (1976) asked a group of adults to rate the emotional behaviour of 9-month-old infants. One half of the group was told the infant was a boy, the other half that it was a girl. The same baby was thought to display different emotions and different levels of emotional arousal depending on whether the adults had been told it was a boy or a girl. When the infant was presented with a 'jack-in-the-box', 'girls' were judged to be showing 'fear', while the 'boys' were judged to be showing 'anger'.

Frisch (1977) observed adults interacting with 14-month-olds. In one session, each child was introduced as a boy, and in a second, the same child was introduced as a girl. The adults encouraged more activity and tended to choose male toys when playing with children they thought were boys; while when they thought the babies were girls, the adults interacted in a more interpersonal and nurturant way.

Lyberger-Ficek and Sternglanz (1975) found that nurses caring for newborns gave more attention to fussing and crying boys than fussing and crying girls. They also gave male infants more attention than females during periods when the babies were not crying or fussing.

According to Rubin et al (1974), from the moment of birth boys and girls are seen as different by their parents, girls being seen as smaller, weaker and prettier, boys as firmer, better co-ordinated, stronger and more alert. (Boys do, in fact, tend to be longer and heavier at birth and they also tend to be stronger—but the crucial finding is that they are *perceived* as being different.)

Rheingold and Cook (1975) found that parents provide vehicles, educational materials, sports equipment, machines, toys or real animals and military toys for their sons and decorate their rooms with pictures of animals. Daughters are given dolls, dollshouses, housekeeping toys, and their rooms are decorated with lace, ruffles, fringes and floral designs. Block (1973) and Baumrind (1977/79) found that sons are encouraged to achieve and compete, and daughters to be sociable. Like peers, parents tend to discourage 'sissy' behaviour in their sons much more than they discourage 'tomboy' behaviour in their daughters.

An interesting social class difference has been found by several studies (eg Angristetal, 1977, Morgan, 1982, and Nadelman, 1974). In England and the USA lower Socioeconomic Status children commonly show stronger preferences for sex-typed behaviours and also hold more stereotyped views about gender roles than children from higher SES backgrounds. So in this sense parents of different SES backgrounds may provide different kinds of models for their children.

Despite all the evidence that sex-typing does go on, we cannot be sure that there is a cause-and-effect relationship between this and the gender differences that have been found to exist. That is, we cannot be absolutely certain that, for example, because boys are allowed to be more aggressive, and are given more aggressive-type toys, than girls, that this actually makes boys more aggressive. The evidence is only correlational.

Cultural Relativism

This really represents the most direct challenge to the biological approach. If gender differences do reflect biological differences, then we would expect to find the same differences occurring in different cultures. Any differences that exist between different cultures in relation to gender roles would tend to support the view that gender role is culturally determined (*cultural relativism*), that is, learned.

One of the most famous and influential of all anthropologists has been Margaret Mead (she died in 1980), who, in her *Sex and Temperament in Three Primitive Societies* (1935), concluded that the traits which we call masculine and feminine are completely unrelated to biological sex; just as the clothing, manner and head-dress that are considered to be appropriate in a particular society, at a particular time, are not determined by sex, so temperament and gender role are not biologically but culturally determined.

Margaret Mead studied three New Guinea tribes, who lived quite separately from each other within about a 100-mile radius. The adult Arapesh, who lived on hillsides, she described as gentle, loving and co-operative, boys and girls were reared in order to develop these qualities which in western society, are stereotypically feminine ones. Both parents were said to 'bear a child' and men took to bed while the child was born.

The Mundugumor were riverside dwellers and ex-cannibals. Both males and females were self-assertive, arrogant, fierce and continually quarrelling, and they both detested the whole business of pregnancy and child-rearing. Sleeping babies were hung in rough-textured baskets in a dark place against the wall and when they cried, someone would scratch gratingly on the outside of the basket.

The Tchambuli, who lived on the lakeside, represented the reversal of traditional western gender roles. Girls were encouraged to take an interest in the tribe's economic affairs while the boys were not. The women took care of trading and food gathering while the men, considered sentimental, emotional and incapable of making serious decisions, spent much of the day sitting around in groups, gossiping and 'preening' themselves.

But Tony Booth, in *Growing Up In Society* (1975), proposes that the conclusions which Mead drew from her research may have been influenced by things going on in her private life. She had always been very keen to have a child but was told she was unable to have children, and Booth believes that her perception of the Mundugumor, who did not seem to place great value on children generally, may have been coloured by her own sadness and frustration. Significantly, perhaps, she described the Arapesh after the colonial period, yet referred to the Mundugumor as if they still practised their old forms of warfare—this exaggerated the differences between them. Before colonization, the Arapesh had been quite warlike; according to Fortune (1939), half of the older men claimed to have killed at least one person.

By 1949 (in *Male and Female—a Study of the Sexes in a Changing World*), after she had studied four other cultures (Samoa, Manus, Iatmul and Bali), Mead had rather dramatically changed her views about gender roles. From a rather extreme 'cultural determinism' in the original 1935 book, she now concluded that women are 'naturally' more nurturing than men, expressing their creativity through childbearing and childbirth, and are superior in intellectual abilities requiring intuition. While motherhood is a 'biological inclination', fatherhood is a 'social invention'; the implication is that societies which encourage a gender role division other than that in which dominant, sexually energetic men live with passive, nurturant women, are 'going against nature'. Significantly, by this time she had given birth to a child of her own!

A finding which may seem to support Mead in her search for 'natural' differences is that there is no known society in which the female does the fighting in warfare (eg Scott, 1958) and this includes the Tchambuli and the Arapesh (Fortune, 1939). However, to define aggression in this way is extremely limited—aggression can be expressed in many, more subtle, ways which it is often difficult to measure.

Malinowski (1929) studied the Trobriand Islanders and reported that groups of women, in order to foster their tribe's reputation for virility, would catch a man from another tribe, arouse him to erection and rape him! This 'gang rape' was carried out in a brutal manner and the women often boasted about their achievement. Albert (1963) found many cultures where women do the heavy work because men are thought to be too weak.

These findings, of course, tend to detract from the view that there are biologically (probably hormonally) determined psychological gender differences. Further evidence that gender roles are learned rather than 'natural' comes from Green (1976) who studied the Sakalavas in Madagascar. There, boys who are thought to be pretty are raised as girls and readily adopt the female gender role.

Westermarck (1917) studied the Alentian Islanders in Alaska, who also raise handsome boys as girls. Their beards are plucked at puberty and they are later married to rich men; they too seem to adapt quite readily to their assigned gender role.

Studies of certain North American Indian tribes reveal the possibility of *more* than two basic gender roles. For example, Seward (1946) described the 'berdache', a biological male of the Crow tribe, who simply chose not to follow the ideal role of warrior. Instead, they might become the 'wife' of a warrior but they were never scorned or ridiculed by their fellow Crows. (Little Horse in the film 'Little Big Man', starring Dustin Hoffman, was a 'berdache').

According to Olien (1978), the Mohave Indians recognized *four* distinct gender roles: (i) traditional male; (ii) traditional female; (iii) 'alyha'; and (iv) 'hwame'. The 'alyha' was a male who chose to live as a woman (to the extent of mimicking menstruation by cutting his upper thigh and undergoing a ritualistic pregnancy) and the 'hwame' was a female who chose to become a man.

These exceptions to the general rule of two fundamental gender roles provide further evidence for the shortcomings of the biological approach.

Cognitive-Developmental Theory

We could sum up the social learning theory approach in this way: I want rewards; I am rewarded for doing boy/girl things; *therefore*, I want to be a boy/girl.

Using the same form of argument, we could sum up Kohlberg's cognitive-developmental theory like this: I am a boy/girl; I want to do boy/girl things; *therefore*, the opportunity to do boy/girl things (and gain approval) is rewarding.

For Kohlberg (1966/1969) the child first comes to think of itself as a boy or girl and only then will it selectively attend to (or identify with) same-sex models, ie the child first develops a *gender identity* which determines who it will imitate, which is the *reverse* of the SL theory view. As we shall see below, gender identity develops in stages and reflects the child's general cognitive development.

According to Kohlberg, the child actively constructs its own conception of gender, based on both physical and social sources; the crucial organizer of gender roles, gender role identity and, therefore, gender differences, is the child's categorization of itself as a 'boy' or 'girl'.

Once the child has acquired its gender label, it comes to value positively behaviours, objects and activities which are consistent with it—rewards stem from behaving consistently with one's gender label rather than from what other people consider appropriate.

Stages of Gender Identity

i)   Basic Gender Identity (2/3 to 5 years)

Kohlberg (1966) found that a 2- or 3-year-old boy may be able to tell you that he is a boy, but that he believes he *could* become a girl, or a mummy, if he wanted to, for example, by playing girls' games or wearing dresses or growing his hair long: he lacks gender consistency. Similar results were found by Marcus and Overton (1978) and Slaby and Frey (1975) for 3 to 5-year-olds, and are consistent with Katcher's findings (1955) that the basis for applying gender labels changes as the child gets older. All his 3-year-old subjects could identify the gender of dolls on the basis of hair and clothing cues, but only 12 per cent of them could do so on the basis of genitals. However, 31 per cent of 4-year-olds, 51 per cent of 5-year-olds and 70 per cent of 6-year-olds could use genital differences to classify male and female dolls. Similar results were found by Thompson and Bentler (1971).

ii)   Gender Stability (4/5 to 6 Years)

This involves understanding that you stay the same gender throughout your life; that is, basic gender identity is seen as stable over time, as reflected in the answers to questions such as, 'When you were a little baby, were you a little boy or a little girl'? and, 'When you grow up will you be a mummy or a daddy?'.

iii)   Gender Constancy or Consistency (6 to 7 years)

The child now grasps that gender identity is stable over time *and* across situations, eg someone remains the same gender even though they may appear to change by wearing different clothes or a different hairstyle.

Gender constancy represents a kind of conservation (see Chapter 19) which, significantly, appears shortly *after* the child has mastered conservation of quantity (Emmerich and Goldman, 1972, Marcus and Overton, 1978). The child has to learn that gender is not like other personal characteristics that do change, such as age and size.

Slaby and Frey (1975) found that children at a higher stage of gender constancy were more likely to attend to same-sex models in a film compared with lower-stage children; and this supports Kohlberg's belief that gender constancy is a *cause* of imitation of same-sex models rather than an effect (as the SL theorists would argue).

However, a major problem for Kohlberg's theory is that sex-typing is already well underway before the child acquires a mature gender identity. For example, 2-year-old boys prefer masculine toys before they have even become aware that these are more appropriate for boys, and Kuhn et al (1978) and Maccoby (1980) found that 3-year-olds have learned many gender-role stereotypes and already prefer same-sex activities or playmates long before they begin to attend selectively to same-sex models.

Finally, Money and Ehrhardt's claim (1972) that gender reassignment is very difficult after 3 years of age (which is when, according to Kohlberg, the child is only just beginning to develop a stable and constant sense of its status as boy or girl) seems to pose serious problems for Kohlberg's theory.

Androgyny

This term is a convenient way of drawing together many of the findings and controversies regarding how gender roles are determined and the stereotypes which reflect them.

In *Fluffy Women and Chesty Men* (1975) Sandra Bem points out that the masculine-feminine pair of opposites had traditionally been taken as evidence of psychological health. This is reflected in psychological tests of masculinity and femininity, where a person scores as either one or the other—they do not permit a person to say that he or she is both.

The word 'androgynous' (from 'andro' meaning male and 'gyne' meaning female) is used to refer to the possession and expression of characteristics, behaviours, abilities, values etc, both 'masculine' and 'feminine', by the same person, regardless of biological sex.

Bem, together with a growing number of psychologists and feminists, believes that we need a new standard of psychological health, one that frees us from the strait-jacket of stereotypes and which allows people to be more flexible in meeting new situations, in what they can do and how they do it. Usually, we tend to suppress parts of our personality which might be thought 'unmasculine' or 'unfeminine', for example, men being afraid to be gentle, or to cry, and women being afraid to be assertive. In brief, men are reluctant to do 'women's work' and women are afraid to enter the 'man's world'. Bem points out that there is considerable evidence that traditional sex-typing is unhealthy.

In order to determine whether sex-typed people really are more restricted and androgynous people more adaptable, Bem devised the Bem Sex Role Inventory (BSRI) which consists of a list of 60 personality characteristics, 20 traditionally masculine (ambitious, self-reliant, independent, assertive), 20 traditionally feminine (affectionate, gentle, understanding, sensitive to the needs of others) and 20 neutral (truthful, friendly, likeable). The subject has to rate each of the 60 characteristics in terms of the extent to which they apply to them personally. If masculinity and femininity scores are approximately equal, the individual is judged to be androgynous.

After assessment on the BSRI, subjects were assessed for actual behaviours considered either typically masculine or feminine—the masculine behaviours were independence and assertiveness, and the feminine behaviours were concerned with the extent to which a person was willing to be responsible for or helpful toward another living creature. It was predicted that the highly feminine woman would be less independent and assertive than anyone else, while the highly masculine men would be at a disadvantage as far as the feminine, helping, behaviours were concerned. The predictions were confirmed.

Androgyny allows an individual to be both independent and tender, assertive and yielding, masculine and feminine, which can only help them to cope more effectively with diverse situations. The aim is *not* to make boys and girls the same but to give children the freedom to blend the best of masculine and feminine traits—to be truly themselves.

Who raises androgynous offspring? According to Orlofsky (1979) and Spence and Helmreich (1978), androgynous adolescents and college students tend to come from homes where the parents are androgynous also.

However, Baumrind (1982) reports that traditional, sex-typed, parents tend to be more firm and authoritative in their child-rearing than the more permissive and child-centred androgynous parents; and the former's children tend to be more socially assertive and generally competent. Indeed, Baumrind believes that traditional parents make *better* parents.

Coincidental with the 'discovery' of androgyny, during the latter half of the 1970s, was the 're-discovery' of the father as an important figure in the socialization process. Before then, the father was almost totally ignored in the research literature and the use of terms such as 'mothering' and 'maternal deprivation' reflected this bias towards the mother as the major influence in the development of the child's personality (see Chapter 18). But now the father has come into his own as a parent and it is much more common to read about 'parenting' and the effects of father absence etc than it ever was before the mid-1970s.

The amount of father participation in child-rearing is related to how androgynous the father is. Bem (1974), Defrain (1979) and Russell (1978) found that androgynous fathers are more nurturant, more involved in everyday child activities and generally interact with their children more than 'masculine' fathers.

At a rather less scientific level, evidence for androgyny comes in the form of the way the two sexes 'imitate' each other, for example, males wearing their hair long, wearing earrings, make-up and so on, and females wearing trousers, having their hair shaved, being tattooed etc. Pop singers such as David Bowie, and Boy George, far from being effeminate freaks may be seen as personifying the trend towards androgyny—the embodiment of that wish to break down gender role divisions and to realize one's true self, which is likely to include characteristics and behaviours which are both traditionally masculine and feminine.

One final point is worth making: gender roles and gender differences have to be understood not only in a culturally relative way but also in a historically relative way, that is, ideas about what is masculine and feminine change within the same society at different times in its history—the very concept of androgyny is an example of this. Not only does androgyny challenge traditional western gender roles and gender role stereotypes, it also proposes a new way of being a person, where biological sex is no longer one of the fundamental determinants of one's identity, personality, behaviour and relationships with others.

23

Adolescence and Adulthood

Here and in Chapter 24 we turn our attention from the development of behaviour and psychological processes (the focus of the last five chapters) to the years of development themselves.

Measuring Developmental Change: Cross-Sectional and Longitudinal Studies

In discussing the development of attachments, concepts, language, morality and gender, we have drawn on a large number of studies, using a wide range of methods, including experiments (laboratory and field) observation (naturalistic and controlled), case studies, surveys, questionnaires, interviews and testing (see Chapter 2). All of these methods are, of course, used in psychology as a whole and not exclusively in developmental psychology; many of their advantages and disadvantages apply regardless of the age of the subjects, although, clearly, age sometimes dictates which method can be used.

However, in studying development we are interested in the *changes* in behaviour that occur with age—we are comparing performance of some kind at two or more different ages. How do psychologists do this?

Usually they conduct one of two kinds of study—either cross-sectional or longitudinal. These are not methods as such but types of research *design*: both designs may entail any one or more of the methods already described. For example, if we are interested in whether intelligence declines as we get older we might use an IQ (Intelligence Quotient) test, and if we want to know how children's speech develops during the first five years, we might make tape-recordings of the child's spontaneous speech.

But with each of these two examples, there are two ways we can go about *comparing* performance at one age with performance at another: either (i) we can compare the performance of *different* groups of subjects, varying in age, for example, a group of 20-year-olds, 40-year-olds, 60- and 80- year olds, giving them the same IQ test and comparing their average scores, or a group of 1-, 2-, 3-, 4- and 5-year-olds, analysing their spontaneous speech—this is the *cross-sectional* design; or (ii) we can start with the *same* group of adults and measure their intelligence at twenty year intervals, or the *same* group of infants and study their speech at yearly intervals—this is the *longitudinal* (or 'follow-up') design. Both have their advantages and disadvantages.

i) Cross-Sectional Design

Advantages
a) It is relatively simple and quick to carry out—it only takes as long as is needed to find the subjects, collect and analyse the data, since the different age-groups are being tested all at the same time. It is a short-term study and so is relatively inexpensive and requires no continuity of the research team.
b) The data need not be 'frozen' over a long period until the subjects have completed their development and before analysis, interpretation and publication of the findings become possible.
c) There is not the problem of subjects dropping out of the study over an extended period of years.
d) It provides age-related norms, ie average or typical scores for different age-groups.

Disadvantages
a) The major disadvantage is the *cohort* effect—if widely different age-groups or cohorts are being compared then any differences between them could be due *either* to actual change in the variable being studied (eg intelligence) *or* to the fact that the different age-groups represent different generations.

   This could be a problem in our example of changes in intelligence between 20 and 80 years but is not likely to be with speech development in the first 5 years of life. Clearly, 80-year-olds have had very different kinds of education and life experience compared with the other age-groups (including the 60-year-olds); rapid social change makes it difficult even to compare different age-groups of children, for instance, comparing 5-year-olds born in 1945 (at the end of the Second World War) with 10-year-olds born in 1940 (when the war had only recently started).
b) As far as possible, we must try to match subjects in different age-groups on all those variables which might influence the behaviour or ability under study (eg gender, race, social class background, intelligence and so on, just as we do in experiments). But this is often difficult to do and can sometimes prove expensive and time-consuming. Also, a large number of subjects is required.
c) In school populations, increasing age itself tends to operate selectively in important variables, such as intellectual ability (ie many less bright children drop out), so that different age-groups are not necessarily all equally a 'cross-section' of the population.

   Similarly, at the other end of the life-cycle, the 80-year-olds, say, who are studied, may not be typical in the sense that many of their peers have already died, which makes them fitter and stronger and perhaps better cared for etc. (Most people do not live until 80.)

d) Individual differences within each age-group can be a problem, eg a group of 13-year-old girls will include many who are well past puberty and others who have not yet started it, while a group of 70-year-olds will include some who are still very active, physically, socially and mentally, and others who are suffering from senile dementia.

e) It allows us to describe changes in behaviour (answering the *what* questions) but not to explain them (the *how* and *why* questions); in a sense, it raises more questions than it answers. We know that it is not *age* as such which *causes* the changes in behaviour but variables associated with age (eg physical changes or maturation, life-experience); so, at best, cross-sectional studies can tell us that certain changes do occur but cannot give us the reasons.

ii) Longitudinal Design

Advantages
a) There is no cohort problem, since it is the *same* subjects being compared with themselves, at successive intervals during their life-span. This makes the comparability greater and the matching of subjects (for gender, IQ etc) is not necessary.

b) Again, since the same subjects are being compared at different times, data is obtained about individual differences in development (individual growth curves) as well as about average differences between age-groups.

c) It is essential for studying the *consistencies* of behavioural development, against which developmental change can be measured.

d) Certain events occur at different times for different subjects, eg death of a parent, starting school or pre-school, onset of puberty and so on. With longitudinal data, the effects of these events can be measured and added to the data for the other subjects regardless of when those events actually occur. So individual differences are not a problem.

e) When the interval between successive observations or measurements is appropriately small, the longitudinal approach is sensitive to changes which occur quickly; this is necessary where the effects of early experience on subsequent behaviour are being investigated. It is much more reliable than, say, parental reports and other kinds of retrospective data (see above)—it is always best to try to observe the changes as they occur or as soon after they have occurred as possible.

Disadvantages
a) The longitudinal approach is, by definition, time-consuming and expensive; it requires the continuity of the research team, keeping track of subjects over several years, and postponing the publication of the final results for as long as the study lasts (although interim reports are often published).

b) It is difficult to keep the original group of subjects together for the whole duration—this is the 'drop-out' or *attrition* problem, whereby subjects may lose interest, or be withdrawn by their parents, become ill or die or simply 'disappear'.

The data already collected for the drop-outs have to be discarded otherwise different age-levels are no longer comparable. The real concern is that the sample we are left with may be unrepresentative of the original group of subjects, which makes it more difficult to draw general conclusions at the end of the study.

Also, the subjects who remain may be affected in some way by repeated testing over the years; even if the original sample was considered to be representative of the population at large, the subjects who survive will probably not be.

c) Any mistakes made at the beginning of the study (eg unrepresentative sample, omission of crucial variables) must remain and cannot be corrected or omitted once discovered—this would again detract from the comparability of the data from one interval to another.

Similarly, the same methods of study (including tests) must be used throughout the duration of the study, at each time of testing.

Longitudinal studies are becoming more popular, especially with children. But there is also a trend towards 'short-term, longitudinal studies', which combine the best of both cross-sectional and longitudinal designs. In Chapter 24 we shall discuss the work of Schaie and his colleagues, using the 'cross-longitudinal' or 'cohort-sequential' design, whereby subjects of different ages (20 to 70 years) were tested on three separate occasions over a 14-year period. This 'compromise' design permits the study of individual developmental changes over a 14-year period (instead of, say, 50 years), whereby subjects are compared with themselves, as well as generation differences (comparing, say, 30-year-olds born in 1926 with 30-year-olds born in 1936).

Some of the most famous longitudinal studies include: (i) the Study of the Gifted, started by Terman in 1920 at Stanford University, with 1500 3-year-olds who were studied until they were 45 (eg Sears, 1977); (ii) the Berkeley Growth Study, started by Bayley in 1928, with 60 infants studied until they were 30 years old (Macfarlane et al, 1954); and (iii) the Study of Human Development began by Sontag in 1929 at the famous Fels Research Institute, involving 750 infants, studied until they were 33 years old (Kagan and Moss, 1962).

In Britain, one of the largest and most ambitious longitudinal studies has been 'Britain's Sixteen-Year-Olds', published by the National Children's Bureau in 1976. The 16-year-olds (over 14,000 of them) were all born in the same week (3-9 March 1958) in England, Scotland and Wales and so constitute about as representative a group as it is possible to find. They were monitored at regular stages of their development, in infancy and at the ages of 7 and 11. The data on this 'birth-cohort' at 16 have gone quite a long way towards modifying the traditional and stereotyped image of teenagers as rebellious, idle, emotionally unstable and so on.

Adolescence

The word 'adolescence' comes from the Latin *adolescere* meaning 'to grow into maturity'. Traditionally, this stage has been regarded as a prelude to, and a preparation for, adulthood, a transitional period of life between immaturity and maturity.

Probably the earliest theory of adolescence was that of G. Stanley Hall in his book *Adolescence* (1904) and he is generally regarded as the father of adolescent psychology; he was also one of the pioneers of developmental psychology as a whole. Heavily influenced by Darwin's evolutionary theory, Hall believed that each individual's psychological development recapitulates the evolution of the human species, both biological and cultural; in the case of adolescence (12 to 25 years), he saw it as a time of 'Storm and Stress' (or Sturm and Drang) which mirrors the volatile history of the human race during the past 2000 years.

Although the 'recapitulation theory' is only of historical interest, parts of it are consistent with modern theories, in particular, the notion of 'storm and stress', important ingredients of which are the violent swings of mood and other 'contradictory tendencies', such as: (a) energy and enthusiasm versus indifference and boredom; (b) gaiety and laughter versus gloom and melancholy; and (c) idealistic altruism versus selfishness.

While adolescence is generally taken to begin with puberty (which itself is a lengthy process which passes through stages) to say when it ends is more problematic. Usually, the criteria are psychological (rather than physical) and they constitute the beginning of adulthood, for example: (a) the development of a sense of personal identity (Erikson, 1950); (b) the ability to engage in a truly intimate relationship with another person (Dacey, 1982, Erikson, 1950); (c) the achievement of employment, a relatively permanent relationship with another, or both (Abbott, 1981).

Adolescence and the Self-concept

Body-image
Just as the bodily self is the first aspect of the self-concept that emerges in the baby (see Chapter 9), so the bodily-self (or body-image) undergoes a dramatic change with the onset of puberty, which marks the beginning of adolescence.

Prior to the onset of puberty, most children have felt very much at home in their bodies and have been relatively unaware of their bodies as such; they have been more concerned with what their bodies can *do* (or what they can do with the help of their bodies) than what their bodies are like.

But the growth spurt of puberty, together with the dramatic changes in the shape and appearance of the body, plus the new sexual feelings and other sensations that accompany these changes, put an end to all that! Inevitably, it seems, the adolescent has a much stronger and more clearly defined body-image.

Arnhoff and Damianopoulos (1962) showed that 20-year-olds, just beyond adolescence, had a more definite body-image than 40-year-olds. They were all shown a set of six photographs of men dressed only in shorts and with faces blacked out, one of which was themselves; the younger subjects were better at recognizing their own photograph than the older subjects. (When you think of how much time adolescents spend admiring and examining themselves in front of the mirror, these findings do not seem very surprising. But we should also be aware of important individual differences which cut across age-differences.)

Jersild (1952) found that when adolescents were asked what they did not like about themselves, very few mentioned their abilities but about 60 per cent referred to some aspect of their physcial appearance, especially facial defects like skin problems.

The time at which the adolescent growth spurt occurs may have an important effect on the adolescent's self-concept, especially self-esteem. Physical growth can be a source of great anxiety; is it too fast or too slow, too little or too much etc? The rate of physical development often becomes an important basis for adolescents making comparisons between themselves and other adolescents.

The behavioural and emotional effects of early and late maturation on the self-concept seem to be different for boys and girls. Jones and Bayley (1950) picked the most advanced and retarded 14- to 18-year-old boys and studied their personalities and how adults and peers reacted to them. Early maturers were usually seen as more attractive, less childish and less talkative than the late maturers, they showed more interest in girls at 15 and were more likely to be popular and hold positions of responsibility; the late maturers were more childish and attention-seeking. At 17, the early maturers were still more self-confident and less dependent; the later maturers had very strong desires for contact with girls and were more aggressive.

Eichorn (1963) followed up these adolescents when they were 33: the late maturers were more likely to seek aid and encouragement from others, were more impulsive and touchy but showed more insight into the problems of others.

Weatherley (1964) found that boys who developed at an average age were very similar to those who matured early, and both groups differed from the late maturers who scored significantly lower in self-esteem. This suggests that it is only late maturation that causes difficulties (while early maturation does not necessarily confer any advantage).

In the case of girls, the effects of rate of maturation, whether early or late, seem to be much less marked than with boys. Mussen and Jones (1957) compared early and late maturing 17-year-old girls in terms of self-concept, motivation and interpersonal attitudes. Early maturers had more favourable self-concepts and less dependency needs than the late maturers, but the differences were far less clear-cut than for boys. However, an interesting finding reported by Argyle (1973) is that girls who are taller than average at 13 still see themselves as tall later in life, even though they are only average by the time they have stopped growing.

The gender differences may be accounted for by the fact that females in our culture are expected to make themselves look attractive and are judged according to how they look; they can 'manipulate' their appearance in various ways (eg make-up). Males, on the other hand, are expected to be strong and to perform athletic and other physical feats and it is much more difficult to manipulate these; their appearance is relatively less important than for females and it is generally more difficult for males in our culture to alter their appearance. A number of studies all show that a large or strong stature is a central part of the male's ideal bodily self. (This does not necessarily indicate what females regard as an ideal male physique!)

For example, Jourard and Secord (1955) found that males were more satisfied with their bodies when they were large, while females were satisfied if their bodies were smaller than average (although many of the latter were happy with a larger than-average bust). Dwyer and Mayer (1969) and Lerner

(1969) found that muscular males were rated as being more popular and having a better personality than males with other body types.

Females are generally more sensitive to obesity in others (Harris and Smith, 1982, Worsley, 1981) and they take more notice of this in themselves, expressing more concern over body shape and wanting to lose weight more often than males (Jakobivitz et al, 1977, Miller et al, 1980). It seems highly probable that we learn what kind of a body we 'should' have and then judge our bodily-self in terms of these cultural ideal-types. The advertising media are largely responsible for presenting particular ideal face and body types and, in the main, these have been aimed at females.

Support for this view comes from studies by Faust (1983) and Garner et al (1980); in the latter study, a trend was found towards thinner female figures since 1970 both in magazine dieting articles and in other media. Furnham and Alibhai (1983) believe that western ideals of physique play a large part in the greater self-consciousness of girls regarding overweight; they found that predominantly slim and borderline anorexic shapes were often rated as highly attractive, and desirable personality traits were more often associated with slim as opposed to obese figures.

Tobin and Richards (1983) found that the more developed a pubescent girl is, the more she tends to be dissatisfied with her weight and the greater satisfaction is associated with feelings of being *under*-weight. Similarly, Davies and Furnham (1986), in a study of 182 11- to 18-year-olds, reported that, although comparatively few at any age were actually overweight, nearly half in each age group wished to lose weight—and considerably fewer wished to put on weight. Dissatisfaction with their weight was also found to increase with age and this was particularly marked between 14 and 16. Further, the numbers wishing to lose weight (at all ages) far exceeded the numbers classifying themselves as overweight, which seems to represent very powerful evidence of the influence of cultural pressures; indeed, Davies and Furnham noted a trend towards exercising as against dieting as a way of losing weight, reflecting the recent 'aerobics revolution'.

Anorexia Nervosa

The pressure to conform to ideal bodily types may partly account for the illness *anorexia nervosa* (literally, 'nervous lack of appetite'), which is suffered mainly by 16- to 19-year-old girls (Crisp, 1975, Palmer, 1982). One study of nine secondary schools in London (Crisp et al, 1976) found that one out of every 100 16- to 18-year-olds had anorexia.

However, some symptoms appear in pre-puberty (Tolstrup et al, 1982) and according to Richards (1982), the number of children who are diagnosed as having anorexia has doubled in each decade over the last 30 years; and Swift (1982) also reports that it is not entirely unusual for anorexia to occur in pre-pubertal children.

Anorexia is commonly understood to be a steady loss of weight, associated with dieting, which, if untreated, will be fatal. But what exactly is it and what causes it?

One long-held theory is that it is a rejection of womanhood and that adolescent girls use it as a way of warding off maturity, of preventing bust growth, menstruation and, thereby, conception. But this is arguable—are all girls aware that their periods will stop when they practise self-starvation? And how long is it before they realize that the bust is less affected by weight loss than other parts of the body?

It is true that women are more prone than men to being teased about puppy fat and obesity and are more likely to be advised or pressurised to diet. One Australian study did, indeed, find these to be among the stresses which precede anorexia.

Dieting itself is not the cause of anorexia but it can act as a trigger. Many may start by wanting to lose a few pounds but carry on if the results are rewarding—an upper limit may then be set and movement towards that causes great distress and guilt. Self-starvation becomes very satisfying and all the girl's energy is channelled into losing weight so that everything else loses its meaning. Another stress that can lead to anorexia is parental pressure to do well at school or university. Significantly, anorexia is highest in the private sector of education and the fathers of anorexics are usually in professional or managerial jobs. Many anorexic girls are often very intelligent and feel that their identity is linked with achievement. When they go to university or college, they might find themselves to be 'a small fish in a big pool' and they have to face greater competition and experience greater stress as a result.

The onset of anorexia may also be a reaction to pressures at home, such as hostility towards one or both parents, a change or disruption in family relationships or a history of psychiatric illness in the family.

Certainly, what all anorexics seem to have in common is a distorted body-image, a belief that they look and are greatly overweight, when, in fact, they are severely underweight. They are also particularly vulnerable to ordinary life events, have rather obsessive personalities, and they tend to avoid situations they fear. They have low self-esteem and seem incapable or afraid of managing their own lives as an adult—it is easier to remain a child and they both want and fear autonomy.

Some anorexics cannot control their desperate need to eat and find a solution in starving, then going on a binge of eating and then, finally, making themselves vomit. (This is known as 'secondary anorexia' or *bulimia*.)

Various medical symptoms are associated with both dieting and anorexia, including ammenorrheoa, ie absence of menstrual periods (Miles, 1982, Nylander, 1971), increased interest in food, depression, childishness and impaired academic performance (Nylander, 1971); this has led to the view that anorexia is at one end of a continuum and so is only quantitatively different from 'normal' dieting (eg Nylander, 1971, Fries, 1974, Button and Whitehouse, 1981). However, others see it as a qualitatively different condition (eg Garner et al, 1984, Thompson and Schwartz, 1982).

Self-identity

Throughout life the individual has to try to maintain a balance between the constant (or invariant) and the changing (or variant) aspects of the self. But across the life-span there are periods when the self-concept undergoes quite dramatic and extensive change, for example, during toddlerhood or the 'terrible twos' ($1\frac{1}{2}$ to 3 years), when starting school (4 to 5) and adolescence (starting with puberty), and at these times the balance is much more difficult to maintain.

A psychologist who has been particularly interested in this balance between a constant and a changing self is Erik Erikson, who sees the life-span as comprising eight developmental stages, at each of which there is a new and different task for the individual to solve; each task has in common the need to resolve a conflict between two opposing forces or components, and in the case of adolescence, the conflict is between Identity (or self-identity) and Role Confusion. (See Chapter 26 for a fuller discussion of Erikson's theory as a whole.)

As with each of the other stages, Erikson believes that the individual exists and develops on three planes and levels simultaneously: (a) the biological (organism); (b) the social (member of society); and (c) the psychological (individual).

a) We have already looked at how the body-image changes in adolescence but a few of Erikson's observations are worth noting. He says that the rapid body growth disturbs the previous trust in the body and mastery of its functions that were enjoyed in childhood. So the adolescent has to learn to 'grow into' the new body, but for a long time it will not feel comfortable and will not seem to 'fit' properly.

Sexual maturity implies the need for other people to fulfil new sexual needs and feelings; masturbation is very common, especially among boys, in early adolescence, and is often accompanied by sexual fantasy, but it can never be totally fulfilling.

The social and psychological counterpart of this is having to decide on a sexual identity, that is, deciding about one's sexual preference or orientation, whether to be heterosexual or homosexual.

b) At the *social* level, western culture has invented adolescence as a 'moratorium', an authorized delay of adulthood (in the form of extended formal education, certain laws relating to marriage, voting and so on) which is aimed at helping the young person to make the difficult transition from childhood to adulthood.

Yet it often creates confusion and conflict at the same time as it reduces them. For example, social and biological abilities and status may not be compatible, as in the case of the 'gym-slip mother' or the teenager who is married and still at school. Teenagers are expected to make decisions about their future (by parents and teachers) but are not allowed to vote and generally they are being kept dependent on adults, while being expected to behave like adults, in an independent and responsible way.

If an adolescent makes their choices too early (what Erikson calls a 'premature foreclosure' of the moratorium), this will be regretted and they are especially vulnerable to identity confusion in later life. Catholic confirmation and the Jewish bar-mitzvah may limit the young person, forcing them into a narrow, negative, identity.

Marcia (1966, 1967, 1968, 1970), inspired by Erikson and based on his own research, identified four states of adolescent identity formation. The two essential factors in the attainment of a mature identity are: (i) the individual must experience several *crises* in choosing among life's alternatives; and (ii) they must finally arrive at a *commitment*, an investment of the self in those choices.

The four states or statuses are:

i) *Identity diffusion*—the person is in crisis and is unable to formulate clear self-definition, goals and commitments;
ii) *Identity foreclosure*—the person has avoided the uncertainties and anxieties of crisis by rapidly committing themselves to safe and conventional goals without exploring the many options open to the self;
iii) *Identity moratorium*—decisions about identity are held in abeyance while the person tries out alternative identities without being committed to any particular one;
iv) *Identity achievement*—the person has experienced a crisis but has emerged successfully with firm commitments, goals and ideology.

Unlike Erikson's eight stages, these four states of identity are not sequential (they are not stages), with the exception that identity moratorium is a prerequisite for identity achievement.

Traditionally, the 'world of work' and the 'adult' world have been virtually synonymous and this is what most young people aim at, either through gaining relevant qualifications or by wanting to leave school at the earliest opportunity in order to assume adult status and to earn money and become self-supporting. With unemployment being the problem it is, the purpose of schooling and the expectations regarding their entry into the adult world must be much more blurred than ever before for many young people (see below).

Quite clearly, there is no well-defined initiation into adulthood in our culture as there is in many non-western cultures where, at a certain age, ritualized puberty rites or initiation ceremonies take place, marking the end of childhood and the start of adulthood. In these other cultures, adolescence, as such, does not exist, and while puberty is a biological fact, adolescence is very much a socially constructed phenomenon.

c) At the *psychological* level, the adolescent re-experiences the conflicts of early childhood, particularly the early encounter with parents as authority figures (focused around toilet training) and the Oedipus and Electra complexes (see Chapter 21).

Related to this is the typical adolescent mood swings and ambivalence, whereby they are sometimes very co-operative with parents and other adults and at other times 'dig in their heels' and disobey, almost for the sake of it. (This ambivalence is also typical of the 3-year-old.) This is very difficult for parents to cope with, especially when they need to remain stable, firm and predictable for the sake of their adolescents.

As we saw when discussing Piaget in Chapter 19, adolescents, having obtained formal operational thought, can think in abstract and hypothetical terms about what might be (and not just about what does exist), about other people's thinking and, particularly, what others think about them. They can conceive of ideal families, religions and societies, which can then be compared with what they have themselves experienced. They can also construct theories and philosophies designed to bring all the varied and conflicting aspects of society into a working, harmonious and peaceful whole. To quote

David Elkind (1970), the adolescent is, 'an impatient idealist, who believes that it is as easy to realize an ideal as it is to imagine it'.

Elkind also draws a very significant and intriguing parallel between the child and the adolescent in terms of egocentrism: even though the adolescent is cognitively able to understand that their view of things is not the only possible view of things,

> Since he fails to differentiate between what others are thinking about and his own mental preoccupations ... he assumes that other people are as obsessed with his behaviour and appearance as he is himself. It is this belief that others are preoccupied with his appearance and behaviour that constitutes the egocentrism of the adolescent. (Elkind, 1967)

Piaget and Inhelder (1958) make similar comments. Elkind goes on to say that adolescents are forever playing to (imaginary) audiences, think they are special, have a sense of immortality and 'personal fable', a story which they tell themselves but which is not true.

The major developmental task of adolescence is to develop a sense of identity, that is, to bring together all the things we have learned about ourselves as a son/daughter, brother/sister, friend, student and so on, plus all our past experiences, thoughts and feelings, to integrate these different and varied images of ourselves into a whole which makes sense and which has continuity with the past while preparing for the future. If the young person is successful, they will emerge from this developmental stage with a sense of psychosocial identity (the positive component), a sense of who they are, where they have been and where they are going.

The influence of parents is much more indirect than it has been in previous stages; it is more a question of how they influenced earlier stages (trust versus mistrust, initiative versus guilt, industry versus inferiority), rather than how they directly influence the search for identity versus role confusion (the negative component). So, the more positive the outcome of the earlier stages, the more likely it is that the adolescent will achieve an integrated psychosocial identity.

David Elkind (1970) points out that this will also depend on the social milieu in which the adolescent grows up. For example, in a society where women are second-class citizens, it may be more difficult for females to arrive at a sense of psychosocial identity. Likewise, at times of rapid social and technological change, such as the present, where there is a breakdown of many traditional values, it may be more difficult for young people to find continuity between what they learned and experienced as children and what they learn and experience as adolescents. This may lead them to seek causes (political, religious, humanistic) which give meaning and direction to their lives.

Typically, the adolescent will experiment with several different identities which may involve taking very extreme views on certain issues; whereas children merely play at social roles, the adolescent actually tries them out.

The negative component, role confusion, involves not knowing what you are, where you belong or to whom you belong. Such confusion is a frequent symptom in juvenile delinquents (including promiscuous delinquent girls); some young people seek a 'negative identity' (eg delinquent, hippie, punk), one opposite to what their family would want from them, not as an act of rebellion, but as a way of achieving some identity—a negative identity may sometimes be preferable to having no identity at all.

Whatever the final outcome of this stage Erikson believes that some form of stress or turmoil or disturbance of identity is inevitable (the 'normative crisis' or 'identity crisis'); he says, 'at no other phase of the life-cycle are the pressures of finding oneself and the threat of losing oneself so closely allied'.

Failure to establish a clear sense of personal identity at adolescence does not necessarily mean perpetual failure; equally, the person who attains a greater sense of identity than role confusion will inevitably encounter challenges and threats to that identity as they move through life.

Erikson stresses that life is constant change and that confronting problems at one stage of life is no guarantee against the re-appearance of these problems at later stages, or against the finding of new solutions to them. As far as a sense of identity is concerned, the optimum time to achieve it is during adolescence; to have a sense of self-identity is to have a 'feeling of being at home in one's body, a sense of knowing where one is going and an inner assurance of anticipated recognition from those who count'.

Work as a Source of Identity

Given that definitions of adolescence (like those we considered earlier) emphasize the part played by work in marking the end of adolescence and the achievement of an adult identity, it is important to consider the influence on identity formation of the inability to find work—or the loss of a job for those who have been working. Although the importance of leisure-time has been growing in the last few decades, Erikson (1968) believes that the jobs people choose still play a major role in their representation of themselves to society.

According to Kelvin (1981), if work is crucial to an individual's self-concept, it will also be crucial to their relationships with others. In introducing the subject of psychology at the beginning of Chapter 1, I suggested a scenario in which two people meet at a party and one asks the other 'What do you do?'. People normally understand that this means 'what job do you do?', and the reason why this is often one of the first bits of information we try to obtain about another is that it is highly illuminating: according to Brown (1978), a person's work (or the fact that they do not or cannot work) tells us so much else about their social situation and likely life experiences. 'An occupation is a socially recognized set of work activities... it, therefore, implies... a place in the social division of labour,' (Brown, 1978).

Garraty (1978) maintains that to be unemployed places a person outside the accepted, taken-for-granted, system and sets them apart from those who are in work. Kelvin (1981) argues that the unemployed generally withdraw from much of their previous network of wider social activities, partly for financial reasons but also partly because of a subjective sense of inadequacy, a feeling 'that one is not quite a full member of society in which social life takes place'; the outcome is 'retreatism' (Merton, 1968). In losing our job, we lose much of our social identity (Kelvin, 1981).

Erikson (1956) claims that a state of acute identity confusion (or diffusion) usually manifests itself at a time when the young person is faced with a combination of experiences which demand simultaneous commitment, including occupational choice. If such a choice is denied the school-leaver, the opportunity to engage in other activities vital to the development of a sense of personal identity may be denied as well; failure to achieve identity may prevent the development of intimacy (along with work, the other major criterion of adulthood).

According to Hill (1977), one of the main problems for the young person out of work might be that unemployment extends the period of stay at home and increases dependence on parents at a time when the main psychosocial task is to achieve independence. For many young people, therefore, unemployment may represent an enforced and prolonged moratorium. What are the psychological consequences?

In a survey of 15-year-olds, Porteous (1979) found that not being able to find a job was one of the main concerns of this age-group. Catalano and Dooley (1977) reported a significant association between economic conditions and psychological well-being, and unemployment is related to both depressed mood and stressful life events (Dooley and Catalano, 1979). The economic change which results from losing one's job precipitates behavioural problems and causes distress by increasing the number of adaptation-requiring life events (Catalano, 1975).

Jahoda (1979) believes that a change of economic status is not the only consequence of unemployment; a loss of *structured* activity, social contacts and a sense of identity and purpose are also suffered. Indeed, the young school-leaver is unlikely to experience a significant change of economic status at all (if anything they will be better off by becoming eligible for social security benefits) and yet their distress may be as great as that of any adult faced with redundancy.

This lack of structure etc is, according to Kelvin (1981), a problem of 'not being in work' (as opposed to being unemployed as such) because its ill-effects are found amongst the retired too (Jahoda et al, 1933, Friedlander and Havighurst, 1954, Hill, 1978, Marsden and Duff, 1975). (See Chapter 24.) Leisure activities are usually no substitute for the *interdependence*, on a continuing basis, which is the essence of most work relationships (Kelvin, 1981).

Stafford et al (1980) studied school leavers in the north of England and found that those who did not find work showed higher levels of minor psychiatric problems. Similar results were found by Donovan and Oddy (1982) and Banks and Jackson (1982); in the latter study, youngsters were studied while still at school until after leaving and finding (or not finding) work and while there were no significant differences between them prior to leaving school, 'the experience of unemployment (is) more likely to create increased symptoms rather than the other way round' (Banks and Jackson, 1982).

Donovan et al (1985) compared 800 15-year-olds while still at school and then again six to eight months after leaving school. Of the 131 who were studied on the later occasion, 45 were employed, 43 were unemployed and 43 were participating in a government training scheme (YOPs). Based on a general health questionnaire and measures of anxiety and depression, present life satisfaction, self-esteem and self-adjustment, the unemployed were found to show the greatest number of psychological symptoms, to have the lowest degree of satisfaction with their lives and to experience poorer family and social relationships, and these differences held good after allowance was made for individual differences, gender, socioeconomic status and educational attainment.

Donovan et al attributed the psychological symptoms directly to the decreased rate of positive reinforcement which is normally provided by employment and found support for Jahoda's interpretation of the harmful effects of unemployment. If psychological well-being is taken as a measure of the effectiveness of YOPs schemes, then they obviously work up to a point: the YOPs group fell mid-way between the employed and unemployed groups on most measures.

Other Theories or Adolescence

Erikson's psychosocial theory is probably the most famous psychological theory of adolescence and the most influential. Erikson was trained as a psychoanalyst but was also very much influenced by the anthropological studies of Ruth Benedict and Margaret Mead and he carried out anthropological research himself (see Chapter 26).

a) Psychoanalytic Theories

Both Sigmund Freud and his daughter, Anna, saw adolescence as a stage in which the balance within the personality of the child becomes disturbed. During the latency period (5 or 6 to puberty), the id, ego and superego are in relative harmony but the new id urges which arise at puberty are very powerful and the superego is 'in the melting pot', that is, there is a bid for independence (whereby the identification with the same-sex parent is weakened) but at the same time there is a renewed dependence on the opposite-sex parent.

So there is a re-emergence of strong Oedipal feelings and the adolescent's task is to restore the psychic balance. Anna Freud (*The Ego and the Mechanisms of Defence*, 1937) believed that her father had overemphasized the development of sexuality early in life and neglected its adolescent manifestation; she also regarded the ego defence mechanisms (see Chapter 26) which were used prior to puberty as no longer adequate to deal with the upsurge of instincts and she identified two new adolescent defences (a) *asceticism*, whereby adolescents deprive themselves of pleasurable experiences and activities (particularly sexual ones); and (b) *intellectualization*, whereby anxiety-provoking subjects are discussed and read about at great length (typically, adolescents spend more time talking about sex than enjoying it).

More recently, Peter Blos (1967) has described adolescence as a, 'second individuation process', that is, the process of becoming a separate person (the first individuation process having occurred at the end of the child's third year).

The adolescent *disengages*, that is, renounces their dependency on the family and loosens early childhood ties which until puberty were the main source of emotional sustenance. This, in turn, produces 'affect and object hunger', a means of coping with the 'inner emptiness' which results from the breaking of childhood ties. Affect and object hunger are satisfied by: (i) group experiences (a family substitute); (ii) doing exciting things, 'just for kicks', (iii) frequent and abrupt changes in relationships; and (iv) drug-induced and mystical experiences.

Disengagement also produces regression, which can take the form of 'hero worship' (of rock stars, sporting personalities etc) and the 'homosexual crush' (on a same-sex teacher or friend of the parents) both involving the search for substitute parents, absorption in politics, religion and philosophy etc, and ambivalence. Ambivalence underlies relationships with parents in early childhood and involves a fluctuation between loving and hating, dependent and independent, co-operative and uncooperative and so on; according to Blos, ambivalence is reactivated in adolescence in an extreme form and accounts for much of the aggressive, negative and generally unpredictable behaviour which parents in particular, and adults in general, find so hard to understand.

Blos believes that regression is actually necessary for progress to take place and the non-conformity of adolescents is, in fact, a very adaptive defence against the temptation to become dependent again on the parents and other adults. He also sees transient maladaptive behaviour (what Erikson calls the 'psychopathology of everyday adolescence') as inevitable.

b) Cultural Relativism: the Contribution of Cultural Anthropology

The theories of Ruth Benedict (1934, 1954) and Margaret Mead (1942, 1944, 1961) were partly a reaction against the instinctive theories of Freud (as we saw in Chapter 22); any conflict, stress or problem experienced by young people cannot usefully be understood in isolation from the cultural norms and institutions to which they are related.

While it is universal for children to move from a state of dependence upon older people to relative independence, how this takes place varies greatly from one society to another. In some (such as the Cheyenne Indians studied by Benedict, 1934), the transition is smooth, gradual and continuous, eg a Cheyenne boy's hunting prowess is recognized by adults and his contribution to the feast is valued alongside the father's.

However, in western culture, many adult activities are forbidden to children and a great deal of behaviour which is thought appropriate for children must be 'unlearned' when we 'grow up'; we make fairly sharp distinctions between 'being mature' and 'being immature' and the unlearning which this involves produces inevitable strain which lies at the root of adolescent difficulties.

Specifically, there are three types of *discontinuity* in western culture, namely those centring around: (i) responsible and non-responsible roles; (ii) dominant and submissive roles; and (iii) sexual roles. Related to these are three kinds of unlearning: (a) play attitudes when moving into the world of work; (b) submissive attitudes when assuming positions of authority; and (c) the taboo on sex when moving into marriage.

Although Mead (like Erikson) acknowledged the part played by biological changes at puberty, she believed that adolescent problems are mainly due to social factors, in particular, the wide range of choices open to the individual in a rapidly changing world. If the primary task of adolescence is to establish a meaningful identity, the obstacles to doing this are greater now than ever before; there is no enduring frame of reference, no single set of values (religious, political, ideological etc) by which the adolescent can make sense of the world.

c) Coleman's Focal Theory of Adolescence (1978, 1980)

The 'classical' picture of adolescence which emerges from the theories we have considered (and many which we have not) has three main components: (i) *storm* and *stress*: (ii) *identity crisis*; and (iii) *generation gap*. However, Coleman believes that the actual empirical data paint a very different picture.

i) Storm and Stress
Westley and Elkin (1957) studied a small, middle-class, sample of teenagers in Montreal, Canada, and described their adolescence as being, on the whole, peaceful and tension-free. This was confirmed, using more representative samples, by Douvan and Adelson (1966), Bandura (1972) and Offer and Offer (1975).

In a study of adolescents on the Isle of Wight, Rutter et al (1976) found hardly any difference in the number of 10-year-olds, 14-year-olds and adults who were judged as having psychiatric disorders (10.9 per cent, 12.5 per cent and 11.9 per cent, respectively) and a substantial proportion of these 14-year-olds with problems had had problems since childhood. Again, when difficulties did first appear during adolescence they were mainly associated with stressful situations, such as the parents' marital discord. Only 20 per cent of teenagers agreed with the statement, 'I often feel miserable or depressed'.

The National Children's Bureau study (1976) of all the 16-year-olds born in a single week in 1958 in England, Scotland and Wales concluded that it is a 'difficult' age, at least for parents. Parents most often described their 16-year-olds as solitary, then came irritable ('quick to fly off the handle'), then 'fussy or overparticular'; very few were described as destructive or aggressive to others or frequently disobedient; 12 per cent were thought to be untruthful on some occasions, 2 per cent still sucked their thumbs, 3 per cent suffered emotional problems, 15 per cent were nailbiters, 11 per cent suffered from migraine or recurrent headaches, 3 per cent had a stammer or stutter and 1 per cent were still wetting the bed.

ii) Identity Crisis
Many of Erikson's notions surrounding identity crisis are difficult to translate into empirically meaningful terms but many researchers have used measures of the self-concept (in particular, self-esteem) as indicators of crisis.

We have already discussed self-esteem in relation to *body-image*, including early and late maturation and satisfaction with body weight, particularly in girls. In a longitudinal study, Engel (1959) tested boys and girls of 13 and 15 years and tested them again two years later; 80 per cent showed a fairly stable self-image over that two-year period and this was confirmed by two cross-sectional studies with 12- to 18-year-olds (Tomé, 1972, Monge, 1973).

Offer and Howard (1972) and Simmons and Rosenberg (1975) found that lowered self-esteem is more common during early adolescence than either late childhood or later adolescence, and this was more evident in girls than boys. For example, 32 per cent of 12- to 14-year-old girls had lower self-esteem (26 per cent of boys) and 43 per cent of girls had a more unstable self-image (30 per cent of boys), a finding which Maccoby and Jacklin (1974) suggest could reflect the greater willingness of girls to disclose negative aspects of themselves. In the Simmons and Rosenberg study, half the pre-pubescent girls were satisfied with their physical appearance, compared with one-quarter of the early adolescents and one-sixth in late adolescence. Simmons et al (1973) concluded that self-esteem is directly related to perception of physical appearance.

Perhaps what we have said about the harmful effects of unemployment could be interpreted as supporting the notion of an identity crisis; but the point is that the 'classical' view of adolescence sees crisis as an *inherent* feature of the period, not something induced by environmental forces and which can induce similar distress in other age-groups.

iii) Generation Gap

Bandura (1972) found no support for the 'classical' view that adolescents are trying to emancipate themselves from parental ties. However he did find that independence from the parents is more or less completed by 13 or 14 years (*not* just beginning) and that the autonomy of adolescents seems to pose more problems for adults than the adolescents themselves.

Instead of parents becoming more restrictive and controlling, Bandura found the reverse; relationships were seen by both sides as becoming easier with more mutual trust. He also found that adolescents were very selective in their choice of reference groups and there was little evidence of the 'slavish conformity' to the peer group which is another feature of the 'classical' view. In general, peer group values and parental values were *not* in direct opposition and peer group membership did not necessarily generate family conflict. Similarly, Offer and Offer (1975) conclude that peer group values are likely to be extensions of parental values.

Many studies have confirmed this picture (eg Gustafson, 1972, Jennings and Niemi, 1975, Douvan and Adelson, 1966); regarding basic attitudes towards politics, religion, sex and marriage, teenagers tend to be much more 'conventional' than the 'classical' view would have us believe. In the National Children's Bureau study, for example, the majority of both parents and 16-year-olds reported harmonious family relationships; only 3 per cent of the teenagers were totally against marriage, and the vast majority believed the ideal age for getting married is between 20 and 25 with two children as the ideal family.

Where conflicts do arise, these tend to centre around physical appearance (especially clothes and hairstyle), time of getting home at night and going to bed and homework (National Children's Bureau, 1976), noisiness and tidiness (Coleman et al, 1977).

So if the 'classical' view and the empirical data present two contradictory pictures, how can we reconcile them?

Coleman's solution, essentially, is to see the truth as lying somewhere between these two versions:

i)   Psychoanalytic theories have tended to be built upon clinical data, so that a distorted picture of the 'typical' adolescent emerges from an atypical sample of emotionally disturbed patients (see Chapter 26).

ii) Researchers who have conducted large-scale surveys have probably over-estimated the individual teenager's ability and/or willingness to reveal their innermost feelings and this had led to an *under*-estimation of adolescent crisis.

iii) The media have contributed to the popularity of the 'classical' picture by giving disproportionate coverage of the antisocial, deviant (and minority), threatening activities of youth.

iv) Coleman's *Focal theory* (1978, 1980) maintains that the adolescent is *not* overwhelmed by trying to resolve all areas of personal uncertainty simultaneously but instead focuses on problematical aspects of the self *in turn*.

The theory grew out of a study of 800 boys and girls aged 11, 13, 15 and 17 (Coleman et al, 1977) which found that concern about different issues (self-image, being alone, heterosexual relationships, parental relationships etc) reached a *peak* at different stages of the adolescent process (for both sexes).

At different ages, particular sorts of relationship patterns come into focus (that is, they are the most prominent) but no pattern is specific to one age only; the patterns overlap and there will also be individual differences, so that just because an issue is not the predominant feature of a particular age, this does not mean that it will not be critical for some individuals.

So, according to the focal theory, the process of adaptation is spread over a number of years, solving one issue first before tackling the next; problems are most likely to occur when issues 'accumulate', such as the late maturer who may have bodily and other changes to deal with at the same time.

Another way of coping is to see certain issues as residing in the *future* (eg Douvan and Adelson, 1966) so that they do not have to be dealt with *now*. Porteous (1984) showed that for 12- to 16-year-olds living in the north of England and Eire problems which are prevalent in early adolescence (eg about rules, permissiveness, adult criticism, bullying and friendships) decline and are replaced by worries about employment and, in some cases, worries about their worth as an individual; Porteous also found that with increasing age self-awareness increases and there is a growing tendency to be self-critical and to make comparisons between self and others (see Chapter 9), particularly in the case of girls.

Coleman concludes that:

> Adolescence is not an either/or phenomenon, but, as the evidence shows, is a period in the life cycle which contains difficulties and where stress is experienced, though of a minor rather than a major nature. There is conflict with parents, over mundane domestic issues, rather than over fundamental values. Many young people experience feelings of unhappiness but on the whole these go unnoticed by parents and teachers. Adolescents do worry over their future identities as they become older but these worries rarely cause an identity crisis (Coleman, 1980).

Adulthood

In discussing adolescence we have, unavoidably, touched on adulthood and have mentioned *intimacy* as a criterion of having attained the psychosocial state of adulthood. For Erikson, the attainment of identity by the end of adolescence is a pre-requisite for the ability to become intimate with another person; by this, he means much more than just making love and means the ability to share with, and care about, another person, 'without fear of losing oneself in the process' (Elkind, 1970), the essential ability to relate our deepest hopes and fears to another person and to accept another's need for intimacy in turn (Dacey, 1982). Indeed, intimacy need not involve sexuality at all and describes the relationship between friends as much as that between husband and wife.

Our personal identity only becomes fully realized and consolidated through sharing ourselves with another and if a sense of intimacy is not established with friends or a marriage partner, the result, in Erikson's view, is a sense of *isolation*, of being alone without anyone to share with or care for.

Intimacy is normally achieved, according to Erikson, in our twenties (young adulthood), after which we enter middle age (our thirties, forties and fifties) which brings with it either *generativity* or *stagnation* (self-absorption). Generativity means that the person begins to be concerned with others beyond the immediate family, with future generations and the nature of the society and world in which those generations will live. Generativity is not confined to parents but is displayed by anyone who is actively concerned with the welfare of young people and with making the world a better place for them to live and work, such as teachers, youth workers, community workers and so on.

Failure to establish a sense of generativity results in a sense of stagnation in which the individual becomes pre-occupied with their personal needs and comforts; such people indulge themselves as if they were their own (or another's) only child.

Many writers believe that most adults never attain generativity and that men get 'stuck' in the industry stage (7 to 12) and women in the adolescent stage (eg Roazen, 1976). (See Chapter 26.)

According to Gould (1978), the major task of *women* during their mid-forties is to deal with the persisting assumption that they need a 'protector' to survive; it is a time for women to reach full independence for the first time.

Sangiuliano (1978) interviewed women in depth and concluded that they achieve identity and intimacy in *reverse* order; agreeing with Gould, she found that a full occupational identity is not achieved until much later than is typical for men. Indeed, the typical life course for women is to pass directly into a stage of intimacy without achieving personal identity; most women submerge their identity into that of their partner and only at mid-life do they emerge from this to search for their own, separate, identity.

However, her sample was very small and unrepresentative and, despite some empirical support from Hodgson and Fisher (1979), there are some important qualifications that need to be made to her conclusions. In particular, there are major *social class* differences, which apply to men and women.

Working-class men and women tend to marry earlier and their careers may 'top out' sooner; this may change the *pace* of the sequence of stages compared with middle-class men and women.

Neugarten (1975) found that working-class men see an early marriage as part of the normal or 'good' life pattern; their young adulthood (twenties) is a time for settling down, having a family and working steadily. But middle-class men and women see their twenties as a time for exploration, trying out different occupations; marriage comes later and settling down is postponed until the thirties.

Therefore it seems necessary to describe developmental patterns for gender and social class-groups separately; it is more difficult to describe universal stages for adults than it is for children and even adolescents and adult development seems to be very much influenced by *social* definitions of roles (Bee and Mitchell, 1980). Nevertheless, some stage theories of adulthood have been proposed in the last decade.

Stage Theories of Adulthood

a) Levinson et al (1978)
They describe the 'seasons of a man's life', based on the in-depth study of 40 men, aged 35 to 45, from a variety of occupations. The six major seasons are summarized in Table 23.1 over the page.

'Seasons' is used instead of 'stages' because life-changes do not go from 'worse' to 'better' (which 'stage' usually implies); movement from one season to the next is the product of both external events (eg success or failure in a job, marriage, divorce) and internal ones (eg satisfaction or dissatisfaction with the life structure one has created). The emphasis is very much on external factors, particularly the influence of a man's occupation, but, as Bee and Mitchell (1980) point out, occupation and career are not the be-all and end-all of life. Clearly, the theory is also unbalanced, because it focuses exclusively on male development.

b) Gould (1978)
Like Levinson et al, Gould sees occupation (together with the family) as a major stimulus to change, with a major transition at about 30 and another at about 40. Adult development is seen as a process of movement from childhood to adult consciousness; the former, essentially, amounts to feelings of anxiety, depression, fear, inadequacy, self-doubt and so on which prevent us from using our talents to the full and achieving self-fulfillment. We must overcome childhood consciousness through our own efforts and insight (it is not just 'outgrown') and real psychological growth (or 'transformation') comes from making use of the crises and change we all experience in order to enhance our self-understanding.

Unlike the 'seasons' of Levinson et al, Gould's stages are *hierarchical*, that is, they go from 'worse to better'; the process of adult growth is a dismantling of the old, childish, structure, and replacing it with a stronger one (see Table 23.2 on page 599).

Clearly, both these theories presuppose the full availability of employment and a full range of choices across different social class groups. However, any

Table 23.1 The 6 'Seasons of a Man's Life' (Levinson et al, 1978) (summary based on Bee and Mitchell, 1980)

Season	Age	Major tasks
Early adult transition	17–22	Move out of the pre-adult world and make preliminary steps into the adult world. Explore possibilities and make preliminary choices.
Entering adult world	22–28	Create a first major life structure, usually marriage and own home. Create a stable life structure but also explore options.
Age 30 transition	28–33	Work on imperfections of first life structure. Reconsider choices of early 20s and make necessary changes.
Settling down	33–40	Create major new life structure, more stable than first. Usually involves heavy commitment to occupational success. Importance of a 'mentor' who can advise and support in the job.
Mid-life transition	40–45	Bridge from early to middle adulthood. Must re-examine settling down structure and modify it. 'What have I done with my life?'
Entering middle adulthood	45–50	Create new life structure. Focus is on new relationships with children and new occupational tasks, including acting as mentor for younger colleages.

adequate theory of adult development must take account of: (i) the very real impact of unemployment; and (ii) the changing pattern of gender roles (including female employment).

An Evaluation of Stage Theories of Adulthood

Fiske (1980) conducted a longitudinal study of several hundred adults and found that many of the mainstream working and middle-class population do *not* 'grow' or change in systematic ways; instead of an ebb and flow of stability followed by transition, followed by a further period of stability and so on, Fiske observed many rapid fluctuations, depending on the individual's relationship, work demands and other life stresses at each moment. To talk about stages, which are sequential and predictable, would seem inappropriate in the light of such data.

Costa and Macrae (1980) and Block (1981) see considerable *continuity* of

Table 23.2   The 4 stages of transformation from childhood to adult consciousness
(summary based on Bee and Mitchell, 1980) (Gould, 1978)

Stage	Age	Major changes
Leaving our parents' world	16–22	Leaving the protective 'blanket' of our family and giving up idea that parents will rescue us if necessary.
'I'm nobody's baby now'	22–28	Developing an independent, competent, identity; coming to terms with idea that things will not necessarily work out perfectly just because we follow our parents' rules.
Opening up to what's inside	28–34	Turning inward to discover additional facets of ourselves besides competence and independence, eg tenderness, compassion, fears etc.
Mid-life decade	35–45	Accepting our own mortality, realizing we have to get on with anything still left to do. Achieving sense of freedom and responsibility for oneself.

personality during adult life and do not accept the existence of developmental stages of any kind; this is consistent with the popular stereotype which sees middle adulthood as a time when the person is responsible, settled, contented and at the peak of their achievement (eg Hopson and Scally, 1980). As with other stereotypes, the experience of being adult is affected by these age stereotypes and people who find that they simply do not conform to expectations tend to blame themselves rather than seeing the stereotype as simply wrong (Schlossberg et al, 1978).

Schlossberg et al (1978) suggest that a 'social clock' is used by adults to judge whether or not they are on time with respect to a particular life event (marriage, having children etc); to be 'off-time' (either early or late) is to be an age-deviant and, like other forms of deviancy, can result in social penalties.

There is remarkable agreement between people of different ages as to what age is appropriate for particular behaviour. For instance, in one study (Neugarten et al, 1965), there was 80 per cent agreement regarding the age at which a man should marry (20 to 25), the age at which a woman should marry (19 to 24), the age at which people should complete their education (20 to 22) and the age at which they should retire (60 to 65).

Is the 'Mid-life Crisis' a Developmental Stage?

In *Passages—Predictable Crises of Adult Life* (1976), Gail Sheehy describes a shift in our forties when men begin to explore and develop their more 'feminine' selves (eg they become more nurturant, affiliative and intimate) while women are discovering their more 'masculine' selves (eg they become more action-oriented, assertive and ambitious). This passing-by, in opposite directions, produces distress and pain which are the 'mid-life crisis'.

Collins (1977) argues that it is *not* a stage through which everyone must pass; it can stem from a number of sources, including the ineffective adjustment to the normal stresses of growth and transition in middle age, and the reaction of a particularly vulnerable person to these stresses.

Hopson and Scally (1980) also take this position and they prefer not to talk about stages or cycles, seasons or passages, at all. Because of the diversity of adult experience, these terms are too restrictive and instead they describe *themes*; these include the changing nature of roles, adaptation to life transitions, adjustment to biological ageing and so on. More specifically, they might refer to concepts such as 'mid-life crisis', the 'empty nest syndrome' and 'age-30 transition'.

Conclusions

Bee and Mitchell (1980), in trying to draw the various theories and concepts of adult development together, suggest that, in any particular society, there are particular ages at which a large number of stressful life-changes (biological, social and psychological) are likely to happen together, so that most people will experience a transition or crisis at roughly the same time in their life-cycle. Individuals will differ in how much stress they can tolerate before a 'crisis' is experienced and in how they respond to it when it does occur. One potential response is personal growth, so that another piece of 'childhood consciousness' is removed (in Gould's terms); another response is to change major 'external' aspects of one's life, such as change jobs, get divorced, move house (which are emphasized by Levinson et al.)

Exploration of these individual differences in response to life-crisis, according to Bee and Mitchell (1980), seems to be at the heart of understanding adult development.

24

Ageing

While 'growing-up' is normally taken to be something desirable and almost an end in itself, 'growing old' has, traditionally, had very negative connotations. This negative view of ageing is based on the Decrement Model, which sees ageing as a process of decay or decline of our physical and mental health, our intellectual abilities and our social relationships.

In contrast, the Personal Growth Model stresses the potential and advantages of old age and this much more positive attitude is the way in which ageing is studied within the life-span approach. For example, Kalish (1979/1982) emphasizes the increase in leisure time, the reduction in many day-to-day responsibilities and the ability to pay attention only to matters of high priority among the elderly. Older people respond to the reality of a finite and limited future by ignoring many of the inconsequential details of life and channelling their energies into what is really important.

Ageism

It will take time for the balance between the decrement and personal growth models to shift; our prejudice against ageing and the aged (ageism) runs very deep (reflecting, perhaps, our deep-seated fear of death) and is mirrored in our language and our behaviour.

In an article called '"Old" is not a Four-Letter Word' (1978), Anderson claims that old people face a painful wall of discrimination that they are often too polite or too timid to attack. They are not hired for new jobs, and are eased out of old ones (because they are considered rigid or feeble-minded), they are shunned socially (because they are considered 'senile' or boring) and they are edged out of family life (because their children often regard them as sickly or parasitic).

In many ways they are treated as if they were no longer real people. Barrow (1976) found that college students generally felt disgust or repulsion about growing old. Chitwood and Bigner (1980) showed pre-schoolers photographs of young, middle-aged and old people and asked them to indicate which of the photographs went with each of a list of adjectives; 'sad', 'bad', 'ugly', 'poor' and 'dirty' were linked much more often with old people than with the young or middle-aged.

Another form that ageism takes was demonstrated by Palmore (1977); he found a preference among workers in the caring professions to work with children or younger adults. Similarly, Sudnow (1967) found that in hospital emergency rooms old people are less likely to receive a thorough examination or to elicit the fullest efforts of the medical staff; they are also more likely to be declared 'dead on arrival' compared with younger age-groups.

Even those psychologists who study ageing and try to present the positive features of growing old may, inadvertently, be guilty of ageism. For example, Kalish (1975) defined 'successful ageing' as continuing to behave as we did when we were younger (ie middle-aged). This assumes that one age group's pattern of behaviour is somehow inherently superior to that of another and is, therefore, a value-judgement (rather than an objective observation) which merely reinforces the idea of 'younger' being more desirable than 'older'.

Our prejudices against the elderly are built into everyday expressions (as are our racial, religious and gender-related prejudices), such as 'dirty old man' and 'old hag', which we often use without being aware of the attitudes on which they are based.

Undoubtedly, the elderly enjoy a very low status compared with both children and younger adults, and this inevitably influences the self-concept of those who are nearing the latter part of their lives. In turn, this change in self-concept may partly determine the behaviour of the older person. But how much are these changes an inherent part of the ageing process itself?

Is there any foundation for our very negative attitude towards growing old?
How much evidence, if any, is there to support the decrement model?
Is growing old inevitably and necessarily a period of decay and decline?
Are our fears of and resistance to growing old justified?
Just what are the facts of ageing (as far as they are known) and how can we account for them?

These are some of the major questions investigated by *gerontology* (from the Greek words *geron* and *ontos* meaning 'old man') which is a multi-disciplinary field of scientific research concerned with the ageing process and which we shall be discussing in the remainder of this chapter.

The Ages of Me

Can 'age' have more than one meaning? Can we be more than one age at the same time? These may seem rather strange questions to ask until you begin to think about them a little more carefully.

If age is an important part of our self-concept and if society generally seems to value 'younger' much more positively than 'older', then how old (or young) we perceive ourselves as being is going to have a significant effect on how we value ourselves (ie our self-esteem).

Robert Kastenbaum, in *Growing Old—Years of Fulfilment* (1979) has devised a questionnaire (called 'The Ages of me') which assesses how we see ourselves at the present moment in relation to our age.

My *chronological* age is my actual or official age, dated from the time of my birth. (Interestingly, this is not a universal method—in some cultures, a year is added on so that we are one when we are born.) Again, different people (according to their actual age) will define what is—chronologically—old very differently; children will probably see anyone over 16 as old, while the 70-year-old will regard those over 80 as old, and not themselves! Chronological age itself, therefore, is a very unreliable measure of 'old-ness'; what is old is a very relative matter!

My *biological* age refers to the state and appearance of my face and body (on the questionnaire, this is indicated by the items (a) 'In other people's eyes, I *look* as though I am about____years of age' and (b) 'In my own eyes, I judge my body to be like that of a person of about____years of age').

Subjective age is indicated by, 'Deep down inside, I really feel like a person of about____years of age'. This corresponds, of course, to the popular expression 'you're as old as you feel'.

My *functional* age, which is closely related to my *social* age, is the kind of life I lead, what I am able to do, the status I believe I have, whether I work, have dependent children, live in my own home, etc. Thus (a) 'My thoughts and interests are like those of a person about____years of age' and (b) 'My position in society is like that of a person of about____years of age'.

Of course, because of official retirement, society makes it very difficult for people over 60 or 65 to be in work, even if they are fit and willing to go on working. This contributes to what is probably a fairly high correlation between functional, social and chronological age (that is, there is quite a high correspondence between them, so that the older we are—at least beyond 60 or 65—the lower our social status, for example). If people were allowed to go on working until they decided to stop, or until they become physically unfit to do so, the correlation would be much lower, that is, the relationship between functional, social and chronological age would be much less clear-cut. Some people may decide to stop working in their fifties, others not until they were in their seventies or even beyond. One of the features of mass unemployment is the trend towards early retirement, which probably serves to reduce the correlation even further.

In practice, few people, at any chronological age, describe themselves consistently (ie give the same answer to all the items). One of the most typical differences occurs between subjective and chronological age: people in their twenties and above usually *feel* younger than their official age (and this includes many in their seventies and eighties) and also *prefer* to be younger, that is to say, they consider themselves to be *too* old. Very few people say they want to be older, which seems to confirm the aversion to old age that we have already discussed.

Two people of the same chronological age may behave quite differently and have very different subjective, biological, functional and social ages. The range of individual differences between people in their sixties and above is probably as great as that between children and younger adults, and knowing a person's chronological age tells us really very little about them. Yet one of the dangerous aspects of ageism is that actual age is taken as an accurate indicator of all the others, so that we tend to infer that people over 60 all have certain characteristics which, together, make up the decrement model ('past it', 'over the hill' etc). Recognizing the different 'ages of me' should help us to break down this idea of ageing as decaying and to look more analytically and more positively at old age.

Life-span and Life-expectancy

There is no doubt that people are living longer, that is, life-expectancy is increasing. For example, in 1900, the average life-expectancy (at birth) was 49 years, while in 1976 it was 73; females can expect to live a little longer than males (75 versus 69 years respectively).

Clearly, these gains are the result of advances in the prevention and treatment of childhood and other killer diseases; only 41 per cent of the babies born in 1900 reached 65 years old, compared with 74 per cent in 1974. Further, a man who reaches 65 today can expect to live to almost 79 and a woman to 83. But these gains in life-expectancy after 65 are quite modest compared with the gains made in the chances of surviving as far as 65. Again in 1900, 33 per cent of those who reached 65 survived to 80, in 1974 the figure was 51 per cent.

Nevertheless, it means that the elderly represent an increasingly large proportion of the population. For example, they made up 4 per cent of the total American population in 1930, 10 per cent in 1980 and will be an estimated 13 per cent in 2020. In Britain in 1972 there were 1300 people who lived to be 100 or beyond (1000 of them were women) and 8 million people over 65 (about 14 per cent of the population), compared with 2 million in 1900.

But is there an upper limit to how long human beings can live? This is the question of life-span (as distinct from life-expectancy).

All forms of life have some upper limit to how long they live; for example, ten to twenty days for the house-fly and up to 2000 years for some trees. Our increasing longevity (long life) reflects the fact that we are now able to live out a greater portion of our intrinsic life-span; that is, our life-expectancy has increased and has moved closer to the life-span of our species. Life-span itself—the inherent length of life of a particular species—has remained unchanged for humans during this century and, apparently, throughout recorded history. Humans live longer than other mammals; Medvedev (1975) estimates a maximum life-span of 110. (As I write, Britain's oldest person has just celebrated her 113th birthday!)

Perhaps life-expectancy has increased to the detriment of the quality of those extra years; society seems not to have been prepared for the increased life-expectancy of this century and, as a result, too many elderly people have spent their 'golden years' poor, dependent and sick.

According to Aschoff (1938), natural death in humans never occurs, or only in rare instances; the majority of deaths, he claimed, are caused by pathological factors (disease etc). As we learn to prevent or treat more and more diseases which are commonly associated with old age, we move closer to the point where ageing, and not disease, becomes the limiting factor in life-expectancy.

Before we try to answer the questions as to why we grow old and whether or not ageing is an inevitable process, we must first summarize the major physcial characteristics of ageing.

Physical Aspects of Ageing

According to Bee and Mitchell in *The Developing Person* (1980), because growth essentially comes to an end in the late teens and early twenties, we are inclined to think that body change and development also stop. But all the organ systems in the body show normal and predictable changes in structure and function during the adult years. Yet much less is known about these changes compared with what is known about infancy, childhood and adolescence and it is also more difficult to specify the age at which changes can be expected to occur; in adults, physical changes are less tied to chronological age and maturation and more to social and interpersonal factors.

It is interesting to note that *geriatrics* (from the Greek words *geras* meaning 'old age' and *iatros* meaning 'physician') which is the branch of medicine concerned with the diseases and care of the elderly, is more recent, has much less money spent on it and is generally less attractive and respected than paediatrics, which is concerned with the diseases of childhood. (This is another example of ageism.)

Bee and Mitchell summarize the major physical changes that occur in old age under five headings: smaller, slower, weaker, lesser and fewer.

i) Smaller

Height tends to decrease, due not to the long bones of the body (arms and legs) becoming smaller but rather to the connective tissues that hold them together (tendons, ligaments and muscles) becoming compressed and flattened (this is especially true of the bones of the spine). Related to these spinal changes is the stooped posture of the elderly.

Weight decreases too; the average male weight is 167 lbs (in the late thirties), compared with 155 lbs (after 65). Calcium tends to be lost from the bones (especially in women) so that bones account for a smaller percentage of total body weight than in younger people.

Muscle mass is reduced too, apparently because some muscle cells are replaced by scar tissue. Some body organs get smaller too, the uterus and vagina may shrink to their pre-adolescent size and the testes get smaller, as does the bladder.

ii) Slower

Electrical nerve impulses (the form in which information is communicated in the nervous system) travel more slowly to and from the brain (about 15 to 20 per cent slower in an 80-year-old compared with a 20-year-old); this partly accounts for slower response or reaction time. Some basic reflexes (eg bladder control) may also slow down.

As far as homoeostasis is concerned (maintenance of the body's internal environment), there is no substantial difference between younger and older people under normal conditions, but under stress, older people show much slower recovery.

Fractures may also take longer to heal in the elderly (partly due to the loss of calcium) and a simple break may result in a serious or complicated disability. The rate of renewal of liver and skin cells also slows down.

iii) Weaker

Bones become more brittle and break more easily, partly due, again, to the loss of calcium and partly to wear and tear. This applies to all bones, including the small bones of the middle ear (the ossicles) which can result in impaired hearing, especially the ability to hear high-pitched sounds.

Muscles also become weaker, including those of the arms, legs, chest, diaphragm (crucial for breathing), face (crucial for chewing and facial expressions), bladder (crucial for bladder control). Overall, muscle strength is reduced by 25 per cent in an 80-year-old compared with a 20-year-old. After about 30, there is a gradual reduction in the speed and power of muscles and decreased capacity for sustained muscular effort. Muscular effort is also limited by stiffer and more restricted movements of the joints. Generally, the senses become less efficient. In the case of vision, convergence becomes less efficient, the iris fades, the cornea thickens and loses its lustre and becomes less transparent, thus making the projection of light from objects onto the retina more difficult and the image less clear. The retina also receives a poorer blood supply.

iv) Lesser

The gradual lessening of the elastic tissue in the skin causes wrinkling and sagging. The eardrum loses some of its elasticity, which mainly affects hearing high frequency sounds, as does the lens of the eye, which produces poor accommodation to short distances and hence a tendency towards far-sightedness.

Blood vessels also become less elastic which can give rise to circulatory problems.

In women, the ovaries stop producing eggs and so reproductive ability (fertility) is totally lost; this represents the most dramatic change associated with the menopause (or climacteric) and, of course, means the end of menstruation. For most women, this occurs sometime during the late forties and early fifties but there is considerable variation depending on a number of factors, including race, living standards, whether or not the woman has had any children, when she started menstruating and her weight.

The major cause of all the changes related to the menopause (including the 'hot flushes', depression and weight gain) is the reduced level of oestrogen.

Men too show 'menopausal' symptoms during middle age, such as insomnia, depression and weight gain. Although the production of testosterone declines, there is no equivalent in men to the cessation of menstruation; in fact, they never stop producing sperm and are usually capable of reproducing right up until their death.

v) Fewer

Body hair gets more sparse and the number of teeth and taste-buds is reduced; hence different foods tend to taste rather more alike.

After 30, neurons (nerve-cells) die at an estimated rate of 30 per minute within the central nervous system, but we do have an estimated 10 billion of them! Loss of brain weight is about 20 per cent between the ages of 20 and 80.

When the rate of brain cell death reaches certain proportions, senile dementia occurs, but this applies to only a small minority of old people and it is not an inevitable part of ageing. Yet these changes in the brain may account for changes in memory, intelligence and reaction time (see below).

Most of these physical changes have been taking place, gradually, since about 30, but we are more likely to become aware of them after about 60 than we were before. Also, the range of individual differences in ageing is very great and ageing generally is not a process of rapid and drastic physical decline.

The specific factors that may increase human life-expectancy have been suggested by studies of communities where it is not uncommon for people to live to ripe old ages, even 120 and above. This, of course, challenges the figure of 110 which Medvedev takes to be the human life-span. So can the kind of life we lead increase not just our life-expectancy but also the life-span of the species too?

The communities that were studied were Vilcabamba, an Andean village in Ecuador (South America), a village in Kashmir, and a village in Georgia (in the USSR); in Vilcabamba, out of a population of 819, 9 were over 100 years old (1.1 per cent compared with 0.003 per cent in the American population).

What did these three villages all have in common which might account for the unusual longevity of their inhabitants?

i)   They were all located at high altitudes, in rugged mountainous areas, where the air was clean and bracing.

ii) The work done was very rugged and went on mainly outdoors.

iii) Men and women continued to work well into their eighties and sometimes beyond, which gave them a sense of usefulness and purpose —there was no such thing as compulsory retirement.

iv) The elderly enjoyed a high social status, mainly related to their being seen as a repository of wisdom. (This is quite common in societies which undergo relatively little change from one generation to the next, unlike western culture.)

v)   The elderly belonged to an extended family, they were all cared for (if necessary) within the family structure. (There were no institutions specially set up for the purpose.) There was also the expectation of longevity.

vi) All the centenarians had at least one parent and/or one sibling who had also lived to 100 or more. This suggests that there is some genetic predisposition towards long-life, although there is no known 'long-life' gene; more likely is an absence of 'bad' ones. (This is probably also true of the greater life-expectancy of women in our society—they are more resistant to heart disease and certain forms of cancer.)

vii) As far as diet is concerned, in Vilcabamba and the Kashmir village, meat and dairy produce represented a very small percentage of the overall diet. Protein and fat were derived mainly from vegetable sources and there was little obesity or under-nutrition. So the inhabitants were mainly vegetarians and they also drank river-water.

An interesting study was made in 1965 of 23 Hungarian centenarians, most of whom were vegetarians. They were put into an old people's home and given a traditional diet which included meat and other dairy produce. They quickly started to deteriorate, began fumbling, had trouble remembering things and usually died from thrombosis.

viii) In the Georgian village, some of the oldest amongst them smoked, drank and showed an interest in the opposite sex. Extreme old age was attained by the married.

It seems then that there are a number of factors which are related to longevity.

However, the study has been criticized. For example, Mazess and Forman maintained that those people claiming to be centenarians in Vilcabamba were, in fact, not. In co-operation with Ecuadorian scientists, Mazess and Forman studied naming patterns, observed the frequency of age exaggeration, studied population migration patterns and explored civil and church records. Based on this research, they compiled a list of persons born before 1900—and the oldest was 96!

It seems that much of the confusion stems from the custom of passing a family name from one generation to the next. Because of this, the actual recorded birth dates of these people living in Valcabamba are often confused with those of their parents and grandparents. Another common practice is to give a surviving child the same name as that of a sibling who has died; consequently, a person's age is often the sum total of more than one family member.

They also found a tendency to exaggerate age once the inhabitants reached 60 and the world-wide attention which has been focused on the village has made this even more likely to happen. Apparently, one woman told an Italian television crew that she was 146 and that she had had her last child when she was 115!

However, more reliable data relating to geographical, ethnic and racial variations in life-expectancy, especially in the USA, suggest that more research into the interplay between biology, social status and environment in longevity could prove very valuable, both practically and scientifically.

Having discussed some of the possible social and other environmental factors that may extend our life-expectancy, we now turn to the more fundamental question of life-span.

Is ageing inevitable? Are we programmed to die? What are the mechanisms which underlie our growing old, and is it possible (and desirable) to interfere with those mechanisms, so that our life-span can be extended, if not indefinitely, then at least significantly beyond the 110 years suggested by Medvedev?

Theories of Ageing

According to Strehler, there is no absolute principle in nature which dictates that individual living things cannot live for indefinitely long periods of time in optimum health; he belongs to a school of thought amongst gerontologists who share four basic beliefs:

i) There exists within each of us a 'clock of ageing', a genetically determined mechanism that dictates that we will age and die as well as the rate at which this will occur.

ii) We have an excellent chance of discovering the location(s) of the ageing-clock as well as how it works and how to interfere with it to our own advantage.

iii) This can begin to happen now, not at some unspecified time in the future, if only the research can be carried out.

iv) Senescence (growing old) may eventually become obsolete.

When the first anti-ageing drugs are tested, they will almost certainly be tried initially in vitro, that is, on cells kept alive, through many generations, in artificial laboratory preparations or cultures. A few substances, in fact, already seem to be capable of increasing the life-span of cultured cells.

But do cells in culture truly age? And if so, is the process involved the same as the one that takes place in vivo, that is, in the living organism? In other words, can the study of cells in culture tell us anything about the physiological deterioration and death of human beings?

This is currently a matter of controversy amongst gerontologists.

One of the leading opponents of the study of cells in vitro is Denckla, who also believes that the clock of ageing is located in the brain and is hormonal in nature. Another controversial issue is to do with the location of the clock —is it found inside the nucleus of each cell or in the brain? (In either case, it is a genetically determined process.)

Intelligence, IQ and Ageing

Until recently, psychologists believed that our intellectual capacity reaches a peak in our late teens or early twenties, and then levels off in our twenties and thirties (reaches a plateau), before starting to decline fairly steadily during middle age and more rapidly in old age.

But this general picture of decline seems to be based upon a number of factors, in particular:

a) The way that intelligence is defined;
b) The type of tests used to measure intelligence and the way the results are analysed;
c) The kind of study used to compare intelligence at different ages (cross-sectional versus longitudinal).

The Definition of Intelligence

This has always been a matter of disagreement and controversy among psychologists and will be looked at in detail in Chapter 27. Psychologists cannot agree on a single definition of intelligence, and whether intelligence tests reliably and validly measure intelligence is still hotly debated. Suffice it to say here that intelligence (at any age) is best understood as multi-dimensional, that is, it is composed of a number of different abilities and each of us has a different pattern or profile, so that we are better at some than at others (compared with ourselves and with others). Also, this pattern may change over time, both for individuals and for age-groups as a whole. This way of thinking about intelligence makes it possible that, as far as certain abilities are concerned, the traditional picture of decline may be fairly accurate, but as far as others are concerned intelligence may actually go on increasing.

One way of classifying these various abilities is in terms of *fluid* and *crystallized intelligence*, a distinction made by Cattell. Fluid intelligence refers to the ability to solve novel and unusual problems (ones which the individual has not come across before) and involves memory span and mental agility, that is, the speed of thought needed, for example, to find the pattern in a string of letters, visualizing an object in space or doing jigsaws. So it is not based on specific knowledge or any particular previous learning. It can also be thought of as the capacity or aptitude to learn.

Crystallized intelligence, on the other hand, refers to knowledge and skills acquired through living in society and includes the ability to define words, verbal skills in general, and the effective use of the skills and knowledge which formal education is primarily concerned with.

Since fluid intelligence is thought to be more sensitive to changes in the central nervous system, and since ageing involves such changes, we might expect it to decline with age, and since crystallized intelligence is more dependent on ongoing experience, we might expect that it will go on improving. This is exactly what has been found.

Most people show decline in fluid intelligence during the second half of their lives—it seems to reach a peak in adolescence and then drop fairly sharply afterwards; it has been estimated that the average 30-year-old has already lost about 50 per cent of the measurable fluid intelligence that they will have lost by age 60.

A test which attempts to measure these two different kinds of intelligence is the Primary Mental Abilities (PMA) test, based on the work of Thurstone (1938). Fluid intelligence is measured by response speed (for example, writing down, within a specific time limit, all words beginning with a particular letter), memory span and non-verbal reasoning. These do show a

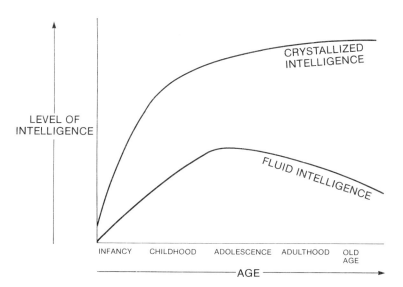

Figure 24.1 Changes in fluid and crystallized intelligence with age

decline with age. Crystallized intelligence is measured by reading comprehension and vocabulary and these show no decline with age.

Botwinick (1978), for example, found that fluid intelligence begins a gradual decline in middle age and may drop more sharply for many people in later adulthood, while Nesselroade, Schaie and Baltes (1972) found that crystallized intelligence remains the same or actually improves at least until the early eighties. (See Figure 24.1.)

Intelligence Tests

The most widely used test of adult intelligence is the Wechsler Adult Intelligence Scale (WAIS), designed by Wechsler in 1958. It consists of two separate scales, a *verbal* scale and a *performance* scale, and each of these produces a separate IQ (Intelligence Quotient); the scales can be combined to produce a third, total or overall IQ.

The verbal scale (so called because all the questions are given verbally and require verbal answers) comprises a number of tests (information, comprehension, arithmetic, similarities, digit span and vocabulary).

The performance scale (so called because the testee actually has to do something) also comprises a number of tests (digit symbol, picture completion, block design, picture arrangement and object assembly or jigsaw puzzles).

The test was originally standardized on 2000 men and women, 16 to 75 years old, that is, it was given to those subjects in order to determine how people typically score at different ages. The highest overall scores were obtained by 25 to 29 year olds and the younger subjects tended to have an overall IQ that was more evenly determined by the verbal and performance scales compared with older subjects, whose verbal ability contributed a much larger proportion of their total IQ. Another way of putting this is to say that, while total IQ seems to decline with age, verbal IQ does not (at least not until after 60); performance IQ seems to follow the pattern for total IQ. (This is equivalent to the findings for fluid and crystallized intelligence.)

However, there are certain important differences within each scale. As far as digit span is concerned, while there is very little deterioration for recalling digits in the order in which they are presented, there is more when they have to be remembered in reverse order (especially after 45 years). There is usually more decline for mental arithmetic, where marks are given for speed and accuracy. There is some decline on similarities, even though speed is not important here. On the digit symbol test, what is mainly needed are speed of writing and of eye movements, as well as the ability to hold information in short-term memory. The ability to concentrate is important too and in all these respects older people tend to be at a disadvantage.

Cross-Sectional Versus Longitudinal Studies

These findings for the WAIS and those referred to earlier for the PMA, are based mainly on cross-sectional studies which involve studying different age-groups, at the same time, so that, say, 20-year-olds are a different group from the 50-year-olds, who are a different group from the 70-year-olds, and so on (see Chapter 23).

The traditional view of intelligence as declining steadily with age has emerged from these cross-sectional studies, in which an overall IQ on the WAIS or the PMA is compared for different age-groups, or where group tests (pencil-and-paper tests, often computer-marked, giving just an overall IQ) have been used. But there are serious problems associated with this method of study, in particular, what is known as the cohort effect. This refers to the fact that differences between, say, 20-year-olds and 80-year-olds, are not confined merely to age, but include all those features of their upbringing and experience (eg wars, poverty and education). The two age-groups represent different cohorts and so we cannot draw any simple conclusions about how intelligence changes with age on the basis of differences in IQ between the two groups—we know how a whole range of environmental and social factors can influence the development of intelligence, and, hence of IQ.

As Labouvie-Vief (1979) has pointed out, younger subjects are born in a time of greater educational opportunity which almost certainly contributes to their higher scores on IQ tests.

We should also note that younger subjects are more likely to have already been given an IQ test while many of the elderly subjects will be doing one for the first time. Also, the elderly are likely to be less confident and less motivated; the test will probably have little meaning or relevance for them and they tend to take fewer risks and so take longer over any one test item. These last three differences are to do with personality but will significantly affect the score on the test. Yet the test has no way of measuring their effects separately from the effects of intellectual ability.

Longitudinal studies do not face this difficulty; since the same individuals are tested and re-tested at various times during their lifetime, we are always comparing them with themselves (ie there is only one cohort involved).

However, it is practically very difficult to carry them out: the study has to last at least 60 years in the case of intelligence and ageing, and so, not surprisingly, there are very few such studies covering the full adult life-span. But those that have been conducted, according to Botwinick (1978), show less decline in intelligence with age than cross-sectional studies and the decline tends to occur late in life.

However, there is a kind of compromise method of study (the cross-longitudinal method) which attempts to combine the advantages of both while reducing the disadvantages; groups of subjects, of different ages, are followed up over as long a period of time as possible.

One study of this kind was reported by Schaie and Strother (1968) and Schaie and Labouvie-Vief (1974). In 1956, Schaie gave the PMA test to a large group of subjects, aged 20 to 70, and in 1963, and again in 1970, he retested as many as possible (161 in all). They were divided into age-groups (on the basis of their age at the start of the study), ranging from 25, 32, 39 and so on up to 67. Each group was a cohort and test scores for each cohort can be viewed as a small longitudinal study of a particular 14-year-long 'slice' of adulthood. These overlapping slices could then be combined.

On verbal meaning (vocabulary) for the 25- and 32-year-old groups, scores actually got better; for the two oldest groups (60 and 67) the scores got worse. Overall, scores increased or remained stable up to 60 and then began to decline. Fluid intelligence (eg measured by word fluency) showed a decline for all age-groups.

Cognitive Changes in Adulthood and Old Age

Some fascinating research in the USA during the 1970s has attempted to answer the question as to whether there might be a fifth stage of cognitive development.

You will remember from Chapter 19 that Piaget argues that, although adults may become increasingly knowledgeable and skilful in the use of logical thinking, he believes that there is no new *kind* of thinking that develops after about 15 years of age. Indeed, many adults never attain formal operational thinking at all and of those who do, many do so only in relation to their own particular area of expertise and experience.

But many psychologists have pointed out that the mental abilities related to formal operational thought are all focused on problem-solving of one kind or another, whereby several pieces of information must be brought together in order to find the solution to a problem; this is known as *convergent* thinking. (This is also the kind of thinking assessed by IQ tests.)

Yet many problem situations in real life require *divergent* thinking, whereby for example, a solution is found by approaching the problem in an original or unconventional way and where a number of possible solutions may be required and not just one. This kind of approach is not covered by Piaget's theory.

Patricia Arlin (1975/1977) has suggested that there is a fifth stage of development, corresponding to this ability to think divergently, which she calls problem-finding. However, the evidence is conflicting.

Riegel (1973), on similar lines to Arlin, advocated that we should de-emphasize formal thought and study 'mature' thought in adults instead; mature thought is the acceptance that some things can be both true and not true at the same time. For example, to the person using concrete operations, it would mean understanding that two lumps of plasticine are simultaneously the same (quantity) *and* different (shape). But in Piaget's conservation tasks, only one or other can be true, that is, they are either judged to be the same (despite their different appearance), in which case the individual displays conservation, or they are judged as being different (despite the fact that nothing has been added or taken away), in which case the individual does not display conservation.

In Piaget's theory, the emphasis is on how the child tries to resolve the contradiction by building new cognitive structures. But Riegel suggests that, instead of resolving the contradiction, the child needs to learn to accept it—concrete operations can be used skilfully and flexibly.

Another question which fairly recent American research has investigated is whether or not there is cognitive regression in old age, that is, do the elderly return to earlier, less complex, ways of thinking and reasoning? Some of the research has involved the use of Piaget's conservation tasks.

Papalia (1972), for instance, gave 6- to 7-year-olds tests of number, substance, weight and volume conservation. All the subjects, except the 6-year-olds, could do the number task, while the conservation of volume was the most difficult at all ages. Overall, the 18- to 19-year-olds, and the 55- to 64-year-olds did fairly well, while the oldest subjects did very poorly indeed. But this was a cross-sectional study and can be criticized for the same reasons as those concerned with ageing and IQ.

Douglas and Nancy Denney (1973) played 'twenty questions' with 26- to 46-year-olds and 75- to 90-year-old women. Younger children typically make guesses, one at a time, until they hit the correct answer, while older children use their ability to classify objects hierarchically, that is, they narrow down the range of possible answers by asking about categories or classes of items ('constraint questions'), such as, 'is it animal, vegetable or mineral?'. Among the Denneys' subjects, the 75- to 90-year-olds were much more likely to guess (85 per cent) compared with the 26- to 46-year-olds (35 per cent) and were also much less likely to ask constraint questions (3 per cent compared with 58 per cent). So, in this respect, older women acted like younger children, while the younger women acted like older children.

But Hornblum and Overton (1976) found evidence to suggest that the elderly may be capable of much more advanced performance than they actually demonstrate. Being capable of doing something (competence) does not guarantee that the ability will be used (performance); so perhaps the elderly are capable of more complex cognitive strategies than they often reveal in experiments.

Institutional Life and Cognitive Abilities

Rubin (1973) compared groups of elderly people living independently with another group who had chosen to live in a residential home. They were about equal in educational background and the institution studied was designed for the healthy, as opposed to the convalescing or senile elderly. They were all given tests of conservation and egocentrism.

Those living independently were less egocentric and did better on the conservation tasks as well.

Many institutions for the elderly are similar to orphanages, residential nurseries and other institutions for children as far as social deprivation is concerned: residents are given very little individual attention by the staff and receive little physical affection, stimulation or social interaction of any kind. This kind of atmosphere could impair cognitive functioning in the same way as it does in infant development.

DeCarlo (1971) and Spirduso (1975) both make the point that the degree to which the older person has the opportunity to be physically active and intellectually stimulated, to use their minds and bodies, is as crucial as for other stages of development, if not more so. Why it may be more important is because of what we said earlier about ageism and the popular sterotype of ageing, which regards the elderly as not needing to think or to be stimulated, since they have reached the 'end of the road'.

At least we recognize that children can be helped to develop and so we provide what they need; the elderly may have to look after themselves in this respect! (This is another instance of 'growing up' versus 'growing old'.) In adults, as in children, depression, despair, and a sense of worthlessness can all detrimentally affect physical and mental well-being.

Ageing and Memory

If a list of seven letters or digits is read out, at a rate of one per second, and the subject has to recall the list immediately, older people, on average, recall slightly fewer correctly than younger people. But if some kind of interference task is given before recall (eg having to count backwards from 100), older people perform significantly worse than younger people. Also, if the list has to be recalled in reverse order, the older person (over about 45) is at much more of a disadvantage than the younger person (Bromley, 1958).

It seems that, as we get older, the co-ordination between STM and LTM deteriorates (see Chapter 6); each part of the memory system may be all right in itself but we are unable to transfer information from STM to LTM as efficiently as we could when younger. Tasks in which there is a time limit, or which require information to be retrieved from memory quickly, are especially difficult.

Also, STM in the elderly is likely to be hindered by a task requiring a division of attention. For example, older people have more difficulty performing two tasks at the same time, as when having to sort triangles according to colour, say, and circles according to size. Here, you have to keep a lot of information in your head at the same time.

Kirchner (1958) put subjects in front of a panel of 12 light bulbs and 12 keys and each time a light came on, subjects had to press the key immediately below it—this turned the light off, and another would come on. Old and young subjects performed equally well on this task. But if subjects had to press the key beneath the previously-lighted bulb, older subjects did less well; this required a division of attention because they had to remember the position of two bulbs at a time.

As measured by Reaction Time or RT (the time interval between the onset of light—the stimulus—and the pressing of the key—the response), the older subject is again at a disadvantage and this increases in proportion to the number of bulb positions which have to be remembered; the greater the number of bulbs involved, the more complex the task.

RT, in turn, seems to be related to the speed of Decision Time (DT), so that the greater the one, the greater the other. Although it is true for all age-groups that the more complex the task, the longer the DT, the DT is relatively longer for older than for younger subjects, particularly at higher levels of complexity. But again, we must remember that these findings are based on cross-sectional studies. However, these STM deficits are not large and their effects are not especially detrimental to the ability to function effectively; outside the laboratory, many of the differences described above may be hardly detectable.

As far as LTM is concerned, the popular belief that the elderly have little trouble recalling events from their youth and early adult life has some empirical support. But Warrington and Sanders (1971), for example, found that older adults had rather more difficulty recalling news events from the distant past compared with younger adults, although the differences were not dramatic.

When questioned about major news events from one to 24 months earlier, subjects of all age-groups recalled less information as the number of months which had elapsed since the event increased. Perhaps the elderly have relatively less trouble remembering incidents that occurred in their own lives, and since they have so much more to remember and the time-span is so much greater than for younger people, this feat seems all the more impressive!

Older People at Work

A. T. Welford in *Ageing and Human Skill* (1958) pointed out that the decline with age of STM and speed of RT and DT have a great influence on the performance of older people at work.

An older worker can still perform satisfactorily but will be working nearer to their full capacity; with age, STM or RT will put a limit on performance. If the job involves having to make frequent and speedy decisions, a decline in performance will probably occur, as predicted by what we noted above about memory. Similarly, if the job makes demands on STM, by requiring something to be held in STM while doing something else and then recalling it, or by having to remember a set of elaborate instructions, performance will also decline.

At the same time, however, the more experienced we become, the greater our store of knowledge becomes; 'tricks of the trade' may help to compensate for some of the deficits of STM and RT. But this can produce its own problems; for example, we may have many more responses to choose from than someone who is less experienced and this may slow down DT and hence RT. Also, this extra knowledge and experience may make us less rather than more flexible and adaptable. So just how easy or difficult is it to 'teach an old dog new tricks'?

Belbin and Belbin (in *Problems in Adult Retraining*, 1972) found that when older workers are compared with 20- to 40-year-olds, they often learn new tasks considerably less well. But this may be due not to their inability to learn but to the unsuitability of the training methods involved: younger and older people may require different methods.

They decided that three aspects of conventional methods pose problems for older workers:

i)   Having to translate a series of verbal instructions into action;
ii) Understanding instructions, especially if they are new, long and complex;
iii) 'Unlearning' incorrect habits or inappropriate procedures.

Therefore they carried out an experiment at a wool mill which involved training workers to mend miswoven fabric. The traditional method was for trainees to sit next to an experienced mender who carried out the repair and explained to the trainee what to do.

The Belbins believed that older trainees should be encouraged to carry out the repair from the start of training; that is, instead of being instructed verbally on what was required, trainees should be able to see, visually, what they had to do, thus avoiding the need to translate from verbal instructions into actions.

So the older trainees were allowed to practise mending fabric with larger-scale weaves which were specially made of thick elastic, so that errors in the weave could easily be seen and were quite easy to mend. When they moved on to the actual thread weaves, they used a magnifying glass. The results were quite dramatic. After 8 hours of guided instruction and practice on the enlarged weaves and 12 hours of solo practice (a total of 20 hours), the older workers could mend most types of weave in about three to five minutes. By contrast, groups of 15-year-old school-leavers took between three and ten weeks to reach the same level of proficiency (using either the traditional method or the modified one used to train the older workers).

In another study, tram drivers were retrained to drive buses, being given 3 weeks (or 4 if needed) of training, consisting of 40 hours at the wheel and 8 hours in the classroom (using a simulated or 'mock' bus). They were not given marks but either passed or failed, but they could repeat the whole course. Results showed a steady decline after 20, especially poor control, poor road sense, difficulty with the gear-box and poor rearside judgement (too much or too little space left).

However, the majority who failed first time passed second time and even of those in their sixties, two-thirds passed (eventually). Experience with other vehicles seemed to help but many of those who were 50 or older passed without it.

Clearly, training or learning methods must be tailored to suit the needs of the trainee or learner, young or old. A general principle which seems to be especially applicable to the older student is that the pace of learning should be dictated by the learner, that is, they must learn in their own time—this will generally be longer for the older learner. Another general principle which, again, perhaps, has special relevance for the older learner, is to utilize, positively, the knowledge and experience the learner brings to the learning situation.

Social Changes in Old Age

One of the most significant social changes associated with growing old is, of course, retirement. But unlike other life-markers or landmarks, it seems to signal an ending rather than a new beginning.

However, as long as individuals maintain their health and have an adequate income, they can find retirement a satisfying stage of their lives. Barfield and Morgan (1978) asked a number of retired men and their wives how they felt about retirement and their negative responses were usually related to poor health.

Of course, it takes time to adapt to a basically leisure-oriented life, as opposed to a work-oriented one, and still feel important and worthwhile; one of the major criticisms made of compulsory retirement is precisely its 'scrap-heap' connotations, something unknown in Vilcabamba and the Kashmir and Georgian villages discussed earlier. Yet, according to Haynes et al (1978), retirement does not constitute a threat to the psychological health of most people, nor do most people miss their work. And Maddox (1968) concludes that, by and large, the retired regret only their reduced incomes.

According to Stevens-Long (1979), there are three conditions that must be met before the retired can be completely comfortable with their leisure-centred life: (i) they must have enough money to spend on leisure pursuits; (ii) they must develop a new ethic, based on the belief that leisure is as important and valuable as work; and (iii) they must learn to use their time in a new and appropriate way.

One very important change that many old people will experience is the loss of a spouse, their life-partner of up to 60 or 70 years standing. According to Hendricks and Hendricks (1977), most married women will outlive their husbands, so there are many more widows than widowers. More than half the married women in the USA are widowed by their early sixties and 80 per cent by their early seventies. Among people over 65, widows outnumber widowers by 4 to 1.

As well as putting a severe financial strain on the survivor (especially women), the loss of a spouse can also shatter the person's social world and lead to social isolation: 75 per cent of widowed adults also live alone, thus experiencing physical isolation too. Significantly, Gubrium (1974) found that people who had remained single all their lives felt more satisfied in late adulthood than widows or widowers of the same age.

Similarly, Barrett (1978), who studied over 400 people over 62, found that widowers felt more lonely, had a harder time with routine household chores, and were generally less happy with their lives than widows. Widowers were more likely to be emotionally dependent on their spouse and for the running of the house etc. As might be expected from this, widowers are considerably more likely to remarry (and do so sooner) than widows.

Relationships with children also change; children have established their own, independent, lives and parents may make demands for time and assistance that children find difficult, or are reluctant, to meet. Children may also make too many demands themselves or they may seem detached and aloof. But there are important rewards too, especially in the form of grandchildren.

Robertson (1977) found that grandparents can enjoy seeing the grandchildren grow up without having to deal with all the day-to-day problems and responsibilities of child-rearing.

Friendships too are likely to change. Although Lowenthal and Robinson (1977) found that people who had previously led relatively private lives usually continued to so in late adulthood, and that those who had many friends tended to continue their social pattern, Fischer and Fischer (1981) found that, on the whole, social contacts are reduced as we get older.

Again, Perlman et al (1978) reviewed a number of studies showing that relationships with friends remain very important to the elderly and that friends actually play a larger role than relatives in preventing loneliness. Like all other age-groups, the elderly tend to prefer people of their own age.

For many elderly (about 5 per cent in the USA), the last years of their lives are lived out in some kind of residential home. We discussed the effects of institutionalization on intelligence and cognitive abilities earlier in the chapter. At their worst, they can deprive the elderly of independence and dignity; at their best, they can provide the companionship, security and physical comforts which can help them in their task of reviewing and evaluating their life as a whole.

Social Disengagement Theory

A major theory of what happens to us socially as we get older was put forward by Cumming and Henry in *Growing Old—The Process of Disengagement* (1961). Social disengagement refers to the mutual withdrawal of society from the individual (compulsory retirement, children growing up and leaving home and starting families of their own, the death of spouse and friends etc) and of the individual from society (reduced social activities and a more solitary life). The theory also considers that this mutual withdrawal is the most appropriate and successful way to age.

Cumming and Henry also claim that most people, regardless of their attitudes towards retirement before the event, will, in practice, feel fearful and rejected when it actually happens to them. Since our lives usually revolve around our work and colleagues, our social relationships are much more difficult to maintain after retirement. It also becomes more difficult physically to travel in order to see family and friends and so in this way also the number of friends begins to decrease.

The disengaging person retreats from the social world as if preparing for their eventual death and it is a process resulting from both external (economic and social) and internal (physical and developmental) factors; the latter include increased pre-occupation with the self and decreased emotional investment in other people and objects and, to this extent, disengagement is a natural process rather than an imposed one. The older person who has a sense of psychological well-being will usually have attained a new equilibrium characterized by greater psychological distance, altered types of relationships and decreased social interaction.

Cumming and Henry's older subjects often seemed to be less involved with other people than did younger subjects; many seemed to accept or even welcome comparative isolation and this led them to a view of ageing people as naturally and voluntarily withdrawing from too much involvement with others, cutting down on their emotional involvement with others and being satisfied with relatively superficial social contacts.

But is this process of disengagement inevitable? Indeed, is it the one which most accurately describes and accounts for what happens to us when we get older?

Lowenthal and Boler (1965) agreed that a cutting down of social contacts often does take place in old age but questioned how far this was voluntary. Some people, at least, have disengagement forced upon them and when this happens they tend to be unreconciled to it for quite a while. Also, there are some disengaged people who are not the victims of environmental pressures (in particular retirement, death of a spouse and physical illness or disability) and who seem to be quite happy with their withdrawn state.

Activity Theory

The major alternative to Social Disengagement theory is Activity Theory (eg Havighurst, 1964). Except for the inevitable changes in biology and health, older people are the same as middle-aged people with essentially the same psychological and social needs.

Decreased social interaction in old age results from the withdrawal by society from the ageing person and happens against the wishes of most elderly people—so the withdrawal is not mutual, as maintained by social disengagement theory.

Optimal ageing, therefore, involves staying active and managing to resist the 'shrinkage' of the social world by maintaining the activities of middle age for as long as possible and then finding substitutes for work or retirement and for spouse and friends upon their deaths. In particular, it is important for the old person to maintain their 'role count', that is, to ensure that they always have several different roles to play.

Neugarten and Havighurst (1969) found that those elderly people who are socially active and involved with their families and communities are usually the most satisfied with their lives.

However, Havighurst (1968) has also pointed out the shortcomings of the activity theory, in particular, the many exceptions to the rule that the greater the level of activity the greater the degree of satisfaction. By the same token, there are some elderly people who seem satisfied with disengagement and this suggests that activity theory on its own is not an adequate theory of successful ageing. So what else is involved?

Havighurst et al (1964) and Neugarten (1965) see the role of personality as crucial in determining the relationship between levels of activity and life satisfaction; according to Neugarten et al (1972) an individual will select a style of ageing that is best suited to their personality and past experience or lifestyle—there is no single way to age successfully.

Some people may actually develop new interests or pursue in earnest those for which they did not have too much time during their working lives, many will be developing relationships with grandchildren (or even great-grandchildren), some will be re-marrying (or even getting married for the first time) and some will go on working part-time or in a voluntary capacity in their local community.

Social Exchange Theory

Dyson (1980) has criticized both major theories of ageing for not taking sufficient account of the physical and economic factors which might limit the individual's choice of how they age; both theories are, therefore, *prescriptive*, that is, they say what the elderly should be doing during this stage of life rather than accounting for how most people do, in fact, age.

Dyson suggests that a more useful approach is to see the process of adjusting to retirement in particular, and ageing in general, as a sort of contract between the individual and society. Dowd (1975), for instance, proposed that we give up our role as an economically active member of society when we retire but, in exchange, we receive increased leisure time, less responsibility and so on. The contract is, for the most part, unwritten and not enforceable, but most people will probably conform to the expectations of the elderly which are built-in to social institutions and stereotypes.

Perhaps a more valid and useful way of looking at what all elderly people have in common is to look at the psychological importance of old age as a stage of development, albeit the last that we shall go through—indeed, this is precisely where its importance lies. This brings us, almost full circle, to the Personal Growth model, which stresses the advantages and positive aspects of ageing. The original and perhaps still the most influential representative of this view is Erik Erikson. In old age ('maturity') there is a conflict between Ego Integrity (the positive force) on the one hand and Despair (the negative force) on the other and the individual's task is to end the stage, and hence their life, with greater ego integrity than despair. The achievement of this represents, for Erikson, successful ageing.

But as with all the other seven stages, we cannot avoid the conflict which is an unavoidable outcome of biological, psychological and social forces. The important thing is how successfully we resolve it. The task of ageing is to take stock of one's life, to look back over it and assess and evaluate how worthwhile and fulfilling it has been.

What exactly does Erikson mean by ego integrity?

a)   The conviction that, in the long-term view, life does have a purpose and a meaning and does make sense;
b)   The conclusion that, within the context of one's life as a whole, what happened was somehow inevitable and could only have happened when and how it did;
c)   The belief that all life's experiences offer something of value, ie there is something to be learned from everything that happens to us, including the bad times. Looking back, we are able to see how we have grown psychologically as a result of life's ups and downs, triumphs and failures, calm and crisis;
d)   Coming to see our own parents in a new light and being able to understand them better because we have lived through our own adulthood and probably have raised children of our own;
e)   Coming to see that what we share with all other human beings, past, present and future, is the inevitable cycle of birth and death. Whatever the differences, historically, culturally, economically etc, all human beings have this much in common; in the light of this, 'death loses its sting'.

Lack or loss of this ego integrity is signified by a fear of death, which is the most conspicuous symptom of despair; despair expresses the feeling that it is too late to undo the past, to put back the clock, in order to do what one has omitted to do or to put right the wrongs. Life is almost over and it is the only chance you get! This despair is, in fact, a form of basic mistrust, a fear of the unknown which follows death. (This mistrust is also the negative component of the conflict involved in infancy, the first of Erikson's Eight Ages of Man, and so here is an important link between infancy and old age within Erikson's psychosocial theory, see Chapter 26.)

According to Butler (1963), much of the reminiscing common in later life may be a valuable way of 'sorting out' the past and the present. Prompted by the recognition of impending death, the elderly re-examine old conflicts, consider how they have treated others and come to some conclusions about themselves and their lives. This 'life review' may result in a new sense of accomplishment, satisfaction and peace (equivalent to Erikson's ego integrity).

Boylin et al (1976) found that people who reminisced often were better adjusted (on a measure based on Erikson's theory) than those who did less reminiscing. But, of course, the life review can also lead to a sense of self-hate and despair.

Neugarten (1976) observed that as we grow older we show increased 'interiority', that is, greater concern with our inner life, introspection and conscious re-appraisal: 'life is restructured in terms of time left to live rather than time since birth,' and we become aware of death as, 'a real possibility for the self; it is no longer the magical or extraordinary occurrence that it appears to us to be in our youth.'

The transition to old age is not always easy but many people cope with major life-changes without undue stress. Barfield and Morgan (1970) found that 70 per cent of men who retired as planned were content with their new status compared with less than 20 per cent who had retired unexpectedly, due to redundancy or ill-health.

Similarly, Lieberman and Caplan (1970) reported that those elderly people living in familiar and stable surroundings were less afraid of dying than those about to be admitted to a residential home. So long as the expected rhythm of the life cycle is not disrupted too much or too suddenly, most adults cope successfully with life, even in its final stages.

Some individuals review their lives privately or internally, others share their memories and reflections with others. For the latter, this serves a double purpose: (i) it helps them to organize a final perspective on their lives for themselves; (ii) it leaves a record that will live on with others after their death.

Clearly, however we may go about it, one task of life, especially during our 'twilight years', is to prepare for death.

Bereavement, Grief and Mourning

Preparing for our own death may be a major development task of old age, but another feature of growing old is that it becomes increasingly likely that we will suffer the loss, through death, of loved ones, parents, husbands and wives, siblings and friends.

Suffering such losses is referred to as bereavement, while grief is the complex set of psychological and bodily reactions commonly found in people who suffer bereavement. Parkes and Weiss (1983) define grief as, 'a normal reaction to overwhelming loss, albeit a reaction in which normal functioning no longer holds'; they distinguish between grief and mourning, the latter being the, 'observable expression of grief'. (Mourning is also used in a different sense to refer to the social customs and conventions surrounding death, such as funerals, wearing dark clothes, cancelling social engagements and so on; we talk about a 'period of mourning' in which grieving is 'official' and largely public.) What constitutes a normal pattern of grieving?

A number of writers (including Freud, Engel and Parkes) have described the characteristic stages or phases of the grieving process. Engel (1962), for example, uses the concept of *grief work* to refer to the process of mourning through which a bereaved person readjusts to their loss and it comprises three phases:

i) Disbelief and shock, the initial reaction to the loss, which can last for up to a few days and involves the refusal to accept the truth of what has happened.

ii) Developing awareness, the gradual realization and acknowledgement of what has happened, often accompanied by pangs of grief and guilt. Apathy, exhaustion and anger are also common, the last being closely related to self-blame and guilt and at this time it is important that there are people around who are willing simply to listen and tolerate the expression of all these feelings.

iii) Resolution, which involves the establishment of a new identity, the full acceptance of what has happened, and marks the completion of grief work. The bereaved person takes a realistic view of their situation and resolves to cope without the loved one and begin a new life.

All grief theorists agree that grief must be worked through—there is some sort of natural progression and blending of feelings which must be experienced if a healthy adjustment to the loss is to be achieved.

However, some prefer to talk about *components* of *grief* instead of stages; the latter implies a clear-cut, orderly, pre-determined set of events which is the same for everyone. Yet this is not the case—the 'stages' are not separate, may not be successive and it is not certain that everyone has to experience each and every one of them.

Ramsay and de Groot (1977) describe nine components, some of which tend to appear earlier in the grief process, some of which come later (see Table 24.1 overleaf).

Parkes (1965), in a study of a number of bereaved people who needed psychiatric treatment, found that one-quarter showed considerable animosity towards the doctor or clergy, making wild accusations of neglect or incompetence which were usually quite unjustified.

In a later study (1970), Parkes reported that most widows experiencing apparently normal reactions to bereavement had periods of irritability and bitterness, tending to blame others, God and sometimes the deceased themselves.

Marris (1958) interviewed widows and found that many spoke of feeling that their husbands were still present; about half a sample of bereaved psychiatric patients had a similar impression (Parkes, 1962). Similarly, Rees (1971) reported that 1 in 8 widows and widowers had hallucinations of hearing their dead spouse speak and a similar proportion claimed to have seen the deceased. They also referred to this general sensation of the presence of the dead person, which could continue for years, and they found it helped them; significantly, it was reported more often by those who had been happily married.

Normal and Abnormal Grieving

One problem involved in trying to distinguish normal from abnormal or pathological grief is the enormous variation in the grieving patterns of different individuals (even though the components may be similar). As far as the duration of grieving is concerned, Hinton (1975) claims that the more

Table 24.1   Ramsay and de Groot's 9 components of grief

1. *Shock*	Usually the first response, most often described as a feeling of 'numbness'. However, feelings can include pain or calm, apathy, depersonalization and derealization. It is as if the feelings are so strong that they are 'turned off' and this can last from a few seconds to several weeks.
2. *Disorganization*	The bereaved person may be unable to do the simplest thing or, alternatively, may be able to organize the entire funeral—and then collapses.
3. *Denial*	Usually an early feature of grief but this defence against feeling too much pain at once may recur at any time throughout the entire process. A common form of denial is searching behaviour, eg waiting for the deceased to come home, looking for them in the street and having hallucinations of seeing or hearing them. In denial, the bereaved behaves as if the deceased were still alive.
4. *Depression*	Emerges as the denial breaks down and can also occur throughout the entire grieving process but it tends to become less frequent and intense. Two forms of this are: (i) 'desolate pining', an active feeling of yearning and longing, an emptiness 'interspersed with waves of intense psychic pain', and (ii) 'despair', a feeling of helplessness and hopelessness, the blackness of the realization of powerlessness to bring back the dead.
5. *Guilt*	Can be both real and imagined, for actual neglect of the deceased when they were still alive or for angry thoughts or feelings.
6. *Anxiety*	May take the form of fear of losing control of one's feelings, of going mad, or more general apprehension about the future (changed roles, increased responsibilities, financial worries, etc).
7. *Aggression*	Can range from irritability towards family and friends to outbursts of anger towards God or fate, doctors and nurses, the clergy or even the person who has died.
8. *Resolution*	As the emotions die down, an acceptance of the death emerges; a 'taking leave of the dead and an acceptance that life must go on'.
9. *Re-integration*	Acceptance is put into practice and the bereaved reorganizes their life in which the dead person has no place. (However, pining and despair and other components may re-appear on occasions, eg anniversaries, birthdays, etc).

severe mental pain will have largely eased within one, two or perhaps a few more weeks and that it is generally assumed that the grief will have largely abated within six months.

However, Marris (1958) found that a majority of the widows he studied were still distressed one year later and Maddison and Viola (1968) reported that 20 to 30 per cent of a sample of American and Australian widows were experiencing some psychological or physical ill-health a year after their husband's death (compared with 7 per cent of a sample of women whose husbands were still living).

Parkes (1965) believes that prolonged, incapacitating grief ('chronic grief') is the commonest variant of the usual pattern of grieving and later reported that people who at first do not show their grief may later show this disturbed, chronic, form of mourning (Parkes, 1970).

What are some of the other abnormal patterns of grieving?

Hinton (1975) identifies three: (i) exaggeration of the numbness associated with the shock of the loss; (ii) shading of some of the more immediate responses into neurotic forms of emotional distress; and (iii) the appearance of physical symptoms, sometimes merely accompanying, sometimes over-shadowing, the emotional disturbance.

Looking at these in more detail:

(i) Some bereaved people continue going about their everyday business for many days or even weeks as if the fact of the loss had never really registered. If it does lie hidden for a while, it may finally erupt some weeks later or may appear on a much later but emotionally salient occasion, such as the anniversary of the death or the dead person's birthday. There is also some evidence that a psychological illness is likely to develop when a person reaches, for example, the age at which their parent died or when their own child reaches the age at which they themselves suffered a bereavement (Hilgard and Newman, 1959), and it is also quite common for people to experience anxiety about not living beyond the age at which one of their parents died.

(ii) According to Parkes (1970), occasional feelings of panic are so common-place that it could be considered a normal reaction. Other illogical fears may include being alone, claustrophobia, dirt and death. Roth (1959) described depersonalization among the bereaved, a sense of being unreal or unfamiliar to oneself. Obsessions also may become more likely.

(iii) Fatigue, insomnia, loss of appetite, weight loss, headaches, breathless-ness, palpitations, blurred vision and exhaustion are among the many physical symptoms of which widows complain to their doctors. Parkes (1964) found that widows needed to consult their GPs much more often than usual during the first six months of widowhood, both for physical and psychological symptoms, and this has been confirmed by Clayton et al (1968) and Maddison and Viola (1968).

Stern et al (1951) found that elderly people who suffer bereavement are especially likely to experience their distress as predominantly physical.

Widows and widowers, for some time after the death of their spouse, in fact run a greater risk of suffering serious illness and themselves dying than married people of similar age, with widowers being at a relatively greater risk (eg Cox and Ford, 1964).

Rees and Lutkins (1967) reported a ten-fold increase in mortality among a Welsh sample of widows and widowers during the year following their loss. Parkes et al (1969) believe this risk is largely confined to the first six months after the bereavement and identify three main factors that are responsible: (a) self-neglect; (b) suicide; and (c) cardiac disease ('broken heart') and (in the case of widowers) death through a disease similar to that of the wife.

Interestingly, it is younger adults (up to their mid thirties), especially men, who are most at risk (eg Kraus and Lilienfield, 1959).

The Causes of Pathological Grief

According to Parkes and Weiss (1983) most of the psychological symptoms that bring the bereaved into the care of their doctors can be seen as distortions or exaggerations of the normal process of grieving and this leads us to look more closely at the day-to-day factors which normally influence the course of grief. Given the range of individual differences in the intensity, duration and pattern of grieving, and that most of these variations are within the range of normality, it may well be that the pathological variations are simply the extreme responses to particularly unfavourable circumstances.

Parkes and Weiss identify two main groups of factors which are likely to complicate the course of the grieving process: (i) those which discourage the *expression* of grief; and (ii) those which discourage the *ending* of grief.

i) The mode of death is of particular importance; a sudden and untimely death will produce greater shock and set in motion more psychological defences (which probably explains why younger widows and widowers are especially susceptible). Volkan (1970) found that of 23 psychiatric patients suffering 'pathological grief', *all* had experienced the death as sudden, either because it actually was or because they were unprepared for it for other reasons.

   The immediate family may encourage or discourage the bereaved to express or inhibit their grief, and society at large may also influence grieving through religious and other rituals (eg Maddison and Walker, 1967).

   Parkes (1970) describes seven widows who expressed very little distress during the first week of bereavement, did not wear mourning dress and failed to visit their husband's grave; they were significantly more distressed three months later than 18 other widows who had expressed grief and mourned actively from the start.

ii) Grief is not only a psychological reaction to bereavement but a duty to the dead; some may feel that to engage in perpetual mourning is a tribute to the dead. It may also be a way of making restitution for some failure or neglect of the dead.

Parkes (1962), in a study of 98 bereaved psychiatric patients, found that 21 per cent of those whose illness was evidently a pathological form of grief had mixed feelings of fondness and hostility towards the deceased, compared with

6 per cent of those who showed little evidence of problematic grief at the time of admission. Parkes also found a high incidence of previous depressive illness among the bereaved psychiatric patients, and Wahl (1970) noted that bereavement may aggravate pre-existing neurotic problems.

Family and friends may put pressure on the bereaved to come out of mourning, even though grieving continues, and some may fear social ostracism if they continue to be seen as 'in mourning' and so conceal their grief.

Finally, the more unsatisfactory the relationship with the deceased while they were alive, the more disturbed the grieving process will be; as Krupp (1962) puts it, 'if one can learn how to live with the living, then one can manage to live with the dead'.

25

Personality (1) Psychometric and Other Non-psychodynamic Approaches

Introduction

As we saw in Chapter 1, 'personality' is one of those terms which, while commonly used in everyday language, has been given a special technical meaning by psychologists, which is why, in any psychological discussion, it makes no sense to say that a person has 'lots of personality'.

We also saw in Chapter 1 that 'personality' is a hypothetical construct, something which cannot be directly observed but only inferred from behaviour in order to make sense of it.

In Chapter 8 we discussed the ways in which our perception of other people (and, to that extent, our interaction with them) is influenced by 'implicit personality theories', in particular, stereotypes, our beliefs about which characteristics or traits tend to cluster together in individuals. If, indeed, we predict how someone is going to behave on the basis of what we believe they are like, and if our behaviour towards that person is likewise influenced, then this suggests that personality is not merely an abstraction which helps to explain an individual's behaviour in isolation but a concept which has real meaning in the context of interpersonal behaviour.

Another interesting connection with other topics is that of Self-concept. You will remember from Chapter 9 that one of the major categories to emerge from studies of people's self-image is personality traits and we also saw how important the reaction of others and comparison with others are in the development of the self-concept. To this extent, personality is not something a person 'has' (it is not a 'thing') but rather is to do with *how* we relate to other people and generally deal with the world.

One definition of personality which makes this point quite explicit is that of Goodstein and Lanyon (1975): personality is, 'the enduring characteristics of the person that are significant for interpersonal behaviour'.

The Place of Personality in Psychology as a Whole

The study of personality is, probably, what many potential students of psychology imagine the subject to be about and, to a certain extent, they are right: personality does enter into other topic areas (as we have noted above), some of the major theoretical schools of psychology (in particular, psychoanalytical theories) are mainly concerned with personality, and the largest single group of psychologists are clinical psychologists whose work brings them into contact with a wide range of personalities, many of which are regarded as abnormal or pathological (see Chapter 28).

Fontana (1982) goes so far as to claim that, 'of all the areas of psychology, the study of personality is the most important', although many would disagree. However, even if we did accept Fontana's claim, it would still be true that personality is conceptualized and studied in a variety of different ways according to the persuasion of the psychologist and, because of this diversity, two chapters are devoted to the topic; here we shall discuss some of the general theoretical and methodological issues relating to the study of personality as well as the theories of Eysenck, Cattell, Kelly and Maslow, and Chapter 26 will be devoted to discussion of the psychoanalytic theories of Freud, Jung, Adler and Erikson.

How Do Theories of Personality Differ?

Because of the diversity of theories, it is virtually impossible to find a definition which all psychologists would accept. However, if our aim is to highlight some of the dimensions along which different theories differ, then a useful definition of personality would be:

> . . . those relatively stable and enduring aspects of an individual which distinguish them from other people, making them unique, but which at the same time permit a comparison between individuals (see Chapter 1).

The definition brings into focus two central issues: (i) is personality enduring and permanent? And (ii) is the study of personality the study of unique individuals or is it aimed at comparing individuals and discovering the factors which constitute personality in general? (See Table 25.1 overleaf.)

i) Those psychologists who answer 'yes' to the first question and who are interested in personality in general belong to the *psychometric* tradition and are known as *type* and *trait* theorists. They make great use of personality questionnaires and the results from these are analysed using a statistical technique called *Factor Analysis*. In trying to establish factors in terms of which everyone can be compared, they adopt a *nomothetic* approach and the major figures are H. J. Eysenck and R. B. Cattell. (See Chapter 2.)

ii) Those who believe in the uniqueness of every individual represent the *idiographic* approach, but beyond this it is not easy to say what else they have in common; for example, they may or may not see personality as permanent or may differ as to how much or what kind of change is possible. G. Allport is probably the most ardent advocate of the idiographic approach, although,

Table 25.1 A classification of personality theories

	Behaviour seen as consistent due to enduring personality traits/personality change unlikely or impossible	Behaviour seen as variable due to the influence of situational factors/personality change is possible
Nomothetic	←———————— *Psychoanalytical theories* ——————————→ eg Freud, Jung, Adler and Erikson	
	Type and Trait Theories eg Eysenck and Cattell	
		'Situationalism' eg Mischel
	Interaction-ism — eg Mischel and Endler	
Idiographic	*Allport's Trait Theory*	*Humanistic theories* eg Rogers and Maslow
	←———————— *Kelly's Personal Construct Theory* ——————————→	

ironically, he puts forward a trait theory of personality (but one that is very different from that of Cattell, for example).

G. Kelly's Personal Construct Theory is perhaps the most radical of all in so far as it is not so much a theory of personality as a total psychology; according to Fransella (1981), 'Kelly sought to incorporate within the same theoretical framework those areas in psychology usually coming under separate chapter headings' (learning, cognition, motivation, emotion, psychophysiology) and, to this extent, the theory provides a total psychology about the total person.

The other major representatives of the idiographic approach are the Humanistic psychologists, in particular A. Maslow and C. Rogers; we looked at Rogers' Self-Theory in detail in Chapter 9.

What they share is a concern for those characteristics of people which make us distinctively human, including our experience of ourselves as persons.

The kinds of methods used include case studies, biographical studies, rating scales, the Rep Grid (developed by Kelly) and the Q-Sort, developed by Stephenson in 1953 and used extensively by Rogers in his study of the effects on the self-concept of his client-centred therapy (see Chapters 9 and 29). The Rep Grid is also used to evaluate the progress of therapy (see Chapter 29).

iii) The psychoanalytical theories of Freud, Jung, Adler and Erikson are clearly idiographic in that they are based on case studies of patients in the clinical context of psychotherapy and they are not attempting to measure personality in any sense. However, they are concerned with the nature of personality in general, and Freud and Jung especially are also trying to account for individual differences; it was Jung, for example, who first distinguished between introverts and extroverts, which Eysenck later investigated in depth and measured in his personality questionnaires.

As far as the enduring nature of personality is concerned, the psychoanalytic theorists all allow for the possibility of change, primarily through psycho-therapy, although at any point in time behaviour is essentially the reflection of a person's characteristics and habitual ways of dealing with the world. Chapter 26 is devoted to these four major theorists.

The Nomothetic versus Idiographic Approach: Individual Differences or Unique Individuals?

According to Kluckhohn and Murray (1953), 'every man is in certain respects like all other men, like some other men and like no other men'. What we have in common with all other human beings is the subject-matter of experimental or 'general' psychology, which studies cognitive and physiological processes and learning; much of developmental and social psychology too are concerned with discovering 'universal norms' which apply equally to all individuals.

What we have in common with some other human beings is that which the area of psychology known as individual differences (or differential psychology) has traditionally concentrated on; personality differences represent one kind of 'group norm', others being age, gender, ethnic and cultural background and intelligence. It is the study of 'how and how much a particular individual is similar to or differs from others' (Shackleton and Fletcher, 1984) which constitutes the factor-analytic/psychometric approach; as we have seen, this is also a nomothetic approach.

Finally, what we have in common with no other human beings is what makes us unique and, of course, this is an expression of the idiographic approach which attempts to discover 'idiosyncratic norms'.

Allport's Trait Theory (1961)

Allport and Odbert (1936) found over 18,000 terms describing personal characteristics and, even after omitting evaluative terms and transient states, there remained between four and five thousand. Allport believed that this large number of trait words could be reduced further, in fact, to two basic kinds:

i) *Common traits*—These are basic modes of adjustment which are applicable to all members of a particular cultural, ethnic or linguistic background. For instance, since we must all interact in a competitive world, we must each develop our own most suitable level of aggression and each of us can be placed somewhere along a scale of aggressiveness.

ii) *Individual traits*—These are a unique set of personal dispositions based on unique life experiences and are unique ways of organizing the world; they are *not* dimensions which can be applied to all people. They cannot be measured by a standardized test and can be discovered only by careful and detailed study of individuals.

Individual traits can take one of three forms:

a) *Cardinal traits*—These are so all-pervading that almost all of an individual's behaviour is dictated and directed by their cardinal trait, for instance, someone who is consumed by greed, ambition or lust. However, such traits are quite rare and most people do not have one, predominant, trait.

b) *Central traits*—These are the basic building-blocks which make up the core of personality and which constitute the individual's characteristic ways of dealing with the world (eg honest, loving, happy-go-lucky). Usually, a surprisingly small number of these is sufficient to capture the essence of a person.

c) *Secondary traits*—These are less consistent and less influential than central traits and refer to tastes, preferences, political persuasions, reactions to particular situations and so on.

Clearly, common traits are the subject-matter of the nomothetic approach and individual traits the subject matter of the idiographic approach.

Allport believed that the unique individual cannot be studied scientifically, since science deals with the general (see Chapter 2); the nomothetic approach, for example, ignores the 'novelty' that results from an interaction of an individual's traits and an individual cannot be reduced to a combination of numerous, unrelated, attributes. However, are the idiographic and nomothetic approaches necessarily opposed in this way?

In terms of Popper's (1945) distinction between the descriptive sciences (which include history and biography) and the generalizing sciences (which include the natural sciences), Allport's argument does not appear to be valid; only if *all* science were of the generalizing kind would the study of the individual *per se* be inconsistent with scientific methods. According to Kirby and Radford (1976), Allport was engaged in a different activity from the study of 'individual differences', which, as Bannister and Fransella (1971) correctly point out in their criticism of the nomothetic approach, is, in fact, the study of 'group sameness'; Allport was concerned with 'idiography' or 'idiodynamics', as Rosenzweig (1958) termed the study of individual norms.

Perhaps a more incisive criticism is that of Holt (1962) who argues that the idiographic–nomothetic issue is based on a false dichotomy: all description involves some degree of generalization, so that to imagine that we can describe an individual in terms which make no reference to any other individual is a fallacy. To describe a person *as* a person, we must use descriptive terms which apply to others as well, hence, in principle, assimilating the individual to the general. As Kirby and Radford (1976) argue, a 'truly unique individual would be incomprehensible, in fact not recognizable as an individual'.

Holt also argues that Allport's so-called idiographic methods are just more or less nomothetic ones applied to individual cases, and Kline (1981) believes that the existence of personality scales or questionnaires is not incompatible with the notion of uniqueness; in any one sample individuals will have very different profiles across a range of scales, but this does not mean that they will not share certain characteristics or groups of characteristics in common with other members of the sample.

Behaviour—Is it the Product of Personality or the Situation, or Both?

Most definitions of traits focus on their stability and permanency which, in turn, implies that an individual's behaviour is *consistent* over time and from one situation to another. Guilford (1959), for example, defined a trait as, 'any relatively enduring way in which one individual differs from another' and Hall and Lindzey (1957) defined it, 'as a determining tendency or predisposition to respond'.

When discussing the attribution process (Chapter 8) we noted that there is a tendency to attribute other people's behaviour primarily to their dispositional qualities (including personality traits) as opposed to situational factors (Fundamental Attribution Error) while we tend to see our own behaviour primarily as a response to the situation (Actor-Observer Effect). It follows from this that we are likely to regard the behaviour of others as more consistent (and, hence, more predictable) and to regard our own as more variable from situation to situation (and, hence, less predictable).

Seeing behaviour as primarily caused by personality traits (the *trait approach*) is usually opposed to what has become known as *situationalism* (Mischel, 1968), the view that behaviour is largely determined by situational factors.

Mischel, a social learning theorist (see Chapters 3 and 21), wrote a book in 1968 called *Personality and Assessment*, in which he threw doubt on the validity of the trait approach by reviewing a large number of studies which showed that correlations between scores on personality tests and measures of behaviour in various situations rarely exceeded 0.3. This lack of cross-situation consistency was taken by Mischel to indicate the importance of the situation in determining behaviour; for example, if people have been reinforced for behaving in particular ways in particular kinds of situation, or if different kinds of models have been available, then we would expect people to behave differently in different situations and there is no longer any need to appeal to traits since they are used to account for consistency which Mischel believed is lacking.

However, intuitively there seems to be something wrong with situationalism, at least in its extreme form; surely different people behave differently even within the same situation and, conversely, are we not recognizably the *same* person from one situation to another?

Eysenck and Eysenck (1980) and Kline (1983) cite a number of studies which demonstrate consistency between scores on questionnaires and rating scales on the one hand and behaviour on the other, with average correlations of around 0.8 and Bowers (1973) criticized the social learning theorists for favouring an experimental design which is intended to emphasize the role of situational determinants of behaviour (situation-specificity) relative to behavioural consistency or stability.

A number of writers have pointed out that to regard behaviour as being caused *either* by situational factors *or* by personality traits is an oversimplification of a complex issue. Bowers (1973), Endler (1975) and Pervin and Lewis (1978) all advocate an *interactionist* position, which stresses the mutual influence of situational and dispositional variables.

Bowers, for instance, reviewed 11 studies covering a wide range of behaviour including aggression in young boys, anxiety in students and resistance to temptation in children and concluded that 13 per cent of the variance in subjects' behaviour was due to *person* variables, 10 per cent to *situational* variables and 20 per cent to an *interaction* between the two.

Mischel has himself moved towards a more interactionist position (eg,

1973) but prefers to talk about 'person' variables (as we saw in Chapter 21) as opposed to traits, the former being more cognitive, the latter being more related to temperament. Mischel believes that the 'same' situation can have different meaning for different individuals, depending on past learning experiences; this determines how we select, evaluate and interpret stimuli and, in turn, how particular stimuli will affect behaviour. It follows that situational factors cannot account adequately for human behaviour on their own since they do not exist *objectively*, independently of the actor; based on a study of children's ability to resist temptation when looking at attractive sweets, Mischel concluded that, 'the results clearly show that what is in the children's heads—not what is physically in front of them—determines their ability to delay' (Mischel, 1973).

Bem and Allen (1974), while recognizing the validity of Mischel's criticisms of trait theory, also stressed the considerable importance of trait theory. They argued that our intuitions are not entirely wrong—each person will show consistent behaviour as far as a few traits are concerned but which traits they are will vary from person to person.

Students were asked to rate themselves on their consistency of 'friendliness' and 'conscientiousness' and for each trait they were divided into two groups, one which rated themselves as consistent and one which rated themselves as quite inconsistent. These self-ratings were then compared with ratings from subjects' parents and friends and with the ratings of two independent observers who rated their behaviour in group discussions and other situations.

The crucial finding was that subjects who rated themselves as consistent on one or other trait were also rated as being consistent by others on that trait (for instance, for friendliness, the correlation was 0.73) while those who described themselves as inconsistent were rated in this way by others too (0.3).

Not only were subjects quite accurate in assessing their own behaviour, but subjects who showed consistency on one trait were not necessarily consistent on the other, showing that people vary in their consistency on different traits. As Hilgard et al (1979) point out, if a random selection of subjects is taken in an attempt to demonstrate high cross-situational consistency (as would be predicted by a trait theorist), this is bound to fail, because some subjects will be highly consistent on that trait while others will be low on consistency. (We should also note that those traits on which individuals rate themselves as consistent—and on which they are consistent as rated by others—are likely to be an important part of their self-image and, in Allport's terms, are likely to be central traits.)

Bem and Allen (1974) conclude that we must take internal and external forces into account, the former including the person's perception of the situation. Similarly, Kenrick and Stringfield (1980) argue that in order to predict behaviour we must assess people *and* situations, since what is taken to be subjects' behavioural inconsistency may be due as much to the investigator's ignorance of how they perceive or construe situations as to their ratings on particular traits.

Finally, Smith et al (1982) define personality itself as, 'an organization of characteristics that functions in a certain way and interacts with the environment', making explicit the reciprocal relationship between the person and the situation.

The Type and Trait Approach—Eysenck and Cattell

To understand the similarities and differences between these two psychometric theorists, we need to say something about Factor Analysis (FA) which is an essential part of this approach.

The Use of Factor Analysis

Factor analysis is a statistical technique, based on correlation, which attempts to reduce a large amount of data (scores on personality questionnaires, objective tests and other measuring devices) to a much smaller amount. Essentially, the aim is to discover which test items correlate with one another and which do not and then to identify the resulting correlation clusters (or factors); put another way, what is the smallest number of factors which can adequately account for the variance between subjects on the measures in question?

Assuming that the tests are 'good' tests, the researcher is trying to discover the fundamental components of personality which apply to everyone and in terms of which everyone can be compared; as measured by the tests, individuals will differ in the degree to which they display these components. But what is meant by a good test?

a) A good test should have *discriminatory power*, that is, it should produce a wide distribution of scores;

b) A good test should be properly *standardized*, that is, it should have been tried out with a large, representative, sample of the population for whom the test is intended so that the resulting norms (typical scores or distribution for those groups) can be legitimately used when assessing an individual's score;

c) A good test should be *reliable*, that is, it should consistently measure the variable it measures;

d) A good test should be *valid*, that is, it should actually measure what it claims to measure. (These are discussed further in relation to intelligence tests, see Chapter 27.)

Just as there are different kinds of reliability and validity, so there are different kinds of FA. One of the most important distinctions is between *orthogonal* and *oblique* methods: an *orthogonal* method aims to identify a small number of powerful factors which are independent of each other (uncorrelated), and this is the method preferred by Eysenck; while an *oblique* method aims to identify a larger number of less powerful factors which are not independent (ie they are correlated to some degree), and this is the method preferred by Cattell.

Since it is possible to carry out a further FA of oblique factors, they are referred to as *first-order factors* and the resulting re-grouping of the oblique factors as *second-order factors*; in fact, Cattell has discovered a small number of second-order factors which correspond closely to Eysenck's three major second-order factors (see below).

Eysenck's second-order factors are referred to as *types* (what Cattell calls Surface Traits) and Cattell's first-order factors as *traits* (what Cattell calls

Table 25.2 Differences between Eysenck and Cattell regarding factor analysis

	Eysenck	*Cattell*
Preferred method of Factor Analysis	Orthogonal	Oblique
Level of analysis	Second order	First order
Description of Factors	Types ('Surface Traits')	Traits ('Source Traits')

Source Traits). The differences between the two theorists are summarized in Table 25.2.

What is it that determines which method is chosen by a particular researcher? Is one superior to the other?

Ultimately, the method used depends on the taste or preference of the researchers; both Cattell and Eysenck believe that their method is the one which best reflects the psychological reality of personality, and there is no objective way of establishing that one is right and the other wrong.

Because there is an infinite number of possible solutions, Heim (1975) believes that FA should not be used at all. However, Thurstone (1947) had argued that rotation to simple structure could overcome this difficulty and Cattell (1966) and Cattell and Kline (1977) support this view. Simple structure means that each factor will have a few high loadings (ie correlate quite highly with a few other factors) and a large number of low or nil loadings (very little or no correlation with a large number of factors), making each factor simple to interpret; the rationale behind simple structure is the law of parsimony, the most economical solution to the problem. As Kline (1981) suggests, if each FA solution is regarded as a hypothesis accounting for the correlations, the most simple is to be preferred. Cattell argues that an orthogonal technique prevents the attainment of simple structure.

Guilford (1959), on the other hand, believes that a set of uncorrelated factors is more simple than a set of oblique or correlated ones, which is why Eysenck opts for an orthogonal technique.

According to Kline (1981), most factor analysts, in practice, prefer oblique factors.

Eysenck's Type Theory

The use of the term 'type' (since it is based on second-order FA) to describe Eysenck's theory is, in fact, a misnomer, since he proposes major *dimensions* of personality which represent continuums along which everyone can be placed; by contrast, a true type theory places people in categories so that any individual can only belong to one or another.

One of the earliest type theories (and, indeed, one of the first theories of personality of any kind) was Galen's theory of the four Humours (put forward in the second century AD); these are included in the inner circle of Eysenck's diagram shown in Figure 25.1.

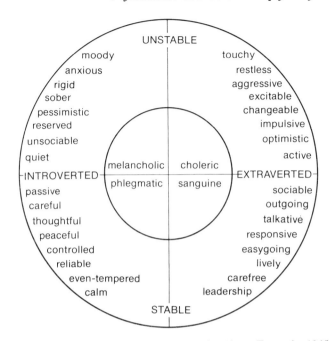

Figure 25.1 Dimensions of personality (from Eysenck, 1965)

Eysenck's dimensions in fact constitute the highest level of a *hierarchy* (Cattell's 'surface' traits) with a number of traits at the next level down (Cattell's 'source' traits), and below that a set of habitual responses (typical ways of behaving) linked to a particular trait. At the lowest level is a specific response (a response on one particular occasion). (See Figure 25.2.) This hierarchical model is similar to Vernon's 1950 model of intelligence, to which Eysenck would subscribe—see Chapter 27.

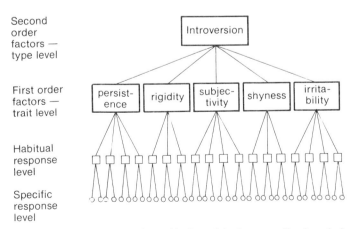

Figure 25.2 Eysenck's hierarchical model of personality in relation to the introversion dimension (after Eysenck, 1953)

Introversion–Extroversion, Neuroticism and Psychoticism

Eysenck (1947) factor analysed 39 items of personal data for each of 700 neurotic soldiers, screening them for brain damage and physical illness; the items included personality ratings. Two orthogonal (uncorrelated) factors emerged, Introversion–Extroversion (E) and Neuroticism or Emotionality–Stability (N). These two dimensions are assumed to be normally distributed, so that most people will score somewhere in the middle of the scale and very few at either extreme. The following descriptions are of 'typical' introverts and extroverts, and are 'idealized extremes':

> The typical introvert is a quiet, retiring sort of person, introspective, fond of books rather than people; he is reserved and distant except to intimate friends. He tends to plan ahead, 'looks before he leaps' and distrusts the impulse of the moment. He does not like excitement, takes matters of everyday life with proper seriousness, and likes a well-ordered mode of life. He keeps his feelings under close control, seldom behaves in an aggressive manner, and does not lose his temper easily. He is reliable, somewhat pessimistic, and places great importance on ethical standards.

> The typical extrovert is sociable, likes parties, has many friends, needs to have people to talk to, and does not like reading or studying by himself. He craves excitement, takes chances, often sticks his neck out, acts on the spur of the moment, and is generally an impulsive individual. He is fond of practical jokes, always has a ready answer, and generally likes change; he is carefree, easy-going, optimistic and likes to 'laugh and be merry'. He prefers to keep moving and doing things, tends to be aggressive and lose his temper quickly; altogether his feelings are not kept under tight control, and he is not always a reliable person. (Eysenck, 1965.)

As regards Neuroticism, the typical high N scorer could be described as:

> . . . an anxious, worrying individual, moody and frequently depressed; he is likely to sleep badly and to suffer from various psychosomatic disorders. He is overly emotional, reacting too strongly to all sorts of stimuli and finds it difficult to get back on an even keel after each emotionally arousing experience.

By contrast, the stable individual 'tends to respond emotionally only slowly and generally weakly and to return to baseline quickly after emotional arousal; he is usually calm, even-tempered, controlled and unworried.' (Eysenck, 1965.)

Since the original 1947 study, the existence of E and N has been supported by further research involving literally thousands of subjects.

In 1952, a study of psychiatric patients uncovered a third dimension, Psychoticism (P), also unrelated to E and N. Although P is less well-established than the other two dimensions, Eysenck (1975) offers the following description:

> A high scorer, then, may be described as being solitary, not caring for people; he is often troublesome, not fitting in anywhere. He may be cruel and inhumane, lacking in feelings and empathy, and altogether insensitive. He is hostile to others, even his own kith and kin, and aggressive, even to loved ones. He has

a liking for odd and unusual things, and a disregard for danger; he likes to make fools of other people, and to upset them. (Eysenck and Eysenck, 1975.)

Unlike E and N, P is not normally distributed—both normals and neurotics score low on P. Eysenck also believes that P overlaps with (other) psychiatric labels, in particular, 'schizoid', 'psychopathic', and 'behaviour disorders' (see Chapter 28). However, there is only a *quantitative* difference between normals and psychotics (and this applies equally to differences between normals and neurotics).

Personality Questionnaires

How 'good' are they?

The original questionnaire was the Maudsley Medical Questionnaire (MMQ), first used in 1952, which only measured N; this was replaced in 1959 by the Maudsley Personality Inventory (MPI) which measured both E and N. The Eysenck Personality Inventory (EPI) added a Lie Scale, which measures a person's tendency to give socially-desirable answers and which Eysenck believes is a stable personality dimension (Eysenck and Eysenck, 1964); and finally, the Eysenck Personality Questionnaire added a P scale (Eysenck and Eysenck, 1975). There are also junior versions of these questionnaires for use with nine-year-olds and over.

The scales all comprise items of a 'yes/no' variety. They are essentially intended as research tools (as opposed to diagnostic tools for use in clinical settings) and, as such, they are generally regarded as acceptable, reliable and valid (eg Kline, 1981, Shackleton and Fletcher, 1984), the main exception being the P scale which Eysenck himself admits is psychometrically inferior to other scales.

An important way in which Eysenck has attempted to validate his scales is through *Criterion analysis*. This involves giving the questionnaires to groups of individuals who are known to differ on the dimensions in question; for example, although the test is not meant to diagnose neurosis, we would still expect diagnosed neurotics to score very high on N compared with non-neurotics, and generally this is found to be the case. Eysenck also believes that criterion analysis overcomes the problem of the arbitrary nature of the labels given to the factors that emerge from FA (see Chapter 27).

The Biological Basis of Personality

Eysenck's theory attempts to explain personality differences in terms of differences in the kinds of nervous system that individuals possess; in turn, these nervous system differences are inherited. As far as E is concerned, it is the balance between *excitation* and *inhibition* processes in the central nervous system that is crucial, specifically the Reticular Activating System (RAS). (See Chapter 15.) The RAS is located in the central core of the brain-stem and its main function is to maintain an optimum level of alertness or 'arousal'; it can do this either by enhancing the incoming sensory data to the cortex through the excitation of neural impulses or it can 'damp them down' through inhibition.

In these terms, extroverts have a 'strong nervous system'; their RAS is biased towards the inhibition of impulses, inhibition builds up quickly and strongly and it dissipates only slowly, with the effect of reducing the intensity of any sensory stimulation reaching the cortex.

For introverts, the bias is in the opposite direction; for them, excitation builds up strongly and rapidly and inhibition develops slowly and weakly, with the effect of increasing the intensity of any sensory stimulation reaching the cortex.

As far as N is concerned, it is the reactivity of the Autonomic Nervous System (ANS) that determines a person's standing on the scale and, in particular, differences in the limbic system, which controls the ANS. Especially important is the sympathetic branch of the ANS which is activated by frightening or stressful experiences ('fight or flight syndrome'), resulting in increases in heart-rate, breathing rate, blood pressure, sweating, adrenalin production and so on (see Chapter 15).

The person who scores high on N has an ANS which reacts particularly strongly and quickly to stressful situations compared with less emotional or more stable individuals.

Finally, regarding P, the biological basis is much more uncertain but Eysenck (1980) has suggested that it may be related to levels of the male hormone, androgen, and/or other hormones. Is there any evidence to support this part of Eysenck's theory?

Eysenck (1967) linked the concepts of inhibition and excitation to 'psychical fatigue', so that extroverts (who are characterized by *low arousal*) 'tire' more easily than introverts (who are characterized by *high arousal*.) According to Kline (1983), there should be clear differences between introverts and extroverts on long and tedious jobs: extroverts should start better than introverts, do worse in the middle and then improve again towards the end, while introverts would work much more steadily throughout. Evidence to support these hypotheses comes from Eysenck (1967 and 1971) and further support from Harkins and Green (1975), who found that introverts do better at vigilance tasks, which require prolonged periods of concentration.

Wilson (1976) points out that we would expect introverts to be more difficult to sedate using a drug such as sodium amytal since they are supposed to be more aroused. He cites a study by Claridge and Herrington (1963) in which introverted neurotics (dysthymics) were more difficult to sedate than extroverted neurotics (hysterics), the latter being more easily sedated than normal subjects.

Again, regardless of an individual's normal position on the scale, stimulant drugs should shift behaviour in an *introverted* direction while depressant drugs should have the opposite effect, pushing behaviour in an *extroverted* direction and Eysenck (1967) claims to have found considerable support for these hypotheses.

According to Eysenck (1970), the greater sensitivity of introverts to stimuli is matched by their relative dislike of strong stimuli; everyone has an optimum level of stimulation but this is *lower* for the more highly aroused introvert. Introverts have lower pain thresholds and extroverts are more susceptible to the adverse effects of sensory deprivation. Weisen (1965) demonstrated the 'stimulus-hunger' of extroverts when he found them willing to go to great lengths to obtain a 'reward' of loud jazz music or bright lights which introverts worked hard to *avoid*.

However, Claridge (1967) could not find a simple relationship between E and physiological arousal; instead, there seems to be a complex interconnection between arousal and the individual's position on E and N (as the Claridge and Herrington, 1963, study using sodium amytal, shows).

The Relationship between Personality and Conditionability

From a strictly psychological point of view, the importance of the biological aspects of Eysenck's theory is how they are related to individual differences in conditionability. Because extroverts require a stronger stimulus to make an impact (they are 'stimulus-hungry') compared with the more easily stimulated introvert, and because the learning of S–R connections is best achieved by a strong and rapid build-up of excitation in the nervous system (which is characteristic of introverts), introverts are more easily conditioned than extroverts. Does the evidence support Eysenck?

Despite Eysenck's strong claims to the contrary, the evidence is equivocal; for instance, about half the studies he reviewed in 1967 support his predictions while the other half do not. Vernon (1964) argues that Eysenck assumes that conditionability is a *unitary* trait, that is, if an introvert is easily conditioned to one kind of stimulus, they will also condition easily to a range of other stimuli. However, such a general trait has never been demonstrated and the experimental evidence mainly involves three conditioned responses—the GSR (Galvanic Skin Response), the eye-blink and simple verbal conditioning. According to Kline (1983), until such a general dimension is discovered, this part of the theory remains weak and, in addition, extrapolation from laboratory studies to real-life situations is a dangerous business.

Personality and Criminality

In view of the criticisms of conditionability, it becomes all the more important to 'test' the theory in the 'real world' and one way in which Eysenck has done this is by advancing a theory of criminality. For Eysenck, the criminal is a neurotic extrovert; because the extrovert is more difficult to condition, and because 'conscience' is nothing more than a series of conditioned anxiety responses (see Chapter 21), the neurotic extrovert is undersocialized and has an under-developed conscience.

Cochrane (1974) reviewed a number of studies in which prisoners and control groups were given EPI questionnaires; although prisoners are generally higher on N, they are *not* higher on E and, indeed, several studies have shown criminals to be *less* extroverted (and so *more* introverted) than controls. Given the crucial part played by conditionability in Eysenck's theory, these findings would appear to seriously undermine it. Eysenck (1974) retorted by claiming that the EPI largely measures the 'sociability' component of extroversion rather than the 'impulsivity' component which is the more relevant to conditionability; here, he is certainly changing his earlier position whereby he equated 'sociability' (ie capacity for socialization) and 'conditionability'. Cochrane concludes that, at least in its original form, the theory has been discredited.

Even if prisoners were uniformly more extroverted and neurotic than non-prisoners, it could still be possible to explain these differences by reference to factors other than personality: for example, offenders who are caught (or found guilty) might differ in certain significant ways from those who are not (or who are not found guilty), such as the nature of the offence and the 'offender's' social status.

Hampson (1982), in a review of the research, concludes that, although there is some evidence that criminals are highly neurotic, the neurotic–extrovert theory is not supported (thus agreeing with Cochrane) and any attempt to identify any personal trait or dimension which differentiates criminals from non-criminals has been singularly unsuccessful.

A final criticism comes from Heather (1976), who argues that:

> The notion that such a complex and meaningful *social* phenomenon as crime can ever be explained by appealing to the activity of individual nervous systems would be laughable were it not so insidious.

What makes the theory insidious, he says, is that it, 'places the fault inside individuals rather than in the social system where it almost always belongs'.

Psychiatric Diagnosis

Eysenck argues for a dimensional (as opposed to a categorical or classificatory) approach to psychiatric diagnosis, with two independent dimensions of N and P each forming a continuum from extreme abnormality to normality.

However, the whole status of P as a separate dimension has been seriously questioned (eg Bishop, 1977, Black, 1978). Claridge and Chappa (1973) did find evidence that P is a normal personality dimension (ie continuous between normals and psychiatric patients) but they also found considerable overlap between low N subjects and high P subjects on several psychological and physiological measures.

Within the broad group of neurotic disorders, Eysenck distinguishes between *dysthymic* disorders, such as depression, obsessions and phobias (related to high N and low E scores) and *hysterical* disorders (related to high N and high E scores). Patients who are high on P and low on E are likely to develop a psychotic, schizophrenic, disorder. According to McGuire et al (1963), hysterics tend to be rather lower on N than dysthymics but normal on E, that is, neither highly introverted nor highly extroverted.

Although the theory hinges on the differences in conditionability between different groups of neurotic patients (a phobia, for instance, being seen as a conditioned anxiety response to a previously neutral stimulus through classical conditioning), and despite the major contribution which Eysenck himself has made to behaviour therapy (see Chapter 29), most behaviour therapists to not seem to use the concepts of E and N at all. According to Peck and Whitlow (1975), lack of evidence has led to a general disillusionment with standardized tests (such as the EPI and EPQ) as predictors of response to treatment or as a measure of change.

An Evaluation of Eysenck's Theory as a Whole

1.   One of the most serious weaknesses seems to be the failure to produce any convincing evidence that introverts do, in fact, condition more easily than extroverts. Conditionability is a vital part of the overall theory because it 'points inwards' towards the biological (including genetic) basis of personality and 'outwards' towards the socialization experiences of different individuals (behaviour always being the product of an interaction between a nervous system and an environment).

2.   From his biological theory, it follows that there should be some overlap with mammalian personality in as much as any similarity of physiology between humans and mammals exists. Emotionality (defined as faecal counts) has been studied in rats by Broadhurst (1975) and E, N and P have been identified in monkeys (Chamone et al, 1972).

3.   Heim (1970) has criticized the EPI (and, by implication, the EPQ) because of its forced-choice ('yes/no') form; she argues that a few, simple yes/no questions can hardly be expected to do justice to the complexities of human personality and she has criticized the Lie Scale for its lack of subtlety.

4.   Validation of the scales, as we have seen, has involved the use of criterion groups, for instance, groups of neurotics who tend to score at the extreme ends of the scale. But can we assume that the scale is 'valid' for the majority of people who lie somewhere in the middle? Gibson (1971) tried to overcome this by asking students to complete the EPI to rate an unselected group of their friends and he found significant overall correlations between these ratings and their friends' self-ratings on the E and N scales. This offers some support for the validity of the EPI when used with unselected subjects who may score at any point along the scale.

5.   Shackleton and Fletcher (1984) have pointed out the vast amount of research Eysenck's theory has generated: 'whilst the theory as it now stands is not adequate, some aspects of it, maybe even most, may well survive the test of time.'

Cattell's Trait Theory

As we have seen, Cattell's factors are first-order, oblique, source traits, which he believed to be the fundamental dimensions of personality, the underlying roots or causes of clusters of behaviour that are surface traits. Whereas surface traits may correspond to commonsense ways of describing behaviour, and may sometimes be measured by simple observation, they are, in fact, the result of interactions among the source traits; valid explanations of behaviour must concentrate on source traits as the structural factors which determine personality.

Cattell identified three sources of data relevant to personality, L-data (L for 'Life'), Q-data (Q for 'Questionnaire') and T-data (T for 'Tests').

1)   *L-data* refer to ratings by observers which Cattell regarded as the best source but which he also recognized are notoriously difficult to make; great

skill and time are needed to make accurate ratings. His research began by identifying all the words in the English language which describe behaviour (trait elements), including the more technical terms from psychology and psychiatry, and after removing all the synonyms, a small sample of students was intensively studied for six months by trained personnel who rated each subject on all the trait elements.

The resulting data was factor analysed, producing 15 first-order traits or source traits (also called primary traits by Cattell).

2) *Q-data* refers to scores on personality questionnaires. Based on the original 15 source traits, a large number of questionnaire items were assembled and given to large numbers of subjects. When their scores were factor analysed, 16 source traits emerged, composed of 12 of the original L-data factors plus 4 new ones. These 16 factors were measured by the widely used Cattell 16PF (Personality Factor) Questionnaire, which is intended for adults; as shown in Table 25.3 the first 12 are found in L-data and Q-data, while the last 4 (Q1–Q4) are based on Q-data only.

The Pre-School Personality Quiz (PSPQ) is designed for 4- to 6-year-olds, the Child's Personality Quiz (CPQ) for 6- to 11-year-olds and the High School Personality Questionnaire (HSPQ) for 12- to 15-year-olds.

From Table 25.3 you will notice that there is no D-factor (excitability versus undemonstrativeness) or J-factor (individuality versus liking for group action): these are adolescent factors which appear in the HSPQ but not in the 16PF. (Conversely, Factors L, M and Q1 appear in the 16PF but not in the HSPQ.) There is also a Clinical Analysis Questionnaire (CAQ) designed for use with psychotic patients.

Unlike Eysenck's questionnaires, Cattell's scales are not exclusively of the 'yes/no' variety; for instance, there may be three choices—yes/occasionally/no. However, there is the problem of social desirability (which Eysenck tries to measure by inclusion of an L-scale) and also acquiescence, a kind of 'response set' in which the subject tends to put 'yes' rather than 'no' or to agree with the questionnaire items.

Although intended mainly as a research instrument, the 16PF has been used in clinical work, as well as occupational selection and assessment. However, Williams et al (1972) believe that its validity is insufficient for its use as a diagnostic tool in a clinical setting.

Five alternative forms of the 16PF have been developed (Cattell et al, 1970) of which A and B are the most widely used; alternative forms are very important when the reliability of the test is being investigated (see Chapter 27).

3) *T-data* refer to objective tests specially devised to measure personality; for instance, the Objective–Analytic (O–A) test battery measures, amongst other things, GSR, reaction time, body-sway and suggestibility. T-data are objective primarily in the sense that the purpose of the test is concealed from the subject. Factor analysis of these has yielded 21 factors altogether (the O-A battery measuring just 12 of these) and some of these correspond to a number of second-order factors obtained from Q-data.

Table 25.3 The 16 source traits measured by Cattell's 16PF questionnaire (after Cattell, 1965)

Description	Name of trait	Description
Warm-hearted, outgoing, easygoing, sociable	A Affectia v. Sizia	Reserved, cool, detached, aloof
High score: abstract-thinker, intellectual interests	B Intelligence	Low score: concrete-thinker, practically-minded
Emotionally stable, calm, mature, stable	C Ego-strength v. Dissatisfied emotionality	Emotionally unstable, easily upset, immature
Assertive, aggressive dominant, competitive	E Dominance v. Submissiveness	Submissive, mild, modest, accommodating
Happy-go-lucky, enthusiastic, unworrying	F Surgency v. Desurgency	Pessimistic, subdued, sober, cautious, serious, taciturn
Persevering, conscientious ⎱ High moralistic, straight-laced ⎰ score	G Super-ego strength	Expedient, disregards rules, ⎱ Low feels few obligations, law ⎰ score to oneself
Adventurous, gregarious, uninihibited, socially bold	H Parmia v. Threctia	Shy, restrained, timid, diffident, inhibited
Tender-minded, sensitive, gentle, clinging	I Premsia v. Harria	Tough-minded, self-reliant, practical, realistic, no-nonsense
Suspicious, jealous, self-opinionated	L Protension v. Alaxia	Trusting, understanding, adaptable, easy to get along with
Unconventional, imaginative, strong subjective life, bohemian	M Autia v. Praxernia	Conformist, conventional, influenced by external realities
Shrewd, calculating, worldly, penetrating	N Shrewdness v. Naivety	Simple, artless, natural, unpretentious, lacking insight
Insecure, worrying, self-reproaching	O Guilt proneness	Self-assured, confident, complacent, spirited.
Liberal, free-thinking	Q1 Radicalism v. Conservatism	Conservative, traditional
Prefers own decisions	Q2 Self-sufficiency v. Group dependence	Group dependent, a follower
High score: ⎰ Controlled, ⎱ socially precise	Q3 Self-sentiment strength	Low score: ⎰ Undisciplined, ⎱ careless of social rules
High score: ⎰ Relaxed, ⎱ composed	Q4 Ergic tension	Low score: ⎰ Overwrought, ⎱ tense, frustrated

First- and Second-Order Factors: Cattell and Eysenck compared

As we have seen, first-order (oblique) factors correlate with each other to some degree and, indeed, Cattell argues that overlapping factors are what would be expected since, for example, an intelligent person (B-factor) is also likely to be shrewd and worldly (N-factor). We should note here that whereas Eysenck does not include intelligence amongst his three major personality dimensions, Cattell does include it in his 16 primary factors, although it assumes a rather different meaning in the 16PF than it does in his distinction between fluid and crystallized intelligence (see Chapters 24 and 27).

However, Cattell has carried out a second-order factor analysis of his 16 primary factors which yields a number of surface traits, the two most important being *exvia(–invia)* and *anxiety*, which seem to correspond to Eysenck's E and N respectively (see Figure 25.3). Others include *radicalism* (aggressive and independent), *tendermindedness* (sensitivity, frustration and emotionality) and *superego* (conscientious, conforming and persevering).

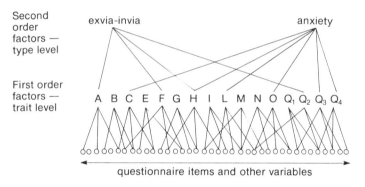

Figure 25.3   The hierarchical organization of personality resulting from a second-order analysis of the first-order 'source traits' (after Cattell, 1965)

Another important difference is that Cattell believes that there is a fundamental discontinuity between normals and, say, schizophrenics, that is, there is a qualitative difference and not merely a quantitative one as Eysenck maintains. For instance, Q-data used with psychiatric patients produce 12 factors which discriminate psychotics as a group (eg paranoia, suicidal disgust, schizophrenia and high general psychosis), who score very high on these compared with normals. A second-order FA of Q-data from psychiatric patients yields 3 factors, one of which resembles Eysenck's P.

Altogether, using L and Q-data, Cattell has identified 23 primary factors, although the 16 shown in Table 25.3 are still the best established, plus 8 surface traits in normal subjects, as well as the 12 source and 3 surface traits in abnormal subjects (Cattell and Kline, 1977).

Evaluation of the 16PF

As far as test/re-test reliability is concerned (ie how consistently subjects score when they do the test on a subsequent occasion), no data are presented, since Cattell assumes that normal variations in traits occur over time and so low test/re-test correlations are only to be expected.

As for its validity, this has been challenged by Eysenck and Eysenck (1969), Vagg and Hammond (1976), Saville and Blinkhorn (1976) and Browne and Howarth (1977), all of whom found a smaller number of source traits than Cattell.

Again, Howarth and Browne (1971) failed to find any kind of clear-cut factor structure using a sample of over 500 students. However, Kline (1981) has pointed out that different investigators have used different techniques and so it is not always possible to make meaningful comparisons.

As we have already seen, the agreement between Cattell and Eysenck as far as certain second-order factors are concerned tends to enhance the validity of the 16PF and Cattell believes that many of these criticisms no longer apply to the improved 1974 version of the questionnaire.

Personality and Behaviour

Does behaviour equal personality?

Although clearly belonging to the nomothetic approach which sees behaviour as reflecting a relatively enduring personality (see Table 25.1) Cattell, much more than Eysenck, acknowledges the way that behaviour can fluctuate in response to situational factors.

His definition of personality as 'what determines behaviour in a defined situation and a defined mood' (Cattell, 1965) implies that behaviour is never totally determined by source traits: although personality factors remain fairly stable over time, they constitute only one kind of variable influencing overt behaviour. So what other kinds are there?

Cattell in fact makes the distinction between: (a) Mood and State factors (eg depression, arousal, anxiety, fatigue and intoxication), which are measured by the Eight State Questionnaire; and (b) Motivational factors, measured by the Motivational Analysis Test (MAT). The MAT involves a series of objective tests which indirectly measure motivation by studying the effects of interests or drives through their effect on memory, perception, speed of decision-making and so on.

Cattell distinguishes two kinds of motivational factors: (i) *ergs*, which are the innate, biological, drives (the ten so far identified are food-seeking, gregariousness, mating, narcissism, acquisitiveness, parental, pugnacity, security, exploration and assertiveness); and (ii) *sentiments*, which are culturally acquired drives, the six main ones being self-sentiment, superego, religious and professional, career, home-parental and sweetheart-spouse. The MAT measures five of each type of motive and there are versions of the test designed for children (the School MAT and the Child MAT).

Cattell also identifies seven main components of a motive, three of which are: *alpha*, the 'id' component, corresponding to 'I want'; *beta*, the 'ego' component, concerned with knowledge and information; *gamma*, the 'superego' component, corresponding to 'I ought'.

Although an ardent behaviourist, Cattell was influenced by Freud's psychoanalytic theory, at least to the extent that three of the 16PF names are derived from Freudian terminology (C—Ego Strength, G—Superego Strength and Q4—Ergic or Id Tension) together with the three components of a motive which we have just discussed.

When we discuss Freud's theory, in Chapter 26, we shall discuss the relationship between this and factor-analytic concepts.

Kelly's Personal Construct Theory

As Table 25.1 shows, Kelly's Personal Construct Theory (PCT) is an idiographic approach, stressing the uniqueness of each individual; it is also a phenomenological approach, in that it attempts to understand the person in terms of their experience and perception of the world, a view of the world through the person's own eyes and not an observer's interpretation or analysis which is imposed on the person.

Kelly's dissatisfaction with both Freudian and behaviourist theories led him to propose a model of the human being which was radically different from any model previously proposed, namely 'man the scientist'. (This was a notion we discussed in relation to interpersonal perception—see Chapter 8.) What does Kelly mean?

We are all scientists in the sense that we put our own interpretation (or theories) on the world of events and from these personal theories we produce hypotheses which are predictions about future events. Every time we act we are putting our hypotheses to the test and in this sense, behaviour is the Independent Variable, it is the experiment. Depending on the outcome, our hypotheses are either validated—or not—and this will determine the nature of our subsequent behavioural experiments (Fransella, 1981). But what exactly are these personal theories from which we derive our hypotheses?

In order to answer this question, we need to discuss Kelly's philosophy of *Constructive Alternativism*. Although a real world of physical objects and events does exist, no one organism has the privilege of 'knowing' it; all we can do is place our personal constructs upon it and the better our constructs 'fit' the world, the better will be our control over our own, personal world. To quote Kelly:

> Man looks at his world through transparent patterns or templates which he creates and then attempts to fit over the realities of which the world is composed. The fit is not always very good. Yet without such patterns the world appears to be such an undifferentiated homogeneity that man is unable to make any sense of it. (Kelly, 1955.)

In other words, there is no way of getting 'behind' our interpretation of the world to check if it matches what the world is *really* like: all we have are our own interpretations (compare this with Gregory's definition of perception—see Chapter 4) and so we necessarily see the world 'through goggles' which cannot be removed. However, these goggles or *constructs* are not fixed once and for all; the person as scientist is constantly engaged in testing, checking, modifying and revising their unique set of constructs which represent their working hypotheses.

Each person's construct system is organized in a hierarchical way, with some broad constructs (superordinate) subsuming other, narrow constructs (subordinate).

The Repertory Grid Technique

The original test used for eliciting personal constructs was the Role Construct Repertory Test ('Rep Test') which was designed for individual use by a clinical psychologist. This has been succeeded by the Repertory Grid Test ('Rep Grid') which is used as a major research instrument.

The basic method involves the following steps:

1) The person is asked to name the most important figures in their life (*elements*).
2) They are then presented with three of these elements, the names being written on separate cards.
3) They are asked, 'In what ways are two of these alike and different from the third?' The descriptions given (eg 'My mother and girlfriend are affectionate, my father is not') constitute a construct which is expressed in a *bipolar* way, ie 'affectionate–not affectionate'.
4) This first construct is then applied to all the remaining elements; each element can only be assigned to one or other end (pole) of the construct.
5) Then another set of three elements is selected and the whole process is repeated. It continues until either the person has produced all the constructs they can (which is usually no more than 25 with one set of elements) or until a sufficient number has been produced as judged by the investigator.

All this information can be collated in the form of a *grid*, with the elements across the top and the constructs down the side and a tick or cross indicating which pole of the construct is applicable (for example, a tick indicates 'affectionate' and a cross indicates 'not-affectionate').

The Rep Grid is a very flexible instrument and there are different ways in which it can be used. Kelly himself suggested that 24 role titles (elements) might provide a representative sample of 'significant others' and eight different ways in which triads of role titles can be compiled. However this may be done, the Rep Grid is an attempt to help the individual discover the fundamental constructs they use for perceiving and relating to others.

The grid can be factor analysed and this often reveals that many constructs overlap, that is, they mean more or less the same thing; probably between three and six major constructs cover most people's construct system. It can be used nomothetically, as Bannister and Fransella have done with thought-disordered schizophrenics; their Grid Test of Thought Disorder (Bannister and Fransella, 1966/67) has standardized elements and constructs (that is, they are supplied by the researcher) and the test has been standardized on large numbers of similar patients so that an individual score can be compared with group norms. However, this is probably rather far removed from how Kelly intended the technique to be used. It has also been used to study how patients participating in group psychotherapy change their perception of each other (and themselves) during the period of therapy, where the group members are themselves the elements and a number of constructs are supplied (eg Fransella, 1970). Fransella (1972) has used it extensively with people being treated for severe stuttering.

However, its uses are not confined to clinical situations. Elements need not be people at all, but could be occupations, religions, cars and so on, and Shackleton and Fletcher (1984) argue that the Rep Grid stands on its own as a technique, that is, you do not have to believe in Kelly's PCT in order to use it.

However, neither the Rep Grid nor the theory has been without its critics. Some of the most common criticisms have been to do with the reliability and validity of the Rep Grid. Gathercole et al (1970), for example, studied 'parallel-form' reliability (in which different persons were put into the same role titles) as well as test/re-test reliability of various types of Rep Grid in general use. They concluded that generalizations about individuals based on single grids, especially if the constructs are elicited from the subject, should only be made with extreme caution since the results are likely to be unreliable.

However, Bannister and Mair (1968) believe that the concepts of reliability and validity are not strictly relevant or applicable since the Rep Grid is primarily a methodology rather than a standardized test.

An Evaluation of PCT

Unfortunately, we have only been able to scratch the surface of Kelly's very complex and challenging theory, which essentially comprises a Fundamental Postulate (which states that, 'a person's processes are psychologically channelized by the ways in which he anticipates events') plus 11 corollaries. Two excellent summaries are Bannister and Fransella, *Inquiring Man* (1980) and Fransella (1981).

As Bannister and Fransella (1980) point out, the theory is deliberately stated in very abstract terms so as to avoid the limitations of a particular time and culture; it is an attempt to redefine psychology as a psychology of persons and is 'content-free'. As we noted earlier in the chapter, PCT is not so much a personality theory, more a total psychology: Kelly is not concerned with separate sub-divisions of psychology as dealt with in most textbooks because he believes these can all be dealt with by the fundamental postulate and 11 corollaries.

For instance, Kelly believes that the traditional concept of motivation can be dispensed with. We do not need concepts like drives or needs or psychic energy (see Chapters 17 and 26) to explain what makes people 'get up and go'—man is a form of motion and a basic assumption about life is that 'it goes on': 'It isn't that something *makes* you go on, the going on is *the thing itself*' (Kelly, 1962).

Various aspects of emotion are dealt with in terms of how an individual's construct system is organized and how it changes; for instance, 'anxiety' is the awareness that what you are confronted with is not within the framework of your existing construct system—you do not know *how* to construe it.

(This is discussed further in Chapter 29.) For some, this is far too cognitive and rational an approach; what about the subjective experience (the gut feeling) that we call anxiety? It is almost as if emotional experiences and 'behaviour' itself are being drowned in a sea of constructs.

Peck and Whitlow (1975) believe that Kelly trivializes important aspects of behaviour, including learning, emotion and motivation, as well as neglecting situational influences on behaviour; PCT, they say, appears to place the person in an 'empty world'.

However, they conclude by saying that, 'Personal Construct Theory constitutes a brave and imaginative attempt to create a comprehensive, cognitive, theory of personality.' (Peck & Whitlow, 1975.)

Maslow's Humanistic Theory

'Humanistic' is an umbrella term (first coined by Cantril in 1955) referring to a group of theories which all share the belief that scientific attempts to study human beings are misplaced and inappropriate, since, 'to see man at second hand through his behaviour as against his experience is ultimately to see ourselves at second hand and never be ourselves' (Evans, 1975).

Maslow introduced the notion of a 'third force' in psychology in 1958, Behaviourism and Psychoanalytic theory being the first and second forces, and it is he and Rogers who are the best known humanistic psychologists.

Humanistic theories (and Kelly's PCT) have their philosophical roots in phenomenology and existentialism and, some would say, they justify the label 'philosophical' more than they warrant the label 'psychological'. They are concerned with characteristics that are distinctively and uniquely human, in particular, experience, uniqueness, meaning, freedom and choice; we have first-hand experience of ourselves as persons and Rogers's particular theory is centred around the self-concept (see Chapter 9).

What Rogers and Maslow have in common is their positive evaluation of human nature, a belief in the individual's potential for personal growth, what they call *self-actualization*.

Maslow's Hierarchy of Needs

Self-actualization represents the top-most level of a hierarchy of human needs, which Maslow first proposed in 1954 (see Figure 25.4 overleaf). Because he is describing 'needs', Maslow's hierarchy is often discussed in the context of motivation and is not as 'pure' a personality theory as say, Eysenck's or Cattell's.

According to Maslow, we are subject to two quite different sets of motivational states or forces: (a) those which ensure *survival* by satisfying basic physical and psychological needs (physiological, safety, belongingness and love and esteem needs); and (b) those which promote the person's *self-actualization* that is, realizing one's full potential, 'becoming everything that one is capable of becoming' (Maslow, 1970), especially in the intellectual and creative domains.

While behaviours which relate to survival or deficiency needs are engaged in because they satisfy those needs (a means to an end), those which relate

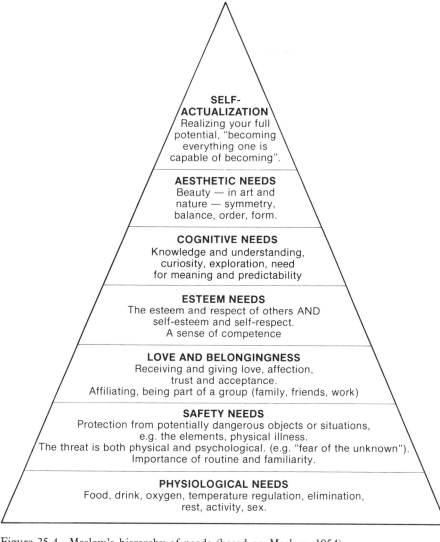

Figure 25.4 Maslow's hierarchy of needs (based on Maslow, 1954)

to self-actualization are engaged in for their own sake, because they are intrinsically satisfying.

The hierarchical nature of Maslow's theory is intended to emphasize the following points.

1) Needs lower down in the hierarchy must be satisfied before we can fully attend to needs at the next level up; for instance, physiological needs must be met before we concentrate on safety needs. If you are trying to concentrate on what you are reading while your stomach is trying to tell you it is lunchtime, you probably will not absorb much about Maslow; similarly, if you are very tired or in pain.

Yet it is possible to think of exceptions: the starving artist who finds inspiration despite hunger or the mountain-climber who risks their life for the sake of adventure (what Maslow would call a 'peak' experience —pun intended!).

2) Higher-level needs are a later evolutionary development, that is, in the development of the human species (phylogenesis), self-actualization is a fairly recent need to have appeared. This applies equally to the development of individuals (ontogenesis); clearly, babies are much more concerned with their bellies than their brains. However, it is never a case of one need being present and another being absent but rather one predominating over another; this applies at any stage of development.

3) The higher up the hierarchy we go, the greater the need becomes linked to life experience and the less the biological character of the need. Individuals will achieve self-actualization in different ways, through different activities and by different routes and this is related to experience, not biology.

4) Following on from (3), the higher up the hierarchy we go, the more difficult the need is to achieve. Many human goals are remote and long-term, and can only be achieved in a series of steps; this pursuit of ends which lie very much in the future is one of the unique features of human behaviour and individuals differ in their ability to set and realize such goals.

Who Achieves Self-actualization?

Although we are all, theoretically, capable of self-actualizing, most of us will not do so, or only to a limited degree. Maslow was particularly interested in the characteristics of people whom he considered to have achieved their potential as persons; his list included Einstein, William James, Eleanor Roosevelt, Abraham Lincoln, Spinoza, Thomas Jefferson and Walt Whitman, and some of the characteristics of self-actualizers and some of the behaviours leading to self actualization are shown overleaf in Table 25.4.

One way of measuring self-actualization is to study people's *peak experiences*, moments of ecstatic happiness when people feel most 'real' and alive. Maslow (1962) interviewed several people, many of whom were successful in their chosen field; his view was confirmed that at such moments, the person is concerned with 'being' and is totally unaware of any deficiency needs or the possible reactions of others.

Empirical Studies of Self-actualization

Czikszentmihalyi (1975) interviewed a wide range of prominent sportsmen and reported experiences, similar to those reported by Maslow, of ecstatically losing themselves in the highly skilled performance of their sport.

Such peak experiences cannot, normally, be consciously planned and yet, as Smith (1981) observes, for many, the growth of humanistic psychology is almost synonymous with *deliberate* attempts to enhance personal growth through encounter groups and other short, intensive, group experiences. (See Chapter 29.)

Table 25.4   Characteristics of self-actualizers and behaviour leading to self-actualization (after Maslow 1962/70)

	Characteristics of self-actualizers
(i)	They perceive reality efficiently and can tolerate uncertainty;
(ii)	Accept themselves and others for what they are;
(iii)	Spontaneous in thought and action;
(iv)	Problem-centred (not self-centred);
(v)	Good sense of humour;
(vi)	Able to look at life objectively;
(vii)	Highly creative;
(viii)	Resistant to enculturation, but not purposely unconventional;
(ix)	Concerned for the welfare of mankind;
(x)	Capable of deep appreciation of basic life-experiences;
(xi)	Establish deep satisfying interpersonal relationships with a few people;
(xii)	Peak experiences.
	Behaviour leading to self-actualization
(a)	Experiencing life like a child, with full absorption and concentration;
(b)	Trying new things instead of sticking to safe paths;
(c)	Listening to your own feelings in evaluating experiences instead of the voice of tradition or authority or the majority.
(d)	Avoiding pretence ('game playing') and being honest;
(e)	Being prepared to be unpopular if your views do not coincide with those of the majority;
(f)	Taking responsibility and working hard;
(g)	Trying to identify your defences and having the courage to give them up.

A questionnaire that is widely used to assess the effect of encounter groups etc is the Personal Orientation Inventory or POI (Shostrom, 1966), which claims to be a measure of self-actualization. It is a self-report questionnaire in which the subject has to choose between 150 pairs of statements describing oneself, and is based on Maslow's descriptions of how a self-actualized person will act and feel. It comprises two major scales—'Time-Competence' and 'Inner-Directed Support': a time-competent person is engrossed neither in the past nor the future but makes choices about what to do on the basis of present experience; and a person with inner-directed support decides what to do by referring to their own inner feelings and goals rather than the possible demands and reactions of others.

Smith (1981) notes that the POI treats self-actualization as an attribute that people have to some degree or other, as opposed to a variable state which we might experience more or less frequently under certain special conditions, which is how Maslow and Rogers would describe it.

Several dozen studies have used the POI to test for increased self-actualization after encounter groups and most have shown increased scores following the group experience. However, some did not use control groups, and in some of those that did, increases were found among the controls too!

There is also some evidence that completing the POI may in itself induce changes: Knapp (1976), reviewing the literature, concludes that POI scores can increase after a wide range of experiences, including drugs, and studying courses in humanistic psychology!

Conclusions

Whatever the empirical support or otherwise for Maslow's theory, there is no doubt that it represents an important balance to the nomothetic approach of Cattell and Eysenck by attempting to capture the richness of the personal experience of being human.

26

Personality (2)
Psychodynamic Theories

Introduction

As we saw in Chapter 25, theories like those of Eysenck and Cattell see personality as fairly stable and enduring and, to this extent, they conceptualize it as being *static*. Contrast this with the theories of Freud, Jung, Adler and Erikson, which, collectively, are referred to as *Psychodynamic*, stressing the *active* forces within the personality, the inner causes of behaviour which include feelings, conflicts, instinctive drives and a variety of unconscious motivational factors. Freud's was the first of these theories to be formulated and all psychodynamic theories stem, more or less directly, from Freud's work. Collectively, these theories are also known as *Depth psychology*.

Freud's Psychoanalytic Theory

Freud's work represents much more than just an account of human personality; it also comprises a theory of personality development, a motivational theory and an approach to the treatment of mental illness. It is quite common to refer to all of these as 'psychoanalysis' but it might be helpful to reserve that term to denote Freud's form of psychotherapy and to use the term 'psychoanalytic theory' when discussing his theories.

The sheer volume of Freud's work, the fact that his theories were intended to cover all aspects of human behaviour and the great influence his work has had within psychology as a whole, makes it impossible to do him justice in part of one chapter, although we have, of course, discussed some of his developmental theory in Chapters 21, 22 and 23 and in Chapter 29 we shall be discussing psychoanalysis.

Biographical Sketch

Sigmund Freud was born in Moravia, in present day Czechoslovakia, in 1856 (then part of the Austrian Empire) and spent most of his life in Vienna, from where he fled, in 1937, when the Nazis invaded. Neither Freud himself, being Jewish, nor his theories, were very popular with the invaders and he escaped to London, where he died in 1939. He had wanted to be a research scientist but anti-Semitism forced him to choose a medical career instead and he worked in Vienna as a doctor, specializing in neurological disorders (disorders of the nervous system). He constantly revised and modified his theories right up until his death but much of his psychoanalytic theory was produced between 1900 and 1930. Most of what is discussed in this chapter represents the 'final version' of the theory.

Influences on Freud's Thought

Freud originally attempted to explain the workings of the mind in terms of physiology and neurology and he thought in the manner of a natural scientist. Helmholtz, one of the leading physicists of his day, had formulated the law of Conservation of Energy which states that energy (like mass) can be transformed but not destroyed. In 1874, Brücke, an eminent physiologist, argued that the living organism is a dynamic system to which the laws of physics and chemistry apply. Freud was to put these two principles together and extend them by applying them to the (non-physical) personality.

Quite early in his treatment of neurological patients, Freud realized that symptoms which had no organic or bodily basis could imitate the 'real thing' and that they were as real for the patient as if they had been neurologically caused. So began Freud's search for psychological explanations of these symptoms and ways of treating them.

In 1855 he spent a year in Paris learning Charcot's method of hypnosis which he then started using with his patients in Vienna. However, he found its effects to be only temporary, at best, and it did not usually get to the root of the problem; nor was everybody a suitable subject.

An alternative approach was being developed by Breuer, a Viennese doctor like Freud. Breuer was using the cathartic method, where patients would talk out their problems; Freud adopted Breuer's method and called it 'free association' which became one of the three fundamental tools of psychoanalysis (see Chapter 29).

Freud began his self-analysis during the 1890s and in 1900 had published *The Interpretation of Dreams* in which he outlined his theory of the mind, followed by *The Psychopathology of Everyday Life* (1904), *A Case of Hysteria* and *Three Essays on the Theory of Sexuality* (1905).

Two of Freud's closest colleagues, Carl Jung and Alfred Adler, helped him form the psychoanalytic movement and the first International Psychoanalytic Congress was held at Salzburg in 1908. The *Journal of Psychoanalysis* was first published in 1909 and, in that year, Freud and Jung made a lecture tour of the USA.

Psychoanalytic Theory

We will start our investigation into Freud's psychoanalytic theory with a look at the structure of personality, the 'psychic apparatus'.

1) The Structure of Personality

The personality or 'psychic apparatus' consists of three parts (which must not be thought of as parts of the brain or in any way physical), the Id, Ego and Superego.

a) The Id

Although part of the personality, the id responds directly to the instincts, those demands arising from within the body itself, for instance, the biologically-based needs for food, warmth, sexual gratification and so on.

For Freud, the human organism is a complex energy system and the kind of energy needed to fuel or operate the psychic apparatus is *psychic energy*, which performs psychological work; the source of psychic energy is the id. The id, 'contains everything that is inherited, that is present at birth, that is laid down in the constitution—above all, therefore, the instincts'.

The wishes and impulses arising from the body's needs build up a sort of pressure or tension (excitation) which demand immediate release or satis-faction; when this happens, we experience pleasure but when it is prevented, we experience pain or frustration. Since the id is in closer touch with the body than with the outside world, and since it is not affected by logic or reason, and its sole aim is to reduce excitation to a minimum, it is said to be governed by the *Pleasure principle* (seeking pleasure and avoiding pain). For this reason, the id can be thought of as the infantile part of the personality, what we are before the environment has begun to exert any influence over us (including other people), the *pre-socialized* part of our make-up.

At birth, we are 'bundles of id' and the id retains its infantile character throughout our lives; whenever we act on impulse, selfishly, or demand something 'here and now', it is our id controlling our behaviour at those times (it is 'the spoiled child' of the personality).

In its earliest, most primitive form, the id acts in a reflex way to release tension, for example, blinking the eye or the eye watering to remove dust or dirt, sneezing to remove an irritation from the nostril and automatic opening of the bladder when pressure on it reaches a certain level. However, not all tension can be released in this reflex way, for instance, hunger does not automatically produce food but only irritability and crying etc; these signals have to be interpreted by another person if the child is not to starve to death.

Indeed, if the id were capable of satisfying the body's needs in a reflex way, there would not be any need for psychological development—so not only is some degree of frustration and discomfort inevitable, they are also necessary for development beyond the reflex level.

The main development that occurs in the id is the *primary process*, a form of thinking in which an image of the object needed to reduce tension is pro-duced. So, for example, through repeated association of food and hunger-reduction, the hungry baby, if not fed immediately, may conjure up an image of food. However, the id is incapable of distinguishing between the subjective memory-image and the real thing—that is left to the ego.

b) The Ego

The ego is, 'that part of the id which has been modified by the direct influence of the external world through the medium of conscious perception' (Freud, 1923); it gradually develops (starting at a few months) as psychic energy is 'borrowed' from the id and directed outwards towards external reality.

The ego can also be described as the 'executive' of the personality, the planning, decision-making, rational and logical part of us, which engages in *secondary process thinking* which is roughly equivalent to the cognitive processes of perception, attention, memory, reasoning, problem-solving and so on. It enables us to distinguish between a wish and reality, inside from outside, subjective from objective and so on, and is governed by the *Reality principle*.

While the id demands immediate gratification for some need arising within the body, the ego will postpone its satisfaction until the appropriate time and place ('deferred gratification'). However, this does not imply any kind of moral code—what the ego considers 'right' or 'correct' is what others would find acceptable or what is objectively possible in the situation—it is the consequences of the act rather than the act itself which is the ego's priority. For example, whereas the id would have us scratch wherever and whenever an itch arises, the ego takes reality into account by deciding that scratching in public might offend others and may lead to our being ostracized, which most of us would not like to happen. So the ego, like the id, is amoral, but the feelings, needs, reactions and so on of other people *are* taken into account; again, while the id is concerned only with *what* it wants, the ego is equally concerned with *how* it is to get it.

c) Superego

Not until the superego has developed can we describe the person as a moral being; it involves the internalization of a set of moral values which determine that certain behaviour is good or bad, right or wrong, *in itself*. So the superego represents the moral or judicial branch of the personality and its development was discussed in detail in Chapter 21. It comprises two components: (i) the *conscience*, which threatens the ego with punishment (in the form of guilt) for bad behaviour; and (ii) the *ego-ideal*, which promises the ego with rewards (in the form of pride and high self-esteem) for good behaviour.

Conflict and the Ego

As shown in Figure 26.1 overleaf, the ego can be viewed as 'located' square in the middle of the psychic apparatus, the point of convergence of conflicting demands from three sources—external reality, the id and the superego. Where external reality makes demands on the ego (eg someone threatening you with a knife) the resulting conflict is called *external* or *reality conflict*, when the ego fears being overwhelmed by the power of the id's demands for instinctual gratification, the result is *neurotic conflict*, and where the ego feels threatened by punishment from the conscience, the result is *moral conflict*.

Freud believes that conflict is inevitable; we live in society which, for its own survival, cannot allow us to give free expression to our id impulses and our ego develops in order to ensure that the individual acknowledges social and material reality. The superego develops in order to assist the ego in keeping the very powerful id in its place but it can only do so by making demands on the ego—there is no direct 'contact' between the id and the superego. Consequently, the ego, the person's conscious self, is caught in the middle of opposing sets of demands, it is the battleground on which three opposing factions (reality, the id and the superego) fight for supremacy. But the ego

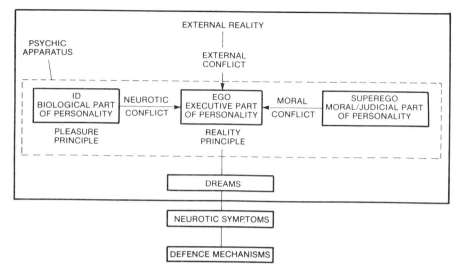

Figure 26.1   The psychic apparatus, showing sources of conflict and ways of resolving it

is, at the same time, the arbitrator and has to find ways of keeping all the factions 'happy', of satisfying all their demands and not responding to some at the expense of others! How is this achieved?

For Freud, all behaviour is a *compromise* which can take three major forms —Dreams, Neurotic Symptoms and Defence Mechanisms.

Dreams

'A dream is a (disguised) fulfilment of a (suppressed or repressed) wish' (Freud, 1900) and so is another example of the id's primary process thinking; it represents a compromise between forbidden urges and their repression. What we dream about and are conscious of upon waking (what we report) is called the *manifest content*, while the meaning of the dream (the wish being fulfilled) is the *latent content*.

The manifest content is often the product of the weaving together of certain fragments from that day's events ('day residues') and the forbidden wish and is, essentially, a hallucinatory experience (predominantly visual for most people). It often appears to be disjointed, fragmentary and often bizarre and nonsensical; dream interpretation (a second major technique involved in psychoanalysis) aims to make sense of the manifest content by 'translating' it into the underlying wish fulfilment.

Dreams come into being through *dream work*, which converts the underlying (latent) wish into the manifest content and comprises Displacement, Condensation and Concrete Representation; it is controlled by the ego.

Displacement refers to the role of *symbols* in dreams, whereby something (eg a king) appears in the manifest dream as a substitute for something or somebody involved in the wish (eg the dreamer's father).

Condensation involves the same part of the manifest dream representing different parts of the latent wish. For example, a king may represent not only the dreamer's father but authority figures in general or very wealthy and powerful people. So more than one dream idea may be 'condensed' into a single manifest image and Freud would say the manifest image is 'over-determined' (see below).

Concrete representation refers to the expression of some abstract idea in a very concrete way; the concrete image of a king, for example, could represent the abstract notion of authority, power or wealth.

The importance of dream work as a whole is that it permits the expression of a repressed (and, therefore, forbidden and disturbing) wish and at the same time allows the dreamer to go on sleeping; the compromise involved in dreaming takes the form of disguising the true nature of the dream (ie wish-fulfilment), for if the wish were not disguised, the dreamer would wake up in a state of shock and distress. Hence, 'the dream is the guardian of sleep'.

Dream interpretation is also the 'royal road to the unconscious', reversing the dream work and unravelling the wish from the manifest content can provide invaluable information about the unconscious mind in general and about the dreamers in particular. (Free-associating to his own dreams was a major part of Freud's self-analysis.)

So what happens when we have a nightmare (or 'anxiety dream')? Freud says that the ego normally acts as a 'censor' of what is consciously experienced but is less alert and on guard when we are asleep. Occasionally, the dream work is less effective than usual in disguising the repressed wish so that it becomes too clear and, therefore, too dangerous; consequently, the dream awakens the sleeping ego and brings the undisguised wish-fulfilment to an abrupt end.

Neurotic Symptoms

Symptoms have much in common with dreams; they are essentially the expression of a repressed wish (or memory) which has become disguised in ways that are very similar to those involved in dream work:

i)   The symptom in some way symbolizes the wish to which it is linked; for example, one of Freud's patients (cited by Wollheim, 1971) suffered from hysterical hand-twitching which was related to her memories of being badly frightened while playing the piano (*displacement*).
ii) A symptom can be over-determined, for example, this same patient's hand-twitching was traced to two other memories—receiving a disciplinary strapping on the hands as a schoolgirl and being forced to massage the back of a detested uncle (*condensation*).
iii) The symptom is often something 'physical' while the underlying cause is something 'mental' (*concrete representation*).

Most of Freud's patients were suffering from 'hysterical conversion neurosis', whereby emotional energy is converted into physical energy, so that the manifest problem is paralysis, blindness, deafness, headaches and a whole variety of other 'physical' symptoms. Through displacement and concrete representation in particular, the symptom deflects the patient's attention (and that of others) away from the repressed material—it is acceptable to consult a doctor about the symptom but not about the unconscious wish. It is in this way that symptoms, like dreams, are compromises—every symptom must comply with the demands of the ego or it too would be repressed. Freud and Breuer (1895) called these underlying wishes and memories *pathogenic* ('disease-producing') *ideas*, and Freud later reached the conclusion that *all* symptoms are caused by pathogenic ideas of a *sexual* nature (although not every dream).

Defence Mechanisms

These represent the third major form of compromise used by the ego in the face of inevitable conflict. The defence mechanisms of the ego are, by definition, unconscious, and this is partly how they derive their effectiveness: if we knew about them (at the time) we would in most cases, be unable to go on using them. They also share the characteristic of involving some degree of self-deception (which is linked to their being unconscious) and this, in turn, is related to their distortion of 'reality', both the internal reality of feelings etc and the external reality of other people and the physical world.

Table 26.1 Some of the major ego defence mechanisms

Name of defence	Description	Example(s)
1. *Repression* (motivated Forgetting see Chapter 6)	Forcing a dangerous/threatening memory/idea/feeling/wish etc out of consciousness and making it unconscious. Often used in conjuction with one or more other defences and one of the earliest to be used.	A 5 to 6-year old child repressing its incestuous desire for the opposite-sex parent as part of the Oedipus/Electra complex (see Chapter 21).
2. *Displacement*	Choosing a substitute object for the expression of your feelings because you cannot express them openly towards their real target. You transfer your feelings onto something quite innocent, or harmless, because it is convenient in some way.	Anger with your boy/girl friend is taken out on your mother/father/brother/sister, or you slam the door (or kick the cat). Phobias (see Chapters 28 & 29). Prejudice (see Chapter 11).
3. *Denial*	Refusing to acknowledge certain aspects of reality, refusing to perceive something because it is so painful or distressing.	Refusing to accept that you have a serious illness or that a relationship is 'on the rocks' or that you have an exam tomorrow. A common component of grieving (see Chapter 24).
4. *Rationalization*	Finding an acceptable excuse for something which is really quite unacceptable, a 'cover story' which preserves your self-image or that of someone close to you. Justifying your own and others' actions to yourself — and believing it!	'Being cruel to be kind.' 'I only did it for you.' 'It was in your best interests.' 'I did so badly because I didn't revise properly.'

Continued

Table 26.1 (*Continued*)

Name of defence	Description	Example(s)
5. *Reaction-formation*	Consciously feeling or thinking the very opposite of what you (truly) unconsciously feel or think. The conscious thoughts or feelings are experienced as quite real.	Being considerate/polite to someone you cannot stand, even going out of your way to be nice to them. This 'display' may be quite suspicious to an observer. Obsessive–compulsive neurosis, eg compulsive cleanliness as an attempt to cancel out an obsession with dirt (see Chapter 28).
6. *Sublimation*	A form of displacement where a substitute activity is found to express an unacceptable impulse. The activity is usually socially acceptable — if not desirable. One of the most positive/constructive of all defences.	Playing sport to re-channel aggressive impulses. Doing sculpture or pottery or gardening to re-channel the desire to play with faeces. All artistic and cultural activities.
7. *Identification*	The incorporation or *introjection* of an external object (usually another person) into one's own personality, making them a part of oneself. Coming to think, act and feel as if one were that person. Involves imitation and modelling.	A young boy's assumption of the male role and acquisition of a conscience in order to avoid castration (*identification with the aggressor*) (see Chapters 21 & 22). A common component of grieving (see Chapter 24).
8. *Projection*	Attributing your own, unwanted, feelings and characteristics onto someone else. The reverse of Identification.	Suspecting or accusing someone of dishonourable motives based on your own (unconscious) dishonourable motives. 'I hate you' becomes 'You hate me'. The basis of paranoia (see Chapter 28).
9. *Regression*	Engaging in behaviour characteristic of an earlier stage of development. We normally regress to the point of fixation (see text).	Taking to your bed when upset, crying, losing your temper, eating when depressed, wetting yourself if extremely frightened.
10. *Isolation*	Separating contradictory thoughts or feelings into 'logic-tight' compartments so that no conflict is experienced. Separating thoughts and emotions which usually go together. A form of dissociation.	Calmly and clinically talking about a very traumatic experience without showing any emotion (or even giggling about it, as in schizophrenia). (See Chapter 28.)

Partly because of this distortion and deception, and partly despite it, the defences help us deal with anxiety; they prevent us from being overwhelmed by temporary threats or traumas and can provide 'breathing space' in which to come to terms with conflict or find alternative ways of coping. As short-term measures, they are advantageous, necessary and 'normal', but as long-term solutions to life's problems they are usually regarded as unhealthy and undesirable. Some of the major defence mechanisms are shown in Table 26.1.

2) Theory of the Mind (Levels of Consciousness)

Freud believed that thoughts, ideas, memories and other psychic material could operate at one of three levels: conscious, pre-conscious and un-conscious. These levels of consciousness do not correspond to areas or layers of the mind or brain but refer to how accessible the thought etc is to the thinker.

What we are consciously aware of at any one time represents the mere tip of an iceberg—most of our thoughts and ideas are either not accessible at that moment (pre-conscious) or are totally inaccessible (unconscious), at least without the use of special techniques such as free association and dream interpretation. The ego represents the *conscious* part of the mind, together with some aspects of the superego, namely those moral rules and values that we are able to express in words.

The ego also controls the *pre-conscious*, a kind of 'ante-room', an extension of the conscious, whereby things we are not fully aware of right now can become so fairly easily if our attention is directed to them. For example, you suddenly realize that you have been in pain for some time or you notice a ticking clock which has been ticking away all the time. The pre-conscious also processes ill-defined id urges into perceptible images and part of the superego may also function at a pre-conscious level.

The *unconscious* (the most contentious part of Freud's theory of the mind) comprises: (i) id impulses; (ii) all repressed material; (iii) the unconscious part of the ego (the part which is involved in dream work, neurotic symptoms and defence mechanisms); and (iv) part of the superego, for example, the free-floating anxiety or vague feelings of guilt or shame which are difficult to account for, and behaving in ways which seem to reflect parental standards but not being able to say what these standards are.

Freud depicted the unconscious as a *dynamic* force and not a mere 'dustbin' for all those thoughts etc which are not important or too weak to force themselves into awareness; this is best illustrated by the process of repression, whereby what is threatening is actively forced out of consciousness by the ego (R. Murray Thomas 1985).

'Our Reasons' versus 'The Reasons'

We discussed overdetermination earlier in relation to dream work and symptomatology. Freud also used the term in a more general way to refer to the fact that much of our behaviour (and our thoughts and feelings) has multiple causes, some conscious, some unconscious. By definition, we only know about the conscious causes and these are what we normally take to be *the* reasons for our actions. However, if the causes also include unconscious factors, then the reasons we give for our behaviour can never tell the whole story and, indeed, the unconscious causes may be the more important.

This view of the individual as never being fully aware of all the reasons for their behaviour is one of *irrational man*—we do not know ourselves as well as we would like, or as well as we think we do.

Overdetermination is one aspect of *psychic determinism*, the view that all behaviour is purposive, or goal-directed, and that everything we do, think and feel has a *cause* (often unconscious). It follows that what we often call 'accidents' (implying a chance occurrence, something which 'just happens'), do have a cause after all and, taking this a step further, that the cause (or contributory cause) may actually turn out to be the 'victim'. For instance, the 'accident-prone' person is *not*, according to Freud, an unfortunate victim of circumstance but is, unconsciously, bringing about the accidents—perhaps in an attempt to punish themselves in some way. Freud did not deny the existence of events which lie beyond the control of the victim but these are rare occurrences; it is more common for an 'accident' to be the consequence of our own, unconscious, wishes and motives.

The Psychopathology of Everyday Life

We have seen how the unconscious reveals itself through dreams and neurotic symptoms and the major aim of psychoanalysis is to make the unconscious conscious. But Freud believed that there is another important way in which our everyday behaviour provides us with glimpses of the unconscious at work and that is what he called 'parapraxes', the all-too-common slips of the tongue, slips of the pen, forgetting things (including words and people's names), leaving things behind and 'accidents'. Parapraxes have come to be known as 'Freudian slips', an indication of how Freud's theories have permeated our everyday language and thinking.

3) Freud's Instinct Theory

Psychoanalytic theory is often described as an instinct theory; from what we have said about the id, it should be evident that Freud believed that personality is based on biological drives, mainly sexual and aggressive in nature, rooted in the body with its unalterable hereditary constitution.

However, this needs to be qualified in two main ways. First, although he saw personality development as largely bound up with development of the sexual instinct (libido) which passes through a maturational, biologically determined sequence of stages, Freud also stressed the influence of the reactions of significant others (especially parents) on the child's behaviour as it passes through the stages. As we shall see below, Freud's theory of how adult personality types arise is directly linked to experiences the child has had at a particular developmental stage. Secondly, Freud's concept of an instinct was very different from the earlier view of unlearned, largely automatic (pre-programmed) responses to specific stimuli (based on instincts in other species). He saw instincts as relatively undifferentiated energy, capable of almost infinite variation through experience; indeed, instead of using the German *Instinckt*, he used *Trieb* which is most accurately translated as 'drive'.

Although Freud emphasized the role of the sexual instinct in personality development, this was by no means the only one he identified. In *Beyond the Pleasure Principle* (1920), he distinguished two main groups of instincts: (i) the Life Instincts (*Eros*) which include libido (sexual energy); and (ii) the Death Instincts (*Thanatos*), comprising, primarily, aggression. Libido later came to refer to *all* kinds of psychic (drive) energy, the principal components of which are sexual; however, Freud never maintained that no other instincts exist or that 'everything is sex' (see Chapter 13).

4) Psychosexual Development

One of the most radical aspects of Freud's theories is the notion of *infantile sexuality*, the view that babies and young children (and not just adolescents and adults) have sexual experiences and are capable of sexual pleasure. As a way of trying to illustrate how revolutionary this part of the theory was, Table 26.2 compares the Victorian concept of sexuality (the 'official' view) with Freud's in terms of the four major components of an instinct, namely, source, impetus or force, aim and object.

As Table 26.2 shows, according to Freud sexuality is not confined to adults but is evident from the moment of birth. In order to understand Freud's theory of infantile sexuality we must understand his use of the term sexuality: he used it to describe the desire for physical, sensuous, pleasure of any kind and, far from being a highly specific drive towards heterosexual gratification (ie genital stimulation), sexuality can be satisfied in a variety of ways. The essence of sexual pleasure lies in the rhythmical stroking or stimulation of virtually any part of the body and, accordingly, he describes the baby as 'polymorphously perverse'.

Why did he define sexuality in this unusual way?

a) In sexual perversions, adult behaviour may be directed towards persons of the same sex, the individual, animals, inanimate objects etc, so sexual desire is not necessarily aimed exclusively at adult members of the opposite sex.

b) Even with adult members of the opposite sex, genital intercourse is not the only form of sexual behaviour enjoyed.

c) Infants often show behaviour similar to adult perverts, eg interest in urination and defecation, thumb-sucking, exposing their naked body and enjoying seeing others naked.

Freud believed that current (adult) neuroses are the result of inadequate solutions to the problems experienced in childhood at one or more psychosexual stage. Each state (the sequence being maturationally determined) involves a particular mode or means of achieving gratification and the degree and kind of satisfaction which the child experiences at each stage will depend on how the child is treated by its parents (in particular).

Table 26.2 Comparison between Freud's theory of infantile sexuality and the Victorian view of sexuality

Components of an instinct	*The Victorian view of sexuality*	*Freud's view (infantile sexuality)*
Source Where in the body does it arise?	Arises exclusively in the genital area, and so does not appear before puberty.	Present at birth and passes through a series of pre-determined stages, each one focused on a different part of the body (*Erogenous/erotogenic zone*): Stages of psychosexual development: Oral (0–1), Anal (1–3), Phallic (3–5/6), Latency (5/6 to puberty), Genital (puberty to maturity)
Impetus or *force* How much excitement is produced?	It varies, in adults, from one time to another; gratification reduces it to a minimum. Frustration increases the impetus. In children it is absent so there is zero impetus.	It can be as strong in a baby (oral stage) as in an adult (genital stage). In itself, one kind of sexuality is no more or less strong than any other. Difference between stages is *qualitative*.
Aim What is it for? What is its purpose?	*Primary aim*: Procreation (reproduction) *Secondary aim*: Release of tension	*Primary aim:* Release of tension (ie pleasure) Procreation is almost incidental.
Object What or whom is needed in order to satisfy it?	Legal spouse	At first, ourselves, eg sucking, later masturbation (ie auto-erotism). From the genital stage on-wards, we need an adult of the opposite sex.

According to Freud, both excessive gratification and extreme frustration can produce permanent consequences for the individual (*fixation*) and the nature of these consequences is a function of the particular stage at which it occurs and the form it takes. The most satisfactory balance is between gaining enough pleasure to be willing to move on to the next stage but not so much that the individual is content to stay there!

Development for Freud is a complex interaction between a biologically-programmed timetable of change and the environmental or social context in which it happens, and if we want to understand the adult we need to retrace their childhood, hence, 'the child is father to the man'.

Oral Stage (0 to 1 year)

It is through the mouth that the newborn must obtain life-sustaining nourishment; the nerve endings in the lips and mouth are particularly sensitive so that the baby derives pleasure from sucking quite independently of the feeding process (non-nutritive sucking). The mouth is also important for finding out about objects.

The oral stage is divided into two: the earlier, receptive or incorporative sub-stage (lasting for the first few months); and the later, biting or aggressive sub-stage. In the former, the baby is passive and almost totally dependent and the major oral activities are sucking, swallowing and mouthing; in the latter, gums are hardening and teeth erupting and biting and chewing become the most important activities. Biting the breast, or fingers etc can express the baby's *ambivalence*, its experience of both loving and hating the same object (ie the mother) at the same time.

Anal Stage (1 to 3 years)

The most sensitive and pleasurable body zone is now the anal cavity, the sphincter muscles of the lower bowel and the muscles of the urinary system (because the urinary functions are involved as well as the anal, it is sometimes called the anal–urethal stage). The primary concern is with expelling and retaining faeces and this stage also divides into two sub-stages: the earlier, expulsion, and the later, retention, sub-stages. In the former, the child experiences its first encounter with external restrictions on its wish to defecate where and when it pleases, in the form of parents trying to potty-train it. This represents a crucial time for the child to learn to earn praise and approval—love from parents is no longer unconditional but now depends on how the child *behaves*. It is also a crucial time for developing (general) attitudes towards authority. In the latter, the child has learned to retain faeces and urine at will and now sensuous pleasure can be derived from holding in or holding onto these bodily 'products' or 'creations'.

Phallic Stage (3 to 5 or 6 years)

Sensitivity now becomes concentrated in the genitals and masturbation (in both sexes) becomes a new source of pleasure. The child becomes aware of anatomical sex differences, which sets in motion the conflict between erotic attraction, resentment, rivalry, jealousy and fear which Freud called the Oediupus complex (in boys) and the Electra complex (in girls). These have been discussed in detail in Chapters 21 and 22.

Latency (5 or 6 to puberty)

Freud used the term 'latency' to indicate that only quantitative changes occur in the libido during these few years prior to puberty—there are no new qualitative changes as in the earlier stages. Although this does not mean that the child is asexual, it falls 'victim' to 'infantile amnesia' and represses the sexual preoccupations of the earlier years, allowing social and intellectual development to proceed. Much of the child's energies are channelled into developing new skills and acquiring new knowledge and play becomes largely

---

Box 26.1: Freud's Theory of Play (based on Millar, 1972)

1. Like *all* behaviour, play is motivated behaviour (ie caused by the child's feelings and emotions, both unconscious and conscious).

2. In common with dreams and fantasy, play is determined by *wishes*. The child *can* distinguish play from reality but uses objects and situations from the real world to create a world of its own in which to *repeat* pleasant experiences at will and to order and alter events in the way that it finds most pleasing. For instance, children want to be grown up and do what adults do—in play this is possible.

3. But how does this account for the frequency with which *unpleasant* experiences are repeated in play? For example, children who hate taking medicine dose their dolls or they graphically re-enact a frightening accident or event. Given that we try to keep excitation to a minimum, so that all increases in excitation are felt as unpleasant and all decreases as pleasurable, repeating distressing or upsetting experiences in play is, in fact, an attempt to feel pleasure, since repetition *reduces* the excitation associated with them.

4. This impulse to repeat (*repetition compulsion*) is part of the urge to return to an earlier, more stable, tension-free state (ie death). (See section (3) on Freud's Instinct Theory.)

5. Through play the child can *master* disturbing experiences by *actively* bringing them about rather than being a passive and helpless victim; this view contributed to the development of *play therapy* and the use of *projective* tests of personality (see Chapters 28 and 29).

6. *Play* and the *Defence mechanisms.*
   Given that conflict and frustration are inevitable, then much play can be seen as the special use of:

i) *Projection*—dolls, imaginary companions, evil witches etc behave maliciously.

ii) *Displacement*—immersing doll-baby or toy in water or throwing it about helps relieve a jealous sibling's feelings without harming the new baby brother or sister;

iii) *Regression*—blowing bubbles may represent a return to oral over-indulgence or frustration.

iv) *Sublimation*—sand and water play are acceptable, while playing with faeces is not.

7. Different kinds of play will be associated with different psychosexual stages, eg the example of sublimation above, or playing roles reflecting identification with same-sex parent during phallic stage.

---

confined to other children of the same gender (helping the child to control sexual thoughts). Freud's theory of play is summarized in Box 26.1.

In relative terms, the balance between the id, ego and superego is greater during latency than at any future time in the child's life; indeed, latency represents the calm before the storm of puberty, which marks the beginning of the *genital stage*. The relative harmony within the child's personality is now disrupted and the id begins to make powerful new demands in the form of heterosexual desires, so that members of the opposite sex are now needed to satisfy the libido. (See Chapter 23.)

Psychosexual Development and Personality Types

We noted above that both excessive gratification *and* extreme frustration (especially during the oral stage) could produce long-lasting consequences, notably, the kind and combination of personality characteristics that the identified two major personality types—the oral and the anal; some of the trated in activities associated with one or other stage and the process by which this happens is called *fixation*.

Fixation
However, fixation is not an all-or-none thing, it can vary in degree. There are many examples of how commonplace oral fixation is, for example, smoking, nail-biting, pen-sucking and kissing are all 'oral' activities, while many swear words make reference to anal-urinary activities ('crap', 'shit', 'piss', for example). These examples show that the early stages of development all leave their mark or imprint to varying degrees.

Freud was equally interested in more extreme examples of fixation and identified two major personality types — the oral and the anal; some of the major traits associated with these, together with traits and activities resulting from the use of defence mechanisms, are shown in Table 26.3.

5) Empirical Studies of Freud's Theories

There have been literally thousands of empirical studies of various aspects of Freud's theories.

Two of the major reviews of this research have been carried out by Kline (1972) and Fisher and Greenberg (1977), the latter being perhaps the most comprehensive to date. They conclude that Freud was right in some areas, wrong in others and too vague to be tested at all in still others. Psychoanalytic theory cannot be accepted or rejected as a total package, 'it is a complex structure consisting of many parts, some of which should be accepted, others rejected and the rest at least partially re-shaped,' (Fisher & Greenberg 1977).

Three basic kinds of study have been carried out: (i) *validational*, which try to test directly various parts of the theory, mainly in the laboratory; (ii) those which try to investigate some of the *underlying mechanisms* involved but which are not direct tests of the theory, again mainly laboratory experiments; (iii) those which study the *effects* of *psychoanalysis* as therapy (these will be discussed in Chapter 29).

Fonagy (1981) asks whether it is conceivable that laboratory studies could 're-create' the clinical concepts and experiences that Freud describes and, therefore, questions the usefulness of validational studies. He also queries the relevance of studies of treatment-effectiveness as a way of 'testing' the theory —he says it is equivalent to the relevance of the effectiveness of aspirin to a theory of headaches!

i) Validational Studies

Many of these have been concerned with Freud's theory of personality types, especially the Oral and Anal. First, what is the evidence that the oral personality exists? (See Table 26.3.)

Table 26.3 Relationship between fixation at psychosexual stages and adult personality types

Oral (0–1)	Incorporative	Fixation through over-indulgence	Passive —	1. Cheerful unrealistically optimistic; 'life is easy.' 2. 'I am the centre of the universe'; self-centredness. 3. Dependent—can't bear others' disapproval. Through *sublimation:* interest in languages, compulsive talker, ventriloquist, 'thirst for knowledge'.
		Fixation through frustration	Dependent	1. Greedy, acquisitive. 2. Envious, pessimistic. 3. Addict, parasite. 4. Gluttonous. 5. Thumb-sucker. 6. Smoker.
	Aggressive	Fixation through over-indulgence	Active —	
		Fixation through frustration	Biting	1. Cynical 2. Verbally, 'biting', sarcastic, scornful, disdainful, contemptuous. 3. Nail-biter.
Anal (1–3)	Expulsive	Orderliness could represent a *Reaction formation* against the wish to mess.		
		a) Orderliness	1. Pre-occupation with punctuality, routine; everything must be in its proper place. 2. Obsessive-compulsive behaviour (in extreme cases).	
		'Performing' for others, giving presents, donating to charity etc, could be *sublimations* of wish to 'perform on the potty' for parents. Sculptors, potters, gardeners are all *sublimating* the wish to smear.		
	Retentive	b) Parsimony c) Obstinacy	1. Miserly, thrifty. 2. Wilfully hoarding	*Reaction formation* against this could be feeling compelled to give things away or lose them through gambling or speculation on stock market.
Phallic (3–5/6)		1. Homosexuality 2. Curiosity 3. Exhibitionism 4. Exploitation of others	5. Excessive displays of masculinity/femininity 6. Extreme self-centredness 7. Excessive ambition 8. Narcissism (self-love)	A surgeon may be *sublimating* hostile feelings towards same-sex parent. Writer of pornography may be *sublimating* sexual preoccupations.
Latency (5/6–puberty)		1. Never feeling comfortable with members of the opposite sex; may avoid heterosexual relationships. 2. May perform sexual activities in an emotionally-detached or aggressive way.		

One early study, (Goldman-Eisler, 1948) found that pessimism, passivity, aloofness, verbal aggression and autonomy tend to cluster together (as do their opposites); this was confirmed by Lazare et al (1966).

Kline and Storey (1977) found evidence for two oral characters, one in which dependency, fluency, sociability, liking of novelty and relaxation clustered together ('oral optimistic') and one in which independence, verbal aggression, envy, coldness and hostility, malice, ambition and impatience clustered together ('oral pessimistic'). Storey (1980) found a relationship between these scores and smoking, food preferences and nail-biting.

Fisher and Greenberg (1977) concluded that people who are unusually preoccupied with oral themes tend to crave approval and support from significant others. Also, 'oral people' (eg those sensitive to oral images or dependency themes) use submission and passivity to maintain contact with potential supporters; they also tend to over-eat, smoke, and drink a lot of alcohol.

What about the evidence for the anal personality?

Kline (1972), Fisher and Greenberg (1977) and Pollak (1979) found evidence for the clustering of three major character traits, namely *orderliness*, *parsimony* and *obstinacy*. But Hill (1976) criticized six of the studies reviewed by Kline as being good ones for having major methodological weaknesses.

Better support comes from students where a questionnaire and behavioural measures of anal anxiety have been correlated with specific behavioural measures of the three main anal traits. For example, Rosenwald (1972) found that the amount of anxiety experienced about anal matters predicted how carefully subjects arranged magazines when asked to do so by the experimenter and subjects' obstinacy in shifting their opinion was predicted by the difficulty they experienced in solving a puzzle which involved immersing their hands in a faecal-like substance.

Fisher (1978) found that racial prejudice based on skin colour can be predicted by subjects' attitudes to cleanliness and thrift, implying that colour prejudice is at least partly the consequence of an unconscious connection between skin colour and faeces. As Fonagy (1981) points out, these predictions certainly seem highly counter-intuitive and difficult to account for except in psychoanalytic terms.

However, the fact that there is substantial evidence for the existence of oral and anal personality types does not, of course, mean that these traits come about in the way Freud believes. So what is the evidence that these personality variables are related to early oral/anal experiences?

Fisher and Greenberg (1977) found that the evidence is often contradictory. For example, Goldman-Eisler (1951) found a correlation between her orality factor and length of breast-feeding and Sears et al (1953/65) found dependency to be related to severity of weaning. However, Thurstone and Mussen (1951) found no relationship between dependency and duration of breast-feeding.

However, the measures of feeding-styles used in these studies do not do justice to the complexities of mother-infant interaction and when these are taken into account, the evidence tends to be favourable to Freud. For example, Kagan and Moss (1962) found that protective, warm mothers tend to have boys who are dependent (up to age 10, anyway) while Hernstein (1963), in an 18-year longitudinal study, found that such mothers tend to have children who are less fussy about food and who are generally *more* independent than children of cold mothers. (These apparent contradictions can be reconciled by drawing on the explanatory 'power' of the defence mechanisms—can you think which one in particular?)

Laboratory studies also tend to suggest that the oral person is rather dependent; eg positive correlations have been found between orality and responsiveness to *verbal reinforcement* (Timmons and Noblin, 1963), *verbal advice* (Tribich and Messer, (1974) and *social support* under stress (Sarnoff & Zimbardo, 1961). However, not only do these studies *not* show cause and effect but they all use different measures of orality (eg number of mouth movements, number of ice-creams eaten etc) and how valid are such measures?

As to the anal character, Finney (1963), Hetherington and Brackbill (1963) and Sears et al (1965) all failed to verify that the anal person differs from other types in age of initiation or completion of toilet training or in severity of training procedures.

Defence Mechanisms

Both Wilkinson and Cargill (1955) and Levinger and Clark (1961) found that emotive material is more easily forgotten than neutral material. Repression, displacement and sublimation have been demonstrated under controlled conditions by Miller and Bugelski (1948) and Wallach and Greenberg (1960). Halpern (1977) reported that subjects who denied being aroused by pornography projected more lust onto a disliked person compared with less defensive subjects. Speisman et al (1964) demonstrated intellectualization by measuring subjects' GSR (Galvanic Skin Response) as they watched a stressful film with commentaries intended either to increase or decrease stress.

Hilgard (1965) demonstrated rationalization by putting subjects into a hypnotic trance and telling them that when they woke up they would open the window (at a cue from the experimenter) but would not remember being given the instruction; in trying to preserve their self-image as a 'rational' person, they searched for a reasonable excuse ('Isn't it a little stuffy in here?') and proceeded to open it.

However, Fonagy (1981) points out that in some of these studies the thinking and feeling involved were conscious, while defence mechanisms, as Freud defined them, are unconscious. But these difficulties aside, he believes that much more relevant is the second kind of study, namely those which go beyond trying to replicate clinical phenomena and which instead attempt to identify basic mechanisms or processes which may underlie unconscious phenomena.

Relationship Between Freudian and Factor-analytic Concepts

Although not validation studies as such, the factor-analytic studies of Eysenck and Cattell provide some indirect support for Freud. In a review of these, Kline (1983) argues that studies of Eysenck's N, showing a continuum, indirectly support Freud's view that neurotics are only different in degree from non-neurotics.

As far as psychotics are concerned, Freud argued (1924) that they deny reality and obey their instinctual urges compared with neurotics who deny their urges and obey reality, in other words, there is a discontinuity between psychotics on the one hand and neurotics and normals on the other (hence, a qualitative difference). Eysenck's findings that both normals and neurotics score low on P seems to confirm Freud's view.

As far as Cattell is concerned, we noted in Chapter 25 that he was influenced by Freud in the labels he attached to some of his primary factors: Factor C (ego-strength), Factor G (superego) and Factor Q4 (id tension). According to Freud, neurotics have weak egos: either they feel threatened by id impulses (neurotic conflict) or they have a very strong superego (moral conflict), and this picture has been confirmed by Cattell. For example, on the 16PF, diagnosed neurotics score low on C and high on Q4 and as far as Factor O is concerned (guilt proneness), neurotics also score high.

However, G is no higher in neurotics than normals, suggesting that neurotic conflict may be more important than moral conflict in the aetiology of neurosis (Kline, 1983).

ii) Studies of Underlying Mechanisms Involved in Unconscious Phenomena

Dixon (1971) reviewed several studies which show that verbal stimuli which are too quick or dim to be consciously perceived will nonetheless affect the subject's associative processes.

Marcel and Patterson (1978) found that associations following the subliminal perception of a word were linked to its meaning; Tyler et al (1978) found that subjects' self-ratings on anxiety increased following the subliminal presentation of unpleasant words (eg cancer) and O'Grady (1977) found increased GSRs to the subliminal presentation of emotive picture stimuli (eg of a breast).

The relevance of these is that thoughts in the form of associations may occur in the absence of awareness; also emotions can be elicited from subjects without awareness of their source. This implies that consciousness is not essential to cognition and it only periodically samples the ongoing processing of information, a view highly consistent with Freud's.

Closely related to subliminal perception is *perceptual defence* (see Chapter 4). Studies by Worthingon (1964), Dixon and Haider (1961) and Shevrin (1973) all suggest that subjects perceive words *at some level* in order to recognize their threatening nature and then make a decision *not* to perceive the message after all.

A further source of evidence is neurophysiological psychology. Penfield (1958) directly stimulated the temporal cortex and patients reported phenomenal experiences of 'bygone days', including the entire spectrum of emotions and visual/acoustic components. The central nervous system seems to preserve a record of past experience and perceptions of astonishing detail which is not normally available to consciousness. Perhaps these perceptions, encoded as memories, form the basis of pre-conscious and unconscious systems.

Bogen (1969), Galin (1974) and McKinnon (1979) have all equated the function of the dominant hemisphere of the brain (the left for most people) with secondary process thinking and that of the minor hemisphere with primary process thinking.

Other support for Freud comes from studies of *split-brain* patients (whose left and right hemispheres are no longer physically connected—see Chapters 15 and 16). For example, Hoppe (1977), Zaidel (1978) and Diamond (1979) found that, as the ability to speak is localized in the left (dominant) hemisphere, all phenomenal experiences these patients report refer to the left hemisphere: their dreams are free from primary process distortions and bizareness and lie much closer to ordinary modes of thinking of awake adults. This suggests that dreams and primary process thinking as a whole are normally controlled by the right side of the brain.

Evaluation

1) Is the theory scientific?

We have seen how much research Freud's theories have generated and, in the light of this, it seems very difficult to accept Popper's criticism (see Chapter 2) that they are unfalsifiable and, therefore, unscientific. The theory as a whole (or, at least, many parts of it) does seem testable (even if it is not always shown to be true), although we should note Fonagy's (1981) warning that many validational studies may not be very relevant to an understanding of the clinical phenomena as Freud described them. Perhaps more relevant to Popper's criticism are rather specific parts of the theory, in particular, the defence mechanism of reaction formation.

Scodel (1957) predicted, based on Freud's theories, that highly dependent men would prefer big-breasted women. (Dependency, as we have seen, is an oral trait and the breast can be regarded as a symbol of a state of dependency.) Scodel in fact found the opposite to be true—dependent men tended to prefer *small*-breasted women so Freud's theory, in this respect, seems to have been falsified (on this occasion, at least). However, Kline (1972) invoked the concept of reaction formation in order to show that Scodel had *confirmed* the theory, since a fixation (unconscious) with big breasts may show up as a preference (conscious) for small breasts! According to Kline, then *either* outcome (preference for big *or* small-breasted women) would have shown Freud to be right!

As we saw in Chapter 2, another important scientific criterion is to do with predictability and, at least as far as the concept of reaction formation is concerned, Freud's theory is very bad at predicting particular outcomes; it is very good, however, at accounting for what has already happened in the past. Is there, at least in principle, any way of testing the hypothesis that someone's affection towards another person is, in fact, a reaction formation against their repressed hostility? At the worst, the Freudian would only have to concede (if it was somehow shown that the affection was genuine) that the person's behaviour was 'overdetermined' (ie motivated by conscious affection *and* unconscious hostility).

Eysenck (1973) also points to reaction formation to demonstrate the low status of psychoanalytic theory as a scientific theory; he argues that for the Freudian all behaviour can be explained even if none can be predicted and this is largely because of the retrospective nature of data-collection involved in the case study method which Freud used (see (2) below).

However, it would be a serious mistake to regard reaction formation as typifying Freudian theory; the sheer volume of research suggests that it cannot be dismissed as lightly as Popper and Eysenck would like on the grounds of being 'unscientific'.

2)   How valid is the case study method?
Relying as they do on the re-construction of childhood events, the case study, as used by Freud, is generally considered to be the least scientific of all empirical methods used by psychologists; they are open to many types of distortion and uncontrolled influences. Not only were the memories of his patients part of the basic data but Freud himself made no notes during the treatment sessions themselves but only several hours later—the distortions involved in remembering are notorious (see Chapter 6).

Greenberg and Fisher (1977) point out the tendency to select or emphasize material which supported particular interpretations and nowhere is this more clearly illustrated than in the case of Little Hans (Chapter 21).

3)   How representative were the subjects studied by Freud?
One of the standard criticisms made of Freud's data-base is that his patients were mainly wealthy, middle-class Jewish females, living in Vienna at the turn of the century, and therefore hardly representative of the population to whom his theories were generalized. If these people were also neurotic, how can we be sure that what Freud discovered about them is true of normal individuals? However, as we have seen, Freud regarded neurosis as continuous with normal behaviour, that is, neurotics are suffering only from more extreme problems experienced by all of us.

More serious, perhaps, is the criticism that Freud only studied adults (with the very dubious exception of Little Hans) and yet he put forward a theory of personality development. How many steps removed were his data from his theory? According to R. Murray Thomas (1985): (i) the analyst interprets through his theoretical 'lens', (ii) ostensibly symbolic material derived from (iii) the reported dreams/memories etc of neurotics about (iv) ostensible experiences stemming from their childhood one or more decades earlier. However, this in itself does not invalidate the theory—it merely makes the study of children all the more necessary.

Significantly, although he described most of his patients as neurotics, many writers have subsequently concluded that many of them would today be diagnosed as psychotic (see Chapter 28).

4)   A key issue which divides Freudians and other psychodynamic theorists (Jung, Adler, Erikson and others) is to do with the role of biological factors in personality development. While none of the neo-Freudians denied that biological factors are important, or that all psychic energy must ultimately be rooted in the body, they did deny that all behaviour is directed towards the satisfaction of biological needs in the way Freud believed. For example, although it may be true that hoarding is a trait associated with the anal stage, it is absurd to claim that hoarding is *always* the manifestation of anal fixation (J. A. C. Brown, 1963).

It was Freud's emphasis on the role of sexuality which ultimately led to the split with Jung and Adler, and neo-Freudians such as Erikson stressed the role of socio-cultural influences almost as a counter-balance to Freud's preoccupation with biological factors.

5) Several writers (eg Schafer, 1976) have criticized terms like the id, ego and superego as bad metaphors; they do not correspond to any aspect of psychology or neurophysiology and they encourage *reification*, that is, treating metaphorical terms as if they were 'things' or entities.

However, Bettelheim (1985) points out that much of Freud's terminology was mistranslated and this had led to a misrepresentation of those parts of his theory. For example, Freud himself never used the Latin words *id, ego* and *superego*; he used the German *das Es* ('the it'), *das Ich* ('the I') and *das Über-Ich* (the 'over-I') which were intended to capture how the individual relates to different aspects of the self, whereas the Latin terms tend to depersonalize these and give the impression that there are three separate 'selves' which we all possess! The Latin words (chosen by his American translator to give greater scientific credibility) turn the concepts into cold technical terms which arouse no personal associations; whereas the 'I' can only be studied from the inside (through introspection), the 'ego' can be studied from the outside (as behaviour). In translation, Freud's 'soul' became scientific psychology's 'psyche' or 'personality' (Bettelheim, 1985).

6) More positively, there is no doubting the tremendous impact that Freud has had, both within psychology and outside. The fertility of psychoanalytic theory, in terms of the debate, research and theorizing it has generated, makes it one of the richest in the whole of psychology.

> He [Freud] has provided us with a set of ideas and concepts which, both in literature and everyday conversation, have helped us to formulate questions about ourselves, our inner experience and our social conditioning. He helped explode the myth of 'rational Man' and has brought us face to face with our irrational selves, a new image of ourselves at least as valid as any other major image-of-man that Social Science has offered and perhaps as challenging and disturbing as any it is ever likely to offer (Clift, 1984).

Carl Gustav Jung (1875-1961): Analytical Psychology

Jung 'broke ranks' with Freud in 1913 to form his 'Analytical Psychology'; he disagreed with Freud over a number of fundamental issues and it is these that I shall emphasize here.

Structure of the Personality and Levels of Consciousness

For Jung, the personality as a whole is the *psyche*, the totality of all psychic processes, conscious and unconscious; it embraces all thought, feeling and behaviour and helps the individual adapt to their social and physical environment. The term psyche also includes what is normally called 'soul'. The person is seen as a whole almost from the moment of birth; personality is not acquired piece-by-piece (the 'jigsaw' concept) through learning and experience but it is already there, so that instead of striving to achieve wholeness, our aim in life is to *maintain* it and to prevent the splitting or dissociation of the psyche into separate and conflicting parts. Jung saw the role of therapy as helping the patient recover this lost wholeness and to strengthen the psyche so as to resist future dissociation (see Chapter 28). The psyche comprises three major, interacting, levels: (i) Consciousness, (ii) the Personal Unconscious, and (iii) the Collective Unconscious. The distinction between (ii) and (iii) represents one of the major differences between Jung and Freud.

i) Consciousness

This is the only part of the mind known directly by the individual; it appears early in life through the operation of four basic functions: *thinking* (which tries to understand the world through cognition); *feeling* (which tries to evaluate things in terms of 'pleasant–unpleasant', 'acceptable–unacceptable'); *sensing* (which comprises all conscious experiences produced by stimulation of the sense organs—internal and external); and *intuiting* (which is 'knowing something without knowing how you know it' or 'perception via the unconscious'). While all four functions are constitutionally present in each person, they are not all used to the same degree and one usually predominates; this is what makes the basic character of one person different from that of another.

In addition to these four functions there are two attitudes which determine the orientation of the conscious mind, namely *extroversion* and *introversion*. The extrovert's libido (Jung's term for psychic energy as a whole or life-force) is directed outwards towards the external, objective world of physical objects, people, customs and conventions, social institutions and so on and they are preoccupied with *inter*personal relationships and are generally more active and outgoing. By contrast, the introvert's libido is directed inwards towards the internal, subjective world of thoughts, feelings and so on and they are preoccupied with *intra*personal matters, are introspective and withdrawn and may be seen by others as aloof, reserved and antisocial. Jung believed that a person is predominantly one or the other throughout life, although there may be occasional inconsistencies in different situations; so for Jung, extroversion–introversion represents a *typology* whereas, as we saw in the last chapter, Eysenck's 'adoption' of Jung's terms took the form of personality *dimensions*, or a scale with extreme extroversion at one end and extreme introversion at the other.

Jung believed that the development of consciousness is also the beginning of *individuation*, the process by which a person becomes, psychologically 'in-dividual' that is, a separate, indivisible unity or whole, and from this process emerges the *ego*. The ego refers to how the conscious mind is organized and consists of conscious perceptions, memories, thoughts and feelings. Although it represents only a small part of the psyche as a whole, it plays the essential role of 'gatekeeper to consciousness', that is, it selects important sensations, feeling, ideas etc and allows them through into conscious awareness (much as Freud's pre-conscious does); this prevents us from becoming overwhelmed by the mass of stimulation going on around (and inside) us. (Also see Chapter 4.)

The ego provides a sense of identity and continuity for the individual and it is the central core of the personality.

ii) The Personal Unconscious

The Freudian unconscious, in Jung's terms, is predominantly 'personal', that is, composed of the individual's particular and unique experiences which have been made unconscious through repression; for Jung, repressed material represents only one kind of unconscious content. The personal unconscious also includes things we have forgotten because they were irrelevant (or seemed unimportant) at the time or because they have lost some of their 'energic value' since they happened, as well as all those things which we think of as being 'stored in memory', and things which may not be accessible to conscious recall at a particular time but which are available and could become accessible (see Chapter 6). In these respects, Jung's personal unconscious resembles Freud's pre-conscious.

A major feature of the personal unconscious is that associated groups of feelings, thoughts and memories may cluster together to form a *complex* which represents a quite autonomous and powerful 'mini-personality' within the total psyche; it is from Jung that the term has been 'borrowed' and become a commonly used one in everyday language, together with synonyms such as 'hang-up' (Calvin S. Hall and Nordby, 1973). Freud's Oedipus complex illustrates this constellation of thoughts and feelings. Although not necessarily detrimental, complexes often prevent the complete individuation of a person from taking place and one aim of therapy is to free the patient from the grip of such complexes.

In looking for the origin of complexes, Jung eventually turned to the collective unconscious.

iii) The Collective Unconscious

This part of Jung's theory sets him apart from Freud probably more than any other, since Jung was acknowledging the role of evolution and heredity in providing a blueprint for the psyche just as they do for the body. Freud's id is, of course, part of each individual's 'personal' unconscious and represents our biological inheritance. Ironically, in view of the criticism of Freud that he overemphasized the role of biological factors, Jung could be seen as having given inherited factors an even greater role than Freud by virtue of his collective unconscious.) According to Jung, the mind (through the brain) has inherited characteristics which determine how a person will react to life experiences and what type of experiences these will be.

Whereas for Freud our childhood is of critical importance in making us what we are as adults, Jung attached relatively little importance to our individual past in relation to the personal unconscious but saw the evolutionary history of human beings as a species as being all-important in relation to the collective (or *racial*) unconscious.

The collective unconscious can be thought of as a reservoir of latent images, called *primordial images*, which relate to the 'first' or 'original' development of the psyche, stemming from our ancestral past, both human, prehuman and animal (Calvin S. Hall and Nordby, 1973). These images are not literally pictures in the mind but are predispositions or potentialities for experiencing and responding to the world in the same way that our ancestors

Box 26.2: The Four Major Archetypes of the Collective Unconscious

The Persona ('Mask')
This is the outward face we present to the world, both revealing and concealing the real self; it allows us to play our part in social interaction and to be accepted by others. Jacobi (1980) maintains that the persona is, in fact, part of the ego; he describes it as a kind of cloak between the ego and the objective world. It is very similar to the notion of a social role, which refers to the expectations and obligations associated with a particular social position; Jung describes it as the 'conformity' archetype (see Chapter 8).

Normally, we play a variety of roles and personality as a whole cannot be reduced to any one of them—or to the entire set. However, we sometimes become dominated by a particular role which can take over our entire personality; when the ego identifies with the persona, Jung says that *inflation* is happening.

Anima/Animus
This refers to the unconscious mirror-image of our conscious ('official') gender —if we are male, our *anima* is our unconscious female side and if we are female, our *animus* is our unconscious male side. We all have qualities of the opposite sex/gender—both biologically and psychologically—and in a well-adjusted person both sides must be allowed to express themselves in thought and behaviour.

The anima has a preference for all things vain, helpless, uncertain and unintentional; the animus prefers the heroic, the intellectual, the artistic and athletic. These would be expressed in different ways in different cultures but are universal characteristics (compare them with gender role stereotypes as discussed in Chapter 22). Jung believed that repression of the anima/animus is very common in western culture, where the persona predominates. (What about androgyny? Again see Chapter 22.)

The Shadow
This contains more of our basic animal nature than any other archetype and is similar to Freud's id. Like the id, it must be kept in check if we are to live in society but this is not achieved easily and is always at the expense of our creativity and spontaneity, depth of feeling and insight. So the shadow represents the source of our creative impulses—but also of our destructive urges; if it is too severely repressed it will seek revenge, as in war. When the ego and shadow work harmoniously, the person is full of energy—both mentally and physically. The shadow of the highly creative person may occasionally overwhelm the ego causing temporary insanity (confirming the popular belief that genius is akin to madness).

The Self
This is the central archetype which unites the personality, giving it a sense of 'oneness' and firmness. The ultimate aim of every personality is to achieve a state of selfhood and self-realization (similar to Maslow's Self-Actualization); this is a life-long process, attained by very few individuals, Jesus and Buddha being notable exceptions.

did; for example, we do not have to learn to fear the dark or snakes through direct experience because we are naturally predisposed to develop such fears through the inheritance of our ancestors' fears. (Interestingly, support for Jung comes from studies of conditioning, which, as we saw in Chapter 3, show that it is much easier to induce a fear of snakes, for example, than to induce a fear of flowers. Similarly, clinical psychology shows that naturally acquired phobias of snakes and spiders are the most common amongst adults and of the dark in children.) (See Chapters 28 and 29.)

The contents of the collective unconscious are known as *archetypes* (a prototype or 'original model or pattern'), which, according to Calvin S. Hall and Nordby (1973) are more like a negative (which has to be developed through experience) than an already-developed and clearly recognizable photograph, 'forms without content', potential ways of perceiving and feeling and acting.

Jung identified a large number of archetypes, including birth, re-birth, death, power, magic, the hero, the child, the trickster, God, the demon, the wise old man, earthmother and the giant. Although universal, archetypes are expressed differently by different individuals, within and between racial and cultural groups; they also form the nucleus of a complex. Jung paid special attention to four archetypes: the Persona, Anima/Animus, the Shadow and the Self and these are featured in Box 26.2.

What did Jung base his theory of archetypes on and what is the evidence for their existence?

According to J.A.C. Brown (1963) there are three major sources of evidence: (i) the 'extraordinary' similarity of themes in the mythologies of various cultures; (ii) the recurring appearance, in therapy, of symbols which have become divorced from any of the patient's personal experiences and which become more and more like the primitive and universal symbols found in myths and legends; (iii) the content of fantasies of psychotics (especially schizophrenics) which are full of themes such as death and re-birth, which are similar to those found in mythology.

Many writers do not accept the theory of a collective unconscious, among them an anthropologist and psychoanalyst called Roheim (cited by J.A.C. Brown). Brown himself argues that members of all cultures share certain common experiences and so it is not surprising that they dream or create myths about archetypal themes. The deeper the interpretation, he says, the more likely we are to come up with universal explanations which seem to have an innate or biological basis; less deep, ego interpretations, however, are more likely to reveal the specific features of different cultures, ie cultural differences. (J.A.C. Brown, 1963).

Other Similarities and Differences between Jung and Freud

1) Dream Theory

Jung shared Freud's belief that dreams are the clearest manifestation of the unconscious. However, he certainly disagreed with Freud that all dreams are wish-fulfilments; rather, Jung saw dreams as an important way of attaining self-knowledge which, in turn (together with religious or spiritual experiences) is a path to achieving self-realization (see Box 26.2). However, not all dreams are equally significant in this respect.

The general function of dreams is to restore our psychological balance and to re-establish 'the total psychic equilibrium' and they are just as likely to point to the future (eg by suggesting a solution to a conflict) as to the past. He also believed that Freud's 'disguise' was far too elaborate and preferred to take the dream at face value. Dream symbols do not have a fixed meaning (as they very largely did for Freud) and he also advocated the study of *dream series*, that is, several dreams recorded over a period of time by the same individual.

2) Stages of Development

Jung's theory of personality development is, as we have seen, much less tied up with sexual development than Freud's. Jung identified four major life stages: Childhood (birth to puberty); Youth and Young Adulthood (puberty to 35–40); Middle Age (35–40 to old age); and Old Age. To the extent that he recognized developmental stages beyond Young Adulthood (Freud's genital stage), Jung's theory has more in common with Erikson's than Freud's.

3) Neurosis and Therapy

Repression plays very little part in Jung's theory of neurosis; more important is the conflict between different parts of the personality which have developed unequally. Jungian therapy is much more concerned with future goals than past history and the present situation is the key to neurosis; therapy aims to bring the patient into contact with the healing collective unconscious, largely through dream interpretation. Free association is also important but the Jungian analyst, compared with the Freudian, plays a much more active role and therapy is seen as a co-operative venture between patient and therapist.

4) Scientific Status

Jung is generally regarded as much more difficult to 'pin down' scientifically than Freud and has stimulated relatively little empirical research. However, Eysenck's dimensional interpretation of introversion/extroversion and two tests claiming to measure Jung's four basic functions (combined with introversion and extroversion), the Gray-Wheelwright Inventory (1946) and the Myers-Briggs Type Indicator (1962), represent important exceptions.

Alfred Adler (1870–1937): Individual Psychology

Adler broke from Freud two years earlier than Jung, in 1911; although he agreed with Freud about the importance of unconscious forces, he, like Jung, rejected Freud's emphasis on sexuality as the major influence on the personality and, instead, saw people as being motivated primarily by the drive towards affirmation of their personality, the tendency towards self-preservation, the *will to power* or striving for superiority.

Adler was much more interested than Freud in the social nature of man and, like Jung, he saw the individual as an indivisible unity or whole; any event must be considered in the light of its effect on the whole person if we are to understand it properly.

Adler was impressed by the body's capacity to compensate for organic damage, for example, damage to a kidney or lung may be followed by increased compensatory functioning of the undamaged one, and an undamaged part of the brain may take over the job normally carried out by the damaged area (see Chapter 15). To this extent, the strictly biological basis of Freud's theory was attractive to Adler and he believed that similar processes could be observed in the psychological sphere, for example, painters with imperfect vision, musicians and composers who are deaf, might be compensating for their defect in such a way that their inferiority actually becomes transformed into superiority. Adler saw feelings of inferiority as not only inevitable but as the key to understanding the whole of mental life.

The Origins of Inferiority

Every child spends its early years in a state of dependence on others and experiences all kinds of desires which cannot be satisfied; by comparison, adults seem happier and have more power. As a result, children come to experience their dependence and powerlessness as a state of *inferiority* relative to adults and, in reaction to this, an unconscious drive emerges towards superiority, the *will to power*.

Factors Contributing to Inferiority

Against this common background of inferiority, Adler identified several factors which could influence the degree of inferiority an individual might experience:

(a) Any kind of physical deformity, either congenital (eg harelip) or environmental (scarring as the result of an accident), to the extent that it is experienced psychologically.

(b) Gender—Adler recognized the inequality of men and women in society and believed that the equation between 'masculine' and 'strong and superior' and 'feminine' and 'weak and inferior' is made at an early age. Some boys may be unable to live up to these gender role stereotypes, especially if their fathers attribute them with masculine qualities which they do not possess and this may be at the root of homosexuality and other sexual 'deviations'. The Don Juan character, for example, is continually trying to convince himself of his masculinity (which he equates with sexual prowess); it is usually the 'conquest' rather than the actual sexual experience that matters since his behaviour is motivated not by an insatiable sexual appetite as such but by his underlying sense of inferiority. Women may try to compensate for their inferiority by wishing to be a man (the 'masculine protest') or by exploiting their 'weakness' and their feminine charms.

(c) Birth order, the social and economic status of the family and the length and quality of education can all contribute to a sense of inferiority.

(d) The way parents in particular, and adults in general, react to the child's successes and failures are vitally important; pressure to succeed may be too great and unrealistic for a particular child and its failures can produce anxiety in the parents which, in turn, cause extra pressure and anxiety in the child. (See Erikson's stage of 'initiative versus doubt and shame'.)

(e) A neglected, spoilt or hated child is likely to have very low self-esteem. How do people cope with inferiority?

In general, the more the original feelings of inferiority develop into the unconscious form of an inferiority complex, the greater the drive towards compensation. Each child develops early on in life its own particular strategy for dealing with the family situation as it is perceived; this strategy essentially comprises a set of attitudes which, collectively, form the 'lifestyle' upon which the adult personality is based. The traits we adopt have functional value for us in the earliest years—they were the traits which seemed to give us the best results in terms of power.

In addition, Adler identified three major techniques by which people try to overcome inferiority:

(i) *Successful compensation* involves compensating in a positive and constructive way which is socially advantageous for the individual, for example, intellectual achievement as a compensation for some physical handicap. In general, it refers to a successful adjustment to life's three challenges— Society, Work and Sex.

(ii) *Over-compensation* involves trying too hard so that the underlying motive becomes obvious, that is, aiming for extraordinary achievements and settling for nothing less. Such goals may be achievable only in fantasy and this can result in maladjustment. Less extreme examples are the bumptious little man, or the small man who smokes a huge cigar or drives an enormous car or lives in an enormous house, or the coward who becomes a bully.

(iii) *Escape from combat* is essentially a way of ensuring that failure is impossible (or is reduced to a minimum)—but at the price of any real success. For example, physical symptoms can be 'used' in order to deflect attention away from the real reasons for opting out, which may be fear of failure (very often the fear of failing to achieve impossibly high standards); this retreat into illness or adoption of the sick role can become a way of life and a means of gaining power over others.

Another form this can take is for the individual to go about things so casually that other people form the impression that they are not really trying or doing their best; this 'covers' the person in the event of failure, since the best way of never experiencing a real failure is never to have given yourself completely to the task in the first place.

Neurosis and Therapy

According to Adler, 'every neurosis can be understood as an attempt to free oneself from a feeling of inferiority in order to gain a feeling of superiority'. The neurotic is a person who is unable to gain superiority by legitimate means and so develops symptoms, either as an excuse to avoid situations in which they might be exposed as a failure or as a means of gaining control over others by a sort of emotional blackmail (as we saw in escape from combat).

The essential aim of therapy is to help the patient to understand their secret psychic processes and to gain the courage and self-confidence necessary to exist and develop in a normal way; the analyst points out the patient's style of life with its 'fictive goals' (unrealistic goals) and gives some practical advice regarding a more sensible alternative future lifestyle.

Evaluation

Adler's emphasis on social factors in personality development, his view of the person as a unity, the de-emphasis on sexual influences, and his relative emphasis on the conscious ego (as opposed to unconscious forces) are all significant modifications of Freud's theory which helped to inspire the theories of the neo-Freudians, such as Erik Erikson (born 1902), Karen Horney (1885–1952) and Erich Fromm (born 1900).

However, he seems to have over-emphasized the role of inferiority; as J. A. C. Brown (1963) points out, it is difficult to believe that *all* the non-organic nervous disorders (neuroses) are produced by a 'feeling of inferiority' or that psychoses are the result of complete failure to conquer inferiority, which leads the psychotic to 'refuse to play' the game of life.

According to J. A. C. Brown (1963), Adler's individual psychology has almost ceased to exist as a distinct, independent theory but its influence lives on (although this is not always acknowledged) in the theories of neo-Freudians. We turn to the theory of one of these now, Erik Erikson.

Erik Erikson (born 1902): Psychosocial Development

Apart from representing a significant contribution to psychological theory in its own right, Erikson's theory represents an important way of assessing Freud's theory and putting it into perspective.

Born in Germany in 1902 to Danish parents, Erikson trained as a Montessori teacher and took a teaching post in Vienna in 1927 where he undertook psychoanalytic training with Anna Freud, Sigmund's daughter; she was much more interested in child analysis than her father had been and this rubbed off on Erikson. He fled from the Nazis in 1933 and went to the USA, setting up private practice as a child analyst in Boston, where he came into contact with famous anthropologists such as Ruth Benedict and Margaret Mead, whose discipline was to have such an impact on his theory.

Similarities Between Erikson and Freud
a) He accepted Freud's tripartite theory of the structure of personality (id, ego, superego);
b) He accepted Freud's three levels of consciousness (conscious, pre-conscious and unconscious);
c) He accepted Freud's psychosexual stages as basically valid—as far as they went (but he thought that, as they stood, they did not go far enough).

Differences between Erikson and Freud
a) Erikson saw development as proceeding throughout the life-cycle, with Freud's last stage, the genital, constituting the pre-adult (adolescent) stage, with a subsequent three stages spanning adulthood (early, middle and late) as such. (His 'Eight Ages of Man' were first proposed in 1950.)
b) He believed (as did many other neo-Freudians) that Freud under-emphasized the role of socialization of the individual, particularly the

various patterns of behaviour which different cultures consider desirable and which the individual needs to adopt in order to be accepted by their cultural or sub-cultural group.

c) Erikson believes that the interaction between the individual and the social environment produces eight *psychosocial stages* (as opposed to Freud's psycho*sexual* stages), each of which centres around a developmental *crisis*, involving a struggle between two opposing or conflicting personality characteristics.

d) Erikson was much more concerned than was Freud with *mental health*; this is reflected in the concept of *ego identity* which is achieved by resolving the specified psychosocial crisis at each developmental stage.

e) Erikson is an *ego* psychologist (whereas Freud is an *id* psychologist), believing, for example, that conflict *within* the ego itself (as against conflict between the ego and the id or superego) could produce emotional disturbance and this, in turn, is related to his greater emphasis on social and cultural factors. Indeed, the individual (psychological) aspect of each developmental stage is inseparable from the social and cultural—they are opposite sides of the same coin. At each stage, a new dimension of 'social interaction' becomes possible, and this denotes the person's interaction both with the self and the social environment.

However, Erikson agreed with Freud that there is a biological basis to development—the sequence of stages is genetically determined and so is universal, the same for members of all cultures. Yet even here there is a crucial difference between the two theories: whereas for Freud, the baby begins life as a 'bundle of id' and only gradually becomes socialized, acquiring in turn an ego and superego; for Erikson, the human being is at *all times* an organism (id), an ego and a member of society (superego) and the individual must be biologically, psychologically and socially *ready* to move from one stage to the next; this, in turn, is matched by society's readiness. Although the order of stages is biologically based, the stages constitute the *ego*'s timetable and mirror the structure of the relevant social institutions; in this sense, individuals and society are interdependent.

Erikson's belief in the fixed, pre-determined sequence of the stages is expressed in his *epigenetic principle*, based on embryology, which maintains that the entire pattern of development is governed by a genetic structure common to all humans, whereby the genes dictate a timetable for the growth of each part of the unborn baby. (This biological principle can be seen in post-natal development too, for example, crawling, walking and puberty.)

Erikson extended this principle to social and psychological growth and proposed that personality seems to develop according to steps, 'predetermined in the human organism's readiness to be driven toward, to be aware of, and to interact with, a widening radius of significant individuals and institutions' (Erikson, 1968).

So Erikson believed that it is human nature to pass through a pre-determined sequence of psychosocial stages which are genetically determined. However, the social-cultural environment has a significant influence on the psychosocial modalities (dominant modes of acting and being), 'the radius of significant individuals and institutions' with which the individual interacts, *and* the nature of the crisis which arises at each stage (see Table 26.4).

Table 26.4 Comparison between Erikson's and Freud's stages of development (based on K Murray Thomas 1985/Erikson 1959)

Number of stage	Name of stage (psychosocial crisis)	Psychosocial modalities (dominant modes of being and acting)	Radius of significant relationships	Human virtues ('qualities of strength')	Freud's psychosexual stages	Approximate ages
1	Basic trust versus Basic mistrust	To get, To give in return	Mother or mother-figure	Hope	Oral-Respiratory Sensory-Kinaesthetic	0–1
2	Autonomy versus Shame and doubt	To hold on, To let go	Parents	Willpower	Anal-Urethral Muscular	1–3
3	Initiative versus Guilt	To make (going after), To 'make like' (playing)	Basic family	Purpose	Phallic Locomotor	3–6
4	Industry versus Inferiority	To make things (completing), To make things together	Neighbourhood and school	Competence	Latency	7–12
5	Identity versus Role confusion	To be oneself (or not to be), To share being oneself	Peer groups and outgroups, models of leadership	Fidelity	Genital	12–18
6	Intimacy versus Isolation	To lose and find oneself in another	Partners in friendship, sex, competition, co-operation	Love		20s
7	Generativity versus Stagnation	To make be, To take care of	Divided labour and Shared household	Care		Late 20s–50s
8	Ego integrity versus Despair	To be, through having been, To face not being	'Humankind', 'my kind'	Wisdom		50s and beyond

Erikson's Psychosocial Stages

As we have said, at each stage a conflict arises which centres around two possible and opposing outcomes of the attempt to resolve the problems inherent in that stage; each stage is named by reference to these two opposite outcomes, the first referring to the positive or functional (adaptive) outcome, eg trust, and the second referring to the negative or dysfunctional (maladaptive) outcome, eg mistrust.

However, it is important to stress that these are extremes and it is not an either-or situation but rather every personality represents some mixture of trust and mistrust (and similarly for the other seven stages). Trust and mistrust etc are relative terms and healthy development involves trust outweighing mistrust, the positive outcome, on balance, being greater than the negative outcome.

Although the optimum time for developing a sense of trust is during infancy, Erikson believes it is possible to make up for unsatisfactory early experiences at a later stage, although it becomes increasingly difficult to do so. Conversely, a sense of trust developed during infancy could be shattered or at least shaken if later deprivation is experienced. Either way, Erikson presents a much less deterministic view than Freud: the issue of trust-mistrust is not resolved once and for all during the first year but recurs at each successive stage of development, so there are 'second chances' as well as the danger of positive early outcomes turning out badly later on.

The last four stages, spanning adolescence, adulthood and old age have been discussed in Chapters 23 and 24 so we shall concentrate here on the stages of infancy and childhood.

1) Basic Trust versus Basic Mistrust (0–1)
The quality of care the baby receives determines how it comes to view its mother and other people in particular and the world in general (see Chapter 18)—is it a safe, predictable, comfortable place to be or is it full of hazards? This is linked to the infant's sense of its ability to influence what happens to it and hence to its trust in itself; if the infant's needs are met as they arise and its discomforts quickly removed, if it is cuddled and fondled, played with and talked to, it develops a sense of the world as a safe place to be and of people as helpful and dependable. However, if its care is inconsistent, it develops a sense of mistrust, fear and suspicion, which reveal themselves as apathetic or withdrawn behaviour, a sense of being controlled rather than being able to control; a sense of trust allows the baby to accept new experiences and fear of the unknown is accepted as part and parcel of having new experiences.

2) Autonomy versus Shame and Doubt (1–3)
The child's cognitive and muscle systems are maturing and it is becoming more mobile so that its range of experiences and choices is expanding. The child is beginning to think of itself as a person in its own right, separate from the parents, and this new sense of power is the basis for its growing sense of autonomy and independence. The child wants to do everything itself and parents have to allow it to exercise these new abilities while simultaneously ensuring that the child does not 'bite off more than it can chew'—repeated

failures and ridicule from others can lead to a sense of shame and doubt. The child must be allowed to do things at its own pace and in its own time; parents should not impatiently do things for it 'to save time' or criticize the child for its failures and the inevitable accidents. These 'accidents', and the whole conflict between autonomy and shame and doubt, may have become focused on toilet-training; if it is too strict or starts too early, the child may be faced with a 'double rebellion and a double defeat', feeling powerless to control its bowels and its parents' actions. This may result in regression to oral activities (eg thumb-sucking), attention-seeking or a pretence at having become autonomous by rejecting the help of others and becoming very strong-willed. But firm and considerate training helps the child to develop a sense of 'self-control without a loss of self-esteem'.

3) Initiative versus Guilt (3–5/6)
The child's development proceeds at a rapid pace, physically, intellectually and socially, and the child is keen to try out its developing abilities and skills to achieve all sorts of new goals. If the child is encouraged to ask questions and express its natural curiosity in other ways and is given the freedom to run and jump, ride a bike and to indulge in fantasy and other kinds of play, its sense of initiative will be reinforced. However, if parents tend to find the child's questions embarrassing or difficult intellectually or a nuisance, its motor activity dangerous and its fantasy play silly, then the child may come to feel guilty about intruding into others' lives and activities and may inhibit its initiative and curiosity.

This guilt can be exaggerated by the Oedipus/Electra complex, but whereas for Freud this is the central feature of this stage, for Erikson it is but one feature of a much wider theme.

4) Industry versus Inferiority (7–12 or so)
Industry refers to the child's concern with how things work, how they are made and their own efforts to make things; this is reinforced when the child is encouraged by adults, who now are no longer confined to the parents. Teachers begin to assume a very real significance in the child's life and society requires them to help the child to develop all sorts of new skills valued by society. The peer group also assumes increasing importance relative to that of adults and is a major source of self-esteem; children begin to compare themselves with other children as a way of assessing their own achievements (see Chapter 9).

Self-esteem and the esteem of others stem largely from the successful completion of realistic tasks, being allowed to make things and being given the necessary guidance and encouragement by adults. A child may have potential abilities which, if not nurtured during this period, may 'develop late or never'.

Ego Identity

As we saw earlier, Erikson has emphasized the healthy personality in contrast to Freud, who stressed conflict and the neurotic personality; this difference stems largely from the importance of the ego and the id in their respective theories. For Erikson, 'growing up' is a process of achieving Ego Identity which comprises: (i) an *inner focused* aspect; and (ii) an *outer-focused* aspect. The former is the individual's recognition of their own unified 'self-sameness and continuity in time' (1959), knowing and accepting oneself; while the latter is the individual's recognition of, and identity with, the ideals and essential pattern of their culture and includes sharing 'some kind of essential character with others' (1968).

A healthy mature person combines individual happiness and responsible citizenship; this is similar to Adler's belief in the need for a suitable adjustment to be made in the areas of love, work and society, and Freud's 'Lieben und Arbeiten' (love and work). Again, a healthy person actively masters the environment, shows a unity of personality and is able to perceive the world and self correctly—the new-born displays none of these, the healthiest adult displays them all (Erikson, 1968).

Human Virtues
In 1964, Erikson expanded his basic 1959 picture of positive ego development by describing a set of human virtues or 'qualities of strength', meant to express an integration of psychosexual and psychosocial growth schedules. As can be seen from Table 26.4, they are based on the positive outcomes of each of the eight stages of psychosocial development.

Erikson's theory of *play* is outlined in Box 26.3.

An Evaluation of Erikson's Theory

The criticisms made of Freud's methods of study and his biased and limited samples cannot be made so easily against Erikson; he did not confine his studies to small numbers of neurotic adults from one particular culture but included much larger numbers of both disturbed and healthy individuals of all ages from a variety of cultures. Erikson was a psychoanalyst and teacher in Europe, a child analyst in Boston, he studied normal adolescents in California and spent time living among the Sioux Indians of South Dakota and the Yurok Indians of Northern California.

It was while working with the Indians that Erikson began to notice syndromes which he could not explain within the terms of Freudian theory. Central to many of the Indians' emotional problems was their sense of being uprooted and a lack of continuity between their present lifestyle and the one portrayed in the tribal history. This sense of a break with the past, and an inability to identify with a future requiring assimilation of white cultural values, is an ego-related and culture-related conflict and has little to do with sexual drives.

These impressions were reinforced during the Second World War when he worked at a war-veterans' rehabilitation centre; he saw many soldiers who did not seem to fit the traditional 'shell shock' or 'malingerer' cases of the First World War and instead they seemed to have lost a sense of who and what they were. They suffered an 'identity confusion'—they could not reconcile what they had felt and done as soldiers with what they had known before the war.

Box 26.3: Erikson's Theory of Play

The great emphasis given to play by psychotherapists is based on their recognition that young children are limited in their ability to communicate their problems in the way adults may. So in therapy, play situations are opportunities for the child to *externalize* its problems, work them through and come to terms with them; they are also, of course, opportunities for the therapist to observe and understand those problems.

Play deals with life experiences which the child attempts to repeat, master or negate in order to organize its inner world in relation to the outer one. It also involves self-teaching and self-healing: 'the child uses play to make up for defeats, sufferings and frustrations, especially those resulting from a technically and culturally limited use of language' (1950).

'Playing it out' becomes the child's means of reasoning and allows the child to free itself from the ego boundaries of time, space and reality and yet to maintain a reality orientation because it and others know it is 'just play'.

Play, too, is an important form of self-expression for the ego and helps the child towards new mastery and new developmental stages. For example, play provides a safe island where the child can develop a sense of autonomy within its own boundaries or laws; doubt and shame can be conquered here—'the small world of manageable toys is a harbour which the child establishes to return to when he needs to overhaul his ego' (1950).

But just as Freud defined sexuality in a very broad way, so Erikson defined play very broadly. In *Toys and Reasons* (1977) he makes it clear that play is not limited to childhood but is pursued throughout the life-cycle. Play is not simply what we do when we are not working, not just a non-serious pastime or diversion but rather is often an attempt by the individual to resolve the psychosocial crisis they are currently experiencing. So, for Erikson, the child is playing when it builds a structure with bricks or when it acts out the family drama with dolls and the physicist, too, is playing when putting forward a model of the universe.

Play also has a crucial social quality or dimension: it cannot help us resolve our psychosocial crises unless we can try out possible solutions on others and see how they respond.

Erikson believes that anatomical differences contribute to personality differences between males and females; the 'inner space' or a woman's ability to bear children is a pervasive force in female gender identity. His position is based on observations of the miniature play constructions of boys and girls from 10 to 12 years. Typically, girls construct an interior scene, while boys construct an exterior scene with elaborate walls or facades with protrusions or high towers (contrast the internal and external sex organs of females and males respectively).

One of Erikson's major innovations is his method of *psychohistory* in which he applies his theory of the human life-cycle to the study of famous historical figures; after essays on Gorky, G. B. Shaw and Freud, he devoted whole books to Martin Luther (*Young Man Luther*, 1958) and Gandhi (*Gandhi's Truth*, 1969).

According to Elkind (1970), teaching of Erikson's concepts is on the increase in psychology, psychiatry, education and social work. However, researchers have found his theory rather difficult to test and not everyone agrees with the details of the theory (see Chapter 23 on adolescence), but it is generally agreed that Erikson has inspired the 'life-span' approach in developmental psychology.

27

Intelligence

The concept of intelligence is probably one of the most elusive in the whole of psychology: to try to pin it down and provide a definition which all (or even most) psychologists can agree on seems almost impossible and attempts to measure it are fraught with difficulties (not least of which is not knowing what it is).

Intelligence represents one of the most researched sources of individual differences but it is not just of academic interest—the intelligence test (in one form or another) has impinged on the lives of most of us, whether it is for educational selection, occupational selection or selection for Mensa, the high IQ society. According to Vernon (1979), over 2,000 million tests of intelligence or achievement are given every year in the USA alone.

The near-obsession of western culture with measuring and categorizing people is also highly emotionally charged and politically sensitive, particularly in relation to the question of racial differences in intelligence, which represents another instance of the heredity–environment issue.

Yet unlike the discussion of language or perception, or even personality, the nature–nurture debate in intelligence has become equated with extremes of political viewpoints and the issue highlights the impossibility of completely divorcing the social from the scientific functions of psychology.

Definitions of Intelligence

So diverse are the definitions of intelligence, that Vernon (1960) thought it necessary to identify three broad groups of definition, namely biological, psychological and operational.

Biological definitions see intelligence as related to adaptation to the environment. As we saw in Chapter 19, Piaget studied intelligence as a process and not as a set of capacities, so that he was not interested in how individuals differ from one another but rather in what stages of development all individuals go through.

For Piaget, intelligence is 'essentially a system of living and acting operations, ie a state of balance or equilibrium achieved by the person when he is able to deal adequately with the data before him. But it is not a static state,

Table 27.1   Some psychological definitions of intelligence

1. *Binet* (1905)	'It seems to us that in intelligence there is a fundamental faculty, the impairment of which is of the utmost importance for practical life. This faculty is called judgement, otherwise called good sense, practical sense, initiative, the faculty of adapting one's self to circumstances. To judge well, to comprehend well, to reason well. . . .'
2. *Terman* (1921)	'An individual is intelligent in proportion as he is able to carry on abstract thinking.'
3. *Burt* (1955)	'Innate, general, cognitive ability.'
4. *Wechsler* (1944)	'The aggregate of the global capacity to act purposefully, think rationally, to deal effectively with the environment.'
5. *Heim* (1970)	'Intelligent activity consists in grasping the essentials in a situation and responding appropriately to them.'
6. *Vernon* (1969)	'The effective all-round cognitive abilities to comprehend, to grasp relations and reason.'

it is dynamic in that it continually adapts itself to new environmental stimuli'. And again, 'intelligence constitutes the state of equilibrium towards which tend all the successive adaptations of a sensory, motor and cognitive nature' (1950).

So Piaget represents the *qualitative* approach to intelligence, where the focus is on intelligence itself and not differences in intelligence between individuals.

Psychological definitions, by contrast, represent the *quantitative* or *psychometric* approach, where the emphasis is very much on the measurement of intelligence in order to compare and differentiate between individuals. There are many psychological definitions and some of the best known and most influential are shown in Table 27.1.

The definitions of Terman, Burt and Vernon all stress the purely intellectual aspects of the concept, while Binet's and Wechsler's definitions are much broader and perhaps closer to commonsense understanding.

According to Heim, however intelligence may be defined, 'it is complex and not simple, facets are many and varied' and, consequently, to speak of an individual's 'true' intelligence is meaningless. (We shall take up this point again later when we discuss intelligence tests.)

Heim objects to the use of intelligence as a noun because, she says, it smacks of an 'isolable entity or thing' which is opposed to her belief that intelligence should be regarded as part of personality as a whole (combining cognitive, affective and conative dimensions, the last referring to the 'striving, doing, aspect of experience') which is an integrated unit. Consequently, she prefers to talk about 'intelligent activity' rather than 'intelligence'.

The third kind of definition identified by Vernon, *operational*, simply defines intelligence in terms of tests designed to measure it, that is, 'intelligence is what intelligence tests measure' (eg Miles, 1957). While such a definition is intended to get round the problem of the multiplicity of definitions that exists, it fails to tell us exactly what it is that intelligence tests measure and is, in fact, circular, that is, the concept being defined is part of the definition itself. Miles argues that if we substitute the names of particular tests, then we can break into the circle, but Heim is not convinced, pointing out that this merely decreases the circumference of the circle!

Like Heim, Ryle (1949), a philosopher, believes that 'intelligence' does not denote an entity or an engine inside us causing us to act in particular ways; instead, he argues that any action can be performed more or less intelligently, so it should be used as an adjective and not as a noun.

Factor Analytic Theories of Intelligence: One Factor or Many?

Having looked at some of the major definitions of intelligence, we now turn to more detailed accounts of the nature of intelligence. Not surprisingly, there are sharp divisions of opinion here too but they all have in common the basic assumption that intelligence is a characteristic of a person that can be measured by intelligence tests which, in turn, implies that individuals differ with respect to that characteristic.

We shall be discussing tests later in the chapter and all we need to understand for the moment is that theories of intelligence are based upon analysis of scores of large numbers of individuals on various intelligence tests using a statistical technique called Factor Analysis (see Chapter 25).

Factor analysis involves correlating the scores of a large sample of subjects in order to determine whether scores on certain tests are related to scores on certain other tests, that is, whether some, or any, of the tests have something in common. The basic assumption made is that the more similar the scores on two or more tests (ie the higher the correlation), the more likely it is that these tests are tapping the same basic ability (or factor).

If we find, for example, that people's scores on tests A, B, C, D and E are highly correlated (that is, if they score high on one they tend to score high on the others or low on all five) then it could be inferred that all five tests are measuring the same ability and individuals differ according to how much or how little of that particular ability they have. However, if there is very little relationship between scores on the five tests, then each test may be measuring a distinct ability and when comparing individuals we would have to look at each ability separately.

These two hypothetical outcomes roughly correspond to two theories of intelligence, the first of which is sometimes referred to as the 'London Line' and is associated with Spearman (1904/27), Burt (1949/55) and Vernon (1950), in contrast with the mainly American approach of Thurstone (1938) and Guilford (1959/67). However, as we shall see, there are important differences within each of these approaches.

Spearman's Two-Factor Model

Spearman factor-analysed the results of children's performance on various tests and found that many tests were moderately positively correlated, concluding that all the tests had something in common (a general factor) as well as something specific to each test (a specific factor). Spearman believed that every intellectual activity involves both a general factor (which he called *g* or general intelligence) and a specific factor (*s*) and differences between individuals are largely attributable to differences in their *g*. (This *g* is, in fact, an abbreviation for *neogenesis* which refers to the ability to 'educe relations', as in a common kind of test item which asks 'A is to Y as B is to ?'). Although *g* accounts for why people who are good at one mental ability also tend to be good at others, people also differ according to their specific abilities.

Burt and Vernon's Hierarchical Model

Burt (who was a student of Spearman) agreed that there is a *g* factor common to all tests but also thought that the two-factor model was too simple. He and Vernon elaborated and extended Spearman's model by identifying a series of group factors (major and minor) in between *g* and *s* factors (see Figure 27.1).

According to this model, *g* is what all the tests are measuring, the major group factors (*v:ed* and *k:m*) are what some tests are measuring (some to a greater extent than others), the minor group factors are what particular tests measure whenever they are given, while specific factors are what particular tests measure on specific occasions (Burt, 1970).

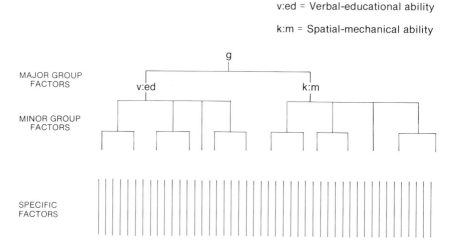

Figure 27.1 The hierarchical model of intelligence (after Vernon, 1950)

Thurstone's Primary Mental Abilities

Using 14-year-olds and college students as his subjects, Thurstone (1938/47) found that not all mental tests correlate equally but appear to form seven distinct factors or groupings, which he called *Primary Mental Abilities* (or PMAs), namely:

Spatial(S)—the ability to recognize spatial relationships.

Perceptual Speed(P)—the quick and accurate detection of visual detail.

Numerical Reasoning(N)—the ability to perform arithmetical operations quickly and accurately.

Verbal meaning(V)—understanding the meaning of words and verbal concepts.

Word Fluency(W)—speed in recognizing single and isolated words.

Memory(M)—the ability to recall a list of words, numbers or other material.

Inductive Reasoning(I)—the ability to generate a rule or relationship that describes a set of observations.

Many researchers have questioned Thurstone's conclusions, pointing out that people who score high on a test of one PMA also tend to score high on most of the others. Indeed, Thurstone himself later admitted that *g* seems to be involved in all PMAs (having carried out a 'second-order' factor analysis on the results of the first).

Guilford's 'Structure of Intellect' Model

This represents the most extreme alternative to Spearman's two-factor theory and totally rejects the notion of a general intelligence factor.

Guilford first classified a cognitive task along three major dimensions: *content* (what must the subject think about?); *operations* (what kind of thinking is the subject being asked to perform?); and *products* (what kind of answer is required?). He identified four kinds of content, five kinds of operation and six kinds of product which, multiplied together yields a total of 120 distinct mental abilities altogether. Guilford's model is presented in more detail in Figure 27.2.

Guilford set out to construct tests to measure each of the 120 abilities; according to Shaffer, writing in 1985, tests have been devised to assess more than 70. However, the scores people get are often correlated, which suggests that the number of basic mental abilities is much smaller than Guilford assumed (Brody and Brody, 1976).

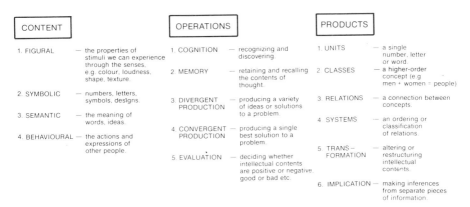

Figure 27.2 A summary of Guilford's 'structure of intellect' model (after Shaffer, 1985)

However, the multi-factorial approach of Guilford (and to a lesser extent that of Thurstone) represents an important counter-balance to the much more restricted model of Spearman. Vernon (1950) concluded that intelligence is *neither* a single general mental ability *nor* a number of more specific, independent, abilities—but both; general intelligence plays a part in all mental activities but more specific abilities are also involved in producing performance. Shaffer (1985) believes that this combined approach is the currently held viewpoint amongst most psychologists.

Criticisms of Factor Analysis

1) How can we account for the conflicting models of intelligence to have emerged from the work of different psychologists, all of whom have used factor analysis?

The simple answer is that there is more than one way of factor analysing a set of data and there is no 'best' way. As we have seen above, Thurstone re-analysed his original data by using a 'second-order' factor analysis which produced a very different pattern of factors. Originally, he had used a form of factor analysis which gives a 'simple structure' solution in contrast to the 'principal component' solutions resulting from Spearman's and Burt's analyses. As Shackleton and Fletcher (1984) point out, these two alternatives are mathematically equivalent and the same data from the same sample can produce a number of different patterns of factors depending on which alternative is used.

2) In practice, however, it seems that the split between the British and American models of intelligence is as much a reflection of the type of subjects used as of the form of factor analysis employed. Thurstone and Guilford used mainly college students, while Spearman, Burt and Vernon used mainly schoolchildren; the former are much more alike in terms of their all-round intelligence ability than the latter, that is, they are a much more homogenous group and so differences between them are likely to reflect differences in particular abilities which are relatively independent of each other.

3) The type and number of tests used (in conjunction with type of subjects) can also determine the pattern of factors that emerges; Shackleton and Fletcher (1984) maintain that if a few, similar tests are used with subjects who vary widely in age, education, cognitive abilities and so on, a picture of intelligence comprising one dominant, general ability, is likely to emerge, while a large number of different types of tests given to a homogenous sample is likely to produce a larger number of independent factors without a general intelligence factor being involved.

4) Even without these problems, there is still the fundamental issue of interpreting the factors which do emerge. All that factor analysis achieves is a cluster of intercorrelations between different tests and parts of tests—it is then up to the researcher to scan these patterns of intercorrelations and to label them. As Radford (1980) says, factors do not come 'ready-labelled' and the labels that are attached to the factors are only 'best guesses' about the psychological meaning of the factors—they may or may not reflect 'psychological reality'.

5) Surely a technique which leaves so much room for subjective interpretation and, hence, disagreement, amongst different researchers, is hardly very objective and several writers have questioned the relevance of the whole technique in providing an account of the structure of intelligence (eg Block and Dworkin, 1974).

Vernon (1979) has attempted to defend factor analysis by arguing that the differences between various models are more apparent than real. However, it is still true that how factors are labelled is an arbitrary act on the part of the researcher, 'merely to label a factor in one way or other is not necessarily to advance our understanding of the nature of intelligence' (Lloyd et al, 1984).

6) Once a factor has been labelled (eg 'verbal ability') there is the danger of believing that it exists in some objective way (this is called *reification*) whereas a factor is merely a statistic.

Alternative Models of Intelligence

a) Although still working within the Factor Analytic approach, Cattell (1963) and Horn and Cattell (1967/1982) have proposed a model which can reconcile the different models discussed above. They argue that the *g* factor can be sub-divided into two major dimensions—Fluid and Crystallized intelligence (see Chapter 24).

Fluid intelligence (gf) is the ability to solve abstract relational problems of the sort that are not taught and which are relatively free of cultural influences. It increases gradually throughout childhood and adolescence as the nervous system matures, then levels off during young adulthood and after that begins a steady decline.

By contrast, *crystallized* intelligence (gc) increases throughout the life-span and is primarily a reflection of one's cumulative learning experiences. It involves understanding relations or solving problems which depend on knowledge acquired as a result of schooling and other life experiences (eg general knowledge, word comprehension and numerical abilities).

As we saw in Chapter 24, many students have confirmed Cattell and Horn's view that gc goes on improving but longitudinal studies have failed to find the steady decline in gf. For instance, studies by LaBouvie-Vief (1977), Schaie and LaBouvie-Vief (1974) and Schaie and Hertzog (1983) all agreed that neither gc nor gf shows an appreciable decline till after 60.

b) Apart from Piaget's qualitative approach, the other major theoretical approach to the study of intelligence is that known as the *information processing approach*. According to Fishbein (1985), this approach sees intelligence as the steps or processes people go through in solving problems; one person may be more intelligent than another because they move through the same steps more quickly or efficiently or they are more familiar with the required problem-solving steps.

Advocates of this view (eg Sternberg, 1979, Hunt, 1983) focus on: (i) how information is internally represented; (ii) the kinds of strategies people use in processing that information; (iii) the nature of the components (eg memory, inference, comparison) used in carrying out those strategies; and (iv) how decisions are made as to which strategies to use.

Like Piaget, they are trying to develop a theory of intelligence which is universal (and so which applies equally to everyone) but like the factor analytic theorists, they are interested in individual differences in information processing. As Fishbein puts it, they see intelligence as neither an 'it' (for example *g*) nor a 'them' (for example, primary mental abilities) but as everything the mind does in processing information.

Attempts to correlate scores on intelligence tests with measures derived from information-processing theories have so far produced only small correlations (eg Hunt, 1980), but perhaps more promising is a recent attempt by Globerson (1983) to integrate the psychometric, Piagetian and information-processing approaches. He tested the concept of 'M-space' or 'Central Computing Space' which refers to the number of schemes an individual can attend to and manipulate within a given time span and which is assumed to grow with maturation and to be relatively independent of specific learning, knowledge or skills; it is a measure of pure cognitive ability.

Intelligence Tests

What do they measure and how do they measure it?

As we have seen, the basic 'data' of the psychometric approach are scores on intelligence tests and it is to these tests that we now turn our attention.

A Brief History of Intelligence Tests

In 1904, Binet and Simon were commissioned by the French government to devise a test which would identify those children who would not benefit from ordinary schooling because of their inferior intelligence and the result was the Simon–Binet (1905) test, generally accepted as the first intelligence test.

The sample of children used for the development of the test (the standardization sample) was very small and it was subsequently revised twice, in 1908 and 1911, with much larger samples being used.

In 1910, Terman began adapting the Simon–Binet test for use in the USA and, since he was working at Stanford University, the test became known as the 'Stanford-Binet' test and is still referred to in this way. The first revision was published in 1916 and was designed to measure normal and superior intelligence as well as subnormal. In 1937, the Terman–Merrill revision appeared, comprising two equivalent forms of the test (L and M) and in 1960 the most useful questions from the 1937 revision were combined into a single form (L–M) and an improved scoring system was used.

Prior to 1960, the Stanford–Binet test was designed for individuals up to age 16 (starting at $2\frac{1}{2}$ to 3) but this was extended to 18 in the 1960 revision. A further revision was published in 1973 and another was due in 1985.

Another major figure in intelligence testing is Wechsler, who developed the most widely used test of adult intelligence, the Wechsler Adult Intelligence Scale (1944), revised in 1958. (It was originally published in 1939 as the Wechsler-Bellvue Intelligence Scale.) Wechsler has also constructed the Wechsler Intelligence Scale for Children, the WISC, first published in 1949 and revised in 1974 (WISC–R), designed for children between 5 and 15 years, and the Wechsler Pre-school Primary Scale of Intelligence—WPPSI —first published in 1963 and designed for 4- to $6\frac{1}{2}$-year-olds.

Another important impetus to the development of intelligence testing was America's involvement in the First World War; a fairly quick and easy method of selecting over one million recruits for suitable tasks was needed and the result were the 'Army Alpha' and 'Army Beta' tests. A recent British test is the British Ability Scales, produced over a 12-year-period at Manchester University (Elliot, 1976), designed for 2 to 17-year-olds.

Individual and Group Tests

Although all the tests mentioned above are tests of intelligence, an importance difference between them is that some are given to one person at a time (eg the Stanford–Binet and Wechsler tests) and so are known as Individual Tests, while others are given to groups of people at a time (eg the Army Alpha and Beta tests) and so are referred to as Group Tests. Related to this distinction are other important differences:

(1) Individual tests are used primarily as diagnostic tests in a clinical setting, for example, they are used to assess the ability of a child who has learning difficulties in school and the Stanford–Binet and Wechsler are the tests most widely used by educational psychologists both in Britain and the USA. Group tests, by contrast, are used primarily for purposes of selection and research; for example, in Britain until the mid-1960s, all children at 11 sat an examination (the Eleven Plus) which would determine the kind of secondary schooling they would receive and this included a group test of intelligence. (Despite the introduction of comprehensive schools, there are still parts of the UK where selection at 11 still takes place.) Again, when large groups of people are being studied as part of a research project, it is very likely that their intelligence will be assessed by using one or other group test.

(2) Because the individual test involves a one-to-one situation, it is clearly more time-consuming than a group test, which, in theory, can be given to as many individuals as can be comfortably accommodated in a particular room.

(3) Although individual tests require that instructions are standardized (the same for all testees) and that the same questions are asked and in the same sequence, there is some degree of leeway on the part of the tester as to exactly how the test is conducted; for example, the child must be put at its ease before the test proper can begin and it is important that a good rapport be established between the child and the tester. How the tester achieves this will probably vary on each occasion; no face-to-face situation can be made totally uniform or predictable, and the psychologist's training will help prepare them for this. Group tests, on the other hand, are presented in the form of written questions, the group is read out a set of standardized instructions and the test is timed; the person administering the test need not be a psychologist and, indeed, may have no special training or familiarity with the particular test and the marking can either be done by using a special marking key or by computer. In this respect, then, group tests are more objective, that is, only one answer is accepted as correct and there is no room for interpretation on the part of the marker.

(4) Individual tests usually involve some *performance* items, that is, the testee has to *do* something (eg a jigsaw puzzle) as well as answer questions

about the meaning of words and do some mental arithmetic etc. By contrast, the group tests are 'pencil-and-paper' tests and in that respect are much like other, written, exams.

Mental Age and IQ

The Stanford–Binet test is based on the assumption that mental ability is developmental, that is, it increases with age through childhood and so consists of a number of age-related scales; each scale comprises a series of questions which are normally answered correctly by a majority of children of that age. So, for example, the 5-year-old scale is what most 5-year-olds could pass comfortably (as well as all children over 5) but which most 4-year-olds could not; hence, a child passing the 5-year-old scale has a *mental* age of 5, that is, the child can do what the average 5-year-old can do. (Some examples of questions from different age-scales are given in Table 27.2.)

In practice, a child is started off on the scale immediately below its chronological age (to determine its *basal age*) and then the scale corresponding to its chronological age and so on, until the child fails to answer any questions correctly on a particular scale.

The concept of Mental Age is useful in that it gives an *absolute* assessment of the child's level of intellectual development, but by itself it does not tell us how bright, average or dull the child is; to establish this we must compare the child's Mental Age with its Chronological (actual) Age (CA). Imagine two children, both of whom do equally well on the test and attain a Mental Age (MA) of 10; can we regard them as equally intelligent? The answer is 'No', because one of them is 10-years-old while the other is only 9, and 9-year-olds are not expected to do as well on the test as 10-year-olds. So, when we take CA into account, we are thereby making a comparison with other children.

For these reasons, Stern introduced the notion of an Intelligence Quotient (IQ) in 1912, in which the MA is expressed as a ratio of CA, multiplied by 100 in order to produce a whole number. The first IQ was, therefore, a *ratio* IQ, such that where MA and CA are the same, IQ is 100 (which, by definition, is average) where MA is greater than CA, IQ is over 100 (and, therefore, above average) and, where CA is greater than MA, IQ is below 100 (and, therefore, below average).

It should be clear from these examples that for IQ to remain stable over time, the MA must increase in step with the CA. However, the concept of MA does not apply beyond 18, since intellectual ability is usually fully developed by that time (according to the 1960 version of the Stanford–Binet, anyway) and consequently, the test IQ is not meaningful beyond a chronological age of 18.

The measurement of adult IQ was discussed fully in Chapter 24 so we shall say no more about it here. However, we should say something about the important differences between the Stanford–Binet and the Wechsler tests.

The WAIS is the most widely used test of adult intelligence (16- to 75-year-olds) and is structured in a similar way to the WISC. The test comprises two

Table 27.2 Some items from the Stanford–Binet (1960) test and the 2 scales of the WAIS (1944)

Stanford-Binet	Wechsler Adult Intelligence Scale (WAIS)
Children of 3 should be able to: Point to objects that serve various functions (eg 'goes on your feet'). Repeat a list of 2 words or digits (eg 'can' and 'dog'). *Children of 4 should be able to:* Discriminate visual forms (eg squares, circles and triangles). Define words (eg ball and bat). Repeat 10-word sentences, count up to 4 objects, solve problems (eg 'In daytime it is light, at night it is . . .') *Children of 9 should be able to:* Solve verbal problems (eg 'tell me a number that rhymes with tree'). Solve simple arthmetical problems and repeat 4 digits in reverse order. *Children of 12 should be able to:* Define words (eg 'skill' and 'muzzle'). Repeat 5 digits in reverse order. Solve verbal absurdities (eg 'One day we saw several icebergs that had been entirely melted by the warmth of the Gulf Stream.' What is foolish about that?).	*Verbal Scale* (None of sub-tests is timed 1. *Information*—general knowledge. 2. *Comprehension*—ability to use knowledge in practical settings (eg 'What would you do if you were lost in a large, strange, town?') 3. *Arithmetic* 4. *Similarities*—conceptual and analogical reasoning (eg 'In what ways are a book and TV alike?') 5. *Digit span*—STM (eg repeating a string of digits in the same or reverse order). 6. *Vocabulary*—word meaning. *Performance Scale* (All sub-tests are timed) 1. *Picture completion*—assessment of visual efficiency and memory by spotting missing items in drawings. 2. *Picture arrangements*—assessment of sequential understanding by arranging a series of picures to tell a story. 3. *Block design*—ability to perceive or analyse patterns by copying pictures using multicoloured blocks. 4. *Object assembly*—jigsaw puzzles. 5. *Digit symbol*—ability to memorize and order abstract visual patterns.

separate scales (a verbal scale and a performance scale) each comprising a number of sub-tests, and each producing a separate IQ which can then be combined to yield an overall IQ. By contrast, the Stanford–Binet test includes performance items only for the youngest children (up to age 4–5) when verbal abilities are still relatively underdeveloped (see Table 27.2).

A second important difference between them is that the same items are given to all children (or adults) on the Wechsler tests, so that age-related scales are not used. The questions become progressively more difficult and the testing usually continues until the testee has failed on a predetermined number of items in succession.

The Relationship Between Intelligence and IQ

The Wechsler tests do not use the concept of MA in the way that the Stanford–Binet test does and instead uses a *deviation* IQ, which expresses the test result as a *standard score*, that is, it tells the tester how many Standard Deviations (SDs) above or below the mean of the testee's age-group the score lies.

Before 1960, it was very difficult to compare scores on the two tests because of the difference in the way the IQ was calculated—the ratio IQ of the Stanford–Binet and the deviation IQ of the Wechsler test are not equivalent. However, in the 1960 revision of the Stanford–Binet, the ratio IQ was replaced by the deviation IQ, making scores on the two tests more comparable. However, although all tests are designed in such a way as to produce a normal curve, that is, a symmetrical distribution of IQ scores, with a mean of 100, the standard deviation (or dispersion of the scores around the mean) can differ from test to test.

Fontana (1981) gives the example of two tests, A and B, test A having a SD of 10 and test B having a SD of 20. In both cases, 68 per cent of children would be expected to have scores one SD below or above the mean (ie between 90 and 110 in Test A and between 80 and 120 in Test B). So a particular child might have a score of 110 on test A and 120 on test B and yet the scores would be telling us the same thing.

This suggests that while intelligence is a psychological concept, that of IQ is purely statistical. Put another way, if it is possible for the same characteristic of a person (their intelligence) to be assigned different values according to which test is used to measure it, then instead of asking, 'How intelligent is this individual?' we should ask, 'How intelligent is this individual as measured by this particular test?'. Since the IQ score of the same individual can vary according to the standard deviation of the particular test being used, we cannot equate 'IQ' with 'intelligence'; whereas we can (and usually do) enquire about somebody's height without taking the particular measuring rod or tape measure into account, we cannot do this in the case of a person's intelligence.

The very relationship between 'intelligence' and 'IQ' is problematic in a way that the one between 'height' and 'feet and inches' is not. Normally, we

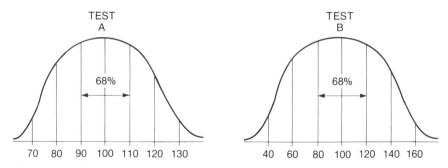

Figure 27.3   Normal curves for 2 hypothetical IQ tests, each with a different standard deviation

are prepared to accept an operational definition of someone's height, that is, height is the number of feet and inches as measured by a tape measure and there is no debate as to the 'true nature of height'. However, as we have seen, an operational definition of intelligence is not satisfactory precisely because there is such a variety of definitions and we feel that IQ is an unwarranted 'reduction' of intelligence, something very diverse and complex, to a single number.

In agreeing with Heim that to name the particular test used is merely to reduce the circumference of the circle represented by an operational definition, we could perhaps take this a step further by saying that for each separate test there exists a separate circle.

In 'IQ—the illusion of objectivity' (1972), Joanna Ryan points out that because intelligence is expressed as a number, the impression is created that IQ tells us in some absolute way about an individual's intellectual ability, in the same way as feet and inches tell us about someone's height. However, there is a fundamental difference between the two measuring scales being used. IQ scores are not 'free-standing' scores in the way that somebody's height is: we can measure a person's height without having to take anybody else's height into account, but IQ only derives its meaning *as a comparison* with other people's scores. This is because intelligence is measured on an *ordinal* scale, which tells us whether one person is more or less intelligent than another but little else. For instance, the difference between an IQ of 100 and 105 appears to be the same as the difference between scores of 105 and 110 and leads some to argue that intelligence tests involve an interval scale (as in temperature); however, Ryan (1972) argues that even this sort of arithmetical move is unjustified, and to claim that someone with an IQ of 150 is twice as intelligent as someone with an IQ of 75 is completely illegitimate, since this requires a *ratio* scale, where there is an absolute zero (as in time and height).

The Criteria of an Intelligence Test

What makes a test a 'good' test?

According to Kline (1982) there are three criteria that all psychological tests must fulfill if they are to be considered good or efficient tests, namely (i) discriminatory power, (ii) reliability, (iii) validity; and to these we can add a fourth—standardization.

i) Discriminatory Power and Standardization

Good psychological tests should be discriminating, that is, they should produce a wide distribution of scores. If everyone scored equally well (or badly) on a particular test it would not be discriminating, ie it would not reveal differences between people with respect to the characteristic or ability being measured.

This requirement of a test is a practical and a statistical one, but it is not a logical one. For example, we want tests to be discriminating because we want to use test scores as a basis for categorizing and selecting people and if our society did not run this way, there would be no problem involved in most people scoring very high (or very low); indeed, in such a society, there might be no need for tests at all. Quite clearly, what is considered a 'good' test depends to a very large extent on the purposes to which the test is put and it cannot be judged independently of the context.

The statistical side of the requirement that a good test be discriminating is related to the kind of distribution of scores that is expected, and here we return to the normal curve and the standard deviation. The assumption is made that intelligence is normally distributed, so that fixed proportions of the population will score so many standard deviations above or below the mean. (This idea is based on the further assumption that intelligence is largely biologically determined—since other characteristics such as height and weight, which are also largely biologically determined are found to be normally distributed, then it is expected that intelligence will also be.)

Starting out with this assumption, when testers are standardizing their tests, that is, trying to establish a set of norms for a particular population against which any individual's score can be compared, they modify the test items in order to fit the requirements of a normal distribution.

For example, if a particular item is passed by all testees it would be considered too easy and probably dropped from the test; similarly, if an item is so difficult that it is passed by nobody, then it too will be dropped. The items that are retained should then discriminate between testees so as to comform with the normal curve.

Of course, once a test has been standardized so as to produce a normal distribution, the tester can use this as evidence that intelligence is, indeed, a biological property. However, many writers have criticized this view of intelligence, including Hilary and Steven Rose in an article called 'The IQ Myth', in which they point out that not all biological properties are normally distributed anyway and that tests reveal, 'as much about the assumptions of their designers and users as about the individuals to whom they are applied'. We have stumbled upon another circle!

Standardization also requires testing a large, representative sample of the population for whom the test is intended, otherwise the resulting norms cannot be used legitimately for certain groups of individuals. Classic examples of improper standardization involve the two most widely-used individual tests of intelligence, the Stanford–Binet and the Wechsler scales, both of which were originally standardized in the USA. In the 1960 revision of the Stanford–Binet, Terman and Merrill took only the population included in the census as their reference group, which excluded many migrant and unemployed workers. More seriously, both tests were standardized on whites only (without any explanation for this from the authors) and yet they would be used with both black and white children; as Ryan (1972) says, these tests are, therefore, tests of white abilities and although we can still compare black and white children, we must be aware that in doing so we are not comparing black and white intelligence 'but instead how blacks do on tests of white intelligence'. In the 1973 revision of the Stanford–Binet, the 2,100 strong standardization sample did include black children but it remains to be seen how this will affect the race and IQ controversy in the future (see below).

Heather (1976) also points out the ideological significance of IQ as illustrated by re-standardization of tests. Before 1937, the mean score of women on the Stanford–Binet was 10 points lower than that of men and it was decided to eliminate this discrepancy by modifying the items so that average scores for men and women were the same. Heather asks why this has not been done with blacks and answers his own question in terms of the predictive efficiency or validity of the test: tests are meant to predict future education and occupational success, so changing a test so as to eliminate racial differences, while not at the same time changing social inequalities (a much longer process, of course), would render the test a less efficient predictive tool. As Heather notes, removing the male–female bias did, in fact, make the test less efficient as a predictor of gender differences in educational and occupational success. (We shall return to the question of validity below.)

ii) Reliability

This refers to how consistently the test measures whatever it is measuring. Consistency can refer either to: (a) the test itself (*internal consistency*); or (b) consistency over time. In (a), each item on the test should be measuring the same variable and to the same extent, that is, they should all contribute equally to the overall test score. One way of assessing internal reliability is the 'Split-Half' method where, for example, scores on the odd-numbered questions are correlated with scores on the even-numbered questions; if the test is reliable, there should be a significant, positive, correlation.

These two sets of scores can be thought of as two forms of the same test and, indeed, there is a method of assessing reliability called Alternate or Parallel Forms (as in the 1937 version of the Stanford–Binet) where scores on one form should correlate very highly with scores on the other. Finally, the Kuder–Richardson method refers to all possible ways in which a test can be split in half. In (b), consistency over time, the most commonly used method is Test-Re-Test reliability, where the same subjects are given the same test on more than one occasion; a reliable test is one which produces very similar scores when repeated.

In relation to intelligence tests, IQ is expected to be stable across time, not just because a good test must be reliable but also because the predominant view of intelligence underlying most tests is that it is largely genetically determined and, hence, unlikely to fluctuate in an individual over time. However, the evidence suggests a rather different picture which we shall discuss later in the chapter in relation to the heredity–environment issue.

Reliability is not only important in itself but is a prerequisite for validity: if a test produces different scores on different occasions, it cannot possibly be valid; yet a test's reliability is no guarantee of its validity.

iii) Validity

A test is valid if it measures what it claims to measure, and there are several ways of assessing it. In relation to intelligence tests, the question is, do they measure intelligence?

(a) *Face* (or *content*) *validity* is a rather superficial type of validity which refers to whether or not the test seems to be testing what it claims to test by looking at the kind of questions it contains. In a sense, this begs the question of just what intelligence is; whereas we can fairly easily determine whether a test measures knowledge of history, for example, and know that it is not a valid history test if the questions deal with geography, the situation is far more complex in the case of intelligence tests precisely because of the failure by psychologists to agree on what intelligence is.

(b) *Concurrent validity* involves trying to correlate scores on an intelligence test with some other, independent, measure or criterion at the same point in time. One method is to correlate scores on a new test with scores on another, well-established test (in practice, this is very often the Stanford–Binet). The circularity of this attempt should be obvious: what independent proof do we have that the well-established test is itself a valid test of intelligence, and not something else? Even if we could get around this problem, the question would arise as to what value the new test has, since, if the correlation between the two tests is very high, they would seem to be measuring the same thing! (Kline, 1982.) Other criteria that might be used include teachers' ratings and the child's current academic performance, both of which seem to create as many problems as they solve and which are most usefully discussed in relation to predictive validity.

(c) *Predictive validity* (which, together with (b), is known as external validity) refers to the correlation of a test with some future criterion measure and is the most commonly used method of establishing validity.

Probably the most common and powerful external criterion is educability or educational success, and Binet started the trend by establishing that scores on his test differentiated between children thought to be bright or dull based on classroom performance. Many, more recent, studies show that well-established tests do, in fact, predict school achievement with considerable accuracy (eg Minton and Schneider, 1980, Crano et al, 1972 and Brody and Brody, 1976).

However, to conclude from these findings that intelligence tests therefore measure some 'pure', cognitive ability called 'general intelligence' is unjustified. Many writers have pointed out that all the variables (including cognitive ability) which contribute to school success also contribute to performance on IQ tests and a high correlation would be expected for this reason; Heather (1976), for example, argues that 'general intelligence' can be called 'school intelligence', the ability to do well at school. Ryan (1972) maintains that to the extent that tests do measure educability, they are measuring something which is influenced to a considerable extent by various social and motivational factors, as shown by studies such as Douglas (1964) and Pidgeon (1970). Although tests are intended to measure only cognitive ability or potential, by trying to validate them against educational success, 'many important social influences are thereby implicitly introduced'. Again, 'IQ tests do not, and could not, assess only the cognitive, as opposed to social and motivational, determinants of school success' (Ryan, 1972). Heim (1970), who advocates a view of intelligence as a part of personality as a whole, would agree.

As we saw when discussing standardization, the predictive validity of tests is closely related to the practical and social purposes to which they are put —so validation is not a purely objective, scientific, process.

Other external criteria that have been used include health, adjustment and general life satisfaction (eg Terman, 1922 and 1954, Terman and Oden, 1959 and Fincher, 1973) and occupational status and income (eg Eysenck, 1973, Brody and Brody, 1976).

(d) *Construct validity* is defined, 'by taking a large set of results obtained with the test and seeing how well they fit in with our notion of the psychological nature of the variable which the test claims to measure' (Kline, 1982). So it embraces both concurrent and predictive validity and normally involves formulating hypotheses about what kind of test results we would expect if the test really does measure intelligence. For example, (i) scores on the test will correlate highly with educational attainment (both currently and in the future) and (ii) scores on the test will correlate highly with scores on other, well-established, tests (concurrent validity).

To the extent that such hypotheses are supported, the construct validity of the test has been demonstrated, and Kline (1982) concludes that most well-known tests of intelligence, 'have now accumulated so much evidence relating to validity that there is no dispute about them'.

Similarly, Heim (1970) concludes that, 'a reputable test is still the best single means of assessing an individual's intelligence, whatever definition is used. It is more objective, consistent and valid as a first approximation than any of the validatory criteria against which tests may be calibrated.'

However, we should also remind ourselves of the diversity of definitions and (perhaps more importantly) theories of intelligence which abound in psychology, and the logical problem of measuring something if we cannot first agree *what* it is that we are measuring.

The Cultural Nature of Intelligence and Intelligence Tests

One of the major criticisms of intelligence tests has been that they are biased in favour of white middle-class children and adults; it follows that it is both unfair and meaningless to compare groups which differ substantially in their social and cultural experience.

However, defenders of tests would appeal to the distinction between attainment and aptitude tests, ie two kinds of ability tests. *Attainment* (or achievement) *tests* are concerned with how much a person knows about a specific subject (eg geography) or with a person's current level of perform- ance (eg reading) and are unambiguously related to actual learning and educational experiences.

Aptitude tests, by contrast, are intended to measure somebody's capacity or potential ability to succeed in a particular task or job of work or academic subject, and are designed to reduce to a minimum the influence of specific learning and experience. Intelligence tests have always claimed to be aptitude tests and, to this extent, test constructors have argued, they are culture-fair or culture-free.

But is the attainment–aptitude distinction a valid one and is it possible to design a test which is completely culture-free?

According to Cronbach, aptitude tests are merely attainment tests in disguise; group tests, in particular, rely on reading and arithmetic which are taught in all schools and so, in practice, at least, it is very difficult to separate aptitude from attainment. It is somewhat easier to distinguish between them in terms of their purpose and ways of trying to validate them; aptitude tests, by definition, are trying to assess some future performance and so involve predictive validity, but we have already seen the problems that this entails.

Ryan (1972) accepts that intelligence tests are very different in content from school attainment tests and to this extent they do eliminate some specific aspects of differing educational experiences. However, they do not and cannot minimize the more general effects of education and upbringing; 'the cumulative effects of different social histories are extremely complex and pervasive and an individual's behaviour will always reflect this'.

She also makes a different kind of criticism, which seems to strike at the heart of the attainment–aptitude distinction, namely that it is logically impossible to measure potential separately from some actual behaviour, ie some of the skills which an individual has developed during their lifetime must be used when they do an intelligence test. 'There is nothing extra "behind" the behaviour corresponding to potential that could be observed independently of the behaviour itself,' (Ryan, 1972). She concludes that the notion of 'innate potential' itself does not make sense.

Given the breakdown of the attainment–aptitude distinction, a number of attempts have been made to produce culture-free tests which usually consist of non-verbal questions; traditionally, the emphasis on language has been one of the more obvious sources of bias in intelligence tests. An example of the kind of questions involved is shown in Figure 27.4 and is based on Raven's Progressive Matrices, one of the most widely used culture-free tests.

Even without any written instructions, you can probably infer what you have to do. However, the very nature of the task is something which is likely to reflect particular cultural experiences; questions must be formulated in words or symbols of some kind and the testee's familiarity with these will

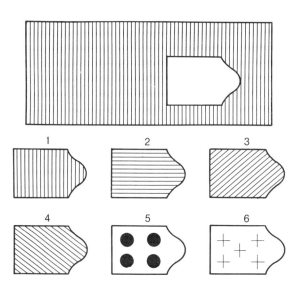

Figure 27.4 A sample item from the Raven progressive matrices test

depend on their life experience. According to Brian Simon (1971), 'the suggestion that human intelligence might be measurable by the development of a new kind of test which actually eliminates all words and symbols is an absurdity', and Owen and Stoneman (1972) believe that because the influence of language is so pervasive, any attempt to devise a culture-fair test by removing 'overt language structures' is doomed to failure. Vernon (1968) argues that, 'we must give up the notion of intelligence as some mysterious power or faculty of the mind which everyone, regardless of race or culture, possesses in varying amounts, and which determines his potentiality for achievement'. He concludes by stating that, 'there is no such thing as a culture-fair test and never can be' and Bruner agrees by maintaining that, 'the culture-free test is the intelligence-free test, for intelligence is a cultural concept'.

Finally, Gillham (1975) concludes that any attempts to 'define' intelligence which do not involve identifying 'specially valued cultural attainments' must fail. The concept of intelligence only derives its meaning within a particular cultural and social context.

Psychophysiological Approaches to Measuring Intelligence

A fairly recent attempt to avoid some of the difficulties discussed above (although not usually discussed in the context of 'culture-free' tests) is to correlate IQ test scores with certain physiological measures, such as electroencephalograms (EEGs), evoked potentials (EPs) and reaction time (RT). Some of the early investigators (eg Ertl, 1971, and Ertl and Schafer, 1969) found only moderate correlations between average evoked potentials (AEPs) and IQ but Hendrickson and Hendrickson (1980) reported much higher correlations; for example, combining the latency of the brain waves with their amplitude (see Chapters 15 and 16) they found a correlation of $0 \cdot 60$ and, using a rather different measuring technique, they found a correlation of $0 \cdot 77$ with scores on the WISC.

Again, Nettelbeck and Lally (1976) asked subjects to say which of two lines was longer when presented at gradually increasing rates via a tachistoscope; the more intelligent they were as assessed by the WAIS, the less time it took them to make a correct judgement and a negative correlation of $0 \cdot 92$ was reported.

However, despite these promising findings, the use of IQ tests as a validating criterion throws up all the difficulties which we have encountered already.

The Heredity–Environment Issue

Why are some people more intelligent than others?

Along with gender differences, the debate about the source of intelligence differences must be the most controversial and divisive in the whole of psychology. Before we begin to consider the relevant evidence, there are a number of preliminary points that should be made.

First, intelligence tests are, in practice, assumed to be valid measures of intelligence, so 'IQ' is used synonymously with 'intelligence' in discussion of the heredity–environment issue.

Secondly, the heredity–environment issue is about how we account for intelligence differences *between* individuals (and, even more controversially, between groups, particularly working-class, middle-class and black–white differences). The impression is sometimes created that the heredity–environment issue is about how much of an individual's intelligence is determined by genetic factors and how much by environmental factors, but this is logically absurd; Hebb (1949) likened it to asking how much of the area of a rectangle is contributed by its width, a meaningless question, since area, by definition, is width times length.

According to McGurk (1975), there are four interrelated propositions which seem to follow from the genetic theory (the belief that IQ differences are largely determined by genetic factors), namely:

Proposition (1) The closer the genetic relationship between any two individuals, the greater should be the correspondence (concordance) between them with respect to intelligence.
Proposition (2) Since the genetic inheritance of each individual is a constant, there should be a high degree of continuity in IQ throughout an individual's life-span.
Proposition (3) Individual differences in early experience should have no fundamental effect on the development of individual differences in intelligence.
Proposition (4) Deliberate attempts to increase the level of intelligence by special enrichment-experience should have no effect.

What is the evidence for and against these propositions?

Proposition (1)

Table 27.3 shows a selection made from Erlenmeyer-Kimling, Jarvik and Jensen's review of 109 studies of different kinship relations, conducted in eight countries, four continents and over more than two generations. How can we interpret these data?

First, we need to understand the difference between MZs and DZs: MZ stands for 'monozygotic' meaning 'one egg'. So MZs are identical twins who have developed from the same, single, fertilized ovum and are usually regarded as being genetically identical and are, by definition, of the same sex. DZ stands for 'dizygotic', meaning 'two egg', so DZs are non-identical (or fraternal) twins who have developed from two quite separately fertilized ova; they are no more alike than ordinary siblings (that is, they have roughly 50 per cent of their genes in common) and can be either of the same or different sex.

Secondly, we can see fairly easily that the closer the kinship relation (and, hence, the greater the genetic similarity), the higher the correlation for IQ. Can we take this as support for the genetic theory? Unfortunately, it is not as simple as this. Notice what else is happening as the genetic similarity increases—the environments are also becoming more similar!

Table 27.3 A sample of IQ correlations for different kinships (based on Erlenmeyer-Kimling, Jarvik and Jensen (1967)

Kinship relation	Number of studies	Median correlation obtained (IQ)	Genetic expectation
MZs reared together	14	0.87	1.00
MZs reared apart	4	0.75	1.00
DZs (like-sex) reared together	11	0.56	0.50
DZs (unlike-sex) reared apart	9	0.49	0.50
Full siblings reared together	36	0.55	0.50
Siblings reared apart	3	0.47	0.50
One parent with one child	12	0.50	0.50
Foster/adoptive parent with fostered/adopted child	3	0.20	0.00
Unrelated children reared together	5	0.24	0.00

Take the case of MZs reared together: not only are they as similar genetically as any two humans can get, but they are much more likely to be treated in the same way than DZs or ordinary siblings. Kamin (1981), for example, points out that even MZs vary in their physical likeness and this seems to be a factor in determining how similarly they will be treated; significantly, the more alike physically they are, the more similar their IQ. He also claims that DZs of the same sex are treated more alike than opposite sex DZs and both are treated more alike than ordinary siblings; even though all these groups are similar genetically, same-sex DZs are most alike in IQ scores.

A study by Lytton et al (1977) shows that it is not parents' belief about their twins' similarity which determines their behaviour towards them but rather the twins' actual similarity. They studied eight sets of parents who had been mis-informed, four sets thinking they had MZs when they really had DZs and vice-versa for the other four. Parents of the mislabelled MZs acted more uniformly towards their twins than parents of the mislabelled DZs.

So it is difficult to draw any conclusions from the fact that MZs reared together are most alike in IQ (0·87) since this would be predicted from both a genetic theory *and* and an environmentalist theory. Yet how would an environmentalist explain the finding that separated MZs are more alike than like-sex DZs reared together (0·75 and 0·56 respectively)? Taken at face value, this would certainly seem to support the genetic argument and, indeed, is generally regarded as the strongest single piece of evidence. But we need to look at studies of separated twins in more detail.

The Rationale of Twin Studies

Why do we need to study separated twins?

As we have seen, MZs reared together do not tell us about the relative importance of genetic and environmental factors, although even here environmental factors must be playing some role, since if only genetic factors were involved in IQ, the correlation would be perfect (ie 1·00). If the differences in IQ due to environmental differences (MZs reared apart) are *smaller* (ie the correlation is higher) than IQ differences due to genetic

Table 27.4   The findings from the 4 major studies of separated identical twins

Name of study	IQ Correlations (numbers of pairs are shown in brackets)		
	MZs reared together	MZs reared apart	DZs (same sex) reared together
Newman, Freeman and Holzinger (1937)	0.91(50)	0.67(19)	0.64(50)
Burt (1955) Burt (1958) Conway (1958) Burt (1966)	0.944(83) 0.944(?) 0.936(?) 0.944(95)	0.771(21) 0.771('Over 30') 0.778(42) 0.771(53)	0.552(127)
Shields (1962)	0.76(34)	0.77(40)	0.51
Juel-Nielsen (1965)		0.62(12)	

differences (DZs of the same sex reared together), then we can conclude that environmental factors are *less* important than genetic factors in causing differences in IQ. So the crucial comparison is between MZs reared apart and DZs of the same sex reared together; in the former case, genetic factors are held constant while environmental factors vary and in the latter the situation is reversed; so twin studies represent an important kind of natural experiment (see Chapter 2).

The four major studies of separated MZs are Newman, Freeman and Holzinger (1937), Burt (1955, 1958, 1966), Shields (1962), and Juel-Nielsen (1965). A summary of the main findings appears in Table 27.4. As can be seen, MZs reared apart turn out to be more alike than DZs of like-sex brought up together (and in the Shields study, they were actually more alike than MZs reared together—a rather strange finding which neither theory would predict). So is the genetic theory proven? According to Kamin (1977, 1981) the answer is a resounding 'No'. Why?

Criticisms of Twin Studies
1)   Perhaps the most damaging criticism is that the 'separated' MZs turn out not to be separated at all. For instance, in the Shields study, the criterion of separation was that the twins should have been reared in different homes for at least five years, even though in some cases the separation did not occur until 7, 8 or 9 years (and very few separations occurred at birth). Out of 40 separated pairs 27 were actually raised in related branches of the parents' families and attended the same school. The most common arrangement was for one twin to stay with the natural mother and the other to go to the maternal grandmother or aunt; the correlation for these 27 pairs was 0·83. The remaining 13 pairs were, in fact, raised in unrelated families (although these often were friends of the mother) and their correlation was 0·51.

Jessie and Winifred were 8-years-old when studied and had been 'separated' at 3 months, but they were 'brought up within a few hundred yards of each other . . . told they were twins after the girls discovered it for themselves, having gravitated to one another at school at the age of 5. They played together quite a lot . . . Jessie often goes to tea with Winifred. . . . They were never apart and wanted to sit at the same desk.' (Shields, 1962.) Similar cases are reported in the Juel-Nielsen (1965) study.

2) When twins have to be split up, the agencies responsible for placing them will try to match the respective families as closely as possible, which can account for much of the similarity found between the separated MZs. However, when the environments are substantially different, very marked IQ differences are found.

For example, one of the pairs in the Newman et al (1937) study experienced very contrasting upbringings: one girl was raised in a good farming region, went to college and became a teacher and her IQ was 116; her sister was reared in the backwoods, had only two years of regular schooling and, although she later worked in a big city as a general assistant in a printing firm, her IQ was only 92. This 24 point difference was the largest difference found for any of the 19 pairs, which also included differences of 19 and 17 points. Three other pairs had very different educational experiences and the average difference for these was 13 IQ points. Using a rating scale to estimate the educational difference between all 19 pairs, there was an overall correlation of 0·79 between educational difference and IQ difference.

3) These findings also demonstrate the large absolute differences which may exist between pairs of separated MZs; this is important because the use of correlation coefficients tends to emphasize the relative similarities of MZs compared with DZs.

4) Experimenter bias is another problem, especially in the Newman et al and Shields studies. In the Newman et al study, when the twins were tested, the investigators knew which were MZs and which were not. Similarly, Shields tested both members of 35 out of the 40 pairs of separated MZs himself and the overall correlation was 0·84 (with a mean difference of 8·5 points); this compared with 0·11 (and a mean difference of 22·4 points) for the remaining five pairs (one member of which was tested by Shields and the other by another tester).

5) The twin samples were often biased. For instance, in the Newman et al study, volunteers responded to newspaper and radio appeals and then had to send in a questionnaire and a photograph of themselves. When a pair who looked so alike that they were mistaken for each other gave very different answers on the questionnaire, they were judged not to be MZs and were excluded from the study; so it is possible that amongst those who were excluded were MZs who happened to have developed very different personalities. This is a particularly serious criticism since, in 1937, there was no reliable medical test of zygosity (ie whether twins are MZ or DZ) and the reliability of the case histories is very dubious (eg regarding when they were separated).

6) The intelligence tests used differed from study to study, which makes it very difficult to compare different studies. There are also problems with the tests used in particular studies; for example, Newman et al used the 1916

version of the Stanford–Binet which, as we have seen, was designed for people up to 16 and, since the 19 pairs of MZs were mostly adults (age range 11 to 59), the similarity of their IQs were artificially increased.

Similarly, Shields used two tests, the Dominoes Test (a test of non-verbal intelligence) and the Mill Hill Vocabulary Scale, neither of which had been standardized on females, a significant fact when you consider that two-thirds of his sample of MZs were female!

The Danish translation of the WAIS used by Juel-Nielsen had never been standardized on a Danish sample.

7)   As can be seen from Table 27.4, the largest number of separated MZs was gathered by Burt, and Eysenck and Jensen have based their genetic theory largely on Burt's findings. However, it is now generally accepted that Burt actually invented some of his data: Kamin (1977) pointed out, 'a number of puzzling inconsistencies' as well as 'a number of astonishing consistencies' (see the correlation coefficients, expressed to three decimal places, despite differences in the number of twin pairs—Table 27.4). Some of his data was published under the names of fictitious co-workers (eg the Conway, 1958, paper) and Kamin (1977) concludes that, 'the numbers left behind by Professor Burt are simply not worthy of our current scientific attention'.

An Evaluation of Twin Studies

Do they provide a *heritability estimate for intelligence?*

Based on twin studies in general, and Burt's study in particular, Eysenck and Jensen have proposed that 80 per cent of the variance between the IQ scores of individuals are attributable to genetic differences; this is referred to as a *heritability estimate* (of 80 per cent).

In view of all the shortcomings of twin studies, they would appear to be an extremely unreliable basis for drawing such a conclusion, particularly (as pointed out by Kamin and others) when a heritability estimate applies only to a *particular population* at a *particular time*. What does this mean? All the twin studies used white middle-class Americans, Britons or Danes and so we are not justified in applying the heritability estimate to blacks or to working-class populations (something of which both Eysenck and Jensen are guilty); if they tell us anything at all, they tell us about differences *within* the white middle-class population of those particular countries. We have also seen that where environmental differences between separated MZs are quite substantial, there is a correspondingly large difference in their IQs, which means the heritability will be smaller and, indeed, the four studies produce different heritability estimates ranging from 0·62 (Juel-Nielsen) to 0·771 (Burt), with an average of 0·75. So, clearly, the amount of 'room for manoeuvre' which genetic factors have depends very much on the kind of environmental conditions in which they find themselves. (Herrnstein (1982) has observed that heritability estimates vary from 0·50 to 0·80.)

Even within the white middle-class populations that have been studied, Kamin argues that twin studies could be used as a basis for a heritability estimate *only* if:

i)   The twins were genetically representative of the population;

ii) The range of environments to which the twins were exposed was also representative;

iii) There was no tendency for the environments to be systematically correlated (or matched).

According to Bodmer (1972), for example, the difference between members of a DZ pair represents only a fraction of the genetic difference that can exist between any two individuals taken at random; like siblings, they have half their genes in common. MZs, of course, have all their genes in common, and so are even less representative of the population as a whole.

As far as their environments are concerned, Bodmer again argues that the environmental differences between members of a twin pair represent only a fraction of the total environmental differences that can exist between two individuals chosen at random. Even within the same family, the environment of twins (MZ or DZ) will be more similar than for ordinary siblings, as we have seen. We have already seen how similar the environments of separated MZs were, partly because of deliberate matching by the agencies responsible and partly because of the more informal arrangements made by the family.

In the light of this, Kamin concludes that none of the three conditions has been met and so twin studies are not a reliable source of data regarding a heritability estimate for intelligence. Regarding the exposure of Burt's fabrication of his results, Jensen (1974) claims that there is other evidence which is equally supportive of the genetic theory, Scarr and Weinberg (1977) believe that estimates of heritability should be scaled downward, but not drastically, and Vernon (1979) agrees. What is this other evidence which Jensen alludes to?

Fostering and Adoption Studies

The average correlation of $0 \cdot 20$ between fostered/adopted children and their foster/adoptive parents compared with $0 \cdot 50$ between natural children and their parents would seem to indicate a strong genetic component.

The early studies (Burks, 1928, Leahy, 1935, Skodak and Skeels, 1949) have been criticized on methodological grounds (eg Kamin, 1977) and because of important differences between the intelligence of foster/adoptive parents as a group and that of the children they foster and adopt. McGurk (1975), for example, points out that such parents are a carefully selected group of people who tend to be middle class, with better education and higher IQs than parents in general; in addition, the variance of their IQ scores is smaller than that of the children they foster or adopt (many of whom come from working-class, disadvantaged, backgrounds) and the effect of this is to reduce the correlation.

McGurk and others also point out that in terms of *absolute* levels of IQ, adopted children move towards the level of the adoptive parents and, on average, they score significantly above those of the natural parents; ie the adoptive environment raises the child's IQ above what it probably would have been if the child had remained with the natural parents. This is demonstrated by the Skodak and Skeels study and a more recent study by Scarr and Weinberg (1977, 1983).

Scarr and Weinberg, in Minnesota, USA, studied black children adopted by white families in which there was a biological child; their major finding was that the adopted black child and the biological white child resembled the mother equally in IQ, that is, the black child scored just as well as the white child on IQ tests.

Many of these black children (and many of those in the Skodak and Skeels study) came from disadvantaged homes where the biological parents were poorly educated and were below average in IQ. By age 4 to 7, the adopted children were scoring well above average on IQ tests (about 110 in the Scarr and Weinberg study and 112 in Skodak and Skeels), scores that are considerably higher than would have been expected on the basis of the natural parents' IQ and education levels or the IQs of other children from disadvantaged backgrounds. Since the adoptive parents are known to be highly educated and above average in IQ, it seems reasonable to assume that they provide an enriched, intellectually stimulating, home environment which facilitates the cognitive development of the adopted children.

Horn et al (1978) in Texas also found that there was no significant difference in the correlations of adoptive mothers with their adopted or biological child (in fact, there was a marginally higher correlation with the adopted child). Kamin (1981) believes the Horn et al and Scarr and Weinberg studies represent an improved design compared with the early studies and they show that whether or not they share common genes, 'two children who are raised in the same environment resemble each other in IQ to about the same degree'.

Finally, Schiff et al (1978) in France, studied 32 children, born to parents of low social status, who were adopted before they were six months old by parents of high social status. Compared with the IQs of their biological siblings reared by the natural mother, the average IQ of the adopted children was far superior (95 and 111 respectively).

Reaction Range: An Example of Gene–Environment Interaction

A way of summarizing these studies is by reference to the concept of *reaction range*. This refers to the range of possible responses by an individual to the particular environment they encounter; it is unique to that individual and is related to their genetic make-up. So, for instance, your genes might dictate that you grow to be six feet tall but this will only happen if you receive an adequate diet.

As far as IQ is concerned, Scarr-Salapatek (1971) maintains that, assuming the individual is not severely retarded, they have a reaction range of 20–25 IQ points, that is, any individual's IQ score can vary by as much as 25 points (almost two standard deviations) depending on the kind of environment to which they are exposed.

Another classic example of gene–environment interaction is the disease phenylketonuria (PKU) which involves the inheritance of two recessive genes, one from each parent, which prevent the body's production of an enzyme, whose function is to metabolize phenylalanine (a common constituent of many foodstuffs, particularly dairy produce). If untreated, phenylalanine builds up in the bloodstream and poisons the nervous system, causing severe mental retardation and, eventually, death. However, by putting the baby on a low-protein diet (for at least its first ten to twelve years), these effects can be prevented and normal intelligence will develop. This suggests that any talk of 'high or low IQ genes' is meaningless—how particular genes contribute to high or low intelligence depends upon the environment in which they express themselves; in themselves they are neither 'bright' nor 'dull'.

Proposition (2)

(See page 712).

In order to evaluate studies of the stability of IQ, we need to make two important points:

i) There is an important difference between longitudinal and cross-sectional studies—in a longitudinal study, the same group of individuals is studied over a period of time (hence, 'follow-up' study) while in a cross-sectional study, different age-groups are compared, at more-or-less the same point in time. Longitudinal studies are generally the 'method of choice'—since the same individuals are being compared with themselves over time, it is much easier to detect real changes that occur (see Chapter 23).

ii) IQ is not normally used as a measure of intelligence below two years of age; instead a Developmental Quotient (DQ) is used and perhaps the most widely used is the Bayley Scales of Infant Development (Bayley, 1969); designed for 2- to 30-month-olds, it assesses a child's rate of development compared with the 'average' child of the same age.

Generally, the younger a child is when given a developmental test, the lower the correlation between its DQ and its later performance on an IQ test (eg Anderson, 1939, Honzik, 1976, Rubin and Balow, 1979).

Once IQ begins to be measurable, it becomes a better predictor of adult IQ (compared with DQ). However, the evidence is still very mixed.

Honzik et al (1948) studied over 250 children in California, testing them at regular intervals between 2 and 18 years. Some of the important findings are shown in Table 27.5.

Clearly, the closer in time the IQ scores are taken, the higher the correlation and the overall picture is one of little fluctuation over time. However, there were many fluctuations in the short term, often related to disturbing factors in the child's life, and the 'stability coefficients' are based on large groups of subjects, obscuring important individual differences.

Another longitudinal study (the Fels Longitudinal Study of Development, McCall, 1973) studied 140 middle-class children from $2\frac{1}{2}$ to 17 years. The

Table 27.5 Correlations for IQ at ages 4–18 for the same individuals (after Honzik et al, 1948)

Age of child	Correlation with IQ at age 10	Correlation with IQ at age 18
4	0·66	0·42
6	0·76	0·61
8	0·88	0·70
10		0·76
12	0·87	0·76

average change in IQ during that period was 28 points and even the 'most stable' changed an average of 10 points. About 15 per cent shifted 40 points or more (in either direction) and Hindley and Owen (1978) observed that changes of 70 points and over are not unknown.

Finally, the Berkeley Growth Study (Bayley and Shaefer, 1964, Bayley, 1970) continually tested subjects from birth up to 36 years and found changes of up to 15 points in several cases.

Box 27.1: Kagan's (1973) Study of Guatemalan Village Children

A different approach to studying the continuity of IQ is offered by Kagan's (1973) research in a small, remote, farming village in Guatemala, where infants typically spend their first year in an isolated state, in a dark and tiny hut. They are not played with or spoken to and are poorly nourished, experiencing continuous gastrointenstinal and respiratory illness; compared with American babies of the same age, they are mentally retarded.

By their second year, conditions change; they are allowed to move about outside the hut and they begin to develop an interest in people, animals and objects. By 4 or 5 years they are playing with other children and at 8 or 9 assume some responsibilities in the family farm and domestic chores. Yet until 10 they remain inferior intellectually to their American counterparts; they also do more poorly on tests of perception, memory and reasoning compared with other Indian children from a nearby village who are not so completely isolated during their first year. However, by the time they reach adolescence, they do almost as well as Americans on intelligence tests; any remaining differences are likely to be due to relatively poor schooling and general cultural deprivation.

Proposition (3)

A much cited study (which could just as easily be discussed in relation to proposition (4)) is that of Skeels and Dye (1939), and the follow-up by Skeels (1966); these were described in detail in Chapter 18. Perhaps the most directly relevant studies here are those which are concerned with factors which adversely affect intellectual development. Unfortunately, we could easily devote an entire chapter to these alone; instead, Table 27.6 summarizes some of the major variables and some of the key studies.

Proposition (4)

Two books which first appeared in the early 1960s contributed to the deliberate attempt in the USA to close the educational gap between white middle-class children and those from socially disadvantaged backgrounds, particularly those from black and other ethnic minorities.

J. McVicker Hunt's *Intelligence and Experience* (1961) summarized all the evidence showing that intelligence was not a fixed attribute of a person but depended very heavily on environmental experience. Bloom's 1964 *Stability and Change in Human Characteristics* also argued that intellectual ability could be increased by circumstances and that it was essential to give disadvantaged children enriched opportunities early in life.

Table 27.6   Major variables, genetic and environmental, which adversely influence intellectual development

Genetic	Environmental	
	Biological	*Socio-cultural*
(i) *Down's syndrome* (extra 21st chromosome) (ii) Klinefelter's syndrome ('Apparent Males' XXY) (iii) *Turner's syndrome* ('Apparent Females' XO) (iv) *Phenylketonuria* (PKU) (2 recessive genes)	*Pre-natal* 1. Maternal diseases (eg rubella, syphilis) 2. Rh incompatibility 3. X-rays and other radiation 4. Toxic agents (eg lead poisoning, carbon monoxide) 5. Drugs (eg thalidomide, cigarettes, alcohol, barbiturates, heroin) 6. Maternal stress during pregnancy 7. Mother's age 8. Multiple pregnancies 9. Birth order 10. Birth difficulties 11. Prematurity 12. Mother's diet and malnutrition	*Post-natal* Many of these pre-natal variables are correlated with socio-economic status (SES) and race. In the USA, SES and race are more highly correlated than in the UK. eg Belmont & Marolla (1973) Berbaum & Moreland (1980) → FAMILY SIZE eg Rothbart (1971) Marjoribanks & Walberg (1975) eg Nelson (1963) — Africa Richardson (1972) — Jamaica' Winnick et al (1975) — Korean orphans Das and Soysa (1979) — Sri Lanka' McKay (1978) — Columbia

The first of these compensatory pre-school programmes was Operation Headstart, begun in 1965; initially it took the form of an 8-week summer programme and shortly afterwards became a full year's pre-school project. The aim was, literally, to give an educational headstart, but the first follow-up studies (conducted one or two years after starting school) were discouraging: IQ gains, when they did occur, were short-lived and educational improvement was minimal.

However, Hunt (1969, 1972) was critical of Headstart, claiming that it was inappropriate to the needs of the children involved, not providing them with the skills which they had failed to develop at home during their first four years and which are developed by most middle-class children. There was also too much emphasis on IQ as a criterion of success.

Yet these criticisms were, themselves, to prove premature, since the impact of early intervention has been shown to be cumulative, not showing up for several years. One major follow-up of Headstart by Collins (1983) suggests there is a 'sleeper effect'; compared with non-participants:

(a) participants tend to score somewhat higher on tests of reading, language and maths and this 'achievement gap' tends to widen between 6 and 14;

(b) participants are more likely to meet the school's basic requirements, that is, they are less likely to be assigned to special education/remedial classes, to repeat a year in the same grade, or to drop-out of high school;

(c) participants are more likely to want to succeed academically;

(d) their mothers are more satisfied with their children's school performance and hold higher occupational aspirations for their children.

The gains in IQ, which lasted for up to four years after the programme ended, were not sustained and by age 11 to 12 there were no differences between those who had and had not participated. However, Collins believes that the educational benefits have been sufficiently impressive to persuade the Reagan administration to continue funding at a time of severe cutbacks in public spending generally.

Ironically (in view of these subsequent findings for Headstart participants), other compensatory programmes in the 1960s and '70s tried to provide a more appropriate pre-school education, including Bereiter and Engelmann (1966), Blank and Solomon (1965), Klaus and Gray (1968) in Tennessee, Karnes et al (1970) and Garber and Heber (1977) in Milwaukee. In a review of eleven early intervention programmes, Lazar and Darlington (1982) reached similar overall conclusions to those of Collins.

Conclusions: Nature, Nurture or an Interaction?

Much of what we have discussed in relation to each of the four propositions implied by the genetic theory seems to suggest that environmental factors are considerably more important than a heritability estimate of 80:20 suggests.

As long ago as 1949, Hebb suggested that the whole nature–nurture controversy was a result of the 'double reference' to the term 'intelligence'. One meaning of the term (intelligence A) is an, 'innate potential, the capacity for development, a fully innate property that amounts to the possession of a good brain and a good neural metabolism'; in this sense, intelligence is not measurable. Intelligence B is a product of the interaction between intelligence A and the environment and is defined as, 'the functioning of a brain in which development has gone on, determining an average level of performance or comprehension by the partly grown or mature person'. To ask about differences in intelligence is to ask about intelligence B; we can never, in principle, compare people's intelligence A or know how much of their innate potential is reflected in their intelligence B.

However, despite Hebb, the controversy has raged on, particularly since the mid to late 1960s. Vernon, who in 1969 added intelligence C to Hebb's A and B (to refer to IQ test scores, really a sample of B), believes that there are certain observed phenomena which represent very strong arguments in favour of the genetic theory:

(a) The difference in IQ between siblings, sometimes of up to 30 points;

(b) Very bright children being born to relatively dull parents;
(c) Very dull children being born to highly intelligent parents.

He believes that an environmentalist would find it very difficult to explain these while a genetic theorist would predict such phenomena. Reviewing the evidence in all its forms, Vernon (1979) concludes that it demonstrates a strong genetic component in the development of individual differences in intelligence. Although environment has an important role to play, measurable IQ seems to, 'depend more on genetic endowment than on favourable or unfavourable environmental opportunities and learning, at least within white culture'. However, both heredity and environment, 'are essential and neither can be neglected if we are to plan children's upbringing and education wisely'.

Race and IQ

Are some racial groups naturally more intelligent than others?

The figure who is at the centre of the race and IQ controversy is the American psychologist Arthur Jensen. In 1969, in the *Harvard Educational Review*, he published an article called 'How much can we boost IQ and scholastic achievement?', in which he reviewed all the literature which compared black and white IQ scores.

The basic findings, namely that, 'on average, Negroes test about one standard deviation (15 IQ points) below the average of the white population in IQ' is not itself a matter of dispute; it is Jensen's explanation of these findings that constitutes the controversy:

> Genetic factors are strongly implicated in the average Negro–white intelligence differences. The preponderance of the evidence is, in my opinion, less consistent with a strictly environmental hypothesis than with a genetic hypothesis. . . (Jensen, 1969).

Eysenck (1971) and Herrnstein (1971) agree with Jensen.

Some of the evidence upon which Jensen based his genetic theory was the apparent failure of compensatory pre-school programmes such as Headstart, which, as we have seen, was a rather premature conclusion to reach. Perhaps the most fundamental criticism of Jensen is that he bases his view of black–white differences (*between-group* differences) on the heritability estimate of 80:20 which, as we have seen, is based on studies of the white population (and is about *within-group* differences). Several writers, including many biologists (eg Bodmer, 1972) have pointed out the illegitimacy of making this logical jump.

As an example here, suppose we take a bag of seed collected from a wheat field and sow one handful on barren ground, and another on fertile ground. Those sown on fertile ground will clearly grow taller and give a much higher yield per plant than those sown on barren ground. Within each crop there will be differences, which clearly must be related to genetic differences but this has nothing to do with the overall differences between the two crops which have grown in two very different environments (Bodmer, 1972).

Relating this to intelligence, it is perfectly possible that individual differences in IQ (*within*-group differences) are heavily influenced by genetic differences, while group differences (*between*-group differences) are largely or entirely the result of environmental differences.

Jensen's response to this criticism is to appeal to studies in which environmental factors are controlled. For example, Shuey (1966) compared middle-class blacks and whites and working-class blacks and whites and found the same average 15-point difference. But is social class (measured largely in terms of occupation and income) a sufficiently sensitive measure of 'environment' to be very helpful? Should we expect the experience of working-class and middle-class blacks to be equivalent to that of their white counterparts, given the history of slavery and continuing prejudice and discrimination? According to Bodmer (1972), 'measuring the environment only by standard socio-economic parameters is a little bit like trying to assess the character of an individual by his height, weight and eye colour'.

Tobias (1974) points out a further problem with Jensen's argument— when he says that environment has been controlled, he means controlled at the moment in time when the investigation began. Yet the study of a 10-year-old child, for example, when the family may have attained a reasonable status, tells us nothing about the family's position when the child was passing through its critical, formative period (both pre- and post-natally), such as mother's diet, illnesses, emotional stress and other adverse influences on intellectual development (see Table 27.6).

We have already discussed the cultural nature of IQ tests, which represents another stumbling block to Jensen's argument. It is certainly easier to devise tests which are patently biased than to construct a culture-fair or culture-free test and this was demonstrated by Dove, a black American sociologist, who in 1968 published the Dove Counterbalance General Intelligence Test ('Chitling Test'), a parody of the white bias in traditional tests. It draws freely on black language and culture and whites would be expected to emerge as inferior to blacks on such a test. (See Chapter 7 for a discussion of Black English.) Significantly, the gap between American whites and blacks is almost non-existent in the pre-school years (using, eg the Gesell developmental test for 0 to 2-year-olds). Werner (1972) summarized worldwide evidence on psychomotor tests and found that both African and American black children show the highest mean scores of any group tested, while Western whites score lowest of all. It is only at school age, when IQ tests come to rely much more heavily on verbal items, that the gap begins to widen —in the opposite direction.

Mercer (1972) argues that, 'IQ tests are Anglocentric: they measure the extent to which an individual's background matches the average cultural pattern of American society', ie white, middle-class society. Her conclusions, based on studies in Riverside, California, led to legislation in that state making it illegal to determine that a child is retarded on the sole basis of its score on an IQ test; Massachusetts has gone even further and has banned the use of tests in the school system altogether and, likewise, in Washington DC, Philadelphia and New York.

Finally, the whole concept of race itself is problematic; like intelligence, there are various definitions and criteria, but whichever is used (eg blood types) the extent of genetic variation *within* any population is usually far greater than the average difference *between* populations (eg Bodmer, 1972). The same is true of IQ scores and to emphasize average group differences (as

Jensen does) is to overlook the considerable overlap between whites and blacks as well as the even greater differences within each population.

Conclusions

On the basis of their adoption studies, Scarr and Weinberg (1983) believe that genetic differences do not account for most of the IQ differences between racial groups. Loehlin et al (1975) explain racial differences in terms of three interacting, factors:

   i)   the inadequacy and bias of tests;
   ii) environmental differences;
   iii) genetic differences.

It is *how* these factors contribute to racial differences, rather than how much, which is perhaps the crucial question.

28

Psychopathology

So far, the emphasis in this book has been on normal psychological processes and development. However, we have also had occasion to qualify what we have said in two ways: first, by considering examples of abnormality (which often serve to illuminate the normal); and, secondly, by considering individual differences. In discussing psychopathology, we are bringing these two forms of qualification together, since psychological disorders represent a major source of individual differences.

Psychopathology also constitutes the point of contact between psychiatry (a branch of medicine) and psychology, most clearly and importantly in the shape of clinical psychology (see Chapter 1).

Here and in Chapter 29 we shall be looking at the contributions of both disciplines to the understanding and alleviation of psychological disorders and we shall see how radically different their theories and methods are. (This difference is only to be expected in view of the very different training each discipline provides.)

However, within clinical psychology itself there are various approaches which correspond to those we have already discussed throughout the book, namely, the Psychoanalytic, the Behavioural, the Humanistic–Existential, the Neurobiological and the Cognitive; each defines psychological abnormality differently and, accordingly, favours a different way of dealing with it. Before we consider each in detail, we must discuss the concept of abnormality itself.

The Concept of Abnormality

Implicit within each psychological theory of abnormality is the assumption that it is possible, and meaningful, to draw the line between normal and abnormal at all. How, if at all, can the line be drawn?

1) The Statistical Criterion
This represents the literal sense of abnormality, whereby any behaviour which is not typical or usual (ie infrequent) is, by definition, abnormal. Again, 'normal' is 'average', it is what most people do or are like; however, this does not help to distinguish between atypical behaviour which is

desirable (or, at least, acceptable) and that which is undesirable and unacceptable. For example, creative genius (such as that possessed by Picasso) and megalomania (such as that possessed by Hitler) are both statistically rare (and to this extent, abnormal) but the former would be rated as much more desirable than the latter.

Again, there are certain types of behaviour and experience which are so common as to be normal in the statistical sense but which are regarded as constituting psychological disorders, such as anxiety and depression. So the statistical criterion would seem to be neither necessary nor sufficient as a way of defining abnormality.

2) Deviation-From-The-Norm Criterion

If the statistical criterion is insufficient, it is because it is essentially *neutral*, that is, the statistical average is neither good nor bad, desirable nor undesirable (abnormal is defined as deviation-from-the-average). Deviation-from-the-*norm*, however, implies not behaving or feeling as one *should*; 'norm' has an 'oughtness' about it whereby behaviour is expected from individuals occupying particular roles (see Chapter 8) and if those expectations are not met or are positively 'transgressed', a judgement of 'bad' or 'sick' may be passed.

For example, as far as many people are concerned, homosexuality is abnormal not because it is statistically less common than heterosexuality but because the latter represents the 'normal' state of sexual affairs, that is, the 'natural' form of sexual behaviour in human beings (and, they would argue, in other species too) is heterosexual. From a religious–moral perspective, homosexuality might be judged as 'bad', 'wicked', 'sinful' etc (implying, perhaps, the element of choice) while from a more biological-scientific perspective, it might be labelled 'sick', 'perverse', 'deviant' etc (implying perhaps lack of choice and responsibility). Either way, even if it was found that a majority of men and women engaged in homosexual relationships (making *hetero*sexuality abnormal according to the statistical criterion), this would still be considered a deviation from the norm and, therefore, abnormal.

There is a further implication, which is that what is 'normal' is also 'desirable'; unlike the statistical criterion, deviation-from-the-norm does not allow for deviations which are also desirable.

3) The Adequacy or Mental Health Criterion

One way of 'fleshing out' the notion of desirability is to identify characteristics and abilities which people should possess for them to be considered normal; by implication, any lack or impoverishment of these characteristics and abilities constitutes abnormality or disorder.

Jahoda (1958) identified several ways in which mental health has been (or might be) defined, including:

a) The absence of mental illness (clearly, a very negative definition);
b) Being able to introspect about ourselves, being aware of what we are doing and why;
c) Growth, development and self-actualization (as emphasized by Rogers, see Chapter 9 and Maslow, see Chapter 25);

d) Integration of all the processes and attributes of the individual (eg balance between the id, ego and superego in Freud's theory and the achievement of ego identity in Erikson's theory, see Chapter 26);
e) The ability to cope with stress;
f) Autonomy;
g) Seeing the world as it really is (part of Erikson's concept of ego identity);
h) Environmental mastery—the ability to love, to be adequate in love, work and play, to be satisfactory in our interpersonal relationships and the capacity for adaptation and adjustment (Erikson's ego identity again, Adler's belief in the need for an adjustment in the areas of love, work and society and Freud's 'lieben and arbeiten'—love and work).

While many or all of these criteria of mental health may seem valid and are intuitively appealing, that they are intended to be universal and absolute raises three serious problems.

(1) According to these criteria, most of us would be considered maladjusted or disordered, for example, Maslow himself argues that most of us do not achieve self-actualization and so there is a fundamental discrepancy between these criteria and the statistical criterion (Mackay, 1975).

(2) Although there is some overlap between these criteria, and many psychologists would subscribe to them, they are essentially value-judgements, reflecting what is considered to be an *ideal* state of being human. By contrast, there is little dispute as to the precise nature of physical health; according to Szasz (1960), 'the norm is the structural and functional integrity of the human body' and if there are no abnormalities present, the person is considered to be in good health. Judgements about physical health do *not* involve making moral or philosophical decisions; 'what health is can be stated in anatomical and physical terms' (Szasz, 1960) and ideal and statistical criteria tend to be roughly equivalent (Mackay, 1975).

(3) It follows from (2) that what is considered to be psychologically normal (and, hence, abnormal), depends upon the society and culture in which a person lives; psychological normality and abnormality are *culturally* defined (unlike physical normality–abnormality which, Szasz believes, can be defined in universally applicable ways).

Take the example of homosexuality again; for 23 years (up to 1974), homosexuality was defined as a mental disorder by the American Psychiatric Association's official diagnostic manual. Clearly, nothing happened to homosexuality itself during that period—what changed were attitudes towards it, which then became reflected in its official psychiatric status. Put another way, homosexuality *in itself* is neither normal nor abnormal, desirable nor undesirable, and this can be extended to all behaviour.

Again, within the same culture or society, a particular instance of behaviour may be considered normal or abnormal depending on the *situation* or *context*; for example, taking your clothes off is fine if you are about to step into a bath but not in the middle of a supermarket, and what determines judgements of normality/abnormality are the norms (expectations) associated with those situations. Behaviour, of course, always does occur (and can only occur) within particular situational contexts and so can never be judged except in terms of situational norms; behaviour is inherently *social*.

We should also note that situational norms are not the only ones we apply;

there are also *developmental* norms, whereby particular behaviour may be judged as normal or abnormal depending on the developmental age of the person. For instance, regardless of where they occur, we accept temper tantrums as perfectly normal in a 2-year-old but decidedly abnormal in a 32-year-old (even in the privacy of their own home).

Smith et al (1986) argue that people with behaviour disorders:

> are unable to modify their behaviour in response to changing environmental requirements. Thus, their behaviour is maladaptive because it is inflexible and unrealistic. It is also likely to be statistically uncommon and socially deviant, although neither of these characteristics is always present. People whose behaviour is abnormal may or may not seem unhappy about their failure to adapt.

4) The Mental Illness Criterion—Abnormality as Mental Illness

The influence of the *medical model* extends beyond psychiatry and many psychological theories of abnormality or disorder represent a rejection of and alternative to the medical model or, in the case of the neurobiological approach, an attempt to find empirical support for it.

Many writers have pointed out that the vocabulary we use to refer to psychological disorder is borrowed from medical terminology: deviant behaviour is referred to as psycho*pathology* (the title of this chapter), is classified on the basis of *symptoms*, the classification being called a *diagnosis*, the methods used to try to change the behaviour are called *therapies* and these are often carried out in mental or psychiatric *hospitals*. If the deviant behaviour ceases, the *patient* is described as *cured* (Maher, 1966).

It is the use of such vocabulary which reflects the pervasiveness of a 'sickness' model of psychological abnormality (together with terms such as 'syndrome', 'prognosis', 'in remission' and so on); in other words, whether we realize it or not, when we think about abnormal behaviour we think about it *as if* it were indicative of some underlying *illness*. How valid is the medical model?

The Concept of Mental Illness: The Case For and Against

1) Many defenders of the medical model have argued that it is more *humane* to regard a psychologically disturbed person as sick (or mad) than plain bad, that is, it is more stigmatizing to be regarded as morally defective (Blaney, 1975). However, when we label someone as sick or ill we are removing all *responsibility* from them for their behaviour; just as we do not normally hold someone responsible for having cancer or a broken leg, so 'mental illness' implies that something has happened to the person who is a victim and who is, accordingly, put in the care (and often the custody) of doctors and nurses who will take over responsibility. (We should note that stigma may be attached to physical illness, even if responsibility is not—as with cancer).

It could be argued that the stigma attached to mental illness is actually greater than that attached to labels of 'bad' since our fear of mental illness is even greater than our fear of becoming involved in crime or other immoral activities due to our belief that the former is something that 'happens to people' while the latter is chosen in some way.

While it may be considered more humanitarian to care for people in hospitals than to torture them for witchcraft, exorcize their evil spirits or lock them up in prisons, there is a sense in which these past practices were more honest than some of the current abuses of psychiatry. When people were imprisoned, society was saying quite unambiguously, 'We do not approve of your behaviour and will not tolerate it', making its values clear but also not removing responsibility from the person whose behaviour was being condemned. However, when Soviet political dissidents are diagnosed as suffering from schizophrenia (the most 'serious' form of mental illness), that society is saying, 'No one in their right mind could hold the views you express, so you must be out of your mind', thereby bypassing the actual issues raised by the dissident's beliefs and removing responsibility for those beliefs from the 'patient'.

2)   As we have seen in discussing criteria of normality–abnormality, defining psychological health is much more problematic than defining physical health; not only do norms differ between cultures but they change within the same culture from one historical period to another and, for this reason, Heather (1976) believes that the criteria used by psychiatry to judge abnormality must be seen in a *moral* context and *not* a medical one. The fact of cultural relativity, he argues, makes psychiatry an entirely different kind of enterprise from legitimate medicine; psychiatry's claim to be an orthodox part of medical science rests upon the concept of mental illness but far from being another medical speciality, psychiatry is a 'quasi-medical illusion' (Heather, 1976).

3)   Probably the most radical critic of the concept of mental illness is Szasz; the titles of his books give an indication of his position, for example, *The Myth of Mental Illness* (1962), *The Manufacture of Madness* and *Ideology and Insanity* (1974).

According to Szasz, the basic assumption made by psychiatrists is that 'mental illness' is caused by diseases or disorders of the nervous system (in particular, the brain) which are revealed in abnormal thinking and behaviour. If this is the case, it would be better to call them 'diseases of the brain' or neurophysiological disorders; this would then get rid of the confusion between any physical, organic, defect (which must be seen in an anatomical and physiological context) and any 'problems in living' the person may have (which must be seen in an ethical and social context).

The vast majority of cases of 'mental illness' are, according to Szasz, actually cases of problems of living and they should be referred to as such. It is the exception to the rule to find a 'mentally ill' person who is actually suffering from some organic brain disease (as in senile dementia, alcoholic poisoning etc) and this fact is recognized by psychiatrists themselves when they distinguish between *organic psychosis* and *functional psychosis*; 'functional' means that there is no demonstrable physical basis for the abnormal behaviour and that something has gone wrong with the way the person functions in the network of relationships which made up their world (Bailey, 1979).

Although this distinction between organic and functional psychosis is made, organic psychiatrists believe that medical science will, in time, identify the physical causes of the latter (which include schizophrenia and psychotic depression). However, as Heather (1976) points out, this belief does not constitute evidence and even if such evidence were forthcoming it would still leave major categories of mental disorder (in particular, neurosis and personality disorder) which even the organicists admit are *not* bodily diseases in any sense!

If it is not the brain which is diseased, we are left asking in what sense can we think of the mind as being diseased? Szasz answers this by saying that only *metaphorically* can we attribute disease to the mind; in a literal sense, it is logically impossible for a non-spatial, non-physical, mind to be suffering from a disorder of a physico-chemical nature (unless, of course we identify the mind with the brain—see the discussion of reductionism in Chapter 2).

According to Bailey (1979), medicine began by classifying such things as syphilis, TB, carcinoma and typhoid as illnesses, all sharing the common feature of reference to a state of disordered structure and/or functioning of the human body as a physico-chemical machine; the mistake was to keep adding to this list additional items which are *not* illnesses in this sense. Agreeing with Szasz, Bailey maintains that: (a) *organic* mental illnesses are *not* mental illnesses at all but *physical* illnesses in which mental symptoms are manifested and which aid diagnosis and treatment; (b) *functional* mental illnesses are *not* mental illnesses but *disorders* of *psychosocial* or *interpersonal functioning* (Szasz's 'problems in living') in which mental symptoms are important in deciding the type of therapy the patient requires.

4) An important difference between diagnosis in general medicine and psychiatry is to do with the role of *signs* and *symptoms*. While a doctor looks for *signs* of disease (ie the results of objective tests, such as blood tests, X-rays and so on and physical examination) as well as *symptoms* (the patient's report of pain etc) they tend to attach more weight to the former when forming a diagnosis.

By contrast, the psychiatrist is much more at the mercy of symptoms; although psychological tests are the psychiatric equivalent of blood tests and X-rays, they are nothing like as reliable and valid (see Chapters 11, 25 and 27) and, in practice, the psychiatrist will rely to a large extent on the patient's own description of the problem.

Whether or not the patient's claim that he is Napoleon, for example, will be judged by the psychiatrist to be a symptom depends on whether the psychiatrist believes that the patient means it or not, their overall impression of the patient, their comparison of the patient's statement with their *own* beliefs and their interpretation of the norms of the society in which they live (Fransella, 1975).

In trying to describe the *norms* from which the mentally ill are thought to deviate, Szasz (1962) found that they have to be stated in psychological, ethical and legal terms and yet the remedy is sought in terms of *medical* measures. For this reason, Szasz believes that the concept of mental illness has replaced beliefs in demonology and witchcraft; 'mental illness thus exists or is "real" in exactly the same sense in which witches existed or were real' (Szasz, 1962) and serves the same political purposes. What might these be?

In *Ideology and Insanity* (1974), Szasz argues that whenever people wish to exclude others from their midst, they attach to them *stigmatizing labels* (eg 'foreigner', 'criminal', 'mentally ill' etc).

Unlike people suffering from physical illness, most people considered to be mentally ill (especially those 'certified' or 'sectioned' and so legally mentally ill) are so defined by others (relatives, friends, employers, police etc), *not* by themselves. They have upset the social order (by violating or ignoring social laws and conventions) and so society labels them as mentally ill and (in many cases) punishes them by commitment to a mental hospital.

However, punishment is the last thing that psychiatrists would admit to giving their patients; as doctors, they must believe that what they give is help, care, treatment etc, which are all in the patients' best interest. The patient soon learns that until they change their behaviour (in the way required by the hospital) they will remain segregated from society. However, even if this happens and the patient is 'let out', their 'record' goes with them (much like a criminal record); stigmatizing labels become very firmly attached!

Because of the over-emphasis on the therapeutic potentialities of psychiatry, and the under-emphasis of its punitive functions, Szasz believes that there has developed a distorted relationship between psychiatry and the law (in the USA, at least). People accused of serious crimes used to be advised to *plead insanity* (which would reduce their prison sentence or require them to receive psychiatric help rather than imprisonment) but now they are often being *charged* with it and being branded 'insane' may result in incarceration for *life* in a psychiatric institution. This is what happened to a filling-station operator whom Szasz calls Joe Skulski:

> When he was told to move his business to make way for a new shopping centre, he stubbornly resisted eviction. Finally the police were summoned. Joe greeted them with a warning shot in the air. He was taken into custody and denied bail, because the police considered his protest peculiar and thought he must be crazy. The district attorney requested a pre-trial psychiatric examination of the accused. Mr Skulski was examined, pronounced mentally unfit to stand trial, and confined in the state hospital for the criminally insane. Through it all, he pleaded for the right to be tried for his offence. Now in the mental hospital, he will spend years of fruitless effort to prove that he is sane enough to stand trial. If he had been convicted, his prison sentence would have been shorter than the term he has already served in the hospital. (Szasz, 1974.)

Underlying the labelling process, according to Szasz, is the need to *predict* other people's behaviour; people who get labelled 'mentally ill' are far less easy to predict and others find this disturbing. Attaching a diagnostic label represents a *symbolic recapture* and this may be followed by a *physical capture* (hospitalization, drugs etc). (R. D. Laing also observes that it is usually *we* who are disturbed by the patient's behaviour, rarely the patient.) While medical diagnosis usually focuses only on the damaged or diseased parts of the body (eg someone has a broken leg or lung cancer), psychiatric diagnosis describes the *whole person*—someone does not have schizophrenia but is *schizophrenic*, this represents a new and total identity which not only describes the person but prescribes how they should be regarded and treated by others.

Psychiatric diagnosis, therefore, is a form of *action*. But in what ways are schizophrenics unpredictable and what kinds of rules are they breaking?

According to Scheff (1966), they are breaking *residual rules*, the 'unnameable' expectations we have regarding such things as 'decency' and 'reality'. Because these rules are themselves implicit, taken-for-granted and not articulated, behaviour which violates them is not easily understood and is also difficult to articulate; hence, it is found strange and frightening.

According to Becker (1963), the values on which psychiatric intervention is based are, generally speaking, middle-class values regarding decent, reasonable, proper behaviour and experience and which are applied to working-class patients who constitute the vast majority of the inmates of psychiatric hospitals. In *Asylums* (1968), Goffman describes the 'career' of psychiatric patients, by which he means any social strand in a person's journey through life; the progress of an individual from being a member of society with a full range of rights and privileges to a patient dispossessed of almost all of those rights and privileges can be thought of as a developing career. Related to this is the patient's *moral* career, by which he means the changes in the patient's view of themselves and others.

Psychiatric hospitals (like prisons and boarding schools) are *total institutions*, that is, they encompass all aspects of an inmate's life and like all institutions, they have an overt, official purpose as well as a covert, unofficial, purpose: the former is to help the mentally ill recover from their illness, while the latter is to destroy the patient's previous personal identity and to re-mould it into a form required by the institution.

In this way, psychiatric hospitals operate as agencies for *social control*. As Szasz (1970) observes, persons are deprived of their civil liberties who have not broken the law.

5) An integral part of the medical model is the *classification* of *mental illness* and the related process of diagnosis.

All systems of classification stem from the work of Emil Kraepelin (1913) who claimed that certain groups of signs and symptoms occur together sufficiently often to merit the designation 'disease' or syndrome; he then described the diagnostic indicators associated with each syndrome.

Kraepelin's classification is embodied in the 1959 Mental Health Act, although the latter is much broader and, in fact, is concerned with mental *disorders* (including mental illness). The classification system currently used in the UK is the Mental Disorders Section of the Ninth Revision of the International Classification of Diseases (ICD-9), published by the World Health Organization. The major categories of Mental Disorder are shown in Figure 28.1 over the page.

In the USA, the American Psychiatric Association's official classification system is the Diagnostic and Statistical Manual of Mental Disorder (DSM); DSM-I was published in 1952, DSM-II in 1968 and the most recent, DSM-III, in 1980.

As can be seen from Table 28.1 on page 735, DSM-III comprises a number of major categories each with a number of specific disorders. Compared with DSM-II, DSM-III:

i) uses more specific criteria for diagnosis, with extensive and highly detailed descriptions for the different diagnostic categories;
ii) requires much more information about the patient for a diagnosis to be made; whereas DSM-II required only a simple diagnostic label, DSM-III instructs the diagnostician to evaluate the patient on five different

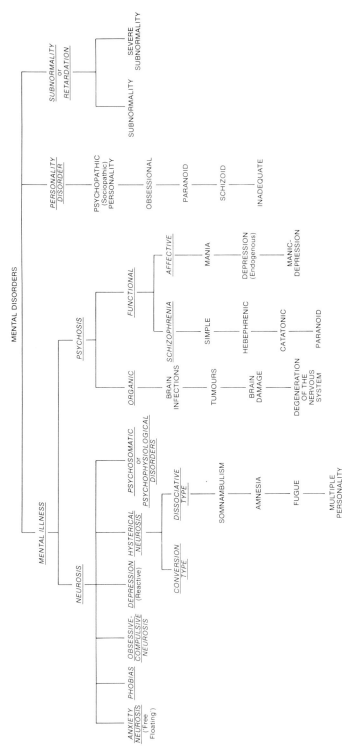

Figure 28.1 Classification of mental disorders (based on the 1959 Mental Health Act and ICD-9)

Table 28.1 Some of the major categories of mental disorder used in DSM-III (1980).

Category name	Examples of specific disorders included within the category
1. Disorders usually first evident in infancy, childhood or adolescence	1. Mental Retardation 2. Attention Deficit Disorder (Hyperactivity) 3. Conduct Disorder 4. Anxiety Disorders of Childhood and Adolescence. 5. Eating Disorders (eg Anorexia Nervosa). 6. Pervasive Development Disorders (eg Infantile Autism).
2. Organic mental disorders	1. Senile dementia 2. Korsakoff's syndrome
3. Substance-use disorders	1. Alcohol dependence 2. Amphetamine dependence 3. Heroin dependence
4. Schizophrenic disorders	1. Disorganized (Hebephrenic) 2. Catatonic 3. Paranoid 4. Undifferentiated
5. Paranoid disorders	1. Paranoia
6. Psychotic disorders not elsewhere classified	1. Schizophreniform Disorder 2. Brief Reactive Psychosis
7. Affective disorders	1. Depression 2. Manic-Depression
8. Anxiety disorders	1. Anxiety attacks 2. Phobias 3. Obsessive—compulsive disorders
9. Somatoform disorders	1. Hysterical Neurosis (Conversion Type) 2. Psychogenic pain 3. Hypochondriacal Neurosis
10. Dissociative disorders (hysterical neurosis — dissociative type)	1. Amnesia 2. Sleepwalking (somnambulism) 3. Multiple Personality 4. Fugue
11. Psychosexual disorders	1. Impotence 2. Transsexualism 3. Sado-masochism 4. Exhibitionism 5. Voyeurism 6. Paedophilia
12. Factitious disorders	Physical or psychological symptoms voluntarily produced by the patient, often involving deliberate deceit
13. Disorders of impulse control not elsewhere classified	1. Pathological gambling 2. Kleptomania (chronic stealing) 3. Habitual fire-setting
14. Adjustment disorders	Impairment of functioning due to identifiable life stresses, eg family and financial problems and crises
15. Personality disorders	1. Antisocial (psychopathy) 2. Paranoid 3. Schizoid

axes which represents different areas of functioning. (The inclusion of these axes reflects the assumption that most disorders are caused by the interaction of biological, psychological and sociological factors.)

iii)   the category of 'neurosis' is dropped (with neurotic disorders dispersed among several categories, eg anxiety disorders, dissociative disorders and somatoform disorders) and the distinction between neurotic and psychotic has been dropped.

Instead of simply placing someone in one category (eg schizophrenia), each patient's behaviour is evaluated in terms of several clinically important factors. There are five axes in all (hence DSM-III uses a *multiaxial* classificatory system), with axes 1 to 3 being used in *all* cases and 4 to 5 being optional:

Axis 1: *Clinical syndromes* and other conditions—the patient's specific psychological disorder at the time they come for assessment (eg heroin addiction);

Axis 2: *Personality disorders* and specific developmental disorders—a set of deeply ingrained, inflexible and maladaptive traits which significantly impair an individual's psychological and social functioning, may occur quite independently of the Axis 1 syndrome and may affect response to treatment (eg paranoid personality);

Axis 3: *Medical disorders* which seem relevant (eg heart attacks);

Axis 4: *Severity of psychosocial stressors*—stressful events which have occurred within a year of the current problem which are judged to be a possible contributory factor and which might influence the course of treatment (eg divorce or death of a parent); these are rated on a scale of 1 to 7 (from 'none' to 'catastrophic');

Axis 5: *Highest level* of *adaptive functioning*—how well the patient has performed during the previous year in social relationships, occupational activities and leisure time. Again a 7-point scale is used ('superior' to 'grossly impaired') and the rating gives an indication of the patient's potential for recovery (prognosis).

Although optional, the importance of Axes 4 and 5 can be seen by the fact that the similar behaviours of two severely disturbed people would probably be interpreted—and even treated—quite differently according to their ratings (Smith et al, 1986).

Description of Mental Disorders

In describing separate disorders, I shall follow the sub-divisions shown in Figure 28.1 but before we do this, an overall comparison of neurosis and psychosis (the two major categories of mental *illness*) will be helpful—this is shown in Table 28.2.

Neurosis

There are six types of neurosis to consider here.

Table 28.2 A comparison between neurosis and psychosis

Neurosis	*Psychosis*
1. Only a *part* of the personality is involved/affected.	1. The *whole* personality is involved/affected.
2. Contact with reality is *maintained*.	2. Contact with reality is *lost*.
3. The neurotic has *insight* (ie recognizes that they have a problem).	3. The psychotic has *no* insight.
4. Neurotic behaviour is understandable as an exaggeration of 'normal' behaviour (so there is only a *quantitative* difference).	4. Psychotic behaviour is discontinuous with 'normal' behaviour (so there is a *qualitative* difference).
5. Often begins as a response to a stressor.	5. There is usually *no* precipitating cause.
6. The neurotic disturbance is related to the person's personality prior to their 'illness' (the pre-morbid personality).	6. The psychotic disturbance is *not* related to the person's personality prior to their 'illness'.
7. Treated mainly by *psychological* methods.	7. Treated mainly by *physical* methods (particularly early on).

1) Anxiety Neurosis ('Free-floating anxiety')

The person experiences a generalized, diffused, anxiety which is not aroused by any particular situation or object and in the absence of any realistic threat or danger. The person is typically jumpy, irritable, finds it difficult to concentrate and make decisions, has trouble sleeping, a poor appetite and may experience a whole range of physical symptoms.

The person may experience occasional *anxiety attacks* (which may last from 15 minutes to an hour) in which there are feelings of inescapable danger which can leave them feeling exhausted. An extreme form of anxiety attacks are *panic reactions* which may last for days, producing a state of disorganization and disorientation.

2) Phobias

A phobia is defined as an extreme, irrational, fear of some specific object or situation. Typically, the phobic acknowledges that the object of fear is harmless but the fear is experienced nonetheless (this is the irrational element) and trying to hide the phobia from others may induce further anxiety, guilt and shame. The phobic will try to avoid the feared object or situation at all costs, and it is this avoidance behaviour which can interfere with the person's normal functioning and which distinguishes a phobia from a milder fear or mere dislike of something.

Almost anything may become the object of a phobia but some phobias are much more common than others. The most common of all is *agoraphobia* (usually defined as fear of open places), accounting for about 60 per cent of all phobic patients (and about 6 per 1000 of the general population), followed by *social* phobias, including fear of having to eat or drink in public, talking to members of the opposite sex or having to speak or write in front of others, which account for another 8 per cent and *animal* phobias or zoophobia (with some much more common than others, eg snakes and spiders) accounting for a further 3 per cent (Marks, 1970). (See Chapter 3 and Chapter 29 for a discussion of 'preparedness'.)

Marks (1970) conducted a 10-year retrospective study of out-patients seen at the Maudsley Hospital in London and found that phobic disorders represented 5 per cent of all cases seen; this compares with the figure of 2 to 3 per cent of all neurotic patients seen in both the UK and the USA (Torgersen, 1979). Because of its common occurrence, much attention has been given to agoraphobia. According to Mitchell (1982), although some patients are terrified of being alone in wide open spaces (such as fields, deserted moorland and so on), what all agoraphobics share is a fear of being alone *anywhere* and they are probably suffering from a form of separation anxiety, fearing that something unpleasant will happen to them because there is no one there who could come to their assistance.

The *primary* fear, says Mitchell, is leaving the safety and security of home and/or companions; fear of being in public places (shops, on buses, in the street etc) represents a *secondary* fear but, significantly, the patient is usually aware only of the latter.

Agoraphobia occurs predominantly in women, while most other phobias tend to be fairly evenly divided between the sexes. Other phobias include acrophobia (fear of heights), school phobia or 'school-refusal', algophobia (fear of pain), astraphobia (fear of thunder and/or lightning), hydrophobia (fear of water), nyctophobia (fear of darkness, which is quite normal in young children), xenophobia (fear of strangers), and, would you believe, phobophobia (fear of fear!).

3) Obsessive-Compulsive Neurosis

Obsessions are recurring irrational thoughts or ideas over which the person has no control, while compulsions are actions which the victim feels compelled to repeat over and over again (a common example being compulsive hand-washing).

Obsessions and compulsions are often related, the latter representing an attempt to counteract the former; for example, compulsive hand-washing may be an attempt to remove the obsessive pre-occupation with contamination by dirt or germs, either as agent or victim (hence obsessive-compulsive neurosis). Howard Hughes was a well-known neurotic of this kind.

An example of an obsession occurring without compulsive behaviour is sexual jealousy, an extreme case of which is described by Stuart Sutherland in *Breakdown* (1976). Sutherland was a well-known British experimental psychologist who had been happily married for several years when his wife suddenly revealed that she had been having an affair (but had no wish to end their marriage). At first, he was able to accept the situation and, indeed, found that the increased honesty and communication actually improved their marriage; however, after asking his wife for further details of the affair, he become obsessed with vivid images of his wife in moments of sexual passion with her lover and he could not remove these thoughts from his mind, day or night. Finally, he had to leave his teaching and research duties and it was only after several months of trying various forms of therapy that he managed to reduce those obsessive thoughts sufficiently to be able to return to work.

4) Neurotic (Reactive) Depression

As we noted earlier, depression is so common that it may be regarded as 'normal' (at least in a statistical sense) and the difference between 'normal' and neurotic depression is clearly one of degree only. Its onset is usually the reaction to something which happens in the person's life, such as a relationship breaking up, losing a job, becoming physically ill and so on but the depression lasts well beyond the 'normal' recovery period and with a greater intensity (see Chapter 24 for a discussion of abnormal grieving).

A prolonged state of sadness and dejection is accompanied by an inability to face the future, a lack of energy, difficulties in concentration and getting off to sleep at night, a preoccupation with unpleasant thoughts and a general 'slowing down'. Because of these kinds of symptoms, some writers have questioned the distinction between neurotic and psychotic (endogenous) depression (eg Kendall, 1968).

5) Hysterical Neurosis

In the *conversion type* of hysterical neurosis (which was the 'model' of neurosis on which Freud based his psychoanalytic theory) a simulation of physical symptoms occurs, that is, the person experiences physical symptoms for which there is no detectable physical or bodily cause. According to Mackay (1975), these are usually one of three kinds:

i) *Sensory symptoms*—anaesthesia (complete loss of sensation to pain) or paraesthesia (tingling or other unusual sensations), hysterical blindness or deafness.

ii) *Motor symptoms*—paralysis, aphonia (inability to talk above a whisper) and mutism (complete inability to talk).

iii) *Visceral symptoms*—pseudo-appendicitis, malaria, TB, pregnancy, coughing fits, black-outs, severe headaches.

There are usually three 'tell-tale' signs: first, a lack of concern about the symptoms ('la belle indifférence'); secondly, the selective nature of the dysfunction (for example, the patient is mute only in the presence of certain people); and thirdly, the inconsistency in the symptomatology (for example, the paralysed arm which does not atrophy or wither). Also, symptoms often appear and disappear quite suddenly (unlike genuine symptoms). These apparently physical symptoms will still demand a great deal of attention from doctors and relatives etc and they may also ensure that the person will avoid certain unpleasant situations; these advantages of being 'ill' are known as 'secondary gain'.

In the *dissociative type* of hysterical neurosis, psychological rather than physical dysfunction occurs and takes the form of a separation, or dissociation, of one part of the self from the other parts. (This has led to the common confusion between multiple personality, one kind of dissociative disorder, and schizophrenia, in which a splitting occurs but is different in character from dissociation—we shall return to this point when we discuss psychosis.)

In *somnambulism* (sleepwalking), one part of the personality takes over control of behaviour while the 'ordinary' personality becomes inactive or sleeps; these daze-like states occur during the day or night, with the eyes open or closed.

Amnesia often appears 'out of the blue' (with nothing to account for it, such as a blow on the head) and may disappear just as suddenly. The forgetting is very selective and the forgotten material can often be recovered under hypnosis or will be recognized when presented (which would not be true of a brain-damaged patient). *Fugue* ('flight') may be thought of as an extension of amnesia, in which the patient flees from home and self by wandering off on a journey, not knowing how they got there and unable to recall their true identity. The person assumes a new identity but, unlike many amnesia patients, does not experience confusion and disorientation. It is usually a brief episode, lasting from hours to days rather than weeks; like amnesia, it may often be triggered by severe psychological stress and in both cases recovery is usually rapid and complete and recurrence is rare.

Multiple personality involves two or more integrated personalities 'residing' within the same body, each dominating at different times. The 'original' personality is usually not aware of the other(s) although these others may be (at least partly) aware of the first. Often, the other personalities embody parts of the first personality which have become repressed and so have remained unexpressed; for example, a shy and sexually inhibited person may develop a second personality who is flirtatious and sexually promiscuous. Shifts from one to the other may be sudden and dramatic and multiple personality may be accompanied by fugue.

The 'original' case was Robert Louis Stevenson's 'Dr Jekyll and Mr Hyde'. True-life cases (which are very rare) include 'The Three Faces of Eve' (Thigpen and Cleckley, 1954) and the truly staggering 'Sybil' (Rheta-Schreiber, 1973) who had 16 separate personalities—the case must be read to be believed!

6) Psychosomatic (or Psychophysiological) Disorders
These are not always included under the general category heading of neurosis, but it is convenient to do so because of the part played by anxiety which is really the 'hallmark' of neurosis in general. The symptoms involved here (unlike those of hysterical conversion neurosis) are real and are confirmed by medical examination ('signs'); they include ulcers, high blood pressure, asthma, migraine headaches, heart attacks etc, and are clearly stress-induced or stress-related (see Chapter 17).

Psychosis: Organic

Organic psychosis is the only kind of mental disorder in which there are known, identifiable, organic causes.

Brain infections include general paresis ('general paralysis of the insane'), a major psychiatric disorder caused by untreated syphilis and which is terminal, while *brain tumours* may not always give rise to psychotic symptoms and their effects will always depend on their precise location.

Brain damage is acute when caused by high fevers, hormonal disturbances, excessive drug intake and severe nutritional deficiencies and is usually only temporary; chronic brain damage, however, is more severe and is basically irreversible. Some of the clinical signs of brain damage include: (a) memory dysfunction (eg confabulation, see Chapter 6); (b) affective changes (eg an increase in emotional instability); (c) general intellectual impairment (eg less capable of abstract thought, understanding new ideas or making decisions); (d) disorders of attention (eg more easily distracted and less able to concentrate); (e) personality changes (which are usually related to the pre-morbid personality); and (f) epileptic fits.

Degeneration of the *nervous system* includes senile dementia, Huntington's Chorea, Pick's Disease, Alzheimer's Disease and Parkinson's Disease.

Psychosis: Functional

Here we will consider the two main sub-divisions in the category of functional psychosis: schizophrenia and affective psychosis.

1) Schizophrenia

What we now call schizophrenia was originally called *dementia praecox* ('senility of youth') by Kraepelin (1902), who believed that the typical symptoms (namely, delusions, hallucinations, attention deficits and bizarre motor activity) were due to a form of mental deterioration which began in adolescence.

Bleuler (1911) observed, however, that many patients displaying these symptoms did *not* go on deteriorating and that illness often begins much later than adolescence. Consequently, he introduced the term *schizophrenia* instead (literally 'split mind' or 'divided self') to describe an illness in which 'the personality loses its unity'.

According to Clare (1976), the diagnosis of schizophrenia in the UK relies greatly on what Schneider (1959) called *first rank symptoms*; in the presence of one or more of these (and in the absence of brain disease etc) a diagnosis of schizophrenia is usually made. But even in their absence the diagnosis may still be made, since in the very early and acute stages of the illness, and in the chronic 'defect' state of the severely disturbed patient, first rank symptoms are often not apparent (Clare, 1976). Schneider's first rank symptoms are shown in Table 28.3 over the page.

Slater and Roth (1969) regard hallucinations as the least important of all the major symptoms because they are not exclusive to schizophrenia; in addition to Schneider's first rank symptoms, Slater and Roth identify: (i) thought process disorder; (ii) disturbances of affect; (iii) psychomotor disorders; and (iv) lack of volition as the key symptoms. These are described in Table 28.4 on page 743.

Usually four kinds of schizophrenia are distinguished—Simple, Hebephrenic, Catatonic and Paranoid.

Table 28.3   Schneider's (1959) first rank symptoms of schizophrenia

1. *Passivity experiences and thought disturbances*
Thoughts, emotions, impulses or actions are experienced as under external, alien, control, including 'made' experiences which the patient believes are imposed on them or in which their will seems to be taken away. Certain thought-control disturbances are included: *Thought insertion* (thoughts are inserted into one's mind from outside and are under external influence); *Thought withdrawal* (thoughts are removed from one's mind and are under external control); *Thought broadcasting* (thoughts are broadcast to—or otherwise made known to—others). External forces may include the Martians, the Communists and 'the Government' and such experiences are sometimes referred to as *delusions* (see below).
2. *Auditory hallucinations (in the third person)*
Hallucinatory voices are heard discussing one's thoughts or behaviour as they occur (a kind of 'running commentary') or they are heard arguing about one in the third person (or using one's name) or repeating one's thoughts out loud or anticipating one's thoughts. 'True' hallucinations involve the voices being experienced as alien or under the influence of some external source. (Hallucinations experienced by patients with organic psychoses tend to be visual.)
3. *Primary delusions*
Delusions are false beliefs which are maintained in the face of contradictory evidence. Two major kinds are delusions of *grandeur* (eg 'I am Napoleon' or, 'I am God') and delusions of *persecution* (eg 'my mother is trying to poison me' and the beliefs regarding thought-control). A 'primary' delusion appears suddenly and in a moment of clear consciousness and is accompanied by a strong feeling of conviction; it is often of the grandiose type.

(a)   *Simple schizophrenia* often appears during late adolescence and has a slow, gradual, onset. The main symptoms are gradual social deterioration, withdrawal of interest from the environment, an increase in apathy, difficulty in making friends and a decline in academic or occupational performance. Such people may become drifters or tramps and are often regarded by others as idle and a 'layabout'.

(b)   *Hebephrenic schizophrenia* is probably the nearest thing to many people's beliefs about what a 'mad' or 'crazy' person is like and typically makes a gradual appearance between 20 and 25 years of age. The hebephrenic will typically display many of the symptoms described in Tables 28.3 and 28.4, including hallucinations, delusions, thought process disorder and disturbances of affect. Behaviour is often silly or mischievious, childish or bizarre and sometimes may be violent (if, for example, the patient is approached while hallucinating).

Table 28.4 Other major symptoms of schizophrenia (based on Slater and Roth, 1969)

1. *Thought process disorder*
The inability to keep to the point, being easily distracted and side-tracked, especially in the form of *clang associations* (eg 'big', 'pig', 'twig'), where words are 'thrown' together by virtue of their sounds rather than their meaning (producing an apparently incoherent jumble of words, or 'word salad'), being unable to finish a sentence and sometimes stopping in the middle of a word ('thought-blocking'). Also making up new words (neologisms) and interpreting language very literally (eg proverbs).
2. *Disturbances of affect*
A 'flattening of affect', in which they may appear insensitive, inconsiderate or indifferent to other people's feelings and experiences and 'incongruity of affect', a loss of appropriate emotional responses, such as laughing or getting angry without any apparent reason, changing very suddenly from one mood or emotional state to another, feeling happy but non-verbally (eg through facial-expressions) conveying dejection and misery, or giggling when given bad news.
3. *Psychomotor disorders*
Catelepsy (muscles in a state of semi-rigidity), grimacing of facial muscles, twitching of limbs, stereotyped behaviours (such as constant pacing up and down) or catatonic stupor (assuming a fixed position for long periods of time — several years in some cases).
4. *Lack of volition*
Inability to make decisions or carry out a particular activity, loss of will power or drive, loss of interest in the environment and a loss of affection for loved ones.

(c) *Catatonic schizophrenia* is characterized by excited, sometimes violent, motor behaviour or mute, unmoving, stupors; some patients alternate between these two states but usually one or other dominates. Another symptom which is sometimes displayed is negativism—doing the opposite of what is asked.

(d) *Paranoid schizophrenia* is characterized by either delusions of persecution *or* grandeur (or both). In other respects, the person is less disturbed (the personality is better preserved) than in the other three kinds. It is the most homogeneous of the four categories (ie paranoid schizophrenics are more alike than are catatonics etc) and Venables (1963) believes that the only viable division of schizophrenia is into paranoid and non-paranoid.

DSM-III uses the term 'disorganized' to refer to hebephrenic schizophrenia (see Table 28.1) and does not recognize the sub-category of 'simple' schizophrenia. Also, DSM-III acknowledges what is found so commonly in practice, namely that different patients have so many overlapping symptoms that it is impossible to place them in one of the main sub-categories; the sub-category 'undifferentiated' is the diagnosis which would be made in the case of such patients.

Theories of Schizophrenia

Not only is schizophrenia the most commonly diagnosed form of mental illness (psychosis or neurosis)—some 40 to 50 per cent of all mental patients are labelled schizophrenic and 1 per cent of the whole population will be hospitalized at some point in their lives as schizophrenic—but it has become the focus for the whole controversy surrounding the medical model; many of its most articulate critics, such as Szasz and R. D. Laing, have directed their critique towards schizophrenia as the example par excellence of what the medical model sees as mental illness.

Part of the controversy surrounds the *causes* of schizophrenia and we shall now consider some of the varying theories regarding aetiology.

1) The Genetic Theory

A greal deal of research effort has gone into trying to demonstrate a genetic component in schizophrenia. As with intelligence (see Chapter 27), the two major kinds of study are those involving twins and those involving adopted children. Just as these studies discussed in Chapter 27 presuppose that IQ tests are a valid measure of intelligence, so the studies discussed here presuppose that schizophrenia is a distinct syndrome which can be reliably diagnosed by different psychiatrists; this presupposition has been seriously questioned.

Some of the major twin studies are summarized in Table 28.5.

In most cases, the MZs have been reared together and we saw in Chapter 27 how this tends to confound the relative influence of genetic and environmental factors. Furthermore, the concordance rate for MZs in different studies ranges from 15·5 to 69 per cent (for DZs it is 0 to 26), which suggests that different countries use different criteria for diagnosing schizophrenia. By

Table 28.5   Concordance rates for schizophrenia for MZs and DZs

Study	*Country*	*Concordance rate (%) — MZs*	*Concordance rate (%) — DZs*
Luxenburger (1928)	Germany	58	0
Rosanoff et al (1934)	USA	61	13
Essen-Moller (1941)	Sweden	64	15
Kallmann (1946)	USA	69	11
Slater (1953)	England	65	14
Inouye (1961)	Japan	60	18
Gottesman and Shields (1966, 1972)	England	58	12
Kringlen (1967)	Norway	45	15
Hoffer et al (1968)	USA	15·5	4·4
Fischer et al (1969)	Denmark	56	26
Tienari (1971)	Finland	43	9

the same token, if the highest concordance rate for MZs is 69 per cent, this still leaves plenty of scope for the role of environmental factors; of course, if schizophrenia were totally genetically determined, then we would expect to find a 100 per cent concordance rate for MZs, ie if one member of an MZ pair has schizophrenia, the other twin should also have it in every single case.

However, on the genetic side, the average concordance rate for MZs is five times higher than that for DZs (50 per cent and 10 per cent, respectively) (Kety, 1979, Gottesman and Shields, 1976).

In adoption studies, children born to parents, of whom one or both are schizophrenic, are adopted early in life into a normal family and these children are compared either with biological children of the adoptive parents or other adopted children whose biological parents are not schizophrenic. Two studies using the latter method are Rosenthal et al (1968) and Heston (1966). Heston compared the adopted children of 77 schizophrenic mothers with the adopted children of 50 normal mothers—the former were five times as likely to be hospitalized with schizophrenia than the latter.

Gottesman, Shields and Hanson (1982), reviewing adoption studies, conclude that they show a major role for heredity and Gottesman (1977) believes that twin studies and adoption studies have provided sufficient support for the genetic theory to enable researchers to turn their attention to the *environmental stressors* which activate the genetic predisposition.

While most schizophrenics do *not* have schizophrenic parents or siblings, they *do* tend to have parents or siblings with a wider range of psychological disorders than in the general population. In the Heston (1966) study, for example, those children of schizophrenic parents who did not develop schizophrenia themselves were much more likely than controls to be diagnosed psychopaths, behaviourally disordered or neurotic (as well as to be convicted of a crime).

Zubin and Spring (1977) conclude that what we probably inherit is a degree of vulnerability to exhibit schizophrenic symptoms; whether or not we do will depend on environmental stresses. This very important point is relevant to the equally important distinction between *reactive* and *process* schizophrenia: *reactive* appears quite suddenly and usually later in life (not before adolescence) and is normally seen as a response to extreme stress; while in *process*, pathological symptoms have been evident for many years before the 'breakdown' occurs and genetic factors seem to play a relatively greater role. The distinction was made by Rosenthal (1959) who studied 37 pairs of MZs, one or both of whom were schizophrenic; when *both* twins were schizophrenic, there was a greater incidence of a long history of illness than when only one twin was so diagnosed.

A number of studies have shown that where there is an identifiable precipitating factor, onset is acute, no family history of schizophrenia, a stable personality prior to onset, warm personal relationships and stable family relationships, and prompt treatment, the chances of recovery are greatly enhanced (reactive schizophrenia) compared with process schizophrenia (Clare, 1976).

There is also evidence that people who are later going to develop schizophrenia are disadvantaged educationally, occupationally and in their capacity to make and sustain social and sexual relationships. While it is generally agreed that the lower the social status the higher the incidence of schizophrenia, this can be interpreted in one of two ways—schizophrenia may either be seen as a *cause* of social disadvantage (the *social drift hypothesis*) or an *effect* (the *social causation hypothesis*).

2) The Biochemical Theory

It has been proposed that what directly causes schizophrenic symptoms is an excess of the neurotransmitter dopamine.

The evidence for this hypothesis comes from three main sources: first, post-mortems of schizophrenics show unusually high levels of dopamine, especially in the limbic system, (Iversen, 1979); secondly, the belief that anti-schizophrenic drugs (such as chlorpromazine) work by binding to dopamine receptor sites; and, thirdly, the observation that high doses of amphetamines and L-Dopa (used in the treatment of Parkinson's Disease), both of which enhance the activity of dopamine, can sometimes produce symptoms very similar to those of schizophrenia (see Table 15.2 in Chapter 15).

A word of caution; although schizophrenics may have higher natural levels of dopamine, this could as easily be a *result* of schizophrenia as its cause. Even if dopamine were found to be a causative factor, this could turn out to be indirect, such that abnormal family circumstances give rise to high levels of dopamine which, in turn, trigger the symptoms (Lloyd et al, 1984).

3) Laing and Existential Psychiatry

During the 1950s and '60s, several British psychiatrists, notably R. D. Laing, David Cooper and Aaron Esterson, united in their opposition to existing conditions in state mental hospitals. They rejected the disease model of mental disorder and were hostile to the exclusively organic and genetic explanations of schizophrenia. Like Szasz, they denied the existence of schizophrenia as a disease entity and instead saw it as a metaphor for dealing with people whose behaviour and experience fails to conform to the dominant model of social reality; they thus spearheaded the *anti-psychiatry* movement (Graham, 1986).

Heather (1976) identifies three major landmarks in the development of Laing's thought, corresponding to the publication of three major books.

First, in *Divided Self* (1959), Laing tried to make sense of schizophrenia by 'getting inside the head' of a schizophrenic, by trying to see the world as the schizophrenic sees it. This *existentialist* analysis retained the categories of classical psychiatry but proceeded from the assumption that what the schizophrenic says and does are intelligible if you listen carefully enough and relate to their 'being-in-the-world'.

What Laing found was a split in the patient's relationship with the world and with the self. The schizophrenic (and the schizoid personality, who may well develop full-blown schizophrenic symptoms) experiences an intense form of *ontological insecurity* and everyday events may threaten the very existence of the schizophrenic as they see it.

Specifically, ontological insecurity comprises engulfment, implosion and petrification or depersonalization. *Engulfment* refers to the dread of being swallowed up by others if involvement becomes too close and common expressions of this are, 'being buried, drowned, caught and dragged down into quicksand', being 'on fire, bodies being burned up', feeling 'cold and dry—dreads fire or water'. To be loved is more threatening than to be hated; indeed, all love is a form of hate.

Implosion refers to the fear that the world, at any moment, will come crashing in and obliterate their identity; the schizophrenic feels empty, like a vacuum, and they *are* the vacuum; anything ('reality') can threaten that empty space which must be protected at all costs.

Petrification or *depersonalization* involves fear of being turned to stone (catatonia), fear of being turned into a robot or automaton (thought-control) and fear of turning others into stone. To consider another person as a free agent can be threatening, because you can become an *it* for them; in order to prevent the other depersonalizing you, you may have to depersonalize the other.

Secondly, in *Self and Others* (1961), Laing maintained that 'schizophrenia' does not refer to any kind of entity (clinical, existential or otherwise) but rather refers to an *interpersonal ploy* used by some people (parents, doctors, psychiatrists etc) in their interactions with others (the schizophrenic). According to the *family interaction model*, schizophrenia can only be understood as something which takes place *between* people (and not *inside* them, as maintained by the psychoanalytic model of *Divided Self*).

To understand individuals we must study not individuals but interactions between individuals and this is the subject-matter of *social phenomenology* (see Chapter 8 on Interpersonal Perception). The family interaction model was consistent with research in America, especially that of Gregory Bateson et al (1956), which showed that schizophrenia arises within families which use 'pathological' forms of communication, in particular, contradictory messages ('double-binds') in which, for example, a mother induces her son to give her a hug but when he does so tells him 'not to be such a baby'.

In *Sanity, Madness and the Family* (1964), Laing and Esterson presented 11 family case histories, in all of which one member becomes a diagnosed schizophrenic, in order to make schizophrenia intelligible in the context of what happens within the patient's family and, in so doing, to further undermine the disease model of schizophrenia.

Finally, in *The Politics of Experience* (1967), two new models emerged, the conspiratorial and the psychedelic. The *conspiratorial model* maintains that schizophrenia is a *label*, a form of violence perpetrated by some people on others. The family, GP and psychiatrists conspire against the schizophrenic in order to keep them in check; to maintain their definition of reality (the status quo), they treat the schizophrenic as if they were sick, imprison them in a mental hospital where they are degraded and invalidated as a human being.

Laing now sees the schizophrenic as, in fact, an exceptionally eloquent critic of society and schizophrenia is, 'itself a natural way of healing our own appalling state of alienation called normality'. Again, 'madness need not be all breakdown . . . it may also be breakthrough'; in Bateson's words, the 'patient embarks on a voyage of discovery (death) and returns (re-birth) to the normal world with new insights'. Schizophrenia is seen as a voyage into 'inner space', a 'natural healing process'; unfortunately, the 'natural sequence' of schizophrenia is very rarely allowed to occur because, says Laing, we are too busy *treating* the patient.

This represents the *psychedelic model* of schizophrenia. (We shall say something more about this in Chapter 29.)

2) Affective Psychosis

a)   Mania ('Unipolar')

Mania is a sense of intense euphoria or elation, which many manifest as infectious humour to wild excitement. A characteristic symptom is a 'flight of ideas'; ideas come rushing into the person's mind with little apparent logical connection and there is a tendency to pun and play with words. Manics have a great deal of energy and rush around, usually achieving little and not putting their energies to good use. There is *disinhibition*, which may take the form of a vastly increased sexual appetite (usually out of keeping with their 'normal' personality). They often go on spending sprees, getting through a lot of money, building up large debts. They are constantly talking, on the move, have little need for sleep and may appear excessively conceited (grandiose ideas).

b)   Depression (Endogenous)

The depressive is the complete reverse of the manic: they experience a decreased sex drive and loss of appetite (which can lead to serious malnutrition), a slowing down of thought processes, a sense of hopelessness and despair, worthlessness and ugliness, a general lack of appetite for life and loss of initiative. There may be delusions of physical decay, an expectation of severe punishment and suicide may seem the only way out of a hopeless situation.

c)   Manic-Depression ('Bipolar')

In about 20 per cent of cases, patients experience alternating periods of mania and depression. It is thought 'that depression may be caused by low levels of dopamine, noradrenaline and serotonin in certain brain areas, while mania is associated with excessively high levels (Iversen, 1979).

These neurotransmitter imbalances seem to be inherited (Kety, 1979).

Personality Disorder

a)   Psychopathic (Sociopathic or Antisocial) Personality

The 1959 Mental Health Act defines psychopathy as:

> a persistent disorder or disability of the mind (whether or not including sub-normality of intelligence) which results in abnormally aggressive or seriously irresponsible conduct on the part of the patient, and requires, or is susceptible to, medical treatment.

As Mackay (1975) points out, this reference to susceptibility means that a diagnosis of psychopathy is often made retrospectively; if there is no response to treatment, some other diagnosis would have to be made.

Psychopaths are often of above average intelligence and are charming and socially skilled; their charm can be very disarming and enables them to manipulate and exploit others for their own gain. Whether or not they engage in criminal activities, they are amoral (cannot experience guilt), insensitive to others' feelings, impulsive, stimulus-seeking (needing excitement) and have a low tolerance of frustration. They are unable to develop or maintain

meaningful interpersonal relationships because they are incapable of giving
—or receiving—love and affection (affectionless psychopathy—see Chapter
18).

b) The Obsessional Personality
This person is excessively conscientious, adheres rigidly to rules and routine
and is generally an unbending, rigid and inflexible person.

c) The Paranoid Personality
This personality may (like the paranoid schizophrenic) experience delusions
of grandeur and/or persecution. They are often highly suspicious of others,
hypersensitive to criticism, have an exaggerated sense of self-importance and
tend to blame others for their own shortcomings.

d) The Schizoid Personality
The schizoid may be outwardly quite a successful person but is, in fact, a
solitary, withdrawn figure who cannot relate to people and who prefers to live
in their own private world of fantasies and day-dreams. In terms of ontological insecurity, the schizoid is a potential schizophrenic (Laing, 1959).

e) The Inadequate Personality
The inadequate is unable to cope intellectually, emotionally or physically
with the demands of everyday life.

What all personality disorders have in common is that the deviant behaviour
patterns do not produce a loss of contact with reality (unlike the psychotic)
and (unlike the neurotic) symptoms are completely integrated into the
person's life and so do not cause guilt and anxiety. Often the disorder is
not recognized as such because the problem behaviour is part of the *core*
personality itself; it has become so deeply ingrained as to be 'second nature',
what the person 'is like'.

Subnormality or Retardation

The 1959 Mental Health Act introduced the terms 'subnormality' and
'severe subnormality' to replace the terms 'idiocy', 'imbecility' and 'feeble-
mindedness' (used by the 1944 Education Act). The British Psychological
Society (1963) recommended that an IQ of 55 should be the cut-off point
between the two, although this is not the only criterion used. Severe subnormality is usually associated with brain damage (genetic, eg Down's Syndrome,
or otherwise), while subnormality is usually associated with gross understimulation during infancy and childhood. However, the distinction is
ultimately one of clinical judgement (according to the 1983 Mental Health
Act).

Problems with the Classification of Mental Disorder

One of the most famous studies criticizing basic psychiatric concepts and
practices is that of Rosenhan (1973) which is described in Box 28.1 overleaf.

Box 28.1: 'On Being Sane in Insane Places' (Rosenhan, 1973)

Eight psychiatrically 'normal' people (a psychology student, 3 psychologists, a paediatrician, a psychiatrist, a painter-decorator and a housewife) presented themselves at the admissions offices of eight different psychiatric hospitals in the USA, complaining of hearing voices saying 'empty', 'hollow' and 'thud' (auditory hallucinations). These symptoms, together with their name and occupation, were the only falsification of the truth that was involved at any stage of the study.

All eight were admitted and once this had occurred they stopped claiming to hear voices; they were eventually discharged with a diagnosis of 'schizophrenia in remission' (ie without signs of illness). The only people to have been suspicious of their true identity were some of their 'fellow' patients.

In a second experiment, members of a teaching hospital were told about the findings of the original study and were warned that some pseudo-patients would be trying to gain admission during a particular 3-week period. Each member of staff was asked to rate every new patient as an imposter or not. During the experimental period, 193 patients were admitted, of whom 41 were confidentally alleged to be an imposter by at least one member of staff, 23 were suspected by at least one psychiatrist and a further 19 were suspected by one psychiatrist and one other staff member.

All were genuine patients.

If Rosenhan's conclusions are valid, it appears that psychiatrists are unable to distinguish the 'sane' from the 'insane' and that the traditional psychiatric classification of mental disorders is unreliable, invalid and harmful to the welfare of patients (Spitzer, 1976). But just how valid is the Rosenhan study?

1) Reliability

In the past, up to ten times as many people were diagnosed as being schizophrenic by American psychiatrists as by British ones (Cooper et al, 1972). (This led some wit to recommend that the best and simplest cure for American schizophrenics was to cross the Atlantic!)

Zubin (1967) reviewed the literature and concluded that the degree of agreement between professionals of similar training and experience was too low to justify the continued use of classification systems. Depression, especially, seems to be vague and difficult to recognize unequivocally (Klerman et al, 1979).

According to Ullman and Krasner (1975), although reliability is better than chance for the major categories of disorder, it has been disturbingly low for decisions which have such a great impact on people's lives.

One source of unreliability is clearly the *lack of independence* between different categories (which is true of most classification systems), ie the boundaries between different categories or sub-categories are often very blurred so that in the end the decision to diagnose a patient as one or the other may be quite arbitrary. We have already noted the overlap between the sub-categories of schizophrenia; Guertin (1961) summed this up when he said that, 'it is generally agreed that schizophrenia is such an inclusive label that there is no single behavioural symptom always present in every patient, nor does a group of schizophrenics show much uniformity in traits or symptoms'.

Again, someone whose severe anxiety is associated with fears of a delusional intensity may defy classification as neurotic or psychotic (Shapiro, 1982). Clearly, the categories are *not* mutually exclusive and there is considerable overlap; several different schizophrenics may have *no* symptom in common at all (Fransella, 1975). How valid can such a diagnostic system be?

2) Validity

As we saw when discussing IQ tests, reliability is a pre-condition for validity; if a test (or a classificatory system) is not reliable it cannot be valid. However, there are other grounds for doubting the validity of the classification of mental disorder.

The primary purpose of making a diagnosis is, surely, to enable a suitable programme of treatment to be chosen; treatment cannot be selected randomly but is aimed at eliminating the underlying cause of the disorder (where it is known). However, in psychiatry, as Heather (1976) argues, very few 'causes' are known (except the organic psychoses) and he maintains that there is only a 50 per cent chance of correctly predicting what treatment a patient will receive on the basis of diagnosis. Bannister et al (1964) statistically analysed the relationship between diagnosis and treatment in one thousand cases and found that there simply was no clear-cut relationship. One reason for this seems to be that factors other than diagnosis may be equally important in deciding on a particular treatment.

If the label applied to a patient does not allow the psychiatrist to make a judgement about the causes of the disorder, or a prediction regarding prognosis and response to treatment, how can that diagnostic process be a valid one? (Mackay, 1975.)

Mackay (1975) concludes like this:

> The notion of illness implies a relatively discrete disease entity with associated signs and symptoms, which has a specific cause, a certain probability of recovery and its own treatments. The various states of unhappiness, anxiety and confusion which we term 'mental illness' fall far short of these criteria in most cases.

However, in defence of the psychiatric classification system, it has been argued that in order to put psychiatric diagnosis into perspective, we should compare it with medical diagnosis in general. In one survey, Falek and Moser (1975) found that agreement between doctors regarding angina, emphysema and tonsillitis (diagnosed without a definitive laboratory test) was no better (and sometimes actually worse) than that for schizophrenia.

Clare (1980) argues that the nature of physical illness is *not* as clear-cut as the critics of the medical model claim; while agreeing with criticisms of psychiatric diagnosis, he believes they should be directed at psychiatrists and not the process of diagnosis in general.

Clare (1980) and Clarke (1975) agree that there is a false dichotomy between body and mind: physical suffering is never without psychological aspects and psychological suffering is often expressed physically. Clarke (1975) also argues that treatment does *not* always aspire to 'cure' the patient but often aims simply to alleviate the suffering; knowledge of the cause does not always or necessarily determine treatment and disorders rarely have *single* causes. People are neither mindless bodies nor bodyless minds, he says, and many organic illnesses require psychological treatment.

In recent years, reliability of diagnosis has been improved in a number of ways. Very explicit, practical and exact criteria have been specified ('operational criteria') and have left relatively little room for subjective judgement (Fonagy and Higgitt, 1984). DSM-III in the USA has addressed itself largely to the problem of unclear criteria (which is why diagnoses have been so unreliable in the past, Kendell, 1975). It covers a broader range of disorders, gives more specific categories and uses more precise language than earlier versions; the use of checklists has aided in increasing reliability, whereby the patient must show a specified number of observable symptoms before being diagnosed in a particular way.

ICD-9 as used in the UK has also been improved and the development of structural interviews has made diagnosis less subjective, eg the Present State Examination (PSE), originally used by Wing et al (1967) but which has been revised many times and the Schedule for Affective Disorders and Schizophrenia (SADS) by Endicott and Spitzer (1978) used in the USA.

Robinson et al (1981) report at least 80 per cent agreement among psychiatrists on diagnosis of a patient's principal problem.

Conclusions: To Classify or Not To Classify?

As fundamental as the questions raised by Rosenhan's study might be, the study itself has been criticized, notably by Spitzer (1976).

As a professor of law and psychology, Rosenhan should know that the terms 'sane' and 'insane' are *legal*, not psychiatric, concepts and that no psychiatrist makes a diagnosis of 'sanity' or 'insanity'.

Perhaps more seriously, Spitzer notes that the diagnosis 'schizophrenia in remission' is extremely rare; in addition to his own New York hospital, he examined the records of discharged schizophrenic patients for 12 other US hospitals and found that in 11 cases, 'in remission' was either never used or used for only a handful of patients each year. Spitzer concluded from this that Rosenhan's pseudo-patients were given a discharge diagnosis which is rarely given to *real* patients with an admission diagnosis of schizophrenia and that, therefore, the diagnoses were a *function* of the pseudo-patients' behaviours and *not* of the setting (psychiatric hospital) in which the diagnoses were made (as Rosenhan claimed).

Further, there is a serious problem in generalizing from these eight pseudo-patients to genuine psychiatric patients in general; as Spitzer argues, they are two different populations.

Finally, the evidence regarding the unreliability of medical diagnosis, even when tests are used (eg pulmonary disorders, Fletcher, 1952, electro-cardiograms, Davies, 1958, and even the certification of the causes of death, Markush et al, 1967) does not mean that medical diagnosis is of no value—similarly, with psychiatric diagnosis (Spitzer, 1976).

According to Rosenhan (1973), the issue is the, 'diagnostic leap that was made between the single presenting symptom, hallucinations, and the diagnosis, schizophrenia'. What we need, he argues, is the avoidance of 'global diagnosis', eg 'schizophrenia', 'manic-depressive psychosis'; instead, attention should be directed to, 'behaviours, the stimuli that provoke them and their correlates'.

Finally, Fonagy and Higgitt (1984) believe that:

> Descriptive terms such as anxiety, depression or schizophrenia should be used as theoretical constructs to aid in the making of predictions and the developing of testable hypotheses about psychological disorders rather than to describe diagnostic categories which assume an underlying disease process and other 'medical' concepts.

29

Treatments and Therapies

A Classification of Treatments and Therapies

It is more difficult to say what different treatment approaches have in common, and so classify them in some meaningful way, than it is to describe the aims and techniques of particular approaches. One of the problems is the sheer diversity of therapies and obviously in one chapter we can only attempt to discuss the major ones. So how can we begin to categorize different forms of therapy?

1) As you can see from Figure 29.1, all the major theoretical approaches which have been discussed throughout this book are represented and we have touched on aspects of their methods of therapy in earlier chapters. Table 1.1, page 14, indicates the position of the five major theoretical approaches regarding the causes of disorder, methods of treatment and the goals of treatment; it should be clear by now that the way each approach defines abnormality is logically related to how it defines normality (and this will be further reinforced in this chapter). The relationship between theory and therapy, however, is not quite so straightforward.

Where theory has grown out of clinical practice (ie work with psychiatric patients), theory and therapy are intimately connected (eg Freud's psychoanalysis and Rogers' client-centred therapy). By contrast, behavioural therapies (of which there are many different kinds) are not always directly derived from learning theory, which is sometimes unable to account for therapeutic outcomes and certain aspects of abnormal behaviour. (This is especially true in the case of phobias which we shall discuss in detail.)

2) Some forms of therapy are not directly related to any particular theory (eg Psychodrama and Transactional Analysis) and, in practice, treatment is often 'eclectic', that is, it combines different techniques from different approaches.

3) A major distinction is between *physical* (organic) and *psychological* treatments—what the latter all share is a rejection of the medical model. For example, although Freud distinguished between 'symptoms' and 'underlying pathology', the latter is conceived in psychological terms (not genetic or

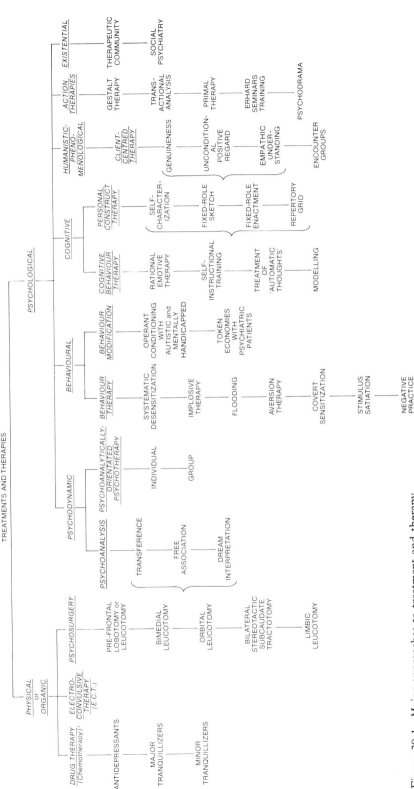

Figure 29.1 Major approaches to treatment and therapy

biochemical) and he was concerned with the individual and not the 'disorder'. Although he used diagnostic labels, he did so as linguistic conveniences rather than as an integral part of his theories and he focused on understanding his patient's problems in their life context rather than on clinical labelling (Mackay, 1975).

4) All psychological therapies are sometimes, misleadingly, referred to as 'psychotherapy' but I prefer to reserve the term for methods based on Freudian psychoanalysis (psychodynamic treatments). Similarly, 'behavioural psychotherapy' is sometimes used to refer to what I will call 'behaviour therapy' (but see page 764).

5) What do different forms of therapy have in common?

According to Oatley (1984), the major common element is that they all take place within a *human relationship*. One aspect of 'technique' which is profoundly important in the therapeutic relationship is whether or not the therapist makes suggestions and gives advice to the patient (or client). In *directive* therapies, concrete suggestions are made and the client is often instructed to do certain things, for example, they may be given 'homework' in between sessions or may have to perform specific exercises under the therapist's supervision. Directive therapy is best illustrated by behaviour therapy, cognitive behaviour therapy, personal construct therapy and Gestalt therapy.

Non-directive therapies, on the other hand, concentrate on making sense of what is going on in the relationship between therapist and client and on understanding the meanings of the client's experience; the best examples are psychoanalysis (and psychodynamic or 'insight' therapies in general) and client-centred therapy.

Directive therapies are generally easier to describe because they seem to comprise procedures which the therapist suggests and which the client either goes along with or not. What distinguishes different directive therapies is *what* they suggest the client does and *how* this leads to the desired change (which, in turn, of course, depends upon what the therapist sees as 'the problem' in the first place). For example, behaviour therapy concentrates directly upon changing people's *behaviour* (and any desired changes in thoughts and feelings will 'look after themselves') while cognitive–behaviour therapy is aimed directly at thoughts and feelings, so that clients are instructed to talk to themselves in different ways, to give themselves instructions for behaviour, to write down their distressing and negative thought patterns and so on.

Non-directive therapies are, by comparison, more difficult to describe because the therapist plays a more passive role and generally does not suggest things to the client but, 'rather listens and takes part with the client in exploring and experiencing what is going on between them' (Oatley, 1984). But as with directive therapies, there are important differences, in particular, how the therapist contributes to that process of exploring and experiencing which, in turn, reflect the therapist's theoretical assumptions about what is wrong.

6) Another important way in which therapies differ is whether they are conducted between a therapist and a client (*individual*) or with several clients at a time, with one or more therapists or leaders (*group*); most of the major

approaches to be described in this chapter are individual but some less well-known therapies are, by definition, group therapies (eg psychodrama, encounter groups and therapeutic communities). We should also note that psychodynamic and client-centred therapies may be individual or group but they will be described here in their individual form.

7) A major development in psychotherapy in the late 1970s and early '80s is the emergence of *family therapies* and *marital/couple therapy*, which seems to reflect the growing awareness by therapists of the important role played by the client's relationships in the development and maintenance of their problems (Dryden, 1984).

This change seems to have been inspired by Laing's *family interaction model* of schizophrenia which has been applied to less 'serious' problems which commonly occur in families and between partners and, generally, where the problem is seen as interpersonal, family, marital/couple or group therapy is likely to be recommended. However, where the problem is seen as 'residing' within the client (*intrapsychic*), individual therapy would be recommended.

Of course, 'the separation of intrapsychic processes and interpersonal processes is quite artificial as these processes are always mutually influencing one another' (Sander, 1979), but Dryden (1984) sees them as separate, independent dimensions, so that both can have a high or low impact (at extreme points on each continuum) on a client's psychological problems. It is not unusual for a client to be involved in some form of individual *and* group or family or marital/couple therapy at the same time.

We will now consider in more detail the seven main approaches, as outlined in Figure 29.1.

1) Physical or Organic Approaches

There are three main approaches to be considered here.

a) Drug Therapy (Chemotherapy)

Table 15.2, page 378, shows the three major groups of *psychoactive* drugs used in the treatment of mental illness: (i) the *antidepressants*, (ii) the *major tranquillizers* (phenothiazines or 'antischizophrenic drugs'); and (iii) the *minor tranquillizers* (benzodiazepines, 'antianxiety drugs' or anxiolytic sedatives).

i) *Antidepressants* were discovered accidentally in 1952 when TB patients were being treated with iproniazid and it was found to produce euphoria in some patients.

Imipramine (tofranil), one of the tricyclic antidepressants, is the most studied and is often used as a standard for comparing other anti-depressants. It is probably most effective with psychotic (endogenous) depression but has also been used successfully with obsessives and patients with bizarre states of pain (Wright, 1976).

The MAO inhibitors (eg phenelzine or nardil) are less effective than the

tricyclics and can cause cerebral haemorrhage by causing the bodily accumulation of amine chemicals. Interestingly, Tyrer (1975) used nardil with 28
patients who had agoraphobia and various social phobias and found it to be
comparable to other treatments; and Mountjoy (1977) believes that nardil can
help phobic patients who have been helped by the minor tranquillizers
valium or librium.

Lithium carbonate (Lithane or Lithonate) is used to treat manic psychosis
and manic-depressive psychosis and can help to restore emotional
equilibrium—but there is the risk of kidney poisoning.

ii) *Major tranquillizers* were first introduced in the early 1950s and are considered to have revolutionized psychiatry by permitting the most disturbed
schizophrenic patients to live outside a psychiatric hospital or to reduce their
average length of stay. However, re-admission rates have increased and many
critics have called these drugs (in particular, chlorpromazine (largactil))
'pharmacological straitjackets' replacing the kind with straps, because of the
'zombie-like' state which they produce.

Chlorpromazine, for example, becomes concentrated in the brain-stem and
is secreted only very slowly, so that the effect on the brain is prolonged. At
first there is a striking sedation effect, which wears off after a few days; it
reduces responsiveness to external stimulation and gross motor activity but
without reducing motor power or co-ordination. It has been shown to be
superior to placebos in controlling hallucinations, excitement, thought
disorder and delusions, but this is often at the expense of a dry mouth,
blurred vision, low blood pressure (which may cause fainting attacks) and
neuromuscular effects (identical to those seen in Parkinson's Disease).

Grinspoon et al (1968) believe that the combination of these drugs with
psychotherapy is the most productive way of treating severely disturbed
patients; drugs cannot produce a 'cure' but can only alleviate some of the
symptoms which may enable the patient to benefit from other forms of
treatment or therapy.

iii) *Minor tranquillizers* reduce anxiety and cause drowsiness by depressing
neural activity, especially in the brain-stem and the limbic system; they are
quite ineffective in the treatment of psychosis and are used mainly for
neurosis, where anxiety is usually the central symptom. Whereas only
psychiatrists would prescribe a major tranquillizer, minor tranquillizers are
commonly prescribed by GPs (far too commonly, many would say) for all
kinds of anxieties and Ray (1978) has described diazepam (valium) as the
most prescribed drug in the world.

b) Electro-convulsive Therapy (ECT)

During 1935–6, Cerletti and his colleagues began to use ECT on the assumption that schizophrenia and epilepsy do not occur together in the same
person; if a grand mal epileptic fit is induced (artificially) this should reduce
or eliminate the symptoms of schizophrenia. This is the logic behind ECT
historically, but it is now used mainly with depressive patients. What
happens?

First, the patient is made comfortable on a bed, clothes loosened and shoes
and dentures removed; atropine is given as a routine pre-anaesthetic medica-

tion (to dry up salivary and bronchial secretions) and then thiopentone, a quick-acting anaesthetic, is given, followed by a muscle relaxant.

An 80–110 volts shock lasting a fraction of a second is then given through electrodes placed on the temples, producing a generalized convulsion (which is detected by facial and limb twitching). Many psychiatrists believe that for severe depression, *bilateral* ECT (one electrode on each side of the head) is preferable as it acts more quickly and fewer treatments are needed; in *unilateral* ECT, an electrode is applied to the non-dominant hemisphere side (the right for most people) and is intended to reduce the side-effects, particularly memory disruption (Benton, 1981).

Side-effects of ECT

Memory disruption includes retrograde amnesia and impaired ability to acquire new memories (see Chapter 6); however, depression is associated with impaired memory function and so it is not clear how much ECT itself is responsible (Benton, 1981). The patient is normally confused for up to 40 minutes following treatment but recall of events prior to treatment gradually returns, although some degree of memory loss may persist for several weeks.

The mortality rate is now quite low, somewhere between 3·6 and 9 per 100,000 treatments (a figure very similar to those resulting from anaesthesia for minor surgery). According to Smith (1977), the Registrar-General's figures for deaths during the 1960s in the UK made ECT one of the safest medical treatments there is (an average of 3 per cent for the whole country) and when the number of suicides resulting from depression are taken into account (one estimate being that, without treatment, 11 per cent of depressives will die from suicide or other causes over a five-year-period), ECT emerges as very low-risk indeed.

However, the possibility of death is only one of the objections made to ECT by, for example MIND (the National Association for Mental Health) and PROMPT (Protect the Rights of Mental Patients in Therapy) in the UK and NAPA (Network Against Psychiatric Assault) in the USA. The main objections are *ethical*, one of them being that since we do not know how it works (*if* it works) it should not be used.

Is ECT Effective?

One problem with trying to measure its effectiveness experimentally is, ironically, also ethical, namely, the problem of the placebo effect or simulated ('dummy') ECT, in which the patient undergoes all aspects of the ECT except that no electrical current is passed through the brain (so no seizure is produced).

Fink (1978) reviewed the literature on ECT, comparing it with a variety of other treatments, including psychotherapy, chemotherapy and simulated ECT and concluded that, for psychotic-depressive patients (and manic patients), success rates were from 60 to 90 per cent. One measure of success is the suicide rate for depressive patients—several studies found that suicide was less frequent in ECT-treated patients than among those who received only psychotherapy.

Several studies have shown that ECT is effective when antidepressant drugs have failed (eg Endler, 1982, Scovern and Killman, 1980) and that

ECT is generally unsuitable for non-depressed patients (eg Scovern and Killman, 1980).

How does ECT Work?

Benton (1981) identifies three proposed explanations:

i) The patient learns that treatment is recommended because of their pathological behaviour and so ECT is seen as a *punishment* which extinguishes the undesirable behaviour. However, equally unpleasant but *sub*-convulsive shocks (ie they do not produce a convulsion) are not effective, which seems inconsistent with the punishment explanation.

ii) *Memory loss* allows the restructuring of the patient's view of life. However, unilateral ECT is intended to minimize memory disruption and so it seems possible to dissociate memory loss from therapeutic advantage.

iii) The shock produces a wide range of *biochemical changes* in the brain (eg the stimulation of noradrenaline) and this effect is more widespread than that produced by antidepressant drugs.

Clearly, there is no generally accepted explanation, only very tentative hypotheses; however, Benton (1981) believes that this does not constitute a reason for not using it since many medical treatments fall into this category (eg aspirin getting rid of headaches).

Anthony Clare (*Psychiatry in Dissent*, 1980) argues that, because it is relatively quick and easy to administer, ECT is much abused and over-used: 'psychiatrists who persist in so abusing it have only themselves to blame if the public conclude that the treatment is a fraud and an anachronism and demand its abolition'. Again, 'it is easier for a psychiatrist, overwhelmed by the sheer number of patients, to reach for the ECT machine than to use more time-consuming and different approaches.'

c) Psychosurgery

Psychosurgery really began with Moniz, a Portuguese professor of neurology, in 1935. This represents the most drastic form of physical intervention and is by far the most controversial of the medical approaches, partly because it is irreversible.

Between 1935 and 1949, Moniz performed about one hundred *pre-frontal lobotomies* or *leucotomies* in which tissue connecting the frontal lobes of the cortex with sub-cortical brain areas is cut, on both sides of the cortex. (Moniz was awarded the Nobel Prize for Medicine in 1949.)

Freeman and Watts pioneered psychosurgery in the USA and it has been estimated that 40 to 50,000 pre-frontal lobotomies have been performed in that country alone since the late 1930s.

In the UK, about 10,000 operations were carried out between 1942 and 1952, two-thirds of which involved schizophrenics and about one-quarter depressives, with the latter responding much more favourably.

Since the 1950s and the widespread use of antischizophrenic drugs, schizophrenics have rarely been treated in this way and psychosurgery has become much more sophisticated, with very small amounts of brain tissue being destroyed in very precise locations ('fractional operations'). Some of these include: (a) *bimedial leucotomy* (first used at the Maudsley Hospital in London in 1951), used mainly with depressive or obsessional patients; (b) *orbital leucotomy*, used with depressives, obsessionals and patients with extreme anxiety; (c) *bilateral stereotactic subcaudate tractotomy*, used mainly with patients suffering from severe and intractable depression; and (d) *limbic leucotomy*.

The first two (together with the original pre-frontal lobotomy) involved serious side-effects, including death and significant personality changes. The third technique (c) is considered much safer; for example, the risk of post-operative epileptic fits is about 1 per cent, which is no higher than for any operation inside the skull (Bridges and Williamson, 1977).

Limbic leucotomies involve the destruction of tissue in a variety of sites; when used with patients who are abnormally aggressive, the neural circuit connecting the amygdala and the hypothalamus is destroyed (based on Kluver and Bucy's work with cats—see Chapter 13). This is perhaps the most controversial of all psychosurgical techniques, partly because the patient is not usually suffering, partly because it is often used with subnormal aggressive patients (so informed consent is unlikely to be given) and partly because, although the surgery has a 'marked calming effect' in 95 per cent of cases, it has, 'failed to entirely eliminate episodes of terror and outbursts of violence' (Bridges and Williamson, 1977).

2) Psychodynamic Approaches

There are two main categories to be considered under this approach, which (like the following approaches to be looked at) is psychological as opposed to physical or organic.

a) Freud's Psychoanalysis

Freud's Theory of Psychological Disorder
In Chapter 26, neurotic symptoms were described as compromises (as were dreams and defence mechanisms) between the opposing demands made on the ego by the id and the superego; symptoms, dreams and defences are all expressions of the inevitable conflict which arises from these opposing demands and are, at the same time, attempts to deal with it.

When the person experiences anxiety, the ego is signalling that it fears being overwhelmed by an all-powerful id (neurotic anxiety) or superego (moral anxiety) and so must mobilize its defences. Anxiety is the hallmark of most neurotic disorders but, except in 'free floating anxiety' it becomes redirected or transformed in some way (depending on which particular defence is used), so that the resulting symptom makes it even less likely that the true nature of the problem (ie the underlying conflict) will be spotted.

Phobias, for example, involve *repression* (as do all neuroses) plus *displacement* and *projection*. Little Hans, for example (see Chapter 18), had a phobia of being bitten by a horse, which could be explained in terms of: (i) repressing his jealous anger and hatred felt towards his father; (ii) projecting these feelings onto his father, thus seeing him as a threatening, murderous man;

and (iii) displacing this perception of his father onto a 'safer' target, namely, horses. Phobic objects, according to Freud, are not arbitrarily chosen but in some way symbolically represent the object for which they are a substitute. (For further examples see Table 26.1, page 662.)

Neuroses, therefore, are maladaptive solutions to the problems faced by the person, that is they do not help them resolve the conflict but merely help to avoid it (both in thought and behaviour). So neurotics adopt self-defeating strategies; far from solving problems, the neurotic's behaviour usually creates its own distress and unhappiness (the 'neurotic paradox'). How can we account for such paradoxical behaviour? One answer is that it permits *immediate* tension release, even if it only adds to the neurotic's problems in the long-term. (This is an explanation that easily fits the learning theory principle of reinforcement, which we shall discuss in detail in the next section.)

Psychoneurotic symptoms, therefore, are indicative of deep-seated, unresolved, unconscious conflicts, usually of a sexual and/or aggressive nature, which stem from childhood feelings, memories, wishes and experiences which have been repressed and defended against in other ways; however, these defences are not effective ways of dealing with the conflict and they create their own distress and anxiety.

The Aims of Psychoanalysis

The basic goal of psychoanalysis is to make 'the unconscious conscious', to undo unsatisfactory defences and through a 'therapeutic regression' (Winnicott, 1958) to re-experience repressed feelings and wishes which have been frustrated in childhood in a safe context and to express them, as an adult, in a more appropriate way, 'with a new ending' (Alexander and French, 1946).

Again, the aim of therapy is to provide the client with *insight*, self-knowledge and self-understanding.

Therapeutic Techniques: How are the Aims Achieved?

i) In classical psychoanalysis, the analyst is meant to remain 'anonymous', that is, they should not show any emotion, should not reveal any personal information and should not make any value-judgements regarding anything the client might say or do. Instead, the analyst tries to become an 'ambiguous object' onto which the client can project and displace repressed feelings, in particular, those concerning parents. (In a similar way, projective tests of personality, such as the Thematic Apperception Test, TAT, and the Rorschach Inkblot Test, require the subject to interpret an ambiguous stimulus by projecting onto it their unconscious feelings and wishes.)

The anonymity of the analyst is aided by the client lying on a couch with the analyst sitting behind, out of the client's (analysand's) field of vision, and the client's projection and displacement onto the analyst is called *transference*. According to Sandler et al (1970), Freud viewed transference as, 'the displacement of libido from the memory of the original object to the person of the analyst, who becomes the new object of the patient's sexual wishes, the patient being unaware of this process of displacement from the past.'

The analyst has gone through their own psychoanalysis in order to prevent the *counter-transference* of their own repressed childhood feelings and wishes onto the client.

ii) To enable the client to understand the transference and how it relates to childhood conflicts, the analyst must *interpret* it, that is, tell the client what it means, its significance in terms of what has already been revealed about the client's childhood experiences. Because this is likely to be painful and distressing for the client, they use another form of defence called *resistance*, an attempt to escape from, or avoid, these self-revelations; it may take the form of 'drying up' when talking, changing the subject, dismissing some emotionally highly significant event in a very flippant way, even falling asleep or arriving late for therapy. All forms of resistance are extremely significant items and themselves require interpretation.

iii) Despite what we have said about the anonymity of the analyst, it is essential that there is a 'working alliance' with the client, whereby the client's ego is strengthened sufficiently to be able to cope with the anxiety caused by the return to consciousness of repressed feelings and memories. According to Jacobs (1984), the working alliance consists of two adults co-operating to understand the 'child' in the client; the analyst adopts a quiet, reflective, style, intervening when they judge the client to be ready to make use of a particular interpretation. This is an art, says Jacobs, and does *not* involve fitting the client into psychoanalytic theory as some critics suggest. Throughout the process of analysis, the analyst remains a real person; the client moves from transference relationships to forming an accurate perception of the analyst as a person in their own right (Guntrip, 1971).

iv) Apart from transference, the two other major techniques used to reveal the client's unconscious mind are *dream interpretation* (which we discussed in Chapter 26) and *free association*, in which the client says whatever comes to mind, no matter how silly, irrelevant or embarrassing it may seem. (These may both lead to resistance which, like transference, will in turn be interpreted by the analyst.)

The Concept of Cure—How do You Know When to Stop?

According to Jacobs (1984), the goals of therapy are limited by what the client consciously wants to achieve and is capable of achieving, together with their motivation, ego strength, capacity for insight, ability to tolerate the frustration of gradual change, financial cost and so on. These factors, in turn, will determine how a cure is to be defined and assessed.

In practice, psychoanalysis ranges from 'psychoanalytical first aid' (Guntrip, 1968) or symptom relief to different levels of more intense work. However, Anthony Storr (1966) believes that a quick, complete 'cure' is very much the exception rather than the rule and the majority of people who present themselves for psychoanalysis cannot expect that their symptoms will easily disappear or, even if this should happen, that they will be freed of emotional problems. This is because of what we have already noted about the distinction between symptoms and underlying pathology: neurotic symptoms are merely the outward and visible signs of an inner, less visible, distortion of the client's total personality, and exploration and analysis of the symptoms inevitably lead to an analysis of the whole person, their development, temperament and character structure.

In trying to assess the effectiveness of psychoanalysis, the usual practice is to assess the extent to which clients experience relief of their symptoms, but

Storr believes this is an inappropriate way of thinking of 'cure', partly because of symptom analysis being only the *start* of the analytic process and also because a majority of clients do not have clear-cut symptoms anyway. (We shall return later on to the debate about the effectiveness of psychoanalysis compared with other approaches.)

b) Psychoanalytically-orientated Psychotherapy

Classical psychoanalysis requires the client to attend five 50-minute sessions per week for several years which, for many people, is far too expensive as well as too time-consuming.

In a modified form of analysis, therapist and client meet once or twice a week for a limited period; for example, Malan (1979) at the Tavistock Clinic in London uses *brief focal therapy* (one session per week for about 30 weeks), in which the focus is on fairly specific psychological problems, such as a single conflict area or relationship in the client's current life.

Although all the basic techniques of psychoanalysis may be used, there is considerably less emphasis on the client's past and client and therapist usually sit in armchairs face-to-face; this form of psychotherapy is practised by many clinical psychologists (as well as psychiatrists and social workers) *without* receiving a full-blown psychoanalytic training (Fonagy and Higgitt, 1984).

Finally, another form of this is psychoanalytically-orientated *group* psychotherapy.

3) Behavioural Approaches

Treatment methods based on classical learning theory (ie conditioning) are often referred to interchangeably as 'behaviour therapy' and 'behaviour modification'. However, I shall distinguish between them in the way proposed by Walker (1984), namely:

a) *Behaviour therapy* refers to techniques based on *classical conditioning* and developed by psychologists such as Wolpe and Eysenck in order to extinguish maladaptive behaviours and substitute adaptive ones;
b) *Behaviour modification* refers to techniques based on *operant conditioning* and developed by psychologists such as Allyon and Azrin to build up appropriate behaviour (where it did not previously exist) or to increase the frequency of certain responses and decrease the frequency of others.

Models of Psychological Disorder
i) Both behaviour therapy and modification regard *all* behaviour, whether adaptive or maladaptive, as acquired by the same principles of classical and operant conditioning respectively (see Chapter 3).
ii) The medical model is completely rejected, including any distinction between 'symptoms' and underlying pathology; according to Eysenck (1960), if you 'get rid of the symptom ... you have eliminated the neurosis', ie what you see is what there is! However, Mackay (1975)

observes that some behaviour therapists make use of the formal diagnostic categories or 'syndromes' and try to discover which techniques are most effective with particular diagnostic groups; key figures in this nomothetic approach are Eysenck, Rachman and Marks, and Mackay refers to it as *behavioural technology*.

Other behaviour therapists, however, believe that therapists should isolate the stimuli and consequences which are maintaining the inappropriate behaviour in each individual case and that, accordingly, any treatment programme should be derived from such a 'behavioural analysis' (or 'functional analysis'). Mackay calls this idiographic approach, associated with Yates, Meyer and others, *behavioural psychotherapy*.

iii) Part of the functional analysis is an emphasis on *current* behaviour–environment relations, in contrast to the Freudian emphasis on past events (particularly early childhood ones) and unconscious (and other internal) factors. Psychological problems are behavioural problems which need to be *operationalized* (ie described in terms of observable behaviours) before we attempt to change them.

iv) According to Eysenck and Rachman (1965), the case of Little Albert (Chapter 3) exemplifies how *all* abnormal fears are acquired (ie through classical conditioning). Evidence to support this view comes from many sources, for example, phobics often recall an earlier traumatic experience associated with the onset of their phobia (eg a dog phobic recalling being attacked by a large Alsatian, Rimm et al, 1977) and laboratory studies with humans and animals have shown that if the UCS is highly traumatic, a single pairing of the CS and UCS may be sufficient to induce a long-lasting CR, (eg Garcia's *taste aversion studies*—see Chapter 3).

However, there is also considerable evidence *against* Eysenck and Rachman. Several studies have shown that phobics are often unable to recall any traumatic experience involving the object of their fear (eg Lazarus, 1971) and, conversely, people may experience profound traumas without developing any obvious phobias (eg the concentration camp survivors, studied by Freud and Dann, 1951—see Chapter 18).

We noted in Chapter 3 that some phobias are easier to induce in the laboratory (in subjects who do not already have them) and it is well-known that certain naturally-occurring phobias are more common than others. For example, rats, jellyfish, cockroaches, spiders, and slugs are consistently rated as frightening and rabbits, ladybirds, cats and lambs as non-frightening, and the crucial perceptual qualities seem to be ugliness, sliminess, and suddenness of movement (Bennett-Levy and Marteau, 1984).

These and similar findings are consistent with the concept of *preparedness* (Seligman, 1971, Ohman et al, 1979) which was discussed in Chapter 3. However, these findings have not always been replicated; for example, induced phobias of snakes and corpses are no harder to extinguish through treatment than phobias of chocolate and in a review of the literature, McNally and Reiss (1982) concluded that there is little evidence to support the concept of preparedness.

It is the persistence of naturally-occurring phobias (ie their failure to extinguish) which poses one of the greatest difficulties for the classical conditioning explanation and the major theoretical attempt to account for this phenomenon has been the two-process/two-factor model (see Chapter 3), whereby the reduction of fear brought about by escaping or avoiding the feared object or situation negatively reinforces the escape or avoidance behaviour so that it tends to be repeated (this is the operant conditioning factor). The fear may have been acquired initially through classical conditioning (the other 'factor') but, on its own, classical conditioning cannot explain its persistence.

The persistence of neurotic behaviour may also be accounted for in terms of what Freud (1926) called 'secondary gain', whereby other people may, inadvertently, *positively* reinforce it; because of the role of positive and negative reinforcement in maintaining neurotic behaviour, Ullman and Krasner (1975) refused to accept that neurosis is, in any sense, paradoxical.

We should note that the 'two-process/factor' model has itself come in for criticism (see Fonagy and Higgitt, 1984). One important alternative to it is the *safety-signal hypothesis* which maintains that avoidance is motivated *not* by the reduction of anxiety but by the *positive* feeling of safety. According to Rachman (1984), agoraphobia is motivated by seeking signals of safety and the safety-signal hypothesis provides a better explanation of why agoraphobics find it easier to go out with, or be driven by, someone they trust and to take certain routes to their destination than the two 'process/factor' model—perhaps trusted individuals and certain streets and situations etc act as safety signals. It may also explain why the loss of a close relative so often marks the onset of a phobia (Fonagy and Higgit, 1984).

a) Behaviour Therapy

i) Systematic Desensitization (SD)

As we saw in Chapter 3, the case of Little Peter represents perhaps the earliest attempt to remove a phobia using SD (and, indeed, the earliest attempt at any kind of behavioural treatment).

Wolpe (1958) defined behaviour therapy as a whole as 'the use of experimentally established principles of learning for the purpose of changing unadaptive behaviour' and he is perhaps best known for his use and development of SD.

Wolpe was very much influenced by the theory of Hull (see Chapter 17) and the key concept in SD is that of *reciprocal inhibition* (taken from Sherrington's work on the spinal cord); as applied to phobias (for which SD is mainly used), this maintains that it is impossible for two opposite emotions (eg anxiety and relaxation) to exist together at the same time. Accordingly, a patient with, for example, a spider phobia, is taught to relax through deep muscle relaxation in which different muscle groups are alternately relaxed and tensed, (alternatively, hypnosis or tranquillizers might be used) so that relaxation and fear of the object or situation 'cancel each other out' (this is the 'desensitization' part of the procedure).

The 'systematic' part of the procedure involves a gradual, step-by-step, contact with the phobic object (usually by *imagining* it) based on a *hierarchy*, running from the least to the most feared possible contact, drawn up together by the therapist and the patient. Starting with the least feared contact, the patient, while relaxing, imagines it until this can be done without feeling any anxiety at all; then and only then, will the next least feared contact be dealt with, in the same way, until the *most* frightening contact can be imagined with no anxiety.

For example, imagining the word 'spider' on a printed page may cause very little anxiety while imagining a large, hairy, spider running all over your body might be very frightening indeed!

Rachman and Wilson (1980) and McGlynn et al (1981) believe that SD is, beyond doubt, effective, although it is most effective for the treatment of *minor* phobias (eg animal phobias) as opposed to, say, agoraphobia (see Chapter 28), and for patients who are able to learn relaxation skills and have sufficiently vivid imaginations to be able to conjure up the sources of their fear (Emmelkamp, 1982). Another limitation of SD is that some patients may have difficulty transferring from the imaginary stimulus to real-life situations (Blakey and Greig, 1977).

Again, there is some debate as to whether or not either relaxation or the use of a hierarchy is actually necessary at all. Lang and Lazovik (1963) found that snake phobias were effectively dealt with by relaxation *plus* a hierarchical presentation of 'snake scenes' but relaxation *alone* proved ineffective. However, Waters et al (1972) found no difference between the use of a hierarchy with or without relaxation (suggesting that relaxation is not necessary) and Welch and Krapfl (1970) found no difference when a hierarchy was presented in the standard way (least to most frightening), in reverse (most to least frightening) or randomly (suggesting that a hierarchy is not necessary). The two studies combined suggest that what is probably the essential ingredient is *exposure* to the feared object. According to Kazdin and Wilcoxin (1976), neither reciprocal inhibition nor relaxation is necessary for therapeutic benefit and the use of real objects makes the use of a graded hierarchy unnecessary (Bandura, 1977, Leitenberg, 1976).

ii) Implosive Therapy (or Implosion) and Flooding

The essence of *implosion* is to expose the patient to what, in SD, would be at the top of the hierarchy; there is no gradual exposure accompanied by relaxation but the patient is 'thrown in at the deep end' right from the start. This is done by getting the patient to imagine their most terrifying form of contact (the big, hairy spider let loose, again) with vivid verbal descriptions by the therapist ('stimulus augmentation') to supplement the patient's vivid imagery. How is it meant to work?

a) The patient's anxiety is maintained at such a high level that eventually some process of exhaustion or stimulus satiation takes place—the anxiety level can only go down!

b) Extinction occurs by preventing the patient from making their usual escape or avoidance responses (Mowrer, 1960) and so implosion—and flooding—represent 'a form of forced reality testing' (Yates, 1970).

Flooding is exposure which takes place *in vivo* (eg with an actual spider). Marks et al (1971) compared SD with flooding and found flooding to be superior and Gelder et al (1973) compared SD with implosion and found no difference. These findings suggest that it is *in vivo exposure* which is crucial, and several writers consider flooding to be more effective than implosion (eg Mathews et al, 1981, Emmelkamp and Wessels, 1975).

Emmelkamp and Wessels (1975) and Marks et al (1981) used flooding with agoraphobics very successfully and other studies have reported continued improvement for up to nine years after treatment without the appearance of 'substitute' problems (Munby and Johnston, 1980, Cohen et al, 1984). Hodgson et al (1972) used flooding with obsessive–compulsive patients in which they were deliberately exposed to situations in which certain compulsive rituals would normally be performed and then *prevented* from performing them. Wolpe (1960) forced an adolescent girl with a fear of cars into the back of a car and drove her around continuously for four hours; her fear reached hysterical heights but then receded and, by the end of the journey, had completely disappeared.

Marks (1981), in a review of flooding studies, found it to be the most universally effective of all the techniques used to treat fear.

iii) Aversion Therapy and Covert Sensitization

In *aversion therapy* some undesirable response to a particular stimulus is removed by associating the stimulus with another, aversive, stimulus. So, for example, alcohol is paired with an emetic drug (which induces severe nausea and vomiting) so that nausea and vomiting become a conditioned response to alcohol.

ie   (UCS) Emetic drug ——————→ Nausea/vomiting (UCR)
              (Antabuse or apomorphine)
(CS) Alcohol + (UCS) emetic drug ——————→ Nausea/vomiting (UCR)
              (CS) Alcohol ——————————→ Nausea/vomiting (CR)

The patient would, typically, be given warm saline solution containing the emetic drug; immediately before the vomiting begins, they are given a 4-ounce glass of whisky which they are required to smell, taste, and swill around in the mouth before being swallowed. (If vomiting has not occurred, another straight whisky is given and in order to prolong nausea, the patient is given a glass of beer containing emetic.) Subsequent treatments involve larger doses of injected emetic or increases in the length of treatment time or a widening range of hard liquors (Kleinmuntz, 1980). (Between trials, the patient may sip soft drinks in order to prevent generalization to all drinking behaviour and to promote the use of alcohol substitutes.)

Meyer and Chesser (1970) found that about half their alcoholic patients abstained for at least one year following treatment and that aversion therapy is better than no treatment.

More controversially, aversion therapy has been used with homosexuals, fetishists, male transvestites, and sadomasochists, and Marks et al (1970) reported desired changes for up to two years after treatment. In a typical treatment, slides of nude males are presented to male homosexuals and then quickly followed by electric shock; the conditioned response to the slides is intended to generalize to homosexual fantasies and activities outside the treatment sessions. More recently, attempts have been made to replace homosexual responses with heterosexual ones by showing slides of naked females; any sexual response will terminate the shock.

Covert sensitization is a variant of aversion therapy (Gottman and Leiblum, 1974, Cautela, 1967) which also includes elements of SD. 'Covert' refers to the fact that both the behaviour to be removed and the aversive stimulus to be associated with it are *imagined* by the patient who has to visualize the events leading up to the initiation of the undesirable behaviour: just as this happens they have to imagine nausea or some other aversive sensation. 'Sensitization' is achieved by associating the undesirable act with an exceedingly disagreeable consequence (Kleinmuntz, 1980). The patient may also be instructed to rehearse an alternative 'relief' scene in which the decision *not* to drink or whatever is accompanied by pleasurable sensations. (This is generally preferred to aversion therapy on humanitarian grounds.)

iv) Stimulus Satiation

In stimulus satiation, a patient who hoards things would be *given* as many of the hoarded objects as they can 'tolerate' until they begin to refuse them (Allyon, 1963). *Negative practice* (Meyer and Chesser, 1970) is often used with nervous tics where the patient is told to produce the tic deliberately, as accurately and frequently as possible for several minutes at a time; eventually (it is hoped) fatigue will produce extinction.

b) Behaviour Modification

i) Operant Conditioning with Autistic Children and the Mentally Handicapped

Lovaas et al (1967) pioneered operant conditioning with autistic children who normally have little or no normal speech. They used a shaping technique: (1) the first step was to pair verbal approval with a bit of food whenever the child made eye-contact or merely attended to the therapist's speech or behaviour (which is also unusual for autistic children), this reinforces attention and associates a positive social gesture with food so that verbal approval eventually becomes a conditioned reinforcer; (2) the next step was to reinforce the child with food and praise whenever it made any kind of speech sound or even tried to imitate the therapist's actions; (3) once this occurred without prompting, the therapist gradually withheld reinforcement until the child successfully imitated complete actions or uttered particular vowel or consonant sounds, then syllables, then words and, finally, combinations of words.

Sometimes hundreds or even thousands of reinforcements were necessary before the child began to label objects appropriately or imitate simple phrases and even when children have received extensive training they are likely to regress if returned to a non-supportive institutional setting. Even under optimum conditions, they never achieve the creative use of language and broad range of social skills of normal children (R. Murray Thomas, 1985). However, Lovaas et al (1976) believe that many therapeutic gains can be retained (and even some modest improvements shown) at home if parents have been trained to use the shaping techniques.

Burgio et al (1983) cite many striking examples of successful modification programmes with the mentally handicapped (or impaired), both adults and children. In one large-scale study, Matson et al (1980) reported substantial improvements in the eating behaviour of profoundly impaired adults; they used peer and therapist modelling (see below), social reinforcement, verbal prompts to shape eating, the use of utensils, table manners etc. Reinforcers included going to meals early and having one's own table-mat and there was a significant improvement in the treated group even four months after the end of treatment, compared with an untreated control group.

Senatore et al (1982) used *social skills training* with mentally impaired adults; the therapist initially modelled appropriate social responses in a number of situations and used social reinforcements to shape them; improvement was maintained six months after treatment.

Azrin and Foxx (1971) and Foxx and Azrin (1973) produced a toilet-training 'package' in which: (1) the client is taken to the toilet every half hour and given extra fluids, sweets, biscuits, praise and attention when it is used successfully; (2) the client is strapped into a chair for half an hour, away from other people, if they have an accident (this is *not* a punishment procedure but '*time out*', that is, a time away from positive reinforcement).

As with speech training in autistic children, there are problems of generalizing from hospital-based improvement to the home situation (Rutter, 1982) but if parents continue the programme at home, there can be short and long-term benefits (Howlin, 1981).

(ii) Token Economy Programmes with Chronic Psychiatric Patients

The *token economy* (Allyon and Azrin, 1968) is based on the principle of secondary reinforcement, whereby tokens (conditioned reinforcers) are given for socially desirable/acceptable behaviours as they occur; the tokens can then be exchanged for certain 'primary' reinforcers. (For example, making one's own bed is worth one token, brushing teeth once a day, one token, and washing up for 10 minutes, six tokens; 20 tokens can 'buy' a private consultation with the ward psychologist and three tokens, choosing a favourite TV programme.)

If the introduction of chlorpromazine and other antischizophrenic drugs in the 1950s marked a revolution in psychiatry, the introduction of token economy programmes during the 1960s was, in its way, equally revolutionary, partly because it drew attention to the ways in which nursing (and other) staff were inadvertently maintaining the psychotic, 'mad' behaviour of many chronic schizophrenics by giving them attention, thus reinforcing unwanted behaviour.

There seems little doubt that well-run token economy programmes do produce behaviour change, in the required direction, even among chronic, institutionalized schizophrenics (Walker, 1984). However, a number of doubts have been raised and questions asked:

a) There is the problem of transferring the control of behaviours from tokens to social reinforcers both within and, ultimately, outside the hospital; the former is normally achieved by gradually 'weaning' patients off the tokens and the latter by transferring patients to halfway houses and other community live-in arrangements. However, O'Leary and Wilson (1975) noted a high re-hospitalization rate for such patients.

b) Within the hospital itself, a recent preoccupation has been with maintaining new behaviours once the formal token economy programme is finished. Woods et al (1984) did find long-term behaviour change for those patients whose newly acquired behaviours were 'trapped' by natural social reinforcers; for example, some patients were so incapable of behaving in a socially appropriate way that they were avoided by staff prior to the start of the programme but the programme produced such marked changes in their behaviour that they were actually invited home to tea by the staff! Such reinforcement was sufficient to maintain the newly acquired social behaviour.

c) What this study suggests is that a crucial factor in the effectiveness of token economies might be the changes which take place at the *staff* level as opposed to the patients themselves! Bernstein (1982) reported that behaviour modification to change staff behaviour can be very effective and Burgio et al (1983) found that selectively reinforcing staff for verbal interaction with residents produced a reliable improvement in the residents' behaviour.

Feedback which staff receive about their own effectiveness seems to be another crucial factor, eg Pommer and Streedbeck (1974) and Pomerleau et al (1973) found that if ward staff know how well they are doing with their patients' behaviour, then they will tend to keep up the kind of interaction with these patients which will maintain the acceptable behaviours.

d) What these studies suggest is that the fact that token economies work does not in itself prove that they work because of reinforcement; other, confounding, variables may include improvement in nurse–patient ratio, increase in staff morale and an overall more optimistic and enthusiastic approach to patients. Any one of these could, on its own, account for at least some of the improvements commonly found, so that, as with other successful behavioural interventions, the reason for the effectiveness of token economy programmes may be quite unrelated to learning theory principles (Fonagy and Higgitt, 1984).

4) Cognitive Approaches

Here we will consider two main approaches: cognitive–behaviour therapy and personal construct therapy.

a) Cognitive–Behaviour Therapy (CBT)

Model of Psychological Disorder

According to Mahoney (1974) and Meichenbaum (1977), many (if not the majority) of clinical problems are best described as disorders of thought and feeling; and since behaviour is to a large extent controlled by the way we think, the most logical and effective way of trying to change maladaptive behaviour is to change the maladaptive thinking which lies behind it.

Wessler (1986) defines CBT as a 'collection of assumptions about disturbance and a set of treatment interventions in which human cognitions are assigned a central role'; it is derived from various theoretical and therapeutic sources and the way that cognition is defined and operationalized differs according to particular approaches. However, Wessler stresses that the attempt to change cognition (*cognitive restructuring*) is always a *means* to an end, that end being the 'lasting changes in target emotions and behaviour' (Wessler, 1986).

(i) Rational Emotive Therapy (RET) (Ellis, 1962, 1973)

Ellis believes that *irrational thoughts* are the main cause of all types of emotional distress and behaviour disorders. Irrational thinking leads to a self-defeating internal dialogue, comprising negative self-statements and these are seen as 'covert' behaviours which are subject to the same principles of learning as overt behaviour. Phobias, for example, are linked to 'catastrophizing self-statements' and, like all other disorders, the aim of therapy is to replace these irrational, unreasonable, beliefs and ideas with more reasonable and realistic ones.

In its simplest form, patients are told to look on the bright side, stop worrying, pull themselves together and so on; as Walker (1984) observes, 'rational' should not be taken too literally as sometimes counter-productive thoughts and beliefs may be replaced by more positive and helpful but equally irrational ones. For instance, it is not necessarily more rational to be an optimist than a pessimist but it is usually more productive and should be encouraged in depressed patients (Walker, 1984).

Ellis (1962) identified 11 basic irrational beliefs or ideas which tend to be emotionally self-defeating and which are commonly associated with psychological problems, including, 'I must be loved and accepted by absolutely everybody', 'I must be excellent in all possible respects and never make mistakes—otherwise I'm worthless' and, 'I am unable to control my emotions'. In RET, the patient is challenged to *prove* that they are worthless because they make mistakes etc, or to say exactly *how* making mistakes makes one a worthless person. Patients may be explicitly directed to practise certain positive/optimistic statements and are generally urged to 'look for the "musts" when they experience inappropriate emotions' (Wessler, 1986).

(ii) Self Instructional Training (SIT) (Meichenbaum, 1973)

Meichenbaum believes that neurotic behaviour is due, at least partly, to 'faulty internal dialogues' (internal speech), in which the patient is failing to *self-instruct* successfully. The underlying rationale for SIT is a study by Meichenbaum and Goodman (1971) in which impulsive and hyperactive children were trained to administer self-instructions for tasks on which they had previously made frequent errors, firstly by talking aloud, then covertly, without talking, but still moving their lips and, finally, without any lip movements. This 'silent speech' is the essence of verbal thought (see the discussion of Vygotsky's theory of thought and language in Chapter 7).

Patients are made aware of the maladaptive nature of their self-statements and are then helped to develop coping skills in the form of coping self-statements, relaxation and plans for behaviour change. For instance, a patient might write down a strategy for dealing with a particular social interaction (eg asking someone to dance at a disco) and then role-play it with a continuous commentary on self-statements before actually doing it 'for real'; as well as these advance preparations, the patient may give on-the-spot warnings and self-debriefings once it is over.

Wolpe (1978) argues that these techniques are not very useful in cases of severe anxiety since many strong neurotic fears are triggered by objects and situations which the patient *knows* are harmless—this is why phobias are irrational! So Wolpe has used a technique called *thought-stopping* (mainly with obsessive–compulsive patients) in which the patient is told to dwell on their obsessive thoughts and while this is happening the therapist shouts *stop*; the patient then shouts the command and eventually this is done sub-vocally.

(Covert sensitization, which we discussed in the section on Aversion Therapy, is a form of self-instruction or self-training.)

(iii) Treatment of 'Automatic Thoughts' (Beck, 1963)

Beck believed that depressives see themselves as victims (based largely on interpretation of their dreams); the key elements in depression are negative thoughts about oneself, the world and the future (the 'cognitive triad' of depression) and these thoughts seem to come automatically and involuntarily. The source of such thoughts are logical errors based on faulty 'data' and, once negative thinking has been identified, it can be replaced by collecting evidence against it; accordingly, Beck sees the client as a colleague of the therapist who researches verifiable reality (Wessler, 1986).

For example, if a client expresses the negative thought, 'I'm a poor father because my children are not better disciplined', Beck would take the second part of the statement and seek factual evidence about its truth; he would also focus on the evaluative conclusion that one is a *poor* father because one's children sometimes misbehave. In these and other ways, clients are trained to distance themselves from things, to be more objective, to distinguish fact from fiction and fact from evaluation, to see things in proportion and not to see things in such extreme terms.

(iv) Modelling (Bandura, 1968, 1977)

Modelling, of course, is a direct application of Social Learning Theory (discussed in Chapters 3 and 21). In a famous demonstration of therapeutic modelling (Bandura and Menlove, 1968), 48 nursery school children with dog phobias were divided into three groups:

Group 1, the *single model condition*, saw eight 3-minute films (two per day for four days) in which a 5-year-old boy engaged in progressively bolder interactions with a cocker spaniel;

Group 2, the *multiple model condition* saw similar films, but several boys and girls were seen interacting with a number of dogs ranging in size from very small to quite large;

Group 3, the *control group* saw a film about Disneyland and Marineland.

The day after the final film, the children were asked to perform 14 acts as a test of their fear of dogs; compared with a pre-test performance, the control group showed no fear reduction but groups 1 and 2 were much more willing to approach and interact with a real dog and one month later the differences remained. (Also, Group 2 children were much more willing to initiate very intimate contact than Group 1 children.)

Bandura argues that: (a) modelling is more effective for treating phobias than counterconditioning (based on classical conditioning); (b) symbolic modelling (films) is *less* powerful than live demonstrations; and (c) the age of the model seems to be irrelevant (Bandura and Barab, 1973). Bandura (1969) claimed a 90 per cent success rate in curing snake phobias and similar success for dog phobias. However, it seems to be mainly effective with children (although it may form part of behaviour therapies with adults) and with simple (eg animal) phobias; it may work simply by persuading the child to *expose* itself to the object of its fear (Marks, 1978).

According to Kazdin and Wilcoxin (1976), the crucial ingredients of therapy (whatever techniques are involved) are: (i) the patient is influenced to *expect* success; and (ii) the patient's *self-concept* changes, whereby they come to believe (through supervised practice) that the previously feared object or situation *can* be coped with. Bandura (1977) has integrated a number of findings into the proposal that the central element in psychological therapy is the cognitive change towards *self-efficacy*, that is, the belief that one can perform desired behaviour effectively and this is brought about most effectively through actual experience in facing previously feared or avoided situations.

b) Personal Construct Therapy (PCT) (Kelly, 1955)

Kelly's Personal Construct Theory was discussed in Chapter 25 (page 648).

Model of Psychological Disorder

Kelly completely rejects the medical model and with it all notions of 'illness' and 'health'. Instead, he uses the concept of *functioning*: a person who is functioning fully is able to construe the world in such a way that predictions are, most of the time, confirmed or validated but who, when they are not validated, is able to change their personal construct system accordingly (things are put down to 'experience', Fransella, 1984).

If our constructs are repeatedly invalidated, we may consider we have 'a problem' and a psychological disorder is defined as 'any personal construction which is used repeatedly in spite of consistent invalidation' (Kelly, 1955). Symptoms serve to give structure and meaning to the chaotic experience which arises out of the use of invalidated constructs (Laudfield and Leitner, 1980); for instance, anxiety is an indication that an individual's personal construct systems are inadequate for, or inappropriate to, the events to which they are applied, ie those events lie outside its *range* of *convenience*. One response to anxiety is to *loosen* our constructs, so that more events can be accommodated by them—our predictions become less specific and so there is less chance of our being wrong.

According to Bannister (1963, 1965), schizophrenia represents an extreme form of loosening—constructs which are normally interlinked come to 'hang together' in an almost random way. Obsessive–compulsive symptoms represent the opposite way of dealing with anxiety, namely an extreme *tightening* of the construct system, an attempt to ensure that predictions are never invalidated.

The Aims of Therapy

The basic aim of PCT is to change the client's way of construing the world so that they can make better sense of it and predict it more accurately: the constructs of a loose construer need to be tightened and those of a tight construer loosened.

Therapeutic Techniques

It is much more difficult to identify specific techniques than it is in most other approaches and the therapist may well use techniques from other approaches; for example, if a client is a tight construer, free association, dream interpretation, Gestalt therapy and some aspects of Rogers' client-centred therapy may be used (see below) while a loose construer may undergo behaviour therapy (Mackay, 1975). More specifically, the client-therapist relationship, self-characterization and fixed role therapy (sketch and enactment) constitute the basic ingredients of PCT.

a) The *relationship* between client and therapist is seen, essentially as comparable to that between a PhD student and their supervisor; together, they struggle to understand why one of them is failing to solve the problems that they encounter in life. The therapy room is a laboratory and the therapist is a *validator* of the client's behavioural experiments; they can help the client to see alternative ways of construing the world (Fransella, 1984).

b) A client's problem is that their construct system has not adapted to deal with certain vital aspects of life; therefore, 'diagnosis' involves trying to understand the problem *as the client sees it* and a method of trying to achieve this is *self-characterization* (which, together with Fixed Role Therapy, is the only really original treatment device, according to Mackay, 1975).

The client is asked to write a character sketch about themselves, in the third person, 'just as if she were the principal character in a play. Write it as if it might be written by a friend who knew her *intimately* and very *sympathetically*, perhaps better than anyone ever really could know her ...' (Fransella, 1984).

c) The therapist then writes a second version of the client's original self-characterization (called a *fixed role sketch*) which, ideally, lies somewhere between the client's self-portrait and its exact opposite, eg if the client uses the construct 'aggressive–submissive' in relation to their boss, the therapist will use 'respectful' (Fransella, 1984). The client and therapist discuss the fixed role sketch together and modify it until it describes a person the client feels it is possible to be; the client then goes away and lives the life of that person for a few weeks (*fixed role entactment*) with frequent meetings during this period *in the prescribed role*.

The purpose of fixed role enactment is to show the client that we can, indeed, change ourselves.

d) The *repertory grid* (see Chapter 25), which can be used without subscribing to Kelly's personal construct theory, may be used in a variety of ways: (i) to measure the client's construct system; (ii) to measure the therapist's construct system, eg how they construe the client; and (iii) to monitor the therapeutic process, for example, the client can provide a series of self-ratings and the selves as rated can form the elements of a grid which can then be combined to make a grid which can provide a summary of the change, through time, of the therapeutic process (Ryle, 1975).

5) Humanistic-Phenomenological Approaches

Here we will look at Rogers' (1951) approach.

Client-Centred Therapy (CCT)

Model of Psychological Disorder

As we saw in Chapter 9, when a person is aware of a lack of *congruence* between their experience and self-concept, *threat, anxiety* or *depression* is experienced. Because of our need for positive regard, we may behave in ways which are discrepant with the values of our self, and feeling threatened anxious or depressed is the price we pay. As defences against these unpleasant feelings, we use *denial* and *distortion*, whereby part of reality is prevented from entering consciousness and is, consequently, unable to contribute to our self-concept. As a result, our self-concept becomes increasingly incongruent with reality which, in turn, increases anxiety and makes the need for defences all the greater—a vicious circle has been created.

Where the incongruence is severe and/or persistent, the resulting threat, anxiety or depression may interfere with the person's life in a *neurotic* way; where it is so great as to defy denial and distortion, the incongruent experience is accurately symbolized at a conscious level and this leads to the disintegration of personality (characterized by bizarre, crazy, behaviour) which is commonly called *psychotic*.

However, Rogers regards individuals as *unique* and human personality is so complex that no diagnostic labelling of persons can ever be fully justified; indeed, he has recently come to reject all diagnostic labelling (Rogers, 1977).

The Aims of Therapy

Therapy is a process where the individual has the opportunity to re-organize their subjective world so as to integrate and actualize the self; the key process, therefore, is facilitation of their experience of becoming a more autonomous, spontaneous and confident person (Graham, 1986).

The person has within themselves an inherent capacity for, and tendency towards, self-understanding and self-actualization *but* the conditions for facilitating its development reside in the *relationship* between the client and the therapist. The word 'client' is used to emphasize the person's self-responsibility (while 'patient' implies the opposite) and 'client-centred' implies that the client is encouraged to direct the whole therapeutic process —any changes which occur during therapy are brought about by the client.

The Therapeutic Process

The therapist's main task is to create a *therapeutic atmosphere* in which clients can become fully integrated again—but this can only be achieved if they reduce their conditions of worth and increase their unconditional positive self-regard.

The therapist's job is to create a situation in which clients can change themselves and this is aided by an emotionally warm, accepting, understanding and non-evaluative relationship in which the person is free from threat and has the freedom to be 'the self that he really is' (Graham, 1986).

There are three particularly significant qualities to the relationship or *attitudes* on the part of the therapist who must effectively communicate them to the client as both a necessary and sufficient condition for therapeutic change (Rogers, 1980):

1) *Genuineness* (Authenticity or Congruence)—the therapist must show themselves to be a *real* person, with feelings which should be expressed where appropriate. The client needs to feel that the therapist is emotionally involved and not hiding behind a facade of professional impersonality; the therapist must be 'transparent'. This is the most important of the three qualities or attitudes.

2) *Unconditional positive regard*—the therapist must show complete acceptance of, and respect for, the client, as a separate person in their own right. The therapist must have a deep and genuine caring for the client *as they are now* in a non-judgemental way.

3) *Empathic understanding*—the therapist must try to enter the client's inner world through a genuine, attentive listening, which involves intense concentration. This may involve re-stating what the client says as a way of trying to clarify its emotional significance (rather than its verbal content) and this requires the therapist to be sensitive to what is currently going on in the client and of meanings which are just below the level of awareness.

Thorne (1984) believes that this is the most 'trainable' of the three therapist attitudes but is at the same time remarkably rare; he also suggests that a fourth attitude, *tenderness*, could be added to Rogers' three.

If these therapeutic conditions are established, clients will talk about themselves more honestly and this will bring about a re-establishment of congruence which will be sufficient to produce changes in behaviour (Fonagy and Higgitt, 1984).

Unlike most other humanistic therapists, Rogers has attempted to validate his therapy empirically (and has encouraged others to do so). A form of assessment devised by Rogers is the *Q-sort*, which comprises a number of cards with statements referring to the self (eg 'I am a domineering person'); the client is asked to arrange them in a series of ten piles ranging from 'very characteristic of me' to 'not at all characteristic of me' (describing the self-image) and the process is repeated so as to describe the ideal self. The two Q-sorts are then correlated to determine the discrepancy between self-image and ideal self—the lower the correlations, the greater the discrepancy. The whole procedure is repeated at various intervals during the course of therapy (in a similar way to the use of the Repertory Grid in Kelly's PCT).

One way of assessing the importance of the three qualities or attitudes of the therapist is to give trained judges transcripts or tape-recordings of therapy sessions which they have to rate; Truax and Mitchell (1971) found that therapists who were rated high were much more likely to be associated with desirable changes in their clients and low-rated therapists actually worsened their clients' condition. Strupp and Hadley (1979) found that the therapists' personal characteristics are likely to be more important than any specific techniques used.

However, results have generally been mixed (Mitchell, 1977).

CCT and Counselling

Barker (1983) believes that, despite their questionable empirical basis, Rogers' ideas about ideal therapeutic relationships and attitudes have become

part of the accepted clinical wisdom of psychologists of all theoretical orientations. Essentially, Rogerian therapy provides a situation in which the client
learns to be free and, as such, it is an *educational* process which Rogers
believes can be as effective in the classroom as in the clinic (*Freedom to Learn*,
1969). He is generally regarded as having inspired the *counselling* movement,
especially in the UK, which is a product of his involvement with therapy *and*
education (Graham, 1986).

Encounter Groups

Another spin-off of CCT is the encounter or personal growth movement,
originally very much an American (particularly Californian) phenomenon of
the 1960s and '70s. These were originally developed by Rogers, 'as a means
whereby people can break through the barriers erected by themselves and
others in order to react openly and freely with one another' (Graham, 1986).

Participants (not 'clients') are encouraged to act out their emotions (not
just talk about them) through body contact and structured activities and
'games'; the leader (or facilitator) attempts to create a climate of mutual trust
in which people (usually between 8 and 18 in number) feel free to express
their true feelings—both positive and negative—thereby reducing defen-
siveness and promoting self-actualization (Rogers, 1973).

Variants of encounter groups include T-groups or Sensitivity Training
Groups (Marrow, 1969); how effective these actually are in bringing about
change is very unclear and, indeed, many writers have warned against the
dangers of such groups. Blanchard (1970), for example, claims that they can
cause—or at least precipitate—various sorts of psychological disturbance
and Yalom and Lieberman (1971) reported 16 'casualties' out of a total of 209
undergraduates who had participated in encounter groups, including
'psychotic' reactions, depression, withdrawal and poorer interpersonal relationships. Aggressive and highly charismatic, authoritarian, leaders are the
most likely to have casualties in their groups.

One of their destructive characteristics, according to Blanchard (1970), is
the pressure to have some ecstatic or 'peak' experience, which is seen as
necessary for continuing mental health; but Maslow would say that such
experiences are relatively uncommon and certainly cannot be produced 'on
demand' (see Chapter 25).

6) Action Therapies

These refer to a diverse set of therapeutic approaches which are derived from
an equally diverse set of theoretical perspectives. Encounter groups are, of
course, action-based and are quite closely related to Rogers' theory of self.
The others that I shall briefly describe in this section are Gestalt therapy,
Transactional Analysis, Primal therapy, EST and Psychodrama.

a) Gestalt Therapy (Fritz Perls, 1969)

Based on the Gestalt theory of perception (see Chapter 4), Gestalt therapy
helps people to become *whole* by putting them in touch with their *entire* selves

and their surroundings. We tend to block awareness of aspects of ourselves and only by acknowledging every part of ourselves can the self emerge as a unified *figure* against its environmental *ground* or field.

The client is required to play *all* the roles of a drama alone, either by acting each part in turn or in the form of dialogues between the various parts (including physical props); one popular method is the 'empty chair technique' in which the client projects into an empty chair any part of the drama in order to confront it (eg aspects of the client's self which are normally unexpressed, or other people—real or imagined). The overall aim is, by bringing these elements into the open, to enable people to identify and integrate the various diverse parts of themselves and, thereby, to achieve an individual *gestalt* (Graham, 1986).

b) Transactional Analysis (TA) (Eric Berne, 1968)

Influenced very much by psychoanalytic theory, TA sees personality as comprising three ego-states—*parent*, *child* and *ego*, corresponding to the Superego, Id and Ego respectively.

Through role-play, an individual's ego states are identified as they are used in various personal transactions; this 'structural analysis' enables the person to understand their behaviour and change it in a way which will give them greater control over their life. This is usually conducted on an individual basis initially, after which the person is free to participate in group transactions or TA proper.

In the group, participants are encouraged to experiment by enacting more appropriate ego states and observing their effects on themselves and others. The focus is on the individual's tendency to manipulate others in destructive and non-productive ways. Berne (*The Games that People Play*, 1968) identified a number of distinct games and strategies which are commonly used in interpersonal relationships and which prevent spontaneous and appropriate behaviour; TA involves analysing an individual's characteristic games and strategies.

c) Primal Therapy (Arthur Janov, 1973)

In *The Primal Scream* (1973), Janov describes how birth represents the primary trauma in an individual's life from which all others stem and which, therefore, is the source of all anxiety; the aim of primal therapy is, to help the person overcome the defences built up against the intolerable pain associated with birth by experiencing the pain while re-enacting the birth process. This is facilitated by careful 'staging'; for example, the client assumes a foetal position, is covered in pillows (representing the birth canal), is encouraged to scream (the 'primal scream') and so on.

'Re-birthing' may symbolically represent the person's desire to make a fresh start in life; it is cathartic, releasing blocked emotions and the pain associated with the birth experience.

d) Erhard Seminars Training (EST) (Werner Erhard)

During the early 1970s, EST became the fastest growing and most contro-versial enlightenment programme in the USA (Graham, 1986). It is very eclectic, drawing on techniques used in many religious and therapeutic disciplines, including Gestalt, psychodrama, encounter groups and sensitivi-ty training.

The aim is to encourage people to take responsibility for themselves; paradoxically, that is achieved by means of manipulative techniques, in-cluding various kinds of deprivation, sensory overload and shock tactics. One of the original and most publicized features is work with *crowds*: spanning two weekends (lasting over sixty hours altogether), 250 people are assembled to be shouted at, bossed around, humiliated, lectured at and coaxed into performing a highly structured programme of exercises and procedures designed to help people realize what life is actually like and to accept it for what it is! (Graham 1986.)

e) Psychodrama (Jacob Moreno)

Moreno was a Viennese psychiatrist and a contemporary of Freud who sought alternative approaches to the predominantly verbal nature of orthodox psychoanalysis but which would facilitate powerful emotional release or catharsis.

He believed that most human problems arise from the need to create and maintain social roles which may conflict with each other and the person's essential self; this conflict is the source of anxiety. Starting in the 1920s, Moreno proposed that within the relative safety of psychodrama, groups of individuals (usually 7 or 8 up to 12) could explore role conflicts, together with those aspects of self which are not expressed through any existing roles, in order to bring about integration and balance within the personality.

The principal actor who is dramatizing their conflicts and problems is the *protagonist*, who is helped to create the atmosphere and circumstances of the situation and 'sets the scene' at a physical level by describing it in words and with the aid of very simple props. The interpersonal events are then recreated by role-play; the protagonist chooses other members of the group to repre-sent the key figures and they are briefed by being given a full description of the role (they are known as *auxiliary egos*). They try to 'feel their way' into the part, *not* by aiming for dramatic excellence but by trying to discover the possible feelings and perceptions that the person they are playing might have in the situation.

Another technique is *role-reversal* in which the protagonist switches roles with the auxiliary egos. In *doubling*, the leader (or some other member) stands with the protagonist and suggests to them feelings, perceptions, motives, etc, which may be operating within them (but which have not yet been identified); and *mirroring* involves group members mimicking or exag-gerating the protagonist's behaviour in order to provide effective feedback. The group leader generally directs proceedings, often intervening with suggestions (eg role-switching) and directions designed to enable the protag-onist to stop and explore their feelings and perceptions.

7) Existential Approaches

The Therapeutic Community

As we saw in Chapter 28, psychiatrists such as Laing, Cooper and Esterson championed the *anti-psychiatry* movement during the 1950s and '60s. They advocated the removal of all diagnostic labels and categories as well as all role distinctions between therapists and clients/patients and the provision of an informal, unstructured, environment where schizophrenics could discover themselves through genuine encounters with others (Graham, 1986).

This was first attempted by Cooper in 1962: 'Villa 21' was an experimental therapeutic ward within a conventional mental hospital and was specifically geared towards the problems of young, recently labelled, schizophrenics. Although short-lived, Villa 21 showed that such radical alternatives to conventional psychiatric care could be established outside the larger institution; such *therapeutic communities* should be somewhere that people *choose* to go, an *asylum* (safe refuge) in the true meaning of the term.

Laing, Cooper and Esterson founded the Philadelphia Association in 1964, a charity which set up the famous Kingsley Hall in the East End of London in 1965. Perhaps the most famous resident was Mary Barnes, who, with the support of her therapist, Joseph Berke, 'went down' into her own madness (she had been diagnosed as schizophrenic 12 years earlier and had been given ECT during a year-long stay in hospital), regressed to infancy and acted out the anger which had been repressed by her family. From a demanding, obsessive child, there emerged a whole, creative, adult human being. Her story is told in *Mary Barnes – two accounts of a journey through madness* (1973).

Although Kingsley Hall closed in 1970, the Philadelphia Association now has a network of similar households in London and offers training in psychotherapy and community therapy. Joseph Berke has helped to establish the Arbours Association, a mental health charity to assist those in emotional distress. It sponsors four long-term communities and a short-stay crisis centre, psychotherapy training and training in social psychiatry.

Social Psychiatry

This essentially means the treatment of psychological disorder outside mental hospitals, in the community; apart from therapeutic communities such as those run by the Philadelphia and Arbours Associations (and other mental health charities), community care facilities include small selective units specializing in alcoholism and drug addiction, day-care units, local authority hostels and halfway houses for the rehabilitation of drug addicts and newly-released psychiatric patients (and prisoners). Any crisis-intervention facility, such as telephone hot-lines (eg the Samaritans) also form an important part of the community care/social psychiatric alternative to psychiatric hospitals.

Treatment Effectiveness: Does Therapy Work?

We have discussed some of the evidence relating to treatment effectiveness as we have examined particular approaches; we need now to refer to some other studies of effectiveness.

Probably the most famous (and controversial) is that of Eysenck (1952) in which he reviewed five studies of the effectiveness of psychoanalysis and 19 studies of the effectiveness of 'eclectic' psychotherapy. He concluded that only 44 per cent of psychoanalytic patients improved and 64 per cent of those who received the 'mixed' therapy. However, since roughly 66 per cent of patients improve without *any* treatment ('spontaneous remission'), Eysenck concluded that psychoanalysis in particular, and psychotherapy in general, simply do not work—they achieve nothing which would not have happened anyway without therapy!

By 1960, he was arguing that behaviour therapy is the *only* kind of therapy worth rational consideration and he inspired an enormous amount of research on therapy outcomes (Oatley, 1984). However:

a) If the many patients who drop out of psychoanalysis are excluded from the 44 per cent quoted by Eysenck (they cannot legitimately be counted as 'failures' or 'not cured'), the figure rises to 66 per cent;

b) Bergin (1971) reviewed some of the papers included in Eysenck's review and concluded that, by choosing different criteria of 'improvement', the success rate of psychoanalysis could be raised to 83 per cent. He also citied studies which showed only a 30 per cent spontaneous remission rate.

c) Bergin and Lambert (1978) reviewed 17 studies of untreated 'neurotics' and found a median spontaneous remission rate of 43 per cent. They also found that the rate of spontaneous remission varies a great deal depending on the disorder—generalized anxiety and depression, for example, are much more likely to 'cure themselves' than phobias or obsessive-compulsive disorders.

d) Smith and Glass (1977) reviewed 400 studies of a wide variety of therapies (including psychodynamic, Gestalt, CCT, TA, SD and eclectic) and concluded that all were more effective than no treatment; for example, the 'average' client who had received therapy scored more favourably on the outcome measures than 75 per cent of those in the untreated control groups.

Smith et al (1980) extended the 1977 study to include 475 studies (an estimated 75 per cent of the published literature); strict criteria for admission into their 'meta-analysis' included the comparison between a treated group (given a specified form of therapy) with a second group (drawn from the same population) given either no therapy, put on a waiting list or given some alternative form of therapy. As with the 1977 results, the effectiveness of therapy was shown to be highly significant—the average client was better off than 80 per cent of the control groups on the outcome measures.

Different therapies had different kinds of effects: (i) the largest overall effects were produced by *cognitive* therapies and *cognitive-behaviour* therapies, which were particularly effective with single, simple phobias, fear and anxiety; (ii) psychodynamic therapies did best with psychotics; (iii) CCT did best with low self-esteem clients; (iv) dynamic eclectic therapy did best with work and school adjustment; and (v) neither behaviour therapy nor psychodynamic therapy emerged as superior to the other.

Conclusions

i) The whole concept of 'cure' is highly complex and is itself defined differently from different theoretical and therapeutic perspectives. For example, as we noted earlier, as far as psychoanalysis is concerned, a 'cure' cannot be defined in terms of symptom removal because the 'real' problem is an underlying conflict and not the symptoms themselves; consequently, if the underlying conflict is not successfully dealt with, other symptoms will replace those which have been removed (*symptom substitution*).

Behaviour therapists, on the other hand, believe that symptom removal constitutes a cure, since symptoms *are* the disorder (and so, no symptom substitution will occur).

However, this way of presenting the issue is probably an oversimplification. Bandura (1969), for instance, argues that behaviour therapists (as well as psychoanalysts) may talk about 'merely treating the symptom', implying that the therapist has been too narrow in their perception of the number of different situations in which the deviant behaviour is used. What may appear to be symptom substitution (as judged by a psychoanalyst) may be the substitution of a response lower down in the person's hierarchy of responses for that situation but which is also socially unacceptable (ie the person has already acquired a hierarchy of *possible* responses). According to Beech (1972), symptom substitution probably does occur in some cases but is relatively uncommon. Sometimes symptoms might be seen in too simple a way (and lead to inappropriate treatment) as when a 'superficial' symptom (eg writer's cramp and stammering) might be related to a more basic and meaningful 'symptom' (eg fear of dealing with people in authority); it is the latter which needs treatment (and, in a way, is equivalent to the 'underlying conflict' of psychoanalysis).

ii) Shapiro (1980) believes that outcome studies in general indicate the effectiveness of *both* (a) specific factors due to the *particular* form of therapy used *and* (b) some non-specific factors, the most important of which might well be the *relationship* with the therapist and the *expectation* of improvement (Oatley, 1984).

iii) To ask, 'Does therapy work?' or, 'Is one form of therapy more effective than another?' is to ask the wrong sorts of questions. According to Ryle (1975), there are two fundamental questions which need to be kept separate; (a) 'What kinds of patient can change in what kinds of ways through what kinds of therapy?' (research into *outcome*); and (b) '*How* does therapy effect these changes?' (research into *process*). In a similar vein, Altrocchi suggests that we ask:

> What therapeutic techniques used by what kinds of therapists, under what conditions, produce what kinds of behaviour changes, in what recipients, with what other effects? (Altrocchi, 1980.)

References

*Particularly recommended

Adams-Webber, J., (1981) Personal Construct Theory: research into basic con-
cepts. In *Personality—Theory, Measurement and Research*, Fransella F. (ed.),
London: Methuen.
* Adorno, T.W., Frenkel-Brunswick, E., Levinson, D.J., and Sanford, R.N.
(1950) *The Authoritarian Personality*, New York: Harper and Row.
Ainsworth, M., Blehar, M., Waters, E., and Wall, S. (1978) *Patterns of Attach-
ment*, Hillsdale, New Jersey: Erlbaum.
* Allport, G.W. (1954) *The Nature of Prejudice*, Wokingham: Addison-Wesley.
* Allport, G.W. (1955) *Becoming—Basic Considerations for a Psychology of
Personality*, Yale University Press.
Allport, G.W. (1971) *Pattern and Growth in Personality*, Holt, Rinehart and
Winston.
Allyon, J., and Azrin, N. (1968) *The Token Economy*, New York: Appleton-
Century-Crofts.
Altrocchi, J. (1980) *Abnormal Behaviour*, New York: Harcourt Brace Jovanovich.
Altschul, A.T. (1980) The care of the mentally disordered : 3 approaches. In
Nursing Times, 13 March, 452–4.
Anderson, A. (1978) 'Old' is not a four-letter word. In *Across the board*, May.
Annett, J. (1972) Programmed learning. In *New Horizons in Psychology 1*, Foss,
B.M. (ed.), Harmondsworth: Penguin.
Argyle, M. (1967) *The Psychology of Interpersonal Behaviour*, Hardmondsworth:
Penguin.
Argyle, M. (ed.) (1973) *Social Encounters—Readings in Social Interaction*,
Harmondsworth: Penguin.
Argyle, M. (1982) Social behaviour. In *Psychology for Teachers*, Fontana, D. (ed.),
British Psychological Society and the Macmillan Press Ltd.
Argyle, M., and Dean, J. (1965) Eye contact, distance and affiliation. In
Sociometry, 28, 289–364.
Aronson, E. (1968) The process of dissonance. In *Attitudes*, Warren, N., and
Jahoda, M. (eds.), Harmondsworth:Penguin.
* Aronson, E., and Mills, J. (1959) The effect of severity of initiation on liking
for a group. In *Journal of abnormal and social psychology*, 59, 177–81.
Asch, S.E. (1946) Forming impressions of personality. In *Journal of Abnormal and
Social Psychology*, 4, 258–90.

Asch, S.E. (1956) Studies of independence and submission to group pressure: 1 A minority of one against a unanimous majority. In *Psychological Monographs*, 70, (9) (Whole No. 416).

Atkinson, R.C., and Shiffrin, R.M. (1971) The control of short-term memory. In *Scientific American*, 224, 82–90.

Atkinson, R.C., and Shiffrin, R.M. (1977) Human memory: A proposed system and its control processes. In *Human Memory: Basic Processes*, Bower, G.H. (ed.), New York, Academic Press.

* Baddeley, A.D. (1976) *The Psychology of Memory*, New York: Harper and Row.

Baddeley, A.D. (1980) Human memory. In *New Horizons in Psychology 2*, Dodwell, P.C. (ed.), Harmondsworth: Penguin.

Bailey, C.L. (1979) Mental illness—a logical misrepresentation? In *Nursing Times*, May 3, 761–2.

Baker, R. (1972) The chronic psychiatric patient—a new hope for treatment? (A study in operant conditioning—1). In *Nursing Times*, 14 September, 1161–3.

Baker, R., Hall, J.N., and Hutchinson, K. (1974) A token economy project with chronic schizophrenic patients. In *British Journal of Psychiatry*, 124, 367–84.

Bandura, A. (1969) *Principles of Behaviour Modification*, New York: Holt, Rinehart and Winston.

* Bandura, A. (1977) *Social Learning Theory*, New Jersey: Prentice Hall.

Bandura, A., Ross, D., and Ross, S.A. (1961) Transmission of aggression through imitation of aggressive models. In *Journal of Abnormal and Social Psychology*, 63, 375–82.

Bannister, D. (1982) Knowledge of self. In *Psychology and People—A Tutorial Text*, Chapman, A.J., and Gale, A. (eds.), British Psychological Society and Macmillan Press Ltd.

* Bannister, D., and Fransella, F. (1980) *Inquiring Man—The Psychology of Personal Constructs*, Harmondsworth: Penguin.

* Barnes, M., and Berke, J. (1973). *Mary Barnes—Two Accounts of a Journey Through Madness*, Harmondsworth: Penguin.

Bartlett, F.C. (1932) *Remembering*, Cambridge: Cambridge University Press.

Bartley, S.H. (1980) *Introduction to Perception*, London: Harper and Row.

Baumrind, D. (1964) Some thoughts on the ethics of research: after reading Milgram's study of obedience. In *American Psychologist*, 19, 421–3.

Beard, R.M. (1969) *An Outline of Piaget's Developmental Psychology*, London: Routledge Kegan Paul.

Beck, A.T. (1967) *Depression: Clinical, Experimental and Theoretical Aspects*, London: Harper and Row.

* Bee, H.L., and Mitchell, S.K. (1980) *The Developing Person—A Life-Span Approach*, London: Harper and Row.

Beech, H.R. (1972) Personality theories and behaviour therapy. In *New Horizons in Psychology 1*, Foss, B.M. (ed.), Harmondsworth: Penguin.

Beech, H.R. (1976) Behaviour modification. In *A Textbook of Human Psychology*, Eysenck, H.J., and Wilson, G. (eds.), MTP Press.

Bell, P.B., and Staines, P.J. (1981) *Reasoning and Argument in Psychology*, London: Routledge Kegan Paul.

Bem, D.J. (1967) Self-perception: an alternative interpretation of cognitive dissonance phenomena. In *Psychological Review*, 74, 183–200.

* Bem, S.L. (1974) The measurement of psychological androgyny. In *Journal of Consulting and Clinical Psychology*, 42, 155–62.

Bem, S.L. (1975) Fluffy women and chesty men. In *Psychology Today*, September.

Benton, D. (1981) ECT—Can the system take the shock? In *Community Care*, 12 March, 15–17.

* Bettelheim, B. (1985) *Freud and Man's Soul*, London: Fontana.

Blakemore, C., and Cooper, G.F. (1970) Development of the brain depends on the visual environment. In *Nature*, 228, 477–8.

Blakey, R., and Greig, K. (1977) Severe cat phobia. In *Nursing Times*, July 21, 1106–8.

Blundell, J. (1975) *Physiological Psychology*, London: Methuen.

Boden, M.A. (1979) *Piaget*, London: Fontana.

* Bodmer, W.F. (1972) Race and IQ: the genetic background. In *Race, Culture and Intelligence*, Richardson, K., and Spears, D. (eds.), Harmondsworth: Penguin.

Booth, T. (1975) *Growing up in Society*, London: Methuen.

Borger, R., and Seaborne, A.E.M. (1966) *The Psychology of Learning*, Harmondsworth: Penguin.

Bower, G.H. (ed.), (1977) *Human Memory: Basic processes*, New York: Academic Press.

Bower, G.H., Clark, M., Lesgold, A., and Winzenz, D. (1969) Hierarchical retrieval schemes, in recall of categorized word lists. In *Journal of Verbal Learning and Verbal Behaviour*, 8, 323–43.

* Bower, T.G.R. (1977) *The Perceptual World of the Child*, London: Fontana.

* Bower, T.G.R. (1977) *A Primer of Infant Development*, San Francisco: Freeman.

Bowlby, J. (1953) *Child Care and the Growth of Love*, Harmondsworth: Penguin.

* Bowlby, J. (1971) *Attachment and Loss, Volume 1*, Harmondsworth: Penguin.

* Bowlby, J. (1975) *Separation—Anxiety and Anger (Attachment and Loss, Vol. 2)*, Harmondsworth: Penguin.

Breakwell, G.M., Foot, H., and Gilmour, R. (eds.), (1982) *Social Psychology—A Practical Manual*, British Psychological Society and Macmillan Press Ltd.

Brehm, J.W. (1956) Post-decision changes in the desirability of alternatives. In *Journal of Abnormal and Social Psychology*, 52, 384-9.

Bridges, P., and Williamson, C. (1977) Psychosurgery today. In *Nursing Times*, 1 September, 1363–7.

Brierley, H. (1975) Choice of gender. In *New Behaviour*, 25 September, 500–501.

Brierley, H. (1979) *Transvestism: A handbook with case studies for Psychologists, Psychiatrists and Counsellors*, Oxford: Pergamon Press.

British Psychological Society, (1978) *Ethical Principles for Research with Human Subjects*, British Psychological Society, April.

Broadbent, D.E. (1958) *Perception and Communication*, Oxford: Pergamon.

Broadbent, D.E. (1964) *Behaviour*, London: Methuen.

Bromley, D.B. (1966) *The Psychology of Human Ageing*, Harmondsworth: Penguin.

Brooks-Gunn, J., and Lewin, M. (1982) The development of self knowledge. In *The Child—Development in a Social Context*, Kopp, C.B., and Krakow, J.B. (eds.), Wokingham: Addison-Wesley.

Brown, H. (1976) *Socialization—the Social Learning Theory approach*, Milton Keynes: Open University Press.

* Brown, H. (1985) *People, Groups and Society*, Milton Keynes: Open University Press.

* Brown, J.A.C. (1961) *Freud and the Post-Freudians*, Harmondsworth: Penguin.

Brown, R. (1973) *A First Language—The Early Stages*, London: Allen and Unwin.

* Brown, R. (Second edition, 1986) *Social Psychology*, New York: Free Press.

Bruner, J.S. (1966) *Towards a Theory of Instruction*, Harvard University Press.

* Bruner, J.S. (1973) *The Relevance of Education*, London: Norton.

Bruner, J.S., and Goodman, C.C. (1947) Value and need as organizing factors in perception. In *Journal of Abnormal and Social Psychology*, 42, 33–44.

* Bry, A. (1975) *A Primer of Behavioural Psychology*, Mentor.

Burns, R.B. (1980) *Essential Psychology*, MTP Press.

* Burns, R.B., and Dobson, C.B. (1984) *Introductory Psychology*, MTP Press.
Burt, C. (1949) The structure of the mind. In *Intelligence and Ability*, Wiseman, S. (ed.), Harmondsworth: Penguin.
Burt, C. (1966) The genetic determination of differences in intelligence, in *British Journal of Psychology*, 57, 137–53.
Butcher, H.J. (1968) *Human Intelligence*, London: Methuen.
Butler, R. (1978) Unravelling the secrets of aging. In *Aging*, July/August.
Campbell, W. (1979) The therapeutic community: a history. In *Nursing Times*, November 15, 1985–7.
Cannon, W.B. (1927) The James-Lange theory of emotions: a critical examination and an alternative. In *American Journal of Psychology*, 39, 106–24.
Cannon, W.B. and Washburn, A.L. (1912) An explanation of hunger. In *American Journal of Psychology*, 29, 441–54.
Carmichael, L., Hogan, P., and Walter, A. (1932) An experimental study of the effect of language on the reproduction of visually perceived forms. In *Journal of Experimental Psychology*, 15, 73–86.
Cartwright, D., and Zander, A. (eds.), (1968) *Group Dynamics*, New York: Harper and Row.
Cattell, R.B. (1963) Theory of fluid and crystallized intelligence: a critical experiment. In *Journal of Educational Psychology*, 54, 1–22.
* Cattell, R.B. (1965) *The Scientific Analysis of Personality*, Harmondsworth: Penguin.
Cattell, R.B. (1971) *Abilities: Their Structure, Growth and Action*, New York: Houghton-Mifflin.
Cattell, R.B., and Kline, P. (1977) *The Scientific Analysis of Personality and Motivation*, London: Academic Press.
Chapanis, N.P., and Chapanis, A. (1964) Cognitive dissonance—5 years later. In *Psychological Bulletin*, Vol. 61, No. 1, 1–22.
* Chapman, A.J., and Gale, A. (1982) *Psychology and People—A Tutorial Text*, British Psychological Society and Macmillan Press Ltd.
* Chomsky, N. (1968) *Language and Mind*, New York: Harcourt Brace Jovanovich.
Chown, S.M. (ed.), (1972) *Human Ageing*, Harmondsworth: Penguin.
* Clare, A. (1976) *Psychiatry in Dissent*, London: Tavistock Publications.
Clare, A. (1976) What is schizophrenia? In *New Society*, 20 May, 410–12.
* Clarke, A.M., and Clarke, A.D.B. (1976) *Early Experience: Myth and Evidence*, London: Open Books.
Clarke, P.R.F. (1975) The 'medical model' defended. In *New Society*, 9 January, 64–5.
Clarke, R. (1979) Assessment in psychiatric hospitals. In *Nursing Times*, 5 April, 590–2.
Clarke-Stewart, A., and Koch, J.B. (1983) *Children—Development Through Adolescence*, Chichester: Wiley.
* Cohen, G. (1975) Cerebral apartheid: a fanciful notion? In *New Behaviour*, 18 September, 458–61.
* Coleman, J.C. (ed.), (1979) *The School Years—Current issues in the socialization of young people*, London: Methuen.
* Coleman, J.C. (1980) *The Nature of Adolescence*, London: Methuen.
Coleman, J.C., Herzberg, J., and Morris, M. (1977) Identity in adolescence: present and future self-concepts. In *Journal of Youth and Adolescence*, 6, 63–75.
* Collins, A.M., and Quillian, M. (1969) Retrieval time for semantic memory. In *Journal of Verbal Learning and Verbal Behaviour*, 8, 240–7.
* Conrad, R. (1964) Acoustic confusion in immediate memory. In *British Journal of Psychology*, 55, 75–84.

Cook, M. (1971) *Interpersonal Perception*, Harmondsworth: Penguin.
* Cook, M. (1979) *Perceiving Others: the psychology of interpersonal perception*, London: Methuen.
Coon, D. (Third edition, 1983) *Introduction to Psychology—Exploration and Application*, West Publishing Company.
Coopersmith, S. (1967) *The Antecedents of Self-Esteem*, San Francisco: Freeman.
Cornwall, D., and Hobbs, Sandy, (1976) The strange saga of little Albert. In *New Society*, March 18, 602–4.
* Cox, T. (1975) The nature and management of stress. In *New Behaviour*, 25 September, 493–5.
* Craik, F., and Lockhart, R. (1972) Levels of processing. In *Journal of Verbal Learning and Verbal Behaviour*, 11, 671–84.
* Craik, F., and Tulving, E. (1975) Depth of processing and retention of words in episodic memory. In *Journal of Experimental Psychology*, 104, 268–94.
Craik, F., and Watkins, M. (1973) The role of rehearsal in short-term memory. In *Journal of Verbal Learning and Verbal Behaviour*, 12, 599–607.
Crider, A.B., Goethals, G.R., Kavanaugh, R.D., and Solomon, P.R. (1983) *Psychology*, Scott, Foresman and Co.
Cromer, R.F. (1980) Normal language development: recent progress. In *Language and Language Disorders*, Hersov, L.A., Berger, M., and Nicol, A.R. (eds.), Oxford: Pergamon Press.
Cumming, E., Dean, L.R., Newell, D.S., and McCaffrey, I. (1960) Disengagement: a tentative theory of ageing. In *Human Ageing*, Chown, S.M. (ed.), Harmondsworth: Penguin.
Dacey, J.S. (Second edition, 1982) *Adolescents Today*, Scott, Foresman and Co.
Danziger, K. (1971) *Socialization*, Harmondsworth: Penguin.
Dawkins, R. (1978) *The Selfish Gene*, Oxford University Press.
* de Villiers, P.A., and de Villiers, J.G. (1979) *Early Language*, Harvard University Press.
* Deese, J. (1972) *Psychology as Science and Art*, New York: Harcourt Brace Jovanovich.
Dember, W.N. (1960) *The Psychology of Perception*, Holt, Rinehart and Winston.
* Dement, W. (1972) *Some Must Watch While Some Must Sleep*, Stanford: Stanford Alumni Association.
Deregowski, J. (1972) Pictorial perception and culture. In *Scientific American*, 227, 82–8.
* Diagram Group (1982) *The Brain—a Users Manual*, New York: G.P. Putnam's Sons.
Diamond, M. (1978) Sexual identity and sex roles. In *The Humanist*, March/April.
Dion, K.K. (1972) Physical attractiveness and evaluation of children's transgressions. In *Journal of Personality and Social Psychology*, 24, 207–13.
Dion, K.K., Berscheid, E., and Walster, E. (1972) What is beautiful is good. In *Journal of Personality and Social Psychology*, 24, 285–90.
Dobson, C.B., Hardy, M., Heyes, S., Humphreys, A., and Humphreys, P. (1981) *Understanding Psychology*, London: Weidenfeld and Nicolson.
* Dodwell, P.C. (ed.) (1980) *New Horizons in Psychology 2*, Harmondsworth: Penguin.
* Donahoe, J.W., and Wessels, M.G. (1980) *Learning, Language and Memory*, New York: Harper and Row.
* Donaldson, M. (1984) *Children's Minds*, London: Fontana.
* Donovan, A., Oddy, M., Pardoe, R., and Ades, A. (1985) Employment status and psychological well-being: a longitudinal study of 16-year-old school-leavers. In *Journal of Child Psychology and Psychiatry*, 27, 65–76.
Doyle, J.A. (1983) *The Male Experience*, Iowa: Wm.C. Brown Co. Publishers.

Drewe, E. (1976) Memory and learning. In *A Textbook of Human Psychology*, Eysenck, H.J., and Wilson, G.D. (eds.), MTP Press.

* Dryden, W. (ed.) (1984) *Individual Therapy in Britain*, London: Harper and Row.

Dryden, W. (1984) Therapeutic arenas. In *Individual Therapy in Britain*, Dryden, W. (ed.), London: Harper and Row.

* Dryden, W., and Golden, W. (eds.), (1986) *Cognitive-Behavioural Approaches to Psychotherapy*, London: Harper and Row.

Durkin, K. (1985) *Television, Sex Roles and Children*, Milton Keynes: Open University Press.

* Dworetzky, J.P. (1981) *Introduction to Child Development*, West Publishing Company.

Eibl-Eibesfeldt, I. (1970) *Ethology: The Biology of Behaviour*, Holt, Rinehart and Winston.

* Elkind, D. (1970) Erik Erikson's Eight Ages of Man. In *New York Times Magazine*, April 5.

* Erikson, E.H. (1965) *Childhood and Society*, Harmondsworth: Penguin.

Erikson, E.H. (1968) *Identity: Youth and Crisis*, New York: Norton.

* Erikson, E.H. (1980) *Identity and the Life Cycle*, New York: Norton.

* Erlenmeyer-Kimling, L., Jarvik, L.F., and Jensen, A. R. (1967) Median correlations for different kinships. In *Psychopathology of Mental Development*, Zubin, J., and Jervis, G. A. (eds.), New York: Grune and Stratton.

Esterson, A. (1972) *The Leaves of Spring—Schizophrenia, Family and Sacrifice*, Harmondsworth: Penguin.

Evans, P. (1975) *Motivation*, London: Methuen.

Evans, P. (1980) Ethological studies I and II; The laboratory analyses of animal behaviour, and Reinforcement. In *A Textbook of Psychology*, Radford, J., and Govier, E. (eds.), London: Sheldon Press.

Evans, P.D. (1982) Motivation in *Psychology and People—A Tutorial Text*, Chapman, A.J., and Gale, A. (eds.), British Psychological Society and Macmillan Press Ltd.

Evans, P.J. (1980) Thinking of Maslow. In *Nursing Times*, 24 January, 163–5.

Eysenck, H.J. (1953) *Uses and Abuses of Psychology*, Harmondsworth: Penguin.

Eysenck, H.J. (1957) *Sense and Nonsense in Psychology*, Harmondsworth: Penguin.

* Eysenck, H.J. (Third edition, 1970) *The Structure of Human Personality*, London: Methuen.

* Eysenck, H.J. (1970) *Crime and Personality*, London: Paladin.

Eysenck, H.J. (1971) *Race, Intelligence and Education*, London: Temple-Smith.

* Eysenck, H.J. (ed.) (1973) *The Measurement of Intelligence*, MTP Press.

Eysenck, H.J., and Eysenck, S.B.G. (1975) *Manual of the Eysenck Personality Questionnaire*, London: Hodder and Stoughton.

* Eysenck, H.J., and Kamin, L. (1981) *Intelligence: Battle for the Mind*, London: Pan Books.

* Eysenck, H.J., and Wilson, G.D. (1973) *The Experimental Study of Freudian Theories*, London: Methuen.

* Eysenck, H.J., and Wilson, G.D. (eds.), (1976) *A Textbook of Human Psychology*, MTP Press.

* Eysenck, M.W. (1984) *A Handbook of Cognitive Psychology*, Lawrence Erlbaum Associates.

* Fancher, R.E. (1973). *Psychoanalytic Psychology—The Development of Freud's Thought*, New York: Norton.

* Fancher, R.E. (1979) *Pioneers of Psychology*, New York: Norton.

* Fantz, R.L. (1961) The origin of form perception. In *Scientific American*, 204 (5), 66–72.

* Faraday, A. (1973) *Dream Power—The use of dreams in everyday life*, London: Pan Books.
Felipe, N.J., and Sommer, R. (1966) Invasion of personal space. In *Social Problems*, 14, 206–14.
* Festinger, L. (1957) *A Theory of Cognitive Dissonance*, New York: Harper and Row.
* Festinger, L., and Carlsmith, J.M. (1959) Cognitive consequences of forced compliance. In *Journal of Abnormal and Social Psychology*, 58, 203–10.
Fiedler, F.E. (1968) Personality and situational determinants of leadership effectiveness. In *Group Dynamics*, Cartwright, D., and Zander, A. (eds.), New York: Harper and Row.
Fiedler, F.E. (1971) Validation and extension of the contingency model of leadership effectiveness: a review of empirical findings. In *Psychological Bulletin*, 76, 128–48.
Fiedler, F.E. (1972) Personality motivational systems and the behaviour of high and low LPC. In *Human Relations*, 25, 391–42.
* Fishbein, H.D. (1984) *The Psychology of Infancy and Childhood—Evolutionary and Cross-Cultural Perspectives*, Lawrence Erlbaum Associates.
Fisher, H. (1980). Developmental psychology; Three accounts of human development; Nature, nurture and development, and Socialization and development. In *A Textbook of Psychology*, Radford, J., and Govier, E. (eds.), London: Sheldon Press.
* Fisher, S., and Greenberg, R.P. (1977) *The Scientific Credibility of Freud's Theories and Therapy*, New York: Basic Books.
* Fiske, S.T., and Taylor, S.E. (1984) *Social Cognition*, Wokingham: Addison-Wesley.
Flake-Hobson, C., Robinson, B.E., and Skeen, P. (1983) *Child Development and Relationships*, Wokingham: Addison-Wesley.
Fogelman, K. (ed.) (1976) *Britain's Sixteen-Year-Olds*, National Children's Bureau.
Fonagy, P. (1981) Research on psychoanalytic concepts. In *Personality—Theory, Measurement and Research*, Fransella, F. (ed.) London: Methuen.
* Fonagy, P., and Higgitt, A. (1984) *Personality, Theory and Clinical Practice*, London: Methuen.
* Fontana, D. (ed.) (1982) *Psychology for Teachers*, British Psychological Society and Macmillan Press Ltd.
Fontana, D. (1982) Play. In *Psychology for Teachers*, Fontana, D. (ed.), British Psychological Society and Macmillan Press Ltd.
Fordham, F. (1953) *An Introduction to Jung's Psychology*, Harmondsworth: Penguin.
* Foss, B.M. (ed.) (1972) *New Horizons in Psychology 1*, Harmondsworth: Penguin.
* Fransella, F. (1975) *Need to Change?* London: Methuen.
* Fransella, F. (ed.), (1981) *Personality—Theory, Measurement and Research*, London: Methuen.
Fransella, F. (1981) Personal construct psychology, and Repertory grid technique. In *Personality—Theory, Measurement and Research*, Fransella, F. (ed.), London: Methuen.
Fransella, F. (1984) Personal construct therapy. In *Individual Therapy in Britain*, Dryden, W. (ed.), Harper and Row.
Freud, A. (1936) *The Ego and the Mechanics of Defence*, London: Chatto and Windus.
Freud, A., and Dann, S. (1951) An experiment in group upbringing. In *Psychoanalytic Study of the Child*, Vol. VI.
* Freud, S. (1914) *Psychopathology of Everyday Life*, Harmondsworth: Penguin.
* Freud, S. (1938) *The Interpretation of Dreams*, London: Allen Unwin.

Freud, S. (1962) Three essays on the theory of sexuality. In standard edition of *Complete Psychological Works of Sigmund Freud*, Vol. 7, London: Chatto and Windus.

Freud, S. (1963) Introductory lectures on psychoanalysis. In standard edition of *Complete Psychological Works of Sigmund Freud*, Vols. 15–16, London: Chatto and Windus.

Freud, S. (1978) *New Introductory Lectures*, Harmondsworth: Penguin.

Friedenberg, E.Z. (1973) *Laing*, London: Fontana.

Friedrich, H. (ed.) (1972) *Man and Animal*, London: Paladin.

Fromm, E. (1941) *Escape from Freedom*, New York: Farrar and Rhinehart.

* Fromm, E. (1962) *The Art of Loving*, London: Unwin Books.

* Fromm, E. (1973) *The Crisis of Psychoanalysis—Essays on Freud, Marx and Social Psychology*, Harmondsworth: Penguin.

Gagné, R.M. (1974) *Essentials of Learning for Instruction*, New York: Dryden Press.

Gagné, R.M. (1977) *The Conditions of Learning*, Holt, Rinehart and Winston.

Gahagan, J. (1975) *Interpersonal and Group Behaviour*, London: Methuen.

* Gahagan, J. (1984) *Social Interaction and Its Management*, London: Methuen.

Gazzaniga, M.S. (1970) *The Bisected Brain*, New York: Appleton-Century-Crofts.

* Gergen, K.J., and Gergen, M.M. (1981) *Social Psychology*, New York: Harcourt Brace Jovanovich.

* Gibson, E.J., and Walk, P.D. (1960) The visual cliff. In *Scientific American*, 202, 64–71.

Gilbert, P. (1984) *Depression—From Psychology to Brain State*, Lawrence Erlbaum Associates.

Gillham, W.E.C. (1975) Intelligence: the persistent myth. In *New Behaviour*, 26 June, 433–5.

Glanzer, M., and Cunitz, A.R. (1966) Two storage mechanisms in free recall. In *Journal of Verbal Learning and Verbal Behaviour*, 5, 351–60.

* Goffman, E. (1968) *Asylums—Essays on the Social Situation of Mental Patients and Other Inmates*, Harmondsworth: Penguin.

Goffman, E. (1968) *Stigma—Notes on the Management of Spoiled Identity*, Harmondsworth: Penguin.

* Goffman, E. (1971) *The Presentation of Self in Everyday Life*, Harmondsworth: Penguin.

Goffman, E. (1972) *Relations in Public—Microstudies of the Public Order*, Harmondsworth: Penguin.

Goldfarb, W. (1943 a) The effects of early institutional care on an adolescent personality. In *Journal of Experimental Education*, 12, 106–29.

Goldfarb, W. (1943 b) Infant rearing and problem behaviour. In *American Journal of Orthopsychiatry*, 13, 249–65.

* Goldwyn, E. (1979) The fight to be male. In *The Listener*, May 24, 709–12.

Golombok, S., Spencer, A., and Rutter, M. (1983) Children in lesbian and single-parent households: psychosexual and psychiatric appraisal. In *Journal of Child Psychology and Psychiatry*, 24, 551–72.

Gottesman, I.I., and Shields, J. (1972) *Schizophrenia and Genetics*, Academic Press.

* Gottesman, I.I., and Shields, J. (1973) Genetic theorizing and schizophrenia. In *British Journal of Psychiatry*, 122, 15–30.

* Graham, H. (1986) *The Human Face of Psychology—Humanistic Psychology in its Historical, Social and Cultural Context*, Milton Keynes, Open University.

Gray, J., and Wedderburn, A. (1960) Grouping strategies with simultaneous stimuli. In *Quarterly Journal of Experimental Psychology*, 12, 180–4.

Grasha, A.F. (Second edition, 1983) *Practical Applications of Psychology*, Boston: Little, Brown and Co.

Green, S. (1980) Physiological studies I and II. In *A Textbook of Psychology*, Radford, J., and Govier, E. (eds.), London: Sheldon Press.

Greenberg, R.P., and Fisher, S. (1978) Testing Dr Freud. In *Human Behaviour*, September.

Greene, J. (1975) *Thinking and Language*, London: Methuen.

Gregg, V. (1975) *Human Memory*, London: Methuen.

Gregor, A.J., and McPherson, D. (1965) A study of susceptibility to geometric illusions among cultural outgroups of Australian aborigines. In *Psychologica Africana*, 11, 1–13.

* Gregory, R.L. (1966) *Eye and Brain*, London: Weidenfeld and Nicolson.

Gregory, R.L. (1970) *The Intelligent Eye*, London: Weidenfeld and Nicolson.

* Gregory, R.L. (1972) Visual illusions. In *New Horizons in Psychology 1*, Foss, B.M. (ed.), Harmondsworth: Penguin.

Gregory, R.L. (1974) Psychology: towards a science of fiction. In *New Society*, May 23, 439–41.

* Gregory, R.L., and Wallace, J. (1963) *Recovery from Early Blindness*, Cambridge: Heffer.

Guilford, J.P. (1959) Three faces of intellect. In *Intelligence and Ability*, Wiseman, S. (ed.), Harmondsworth: Penguin.

* Hall, C.S. (1954) *A Primer of Freudian Psychology*, New York: Mentor.

* Hall, C.S., and Nordby, V.J. (1973) *A Primer of Jungian Psychology*, New York: Mentor.

* Halsey, A.H. (ed.) (1977) *Heredity and Environment*, London: Methuen.

Harlow, H.F. (1949) Formation of learning sets. In *Psychological Review*, 56, 51–65.

* Harlow, H.F. (1959) Love in infant monkeys. In *Scientific American*, 200 (6), 68–74.

Harlow, H.F., and Harlow, M.K. (1962) Social deprivation in monkeys. In *Scientific American*, 207, (5), 136.

Harlow, H.F., Harlow, M.K., and Suomi, S.J. (1971) From thought to therapy: lessons from a primate laboratory. In *American Scientist*, 59, 74–83.

* Harlow, H.F., and Zimmerman, R.R. (1959) Affectional responses in the infant monkey. In *Science*, 130, 421–32.

Hartshorne, H., and May, M. (1930) *Studies in the Nature of Character*, New York: Macmillan.

Havighurst, R.J. (1968) Personality and patterns of ageing. In *Human Ageing*, Chown, S.M. (ed.), Harmondsworth: Penguin.

Hawkins, L.H., and Armstrong-Esther, C.A. (1978) Circadian rhythms and night shift working in nurses. In *Nursing Times*, 4 May, 49–52.

Hayes, N. (1984) *A First Course in Psychology*, London: Harrap.

Hebb, D.O. (1949) *The Organisation of Behaviour*, New York: Wiley.

* Heim, A. (1970) *Intelligence and Personality—Their Assessment and Relationship*, Harmondsworth: Penguin.

Held, R., and Hein, A. (1963) Movement—produced stimulation in the development of visually guided behaviour. In *Journal of Comparative and Physiological Psychology*, 56, 607–13.

Hersov, L.A., Berger, M., and Nicol, A.R. (eds.), (1980) *Language and Language Disorders in Childhood*, Oxford: Pergamon Press.

Hess, R.D., and Shipman, V. (1965) Early experience and the socialization of cognitive modes in children. In *Child Development*, 36, 860–886.

* Hilgard, E.R., Atkinson, R.L., and Atkinson, R.C. (Seventh edition, 1979) *Introduction to Psychology*, New York: Harcourt Brace Jovanovich.

* Hinde, R.A. (1982) *Ethology*, London: Fontana.

Hinton, J. (1975) *Dying*, Harmondsworth: Penguin.

Hofling, K.C., Brotzman, E., Dalrymple, S., Graves, N., and Pierce, C.M. (1966) An experimental study in the nurse-physician relationship. In *Journal of Nervous and Mental Disorders*, 143, 171–80.

Holmes, T.H., and Rahe, R.H. (1967) The social readjustment rating scale. In *Journal of Psychosomatic Research*, 11, 213–18.

Hopson, B., and Scally, M. (1980) Change and development in adult life: some implications for helpers. In *British Journal of Guidance and Counselling*, Vol. 8, (2), July, 175–87.

Horney, K. (1926) The flight from womanhood: the masculinity complex in women as viewed by men and by women. In *Psychoanalysis and Women*, Miller, J.B. (ed.), Harmondsworth: Penguin.

Houston, J.P., Hee, H., and Rimm, D.C. (Second edition, 1983) *Invitation to Psychology*, Academic Press.

* Howe, M.J.A. (1980). *The Psychology of Human Learning*, London: Harper and Row.

Hull, C.L. (1943) *Principles of Behaviour*, New York: Appleton-Century-Crofts.

Hunt, J. McV. (1961) *Intelligence and Experience*, Ronald Press.

Hunter, I. (1957) *Memory*, Harmondsworth: Penguin.

Hunter, I.M.L. (1974). How to play twenty questions. In *New Society*, 26 December, 810–11.

Hutt, C. (1972) *Males and Females*, Harmondsworth: Penguin.

Illman, J. (1977) ECT: therapy or trauma? In *Nursing Times*, 11 August, 1226–7.

Jacobs, M. (1984) Psychodynamic therapy: the Freudian approach. In *Individual Therapy in Britain*, Dryden, W. (ed.), London: Harper and Row.

Jahoda, G. (1966) Geometric illusions and environment: a study in Ghana. In *British Journal of Psychology*, 57, 193–9.

* James, W. (1890) *The Principles of Psychology*, New York: Holt, Rinehart and Winston.

Janis, I.L., and Feshbach, S. (1953) Effects of fear-arousing communication. In *Journal of Abnormal and Social Psychology*, 48, 78–92.

Janis, J.L., and Terwillinger, R.T. (1962) An experimental study of psychological resistance to fear-arousing communication, in *Journal of Abnormal and Social Psychology*, 65, 403–10.

* Janov, A. (1975) *The Primal Revolution*, London: Sphere Books Ltd.

Jenkins, J.G., and Dallenbach, K.M. (1924). Oblivescence during sleep and waking. In *American Journal of Psychology*, 35, 605–12.

* Jensen, A.R. (1969) How much can we boost IQ and scholastic achievement? In *Harvard Educational Review*, 39, 1–123.

* Jones, E. (1964) *The Life and Work of Sigmund Freud*, Harmondsworth: Penguin.

Jones, E.E., and Davis, K.E. (1965) From acts to dispositions: the Attribution Process in person perception. In *Advances in Experimental Social Psychology*, Vol. 2., Berkowitz, L. (ed.), New York: Academic Press.

Jones, E.E., and Nisbett, R.E. (1971) *The Actor and the Observer: Divergent Perceptions of the Causes of Behaviour*, Morristown, New Jersey: General Learning Press.

Jones, H. (1975) Psychiatry and politics. In *New Behaviour*, 14 August, 249–51.

Jones, M.C. (1924 a) A laboratory study of fear: the case of Peter. In *Pedagogical Seminary*, 31, 308–15.

Jones, M.C. (1924 b) The elimination of children's fears. In *Journal of Experimental Psychology*, 7, 382–90.

Jourard, S.M. (1966) An exploratory study of body-accessibility. In *British Journal of Social and Clinical psychology*, 5, 221–31.

Jourard, S.M. (1971) *Self-Disclosure: An Experimental Analysis of the Transparent Self*, New York: Wiley Interscience.

* Joynson, R.B. (1974) *Psychology and Common Sense*, London: Routledge Kegan Paul.

Kagan, J., Kearsley, R.B., and Zelazo, P.R. (1980) *Infancy—Its Place in Human Development*, Harvard University Press.
* Kamin, L.J. (1977) *The Science and Politics of IQ*, Harmondsworth: Penguin.
Karlins, M., Coffman, T.L., and Walters, G. (1969) On the fading of social stereotypes: studies in three generations of college students. In *Journal of Personality and Social Psychology*, 13, 1–16.
Kastenbaum, R. (1979). *Growing Old—Years of Fulfilment*, London: Harper and Row.
Katz, D. (1960) The functional approach to the study of attitudes. In *Public Opinion Quarterly*, 24, 163–204.
Katz, D., and Braly, K. (1933) Racial stereotypes of one hundred college students. In *Journal of Abnormal and Social Psychology*, 28, 280–90.
Katz, E. (1957) The two-step flow of communication. In *Public Opinion Quarterly*, 21, 61–78.
* Kelly, G.A. (1955) *A Theory of Personality—the Psychology of Personal Constructs*, New York: Norton.
Kelley, H.H. (1950) The warm-cold variable in first impressions of people. In *Journal of Personality*, 18, 431–9.
* Kelvin, P. (1981) Work as a source of identity: the implications of unemployment. In *British Journal of Guidance and Counselling*, Vol. 9. (1), January, 2–11.
Kirby, R., and Radford, J. (1976) *Individual Differences*, London: Methuen.
Klaus, H.M., and Kennell, J.H. (1976) *Maternal Infant Bonding*, St. Louis: Mosby.
Kleinmuntz, B. (Second edition, 1980) *Essentials of Abnormal Psychology*, London: Harper and Row.
Kline, P. (1972). *Fact and Fantasy in Freudian Theory*, London: Methuen.
* Kline, P. (1981) The work of Eysenck and Cattell. In *Personality—Theory, Measurement and Research*, Fransella, F. (ed.), London: Methuen.
Kline, P. (1982) Personality and individual assessment. In *Psychology and People —A Tutorial Text*, Chapman, A.J., and Gale, A. (eds.), British Psychological Society and Macmillan Press Ltd.
* Kline, P. (1983) *Personality—Measurement and Theory*, London: Hutchinson.
Koedt, A. (1974) The myth of the vaginal orgasm. In *The Radical Therapist*, Radical Therapist Collective, Harmondsworth: Penguin.
* Koestler, A. (1970) *The Act of Creation*, London: Pan Books.
* Koestler, A. (1970 *The Ghost in the Machine*, London: Pan Books.
* Kohlberg, L. (1969) Stage and sequence: the cognitive developmental approach to socialization. In *Handbook of Socialization Theory and Research*, Goslin, D.A. (ed.), Chicago: Rand McNally.
Kohlberg, L. (1975) The cognitive-developmental approach to moral education. In *Phi Delta Kappan*, June, 670–77.
Kohlberg, L. (1976) Moral stages and moralisation. In *Moral Development and Behaviour*, Lickona, T. (ed.), New York: Holt, Rinehart and Winston.
Kohlberg, L. (1981) *Essays on Moral Development (Vol.1)*, New York: Harper and Row.
Kohler, I. (1964) The formation and transformation of the visual world. In *Psychological Issues*, 3, 28–46 and 116–33.
Kohler, W. (1925) *The Mentality of Apes*, New York: Harcourt Brace Jovanovich.
Kopp, C.B., and Krakow, J.B. (eds.) (1982) *The Child—Development in a Social Context*, Addison-Wesley Publishing Co. Inc.
* Kuhn, T.S. (1962) *The Structure of Scientific Revolutions*, University of Chicago Press.
Kurtines, W., and Greif, E.B. (1974) The development of moral thought: review and evaluation of Kohlberg's approach. In *Psychological Bulletin*, 81, no. 8.

Lahey, B.B. (1983) *Psychology—An Introduction*, Wm. C. Brown Co. Publishers.
* Laing, R.D. (1965) *The Divided Self*, Harmondsworth: Penguin.
Laing, R.D. (1967) *The Politics of Experience and the Bird of Paradise*, Harmondsworth: Penguin.
* Laing, R.D. (1971) *Knots*, Harmondsworth: Penguin.
Laing, R.D. (1971) *Self and Others*, Harmondsworth: Penguin.
* Laing, R.D., and Esterson, A. (1970) *Sanity, Madness and the Family*, Harmondsworth: Penguin.
La Piere, R.T. (1934) Attitudes versus action. In *Social Forces*, 13, 230–7.
Larsen, K.S. (1974) Conformity in the Asch experiment. In *Journal of Social Psychology*, 94, 303–4.
Larsen, K.S. (1982) Cultural conditions and conformity: the Asch effect. In *Bulletin of the British Psychological* Society, 35, 347.
Larsen, K.S., Triplett, J.S., Braut, W.D., and Langenberg, D. (1979) Collaborator status, subject characteristics and conformity in the Asch paradigm. In *Journal of Social Psychology*, 108, 259–63.
* Latané, B., and Darley, J.M. (1968) Group inhibition of bystander intervention in emergencies. In *Journal of Personality and Social Psychology*, 10, 215–21.
Latané, B., and Darley, J.M. (1976) *Help in a Crisis: Bystander Response to an Emergency*, Morristown, New Jersey: General Learning Press.
Latané, B. and Hothersall, D. (1980) Social attraction in animals. In *New Horizons in Psychology 2*, Dodwell, P.C. (ed.), Harmondsworth: Penguin.
Latané, B., and Rodin, J. (1969) A lady in distress: inhibiting effects of friends and strangers on bystander intervention. In *Journal of Experimental Social Psychology*, 5, 189–202.
Laycock, A.L. (1970) *Adolescence and Social Work*, London: Routledge Kegan Paul.
Lazarus, R.S., and McCleary, R.A. (1951) Automatic discrimination without awareness: a study of subception. In *Psychological Review*, 58, 113–22.
* Lea, S.E.G. (1984) *Instinct, Environment and Behaviour*, London: Methuen.
Lefrancois, G.R. (1983) *Psychology*, Wadsworth Publishing Co.
* Legge, D. (1975) *An Introduction to Psychological Science*, London: Methuen.
Legge, D. (1982) How do you know? Psychology and scientific method. In *Psychology and People—A Tutorial Text*, Chapman, A.J., and Gale, A. (eds.), British Psychological Society and Macmillan Press Ltd.
Lenneberg, E.H. (1960) Review of speech and brain mechanisms by W. Penfield and L. Roberts. In *Language*, Oldfield, R.C., and Marshall, J.C. (eds.), Harmondsworth: Penguin.
Lenneberg, E.H. (1967) *Biological Foundations of Language*, Wiley.
Levitas, G. (1976) Second start. In *New York Times*, June 6.
Lewin, K., Lippitt, R., and White, R. (1939) Patterns of aggressive behaviour in experimentally created 'social climates'. In *Journal of Social Psychology*, 10, 271–99.
* Lloyd, P., Mayes, A., Manstead, A.S.R., Meudell, P.R., and Wagner, H.L. (1984) *Introduction to Psychology—An Integrated Approach*, London: Fontana.
* Loftus, E.F. (1979) *Eyewitness Testimony*, Harvard University Press.
Loftus, E.F., Miller, D.G., and Burns, H.J. (1978) Semantic integration of verbal information into a visual memory. In *Journal of Experimental Psychology*, 4 (1), 19–31.
Lorenz, K.Z. (1966) *On Aggression*, London: Methuen.
Luria, A.R. (1959) The directive function of speech in development and dissolution, Parts I and II. In *Language*, Oldfield, R.C., and Marshall, J.C. (eds.), Harmondsworth: Penguin.
* Luria, A.R. (1969) *The Mind of a Mnemonist*, London: Jonathan Cape.
* Luria, A.R. (1975) *The Man with a Shattered World*, Harmondsworth: Penguin.

Luria, A.R., and Yudovich, F.I. (1971) *Speech and the Development of Mental Processes in the Child*, Harmondsworth: Penguin.

Lyons, J. (1970) *Chomsky*, London: Fontana.

* Maccoby, E.E. (1980) *Social Development—Psychological Growth and the Parent–Child Relationship*, New York: Harcourt Brace Jovanovich.

Maccoby, E.E., and Jacklin, C.N. (1974) *The Psychology of Sex Differences*, Stanford: Stanford University Press.

* Mackay, D. (1975) *Clinical Psychology: Theory and Therapy*, London: Methuen.

Mackay, D. (1984) Behavioural psychotherapy. In *Individual Therapy in Britain*, Dryden, W. (ed.), London: Harper and Row.

Magee, B. (1973) *Popper*, London: Fontana.

Maher, B. (1980) Experimental psychopathology. In *New Horizons in Psychology*, 2, Dodwell, P.C. (ed.), Harmondsworth: Penguin.

* Maslow, A. (1962) *Towards a Psychology of Being*, London: Van Nostrand.

Maslow, A. (1972) *The Farther Reaches of Human Nature*, New York: The Viking Press.

Masters, G. (1978) Learning to communicate. In *Nursing Times*, 2 March, 350–2.

McClelland, D.C., and Atkinson, J.W. (1976) *The Achievement Motive*, New York: Irvington Press.

McConnell, J.V. (Fourth edition, 1983) *Understanding Human Behaviour*, Holt, Rinehart and Winston.

McGinnies, E. (1949) Emotionality and perceptual defence. In *Psychological Review*, 56, 244-51.

McGuire, W.J. (1980) Social psychology. In *New Horizons in Psychology 2*, Dodwell, P.C. (ed.), Harmondsworth: Penguin.

McGuire, W.J., and Papageorgis, D. (1961) Effectiveness of forewarning in developing resistance to persuasion. In *Public Opinion Quarterly*, 26, 24–34.

* McGurk, H. (1975) *Growing and Changing*, London: Methuen.

McKellar, P. (1968) *Experience and Behaviour*, Harmondsworth: Penguin.

McNeill, D. (1966) The creation of language. In *Language*, Oldfield, R.C., and Marshall, J.C. (eds.), Harmondsworth: Penguin.

Mead, G.H. (1925) The genesis of the self and social control. In *International Journal of Ethics*, 35, 251–73.

Mead, M. (1962) *Male and Female*, Harmondsworth: Penguin.

* Medcof, J., and Roth, J. (eds.), (1979) *Approaches to Psychology*, Milton Keynes: Open University Press.

Melville, J. (1980) Anorexia—fear eats the soul. In *New Society*, 25 September, 612–13.

Meyer, P. (1970) If Hitler asked you to electrocute a stranger, would you? In *Esquire*, February.

Miles, T.R. (1957) On defining intelligence. In *Intelligence and Ability*, Wiseman, S. (ed.), Harmondsworth: Penguin.

* Milgram, S. (1974) *Obedience to Authority*, New York: Harper and Row.

Millar, S. (1968) *The Psychology of Play*, Harmondsworth: Penguin.

* Miller, G.A. (1956) The magical number seven, plus or minus two: some limits on our capacity for processing information. In *Psychological Review*, 63, 81–97.

* Miller, G.A. (1966) *Psychology—The Science of Mental Life*, Harmondsworth: Penguin.

Miller, G.A. (1968) *The Psychology of Communication—Seven Essays*, Harmondsworth: Penguin.

Miller, G.A., Galanter, E., and Pribram, K.H. (1960) *Plans and the Structure of Behaviour*, Holt, Rinehart and Winston.

Miller, J.B. (ed.) (1973) *Psychoanalysis and Women*, Harmondsworth: Penguin.

Milner, G.B. (1974) Boys will be girls. In *New Society*, 25 July, 215–17.

Mischel, W. (1968) *Personality and Assessment*, New York: Wiley.

Mitchell, R. (1978) Establishing a therapy group. In *Nursing Times*, 2 March, 352–4.

* Mitchell, R. (1982) *Phobias*, Harmondsworth: Penguin.

Morgan, P. (1974) Against clinging: monkeys and mothers. In *New Society*, 29 August, 537–40.

* Murphy, J., John, M., and Brown, H. (eds.), (1984) *Dialogues and Debates in Social Psychology*, Lawrence Erlbaum Associates/Open University.

Muson, H. (1979) Moral thinking—can it be taught? In *Psychology Today*, February.

* Mussen, P.H., Conger, J.J., Kagan, J., and Huston, A.C. (Sixth edition, 1984) *Child Development and Personality*, London: Harper and Row.

Mussen, P.H., and Jones, M. (1957) Self-conceptions, motivations and interpersonal attitudes of late and early maturing boys. In *Child Development*, 28, 243–56.

Napoli, V., Kilbride, J.M., and Tebbs, D.E. (1982) *Adjustment and Growth in a Changing World*, West Publishing Co.

Neisser, U. (1967) *Cognitive Psychology*, New York: Appleton-Century-Crofts.

Neugarten, B.L. (1963) Personality and the ageing process. In *Human Ageing*, Chown, S.M. (ed.), Harmondsworth: Penguin.

Newman, H.H., Freeman, F.N., and Holzinger, K.J. (1937) *Twins: A Study of Heredity and Environment*, University of Chicago Press.

Nichols, K. (1975) Psychodrama. In *New Behaviour*, 7 August, 214–17.

Nicholson, N., Cole, S.G., and Rocklin, T. (1985) Conformity in the Asch situation: a comparison between contemporary British and US university students. In *British Journal of Social Psychology*, 24, 59–63.

Norman, M. (1978) Substitutes for mother. In *Human Behaviour*, February, 112–15.

Oatley, K. (1975) New metaphors for mind. In *New Behaviour*, 1 May, 68–71.

Oatley, K. (1981) The self with others: the person and the interpersonal context in the approaches of C.R. Rogers and R.D. Laing. In *Personality—Theory, Measurement and Research*, Fransella, F. (ed.), London: Methuen.

Oldfield, R.C., and Marshall, J.C. (eds.) (1968) *Language*, Harmondsworth: Penguin.

Olds, J., and Milner, P. (1954) Positive reinforcement produced by electrical stimulation of septal area and other regions of rat brain. In *Journal of Comparative Physiological Psychology*, 47, 419–27.

Olds, S.W. (1977) When mommy goes to work. In *Family Health/Today's Health*, February.

Orne, M.T. (1959) The nature of hypnosis: artifact and essence. In *Journal of Abnormal and Social Psychology*, 58, 277–99.

* Orne, M.T. (1962) On the social psychology of the psychological experiment— with particular reference to demand characteristic and their implications. In *American Psychologist*, 17 (11), 776–83.

* Ornstein, R.E. (1977) *The Psychology of Consciousness*, New York: Harcourt Brace Jovanovich.

Osgood, C.E., Suci, G.J., and Tannenbaum, P.H. (1957) *The Measurement of Meaning*, University of Illinois Press.

Oswald, I. (1966) *Sleep*, Harmondsworth: Penguin.

Paivio, A. (1969) Mental imagery in associative learning and memory. In *Psychological Review*, 76, 241–63.

* Parke, R.D. (1981) *Fathering*, London: Fontana.

* Parkes, C.M. (1975) *Bereavement—Studies of Grief in Adult Life*, Harmondsworth: Penguin.

Parkes, C.M., and Weiss, R.S. (1983) *Recovery from Bereavement*, New York: Basic Books.

* Peck, D., and Whitlow, D. (1975) *Approaches to Personality Theory*, London: Methuen.

Perls, F.S., Hefferline, R., and Goodman, P. (1973). *Gestalt Therapy—Excitement and Growth in the Human Personality*, Harmondsworth: Penguin.

Peterson, L.R., and Peterson, M.J. (1959) Short term retention of individual items. In *Journal of Experimental Psychology*, 58, 193–8.

Piaget, J. (1932) *The Moral Judgement of the Child*, London: Routledge Kegan Paul.

Piaget, J. (1950) *The Psychology of Intelligence*, London: Routledge Kegan Paul.

Piaget, J. (1968) *Six Psychological Studies*, University of London Press.

Piaget, J. (1973) *The Child's Conception of the World*, London: Paladin.

Piliavin, J.A., and Piliavin, I.M. (1972) Effect of blood on reactions to a victim. In *Journal of Personality and Social Psychology*, 23, 353–62.

Piliavin, I.M., Piliavin, J.A., and Rodin, S. (1975) Costs, diffusion and the stigmatised victim. In *Journal of Personality and Social Psychology*, 32, 429–38.

Piliavin, I.M., Rodin, J., and Piliavin, J.A. (1969). Good samaritanism: an underground phenomenon? In *Journal of Personality and Social Psychology*, 13, 289–99.

Porteous, M.A. (1985) Developmental aspects of adolescent problem disclosure in England and Ireland. In *Journal of Child Psychology and Psychiatry*, 26, 465–78.

Postman, L., Bruner, J.S., and McGinnies, E. (1948) Personal values as selective factors in perception. In *Journal of Abnormal and Social Psychology*, 43, 142–54.

* Radford, J., and Burton, A. (1972) Changing intelligence. In *Race, Culture and Intelligence*, Richardson, K., and Spears, D. (eds.), Harmondsworth: Penguin.

Radford, J., and Govier, E. (eds.), (1980) *A Textbook of Psychology*, London: Sheldon Press.

Radford, J. and Kirby, R. (1975) *The Person in Psychology*, London: Methuen.

Radical Therapist Collective, (1974) *The Radical Therapist*, Harmondsworth: Penguin.

* Reich, B., and Adcock, C. (1976) *Values, Attitudes and Behaviour Change*, London: Methuen.

Rice, B., (1979) The brave new world of intelligence testing. In *New Society*, 11 October, 63–6.

* Richardson, K., and Spears, D. (eds.), (1972) *Race, Culture and Intelligence*, Harmondsworth: Penguin.

Robertshaw, S. (1975) Left brain, right brain. In *New Behaviour*, 12 June, 354–7.

Robinson, T. (1975) One man's madness. In *New Behaviour*, 18 September, 452–4.

Roediger, H.L., Rushton, J.P., Capaldi, E.D., and Paris, S.G. (1984) *Psychology*, New York: Little, Brown and Co.

Rogers, C.R. (1951) *Client-centred Therapy, its Current Practices, Implications and Theory*, Boston: Houston.

* Rogers, C.R. (1961) *On Becoming a Person*, Boston: Houghton Mifflin.

Rogers, C.R. (1970) *Encounter Groups*, New York: Harper and Row.

Rokeach, M. (1960) *The Open and Closed Mind*, New York: Basic Books.

* Rose, S. (1976) *The Conscious Brain*, Harmondsworth: Penguin.

Rosenfeld, A. (1978) Are we afraid of living longer? The strange resistance to aging research. In *Saturday Review*, 27 May.

* Rosenhan, D.L. (1973) On being sane in insane places. In *Science*, 179, 250–8.

Rosenthal, G., Andrew, P., and Ineson, H. (1972) The chronic psychiatric patient—a new hope for treatment? (A study in operant conditioning—2). In *Nursing Times*, 21 September, 1182–5.

Rosenthal, R. (1966) *Experimenter Effects in Behavioural Research*, New York: Appleton-Century-Crofts.

Rosenthal, R., and Jacobson, L. (1968) *Pygmalion in the Classroom*, New York: Holt, Rinehart and Winston.

Roth, I. (1976) *Social Perception*, Milton Keynes: Open University.

Rotter, J.B. (1966) Generalized expectancies for internal versus external control of reinforcement. In *Psychological Monographs*, 30 (1), 1–26.

Rubin, Z. (1973) *Liking and Loving*, New York: Holt, Rinehart and Winston.

* Rubin, Z., and McNeil, E.B. (Third edition, 1983) *The Psychology of Being Human*, London: Harper and Row.

* Ruch, J.C. (1984) *Psychology—The Personal Science*, Wadsworth Publishing Co.

* Rutter, M. (Second edition, 1981) *Maternal Deprivation Reassessed*, Harmondsworth: Penguin.

* Ryan, J. (1972) IQ—The Illusion of Objectivity. In *Race, Culture and Intelligence*, Richardson, K., and Spears, D. (eds.), Harmondsworth: Penguin.

* Rycroft, C. (ed.) (1966) *Psychoanalysis Observed*, London: Constable.

Ryle, A. (1975) Psychotherapy research: the role of repertory grid. In *New Behaviour*, 28 August, 326–8.

Ryle, G. (1949) Knowing how and knowing that. In *Intelligence and Ability*, Wiseman, S. (ed.), Harmondsworth: Penguin.

Sagan, C. (1978) The planet of the talking apes. In *Newsday*, 9 April, 108–9.

Sage, W. (1976) The split brain lab. In *Human Behaviour*, June.

Sandford, R.N. (1936) The effects of abstinence from food on imaginal processes. In *Journal of Psychology*, 2, 129–36.

Scarr, S., and Weinberg, R.A. (1976) IQ test performance of black children adopted by white families. In *American Psychologist*, 31, 726–39.

Scarr, S., and Weinberg, R.A. (1977) Intellectual similarities within families of both adopted and biological children. In *Intelligence*, 1, 170–191.

Scarr, S., and Weinberg, R.A. (1978) Attitudes, interest and IQ. In *Human Nature*, April.

Schachter, S., and Singer, J.E. (1962) Cognitive, social and physiological determinants of emotional state. In *Psychological Review*, 69, 379–99.

* Schaffer, H.R. (1971) *The Growth of Sociability*, Harmondsworth: Penguin.

* Schaffer, Rudolph (1977) *Mothering*, London: Fontana/Open Books.

Schaffer, H.R. (1982) Social development in early childhood. In *Psychology and People—A Tutorial Text*, Chapman, A.J., and Gale, A. (eds.), British Psychological Society and Macmillan Press Ltd.

Schaffer, H.R., and Emerson, P.E. (1964) Patterns of response to physical contact in early human development. In *Journal of Child Psychology and Psychiatry*, 5, 1–13.

Schaffer, H.R., and Emerson, P.E. (1964) The development of social attachments in infancy. In *Monographs of the Society for Research in Child Development*, 29, 3 (Serial No. 94).

Sears, R.R., Maccoby, E., and Levin, H. (1957) *Patterns of Child-Rearing*, Evanston, Illinois: Row, Petersen and Co.

Secord, P.F., and Backman, C.W. (1964) *Social Psychology*, McGraw-Hill.

Segall, M.H., Campbell, D.T., and Herskovits, M.J. (1963) Cultural differences in the perception of geometrical illusions. In *Science*, 139, 769–71.

Seligman, M. (1972) *Biological Boundaries of Learning*, New York: Appleton-Century-Crofts.

Selye, H. (1956) *The Stress of Life*, New York: McGraw-Hill.

Serpell, R. (1976) *Culture's Influence on Behaviour*, London: Methuen.

* Shackleton, V.J., and Fletcher, C.A. (1984) *Individual Differences—Theories and Applications*, London: Methuen.

* Shaffer, D.R. (1985) *Developmental Psychology—Theory, Research and Applications*, Brooks/Cole Publishing Co.

Shapiro, D.A. (1982) Psychopathology. In *Psychology and People—A Tutorial Text*, Chapman, A.J., and Gale, A. (eds.), British Psychological Society and Macmillan Press Ltd.

* Sheehy, G. (1976) *Passages—Predictable Crises of Adult Life*, New York: Bantam Books.
Sherif, M., Harvey, O.J., White, B.J., Hood, W.R., and Sherif, C.W. (1961) *Intergroup Conflict and Co-operation: The Roberts Cave Experiment*, University of Oklahoma Press.
Shields, J. (1962) *Monozygotic Twins Brought Up Apart and Brought Up Together*, Oxford University Press.
* Shotter, J. (1975) *Images of Man in Psychological Research*, London: Methuen.
* Siann, G. (1985) *Accounting for Aggression—Perspectives on Aggression and Violence*, Allen and Unwin.
* Simon, B. (1971) *Intelligence, Psychology and Education—A Marxist Critique*, London: Lawrence and Wishart.
Skeels, H.M. (1966) Adult status of children with contrasting early life experiences. In *Monographs of the Society for Research in Child Development*, 31, 3 (Serial No. 105).
Skeels, H.M., and Dye, H.B. (1939) A study of the effects of differential stimulation on mentally retarded children. In *Proceedings of the American Association of Mental Deficiency*, 44, 114–36.
Skinner, B.F. (1938) *The Behaviour of Organisms*, New York: Appleton-Century-Crofts.
Skinner, B.F. (1953) *Science and Human Behaviour*, New York: Macmillan.
Skinner, B.F. (1957) *Verbal Behaviour*, New York: Appleton-Century-Crofts.
* Skinner, B.F. (1973) *Beyond Freedom and Dignity*, Harmondsworth: Penguin.
* Skinner, B.F. (1974) *About Behaviourism*, London: Jonathan Cape.
Skodak, M., and Skeels, H. (1949) A final follow-up study of 100 adopted children. In *Journal of Genetic Psychology*, 75, 85–125.
Skolnick, A. (1978) The myth of the vulnerable child. In *Psychology Today*, February.
* Sluckin, W. (1965) *Imprinting and Early Experiences*, London: Methuen.
Sluckin, W. (1972) Early experience. In *New Horizons in Psychology 1*, Foss, B.M. (ed.), Harmondsworth: Penguin.
Smith, A.C. (1977) The benefits of ECT. In *Nursing Times*, 17 March, 368–9.
Smith, P.B. (1981) Research into humanistic personality theories. In *Personality—Theory, Measurement and Research*, Fransella, F. (ed.), London: Methuen.
* Smith, R.E., Sarason, I.G., and Sarason, B.R. (Third edition, 1986) *Psychology—The Frontiers of Behaviour*, London: Harper and Row.
* Solso, R.L. (1979) *Cognitive Psychology*, New York: Harcourt Brace Jovanovich.
Spearman, C. (1927) The doctrine of two factors. In *Intelligence and Ability*, Wiseman, S. (ed.), Harmondsworth: Penguin.
* Sperling, G. (1960) The information available in brief visual presentation. In *Psychological Monographs*, 74, No. 498.
Spitz, R.A. (1946) Anaclitic depression. In *Psychoanalytic Study of the Child*, 2, 313–42.
* Spitzer, R.L. (1976) More on pseudoscience in science and the case for psychiatric diagnosis, *Archives of General Psychiatry*, 33, 459–470.
Stevens, R. (1976) *Integration and the Concept of Self*, Milton Keynes, Open University.
Stones, E. (1971) *Educational Psychology*, London: Methuen.
Storr, A. (1966) The concept of cure. In *Psychoanalysis Observed*, Rycroft, C. (ed.), London: Constable.
Storr, A. (1968) *Human Aggression*, Harmondsworth: Penguin.
Storr, A. (1973) *Jung*, London: Fontana.
Storr, A. (1976) *The Dynamics of Creation*, Harmondsworth: Penguin.
Stroop, J.R. (1935) Interference in serial verbal reactions. In *Journal of Experimental Psychology*, 18, 643-61.

* Swift, D. (1972) What is the environment? In *Race Culture and Intelligence*, Richardson, K., and Spears, D. (eds.), Harmondsworth: Penguin.

Sylva, K., and Lunt, I. (1982) *Child Development—A First Course*, Oxford: Basil Blackwell.

* Szasz, T. (1972) *The Myth of Mental Illness*, London: Paladin.

Szasz, T. (1973) *The Manufacture of Madness*, London: Paladin.

* Szasz, T. (1974) *Ideology and Insanity*, Harmondsworth: Penguin.

Tajfel, H. (ed.), (1982) *Social Identity and Intergroup Relations*, Cambridge University Press.

Terrace, H.S. (1979) How Nim Chimpsky changed my mind. In *Psychology Today*, November.

* Thomas, R.M. (Second edition, 1985) *Comparing Theories of Child Development*, Wadsworth Publishing Co.

Thompson, C. (1943) Penis envy in women. In *Psychoanalysis and Women*, Miller, J.B. (ed.), Harmondsworth: Penguin.

Thorndike, E.L. (1898) Animal intelligence: an experimental study of the associative processes in animals. In *Psychological Review Monograph Supplement*, 2, No. 8.

* Thorne, B. (1984) Person-centred therapy. In *Individual Therapy in Britain*, Dryden, W., (ed.), Harper and Row.

Thorpe, J.G. (1980) Time out or seclusion? In *Nursing Times*, 3 April, 604.

Thurstone, L.L. (1938) Primary mental abilities. In *Psychometric Monographs*, *No.1*.

* Tinbergen, N. (1951) *The Study of Instinct*, Oxford University Press.

* Tizard, B. (1977) *Adoption: A Second Chance*, London: Open Books.

Tizard, B., and Hodges, J. (1978) The effect of early institutional rearing on the development of eight-year-old children. In *Journal of Child Psychology and Psychiatry*, 19, 99–118.

Tizard, B., and Rees, J. (1974) A comparison of the effects of adoption, restoration to the natural mother and continued institutionalization on the cognitive development of four-year-old children. In *Child Development*, 45, 92–9.

Treisman, A. (1960) Contextual cues in selective listening. In *Quarterly Journal of Experimental Psychology*, 12, 242–8.

* Treisman, A. (1964 a) Verbal cues, language and meaning in selective attention. In *American Journal of Psychology*, 77, 206–19.

* Treisman, A. (1964 b) Monitoring and storage of irrelevant messages in selective attention. In *Journal of Verbal Learning and Verbal Behaviour*, 3, 449–59.

Triseliotis, J. (1980) Growing up in foster care and after. In *New Developments in Foster Care and Adoption*, Triseliotis, J. (ed.), London: Routledge Kegan Paul.

Trotter, R. (1976) Intensive intervention programme prevents retardation. In American Psychological Association Monitor, September/October.

Tulving, E. (1962) Subjective organization in free recall of unrelated words. In *Psychological Review*, 69, 344–54.

Tulving, E. (1972) Episodic and semantic memory. In *Organization of Memory*, Tulving, E., and Donaldson, W. (eds.), New York: Academic Press.

* Tulving, E., and Pearlstone, Z. (1966) Availability versus accessibility of information in memory for words. In *Journal of Verbal Learning and Verbal Behaviour*, 5, 381–91.

Turnbull, C.M. (1961) *The Forest People*, New York: Simon and Schuster.

Turner, J. (1975) *Cognitive Development*, London: Methuen.

* Turner, J. (1984) *Cognitive Development and Education*, London: Methuen.

* Unger, R.K. (1979) Female and Male, London: Harper and Row.

* Valentine, E.R. (1982) *Conceptual Issues in Psychology*, Allen and Unwin.

Vernon, P.E. (1950) The hierarchy of ability. In *Intelligence and Ability*, Wiseman, S. (ed.), Harmondsworth: Penguin.

Vernon, P.E. (1969) *Personality Assessment—a Critical Survey*, London: Methuen.
Vernon, P.E. (1969) *Intelligence and Cultural Environment*, London: Methuen.
* Vernon, P.E. (1979) *Intelligence: Heredity and Environment*, San Francisco: W.H. Freeman.
Vygotsky, L.S. (1962) *Thought and Language*, M.I.T. Press.
Walker, S. (1975) *Learning and Reinforcement*, London: Methuen.
* Walker, S. (1984) *Learning Theory and Behaviour Modification*, London: Methuen.
* Warren, N., and Jahoda, M. (eds.), (Second edition, 1973) *Attitudes*, Harmondsworth: Penguin.
Watson, J.B., (1924) *Behaviourism*, New York: J.B. Lippincott.
Watson, J.B., and Rayner, R. (1920) Conditioned emotional reactions. In *Journal of Experimental Psychology*, 3, 1–14.
Weaver, S.M., Armstrong, N.E., Broome, A.K., and Stewart, L. (1978) Behavioural principles applied in a security ward. In *Nursing Times*, 5 January, 22–4.
Weinreich-Haste, H. (1979) Moral development. In *The School Years*, Coleman, J.C. (ed.), London: Methuen.
* Wessler, R.L. (1986) Conceptualizing cognitions in the cognitive-behavioural therapies. In *Cognitive-Behavioural Approaches to Psychotherapy*, Dryden, W., and Golden, W. (eds.), Harper and Row.
White, D. (1975) The growth of conscience. In *New Society*, 4 December, 538–40.
Wilding, J.M. (1982) *Perception—From Sense to Object*, London: Hutchinson.
Wilson, C. (1979) The development of self. In *The School Years*, Coleman, J.C. (ed.), London: Methuen.
* Wiseman, S. (ed.) (1967) *Intelligence and Ability*, Harmondsworth: Penguin.
Witkin, H.A., Lewis, H.B., Hertzmann, M., Machorer, K., and Wapner, S. (1954) *Personality Through Perception*, New York: Harper and Row.
* Wollheim, R. (1971) *Freud*, London: Fontana.
* Wolpe, J. (1969) *The Practice of Behaviour Therapy*, Oxford: Pergamon Press.
Woodman, D.D. (1980) What makes a psychopath? In *New Society*, 4 September, 447–9.
Worthington, A.G. (1969) Paired comparison scaling of brightness judgements: a method for the measurement of perceptual defence. In *British Journal of Psychology*, 60, (3), 363–8.
Wright, D. (1971) *The Psychology of Moral Behaviour*, Harmondsworth: Penguin.
Wright, D., and Croxen, M. (1976) *Moral Development—A Cognitive Approach*, Milton Keynes: Open University.
Wright, D.S., Taylor, A., Davies, D.R., Sluckin, W., Lee, S.G.M., and Reason, J.T. (1978) *Introducing Psychology—An Experimental Approach*, Harmondsworth: Penguin.
Wright, J.J. (1976) Physical treatments. In *A Textbook of Human Psychology*, Eysenck, H.T., and Wilson, G.D. (eds.), MTP Press.
Zajonc, R.B. (1968) Attitudinal effects of mere exposure. In *Journal of Personality and Social Psychology*, 9, (No. 2, Part 2).
Zimbardo, P.G. (1972) Pathology of imprisonment. In *Society*, April.
* Zimbardo, P.G., Banks, W.C., Craig, H., and Jaffe, D. (1973) A pirandellian prison: the mind is a formidable jailor. In *New York Times Magazine*, April 8, 38–60.

Index